Dictionary of Biblical Criticism and Interpretation

Compiling the results from contemporary and exciting areas of research into one single important volume, this book stands ahead of its field in providing a comprehensive one-stop handbook reference of biblical interpretation.

Examining a wide range of articles on many of the recognized interpreters including Augustine, Luther, and Calvin, up to the modern figures of Martin Hengel and T.W. Manson, Professor Porter gathers contributors who expertly combine the study of biblical interpretation with the examination of the theological and philosophical preconceptions that have influenced it, and survey the history of interpretation from different perspectives.

Key perspectives studied include:

- the historical dimension: addresses how interpretation has developed at various periods of time, from early Jewish exegesis to the historical-critical method;
- the conceptual approach: looks at the various schools of thought that have generated biblical interpretation, and compares and contrasts competing conceptual models of interpretation;
- the personal perspective: addresses the reality of biblical interpretation by individuals who have helped plot the course of theological development.

With relevant bibliographies as a guide to further reading, the *Dictionary* will be an extremely important reference tool held for many years, not only by libraries, but also by students, scholars, clergy, and teachers of this fascinating and high-profile subject.

Stanley E. Porter is an award-winning editor and author. He has edited over forty volumes, including the *Handbook of Classical Rhetoric in the Hellenistic Period* (1997), the *Handbook to Exegesis of the New Testament* (1997) and, with Craig Evans, the *Dictionary of New Testament Background* (2000). He has also written ten books, including *Early Christianity and its Sacred Literature* (2000), with Lee McDonald, and *The Criteria for Authenticity in Historical-Jesus Research* (2000). He is President, Dean and Professor of New Testament at McMaster Divinity College, Hamilton, Ontario, Canada.

Dictionary of Biblical Criticism and Interpretation

edited by Stanley E. Porter

Routledge
Taylor & Francis Group

LONDON AND NEW YORK

First published 2007
by Routledge
2 Park Square, Milton Park, Abingdon, Oxon OX14 4RN

Simultaneously published in the USA and Canada
by Routledge
270 Madison Ave, New York, NY 10016

First published in paperback 2009

Routledge is an imprint of the Taylor and Francis Group, an informa business

© 2007, 2009 Stanley E. Porter, individual contributors their contributions

Typeset in Bembo by
Keystroke, Tettenhall, Wolverhampton
Printed and bound in Great Britain by
TJ International Ltd, Padstow, Cornwall

Library of Congress Cataloging in Publication Data
Dictionary of biblical criticism and interpretation/ed., Stanley E Porter.
p. cm.
Includes bibliographical references and index.
1. Bible—Criticism, interpretation, etc.—Dictionaries. I. Porter, Stanley E Porter., 1956–
BS440.D496 2006
220.3—dc22
2006034336

British Library Cataloguing in Publication Data
A catalogue record for this book is available from the British Library

ISBN10: 0–415–20100–4 (hbk)
ISBN13: 978–0–415–20100–1 (hbk)

ISBN10: 0–415–55274–5 (pbk)
ISBN13: 978–0–415–55274–5 (pbk)

Contents

Preface

This dictionary has been a long time in the making. At last it is released to the world – far from complete (no dictionary could ever be), but willing to take its place as one of the tools in the enterprise of biblical criticism and interpretation. The title of the volume reflects its aim. That is, to provide a dictionary-length guide to major issues, approaches, and people that have been important in the development of biblical criticism and interpretation. Criticism addresses the variety of methods that have been developed, especially since the Enlightenment, to help us as biblical interpreters to come to terms with the issues surrounding reading the Bible. Interpretation addresses the fact that all these various methods, and those who have utilized them – including those preceding modern critical analysis – have been involved in helping biblical readers to gain understanding. The scope of the dictionary includes major time periods of biblical criticism and interpretation, the range of corpora between the two Testaments and other texts as well, critical approaches, methods, and mind-sets of significance, and even a variety of individual critics and interpreters. Whereas we have some confidence that we have covered the major critical periods and most of the significant methods and approaches, it was necessary to be highly selective regarding the individuals included. I apologize here if you think that your favorite biblical scholar – or even you, yourself! – should have been included but was not.

This enterprise began with the idea of Richard Stoneman, editor for Routledge. I wish to thank him for encouraging the development of this project, and for his patience as it took longer than anticipated. My hope is that this dictionary will join the ranks of the significant and growing list of Routledge volumes that have come to be important for understanding the ancient world, of which the Bible is a significant part.

At the outset of this project, I asked my then colleague Dr. Brook Pearson to be a coeditor with me. He gladly undertook this task and initiated correspondence and kept the databases regarding the project. Due to a variety of factors, he has been unable to continue with the project, and I have truly missed his participation. I wish him the best in his own continuing scholarly endeavors. His separation from the project corresponded to a time of transition for me from one continent to another, which has occasioned the delay in completion and publication.

In his stead, and at the last stages, my teaching and research assistant, Andrew Gabriel, joined the project. I wish to thank Andrew for tackling all dimensions of the project so avidly, including the databases, the ever-growing stack of manuscripts, and the electronic files. He has also been of great assistance in corresponding with authors, recruiting last-minute participants, and editing contributions.

My major debt is to the individual contributors. Over the course of the years, a number have wondered whether this project would ever see the black of print. I am pleased to say that that day has finally arrived. I thank you for your patience, and your faith in believing that this project was far from dead. This volume brings together scholars from several different continents, to say nothing of many different countries. One of the results of this has been the ability to benefit from a variety of perspectives reflective of the places in which these scholars do their critical work. Along the way, some potential contributors had to withdraw, and others had to be recruited. Some of these joined at the last minute. I especially appreciate the willingness with which a number of last-minute contributors accepted invitations and returned their contributions in a timely and efficient manner. I am confident that the quality of their contributions has been equal to the others, and that readers will find a surprisingly high degree of consistently fine contributions within this collection. Thank you to each of you for offering your expertise and for being willing to make a contribution to this project.

As a last word, I wish to encourage users and readers of this volume to explore the depths of its riches. As I reviewed articles, it became clear to me that the tapestry of criticism and interpretation of the Bible is complexly woven. The various strands include history, literature, material remains, philosophy, and a variety of other things. Many of the articles, even though the individual contributors were unaware of it, were closely intertwined with other contributions because of their common task of attempting to help us to understand biblical criticism and interpretation. My hope is that this volume helps you also in your biblical interpretation.

STANLEY E. PORTER

McMaster Divinity College
Hamilton, Ontario, Canada

List of entries and contributors

Introduction to Criticism and Interpretation of the Bible

The field of biblical studies is one of the most complex within the humanities disciplines (some would question whether it is a humanities discipline, since it avails itself of a variety of social-scientific methods as well; that is part of the point that I make below). This assessment has been recognized by a number of scholars who recently have undertaken to join, or at least to have conversation with, the field of biblical studies. Few disciplines make such rigorous demands on those who would call themselves experts in the field. The requirements include knowledge of the ancient world, ancient languages, various ancient literatures, and a history of writing, research, and investigation that dates back nearly two millennia in its most inclusive form, and at least to the Enlightenment in its more immediate critical form. Thus, it qualifies as one of the oldest academic and intellectual disciplines. A number of critical disciplines geared to studying the ancient biblical world have been developed, often called historical criticism, in conjunction with which biblical scholars have been forced also to ask theological questions, including addressing such topics as canonicity, revelation, and inspiration. In more recent times, there has been an influx of modern critical methods, which have been appropriated from related (and sometimes not so related) disciplines. These include literary studies, drawing upon work that has been developed in the study of modern literature; classical studies, including but certainly not limited to exploration of the influence of oral culture; social-scientific criticism, with its prescriptive and descriptive models of various societal patterns; linguistics, with its original attention to spoken languages being applied to the written artifacts of past cultures; and others that could be mentioned (and probably are somewhere in this volume). Much of the recent work that has been done in the discipline could have appeared in any number of major modern languages, including, for example, English, German, or French to be sure, but now also Spanish, Italian, or Swedish, among others.

No doubt as a result of its complexities, the field of biblical criticism and interpretation is one that has been increasingly well served in the last several decades. This is not to say that previous decades did not have significant contributions to the field made by a variety of scholars. Clearly, such contributions were made. However, we currently live in a highly self-conscious and methodologically reflective age. Perhaps that is the inevitable result of the accumulation of history and tradition in any given intellectual enterprise. That is, at a particular time one needs to pause, if only momentarily, and critically reflect on what has preceded in order to impel forward movement into new and different areas of intellectual exploration. Nevertheless, it is only within the last several decades that there has been a multiplication of critical methods within the field of biblical studies that has forced interpreters to come to terms with the nature of their discipline. Few interpreters today would want to make the claim that they uncritically accept and utilize a critical interpretive method (there seems to be a contradiction in terms to make such a claim, whether it is inadvertent or not). Instead, most interpreters are forced to scrutinize the methods that they use and to make a conscious effort to defend and buttress the methods that they believe lead to critical insight. As a result, there is a significant difference of opinion among interpreters regarding what the 'best' method is – in fact, I know of few who would be willing to make such a blanket statement, without also offering a number of caveats and qualifiers. Along with the endorsement of particular methods is the acknowledgment and respect given to those who have paved the way and continue to develop such methodological perspectives. Only time will tell, whether the apparent critical panoply is genuine, or whether we are suffering in our critical examination from a critical myopia bred of proximity in time and environment.

The consequence of such critical scrutiny is a number of positive and negative factors. Some of the positive factors include advancement in critical method, including the development of 'new' methods of interpretation. The process of self-analysis and critical interaction has helped to motivate and refine methods of critical interpretation. What once, for example, passed as simple 'literary' readings of the Bible are now much more critically aware, and would perhaps differentiate between formalist, new critical, new historicist, and reader-oriented methods. Another positive result has been the establishment of bodies of critical interpretation regarding these methods. What began as just one or two structuralist interpreters, for example, developed into a body of critical structuralist interpretation. A third result is that the more traditional critical methods – e.g., the so-called historical-critical method – were forced to defend their territory if they wished to retain advocates other than simply those who were too deeply enshrined in their inherited tradition to contemplate anything else. Even though at various times throughout the last century some have forecast the death knell of the historical-critical method, it appears to have survived into this new century. In fact, it not only has survived, but has also expanded its scope of usage, so that it is being utilized by a number of biblical interpreters who perhaps in a previous generation would not have been its advocates. A fourth positive result, and one that follows directly from the previous one, is that some of the boundaries that have insulated the discipline of biblical studies in various quarters have been broken down, so that there is much more mingling of methods and interpretive models. Even the historical-critical method has had to make adjustments as it has been forced to appropriate perceived benefits from other critical methods. Much of its staying power has perhaps been related to its ability to adapt to the demands of the age, and for many of its advocates to adapt along with it.

Whereas there have been a number of positive results of the recent critical discussion, these advantageous consequences have not come without a price. There have been a number of negative results as well. One of these is the clear fragmentation of the discipline of biblical studies that seems to have become a reality. The result of the development of a greater number of critical methodologies has been that it has become increasingly difficult to expect any given interpreter to be able to understand – to say nothing of master – this range of approaches. As a consequence, not only have there continued to be commentaries and monographs that utilize the mainstream range of critical methods, but there are other series that focus specifically on a single critical method. Related to this is the sometimes unconscious (though sometimes explicit) belief that those critical methods that have not been mastered are in some way inherently inferior to those that have been learned. They may be, but not learning about them is not the way to prove that this is the case. Another disadvantage is that a sense of the history of interpretation has been lost. Biblical interpretation used to be a more synchronic enterprise, in which the major thinkers of the past were viewed as still-relevant interpreters in the present. The reason for this was probably that the approaches to biblical interpretation from then to now were similar enough to make past interpretation relevant in the present. However, in recent times, with the development of new and competing models of interpretation, it has become increasingly easy to see past interpreters

as simply artifacts, and their interpretation as antiquated and irrelevant. I am always pleasantly amused to hear someone promote a new interpretation of a biblical text, only to find out or realize that the interpretation suggested was first proposed in the nineteenth century or earlier (unfortunately, this sometimes involves an English-language scholar failing to have noted the work of a non-English language scholar). One of the goals of this volume will have been accomplished if some of the major essays that are concerned with individual periods of biblical interpretation are read and appreciated for the relevance of their content, and the realization that earlier interpreters often struggled with the same issues that we struggle with today. A third negative consequence is the difficulty in arriving at anything that resembles definitive or normative interpretations. This of course implies that such are desirable. The critical postmodernist terrain argues at some levels that such a goal is not only unattainable but not even desirable. Such may be true, but it then would seem to imply that communication between competing interpreters would in many instances not be possible either, since the common ground for discussion of competing interpretations would be lost. For some, that result would lead to little anxiety; in fact, it would be a welcome relief. For others, however, this might be more distressing. It would make it difficult to evaluate individual interpretations and even more difficult to know whether there is any kind of development in levels of understanding as a result (I will refrain from using the idea of progress in interpretation, since many would object to that characterization as well).

Much more could be said about the positives and negatives of recent interpretation. However, a volume such as this has a contribution to make to this discussion in a number of ways. One is in providing a means of introducing the various kinds of interpretations, both to those who are simply curious and to those who have not desired or been willing to invest more than superficial interest in them. The articles contained herein are not meant to be definitive in any absolute or encompassing sense, but to provide means of access. This volume is designed also to overcome the kind of contemporary critical introspection that results in failure to contextualize the contemporary within the broader sweep of history. I do not think that some grand metanarrative can be found that accounts for the history of interpretation, but I am not inherently indisposed to finding some patterns of critical behavior illustrated by past practitioners. With increased specialization, aided if not encouraged by the growing demand for instant interpretation, has come a neglect of some broad and specialized areas of interpretation by some interpreters. Some of these would be those who have been at the task for some time and have failed to be able to keep up with recent developments, and much less to be able to assess where such critical methods fit within the larger stream of biblical interpretation. Others of these would be those who have come to the task more recently, but who have not been exposed to some of the older and perhaps (perceived to be) antiquated methods. This volume is designed to provide historical and methodological introductions to such areas. The inclusion of a number of individual interpreters – several of whom are still alive and writing – is designed to bring such critical method to life in terms of the work of individuals who have made significant and what appear to be lasting contributions to the discipline.

This volume ably and aptly captures the state of play in biblical criticism and interpretation at the turn of the twentieth to the twenty-first centuries. As a number of the articles contained herein make clear, the twentieth century was an important one for biblical interpretation. The historical-critical method came into its own in terms of the major types of criticism (form, source, and redaction), but it also had to fend off and adapt to the introduction of a number of new methods (literary/ narrative criticism, linguistic criticism, social-scientific criticism). By the same token, a number of new methods were explored and were able to establish a beachhead, some of them even being able to make serious if not permanent incursions into the critical continent.

As a result, one might well ask the question of where the twenty-first century will take biblical criticism and interpretation. Of course, such thought is speculative at best. Nevertheless, a number of patterns emerge that could develop into trends and end up shaping the discipline. Perhaps more relevant than speculating on what will happen is forecasting a set of desiderata to aid biblical interpretation in the future. Right now, it seems to me, biblical interpretation is in a period of some stagnation. A number of new methods have been developed – some of which have greatly aided and enhanced traditional historical criticism and some of which have established themselves as independent approaches – but the results of these interpretive methods have not sufficiently filtered through to actual textual interpretation. When one reads and considers exegeses of biblical texts, there are numerous places where knowledge of, or use of, one of the newer methods would have greatly aided interpretation, to the point of helping to avoid critical misjudgments. One desirable future development would be better utilization and incorporation of a number of these new methods into actual interpretation of specific passages. A further desired result, which could come about as a result of this, would be the ability to better evaluate the critical methods on the basis of the productivity and clarity of their readings. I do not take the view that the simple test of a method is its practical payoff. Such a pragmatic and functional view of interpretation would result in methodological stagnation, if not retroversion, if left to its own reactionary devices. However, there does come a valid point where critical methods – whether old or new, recent or traditional – are asked to speak to a text. The resulting reading may not be new in any meaningful sense of the word, and certainly not unique, but it should provide some further critical insight into a passage, even if it is merely to provide a better explanation of a traditional interpretation first arrived at through other means. To date, much of the development of new critical methods has been by biblical scholars who have appropriated – often in simplified or reduced form – methods first developed in other scholarly fields of inquiry. A further desired goal would be for the crossover between disciplines to be more genuine and reciprocal. In such a world, biblical scholars would put forth the energy needed truly to master the cognate field, so that they could be actual practitioners of it. Scholars in these other fields would then be welcome to explore the biblical world, and their readings of the biblical text would be welcome in the discussion – but they too would then be called upon to acknowledge many of the critical issues that biblical studies has raised. A final – but by no means a last – desideratum would be a reintegration of historical and theological disciplines. In recent years, there has been a tendency to bifurcate and bracket out certain questions, as if they are not part of biblical criticism. The history of the disciplines – and the continuing orientation of many of its practitioners – indicates that theological questions are still a valuable part of modern biblical studies. The development of modern critical methods has not rendered questions regarding the divine obsolete. At some point in the not too distant future, it will be necessary to ask the hard questions of how these two worlds of (sometimes in its extreme forms naturalistic and hyperskeptical) criticism and (sometimes pietistic) theology can and must talk to each other.

No single volume can hope to accomplish every idealized task, or even all of the tasks that it might set itself to do. No doubt this volume will fail in this regard also. However, there is much within it that, I believe, will be of significance in addressing many of the issues of current biblical criticism and interpretation. The goal is not a resolution of all of the problems – that would bring discussion to a close – but to provide some historical and contemporary perspective on the major issues and approaches at hand as an aid to the ongoing task.

STANLEY E. PORTER

A

ABELARD, PETER (1079–1142)

The French theologian Peter Abelard was possibly the most brilliant thinker of the twelfth century. He studied under Roscelin (d. *c.* 1125), the nominalist, who believed all *universalia* is pure mental conception. Later he studied under William of Champeaux (*c.* 1070–1121), a realist, who believed that *universalia* is the essence of all existence. Opposing his teachers to find a middle position, Abelard saw *universalia* as a mental concept existing not independently from individuals but also not as arbitrary mental concepts.

He taught at the University of Paris from 1108 to 1118, where large crowds gathered from around Europe to hear him. In 1122, he wrote *Sic et Non* (*Yes and No*) in which 158 theological questions are considered by juxtaposing quotations from biblical passages, early Church Fathers, and other authorities without offering solution. His goal was not to discredit these authorities; rather, he called upon reason to reconcile conflicting authorities. Abelard's approach was to introduce doubt as a method of finding the truth. Accordingly, doubt was not seen as a sin, but rather the beginning of knowledge. Additionally, in his introduction, he notes the importance of recognizing and accounting for the meaning of some words changing over time.

Incorporating the principles of logic in his study of the Bible, he produced treatises of speculative theology in addition to biblical commentaries. However, he did not propose that the doctrines of the Christian faith be proved logically by rational arguments. In contrast, rational arguments could be used in counterattacks directed toward Christian doctrine. Although his comprehension of Greek and Hebrew appears to be no more than the consideration of individual biblical terms, he encouraged others to study the original languages.

Abelard is known for his contribution to the doctrine of the atonement. Contrary to some interpretations, Abelard did not reduce the meaning of the cross to merely a demonstration of God's love. Abelard used commentary on Romans 3:10–26 to discuss the doctrine of the atonement. Abelard is distinctive in that he emphasized the subjective impact of the cross. He followed the Augustinian notion that the incarnation of Christ was a public demonstration of the vastness of God's love for the purpose of evoking a human response. However, Abelard questioned the idea that God paid a ransom to Satan through Christ, and he went so far as to question the entire idea of ransom, by looking for a clearer significance of the cross. Abelard does not provide an adequate theological foundation for why Christ's death is understood as a demonstration of God's love. Nevertheless, he highlighted the subjective impact of the death of Christ, which was ignored or underemphasized by his contemporary writers such as Anselm of Canterbury.

Abelard was summoned to the Council of Sens in 1141 where he expected to debate Bernard of Clairvaux. However, upon arrival the council had met and accused him of heresy. Abelard did not defend himself but appealed directly to the pope. The Venerable Peter mediated for Abelard and he was allowed to spend the rest of his days as a monk in Cluny before dying in 1142.

References and further reading

PL 178 and *CCCM* 11–12.
Boyer, B.B. and R. Mckean (eds.) (1977) *Sic et Non: A Critical Edition*, Chicago: University of Chicago Press.
Grane, L. (1970) *Peter Abelard*, New York: Harcourt, Brace and World.
Luscombe, D.E. (1969) *The School of Peter Abelard: The Influence of Abelard's Thought in the Early Scholastic Period*, Cambridge: Cambridge University Press.
McCallum, J.R. (1948) *Abelard's Christian Theology*, Oxford: Blackwell.
Marenbon, J. (1997) *The Philosophy of Peter Abelard*, Cambridge: Cambridge University Press.
Weingart, R.E. (1970) *The Logic of Divine Love: A Critical Analysis of the Soteriology of Peter Abelard*, London: Clarendon.

KURT A. RICHARDSON

ACTS

'A storm center' (van Unnik 1966). 'Shifting sands' (Talbert 1976). 'A fruitful field' (Gasque 1988). These are but a few of the epithets used to describe the scholarly interpretation of the Acts of the apostles in the twentieth century. The spate of recent commentaries in English and collected essays suggests continued and sustained interest in Acts (commentaries: Johnson 1992; Polhill 1992; Barrett 1994, 1998; Talbert 1997; Fitzmyer 1998; Witherington 1998; collected essays: Tyson 1988; Keathley 1990; Richard 1990; Neyrey 1991; Parsons and Tyson 1992; Marconi *et al.* 1993; Witherington 1996; Marshall and Peterson 1998; Thompson and Phillips 1998; Moessner 1999; Verheyden 1999).

Since van Unnik, surveyors of the Lukan landscape typically categorize the scholarship on Acts in terms of interest in Luke the historian, Luke the theologian, and more recently Luke the *litterateur*. The move from form and source criticism (Dibelius *et al.*), which focused on Luke as a historian, to redaction criticism (Conzelmann *et al.*), which focused on Luke as a theologian, to the newer literary studies, which focus on Luke as a creative writer (Tannehill *et al.*), have been well documented in the surveys of Acts research (see esp. Powell 1991). The attention Acts has generated has not always been positive. As a historian, though he had his defenders (see Ramsay, Gasque, Marshall, Hemer), Luke was routinely criticized for his unreliable depictions of various characters (e.g., P. Vielhauer on Paul) and events (e.g., J. Knox on the Jerusalem conference). As a theologian, Luke was accused, among other things, of advocating a triumphalistic 'theology of glory' that was inferior to Paul's 'theology of the cross' and of replacing the pristine eschatology of early Christianity with a three-stage salvation history – an 'early Catholicism' shaped by the delay of the Parousia that represented a degenerative step away from the primitive Christian kerygma, proclaiming the imminent return of Jesus (so Käsemann). Even Luke's abilities as a writer have been called into question from time to time (see Dawsey 1986).

This rubric of Luke as historian, theologian, and writer remains useful for describing works that have appeared particularly within the last decade or so of the twentieth century, albeit with certain new nuances. Given the sea of literature and the already very competent surveys of scholarship, this article is focused mainly (although not exclusively) on book-length studies of Acts or Luke/Acts (but not Luke alone) that have appeared (including some 1987 publications) since Gasque's 1988 summary or research was written. The article also overlaps to some limited extent with Mark Powell's fine summary of Acts scholarship (see Powell 1991).

1 Luke the historian

While the question of the identity of the author of the Lukan writings no longer invigorates scholarly discussion as it once did, there are still those who give ample attention to defending or refuting the traditional attribution to Luke the physician (see the discussion in Fitzmyer 1989, 1998). Others have departed from the traditional question of authorship to examine the social location of the implied author of Luke/Acts (Robbins in Neyrey 1991) or, accepting the common authorship of Luke and Acts, have probed its implications for the study of the genre, literary patterns, and theological themes of the Lukan writings (Parsons and Pervo 1993).

Though strictly speaking not an issue pertaining to Luke as a historian, the status of the text of Acts is nonetheless a historical question. Most scholars, and especially those responsible for the critical editions of the Greek New Testament, are still persuaded of the priority of the Alexandrian text over the so-called 'Western' text in establishing the 'original' text of Acts. Still, a flurry of activity from a variety of sometimes-conflicting perspectives has served to challenge the *opinio communis* (see Delobel in Verheyden 1999). Among these, the most noteworthy contributions are those by Boismard and Lamouille (of their many contributions, see esp. Boismard and Lamouille 1990) and W.A. Strange (Strange 1992). Though there are many differences in terms of method and argumentation, both works conclude that the Western text reflects a corrupted tradition of a version of Acts earlier than that represented by the Alexandrian text, thus reviving in part a proposal made over a century ago by F. Blass that the Western text ultimately comes from the hand of Luke himself. Though these and other works that question the scholarly received tradition have been (and no doubt will continue to be) subjected to vigorous critique, they represent the vitality of the debate over an issue that is far from settled.

Nor can the question of Luke's historical reliability be considered resolved. On the one hand, are those many erudite scholars who continue, in the spirit of William Ramsay, to defend Luke's reliability. In addition to Hemer (Hemer 1990) and Witherington (Witherington 1998), many of the contributors to the multivolume series on *The Book of Acts in Its First Century Setting* have as one of their goals the defense of Luke's historical accuracy (see Winter 1993–1998). On the other hand, Gerd Lüdemann, in his attempts to separate tradition from redaction in Acts, has claimed that while Luke preserves individual and isolated facts accurately, much of his chronology and framework is secondary, and Lüdemann rejects out of hand all reports of the miraculous (Lüdemann 1989). Such presuppositions on the part of the interpreter inevitably and profoundly shape the conclusions drawn about this historicity of a narrative like Acts (see appendix in Talbert 1997). Critical evaluation of the historicity of Acts continues with the work of the Acts Seminar, a group of scholars convened by the late Robert Funk and the Westar Institute, to evaluate the reliability of early Christian history as depicted by Luke, in ways analogous to what the Jesus Seminar (sponsored by the same institute) attempted with the historical Jesus.

More recently, some have turned away from questions of history in Acts to the place of Acts in history. In a collection of essays edited by Jerome Neyrey (Neyrey 1991), various contributors examine sociological aspects of the Lukan writings, from the role of ritual and ceremony in Acts to the significance of the social relations in preindustrial cities or the countryside to the importance of the social values of honor/shame for reading the Lukan writings. Others have employed sociological criticism to examine Luke/Acts as a document of 'political legitimation' for the early Christian movement (Esler 1987). Still others have examined the cultural context of Acts for understanding such topics as magic and miracle in Luke/Acts (Garrett 1989). These studies have profitably used the narrative of (Luke and) Acts to open up the sometimes unspoken cultural codes, mores, and values that nevertheless pervade the text and shape our reception of it. Finally, others have attempted to situate (Luke/)Acts in its larger literary and intellectual environment (see e.g., Alexander 1993; Squires 1993). Attention to the reception of Acts in subsequent history, especially in the 'premodern' period, also fits under this rubric of 'Acts in history' (one eagerly awaits, for example, the contribution on Acts in the 'Ancient Commentary on Scripture' series). The relationship between Acts and history is much more broadly conceived these days than it once was.

2 Luke the theologian

Studies on various aspects of Lukan theology continue to pour out, confirming C. Talbert's observation a quarter century ago that H. Conzelmann's theological synthesis no longer held a consensus among scholars (Talbert 1976). Conzelmann's failure has not totally discouraged others from making similar attempts to synthesize Luke's theology (e.g., Fitzmyer 1989; Jervell 1996; Pokorný 1998), although far more prevalent are studies that deal with specific aspects of Luke's theology (Marshall and Peterson 1998; see the bibliography in Verheyden 1999: 22–45). One notes also that these studies employ a plethora of methodologies to characterize Luke's theology.

The end of the twentieth century has also witnessed a turn in some quarters of biblical scholarship from theology understood in redaction-critical terms to ideology shaped by advocacy criticism. This turn has had its impact on Acts scholarship. Feminist scholars have examined anew the Lukan writings for their perspective on gender. In *The Women's Bible Commentary*, Jane Schaberg reaches the radical conclusion that Luke (and by extension Acts) is the 'most dangerous book in all the Bible' (Schaberg in Newsom and Ringe 1992). This view is balanced by more judicious studies of gender in Luke (in addition to various articles, see the book-length studies by Seim 1994; Reimer 1996; Arlandson 1997). The question of Luke's 'anti-Judaism' has been taken up again by Joseph Tyson (Tyson 1999). Though calling Tyson himself an 'advocacy critic' would be a misnomer, he does chronicle the anti-Jewish (both intentional and inadvertent) attitudes prevalent in much of the history of Lukan scholarship, though given Luke's characterization of the Christian movement in Acts as a Jewish sect one might rightly question Tyson's assertion that Luke himself was anti-Jewish in any modern sense of the term. Again, interest in the theological shape of Acts has not diminished, but there is little agreement on the most appropriate methods for describing that theology and for assessing its hermeneutical value for contemporary communities.

3 Luke the writer

The explosion of new literary approaches in New Testament studies that began in the 1980s has certainly left its mark on the study of Acts. In the last decade alone, too many narrative and literary-critical studies have appeared to enumerate (but see especially Tannehill 1990; Gowler 1991; Darr 1992; Kurz 1993; Shepherd 1994; Brawley 1995; Matson 1996). Despite the widely acknowledged achievements of these studies in refocusing our attention on the narrative as a whole (and the attendant issues of plot, characterization, and intertextuality, *inter alia*), the limitations are well known as well. Drawing its methodology largely from the secular field of literary criticism, narrative criticism uses terminology to describe techniques and literary phenomena that might be appropriate for nineteenth- and twentieth-century novels, but not necessarily appropriate for first-century narratives. This problem is often acknowledged but seldom addressed.

Given this oft-cited criticism of applying modern theory to ancient narrative, it is surprising, perhaps, to note the lack of studies that attend to Acts from the perspective of ancient rhetorical criticism. Such studies are not altogether missing, especially on the speeches in Acts (Soards 1994; Witherington 1998). These studies (as well as numerous articles) have advanced convincing arguments regarding Luke's knowledge of rhetorical conventions in the speeches. Thus, it would appear that studies that read the narrative portions of Acts in light of ancient rhetoric, and especially in light of ancient *progymnasmata* (elementary rhetorical exercises for speaking and writing), would hold great promise in further illuminating Luke's rhetorical strategies employed not only in the composition of the Third Gospel (see, e.g., Robbins in Moessner 1999; and O'Fearghail 1991), but Acts as well.

The study of the author of Acts as a writer continues to include consideration of its genre, although no consensus has been reached. In addition to those who maintain that Acts represents anything from a *sui generis* to a *genus mixtum*, advocates for (Luke/)Acts as ancient biography (see recently Talbert 1988), some form of ancient historiography (Sterling 1992), or a kind of ancient novel (Pervo 1987) can still be found. Finally, while the search for oral and/or written sources in Acts has subsided, the interest in Luke's use of scripture as a key to his hermeneutic and theology has increased (in addition to Brawley 1995 and Moessner 1999 already cited, see Bock 1987; Evans and Sanders 1993). How best to appreciate Luke's literary prowess is no less contested than are issues of history and theology in relation to the Lukan writings.

4 Conclusion

Long ago W.C. van Unnik rightly warned against the biblical scholar playing the role of prophet in trying to predict the future shape of Lukan studies (van Unnik 1966). Given what transpired in the intervening decades between van Unnik's caveat and now, his words seem even more prudent. Nevertheless, it is safe to say that work on Luke as historian, theologian, and writer, with all the mutations noted above, will continue. Studies that explore the rhetorical shape of social conventions (e.g., hospitality, friendship, and benefaction) in terms of how they illuminate Lukan theological perspectives will be especially welcome.

References and further reading

Alexander, Loveday (1993) *The Preface to Luke's Gospel: Literary Convention and Social Context in Luke 1.1–4 and Acts 1.1*, SNTSMS 78, Cambridge: Cambridge University Press.

Arlandson, J.M. (1997) *Women, Class, and Society in Early Christianity: Models from Luke-Acts*, Peabody, MA: Hendrickson.

Barrett, C.K. (1994, 1998) *Acts*, ICC, 2 Vols., Edinburgh: T.&T. Clark.

Bock, Darrell L. (1987) *Proclamation from Prophecy and Pattern: Lucan Old Testament Christology*, JSNTSup 12, Sheffield: Sheffield Academic Press.

Boismard, M.-É. and A. Lamouille (1990) *Les Actes des deux Apôtres*, 3 Vols., Paris: Gabalda.

Brawley, Robert L. (1995) *Text to Text Pours Forth Speech: Voices of Scripture in Luke-Acts*, Bloomington: Indiana University Press.

Darr, John A. (1992) *On Character Building: The Reader and the Rhetoric of Characterization in Luke-Acts*, Louisville, KY: Westminster/John Knox.

Dawsey, James (1986) *The Lukan Voice*, Macon, GA: Mercer University Press.

Esler, Phillip (1987) *Community and Gospel in Luke-Acts: The Social and Political Motivations in Lucan Theology*, SNTSMS 57, Cambridge: Cambridge University Press.

Evans, Craig and James A. Sanders (1993) *Luke and Scripture: The Function of Sacred Tradition in Luke-Acts*, Minneapolis: Augsburg Fortress Press.

Fitzmyer, Joseph A. (1989) *Luke the Theologian: Aspects of His Teaching*, New York: Paulist Press.

—— (1998) *The Acts of the Apostles*, AB 31, New York: Doubleday.

Garrett, Susan R. (1989) *The Demise of the Devil: Magic and the Demonic in Luke's Writings*, Minneapolis: Fortress Press.

Gasque, W. Ward (1988) 'A Fruitful Field: Recent Study of the Acts of the Apostles,' *Interpretation* 42: 117–31.

Gowler, David B. (1991) *Host, Guest, Enemy and Friend: Portraits of the Pharisees in Luke and Acts*, ESEC 2, New York: Peter Lang.

Hemer, Colin J. (1990) *Book of Acts in the Setting of Hellenistic History*, WUNT 49, Winona Lake, IN: Eisenbrauns.

Jervell, Jacob (1996) *The Theology of the Acts of the Apostles*, Cambridge: Cambridge University Press.

Johnson, Luke Timothy (1992) *Acts*, SP 5, Collegeville, MN: Liturgical Press.

Keathley, Naymond H. (ed.) (1990) *With Steadfast Purpose: Essays in Honor of Henry Jackson Flanders*, Waco, TX: Baylor University Press.

Kurz, William S. (1993) *Reading Luke-Acts: Dynamics of Biblical Narrative*, Louisville, KY: Westminster/John Knox.

Lüdemann, Gerd (1989) *Early Christianity according to the Traditions in Acts: A Commentary*, Philadelphia: Fortress Press.

Marconi, Gilberto *et al.* (eds.) (1993) *Luke and Acts*, New York: Paulist Press.

Marshall, I. Howard and David Peterson (eds.) (1998) *Witness to the Gospel: The Theology of Acts*, Grand Rapids, MI: Eerdmans.

Matson, David L. (1996) *Household Conversion Narratives in Acts: Pattern and Interpretation*, JSNTSup 123, Sheffield: Sheffield Academic Press.

Moessner, David P. (ed.) (1999) *Jesus and the Heritage of Israel: Luke's Narrative Claim upon Israel's Legacy*, Harrisburg, PA: Trinity Press International.

Newsom, Carol A. and Sharon Ringe (eds.) (1992) *The Women's Bible Commentary*, Louisville, KY: Westminster/John Knox.

Neyrey, Jerome (ed.) (1991) *The Social World of Luke-Acts*, Peabody, MA: Hendrickson.

O'Fearghail, Fearghus (1991) *The Introduction to Luke-Acts, A Study of the Role of Lk1.1–4.44 in the Composition of Luke's Two-Volume Work*, AnBib 126, Rome: Pontifical Biblical Institute.

Parsons, Mikeal C. and Richard I. Pervo (1993) *Rethinking the Unity of Luke and Acts*, Minneapolis: Ausburg/Fortress Press.

Parsons, Mikeal C. and Joseph B. Tyson (eds.) (1992) *Cadbury, Knox, and Talbert: American Contributions to the Study of Acts*, Atlanta: Scholars Press.

Pervo, Richard I. (1987) *Profit with Delight: The Literary Genre of the Acts of the Apostles*, Philadelphia: Fortress Press.

Pokorný, P. (1998) *Theologie der Lukanischen Schriften*, FRLANT 174, Göttingen: Vadenhoeck & Ruprecht.

Polhill, John B. (1992) *Acts*, NAC, Nashville: Broadman Press.

Powell, Mark A. (1991) *What Are They Saying About Acts?* New York: Paulist Press.

Reimer, I. Richter (1996) *Women in the Acts of the Apostles*, Minneapolis: Fortress Press.

Richard, Earl (ed.) (1990) *New Views on Luke and Acts*, Collegeville, MN: Liturgical Press.

Rothschild, Clare K. (2004) *Luke-Acts and the Rhetoric of History: An Investigation of Early Christian Historiography*, WUNT 2.175, Tübingen: Mohr Siebeck.

Seim, Turid Karlsen (1994) *The Double Message: Patterns of Gender in Luke-Acts*, Nashville: Abingdon Press.

Shepherd, William H. Jr. (1994) *The Narrative Function of the Holy Spirit as a Character in Luke-Acts*, SBLDS 147, Atlanta: Scholars Press.

Soards, Marion L. (1994) *The Speeches in Acts: Their Content, Context, and Concerns*, Louisville, KY: Westminster/John Knox.

Squires, John T. (1993) *The Plan of God in Luke-Acts*, SNTSMS 76, Cambridge: Cambridge University Press.

Sterling, Gregory L. (1992) *Historiography and Self-Definition: Josephos, Luke-Acts and Apologetic Historiography*, NovTSup 64, Leiden: Brill.

Strange, W.A. (1992) *The Problem of the Text of Acts*, SNTSMS 71, Cambridge: Cambridge University Press.

Talbert, Charles H. (1976) 'Shifting Sands: The Recent Study of the Gospel of Luke,' *Interpretation* 30: 381–95.

—— (1988) 'Once Again: Gospel Genre,' *Semeia* 43: 53–73.

—— (1997) *Reading Acts: A Literary and Theological Commentary on the Acts of the Apostles*, New York: Crossroad.

—— (2003) *Reading Luke-Acts in its Mediterranean Milieu*, NovTSup 107, Leiden: Brill.

Tannehill, Robert C. (1990) *The Narrative Unity of Luke-Acts: A Literary Interpretation*, Vol. 2, *The Acts of the Apostles*, Minneapolis: Fortress Press.

Thompson, Richard P. and Thomas E. Phillips (eds.) (1998) *Literary Studies in Luke-Acts: Essays in Honor of Joseph B. Tyson*, Macon, GA: Mercer University Press.

Tyson, Joseph B. (ed.) (1988) *Luke-Acts and the Jewish People: Eight Critical Perspectives*, Minneapolis: Augsburg/Fortress Press.

—— (1999) *Luke, Judaism, and the Scholars: Critical Approaches to Luke-Acts*, Columbia, SC: University of South Carolina Press.

Tuckett, Christopher M. (ed.) (1996) *Luke's Literary Achievement: Collected Essays*, JSNTSup 116, Sheffield: Sheffield Academic Press.

Van Unnik, W.C. (1966) 'Luke-Acts: A Storm Center in Contemporary Scholarship,' pp. 15–32 in *Studies in Luke-Acts*, Leander E. Keck and J. Louis Martyn (eds.), Philadelphia: Fortress Press.

Verheyden, Jozef (ed.) (1999) *The Unity of Luke-Acts*, Leuven: Leuven University Press/Peeters.

Winter, Bruce (ed.) (1993–1998) *The Book of Acts in Its First Century Setting*, 6 Vols., Grand Rapids: Eerdmans.

Witherington, Ben (1998) *The Acts of the Apostles: A Socio-Rhetorical Commentary*, Grand Rapids: Eerdmans.

—— (ed.) (1996) *History, Literature and Society in the Book of Acts*, Cambridge: Cambridge University Press.

MIKEAL C. PARSONS

ALLEGORICAL INTERPRETATION

Allegory is a Greek word that takes its roots from ἄλλα and ἀγορεύω (literally): to speak other things; in a technical sense ἀλληγορέω means: to speak or interpret allegorically.

Greek philosophers have used allegorical interpretation to explain and justify troubling passages in Greek poetry, particularly in the works of Homer and Hesiod. In the classical period other terms, such as ὑπόνοια (the underlying meaning or deeper sense), were used to express this method of interpretation, and only in the Hellenistic period did the terms ἀλληγορέω, ἀλληγορία, and related words emerge. Another term is metaphor (μεταφορά), which means literally: a transference (to a new sense). The usual distinction between a metaphor and an allegory is that the allegory represents a sequence of metaphors or a continuation of metaphoric speech (see Quintilian, *Inst. Or.* 8.6.44; Clement of Alexandria, *Strom.* VI 126.1–4).

Early attempts to allegorize can be found in the works of the Milesian geographer and history writer Hecataeus and in the writings of Theagenes of Rhegium, both dating to the end of the sixth century BC. The fragmentary remains of their works contain allegorical interpretations of the battle of the gods (θεομαχία) and the struggle between the gods and the elements (see Diels and Kranz 1951–1954). Theagenes interpreted the names of the gods as the various elements of nature;

9

thus Apollo, Helios, and Hephaistos stand for fire; Poseidon stands for water; and Hera for air. Nature and cosmology continued to be suitable subjects for allegorical interpretation also in later times.

A second fruitful domain for allegorical exploration was the area of ethics. Anaxagoras may have been one of the first to mention that Homeric poetry was, in fact, about 'virtue and justice' (see Diogenes Laertius 2.3.11). Metrodorus of Lampsakos can be considered the most important philosopher of this early stage of allegorical interpretation. He compared the Homeric gods with the foundation of the natural order and the orderly arrangement of the elements. He also interpreted the Trojan heroes allegorically, so that Agamemnon stands for the upper regions of the air, Achilles for the sun, Helen for the earth, Paris for the air, and Hector for the moon (see Diels and Kranz 1951–1954). Metrodorus continued to influence later philosophy, particularly the Stoa.

Although Plato did not deny that mythology could have a deeper meaning, he did not give allegorical interpretation a strong endorsement in his search for the truth. In the *Phaedrus* Socrates brings up the story of Oreithyia, who was carried off by Boreas; he prefers to understand the myth in a rational way, just as he wants to give a rational explanation to the Centaurs, the Chimera, the Gorgons, or other 'extraordinary and strange creatures.' He considers nonrational speculation a 'rustic sort of wisdom,' to which he does not want to apply his mind (see *Phaedrus* 229e).

Allegorization takes on an increased significance in the Stoa. There is once again a tendency to interpret gods and other divine beings in terms of cosmological powers, as seen, for example, in Zeno, who interprets the Titans as elements of the cosmos. Not only Hesiod's cosmology but also stories of Greek heroes offered fertile ground for allegorization; the popular figure of a godman like Heracles gave ample opportunity to allegorize, as the fragments of Cleanthes show (von Arnim 1964). Chrysippus himself offers an abundance of allegorical material, and he often intertwines it with etymologies. He interprets, for example, Rhea as land (γῆ), from which the waters stream (ῥέω). The combination of allegory, etymology, and number speculation is characteristic of later forms of allegorical techniques, particularly as they develop in the works of Jewish and early Christian allegorists, such as Philo, Clement, and Origen.

Two important sources for our knowledge of allegory in antiquity are the works of Cornutus and a certain Heraclitus or Heraclides, who was a grammarian. Cornutus (first century AD) was bilingual, writing both in Latin and Greek. In his *Summary of the Traditions concerning Greek Theology*, he follows Chrysippus and reflects the principles of Stoic criticism of myths, which he explains allegorically.

Following their founder, some of the later Platonists continued to reject allegorical interpretation, but others actively began to engage in it. Although Porphyrius allegorized extensively in his works *About the Cave of the Nymphs in the Odyssey* and *Homeric Inquiries*, he nevertheless attacked the Christians vigorously for their way of using allegories. Even in the fifth century, Neoplatonic philosophers, such as Proclos, who had a great influence on later medieval thought, continued to use allegorical techniques.

Even before Philo, Jewish apologists had used the allegorical method on a limited scale. The fragments of Aristobulus and the *Letter of Aristeas* show influence from Stoic allegories, whether in their commentaries on the Pentateuch in general or in discussions of individual food laws. The pseudepigraphical work *Sapientia Salomonis*, which may have stemmed from Alexandria, shows similar Stoic influence.

Philo forms an important turning point for the use of allegory, since he represents both the end of one tradition and the beginning of another. Like the Stoics, he uses allegory both for interpretations of creation and cosmogeny and for explorations of ethical issues. While most of the works of his predecessors, most notably Aristobulus, are known only in fragmentary form, the majority of Philo's treatises have survived. Philo is also a pioneer in providing a theoretical framework for the use of allegory. In his account of a Jewish sect, the Therapeutae, he describes how they interpreted the underlying or deeper meaning (ὑπόνοια) of sacred scriptures through allegories. They regarded the whole law as resembling a living creature, with its literal disposition as its body and with its invisible meaning stored in its words as its soul. The rational soul starts to contemplate the things that are akin to itself, and by bringing them back to memory, it is able to view the invisible through the visible (*De Vita Contemplativa* 78). This passage shows how strongly this way of thinking was influenced by Platonic thought.

Although in the above-mentioned passage Philo describes this process of allegory as coming from the Therapeutae, the system resembles closely his own way of interpreting scripture. In other parts of his work he explains this process with different words and different images: the literal meanings of the sacred text resemble shadows of bodies, whose meanings represent true realities (*De Confusione Linguarum* 190). Philo's interpretations exploited every detail of the biblical text, and in addition they were linked to a Platonic way of thinking with the rational soul at its center. The soul reports its experiences to memory, and through memory it starts to recognize and to view the invisible realities. Platonic speculation may have been a new element in the interpretation of scripture, one which distinguishes Philo from his predecessors.

In addition to Platonic speculation, Philo also used traditional allegorical techniques. One is number speculation, another is etymology, both of which he fully exploits. He may have found some of his etymologies elsewhere, since they turn up in independent traditions, such as rabbinic sources. Philo may have created others to solve a specific textual problem or to explore a certain theme. Yet other etymologies have to do with translations from Hebrew or Aramaic into Greek. In his discourse every detail of the biblical text counted, and Philo used whatever was convenient for his argument. For this reason it is virtually impossible to assess where all these materials came from.

Changes of names, such as from Abram to Abraham, were for him indicators of more powerful meanings; a small letter change could stand for greater things; visible realities implied intellectual realities (*De Mutatione Nominum* 65). Another favorite subject in Philo's allegorical treatment was the question of anthropomorphic language in the Bible when referring to God. Philo inherited this theme from his predecessors. He pointed out that the divine nature which presents itself to us as visible and comprehensible was in reality invisible and incomprehensible (*De Confusione Linguarum* 138). According to his view, anthropomorphic expressions of God had no other meaning than to explain the supreme being to the human condition, which needs images because of the limitations of human understanding.

Philo's influence did not last in Judaism but was transmitted through the Christian Alexandrian authors, Clement and Origen (see below). The allegorical technique was also used by Philo's contemporary, Paul, as the allegory of Hagar and Sarah in his letter to the Galatians shows (Gal. 4:24–26), and it was equally current among the rabbis. The most famous among them was Rabbi Aqiba, who died about 100 years after Philo (AD 135) and wrote about the mystical relationship between God and Israel in his interpretation of the *Song of Songs*. The latter remained a favorite subject for allegorical interpretation, although not for Philo, who never referred to it. The main focus for his allegories was, after all, the Pentateuch.

A number of second-century Christian apologists, such as Aristides, Tatian, and Athenagoras, opposed allegorical treatment as it had been practiced by Stoic philosophers and rejected the distinction between physical and ethical allegories. Other authors of that period, such as Pseudo-Barnabas and Justin Martyr, employed allegory in a limited way. The argument of using allegories also became a polemical tool, used both by pagan authors against Christians (see Celsus or Porphyrius) or by Christians against their opponents (Origen, Eusebius, Gregory Nazianzus, and Augustine).

In Valentinian circles the application of allegory was of prime importance, as is clear not only from their opponents, such as Irenaeus and Tertullian, but also from direct sources, such as Heracleon's commentary on the Gospel of John. This work was extensively quoted by Origen and was influential on his own treatment of that Gospel. As in Philo's allegorical commentaries, minute details of the biblical text, such as breathing marks, commas, periods, and grammatical case inflections, were all important springboards for Heracleon to plunge into the deeper meaning of a text.

Philo's legacy continued primarily through Christian authors. Clement, who flourished 150 years after Philo's death, is the first known to have quoted him. The allegories that he took over from Philo are connected with stories of the LXX, such as Hagar and Sarah or the Life of Moses. In addition, Clement's treatment of the themes of anthropomorphic expressions of God, knowledge and wisdom, ascent and contemplation and his allegorizing of biblical scenes in terms of virtuous life often run parallel with Philo's allegories, although they are edited and reworked for new purposes.

Both Clement and Origen are successors of Philo in the sense that they combine allegorical interpretation with Platonizing speculation. Origen, however, represents Philo's legacy best and brings allegorical techniques to new heights. Both Philo and Origen present an almost unlimited range of allegorical speculation. Origen includes by-now traditional elements, such as etymologies, number speculations, and anthropomorphisms. In his commentaries and homilies, he touches on an almost unprecedented number of biblical passages, and allegorical treatment forms an intrinsic part of his explorations. In addition, the New Testament stories and parables represent new elements, which he used to support and confirm the allegories on the LXX.

Like his Jewish predecessor, Origen gave his hermeneutics a theoretical basis, which he formulated in the fourth book of his *De Principis*. He also distinguished between the body and soul of the scriptures. The distinction can even be tripartite; the body represents the grammatical, literal, and historical sense, the soul the moral sense, and the spirit the allegorical and mystical senses of the scriptures. Origen gave these concepts a new meaning by putting them in the broad context of the history of salvation. His theory is that, just as Christ came concealed in a body, the whole divine scripture has been 'embodied' (*sicut Christus celatus venit in corpore . . . sic est omnis scriptura divina incorporata*). Since Origen, this concept and this terminology have had a wide diffusion and are inextricably linked to the history of the interpretation of scripture. The stages of scriptural interpretation are for Origen (as for Clement before him) related to the various stages of the faithful; the more advanced are more apt by their training, interest, and way of life to grasp the deeper meaning of the truth.

Origen had many followers in Alexandria itself and in the East, although their interpretation of scripture often balanced the literal with the spiritual sense more than Origen himself had done; one can think of authors, such as Methodius of Olympus and the Cappadocians; Gregory of Nyssa in particular used the method in his

Commentary on the Canticum. In Alexandria, Cyril favored the allegorical method in his interpretation of the LXX, and Didymus the Blind usually started his biblical commentaries with a literal explanation but subsequently went on to allegorical interpretation.

The most strongly opposed to the 'Alexandrian' allegorical tradition was the school of exegesis in Antioch, founded in the third century by Lucian of Samosata. Antiochene tradition favored a more historical and grammatical approach and sometimes targeted the methods of Origen directly, as the works of Eustathius of Antioch show (see *De Engastrimutho*). Others in the Antiochene tradition were Ephrem, who founded his own school in Edessa, and Diodore of Tarsus, the teacher of John Chrysostom. Diodore offered a substitute for allegorical interpretation by introducing a typological model, in which the historical sense of the Hebrew Bible was brought in line with passages that spoke about Christ and his kingdom. Unfortunately Diodore's treatise entitled *What is the Difference between Contemplation and Allegory* has been lost. In another lost work Theodore of Mopsuestia wrote extensively against the 'Allegorists,' and Chrysostom was also influenced by this tradition.

In the West literal interpretation of scripture remained strong, and Hilary of Poitiers may have been an exception in his use of allegory (see his *Commentary on Matthew*). Ambrose, who was strongly influenced by Philo, is another example of someone who applied the allegorical method to exegetical works. Jerome switched his preferences according to his changing sympathies for Origen and his works. Augustine was not opposed to the allegorical method and even maintained that allegory was sometimes the only means by which the real sense could be transmitted (*De Doctrina Christiana* 3.5.9). In general he applied the historical sense to his biblical commentaries, while the allegorical sense was more present in his *Homilies* and the so-called *Ennarationes*. Later authors, such as Eucherius of Lyon and Gregory the Great, made extensive use of allegory. A work that can be considered pure allegory is the *Psychmachia* of Prudentius, which presents Christian asceticism as an allegory of spiritual warfare.

References and further reading

Barr, J. (1966) 'Typology and Allegory,' pp. 103–48 in *Old and New in Interpretation: A Study of the Two Testaments*, London: SCM Press.

Bloomfield, M.W. (ed.) (1981) *Allegory, Myth and Symbol*, Cambridge, MA: Harvard University Press.

Dawson, D. (1992) *Allegorical Readers and Cultural Revision in Ancient Alexandria*, Berkeley: University of California Press.

Diels, H. and W. Kranz (1951–1954) *Die Fragmente der Vorsokratiker*, Berlin: Weidmann.

Geffcken, T. (1908–1927) 'Allegory, Allegoric Interpretation,' *ERE* 1, 327–31.

Hanson, R.P.C. (1959) *Allegory and Event*, London: SCM Press.

Joosen, J.C. and J.H. Waszink (1950–) 'Allegorese,' *RAC* 1, 283–93.

Kurtz, G. (1982) *Metapher, Allegorie, Symbol*, Göttingen: Vandenhoeck & Ruprecht.

Lamberton, R. (1986) *Homer the Theologian*, Berkeley: University of California Press.

Tate, J. (1927) 'The Beginnings of Greek Allegory,' *Classical Review* 41: 214–15.

von Arnim, H.F.A. (1964) *Stoicorum vetrum fragmenta*, Stuttgart: Teubner.

ANNEWIES VAN DEN HOEK

ANTHROPOLOGY AND INTERPRETATION

If the mid-eighteenth century roughly marked the beginning of the modern critical study of the Old and New Testaments, it also brought the attempt by biblical scholars to use anthropology in a more rigorous and methodological way than ever before. The German Old Testament scholar J.D. Michaelis, who sponsored numerous expeditions to the Middle East, epitomized the new spirit. Although he had set out to bring a comprehensive categorization of plants, animals, or types of diseases mentioned in the Old Testament, his remit ranged wider in that he sought to understand the significance of sociocultural conditions behind the scriptures in order to put biblical interpretation on a firm scientific footing. If, he argued, the Old Testament provided the major source for knowledge of ancient Hebrew law and language, and the society of ancient Hebrew and Jewish history in general, then, in turn, an understanding of the scriptures could be enriched by a detailed knowledge of its social and historical contexts (Michaelis 1762).

The quest of those such as Michaelis marked what might be regarded as the first of two 'revolutions' in the anthropological interpretation of the Bible. It was a revolution identified by the increasing legitimacy of anthropology. This proved evident in the employment of expanding subdisciplines in the field: palaeontology (how populations have evolved), biological anthropology, and psychological anthropology among them. All contributed in their own way to a greater understanding of the Hebrew and Greek texts. However, it was perhaps cultural and social anthropology which advanced the greatest claim to legitimacy. The emphasis was increasingly upon the study of historical, political, and economic circumstances, of customs, folklore, and beliefs, art and material culture, and on their symbolic meaning. The value of the growing discipline was in the way it could contribute to a greater appreciation of core themes in the Old and New Testaments.

It could show, for example, how throughout their history the messianic hope of the Jewish people was generated by particular historical contexts, which had helped them to survive under the unique conditions of the Middle-Eastern world and greatly enriched their folklore with messianic legends and stories.

Another aspect of the sociocultural approach carved out by those like Michaelis, which increasingly grew in prevalence, was its comparative and cross-cultural dimension. Michaelis had drawn comparisons between the Arabian Bedouin of his time and the Hebrew patriarchs and, likewise, between levirate marriage in ancient society and the arrangements of tribes in North America, Greenland, and Mongolia. This comparative endeavor was to be taken up in earnest by others. The large majority were nonbiblical scholars with no great theological interest. Rather, their remit was to throw light on general principles of social organization and to show how even the most apparently exotic customs across the globe are simply ways of coping with common human problems which provide distinct social functions.

It was the Old Testament which initially proved most compelling for comparative studies and a wealth of anthropological work related to certain parts of the Hebrew text. Typical was Hubert and Mauss' discussion of the universal function of sacrifice. They concluded that there were clear parallels to be drawn between Judaism and Hinduism in the practice of this ritual. In short, both seemed to amount to an attempt at communication with the divine and were a principal basis through which social laws were given moral authority (Hubert and Mauss 1899). The implication was that religious practices, hitherto unquestionably accepted as uniquely divinely inspired, were exposed as having a universal purpose. These speculations led to an inevitable backlash from conservative theological quarters that feared, above all, that the parallels drawn between Judaism and other religions profoundly devalued the scriptures. Nonetheless, deference to a developing discipline grew for the majority of scholars involved in biblical interpretation. Its indispensability and legitimacy was symbolized by Rogerson's classic work *Anthropology and the Old Testament*, which was written not by an anthropologist but by a biblical scholar who admitted to have 'done a good deal of anthropological reading' (1978: 2).

During the early 1970s, the application of anthropology to biblical studies emerged with a new vigor and authority. It was the beginning of a second revolution and one which confirmed the increasing appeal of the social sciences for biblical scholars. Their apparent preoccupation with the field since that time has largely resulted from a general disillusionment with previous historical studies, which were seen to be limited in scope or theologically motivated. Hence, over the last three decades, the attempts to enhance an understanding

of the social world of the Bible has moved increasingly from the radical fringes of the discipline of biblical studies closer to the mainstream. This second revolution has gone further than merely attempting to probe the aspects of the social world which were not mentioned in the biblical text. Rather, the growing appeal of anthropology, as well as sociology and archaeology for that matter, has been in focusing upon some of the deficiencies in the texts as sources for their own social world. In short, it is increasingly argued that a theological interpretation of the scriptures must be closely identified with understanding the social context in which they are produced (Esler 1995).

The pioneering works of George Mendenhall (1962, 1973) and Norman Gottwald (1979) on the history of Israel were crucial in the early stages of the new movement. Typically, they concentrated upon the more recent anthropological and sociological studies to query numerous taken-for-granted views which had informed the long-accepted account of early Israelite history, above all, the nature of social and political organization and the relationship with Palestine, and the connection of nomadism to sedentary and state societies. The enterprise, for these scholars, was to furnish the tools for reconstructing the whole social system of ancient Israel, which thus complemented purely historical studies. The challenge was to establish clear models of social organization including the functions, roles, institutions, customs, norms, judicial and religious organization, military and political structures, and the materialist aspects of culture which provided insight into the scriptures. Similarly, New Testament scholars also began to apply social-scientific approaches in innovating ways to understand the biblical texts. Those such as Holmberg (1990) administered a more challenging anthropological model to the New Testament in order to expose the meaning of the word in terms of the first-century cultural conditions of Palestine and the Mediterranean world in which they were originally written.

The second revolution also stirred its critics and controversies. The direction of much recent work which concentrated on the social world behind the scriptures tended to draw a sharp distinction between historical reconstruction and theological understandings. This brought considerable unease in many quarters, with some pleading for a greater dialogue between what appeared to be the two separating worlds of theology and anthropology (Arbuckle 1986). Nonetheless, the enterprise found a home particularly with more liberal-minded scholars and provided a critique, as much as an aid to an interpretation. This acceptance, however, has been marred in recent years by a far-ranging set of controversies. Perhaps above all, in keeping with the spirit of the time, a number of profound epistemological questions have come to plague the anthropological quest, and they have threatened to undermine its whole foundation. The key question has been not only how the scriptures should be interpreted, but also how the anthropological evidence should be approached. As biblical studies remain fundamentally historical they have led to interpretations which have frequently constituted ideological approaches, whether feminist, Marxist, or essentially theological. Inspired by the deconstructionist writings of Derrida (1978), the principal question became not so much how could scholars of the scriptures deal with a text that seemed to justify patriarchy or other expressions of social and political power, but whether interpretation could ever step outside the social environment in which it was itself located. The enterprise of anthropology was likewise brought into question – could the utilization of anthropological evidence be free of value orientations and cultural context? These have not, however, been insurmountable problems. Despite recent tendencies to be preoccupied with matters of theory and method, the anthropological endeavor continues to thrive and inspire the current generation of biblical scholars.

References and further reading

Arbuckle, G.A. (1986) 'Theology and Anthropology: Time for Dialogue,' *Theological Studies* 47: 428–47.

Derrida, J. (1978) *Writing and Difference*, London: Routledge.

Esler, P. (ed.) (1995) *Modelling Early Christianity: Social-scientific Studies of the New Testament in its Social Context*, London: Routledge.

Gottwald, N.K. (1979) *The Tribes of Yahweh: A Sociology of the Religion of Liberated Israel, 1250–1050 BC*, London: SCM Press.

Holmberg, B. (1990) *Sociology and the New Testament: An Appraisal*, Minneapolis: Fortress.

Hubert, H. and M. Mauss (1899) 'Essai sur la Nature et la Fonction du Sacrifice,' *Ann. Sociologique* 11, London: Cohen & West.

Mendenhall, G.E. (1962) 'The Hebrew Conquest of Palestine,' *Biblical Archaeologist* 25: 66–87.

—— (1973) *The Tenth Generation: The Origins of the Biblical Traditions*, Baltimore: Baltimore Press.

Michaelis, J.D. (1762) *Fragen an eine Gesellschaft Gelehrter Männer die auf Befehl Ihrer Majestat des Königes von Dännemark nach Arabien reisen*, Frankfurt.

Rogerson, J.W. (1978) *Anthropology and the Old Testament*, Oxford: Blackwell.

STEPHEN HUNT

THE ANTIOCHENE SCHOOL

The school of Antioch is often contrasted with the school of Alexandria. The city of Antioch in ancient Syria (present-day Turkey) was the third largest city in the Roman Empire and flourished in the late fourth and fifth centuries. The New Testament states that when early Hellenistic Jewish Christians were forced out of Jerusalem they began their Gentile mission in Antioch (Acts 11:19–30). The importance of Antioch in the very early church is witnessed by the origination of the title 'Christian,' which began in Antioch. Furthermore, early on Antioch attracted many Christian teachers as well as Gnostic teachers.

The school of Antiochene interpretation has often been characterized as a response to Alexandrian allegory. It is not a uniform interpretive approach but rather expresses a tradition of scriptural exegesis and Christology. Both schools maintained the divine inspiration and authority of scripture but differed on approaches to interpreting scripture. The Alexandrian school, characterized by Origen (c. 185–254), opened up a path for biblical science and criticism, as it attempted to fuse Greek metaphysical thinking with Christian thought. However, the breadth of interpretation was limited to an allegorical reading that appears at times to be more imposition than exposition. By contrast, the Antiochene approach recognized the importance of salvation history in its interpretation, seeing scripture as rich enough in its grammatical and historical sense. With this stress on the literal and historical scope of interpretation, it appears the Antiochene school is the pioneer of modern historical exegesis, however, that is to some extent misleading since it was far from anticipating modern interpretive approaches.

It is difficult to discern the precise influences upon the Antiochene approach to scriptural exegesis. However, possible influences include Antiochene Judaism, since Antioch was well known as a center of rabbinical studies, and the textual interpretation of one of the most preeminent Neoplatonists of the day, Iamblichus, who expanded Neoplatonist thought to include religious themes. Furthermore, there was an interrelation between the Christology of the Antiochene school, which emphasized both Christ's humanity and divinity, and the biblical exegesis of the school.

Some scholars have credited Paul of Samosata and the martyr, Lucian of Antioch, as possible third-century predecessors or founders of the Antiochene school. Paul of Samosata (bishop of Antioch 260–72) gave Antioch a distinct theological character on account of his Logos Christology, emphasizing a Christology from below, by rejecting the Son's preexistence and descent while stressing the ordinary manhood of Jesus. Paul was condemned in a council in 268 for his Christology. As a scholar, Lucian (c. 240–312) edited the Septuagint, which became the standard Old Testament text in Syria, Asia Minor, and Constantinople, and the New Testament text, which is known as the Textus Receptus. However, both Arius and Eusebius of Nicomedia professed that Lucian was influential in their doctrine, thus Lucian was implicated in the Arian controversy. Not enough is known about either Paul of Samosata or Lucian to warrant the claim that they founded the Antiochene school of interpretation.

Eustathius, bishop of Antioch, was one of the anti-Arians at Nicaea and an early opponent of allegorical exegesis. In his homily, *On the Witch of Endor and Against Allegory*, based on 1 Samuel 28, he attacked Origen's interpretation because the allegorization was based on too literal a reading of the story and it did not seriously consider the context of the story.

By the fourth century, Antioch became active, diverse, and controversial in ecclesiastical and theological matters. Diodore of Tarsus (*c.* 330–94) was a bishop in Antioch who founded a monastery and school that can be more narrowly described as Antiochene. As one of the first representatives of the school, and often regarded as the pioneer of the school, he criticized allegory because it made the Bible incomprehensible. Diodore was known for shaping the thought of two of his students, Theodore of Mopsuestia and John Chrysostom. Departing from Alexandrian Christology, Diodore insisted that exegesis focus on the narrative meaning of scripture. For instance, he saw the relation between the Old Testament and the New Testament as more of a typological than a prophetic fulfilment. Diodore also took note of historical events that occurred outside of the biblical narrative such as the peaceful intermingling of various people groups during the age of Hellenism and the Augustan peace that was preparatory for the success of the later Christian mission. Fragments remain from Diodore's commentaries on the Epistles of Paul, while modern scholars have reconstructed his commentary on Psalms.

The most notorious proponent of the Antiochene method of literal interpretation was Theodore of Mopsuestia (*c.* 350–428), who supported the Nicene orthodoxy and opposed Arians and Apollinarians. As a bishop and discerning biblical commentator and theologian, he questioned traditional prophetic and symbolic readings of the Old Testament while giving the Old Testament autonomy. He refused to read the Song of Songs as merely an allegory revealing the marriage relationship between Christ and his bride the church. Furthermore, he sought to find the relationship of the Prophets and Psalms with Israel's history. He believed that David foresaw what was to come for Israel. Consequently, he interpreted the prophecy in Psalms in relation to the whole of Israel and opposed interpreting them as enigmatic foreshadows of the Messiah with the exception of Psalms 2; 8; 45; 110, which he believed were predictions of Christ. He interpreted the Old Testament with not only a narrative meaning but also a spiritual meaning which was typological. These views combined with his Christological views were received as Nestorian, and Theodore was condemned at the second Council of Constantinople in 553. Nevertheless, Theodore's exegetical work on Paul's writings mediated the apostle for the Greek East. Few of Theodore's exegetical writings are preserved; an early commentary on Psalms is partially restored, some commentary on the minor prophets remains in Greek, and some commentary on Paul's Epistles is recorded in Latin and a Syriac translation of a commentary on John.

In *Commentary on John*, Theodore observes the distinct role of the commentator compared with the role of the preacher. The duty of the commentator is to explain the meaning of difficult words while the preacher attends to what is clear in the text for the sake of edification. In his commentaries he makes explicative notes in the midst of short paraphrases. His doctrinal ideas often contribute to his exegesis.

A contemporary of Theodore was the prolific leading orator of Antioch, the beloved John Chrysostom (*c.* 347–407). Hundreds of John's homilies are extant including sermons on Genesis, Psalms, Isaiah, Matthew, John, Acts of the Apostles, and many of Paul's writings. As a pastor he drew moral lessons using literal exegesis as opposed to allegorization while making his sermons applicable for the spiritual and ethical lives of his congregation. His sermons point to his concern for the grammatical and literary character of the text. Chrysostom, who was trained under the Roman sophist Libanius, allowed his rhetorical and literary education to inform his exegesis and as a pastor he required the Antiochene style of exegesis from his congregation.

Antiochene interpretation followed the schools of grammar and rhetoric of the day in regard to the hermeneutical principles of *methodikon* and *historikon*. First, they used linguistic analysis to understand variant readings, style, diction, etymology, and figures of speech. Second, they searched for background information in an effort to understand the text. They were not opposed to spiritual readings of scripture as long as they did not contradict the historicity of the passage. Antiochenes believed that there was no other meaning of a text than what was openly written. They objected to the practice in philosophic schools of claiming a *hyponoia* or words with a 'true sense' that needed to be deciphered. Consequently, they did not deduce morals or doctrine by allegory unless that *allēgoria* was legitimate when it referred to comparing between past and present situations. The issue was that allegory neglected the logic of the *historia* of the text.

Diodore and Theodore were among the first theorists to develop a critical approach to the canon of scripture; however, their work was not well received or adopted. Rather, at the second Council of Constantinople Theodore was charged with failing to recognize the canonical authority of some biblical books. Theodore followed the Syrian churches' tradition of omitting Ezra-Nehemiah and Chronicles from the canon. John Chrysostom worked with the Peshitta Syriac version of the New Testament, which omitted 2 Peter, 2 and 3 John, Jude and Revelation.

It is important to reiterate that the Antiochene school of interpretation did not practice genuine historical criticism and it is too simplistic to characterize the approach as solely reactionary against the allegorical method.

References and further reading

Downey, G. (1961) *A History of Antioch in Syria from Seleucus to the Arab Conquest*, Princeton: Princeton University Press.
—— (1963) *Ancient Antioch*, Princeton: Princeton University Press.
Kugel, J.L. and R.A. Greer (1986) *Early Biblical Interpretation*, Philadelphia: Westminster Press.
Liebeschuetz, J.H.W.G. (1972) *Antioch: City and Imperial Administration in the Later Roman Empire*, Oxford: Clarendon.
Norris, F.W. and B. Drewery (1977) 'Antiochien,' *TRE* 3, 99–113.
Wallace-Hadrill, D.S. (1982) *Christian Antioch: A Study of Early Christian Thought in the East*, Cambridge: Cambridge University Press

KURT A. RICHARDSON

APOCALYPTIC LITERATURE

Unlike the vernacular that refers to a catastrophic event, 'apocalypse,' in biblical scholarship, represents a literary genre. Many scholars have recently begun to stress the distinction of 'apocalypse' from 'apocalyptic,' that is, an adjective used as a noun to denote 'apocalyptic features,' and from 'apocalyptic eschatology,' which represents ideas and motifs thematic of the general movement that is not unique but is found in other genres and social settings. It is also distinguished from 'apocalypticism,' that is, the sociological ideology behind the movement.

The apocalypse genre is well established in Judaism from at least the third century BC on. However, the specific use of the Greek term *apokalypsis* (revelation) as an identification of genre is not definite before the Christian era. The label or title 'apocalypse' does not seem to be explicitly identified with most of what is traditionally held to be Jewish apocalyptic literature. The first text introduced specifically as *apokalypsis* is the New Testament book of Revelation (also called 'The Apocalypse'), but this term may have been used generally for revelation. It was not until the second century AD that the term 'apocalypse' regularly appeared for the genre.

Texts accepted in the corpus of apocalyptic literature, or the 'apocalypse genre,' share a number of traits that distinguish them from other texts and have given rise to this special category of literature. However, few apocalypses are entirely apocalyptic in character. Some have elements commonly found in nonapocalyptic works and some lack typical features of the corpus. Scholarship continues to be divided over how to distinguish the formal features of apocalypses. There are many variations of style within the genre that make it difficult to label entire texts under one pure generic category or identify the genre by a single motif or theme. The most prudent and comprehensive way to identify the genre is by its distinguishing combination of traits rather than its constitution of unique elements.

Typically revelatory with a narrative framework, apocalypses contain esoteric messages of transcendent reality aimed at a human recipient by God but mediated by an otherworldly agent, usually an angelic figure who interprets the message or acts as guide on an otherworldly journey. Employing abundant imagery, signs, and cryptic symbolism, apocalyptic messages are generally imparted through dreams and visions. As revelations of heavenly mysteries, apocalyptic messages are frequently directed to God's loyal people for edification in the midst of crisis. Counterposed to the experienced world of the present, apocalyptic literature emphasizes both a transcendent or supernatural world and a universal or a cosmological outlook that goes beyond specific situations toward the end of history and eschatological salvation. Apocalypses are often pessimistic about God's present working in history and focus on his cataclysmic intervention in bringing history to an end, the final judgment and the destruction of the wicked. While most apocalyptic messages are eschatological, with an emphasis on futurity, some also interpret past or present events.

The apocalypse genre reflects more of a literary than an oral tradition. Authorship was often pseudonymous and while it was not the sole basis for authority, the false ascription of authorship to an ideal figure served to foster confidence in the text. Within the apocalypse genre there are two main types. One type is characterized by visions and a concern for the development of history, while the other is characterized by otherworldly journeys. For example, Daniel and *4 Ezra* are distinctively 'historical' apocalypses that contain historical reviews and developments, while *2 Enoch* is mostly an account of areas traveled in the otherworldly journey. The only apocalypse that combines both elements, historical development and an otherworldly journey, is the *Apocalypse of Abraham*.

The poetic and symbolic language of the genre does not lend itself well to empirical scrutiny or logical investigation. The language can be difficult for contemporary audiences to identify with, particularly in its affirmation of a supernatural world of angels, demons, and an eschatological judgment that are all equally or more real than the perceived world. Even so, apocalyptic language reflects more than just puzzling sets of symbolic ideas or elaborate intellectual formulations. As the reader comes to a closer understanding of the worldview that fostered the genre and a heightened appreciation of the revaluatory interjection of an unseen world, one will be better prepared to understand the language and content of the texts. Apocalypses were generated in social and historical circumstances that sought to influence our attitudes and beliefs, not to verify scientific data or logical argument. Their value should be weighed less in practical terms than in terms beneficial for faith and belief.

Among the difficulties in understanding this fascinating but cryptic genre, the reader should be particularly watchful of imposing present cultural meanings on symbols from the ancient world. The cultural and historical gap should be respected in the reader's efforts to uncover as much of the context of the ancient world and the biblical realities as possible without presuming symbols to be static or formalized in meaning. For example, the image of 'lion' might refer to Judah, Christ, or Satan in different contexts. Some texts interpret their own symbols, such as in Zechariah 6, but many do not.

Apocalypses are demanding to interpret not only because of extensive symbolism but also because the messages are usually only partly revealed. This created further mystery and the need for supernatural aid in interpretation, both for the original recipient and later readers. To appreciate these elements an interpreter must be prepared to maintain many irreducible and dynamic aspects by often avoiding literalistic interpretations. Recent scholarship has attempted to reverse its previous overemphasis on 'historical' apocalypses with the rediscovery and accentuation of the genre's mystical elements.

Apocalyptic literature embodies a rich tradition covering many important biblical themes and ideas that have had significant influence on Judaism and the early stages of Christianity. Unfortunately, many of the primary texts have been given only infrequent attention by biblical scholars. The apocalypse genre is an area open to pioneering scholarship that is willing to work with the mysteries of its revelation and offer fresh insights into a hidden world.

References and further reading

Charlesworth, James H. (ed.) (1983) *The Old Testament Pseudepigrapha. Vol. 1: Apocalyptic Literature and Testaments*, New York: Doubleday.

Collins, John J. (1998) *The Apocalyptic Imagination: An Introduction to the Jewish Matrix of Christianity*, Grand Rapids: Eerdmans, 2nd rev. edn.

Osborne, Grant R. (1991) *The Hermeneutical Spiral: A Comprehensive Introduction to Biblical Interpretation*, Downers Grove, IL: IVP.

J.C. ROBINSON

APOCRYPHA

1 Individual writings
2 Conclusions

Any discussion of the Apocrypha and the Bible must acknowledge two considerations. First, the collection of books known as 'Apocrypha' is a historical accident, a group of disparate writings that came together not because of mutual similarities, common elements, or intrinsic value but because of external factors. There is no particular characteristic that distinguishes writings of the Apocrypha from other early Jewish writings, whether in the Hebrew canon or as a part of the Pseudepigrapha. Second, the writings of the Apocrypha are not necessarily 'postbiblical'; that is, most of the Apocrypha would have been written before the idea of a canon of scripture as we know it had been formulated. Also, most of the writings of the Apocrypha are found in some biblical canons, in which case any discussion is not one of the use of the Bible in the Apocrypha – since the apocryphal books are biblical – but of inner-biblical exegesis.

1 Individual writings

For convenience – and to avoid a long discussion – I include the writings conventionally found in those English Bibles which contain a section called 'The Apocrypha.'

1.1 Esdras

There is currently a major debate on the character of this work. Some decades ago, it was popular to explain this book as a fragment of the 'Chronicler' whose work encompassed 1 and 2 Chronicles, Ezra, and Nehemiah combined. That approach has largely been abandoned, and a number of scholars explain 1 Esdras as a creation produced by taking Ezra and adding to it elements from the end of 2 Chronicles and Nehemiah. Talshir (1999) has recently expounded a variation of this thesis, arguing that the core of the work is the story of Darius' guardsmen (1 Esdras 3) to which was added relevant material from the present canonical 2 Chronicles, Ezra, and Nehemiah. In that case, 1 Esdras would be a type of biblical interpretation, in which the interpretation is effected mainly by recasting the existing text and combining it with another story. Others, however, have taken the view that 1 Esdras reflects a version of an Ezra story which pre-dates and was used by the canonical Ezra-Nehemiah (Grabbe 1998: 109–15; Böhler 1997). If this thesis is correct, 1 Esdras is not an example of interpretation but a source for the canonical version of Ezra-Nehemiah.

1.2 Tobit

Exactly when Tobit is to be dated is a major question, but it could easily be third century BC or even earlier. There is very little in the book that could be connected unambiguously to books of the Hebrew canon. There are many parallels, but it is difficult to find anything that looks like a quote, and the theological and religious concerns of the story are those that could be fully explained as a part of the developing Jewish tradition and practice. Some of the main themes are not those that are obvious in the books of our present Hebrew canon, e.g., the emphasis on burying the dead and almsgiving as important indications of piety. This also applies to other important themes, e.g., the duty that one has to one's kin, which is a concern that arises from a minority (and perhaps beleaguered) community in a foreign environment perceived as unwelcoming at best. Themes such as tithing (1:6–8) and the Jerusalem temple could have come from current belief and practice and do not have to be derived from written scripture. The angel Raphael, who is prominent in the book, is not mentioned in the books of the Hebrew canon.

On the other hand, there is a specific reference to the 'book of Moses' (7:13), the prophets are mentioned by name (1:8; 2:6; 6:13; 7:11–13; 14:3), and a prophecy of the destruction of Solomon's temple and the rebuilding of a new temple occurs (14:3–7). Tobit 2:10–14 reminds one of the exchange between Job and his wife in Job 2:9–10. In 4:3–19 a set of admonitions is listed, with parallels in the Old Testament, but it is not clear that any come from the Bible as such. Tobit's taking of Sarah as a wife 'according to the law and decree written in the book of Moses' is mentioned in 7:12–14. Another possible passage is 8:6, which appeals to the story of Adam and Eve. Although this story is told in Genesis 1–5, it is referred to nowhere else in the canonical and Deuterocanonical books apart from here (Adam's name is mentioned in the genealogy of 1 Chron. 1:1; Eve's not at all). The reference in the Sinaiticus manuscript (14:3–4) to the prophecy of Nahum (NRSV, NEB, REB, JB) is undoubtedly correct (compared with the 'Jonah' of the Vaticanus [AV, RV, RSV]) since it is the Old Testament book which describes an actual fall of Nineveh.

Thus, Tobit seems to know the Pentateuch and some of the Prophets. However, not much in the book could be directly borrowed from the biblical text nor is there much that could be labeled 'biblical interpretation.'

1.3 Ben Sira (Ecclesiasticus)

The book of Ben Sira is possibly our first evidence of a developing body of scripture, though the term 'canon' is probably inappropriate since the concept of a specific and defined set of sacred books seems to have come along much later. In the long section known as the 'Praise of the Fathers' (44–49), Ben Sira shows his knowledge of a significant portion of the present Hebrew canon, including the Pentateuch, the Former Prophets (Joshua–2 Kings), the Latter Prophets (Isaiah, Jeremiah, Ezekiel, the Twelve), and Chronicles.

Ben Sira himself does not normally give explicit quotations, and he can in many ways be considered a continuation of an old wisdom tradition, but there are many passages with parallels to the current Old Testament, not least in Sirach 44–49. He gives a close paraphrase – almost a quote – from a number of passages (e.g., Gen. 5:24; 6:9; 15:18; 1 Sam. 7:10; 12:3–4; Hag. 2:23; and Mal. 3:23–24). The description of the high priestly garments follows closely the account in Exodus 39:1–31. What is surprising is that Ben Sira follows the biblical text in saying that the priesthood had no inheritance among the tribes, even though it is likely that by his own time the priests owned land, collectively and possibly individually (cf. Grabbe 2000: 38–9). When he describes David, some aspects of his description appear to be taken from 1 Chronicles. For example, his emphasis on David's establishment of the cult and the various singers (Sir. 47:9–1//1 Chron. 15:16; 16:4–6; 23:5, 31–32).

1.4 Baruch

Written in the form of a letter by Jeremiah's scribe Baruch in exile to those remaining in Jerusalem, the exact dating of the book is uncertain: sometime in the second century BC is the most likely time of writing. The book is made up of disparate sections, some of which show interesting parallels with sections of the Hebrew canon. The focus of 1 Baruch is on the return from exile as a sort of second exodus (cf. Isa. 51:10–11). The 'letter' of Baruch (1:1–14) should be compared with Jeremiah 24 (which compares the exiles to good figs and those remaining in the land to bad) and Jeremiah 29 (which contains a letter in the name of Jeremiah encouraging the exiles to settle and make the best of it). A good portion of the book is a prayer of confession over sins (1:15–3:8), apparently based on or having much in common with Daniel 9:4–19. There is also a poem on Zion (4:5–5:9). The image of wisdom is an important section (3:9–4:4). Like Ben Sira 24, wisdom is equated with the Torah (4:1), though much of the poem seems to draw on (or be parallel to) Job 28:12–28 about the inaccessibility of wisdom.

In the end, there are many parallels with other biblical passages (e.g., 4:37 and 5:5//Isa. 43:5 and 60:4; 4:15//Deut. 28:49–50; 5:7//Isa. 40:4). Although interpretation of specific passages is difficult to demonstrate, much still appears to be derived from passages in various books of the Hebrew canon.

1.5 Judith

Many standard practices of Jewish religion are pictured in the book of Judith. The dietary laws are an important theme in the book, including the heroine's argument that violation of them would cause the city to fall

(11:12–15; 12:1–4, 17–19). The book places a great deal of emphasis on prayer (9; 12:6–8), which is one of the chief means by which Judith expresses her piety. Fasting and wearing sackcloth also occur (4:11–15). This was a common reaction to times of crisis in ancient Israel. Judith follows the old sense when Jerusalem is threatened (cf. Isa. 56, which makes fasting a means of expressing humility); however, a new attitude to fasting is attested here, perhaps for the first time: habitual fasting as an act of piety. Before this crisis arose Judith fasted all the days except for the sabbaths and holidays and the preparation day ('eve') before each festival (8:6) as a normal part of her lifestyle. Another possible ascetic act is her remaining unmarried, despite many opportunities to remarry (16:22). This might be simply out of loyalty to her first husband, but it could also suggest another element in an ascetic lifestyle. The book also accepts the temple, cult, and priesthood (4:2–3, 12, 14–15; 8:21, 24; 9:8, 13; 11:13; 16:16–20). The high priest acts as the leader of the nation (4:6–8), though a reference is also made to the *gerousia*, 'council of elders,' in Jerusalem, which is able to make important decisions (11:14).

Yet none of this necessarily shows acquaintance with the biblical text: it could all come from current belief and practice in the Jewish community. One example that may show knowledge of the biblical text is the main event of the book: Judith's seduction and execution of Holophernes. This is strongly parallel to the figure of Jael in Judges 4, as commentators have long pointed out. Although one cannot be dogmatic that Judges 4 served as a literary model for Judith's actions, this is still a strong possibility. In sum, there is little in Judith that has to be scriptural interpretation, though a number of points could depend on biblical passages.

1.6 First Maccabees

Determining possible dependence on or allusion to the Hebrew canonical books is difficult for two reasons: first, 1 Maccabees was clearly originally written in Hebrew, whereas we have only the Greek translation; second, many of the phrases that parallel similar usage in the Hebrew Bible were also probably a part of the common stock of literary Hebrew and may not necessarily indicate direct dependence on particular biblical verses. For example, 'his heart was lifted up' (1:3) is also found in Daniel 11:12, but the expression was evidently a common idiom (Hosea 13:6; 1QpHab 8:10). Compare also 'many evils have found us' (1:11//Deut. 31:21); 'they sold themselves to do evil' (1:15//1 Kings 21:20); 'after two years of days' (1:29//Gen. 41:1). However, 'a heavy crowd' (1:17), meaning 'a great army,' looks more like a possible allusion to Numbers 20:20.

It is difficult to find exact biblical quotations in 1 Maccabees; 7:17 is very similar to Psalm 74:2–3, though it is only a partial quote. One of the problems is that several passages which look like poetic quotations

(1:25–28; 1:36–40; 2:7–13; 3:3–9) are not taken from any Old Testament passage, even though some of the language is reminiscent of such passages as Job (8:22; 30:31); Lamentations (1:4, 18, 19; 2:10, 20; 5:13), and the Psalms (35:26; 109:24; 132:18). First Maccabees 2:26 is not a quotation but strongly suggests dependence on Numbers 25:14, which describes the sin of Zimri and the consequent actions of Phinehas. When the temple was cleansed by Judas and his colleagues, they set up an altar of unhewn stones, which matches the instructions of Exodus 20:25 and Deuteronomy 27:6. Some phrases known from the Septuagint text also occur in the Greek text of 1 Maccabees. One of the most striking is the translation of the Hebrew phrase 'abomination of desolation' (*šiqqûṣ haššōmēm*) by the same expression as found in the Septuagint Daniel (*bdelugma tōn erēmōseōn/tēs erēmōseōs*: Dan. 9:27; 11:31; 12:11; 1 Macc. 1:54; 6:7).

References to physical copies of the 'book of the law' or 'book of the covenant' (1:56–57; 3:48) are almost certainly references to the Pentateuch. The general narrative style of the book reminds one of such biblical books as Judges, 1 and 2 Samuel, and 1 and 2 Kings, suggesting that the original Hebrew text of 1 Maccabees was influenced by the biblical narrative style. Although this is a reasonable deduction, one could argue that Hebrew narrative follows a particular style that happens to be found not only in biblical narrative books but also in other Hebrew narrative books such as 1 Maccabees. Perhaps the most striking parallel is in the last few verses of the book. It ends with a statement about John Hyrcanus' reign (16:23–24) that is reminiscent of the Deuteronomistic formulae summarizing the reigns of kings (e.g., 1 Kings 20:20; 2 Kings 10:34–36). The writer also has a penchant for using biblical names for certain surrounding peoples. He uses 'Israel' quite consistently for the Jewish people, even though the documents always speak of 'the Jews' (e.g., 11:30; 12:5). He speaks of the 'Philistines' (3:41; 4:22), who had long since disappeared, and even of the 'Canaanites' (9:37). He employs the 'sons of Esau' for the inhabitants of Idumea (5:3).

To sum up, the writer of 1 Maccabees is likely to have known the Pentateuch and at least a number of the books from the Prophets and the Writings, to which he now and then alludes. He seldom quotes directly, either because that is not his style or perhaps because his quotations are from memory and not meant to be exact. For the most part, he is trying to tell the story of the Maccabees. The biblical books come into the picture mainly as literary embellishment, via allusions and the use of familiar phraseology that readers would have recognized.

1.7 Second Maccabees

Second Maccabees has two main divisions: 1–2 are alleged letters, prefaced to the book in its present form but likely to have a separate origin from the main narrative, 3–15. The second verse of the book (1:2) refers to the covenants with the three patriarchs Abraham, Isaac, and Jacob, information that could have come from the stories in Genesis; however, since it refers to calling these covenants to mind, it looks like a loose quotation of Leviticus 26:42. A long section (1:18–2:15) discusses Nehemiah and the rebuilding of the temple, but this story is quite different from the book of Nehemiah in the Hebrew canon. This does not say anything about knowledge of other biblical books, though, since the various sources differ as to which particular Ezra-Nehemiah story they accept (see above under '1 Esdras'). An alleged prayer of Nehemiah has some resemblance to several biblical passages (e.g., Isa. 49:7, 25–26; Exod. 15:17) but is not clearly a quote from any known text. References are made to Moses and Solomon (2:8–12) that probably have certain biblical passages in mind even if no exact quotation is made (Lev. 9:22–24; 2 Chron. 7:1); on the other hand, the biblical text makes no reference to an eight-day dedication (2:12), though this could be based on a misunderstanding of 2 Kings 8:65 (cf. 2 Chron. 7:9). The statement quoted in the name of Moses (2:11) does not match any Old Testament passage, though it resembles Leviticus 10:16–19.

In the narrative part of 2 Maccabees (3–15) there is little that could be considered biblical reference or interpretation, except that 8:19 refers to events from Sennacherib's invasion, information most likely taken from 2 Kings 19:35.

We can conclude that 2 Maccabees knows some biblical passages, especially from the Pentateuch and the Prophets, but also from Chronicles. 'Parabiblical' traditions are also known and preferred to those in our present Hebrew canon (especially regarding Nehemiah). Much of the book is an account of the exploits of the Maccabees, though, and much reference to the biblical text would not be expected anyway.

1.8 Wisdom of Solomon

The knowledge of and dependence on the books of the Hebrew canon by the Book of Wisdom or Wisdom of Solomon seems beyond dispute. This is especially true in the long midrash in 10–19, which includes references to various patriarchal figures and also contains a long midrash on the Exodus from Egypt. There are actually two midrashim in Wisdom 10–19, though the one runs without a clear break into the second. The first covers only chapter 10 and follows the fortunes of biblical history to the time of Moses. The emphasis is on the activity of Wisdom, and the individuals named are not all 'heroes' (e.g., Cain). Nevertheless, there is some affinity with the lists of the 'great men of Israel,' the prime example of which is the list in Ben Sira 44–50.

Although the midrash on the plagues of Exodus 7–12 (11:1–14; 16:1–19:22) follows seamlessly from the survey of history in Wisdom 10, it has a different literary form and can for this reason be considered a separate midrash. It is in the form of a *synkrisis*, a set of antitheses contrasting the sufferings of the Egyptians in the plagues with the benefits to the Israelites. It was a form highly developed in the Graeco-Roman literary context. There are ten plagues in the book of Exodus, but the writer draws on only part of them, apparently using three basic principles: (a) the Israelites benefit by the very things which serve to punish their enemies (11:5); (b) the *lex talionis* or principle of punishment by the means of the sin (11:16); and (c) Israel itself should suffer a mild form of the punishments of her enemies, so that she might understand the mercies of God (cf. 16:4).

Another passage hinted at in Wisdom of Solomon 11–19 seems to be Exodus 15. The key is the allusion to Exodus 15 at Wisdom 10:20–21 and 19:9. Psalm 2 seems to underlie a number of passages in the section known as the 'Book of Eschatology' (Wis 1–6). Another possible midrash may be found in Wisdom 2:10–5:23, based on the Fourth Servant Song in Isaiah 52:13–53:12. There is also a convincing case for suggesting that Daniel was used by the author of the Wisdom of Solomon in a number of passages.

It is not surprising that a late book such as the Wisdom of Solomon shows a good acquaintance with the biblical text. What is more, it is probably the best example of a writing in the Apocrypha that attempts in one way or another to interpret preexisting biblical texts.

1.9 Ezra (2 Esdras)

The Apocalypse of Ezra or *4 Ezra* or *2 Esdras* draws on the figure of Ezra known from the Hebrew book of Ezra-Nehemiah and 1 Esdras, yet it is not clear that it is based on either of these texts. It bears such little resemblance to the biblical Ezra that it could be derived from a completely independent tradition; this seems the more likely case and might explain why its figure of Ezra is dated to the time shortly after the Babylonian captivity rather than well into the Persian period as is the biblical Ezra. The story of Ezra's restoring the law that had been lost (14) goes against most of the books of the Hebrew canon. On the other hand, since little more than the name Ezra is used, it is certainly possible that the writer has taken the name from the biblical books and developed his own story without much reference to the details of the Hebrew or Greek book (on the tradition of Ezra in *4 Ezra*, see Grabbe 1998: 90–1).

Within the book there are many echoes of biblical passages: 3:4–27 surveys biblical history from Adam to David; 5:4–5 looks like a biblical quote but is not (though one phrase echoes Hab. 2:11); 6:56 reminds one a bit of Isaiah 40:15, while 7:97, 125 have similar language to Daniel 12:3. *Fourth Ezra* 7:132–40 gives a list of divine characteristics, some of which are also listed in Exodus 34:6–7; 8:58 has the same idea as Psalms 14:1 and 53:1 but is not clearly a quotation. Since the book was written at a time when the present Hebrew canon may have been more or less established, at least in some circles, it is easy to imagine that the passages are deliberate allusions to biblical passages. This may be true; however, it must also be acknowledged that much in the book is not taken directly from the canonical books but is part of the common apocalyptic store of beliefs, motifs, and language. As already noted, the story of how Ezra restored the law that had been lost is contrary to the Hebrew canon. Thus, although there are lots of details that could be derived from the biblical text, the book of *4 Ezra* did not originate primarily from interpretation of the Ezra account in the Hebrew Bible.

2 Conclusions

What can we say about biblical interpretation in the Apocrypha? No blanket statement can be made because there are large differences between the various books of the Apocrypha. Some major principles arise when investigating the individual books, however, and can be summarized as follows:

(1) The 'Apocrypha' are not separate from the Bible; most of these books are included in someone's canon (e.g., Roman Catholic, Greek Orthodox). Therefore, rather than speaking of the Apocrypha's 'biblical interpretation,' we really should consider its interpretation in the same context as inner-biblical interpretation. Some of the same resulting principles apply.

(2) Some of the books of the Apocrypha were written before some of the books of the Hebrew canon, and the Hebrew books may in some cases be drawing on books now a part of the Apocrypha.

(3) A number of the books in the Apocrypha show little interest in the Bible as such but are interested in telling a particular story. Thus, even though some of the biblical content may be presupposed, they are not interested in biblical interpretation as such. Current Jewish belief and practice may be more important than a written text (e.g., Judith).

(4) At the time when most of these books were written, canon as it came to be conceived was unknown. That is, certain books were considered authoritative in some way, but the idea of a closed canon of books, with specific ones included and excluded, did not develop until later (cf. Grabbe 2000: 152–7). Reference to other books and traditions was done more loosely and freely than when a closed canon had developed.

(5) Most of the Apocrypha show knowledge, in some way or other, of the Pentateuch. The suggestion is that it was probably authoritative for all who cite or refer to it. Ben Sira and other sources indicate that it probably had such a status by the end of the Persian period (see Grabbe 2000: 156–7).

(6) The various books of the Former Prophets (Joshua to 2 Kings) and the Latter Prophets (Isaiah, Jeremiah, Ezekiel, the Minor Prophets) were also known to many or all the writers, though their lack of citation in some books means that we cannot be sure of their status in such instances.

(7) There was clearly a body of books (and traditions), some of them variants of one another, that did not have a universal status. For example, a number of traditions relating to the 'restoration' after the exile were extant, but which ones were accepted and which were rejected (or simply unknown) varies from writer to writer. Ben Sira clearly did not know – or did not regard as authoritative – the Ezra tradition in any form. Second Maccabees has a Nehemiah story that contradicts both the Hebrew Ezra-Nehemiah and the Greek 1 Esdras. This situation appears to reflect the developing idea of canon in which the Pentateuch and then the Prophets became authoritative first, with the contexts of the Writings having a developing status. Of course, there were different versions of some books as well, so that a book's being canonical for a particular writer would not automatically tell you which version was in mind.

(8) The one book of the Apocrypha most clearly exhibiting passages that are directly the result of interpreting earlier biblical passages is the Wisdom of Solomon, though 1 Baruch may also have arisen as mainly biblical interpretation.

References and further reading

Böhler, Dieter (1997) *Die heilige Stadt in Esdras α und Esra-Nehemia: Zwei Konzeptionen der Wiederherstellung Israels*, OBO 158, Freiburg (Schweiz): Universitätsverlag; Göttingen: Vandenhoeck & Ruprecht.

Grabbe, Lester L. (1997) *Wisdom of Solomon*, Guides to Apocrypha and Pseudepigrapha, Sheffield: Sheffield Academic Press.

—— (1998) *Ezra-Nehemiah*, Readings, London and New York: Routledge.

—— (2000) *Judaic Religion in the Second Temple Period: Belief and Practice from the Exile to Yavneh*, London and New York: Routledge.

Talshir, Zipora (1999) *I Esdras: From Origin to Translation*, Society of Biblical Literature Septuagint and Cognate Studies Series 47, Atlanta: Scholars Press.

Tov, Emanuel (1992) *Textual Criticism of the Hebrew Bible*, Assen and Maastricht: Van Gorcum; Minneapolis: Fortress.

LESTER L. GRABBE

APOCRYPHAL INTERPRETATION

> 1 Gospels
> 2 Acts
> 3 Apocalyptic

The early noncanonical Christian literature commonly called New Testament apocrypha makes use of the characters and events in the New Testament proper. The motive for much of the writing is to fill perceived gaps in the New Testament narratives, and to that extent the writings may be read as interpretative of Christianity's foundational documents. The contents of some of them may be summarized under three conventional genres: Gospels, Acts, and Apocalyptic.

1 Gospels

The *Protevangelium of James* is principally concerned with Mary's upbringing; the story of her birth owes much to an interpretation of Samuel's birth in 1 Samuel. The Arabic Infancy Gospel tells of the Holy Family's sojourn and miracles in Egypt. The *Infancy Gospel of Thomas* is taken up with miracle stories set in Jesus' boyhood. Other apocryphal gospels fill in gaps at the end of Jesus' career: the Gospel of Nicodemus rewrites the events of the Passion, and in its second part interprets 1 Peter 3:19 by detailing Jesus' descent to the underworld. Fringe characters in the New Testament, such as the good and bad thieves and the woman cured of a haemorrhage, are given more prominent roles in these apocrypha. Christians' curiosity about the fate of Pilate resulted in several apocrypha detailing his death.

2 Acts

The apocryphal Acts, such as the *Acts of Thomas* or the *Acts of John*, treat of the journeys, preaching, miracles, and deaths of their eponymous heroes. The names of New Testament apostles and occasionally perhaps historical reminiscences about their lives are used in these imaginative and often racy novels. The relevance of these founding fathers of the faith as models for Christians is such that their presence in the New Testament was seen to be in need of elaboration and thus interpretation in the apocrypha. These apostles are depicted as imitators of Christ, successful evangelizers and typically martyrs for their faith.

3 Apocalyptic

The tantalizingly oblique reference in 2 Corinthians 12 to Paul's apparent journey to the heavens is the inspiration behind Paul's tours of heaven and hell in the Apocalypse of Paul. Other apocalypses concern the endtime or the fate of the dead – themes found in the New Testament but deemed to be in need of expanding.

Many of these Christian apocrypha date from the second to the fourth centuries AD and so it is somewhat anachronistic to separate them from the canon of Christian scriptures, which was not finalized until the end of this period. Similarly, words like 'orthodox' or 'heretical' are not always appropriate when used of early compositions. Occasionally, however, the interpretation of the Christian story seems to be Gnostic. Parts of the Acts of John, 87–105 in particular, interpret the Passion story in a docetic way. Similarly, several of the 114 logia of Jesus in the *Gospel of Thomas* are capable of Gnostic interpretation. However, several sayings in the *Gospel of Thomas* are close to, although seldom exactly parallel to, a saying in the Synoptics. Differences in wording may sometimes be seen as interpretative theological changes, comparable to differences observed in a Gospel Synopsis or to deliberate scribal variants in the New Testament manuscript tradition. All such change may signify the way in which the early church continually reinterpreted its store of dominical sayings, because they were seen and used as living texts.

A consistent interpreting of the Bible is not to be found in the Christian apocrypha mainly because these are an amorphous collection of writing from many periods and places and come from diverse groups. The Bible stories are accepted uncritically and imitative. That, however, does not prevent imaginative rewriting. The *Gospel of Peter* for instance retells the canonical accounts of Jesus' Passion and adds some new features (possibly of Gnostic origin).

The use of the Old Testament in these apocrypha, principally the Psalter and Isaiah, is similar to its use in the canonical New Testament. The *Gospel of Pseudo-Matthew* for example includes Old Testament passages (Isa. 1:3; Hab. 3:2) prophesying the appearance of animals at Jesus' birth: this interpretation of Old Testament passages continues the tradition of reading the Jewish scriptures as vaticinal of events in Christian origins. Several apocrypha, often erroneously labeled Old Testament apocrypha (i.e. pseudepigraphical) writings because they treat of an *Old* Testament worthy, such as Moses or Elijah, are in fact Christian writings or adaptations of Jewish stories. They too are interpretative by purporting to be sequels to and expansions of events in the Bible.

References and further reading

Charlesworth, J.H. (1983, 1985) *The Old Testament Pseudepigrapha*, 2 Vols., London: Darton, Longman & Todd.

Elliott, J.K. (1993) *The Apocryphal New Testament*, Oxford: Clarendon.

Sparks, H.F.D. (1984) *The Apocryphal Old Testament*, Oxford: Clarendon.

J.K. ELLIOTT

AQIBA (d. *c.* 135 BC)

Rabbi Aqiba ben Joseph was one of the greatest rabbis of the Tannaitic period. He flourished from late first century to early second century AD. Rabbinic legend has it that he was burned at the stake (*c.* 135 AD or later) for refusing to deny his faith and for having supported the Bar Kochba revolt (*b. Berakot* 61b).

Aqiba's most important contribution was the development of the oral law that two or three generations after his time was edited and written down as the Mishnah (*c.* 220 AD). More legal statements (*halakoth*) are attributed to Aqiba than to anyone else of his time. Indeed, many rabbis of later periods assumed that it was Aqiba himself who produced a preliminary edition of the Mishnah that would later serve as the principal source for the final edition produced under the direction of Rabbi Judah the Prince (cf. *t. Zabim* 1.5; *b. Sanh.* 86a; *Abot R. Nat.* §18).

Aqiba held to a high view of scripture, maintaining that it derived from God, that it contained no redundancies, and that every detail of the text, including spelling, held meaning. His haggadic exegesis, especially touching messianism, proved controversial and stood in need of correction by later authorities.

According to Aqiba, the plural 'thrones' of Daniel 7:9 referred to a throne for God and a throne for David (i.e., probably in reference to the Messiah, the son of David). We are told that Rabbi Yose immediately rebuked the great rabbi, 'Aqiba, how long will you profane the Divine Presence? Rather, one (throne) is for justice and one for mercy.' Aqiba then accepts Yose's interpretation, with Eleazar ben Azariah adding, 'Aqiba, what do you have to do with Aggadah? Occupy yourself with Nega'im and Ohaloth' (*b. Sanhedrin* 38b). Eleazar's point is that Aqiba should give up his messianic speculations and concentrate on legal interpretation, for which he is so well known. Aqiba's interest in messianism, however, is deeply attested in the tradition (cf. *Midr. Tanh.* B on Lev. 19:1–2 [*Qedoshin* §1], where Aqiba is again a participant in the discussion of the meaning of the plural 'thrones').

Most controversial of all was Aqiba's recognition of Simon ben Kosiba as the Messiah, based on a wordplay between Simon's name and the Aramaic of the definite form of 'star': 'Rabbi Simeon ben Yoḥai taught: "Aqiba, my master, used to interpret 'a star [*kōkhab*] goes forth from Jacob' [Num. 24:17] – *Kōzeba'* goes forth from Jacob.'" Rabbi Aqiba, when he saw Bar Kozeba, said: 'This is the King Messiah.' Rabbi Yoḥanan ben Torta said to him: 'Aqiba! Grass will grow on your cheeks and still the son of David does not come!' (*y. Ta'an.* 4.5 [8] = Lam. Rab. 2.2 §4; *b. Sanh.* 93b; on messianic interpretation, cf. *y. Ned.* 3.8). Two features of this tradition are clearly secondary. First, the reference to Simon as *Kōzeba'* (lit. 'liar'), instead of Kosiba (Simon's actual name), reflects the later, post-Aqiba neg-

ative assessment of the leader of the revolt. After all, Aqiba would hardly hail the man he believed to be the fulfilment of Numbers 24:17, which in the Targums and earlier traditions (e.g., 1QM 11.4–7; 1QSb 5.27–29; CD 7.18–21) is understood in explicit messianic terms, as the 'liar' who 'goes forth from Jacob.' Second, the immediate rebuke by Yoḥanan ben Torta, like the rebukes by Yose and Eleazar, is probably artificial and represents a later 'correction' of the famous rabbi. It is more probable that Aqiba's recognition of Simon was widely shared, at least initially, as indicated by the great difficulty Rome had in putting down the rebellion and in the enormous losses suffered by both sides.

References and further reading

Finkelstein, L. ([1936] 1962) *Akiba: Scholar, Saint and Martyr*, Philadelphia: Jewish Publication Society.

Goldenberg, R. (1992) 'Akiba, Rabbi,' *ABD* 1.137–38.

Pearson, B.W.R. (1997) 'The Book of the Twelve, Aqiba's Messianic Interpretations, and the Refuge Caves of the Second Jewish War,' pp. 221–39 in *The Scrolls and the Scriptures: Qumran Fifty Years After*, S.E. Porter and C.A. Evans (eds.), JSPSup 26, Sheffield: Sheffield Academic Press.

Schäfer, P. (1980) 'Rabbi Aqiva and Bar Kokhba,' pp. 113–30 in *Approaches to Ancient Judaism*, Vol. 2, BJS 9, Chico: Scholars Press.

Urbach, E.E. (1973) *The Sages: Their Concepts and Beliefs*, Cambridge, MA: Harvard University Press, pp. 258–70.

CRAIG A. EVANS

AQUINAS, THOMAS (1225–1274)

Known as the 'Angelic Doctor' and the 'Prince of Scholastics,' he was sent by his family at age five into the monastic life of Montecassino and was soon dedicated by his supervisors to a life of study. From 1245–1252 he received instruction from Albertus Magnus in Cologne, and later took up a post in Paris to teach at the Dominican *studium generale*. It was in Paris that he became a priest and began to teach at the University of Paris in 1252. Aquinas read very widely: newly available Aristotle texts, the Jewish philosopher Maimonides as well as Muslim scholars Averroës and Avicenna. His chastened realist philosophy held to universals as strictly mental objects while rejecting radical forms of nominalism.

Thomas' study of Aristotle and his admission to the Order of Preachers or Dominicans would lead him eventually to Rome. Toward the end of his life he had to face charges of heterodoxy, which would be dropped after his death. Given to mystical experiences, his humility regarding his intellect and understanding are everywhere evident in his writings. Aquinas adopted Aristotle's account of sense perception and intellectual knowledge. But his other influences include Augustine, Boethius, Pseudo-Dionysius, and Proclus for Neo-platonic elements, which are also evident in his theology. As one of the most prolific theologians of medieval Christianity his writings include a number of exegetical works, particularly: Commentaries on Job, Psalms, probably Isaiah; his *Catena aurea*, elaborating on the four Gospels, probably a Commentary on Song of Solomon, and on Jeremiah; and on John, Matthew, and the Epistles of Paul, and perhaps the better part of the Epistle to the Hebrews. Since the mid-nineteenth century, numerous popes have extolled Aquinas and commended his work as the singular standard for Roman Catholic dogmatics and theology.

Aquinas carefully distinguished between philosophy and theology where the latter draws its knowledge entirely from the revelation of scripture. Nevertheless, he also sought to bring philosophy under the authority of scripture where metaphysical knowledge – 'divine things,' which is what revelation delivers – is required for all other knowledge to progress and to achieve certainty. Aquinas regards the knowledge of divine causation as extremely fruitful in producing a metaphysics which stands behind all knowledge, including that which is derived from revelation itself, since such knowledge is also dependent upon revelation. Through such integrative models of theological knowledge Aquinas was able to create a kind of coherency among all his works, particularly the scripture commentaries, which reflected a unique type of theological exegesis.

In the *Summa Theologica*, Thomas deals quite considerably with hermeneutical issues in his discussion of the nature of 'sacred doctrine.' He argues in favor of a literal sense of scripture which contains multiple senses. His reasoning is based upon several claims. First, scripture uses metaphors to represent divine truth. Certain metaphors are used repeatedly in scripture and receive rich determinations of meaning. Little concerned with problems of anthropomorphism, Thomas effectively claims that the more mundane the metaphor the truer it is to its sources in the natural world and not at all to be confused with the actual nature of God. Indeed, the hiddenness of the divine nature behind the metaphors of scripture might even be necessary obscuration of truth to unbelievers. Citing Augustine, Thomas goes on to affirm historical or literal, allegorical, tropological, or moral, and anagogical or eschatological senses of a single passage of scripture. Whether through Christian interpretations of Old Testament passages or spiritual readings of the New Testament, using arguments from the Fathers and Pseudo-Dionysius, Thomas agrees that scripture passages convey transcendent as well as proximate or literal meanings. This is because two levels of signification inhabit a passage: words signifying things and these things signifying other things, which he gen-

erally describes as the spiritual sense of scripture. Within the spiritual sense Thomas further identifies the three senses beyond the literal: allegorical (e.g., typologies from Old Testament to New Testament), moral (tropological), and eternal (anagogical). Thomas speaks of authorial intent and since God is the author, he declares unproblematic that several meanings should be contained within the literal sense of scripture. Thomas resists the charge of ambiguity, which he takes seriously, distinguishing between verbal signification – words mean only one thing in a given passage, and metaphorical significations – things or images in the text are what can bear multiple senses or meaning. In this way Thomas claims that all the other senses of scripture are contained within its literal sense.

References and further reading

Aquinas, Thomas (1966–1980) *Aquinas Scripture Commentaries*, Albany: Magi Books.
—— (1997) *Summa Theologica*, Notre Dame, IN: Thomas More.
Chenu, M.D. (1964) *Towards Understanding St. Thomas*, Chicago: University of Chicago Press.
Davies, Brian (1992) *The Thought of Thomas Aquinas*, Oxford: Oxford University Press.
Kretzmann, Norman and Eleonore Stump (eds.) (1993) *The Cambridge Companion to Aquinas*, Cambridge: Cambridge University Press.
McInerny, Ralph (trans.) (1998) *Exposition of Paul's Epistle to Philemon*, Harmondsworth: Penguin.
Pesch, Otto (1972) *The God Question in Thomas Aquinas and Martin Luther*, Philadelphia: Fortress Press.
Weisheipl, James A. (1974) *Thomas D'Aquino: His Life, Thought and Work*, Washington, DC: Catholic University of America Press.

KURT A. RICHARDSON

ARCHAEOLOGY AND THE BIBLE

1 Introduction
2 The Bible interprets archaeology
3 Archaeology interprets the Bible

1 Introduction

Sophisticated archaeological methods have increased the value and usefulness of studying the material remains of the ancient world. These remains include the written products of the ancient world (papyri, inscriptions, and other written documents, such as clay tablets; see Papyrology and Epigraphy), as well as other physical objects, such as buildings, sculptures (freestanding and bas-reliefs), pottery, glass, and other ceramic objects, and jewelry; all of which give insight into the life and times of the ancients. What was once a casual exercise for those with time and money has given way to a much more intentional and scientific enterprise. Whether one considers archaeology as a science in its own right or as a subcategory of anthropology or history, it avails itself of many of the latest advances in scientific and related technology. Modern archaeological excavations identify and scrutinize a potential site and what is discovered at such a site, using radar, infrared, magnetic, neutron, and electronic surveying techniques; ground and aerial photography, including three-dimensional photography; ground surveying, soil sampling, and petrography; and other means. Once the site has been identified and the surface surveyed, the dig itself is regulated and recorded, and the findings documented. In conjunction with this study, other areas of study are regularly drawn upon.

The two major techniques that are used by archaeologists are the stratigraphic method of excavation and the typological method of classification. The stratigraphic method involves a systematic and controlled means of uncovering a chosen site. The method includes dividing up the site into diggable units, careful record keeping of what is uncovered and where, and the ability to develop the site as appropriate in the light of what is discovered – while trying to control unnecessary disruption of other areas of the site. The typological method is a means of classifying objects on the basis of comparison with other similar objects, in order to determine, for example, the age of the items found, such as pottery, so that the history and development of a culture can be established (see Vos 1977: 9–29; McRay 1991: 20–34).

2 The Bible interprets archaeology

Much biblical archaeology has been done under the ideological influence of the biblical theology movement (see Biblical Theology and Lexicons [Theological]). According to this movement, there was a link between the historical basis of Christianity and archaeology, a historical discipline. The biblical human expressed his or her faith in relation to historical events and their related narratives. The Bible was an account, not only of religious notions (as important as these are), but also of a particular people who lived in a particular time and place, and who had seen God's hand at work in their history. Their faith, therefore, was transmitted by means of historical narratives, and hence archaeology was a necessary partner for interpreting the significance of the Bible as a complex theological and historical document (see Wright 1957: 17–19). In many ways, the biblical theology movement has been shown to have maintained a mistaken notion of the relationship between conceptions of person, language, history, and theology. As a result, there is now far less of an attempt

made to see a direct correlation between the Bible as a theological book and archaeology as an historical discipline, as if the one speaks directly to the other. Nevertheless, this does not mean that the Bible does not play an important role in archaeology. Apart from written remains – and these too require interpretation – archaeological data are mute and require interpretation. The Bible, as one important source giving access to the ancient world, has a role to play in helping to understand the physical, material, and cultural elements of the ancient world, besides the historical and written ones.

3 Archaeology interprets the Bible

Vos (1977: 13–17) enumerates the functions of archaeology as providing insight into humanity's past, aiding appreciation of that past, and having an impact upon interpreting the Bible. Various specific archaeological discoveries have had clear value in opening up areas of biblical interpretation that have been unknown, including such things as the potential dates and nature of the Exodus, and the kind of environment that was to be found in first-century Corinth, to name but two. However, there are also limitations to the knowledge that one can gain from archaeology in terms of interpretation of the Bible. As Meyers and Strange point out (1981: 30), archaeology provides what amounts to raw data, in terms of the uninterpreted physical remains of human life and habitation. These elements are vitally important for understanding ancient life, history, and culture, but they are only one part of the data that must be taken into account; they cannot of themselves provide definitive proof of the accuracy of the biblical account, and certainly cannot of themselves prove the inspiration of scripture (see McRay 1991: 19). There are even further occasions when the material remains appear to be contradictory to the biblical account. The famous conflict between Garstang and Kenyon over the evidence regarding the fall of Jericho, or the dating of the census of Quirinius, provide two examples. There have been two unhealthy tendencies when such conflicts arise. One is to sacrifice the archaeological data in the light of what appears to be the biblical account, and the other is to sacrifice the biblical account to the apparent archaeological data. Often the most useful solution is to hold the two in tension while further understanding is gained through ongoing textual, historical and archaeological study. Work at the ancient city of Sepphoris is a case in point, where a place not mentioned in the New Testament is increasingly seen to have significance for understanding ancient Galilee, and with it the world in which Jesus grew up (see Reed 2000).

References and further reading

Finegan, J. (1992) *The Archeology of the New Testament*, Princeton: Princeton University Press.

McRay, J. (1991) *Archaeology and the New Testament*, Grand Rapids: Baker.

Meyers, E.M. (ed.) (1997) *The Oxford Encyclopedia of Archaeology in the Near East*, 5 Vols., New York: Oxford University Press.

Meyers, E.M. and J.F. Strange (1981) *Archaeology, the Rabbis and Early Christianity*, Nashville: Abingdon Press.

Reed, J.L. (2000) *Archaeology and the Galilean Jesus*, Harrisburg, PA: Trinity Press International.

Vos, H.F. (1977) *Archaeology in Bible Lands*, Chicago: Moody.

Wilson, C.A. (1977) *Rocks, Relics and Biblical Reliability*, Grand Rapids: Zondervan.

Wright, G.E. (1957) *Biblical Archaeology*, Philadelphia: Westminster Press.

Wright, G.E., D.N. Freedman and E.F. Campbell, Jr. (eds.) *The Biblical Archaeologist Reader*, 3 Vols., New York: Doubleday.

STANLEY E. PORTER

ARISTOTLE (384–322 BC)

Recent analyses of the New Testament have drawn upon Aristotle in respect to moral lists (*Haustafeln*) and rhetoric.

Aristotle's influence on later Greek reflections regarding moral philosophy is found in the *Politics* and the *Nicomachean Ethics*. The *Politics* was probably written about 338 BC when Aristotle was in Macedonia, and the *Nicomachean Ethics* in the later Athenian period or about 330 BC.

In these documents Aristotle discussed 'household management' (*peri oikonomias*) and indicated how these patterns also influenced the state. David Balch in 'Let the Wives be Submissive' (n. 2), wrote:

> Aristotle gave the philosophical discussion of 'household management' (*peri oikonomias*) a particular outline that does not occur elsewhere, for example, not in the Hebrew Bible, not in Plato, and not among the Stoics. He observed that a 'house' includes three relationships, 'master and slave, husband and wife, father and children' (Pol I 1253b 1–14; see NE V 1134b 9–18).

While one cannot argue that the *Haustafeln* in Colossians 3:18–4:1 and Ephesians 5:21–6:4 are directly dependent upon a reading of Aristotle, yet the structure apparently ultimately has an Aristotelian source.

The *Rhetoric* of Aristotle was probably completed about 335 BC, just before Aristotle returned to Athens to found the Lyceum. He had commenced lecturing on rhetoric in Plato's Academy about 355 BC. The five classical divisions of rhetoric, especially in the Roman period, were: (a) invention, so called by later writers, i.e., *heurēsis*; (b) arrangement; (c) style; (d) delivery; and (e) memory. Of these, Aristotle in the *Rhetoric* discussed three of the five, set forth here in the order of the space to which he assigned them: invention, i.e., in Aristotle's terminology, 'proofs' (*pisteis*), then style (*lexis*), and finally arrangement (*taxis*). In another important observation, Aristotle declared that there are three rhetorical genres (*tria genē*) corresponding to three types of hearers: deliberative (*sumbouleutikon*), forensic or juridical (*dikanikon*), and epideictic or demonstrative (*deiktikon*).

The means of persuasion (*pisteis*) were divided into nonartistic (*atexnoi*) and artistic (*entexnoi*). The former consisted of what in the courtroom are called exhibits such as objects, contracts, and witnesses. The speaker or writer invents artistic proofs, that is, he selects the means by which he hopes to persuade the specific audience. There are three types of artistic proofs: the speaker's character (*ēthos*), logical argument and evidence (*logos*), and emotive appeal (*pathos*). In popular speeches arguments take the form of enthymemes (*enthumēmata*). These have their power because they commence from premises accepted by the auditors.

Biblical critics have employed various of Aristotle's categories and observations to analyze the documents of both the Old and New Testaments. Aristotle, however, did not write the *Rhetoric* for critics, but for rhetorical practitioners, which means that rhetorical critics are forced to extrapolate a method of criticism from his work.

In recent years rhetorical analysis of the scriptures has come to the forefront. Various kinds of rhetorical criticism, both ancient and modern, have been employed, and many of these are dependent upon Aristotle. The question remains as to whether Aristotle and his rhetoric may have influenced the writers of the New Testament. It is extremely doubtful that any of the writers of the New Testament were acquainted at first hand with the *Rhetoric*. However, it is conceivable that certain authors may have been influenced by rhetorical handbooks which drew upon Aristotle. Many features of Aristotelian rhetoric may be found in the New Testament, but then, since Aristotle was making universal observations about the discourse of the public arena, any document should exhibit these characteristics.

References and further reading

Balch, D.L. (1974) '"Let the Wives be Submissive . . ." The Origin, Form, and Apologetic Function of the Household Duty Code (Haustafel) in I Peter,' Ph.D. Dissertation, Yale University.

Fitzgerald, J.T. (1992) 'Haustafeln,' *ABD* 3.80–81.

Kennedy, G.A. (1984) *New Testament Interpretation Through Rhetorical Criticism*, Chapel Hill: University of North Carolina Press.

—— (1991) *Aristotle, On Rhetoric: A Theory of Civic Discourse*, trans. with introduction and notes, New York: Oxford University Press.

Lührmann, D. (1980) 'Neutestamentliche Haustafeln und antike Ökonomie,' *New Testament Studies* 27: 83–97.

Olbricht, T.H. (1990) 'An Aristotelian Rhetorical Analysis of 1 Thessalonians,' pp. 216–36 in *Greeks, Romans, and Christians, Essays in Honor of Abraham J. Malherbe*, D.L. Balch, E. Ferguson, and W.A. Meeks (eds.), Minneapolis: Fortress Press.

Porter, S.E. (ed.) *Handbook of Classical Rhetoric in the Hellenistic Period 330 BC–AD 400*, Leiden: Brill.

Watson, D.F. and A.J. Hauser (1994) *Rhetorical Criticism of the Bible: A Comprehensive Bibliography with Notes on History and Method*, Leiden: Brill, 1994.

T.H. OLBRICHT

ART AND INTERPRETATION

The search for meaning in our temporal existence has been nourished over centuries of human endeavor by the creativity of the visual artist; for images, like words, possess the power not simply to portray ideas and thoughts, but also to inspire and shape them. In Judaeo-Christian history, the pivotal tool in the search for self-understanding has been the Bible. As such, the sacred texts have underscored not just human thought but also, as a direct consequence, much of Western art prior to the late nineteenth century. In acknowledgment of its central role, the Bible accordingly earned from William Blake the consummate appellation: 'The Great Code of Art.'

Whilst not all religious art is text-based, an immense body of visual art, both sacred and profane, has been inspired by those events recounted in the Old and New Testaments. Although the precise date of origin is disputed, archaeological evidence attests that the practice of producing biblical imagery had become well established amongst Jewish communities in Israel and the Diaspora, and amongst Christian communities across the Roman Empire, at least by the early third century of the Common Era. Drawing on the stories, moral teachings, and theological doctrines contained in the Bible, visual art was employed by these pioneering religious communities not simply for the adornment of worship space, liturgical accouterments, sacred texts, and private devotional objects. Nor was it merely used for the narration of text. Art also served for the instruction of the faithful, who were often illiterate. Nevertheless, the role of the artist in creating biblical imagery was not, and has at no time since been, limited to passive illustration.

From the outset, the artist played a crucial role in directing the viewer toward a particular understanding of a given textual episode. Regardless of the inherent entertainment value of many biblical stories, their meaning could be transformed by the interpretation given them by the artist. The process of interpretation, which began with the initial choice of a subject for portrayal, could continue with the choice of narrative elements to emphasize or omit the method of execution, and the final placement of the image within a particular decorative scheme or sacred context. The visual representation was further influenced by a miscellany of external factors, including contemporary theological debates, the political and social climate, civil unrest, war, and so on. As the fruit of the convergence of these factors, the completed image may be seen to be strongly influenced, but in no way limited by, biblical text. This has continued to be true of that biblical art created by, or increasingly commissioned from, contemporary artists for use in churches and synagogues today.

It remains unclear as to when and where the first illustrations of the Old and New Testaments were created. Whilst we know that a tradition of Jewish narrative art existed, questions persist regarding when it began and whether it emerged in and was circulated via now lost illustrated biblical texts (Weitzman and Kessler 1990). The wider inquiry into its origins has been persistently hampered by the long-held assumption that the development of visual art in the first centuries of the Common Era was severely retarded by the strict adherence of Jews, and subsequently Christians, to the Mosaic prohibition of images (Exod. 20:4). Certainly, the evolution of Jewish biblical art has been shaped by ongoing reservations about images, expressed pointedly in negative rabbinical statements throughout the Middle Ages and in the cautious attitude of Orthodox Jews, with their continued abstinence from figural art in the modern period. Nevertheless, the popularity of figural images for the decoration of Jewish synagogues and prayer books in Christian Europe, and the continued use of figural art in the homes and synagogues of Reform and Conservative Jews, suggests that multiple understandings of the biblical injunction have emerged in the course of Jewish history, often as a result of Jewish interaction with surrounding cultures (Gutmann 1989). Similarly, whilst pockets of circumspection have existed within Christianity, flaring most notoriously in the Iconoclastic controversy of the eighth and ninth centuries, it can no longer be assumed that Christian art grew from the shadows of a resolute and uniform opposition to images in the early church (Murray 1977).

From at least the third century, Jews and Christians have pictorialized the Hebrew scriptures in divergent ways. Initially, Jewish text-based art was primarily synagogal, and it explicated in visual form the significance of specific biblical events for the Jewish people; in late antiquity, Jewish representations of the Hebrew narratives were therefore visually descriptive and often intricately detailed. In addition, despite the comprehensive selection of narrative biblical themes in the synagogue at Dura Europos, Syria (*c.* 244–245) – including the Crossing of the Red Sea, the Anointing of David, and the Infancy of Moses – the scenes chosen for portrayal were generally taken from a core selection: the Binding of Isaac, Noah's Ark, Daniel and the Lions, the Twelve Tribes, or King David. By contrast, extant Christian art of the same epoch is predominantly funereal, its chief concern being to evoke a broad message of salvation as opposed to outlining the constituent narrative elements of a given story. The text-based images popularly chosen for depiction – including scenes from the Life of Jonah, Noah's Ark and the Three Hebrews in the Fiery Furnace – were pared down to their essential visual elements and illustrated as abbreviated images of multivalent meaning rather than highly detailed narratives of singular import. Hence, the incident of the three Hebrews, whilst testifying to the salvific efficacy of belief in God, could simultaneously foretell of the Christian Trinity.

Whilst the nascent Christian church drew heavily on the Hebrew scriptures, which it appropriated and illustrated to articulate its belief in itself as the fulfilment of Judaism, the New Testament also proved a vigorous stimulant for imagery. As illustrated in the formative pictorial cycles of the catacombs and on sarcophagi of the fourth and fifth centuries, Christians were interested in the Gospel records of Jesus' life for their revelation of divine truth and not simply for their historical value. Yet the message of redemption through the power and grace of God, eloquently expressed in a variety of biblical imagery from the literal to the symbolic, was successfully explored beyond funerary art. In the wall paintings from the Christian baptistery at Dura Europos (*c.* 240), the theme of original sin, captured in the figures of Adam and Eve, is strikingly juxtaposed with that of redemption, embodied in the symbolic figure of the Good Shepherd (Grabar 1980).

Christian artistic expression developed in tandem with the theological, intellectual, and material maturing of the church. Hence, the careful practice in biblical exegesis of drawing symbolic or typological parallels between Old and New Testament events or characters profoundly influenced the design and content of various types of religious imagery: the schemes of thematically related scenes on early Christian sarcophagi (notably that of Junius Bassus, *c.* 359), the cycles of mosaics in Byzantine basilicas, some twelfth-century biblical manuscripts, and the vivid stained-glass illustrations of the late twelfth to mid-fifteenth centuries. In the series of frescoes on either side of the Sistine Chapel, the direct comparison between the Life of Christ and the Life of Moses (1481–1482) illustrates the way in which the artistic presentation of Old Testament events aided the Christian comprehension of their import. To behold an image or series of images was as much an intellectual experience as a sensory and spiritual one.

Invariably, religious controversies affected the visual presentation of a biblical event, whether conflicts between Catholic Christians or Protestants, esoteric disputes arising from contradictory textual interpretations, or interfactional arguments. Even religious reform impacted on the contemporary visual interpretation of scripture, as manifest in the woodcuts and engravings of biblical subjects by Dürer at the time of the Protestant Reformation. The political views or machinations of ecclesiastical and secular groups have also affected the artistic representation of sacred texts, and leaders associated themselves, or have been associated with, biblical figures in works of art in order to gain authority and approval for their actions: hence the episode of Moses crossing the Red Sea could act in the fourth century as a reminder of Constantine's celebrated defeat of the enemy at the Battle of the Milvian Bridge in 312. In this way, art has been manipulated to bestow religious significance on secular actions. Biblical subjects have also embraced national aspirations, as in the case of the Binding of Isaac, which for Jews alluded to the covenant between God and the people of Israel.

The meaning of a given biblical episode is therefore subject to the vicissitudes of the era in which it is visually portrayed. The physical context in which an image appears also influences the manner in which it should be viewed. So representations of the Binding of Isaac, popular in the Jewish as well as Christian artistic tradition, must be read according to the circumstances of their production: whether as a floor mosaic in the sixth-century Bet Alpha Synagogue, Israel, a thirteenth-century sculpture in the north porch of Chartres Cathedral, France, or a seventeenth-century oil painting by Caravaggio (*c.* 1603), the aspects of the story that artists of various faiths, ages, nationalities, cultures, and political climes have chosen to emphasize provide the clues to understanding the visually rendered interpretation of a biblical event. In some instances the artist, as biblical interpreter, might disregard the rabbinical or ecclesiastical interpretation of a text and so present a bolder reading than officials of church or synagogue might proffer.

Occasionally, biblical imagery has presented an intermingling, often subconscious, of narrative details with those derived from extratextual or oral sources, including the midrashic or patristic literary traditions. In the version of the Binding of Isaac in the Durene Synagogue, the main elements of the Hebrew story appear alongside details possibly derived from homiletic rabbinical literature, such as the hand of God portrayed instead of an angel. In the case of New Testament events, visual interpretations sometimes present a picture which draws elements from all four Gospels. Certain variations in the depiction of a biblical subject can simply relate to differences or inaccuracies in textual translation. Claus Sluter's portrayal of Moses in the *Puits de Moïse*, Champmol, Dijon (1395–1403), seems to follow the twelfth-century mistranslation of Exodus 34:30 in which Moses is described as descending from Mount Sinai not with a shining face, according to the common translation, but with horns growing from his head. The method chosen to present such a story, and to show the passage of time in dramatic action, also impacts on artistic interpretation of biblical text. These methods may vary according to the artistic conventions of the time and factors relating to the story chosen for depiction.

In approaching a textual episode for visual explication, the artist has recourse to the Bible for the narrative substance of the image, while theologians, writers, and preachers furnish templates for the interpretation of the story. However, the final rendering of a specific textual passage in art is ultimately dependent upon the inner vision of the artist, and as such may present a divergence from the sacred text. This is pointedly clear when examining illustrations produced to accompany scripture, but equally so in an image such as Grünewald's *Crucifixion* for the Isenheim Altar (1513–1515), where narrative components of the scene are completely transformed by the artist's intensely personal conception of Christ's suffering. Likewise, the artist may render gestures that have no textual basis but which transform the original narrative, as achieved by Rodin in his portrayal of Mary Magdelene clinging to the crucified Jesus (*Christ and Mary Magdelene c.* 1894). In effect, the artist's vision of a particular episode may be shaped by a variety of influences to which he may be receptive, and by his personal response to those influences.

Despite the waning of the role of religion in postmedieval society, the place of the Bible in human thought and conceptualizing has continued into the present day, a testimony to the universality and accessibility of its moral and anecdotal content. Old Testament episodes in particular have proven inherently flexible for use as visual commentaries on contemporary matters, with the recognizability of the human situations and emotional crises contained therein ensuring the endurance of the Old Testament as a quarry for artistic inspiration. Examples that spring to mind might be Adam and Eve succumbing to temptation; Sarah's infertility; David's adultery; or Job's successive afflictions. Tales of human experience that trigger a universal response of recognition, whilst more frequently occurring in the Hebrew narrative, are also found in the Christian Gospels: Judas' treacherous kiss, or the Doubting of Thomas. Thus has the Bible found continued interpretation at the hands of visual artists from various religious persuasions, and from none.

References and further reading

Grabar, André (1980) *Christian Iconography: A Study of its Origins*, London: Routledge & Kegan Paul.

Gutmann, Joseph (1989) *Sacred Images: Studies in Jewish Art from Antiquity to the Middle Ages*, Northhampton: Variorum Reprints.

Murray, Charles Sr. (1977) 'Art and The Early Church,' *Journal of Theological Studies*, NS, 28: 303–45.

Schiller, Gertrud (1966–1976) *Ikonographie der christlichen Kunst*, 5 Vols., Gütersloh: Gütersloher Verlagshaus Gerd Mohn. (TE of Vols. 1–2, London: Lund Humphries.)

Weitzmann, Kurt and Herbert Kessler (1990) *The Frescoes of the Dura Synagogue and Christian Art*, Dumbarton Oaks Studies 28, Washington DC: Dumbarton Oaks.

FELICITY HARLEY

AUGUSTINE (354–430)

Aurelius Augustinus, doctor of the church and bishop of Hippo Regius, was born in Tagaste (Souk Ahras, Algeria) to a non-Christian father, Patricius, and a Christian mother, Monica. He went to school in Madaura and took lessons in rhetoric in Carthage. In his early years he led a turbulent life, having a relationship with a woman whom he could not marry for social reasons but by whom he had a son, Adeodatus (372). His intellectual life went through various phases. Reading Cicero's lost dialogue *Hortensius* inspired him to take up philosophy (373), and shortly thereafter he joined the Manicheans and remained attached for nine years. His rhetorical career brought him to Rome (383) and subsequently to Milan (384). There he met Ambrose and was attracted to his sermons, at first because of their rhetorical qualities and later because of their substance. In the fall of 386 he converted to Christianity in a dramatic episode, which, like other events of his life, he described in his *Confessions*. After spending time with friends in the countryside as preparation, he was baptized by Ambrose during the night of Easter 387, together with his son and Alypius, one of his close friends. In 388 while returning to North Africa, his mother died in Ostia. Back home he did not want to become bishop immediately, and he avoided places with empty sees, intending to start a kind of monastic life with some friends. While visiting Hippo (Bône, Algeria), Augustine was pressed by the people there to become a priest (391), and the old bishop, Valerius, provided the inducement of his garden as a place to realize his monastic ideals. In 395 Augustine became co-bishop with Valerius and a year later his successor, remaining in that position until his own death in 430.

Augustine was a prolific writer and preacher. Many of his *Sermons* have been preserved, and new sermons still turn up on occasion. In the period preceding his baptism, he wrote some philosophical treatises, such as *De Beata Vita, De Ordine, Contra Academicos* and the *Soliloquia*. Among his apologetic works, *De Civitate Dei* has been particularly influential. The work was written to rebut those who maintained that the conquest of Rome by Alaric in 410 was a result of the abandoning of traditional religion. Augustine's *Confessions* created a new genre and have become one of the world's most celebrated literary works. Of his dogmatic writings the fifteen books *On the Trinity* are the most significant; in them Augustine approaches trinitarian questions from analogies in creation, particularly human creation, relating them to the human soul. He gave a small but comprehensive survey of Christian doctrine in his *Enchiridion ad Laurentium*. He wrote various exegetical works, usually on the basis of the old Latin translation current in North Africa, the *Vetus Latina*. An important theoretical work in this respect is *De Doctrina Christiana*. Other writings were directed against various rival religious groups, such as Manichaens, Donatists, and Pelagianists; they include *Contra Faustum Manichaeum, De Baptismo contra Donatistas, De Spiritu et Littera*. As a celebrated teacher, practical religious questions were pressed upon him. The deacon Deogratias, for example, wished to know how to instruct catechumens, leading to a small treatise, *De Catechizandis Rudibus*. As a founder of an ascetic community, Augustine wrote the oldest monastic rule in the West. His influence was long-lasting, particularly on Christian mysticism, early scholastic theology, intellectual scholarship, and thinking about church and state. The development of medieval and reformation theology would be unthinkable without his influence. His feast day is August 28.

References and further reading

Brown, Peter (1972) *Religion and Society in the Age of Saint Augustine*, London: Faber and Faber.

—— (2000) *Augustine of Hippo: A Biography*, Berkeley: University of California Press (new edition with an epilogue).

Marrou, H.-I. (1958) *Saint Augustin et la fin de la culture antique*, Paris: E. Boccard.

—— (1973) *Saint Augustin et l'augustinisme*, Paris: Editions du Seuil.

Rotelle, John E. (ed.) (1990–) *The Works of Saint Augustine: A Translation for the 21st Century*, Brooklyn, NY: New City.

Van der Meer, Frits (1961) *Augustine the Bishop: The Life and Work of a Father of the Church*, London and New York: Sheed and Ward.

ANNEWIES VAN DEN HOEK

AUTHORITY OF SCRIPTURE

The expression 'the authority of scripture' suggests two sorts of questions. One set concerns the location of *authority* in Christian faith – does it lie in scripture or somewhere else? The other concerns the intrinsic nature of *scripture* – how far does the notion of authority illumine scripture's nature and function?

Although the New Testament itself talks about authority and also talks about scripture (i.e., what came to be known as the Old Testament), it does not explicitly relate these two to each other. Such linkage came about in the context of modernity and of the existence of rival understandings of the nature of Christian faith. In a premodern context, Christian theologians such as the Church Fathers simply assumed that the scriptures should determine the nature of Christian faith and life. This was not a matter of controversy and thus not a topic of reflection. In the context of modernity, thinkers asked what was the authority for forms of belief and behavior. They wanted to be sure that the theological and ethical edifice was built on secure foundations. One way of attempting to do that was to see the scriptures as the foundation of all else. If the scriptures have authority, then beliefs and behavior built on them are secure.

This approach is vulnerable to two major difficulties. The first is that we cannot establish why the scriptures of the Old and New Testaments (with or without the Apocrypha or Deuterocanonical writings) should have this authority. If we treat them as a whole, we may be able to establish that they claim authority and tell us that God gives this authority to them, but we cannot test such claims. We must simply either accept or reject them, either on the basis of our own experience or act of faith, or on the basis of ascribing authority to some other entity such as one or other of the branches of the church whose own faith statement we commit ourselves to accept. Thus we cannot tell if the foundation of Christian faith and lifestyle is built on sand or on rock.

The nearest we can get to evading this dilemma involves appealing to the attitude of Christ as suggested by the New Testament writings (which for these purposes do not need to be treated as scripture, by way of circular argument, but simply as a historical source for Christ's attitudes). Although he did not directly speak of the 'authority' of scriptures, he did frequently quote from the Jewish scriptures, and he used phrases such as 'it is written,' which imply that they had authority for him and should have authority for other people. It is difficult to treat this important strand in his thinking as merely a harmless error, or a harmless concession to the beliefs of his contemporaries, or an interpolation from those beliefs (see Packer 1958/2001).

The second difficulty is that even people who agree on the authority of scripture do not agree on the nature of Christian faith and life. They can be in quite radical disagreement about important Christian doctrines such as the nature of God's sovereignty and human free will, or about issues in spirituality such as the question whether we may expect God to heal people today, or about important aspects of behavior such as the question whether Christians may fight in wars. It transpires that even if the foundation is secure, several different buildings can be erected on it. The authority of scripture does not work.

This links with the issues that are raised by the existence of rival understandings of Christian faith. The Protestant Reformation brought Christian thinkers more inescapably face-to-face with the existence of different forms of faith, such as those of Catholics, Protestants, and Anabaptists. One way of articulating the basis for these differences was to suggest that they reflected differences in where people located authority in Christian faith. Does authority lie in scripture? Or does it lie in the traditions that most of the church officially believes, such as those articulated in the creeds and in the doctrine of the Trinity? Or does it lie in the church's right to teach about the nature of Christian faith and the right interpretation of scripture (the *magisterium*)? Or does it lie in the gift of reason that God has given to humanity? Or does it lie in the religious experiences that God gives to people? Or does it lie in the insights of feminism regarding the true nature of humanity? Or does it lie in a commitment to sociopolitical liberation?

Although these are often articulated as alternatives, in practice all forms of Christian faith combine a number of them. All can be sources of truth. The question is, what is the relative importance of each locus of authority, and what do we do when they clash? To emphasize the 'supreme and final authority of scripture' is to affirm two convictions about scripture in relation to these other resources. One is that scripture is of paramount importance for the proactive development of Christian faith and life. It might seem to a sixteenth-century Protestant, for instance, that the worship and spirituality of the medieval church had allowed itself to become distanced from scripture. The reading and exposition of scripture was not central there as it was (for instance) in the synagogue, and this was an outward sign that scripture was not the key dynamic force in the church's life. Similarly, it might seem to a twenty-first-century Roman Catholic that charismatic worship often has similar characteristics to medieval worship. Here, too, the reading and exposition of scripture is not central to worship as it is in the lectionary-based worship of many churches, and in the synagogue. Both examples raise the question whether in their cases, the practice of Christians corresponds to their theoretical commitment to the supreme authority of scripture.

The other conviction is the one implied in the notion of the 'final authority of scripture.' When there is a clash between the authorities, scripture is to be followed. Scripture is the church's 'canon' or measuring line for testing what people say or do, and specifically for testing what counts as Christian. Thus Martin Luther attacked belief in purgatory on the basis that there was no reference to this in scripture. A twenty-first-century spiritual theologian might attack the Protestant belief that God does not have a change of mind on the basis of the explicit declarations in scripture that God does have a change of mind (which make a vital difference to people's understanding of prayer). Scripture exercises authority by correcting what our own experience or thinking inclines us to believe. And one of the great advantages of a belief in the authority of scripture is then realized. We are faced with something outside ourselves that we treat with absolute seriousness, even when we do not care for what it says. We are delivered from assuming that we are the measure of everything.

Once more, the examples cited show how the question of scriptural authority overlaps with two other sorts of question. One concerns the extent of scripture. The Hebrew scriptures do not refer to purgatory, but the Greek Old Testament does so, and Luther's opponent Johann Eck had claimed scriptural authority for belief in purgatory by appealing to 2 Maccabees 12:43–45, while Luther denied the appeal because this book lies outside the Hebrew scriptures. In which set of scriptures does authority reside? The other question concerns the interpretation of scripture. People who reject the idea of God having a change of mind do not see themselves as evading scriptural authority. They believe that such statements are to be interpreted figuratively.

The second set of questions regarding scriptural authority concerns the meaning and appropriateness of the term 'authority' in connection with a collection of documents such as the Old and New Testaments (see Goldingay 1994).

The notion of authority suggests that these documents focus on telling people what to do, or at least what to believe. Some parts of the scriptures indeed do that, and this notion of the authority of scripture would be meaningful, though it remains less simple than it initially sounds. The scriptures tell people not to eat meat with blood in it (Gen. 9:4), not to lend money on interest to the needy (e.g., Exod. 22:25), not to swear oaths (Matt. 5:34), and to turn the other cheek when we are hit on one cheek (Matt. 5:39). These are examples of authoritative scriptural commands that Christians do not usually feel bound by. Once more, establishing scripture's authority only introduces us to the question of its interpretation. The authoritative nature of the scriptures' teaching does not resolve the question of authority.

Further, in general scripture does not focus on telling us what to do, or even what to believe. Most often it is telling us stories or relating history. It is slightly odd to apply the notion of authority to stories. It can be

31

done, though the notion of authority then has a different meaning from the usual one. If the authority of scripture denotes its capacity to tell us what to believe, then the narrative of scripture has authority insofar as it declares authoritatively what is the nature of Christian faith. It establishes that Christian faith is a gospel, a statement about things that have happened in the story of Israel and in the story of Jesus that constitute good news for readers. It is not primarily a set of statements about the being of God or about obligations that Christians have, but a story about what God has done. The authority of scripture is thus built into the nature of Christian faith as a gospel. Although its statements are not more true than many other statements, they have a distinctive status that derives from the nature of the gospel as a story. The scriptures are the documents that tell this story. We might like to decide for ourselves how well they do, but we are not able to do so. We are the heirs to a process that was itself part of this story, a process whereby Jews and Christians decided what were the documents that best witness to this story (see Barr 1980).

To submit one's thinking and life to the authority of scripture is then an act of faith analogous to faith in Christ itself. It is not a leap of faith without evidence but it involves an act of faith that goes beyond what can be demonstrated to be true before the taking of the actual step. One piece of evidence that the decision was correct is then its fruitfulness in a person's life.

But it remains noteworthy that 'authority' is not a word that scripture uses when making statements about its own nature. The New Testament talks about 'authority' in various ways, but not about the 'authority' of the Old Testament. That reinforces the sense that 'authority' is not an obvious word to use in articulating the status of scripture.

This in turn links happily with a fact about the context of Christian thinking in the twenty-first century. 'Authority' became a key concept to apply to scripture because it became a key question in theology and philosophy in the context of modernity and the Enlightenment. We now live in a context in which questions of truth (if they can arise at all) cannot be determined by appeal to authority. The question whether authority lies in scripture, or in reason, or in the church's tradition, or in our experience, or in our commitments, is a question from the past. If scripture talked more in terms of authority, this might raise a problem for us. As it does not do so, the passing of modernity frees us to look at the status and function of scripture in ways that correspond more to its own nature and its own way of articulating theological questions.

References and further reading

Barr, James (1980) *The Scope and Authority of the Bible*, Explorations in Theology 7, London: SCM Press/Philadelphia: Westminster Press.

Goldingay, John (1994) *Models for Scripture*, Grand Rapids: Eerdmans/Carlisle: Paternoster.

Packer, James I. (1958) *'Fundamentalism' and the Word of God*, London: IVF (new edn. Grand Rapids: Eerdmans, 2001).

Reventlow, Henning Graf (1984) *The Authority of the Bible and the Rise of the Modern World*, ET London: SCM Press (US edn. Philadelphia: Fortress Press, 1985).

JOHN GOLDINGAY

B

BARR, JAMES (1924–)

Born March 20, 1924, in Glasgow, Scotland, he was exposed to biblical scholarship by his father Allan Barr, a minister and New Testament professor. Barr received his education from Edinburgh University (M.A., B.D.), Manchester University (M.A.), and Oxford University (M.A., D.D.). He was ordained by the Church of Scotland and served briefly as a pastor. He taught biblical and language studies at several universities, including Manchester, Edinburgh, Princeton, with his longest tenure occurring at Oxford University. Recipient of numerous honorary doctorates, Barr traveled the world giving lectures and reading papers, the content forming the chapters in several of his books geared toward specialists in biblical and linguistic studies.

In 1961, Barr published *The Semantics of Biblical Language*, which established him as a critical analyst of trends in biblical interpretation and language studies. He wrote it to counter what he saw within the field of 'biblical theology' as a mishandling of linguistic evidence concerning the Hebrew and Greek languages. Barr's criticism focused on three areas. First, he contended that the emphasis placed on the differences between Hebrew (Old Testament) and Greek (New Testament) thought as a guide for interpreting scripture was oversimplified and overstated. He demonstrated that while the New Testament was written in Greek the mind-set behind the words was Hebrew and consequently the entire Bible must be understood from a Hebrew perspective. Second, he stated that the etymology of a word is not a reliable guide to its meaning. He criticizes the methodology of G. Kittel's *Theological Dictionary of the New Testament* for failing to discover what the word meant in context and for its corresponding dependence upon associations of words. In *Comparative Philology and the Text of the Old Testament*, he expanded on this thought in refuting a related trend – that of deriving meaning for Hebrew words from the meaning of similar words in other ancient Semitic languages. Third, Barr suggests that a better method would be to discover the meaning from within the sentence. Meaning is found in the sentence, not the word, based on the unique arrangement of words in different combinations. He held that from this perspective biblical theology is possible because it is here that you gain insight into the biblical style.

Barr writes with a critical mind in various fields of biblical thought including the origin of scripture, canon, biblical authority, and biblical theology. However, Barr frequently targets fundamentalism. He explains the key to understanding fundamentalists is their insistence on biblical inerrancy not literal interpretation. Fundamentalists appeal to inspiration, revelation, harmonization, and metaphor to preserve historical and theological accuracy. Barr argues that the fundamentalist's hermeneutic is grounded in an improper interpretation of scripture. The Bible does not claim to be infallible or inerrant and therefore should not be the starting point for interpretation. Barr suggests rather than viewing the Bible as perfect, the Bible should be viewed as a fallible human book open to historical, critical, and literary analysis and interpretation, and be accepted for its theological significance not for its historical accuracy.

References and further reading

Barr, James (1961) *The Semantics of Biblical Language*, London: Oxford University Press.
—— (1966) *Old and New in Interpretation*, London: SCM Press.
—— (1968) *Comparative Philology and the Text of the Old Testament*, Oxford: Clarendon.
—— (1973) *The Bible in the Modern World*, London: SCM Press.
—— (1977) *Fundamentalism*, London: SCM Press.
—— (1980) *The Scope and Authority of the Bible*, Philadelphia: Westminster Press.
—— (1983) *Holy Scriptures*, Oxford: Clarendon.
—— (1984) *Beyond Fundamentalism*, Philadelphia: Westminster Press.
—— (1999) *The Concept of Biblical Theology: An Old Testament Perspective*, Minneapolis: Fortress Press.

H.C. JORGENSEN

BARTH, KARL (1886–1968)

Karl Barth came to prominence with his commentary on Romans (1919), which evolved out of his struggles to articulate the content of scripture for his parishioners at Safenwil. Although the first edition of the commentary received favorable reviews these in fact dismayed Barth and he recognized, mainly thanks to Brunner's criticisms, hermeneutical weaknesses that he repudiated in the second edition (1921). Here Barth shifted from a salvation history which allowed for an understanding of exegesis as an innate ability to hear God ('pneumatic exegesis') to a dialectical theology which contraposed our inability to hear God with God's merciful giving of himself to be known (Robinson 1968: 23–89). In the second edition Barth disowned his teachers, such as Herrmann, more vigorously, using dialectical (God is only spoken of where in Christ his 'yes' steps into our 'no') in preference to dogmatic ('there it is, believe it,' McCormack 1995: 309) and critical methods (speaking of God by negating humanity).

Barth continually pitted statement against statement in the hope that the truth of God himself speaking would emerge in the clash of words. In *Die kirchliche Dogmatik* (1932–1965, ET *Church Dogmatics*, 1956–1969) Barth modified his hermeneutics and tended to subordinate dialectical to dogmatic, the critical method falling into disuse. He was primarily concerned to establish the meaning of the author in order to guide his theological programme but the two purposes were not always clearly separated and each influenced the other. He sharply criticized the historical-critical method of his day and sought rather to write *with* not *about* Paul, turning to scripture as a theological resource. He believed that the aim of historical-critical research to get behind the texts, as in the case of the quest for the historical Jesus, was mistaken.

Theology begins where historical-critical methods end. The canon was seen as the final form of the texts and therefore the context in which theology must be done; the structured whole with the self-revelation of the triune God in Christ at the center (Barth 1956–1969: III/1, 24). Jesus unites scripture as the one to whom the Old Testament points and the New Testament witnesses. Barth's method of writing large sections of continuous exegesis in *Church Dogmatics*, where he piles up text after text to support his line of argument, is both impressive and creative but not always convincing, the latter point being something he shares with other exegetes. He refused to separate form and content (Barth 1956–1969: I/2, 493) but regarded the texts as the 'irreducible witness to a divine-human history' (Watson 1994: 230) given to be understood by, not innate to, the interpreter's humble 'thinking after' the narratives as the Spirit enabled (*nachdenken*). His concept of the three-fold form of the word of God (Barth 1956–1969: I/1, 88f.) where proclamation and scripture only become the word of God as they witness truthfully to Jesus Christ represents Barth's goal to let God himself speak. 'If I understand what I am trying to do in the Church Dogmatics, it is to listen to what Scripture is saying and tell you what I hear. What can be made of

this simplistic, obviously heuristic ploy? I wish to suggest that it be taken seriously' (Barth, cited in Ford 1981: 11).

References and further reading

Barth, K. (1956–1969) *Church Dogmatics*, trans. Geoffrey Bromiley, Edinburgh: T.&T. Clark.

Burnett, Richard E. (2001) *Karl Barth's Theological Exegesis: The Hermeneutical Principles of the Römerbrief Period*, WUNT 2. 145, Tübingen: Mohr Siebeck.

Demson, David E. (1997) *Hans Frei and Karl Barth: Different Ways of Reading Scripture*, Grand Rapids: Eerdmans.

Ford, D. (1981) *Barth and God's Story: Biblical Narrative and the Theological Method of Karl Barth in the Church Dogmatics*, Frankfurt: Peter Lang.

McCormack, B.L. (1995) *Karl Barth's Critically Realistic Dialectical Theology: Its Genesis and Development 1909–1936*, Oxford: Oxford University Press.

McGlasson, Paul (1991) *Jesus and Judas: Biblical Exegesis in Barth*, American Academy of Religion Academy Series 72, Atlanta: Scholars Press.

Robinson, J.M. (ed.) (1968) *The Beginnings of Dialectical Theology, Volume 1*. Virginia: John Knox Press.

Watson, F. (1994) *Text, Church and World: Biblical Interpretation in Theological Perspective*, Edinburgh, T.&T. Clark.

SHIRLEY MARTIN

BAUR, FERDINAND CHRISTIAN (1792–1860)

Ferdinand Christian Baur was the founder of what is generally known as the Tübingen School, a group of young scholars who gathered around him and who during the middle years of the nineteenth-century (roughly 1835 to 1860) enunciated the fundamental principles of the movement which became known as 'higher criticism.' Baur himself was born in Schmiden near Stuttgart in the province of Württemberg in 1792. He studied at Tübingen University and after teaching for ten years at the lower seminary at Blaubeuren, he was appointed professor of New Testament at Tübingen in 1826. Here he remained until his death in 1860.

In 1835 the theological world was rocked by Baur's pupil David Friedrich Strauss (1808–1874), whose two-volume *Life of Jesus* cut through the traditionally conservative view of Jesus as the divine Son of God. Up until this time objections to the traditional view of the Christian faith had been generally confined to freethinkers and rationalists, who had attempted to interpret this or that story according to more rationalistic criteria of reason. Strauss, however, repudiated such interpretations and argued that the Gospel stories were myths, composed in accordance with Old Testament prophesies in order to show that Jesus was the Messiah. He thought that there might have been some historical core, but that this was very difficult to determine with any certainty.

Strauss' book raised a storm throughout Germany, and Baur, as Strauss' teacher, fell under suspicion of heresy. For the next three decades the name Tübingen became notorious and synonymous with 'unbelief.' Baur himself at this time had not yet espoused such radical views, but he had already begun to formulate the principles which later became known as the Tübingen historical viewpoint. He detected a struggle between two main factions in the early church, between a party led by the apostle Peter and one led by the apostle Paul. These two factions, he believed, stood in bitter hostility to each other through the years, fighting for supremacy, until finally they were submerged into a third party led by adherents of the apostle John. Baur alleged that only four of Paul's letters were genuine – Romans, Galatians, and the two Corinthian letters. On this interpretation of history, he and his pupils (preeminently Eduard Zeller and Albert Schwegler) set out to reexamine the whole New Testament.

But behind this *historical* viewpoint lay an even more important *theological* viewpoint in which the New Testament was interpreted by purely 'natural' criteria, which, in effect, excluded the supernatural. Wherever a miracle occurred, declared Baur, the narrative was inauthentic and fictional. On this foundation the higher-critical principles which interpreted the Bible according to these nonsupernatural and nonmiraculous categories of criticism gradually developed. Whereas Baur's *historical* viewpoint was later demonstrated to be untenable, the *theological*, or more accurately *a-theological*, viewpoint, which excluded the supernatural, continued on in the works of Albrecht Ritschl, von Harnack, and Lietzmann, and to an even greater degree in the history of religions school.

References and further reading

Relevant entry from the *Oxford Dictionary of the Christian Church*, p. 171.

Harris, H. (1990) *The Tübingen School*, Grand Rapids: Baker.

Hodgson, P.C. (1966) *The Formation of Historical Theology: A Study of Ferdinand Christian Baur*, Makers of Modern Theology, New York: Harper & Row.

HORTON HARRIS

BIBLICAL THEOLOGY

In one sense, any sort of disciplined theological reflection on the Bible might usefully be labeled 'biblical theology.' But so far as our sources go, the expression was first used in the title of a book by W.J. Christmann, published in 1607 (*Teutsche biblische Theologie*). The work is no longer extant, but was apparently a compilation of prooftexts drawn from the Bible to support Protestant systematic theology. This usage continued for at least a century and a half, culminating in the learned five-volume work of G.T. Zachariae (*Biblische Theologie oder Untersuchung des biblischen Grundes der vornehmten theologischen Lehren*, 1771–1786). More exegetically rigorous than the little volume by Christmann, this work nevertheless belonged to the same approach, displaying very little awareness of historical development within the canon.

Overlapping with this usage of biblical theology Philip Jacob Spener introduced a new overtone. In his famous *Pia Desideria* (1675) Spener distinguished *theologia biblica*, his own theology suffused with piety, from *theologia scholastica*, the prevailing Lutheran orthodoxy that had returned to the Aristotelianism Luther had rejected. Thus biblical theology took on the flavor of protest. Spener's theology was claiming to be more 'biblical' than the prevailing dogmatics.

The same flavor of protest soon attached itself to a rather different use of 'biblical theology.' Influenced by English Deism and the German *Aufklärung*, this movement, in the second half of the eighteenth century, opposed the prevailing dogmatics in favor of rationalism rather than pietism. In several works the aim was to extract from the Bible timeless truths in accord with autonomous reason, truths that were still largely acceptable to the orthodoxy of the ecclesiastical establishment. J.P. Gabler belonged to this group, and it was his 1787 inaugural lecture at the University of Altdorf that captured the mood and prepared the way for the next developments. Contrary to what is often claimed, his lecture, 'An Oration on the Proper Distinction Between Biblical and Dogmatic Theology and the Specific Objectives of Each,' was not primarily an insistence that the Bible must first be read historically, or that its documents need to be set out in historical sequence (though some of this is implicit in his argument). Rather, convinced that dogmatics as a discipline was too far removed from scripture and that dogmaticians were endlessly disputing matters that could not be resolved when their discipline was so divorced from scripture, Gabler proposed a mediating discipline: biblical theology. By this, Gabler meant a largely inductive study of the biblical texts. This sort of study, he argued, was much more likely to generate widespread agreement amongst godly, learned, cautious theologians. Such results could then usefully serve as the foundation on which a more precise and broadly acceptable dogmatic theology might be built. Intrinsic to the proposal was the assumption that biblical theologians would go about their study of scripture with a minimal sense of being bound by dogmatic considerations. The unambiguous articulation of these priorities has earned for Gabler the sobriquet 'father of biblical theology.'

How much Gabler really wanted the fruits of biblical theology to serve as the basis for a revitalized systematic theology, and how much this part of his appeal was little more than a sop for the establishment, it is difficult to tell. Certainly that part of his proposal was not seriously taken up, while the first and fundamental part, inductive study of the biblical texts, assuming a ruptured link between biblical study and confessional application – was soon widely adopted. The effect was to tilt biblical study toward a recognition of scripture's diversities, with diminishing interest in building a coherent 'system.' By 1796, G.L. Bauer had written not a biblical theology but an Old Testament theology, followed shortly by a two-volume New Testament theology (1800–1802). Biblical theologies of the entire Christian canon continued to be written during the nineteenth century and even in the twentieth (see below). The most influential during the nineteenth century was doubtless that of J.C.K. von Hofmann (1886), whose work contributed significantly to the thinking of Adolf Schlatter. But the tide was flowing in another direction.

Throughout the nineteenth century, a diminishing number of scholars conceived of their work in biblical theology as the foundation for a larger systematic or dogmatic synthesis. That stance tended to be associated with theological conservatives, who still confessed one Mind behind scripture. But there were notable exceptions. W.M.L. de Wette, for instance, tried to spell out the bearing of his work on dogmatics (1813–1831), though his vision was a synthesis of faith and aesthetics, of faith and feeling – an attempt to isolate the timeless and the general while the hard data of the New Testament could be stripped out and jettisoned as the particular phenomenon of one phase or other of the history of religions. In any case, attempts at synthesis were against the grain: the tendency in biblical theology was toward the atomistic, cut off from any obligation to confessional dogmatics. This drift toward fragmentation soon meant that even categories like 'New Testament theology' and 'Old Testament theology' were much too broad, except as boundary definitions of sources. One had to focus on the theology of the Pentateuch, or of the sources of the Pentateuch; on the theology of Wisdom, or of the various Wisdom books; on the theology of the Synoptics, or of each Synoptic Gospel individually, or of its sources, including the theology of Q (Quelle, an ostensible sayings source used by Matthew and Luke); on the theology of Paul, and of each document linked to his name. In short, so far as substance is concerned, we must deal with Old Testament theologies and New Testament theologies. This approach to biblical theology still governs much of the discipline, and across a very wide theological spectrum (e.g., compare Ladd 1974 and Strecker 1995).

The first half of the twentieth century witnessed the flowering of these developments, and some reactions against them. A 'whole Bible' biblical theology could still be produced (e.g., Vos 1948), but it was very much out of vogue. One may usefully distinguish four overlapping movements.

The *first* may be labeled the historicist impulse. Historical criticism, with roots reaching as far back as Spinoza and Richard Simon, became part of establishment academic scholarship during the nineteenth century. In no small measure it was stimulated by the work of F.C. Baur and the Tübingen school, whose influence extended far beyond the rather simplistic law/grace, Peter/Paul dichotomies that lay at the heart of their historical reconstructions. In 1864, Baur's New Testament theology was published posthumously, and it marks the beginning of a commitment by many biblical theologians to a developmental view of critically reconstructed history. Invested with a fair degree of naturalism (for which Darwin's discoveries provided substantial reinforcement in later decades), the biblical documents tended less and less to be thought of as revelatory, still less as theologically binding. They merely provided information about the first century and earlier. They were therefore to be studied as part of the development of religious thought in general. The history-of-religions school, which controlled much of the discussion at the end of the nineteenth and the beginning of the twentieth century, aspired to a cool neutrality, to an approach that was usually comparative, synchronically descriptive, and interested as well in diachronic development.

The primacy of a developmental view of history in the interpretation of biblical documents shaped not only the best of the liberal biblical theologians (e.g., Holtzmann 1897, 1911) but the best of the conservative ones as well (e.g., Weiss 1868, 1903). Increasingly, however, a narrow definition of history prevailed, i.e., one that excludes any possibility of accepting as true any biblical affirmation that talks of God acting in history. Its assumptions are naturalistic. Of course, it does not deny the possibility of the existence of God, but denies that history can find any evidence of him. History is by definition a closed continuum. Under such a regimen biblical theology can never be more than the study of what various groups thought about God and related matters at various times. Hence the cheeky title of the influential work of W. Wrede (1897), *Über Aufgabe und Methode der sogenannten neutestamentliche Theologie* (*Concerning the Task and Method of So-Called New Testament Theology*).

Reacting to the sterility of the history-of-religions school, Barth generated the *second* movement. His commentary on Romans (1933) threw down a gauntlet: it was a profoundly theological work, an approach progressively eroded by the history-of-religions school. For many, Barth's reduction of the importance of historical and comparative research for the meaning of the Bible, and his elevation of the theological, was an oasis in a parched land; for others, it was a form of theological escapism that could not long endure.

Moreover, Barth convinced Bultmann that classic theological liberalism had to be abandoned. But instead of joining Barth's crusade, Bultmann introduced and led a *third* movement that dominated discussion (especially in the realm of New Testament theology) for almost half a century. At one level, the naturalism and historicism of Wrede persisted; but at another level, instead of eschewing theological formulation or dogmatic synthesis, Bultmann 'demythologized' what he thought 'modern man' could no longer believe, in order to isolate the real, unchanging gospel in terms that could still be believed. In that sense Bultmann abandoned the historicism of Wrede to produce a kerygma that is remarkably similar to Heideggerian existentialism. Along the way, revelation, God, faith, and much else were redefined. The gain, however, from Bultmann's perspective, was a theological grasp that was utterly independent of historical criticism. His enormously influential *Theology of the New Testament* (1948–1953; ET 1952–1955) provided a faith whose object is not tied to historical revelation, a Jesus about whom little can be said except for a raw *Dass*, a resurrection whose significance lies not in its ostensible historical reality but in the psychological faith of the community, and so forth.

Today his views are largely abandoned. This is not only because it is increasingly difficult to accept as normative Heideggerian existentialism, and still more difficult to see it as somehow at the core of biblical revelation (thus the demythologizing project is seen as obsolete on the one hand and anachronistic on the other), but also for a stronger reason. Once allowance is made for the conceptual structures that prevailed when the biblical documents were written, many passages in both Testaments (e.g., Luke 1:1–4; 1 Cor. 15:6) approach what we mean by scientific history, i.e., tight linking of the textual witness to what actually happened. Christianity is not Buddhism; its claims are in part irreducibly historical. Contemporary scholars may judge that witness to be true, and advance their reasons, or they may hold it to be false, and justify their skepticism. But biblical theologians cannot disallow historical reflection as part of their task of understanding the biblical documents, or relegate such reflection to a compartment hermetically sealed off from theology.

The *fourth* movement was the short-lived but widely influential biblical theology movement which was strong in the 1930s to 1950s in Britain and Europe, and in the 1940s to 1950s in America. Perhaps its most influential figure was Oscar Cullmann. His emphasis on salvation history (*Heilsgeschichte*) as the unifying theme of scripture sought to bring together the themes that had been flying apart since the turn of the century. Moreover, his influence was magnified by his determination to write in an edifying way. Inevitably, those who constructed the 'history' inherent in 'salvation history' a little differently raised many objections.

This was not the only stream of the biblical theology movement. Another stream focused on 'the mighty acts of God' (esp. G. Ernest Wright) as the unifying theme of scripture, though acts apart from an authoritative interpretation of their significance can prove very plastic. R. Morgan (*ABD* 6.479) includes Kittel's *Theological Dictionary of the New Testament* (1933–1974; ET 1964–1974) within the biblical theology movement: after all, it was dedicated to Schlatter.

But the biblical theology movement soon suffered catastrophic criticism. The relation between the mighty acts of God and the biblical texts was less than clear. The attempt to erect entire theological structures on word studies soon faced the withering attack of James Barr (1961). The meaning of *Heilsgeschichte* proved slippery, with quite different emphases from writer to writer. Hesitation about the movement climaxed in the criticism of Childs (1970).

The last fifty years have witnessed extrapolations of most of the earlier stances regarding biblical theology, plus some new developments. We may summarize as follows:

(1) Some of the most straightforward extrapolations have yielded works of great influence. For instance, in the field of Old Testament theology, Eichrodt (1959–1964), though he himself insisted that the discipline should not be shaped by any 'dogmatic scheme,' nevertheless sought a theological center in the documents. On the one hand, he developed a triple division: God and the people, God and the world, God and the individual; on the other hand, the controlling concept in his work was the covenant — an approach which, if nothing else, generated prolonged discussion regarding the 'center' of Old Testament theology. By contrast, von Rad's complex and influential work (1957–1960) rejects any attempt to elaborate the structure of the Old Testament 'world of faith.' Because the Old Testament documents present *Heilsgeschichte*, a history of salvation, Old Testament theology worthy of the name must in the first instance retell this history. But von Rad does not want to return to the sterile 'narrow' history against which Eichrodt and others reacted. Rather than creating a history of Israelite religion, von Rad develops a sequential ordering of the theological witnesses that build up an account of Yahweh's action in history – depending, as he goes, on more-or-less standard historical-critical reconstructions of the sources and their dates.

Similarly in the domain of New Testament theology: some lines of extrapolation from earlier work are plain enough, and show up in various configurations. Some (e.g., Kümmel 1974) begin with a reconstruction of the teaching of Jesus as that can be extracted from the Synoptic Gospels on the basis of standard historical-critical givens. This is followed by an analysis of the primitive church's beliefs, so far as they can be reconstructed on form-critical grounds. There follows in turn the theology of the New Testament corpora, on roughly chronological grounds, starting with Paul. Although the judgments and results vary considerably, the same methodological approaches are followed by many (e.g., Stuhlmacher 1992; Hübner 1990–1995). A more conservative biblical theologian such as Ladd (1974) varies this procedure by starting with the Synoptic Gospels rather than with the historical Jesus *behind* the Synoptics, since he is persuaded that the Synoptics bear faithful witness. None of these writers, however, makes much of an attempt at synthesis. Guthrie (1981) attempts to escape the lack of synthesis by tracing a rich variety of themes across the New Testament corpora. This produces a certain gain in perspective, but at the very considerable expense of losing sight of the distinctive emphases and contributions of each corpus. Caird's conference-table approach (1994) is more creative, but shares Guthrie's methodological limitations.

(2) Approaches that rely on a fairly radical application of historical criticism, usually tied to a 'narrow' understanding of history, tend to produce idiosyncratic results. The work of Schmithals (1994), for instance, is less a New Testament theology than an independent reconstruction of early Christianity (shades of Wrede) into which the New Testament is squeezed. Attempting to find a reason why the traditions about the historical Jesus should have been connected with the post-Easter kerygma, he fastens on such passages as 1 Corinthians 15:20–28 and links between the theme of the kingdom of God in Jesus' teaching and Paul's theology. From this base Schmithals develops a fundamental polarity between Antioch theology (typically apocalyptic, focused on the righteousness of God, and with gnostic tendencies) and Damascus theology (characterized by high Christology, real incarnation, a radical view of sin, realized eschatology) – a polarity which is then traced in various ways through the New Testament documents and on into the Apostolic Fathers. Berger's large volume (1994) develops the analogy of the tree: New Testament thought is like a tree with roots in Jerusalem, but with the primary branching taking place in Antioch. The Jerusalem believers shaped the early Roman church and the Epistle of James; believers more influenced by Hellenism moved to Antioch and became the source of the Pauline and Johannine streams. A secondary node in the Antioch branch generates the Synoptic Gospels, including Mark, Q, and John (which according to Berger antedates Matthew and Luke). All this Berger lays out before his systematic examination of the New Testament documents. The examination itself places the documents within the established grid. Berger thinks he can detect how the various branches repeatedly cross and influence one another. There is no significant attempt to seek out what is unifying in New Testament thought.

(3) Roman Catholic contributions to the discipline were negligible until 1950. The earlier popular and confessional works of Lemonnyer (1928) and Küss (1936) broke little new ground. Since the publication of *Divino Afflante* (1943), however, Catholic scholars have gradually come to display the diversity of approaches to biblical theology that characterize their Protestant colleagues. Meinertz (1950) works inductively and descriptively with the New Testament corpora, but attempts no evaluation of their chronological order or historical development. Bonsirven (1931–1951) is not dissimilar, but is suffused with gentle piety. It was Schnackenburg (1962–1965) who, in the domain of New Testament theology, broke into the main stream of discussion. After first dealing with the kerygma and the theology of the primitive church, he reconstructs the teaching of Jesus according to the Synoptics, summarizes the contribution of the individual synoptists, and then progressively examines Paul, John, and the rest of the New Testament writings.

Meanwhile, Roman Catholic Old Testament theologies were written by van Imschoot (1954–1956), J.L. McKenzie (1974), and Mattioli (1981). Both Schelkle (ET 1968–1976) and Harrington (1973) wrote a biblical theology of the entire Christian Bible – the former a four-volume work structured more-or-less in traditional dogmatic categories, but concerned to trace those categories from the Old Testament through Second Temple Judaism to the New Testament. By the end of this period, mainstream Roman Catholic biblical theologies could not easily be distinguished from, their Protestant counterparts (e.g., Goppelt 1981–1982, Thüsing 1981, Gnilka 1989).

(4) Biblical theology has been increasingly shaped by various perspectives on the canon or on 'canon criticism.' The last twenty years have witnessed a gentle revival of what the Germans call *eine gesamtbiblische Theologie*, a 'whole Bible theology,' what Barr (somewhat dismissively) refers to as 'panbiblical theology.' Sometimes this is the product of strong confessionalism: if the canon is considered in any sense to be the product, ultimately, of one Mind or Actor, then scholars may responsibly pursue its unity within its diverse movements.

But two movements have most commonly been tied to the rubric 'canon criticism.' The *first* is the communitarian stance of J.A. Sanders and his disciples. Sanders does not content himself with the final form of the canonical documents. It is precisely their growth and development that interest him, and in particular the changing communitarian experiences and interests that such changes reflect. The *second* (and more influential) form of canon criticism is found in the work of Brevard Childs and his followers (though Childs himself does not now use the category for his own work). Childs allows only the final form of the canon to shape his theological synthesis. Unlike Sanders, Childs is little interested in delineating the communitarian interests that produced our documents, and not at all interested in ostensible extracanonical influences. The Christian church recognizes a restrictive canon (whose borders are a little fuzzy as one moves from group to group), and if we are Christians that must be the framework in which we do our theological reflection. Ultimately, Childs is interested in using the biblical documents of both Testaments to show how, together, they justify a more-or-less traditional, orthodox theology, as expressed in postbiblical categories. Although much of his work is fresh and stimulating, he has sometimes been charged with 'canonical fundamentalism' because his reason for using the canon as his boundary is not well defended (since he rejects any traditional view of scriptural authority). Childs emerges with a unity of result, but it is less than clear how he gets there as long as the unity of the foundation documents is affirmed by little more than the results (cf. Noble 1995).

(5) The impact of postmodernism on the discipline of biblical theology has begun to be felt, and will certainly increase in years ahead. Some postmodernists criticize the earlier 'biblical theology movement' for being too 'modernist' in its epistemology (e.g., Penchansky). Jeanrond provides a definition of biblical theology that 'maximizes diversity and competing perspectives, rebukes all systematic theology, encourages all nondogmatic models and paradigms,' and eschews any hint of unity. Brueggemann's recent Old Testament theology (1997), wonderfully stimulating and innovative, greatly stresses the virtue of imagination, constantly insists on interpreting individual biblical narratives independently of the larger narrative of its corpus (still less of the biblical metanarrative), and builds into its very structure mutually contradictory options. In other words, it organizes its material into core testimony, countertestimony, unsolicited testimony, and embodied testimony. An example of the outworking of the first two (core testimony and countertestimony) occurs in Brueggemann's treatment of Exodus 34:6–7. This 'credo,' according to Brueggemann, embraces a 'besetting tension not between opposing theological traditions, but in the very life, character, and person of Yahweh': between, on the one hand, Yahweh's solidarity with his people and gracious fidelity and, on the other, his sovereign, sometimes excessive and destructive self-regard. The net result, of course, is a picture of a god whom Brueggemann is happy to embrace, but scarcely one that can reform his perspectivalism.

(6) Despite repeated pronouncements that the 'biblical theology movement' of the first half of the century was dead, biblical theology has renewed itself and begun to flourish anew in the closing decades of the twentieth century. The journal *Jahrbuch für biblische Theologie* has been published for over fifteen years, *Horizons in Biblical Theology* for more than twenty. Major volumes in the field are complemented by countless others. Although enormous diversity of perspective is still the order of the day, the best of this work is enriched by fresh thinking about literary genre, speech act theory, intertextuality, and, more broadly, the use of the Old Testament in the New.

(7) At the same time, one cannot ignore the condemning voices who view askance all or part of the biblical theology project. We may mention two of the more articulate of these voices. Räisänen (1990) is convinced that New Testament theology in any integrative sense is a chimera: the divergences are so great that the pursuit of unity is futile. Barr's recent volume (1999), though it pursues certain biblical theologians intemperately (especially Childs), is at best cautious about the rest of the discipline, especially if it attempts to clothe itself in anything that smacks of the normative or the revelatory.

At the beginning of a new millennium, biblical theology stands on the threshold of major advance. On the one hand, the diversity of the traditions and hermeneutical assumptions that have gone into its history has left the movement in some serious disarray. There is still no broad agreement on such major issues as the nature of revelation, the significance of the canon, the relationships between theological reflection and history, and much more – all of which bear on the very definition of the enterprise. On the other hand, enough groundbreaking work has been done that a path has been cleared for major, creative syntheses to take place, syntheses that do not for a moment downplay the diversities of the biblical corpora but that refuse to succumb to the minimalism of those who think 'whole Bible' biblical theology is a chimerical vision.

References and further reading

Adam, A.K.M. (1995) *Making Sense of New Testament Theology: Modern Problems and Prospects*, StABH 11, Macon, GA: Mercer University Press.

Balla, Peter (1997) *Challenges to New Testament Theology: An Attempt to Justify the Enterprise*, WUNT 95, Tübingen: J.C.B. Mohr and Paul Siebeck.

Barr, James (1961) *The Semantics of Biblical Language*, Oxford: Oxford University Press.

—— (1999) *The Concept of Biblical Theology: An Old Testament Perspective*, Minneapolis: Fortress Press.

Barth, Karl (1933) *The Epistle to the Romans*, Oxford: Oxford University Press (orig. 1919, 1921).

Bauer, G.L. (1796) *Theologie des Alten Testaments*, Leipzig: Weygand.

—— (1800–1802) *Biblische Theologie des Neuen Testaments*, 2 Vols., Leipzig: Weygand.

Baur, F.C. (1864) *Vorlesungen über neutestamentliche Theologie*, Leipzig: Fues's Verlag.

Berger, K. (1994) *Theologiegeschichte des Urchristentums*, Tübingen. Francke.

Bonsirven, J. (1963) *Theology of the New Testament*, London: Burns and Oates (orig. 1951).

Brueggemann, Walter (1997) *Theology of the Old Testament: Testimony, Dispute, Advocacy*, Minneapolis: Augsburg Fortress Press.

Bultmann, Rudolf (1952–1955 [1948–1953]) *Theology of the New Testament*, London: SCM Press.

Caird, G.B. (1994) *New Testament Theology*, L.D. Hurst (ed.), Oxford: Clarendon.

Carson, D.A. (1997) 'New Testament Theology,' pp. 796–814 in *Dictionary of the Later New Testament and Its Developments*, Ralph P. Martin and Peter H. Davids (eds), Downers Grove: IVP.

—— (2000) 'Systematic Theology and Biblical Theology,' pp. 89–104 in *New Dictionary of Biblical Theology*, T.D. Alexander and Brian Rosner (eds.), Leicester: IVP.

Childs, Brevard (1970) *Biblical Theology in Crisis*, Philadelphia: Westminster Press.

—— (1992) *Biblical Theology of the Old and New Testaments*, London: SCM Press.

Cullmann, Oscar (1951) *Christ and Time*, London: SCM Press.

—— (1967) *Salvation in History*, London: SCM Press.

Davies, Philip R. (1995) *Whose Bible Is It Anyway?*, JSOTSup 204, Sheffield: Sheffield Academic Press.

de Wette, W.M.L. (1831) *Lehrbuch der christlichen Dogmatik in ihrer historischen Entwicklung dargestellt. Erster Teil: Die biblische Dogmatik, enthaltend biblische Dogmatik Alten und Neuen Testaments. Oder kritischer Darstellung der Religionslehre des Hebraismus, des Judenthums, und Urchristentums*, Berlin: G. Reimer, 3rd edn. (1st edn. 1813).

Dohmen, Christoph and Thomas Söding (eds.) (1995) *Eine Bibel zwei Testamente: Positionen biblischer Theologie*, Paderborn: Schöningh.

Eichrodt, Walter (1961–1967) *Theology of the Old Testament*, 2 Vols., London: SCM Press (orig. 1959–1964).

Gabler, J.P. (1831) 'Oratio de iusto discrimine theologiae biblicae et dogmaticae regundisque recte utriusque finibus,' pp. 179–98 in Vol. 2 of *Kleinere theologische Schriften*, T.A. Gabler and J.G. Gabler (eds.), Ulm: Verlag des Stettinischen Buchhandlung (available in English in J. Sandys-Wunsch and L. Eldredge (1980) 'J.P. Gabler and the Distinction Between Biblical and Dogmatic Theology: Translation, Commentary and Discussion of His Originality,' *Scottish Journal of Theology* 33: 133–58.

Gnilka, J. (1989) *Neutestamentliche Theologie: Ein Überblick*, Würzburg: Echter Verlag.

—— (1994) *Theologie des Neuen Testament*, Freiburg: Herder.

Goppelt, L. (1981–1982) *Theology of the New Testament*, 2 Vols., Grand Rapids: Eerdmans (orig. 1975–1976).

Guthrie, Donald (1981) *New Testament Theology: A Thematic Study*, Leicester: IVP.

Harrington, W. (1973) *Path of Biblical Theology*, Dublin: Gill and Macmillan.

Holtzmann, H.J. (1897, 1911) *Lehrbuch der neutestamentlichen Theologie*, Tübingen: J.C.B. Mohr and Paul Siebeck.

Hübner, Hans (1990–1995) *Biblische Theologie des Neuen Testaments*, 3 Vols., Göttingen: Vandenhoeck & Ruprecht.

Jeanrond, Werner (1998) 'The Significance of Revelation for Biblical Theology,' *Biblical Interpretation* 6: 243–57.

Kraftchick, S.J., C.D. Myers, Jr., and B.C. Ollenburger (eds.) (1995) *Biblical Theology: Problems and Perspectives*, Nashville: Abingdon Press.

Kümmel, W.G. (1974) *The Theology of the New Testament According to Its Major Witnesses*, London: SCM Press (orig. 1969).

Küss, O. (1936) *Die Theologie des Neuen Testaments: Eine Einführung*, Regensburg: Pustet.

Ladd, George E. (1974) *A Theology of the New Testament*, Grand Rapids: Eerdmans (rev. edn. 1993).

Lemonnyer, A. (1928) *La théologie du Nouveau Testament*, Paris: Bloud & Gay.

McKenzie, J.L. (1974) *A Theology of the Old Testament*, Garden City: Doubleday.

Mattioli, A. (1981) *Dio e l'uomo nella Bibbia d'Israële: Theologia dell' Antico Testamento*, Casale Monferrato: Marietti.

Meinertz, M. (1950) *Theologie des Neuen Testaments*, 2 Vols., Bonn: P. Hanstein.

Morgan, Robert (1973) *The Nature of New Testament Theology*, London: SCM Press.

—— (1992) 'Theology (New Testament),' *ABD* 6.473–83.

Noble, Paul R. (1995) *The Canonical Approach: A Critical Reconstruction of the Hermeneutics of Brevard S. Childs*, BIS 16, Leiden: Brill.

Perichansky, David (1995) *The Politics of Biblical Theology: A Postmodern Reading*, StABH 10, Macon: Mercer University Press.

Räisänen, Heikki (1990) *Beyond New Testament Theology: A Story and a Programme*, London: SCM Press.

Sanders, J.A. (1972) *Torah and Canon*, Philadelphia: Fortress Press.

—— (1987) *From Sacred Story to Sacred Text: Canon as Paradigm*, Philadelphia: Fortress Press.

Schelkle, K.H. (1971–1978) *Theology of the New Testament*, 4 Vols., Collegeville: Liturgical (orig. 1968–1976).

Schlatter, Adolf (1997) *The History of the Christ: The Foundation of New Testament Theology*, Grand Rapids: Baker (orig. 1909).

—— (1998) *The Theology of the Apostles: The Development of New Testament Theology*, Grand Rapids: Baker (orig. 1910).

Schmithals, W. (1994) *Theologiegeschichte des Urchristentums*, Stuttgart: Kohlhammer.

Schnackenburg, Rudolf (1965) *The Moral Teaching of the New Testament*, London: Burns and Oates (orig. 1962).

Strecker, George (1995) *Theologie des Neuen Testaments*, Berlin: de Gruyter.

Stuhlmacher, Peter (1992) *Biblische Theologie des Neuen Testaments*, Göttingen: Vandenhoeck & Ruprecht.

Thüsing, W. (1981) *Die neutestamentlichen Theologien und Jesus Christus*, Band 1: *Kriterien auf Grund der Rückfrage nach Jesus und des Glaubens an seine Auferweckung*, Düsseldorf: Patmos.

Van Imschoot, Paul (1954–1956) *Théologie de l'Ancien Testament*, 2 Vols., Tournai: Desclée.

Von Hofmann, J.C.K. (1886) *Biblische Theologie des Neuen Testaments*, Nördlingen: Beck.

Von Rad, Gerhard (1962–1965) *Old Testament Theology*, 2 Vols., Edinburgh: Oliver and Boyd (orig. 1957–60).

Vos, Geerhardus (1948) *Biblical Theology: Old and New Testaments*, Grand Rapids: Eerdmans.

Weiss, B. (1868) *Lehrbuch der Biblischen Theologie des Neuen Testaments*, Berlin: Teubner.

Wrede, W. (1897) *Über Aufgabe und Methode der sogenannte neutestamentliche Theologie*, Göttingen: Vandenhoeck & Ruprecht.

Wright, G. Ernest (1952) *God Who Acts*, London: SCM Press.

Zachariae, G.T. (1771–1786) *Biblische Theologie, oder Untersuchung des biblischen Grundes der vornehmsten theologischen Lehren*, Tübingen: Frank & Schramm.

D.A. CARSON

BROWN, RAYMOND EDWARD S.S.
(1928–1998)

Raymond E. Brown was an influential and leading Roman Catholic biblical scholar of the twentieth century, who was born in New York City on May 22, 1928. He studied under W.F. Albright and became Professor of New Testament at the Union Theological Seminary in New York (1971). He had earlier studied at the Catholic University of America (Washington), receiving his bachelor's and master's degrees, and subsequently at St. Mary's Seminary (Baltimore) and Johns Hopkins University, receiving doctorates in Sacred Theology and Semitic Languages respectively. He died August 8, 1998.

Brown was the first Catholic in a tenured position at Union Theological Seminary, an historically Protestant institution, where he taught for two decades and was one of the pioneers of biblical criticism in New Testament studies with his defining work on the *Sensus Plenior of Sacred Scriptures*. He wrote very widely and was the author of many articles and nearly forty books, many of them commentaries on the New Testament including detailed studies on the Gospel accounts of Jesus' birth and death.

Although his writings were intended for nonspecialists and thus were intelligible to a variety of audiences, i.e., scholars, students of theology, and interested Christians, this, however, did not compromise his high standards of exegesis and care for detail, evidenced by treatment of detailed technical issues and general comments in the footnotes of all his writings.

In his *Birth of the Messiah*, a commentary on the infancy narratives in Matthew and Luke, Brown writes a convincing 'masterwork' of exegesis covering all aspects of the background and interpretation of the narratives to show that they are a key to the interpretation of the gospel message. In the *Death of the Messiah*, Brown tackles all issues pertinent to the Passion of Jesus and explains in detail what the four evangelists intended to convey to their various audiences. He does this by interpreting the various acts of the Passion and also by providing a comparison with a noncanonical Passion narrative in the Gospel of Peter.

In answer to the question of whether the biblical accounts of Jesus' life and teaching embraced historical truth about Jesus or whether they were the product of early Christian theologians writing decades after the Crucifixion, he wrote what he called a 'new and bold thesis' to bring some balance and direction to biblical studies, *An Introduction to the New Testament*. The *Introduction* addresses religious, spiritual, and ecclesiastical issues raised by the New Testament and keeps to the fore the literary power of the books of the New Testament and their message.

His main work was, however, on Johannine literature. His two-volume commentary on the Gospel according to John is an indispensable contribution to Johannine studies. In the first volume (chapters 1–12), he manifests an incisive and brilliant mind in the way he interprets the Gospel, showing expert knowledge of the Dead Sea Scrolls, the Palestinian and the Gnostic backgrounds in the presentation of Jesus' divinity, ecclesiology, sacramentalism, eschatology, and other motifs. In the second volume (chapters 13–21), the emphasis is on the book of signs stressing an independent tradition underlying John's Gospel. In the commentary on the Epistles of John, Brown delineates the history of the Johannine community (cf. *Community of the Beloved Disciple*).

In the contentious field of biblical studies Brown epitomized the broadly learned, disciplined, fair-minded scholar who was not only a rigorous and exacting scholarly mind but also a centrist, a man of the church who strongly believed that the Gospel accounts were products of the church and that they were basically trustworthy, and also showed that contemporary interpretation of the New Testament could be built on a solid historical analysis of ancient texts.

References and further reading

Carson, Donald A. (1993) *New Testament Commentary Survey*, Leicester: IVP.

Niebuhr, Gustav (1998) 'Raymond E. Brown, 70, Dies; A Leading Biblical Scholar,' *The New York Times*, Tuesday August 11 Section B, p. 8, Column 5.

HUDSON N. ZIMBA

BRUEGGEMANN, WALTER (1933–)

Walter Brueggemann, a major American Old Testament scholar, was born March 11, 1933 in Tilden, Nebraska, the son of a Methodist minister. He is married to Mary Miller, also an ordained minister. They have two sons: James and John. His education included A.B. Elmhurst College (1955), B.D. Eden Theological Seminary (1958); Th.D. Union Theological Seminary (1961), where he studied under Professor James Muilenburg; and Ph.D. St. Louis University (1974).

Walter Brueggemann is an ordained minister of the United Church of Christ. He served as Professor of Old Testament (1961–1986) and Dean (1968–1982) at Eden Theological Seminary in Kansas City, Missouri. Since 1986 he has been William Marcellus McPheeters Professor of Old Testament at Columbia Theological Seminary in Atlanta, Georgia. His felicitous manner of lecturing on Old Testament subjects has made him a popular speaker for students and churches. He is able to present very serious and deep subjects in ways that delight popular audiences and students at all levels. Many of his books record his lectures which made scholarly approaches to biblical literature understandable to all readers. His works are major examples of the renaissance of biblical studies in theological education during the twentieth century.

He has been active in the work of the Society of Biblical Literature, serving as its president in 1990.

He is a prolific author of books and articles, principally on the Old Testament. He has written over fifty books and over 350 articles – from technical Old Testament works, to articles in church and religious magazines, and study guides. He has been active as an editor of books for Fortress Press and served on editorial boards for the *Journal of Biblical Literature, Interpretation, Theology Today, Sojourners, Journal for Preachers* and the *Christian Century*. Brueggemann has been invited to present prestigious lectureships including the Beecher Lectures (Yale University), the Caldwell Lectures (Louisville Presbyterian Seminary), the Cole Lectures (Vanderbilt Divinity School), the James Reid Lectures (Westminster College, Cambridge, UK) and the Sprunt Lectures (Union Theological Seminary, Richmond, VA).

Among his honors and awards are: LL.D. DePauw University 1984, D.D. Virginia Theological Seminary 1988, D.H.Litt. Doane College 1990, D.D. Jesuit School of Theology 1993, D. Litt. Colgate University 1997, and D.H.Litt. Elmhurst College 1997. There is also a festschrift in his honor: *God in the Fray: A Tribute to Walter Brueggemann* (eds. Tod Linafelt and Timothy K. Beal, Minneapolis: Fortress Press).

References and further reading

Brueggemann, Walter (1977) *The Land: Place or Gift, Promise, and Challenge in Biblical Faith*, Philadelphia: Fortress Press.
—— (1978) *The Prophetic Imagination*, Philadelphia: Fortress Press.
—— (1982) *Genesis*, Interpretation: A Bible Commentary, Atlanta: John Knox.
—— (1986) *Hopeful Imagination*, Philadelphia: Fortress Press.
—— (1989) *Finally Comes the Poet: Daring Speech for Proclamation*, Minneapolis: Fortress Press.
—— (1997) *Theology of the Old Testament: Testimony, Dispute, Advocacy*, Minneapolis: Fortress Press.
—— and H.W. Wolff (1982 [1975]) *The Vitality of Old Testament Traditions*, Atlanta: John Knox Press.

JOHN D.W. WATTS

BULTMANN, RUDOLF (1884–1976)

English-speaking readers often find Bultmann initially a perplexing enigma. He appears in the guise of a radical skeptic with regard to issues of the historicity of early Christian traditions. Yet in his insistence that critical historical inquiry 'stands in the service of the interpretation of New Testament writings under the presupposition that they have something to say to the present' (1955: 251) alongside his approval of the kerygmatic significance of Karl Barth's *Romans*, we see a Christian pietist who broadly stands in the tradition of Martin Luther.

Bultmann drew on Neo-Kantianism, Kierkegaard, and especially Martin Heidegger for the conceptual frame in terms of which this kerygmatic gospel should be expressed and interpreted today. It is far too simple to suggest that Bultmann replaced the New Testament message by Heidegger's philosophy of existentialism. Bultmann insists that he learned from him not *what* theology has to say but *how* it may best say it (Bultmann 1964: 24–7).

Bare historical 'facts' (with certain exceptions, see below) become for Bultmann in some cases irrelevant and in other cases even misleading if the purpose of New Testament interpretation is (as he believes) to proclaim the *kerygma* and thereby to awaken self-understanding and faith. To view the biblical texts as largely or primarily a report of 'facts' would be to describe only phenomena within the world rather than to listen for divine address. Still more poignantly, Bultmann is committed to a nineteenth-century understanding of Luther's theology, which sees any attempt to trust in biblical reports of descriptions of 'objective' events as an attempt to work one's way to God by intellectual effort (even if one has rejected the notion of justification on the basis of 'moral' works of achievement).

Hence Bultmann introduces a proposal to 'demythologize the New Testament.' Bultmann confuses his own case and his own proposals by using the term 'myth' in three quite different (often inconsistent) ways. In brief, he begins with the notion of a primitive mythological worldview in which angels, spirits, and demons intervene in human life (Bultmann 1964: 1–8). Next he proceeds to speak of 'myth' as if the term simply denoted 'analogy' (1964: 10, 2, 102–4). Finally, he reaches the heart of the matter in defining myth as 'objectification,' i.e., as using language which normally denotes objects, report, or description to convey modes of being, address, or challenge (1964: 10–11, 33–44).

Bultmann asserts that this has nothing to do with a liberal programme of making certain truths easier to accept. Within the New Testament the kerygmatic message is 'impeded and obscured by the terms in which it is expressed' (1964: 11). Thus, for example, he agrees that language about the last judgment is not a predictive description of an event in time, but a way of calling humankind to responsibility and account for their actions. The mythical language derives from apocalyptic.

It would be a serious mistake to imagine that this mode of interpretation has little or nothing to do with Bultmann's earlier work on form criticism and traditions in the Synoptic Gospels. At the heart of his early work lay the conviction that traditions behind the Gospels served not to report facts of history but to transmit the testimonies of the early Christian communities *to what Christ meant to them*. He begins his *History of the Synoptic Tradition* with the assertion that Mark shaped his material 'in the light of the faith of the early Church' (Bultmann 1968 [1921]: 1). In his *Jesus* he observes, 'Interest in the personality of Jesus is excluded . . . We can now know almost nothing concerning the life and personality of Jesus, since the early Christian sources show no interest in either' (Bultmann 1958 [1926]: 14). Bultmann does recognize, however, that the kerygma *presupposes* the historical Jesus.

Many of Bultmann's assumptions have been decisively called into question. J. Macquarrie urges, for example, 'Does it . . . make sense to talk of 'dying and rising with Christ' without an assurance that, in some cases, Christ actually died and rose?' (Macquarrie in Kegley 1966: 141.) The inconsistencies entailed in Bultmann's varied uses of 'myth' are well known. Furthermore, critics from the 'right' (Macquarrie, Cairns, Thielicke) and from the 'left' (Buri, Braun, Jaspers) agree that Bultmann's attempt to locate a 'boundary' to demythologizing remains arbitrary.

How then, does Bultmann occupy such a prominent place in New Testament scholarship? First, his hermeneutical proposals, although seriously flawed, have served to call attention to the need to ask about 'the point' of much New Testament language. Second, while his overly-neat categorizations between Jewish, Hellenistic, and Gnostic settings no longer command consent, Bultmann rightly called attention to the role of confession and testimony in the New Testament, even if his overly-sharp polarization between faith and history was overdrawn. Third, although existentialism no longer remains in vogue and seduced Bultmann into undue individualism, Bultmann offers a positive model of a New Testament specialist who perceived that interpretation cannot be undertaken responsibly without some engagement with the philosophy of language and wider hermeneutical theory.

References and further reading

Bultmann, R. (1952, 1955) *Theology of the New Testament*, 2 Vols., London: SCM Press.

—— (1958 [1926]) *Jesus and the Word*, London: Fontana.

—— (1962, 1964) (ed.) 'New Testament and Mythology' and 'Bultmann Replies to his Critics,' pp. 1–44, 191–211 in vol. 2 of *Kerygma and Myth*, H.W. Bartsch (ed.), 2 Vols., London: SPCK, 2nd edn. (also in S. Ogden (ed.), *New Testament and Mythology and Other Basic Writings*, Philadelphia: Fortress Press, 1984).

—— (1963) *History of the Synoptic Tradition*, Oxford: Blackwell (2nd edn. ET 1968; orig. 1921).

—— (1964) *Existence and Faith: Shorter Writings*, London: Fontana.

—— (1966) 'Reply,' pp. 257–87 in *The Theology of Rudolf Bultmann*, C.W. Kegley (ed.), London: SCM Press.

—— (1969) *Faith and Understanding I*, London: SCM Press.

Fergusson, D. (1992) *Bultmann*, Collegeville, MN: Liturgical Press.

Johnson, R.A. (ed.) (1987) *Rudolf Bultmann: Interpreting Faith for the Modern Era*, London: Collins.

Jones, G. (1991) *Bultmann: Towards a Critical Theology*, Cambridge: Polity Press.

Kegley, C.W. (ed.) (1966) *The Theology of Rudolf Bultmann*, London: SCM Press.

Macquarrie, J. (1960) *The Scope of Demythologizing*, London: SCM Press.

Painter, J. (1987) *Theology as Hermeneutics: Rudolf Bultmann's Interpretation of the History of Jesus*, Sheffield: Almond Press.

Schmithals, W. (1968) *An Introduction to the Theology of Rudolf Bultmann*, London: SCM Press.

Thiselton, A.C. (1980) *The Two Horizons*, Grand Rapids: Eerdmans/Exeter: Paternoster.

ANTHONY C. THISELTON

C

CADBURY, HENRY J. (1883–1974)

Ernst Haenchen, himself an Acts luminary, once called Henry Cadbury 'the doyen of Anglo-Saxon research on Acts' (Haenchen 1971: 43). Such acclamation, echoed by many others over the past half century, is certainly richly deserved. Cadbury's first major work, *The Style and Literary Method of Luke*, focused, as the title suggests, on the vocabulary and literary style of the Lukan author in the context of Attic Greek. Cadbury showed that Luke's so-called medical vocabulary was not exclusively or uniquely used by medical writers of antiquity, thus, disproving the then widely-held thesis that Luke's 'medical' vocabulary could be taken as evidence that Luke was a physician. Despite the fact that Cadbury's students used to jest that Cadbury had gained his doctorate by taking Luke's away, he also clearly argued that neither did the evidence prove that Luke was *not* a physician. The tradition that Luke the physician was the author of Luke and Acts would have to be examined on different grounds.

Cadbury took up this question of authorship in one of his many contributions to the monumental study of Acts, *The Beginnings of Christianity* (Cadbury 1922). This work continues to assert influence on Acts scholarship and to be a requisite read for any serious study of Acts. In the midst of these contributions, Cadbury also published *The Making of Luke-Acts* (1927). Not only did Cadbury coin the hyphenated phrase, 'Luke-Acts,' he also established the necessity of treating Luke and Acts together as a single, continuous work. Though some have called for clarification and nuancing of the phrase, 'Luke-Acts' (see Parsons and Pervo 1993), that the two documents must be read in light of each other is the *opinio communis* of current scholarship. With *The Book of Acts in History*, Cadbury deliberately turned away from the modern obsession over the historical reliability of Acts to address Acts within its 'concentric cultural environments' of Greek, Roman, Jewish, and Christian.

Over the course of a fifty-five year career of scholarship and publication, Henry Cadbury has left an impressive legacy. Some have viewed Cadbury's work as a forerunner of redaction criticism, though in some respects the success of Conzelmann and others may have briefly eclipsed Cadbury's contributions during the 1960s. Newer literary criticism also found a friend in Cadbury's earlier work, though such a trajectory must be cautiously evaluated (see Gaventa in Parsons and Tyson 1992). Through his pioneering work in placing the Lukan writings securely within the literary environment of antiquity, Cadbury's influence on subsequent scholarship is clearly seen in the contemporary work by C. Talbert, R. Pervo. D. Balch. E. Plümacher, and others.

Any note on Henry Cadbury would be remiss to omit reference to his humanitarian contributions. Most notable was his participation in his faith community, the Society of Friends (Quakers), on whose behalf he received the 1947 Nobel Peace Prize and whose position on pacifism (which he shared) cost him his faculty position at Haverford College (Bacon 1987). Cadbury saw a certain coherence in his professional and confessional life, once remarking that in all these efforts he was 'still trying to translate the New Testament.' He encouraged others to do likewise, and in his 1937 SBL Presidential Address Cadbury called on New Testament scholars to take seriously the social consequences of their work and made explicit reference to the emerging threat of Nazism on the German horizon.

Students of Cadbury's life and work are aware that he would often greet colleagues and students with the question, 'What have you learned that I ought to know?' The aspiring student, hopeful of increasing his or her understanding of the Lukan writings, who approaches the scholarly corpus of the 'great doyen' with that question clearly in mind will never be disappointed!

References and further reading

Bacon, Margaret Hope (1987) *Let This Life Speak: The Legacy of Henry Joel Cadbury*, Philadelphia: University of Pennsylvania Press.

Cadbury, Henry J. (1920) *The Style and Literary Method of Luke*, Cambridge: Harvard University Press.

—— (1922) 'The Identity of the Editor of Luke and Acts: The Tradition,' 2:209–264 and 'Commentary on the Preface of Luke,' 2:489–510 in *The Beginnings of Christianity*, Part I, *The Acts of the Apostles*, F.J. Foakes Jackson and Kirsopp Lake (eds.), 5 Vols., London: Macmillan.

—— (1927) *The Making of Luke-Acts*, New York: Macmillan.

—— (1955) *The Book of Acts in History*, New York: Harper.

Haenchen, Ernst (1971) *The Acts of the Apostles: A Commentary*, trans. Bernard Noble and Gerald Shinn, Philadelphia: Westminster Press.

Parsons, Mikeal C. and Richard I. Pervo (1993) *Rethinking the Unity of Luke and Acts*, Minneapolis: Augsburg/Fortress Press.

—— and Joseph B. Tyson (eds.) (1992) *Cadbury, Knox, and Talbert: American Contributions to the Study of Acts*, Atlanta: Scholars Press (see especially the essays by B. Gaventa, D. Jones, and R. Pervo).

MIKEAL C. PARSONS

CALVIN, JOHN (1509–1564)

The great second-generation Reformer, biblical exegete, and theologian of Geneva. Trained as a humanist and lawyer, Calvin's great analytical skills were turned to the interpretation of scripture and its applications in evangelical doctrine and church order. As a theologian, Calvin was an autodidact, training himself in biblical languages and reading assiduously the historic works of Christian thought. With a deep historical sense for the writings of scripture, Calvin was especially a student of the Church Fathers, particularly Augustine. His many doctrinal controversies with Roman and heretical theologians often centered upon interpreting both scripture and the Fathers. Doctrine, however, was the crystallization of scriptural truths and he wrote his great *Institutes* in their numerous editions as a brief introduction to biblical doctrine.

Calvin's exegetical method was first stated in the introduction to his commentary on Romans (1539), where he declared that he had written it for the public good and according to the chief principles of clarity and brevity. Indeed, he had written in such a sparse way theologically that he was accused of being Judaist and Arian in his approach. In referring to the plurality of the biblical name for God he had not mentioned the Trinity. In other writings he would clarify himself as to orthodox doctrine but his commentaries took on the character of irenic and universal expositions of the text, melding together ancient Catholic and contemporary humanist sources. He was particularly indebted to the works of Cicero and Seneca – indeed, his first commentary writing was actually on a text by the latter, 'On Clemency,' in which Calvin first executed his general hermeneutical principles.

Calvin read scripture in light of ancient Christian creeds and commentaries, and his doctrine of scripture loomed large behind his own commentary writing. This could be expressed as his concern with the believability of scripture whereby its authority was not grounded outside of itself – in the church – but on account of the testimony of the Holy Spirit. The same Spirit which had inspired the original authors of the text constantly acted in every contemporaneous reader to illumine the understanding of that text. This illumination meant that God truly spoke through the text making it a living, communicative Word of God. In a complementary way, the same Spirit did not speak to and through the believer and the church apart from the instrumentality of the scriptural text. Calvin constantly emphasized the inseparability of Word and Spirit. Calvin categorized Roman Catholic and Baptist theologians as both claiming an authoritative source of the Spirit apart from scripture; in the case of the former, in tradition and institution, and the case of the latter, in the experience of regeneration. Calvin was not opposed to tradition or the work of God in the heart; he, however, rejected any authoritative claims for either of these sources.

Calvin wrote forty-five volumes of biblical commentary, thirty on the Old Testament and fifteen on the New Testament; only 2–3 John and Revelation are absent from the latter. The Old Testament commentaries were delivered primarily as lectures recorded by students and edited by him. Calvin's use of the original languages in exegesis betrayed extensive knowledge of the generic features of the original texts, utilizing Targums, LXX, and the Church Fathers for acquiring accurate readings of the Masoretic and Erasmian editions. Even still, he could critically interact with editorial judgments. In many respects, Erasmus' influence upon Calvin was decisive for his exegetical method with regard to scripture: seeking the plain sense, alertness to the text's moral force, reliance upon the Holy Spirit for the understanding of faith, critical openness toward church authorities, and even certain of the canonical contents. As his commentaries unfold, he pays attention to historical and geographical details as they might have been available to virtually anyone in his day. His use of secular sources in this regard was unhesitating. Above all, his concern that his students and readers might become well informed for the explicit purpose of preaching the biblical text is everywhere evident. His range of knowledge and the allusions and cultural criticism of his exposition make the commentaries a veritable feast of Christian learning and are virtually timeless in their value.

References and further reading

Battles, Ford Lewis (ed.) (1997) *Interpreting John Calvin*, Grand Rapids: Baker.

Calvin, John (1994–1996) Calvin's Old Testament and New Testament Commentaries Series, multiple editors, Grand Rapids: Eerdmans.

—— (1995) *Institutes of the Christian Religion*, 2 Vols., Atlanta: Westminster/John Knox.

De Boer, E.A. (2003) *John Calvin on the Visions of Ezekiel: Historical, Hermeneutical, and Exegetical Studies in Calvin's Sermons Inedits, Especially on Ezek, 36–48*, Leiden: Brill.

McKim, Donald K. (ed.) (2004) *Cambridge Companion to John Calvin*, Cambridge: Cambridge University Press.

Parker, T.H. (2002) *The Oracles of God: An Introduction to the Preaching of John Calvin*, Cambridge: Clarke.

Puckett, David (1995) *John Calvin's Exegesis of the Old Testament*, Columbia Series in Reformed Technology, Louisville: Westminster/John Knox.

Tamburello, Dennis E. (1995) *Union with Christ: John Calvin and the Mysticism of St. Bernard*, Atlanta: Westminster/John Knox.

Torrance, Thomas F. (1997) *Hermeneutics of John Calvin*, Edinburgh: Scottish Academic Press.

KURT A. RICHARDSON

CANONICAL CRITICISM: CHILDS' APPROACH

Canonical criticism, an interpretative strategy that focuses on reading the final form of the biblical text in relation to its context in the biblical canon, constitutes one of the major critical methodologies that has challenged the predominance of historically based or diachronic biblical exegesis in the latter portion of the twentieth century. Its primary exponent is Brevard S. Childs.

Childs' earliest publications already demonstrate his attempts to wrestle with diachronic interpretative paradigms that focus on the reconstruction of the earlier stages in the compositional history of biblical texts and the events on which they are based. Each focuses respectively on the theological significance of the mythological (Childs 1960), historical (Childs 1962), and literary (Childs 1967) construction of reality in the Hebrew Bible.

Childs' 1970 volume, *Biblical Theology in Crisis*, constitutes a fundamental challenge to the so-called 'biblical theology movement,' which posits that the theological significance of the Bible must be sought in relation to the historical circumstances and concerns in which it was written. The movement posited that God was revealed in historical events and that the Bible articulated a distinctive faith in relation to its ancient Near-Eastern and Graeco-Roman neighbors. According to Childs, however, the biblical theology movement came to an end with the publication of J.A.T. Robinson's *Honest to God* (1963) and other works which posited God as an ontological category or 'ground of being' in a fully human, secular world.

As a result, Childs advocates a new type of biblical theology that will analyze, synthesize, and develop a picture of the whole Bible; engage in both the descriptive task of historical research and in the constructive task of theology and homiletics; provide guidance to the church so that it might address the social and political concerns of contemporary life; and address the needs of the contemporary Christian pastors.

In Childs' view, a new biblical theology therefore requires several prominent features. In contrast to the prior emphasis on the historical contexts of the ancient Near-Eastern or Graeco-Roman worlds, biblical interpretation must take place in relation to the context of the Christian canon, including both the Old and the New Testaments, as the normative scriptures of Christianity by which God addresses the world. The emphasis on the context of the canon therefore entails a dialectical relationship between the two testaments in which the interpreter is obligated to bring the various portions of the Bible into conversation with each other by determining both the unique witness of a given passage from either Testament and its interrelationship with the whole. Biblical theology must also account for the contexts in which the Bible is read, including the traditions of both Christian and Jewish interpretation of the Bible, so that the exegete might come to understand other perspectives of faith while specifying one's own.

Childs attempts to implement this programme in several subsequent publications. His 1974 commentary on Exodus provides a theological reading of the book in relation to earlier historical-critical exegesis as well as to the canonical contexts of the Old and New Testaments and the later interpretative traditions of Judaism and Christianity. His 1979 introduction to the Old Testament and his 1984 New Testament introduction present canonical readings of the individual books of each Testament which first point to the issues and problems of traditional historical-critical exegesis and then treat the final form of each book as a literary and theological whole. His 1986 study of Old Testament theology focuses on the revelatory character of the Old Testament and employs an intertextual reading strategy so that texts from the three major portions of the canonical Hebrew Bible might be read in relation to each other as normative, revelatory scripture.

Childs' mature thought is expressed in his comprehensive 1993 study of biblical theology, in which he focuses on a search for a new approach to the field. He first addresses the problem of the Christian Bible by noting the variety of canonical forms of the Bible throughout Christianity and Judaism. He also notes that the early church used a much wider Old Testament canon than that of Judaism by virtue of its reliance on the Septuagint and that the Christian concept of canon functions very differently from the Jewish canon because it ultimately bears witness to Christ. Although the New Testament employs the LXX, it ultimately transforms the meaning of the Old Testament. This points to the church's ongoing search for the Christian Bible, which biblical theology must address.

A canonical approach to biblical theology must emphasize the unity of the Christian Bible composed of two distinct Testaments, the Old Testament and the New Testament. Past Christian biblical theology demonstrates a tendency to allow the Old Testament to collapse into the New Testament, resulting in biblical theology becoming de facto New Testament theology. In order to prevent such an occurrence and to affirm the role of the Old Testament as sacred Christian scripture, biblical theology must accept the Old Testament as a distinctive witness to Jesus Christ, not because it speaks explicitly of Christ but because it stands in relation to the New Testament in the context of Christian scripture. In order to articulate the revelatory character of each Testament, biblical theology must move from a description of the biblical witnesses to the subject matter, substance, or res, toward which these witnesses point. The Bible avoids philosophical concepts, such as *substantia* or 'the essence of a thing,' and points instead to the reality of God in communion with God's own self and with creation. Insofar as the reality of God lies in loving, grounded in a freely given commitment toward humanity, biblical theology constitutes theological faith that seeks understanding in relation to divine reality. Childs therefore rejects the Pauline assumption that the Old Testament has lost its theological significance, as such an understanding ultimately undercuts the role of the Old Testament as sacred scripture and avoids theological reflection on the hermeneutics of scriptural interpretation. Interpretation is not just explanation, but also a serious wrestling with the content of scripture. Through an extended discussion of both the Old Testament and the New Testament, he attempts to demonstrate the importance of establishing the initial setting of a witness within the history of Israel, the need to follow a trajectory of its use and application, and the need to discern both the unity and diversity of Israel's faith within the Old Testament.

Childs' proposals have been subjected to sustained critique for not accounting adequately for later textual traditions and alternative canonical forms, and for presenting an essentially Barthian theology with biblical prooftexts. Nevertheless, he has succeeded in prompting interpreters to take seriously the biblical canon, however it might be understood, and its theological character as an essential concern of biblical theology.

References and further reading

Childs, Brevard S. (1960) *Myth and Reality in the Old Testament*, SBT 27, London: SCM Press.
—— (1962) *Memory and Tradition in Israel*, SBT 37, London: SCM Press.
—— (1967) *Isaiah and the Assyrian Crisis*, SBT, Second Series, 3, London: SCM Press.
—— (1970) *Biblical Theology in Crisis*, Philadelphia: Westminster Press.
—— (1974) *The Book of Exodus: A Critical, Theological Commentary*, OTL, Philadelphia: Westminster Press.
—— (1979) *Introduction to the Old Testament as Scripture*, Philadelphia: Fortress Press.
—— (1984) *The New Testament as Canon: An Introduction*, Philadelphia: Fortress Press.
—— (1986) *Old Testament Theology in a Canonical Context*, Philadelphia: Fortress Press.
—— (1993) *Biblical Theology of the Old and New Testaments: Theological Reflection on the Christian Bible*, Philadelphia: Fortress Press.
—— (2001) *Isaiah: A Commentary*, OTL, Louisville: Westminster/John Knox.

MARVIN A. SWEENEY

CANONICAL CRITICISM: SANDERS' APPROACH

James A. Sanders' approach to canonical criticism resembles that of Brevard Childs in that it calls for reading biblical texts in relation to their canonical contexts, but it differs by emphasizing a much broader understanding of canon. Childs focuses on the Protestant canon, including both the Old and New Testaments, and emphasizes the Masoretic text (MT) of the Hebrew Bible as the basis for his understanding of the Old Testament. Sanders, however, notes the plurality of canons, including not only the Jewish Tanakh represented by the MT, but the various forms of the Old Testament (and the New) found in Protestant Christianity, Roman Catholicism, Eastern Orthodox Christianity, and others, as well. Sanders therefore gives greater attention to historical factors and hermeneutics involved in the formation and reading of the biblical canon, including both individual books and the canon(s) as well as their various textual versions.

Sanders' interest in this field is evident in his early works on the Psalms Scrolls from Qumran (1965, 1969). This work is especially influential because it points to a very different understanding of the book of Psalms in the late-Second Temple period. The Cave 11 Psalms manuscripts present a different arrangement of the Psalms from that of the MT as well as various Psalms that did not appear in the MT at all, including some known from the Syriac Psalter and some otherwise unknown. Sanders therefore concludes that the Qumran Psalter manuscripts demonstrate both stability, insofar as they appear to constitute a stable proto-Masoretic text, and fluidity, insofar as they constitute a very different version of the Psalter. Such an observation challenges earlier notions of a single and authoritative biblical canon in antiquity.

Sanders' 1972 call for 'canonical criticism' stems from a concern that Enlightenment-based historical study of the Bible had produced a 'quasiscience' that focused exclusively on identifying the earliest or 'original forms of the biblical texts and the ideas that they contained as the true authoritative basis for scripture. Unfortunately, the rather specialized and sophisticated training necessary to engage in such work effectively removed the Bible from the pulpit and congregation, and placed it in the scholar's study where it was largely removed from the experience and concerns of contemporary readers.

Sanders instead intends to pursue a holistic reading of the Bible in an effort to describe its shape and function in relation to the communities that formed and read it as sacred scripture. Fundamental to his reading of the Bible is the recognition that it is based in Torah, which means 'instruction' or 'revelation' rather than the common and erroneous translation as 'law.' Torah provides the basic narrative or instruction in the identity of the ancient Israelite nation and its relationship to God. It may change or adapt to new circumstances, as indicated by the insertion of Deuteronomy and later priestly materials into earlier narratives of Israel's origins and the rereadings of the basic narratives that result. Indeed, that adaptability was essential to Israel's rebirth following the Babylonian Exile. The Prophets and the wisdom literature facilitated Israel's rebirth in the aftermath of the destruction of the first Temple by the Babylonians in 587 BC by providing perspectives concerning the disaster and bases for continuity with the older traditions and restoration once the disaster had passed. Likewise, the reading of this canonical literature in the aftermath of the destruction of the Second temple by the Romans in AD 70 provided the basis for the restoration of Israel as rabbinic Judaism and early Christianity.

Sanders' subsequent studies, including a brief introductory handbook (1984), a variety of articles (key articles from 1975 to 1982 are republished in Sanders 1987), and collaborative projects (Barthélemy et al. 1982–1992), address the conceptualization and reading of canonical literature, in both its precompositional and postcompositional forms. The reading of canonical literature may take place during the process of its formation as a text or during its resignification as an established text that is reread without further composition, in the context of literary redaction or reformulation, and in the context of biblical canons and translations. Throughout his work, Sanders stresses two major foci: canonical process and canonical hermeneutics (1984: 21).

Canonical process addresses the history of the canon, particularly its function and formation within the ancient Israelite and later Jewish and Christian communities (1984: 21–451 1987: 939). Although he acknowledges his dependence on critical methodologies, such as tradition, form, and redaction cnticism, etc., to trace the development of biblical literature in the context of the communities that formed it (1991), he tends to focus primarily on function, particularly the stability and adaptability of scripture as it is employed in a variety of historical and social contexts. Scripture is multivalent in that it might mean different things to ancient communities depending upon their needs. Thus, the list of David's mighty men in 2 Samuel 23:8–39 might function as a recollection of past glory, a sign that the monarchy will be restored, an indicator of eschatological expectations, etc. On a larger scale, the Samuel-Kings narrative is rewritten and resignified in Chronicles, and the Gospels employ similar traditions to provide four different perspectives on Jesus. In all cases, elements of selectivity and repetition appear insofar as older traditions are selected, reread, and reinterpreted in relation to newer contexts and needs.

Canonical hermeneutics address the reading and interpretation of biblical texts in relation to the social settings and needs of the interpretative communities (1984: 46–60; 1987: 61–73). This entails consideration of the 'hermeneutical triangle,' in which hermeneutics stand between the texts or traditions that are read and contexts or situations in which they are read (1987: 87–105). In all cases, the biblical canon betrays a broad theocentric hermeneutic (1984: 52), which attempts to identify divine action in the past, present, and future. Thus, a prophet (Jeremiah) might challenge the prophecy of another (Hananiah) whose message may have been pertinent in the past (see Isaiah), but no longer pertains to the circumstances of the present or future (Jer. 27–28). The Gospels and Paul reread earlier biblical texts in relation to their understanding of the significance of Jesus as Christ (1987: 41–60, 107–123). The hermeneutics by which biblical texts are reread and reapplied to new situations are especially evident in the textual versions, such as the Qumran texts, Septuagint, Targums, Peshitta, and Vulgate, each of which renders the earlier Hebrew text in relation to its own understanding of what it meant and means. Text criticism can no longer be preoccupied solely with the reconstruction of original texts; it must entail a reading of the versions as scripture in their own right (1987: 125–51, 1995, 1997).

Reference and further reading

Barthélemy, Dominique et al. (1982–1992) Critique textuelle de l'Ancien Testament. I–III, Fribourg: Éditions Universitaires/Göttingen: Vandenhoeck & Ruprecht.

Sanders, James A. (1965) The Psalms Scroll of Qumrân Cave 11 (11QPsa), Discoveries in the Judaean Desert of Jordan 4, Oxford: Clarendon.

—— (1969) 'Cave 11 Surprises and the Question of Canon,' in New Directions in Biblical Archaeology, D.N. Freedman and J.C. Greenfield (eds.), Garden City: Doubleday.

—— (1972) Torah and Canon, Philadelphia: Fortress Press.

—— (1984) *Canon and Community: A Guide to Canonical Criticism*, Philadelphia: Fortress Press.

—— (1987) *From Sacred Story to Sacred Text*, Philadelphia: Fortress Press.

—— (1991) 'Stability and Fluidity in Text and Canon,' in *Tradition of the Text*, G.J. Norton and S. Pisano (eds.), Göttingen: Vandenhoeck & Ruprecht.

—— (1995) 'The Hermeneutics of Text Criticism,' *Textus* 18: 1–26.

—— (1997) 'The Task of Text Criticism,' in *Problems in Biblical Theology*, H.T.C. Sun *et al.* (eds.), Grand Rapids: Eerdmans.

MARVIN A. SWEENEY

CANONICAL DEVELOPMENT

1 The canon: term and concept

General titles for the scriptures began to appear by the second century BC (1 Macc. 12:9; Sirach, prologue), but 'canon' was not among the earliest of them. It was in the latter part of the fourth century AD that Christian writers began to refer to the collection or list of the scriptures as a 'canon,' using a Greek term for a straight rod or rule, and thus a criterion. Earlier titles for the collection, such as 'the Holy Scriptures,' 'the Old Testament,' 'the New Testament,' continued to be used, but 'canon' added the idea of correctness in the collection, and has since become a technical term.

The canon comprises the basic literature of the Jewish and Christian religions. It is basic, first, in its antiquity: in being, to all intents and purposes, the oldest literature of Judaism and the oldest literature of Christianity (allowing, at most, for a slight overlap with the earliest Apocrypha and Pseudepigrapha in the case of the Old Testament, and with the earliest writings of the Apostolic Fathers in the case of the New).

It is basic, secondly, in its literary content: in setting forth the known facts and received understanding of the Jewish and Christian religions. It is therefore used for teaching purposes, and much of it is read in public worship. It is also used for apologetic purposes, to defend the religion it expounds against corruption or misinterpretation.

Finally, the canon is basic in its theological authority. It records the self-revelation of God, as the creator of the world and the savior of his people, through the call of Abraham, the deliverance from Egypt, the giving of the Law, the sending of the prophets, and then through the coming of God's Son, and the mission of his apostles into all the world. The canon also professes itself to partake of the character of revelation, by being divinely inspired. The idea of biblical inspiration, which has its beginning in the prophetic language of the Old Testament, became fully developed in the intertestamental period and was inherited by the New Testament Christians. It has consequently always been seen as a significant characteristic of canonical scripture.

2 The state of the canon in antiquity

We who have a Bible or Testament between two covers can easily forget that nothing of the kind existed before the great codices of the fourth century AD were produced. At Qumran, each biblical book, or regular grouping of books, occupied its own leather scroll. There were no large groupings: the Pentateuch was not collected in a single scroll before the Christian era. The papyrus scrolls of the LXX were even less capacious: Deuteronomy, for example, might extend to two scrolls. At the turn of the era, codices with leaves began to come into use, but these too were at first of limited size. No manuscript surviving from pre-Nicene times contains more than a few of the larger biblical books. How, then, were the canonical books distinguished from others? The manuscripts containing them could of course be placed together, but might easily get separated. The real safeguard was lists. Christian lists have survived from the second century AD onwards (Melito and the Muratorian Fragment), and the oral Jewish list, recorded as a quotation in the Babylonian Talmud (*Baba Bathra* 14b), may well be older still.

Since the Old Testament canon was inherited by the church (and, as we shall see, was inherited complete), whereas the New Testament canon was assembled by the church, development in regard to the New Testament canon moved in the direction of increasing certainty, while development in regard to the Old Testament canon could only move in the opposite direction. This is in fact what happened. The New Testament canon was effectively settled in the East and West by the end of the fourth century, but there was by then some uncertainty about the Christian Old Testament canon. Because of the breach with Jewish tradition, it had become possible, by a gradual process, for more or less of the Apocrypha to creep into Christian lists and manuscripts, beginning with Tobit, Wisdom, and Sirach, followed more slowly by the other books. Only Fathers with Palestinian connections, such as Melito and Cyril of Jerusalem, or with Jewish knowledge, such as Origen, Epiphanius, and Jerome, made a conscious effort to keep them out, and even they sometimes made allowances for appendices to biblical books, like Baruch and the Epistle of Jeremy, appended in the Greek and Latin Bible to Jeremiah. This situation continued throughout the Middle Ages, in both East and West.

3 The study of the canon in modern times

In the period of the Reformation and for about two centuries thereafter, the historical development of the canon seemed a straightforward matter. The Old Testament canon, said the Reformers, was the canon of the Hebrew Bible, which Jesus and the apostles used and commended to their followers. Gradually, over subsequent years, additional Jewish books (the Apocrypha) had been allowed to find their way into the Greek and Latin Old Testaments: in part at least these books were edifying, but they were not scripture and should be kept separate. Here the Reformers parted company from the Church of Rome, which was determined to endorse the prevailing beliefs and practices of the Middle Ages, in this and other matters, and did so at the Council of Trent (session 4). The New Testament canon, said the Reformers, had never been a subject of controversy, except insofar as seven of its books had been slower in achieving recognition than the others. Luther thought that this longer period of uncertainty was grounds for treating the seven books as less authoritative, but his view did not prevail.

Since the eighteenth century, however, and especially in the last 150 years, this straightforward account has been progressively unsettled. It has been suggested that the wider Old Testament canon of the Middle Ages goes back to the Hellenistic Judaism of Alexandria, and that the infant Christian church, which was mainly Greek-speaking, took it over at the outset as its own canon. It has also been suggested that the three sections of the Hebrew Bible (the Law, the Prophets, and the Hagiographa) are just accidents of history, reflecting the different periods when the Jews accepted new groups of scriptures; also that the third section was not accepted until the Council of Jabneh or Jamnia, about AD 90, after and not before the time of Christ, as is shown by the continuing rabbinical disputes about the inspiration of five of the books included (Ezekiel, Proverbs, Ecclesiastes, Song of Songs, Esther). Finally, it has been suggested that at least one Jewish school of thought, the Qumran Essenes, had some of the Pseudepigrapha in their canon, notably the book of Enoch, which is also quoted in the Epistle of Jude. On grounds like these, it has been concluded that the Old Testament canon was not closed when Christians took it over, and has never really been closed in the Christian church thereafter, even if it eventually was in the Jewish synagogue. As to the New Testament canon, its closing has been thought by some too late to be secure.

4 The Old Testament canon

After this long period of agnosticism, recent scholarship is tending to return to more traditional positions. The idea of a wider Alexandrian Jewish canon is ruled out by the silence of Philo, and the idea that it was taken over by the primitive Christian church is ruled out by the silence of the New Testament. Both Philo and the New Testament quote many Old Testament books as scripture, but none of the Apocrypha. Certainly the primitive church took over the religious reading matter of Hellenistic Judaism, and from time to time reflects a knowledge of it, but it was only very slowly, and under protest, that it began to treat any additional parts of this reading matter as scripture.

The three sections of the Hebrew Bible are not accidents of history but works of art, as is shown by the traditional arrangement of the books within the sections, recorded in the Talmud (*Baba Bathra* 14b). The arrangement is chronological in the case of narrative books, while the other books (oracular in the case of the Prophets, lyrical and sapiential in the case of the Hagiographa) are arranged in descending order of size. Anomalies are easily explained. Ruth is prefixed to Psalms, as ending with the genealogy of the psalmist David. Daniel is treated as a narrative book because of its first six chapters. Chronicles ends the canon, as summing up the whole of biblical history, from Adam to the return from the Exile.

There was no 'Council of Jamnia,' simply a discussion in the academy of Jamnia, which confirmed the canonicity of two books (Ecclesiastes and Song of Songs), not five. The disputes about some of the five books went on long after AD 90, and were aimed at removing books from the canon, not adding them to it: needless to say, they did not succeed in doing this, or even in withdrawing them from use. Moreover, as one of the five books was Ezekiel, the disputes did not simply relate to the Hagiographa but also to the Prophets, a section of the canon which (*ex hypothesi*) was closed much earlier.

The men of Qumran indeed cherished *Enoch, Jubilees,* and similar works, but seem to have placed them in an interpretative appendix to the canon, not in any of its three sections (4QMMT). This is probably related to the fact that the inspiration claimed at Qumran was an inspiration to interpret the scriptures, not to add to them. There is no reason to think that Jude would have claimed more for *Enoch* than the men of Qumran did.

In reality, the Jewish canon was probably closed not later than the mid-second century BC. As early as the third century BC, the devisor of the calendar of Enoch (*1 Enoch* 72–82) seems to have assigned a day of the week to each of the dated events of the Old Testament, avoiding sabbaths. About 180 BC, Ben Sira drew up his catalogue of the famous men of the Old Testament (Sir. 44–49), summing up his catalogue at the end before moving on to a nonbiblical figure in chapter 50. In both cases, a large number of Old Testament books were drawn upon, though not Esther or perhaps Daniel. By the time Ben Sira's book was translated into Greek and the prologue added, about 130 BC, the scriptures had been organized in their three sections and similarly translated, though the third section did not yet have a settled name. The threefold organization involves a standard order for the books (as we have seen) and therefore a standard number, so their identity was probably now fully agreed, though the standard order and number is not explicitly recorded until the first century AD. The final additions to the canon may have been made when Judas Maccabaeus collected the scattered scriptures after Antiochus' persecution (1 Macc. 1:56f.; 2 Macc. 2:14f.).

The divergent canon of the Samaritans, consisting only of the Pentateuch, was once thought to reflect the limits of the Jewish canon in the sixth century BC, when the Samaritan schism took place. The Dead Sea Scrolls, however, have provided evidence that the Samaritans, for their part, maintained strong links with the Jews and conformed to most of their customs until the late second century BC, when the Jews caused a permanent alienation by destroying the Samaritan temple on Mount Gerizim. The Samaritans, it appears, reacted by rejecting the Prophets and Hagiographa, because of the recognition they give to the Jewish temple at Jerusalem. By this stage, the Prophets and Hagiographa were evidently unified enough to be accepted or rejected as a whole.

5 The New Testament canon

The Old Testament canon having been closed for more than two centuries before the New Testament canon was opened, it provided a providential model for the development of the latter. By the first century, the authors of the Old Testament books were all normally thought of as prophets, and this made their position unique, for there had been a cessation of prophecy (in the full sense of that word) during the intertestamental period, as 1 Maccabees, Josephus, and the rabbinical literature all agree. Under the gospel, however, prophecy was revived (Matt. 11:9; Acts 2:16–18; 11:27f.; 13:1, etc.), including written prophecy (Rev. 1:3; 10:11; 22:6f., 9f., 18f.). With the New Testament prophets were linked the apostles (Luke 11:49; 1 Cor. 12:28f.; Eph. 4:llf.), as joint depositaries of the mystery of the gospel and joint foundation stones of the Christian church (Eph. 2:20; 3:5), and Jesus himself was the greatest prophet of all, the prophet like Moses (Mark 6:4; Luke 13:33; 24:19; Acts 3:22f.; 7:37).

The earliest Fathers often quote the sayings of Jesus and the writings of the apostles alongside the Old Testament scriptures, not as scriptures themselves but as having a similar authority. The name of Scripture is

first given to Christian writings in 1 Timothy 5:18 and 2 Peter 3:16, but the command to read them publicly in the congregation may also imply scriptural status (1 Thess. 5:27; Rev. 1:3; cf. 22:18f.). To speak of them as scripture becomes more and more common in the course of the second century and is normal by the end of it. The three criteria which the Fathers are known to have applied to New Testament writings are origin in the apostolic circle, continued use, and orthodoxy, but without the presence of the Old Testament canon before their eyes they might not have concluded that they were dealing with a second body of scriptures. As it was, widespread agreement was reached by the end of the second century to accept as scripture the Four Gospels, the Acts of the Apostles, the thirteen Epistles of Paul, 1 Peter, and 1 John. The remaining seven books (Hebrews, James, 2 Peter, 2 and 3 John, Jude, Revelation) were accepted more slowly, and agreement about them was not reached until the end of the fourth century. A few additional books, which for a time were under consideration, had by that stage been excluded.

The reason for the delay with the seven 'Antilegomena' (books spoken against) is that they all presented particular problems. With five of them, there was doubt about apostolic authorship. Hebrews differed stylistically from the Pauline Epistles, 2 Peter from 1 Peter, and Revelation from the other writings of John. The author of 2 and 3 John called himself 'the elder.' The support that the Montanists claimed to find in Revelation was another cause of hesitation about it. Jude quoted the book of Enoch. Why James was problematic is not recorded, but since the Judaizers regarded James as their champion, the teaching his Epistle gives on justification may have been thought suspect. In the long run, the church did not find these problems insuperable, but the delay they caused is easy to understand.

Probably all these books were accepted as scripture from an early period in some part of the church, even when this is not on record. Otherwise we would have to imagine that, at the end of the fourth century, some of them leaped suddenly from being canonical nowhere to being canonical everywhere – an unlikely hypothesis.

The Syrian New Testament canon, which is singular in that it includes only two of the Antilegomena, can be regarded as the canon in a state of arrested development. When the Peshitta, the standard Syriac translation of the Bible, was made in the fourth century, debate about the Antilegomena was still in progress, so only two of them, Hebrews and James, were included in the translation. The isolation of the Syrian churches, due to language and politics, was greatly accentuated by the Nestorian and Monophysite schisms of the fifth century, in which much of Syrian Christianity became separated for doctrinal reasons from the rest of the Christian church, and this has caused the status of the remaining five Antilegomena in the Syrian churches to remain permanently in doubt.

References and further reading

Beckwith, R.T. (1985) *The Old Testament Canon of the New Testament Church*, London: SPCK/Grand Rapids: Eerdmans.

—— (1991) 'A Modern Theory of the Old Testament Canon,' *Vetus Testamentum* 41: 385–395.

Bruce, F.F. (1988) *The Canon of Scripture*, Glasgow: Chapter House.

Leiman, S.Z. (1991) *The Canonization of Hebrew Scripture*, New Haven: Yale University Press.

Lewis, J.P. (1964) 'What do we mean by Jabneh?,' *Journal of Bible and Religion* 32: 125–32.

Metzger, B.M. (1987) *The Canon of the New Testament*, Oxford: Clarendon.

Purvis, J.D. (1968) *The Samaritan Pentateuch and the Origin of the Samaritan Sect*, Cambridge, MA: Harvard University Press.

Sundberg Jr., A.C. (1964) *The Old Testament of the Early Church*, Cambridge, MA: Harvard University Press.

ROGER T. BECKWITH

CHRONOLOGY (NEW TESTAMENT)

1 Introduction
2 Chronology in the Graeco-Roman world
3 Jesus
4 Paul
5 Implications for biblical interpretation

1 Introduction

Matters of chronology are some of the most vexing that an interpreter confronts. The reasons for this are numerous. They include the fact that timekeeping was viewed differently by the ancients, with an alternative set of priorities. Another factor is that different mechanisms are available now than there were in the ancient world, and these mechanisms help to create expectations regarding the relative timing of events. A third factor is that the scope of the ancient world was more constricted, which means that there was a means of establishing relative time markers within the local context, but these do not have pertinence outside of that context. A final factor is that the documentation from the ancient world is haphazard at best. In other words, even if there were similar, precise methods of establishing chronology in the ancient world as in the modern world, the lack of crucial pieces of evidence has meant that there are difficulties in establishing this chronology. After briefly discussing the nature of chronology in the ancient world, this article examines various means of calculating key dates regarding Jesus and Paul.

2 Chronology in the Graeco-Roman world

There are a number of ways that chronology was established in the Graeco-Roman world, according to both relative and absolute means (for which see Bickerman 1980: esp. 62–79). Relative means of chronology are clearly the oldest, and include means by which events are related to each other relatively, on the basis of some fixed point. This fixed point could include a particularly memorable event, such as a battle, or could be in relation to a significant human accomplishment, such as the birth of a key individual. From that fixed point, relative units are counted. The year is a unit of relative chronology, as is even the calendar, since calendars were calculated differently for different purposes in different places. For example, a year might have been the length of a ruler's term of office, but if the ruler left office after six months rather than one year, that would still be considered a year's rule. Similarly, years began or were calculated on the basis of festival and feast days, whose dates were set by reference to fixed points, such as the new moon. During Roman times, the calendar was originally lunar, until Julius Caesar instituted a solar calendar in 46 BC. The lunar calendar required constant adjustment according to the fixed points found in nature, such as the seasons. One of the best-known units of relative measure is the genealogy, which dates successive generations from a significant individual. Other units of relative measure besides years were days (night was often not counted; and various peoples calculated from sunup to sundown or sunup to sunup), eras, and indictions (when delivery of food was required). Relative chronology was used widely in the ancient world, but was dependent upon being able to establish a fixed point and having units for calculation. Besides the biblical writers, many ancient historians, such as Thucydides and others, used relative chronology.

Absolute chronology is determined on the basis of a variety of natural phenomena, so as to establish definite and fixed units of time, rather than the kind of relative units usually used by the ancients. These would include fixed natural cycles such as revolutions of the sun or the various phases of the moon.

3 Jesus

The New Testament uses relative chronology to establish key events in the life of Jesus. These are grouped around several key periods in Jesus' life. Those events surrounding his birth utilize the following chronological indicators: the genealogies (Matt. 1:1–16; Luke 3:23–38), in which Matthew uses three sets of fourteen generations, and Luke includes several women in Jesus' line, both to establish Jesus' relationship to Abraham or Adam; the rule and death of Herod, including his killing of the infants in Bethlehem (Matt. 2:1, 15; Luke 1:5), the calculation of whose death is dependent upon references in Josephus regarding the rule of Antigonus, an eclipse of the moon, and when Passover occurred; and the census of Quirinius, governor of Syria (Luke 2:1–5), in which the grammar of the Lukan passage may indicate a census before Quirinius was governor (see Porter 2002).

Those temporal indicators surrounding the beginning of Jesus' ministry include: the beginning of Jesus' ministry during the fifteenth year of Tiberius' reign, during the procuratorship of Pontius Pilate (AD 26–36), while Herod Agrippa was tetrarch of Galilee, Philip was tetrarch of Ituraea and Trachonitis, and Lysanias was tetrarch of Abilene, and during the high priesthood of Annas and Caiaphas (Luke 3:1–2), dates that depend on a number of factors, including which calendar is used and whether Tiberius co-ruled with Augustus; reference to Jesus as being about thirty years old at the outset of his ministry (Luke 3:23); and reference to the temple having taken forty-six years to complete (John 2:13–3:21), utilizing Josephus' relative chronology related to the reign of Herod. There are several temporal indicators concerning the length of Jesus' ministry. These include: references to Passover in the Synoptic Gospels (Matt. 26:17; Mark 14:1; Luke 22:1) and in John (John 2:13, 23; 6:4; 11:55).

The final set of temporal indicators focuses upon the death of Jesus. One set of controversies revolves around the day of Jesus' death and the other around the year of his death. Those around the day of his death weigh whether it occurred on Passover (Matt. 27:62; Mark 15:42; Luke 23:54) or on the day before Passover (John 19:14, 16), and whether there are two relative chronologies at work regarding how the day is calculated. The other concerns the year of Jesus' death, which is dependent upon determination of the day of his death, and must fit within the reigns of Pilate, Herod Antipas, and Caiaphas as chief priest.

4 Paul

Pauline chronology is dependent upon three sets of data, including Paul's own letters, the book of Acts, and knowledge of extrabiblical people and events. The letters provide few specific temporal references (but see Gal. 1:18; 2:1), but are useful for their references to people and hints at various events.

Use of the book of Acts depends upon a relative and usually sequential chronology that tries to find its fixed point within the narrative. Paul is seen as a 'young man' (Acts 7:58), who is converted and then stays in Damascus (Acts 9:1–25), makes a trip to Jerusalem, Tarsus, and Antioch (Acts 9:26–30; 11:25–26), and then a second trip to Jerusalem (Acts 11:27–30; 12:25). He then undertakes what appear to be three missionary journeys, each one beginning from Antioch, including a trip to Jerusalem, and then returning to Antioch (Acts 13:1–14:28, followed by the Jerusalem Council in

Acts 15:1–35; 15:35–18:22; 18:23–21:16, but ending in Jerusalem, when he is arrested). Paul is then imprisoned for two years by the Roman governors Felix and Festus (Acts 23:12–26:32), before he is sent to Rome, where he is further imprisoned for two years (Acts 27:1–28:31). Apart from the procuratorships of Felix and Festus, and even these are disputed (see below), there are few fixed points within this chronology.

Extrabiblical people and events are more useful for establishing Pauline chronology. There are at least eight complexes of events that are worth closer analysis: reference to Aretas being king of Damascus (2 Cor. 11:32–33), a date that is disputed by scholars (between AD 38 and 40); the famine referred to in Acts 11:28, since there were many famines at this time during the reign of Claudius (AD 41–54), with dates having been proposed in AD 45, 46, 48 or after 51; Herod Agrippa's death (Acts 12:20–23), which is placed between Petrine and Pauline episodes in Acts, but probably occurred around AD 44; the proconsulship of Cyprus by Sergius Paulus (Acts 13:7), a name known from inscriptions even though this Sergius Paulus is not; the expulsion of the Jews from Rome in AD 49 (Acts 18:2), which is based upon relative chronology concerning several later witnesses (e.g., Orosius) and comparison with other expulsions and related events concerning the Jews (e.g. in Dio Cassius); the date of Gallio's governorship of Cyprus (Acts 18:12), which probably occurred in AD 51/52, a date that is based upon interpretation of an inscription of Claudius found at Delphi; Paul's appearance before the high priest Ananias (Acts 23:2; 24:1), who was apparently appointed in AD 47 and probably continued in that office until AD 59 (despite a brief interruption); and Paul's Roman custody (Acts 23:24–26:32) under Felix, who took up his office around AD 52/53 but is variously interpreted to have left office anywhere from AD 55 to 62, and Festus, who took up his position anywhere from AD 56 to 61.

5 Implications for biblical interpretation

The New Testament chronology relies heavily upon relative chronology, supported by several significant events for which more precise and fixed dates can be established. The resulting chronology is subject to much reinterpretation on account of two factors. The first is that the very few specific temporal terms found in the materials make it difficult to create a precise relative chronology, and the second is that the supposed fixed points in time are themselves often highly disputed due to the nature of the ancient evidence. The result of such an evidential situation is not necessarily to doubt the veracity of the events themselves, even if precise and secure chronological evidence cannot be provided, but to exercise caution in the firmness with which such chronologies are asserted and such fixed dates are set.

References and further reading

Bickerman, E.J. (1980) *Chronology of the Ancient World*, Ithaca: Cornell University Press, 2nd edn.

Porter, S.E. (2000) 'Festivals and Holy Days: Greco-Roman,' pp. 368–71 in *Dictionary of New Testament Background*, C.A. Evans and S.E. Porter (eds.), Downers Grove: IVP.

—— (2000) 'Chronology, New Testament,' pp. 201–8 in *Dictionary of New Testament Background*, C.A. Evans and S.E. Porter (eds.), Downers Grove: IVP.

—— (2002) 'The Reasons for the Lukan Census,' pp. 165–88 in *Paul, Luke, and the Graeco-Roman World: Essays in Honour of Alexander J.M. Wedderburn*, A. Christophersen, C. Claussen, J. Frey and B.W. Longenecker (eds.), Sheffield: Sheffield Academic Press.

Salzman, M.R. (1990) *On Roman Time: The Codex-Calendar of 354 and the Rhythms of Urban Life in Late Antiquity*, Berkeley: University of California Press.

STANLEY E. PORTER

CHRONOLOGY (OLD TESTAMENT)

The chronology of the Old Testament bristles with problems. Methodologically, there is no agreed-upon basis for determining the dating of most of the events recorded in the narratives of the Hebrew Bible. This was as true in ancient times as it is today. An examination of the ages in the lines of Seth and Shem in Genesis 5 and 11 demonstrates wide differences when the MT and the LXX numbers are compared:

NAME	MT	LXX
Adam	930	930
Seth	912	912
Enosh	905	905
Kenan	910	910
Mahalel	895	895
Jared	962	962
Enoch	365	365
Methuselah	868	969
Lamech	777	753
Noah	950	950
Shem	600	600
Arpachshad	438	565
Cainan	not listed	460
Shelah	433	460
Eber	464	504
Peleg	239	339
Reu	239	339
Serug	230	330
Nahor	148	208
Terah	189	199

Not only are many of the total ages different, but even where they agree there is often a dispute regarding the age at the birth of the next generation. Further, the LXX includes a Cainan (also found in Luke 3:36) who is not listed in the MT.

All this suggests two points. First, the genealogies and other chronological sequences in the Bible are not necessarily complete. Generations may have been omitted. Second, there is early disagreement regarding the values of numbers that could be used for chronological determination. This may be due to problems in textual transmission as, for example, the MT of 1 Samuel 13:1 which states, 'Saul was a year old when he became king. He reigned over Israel for 12 years.' More frequently, the numbers are intended as symbolic representations of the quantity of time that they wish to describe. An illustration of this occurs already in Genesis 15. God describes to Abram the period of Israel's time in Egypt. In v. 13 this period is described as 400 years. However, in v. 16 the same period of time is designated as four generations. Texts such as Exodus 4:16–20, where Moses and Aaron are four generations from Levi, suggest that each 100 years is symbolic of a generation (rather than vice versa).

The examples so far discussed deal with relative chronology. That is, the chronological sequence and relationship of characters and events within the broad sweep of the biblical story. While this is useful, biblical historians are also interested in another scheme, absolute chronology. This is the means by which it is possible to determine the precise date before the present when an event took place. In order to do this it is necessary to connect biblical dates to events recorded outside the Bible. Although debate remains regarding the precise dating of many events in the second millennium BC, greater accuracy can be obtained for the first millennium due to the presence of limmu lists and the eponym canon, especially in Assyrian sources (Millard 1994). These provide records by designating each year according to significant events or persons related to it. The whole can be tied into an absolute chronology due to the presence in these records of astronomical phenomena that can be precisely dated. For example, the solar eclipse of June 15, 763 BC provides a foundation for absolute dates for the Assyrian and Babylonian kings and events. Through synchronisms of these with biblical events various scholars have determined dates for the Judaean and Israelite kings and the history portrayed in the Old Testament.

The Old Testament outlines six major chronological periods in its narratives. These may be suggested with the following possible dates: the pre-Abram period of Genesis 1–11 (before 2000 BC); the patriarchal period of Genesis 12–50 (2000–1500 BC); the exodus/wilderness/conquest period of Exodus to Joshua (1500–1150 BC); the Judges period (1200–1000 BC); the monarchy period (1 Samuel to 2 Chronicles; 1000–586 BC); and the exilic/postexilic period (Ezra and Nehemiah; 586–331 BC). Each of these presents its own distinctive questions and problems. In the next section a sampling of chronological issues will be identified from some of these time divisions.

The pre-Abram period includes the genealogies and narratives of Genesis 1–11. This period lies outside of any known extrabiblical historical context. The major issue is the large numbers by which so many of the lifespans are described. There is no simple explanation for this. However, these texts are not unique. The Sumerian King List provides a list of kings who reigned 'before the Flood' (Jacobsen 1939; Hess 1994c). The lengths of their reigns are also far longer than normal human lifespans. Whereas the Genesis account describes people's lives in terms of hundreds of years, the king list defines the lengths in terms of tens of thousands of years. Thus both texts preserve a memory of longer than normal lifespans for people living before the Flood.

The second period, that of the patriarchs, raises issues about the time in which the stories were intended to take place. Although the question continues to be debated as part of concerns about the historicity of the narratives (Van Seters 1975, 1983, 1992; Thompson 1974, 1992; Lemche 1998; Redford 1990, 1997), the most likely time period for many of these narratives may remain the first half of the second millennium BC, i.e., the Middle Bronze Age. Archives at Mari, Nuzi, Alalakh, and elsewhere attest to customs such as treaties/covenants made by killing animals; a marriage arrangement involving a seven-year period, using names such as Abram, Isaac, and Jacob, and the general ability of the patriarchs to live a nomadic life and yet remain in relatively good relations with the local urban centers (Hess 1994a, 1994b; Kitchen 1994, 1995). With respect to Joseph, details such as the price of his sale into slavery, as well as the general context of a West Semitic ruler in Egypt, which resembles the Hyksos rule of 1750–1550 BC, provide parallels with the early second millennium BC world (Kitchen 1977, 1994, 1995).

The exodus/wilderness/conquest period focuses on the major biblical event of that age, the Exodus of Israel from Egypt. For those who find some historical tradition behind this account, there remains disagreement about the date of the event. The proponents of the early date accept 1 Kings 6:1 as literal and do their math to arrive at a 1447 BC date. Those who focus on the archaeological evidence and clues provided in the Exodus narrative itself are prepared to see a symbolic number in 1 Kings and to accept a thirteenth- or (less frequently) a twelfth-century BC date. The later option is supported by, among other things, the absence of any mention of Israel in the fourteenth-century BC. Amarna letters from Canaanite rulers in Palestine, the thirteenth-century burn layer at Hazor (Josh. 11:13), and the name Ramesses that was common in the thirteenth century BC and was applied to a city such as the one the Israelites

constructed, but was rare in the fifteenth century (Hess 1993; Hoffmeier 1997; Kitchen 1994). The mention of Israel in the 1209 BC Merneptah stele argues against the twelfth-century BC date unless one accepts the presence of two groups of people who become Israel.

If a later date is accepted the question arises as to how the judges are to be dated. There are so many of them who judged numerous years that a sequential order would be impossible to correlate with these later dates. Many scholars regard the period of the judges, as described by the Bible, to focus in the twelfth and eleventh centuries BC. This was a time of the sudden appearance of hundreds of small villages in the hill country of Palestine, some or most of which can be identified with Israel (Finkelstein 1988). Thus the village life reflected in Judges, Ruth, and 1 Samuel matches these two centuries much better than it does the thirteenth and fourteenth centuries BC. The periods of the judges are therefore best understood as overlapping and simultaneous (Hess 1993).

The monarchy is well represented in the Bible, with detailed narratives found in 2 Samuel, 1 and 2 Kings, and 1 and 2 Chronicles. There is a constant reference to chronology. A reading of this material demonstrates what appear to be contradictions and hopeless complexities in identifying dates for the kings of the northern and southern kingdoms. Edwin R. Thiele (1951, 1977) has argued that these can be analyzed and form a consistent dating scheme when it is accepted that there were two systems of dating, one from Egypt and the other from Mesopotamia. These differ according to whether the year begins in the autumn or spring and, more importantly, whether a newly crowned monarch counts the remainder of the year of the coronation as the first year of the new reign, or whether the first year begins to be counted at the start of the new year (in the autumn or spring). These assumptions, along with the possibility of co-regencies, allowed Thiele to create a complete and persuasive chronology for all the kings of Israel and Judah. Although some would prefer to see transmission errors where Thiele invokes the above principles, his chronology remains the starting point for all discussions of this debate.

Thus chronological issues remain a significant part of the debate that is so closely tied with questions of the history of ancient Israel.

References and further reading

Finkelstein, Israel (1988) *The Archaeology of the Israelite Settlement*, Jerusalem: Israelite Exploration Society.

Hess, Richard S. (1993) 'Early Israel in Canaan: A Survey of Recent Evidence and Interpretations,' *Palestine Exploration Quarterly* 126: 125–42.

—— (1994a) 'Alalakh Studies and the Bible: Obstacle or Contribution?' pp. 199–215 in *Scripture and Other Artifacts: Essays on the Bible and Archaeology in Honor* of *Philip J. King*, M.D. Coogan, J.C. Exum, and L.E. Stager (eds.), Louisville: Westminster/John Knox.

—— (1994b) 'The Slaughter of the Animals in Genesis 15: Genesis 15:8–21 and Its Ancient Near Eastern Context,' pp. 55–65 in *He Swore an Oath: Biblical Themes from Genesis 12–50*, R. Hess, G. Wenham, and P. Satterthwaite (eds.), Carlisle: Paternoster/Grand Rapids/Baker, 2nd edn.

—— (1994c) 'The Genealogies of Genesis 1–11 and Comparative Literature,' pp. 58–72 in *'I Studied Inscriptions from before the Flood': Ancient Near Eastern, Literary, and Linguistic Approaches to Genesis 1–11*, Sources for Biblical and Theological Study Volume 4, R.S. Hess and D.T. Tsumura (eds.), Winona Lake, IN: Eisenbrauns.

Hoffmeier, James K. (1997) *Israel in Egypt: The Evidence for the Authenticity of the Exodus Tradition*, Oxford: Oxford University Press.

Jacobsen, Thorkild (1939) *The Sumerian King List*, AS No. 11, Chicago: University of Chicago Press.

Kitchen, Kenneth A. (1977) *The Bible in Its World*, Exeter: Paternoster.

—— (1994) 'Genesis 12–50 in the Near Eastern World,' pp. 67–92 in *He Swore on Oath: Biblical Themes for Genesis 12–50*, R. Hess, G. Wenham, and P. Satterthwaite (eds.), Carlisle: Paternoster/Grand Rapids/Baker, 2nd edn.

—— (1995) 'The Patriarchal Age. Myth or History?' *Biblical Archaeology Review* 21/2 (March/April): 48–57, 88, 90, 92, 94–5.

Lemche, Niels Peter (1998) *Prelude to Israel's Past: Background and Beginnings of Israelite History and Identity*. Trans. E.F. Maniscalco, Peabody, MA: Hendrickson.

Millard, Alan R. (1994) *The Eponyms of the Assyrian Empire: 910–612 BC*, State Archives of Assyria Studies Volume II, Helsinki: University of Helsinki Press.

Redford, Donald B. (1990) *Egypt, Canaan, and Israel in Ancient Times*, Princeton: Princeton University Press.

—— (1997) 'The Sojourn of the Bene-Israel,' pp. 57–66 in *Exodus: The Egyptian Evidence*, E. Frerichs and L. Lesko (eds.), Winona Lake, IN: Eisenbrauns.

Thiele, Edwin R. (1951) *The Mysterious Numbers of the Hebrew Kings*, Chicago: University of Chicago Press.

—— (1977) *A Chronology of the Hebrew Kings*, Contemporary Evangelical Perspectives, Grand Rapids: Zondervan.

Thompson, T.L. (1974) *The Historicity of the Patriarchal Narratives: The Quest for the Historical Abraham*, BZAW 133, Berlin: Harrassowitz.

—— (1992) *Early History of the Israelite Peoples from the Written and Archaeological Sources*, SHANE 4, Leiden: Brill.

Van Seters, J. (1975) *Abraham in History and Tradition*, New Haven: Yale University Press.

—— (1983) *In Search of History: Historiography in the Ancient World and the Origins of Biblical History*, New Haven: Yale University Press.

—— (1992) *Prologue to History: The Yahwist as Historian in Genesis*, Louisville: Westminster/John Knox.

RICHARD S. HESS

CHRYSOSTOM, JOHN (c. 347–407)

Considered the greatest preacher of the patristic era, John was born and raised in Syrian Antioch. He studied rhetoric and classical Greek literature under the renowned Roman sophist Libanius. John trained for a career in law and imperial service before abandoning his 'vain verbosity' to study scripture and to enter the clergy. Following his baptism by Bishop Meletius, he became a lector, and studied scripture under the leading teacher of Antioch, Diodore. Under Diodore, John learned the Antiochene approach to scripture of historical and grammatical exegesis, an approach characterized by its reaction to the allegorical approach of Alexandria.

John lived the ascetic life in the nearby Syrian countryside for six years, for three of which he lived in isolation, before returning to clerical ministry in Antioch in 378. In 381 he was ordained deacon and five years later, presbyter.

Over the following twelve years as a presbyter John wrote prolifically and preached regularly to the people of Antioch. John's elegance as a leading pulpit orator earned him the epitaph of *Chrysostomos* – 'golden-mouthed.' Most of his works are homilies on the Bible, hundreds of which are extant. Of notable importance are his sermons on Genesis, Psalms, Isaiah, Matthew, John, Acts of the Apostles, and most of Paul's writings (including Hebrews). These works unite his ability to see the spiritual meaning of the author along with immediate practical application. His exposition of the scriptures is straightforward and historical. His exegetical homilies are beneficial because of John's concern for the grammatical and literary character of the texts.

In 398, John was forced by the emperor's order to accept the position as bishop of Constantinople. He produced fewer sermons in Constantinople than he had at Antioch. His failed diplomacy with the imperial court, along with the unreceptive activity of Theophilus, bishop of Alexandria (a rival Episcopal see) led to the termination of John's office and his exile. John lived his last days in exile and on September 14, 407 John Chrysostom died in a village in Asia Minor.

John's biblical preaching was strongly influenced by his rhetorical education, ascetic ideals, and exegetical formation. His sermons utilized vivid imagery and his audience expected a rhetorical exhibit like that of a secular orator. During the homilies he frequently digressed; it is generally believed that he preached extempore. He, along with other Christian orators, adapted the ancient rhetorical genre of *encomium*, which although common in the fourth century appears artificial to modern readers for its gross exaggerations and repetition. As a pastor, he drew moral lessons from the scriptures opposing the use of allegorization while stressing the literal exegesis, as he understood it. He was concerned with applying scripture to the spiritual and ethical lives of his congregation. The Bible provided the standard for imitation and he strove to make scripture accessible for the general public. In his homilies he exhorted hearers to repeat his message to their households. John was primarily pastoral, reflecting the orthodox doctrines of the church during the crises of Arianism and Nestorianism.

References and further reading

Baur, C. (1960) *John Chrysostom and His Time*, 2 Vols., London: Sands.

Kelly, J.N.D. (1996) *Golden Month: The Story of John Chrysostom: Ascetic, Preacher, Bishop*, Ithaca: Cornell University Press.

Shatkin, M.A. (1987) *John Chrysostom as Apologist*, Thessalonica: Patriarchiken Hidryina Paterikon Meleton.

DALLAS B.N. FRIESEN

COMMENTARY (NEW TESTAMENT)

1 History
2 Aims and contents of a New Testament commentary
3 The modern commentary

1 History

The writing of explanatory notes on a Greek text was not practiced first by Christians. Grammarians and stylists wrote notes on obscure passages in Homer, Hesiod, and others. These were recalled and written in the margins of Byzantine manuscripts as scholia, but the substance of many of these goes back to a much earlier date. Again, every translation of a text is to some extent a commentary, and the Greek (e.g., the LXX) and the Aramaic (Targumim) translations of the Old Testament are to this extent commentaries. More explicitly commentaries in form and substance are the midrashim, which expound books of the Old Testament, applying them to the practice of Judaism in later times. Targumim and midrashim as we have them today are of various dates, but they go back to translations and comments old enough to have provided precedents for Christians who commented on Christian texts, With these may be classed those Qumran manuscripts which interpret Old Testament books in relation to events in the life of the Qumran sect.

The writing of commentaries on books of the New Testament is unlikely to have begun before the beginnings of a New Testament canon, a collection of books recognized as having a special authority and as thereby providing a basis for Christian preaching. Earlier (before, roughly, AD 175) Christians occasionally referred to and expounded passages from New Testament books, but not systematically or in consecutive form. Origen may perhaps count as the first, and certainly one of the greatest, of Christian commentators. He taught biblical exegesis as well as philosophy and theology in Alexandria and Caesarea, and, with the aid of stenographers and copyists, produced works on many books of both Testaments. Of these, some consisted of scholia, some were delivered orally as homilies, and some were commentaries, dealing especially with theological questions, often using allegory.

Many of the ancient commentaries that we possess were in the first instance, like Origens, spoken homilies or sermons. Outstanding authors were Chrysostom and Augustine. Chrysostom combined with unusual success lexical and grammatical explanation with practical application. Unlike Origen, Chrysostom was an Antiochian and made little use of allegory. Augustine, too, was a pastoral preacher who applied the biblical message in practical terms, but he was also a philosophical theologian and showed this in his comments.

Augustine's two interests persisted in medieval exposition of scripture. There was little of the linguistic investigation that was natural to Chrysostom. Comments tended to become stereotyped in the monastic and other schools, notaby in the *Glossa Ordinaria*, for which Anselm (*c.* 1050–1115) and Radulph of Laon were to a great extent responsible. This was written in biblical manuscripts in the form of marginal or interlineary notes, but there were also homiletical expositions by preachers and theologians.

Scriptural exegesis continued in these forms until the Reformation. Luther's early commentaries (notably on Romans) were prepared by him in the form of the *Glossa*, that is, in notes written on the pages of the text in question. From these notes he lectured. His later commentaries have the appearance of spoken homilies, and no doubt often were in the first place sermons.

It was in part the requirements of controversy that led to the development of commentaries in something more like the form familiar in our own time. At the time of the Reformation each side found it important to be supported by the authority of scripture, and sought to establish exactly what the scripture said. It is convenient, and scarcely an exaggeration, to take Calvin as the earliest example of this kind of commentator. He wrote commentaries on nearly every book of the New Testament; the commentaries are no doubt related to his regular lecturing and preaching in Geneva, but they are literary products. There is no doubt that Calvin's primary interest is theological; he wishes to know how the New Testament bears witness to the Christian Gospel; occasionally this leads him into the error of importing theological matter into passages that do not contain it. But he is well aware of the fact that texts on which he comments are historical documents, and he discusses the history they record with some critical freedom. His wide knowledge of Greek and Latin literature and history is frequently apparent.

Two more commentators may be mentioned as introductory to the modern period. They were nearly contemporary: J.A. Bengel (1687–1752) and J.J. Wettstein (1693–1754). Bengel was in the first instance a textual critic, collecting, analyzing, classifying variant readings, and enunciating the principle, *difficilior lectio placet*. The text established, he went on, in another work (*Gnomon Novi Testamenti*), to explain it word by word. He is still a useful guide, and his epigrammatic Latin often hits off the meaning of a Greek phrase very successfully. Wettstein does less to explain the text, but he provided not only a critical apparatus, which showed both a conspectus of variants and his own preferred readings, but also an extensive collection of illustrative passages, from Greek, Latin, and Jewish sources. Like Bengel's *Gnomon*, Wettstein's *Novum Testamentum* is still a valuable resource for the student.

2 Aims and contents of a New Testament commentary

(1) The first task of the writer of a commentary is to establish the text of the document with which he is dealing. The books of the New Testament are known from many Greek manuscripts, from translations into other ancient languages, notably Latin, Syriac, and Coptic, and from quotations in the works of the Church Fathers. All these sources must be classified and assessed, the variants considered, and the original form of the text determined. The commentator will of course at the present time find that most of the work has already been done; good texts are readily available. There will always, however, be doubtful points to discuss.

This point overlaps with the next, for copyists are always likely to 'improve' an author's grammar, and a reading that accords with an author's recognizable style has much to commend it.

(2) The text once ascertained, its meaning must be determined. Every translation is in fact a commentary without notes, for it is ideally a transposition of the original Greek into a new language. This requires as good an understanding of the Greek language as the commentator can provide. Passages chosen to illustrate the text must be carefully chosen and their dates borne in mind; languages change with time. Other languages may have influenced the Greek text – Hebrew, Aramaic, Latin.

The understanding of Greek is not a static discipline,

and a commentator, even when commenting upon the English text, must keep up with it.

Grammar and vocabulary are fundamental, but style too is important. The style is the man; the commentator wishes to know his author and the author's style is an important indicator. Style also facilitates comparison between one book of the New Testament and others; such comparisons may be important. With style goes form, which may help to define the purpose or aim of a book and thus affect its interpretation. Consideration may be given to the several rhetorical forms that were distinguished in antiquity, and to their application in New Testament books.

(3) Language and its correct evaluation provide the indispensable foundation of every commentary but they are not the whole building. When the exact sense of words and sentences has been settled, their historical and theological significance will be discussed, in relation to any other sources that may be relevant. Books of the New Testament call for the same historical and theological criticism that would be applied to other books; this is not inconsistent with a high view of their authority. History may include biography and the history of institutions. The theological significance of the text may be given directly in theological affirmations or arguments, or be implicit in historical events, out of which it must be deduced, as the motivation or outcome of recorded incidents. Particular aspects of theology, such as liturgy or ethics, may be emphasized. These processes provide the constitutive material out of which the history and thought of New Testament Christianity, and its relation with other forms of thought and of society, may be reconstructed. A special interest characteristic of some of the most recent commentaries is sociology. This has included not only an increased interest in social history, but also an application of the methods of sociology.

(4) A commentary may contain information relating to the history of interpretation. An account of the way in which a text has been understood at various points in the past is interesting and important in its own right; it will often provide guidance, negative as well as positive, for the latest commentator. Not every commentary will deal with this at length, but there is no commentator who has nothing to learn from earlier expositions, in both the recent and more distant past.

(5) Parallel to the history of interpretation (*Auslegungsgeschichte*) is the history of the influence or effect (*Wirkungsgeschichte*) of the text studied, The influence may be theological; the effect of Romans on and through Luther, and again later through the commentary by Karl Barth may be recalled. It may be ethical, through such passages as the Sermon on the Mount; it may be negatively ethical, for there are those New Testament passages that have been invoked, justly or unjustly, in the interests of anti-Semitism.

(6) In recent years new methods have been applied to the study of the books of the New Testament.

The use of sociology and of rhetorical studies has been mentioned above. New methods developed in general literary criticism have also been used. Among the earliest of these was structuralism. Another has meant distinguishing between actual author or apparent author, actual readers and apparent readers. The distinction is of less value in the study of the New Testament than in some other fields of literature because, in the New Testament, actual authors are scarcely known except through the works they wrote and read. Reader-response criticism asserts that readers as well as authors contribute to the full meaning of any work of literature. What is of value in this is mostly contained in the history of interpretation. Readers who have made their opinions available to us may help us; but they may also be mistaken and lead us away from the meaning intended by the author, which (whether we agree or disagree with it) should be regarded as the commentator's primary aim.

(7)   At the end, one comes back to what was probably the beginning of New Testament commentary – the work of preaching. A commentary itself is not necessarily, and perhaps should not be, preaching (though some classical commentaries are transcripts of discourses), but it represents the necessary presupposition of preaching, for in it the thought of the writer is brought out and erroneous interpretations are rejected. Between this exposition of the writer's intention and the preached sermon lies the business of hermeneutics, to which, it should be added, modern methods of interpretation are intended to contribute, To make ancient texts equally relevant to hearers in the twenty-first century calls for heavy hermeneutical toil, in which a gain in accessibility and a loss in authority have to be balanced against each other.

3 The modern commentary

Here only a fragmentary sketch is possible. The commentaries by J.B. Lightfoot (on Galatians, Philippians, Colossians, and Philemon), though a century and a half old, are still indispensable as tools and as models of textual, historical, and theological work, The International Critical Commentary, from the 1890s but now in process of renewal, originated in Britain but with an important American contribution. The Anchor Bible and Hermeneia are among series that originated in America.

Roughly contemporary with Lightfoot, H.AW. Meyer founded in 1829 the 'Kritisch exegetischer Kommentar zum Neuen Testament' series which from the first aimed at being purely historical and philological, but has found itself obliged – by its own principles – to enter the field of theology. It contains some of the greatest commentaries, for example, Rudolf Bultmann's *John*, Also in German is the slighter but highly concentrated *Handbuch zum Neuen Testament*.

In French it may suffice to mention the commentaries in the 'Etudes Bibliques' series, initiated by the great commentaries on the Gospels by M.J. Lagrange.

There are excellent commentaries in other series, and in no series, but these will give the reader a good impression of modern New Testament commentaries.

C.K. BARRETT

COMMENTARY (OLD TESTAMENT)

A commentary exists to provide critical explanation and analysis of a biblical text. It seeks to put the reader in closer contact with the language, context, and ideas of the book under examination such that its message is 'led' out of the text (exegesis). Having stated this, every commentary or series of commentaries is as individual as the people involved in the writing and editing. Even a cursory glance over the introductions to various modern commentaries makes patently clear the variety of agendas they bring to the task of commenting on biblical texts, e.g., 'Commitment to scripture as divine revelation, and to the truth and power of the Christian gospel' (*Word*), 'believing criticism' (*NIBC*), 'no systematic-theological perspective' (*Hermeneia*); the contributors to the series: 'scholars representing a wide cross section of American Protestant Christianity' (*Wycliffe Bible Commentary*), 'international and interfaith' (*Anchor*); as well as the readership they are addressing: 'students, teachers, ministers, and priests' (*Interpretation*), 'the general reader' (*Anchor*). Some commentaries contain new translations of the biblical text; others rely upon a widely circulated translation or version. Some approach the text line-by-line, some address whole passages with interpretative commentary, whilst others are technical and philological.

Although distance of time (roughly two millennia) culture (ancient Near East), and languages (Hebrew and Aramaic with numerous loan words from neighboring cultures) separate the modern reader from the origins of the Old Testament biblical texts, the same did not obtain for the earliest commentaries, which can be found within the Bible itself. A classic example is the Chronicler's History. Whether the Chronicler simply reworked the material of Samuel-Kings or worked with an independent source alongside the former is beyond the scope of this article. However, the theological conclusions offered in 1 and 2 Chronicles are not simply a rewritten text or parallel history, but also a commentary on the preeminent place of the Davidic house within the history and faith of Israel. An example of commentary by direct quotation of a biblical text is found in Daniel 9:l–7a, 24–27. Here we see that Jeremiah's prophecy, that the exile and desolation of Jerusalem were to last seventy years, is both expounded upon and reinterpreted. The 'seventy weeks' of Daniel 9:24 are understood as seventy weeks of years, or 490 years. On first reading, this is simply a rejection of the Chronicler's view that

Jeremiah's prophecy was indeed fulfilled by the restoration decreed by Cyrus (2 Chron. 36:21–23; Jer. 25:11–12). However, the Chronicler has already interpreted Jeremiah's prophecy with obvious reference to Leviticus 25–26. The jubilee year, as set out in Leviticus 25, stipulates seven sabbaths (weeks) of years as the maximum period that land could remain outside the possession of its original owner or heirs. In 2 Chronicles 36:21 it is stated that 'the land of Israel ran the full term of its sabbaths. All the time that it lay desolate it kept the Sabbath rest, to complete seventy years' – an interpretation clearly based on Leviticus 26:34–35. Daniel's extension of the period of desolation to seventy weeks of years is equivalent to ten jubilees. This extension of the period of desolation also has a basis in Leviticus. First, it has been inferred that the reference to 'seventy' was *sabbatical* years, thus seventy weeks of years. Second, Leviticus 26:18, 21, 28 state God's threat to punish the people sevenfold for their transgressions, thus yielding another explanation for the extension of Jeremiah's prophecy (Collins 1993: 352). It would seem that from the time the scriptures originated there arose the 'concern to preserve, render contemporary, or otherwise reinterpret these teachings or traditions in explicit ways for new times and circumstances' (Fishbane 1985: 8). Though beyond the particular scope of this article, it is worth briefly mentioning that the most basic way the scriptures were interpreted was through translation, which by its very nature involves an interpretative process. Translation consists of moving from one language and cultural context to another, in the light of the convictions of the community doing the translating. The Aramaic Targums and the Greek Septuagint are among the earliest examples of this process.

The earliest commentaries on biblical texts outside the Bible are to be found in the *pesharim* (plural of Hebrew *pesher*) of the Dead Sea Scrolls from Qumran. The *pesharim* generally take two forms: 'continuous' and 'thematic.' The former are based on continuous commentaries on individual books and usually consist of a citation of a biblical passage, followed by a formula such as: 'its interpretation concerns. . .'. The continuous *pesharim* are eschatological in character with clear reference to 'the last generation' and 'the final period.' The latter type bring together passages from different books on a particular theme and are also strongly eschatological. In both types of commentary, the *pesharim* are characterized by the notion that scripture is a mysterious code, allegorical by nature, and the *pesher* is the means for solving the mystery. In that regard *pesher* reflects its Akkadian cognate *pišru* ('release, interpretation') especially as used in relation to the interpretation of dreams and omens, whereby their mystery or portent is 'solved' (Oppenheim 1956: 219).

Within the rabbinic tradition of Judaism, the task of interpretation of scripture has taken center stage, with God being the prototypical scholar. 'The early rabbis

actually portrayed their God midrashically as a scholar of his own Torah and as subordinate to the decisions made by the disciples of the wise!' (Fishbane 1985: 21 citing *Ber.* 8b, 63b, *Abod Zar.* 3b, *B. Mes.* 59b). As odd as this might sound to some modern ears, it is based on the theological assumption that 'the contents of interpretation *are part* of the written divine revelation (implicitly or explicitly)' (Fishbane 1985: 4). This interpretative tradition is found within the two Talmuds (Babylonian and Palestinian), which are compendia of debate and discussion over Jewish law.

They comprise the Mishnah and Gemara. The Mishnah is a code of Jewish law, topically arranged in sixty-three tractates, which seeks to work out the implications of scriptural laws in such a way that they could permeate and influence daily life. It reached its present form around the early part of the third century AD. The Gemara consists of the discussions/debates regarding the meaning and interpretation of the laws in the Mishnah. The Palestinian Gemara was completed near the end of the fourth century AD and the Babylonian (much larger and more authoritative) at the end of the fifth century. Taken as a whole, the Talmud is chiefly a work of biblical interpretation and commentary, which has been and remains foundational for Judaism. Concomitant with the development of the Talmuds and continuing into medieval times is the Jewish midrashic activity. Midrash is a very broad term, referring to the process of hermeneutics, a particular compilation of the results of hermeneutics on a biblical book, and the written results of an exegesis on a particular passage. Here I refer particularly to the midrashic activity and resultant literature from the Talmudic and early medieval period. The term 'midrash' is derived from the root *darash*, meaning to 'seek, investigate, enquire into.' As a genre it can be divided into three different approaches: *halakhic*, *aggadic*, and homiletic. The *halakhic* midrashim comprise reflections on the legal portions of scripture and the manner in which they are to be fulfilled in daily life: notably the *Mekhilta* (on Exodus), *Sifre* (on Numbers and Deuteronomy), and *Sifra* (on Leviticus). The *aggadic* midrashim are collections of parables and anecdotes dealing primarily with the narrative portions of scripture (notably *Genesis Rabbah* and *Ecclesiastes Rabbah*). The homiletic midrashim are based upon the weekly Torah portions, examples being *Pesiqta* and *Tanḥuma*. Midrash was carried out using one or all of the exegetical methods designated by the acronym *pardes*: *peshat* (the literal translation), *remez* (the implied meaning), *derash* (homiletic exposition), and *sod* (the allegorical/mystical meaning). Of the four methods *peshat* and *derash* are the most popular while the other two have been used largely in mystical and kabbalistic approaches. The application of the literal and homiletic approaches – especially *peshatm* gained in importance in the Middle Ages, both through concern to teach Judaism to the Jewish community, which was under great pressure both from Christians and Muslims, but also as a reaction to the largely allegorical/Christological usage of Hebrew scriptures by Christian commentators. Two great exponents of this approach were Saadya Gaon (880–942) and Rashi (1040–1105). Gaon believed that the literal reading of the text should always take precedence over any implied or allegorical meaning unless the literal reading ran counter to received tradition or reason. Rashi's stated aim was to exegete a text according to its plain meaning, and, if that meaning were not easily arrived at, then according to the closest *aggadic* interpretation. The ascendancy and predominance of the literal over allegorical interpretation of scripture did not prevent the interest in philosophical interpretation. Maimonides' *Guide of the Perplexed* was largely an attempt to reconcile the Bible with the philosophy of Aristotle, which was enjoying a resurgence in Western Europe.

As regards Christian commentary of the Old Testament, that the New Testament contains commentary on the scriptures of the Old Testament is certainly a truism. However, it must be stressed that the primary purpose of the New Testament writings was not to provide interpretative commentary on the Old. Although some of the New Testament authors wrote with the specific intent of interpreting the Old Testament in terms of the new revelation in Jesus, their commentary consisted in showing how the events in his life fulfilled prophecies/expectations found in the Hebrew Bible. The New Testament does not provide any formal or continuous commentary on any book of the Old Testament, rather it declares a new teaching which incorporates the former scriptures. The teaching which the New Testament depicts as coming from the mouth of Jesus does not usually start with the citation of scripture: rather he characteristically begins with a parable, which is itself a comment about the way life is (Barr 1983: 69). Although in Matthew's Gospel, for instance, a number of pesher-style exegeses can be found, they are usually pointers to the way in which Jesus has fulfilled messianic prophecies and not exposition of a biblical text (Stanton 1988: 208). It is more appropriate to say that the Old Testament was used to interpret the events related in the New, e.g., the writer of Hebrews strings one Old Testament citation after another with the purpose of interpreting Christ in terms of the Jewish cultus (Hanson 1988: 300). In this regard both Jewish and Christian commentary on the Hebrew canon began at roughly the same time – but with different purpose. The rabbis turned to the scriptures as the basis of the Torah which guided Jewish faith and life. The Christian writers looked to the Hebrew canon both for its moral guidance but also and especially for its predictive aspects which they found fulfilled in Jesus.

It is with the patristic period that Christian commentary writing comes into its own. Writing early in the third century AD. Origen was the first prominent Christian scholar to engage in continuous commentary on scripture. Not unlike much rabbinic interpretation, he is known for allegorizing the scriptures. Origen based his hermeneutics on a threefold sense of scripture: (1) the literal sense – statements of scripture were 'earthen vessels' which preserved the true meaning, which had both (2) moral sense (the soul) and (3) spiritual sense (the spirit), the highest being the spiritual. The latter two senses of scripture were embedded in allegory, which yielded the highest understanding of scripture. In Song of Songs, for instance, the eroticism is interpreted as the soul's intercourse with the divine Logos. Although he did not read Hebrew, Origen was a keen student of the various Greek translations (which made up his critical six-columned *Hexapla*), and scrutinized the texts for their differences from the church's Septuagint. As regards the Septuagint itself, Origen recognized that there were inconsistencies within the narratives, but these were placed in the text deliberately in order to conceal the true meaning from the simple. In fact the scriptures had their own internal consistency, which could only be found by reading both the Old and New Testaments as a unity, one continuous testament to God's wide-ranging revelation. Origen's work cast a long shadow over the development of Christian interpretation. There were those after him, e.g., Theodore of Mopsuestia and John Chrysostom, who took greater account of the literal sense of scripture, but allegorical interpretation remained strong. In the early Middle Ages commentators expanded Origen's three senses of scripture into four. The spiritual sense was divided into the allegorical, which put forward the true meaning of the text, and the anagogical, which related to the coming world.

From the late patristic period, until the rise of scholasticism in the thirteenth century, the dominant type of interpretation was based upon direct or indirect quotation of patristic literature. In time this became best represented by the *Glossa Ordinaria*, a digest of extracts from the Fathers and early medieval doctors of interpretation. It reached its definitive form by the mid-twelfth century and exerted a normative influence over subsequent interpretation, including the work of Thomas Aquinas who cites it prodigiously.

The authoritative figure of the scholastic period, Thomas Aquinas, regarded the literal sense of scripture as that which the author intended. The literal text carried with it the other three senses (see above), which God, as ultimate Author, inspired the writer to include – both for his contemporaries and for future readership. In that regard the Old Testament authors could not always understand the true significance of their work, as it depended upon later revelation. Thus the other three senses of scripture helped the reader comprehend the true, doctrinal meaning of the text. Whilst this Thomist treatment of scripture gained general acceptance, there were those who sought to get as close to the original text as possible, notably Hugh of St Victor (Paris) and his student Andrew (both twelfth-century) whose work profited greatly by direct study of Hebrew texts. So too with Robert Grosseteste of Lincoln (d. 1253), who worked with both the Septuagint and Hebrew manuscripts. For all these scholars, technical and linguistic matters aided in the exegesis of scripture.

The Protestant Reformation of the sixteenth century was marked by an iconoclasm not only toward church buildings but also toward the edifice of magisterial interpretation which had gained a near 'canonical' status over the centuries. What had become the preserve of monastery and university was wrested back into the hands of churchmen such as Martin Luther and John Calvin. The emergence of new hermeneutical tools (e.g., textual and philological) gave the Reformers the leverage they needed to topple the predominant interpretation of scripture, especially the assumption that scripture could be identified with the Vulgate text. In his interpretation Luther followed a policy not unlike that of Rashi, dismissing allegory unless reason could discern no plain meaning. As regards the Old Testament, Luther made a distinction between the 'literal-historic sense' (how the text pertains to historic Israel) and the 'literal-prophetic sense' (the way the same text stands as a prophetic witness to Jesus Christ). Calvin is primarily known today as a consummate systematic theologian. However, his power as a theologian arose from his philological-historical interpretation of biblical texts and his immersion in biblical thought.

The explosion of commentary writing which began in the sixteenth century has continued unabated ever since. These have been led by religious movements (e.g., the Reformation), personal piety (e.g., Matthew Henry), theology (e.g., Karl Barth), and a host of other interests. The rise of various critical schools of interpretation – historical, form, textual, and literary criticism, deconstructionism, post-modernism to name only some of the major movements – has also brought new style commentaries in their wake. There have also been commentaries in reaction to various movements, as well as commentaries from those hostile to the religion proclaimed within the biblical texts. Certainly there is a real tension in secular Western society between the types of commentaries required by communities of faith and those for whom faith is a matter of indifference or its 'cultured despisers.' Whatever the stance taken and whatever the philosophy, most commentators today make use of a combination of their predecessors' work: account is taken of language, grammar, style, historical context, etc.

We all bring a certain amount of 'baggage' to the reading of a biblical text: religious, cultural, linguistic, national. Biblical commentators are no exception. For this reason the commentator's role becomes decisive in textual interpretation. However, a good commentary should help us to leave some of our baggage at the door of the text. Thus, we end where we began: with

the various agendas different series of commentaries bring to the task of biblical interpretation. As no one can escape his or her cultural/historical condition, commentaries which state their aim in interpreting the Old Testament for today's readership at least make clear the point at which exegesis might stray into eisegesis or reading *into* a text one's assumptions, interests, etc. Furthermore, no matter how assiduously a text is examined, no commentary will be able to make that text yield up all the gems it contains. This fact, coupled with the changing needs of religious communities, students, and scholars will most likely ensure a continuing place for the biblical commentary.

References and further reading

Barr, James (1983) *Holy Scripture: Canon, Authority, Criticism*, Oxford: Clarendon.

Collins, John J. (1993) *Daniel*, Minneapolis: Fortress Press.

Fishbane, Michael (1989) *Biblical Interpretation in Ancient Israel*, Oxford: Clarendon.

Hanson. A.T. (1988) 'Hebrews', pp. 292–302 in *It Is Written: Scripture Citing Scripture*, D.A. Carson and H.G.M. Williamson (eds.), Cambridge: Cambridge University Press.

Oppenheim, A. Leo (1956) *The Interpretation of Dreams in the Ancient Near East*, Philadelphia: The American Philosophical Society.

Stanton, Graham (1988) 'Matthew,' pp. 205–19 in *It Is Written: Scripture Citing Scripture*, D.A. Carson and H.G.M. Williamson (eds.), Cambridge: Cambridge University Press.

JACK N. LAWSON

CULLMANN, OSCAR (1902–1999)

A lay Lutheran from Alsace, Cullmann taught both at Basel, as Professor of New Testament and Ancient Christian History (1938–1972), and at the Sorbonne, Paris, as Professor of Protestant Theology (from 1948).

His scholarly work was marked by a long-term interest in eschatology. In an early study, 'Le caractère eschatologique du devoir missionaire et de la conscience apostolique de S. Paul' (*RHPR* 16, 1936), on 2 Thessalonians 2:6–7, Cullmann was the first to draw attention to the eschatological nature of Paul's apostleship. But his most significant writings in this area were undoubtedly *Christ and Time* (ET 1950) and *Salvation in History* (ET 1967). In these he developed the idea that running through the course of world history has been a narrower stream of salvation history which provides the clue to understanding the whole of history. This redemptive history forms a single (though not straight) line running from Creation through to the eschatological climax. At its center or midpoint is the Christ event, which both anticipates and ensures the eschatological climax, setting up the classic (particularly Pauline) tension between the 'already' and the 'not yet' of the salvation process. In this scheme the delay of the Parousia is of less moment, since the weight of eschatological significance has already been placed on the resurrection of Christ.

More lastingly influential in both New Testament and systematic theology has been Cullmann's *The Christology of the New Testament* (ET 1959). As the first of the Christological studies which focused more or less exclusively on the titles used for Jesus in the New Testament it set the dominant trend for a generation. It was also one of the more conservative and extensive studies of its type. In his earlier work, *The Earliest Christian Confessions* (ET 1949), he had already argued effectively that 'Jesus is Lord' was the earliest Christological confession.

Cullmann himself would probably have given more weight to the contributions which sprang from and expressed his deeply rooted ecumenical concerns (since the 1920s) to improve relations between the Protestant and Catholic churches. Influential on discussions of the sacraments at the time was his high view of baptism in *Baptism in the New Testament* (ET 1950) and his strong sacramental reading of John's Gospel in *Early Christian Worship* (ET 1953). His treatment of Peter, in *Peter – Disciple, Apostle, Martyr* (1952), with its positive evaluation of Matthew 16:17–19, was well received in the Vatican. However, his *Unity Through Diversity* (1986), which summed up his lifetime's work in this area, made it clear that in his view the appropriate ecumenical goal is a 'community of autonomous churches.'

Among his shorter contributions, gathered in his collection of essays, *The Early Church* (ET 1956), mention should be made particularly of 'The Plurality of the Gospels as a Theological Problem in Antiquity' (an issue which has evoked surprisingly little discussion), and 'The Tradition,' in which he dealt sensitively from a Protestant angle with the issue of canon and tradition. The essay on 'Samaria and the Origins of the Christian Mission' was subsequently taken up in the short monograph *The Johannine Circle* (ET 1976) and anticipated the growth of interest in a Samaritan phase of Christian mission as reflected also in the Fourth Gospel.

His last book was *Prayer in the New Testament* (1994).

References and further reading

Cullmann, Oscar (1936) 'Le caractère eschatologique du devoir missionaire et de la conscience apostolique de S. Paul,' *Revue d'histoire et de philosophie religieuse* 16.
—— (1949) *The Earliest Christian Confessions*, London: SCM Press.
—— (1950a) *Baptism in the New Testament*, London: SCM Press.
—— (1950b) *Christ and Time*, London: SCM Press.
—— (1952) *Peter – Disciple, Apostle, Martyr*, London: SCM Press.
—— (1953) *Early Christian Worship*, London: SCM Press.
—— (1956) *The Early Church*, London: SCM Press.
—— (1959) *The Christology of the New Testament*, London: SCM Press.
—— (1967) *Salvation in History*, London: SCM Press.
—— (1976) *The Johannine Circle*, London: SCM Press.
—— (1986) *Unity Through Diversity*, London: SCM Press.
—— (1994) *Prayer in the New Testament*, London: SCM Press.

JAMES D.G. DUNN

CULTURAL RELATIONSHIPS IN THE OLD TESTAMENT PERIOD

1 The extrabiblical context
2 The Pentateuch
3 Historical books
4 Poetry
5 Wisdom literature
6 Prophetic literature

1 The extrabiblical context

It is impossible to read the Old Testament without encountering the presence of cultural forms and items. On every level there are cultural influences from the surrounding countries of Egypt to the south, the Hittites and Aramaeans to the north, Babylonia and Assyria to the east (and later Persia), and the immediate environs of the Canaanites and Philistines, Ammonites, Edomites, and Moabites. Archaeologically, the inhabitants of the Palestinian hill country, where Israel first settled and where its center remained throughout the monarchy and later, inherited Canaanite forms in their early settlements. These included collared rim pithoi, four-room houses, and the use of terraces and cisterns (Hess 1993a). It is true that the period associated with the Israelite settlement saw a significant increase in these cultural forms, but this is on the level of a transformation of existing forms rather than a completely new innovation. The same is true of the Hebrew writing system and language. The alphabet is an adaptation of the Phoenician/Canaanite script and the language is firmly rooted in West Semitic Canaanite dialects already found in the Amarna texts and attested in Phoenician, Moabite, Ammonite, and Edomite (Rainey 1996). The use of the alphabet provided a revolution in media and may have brought about a democratization of written communication as far more people were able to read and write. This is clearer in Israel and Judah than in any other surrounding nation. These two kingdoms have a far greater percentage of their seals (used to identify individuals) with the name of the bearer actually written on the seal. Again, the forms are transformed.

This same transformation is evident in the Hebrew Bible, both in its description of the Israelite people and their lifestyle, and in the literary forms of the texts themselves. While it is true that ascetic groups (Rechabites), reforming kings (e.g, Jehu and Josiah), and many of the writing prophets condemned cultural syncretism and assimilation, the opposite also occurred. Solomon did build a temple that closely resembled Syrian predecessors (Monson 1999; 2000). Jehu is seen bringing tribute and bowing before the Assyrian king on the Black Obelisk of Shalmaneser III. The postexilic community, for all its exclusivity, copied the 'civic temple community' model so common throughout the Persian Empire (Blenkinsopp 1991).

It is in the area of biblical Hebrew literature itself, however, that cultural forms have their greatest impact. Repeatedly the Bible bears witness to the transformation of cultural forms in order to convey a distinctive message to its readers in ways that would be most understandable. There is here an exemplary use of media to create an impact and to persuade those who perceived it of the truthfulness of the message.

2 The Pentateuch

Thus the Creation stories of Genesis 1 and 2 have similarities with Akkadian models (Enuma Elish) but their presentation is altogether transformed by the centrality of humanity in the accounts and by the seven-day sabbath structuring of Genesis 1 (Hess and Tsumura 1994). The genealogies resemble the Sumerian and other king lists but are unique in their forward movement of history (Hess 1994b). The Flood story of Genesis 6–9 has too many points in common with Mesopotamian accounts to be coincidental. Yet only in the Bible is the issue of moral evil addressed as a cause of the Deluge. The patriarchal accounts borrow many social customs from surrounding Syrian culture. However, they alone weave this material into stories of God's dealings with a family.

As a nation Israel is introduced to a covenant that is repeated and reaffirmed by the people (Exod. 20–24; Deut.; Josh. 8:30–35; 24). Without doubt the structure of this covenant resembles legal codes and treaties, especially those of the second millennium BC (Kitchen 1979, 1989). Even here God uses a familiar means of formalizing a relationship between two groups as a way of communicating a relationship with Israel. The similarities of the legal codes also betray a difference in values, one that places the importance of human life first in priority in the Bible (Hess 1980). The cultic laws and rituals have similarities with cultic texts from the Hittites, Ugarit, Emar, and elsewhere (Fleming

1998). However, the Bible simplifies cultic regulations to a far greater extent than Israel's neighbors. The emphasis can be on the heart and attitude of the worshipper rather than on the performance of specific rituals.

3 Historical books

Israel's conquest of the land, as recorded in Joshua, includes several new features, but many similarities to other documents. Thus the conquest and distribution of land has been compared to other nations' founding legends (Weinfeld 1988). Miracles of walls collapsing (Josh. 6) and hailstones from heaven (Josh. 10) have their precedents in other ancient Near-Eastern conquest accounts (Younger 1990), as does the annalistic style of Joshua 10. The distribution of the land, in terms of boundary descriptions and town lists, has parallels in documents from Ugarit and Alalakh. As with Joshua 13–21, which is positioned between two covenant-renewal ceremonies, the boundary descriptions occur in a similar context of land-grant treaties (Hess 1994a, 1994c). The town lists can be compared with administrative documents that provide clues to the ongoing purpose of these texts (Hess 1996).

The motif of an individual chosen to lead but having to gain rulership from an obscure position, often with divine assistance, is found in the biblical narratives of Moses, Jephthah, Gideon, and especially David. Similar themes occur in the legend of Sargon, the rise of the Alalakh king Idrimi, and the Apology of Hattusili III. These narratives, which recognize the role of divine aid, nevertheless describe authentic elements of early second-millennium narrative with character development and plot definition. The biblical distinction is a theological one in which the themes and plots are transformed to glorify the God of Israel as one who preserves that nation and who elects those who are least likely to succeed in human eyes.

The similarity of Solomon's temple has already been noted. However, the texts that describe it (I Kings 6–9) also have parallels in terms of temple-construction accounts that occur elsewhere in a variety of contexts (Hurowitz 1992). The parallels demonstrate Solomon's achievement as one who builds a temple to his deity, but they are transformed as God directs the builder and refuses to accept the temple as a substitute for a fully committed heart. The Solomon account also includes an administrative list (1 Kings 4) that parallels other such lists in details of form, even to the point of making the last entry on the list different from the others (as with Judah in Solomon's list; Hess 1997a).

In some places, the narratives of Kings and Chronicles resemble annalistic accounts of rulers of other ancient Near-Eastern countries. In particular, the Mesha stele and the Tel Dan stele include accounts of wars with Israel and Judah that use similar language of warfare as well as attribution of victory to the deity. The biblical chronicles are distinct in their critical attitude toward the leaders of Israel and Judah, and in the way in which they judge those kings.

4 Poetry

The poetry of the Old Testament shares features with adjacent cultures. The discovery of the archives from the Late Bronze Age city of Ugarit in 1929 uncovered many mythological texts that contained stories about Baal, Asherah, El, and other Canaanite deities. These myths were written in poetry. A close examination of that poetry revealed many similarities with the Hebrew poetry of the Old Testament, especially the Psalms. The basic unit of poetry in both cultures was the two lines, where the second line in some way paralleled and reinforced the idea expressed in the first line. In addition to synonymous parallelism, one could find antithetic parallelism, ascending lines, threefold repetition, and chiastic structures (Watson 1984). Most important are the word pairs, a repertoire of vocabulary pairs from which the poet can draw to creatively weave together a poem. These parallels included larger levels of expressions and groups of phrases. One of the best examples of this is Psalm 29 where there are many close parallels with Ugaritic poetry (Craigie 1971, 1983). The difference is that, while at Ugarit, Baal was the object of adoration using these expressions, in Israel it was Yahweh who received the praise. Thus the earlier Ugaritic myth poetry uses the same expressions (applied to Baal) as are found in later biblical poetry, where they are applied to God. Again, there is evidence of taking on cultural forms and transforming them. Here the transformation involves the elimination of the epic myth context of much of Ugaritic poetry, with its lengthy poetic narratives. The Bible replaces this with shorter psalms of lament and praise to Israel's God.

Insofar as the Psalms are addresses by the psalmist to a sovereign God, they may be compared to much of the fourteenth-century BC Amarna correspondence written by vassal rulers of cities throughout Canaan to their sovereign pharaoh in Egypt. These letters, though not poetic in form, contain rhetorical devices of the same sort as can be found in the poetry: synonymous and antithetic parallelisms, threefold repetitions, and chiasms (Hess 1989). In addition, phrases such as 'the strong arm' of pharaoh, and pharaoh having 'set his name' over the city of Jerusalem occur in the correspondence from the leader of Jerusalem. They are identical to similar expressions used of God in the Psalms and elsewhere. This coincidence argues for the presence of a continuing Canaanite scribal tradition in Jerusalem from before the Israelite presence until well after its appearance. The transformation is the use of these rhetorical forms and expressions in praise of God.

The book of Lamentations records mourning for the fallen city of Jerusalem. It stands within a tradition of lamentations for defeated or destroyed places (Dobbs-Allsopp 1993). One of the earliest of these is the Lamentation over the Destruction of Ur, dating from soon after the city's fall c. 2000 BC. The Song of Songs preserves texts that have been compared to Egyptian love poems in form and content (Murphy 1990).

5 Wisdom literature

Wisdom literature is attested throughout the ancient Near East. Many of the biblical Proverbs have parallels. Indeed, there is a precise and repeated set of parallels between Proverbs 22:17–24:22 and the Egyptian Instruction of Amen-em-opet (Shupak 1993). This gives evidence of the universal character of wisdom literature as found throughout the ancient Near East. The occurrence of proverbial literature is attested in Mesopotamia and in Canaan itself. The Amarna correspondence from Shechem contains a proverb about ants, who also figure in the biblical book of Proverbs (Hess 1993b). The biblical wisdom literature, which consistently shares in the international wisdom corpus of the ancient Near East, is perhaps the closest cultural form of any in the Old Testament. It also has undergone transformation, but more by adding introductory, concluding, and other editorial remarks. Thus Proverbs 1:7 affirms that the fear of Yahweh is the beginning of wisdom.

The book of Job is an example of the disputation type of wisdom literature in which the question of suffering is explored. In Mesopotamian and Egyptian texts, this debate sometimes takes the form of a monologue. At other times it is a dialogue. However, in no case do the parallels resolve the issue as it is done in the Bible, through the direct appearance and address of God to Job (Terrien 1978). The poetical text is unique in its language in the Hebrew Bible.

The results of this survey suggest that the predominant method by which Israel appropriated cultural forms of which they were aware and applied these forms to the special needs of their life and faith was transformation. In so doing, they dramatically transformed some while they maintained others with minimal change.

6 Prophetic literature

The writing Prophets represent a synthesis of poetry and history, describing and critiquing the events and faith of Israel and Judah. Nevertheless, the use of prophecy, even in a predictive sense, was not unknown in the ancient Near East. From the early second millennium BC until after the writings of many of the Israelite prophets, dozens of prophetic texts have been found, along with descriptions of prophets, in Semitic societies (Nissinen 2003). This activity was most often directed toward the king and especially regarding decisions of war. In this there are many parallels with the biblical prophets. However, the latter transform what is known of prophecy by indicting the whole people as well as the king for lapses of belief (Hosea) and of cultic practice (Malachi). They also address the moral and ethical ills of the society (Isaiah, Amos) and prepare the people as much for defeat as they do for victory (Jeremiah, Ezekiel).

References and further reading

Blenkinsopp, J. (1991) 'Temple and Society in Achaemenid Judah,' pp. 22–53 in *Second Temple Studies: 1. Persian Period*, JSOTSup 117, P.R. Davies (ed.), Sheffield: Sheffield Academic Press.

Craigie, Peter C. (1971) 'The Poetry of Ugarit and Israel,' *Tyndale Bulletin* 22: 3–31.

—— (1983) *Ugarit and the Old Testament*, Grand Rapids: Eerdmans.

Dobbs-Allsopp, F.W. (1993) *O Daughter of Zion: A Study of the City-Lament Genre in the Hebrew Bible*, Biblica et Orientalia 44, Rome: Pontifical Biblical Institute.

Fleming, Daniel E. (1998) 'The Biblical Tradition of Anointing Priests,' *Journal of Biblical Literature* 117: 401–14.

Hess, Richard S. (1980) 'The Structure of the Covenant Code: Exodus 20:22–23:33,' Unpublished Master of Theology thesis, Trinity Evangelical Divinity School.

—— (1989) 'Hebrew Psalms and Amarna Correspondence from Jerusalem: Some Comparisons and Implications,' *Zeitschrift für die alttestamentliche Wissenschaft* 101: 249–65.

—— (1993a) 'Early Israel in Canaan: A Survey of Recent Evidence and Interpretations,' *Palestine Exploration Quarterly* 126: 125–42.

—— (1993b) 'Smitten Ant Bites Back: Rhetorical Forms in the Amarna Correspondence from Shechem,' pp. 95–111 in *Verse in Ancient Near Eastern Prose*, AOAT 42, J.C. de Moor and W.G.E. Watson (eds.), Kevelaer: Butzon & Bercker; Neukirchen-Vluyn: Neukirchener.

—— (1994a) 'Asking Historical Questions of Joshua 13–19: Recent Discussion Concerning the Date of the Boundary Lists,' pp. 191–205 in *Faith, Tradition, History: Old Testament Historiography in Its Near Eastern Context*, A.R. Millard, J.K. Hoffmeier, and D.W. Baker (eds.), Winona Lake: Eisenbrauns.

—— (1994b) 'The Geneaologies of Genesis 1–11 and Comparative Literature,' pp. 58–72 in *'I Studied Inscriptions from before the Flood': Ancient Near Eastern, Literary, and Linguistic Approaches to Genesis 1–11*, Sources for Biblical and Theological Study 4, R.S. Hess and D.T. Tsumura (eds.), Winona Lake: Eisenbrauns. (Reprint of 'The Genealogies of Genesis 1–11 and Comparative Literature,' *Biblica* 70 [1989]: 241–54.)

—— (1994c) 'Late Bronze Age and Biblical Boundary Descriptions of the West Semitic World,' pp. 123–38 in *Ugarit and the Bible: Proceedings of the International Symposium on Ugarit and the Bible. Manchester, September 1992*, UBL Band 11, G. Brooke, A. Curtis, and J. Healey (eds.), Münster: Ugarit-Verlag.

—— (1996) 'A Typology of West Semitic Place Name Lists with Special Reference to Joshua 13–21,' *Biblical Archaeology* 59/3: 160–70.

—— (1997a) 'The Form and Structure of the Solomonic District List in 1 Kings 4: 7–19,' pp. 279–92 in *Crossing Boundaries and Linking Horizons: Studies in Honor of Michael C. Astour*, G.D. Young, M.W. Chavalas, and R.E. Averbeck (eds.), Bethesda: CDL.

—— (1997b) 'West Semitic Texts and the Book of Joshua,' *Bulletin for Biblical Research* 7: 63–76.

—— (2001) 'The Old Testament as a Model for Cultural Transformation: Perspectives from Archaeology', *Near East Archaeological Society Bulletin* 46: 1–7.

Hess, Richard S. and David T. Tsumura (eds.) (1994) *'I Studied Inscriptions from before the Flood': Ancient Near Eastern, Linguistic and Literary Approaches to Genesis 1–11*, Sources for Biblical and Theological Study 4, Winona Lake: Eisenbrauns.

Hurowitz, Victor (1992) *I Have Built You an Exalted House: Temple Building in the Bible in Light of Mesopotamian and Northwest Semitic Writings*, JSOTSup 115, JSOT/ASOR Monograph 5, Sheffield: Sheffield Academic Press.

Kitchen, Kenneth A. (1979) 'Egypt, Ugarit, Qatna, and Covenant,' *Ugarit Forschungen* 11: 453–64.

—— (1989) 'The Rise and Fall of Covenant, Law and Treaty,' *Tyndale Bulletin* 40: 118–35.

—— (1994a) 'Genesis 12–50 in the Near Eastern World,' pp. 67–92 in *He Swore an Oath: Biblical Themes from Genesis 12–50*, R.S. Hess, G.J. Wenham, and P.E. Satterthwaite (eds.), Grand Rapids: Baker/Carlisle: Paternoster, 2nd edn.

—— (1994b) 'The Tabernacle – A Bronze Age Artefact,' *EI* 24: 119–129.

Monson, John (1999) 'The Temple of Solomon: Heart of Jerusalem,' pp. 1–22 in *Zion, City of Our God*, R.S. Hess and G.J. Wenham (eds.), Grand Rapids: Eerdmans.

—— (2000) 'The New 'Ain Dara Temple: Closet Solomonic Parallel,' *BAR* 26/3: 20–35, 67.

Murphy, Roland E. (1990) *The Song of Songs: A Commentary on the Book of Canticles or The Song of Songs*, Hermeneia, Minneapolis: Fortress Press.

Rainey, Anson F. (1996) *Canaanite in the Amarna Tablets: A Linguistic Analysis of the Mixed Dialect Used by the Scribes from Canaan. Volume I, Orthography, Phonology, Morphosyntactic Analysis of the Pronouns, Nouns, Numerals. Volume II, Morphosyntactic Analysis of the Verbal System. Volume III, Morphosyntactic Analysis of the Particles and Adverbs. Volume IV, References and Index of Texts Cited*, Handbook of Oriental Studies: The Near and Middle East, Leiden: Brill.

Shupak, Nili (1993) *Where Can Wisdom Be Found? The Sage's Language in the Bible and in Ancient Egyptian*

Literature, OBO 130, Fribourg: University Press Göttingen: Vandenhoeck & Ruprecht.

Terrien, Samuel (1978) *The Elusive Presence: Toward a New Biblical Theology*, San Francisco: Harper & Row.

Watson, Wilfred G.E. (1984) *Classical Hebrew Poetry: A Guide to Its Techniques*, JSOTSup 26, Sheffield: Sheffield Academic Press.

Weeks, Stuart (1994) *Early Israelite Wisdom*, Oxford Theological Monographs, Oxford: Clarendon.

Weinfeld, Moshe (1988) 'The Pattern of the Israelite Settlement in Canaan,' pp. 270–283 in *Congress Volume: Jerusalem 1986*, VTS 40, J.A. Emerton (ed.), Leiden: Brill.

Westermann, Claus (1994) *Lamentations. Issues and Interpretation*, trans. C. Muenchow, Minneapolis: Fortress Press.

Younger, Jr., K.L. (1990) *Ancient Conquest Accounts: A Study in Ancient Near Eastern and Biblical History Writing*, JSOTSup 98, Sheffield: Sheffield Academic Press.

RICHARD S. HESS

CULTURAL RELATIONSHIPS IN THE WORLD OF THE NEW TESTAMENT

1 Kinship and the 'household'
2 Friendship and patronage
3 Relationships beyond the extended household

Relationships in the New Testament world were conceptualized largely in terms of the 'household.' This concept was sufficiently broad to encompass natural kin and slaves who constituted the household in its most basic sense, but also to encompass the relationship between the head or other members of a household and client-dependents. In its broadest form, the empire could be conceptualized in terms of the extended household of the emperor, the 'Father of the Fatherland' (*Pater Patriae*), whose own slaves and clients were to be found administering the empire at all levels. The starting point for an individual's identity was the household and family to which he or she belonged. A person was not taken on his or her own merits so much as the collective merits of the family, so that a person's 'household' in its current and historical dimensions was an important factor in most relationships.

1 Kinship and the 'household'

The basic household consisted of a husband and wife, their children, and slaves (Aristotle, *Pol.* 1.3 [1253b2–7]; cf. 1 Esd. 5:1). The male was the central hub of the household, as classical discussions of household roles (father and children, husband and wife, master and slaves) all take the *paterfamilias*, the male head of the family, as the fixed point of reference. The household was often a unit of production as well as consumption. That is, a household would be involved in some kind of business enterprise together; the elites left the management of agricultural estates to slaves, while the more typical household engaged in all aspects of production and marketing together. Homes were constructed with a view not only (or even primarily) to providing private living spaces for the household, but also to providing spaces for networking with associates and selling the household's produce.

Marriage was undertaken mainly with a view to procreation and the preservation of lines of inheritance. A mark of honor within marriage was not to use it as a license for unbridled lust, even to the extent that Plutarch would advise a wife to consider it a token of respect for her if her husband turned elsewhere to satisfy his baser desires ('Advice on Marriage' 16). It was often arranged by the parents of both parties, or between adult males and the parents of younger brides. Jews tended to follow a strategy of endogamy, marrying within the Jewish *ethnos* and even within one's tribe or extended family. Greeks and Romans tended to pursue exogamic strategies, using marriage as a means of forming a strategic alliance that would strengthen or further stabilize a family's status. Divorce could be initiated by either partner in Greek and Roman culture, by the husband only in Jewish culture.

Women remained largely under the authority of some male throughout their lives – the father until marriage, the husband after marriage (although in some Roman marriages, a father could choose to retain authority over a married daughter). Ancient ethicists urge that this authority be used for the beneficent direction of the female rather than for her harm (Aristotle, *Pol.* 1.13 [1260a17–18]; Seneca, *Ben.* 2.18.1–2; Callicratidas, *On the Happiness of Households* 106.1–5, quoted in Balch 1981: 56–7), but even the most enlightened discussion is still based on the premise that the male is, by nature, fitted to rule while the female is fitted to be ruled (Aristotle, *Pol.* 1.2 [1252a25–32]. The ideal wife was to submit to her husband's authority, to keep herself from the sight, hearing, and touch of any man other than her husband as much as possible, with the result that a woman is urged to remain within the private spaces of the household (Xenophon, *Oec.* 7.16–41; 10.2–13; Sir. 26:14–16; *4 Macc.* 18:6–9; Philo, *Hypothetica* 7.3; *Spec. Leg.* 3.169–171; Plutarch, 'Advice on Marriage' 9, 11, 31–32). A woman, nevertheless, still had considerable authority within the household over which her husband was the head (Xenophon, *Oec.* 3.10–15; 9.14–15).

Parents, particularly the father, had considerable authority over the lives of their children. Considered to owe their parents for the gift of life itself, not to mention upbringing and nurture during their weak and vulnerable childhood, children were indebted to their parents until death (Plutarch, 'On Affection for Offspring' 2–4 [*Mor.* 495 A–C]). Strong cultural sanctions promoted care for one's parents in their old age and in any need. Rather than seeking to 'find their own identity' apart from their parents, children were seen as reflections of their parents – 'like parent, like child' (*4 Macc.* 15.4; Sir. 41:14). Education began in the home (for women, it tended to remain in the home); slaves called 'pedagogues' would usher the children of more elite families back and forth from their lessons and ensure that they kept up with homework. For most, education meant learning the skills necessary to continue the business of the household.

Slaves made up about one-quarter of the population of the Roman Empire. They were indeed regarded and treated as property, as 'living tools' (Aristotle, *Pol.* 1.4 [1253b27–33]). A slave's quality of life was completely dependent upon the virtue or baseness of the master, and ethicists made a great deal of promoting the kind treatment of slaves as extensions of oneself, and of nurturing a relationship of reciprocity to mitigate the power imbalance (Philo, *Decal.* 167; Ecclus, *On Justice* 78.10–11, cited in Balch 1981: 53, 58). Slaves could not enter into legal marriages, and families could be broken up at the whim of the householder. Slaves were to be found performing a great variety of tasks, from the torturous mines and galleys to agricultural estates to domestic environments to high-level administration within the empire.

Hospitality was a sacred obligation, and guests became a part of the household at least for the time of their stay. The cultural commitment to hospitality was especially important for the development of the early church, which depended on the willingness of householders to open their homes for the meetings of the Christian assembly (Acts 5:42; 12:12; 20:20; Rom. 16:3–5, 23; 1 Cor. 16:19; Col. 4:15) and for the support of itinerant missionaries and messengers/envoys (Matt. 10:11–13; Acts 16:15, 40; 21:8, 16; 2 Tim. 1:16; Philem 22; 3 John 5–8). That hospitality could become burdensome is reflected in the attention authors need to give to shoring up commitment to keeping the household fluid with regard to the constant influx of guests (Heb. 13:2; 1 Pet. 4:9).

Classical and first-century ethicists had developed a well-articulated ethos to guide relationships between kin, especially under the heading of 'sibling affection' (*philadelphia*; see Plutarch, 'On Fraternal Affection'; Aristotle, *Eth. Nic.* 8.12). Foremost in these discussions is the value of harmony and agreement between kin, reflecting their common nurture in the same values and by the same parents. This harmony should be enacted through cooperation wherever possible, since the success of one member of a family was a success for the whole family. The image of the fingers of a single hand or other parts of a single body working together was often employed as a model for kin. While competition was appropriate with people outside of the household, it was regarded as destructive within the family. The sharing of material and intangible resources (such as using one's influence to help kin) was another important manifestation of harmony and unity. Trust would be appropriately bestowed upon kin (making betrayal of trust far more heinous), and forgiveness and forbearance were to replace agonistic responses to challenges. The adoption of the language of kinship within the Christian movement, and the formation of a fictive kinship group that extended (or sometimes replaced) one's natural household, resulted naturally in the promotion of this kinship ethic throughout the early church.

2 Friendship and patronage

Perhaps the most important sets of relationships in this world, beyond relationships within the traditional family, involved the relationships of patrons and clients or, as they were known between social equals, friendship relations. Seneca called the formation of such relationships the 'practice that constitutes the chief bond of human society' (*Ben.* 1.4.2). This would be true not only in Roman society, but Greek, Jewish, and other provincial societies as well (though the image of clients gathering outside a patron's house for the morning *salutatio* is a peculiarly Roman ritual attached to patronage). Access to goods, to opportunities, and to many other forms of assistance came not through impersonal channels, but through extremely personal channels. Frequently, this assistance took the form of introducing the client's request to one of the patron's own patrons or friends, the latter being the ones in a position to fulfil the client's fundamental request. The favors that a patron or friend could provide were often necessary for achieving one's personal objectives and securing one's family's well-being.

The value of reciprocity provided the social glue for these relationships (Seneca's *De beneficiis* is the classic textbook on the dynamics of these relationships). A patron might freely grant a petitioner his or her request, supplying whatever particular assistance was being sought. The recipient of this assistance, however, walked away not only with the sought-for aid; he or she also incurred an obligation to show gratitude toward this patron in some very real and public ways. The gift might never be 'repaid' in kind, but it would be returned in the form of respect, public testimony, loyalty, and timely services. In giving a first time, a patron also accepted the obligation to continue to be available to help the client; the latter found a place, conceptually speaking, in the 'household' of the former. A long-term relationship would thus potentially be formed. Relationships between friends tended to proceed on a more equal basis, with exchange and mutual commitment to help one another still guiding the relationship.

Matters were rather different in the case of acts of public, general benefaction (e.g., building a portico, giving public entertainments or distributions of food), which did not initiate long-term relationships. For such gifts, the praise and applause of the masses – and often a public announcement with a commemorative inscription or, in exceptional cases, a statue – was all that was expected. Of course, when the benefaction is sufficiently great (e.g., famine relief for an entire city, or the remission of taxes for a year), the ongoing loyalty of the citizenry toward the benefactor (in such cases, normally the emperor) would be appropriate (see Dio Chrysostom, *Oration* 31).

Discussions of 'grace' should be heard primarily in terms of these relationships, the terms *charis* and *gratia* being used to name not only the patron's disposition to help, but also the gift conferred and the response of thanks and gratitude on the part of the recipient. Showing ingratitude toward one's patrons or benefactors was deemed a heinous crime on par with sacrilege. The social sanctions against ingratitude attest to the importance of generosity – the willingness of the rich to be generous toward both private individuals and the public – for the continued well-being of the state.

Reciprocal relations would be found at all levels of ancient society. Small landholders had just as much need and opportunity for mutual assistance (see Hesiod, *Works and Days* 342–51, 401–4) as the 'political players' in local and imperial politics. Priests were revered as those who mediated the patronage of the divine, securing the favor of the foundational patrons for Graeco-Roman and Jewish society. At the high political level, of course, ties of clientage bound client kings and senatorial proconsuls to the emperor.

3 Relationships beyond the extended household

In day-to-day life, people encountered many who would not be considered part of their household nor related by a 'grace' relationship. Nevertheless, it was often strategic to cooperate with these 'others' for their mutual advantage and security. People might form formal contractual relationships (e.g., between landowners and tenant farmers, the social inequality also demanding respect and loyalty on the part of the latter) or informal agreements and alliances with business associates. As long as the relationship remained mutually advantageous, it would continue. On the opposite side, people also found themselves in competition with each other for the acquisition of desired goods or objectives (whether material or intangible). It is within such relationships that one finds parties challenging one another's honor in an attempt to gain precedence over them, attempting to preserve their honor and standing in the community against all such assaults, and engaging in the social conventions of enmity (Malina 1993; Marshall 1987). Competition and agonistic relationships were

counterbalanced, however, by the cultural values of harmony and unity as political ideals at the civic level as well as the domestic level (Dio Chrysostom, *Oration* 48). This provided a kind of 'check' to any impulses toward unbridled factionalism and competition, thus preserving the fabric of society.

References and further reading

Adkins, Arthur W. (1960) *Merit and Responsibility: A Study in Greek Values*, Oxford: Clarendon.

Balch, David L. (1981) *Let Wives Be Submissive: The Domestic Code in 1 Peter*, SBLMS 26, Missoula, MT: Scholars Press.

Danker, Frederick W. (1982) *Benefactor: Epigraphic Study of a Graeco-Roman and New Testament Semantic Field*, St Louis: Clayton Publishing House.

deSilva, D.A. (1995) *Despising Shame: The Social Function of the Rhetoric of Honor and Dishonor in the Epistle to The Hebrews*, SBLDS 152, Atlanta: Scholars Press.

—— (1998) *4 Maccabees*, Guides to the Apocrypha and Pseudepigrapha, Sheffield: Sheffield Academic Press.

—— (1999) *The Hope of Glory: Honor Discourse and the New Testament*, Collegeville: Liturgical Press.

—— (2000) *Honor, Patronage, Kinship and Purity: Unlocking New Testament Culture*, Downers Grove, IL: IVP.

Finley, Moses (1973) *The Ancient Economy*, Berkeley: University of California Press.

Klanck, H.-J. (1990) 'Brotherly Love in Plutarch and in 4 Maccabees,' pp. 144–56 in *Greeks, Romans, Christians*, D.L. Balch, E. Ferguson, and W.A. Meeks (eds.), Minneapolis: Fortress Press.

Malina, Bruce J. (1993) *The New Testament World: Insights from Cultural Anthropology*, Louisville: Westminster, John Knox Press. rev. edn.

Marshall, Peter (1987) *Enmity in Corinth*, WUNT 2.23, Tübingen: Mohr Siebeck.

Moxnes, Halvor (1997) *Constructing Early Christian Families: Family as Social Reality and Metaphor*, London: Routledge.

Neyrey, Jerome H. (ed.) (1991) *The Social World of Luke-Acts: Models for Interpretation*, Peabody, MA: Hendrickson.

Osiek, Carolyn, and David L. Balch (1997) *Families in the New Testament World: Households and House Churches*. Louisville: Westminster John Knox Press.

Saller, Richard P. (1982) *Personal Patronage Under the Early Empire*, Cambridge: Cambridge University Press.

Stambaugh, John E., and David L. Balch (1987) *The New Testament in Its Social Environment*, Philadelphia: Westminster Press.

Wallace-Hadrill, Andrew (1989) *Patronage in Ancient Society*, London: Routledge.

Williams, Bernard (1993) *Shame and Necessity*, Berkeley: University of California Press.

DAVID A. DESILVA

D

DEAD SEA SCROLLS

The first discoveries of Dead Sea Scrolls in 1947 included two copies of the book of Isaiah (1QIsaᵃ and 1QIsaᵇ). It was immediately apparent that the transmission of the text of the biblical books in the late-Second Temple period was a far more complex affair than had been previously recognized. This short article will attempt to draw out some key challenges which have arisen from the so-called biblical manuscripts found in the Qumran caves.

1 Terminological problems

It is increasingly acknowledged that the terms 'Bible' and 'biblical' are entirely anachronistic for the pre-AD 70 period. These labels imply something far more fixed and stable, like a canon, than was the case. 'Authoritative scripture' is more suitable terminology, implying a composition which was considered both sacred and a reference point for belief and practice, but which was not necessarily part of a fixed list in a fixed form (Ulrich 1999: 51–78). It is also difficult to know exactly which manuscripts might be classified as 'authoritative scripture'; some which have been so classified, such as 4QDeutʲ, have been reclassified as excerpted texts, probably for liturgical use, whilst others which were initially considered as 'nonbiblical,' such as the Reworked Pentateuch (4Q158, 4Q364–67), may have been deemed authoritative by their copyists since they are akin to the Samaritan Pentateuch in many ways. All the books later contained in the Jewish canon are known at Qumran, even Esther whose distinctive terminology is visible in some sectarian compositions, although no copy of the work was found in the Qumran caves; in addition, several compositions found at Qumran, such as Jubilees and the Temple Scroll, claim authoritative

status for themselves. Use of the label 'authoritative scripture' allows for the flexibility which the evidence requires.

The term 'Bible' also suggests an object which has no context of its own. The manuscripts from Qumran show that most, if not all, manuscript copies of authoritative scriptures were copied for a purpose, to be used in prayer and worship or in school settings at all levels, or for other uses; they were not produced just for their own sakes.

2 The plurality of the evidence

The manuscripts found at Qumran show us that in the case of many scriptural books there is a remarkable degree of similarity between the evidence from the late-Second Temple period and that of the medieval period upon which Jewish and most Western Christian Bibles are based. However, it must also be stated clearly that, apart from the possibly coincidental evidence of a very few small fragments, none of the manuscripts from Qumran which might be designated anachronistically as biblical agrees in every detail with a previously known medieval witness. In the more than 200 scriptural manuscripts from Qumran there are several thousand variant readings.

Furthermore, the textual diversity within the evidence cannot be explained through standard text-critical procedures which attempt to explain all variations as the result of the scribal corruption of an original text over the centuries. It is clear that many of the manuscripts attest the deliberate alteration of authoritative scriptures in order to improve them for each successive generation. The evidence from Qumran also shows plainly that at the time no inspiration was attached to the letter of the text, though possibly works as a whole were considered as revelation or their authors as inspired.

3 Rethinking text criticism

The principal goal of the text criticism of the Hebrew Bible, the reconstruction of the original text, is undermined by the evidence of the manuscripts from Qumran containing scriptural texts. For many biblical books the variety of the evidence is such that it is simply no longer possible to conceive of what a supposed original may have contained. Scholars need to focus on the diversity in itself rather than try to explain it away and they need to move away from considering the rabbinic Masoretic Text as in some way textually normative for the prerabbinic period.

Traditionally text critics have explained textual variety through an appeal to the errors which can occur during the scribal transmission of texts. The language that text critics have used to describe such a process has usually been very heavily evaluative; the scriptural texts from Qumran have changed that so that text-critical terminology is rightly increasingly becoming more neutral and descriptive. No longer are particular readings necessarily judged as 'better' or 'worse.'

Text critics have usually grouped manuscripts that share certain features into families which are related to one another through family trees (stemmata). The diversity of the evidence from Qumran prohibits this for the Hebrew Bible, since most manuscripts contain a complex set of agreements and disagreements with other witnesses. For Qumran several alternative attempts have been made to describe the complicated diversity of the evidence in the scriptural manuscripts and how it came about. F.M. Cross has focused on a theory of local texts first suggested by W.F. Albright: the traditional text (Masoretic Text) emerged from Jews in Babylonia, the Hebrew behind the Greek translation was promulgated by and for Jews in Egypt and the Samaritan Pentateuch reflected a form of the texts known to Jews in Palestine (Cross and Talmon 1975: 193–5, 306–20) and each Qumran biblical manuscript can be aligned with one of these local texts. Talmon has argued that the diversity is best explained in terms of the concerns of the groups which passed them on (Cross and Talmon 1975: 321–400). Tov has suggested that while some manuscripts can be variously allocated to the emerging text traditions represented later by the Masoretic text, the Septuagint, and the Samaritan Pentateuch, there are two further classes of biblical manuscript, witnesses to independent traditions of transmission and those written in a fuller form of spelling which also predominates in the manuscripts containing the sectarian compositions found at Qumran (1998: 292–301). More recently, on the basis of noting that at least for Exodus, Samuel, Jeremiah, and the Psalms there are two or more literary editions in the late-Second Temple period, Ulrich has rightly insisted that the history of the transmission of each scriptural book should be considered by itself (1999: 99–120).

4 A fresh appreciation of the MT

From the Qumran evidence it emerges that the traditional Hebrew text (MT) actually contains some intriguing features. Sometimes the MT preserves a form of a scriptural book that is clearly less original than another which is now known: this is certainly the case for Jeremiah for which the scrolls now provide Hebrew exemplars of the earlier and shorter form known previously from the Septuagint. Sometimes the MT, apparently deliberately, preserves divergent forms: it is well known that Samuel-Kings presents a rather different form of many incidents which are also related in 1 and 2 Chronicles, but it is less well known that in the late-Second Temple period there was a form of Samuel in circulation in Palestine (as in 4QSamᵃ) in which the differences were far less accentuated. Sometimes the MT preserves a partisan text: 4QJoshᵃ contains a more logical account of the building of the altar (at Gilgal; at the start of Josh. 5) than does the MT, which locates it on Mt Ebal (Josh. 8:34–35) apparently in deliberate opposition to the one on Mt Gerizim. Sometimes the MT contains errors. This has been acknowledged in a few cases for centuries, but it is now increasingly apparent. For example, Psalm 145 is an acrostic, each verse beginning with a successive letter of the alphabet; the nun verse is missing in the MT, but there is a nun verse in a Qumran psalter (11QPsᵃ 17:2–4): it may be that a Qumran scribe has created the verse to fill an obvious gap, but it is more likely that the reading represents what originally stood in the Psalm. Modern translations have already begun to use the evidence from Qumran to provide improved biblical readings, despite the fact that no religious authority has given permission for this move away from the MT.

5 An emerging canon

The manuscripts from Qumran pose many questions for the understanding of an emerging canon of Hebrew scriptures. In the first place it is difficult to know if any particular manuscript copy of a scriptural book should be deemed authoritative. For example, 1QIsaᵃ is poorly copied with many errors, the majority of which are corrected with supralinear and marginal annotations: it is hard to determine whether this was produced as an authoritative representative of the text of Isaiah or with some other purpose in mind.

Second, it is clear that in many ways during the life of the movement of which the Qumran community was a part, the limits of the canon were not clearly defined. We can guess at what was taken as authoritative from a number of factors: the number of copies of the work, the fact that a work may be explicitly quoted in other compositions (VanderKam 1998: 391–6), the fact that it may be alluded to in other compositions, the fact that it may form the base text of a running commentary (Isaiah, Psalms, the Twelve), and the likelihood that it was included under one of the common designations for authoritative scriptures, such as what was commanded through 'Moses' and 'the prophets' (1QS 1:1–3).

Third, we can learn something from what seems to belong at the heart of the scriptural worldview of the members of the sect. Four books seem particularly significant to them: Genesis for the patriarchal authority it gave to some of their outlook, Deuteronomy for its explicit hard-line view of how the law should be obeyed by those living in the land, Isaiah for its ability to confirm the community as the elect, and the Psalms as spiritual support (Brooke 1997: 251–8). In addition to these texts and others which are now in Jewish and Christian Bibles, several other compositions were considered sacred and authoritative by the Qumran community but are not now part of the canonical tradition of Judaism or Christianity (except for *Enoch* and *Jubilees* in the Ethiopic Church): the *books of Enoch* (extant in at least fifteen manuscripts, and possibly appealed to as an authority in CD 2:17–21 and 4Q247), the *book of Jubilees* (extant in at least fifteen manuscripts, and appealed to as an authority in CD 16:3–4 and 4Q228), a *Testament of Levi* (appealed to in CD 4:15–17), the *Apocryphon of Joshua* (4Q378–379, cited on equal terms with Exodus, Numbers, and Deuteronomy in 4QTestimonia), and the *book of Hagu* (1QSa 1:7; CD 10:6; 13:2), as yet not firmly identified.

Overall, the Qumran evidence displays hints of an emerging collection of authoritative scriptures, but there is no fixed list of such works and the form of their text has not been determined.

References and further reading

Brooke, G.J. (1997) '"The Canon within the Canon" at Qumran and in the New Testament,' pp. 242–66 in *The Scrolls and the Scriptures: Qumran Fifty Years After*, JSPSup 26, Roehampton Institute London Papers 3, S.E. Porter and C.A. Evans (eds.), Sheffield: Sheffield Academic Press.

Cross, F.M. and S. Talmon (eds.) (1975) *Qumran and the History of the Biblical Text*, Cambridge, MA: Harvard University Press.

Tov, E. (1998) 'The Significance of the Texts from the Judean Desert for the History of the Text of the Hebrew Bible: A New Synthesis,' pp. 277–309 in *Qumran between the Old and New Testaments*, JSOTSup 290, Copenhagen International Seminar 6, F.H. Cryer and T.L. Thompson (eds.), Sheffield: Sheffield Academic Press.

Ulrich, E.C. (1999) *The Dead Sea Scrolls and the Origins of the Bible*, Grand Rapids: Eerdmans/Leiden: Brill.
—— (2000) 'Canon,' pp. 117–20 in *Encyclopedia of the Dead Sea Scrolls*, New York: Oxford University Press.

VanderKam, J.C. (1998) 'Authoritative Literature in the Dead Sea Scrolls,' *Dead Sea Discoveries* 5: 382–402

GEORGE J. BROOKE

DEISSMANN, GUSTAV ADOLF (1866–1937)

Deissmann was arguably the internationally most influential German professor of New Testament between the two World Wars, and prior to that a contributor of seminal importance to the contextualizing of the social world of early Christianity and to the understanding of the linguistic matrix of the LXX and New Testament.

The son of a Lutheran pastor, Deissmann was educated at a Gymnasium in Wiesbaden, university studies at Tübingen (1885–1887) and Berlin (1888), followed by his Habilitation at Marburg; Privatdozent 1892. Ordained in 1890, he rejected an approach in 1921 to become diocesan bishop of Nassau.

Three distinct facets of Deissmann's adult career and interests may be identified: postclassical Greek, the archaeological and social context of primitive Christianity, and international ecumenism. *Bibelstudien* and *Neue Bibelstudien* were trailblazers for their quarrying of inscriptions to illuminate features of the Greek of the LXX, and were an earnest of his plan to produce a lexicon of the New Testament, as emerges most clearly in some of his letters to J.H. Moulton (q.v.), his closest English friend (Horsley 1994). This dictionary was to be his *opus vitae*, and in conjunction with various other publications shows him to have been a philologist *manqué* rather than a typical New Testament professor focused on theology. Deissmann's collegial friendship with Ulrich Wilcken (1862–1944), arguably the preeminent papyrologist of his generation, stimulated his interest in the papyri and ostraca as they began to emerge in increasing numbers from the sand and ancient rubbish tips of Egypt. The marriage of this interest with his LXX concerns led directly to his publication of the first volume of the Heidelberg papyri, which included numerous LXX and early Christian texts. His friendship since schooldays with Theodor Wiegand (1864–1936), excavator of Miletos and Priene, and later Director of the Antiquities Section of the Prussian Museum in Berlin, was revised when Deissmann was able to join classical philologists on a study tour to various archaeological sites in 1906. This combination of interests in the *realia* of ancient places, their nonliterary texts, and in the forms of Greek in use at the turn of the era all came together in his remarkable *Licht vom Osten*, a book which was as influential as any on early Christianity to come out of Germany last century because of his gift to popularize his subject (Deissmann's regular visits to Britain ensured a ready readership in English as well for this book), while at the same time providing a substantial new perspective on the social level of the Christian groups. That perspective can now be seen to be distorted partly by his own situation in early twentieth-century Germany and his early links with the Nationalsozialer Verein (Horsley 1994: 200). On the other hand, his views of the nature of the Greek of the Bible were largely set aside by a renewed and exaggerated assertion of the Semitic background to the language of the New Testament. While the first Christians were not necessarily mostly lower-middle-class workers as Deissmann proposed, his appreciation of the language situation still deserves to be taken seriously. In the centuries-long debate between Purists and Hebraizers, Deissmann was certainly not the latter; but neither can he be neatly classified as the former (Horsley 1989: 38–40).

As a provincial, Deissmann felt out of place in Berlin initially, and in a letter to Moulton soon after he arrived there in 1909 he described it as a 'vampire' because he could not make progress on his lexicon (Horsley 1994: 206–10). However, the change of direction which the war effected on his life — his *Evangelischer Wochenbrief* was a conscious attempt to keep open channels of communication between Christians on both sides of the conflict — meant that Berlin as the intellectual and political center was the place for an international figure to be; and to that extent he embraced it as he became increasingly engaged in ecumenical work after the war (Markschies 2005). It was the latter turn in his career rather than the move to Berlin which put paid to his lexicon being completed. Instead W. Bauer's second (1928) and third (1937) editions of the New Testament lexicon, building substantially on E. Preuschen's first edition (7 fasc. 1908–10, which Deissmann reviewed antipathetically; complete one vol. edn. 1910), appeared in his lifetime and were recognized by Deissmann to be a considerable advance in New Testament lexicography.

Yet his ancient world interests were not abandoned entirely. Deissmann was the prime mover in raising funds for the renewal of excavations at Ephesus by the Austrian Archaeological Institute after the war; his close friendship with Joseph Keil (1878–1963) ensured the successful resumption of work there (of which Deissmann was himself an active participant) from 1926 (Gerber 2005).

Before the end of the 1930s Deissmann's academic influence was on the wane, with deprecatory allusions by others to 'Deissmannism' (Ros 1940: 34–44; Horsley 1989: 39, 82); yet some reassessment is warranted to recognize him as a pioneer in his area of research and in his influence on others (Horsley 1989: 37–40). A biography covering both his scholarly and ecumenical endeavors in progress.

References and further reading

Deissmann, G.A. (1895) *Bibelstudien*, Marburg: Elwert.
—— (1897) *Neue Bibelstudien*, Marburg: Elwert (ET of *BS* and *NB* in one vol., Edinburgh: T.&T. Clark, 1923).
—— (1905) *Die Septuaginta-Papyri und andere altchristliche Texte*, Veröffentlichungen aus der Heidelberger Papyrus-Sammlung, 1, Heidelberg: Winter.
—— (1908) *The Philology of the Greek Bible*, London: Hodder & Stoughton.
—— (1909) *Licht vom Osten*, Tübingen: Mohr, 4th edn. 1923 (repr. Milan: La Goliardica, 1976; ET of that edn, London: Hodder & Stoughton, 1927).
—— (1911) *Paulus. Eine kultur- and religionsgeschichtliche Skizze*, Tübingen: Mohr, 2nd edn. 1925 (Swedish edn. already pub. Stockholm: Olaus Petri Foundation, 1910; ET of 1st German edn. London: Hodder & Stoughton, 1912; ET of 2nd German edn. 1927).
—— (Dec. 1914–Dec. 1921) *Evangelischer Wochenbrief*, privately printed (ET: *Protestant Weekly Letter*, 1914–17).
—— (1927) *Die Stockholmer Bewegung. Die Weltkirchenkonferenzen zu Stockholm 1925 und Bern 1926 von innen betrachtet*, Berlin: Furche.
—— (1930) *Die Schicksale des Neuen Testaments. Rede zum Antritt des Rektorats der Friedrich-Wilhelms-Universität zu Berlin am 15. Oktober 1930*, Berlin: Preussische Druckerei- und Verlags-Aktiengesellschaft.
—— (1936) *Una Sancta. Zum Geleit in das ökumenische Jahr 1937*, Gütersloh: Bertelsmann.
—— and G.K.A. Bell (1930) *Mysterium Christi. Christological Studies*, London, Hodder & Stoughton (German trans. Berlin: Furche, 1931).
Gerber, A. (2005) 'Gustaf Adolf Deissmann (1866–1937): Trailblazer in Biblical Studies, in the Archaeology of Ephesus, and in International Reconciliation', *Buried History* 41: 29–42.
Harder, G. and G. Deissmann (1967) *Zum Gedenken an Adolf Deissmann, 7 November 1866 – 5 April 1937*, Bremen: privately printed (includes further bibliography by D.)
Horsley, G.H.R. (1989) *New Documents Illustrating Early Christianity, vol. 5: Linguistic Essays*, Sydney: Macquarie Univ. Ancient History Documentary Research Centre.
—— (1994) 'The Origins and Scope of Moulton and Milligan's *Vocabulary of the Greek Testament*, and Deissmann's planned New Testament lexicon. Some unpublished letters of G.A. Deissmann to J.H. Moulton,' *Bulletin of the John Rylands Library* 76(1): 187–216.
Markschies, C. (2005) 'Adolf Deissmann — ein heidelberger Pionier der Ökumene', *Zeitschrift für neuere Theologiegeschichte* 12: 47–88.
J. Ros (1940) *De Studie van het Bijbelgrieksch van Hugo Grotius tot Adolf Deissmann*, Nimwegen: Dekker & van de Vegt.

G.H.R. HORSLEY

DERRIDA, JACQUES (1930–2004)

French philosopher Jacques Derrida was one of the most influential and controversial of contemporary continental thinkers. Derrida was born in El-Biar, Algeria. In 1952 he began studying philosophy at the École Normale Supérieure, one of France's most prestigious schools, where he later taught from 1965 to 1984. From 1960 to 1964 he taught at the Sorbonne in Paris. He has also taught at American universities such as Johns Hopkins and Yale. Derrida finished his career as Professor of Philosophy and Directeur d'Études at the École des Hautes Études en Science Sociales in Paris, and Professor at the University of California, Irvine.

The movement that has come to be known as 'deconstruction' is associated with Derrida, and was dominant in American universities through the 1970s and early 1980s, and continues to find a wide audience throughout the world. It has been influential in shaping philosophy, literary theory, religious studies, art criticism, even legal studies, and architecture. Derrida introduced his deconstruction thought in 1967 with the coinciding publication of *Speech and Phenomena*, *Of Grammatology*, and *Writing and Difference*.

Derrida was influenced by prominent thinkers that include Nietzsche, Freud, Marx, Levinas, and particularly Heidegger with his *Destruktion* (de-structuring), and his analysis of the structure and history of traditional ontology. As the name implies, many assume deconstruction to be negative but Derrida characterized it as affirmative (not positive). Like Heidegger's analysis that is not an abrogation or destruction of ontology, Derrida's deconstruction is not an annihilation or demolition but a method or theory, more accurately an 'experience.'

Deconstruction has been particularly influential in philosophy and literary criticism as the theory, method, or general analysis that seeks to uncover hidden assumptions (not meanings) and contradictions that shape a text. However, because deconstruction has no simple definition or 'univocal signification' it is often misunderstood and misapplied. Deconstruction is not a set of postulations or beliefs but a way of reading texts, particularly philosophy texts. Even calling it a method or analysis says too much. It is, strictly speaking, not reducible to methodological instrumentality, sets of rules or techniques. It has often been stressed as a method of critique, but it is not. For Derrida, what he is doing is not even hermeneutics. Whatever defining concepts are used for deconstruction are, themselves, subject to deconstruction. Thus, it is best to think of it more as an event or experience rather than an operation or act.

As part of the poststructuralist movement, Derrida's deconstruction radically criticizes accepted notions of the referentiality of language and the objectivity of structures as the false assumptions of traditional Western metaphysics. Deconstruction is not merely postfoundational but antifoundational and critically undermines conventional notions of truth, reality, and knowledge. For Derrida, there is no transcendentally signified (e.g., transcultural, transhistorical) truth or grounding like the sort traditional metaphysics has conceived. There is only a 'play' that connects signs to other signs. Meaning is always contextual, deferred, provisional, and incomplete. Texts have no decidable meaning but are full of internal tensions and contradictions that make their truth claims, even an author's intended meaning, no more than the reflections of the free play of language – an infinite play of signs. However, while words do not refer to fixed truths or meanings but to other words, Derrida believed there can still be indeterminate meaning.

References and further reading

Caputo, John D. (ed.) (1997) *Deconstruction in a Nutshell: A Conversation with Jacques Derrida*, New York: Fordham University Press.

Cohen, Tom (ed.) (2002) *Jacques Derrida and the Humanities*, New York: Cambridge University Press.

Kamuf, Peggy (ed.) (1991) *A Derrida Reader*, New York: Columbia University Press.

Word, David (ed.) (1992) *Derrida: A Critical Reader*, Oxford: Blackwell.

J.C. ROBINSON

DILTHEY, WILHELM (1833–1911)

Born at Biebrich, Dilthey enrolled in 1852 to study theology at Heidelberg but after one year he left to study history and philosophy at Berlin. In 1864, Dilthey defended his doctoral dissertation on Schleiermacher's moral principles. He briefly taught at Berlin, was called to Basel in 1867, Kiel in 1868, and accepted a chair at Breslau in 1871. In 1882, he returned to Berlin as successor of Hermann Lotze to take up the chair that Hegel once occupied. In 1883, Dilthey published the first part of his major philosophical work, *Introduction to the Human Sciences* (*Einleitung in die Geisteswissenschaften*). Dilthey fully retired from teaching in 1907.

Dilthey's works and influence are substantial despite him being little known during his own time. He produced important studies in literary criticism, and made contributions to metaphysics, aesthetics, moral philosophy, epistemology, and more. As a unique historical thinker, Dilthey is best known for his epistemological analysis of the human studies, and as one of the first to make the distinction between the 'human sciences' (*Geisteswissenschaften*) and the 'natural sciences' (*Naturwissenschaften*) that is now standard terminology.

For Dilthey, the human sciences have a distinct subject matter that is empirical, objective, and scientifically valid like the natural sciences. However, unlike the natural sciences, the starting point for a methodology of the human studies is the historical world constituted and formed by the human mind. Dilthey approaches the problems of interpreting human phenomena with a methodology that seeks a deeper historical consciousness and appreciation of life itself. He rejects the reductionist, mechanistic, and ahistorical approaches of the natural sciences on the basis that imposing external categories of interpretation based on the methods of the natural sciences cannot do justice to the fullness of experience. Instead, Dilthey's foundational science for the human studies developed as a method for gaining concrete and historical knowledge of 'expressions of inner life' that makes conclusions as objectively valid as those of the natural sciences. To understand life, Dilthey proposed, one must understand it from categories intrinsic to the complexities of life experiences themselves.

Dilthey's historical paradigm is not merely a particular discovery of facts or an abstraction of sense perception structured in reference to causal laws, but a world of historically constituted experiences – the inner historicity of experiences. Historical science is possible because we are ourselves historical beings. As a strict empiricist, Dilthey's methodology focuses on particular historical individuals bound to particular contexts. While Dilthey treats humans as being more than just biological facts to be quantified this does not mean there is something behind life. There are no universal subjects that can be located in any sort of transcendentalism or metaphysical ultimate. There are only historical individuals in whom life unfolds – contingently and changeably. Consequently, understanding in the human sciences is more like interpreting a poem than doing physics.

Concepts of 'understanding' and 'expression' are particularly important to Dilthey's philosophy and his understanding of interpretation. 'Understanding' (*Das Verstehen*) is used by Dilthey in a specific way which is unlike the merely explanatory knowledge of the natural sciences. Understanding in this sense is a comprehensive awareness of mental content (idea, intention, feeling) that manifests in given expressions (texts, words, gestures, art, etc.). To understand a text, like understanding an expression, involves a circular working from a text to the author's biography, and particular historical context, and then back again – not as a vicious circle leading to tautologies but as a spiral toward wider understandings. Meaning is always contextual. Interpretation, as the application of understanding to a text, reconstructs the environment in which it was composed and places the text within it. Interpretation becomes more effective as one acquires more knowledge about the author. Thus temporal and cultural distance from an author make reliable interpretations more difficult, but not impossible.

References and further reading

Palmer, Richard E. (1969) *Hermeneutics: Interpretation Theory in Schleiermacher, Dilthey, Heidegger and Gadamer*, Evanston: Northwestern University Press.

Plantinga, Theodore (1980) *Historical Understanding in the Thought of Wilhelm Dilthey*, Toronto: University of Toronto Press.

Makkreel, Rudolf A. (1992) *Dilthey: Philosopher of the Human Studies*, New Jersey: Princeton.

J.C. ROBINSON

DODD, C.H. (1884–1973)

Charles Harold Dodd (1884–1973) was a distinguished British New Testament scholar. He was born and brought up in North Wales, in a Nonconformist background. After classical study at Oxford, he began teaching and research in classical studies, then studied for the Congregational ministry. After a short time in ministry he became lecturer and subsequently Professor of New Testament at Mansfield College, Oxford, teaching also New Testament and the Septuagint in the university. In 1930 he moved to Manchester University to the Rylands Chair of Biblical Criticism and Exegesis. Five years later he went to Cambridge, the first non-Anglican to occupy a divinity chair there, remaining until retirement in 1949, thereafter engaging in writing and involvement in the New English Bible translation.

Dodd contributed to a quest in continental and British scholarship for a theological approach to the New Testament. He was a leading figure in the rise of biblical theology. He stressed a unity in the New Testament, from the teaching and life of Jesus through oral tradition to the written documents, and helped promote confidence in its historical reliability and usefulness for Christian theology.

Dodd taught 'realized eschatology': Jesus preached that the Kingdom of God had come in his life and ministry. Dodd disagreed with Schweitzer who held that Jesus spoke of a future Kingdom. Dodd followed continental scholars Rudolf Otto and Gustaf Dalman. Dodd acknowledged that the Kingdom was not fully 'realized' during the lifetime of Jesus, particularly in his later writings, but it was for his interest in 'realized eschatology' that he was remembered. The argument is well stated in *The Parables of The Kingdom* (1935, and many reprints). The book drew on developments in New Testament scholarship, including form criticism. Dodd improved upon the work of a colleague at Mansfield College, the Congregationalist A.T. Cadoux, author of *The Parables of Jesus* (1931).

Another area of investigation associated with Dodd is the distinction between ethical teaching (*didache*) and the proclamation of the Gospel (*kerygma*). He extended the field of form criticism into the epistles, finding traces of a common stock of belief statements about Christ, the *kerygma*, behind which Old Testament ideas were evident.

Dodd wrote extensively on the Gospel of John, investigating the background of ideas in the Hellenistic world. He argued against the influence of a myth of a heavenly man. Rather, the Fourth Gospel reflected authentic Jesus material. Dodd came to believe that it was independent of the Synoptic tradition, taking a lead from a colleague in Jesus College, Cambridge, P. Gardner-Smith, where Dodd held a fellowship.

Another area of interest was the atonement. Partly on linguistic grounds, he held that propitiation was not part of New Testament theology, and cast doubt on the idea of wrath as a divine attribute, stressing, in line with some other British theologians, the idea of a divine moral order, and Christ as representative, rather than as substitute.

Dodd abandoned many older dogmatic presuppositions, including biblical inerrancy, redefining the basis for theological truth. Some of his thought is characterized by the liberalism and idealism of British theology of the first quarter of the twentieth century, notably his *The Meaning of Paul for Today* (1920). However, from the 1930s Dodd emphasized the objective, historical saving events of the life, death, and resurrection of Christ, and as such belongs within the development of biblical theology. He followed Bultmann in stressing that God calls people to decision through the crisis brought about through the presence of Christ in history.

While most of Dodd's conclusions have been shown to require restatement, his accomplished scholarship and knowledge of the linguistic and religious background to the New Testament ensure an abiding legacy and influence.

References and further reading

Barnes, O.G. (1992) 'The Edifice of Exegesis. The Structure of C.H. Dodd's Biblical Theology,' Ph.D., University of Edinburgh.
Bruce, F.F. (1966) 'C.H. Dodd,' in *Creative Minds in Contemporary Theology*, P.E. Hughes (ed.), Grand Rapids: Eerdmans.
Caird, G.B. (1974) 'C.H. Dodd,' *Proceedings of the British Academy* 60: 497–510.
Dillistone, F.W. (1977) *C.H. Dodd Interpreter of the New Testament*, London: Hodder & Stoughton.
Dodd, C.H. (1920) *The Meaning of Paul for Today*, London: Swarthmore (reprinted, London: Fontana, 1958).
—— (1928) *The Authority of the Bible*, London: Nisbet (revised 1938 and many reprints).
—— (1932) *The Epistle of Paul to the Romans*, London: Hodder & Stoughton.
—— (1935a) *The Parables of the Kingdom*, London: Nisbet.

—— (1935b) *The Bible and the Greeks*, London: Hodder & Stoughton.
—— (1936) *The Apostolic Preaching and Its Developments*, London: Hodder & Stoughton.
—— (1946) *The Bible To-day*, Cambridge: Cambridge University Press.
—— (1952) *According to the Scriptures: The Sub-Structure of New Testament Theology*, London: Nisbet.
—— (1953) *The Interpretation of the Fourth Gospel*, Cambridge: Cambridge University Press.
—— (1963) *Historical Tradition in the Fourth Gospel*, Cambridge: Cambridge University Press.
—— (1971) *The Founder of Christianity*, London: Collins.

MALCOLM A. KINNEAR

DUNN, JAMES DOUGLAS GRANT (1939–)

New Testament lecturer at Nottingham (1970), and Lightfoot Professor of Divinity, Durham, UK (1982), Dunn was a leading figure in New Testament studies in the final quarter of the twentieth century and beyond, publishing a number of key works, promoting and advancing British New Testament scholarship, and taking an active role in international New Testament scholarship.

Early works include: *Baptism in the Holy Spirit* (1970); *Jesus and the Spirit* (1975); and *Christology in the Making* (1980; second edition 1989). These variously interconnected works betray a career-spanning interest in New Testament Christology and pneumatology (and the eschatological participation/anticipation dialectic that cuts across both), with a distinctive 'minimalistic' approach to 'preexistence' and baptism, culminating in two volumes of collected essays, *The Christ and the Spirit* (1998). A synthetic study in New Testament history/theology, *Unity and Diversity in the New Testament* (1977; second edition 1990), unites the diverse expressions of earliest Christianity in the identification of the historical Jesus with the exalted Christ, revealing an ecumenical aspect to Dunn's work.

Paul, conspicuously present in these early works, becomes the major focus of Dunn's later work, particularly with regard to the law and Judaism. To the extent that these issues enter the earlier work, Jesus and Paul are conventionally set over against a 'legalistic' Judaism (Dunn 1977: 61–70; cf. 1990: xvii, 61–70). But with the catalyst of the work of E.P. Sanders (and its further application to Paul in the early work of N.T. Wright), Dunn began to articulate a 'new perspective on Paul' over the course of a number of works: *Jesus, Paul, and the Law* (1990), which includes the 1982 Manson Memorial Lecture 'The New Perspective on Paul'; *Romans* (1988); *The Epistle to the Galatians* (1993a); *The Theology of Paul's Letter to the Galatians* (1993b); and *The Theology of Paul the Apostle* (1998b). This 'new perspective' argues for an essential continuity between Paul and the law/Judaism, limiting Paul's critique to a Jewish ethnocentric misuse or perversion of the law (encapsulated in the phrase 'works of law') and the covenant (restricted along ethnic lines). A second synthesis of New Testament history/theology, *The Partings of the Ways between Christianity and Judaism* (1991), reveals an interest in Jewish/Christian dialogue.

Dunn's earlier work gave pioneering attention to the religious experience and unity-within-diversity of early Christianity. His later work on Paul is a monumentally sustained research programme, its innovative social orientation of the issues forming one of the major options on 'Paul and the law' at the close of the twentieth century. Questions faced at the turn of the century concern the cogency of the central thesis regarding the Jewish 'misunderstanding' of the law/Israel putatively criticized by Paul, and of the biblical-theological continuity achieved with this thesis. Dunn's latest work is an attempt at synthesis of the various strands of early Christian thought, beginning with Jesus (2003). The first volume of a projected three-volume work, *Jesus Remembered*, champions the importance of the oral performance of the Jesus tradition in discerning the impact made by Jesus on his first disciples.

References and further reading

Dunn, James Douglas Grant (1970) *Baptism in the Holy Spirit*, London: SCM Press.
—— (1975) *Jesus and the Spirit*, London: SCM Press.
—— (1977) *Unity and Diversity in the New Testament*, London: SCM Press (2nd ed. 1990).
—— (1980) *Christology in the Making*, London: SCM Press (2nd edn. 1989).
—— (1988) *Romans*, 2 Vols., Dallas: Word.
—— (1990) *Jesus, Paul, and the Law*, London: SPCK.
—— (1991) *The Parting of the Ways between Christianity and Judaism*, London: SCM Press/Philadelphia: Trinity Press International.
—— (1993a) *The Epistle to the Galatians*, London: A.&C. Black.
—— (1993b) *The Theology of Paul's Letter to the Galatians*, Cambridge: Cambridge University Press.
—— (1998a) *The Christ and the Spirit*, Edinburgh: T.&T. Clark.
—— (1998b) *The Theology of Paul the Apostle*, Grand Rapids: Eerdmans.
—— (2003) *Jesus Remembered*, Christianity in the Making I, Grand Rapids: Eerdmans.
Matlock, R.B. (1998) 'Sins of the Flesh and Suspicious Minds: Dunn's New Theology of Paul,' *Journal for the Study of the New Testament* 72: 67–90 (followed by a response from Dunn).

R. BARRY MATLOCK

EARLY CHURCH INTERPRETATION

1 Introduction

The study of the interpretation of the Bible in the New Testament is a vitally important one. Historically, differences between Judaism and Christianity can, in large measure, be traced back to and understood in light of their differing exegetical presuppositions and practices. And personally, it is of great importance to appreciate something of how the Bible was interpreted during the apostolic period of the church, and to ask regarding the significance of these interpretations and understandings for one's own convictions, exegesis, and life today.

The study is complicated by a paucity of primary materials in certain areas of importance and frustrated by uncertainties as to the exact nature of the biblical text in its various recensions during the early Christian centuries. It is also, sadly, often bedeviled by (a) the imposition of modern categories and expectations on the ancient texts, (b) desires to work out a monolithic understanding of early Christian interpretation, such as would minimize or discount variations in our sources, and (c) attempts to develop a strictly inner-biblical type of exegesis, such as would ignore or discredit comparisons with the exegetical conventions and practices of the Graeco-Roman world generally and Second Temple Judaism in particular.

2 Jesus

The New Testament reflects an original and highly creative treatment of the Jewish scriptures. It is an approach that bases itself on a Jewish understanding of God, builds on a Jewish appreciation of God's desire for the redemption of humanity, and parallels in many ways the exegetical principles and procedures of Second Temple Judaism. But it is also an approach that evidences a distinctive outlook, a different selection of passages, a creative exegesis, and a unique interpretation. Dodd concluded in words that cannot be improved on: 'To account for the beginning of this most original and fruitful process of rethinking the Old Testament we found need to postulate a creative mind. The Gospels offer us one [i.e., Jesus of Nazareth]. Are we compelled to reject the offer?' (Dodd 1963: 110). It is necessary, therefore, to begin our study of the interpretation of the Bible in the New Testament with Jesus' use of scripture.

2.1 Literal and midrash interpretation

A number of times Jesus is portrayed in the Gospels as interpreting scripture in a quite straightforward, literal manner, particularly when dealing with matters related to basic religious and moral values. For example, in answer to a scribe who asked regarding the greatest of the commandments he quoted Deuteronomy 6:4–5 (the first words of the *Shema*): 'Hear, O Israel, the Lord our God is one Lord. And you shall love the Lord your God with your whole heart, and with your whole soul, and with your whole mind, and with your whole strength' (Mark 12:29–30; Matt. 22:37; Luke 10:27). Then, lest it be thought that God's commandments apply only to a person's vertical relationship and not also to his or her attitudes and actions on the horizontal level, he went on to quote Leviticus 19:18: 'You shall love your neighbor as yourself' (Mark 12:31; Matt. 22:39; Luke 10:27).

Likewise in his teachings on human relationships, Jesus is represented as using scripture in a straightforward manner, with only minor variations in the texts cited. For example, on settling disputes between brothers, he advised that the wronged party confront the other in the presence of one or two others, for, quoting Deuteronomy 19:15, 'by the mouth of two or three witnesses shall every word be established' (Matt. 18:16).

2.2 Pesher interpretation

But while the evangelists record a number of rather literal treatments of scripture on the part of Jesus (as well, it must be noted, as the use of then current midrash syllogisms in outclassing his opponents on their own grounds) his most characteristic use of scripture is portrayed in the Gospels as being a 'pesher' type of interpretation. Pesher interpretation applies scripture to the current situation in a 'this is that' manner. Its point of departure is the present situation ('this'), which it then relates to and finds justification for in a particular biblical text ('that') — (in contrast to 'midrash' interpretation, which starts with the biblical text ('that') and seeks to spell out that text's relevance for the present situation ('this'). Pesher interpretation is not just a commentary on scripture with a present-day application, as found in midrash exegesis ('that applies to this'). Rather, it assumes a revelatory stance and highlights eschatological fulfilment in showing how the present situation is foretold and supported by the ancient biblical text ('this is that').

According to Luke's Gospel, Jesus began to expound the scriptures in terms of a fulfilment theme very early in his ministry. In Luke 4:16–21 he enters the synagogue at Nazareth and is called on to read the lesson from the prophet Isaiah. He reads Isaiah 61:1–2, rolls up the scroll, hands it to the attendant, sits down to speak, and then proclaims: 'Today this scripture is fulfilled in your ears.' In John's Gospel the theme of fulfilment is just as explicitly stated in Jesus' denunciation of the Pharisees in John 5:39–47. The passage begins with a rebuke of his opponents' false confidence, proceeds to give an unfavorable verdict on their attitudes and interpretations, and climaxes in the assertion: 'If you believed Moses you would have believed me, for he wrote of me.' If we had only these two passages, it would be possible to claim that it was Jesus himself who inaugurated for his followers the impetus for understanding scripture in terms of a fulfilment theme and a pesher type of hermeneutic.

The following instances of Jesus' use of the fulfilment theme and a pesher approach to scripture, however, should also be noted:

(1)   Mark 12:10–11; Matthew 21:42; Luke 20:17, where Jesus concludes his allusion to the well-known parable of the vineyard (Isa. 5:1–7) and his not-so-veiled rebuke of the people's rejection of the son with the quotation of Psalm 118:22–23.

(2)   Mark 14:27; Matthew 26:31, where after the Last Supper he quotes Zechariah 13:7 in regard to his approaching death and the disciples' reactions. The citation is introduced by Jesus with the formula 'it is written,' and its use by him with reference to the desertion of his disciples invokes a 'this is that' pesher motif.

(3)   Matthew 11:10; Luke 7:27 (cf. Mark 1:2–3), where Jesus applies the conflated texts of Malachi 3:1 and Isaiah 40:3 to John the Baptist. The formula used in Matthew's Gospel to introduce these Old Testament texts, 'This is the one about whom it is written,' is a typical pesher introductory formula.

(4)   Matthew 13:14–15, where Jesus quotes Isaiah 6:9–10 in explanation of his use of parables.

(5)   Matthew 15:8–9, where he paraphrases Isaiah 29:13 (possibly also collating Psalm 78:36–37) in rebuke of the scribes and Pharisees from Jerusalem.

(6)   Luke 22:3, where Jesus applies the clause 'he was numbered among the transgressors' from Isaiah 53:12 directly to himself.

(7)   John 6:45, where he alludes to the message of Isaiah 54:13 and Jeremiah 31:33, making the point that the words 'and they shall be taught of God,' as the prophets' message may be rather freely rendered, apply to his teaching and his ministry in particular.

(8)   John 13:18, where he applies the lament of David in Psalm 41:9 (LXX 40:10) to his betrayal by Judas.

(9)   John 15:25, where the lament of Psalms 35:19 and 69:4, 'hated without a cause,' is applied by Jesus to his own person and introduced by the statement 'in order that the word that is written in their law might be fulfilled.'

Jesus is also recorded as pointing out typological correspondences between earlier events in redemptive history and various circumstances connected with his own person and ministry. We have already referred to his application of the laments of Psalms 35:19, 41:9, and 69:4 to his own situation. In three other instances, as well, he is portrayed as invoking a typological or correspondence-in-history theme and applying the incident to himself in pesher fashion: (a) in Matthew 12:40, paralleling the experience of Jonah and that of his own approaching death and entombment; (b) in Matthew 24:37, drawing a relationship between the days of Noah and the days of 'the coming of the Son of man'; and (c) in John 3:14, connecting the 'lifting up' of the brass serpent in the wilderness to his own approaching crucifixion. Jesus seems to have viewed these Old Testament events not just as analogies that could be used for purposes of illustration, but as typological occurrences that pointed forward to their fulfilment in his own person and ministry.

3 The earliest believers

Luke 24:27 recounts that in appearing to two from Emmaus, Jesus 'interpreted to them in all the Scriptures, beginning from Moses and the prophets, the things concerning himself.' Luke 24:45 says that he later met with his disciples and 'opened their minds that they might understand the Scriptures.' And Acts 1:3 tells of Jesus teaching his disciples 'things concerning the kingdom of God' during a forty-day postresurrection ministry. These verses, of course, together with a postresurrection ministry generally, are highly suspect in contemporary studies, due to modern theology's denial of Jesus' physical resurrection and therefore a denial of his postresurrection ministry. At the very least, however, it must be said that in these passages Luke is relating what he believed to be the rationale for the distinctive use of scripture by the earliest believers in Jesus, whether it originated in this specific period or not.

The analogy of the exegetical practices at Qumran is probably pertinent here. For, it seems, the members of the Dead Sea community both passively retained their teacher's interpretations of certain biblical portions and actively continued to study the Old Testament along lines stemming from him — either as directly laid out by him or as deduced from his practice. Likewise, the earliest believers in Jesus continued their study of the scriptures not only under the guidance of the Holy Spirit but also according to the paradigm set by Jesus in his own interpretations and exegetical practices.

3.1 Literal and midrash interpretation

A literal mode of biblical interpretation appears in the accounts of the earliest believers' use of scripture in the Acts of the Apostles. Peter, for example, is portrayed in Acts 3:15 as citing the covenant promise to Abraham quite literally, acknowledging that his hearers gathered in the temple precincts were 'children of the prophets and of the covenant that God made with our fathers' (cf. Gen. 12:3; 18:18; 22:18). All the citations and allusions of Stephen in his detailed tracing of Israel's history in Acts 7 — specifically in verses 3 (cf. Gen. 12:1), 6–7a (cf. 15:13–14), 7b (cf. Exod. 3:12), 27–28 (cf. Exod. 2:14), 32 (cf. Exod. 3:6), 33–34 (Exod. 3:5, 7–10), 42–43 (Amos 5:25–27), and 49–50 (Isa. 66:1) – adhere closely to the plain meaning of the biblical text. Even Stephen's use in Acts 7:37 of Deuteronomy 18:15 ('The Lord your God will raise up for you a prophet like me [Moses] from among your own brothers. You must listen to him!'), which by implication is applied to Jesus, is a straightforward treatment of a prophecy that was widely seen within Second Temple Judaism to have direct reference to the coming Messiah.

Likewise, a midrash treatment of scripture by the earliest believers is depicted at many places in the Acts of the Apostles. The exegetical rule qal wa-homer ('light to heavy'), for example, underlies the use of Psalms 69:25 [MT = 69:26] and 109:8, thereby allowing Peter in Acts 1:20 to assert that what has been said of false companions and wicked men generally applies, a minore ad majorem, specifically to Judas, the one who proved himself uniquely false and evil. Similarly, in Peter's Pentecost sermon Psalms 16:8–11 and 110:1 are brought together in Acts 2:25–28 and 34–35 in support of the resurrection on the hermeneutical principle gezera shawa ('analogy'), since both passages contain the expression 'at my right hand' and so are to be treated together.

3.2 Pesher interpretation

But what appears to be most characteristic in the preaching of the earliest Jewish believers in Jesus are their pesher interpretations of scripture. Addressing those gathered in the temple courts, Peter is portrayed in Acts 3:24 as affirming that 'all the prophets from Samuel on, as many as have spoken, have foretold these days.' Such a view of prophetic activity, particularly when coupled

with concepts of *corporate solidarity* and *typological correspondences in history*, opens up all of the biblical message and all of biblical history to a Christocentric interpretation. Taking such a stance, all that remained for the earliest believers in Jesus was to identify those biblical portions considered pertinent to the messianic age (at least as they understood it) and to explicate them in accordance with the tradition and principles of Christ.

In the majority of the cases of Peter's preaching recorded in Acts, a 'this is that' pesher motif and a fulfilment theme come to the fore, as can be seen in the following examples:

(1) The application of Joel 2:28–32 (MT = 3:1–5) to the Pentecost outpouring of the Spirit in Acts 2:17–21, stating explicitly that 'this is that spoken by the prophet Joel.' The feature of fulfilment is heightened by Peter's alteration of 'afterwards,' as found in both the MT and LXX, to 'in the last days, says God,' and by his breaking into the quotation to emphasize the fact of the restoration of prophecy with the statement 'and they shall prophesy.'

(2) The 'stone' citation of Acts 4:11, quoting Psalm 118:22 and introducing the passage in Acts by the words 'this is the stone.' The midrashic bringing together in 1 Peter 2:6–8 of Isaiah 28:16, Psalm 118:22, and Isaiah 8:14 – all of which passages have to do with a prophesied 'stone' – appears to be a later development.

(3) The statements applied to Judas in Acts 1:20, which are taken from Psalms 69:25 (MT = 69:26) and 109:8. While there is here the use of Hillel's first exegetical rule qal wa-homer ('what applies in a less important case will certainly apply in a more important case'), thereby applying what is said in the Psalms about the unrighteous generally to the betrayer of the Messiah specifically, the aspect of fulfilment, as based on *typological correspondences in history*, gives the treatment a pesher flavor as well.

(4) The application of Psalms 16:8–11 and 110:1 to the resurrection and ascension of Jesus in Acts 2:25–36. While a midrashic understanding has brought the two passages together, it is a pesher understanding that evokes such an introduction as 'David said concerning him ["the Christ"]' and applies the passages directly to Jesus.

3.3 Summation

Many other examples could be cited of the earliest believers' use of scripture, as drawn from their preaching (cf. Longenecker 1975, 1999a: chs 3 and 7) and their confessions (cf. Longenecker 1999b: chs 2–5). But from these few examples it seems evident that (a) the earliest believers blended and interwove literal, midrash, and pesher modes of treatment into their interpretations of scripture, together with the application of then generally accepted prophecy, and (b) they interpreted the scriptures from a Christocentric perspective, in conformity with the exegetical teaching and example of Jesus, and along Christological lines. In their exegesis there is the interplay of Jewish presuppositions and practices, on the one hand, and Christian commitments and perspectives, on the other, which produced a distinctive interpretation of the Old Testament.

4 Paul

Having been trained as a Pharisee, Paul shared with the Judaism of his day many of the then current hermeneutical conventions and procedures. But having been confronted by the risen Christ on his way to Damascus, he came to share with the earliest Christian apostles and believers in Jesus their distinctive Christocentric understanding of the Old Testament. Furthermore, Paul worked exegetically from many of the same Old Testament passages as did the earliest believers (cf. Dodd 1952: esp. 23). Yet while there are broad areas of agreement between Paul and other believers in Jesus, there also appear discernible differences between them in matters of exegetical approach and practice.

The earliest believers, following the teaching and exegetical procedures of their Master, seem to have placed the revelation of God in Jesus the Messiah '*neben dem Text*,' so that both stood starkly side-by-side. Paul's treatment of the Old Testament, however, evidences not quite such a simple juxtaposition, but, rather, a more nuanced exposition of the Jewish scriptures within a larger context of Christological awareness. Of course, both the earliest believers in Jesus and Paul began their newly formed Christian thinking with a deep-seated conviction about the Messiahship of Jesus. But in their exegesis of the Old Testament they seem to have been somewhat different. For whereas the earliest believers began with the proclamation of the Messiahship of Jesus of Nazareth and then to relate this new Christological understanding in pesher fashion to their traditional scriptures, Paul in his major letters usually begins with the biblical text itself and then seeks by means of a midrashic explication to demonstrate Christological significance.

As C.H. Dodd long ago pointed out: 'Paul in the main tries to start from an understanding of the biblical text just as it stands in its context' (Dodd 1952: 23). Likewise, as W.F. Albright once observed — contrasting rabbinic hermeneutics with that of the Qumran covenanters and applying that contrast to the hermeneutics of Paul vis-à-vis what appears in the portrayals of Jesus' use of scripture and at many places elsewhere in writings of other New Testament authors: 'St. Paul's interpretation of the Old Testament follows the Greek hermeneutics of the Mishnah rather than the quite different type of interpretation found in the Essence commentaries on the books of the Bible' (Albright 1966: 51). So while the exegesis of the earliest Christian believers and teachers — even, indeed, of Jesus himself — had its closest parallels known to date with the exegetical conventions of the covenanters at Qumran, as found in the Dead Sea Scrolls, it needs to be noted that Paul's treatment of the biblical texts is more closely related to the hermeneutics of early Pharisaism, as later incorporated into the Jewish Talmud in more codified form.

4.1 Frequency and distribution of the quotations

At least eighty-three biblical quotations appear in Paul's letters – with that number growing to approximately 100 if one disengages conflated texts and possible dual sources, treating each separately. Allusive use of biblical language is also found in all Paul's letters, except Philemon. The Old Testament, as Earle Ellis observes, was for the apostle 'not only the Word of God but also his mode of thought and speech' (Ellis 1957: 10), and so parallels of language are inevitable.

What particularly needs to be noted with respect to the distribution of Paul's biblical quotations, however, is that they are limited to only certain letters — (that is, they appear in Romans (45 times), 1 Corinthians (15 times), 2 Corinthians (7 times), and Galatians (10 times), with six other appearances in Ephesians (4 times), 1 Timothy (once), and 2 Timothy (once), but not in 1 & 2 Thessalonians, Philippians, Colossians, Philemon, or Titus. This phenomenon of distribution, as Adolf Harnack long ago observed, should probably be understood circumstantially (cf. Harnack 1928: 124–41). For the letters to believers at Rome, Corinth, and Galatia may be understood to involve, in one way or another, addressees who had some type of Jewish heritage or were influenced by some type of Jewish teaching. Even 1 & 2 Timothy, if 'Timothy' is the young man of Lystra referred to in Acts 16:1–3, and Ephesians, if it can be postulated that 'Ephesians' was originally intended for a wider audience than believers at Ephesus, could be so considered. But the letters written to the churches at Thessalonica, Philippi, and Colosse, as well as those to Philemon and Titus, were addressed, as far as we know, to believers who were relatively uninformed regarding the Old Testament and relatively unaffected by Jewish teaching or a Judaistic polemic. And in his pastoral correspondence with these latter churches and individuals, Paul, it seems, attempted to meet them on their own ideological grounds, without buttressing his arguments by appeals to scripture.

4.2 Literal and midrash interpretation

There is in Paul's use of scripture a great many rather straightforward, even literalistic, treatments of the ancient biblical texts, such as would be common to any reverential or respectful treatment of the Bible, whether Jewish or Christian, and such as would require comment only if they were absent or spoken against. He agrees, for example, with the psalmist that God is true, just, and prevailing in his judgments (Rom. 3:4, citing Ps. 51:4). He quotes the fifth through the tenth commandments as applying to various ethical situations

(Rom. 7:7; 13:9; Eph. 6:2–3, citing Exod. 20:12–17; Deut. 5:16–21), and asserts that whatever has been left untouched in the sphere of human relations by these divine principles is covered by the précis of Leviticus 19:18: 'You shall love your neighbor as yourself' (Rom. 13:9; Gal. 5:14). For further examples see Romans 4:17–18; 9:7–9; 1 Corinthians 6:16; 2 Corinthians 13:1; Galatians 3:8, 16; and Ephesians 5:31.

More particularly, the seven exegetical rules (*middoth*) attributed by tradition to Hillel, which seem to have been widely practiced by first-century rabbis, underlie Paul's use of scripture at a number of places in his letters. Rule one, *qal wa-homer*, is expressed, for example, in the argument of Romans 5:15–21: If death is universal through one man's disobedience and sin has reigned as a result of that one man's act of transgression (citing the Genesis story of Adam), 'much more' will God's grace and the gift of grace 'supremely abound' and 'reign to life eternal' by Jesus Christ.

It also undergirds Paul's contrasts between the fall and the fullness of Israel in Romans 11:12 and between 'the ministry of death and condemnation' and 'the ministry of the Spirit and righteousness' in 2 Corinthians 3:7–18. The apostle can even reverse the procedure and – in demonstration of his thorough familiarity with this first exegetical principle – argue *a maiori ad minus* in such passages as Romans 5:6–9, 5:10, 8:32, 11:24, and 1 Corinthians 6:2–3.

Hillel's second rule, *gezera shawa* ('analogy'), is abundantly illustrated by Paul's frequently recurring practice of 'pearl stringing' – that is, of bringing to bear on one point of an argument passages from various parts of the Bible in support of the argument. This is most obviously done in Romans 3:10–18, 9:12–29, 10:18–21, 11:8–10, 15:9–12, and Galatians 3:10–13, but it appears as well in Romans 4:1–8, 9:33, 12:19–20, 1 Corinthians 15:54–55, and 2 Corinthians 6:16–18. Hillel's fifth rule, *kelal upherat* ('general and particular'), can be seen in the apostle's discussion of love in action in Romans 13:8–10. For after itemizing the last five of the ten commandments, he goes on to say: 'If there is any other commandment, it is summed up in this word: "You shall love your neighbor as yourself"' (v. 9, citing Lev. 19:18; cf. Gal. 5:14).

Rule six, *kayyose bo bemaqom 'aher* ('as found in another place'), expresses itself in Paul's argument of Galatians 3:8–9 regarding the nature of God's promise to Abraham. Quoting Genesis 12:3, he speaks of Abraham as the immediate recipient of God's promise and of 'all nations' as the ultimate beneficiaries. But by bringing Genesis 22:18 into the discussion, a passage generally similar to the first, he is able to highlight the point that both Abraham and his 'seed' were in view in the divine promise. Rule seven, *dabar halamed me'inyano* ('context'), is probably most aptly illustrated by Paul's observations in Romans 4:10–11 that Abraham was accounted righteous *before* he was circumcised. It appears also in Galatians

3:17, where Paul lays stress on the fact that the promise made to Abraham was confirmed by God 430 years *before* the giving of the Mosaic law.

Midrash exegesis characterizes the apostle's hermeneutical procedures more than any other. Indeed, when he speaks to a Judaizing problem or to issues having Jewish nuances, he sometimes uses midrashic exegesis in an *ad hominem* fashion, as he does particularly in Galatians 3:6–14. But even apart from the catalyst of Jewish polemics, Paul's basic thought patterns and interpretive procedures were those of first-century Pharisaism. The dictum of Joachim Jeremias regarding the apostle's biblical interpretation is, it seems, fully justified: 'Paulus Hillelit war' (Jeremias 1969: 89).

4.3 Allegorical and pesher interpretation

In two passages, however, Paul goes beyond both literal and midrashic exegesis and interprets the Old Testament allegorically – that is, elaborating a secondary and hidden meaning that is claimed to underlie the primary and obvious meaning of a historical narrative. In 1 Corinthians 9:9–10 he goes beyond the primary meaning of the injunction in Deuteronomy 25:4, 'You shall not muzzle the ox that thrashes,' to insist that these words were written for a reason not obvious in the passage itself: 'Is it about oxen that God is concerned? Surely he says this for us, doesn't he? Yes, this was written for us!' And in Galatians 4:21–31 he goes beyond the account of relations between Hagar and Sarah in Genesis 21:8–21 when he argues that 'these things may be taken allegorically, for the women represent two covenants,' (v. 24), and so goes on to spell out symbolic meanings that are seen to be contained in the historical account.

But allegorical exegesis, while prominent in the writings of Philo of Alexandria, was also present in milder forms in all the known branches of Judaism during the first Christian century (cf. Longenecker 1975: 45–8; 1999a: 30–3). And in 1 Corinthians 9:9–10 and Galatians 4:21–31 Paul reflects something of this general Jewish background. More particularly, however, it needs to be noted that while 1 Corinthians 9:9–10 displays an allegorical exegesis such as was undoubtedly part-and-parcel of Paul's own exegetical equipment, Galatians 4:21–31 is probably to be seen as an extreme form of allegorical interpretation that was triggered by polemical debate with the teaching of the Judaizers in Paul's Galatian churches – and so is largely *ad hominem* in nature.

But is there any evidence of a pesher treatment of the Old Testament by Paul? Some have argued that textual deviations in Paul's biblical quotations signal a pesher treatment. But pesher interpretation is wrongly understood if it is defined only on the basis of its textual variations, for rabbinic midrash differs only quantitatively and not qualitatively from pesher at this point.

Others have suggested that the 'this is that' fulfilment motif, which is a feature of pesher interpretation, can readily be found in Paul's writings – as, for example, in 2 Corinthians 6:2, where he asserts that 'the acceptable time' and 'the day of salvation' spoken of in Isaiah 49:8 are present with us 'now,' and in Galatians 4:4, where he speaks of 'the fullness of time' taking place in God's sending of his Son. But only in Acts 13:16–41, in addressing those gathered in the synagogue at Antioch of Pisidia, is Paul represented as making explicit use of the fulfilment theme. And that, of course, is directed to a Jewish audience. Paul's habit in his Gentile mission, it seems, was not to attempt to demonstrate eschatological fulfilment in any explicit manner – except, perhaps, when such a theme was incorporated within his quotation of an early Christian confession, as seems to have been the case in Galatians 4:4–5. Evidently such a procedure carried little weight with those unaccustomed to thinking in terms of historical continuity and unschooled in the Old Testament.

What is significant with respect to Paul's use of pesher interpretation, however, is his understanding of one feature of the prophetic message in terms of a 'mystery' that has been made known by means of a 'revelational understanding' – or, to use the nomenclature derived from the Dead Sea Scrolls, a *raz* ('mystery') that has become known through a *pesher* ('revelational interpretation'). Paul uses 'mystery' (Greek: *mustērion*) some twenty times in his letters, and in a number of ways. But in three instances in his use of the term he seems to be definitely involving himself in a *raz-pesher* understanding of the unfolding of redemptive history:

(1)   In the doxology of Romans 16:25–27, where he identifies 'my gospel' as being 'the preaching of Jesus Christ according to the revelation of the mystery that was kept secret for long ages, but now is disclosed and through the prophetic writings is made known to all nations.'

(2)   In Colossians 1:26–27, where he mentions 'the mystery hidden for ages and generation, but is now made manifest to his saints.'

(3)   And in Ephesians 3:1–11, where he speaks of 'the mystery' that was 'made known to me by revelation,' but 'which was not made known to people in other generations as it has now been revealed to his holy apostles and prophets by the Spirit, . . . the mystery hidden for ages in God who created all things.'

Paul could not claim the usual apostolic qualifications, as expressed in John 15:27 and Acts 1:21–22. His understanding of the Old Testament could not be directly related to the teaching and example of the historic Jesus, as was that of the Jerusalem apostles and many of the earliest believers in Jesus. Rather, he was dependent on the early church for much in the Christian tradition, as his letters frankly indicate. But Paul had been confronted by the exalted Lord, directly commissioned an apostle by Jesus himself, and considered that he had been given the key to the pattern of redemptive history in the present age – that is, that he had been given the

'mystery' to the outworking of divine redemption in this present day by means of a 'revelational understanding.' The Jerusalem apostles had the key to many of the prophetic mysteries; but he had been entrusted with a pesher that was uniquely his. Together, they combined to enhance the fullness of the Gospel.

5 The evangelists

The interpretation of the Bible by the four canonical evangelists in their editorial comments (as distinguished from that of Jesus in their portrayals of him) – especially the editorial comments of Matthew and John – represents a particularly distinctive use of biblical material. While there are definite lines of continuity with both Jewish exegetical conventions and Jewish Christian presuppositions and practices, the Gospels of Matthew and John, in particular, exhibit a unique strand of exegesis among early Christian writings. Furthermore, they evidence a development in Jewish Christian interpretation over what we have seen so far in the apostolic period.

The evangelists' own use of scripture is reflected, at least to some extent, in the arrangement of their respective narratives where they parallel certain biblical features, in their emphases where they highlight certain biblical themes, and in their use of Old Testament language. But it is most aptly seen in their editorial comments where they quote biblical material. One such editorial quotation appears in Mark's Gospel (1:23), eleven in Matthew's Gospel (1:23; 2:15, 18, 23; 4:15–16; 8:17; 12:18–21; 13:35; 21:5; 3:3; 27:9–10, with ten of these being explicitly introduced by a fulfilment formula), three in Luke's Gospel (2:23, 24; 3:4–6), and seven in John's Gospel (2:17; 12:15, 38, 40; 19:24, 36, 37, with four of these being explicitly introduced by a fulfilment formula).

5.1   Editorial quotations in Mark's and Luke's Gospels

The use of the Old Testament in Mark's Gospel has proven difficult to isolate and characterize. Some have interpreted the Gospel as built on biblical typology throughout, and others have argued for the wilderness theme as undergirding the entire presentation. On the other hand, there are those who deny any promise-fulfilment schema or any use of biblical themes in the Second Gospel. But both the attempt to make Mark's Gospel something of a Jewish Christian midrash and the denial to the evangelist of any interest in scripture are extreme positions, which have rightly been widely discounted today.

In his editorial comments, as distinguished from his portrayals of Jesus in the narrative material common to all three Synoptic writers, Mark is very reserved with respect to an explicit use of the Old Testament. Such a use appears only in Mark 1:2–3 where the evangelist cites the conflated texts of Malachi 3:1 and Isaiah

40:3. In Matthew 11:10 and Luke 7:27, of course, Malachi 3:1 is attributed to Jesus' teaching. But Mark cites both Malachi 3:1 and Isaiah 40:3 at the very beginning of his narrative – probably, it may be presumed, in continuity with a developing practice within the early church. Beyond this one conflated citation of scripture, however, there are no further explicit quotations in the editorial material of Mark's Gospel.

A number of features in Luke's Gospel deserve mention with regard to the evangelist's own use of scripture. In the first place, the Lukan birth narrative of 1:5–2:52 clearly anchors the birth of Jesus in the faith and piety of Israel, in the Jewish scriptures, and in the plan and purpose of God. Furthermore, it serves to highlight the fact of the renewal of prophecy at the dawn of the messianic age. Thus, while there are no explicit fulfilment quotations in the evangelist's editorial comments, the biblical allusions and prophetic tone of these first two chapters clearly indicate the author's understanding of the gospel's continuity with and fulfilment of the prophetic message to Israel of old. And the emphasis on the activity of the Spirit – both in the conception of Jesus and in the prophetic responses of Mary, Zechariah, Simeon, and Anna – seems to be Luke's way of saying to his Gentile audience that the time of fulfilment has been inaugurated.

To be noted, however, are two quotations from the Pentateuch – first from Exodus 13:2, 12 and then from Leviticus 12:8 – that appear in Luke 2:23–24. But these quotations are not used in any fulfilment manner; rather, only to explain certain features of Jewish ritual law to a non-Jewish audience. Where the note of fulfilment comes into Luke's editorial use of scripture is at the beginning of his 'common narrative,' where in 3:4–6 the evangelist quotes Isaiah 40:3–5 as having been fulfilled in the ministry of John the Baptist – much, of course, like Mark 1:2–3 quotes Isaiah 40:3, though without reference to Malachi 3:1 and with an extension of the quotation to include the very relevant material for Luke's purposes of Isaiah 40:4–5. But beyond these two explanations of Jewish ritual law and the one inclusion of a traditional prophetic portion, there is a decided lack of explicit biblical material in the editorial comments of Luke's Gospel.

5.2 Editorial quotations in Matthew's Gospel

While Mark and Luke are quite reserved in their editorial use of biblical material, the use of scripture in the editorial comments of Matthew's Gospel goes much beyond what has been called historico-grammatical exegesis – even beyond what was practiced by the earliest believers in Jesus or by Paul. Who would have suspected, for example, apart from a knowledge of Matthew's Gospel, that anything of messianic significance could be derived from God's calling Israel's children out of Egypt (cf. 2:15), Jeremiah's reference to Rachel weeping for her children in Rama (cf. 2:17–18),

a statement regarding the lands of Zebulun and Naphtali (cf. 4:14–16), or the payment to Zechariah of thirty pieces of silver and his subsequent action of giving them to the potter (cf. 27:9–10). All these references might resound in quite a familiar fashion to those reared on the New Testament. But they would never have been guessed apart from Matthew's treatment. And any similar treatment of scripture today would be considered by most Christians to be quite shocking. Such biblical quotations within the editorial comments of Matthew's Gospel, in fact, are quite distinctive in their introductory formulae, their textual variations, and their oftentimes surprising applications. For want of space, the first two of these matters must be left for treatment elsewhere (see Longenecker 1975:140–52; 1999a: 124–35). The third, however, needs to be dealt with here, even though briefly.

In seeking to understand the evangelist's own use of the Old Testament, it is well to remind ourselves of a phenomenon that has been frequently noted and variously explained: that many parallels between the life of Jesus and the experiences of the nation Israel seem to underlie the presentation of the First Gospel – especially in the first half (approximately) of Matthew's Gospel, where the order of material varies noticeably from that of either Mark's or Luke's Gospels. Indeed, Matthew seems to be following a thematic arrangement of material in his portrayal of the life and ministry of Jesus that is guided by and incorporates various reminiscences of Israel's earlier experiences.

Scholars have given various explanations for Matthew's thematic arrangement of material in his Gospel. What can be said with confidence, however, is that (a) behind the evangelist's presentation stand the Jewish concepts of *corporate solidarity* and *typological correspondences in history*, (b) the phenomenon of historical parallelism seen in the First Gospel is a reflection of such conceptualization, and (c) this background is important for understanding Matthew's treatment of specific Old Testament statements and events. For by the use of such concepts, Jesus is portrayed in Matthew's Gospel as the embodiment of ancient Israel and the antitype of earlier divine redemption.

Thus in setting out ten explicit 'fulfilment formula' quotations and one direct use of a widely accepted messianic prophecy in his editorial comments, Matthew expresses both the Jewish concepts of *corporate solidarity* and *typological correspondences in history*, on the one hand, and the Christian convictions of *eschatological fulfilment* and *messianic presence*, on the other. Therefore he quotes in application to the ministry and person of Jesus: (a) Isaiah 7:14 (the Immanuel passage) in 1:23; (b) Hosea 11:1 ('Out of Egypt I called my son') in 2:15; (c) Jeremiah 31:15 (Rachel weeping for her children) in 2:18; (d) probably Judges 13:5–7 and 16:17 (Samson a Nazarite), together with an allusion to Jesus' hometown (Nazareth), in 2:23; (e) Isaiah 9:1–2 (Zebulun and

Naphtali) in 4:15–16; (f) Isaiah 53:3 ('he took our sicknesses and bore our diseases') in 8:17; (g) Isaiah 42:1–4 (the servant's works, withdrawal from conflict, and ultimate success) in 12:18–21; (h) Psalm 78:2 (Asaph's words regarding dark sayings) in 13:35; (i) Isaiah 62:11 and Zechariah 9:9 (Israel's king comes riding on a donkey) in 21:5; and (j) Zechariah 11:12–13, with allusions to Jeremiah 18:1–2 and 32:6–9 (thirty pieces of silver given to purchase a potter's field) in 27:9–10.

In addition, the evangelist quotes the explicit messianic prophecy of Isaiah 40:3 ('the voice of one crying in the wilderness') in 3:3, which is the only one of his eleven editorial quotations not introduced by a fulfilment formula and whose text form is almost identical to the text of the LXX. Here, in concert with Mark and Luke, Matthew is taking a widely used Old Testament text, which was commonly considered within Judaism to have messianic relevance, and applying it in Christian fashion to the ministry of John the Baptist. And in his assertion that 'this is the one spoken of by Isaiah the prophet,' he is invoking a pesher type of interpretation.

In surveying Matthew's use of the Old Testament, one gets the impression that this evangelist believed himself to be working from a revelational insight into the scriptures as given by Jesus himself, following out common apostolic hermeneutical procedures, and explicating further the theme of eschatological fulfilment under the guidance of the Holy Spirit. The question as to whether he acted legitimately or not is, of course, more than a strictly historical issue. It involves faith commitments regarding the distinctiveness of Jesus, the reality and activity of the Spirit, and the authority of an apostle or 'apostolic person.' Such matters cannot be settled here. Suffice it to say that it is Matthew's Gospel, and not Mark's or Luke's Gospels, that develops the pesher approach to scripture in such a distinctive fashion and that bears the name of one of Jesus' chosen disciples.

5.3 Editorial quotations in John's Gospel

Whereas Matthew's portrayal of Jesus seems to have been developed along the lines of the Messiah as the embodiment of the nation Israel and the fulfilment of its typological history, John appears to have thought of Jesus more as central in the life of the nation and the fulfilment of its festal observances. A number of features in support of such a hypothesis are readily apparent in the Fourth Gospel, though they may be variously explained as to their details.

Most obvious in this regard is the prominence given to the festivals of Judaism, particularly the Passover, and the way in which the fourth evangelist portrays Jesus as the fulfilment of Israel's messianic hope and the substance of Israel's ritual symbolism (cf. 2:13; 5:1; 6:4; 7:2; 10:22; 11:55; 12:1; 13:1; 18:28; 19:14). Interwoven into this festal pattern is the presentation of Jesus as the true temple (2:18–22), the antitype of the brazen serpent (3:14–15), the true manna (6:30–58), the true water-giving rock (7:37–39), the true fiery pillar (8:12), the eschatological Moses (6:1–15, 25–71; cf. 1:17; 5:39–47; 14:6), the new Torah (1:1–18; cf. 5:39–47; 14:6), and the true paschal sacrifice (1:29, 36; 19:14, 31–37).

In addition, the fourth evangelist builds his narrative around Jesus' visits to Jerusalem. At Passover he purifies the temple (2:13–17), at 'a feast of the Jews' he comes to Jerusalem as a pilgrim and teaches (5:1ff.), at Tabernacles he presents himself as the substance of the festival's symbolism (7:2–52; 8:12–59), and at another Passover he finalizes his redemptive mission (12:1ff.). The imagery, of course, varies from that of Matthew's Gospel. But the presuppositions are the same and the stress on fulfilment is strikingly similar.

Likewise, the seven biblical quotations of John's editorial material closely parallel in their applications and purpose the eleven editorial quotations of Matthew's Gospel. Underlying the use of the Old Testament in the writings of both evangelists are the Jewish presuppositions of *corporate solidarity* and *typological correspondences in history* and the Christian convictions of *eschatological fulfilment* and *messianic presence*. Furthermore, in John's Gospel, as well as in Matthew's Gospel, a pesher type of interpretation is involved in the demonstration of prophetic fulfilment. Thus in application to the ministry and person of Jesus, John in his editorial comments quotes: (a) Psalm 69:9 ('the zeal of your house has eaten me up') in 2:17; (b) Zechariah 9:9 (Israel's king comes riding on a donkey, with a possible allusion to the 'fear not' of Isaiah 40:9) in 12:15; (c) Isaiah 53:1 ('Lord, who has believed our report?') in 12:38; (d) Isaiah 6:9–10 (blinded eyes and hardened hearts) in 12:40; (e) Psalm 22:18 ('they parted my garments among them and cast lots') in 19:24; (f) Psalm 34:20, with possibly also in mind Exodus 12:46 and Numbers 9:12 ('a bone of him shall not be broken'); and (g) Zechariah 12:10 ('they shall look on him whom they pierced') in 19:37.

From the perspective of the completed ministry of Jesus, as validated by his resurrection and interpreted by the Spirit, the fourth evangelist was able to move back into the Old Testament and to explicate a Christocentric fulfilment theme that involved both direct messianic prophecies and corporate-typological relationships. In so doing, he treated his Old Testament scriptures in continuity with the exegetical practices of Jesus and the earliest believers in Jesus. Yet the degree to which he used pesher exegesis and his development of corporate-typological relationships went somewhat beyond what seems to have been common among early Christian exegetes – perhaps not as extensively as in Matthew's Gospel, but a development in pesher interpretation nonetheless. And as was observed with regard to Matthew's Gospel, it is pertinent here to note that it is John's Gospel (in concert with Matthew's), and not Mark's or Luke's, that develops pesher interpretation of Scripture in such a distinctive fashion and that bears the name of one of Jesus' chosen disciples.

6 Hebrews

Hebrews represents in many ways a hybrid blending of traditional Christian theology, the ideological perspectives and concerns of a particular Jewish Christian community, and an anonymous author's own highly individualized exegesis of the Old Testament. Historically, while its author was a Jewish Christian, he takes his stance outside the Jewish Christian mission and urges his readers to be prepared, if need be, to move beyond their former Jewish allegiances. Theologically, while the thought of the writing is compatible with the proclamation of the gospel within the large Graeco-Roman world, its argument is framed according to the interests of a particular Jewish Christian audience. And exegetically, while it uses a number of distinctly Jewish conventions and expresses a distinctly Christian outlook, it is, as Barnabas Lindars has rightly observed, 'a highly individual biblical study in its own right, so that its scriptural interpretation witnesses more to the outlook of the author than to a previous apologetic tradition' (Lindars 1961: 29).

6.1 Selection, text forms, and introductory formulae

The writer of Hebrews obviously felt himself quite at home in the Old Testament. This is particularly so with regard to the Pentateuch and the Psalms – which were among all Jews 'the fundamental Law and the Book of common devotion' (Westcott 1889: 475). From the Pentateuch he drew the basic structure of his thought regarding redemptive history, quoting some eleven times from ten different passages and alluding to forty-one others. From the Psalms he derived primary support of his Christology, quoting some eighteen times from eleven different passages and alluding to two others. With the exceptions of 2 Samuel 7:14, Deuteronomy 32:43 (LXX), and Isaiah 8:17–18, all of which are taken to be direct messianic prophecies, the biblical portions used to explicate the nature of the person of Christ are drawn entirely from the Psalms. On the other hand, with the single exception of 2 Samuel 7:14, no use is made by the writer of the historical books. And with the exception of Isaiah, only minimal use is made of the prophetic books.

Compared with other New Testament authors in their selection of Old Testament portions, the writer of Hebrews exhibits certain similarities and certain differences. Some of the passages he uses appear elsewhere in the New Testament, and are in those instances elsewhere used rather uniquely – for example, Psalm 110:1 (Mark 12:36 par.; Acts 2:34–35); Habakkuk 2:4 (Rom. 1:17; Gal. 3:11); Psalm 2:7 (Acts 13:33); 2 Samuel 7:14 (2 Corinthians 6:18, possibly); Genesis 21:12 (Rom. 9:7), and Deuteronomy 32:35 (Rom. 12:19). On the other hand, nineteen or twenty of the passages quoted in Hebrews are not cited elsewhere in the New Testament. In addition, even where the writer

agrees with other New Testament authors in his selection of texts, he varies at times from them in the text form he uses or in his application of the passage – for example, most prominently, in his variant wording of Habakkuk 2:4 in Hebrews 10:38 (cf. Rom. 1:17 and Gal. 3:11) and his different application of Psalm 8:6b in Hebrews 2:8 (cf. 1 Cor. 15:27 and Eph. 1:22).

Also significant in Hebrews is the distinctive manner in which the biblical portions are introduced. In the majority of cases, it is God himself who is the speaker (cf. 1:5 [twice], 6, 7, 8–9, 10–12, 13; 4:3, 4, 5, 7; 5:5, 6; 6:14; 7:17, 21; 8:5, 8–12; 10:30 [twice]; 12:26; 13:5). In four quotations drawn from three Old Testament passages the psalmist's or prophet's words are attributed to Christ (cf. 2:12–13 [three times]; 10:5–7) and in three quotations drawn from two passages the Holy Spirit is credited as speaking (cf. 3:7–11; 10:16–17 [twice]) – though it needs also to be noted that these three citations credited to the Spirit appear elsewhere in Hebrews credited to God (cf. 4:7; 8:8–12). In many cases the words quoted are introduced as being spoken in the present, whether cited as words of God (cf. 1:6, 7; 5:6; 7:17; 8:8–12), of Christ (cf. 10:5–7), of the Spirit (cf. 3:7–11; 10:16–17 [twice]), or attributed more generally to 'the exhortation that addresses you' (cf. 12:5–6). The rationale for this phenomenon seems to be, as B.F. Westcott expressed it, that 'the record is the voice of God; and as a necessary consequence the record is itself living. It is not a book merely. It has a vital connexion with our circumstances and must be considered in connexion with them' (Westcott 1889: 477). In only two instances are words credited to a human speaker, in both cases to Moses (cf. 9:20; 12:21). And in two or three instances the material is introduced with a comment so general as to be unparalleled by any other introductory formula in the New Testament: in 2:6–8 (quoting Ps. 8:4–6), 'somewhere someone testified, saying,' and in 4:4 (quoting Gen. 2:2), 'somewhere he has said' – which are echoed to some extent by the introduction in 5:6 (quoting Ps. 110:4), 'in another passage he says.'

6.2 Presuppositions, structures, and procedures

From the perspective of the Messiah's presence among his people in 'these last days' (1:2), Israel's life and worship are viewed by the author of Hebrews as preparatory for the coming of the Lord's Christ. A more profound significance is seen in the prophetic words and redemptive experiences recorded in scripture, and all these biblical words and events are understood to be looking forward to the consummation of God's salvific programme in the person and work of Jesus. For the author of Hebrews, as Westcott has pointed out,

the O.T. does not simply contain prophecies, but ... it is one vast prophecy, in the record of national fortunes, in the ordinances of a national Law, in the expression of a national hope. Israel in its history, in its ritual, in its ideal, is a unique enigma among the peoples of the world, of which the Christ is the complete solution. (Westcott 1889: 493)

In spelling out this consummation theme, the author builds his argument around five biblical portions: (a) a catena of verses drawn from the Psalms, 2 Samuel 7, and Deuteronomy 32 (LXX) on which Hebrews 1:3–2:4 is based; (b) Psalm 8:4–6 on which Hebrews 2:5–18 is based; (c) Psalm 95:7–11 on which Hebrews 3:1–4:13 is based; (d) Psalm 110:4 on which Hebrews 4:14–7:28 is based; and (e) Jeremiah 31:31–34 on which Hebrews 8:1–10:39 is based (cf. Caird 1959). All of the exhortations of chapters 11–13 depend on the exposition of these five biblical portions, and all other verses quoted in the letter are ancillary to these.

These five biblical portions were selected, it seems, because (a) they spoke of the eschatological Messiah and/or God's redemption in the Last Days, either as traditionally accepted within Judaism or as understood within the early church, or both, and (b) they set forth the incompleteness of the old economy under Moses and looked forward to a consummation that was to come. The writer uses in the process of his exegesis a number of procedures and practices that were common in his day – for example, *gezera shawa* ('analogy') and *dabar halamed me'inyano* ('context'), an allegorical-etymological treatment of names, and a concept of fulfilment that included *corporate solidarity* and *typological correspondences in history*. But at the heart of his exegetical endeavors is the quite straightforward query: what do the scriptures mean when viewed from a christocentric perspective?

The author of Hebrews is probably not himself originating a pesher approach to scripture, for in chapter 1 he appears to be only repeating certain pesher interpretations that had been used by the earliest believers in Jesus. Nor is he principally engaged in midrashic exegesis *per se*, though at a number of places he makes use of rather common midrashic techniques. Nor is he attempting to develop an allegorical understanding of the Old Testament, though in chapter 7 he treats two names in a mildly allegorical fashion. Rather, what he seems to be doing is basing himself on an accepted exegetical tradition within the early church – a tradition that both he and his addressees accepted – and rather straightforwardly explicating relationships contained within that tradition and implications for his addressees in light of their circumstances. In so doing, he probably saw himself in continuity with what preceded him in Christian hermeneutics. Nonetheless, comparing his interpretation of the Bible to that of his predecessors, he must be judged as having been rather unique in spelling out certain relationships between the Old and New Testaments and highlighting particular implications drawn from early Christian tradition.

7 General Epistles and Apocalypse

James, 1 and 2 Peter, 1, 2, and 3 John, and Jude, together with the Johannine Apocalypse, make up a group of writings that have many features in common. This is particularly the case with regard to the Semitic cast of their expressions and form of their presentations. In their use of the Old Testament, however, while evidencing continuity with earlier Christian exegesis and a degree of agreement among themselves, there are also significant differences between them.

7.1 Phenomena of biblical usage

The writings in the latter part of the New Testament have a somewhat confusing mixture of biblical quotations, biblical allusions, noncanonical materials, and unidentifiable proverbial maxims. The lines of demarcation between biblical and nonbiblical materials is in some of these writings not as clearly drawn as elsewhere in the New Testament, and the interplay between explicit quotations and more indirect allusions is in some cases heightened. All of this makes any listing of biblical materials for these writings extremely difficult, though probably six explicit biblical quotations are to be identified in James (2:8, 11 [two passages], 23; 4:5, 6), eight in 1 Peter (1:16, 24–25; 2:6–8 [three passages]; 3:10–12; 4:18; 5:5), and one in 2 Peter (2:22).

Biblical quotations in these writings occur almost exclusively in James and 1 Peter. Quoted material is used only once in 2 Peter and once in Jude: in 2 Peter 2:22, citing Proverbs 26:11 in conjunction with an unidentifiable maxim, and in Jude 14–15, quoting *1 Enoch* 1:9 as a prophecy – with both quotations being rather strange when compared with the rest of the New Testament. The Apocalypse is replete with biblical expressions and allusions, but it lacks any clear biblical quotation, while the Johannine Epistles are devoid of either quotations or allusions. A number of problems, of course, come to the fore here – particularly with regard to the use of quoted material in 2 Peter and Jude, as well as the lack of biblical quotations in the Johannine Epistles – for which there are no ready answers. It may be that such phenomena are indicative of pseudonymity. Or it may be that a somewhat larger Old Testament canon was used among some Jewish Christian writers of the first century. Or it may only suggest certain personal idiosyncracies or certain uncharted exegetical developments. In any case, this type of data in such short letters is hardly conclusive in support of any current theory.

7.2 Literal and pesher treatments

The Epistle of James is unique among the writings of the New Testament in its selection of biblical quotations from only the Pentateuch and Proverbs. This is, however, hardly surprising, for James is composed of a series of ethical exhortations and so could be expected to highlight the ethical portions of scripture. Furthermore, the author's treatment of passages from the Pentateuch and Proverbs is consistently literal throughout. Allusions to Isaiah and Psalm 103 also appear in 1:10–11 (Isa. 40:6–7), 2:23 (Isa. 41:8), 5:4 (Isa. 5:9), and 5:11 (Ps. 103:8), but always with an ethical rather than a prophetic thrust.

Examples of literal exegesis in 1 Peter are relatively abundant. In 1:16 there is the reminder: 'It is written, "You shall be holy, for I [God] am holy"' (quoting a conflation of Lev. 11:44; 19:2; 20:7). In 3:10–12 the psalmist's words regarding 'whoever would love life and see good days' (Ps. 34:12–16) are cited, laying out a pattern of proper behavior and giving a God-oriented rationale for such conduct. In 4:18 the words of Proverbs 11:31 regarding the righteous being judged in this life are cited in support of the exhortation to rejoice when one suffers for Christ; while in 5:5 the teaching of Proverbs 3:34, 'God resists the proud, but gives grace to the humble,' is used to buttress the author's teaching on humility.

But while there are many points of similarity between James and 1 Peter in their literal treatments of scripture, the Petrine Epistles and Jude – particularly 1 Peter, though to an extent also 2 Peter and Jude – stand apart from James, the Johannine Epistles, and the Johannine Apocalypse in their use of a pesher type of approach to the Old Testament. This is immediately apparent in 1 Peter 1:10–12, where, after the salutation, a doxology, and the setting of the theme of the writing, the author enunciates a clear-cut pesher attitude toward the nature of biblical prophecy:

> The prophets who spoke of the grace that was to come to you searched intently and with the greatest care concerning this salvation, trying to find out the time and circumstances to which the Spirit of Christ in them was pointing when he predicted the sufferings of Christ and the glories that would follow. It was revealed to them that they were not serving themselves but you, when they spoke of the things that have now been told you by those who have preached the gospel to you by the Holy Spirit sent from heaven – things that even angels long to look into.

Though the terms 'mystery' and 'interpretation' are not used, the thought here is strikingly parallel to the *raz-pesher* motif found in the Dead Sea Scrolls. Furthermore, it is in continuity with the use of scripture by Jesus, the earliest believers in Jesus, Paul in speaking about his Gentile ministry, and the evangelists of the First and Fourth Gospels.

And it is such a pesher understanding that underlies at least three of the Old Testament quotations in 1 and 2 Peter: (a) 1 Peter 1:24–25, quoting Isaiah 40:6–8 ('Everyone is like grass and everyone's glory is like the wild flower'), which applies the passage using the typically pesher phrase 'this is the word' (cf. Acts 4:11) and explicates a fuller meaning in the text from the perspective of eschatological fulfilment; (b) 1 Peter 2:6–8, quoting Isaiah 28:16, Psalm 118:22, and Isaiah 8:14 (the 'stone' passages), which applies these three passages directly to Jesus Christ; and (c) 2 Peter 2:22, quoting Proverbs 26:11 ('A dog returns to its vomit') and another proverb of undetermined origin ('A sow that is washed goes back to her wallowing in the mud'), which declares in good pesher fashion that these proverbs have their fullest application to apostates from Christ. Among the latter writings of the New Testament, only Jude 14–15 contains anything similar in its application of *1 Enoch* 1:9 to apostate teachers: 'Enoch, the seventh from Adam, prophesied about these men, saying . . .'.

Aside from these two instances in 1 Peter, one in 2 Peter, and one in Jude, however, the rest of the General Epistles and the Johannine Apocalypse do not use a pesher type of biblical interpretation. James uses scripture in quite a literal manner throughout; John's letters are devoid of either biblical quotations or allusions. And the Apocalypse, while permeated with biblical expressions and allusions, neither directly quotes the scriptures nor enters into a pesher type of exegesis. Some of these differences, of course, may be due to differing circumstances and a different literary genre. Nonetheless, they are interesting and suggest a somewhat different pattern of biblical interpretation than found elsewhere in the New Testament.

References and further reading

Albright, W.F. (1966) *New Horizons in Biblical Research*, New York: Oxford University Press.

Caird, G.B. (1959) 'The Exegetical Method of the Epistle to the Hebrews,' *Canadian Journal of Theology* 5: 44–51.

Dodd, C.H. (1952) *According to the Scriptures: The Sub-Structure of New Testament Theology*, London: Nisbet.

—— (1963) *The Old Testament in the New*, London: Athlone/Philadelphia: Fortress Press.

Ellis, E.E. (1957) *Paul's Use of the Old Testament*, Edinburgh: Oliver & Boyd/Grand Rapids: Eerdmans.

—— (1977) 'How the New Testament Uses the Old,' pp. 199–219 in *New Testament Interpretation: Essays on Principles and Methods*, I.H. Marshall (ed.), Grand Rapids: Eerdmans.

—— (1978) *Prophecy and Hermeneutics in Early Christianity*, Tübingen: Mohr/Grand Rapids: Eerdmans.

—— (1991) *The Old Testament in Early Christianity: Canon and Interpretation in the Light of Modern Research*, Tübingen: Mohr/Grand Rapids: Eerdmans.

—— (1993) 'Jesus' Use of the Old Testament and the Genesis of New Testament Theology,' *Bulletin for Biblical Research* 3: 59–75.

Harnack, A. (1928) 'Das alte Testament in den paulinischen Briefen und in den paulinischen Gemeinden,' in *Sitzungsberichte der preussichen Akademie der Wissenschaften zu Berlin*, pp. 124–41.

Hay, D.M. (1973) *Glory at the Right Hand: Psalm 110 in Early Christianity*, Nashville: Abingdon Press.

Jeremias, J. (1969) 'Paulus als Hillelit,' pp. 88–94 in *Neotestamentica et Semitica*, E.E. Ellis and M. Wilcox (eds.), Edinburgh: T.&T. Clark.

Lindars, B. (1961) *New Testament Apologetic: The Doctrinal Significance of the Old Testament Quotations*, London: SCM Press.

Longenecker, R.N. (1975/1999a) *Biblical Exegesis in the Apostolic Period*, Grand Rapids: Eerdmans (2nd edn. 1999).

—— (1987a) 'Three Ways of Understanding Relations between the Testaments: Historically and Today,' pp. 22–30 in *Tradition and Interpretation in the New Testament: Essays in Honor of E. Earle Ellis for His 60th. Birthday*, G.F. Hawthorne and O. Betz (eds.), Tübingen: Mohr/Grand Rapids: Eerdmans.

—— (1987b) '"Who Is the Prophet Talking About?" Some Reflections on the New Testament's Use of the Old,' *Themelios* 24: 3–16.

—— (1997) 'Prolegomena to Paul's Use of Scripture in Romans,' *Bulletin for Biblical Research* 7: 145–68.

—— (1999b) *New Wine into Fresh Wineskins: Contextualizing the Early Christian Confessions*, Peabody, MA: Henrickson.

Moule, C.F.D. (1962) 'The Church Explains Itself: The Use of the Jewish Scriptures,' in *The Birth of the New Testament*, London: Black/New York: Harper & Row, pp. 53–85 (2nd edn. 1966).

—— (1968) 'Fulfilment-Words in the New Testament: Use and Abuse,' *New Testament Studies* 14: 293–320.

Vermes, G. (1980) 'Jewish Studies and New Testament Interpretation,' *Journal of Jewish Studies* 31: 1–17.

—— (1982) 'Jewish Literature and New Testament Exegesis: Reflections on Methodology,' *Journal of Jewish Studies* 33: 362–76.

Westcott, B.F. (1889) 'On the Use of the Old Testament in the Epistle,' pp. 471–97 in *The Epistle to the Hebrews*, London: Macmillan.

RICHARD N. LONGENECKER

EBELING, GERHARD (1912–2001)

German theologian, originally Protestant (Lutheran) minister, since 1946 taught at the universities in Tübingen and Zürich, student and friend of Rudolf Bultmann, author of studies inspiring biblical exegesis (the most important are included in the volume *Wort und Glaube*/Word and Faith, 1960, ET 1963), however, his field was systematic theology, ecclesiastical history, and hermeneutics.

Together with Bultmann and 'dialectic theology,' he stressed the existential engagement in interpreting the Bible and he analyzed the role of 'preliminary knowledge' (*Vorverständnis*) in interpretation of ancient texts including the New Testament. The present impact of Jesus Christ through a living proclamation is the decisive level for understanding the biblical text. The earthly and crucified Jesus is immediately important as the 'that' (*daß*), stressing as contrast the 'impossible possibility' of his new presence.

However, in the 1950s, Ebeling dared a second step. In his opinion the most legitimate approach to biblical texts is on the level of language. His hermeneutic strategy was to ask what the text was saying. In other words, how are the texts that deal with Jesus challenging us as texts, as language? This concept broadened the first, existing level. Ebeling investigated the language of the Jesus tradition and discovered the crucial role played by the term 'faith' or 'believe' (Gr. *pistis*, *pisteuein*), which has often been used absolutely, without indicating any object (e.g., Matt. 17:20 or Luke 18:8). According to him, faith is a technical term for the general life orientation, the dimension of life corresponding to God's call and challenge – the foundation of authentic humanity. The analysis of the language level of the kerygma opened for Ebeling the way toward the 'historical Jesus.' This was the turning point in development of the Bultmann school, which marked the beginning of the new quest of the historical Jesus (E. Fuchs, J.M. Robinson, and others). Discovering the specific role of faith in the Jesus tradition opened the way toward analysis of this phenomenon also in a diachronic, historical way: e.g., the special term 'little faith' (*oligopistos*, *oligopistia*) from the Synoptic tradition has no analogy in classical Greek. Ebeling concluded that it was most probably created in order that Greek-speaking Christians might understand some Aramaic or Hebrew expression typical from the most ancient Jesus tradition (*Jesus und Glaube*/Jesus and Faith, 1958, reprinted in Ebeling 1963). Faith is the common denominator of the 'historical Jesus' and the post-Easter church, and therefore interpreting faith was the main topic of Ebeling's works in systematic theology.

Faith is being evoked by the present proclamation, but the interpretation and orientation of faith has always to be derived from the tradition of the historical Jesus: 'The problem of the historical Jesus is the problem of the hermeneutical key to christology' (1962: 52). Ebeling considers Jesus research as providing feedback for Christian proclamation, protecting it from enthusiastic distortion or misuse.

References and further reading

Ebeling, Gerhard (1961) *The Nature of Faith*, trans. Ronald Gregor Smith, London: Collins.

—— (1963) *Word and Faith*, trans. James W. Leitch, Philadelphia: Fortress Press.

—— (1966) *Theology and Proclamation: Dialogue with*

Bultmann, trans. John Riches, Philadelphia: Fortress Press.
—— (1979) *Dogmatic des christlichen Glaubens*. 3 Vols., Tübingen: Mohr.

PETR POKORNÝ

EICHRODT, WALTHER (1890–1978)

Born in Gernshack, Germany on August 1, 1890, Eichrodt studied theology in Bethel, Greifswald, and Heildelberg, receiving his 'license in theology' in 1914. His first dissertation on the source criticism of Genesis was published in 1916. He continued his studies in Erlangen, completing his Habilitation in 1918 under O. Procksch on the hope of eternal peace in ancient Israel, which was later published in 1920. In 1922 he went to the University of Basel to be assistant professor in Old Testament and History of Religion. He became full professor in 1934, retiring in 1960. He served as Rector of the University in 1953. On May 20, 1978, he died in Basel, Switzerland.

Eichrodt's most significant scholarly contribution was his three-volume theology of the Old Testament (1933–1939). It is still regarded as momentous both in its methodology and its content for influencing the agenda of biblical theology of the Old Testament. Methodologically, Eichrodt was dissatisfied with both the approach of those who used the outlines of dogmatic theology to organize and survey Old Testament theology and of those who eschewed any theological perspective using an exclusively history of religions approach (e.g., Gunkel). He used what is called a cross-sectional (topical) approach to combine both an historical and a theological analysis As a theologian, he was certain this combined method could 'present the religion of which the records are to be found in the Old Testament as a self-contained entity exhibiting, despite ever-changing historical conditions, a constant basic tendency and character' (1933–1939, I: 11). For Eichrodt this agenda included postulating the relationship of Old Testament theology with the New Testament: 'the Old Testament religion, ineffaceably individual though it may be, can yet be grasped in this essential uniqueness only when it is seen as completed in Christ' (1933–1939, I: 27). Equally, however, theological examination must take account of historical development in both its continuity and its discontinuity. Yet acknowledging and investigating such development did not mean that a narrow scientific historicism should preclude the possibility of discovering the essential uniqueness of Israel's life and faith. He stated that the ongoing challenge of Old Testament biblical theology was, 'the problem of how to understand the realm of Old Testament belief in its structural unity and how, by examining on the one hand its religious environment and on the other its essential coherence

with the New Testament, to illuminate its profoundest meaning' (1933–1939, I: 31).

With regard to content, Eichrodt firmly established the principle that any core organizing theological concept must come from within the Old Testament itself. He posited the idea of the covenant as a central motif which was traceable through all the various sectors and strata of the Old Testament and which was expressive of the central nature of Israel's religion from the time of Moses onward. For Eichrodt, the concept of the covenant upheld both the doctrine of revelation in which God had been at work in the history of Israel and the sense of Israel's faith as a unique and special relationship with God. Using the covenant as an organizing theme and employing both literary and historical tools, he surveyed the Old Testament according to a three-part outline which he felt was endemic to the Old Testament texts: God and People (the covenant, the name and nature of God, and the instruments of the covenant), God and the World (God's power, cosmology, and creation), God and Man (morality, sin and forgiveness, and immortality).

Scholars criticized Eichrodt's theology on several levels. First, they questioned whether 'covenant' is the appropriate '*Mitte*' (center, middle) of Old Testament theology. The meaning of 'covenant' itself is regarded as ambiguous in the Old Testament. In addition, as a central theme, covenant is not as prominent outside the Pentateuch. Scholars also point out that it is not apparent how covenant acts as an organizing concept in parts two and three of Eichrodt's outline. Second, scholars question whether his attempt to find an organizing center is not, in the end, a philosophical abstraction. Third, many scholars, following A. Alt, M. Noth, and G. von Rad, question whether tradition-historical research prevents positing any unifying theological theme(s).

Despite these criticisms, his theology of the Old Testament remains a landmark study. First, he put Old Testament theology firmly back on the programme for Old Testament studies after Graf-Wellhausen, Second, he identified the key theological problem of trying to find a theological coherence within the context of historical diversity and development. Third, he demonstrated the possibility of combining tradition-historical analysis with theological study to posit a unified or coherent center to Old Testament theology. Finally, he reasserted the importance of the continuity of Old Testament theology with the New Testament.

His commentary on Ezekiel and his book, *Man in the Old Testament*, have also been influential in Old Testament studies.

References and further reading

Bray, G. (1966) *Biblical Interpretations Past and Present*, Leicester: Apollos.

Eichrodt, Walther (1916) *Die Quellen der Genesis in neuem untersucht*, BZAW 31, Giessen: A. Töpelmann.

—— (1920) *Die Hoffnung des ewigen Friedens im Alten Israel*, BFCT 25, 3, Gütersloh: C. Bertelsmann.

—— (1933–1939) *Theologie des Alten Testament*, 3 Vols., Leipzig: J.C. Hinrichs (ET *Theology of the Old Testament*, 2 Vols., Philadelphia: Westminster Press, 1961–1967).

—— (1944) *Das menschenverständis des Alten Testaments*, Basel: H. Majer (ET *Man in the Old Testament*, SBT 4, London: SCM Press, 1951).

—— (1959) *De Prophet Hesekiel: Kap 1–18*, ATD 22, 1, Göttingen: Vandenhoeck & Ruprecht.

—— (1960) *Der Helige in Israel: Jesaja 1–12*, BAT 17, 1, Stuttgart: Calwer Verlag.

—— (1966) *Der Prophet Hesekiel: Kap. 19–48*, ATD 22, 2, Göttingen: Vandenhoeck & Ruprecht (ET *Ezekiel: A Commentary*, Philadelphia: Westminster Press, 1970).

—— (1967) *Der Herr der Geschichte: Jesaja 13–23 und 28–39*, BAT 17, 2, Stuttgart: Calwer Verlag.

Goldingay, J. (1981) *Approaches to Old Testament Interpretation*, Issues in Contemporary Theology, Downers Grove: IVP.

Hayes, J.H. and F.C. Prussner (1985) *Old Testament Theology: Its History and Development*, Atlanta: John Knox.

Knight, D.A. and G.M. Tucker (eds.) (1985) *The Hebrew Bible and Its Modern Interpreters*, The Bible and Its Modern Interpreters, 1, Philadelphia: Fortress Press/Decatur: Scholars Press.

McKim, D.K. (ed.) (1998) *Historical Handbook of Major Biblical Interpreters*, Downers Grove: IVP.

Spriggs, D.G. (1974) *Two Old Testament Theologies: A Comparative Evaluation of the Contributions of Eichrodt and von Rad to our Understanding of the Nature of Old Testament Theology*, London: SCM Press.

DENNIS L. STAMPS

ENLIGHTENMENT PERIOD

1 Pyrrhonism, Cartesianism, and early criticism
2 Arianism, Socinianism, and Sir Isaac Newton
3 English Deism
4 Prophecy, miracles, and truth claims
5 The *Fragments* controversy and the quest of the historical Jesus
6 German biblical scholarship
7 The American Enlightenment

1 Pyrrhonism, Cartesianism, and early criticism

The Age of Enlightenment is frequently located in the eighteenth century in contrast to the Age of Reason in the seventeenth century. However, precise time frames are arbitrary, and the term Enlightenment characterizes attitudes and opinions that can be traced to the sixteenth century. As a heuristic device for identifying Enlightenment biblical interpretation I shall adopt the definition of Immanuel Kant (1724–1804) in his essay 'Answer to the Question: What is Enlightenment?' Enlightenment is release from self-inflicted immaturity, reliance upon external authorities, and from the reluctance to use one's own understanding. The motto of enlightenment is *Sapere aude!* ('Dare to be wise') (*Berlinische Monatsschrift*, 1784, 4/12 – Kant 1959: 85). *Sapere aude*, which was taken from Horace, *Epistles* 1.2.40, had previously been adopted by the Gesellschaft der Wahrheitsfreunden (Society of the Friends of Truth, 1736), whose members pledged themselves not to accept or reject any belief except for 'sufficient reason.'

The following survey will focus on the application of this outlook to biblical interpretation in the period terminating with the death of Kant. It is impossible to follow the modern procedure of dividing the field into separate disciplines. Many protagonists ranged widely over the Bible as a whole. New approaches were advanced not only by biblical scholars, but also by philosophers and scientists who were conscious of how the Bible impinged on worldviews. Enlightened interpretation was characterized by the shift from treating the Bible as inspired revelation to examining it as a collection of historical documents, sometimes resulting in thoroughly secular reinterpretations.

The emergence of Enlightened views of the Bible may be traced to Pyrrhonism and the Cartesian response with its appeal to reason and clear and distinct ideas. Pyrrhonism was a revival of ancient skepticism, so called after Pyrrho whose views were discussed by Sextus Empiricus in his *Outlines of Pyrrhonism*. Sixteenth-century Pyrrhonists took from him a skepticism about the reliability of the senses and the ability of reason to discover truth. In the hands of Catholic apologists like Gentian Henet, Jean Gonter, and François Véron (who taught philosophy and theology at the Jesuit College de la Flèche while Descartes was a student), the 'New Pyrrhonism' became an 'engine of war' forged for the destruction of Calvinism. They ridiculed the subjectivity of Calvinistic appeal to the inner witness of the Holy Spirit as proof of the divine authorship of scripture (Calvin, *Institutes* 1.7.4). Protestant apologists like David-Renaud Bouillier, Jean La Placette, and the Anglican convert from Catholicism William Chillingworth (1602–1644) responded in kind. The claim of the Catholic Church to be the guardian of theological truth was itself vulnerable since it rested on the church's own word. The Protestant thesis was summed up in the words of Chillingworth's *The Religion of the Protestants: A Safe Way to Salvation*, 'The BIBLE, I say, the BIBLE only, is the religion of Protestants!' (Chillingworth, *The Religion of the Protestants*, 1638: 6, 56). The Catholic counterquestion had already been posed by Véron, 'How do you know, gentlemen, that the books of the Old and New Testament are Holy Scripture?' (*La Victorieuse Méthode pour combattre tous les Ministères: Par la seule Bible*, 1621: 45–46).

The influence on biblical interpretation of René Descartes (1596–1650) was substantial but indirect. So-called Cartesian doubt played the Pyrrhonists at their own game. Doubt could not be pushed to the extreme of doubting that one was doubting. Hence, the conclusion: 'I am thinking, therefore I exist' (Descartes 1985: 127). Descartes' *Discours de la Méthode, pour bien conduire la raison, and chercher la vérité dans les sciences* (1637) was primarily concerned with scientific thinking. Descartes adopted four rules (Descartes 1985: 120). The first was never to accept anything as true without 'evident knowledge of its truth.' The second was to divide the difficulties into as many parts as possible in order to resolve them. The third was to move from the simplest and most easily known to the more complex. The fourth was to make such a comprehensive review so that one could be sure that nothing had been left out. Descartes' philosophy was a web of rational inferences undergirding the Catholic faith and the natural sciences. In the hands of others it introduced the ideal of rationality in religion and biblical interpretation that characterized the Enlightenment.

The beginnings of critical interpretation are linked with the denial of Mosaic authorship of the Pentateuch, denial of the authenticity of the text of the Bible, and the questioning of the Bible's account of human history (Popkin 1982: 64). In *Prae-Adamatae* (1655; ET *Men before Adam*, 1656) the eccentric millenarist Isaac La Peyrère (1596–1676) argued that Adam was not the first man. He detected textual problems in the Pentateuch, and denied Mosaic authorship. Nevertheless, the parts of scripture necessary to salvation were not liable to misunderstanding. La Peyrère influenced Thomas Hobbes (1588–1679) and Baruch (or to use the Latinized form of his name, Benedictus) de Spinoza (1632–1677), both of whom introduced critical discussions of scripture into their political treatises.

Hobbes' *Leviathan or the Matter Form and Power of a Commonwealth* (1651) presented a theory of government based on natural law and social contract, following the abolition of the British monarchy. Part 3 discussed a 'Christian Commonwealth.' Hobbes accepted scripture as rules for Christian life, but questioned the authorship of several books (ch. 33). Moses could not have written about his own death (Deut. 34). 'But though Moses did not compile those books entirely, and in the form we have them; yet he wrote all that which he is said to have written.' The books of Joshua, Judges, Samuel, Kings, and Chronicles were all written long after the events that they describe. Some of the Psalms were composed by David, and some of the Proverbs by Solomon, but both books contain later compositions. In light of the warnings of Deuteronomy 13

against being led astray by miracles, Hobbes rejected claims to authority based only on them (ch. 32). In a manner anticipating Hume, he professed not to know of any reported miracle:

that a man endued with but a mediocrity of reason would think supernatural. A private man has always the liberty, because thought is free, to believe or not believe in his heart those acts that have been given out for miracles.... But when it comes to confession of that faith, the private reason must submit to the public; that is to say, to God's lieutenant. (ch. 37)

The Quaker Samuel Fisher (1605–1665) was even more outspoken. *The Rustick's Alarm to the Rabbies* (1660) denied that faith should be based on scripture. Fisher distinguished the eternal Word of God from scripture, the physical copy of this Word, which was written by human beings in specific circumstances. Like Hobbes, he denied that Moses had written the entire Pentateuch. Since scripture does not treat the question of canonicity, Fisher concluded that it was the work of rabbis and church leaders.

Holland was the home of the strict Calvinism canonized by the Synod of Dort (1618–1619). It was also a refuge for many seeking religious and political toleration, including Descartes and the parents of Spinoza who had emigrated from Portugal. Spinoza's reading of Maimonides, Descartes, Hobbes, and La Peyrère fostered an unorthodoxy which led to expulsion from the synagogue (1656). The action served the dual purpose of demonstrating the commitment of the Jewish authorities to the Hebrew Bible and of dissociating their community from the heretic. Spinoza eventually settled in The Hague where he earned his living by grinding lenses. In 1663 he published *Renati Descartes Principiorum Philosophiae, Pars I et II*. It was followed by the anonymous *Tractatus Theologico-Politicus* (1670), which outlined the role of biblical criticism in the political order. His *Ethics* written in the form of geometrical theorems, appeared posthumously (1677). Here he presented his concept of 'God or nature' (*dues sive natura*) in which 'God is the immanent, not the transitive, cause of all things' (Spinoza 1985, 1: 426).

The *Tractatus* (1989: 142–43) contains four rules comparable with those of Descartes. The 'universal rule for the interpretation of Scripture' is 'to ascribe no teaching to Scripture that is not clearly established from studying it closely.' The second was to study 'the nature and properties of the language in which the Bible was written.' The third was to order the pronouncements made in each book so as to have to hand all the texts that treat of the same subject, noting all that are 'ambiguous or obscure, or that appear to contradict one another.' The fourth was to set forth the relevant life, character, and pursuits of the author of every book, its context, and the language in which it was written. The methods used to study nature should also apply to scripture, so as to discover universal principles. What God is in himself must be derived from philosophy. With regard to the miracles, Spinoza insisted that, if anything in scripture could be conclusively proved 'to contravene the laws of Nature,' it must be the work of 'sacrilegious men' (Spinoza 1989: 134).

The major pioneer of the historical-critical method was Richard Simon (1638–1712) who from 1662 until his expulsion on account of unorthodoxy in 1678 was a member of the French Oratory. Simon's *Histoire critique du Vieux Testament* (1678) was suppressed, and few copies of the original survived. However, imperfect French editions were produced in Holland between 1680 and 1685. An English translation, made by 'a Person of Quality,' with the title *A Critical History of the Old Testament*, was published in London in 1682. Simon sought to assimilate a historical understanding of scripture with a Catholic view of tradition. His opening words declared that, 'No one can doubt but that the truths contained in the Holy Scripture are infallible and of Divine Authority; since they proceed immediately from God, who has made use of the ministry of Men to be his Interpreters' (Simon 1678: 1.1). This 'ministry' must be understood through critical study. The scriptures that we now have are copies of lost originals, which were abridged and expanded in the course of transmission. Simon observed that, 'The Catholicks, who are perswaded their Religion depends not onely on the Text of Scripture, but likewise on the Tradition of the Church, are not at all scandaliz'd, to see that the misfortune of Time and the negligence of Transcribers have wrought changes in the holy Scriptures as well as in prophane Authours' (Simon 1678: 1.1).

Simon divided his work into three books, Book 1 gave an account of the text from Moses onwards. The centerpiece was ch. 5: 'Proof of the additions and other changes which have been made in Scripture, particularly in the Pentateuch. Moses cannot be the Authour of the Books which are attributed to him. Several Examples.' Moses was compared with Homer. The Pentateuch was 'a collection' of accounts, which like other parts of scripture repeated the same narrative in different versions. Contradictions were exemplified by the conflicting accounts of the creation of Adam and Eve in Genesis 1 and 2. The Deuteronomic picture of Moses reading the entire Torah to the people of Israel was highly improbable. Whereas Spinoza assigned the completed Pentateuch to the time of Ezra, Simon offered a nuanced account of the continuous reworking of tradition by 'Scribes.' Book 2 reviewed translations of scripture from the LXX to modern versions. Book 3 discussed different methods of translation, ending with an annotated catalogue. The Amsterdam reprint (1685) contains 546 pages of text, augmented by 121 pages of responses to critics.

Simon's works include *Critical Enquiries into the Various Editions of the Bible* (ET 1684) with an appended reply to Vossius on the Sibylline Oracles. In his later career Simon turned to study of the text of the New Testament. His *Histoire critique du Nouveau Testament* (1689) was followed by *Nouvelles observations sur le texte et les versions du Nouveau Testament* (Paris 1695). The latter was published under the auspices of the Archbishop of Paris. Simon's avoidance of speculation, his critique of Protestant versions, and his attack on the Jansenist, Antoine Arnauld, doubtless contributed to his rehabilitation. His work on the New Testament was introduced into German scholarship by J.S. Semler (*Kritische Schriften über das Neue Testament*, 3 Vols., 1776–1780).

2 Arianism, Socinianism, and Sir Isaac Newton

Whereas Cartesianism led to reassessment of the historical character of scripture, the revival of Arianism and Socinianism questioned the orthodox understanding of the person of Christ and the Trinity. Arius, who denied the deity of Jesus, was condemned by the Council of Nicea (325) with its affirmation that the Son was *homoousios* ('of one substance') with the Father. Socinianism was a form of Unitarianism derived from the teaching of Lelio Sozini (1525–1562) and his nephew Fausto Sozzini (1539–1604). The 1690s saw in England an outburst of tracts renewing debate over the Trinity. Among the protagonists was William Whiston (1667–1752) who succeeded Sir Isaac Newton as Lucasian Professor of Mathematics at Cambridge. His Arianizing views led to his expulsion from the university in 1710. Whiston is best remembered for his translation of Josephus (1737). Other works include *A New Theory of the Earth, from its Original to the Consummation of All Things* (1696), *Accomplishment of Scripture Prophecies* (1708), which argued that prophecies have only one meaning, *Primitive Christianity Revived* (4 Vols., 1711), and *The Life of Samuel Clarke* (1730).

Samuel Clarke (1673–1729) was a notable London preacher and defender of Newtonian natural philosophy. His *Scripture-Doctrine of the Trinity* (1712) embroiled him in life-long controversy. Although accused of Arianism, Clarke was closer to the Alexandrian tradition from Origen, through Eusebius, to the Cappadocian Fathers. His fifty-five propositions focused on the supremacy of the Father and the subordination of the Son, maintaining that in patristic thought the Son was understood to be of the 'same kind of substance' as the Father. Although Clarke was condemned by the Lower House of Convocation of the Church of England, the House of Bishops imposed no formal retraction on condition of Clarke's promise to write no further on the subject.

The greatest scientist of the age, Sir Isaac Newton (1642–1727), was deeply religious. His *Philosophiae Naturalis Principia Mathematica* (1687) contained an argument for the existence of a transcendent, omnipotent, and perfect supreme being, based on the order of the universe. Newton also wrote extensively about the Bible, though the only work he prepared for publication was *The Chronology of the Ancient Kingdoms Amended* (1728). His *Observations upon the Prophecies of Daniel, and the Apocalypse of St. John* (1733) was published by his nephew. Extracts from Newton's theological manuscripts, estimated at one million words (now housed chiefly in Cambridge, Wellesley, MA, and Jerusalem), have been partially published in modern times. Newton had a high regard for the Bible and was a conforming churchman, but he privately questioned the doctrine of the Trinity. His papers include *Queries regarding the Word Homoousios* and *Paradoxical Questions concerning the Morals and Actions of Athanasius and his Followers*. Treatises on revelation and the day of judgment (Manuel 1974: 107–36) illustrate his method of interpretation and vision of the millennium. Newton urged literal interpretation, keeping close to the uniform sense of words, and attention to language and context. He believed that the restitution of all things is found in all the prophets, and that after the day of judgment the earth would continue to be inhabited by mortals for ever.

3 English Deism

Dr. Samuel Johnson's *Dictionary of the English Language* (1755) defined Deism as 'the opinion of those that only acknowledge one God, without the reception of any revealed religion.' Its origins have been traced to Uriel da Costa, who is seen as a precursor of Spinoza. The 'father of English Deism' was Lord Edward Herbert of Cherbury (1583–1648), who served as English ambassador in Paris where he got to know Pyrrhonists and Cartesians. His *De Veritate, Prout distinguitur a Revelatione, a Verisimnili, a Possibili, et a Falso* (1624) was a reply to Pyrrhonism and an alternative to Protestantism and Catholicism. Religion was based on innate principles, independent of revelation. An enlarged edition (1645) criticized bibliolatry, and urged that religion should be investigated historically.

Lord Herbert's posthumous disciple, Charles Blount (1654–1693), is credited with being the author of *Miracles No Violations of the Laws of Nature* (1693), which paraphrased Spinoza's argument in the *Tractatus*. In 1680 he published *The First Two Books of Philostratus Concerning the Life of Apollonius of Tyana*. Henceforth Apollonius figured continuously in discussions of the historical Jesus. As a miracle-working holy man of the first century he appears as a pagan rival to Jesus. Blount's *The Oracles of Reason* (1693) drew on Thomas Burnet's *Archaeologiae Philosophicae* (1693), which advocated a nonliteral interpretation, provoking the satire (*DNB* 3: 409):

That all the books of Moses Were nothing but supposes . . .

That as for Father Adam and Mrs. Eve, his Madame, And what the devil spoke, Sir,

'Twas nothing but a joke, Sir, And well-invented flam.

In 1694 the Licensing Act was allowed to lapse. Although the blasphemy laws remained in force, the event heralded a new era of free speech. In Germany it took another 100 years before such free expression was permitted. One of the first to avail himself of it was John Toland (1670–1722) in *Christianity Not Mysterious, Showing that there is Nothing in the Gospel Contrary to Reason, nor above it; And that No Christian Doctrine can properly be Call'd a Mystery* (1696). Toland had absorbed the teaching of Hobbes, Locke, and a version of Cartesianism acquired in Holland from Locke's friend, Jean Le Clerc. Applying the criterion of clear and distinct ideas to religion, he ascribed Christian mysteries to paganism and priestcraft. The real Jesus was a preacher of simple, moral religion. The book provoked fifty replies, repudiation by Locke, and public condemnation in England and Ireland.

While Toland drifted toward pantheism, Locke's friend Anthony Collins (1676–1729) was preparing an attack on the twin foundations of apologetics: prophecy and miracles. The attack on prophecy was launched in his *Discourse on the Grounds and Reason of the Christian Religion* (1724) and its sequel *The theme of Literal Prophecy Consider'd* (1727). Collins argued that prophecies like Isaiah 7:14 (cf. Matt. 1:23) and Hosea 11:1 (cf. Matt. 2:15) were not predictions of Jesus as the Messiah. They were fulfilled within the lifetime of the prophets who made them, and were useless as legitimation of supernatural truth claims. Christianity was based on allegory derived from rabbinic methods of interpretation.

It fell to the erratic Cambridge scholar, Thomas Woolston (1670–1731), to complete Collins' plan. He did so in six *Discourses on the Miracles of Saviour* (1727–1729), each mockingly dedicated to an Anglican bishop. Miracles were allegories comparable with those detected in prophecy by Collins. Woolston compared the star of Bethlehem to a will-o'-the-wisp. If Apollonius of Tyana had turned water into wine, people would have reproached his memory. If the healings attributed to Jesus had occurred, there must have been natural causes. The resurrection of Jesus was the most barefaced imposture ever imposed on the world. Woolston was prosecuted for blasphemy, and sentenced to a year's imprisonment and a fine of £100.

The Woolston case prompted Bishop Thomas Sherlock (1678–1761), who had earlier delivered six discourses on *The Use and Intent of Prophecy* (1728), to compose a mock trial of the evangelists. *The Tryal of the Witnesses of the Resurrection* (1729) was a piece of popular apologetics in which the disciples were accused in court of bearing false witness. After listening to arguments about their honesty, intelligence, veracity, and motivation, and the feasibility of events which contradicted ordinary experience, the jury duly acquitted the disciples.

The most learned of the Deists was Matthew Tindal (1655–1733), a fellow of All Souls College, Oxford. In 1730 he published a work that came to be regarded as 'the Deists' Bible,' *Christianity as Old as the Creation: Or, the Gospel, a Republication of the Religion of Nature.* Tindal, who claimed to be a Christian Deist, took his title from one of Sherlock's sermons. He thought that nothing could be proved from miracles, and noted the dubious morals of certain Old Testament heroes. True Christianity consists of natural religion, known to all by reason, and the Gospels merely republished the religion of nature. Tindal provoked over 150 replies, including Joseph Butler's *The Analogy of Religion Natural and Revealed to the Constitution and Course of Nature* (1736). Later Deists included Thomas Chubb (1679–1746) and Peter Annet (1693–1769). Chubb continued the attack on miracles, and wrote on 'the true Gospel of Jesus Christ.' Annet composed examinations of the resurrection and of the character of St. Paul.

4 Prophecy, miracles, and truth claims

The concept of revelation played a significant part in the philosophy of John Locke (1632–1704), whose *Essay Concerning Human Understanding* (1690) was completed in exile in Holland, where he enjoyed the company of Arminian theologians. To Locke,

Reason is natural *revelation* whereby the Father of light, the Fountain of all knowledge, communicates to mankind that portion of truth which he has laid within reach of the natural faculties. *Revelation* is natural *reason* enlarged by a new set of discoveries communicated by God immediately, which *reason* vouches the truth of, by the testimony and proofs it gives that they come from God. (*Essay* 4.19.4)

Fulfilled prophecy and miracles supply these proofs. The argument was developed in *The Reasonableness of Christianity* (1695) and is summed up in *A Discourse of Miracles* (1706). '[W]here the miracle is admitted, the doctrine cannot be rejected; it comes with the assurance of a divine attestation to him that allows the miracle, and he cannot question its truth' (1958: 82). The argument was a restatement of the foundationalist argument, which sought to legitimate a belief system by appeal to indubitable facts or truths. Locke's work reinforced the tendency to treat prophecy essentially as supernaturally guided prediction and reduce miracle stories to legitimating acts. In this regard it is characteristic of the debates in the Deistic controversy. But Locke's *Paraphase and Notes on the Epistles of St. Paul* (1705–1707) evidences a broader interest in scripture.

David Hume (1711–1776) advocated a '*mitigated* scepticism' which derived from Pyrrhonism (*Enquiry Concerning Human Understanding*, 1748, 1758, section 12: 129–30). His celebrated discussion of miracles in section

10 of his *Enquiry* dates from the height of the Deist controversy. Hume formulated the argument in the 1730s at La Flèche, where he enjoyed the company of the Jesuit fathers and the use of their ample library. The core of the argument lay in the contention that, 'A miracle is a violation of the laws of nature; and as a firm and unalterable experience has established these laws, the proof against a miracle, from the very nature of the fact, is as entire as any argument from experience can be imagined' (*Enquiry* 10.90). Hume went on to identify four factors which rendered testimony to miracles dubious: lack of credible witness, the human tendency to exaggerate, obscurity of location, and the claim that the miracles of rival religions cancel each other out. While not openly discussing biblical miracles, the entire argument was directed at their value in legitimating truth claims and belief systems. It is now recognized that most of what Hume was saying had already been said by the Deists. The crucial factor here and in subsequent critical history was the concept of 'analogy' and its role in interpreting reported events in the light of their analogy with our worldview and experience (*Enquiry* 10.89). By assigning prophecy and miracles to the function of legitimation (*Enquiry* 10.101), the entire debate lost sight of the narratives themselves.

5 The Fragments controversy and the quest of the historical Jesus

Since publication in 1906 of Albert Schweitzer's *Quest of the Historical Jesus* it has been customary to date the quest of the historical Jesus from Herman Samuel Reimarus (1694–1768). Reimarus was a prominent figure in Enlightened circles in Hamburg, but few knew of his private *Apologie oder Schutzsschrift für die vernünftigen Vereherer Gottes.* The full text was first published in 1972. But extracts were published by the dramatist, Gotthold Ephraïm Lessing (1729–1781), as *Fragments* found by Lessing in his capacity as librarian to the Duke of Brunswick at Wolfenbüttel. He gave them the title *Fragmente eines Ungenannten* (Fragments of an Unnamed [Author]). To throw witch-hunters off the scent he named the Deist, Johann Lorenz Schmidt who had spent the last two years of his life in Wolfenbüttel, as the putative author. Between 1774 and 1778 (when exemption from censorship was revoked) Lessing published seven *Fragments.* The first *Fragment* 'On Toleration of the Deists' presented Jesus as a teacher of rational, practical religion, whose views had been distorted by a religion full of mysteries. The second and third pleaded the case for rational religion. The next two launched a bitter attack on the Old Testament: 'The Crossing of the Israelites through the Red Sea' and 'That the Books of the Old Testament were not Written to Reveal a Religion.' The sixth *Fragment* 'On the Resurrection Story' saw inconsistencies in the Gospel narratives, which undermined their credibility.

Amid the hue and cry provoked by the *Fragments*, Lessing launched the notorious seventh *Fragment* 'On the Intention of Jesus and His Disciples.' Reimarus noted that Jesus left no personal record of his teaching. Nevertheless, the original intent of his call to 'Repent and believe the gospel' (Mark 1:15) could be recovered. In contrast to the Sadducees, Jesus preached personal immortality. In contrast to the legalism of the Pharisees, Jesus strove for the moral elevation of humankind. Jesus had no thoughts of founding a new religion or claiming personal deity. His intention was to purify Judaism. To the Jewish mind, the call to repentance was linked with preparation for an earthly theocratic kingdom to be inaugurated by a messiah.

There were two fatal turning points in Jesus' career. The first came when he embraced political messiahship, the second when he decided to force through his programme at all costs. Unfortunately he miscalculated popular support. The disturbance he created in the temple confirmed the authorities in their decision to liquidate him. Jesus died a broken man, disillusioned with the God who had forsaken him (Matt. 27:46). The Christian religion could well have died at birth but for the imagination and duplicity of the disciples. When it became clear that Jesus' execution was not to be followed by general persecution, they conceived two masterstrokes. The first was to put out the story that Jesus had been raised from the dead. The second was the proclamation that Jesus would return to complete the work of establishing the messianic kingdom. Both were fraudulent, but together they constitute the foundation of Christianity.

The *Fragments* unleashed a pamphlet war, giving Lessing the opportunity to air his own views. Among the protagonists was the Lutheran pastor in Hamburg, Johann Melchior Goeze, whom Lessing mercilessly lampooned. 'On the Proof of the Spirit and of Power' (1777) was addressed to another protagonist, J.D. Schumann, who had restated the traditional appeal to miracles and prophecy as proof of the truth of the Christian religion. For Lessing it was axiomatic (as it was for other Enlightened thinkers) that 'accidental truths of history can never become the proof of the necessary truths of reason.' Historical truths, which are based largely on reports and narratives, belong to a different class of truth from metaphysical affirmations such as 'God has a Son who is of the same essence as himself.' Between the two classes of truth is 'the ugly, broad ditch' over which Lessing found it impossible to leap (Lessing 1956: 53–5). On being prohibited from publishing further writings on religion, Lessing turned to his 'former pulpit,' the theater. *Nathan der Weise* (1779) was an allegory set in the time of the crusades with characters modeled on protagonists in the *Fragments* controversy.

Lessing's posthumous publications include what the author himself considered his best theological work. Lessing's *Neue Hypothese über die Evangelisten als blos men-*

schliche Geschichtschreiber berachtet (1778) argued that a single Hebrew or Aramaic source, the Gospel of the Nazarenes, lay behind the canonical Gospels. Each evangelist drew upon it independently. Matthew was the first Gospel, though the apostle was not its author. Mark was not the abbreviator of Matthew but of the original Gospel. Luke likewise drew on this Gospel, but changed the order and improved the style. Whereas Matthew was 'the Gospel of the flesh,' John is 'the Gospel of the Spirit,' written for the Gentile world and is the sole basis for treating Jesus as divine.

The weightiest reply to the *Fragments* in both bulk and prestige came from Johann Salomo Semler (1725–1791), who is widely regarded as the founder of the historical study of the New Testament. In 1752 he became professor of theology at Halle, which under his leadership became a center of critical theology in the eighteenth century. Semler's *Institutio Brevio ad Liberalem Eruditionem Theologicum* (2 Vols., 1765–1766) gave currency to the term 'liberal theology.' His programmatic *Abhandlung von freier Untersuchung des Canon* (4 parts, 1771–1775) drew a distinction between 'Holy Scripture' and 'Word of God.' Scripture was not equally the Word of God, and not every part of it taught moral truths, valid in every age. The Jews had their mythology like other nations. All scripture, including the Gospels, should be seen in the context of its historical development. In all this, Semler was building on foundations laid by others including William Whiston (on whom he had written a dissertation) and Richard Simon. What Semler urged and achieved was a reverent and judicious acceptance of the new critical approach to scripture. It was precisely this that was lacking in the final *Fragment*, which was causing bewilderment among theological students, some of whom were turning to secular vocations.

Semler's *Beantwortung der Fragmente eines Ungenannten insbesonder vom Zweck Jesu und seiner Jünger* (1779, 2nd edn, 1780) examined the Fragmentist's argument passage by passage in the manner of Origen's *Contra Celsum*. On the question of the kingdom Semler showed that in Jesus' teaching it was different from contemporary expectations. On whether Jesus intended to found a new religion, Semler drew on his knowledge of Philo and rabbinics to show that the idea of a spiritual religion superseding current Judaism was not something invented by the apostles. An important part of Semler's strategy was to outflank the Fragmentist by showing that not only did Jesus transcend the Judaism of his day but so did messianic expectation. Semler's *Beantwortung* worked its way through the episodes in the Gospels, offering at each point an alternative to that of the *Fragment*. The use of Hosea 11:1 in Matthew 2:15 and the play on the word 'Nazarene' were to be seen, not as crude attempts to manipulate prophecy, but as examples of Hebrew hermeneutics with its love of riddles and hidden meanings. The inconsistencies detected by the Fragmentist in the resurrection narratives might be fatal to the old doctrine of biblical inspiration, but history did not depend on harmonizing every detail. To Semler, the resurrection of Jesus was 'no mere physical event,' capable of being seen by the human eye. It was 'a supernatural event' whose intrinsic possibility was granted by the Pharisees and many others. In short, Semler argued, the Fragmentist sought to denigrate Christianity and Judaism alike 'in order to establish himself as a Deist.'

Schweitzer's account of Reimarus and Semler gives the impression of Reimarus as the brilliant initiator of the quest who located Jesus in the world of Judaism, and of Semler as the aging scholar fighting a desperate rearguard action. Neither impression is accurate. Semler's answer was a work of high critical scholarship. Reimarus' interest in the world of Judaism extended no further than his interest in reducing Jesus' mission to a messianic political coup. Schweitzer glossed over Reimarus' debt to the English Deists, whose writings were already well known in Germany. It is now known that Reimarus' library contained the works of most English Deists, and study of the full text of his *Apologie* has shown how deeply his work was indebted to them. If anyone can claim credit for initiating the quest of the historical Jesus, it is not Reimarus but the English Deists. Whether they were successful is another matter.

6 German biblical scholarship

The foremost exponent of the traditional interpretation was Johannes Albrecht Bengel (1687–1752), who brought together pietism, the classical tradition, and textual study. His *Gnomon Novi Testamenti* (1742, ET 1857–1858) gave pithy comments on exegesis and text, and found many admirers including John Wesley. His critical apparatus and distinction between textual families mark the beginning of modern textual study. A pioneer of critical approaches was Johann August Ernesti (1707–1781) who taught at Leipzig. Ernesti's *Institutio interpretis Novi Testamenti* (1761) insisted that interpretation must be guided by philological and grammatical considerations.

The term *Neologie* denotes a movement which reached its zenith between 1740 and 1790 and which sought to transcend both orthodoxy and pietism by restating the Christian faith in light of modern thought. Revelation was confirmation of the truths of reason. The Neologians pioneered moderate criticism, maintaining that Jesus accommodated his teaching to the beliefs and understanding of his hearers. The *Allgemeine Deutsche Bibliothek* (1765–1806), to which the Neologians contributed, was probably the single most influential organ of the German Enlightenment. The Neologians included J.F.W. Jerusalem, G. Less, F.V. Reinhard, A.F.W. Sack, and J.J. Spalding. Also sometimes included are J.S. Semler, J.D. Michaelis, J.J. Griesbach, and J.G. von Herder.

The University of Göttingen, founded in 1737, came to the fore in biblical studies through the work of Johann David Michaelis (1717–1791) and Johann Gottfried Eichhorn (1752–1827). In 1750 Michaelis published his *Einleitung in die göttlichen Schriften des Neuen Bundes*. Originally an elaboration of the work of Richard Simon, by the time it reached the fourth edition in two volumes (1788), it had become a comprehensive investigation of the historical questions of the New Testament. In so doing, it inaugurated the science of New Testament introduction. The question of whether the New Testament books were inspired was not as important as whether they were genuine. Michaelis questioned whether Mark and Luke were inspired in the same way as Matthew, and John. He rejected the idea of literary dependence among the evangelists, tracing their common characteristics to common use of earlier Gospels mentioned in Luke 1:1. Michaelis detected an anti-Agnostic polemics in John, and was the first critic to relate the Fourth Gospel to the Gnostic thought-world.

Eichhorn studied under Michaelis and the classical philologist, C.G. Heyne. After teaching Oriental languages at Jena (1775) he returned to Göttingen (1778), where he pioneered Pentateuchal and Gospel criticism. His numerous works include *Einleitung ins Alte Testament* (3 Vols., 1780–1783), *Einleitung in die apokryphischen Bücher des Alten Testaments* (1795), *Einleitung in das Neue Testament* (5 Vols., 1804–1827), and the founding of the influential *Allgemeine Bibliothek der biblischen Literatur* (1787). Eichhorn was among the first to distinguish between the Yahwist and Elohist sources in Genesis, and identify the priestly code in the Torah. He recognized the late composition of Isaiah 40, the still later date of Daniel, and treated Jonah as unhistorical. Eichhorn and his pupil, Johann Philip Gabler (1753–1826), related Heyne's concept of myth to the Old Testament, and was instrumental in acclimatizing the public to the idea of myth in scripture (*Urgeschichte*, 3 Vols., 1790–1795). With regard to the Gospels, Eichhorn posited several sources traceable to a single Aramaic Gospel. His work brought into focus two critical questions. One was that of the original form of Jesus' words, which he sought to solve by his theory of a single source. The other was the agreements of Matthew and Luke which posited a common written source, thus anticipating the idea of Q. By reconstructing 'the Primal Gospel' freed from later accretions, Eichhorn hoped 'to establish the credibility and truth of the gospel story on unshakable foundations.'

In the meantime an alternative approach was developed by Johann Jakob Griesbach (1715–1812). Griesbach had been a student of Semler, and actually lived with him both in his student days and after his return from an extensive European tour, which included study of the New Testament manuscripts housed in Oxford, Cambridge, and the British Museum in London. During this time he probably acquired Henry Owen's *Observations on the Four Gospels, tending chiefly to ascertain the Times of their Publication; and to Illustrate their Form and Manner of their Composition* (1764). Griesbach appears to be deeply indebted to this work, not least for its anticipation of the 'Griesbach hypothesis' about the priority of Matthew. In 1775 Griesbach accepted a call to Jena, where he became a dominant figure. In 1774 he published the first volume of a critical text of the New Testament in the form of a synopsis. In 1776 it appeared as a separate volume with the title *Synopsis Evangeliorum Matthaei, Marci et Lucae*. The significance of the work was far-reaching. Griesbach's critical text based on ancient manuscripts, drawing also on the Church Fathers, signaled the impending overthrow of the Received Text. It also marked the beginning of the end of Gospel harmonies. It showed that none of the evangelists follows an exact chronological order, and provided the necessary tool for the critical study of Gospel relationships.

In his *Commentatio qua Marci evangelium totum e Matthaei et Lucae Commentariis decerptum esse monstratur* (1789, 1790), Griesbach argued that 'Mark when writing his book had in front of his eyes not only Matthew but Luke as well, and that he extracted from them whatever he committed to writing of the deeds, speeches and sayings of the Saviour.' All but twenty-four verses of Mark could be found in Matthew or Luke. It was inconceivable that the apostle Matthew should rely on a writer who had not been present at the events described. The 'Griesbach hypothesis' found widespread acceptance in the first half of the nineteenth century. D.F. Strauss and F.C. Baur combined it with their radical views, which led them to skepticism regarding the historical value of Mark. But gradually it fell into disfavor for various reasons: its association with Strauss and Baur; the growing conviction that the apostle Matthew was not the author of the First Gospel, thus undercutting the motive for asserting Matthean priority; and Karl Lachmann's 'De ordine narrationum evangeliis synopticis' (*Theologische Studien und Kritiken* 8 [1835]: 570–90]), which argued that from the point of view of order Mark was the common factor between Matthew and Luke.

Johann Gottfried von Herder (1744–1803) studied philosophy with Kant, but turned to literature and religion under the influence of J.G. Hamann (1730–1788). Herder's *Fragmente über die neuere deutsche Literatur* (1767) established his reputation as a literary critic. He saw his mission in life as the study of the history of humankind to discover its future path. His enthusiasm for Shakespeare and folk poetry, which he conceived as the unrepressed utterance of creative genius, led to the Sturm und Drang movement in literature. In 1776 amid doubts about his orthodoxy Herder moved to Weimar, the cultural capital of Germany, as court preacher and superintendent of the Lutheran Church. His *Ideen zur Philosophie der Geschichte der Menschheit* (1784–1791) presented an evolutionary history of humankind which viewed progress as the product of reaction to environment. The cosmos was not to be explained by a literal reading of Genesis. The First Book of Moses should be read as poetry and not as a scientific treatise.

Gott. Einige Gespräche (1787, 2nd edn, 1800) contained dialogues on Spinoza's pantheism. Without God, nothing would exist, but God must be found in the natural order. Herder's chief contributions to New Testament criticism were made in the last decade of his life. They are to be found in the second and third collections of his *Christliche Schriften*, which sharply distinguished the approaches of the Synoptic Gospels and John. *Vom Erlöser der Menschen. Nach unsern drei ersten Evangelien* (1796) proposed that before anything could be said about Jesus, the character of the Gospels should be examined. In a manner anticipating Bultmann's form criticism and demythologizing programme, Herder drew attention to the gulf between the secular thought-world and that of the evangelists with its cosmic conflict in which the Son of God from heaven defeats the demons of hell. The unusualness of much in the Gospels rules them out as history. Herder rejected the idea of an *Urevangelium*, or single primitive Gospel, together with theories of literary dependence. The evangelists were not historians or biographers, but writers in the primitive poetic, Jewish tradition.

In *Von Gottes Sohn, der Welt Heiland. Nach Johannes Evangelium, Nebst einer Regel der Zusammenstimmung unsrer Evangelien aus ihrer Entstehung und Ordnung* (1797) Herder set out his views on John and Gospel origins. Christianity did not begin with Gospel writing but with oral proclamation. Over the years certain patterns of *apostolic sagas* became established. The first three Gospels represent a tradition which shared many of the same parables, miracle stories, and narratives. But John focuses on Jesus as God's Son who gives eternal life as savior of the world. The Fourth Gospel is not to be regarded as history, but as a series of 'speaking pictures,' held together by editorial cement. John is concerned with 'the reality of idea' and not the letter of the word.

The title of Kant's principal work on religion, *Die Religion innerhalb der Grenzen der blossen Vernunft* (1793), is translated in the Cambridge edition of Kant's works as *Religion within the Boundaries of Mere Reason*. In this context *Mere* has the meaning 'pure, unmixed, undiluted' (Kant 1996: 53). The work was part of Kant's grand project to reappraise four areas of human life: metaphysics, morality, religion, and anthropology. In line with Kant's earlier *Critiques* it began by proclaiming that morality rests on the conception of free human beings who bind themselves through reason to unconditional laws. Because of this, they need neither the idea of 'another being' above them to help them recognize their duty nor any 'incentive other than the law itself' (Kant 1996: 57). The name of Jesus never appears in the book. On the other hand, in a passage replete with biblical echoes, 'The Personified Idea of the Good Principle' is said to be 'in him from all eternity.' 'God's only-begotten Son' is 'the *Word* (the *Fiat!*)' through which all other things exist, 'the reflection of his glory.' 'In him God loved the world' means that 'through the adoption of his dispositions can we hope to become children of God' (Kant 1996: 103–4). Kant reproved K.F. Bahrdt, the author of a fictitious life of Jesus, and the Wolfenbüttel Fragmentist of Jesus for imputing false motives to 'the Master' (Kant 1996: 120). He went on to speak of 'the *wise* teacher' (Kant 1996: 122) and to describe the Christian religion as 'natural religion' (Kant 1996: 179). In all this, Kant was presenting a sophisticated form of Deism, adapted to his philosophy. It was an interpretation of the Bible that matched his definition of Enlightenment.

7 The American Enlightenment

European biblical criticism did not make a major impact in America until the nineteenth century, but European philosophy and Deism made themselves felt in the eighteenth. As a student at Yale, Jonathan Edwards (1703–1758) was enthralled by Locke's *Essay Concerning Human Understanding*. His outlook was also shaped by Puritan Platonism and the Newtonian concept of space as the divine sensorium. Edwards' notebook on *Images or Shadows of Divine Things* presents nature as a symbol of God. The universe was the revelation of the divine to created minds. Combining high Calvinism with current philosophy, Edwards developed a panentheistic form of divine determinism. In *Freedom of the Will* (1754) he countered Arminianism and Deism by claiming that 'God orders all events, and the volitions of moral agents amongst others, by such a decisive disposal, that the events are infallibly connected with his disposal' (Edwards 1957–2000, 1:134).

Edwards' nearly 1,200 extant sermons follow a three-fold pattern discussing text, doctrine, and application. In preparation Edwards made extensive notes, including four volumes of *Notes on Scripture*, and extensive *Miscellanies*, comments written on pages inserted into a Bible known as *The Blank Bible*. In two unfinished projects, *A History of the Work of Redemption* and a *Harmony of the Old and New Testament*, Edwards attempted an overview of world history from the perspective of scripture. His worldview combined Enlightened philosophy with precritical biblical interpretation.

Deism exerted a profound influence on the Founding Fathers and other lesser figures who helped to create the United States. Etlian Allen's *Reason the Only Oracle of Man, Or a Compenduous System of Natural Religion* (1784) ridiculed the Bible and blasted institutional Christianity. In *The Age of Reason: Being an Investigation of True and Fabulous Theology* (1794–1795) Thomas Paine depicted the Bible and the church as agents of injustice and repression. Thomas Jefferson (1743–1826) compiled for private use a volume which came to be known as *The Jefferson Bible*. He called it *The Life and Morals of Jesus of Nazareth Extracted textually from the Gospels in Greek, Latin, French & English*. It was literally a scissors-and-paste compilation, consisting of passages from the Gospels arranged in the form of a harmony, which eliminated the supernatural. Jefferson did not hesitate to cut verses in half in order to achieve this result. He included birth narratives, but omitted all reference to the Holy Spirit. The temptation was omitted, as were exorcisms and miracles. The work concludes with the burial of Jesus. A similar compilation, *The Philosophy of Jesus of Nazareth*, was envisaged 'for the use of Indians, unembarrassed with matters of fact or faith beyond the level of their comprehensions.' Jefferson's Jesus is the American version of the Deists' Jesus.

References and further reading

Allison, Henry E. (1966) *Lessing and the Enlightenment: His Philosophy of Religion and its Relation to Eighteenth-Century Thought*, Ann Arbor: University of Michigan Press.

Altmann, Alexander (1973) *Moses Mendelssohn: A Biographical Study*, London: Routledge.

Auvray, Paul (1974) *Richard Simon (1638–1712), Étude bio-bibliographique avec des textes inédits*, Paris: Presses Universitaires de France.

Baird, William (1992) *History of New Testament Research*, 1, *From Deism to Tübingen*, Minneapolis: Fortress Press.

Bradley, James E. and Dale K. van Kley (eds.) (2001) *Religion and Politics in Enlightenment Europe*, Notre Dame, IN: University of Notre Dame Press.

Brown, Colin (1984) *Miracles and the Critical Mind*, Grand Rapids: Eerdmans.

—— (1985) *Jesus in European Protestant Thought, 1778–1860*, Studies in Historical Theology 1, Durham, NC: The Labyrinth Press.

Burns, R.M. (1981) *The Great Debate on Miracles: From Joseph Glanvill to David Hume*, Lewisburg: Bucknell University Press/London and Toronto: Associated University Presses.

Descartes, René (1985) *The Philosophical Writings of Descartes*, 1, trans. John Cottingham, Robert Stoothoff, and Dugald Murdoch, Cambridge: Cambridge University Press.

Edwards, Jonathan (1957–2000) *The Works of Jonathan Edwards*, 18 Vols., New Haven and London: Yale University Press.

Force, James E. and Richard H. Popkin (eds.) (1994) *The Books of Nature and Scripture: Recent Essays on Natural Philosophy, Theology, and Biblical Criticism in the Netherlands of Spinoza's Time and the British Isles of Newton's Time*, International Archives of the History of Ideas 139, Dordrecht, Boston and London: Kluwer Academic Publishers.

Frei, Hans W. (1974) *The Eclipse of Biblical Narrative: A Study of Eighteenth and Nineteenth Century Hermeneutics*, New Haven and London: Yale University Press.

Gay, Peter (1968) *Deism: An Anthology*, Princeton: Van Nostand.

Greenslade, S.L. (ed.) (1963) *The Cambridge History of the Bible*, 3, *The West from the Reformation to the Present Day*, Cambridge: Cambridge University Press.

Hartlich, Christian and Walter Sachs (1952) *Der Ursprung des Mythosbegriffes in der Modernen Bibelwissenschaft*, Shriften der Studiengemeinschaft der Evangelischen Akademien 2, Tübingen: Mohr Siebeck.

Herrick, James A. (1997) *The Radical Rhetoric of the English Deists: The Discourse of Skepticism, 1680–1750*, Columbus, SC: University of South Carolina Press.

Hornig, Gottfried (1961) *Die Anfange der historisch-kritischen Theologie. Johann Salmo Semlers Schriftverständnis und seine Stellung zu Luther*, Göttingen: Vandenhoeck & Ruprecht.

Hume, David (1975) *Enquiries Concerning Human Understanding and Concerning the Principles of Morals*, L.A. Selby-Bigge (ed.), revised by Peter H. Nidditch, Oxford: Clarendon.

Jefferson, Thomas (1983) *Jefferson's Extracts from the Gospels: 'The Philosophy of Jesus' and 'The Life and Morals of Jesus,'* Dickinson W. Adams (ed.), The Papers of Thomas Jefferson, Second Series, Princeton: Princeton University Press.

Joachim-Jungius Gesellschaft der Wissenchaften (1972) *Hermann Samuel Reimarus (1694–1768). Ein 'bekannter Unbekannter' der Aufklärung im Hamburg. Vorträge der Tagung der Joachim-Jungius Gesellschaft der Wissenschaften in Hamburg am 12. und 13. Oktober 1972*, Göttingen: Vandenhoeck & Ruprecht.

Kant, Immanuel (1959) *Foundations of the Metaphysics of Morals and What is Enlightenment?* trans. Lewis White Beck, Indianapolis, New York: Bobbs-Merrill.

—— (1996) *Religion and Rational Theology*, trans. Allen W. Wood and George di Giovanni, The Cambridge Edition of the Works of Immanuel Kant 4, Cambridge: Cambridge University Press.

Kraus, Hans-Joachim (1982) *Geschichte der historisch-kritischen Erforschung des Alten Testaments*, Neukirchen-Vluyn: Neukirchener Verlag, 3rd edn.

Kümmel, Werner Georg (1972) *The New Testament: The History of the Investigation of its Problems*, trans. S. MacLean Gilmour and Howard Clark Kee, Nashville: Abingdon Press.

Lambe, Patrick J. (1985) 'Biblical Criticism and Censorship in Ancien Régime France: The Case of Richard Simon,' *Harvard Theological Review* 78: 149–77.

Lessing, Gotthold Ephraïm (1956) *Lessing's Theological Writings*, Henry Chadwick (trans. and ed.), London: A.&C. Black.

Locke, John (1958) *The Reasonableness of Christianity with a Discourse of Miracles and part of A Third Letter Concerning Toleration*, I.T. Ramsey (ed.), London: A.&C. Black.

—— (1975) *An Essay Concerning Human Understanding*, A.S. Pringle-Pattison (ed.), revised by Peter H. Nidditch, Oxford: Clarendon.

McKane, William (1989) *Selected Christian Hebraists*, Cambridge: Cambridge University Press.

McKim, Donald K. (ed.) (1998) *Handbook of Major Biblical Interpreters*, Downers Grove: IVP.

Manuel, Frank E. (1974) *The Religion of Isaac Newton*, The Freemantle Lectures 1973, Oxford: Clarendon.

Moeller, Bernd (ed.) (1987) *Theologie in Göttingen. Eine Vorlesungsreihe*, Göttingen: Vandenhoeck & Ruprecht.

Newton, Sir Isaac (1950) *Theological Manuscripts*, H. McLachlan (ed.), Liverpool: University of Liverpool Press.

Orr, Robert R. (1967) *Reason and Authority: The Thought of William Chillingworth*, Oxford: Clarendon.

Pfizenmaier, Thomas C. (1997a) *The Trinitarian Theology of Dr. Samuel Clarke (1675–1729): Context, Sources, Controversy*, Leiden: Brill.

—— (1997b) 'Was Isaac Newton an Arian?' *Journal of the History of Ideas* 58: 57–80.

Pons, Georges (1964) *Gotthold Ephraïm Lessing et le Christianisme*, Paris: Didier.

Popkin, Richard H. (1979) *The History of Scepticism from Erasmus to Spinoza*, Berkeley: University of California Press.

—— (1980) *The High Road to Pyrrhonism*, Richard A. Watson and James E. Force (eds.), Indianapolis: Hackett Publishing Company.

—— (1982) 'Cartesianism and Biblical Criticism,' pp. 61–81 in *Problems of Cartesianism*, McGill-Queen's Studies in the History of Ideas 1, Thomas M. Lennon, John M. Nicholas, and John W. Davies (eds.), Montreal: McGill-Queen's University Press.

—— (ed.) (1988) *Millenarianism and Messianism in English Literature and Thought, 1650–1800*, Clark Library Lectures 1981–1982, Leiden: Brill.

—— and Arjo Vanderjagt (eds.) (1993) *Scepticism and Irreligion in the Seventeenth and Eighteenth Centuries*, Brill's Studies in Intellectual History 37, Leiden: Brill.

Porter, Roy (2000) *The Creation of the Modern World: The Untold Story of the British Enlightenment*, New York: W.W. Norton.

Redwood, John (1976) *Reason, Ridicule and Religion: the Age of Enlightenment in England, 1669–1750*, Cambridge: Harvard University Press.

Reimarus, Hermann Samuel (1970a) *The Goal of Jesus and His Disciples*, trans. G.W. Buchanan, Leiden: Brill.

—— (1970b) *Reimarus: Fragments*, Charles H. Talbert (ed.), trans. R.S. Fraser, Philadelphia: Fortress Press.

—— (1972) *Apologie oder Schutzschrift für die vernünftigen Verherer Gottes. Im Auftrag der Joachim Jungius-Gesellschaft der Wissenschaften Hamburg herausgegeben von Gerhard Alexander*, Frankfurt: Suhrkamp Verlag.

Reventlow, Henning Graf (1984) *The Authority of the Bible in the Modern World*, trans. John Bowden, Philadelphia: Fortress Press.

Scholder, Klaus (1966) *Urspünge und Probleme der*

Bibelkritik im 17. Jahrhundert. Ein Beitrag zur Entstehung der historisch-kritischen Theologie, München: Chr. Kaiser Verlag.

Schweitzer, Albert (1968) *The Quest of the Historical Jesus: A Critical Study of Its Progress from Reimarus to Wrede*, trans. W. Montgomery, reprint with introduction by James M. Robinson, New York: Macmillan.

—— (2001) *The Quest of the Historical Jesus: The First Complete Edition*, John Bowden (ed.), Minneapolis: Fortress Press.

Semler, Johann Salomo (1967) *Abhandlung von freier Untersuchungen des Canon*, Texten zur Kirchen – und Theologiegeschichte 5, Gütersloh: Gütersloher Verlagshaus Gerd Mohn.

Spinoza, Baruch (1985) *The Collected Works of Spinoza*, Edwin Curley (ed. and trans.), Princeton: Princeton University Press.

—— (1989) *Tractatus Theologico-Politicus*, trans. Samuel Shirley with introduction by Brad S. Gregory, Leiden: Brill (Gebhardt edn. 1925).

Steinmann, Jean (1960) *Richard Simon et les origins de l'exégèse biblique*, Bruges: Desclée de Brouwer.

Stromberg, Roland N. (1974) *Religious Liberalism in Eighteenth-Century England*, Oxford: Oxford University Press.

Tuckett, C.M. (1983) *The Revival of the Griesbach Hypothesis: An Analysis and Appraisal*, SNTSMS 44, Cambridge: Cambridge University Press.

Wagar, Warren (ed.) (1982) *The Secular Mind: Essays Presented to Franklin L. Baumer*, New York: Holmes and Meier.

Weinsheimer, Joel C. (1993) *Eighteenth-Century Hermeneutics: Philosophy of Interpretation in England from Locke to Burke*, New Haven: Yale University Press.

Williams, Matthew C. (2000) 'The Owen Hypothesis: An Essay Showing that it was Henry Owen who first formulated to so-called "Griesbach Hypothesis,"' *The Journal of Higher Criticism* 7(1): 109–25.

COLIN BROWN

ERASMUS (1466/69–1536)

Erasmus of Rotterdam's influence extended beyond the Roman Catholic Church to, in one way or another, virtually all the Protestant Reformers. While he shared the general humanist commitment to the revival of the liberal arts, he was also a skilled and eloquent theologian whose editions, translations, and interpretations of the biblical and Greek and Latin patristic writers fueled the saying, which he vehemently repudiated, that he had laid the egg which Luther hatched.

In his 1503 *Enchiridion Militis Christiani* (*The Christian Soldier's Handbook*), which gained widespread influence after its 1515 reissue, Erasmus insisted on the study of the New Testament and made it the court of appeal for faith and practice, though he did not go so far as the Reformers in advocating the *sola scriptura* principle, maintaining the importance of tradition as defined by the Roman Catholic Church. However, in the preface to his Greek New Testament he called for the New Testament to be translated into the vernacular for the benefit of the unlearned, but also for its translation 'into all human tongues' so that even 'the Turks and the Saracens could read and study them' (*Paraclesis*, LB V 140C).

In 1514, the scholars in Alcalá (Latin *Complutum*) in Spain completed the New Testament of their polyglot Bible (not published until 1520) and this spurred Erasmus and his Basel printer Johann Froben to rush out their own New Testament on March 1, 1516, which bore the marks of haste in its many printing and editorial mistakes. Arguably Erasmus' greatest work is the *Novum instrumentum omne* (from the second edition of 1519 entitled *Novum Testamentum* – further editions following in 1522, 1527, and 1535). While it is best-known for its provision of the Greek text, it was originally and primarily a Latin text (see de Jonge 1984). Erasmus' Greek translation was based on five manuscripts which were ready to hand in Basel, but these twelfth- and thirteenth-century texts represented the inferior Byzantine text tradition and it was this, more than the many errors which he later sought to correct, which was the 'most serious defect' of his Greek text (Aland and Aland 1989: 4).

Erasmus' work includes important preliminary studies which occupy almost as much space as the New Testament itself: the *Paraclesis* ('Exhortation,' an encouragement to read scripture), the *Methodus* ('Method,' which indicates how the New Testament might be most profitably read) and an *Apologia* ('Apology'). The volume concluded with Erasmus' *Annotationes* ('Annotations,' which later became so extensive that they required a second volume).

Rather than providing a thorough verse-by-verse commentary, Erasmus employed annotations as explanatory notes on passages. At first these were mainly philological comments supporting his translation and textual explanations for his divergence from the Vulgate, but successive editions saw these expand and interact with his critics as well as patristic and medieval exegetes. The importance of the annotations is that they were based on the Greek text and that they appealed to the Fathers and resisted the excesses of medieval allegorical interpretation. In his Latin translation, 'The humanist was intent on conveying the original Greek as accurately as possible, but he did not favour literal translations, of which the Vulgate was sometimes guilty, for they often obscured the sense. Intelligibility and clarity were just as important to him' (Payne 1998: 186).

While the *Annotationes* were academic in purpose and nature, the *Paraphrases* (1517–1524, later revised and published in collections) were popular expositions of the New Testament (excluding Revelation) in which he sought to say 'things differently, without saying different things' (CWE Ep 710: 36). He also published commentaries on eleven Psalms between 1515–1533, but these display his discomfort with Hebrew as a language.

It is principally in his *Ratio* (LB V 124E–127D) that Erasmus sets out his hermeneutic for the correct exposition of scripture, employing philological and spiritual methods (see also his *Ecclesiastae* [1535], written for preachers). The former focused on textual, literary, and historical approaches – seeking to discover the original text while paying attention to both the style, language, and context of passages. To this end the biblical languages, rhetoric, grammar, and history were all important disciplines which the exegete needed to master. When such approaches failed to explain difficult texts, he believed that other clearer passages could elucidate their meaning. But as well as the literal sense, Erasmus also believed that scripture has a spiritual sense. Medieval scholars had employed the *Quadriga*, the fourfold sense of scripture – the literal, allegorical (concerned with matters of faith), tropological (moral), and anagogical (eschatological). Influenced by Origen and Jerome, he had already defended allegory in the *Enchiridion* (LB V 28A–30B/CWE 66 68–69), and while he rejected the excesses to which allegory was often used he felt that it was the only way to discover the meanings of many passages whose literal meaning were deemed either absurd, or contrary to the person of Christ or Christian morality. Further, the tropological sense was particularly useful to Erasmus because it fitted with his understanding of Christianity as the philosophy of Christ, which is clearly expounded in the *Enchiridion*, with its emphasis on the *imitatio Christi* and the inwardness of true religion.

Erasmus' legacy reflects his importance. His New Testament was used, for example, by Martin Luther, William Tyndale (*c.* 1494–1536), and Theodore Beza (1519–1605) in their translations. His writings and method were greatly influential to the majority of Protestant reformers and his philological and text-critical work anticipated in many ways their modern counterparts.

References and further readings

Aland, K. and B. Aland (1989) *The Text of the New Testament: An Introduction to the Critical Editions and to the Theory and Practice of Modern Textual Criticism*, Grand Rapids: Eerdmans, 2nd edn.

Augustijn, C. (1991) *Erasmus: His Life, Works, and Influence*, Toronto: University of Toronto Press.

Bentley, J.H. (1976) 'Erasmus' *Annotationes in Novum Testamentum* and the Textual Criticism of the Gospels,' *Archiv für Reformationsgeschichte* 67: 33–53.

Bouyer, L. (1969) 'Erasmus in Relation to the Medieval Biblical Tradition,' in *The Cambridge History of the Bible. Volume 2: The West from the Fathers to the Reformation*, G.W.H. Lampe (ed.), Cambridge: Cambridge University Press.

de Jonge, H.J. (1984) '*Novum Testamentum a nobis versum*,

The Essence of Erasmus' Edition of the New Testament,' *Journal of Theological Studies* 35: 394–413.

DeMolen, R.L. (1973) *Erasmus*, London: Edward Arnold.

Dolan, J.P. (ed.) (1964) *The Essential Erasmus*, New York: New American Library.

—— (1953) 'Desirderius Erasmus,' pp. 281–379, *Advocates of Reform: From Wyclif to Erasmus* in M. Spinka (ed.), Library of Christian Classics 14, London: SCM Press, 1953.

Erasmus, D. (1703–1706) *Desiderii Erasmi Roterodami Opera Omnia*, J. Leclerc (ed.), 10 Vols., Leiden (LB).

—— (1974–) 'Collected Works of Erasmus', Toronto: University of Toronto Press (CWE).

Evans, G.R. (1985) *The Language and Logic of the Bible: The Road to Reformation*, Cambridge: Cambridge University Press.

Hoffmann, M. (1994) *Rhetoric and Theology: The Hermeneutic of Erasmus*, Toronto: University of Toronto Press.

Payne, J.B. (1998) 'Erasmus, Desiderius (*c. 1466–1536*),' pp. 184–90 in *Historical Handbook of Major Biblical Interpreters*, D.K. McKim (ed.), Downers Grove: IVP.

Rabil, Jr. A. (1972) *Erasmus and the New Testament: The Mind of a Christian Humanist*, San Antonio: Trinity University Press.

Rummel, E. (1986) *Erasmus' 'Annotations' on the New Testament*, Toronto: University of Toronto Press.

ANTHONY R. CROSS

ETHICS AND INTERPRETATION

In the last decade of the twentieth century, trends in biblical studies indicated forms of inquiry which attempt to correct overly atomized and historicized approaches to scripture. This led to questions as to how the texts prescribe and historically narrate moral or ethical formation of persons but also how these texts might function for contemporary readers and religious communities. In addition, a number of guiding questions have emerged which point up the contextualized nature of contemporary biblical studies as too often uncritically Euro- and male-centered exegesis. The necessity of highlighting the particularity of modern exegetical method with its 'scientific' claims of normativity and neutrality turns out to be driven by overreaching universal claims of Western culture-based interpretation. Ascertaining the relationship between the Western guilds of biblical study and students from cultural backgrounds different from those guilds begs the question of the applicability of the interpretive interests of those guilds to other cultures, including noncritical, religious readers. The ethics of interpretation itself then becomes closely linked with the connection between interpretation and ethics.

One of the dominant strategies for linking interpretation and ethics is the study of biblical hermeneutics and texts from a character-ethics perspective. Some of the leading representatives of this approach are Robert Brawley, Walter Brueggemann, Jacqueline Lapsley, William Brown, Daniel Carroll, Lois Daly, Ellen F. Davis, Mark Douglas, Carol Newsom, Terence Fretheim, Ann Jervis, Marcia Y. Riggs, and Ronald Smith. In this context moral formation, identity, and perception become a kind of exegetical grid for the approach to scripture along with constant attention to the role of community in shaping moral identity. One of the characteristics of this approach is to outline the historical lineage of the approach according to three periods of modern interpretation, reflecting upon the contribution of J.I.H. McDonald. In the first period, from the nineteenth to early twentieth century, liberal scholarship appears to reflect new Enlightenment methods of biblical criticism and ethics. In the second period this approach already undergoes deconstruction separating the hard historical content of the ancient biblical text from contemporary cultural reflection typical of mid-twentieth-century skepticism and existentialism. In the third period, postmodernist recovery of texts, ancient or modern, resolves the question of access and cultural utilization of text through an ironic universal axiom of unavoidable interpretive bias which has always radically colored the reading and interpretation of the Bible in every period and in every context. Instead of being a single, universalizing interpretive strategy or set of privileged interpretive strategies, this latter approach seeks to recognize the radical multiplicity of interpretive standpoints without privileging any one perspective – indeed, rejecting the whole notion of a privileged perspective.

If a distinction is made between studying scripture for its clues as to ancient instruction and narration of character formation and its contemporary function in this regard, the interpreter of course has not escaped a particular context of contemporary interpretation but is merely asking a set of fresh questions of the text. Nevertheless, fresh questioning of the text has revealed a rich array of contemporary scholarly output. This includes looking at how ancient Israel employed narrative, liturgy, and ritual in the religiosocial-formation of its young. The rehearsal of epic narrative included the placement of the contemporary readers within decisive historical events for the purpose of defining and shaping the character of a new generation of members of the community of YHWH. Through a complex and lived process of contemporary community embodying a narrative by seeing itself as embedded in that narrative the communal sense of obligation to the God of the commandments was conveyed by that narrative.

The narratives of scripture shift a great deal in terms of their dramatis personae and frequently focus upon a singular individual within the community. The formation of character within the community of YHWH is often highly complex and defies simplistic codification and transmission. The personages of Abraham and Sarah,

Rebekkah and Isaac, Joseph, Moses, and David, include ambiguous and conflicting portrayals which betray the struggle for moral character, and God's intimate involvement in that struggle. These are those who explicitly or implicitly are portrayed as 'friend of God.' An ethical realism pervades these biographical narratives where the judgment of others can be quite negative as against demonstrations of divine favor and forbearance. The guiding characteristic of these narratives is to present a kind of intimacy of relations between the person portrayed and God, often in spite of disparaging judgments concerning this person by the community. In many respects then, the texts of scripture function as depth perceptions on human character.

While the biblical texts portray the irreducible presence of the community in moral formation, the decisive presence of biography is also at play. Character is not in the end a communal but a personal trait which is indicative of the formation of a 'self' possessed of independent moral judgment and action. The composition of the wisdom literatures of the Old Testament, from Proverbs to Qohelet, conveys this interest in the self from multiple perspectives. From optimistic aphorisms to confrontation between the human friend of God and God, these texts portray contexts of lived experience and interpretation in intimate relation with God. There appear two trajectories of moral formation, one in which the human being and the community is the object of divine favor and even chastisement with particular individuals as models not so much of unambiguous faithfulness to God but of God's faithfulness to God's people. The other trajectory is one of *imitatio Dei*, of imitation of God's character, who unilaterally gives and saves sinful people (cf. Ezek. 24:15–27), as motivation for obedience to the Torah and life in the community of God.

In turning to the New Testament, significant attention is paid to the life of Christ and of the apostles in recent scholarship where *imitatio Dei* becomes *imitatio Christi*. Emphasis also upon charismatic experience and the reality of the immanent presence of the Holy Spirit in the life of the first believers is also evident (cf. Gal. 5:22–25). Discipleship texts, didactic and narratival, as displaying Jesus' unique ethics of the Kingdom of God in distinction from other forms of ancient moral vision can be highlighted. The quintessential disciple, one who follows Jesus (Matt. 4:19; 8:19; 10:38; Mark 8:34; Luke 14:27; John 12:26), or who imitates apostles, and others who in turn are imitating Christ (Phil. 3:17; 2 Thess. 3:7, 9; Heb. 13:7; 3 John 1:11) fulfil a process of character building rooted in exemplarity, both positive (John 13:15; Acts 20:35; Rom. 4:12; Gal. 3:15; 1 Thess. 1:7; 1 Tim. 1:16; 4:12; James 5:10; 1 Pet. 2:21) and negative (Col. 2:15; 2 Pet. 2:6; Jude 1:7). Throughout the literature a broad spectrum of interpretation reflects creative inter-textual linkages between the Testaments.

One of the ways in which a bridge is built between a historical rendering of ancient moral formation in the biblical text and contemporary use of the text is ancient Christian interpretation, e.g., martyrdom texts of the second and third centuries, from Polycarp to Perpetua and early interpreters/commentators such as Augustine. Of interest in martyriologies are the theological and moral parallels of endurance which are narratively constructed between the Passion narratives of Jesus and also of Stephen (Acts 6–7) and the portrayal of the lives of the martyrs themselves. Lives of martyrs, as with the lives of Jesus and his first disciples, exemplify the essential moral teachings of the New Testament (cf. Luke 17:25; 1 Cor. 4:12; 1 Cor. 10:13; Col. 1:11; 1 Pet. 2:19) in obviously ultimate ways.

Discussion of the ethical use of scripture as an always interpretive, contextualized endeavor means that it is a self-consciously cross-disciplinary one. Whether as dialogue partner or resource, social sciences, philosophical ethics, global politics, and literatures are all part of the contemporary construction of interpretations. One of the most frequent utilizations of texts is the exploration of moral formation that results in pacific character- and peace-making activity. Particular attention is paid to Jesus' teaching in the Sermon on the Mount where peace-making is frequently considered the sum of all virtues, which include humility, generosity, self-control, compassion, self-scrutiny, commitment to restitution, purity of thought and action. Exploration of the relation between God's action of salvation, justification, and reconciliation (Rom. 5:1–11; Phil. 2:1–11; and Eph. 2) and human imitative action are at the cutting edge of contemporary discussion. In addition, questions of community formation and boundary setting, the understanding of wealth and possessions (e.g., Acts 2:42–47; 4:32–35), the role of women and minorities, of strangers and displaced persons, of former 'deviants' and those who return to their deviancy, of political power and religions outside Judaeo-Christian boundaries find rich resources and complex expression in contemporary literature.

The whole question of the use of scripture as instrument of moral formation is analyzed in this vein. What is the hermeneutical function of a text in view of such authoritative status and also the history of authoritative misinterpretation and failures of interpretation? At the heart of this discussion is the very question of the history of crossdisciplinary interpretation. Are Aristotelian ethics compatible with biblical ethics? What are the continuities and discontinuities of Judaic and Christian biblical ethics? If biblical ethics are a complex arrangement of prescriptive and descriptive elements for purposes of worship and personal understanding, is there a relativity of biblical ethics that tends to be discounted?

References and further reading

Brown, William P. (ed.) (2002) *Character and Scripture: Moral Formation, Community, and Biblical Interpretation*, Grand Rapids, Eerdmans.

Cohen, Richard A. (2001) *Ethics, Exegesis and Philosophy: Interpretation After Levinas*, Cambridge: Cambridge University Press.

Davies, Andrew (2000) *Double Standards in Isaiah: Re-Evaluating Prophetic Ethics and Divine Justice*, Leiden: Brill.

Haney, David P. (2001) *The Challenge of Coleridge: Ethics and Interpretation in Romanticism and Modern Philosophy*, University Park: Pennsylvania State University Press.

McDonald, J.I.H. (1993) *Biblical Interpretation and Christian Ethics*, Cambridge: Cambridge University Press.

Patte, Daniel (1995) *Ethics of Biblical Interpretation: A Reevaluation*, Atlanta: Westminster/John Knox.

Stock, Brian (1998) *Augustine the Reader: Mediation, Self-Knowledge, and the Ethics of Interpretation*, Cambridge: Harvard University Press.

KURT A. RICHARDSON

EUSEBIUS (c. 263–340)

Eusebius, bishop of Caesarea and church historian, was a pupil and protégé of Pamphilus, an aristocrat and scholar from Berytus (Beirut). Pamphilus, who studied in Alexandria and became bishop in Caesarea, was a strong defender of the legacy of Origen in a very concrete sense, preserving and extending Origen's library after his death. Pamphilus trained Eusebius as his assistant, and the two continued their work of copying texts even during Pamphilus' imprisonment at the time of the Diocletianic persecutions. After Pamphilus' martyrdom (309) Eusebius fled to Tyre and later to Egypt, where he was imprisoned himself. Upon his return in 313, he became bishop of Caesarea. Eusebius was a fervent, almost sycophantic admirer of Constantine, and the emperor consulted him often in religious matters. In the Asian controversies Eusebius tried to find common ground and was willing to make many concessions. At the Council of Nicea (325) he proposed the baptismal creed of Caesarea as a compromise with the anti-Arians. When this was rejected for the absence of the word *homoousios* he ultimately signed the Nicene Creed. He participated in the Council of Tyre, at which Athanasius was excommunicated. At Constantine's death in 337, Eusebius wrote a resounding eulogy.

Eusebius' most important role was that of an archivist and historian. He incorporated numerous documents, letters, and other materials in his works, which make them of unparalleled importance for the history of early Christianity. In his *Chronicon*, which came out in 303, Eusebius tried to show that the Judaeo-Christian tradition was older than those of other nations. Only a few fragments of the work survive in Greek but a full Armenian translation of the sixth century is extant. In addition, Jerome made a partial translation, which was of great influence in the West. In his *History of the Church*, Eusebius described the development of the church from the apostolic age to his own time. He considered the ultimate victory of Christianity a sign of its divine origin. The original series, consisting of seven books, was supposedly written before 303, while three more books, which reported contemporary events, were added later. In addition to the original Greek, translations exist in Latin, Armenian, and Syriac. His *On the Martyrs of Palestine* is an account of the persecutions between 303 and 310, of which he was an eyewitness; it is an appendix to the eighth book of the *History of the Church*. His panegyric *Life of Constantine* contains many authentic documents, such as a speech of the emperor. The *Praise of Constantine* is a speech that Eusebius gave on the occasion of the celebration of Constantine's thirty-year reign in 335. Eusebius wrote a number of apologetic works, of which the double work, the *Preparation for the Gospel* and the *Demonstration of the Gospel*, is the most significant. In the former Eusebius argued that Judaism was a preparation for Christianity and that the pagans received their wisdom from the Hebrew Bible. In the latter he dealt with the preparatory character of the Jewish law. Other apologetic writings include *Against Hierocles*, a defense of Christianity directed at a pagan governor of Bithynia, and two books *Against Marcellus*, in which he opposes Marcellus, the bishop of Ancyra. Some other writings only survive in translation, such as the *Theophany*, a work on the incarnation of Christ, preserved in Syriac. *Prophetic Selections* offers a survey of messianic prophecies and is only partly preserved. *On Easter* is a treatise discussing the eucharistic sacrifice.

In his interpretation of the Bible Eusebius was much influenced by allegorical methods. Extant is a rich array of fragments of commentaries on biblical books, including the Psalms, Proverbs, Daniel, and various New Testament books. A *Commentary on Isaiah* is almost complete. Interesting for its etymologies and its geographical and historical information is the *Onomasticon*, a work that offers an alphabetical list of biblical topographical names and that was translated by Jerome into Latin.

References and further reading

Altridge, H.W. and Gohei Hata (eds.) (1992) *Eusebius, Christianity, and Judaism*, Detroit: Wayne State University Press.

Barnes, Timothy D. (1981) *Constantine and Eusebius*, Cambridge: Harvard University Press.

Chesnut, Glenn F. (1977) *The First Christian Histories: Eusebius, Socrates, Solomen, Theodoret and Erasmus*, Paris: Éditions Beau Chesne.

Edwards, Mark, Martin Goodman, and Simon Price (1999) *Apologetics in the Roman Empire: Pagans, Jews, and Christians*, in association with Christopher Rowland, New York: Oxford University Press.

Eusebius (1953) *The Ecclesiastical History*, trans. Kirsopp Lake LCL, Cambridge: Harvard University Press.

Grant, Robert M. (1980) *Eusebius as Church Historian*, Oxford: Clarendon.

Raban, Arner and Kenneth G. Holum (eds.) (1996) *Caesarea Maritima: A Retrospective After Two-Millenia*, Leiden: Brill.

Wallace-Hadrill, David S. (1960) *Eusebius of Caesasea*, London: A.R. Mowbray.

ANNEWIES VAN DEN HOEK

EXISTENTIAL HERMENEUTICS

Søren Kierkegaard (1813–1855) is usually considered to be the founder of existentialism, but some scholars trace existential thought through St Augustine, the Bible, and even back to Socrates. The existential movement has had tremendous influence on twentieth-century theologies and theologians, such as Karl Jaspers, Paul Tillich, Rudolf Bultmann, Gabriel Marcel, and Martin Buber. Friedrich Nietzsche (1844–1900), Martin Heidegger (1889–1976), and Jean-Paul Sartre (1905–1980) are some of the most distinguished existential thinkers. Heidegger and Hans-Georg Gadamer (1900–2002) are largely responsible for the contemporary characterization of hermeneutics.

Existentialism has no clear criteria or credo but encompasses a broad school of thinking in which existence and thought are closely related. The term stands for so much that many of the most pronounced existential thinkers avoided it. In a like manner, existential hermeneutics is more a philosophical disposition toward general concerns rather than a specific body of doctrine. Existential thought is best characterized as a 'philosophy of existence,' and existential hermeneutics as a 'philosophy of understanding and existence.' The two are sometimes difficult to distinguish except where they refer to different historical periods and specific thinkers. That is, where one might think of Nietzsche or Kierkegaard as existentialists, prior to the revival of hermeneutics, one is now likely to think of existentialism in reference to Heidegger and Gadamer as existential hermeneuticians – both fitting awkwardly under the label.

Existentialism is an experiential turn away from mere objectivity. It is both a philosophical and literary movement typified by a stress on individual existence, human freedom, and responsibility. For existentialists, the uniqueness of being human is not having an abstract and conceptual essence. It is true all other beings have essences, but human beings have none. We have no fixed natures or stable essences but we have consciousness and must make our own nature through choice. This major existentialist theme is best defined in Sartre's now-famous words 'existence precedes essence.' We are thrown into a world not of our choosing and even if we refuse all other choices in life, a choice has been made to make no further choices.

Our choice of self-definition always precedes who we are. Anxiety (angst) and despair play important roles in existentialist philosophy. The freedom and responsibility of our acts are the sources of dread and anguish. Moreover, we are always caught between freedom and facticity – fearful that our freedom is threatened by things that impose upon us, e.g., cultural values, physical pain, perhaps even God's sovereignty.

The existentialist's choice implies freedom as well as responsibility for whatever commitments are made. However, there are no universal and objectively rational grounds for making choices or moral decisions. Questions of life cannot be articulated through reason and science, or answered with methods and logic. Instead, each individual must take action passionately toward personal truth. For Kierkegaard, life is ambiguous and even absurd. In response, the individual must live life as committed in a way that it might only be understood by the individual – perhaps even in defiance of society and custom. Kierkegaard's Christian 'leap of faith' is a commitment toward an unfathomable life full of risk, and the only way he believed that one can be saved from despair. This emphasis on the perspective and subjectivity of the individual may seem highly irrational, even unintelligible, but existentialism still has a great deal to offer. Existential thinkers may tend toward nonrational, even irrational, factors in their avoidance of systematic rationality, but their thinking often exemplifies rational clarity and a penetrating awareness of our facticity, that is, the conditions of our situation – the human predicament.

Where existentialism is the characterization of our human condition, existential hermeneutics is the concern for the concept and practice of understanding in it. With Heidegger's and Gadamer's 'philosophical hermeneutics' many of the epistemological concerns of nineteenth-century theories of interpretation have given way to a phenomenological analysis of existence, that is, understanding as an existential awareness of one's own situation. Like the existentialism that came before, hermeneutics continues to emphasize our predicament as 'thrown' into the universe, but with less emphasis on human subjectivity and our capacities for choice. To be 'thrown' is to be finite, dependent, and contingent in changing historical and linguistic contexts. However, while there are no single objective true interpretations or understandings that transcend all perspectives, this does not mean we are restricted to our own subjective viewpoint. The hermeneutical task is to make 'understanding' meaningful for life and thought in light of our life-world without being helplessly relativistic or subjective.

For Heidegger and Gadamer, the two distinguished conditions for understanding, that is, the hermeneutical 'experience' of understanding, are the limits and conditions imposed by our language and history. Where once there was an emphasis on choice preceding self-definition, there is now a heightened appreciation of history and language that precede as conditions for all understanding. This means that we no longer merely make or define ourselves through choice but find ourselves 'effectively conditioned' by language and history prior to our decision and choice making. The term 'historicity' has become key in contemporary hermeneutic thought. It refers to our participation in and belonging to history. Less like the merely subjective perspectivism presented by Kierkegaard, existential hermeneutics is concerned with 'understanding' as an event into which we enter. In it, through the linguistic fusing of our past and present, we come to understand ourselves and our world. This is not historical determinism but shows the limit of our finite nature and the possibilities open to us as conditioned by preunderstandings.

Hermeneutics, then, is an existential analytic of being – 'being studying being.' The hermeneutical experience is the dialogue or conversation that we ourselves are because understanding always implies self-understanding. Human existence itself has a hermeneutical structure that underlies all our interpretations, including those of the natural sciences. Our finite human understanding cannot be objectively grasped or employed as a faculty of the mind because understanding is our fundamental mode of 'being-in-the-world.' We are always already in a world at a certain time and place, working from our existential situatedness to a self-conscious interpretive stance. Consequently, hermeneutics help defend many schools of thought (religious, aesthetic, etc.) against the prejudice that only scientific propositions have claim to validity and that our aims for understanding should be methods of interpretation and objective truths.

References and further reading

Gadamer, Hans-Georg (2002) *Truth and Method*, trans. Joel Weinsheimer and Donald G. Marshall, New York: Continuum, 2nd revised edn.

Heidegger, Martin (1996) *Being and Time*, trans. Joan Stambaugh, New York: State University of New York Press.

Kierkegaard, Søren (1974) *Concluding Unscientific Postscript*, trans. David F. Swenson and Walter Lowrie, Princeton: Princeton University Press.

Sartre, Jean-Paul (1970) *Existentialism and Humanism*, trans. Philip Mairet, London: Methuen.

Shapiro, Gary and Alan Sica (eds.) (1984) *Hermeneutics: Questions and Prospects*, Amherst: University of Massachusetts Press.

Wachterhauser, Brice R. (ed.) (1986) *Hermeneutics and Modern Philosophy*, New York: State University of New York Press.

J.C. ROBINSON

FEMINIST INTERPRETATION

Feminist interpretation is one of the most recent approaches that have developed to interpret the Bible. Although there were previous writings, the feminist approach emerged during the late 1960s and early 1970s because of the modern women's movement. Although there are many definitions of feminism they have a common theme of a movement for social, economic, political, and religious equality, and rights of women. This drive for equality focuses on the struggle of women against domination, exploitation, and oppression. This definition creates the foundation for feminists to make their own interpretations and approaches to the Bible and ultimately provides the goal that they hope to achieve.

All feminist interpretive approaches have at their root a belief that there is inequality between the genders and that the rights of women are being oppressed by the male-dominated culture. This inequality is also perceived to exist within the church and traditional hermeneutical approaches. Feminist interpretations are in response to this inequality, and desire a reshaping of the accepted approaches to interpretation. The feminists' goal is to change church culture and scholarly approaches by challenging accepted methods and promoting equality of gender within a male-dominated field and theology.

There are three major interpretive approaches that are used by feminists today. The first, proposed by Phyllis Trible, is a 'revisionistic' hermeneutic that follows a critical-historical approach. This view sees the existing patriarchal form of the Bible as a 'husk' (the human word) that is distinguishable from the nonpatriarchal 'kernel' (the divine word) of biblical revelation. Underlying this belief is the understanding that the biblical world and the modern world are patriarchal and that everything that is written from these cultures would also be biased against females. A central point for this hermeneutic is that it does not view the Bible as a problem, but the specifically male interpretation of it. An important example that Trible uses is that Paul's injunction against women teaching is directed at specific women and to them only. This should not be expanded upon to include all women, which is a

misinterpretation. Out of this belief, 'gender research' was developed, which brings to light the diverse realities of women living in biblical times. It demonstrates that women did have freedoms and rights in ancient times and that, even though the culture was male dominated, women were afforded status and dignity. Overall this view calls for the reformation of interpretive approaches not only to include the feminist perspective, but also to acknowledge that the traditional interpretation of the Bible was inherently biased against women because of the patriarchal culture. It also seeks to create a new perspective for reading the Bible, which affirms women with theological significance.

The second approach is a far more radical one, and is led by Mary Daly. This approach to interpretation is much more pessimistic about the established traditions and their ability to reform. The underlying belief of this view is similar to that of the revisionist approach in the belief that the Bible is biased against women. However, because of the disbelief in the church's ability to reform, the action called for is a complete rejection of traditional Christian interpretations. This view states that the Bible no longer has authority for women, because the history of the Bible and Christianity can only be viewed as a history of patriarchy. Resulting from this, Daly has sought to redefine God not as 'Father' but as a gender-neutral 'God/ess' (1973: 19–24). In essence Daly is proposing a new spirituality that is gynocentric in nature, but she does not condemn those who believe in patriarchy. The strength of this hermeneutic is that it confronts the claim of the universality of the biblical-Christian tradition and, as a result, requires it to reconsider its beliefs. However, some of the suggestions put forward by Daly are very close to the rejection of Christianity and the creation of a new religion.

By far the most influential feminist writer is Elizabeth Schüssler Fiorenza. Her hermeneutic of liberation is arguably the most popular feminist interpretive approach. This approach is rooted within the modern women's movement and proposes a theology that all human beings are equal in God's sight, regardless of gender. However, Schüssler Fiorenza believes that this is not practiced within the church or its traditions. She emphasizes the role of experience that all women have had, particularly of devaluation, living within a male-dominated society. It is through these experiences that the liberation approach views the Bible and tradition and can serve as a critical paradigm for a critique of sexual ideologies. Consequently, the liberation-hermeneutical approach attempts to combine biblical exegesis and liberating praxis into one cohesive approach to create a feminist, liberation-seeking theology. This approach begins with a 'hermeneutic of suspicion' against the patriarchal monopolization of scripture and traditional interpretation. After suspicion, the next step is a 'hermeneutic of remembrance,' which looks to recognize women and their contribution to Christian origins. This hermeneutic places the text within its historical cultural setting, and through this placement allows the cultural influences and structures of power dominance to be acknowledged. By acknowledging these cultural influences and structures, they can be removed from the text, allowing the true meaning to be placed within the values of the twenty-first century. The goal of this hermeneutic is to expose the hidden power scheme within the Bible and patriarchal cultures and to revise these long-held beliefs to bring equality for women and their viewpoints.

In conclusion, feminist interpretive approaches have affected Christianity and its theological interpretations. One of the most obvious contributions has been seen with the addition of gender-inclusive language within new translations of the Bible. It has also forced the Christian community to recognize that females have the ability to make viable contributions to its belief. This interpretation also questions which ways the tradition needs to be reinterpreted and reshaped, and also asks what God is calling us to do in response to this new understanding of faith.

References and further reading

Daly, M. (1973) *Beyond God the Father: Toward a Philosophy of Women's Liberation*, Boston: Beacon Press.

Jobling, J. (2002) *Feminist Biblical Interpretation in Theological Context*, Burlington: Ashgate.

Jones, S. (2000) *Feminist Theory and Christian Theology*, Minneapolis: Fortress Press.

Schüssler Fiorenza, E. (1983) *In Memory of Her: A Feminist Theological Reconstruction of Christian Origins*, London: SCM Press.

—— (1986) *Bread Not Stone*, Boston: Beacon Press.

—— (1996) 'Feminist Hermeneutics', in *Dictionary of Feminist Theologies*, L. Russell and J. Clarkson (eds.), London: Mowbray.

—— (2001) *Wisdom Ways: Introducing Feminist Biblical Interpretation*, Maryknoll: Orbis.

Trible, P. (1984) *Texts of Terror: Literary-Feminist Readings of Biblical Narratives*, Philadelphia: Fortress Press.

SEAN ADAMS

FILM AND INTERPRETATION

> 1 The importance of film as a new medium of biblical interpretation
> 2 A working model for understanding ways in which the Bible is presented on film

Few would dare argue with the suggestion that we live in a media-dominated society in which cinema and television have surplanted the place of the church in the lives of many people. The world of moving visual entertainment is undoubtedly ours, whether we enter it through the sanctity of a movie theater or the comfort of our living rooms safely snuggled before our television screens. Ours is a world of moving images, so much so that film might legitimately be described as *the* twentieth-century art form.

Such a suggestion invites us to consider the larger issue of how contemporary culture *affects* mythological constructs, including religious perceptions and ideas. At the same time it provides an excellent example for us to examine how readily popular cultural expressions themselves are *affected by* an underlying religious mythology. The point here is that the relationship between popular culture, on the one hand, and religious beliefs and practices, on the other, is one of mutual influence. Traffic continually flows in both directions on this two-way street, despite the fact that proponents of the sacred world often claim to have right of way over the secular and may at times insist that they saw a one-way sign at the beginning of the road. Religion and popular culture inevitably influence one another on the plane of human existence, sometimes in quite unpredictable ways. In short, we should not be surprised to discover religious truths finding cultural expression within modern films.

1 The importance of film as a new medium of biblical interpretation

It is important to recognize that films are legitimate artistic endeavors. Film-making as an art form is just over 100 years old, and attempts to depict the Bible on film are perhaps best viewed as falling within the long-standing tradition of artistic expression within the church. We could even view films functioning for the general population in a way similar to painting, sculpture, and stained glass in medieval churches. At the same time, film is fast becoming a new lingua franca for an ever-increasing worldwide audience. Knowledge of and appreciation for cinema means that film is becoming an important means of communication, particularly for younger generations for whom the cinematic world is a given. The increase of availability of films and ease of access to video recorders and DVD technology no doubt will continue to play a significant role in years to come.

Attitudes toward biblical films are inevitably a reflection of sociological trends and interests. They are two-way mirrors of society, both challenging and illustrating the prevailing values of a culture. The place of cinema within the wider questions of cultural life is a key consideration. For example, *Variety* magazine reported that at the end of the 1950s six of the ten most popular films of the previous decade were biblical epics (*Samson and Delilah*, 1949; *Quo Vadis*, 1951; *David and Bathsheeba*, 1951; *The Robe*, 1953; *The Ten Commandments*, 1956; *Ben-Hur*, 1959). Yet many of these can be interpreted as carrying something of the Cold War agenda. What does this tell us about the role of the Bible today? Clearly it is impossible to assess films without due care and attention to the social and historical context in which they are produced.

Film studies lend themselves to interdisciplinary programmes and have an increasingly important role to play in the academic world. In many colleges and universities, film/cinema studies are crossdisciplinary in nature and promote a healthy interchange between theology and other subjects. Unfortunately, many theological and religious studies faculties lack a vision for such cross-fertilization, although the signs are that this is beginning to change. There is a 'generational factor' which also needs to be kept in mind as part of the equation here: younger people seem more accepting of the legitimacy of film studies than do many of the older generation, who represent institutional interests.

Using the Bible in film is a hermeneutical exercise of considerable importance. Study of the use of the scriptures in film offers a new discipline to the task of biblical interpretation. Indeed, many of the hermeneutical approaches which we apply to the text of the Bible can also be legitimately, and profitably, used in film studies.

2 A working model for understanding ways in which the Bible is presented on film

'Biblical' material on film can be categorized into five major groups. These categories are by no means watertight and there are many films and television programmes which blur the boundaries and have features which fit comfortably within more than one group. Nevertheless, the following five basic categories suggest themselves:

2.1 The historical epic

These films purport to offer an essentially diachronic approach to biblical interpretation in that they attempt to 'present the Bible as it really happened.' On the surface there is a nod in the direction of historicity,

although generally little acknowledgment is made of the hermeneutical complexities raised by historical-critical method. The text is often presented 'as it stands,' although character embellishments and historical adjustments do occur. Examples include DeMille's *The Ten Commandments* (1956), Zefferilli's *Jesus of Nazareth* (1977), Sykes' *Jesus* (1984), the animated retelling of the story of the life of Moses entitled *The Prince of Egypt* (1998), and most recently Gibson's *The Passion of the Christ* (2003). A number of recent American made-for-TV films about Old Testament figures also fit within this category, including Sargent's *Abraham* (1994), Young's *Joseph* (1995), and *Moses* (1996).

2.2 The fictive drama

These films also employ an essentially diachronic approach and generally are set within the time period of the biblical stories themselves. However, a new component is added in the form of a deliberately injected fictive character or characters. Not surprisingly, many of the films in this category are based on modern works of historical fiction, often by well-respected authors. Most of the so-called 'Sword-and-Sandal' flics of the 1950s and 1960s fit within this category. Examples include Koster's *The Robe* (1953), Dieterle's *Salome* (1953), Wyler's *Ben-Hur* (1959), Vidor's *Solomon and Sheba* (1959), Fleischer's *Barabbas* (1962), and the Monty Python comedy classic *Life of Brian* (1979).

2.3 The contemporary parable

These films offer an essentially synchronic approach to biblical interpretation and are generally concerned to present the essence of biblical stories in modern form. Very often they use typological and allegorical means to do this. The historical setting is rarely a biblical one; rather, a contemporary setting is generally used, although the purported setting might be in the past while the setting of the intended audience may be more modern (e.g., Joffe's *The Mission*, 1986). Somewhat remarkably, there is a long-standing interest among foreign film directors in pursuing this kind of film, beginning with the seminal Bergman film *The Seventh Seal* (1957). Other examples include Kieslowski's *Dekalog* (1989), Axel's *Babette's Feast* (1987), Tarkovsky's *The Sacrifice* (1986), and Arcade's *Jesus of Montreal* (1989). Frequently films of this type are produced within a faith community, or at least have identifiable links to one (usually through the director or the screenwriter).

2.4 The passive allusion

These films use religious themes or images as their primary means of bringing the Bible to bear in the world of cinema. Generally they draw upon a 'residual database' of cultural impressions about religious matters including stock biblical phrases and images. Examples include as diverse titles as the Oscar-winning *Lilies of the Field* (1963), Eastwood's western *The Pale Rider* (1985), Title's black comedy *The Last Supper* (1995), and Bay's sci-fi/disaster *Armageddon* (1998). In short, this category might be described as Hollywood's 'pop-theology' with very little attention to historical accuracy or detail in evidence. A prime example is Steven Spielberg's *Raiders of the Lost Ark* (1981), which draws upon standard conventional Old Testament imagery in weaving its anti-Nazi comic-book fantasy. Another astonishing example is the x-rated film produced by *Penthouse* magazine, Guccione's *Caligula* (1979). This controversial film depicts the story of the crazed Roman emperor and opens with a screen graphic of Mark 8:36, 'What shall it profit a man if he should gain the whole world and lose his own soul?' The strength of this particular approach is that it is easily adaptable to virtually any genre of film-making imaginable.

2.5 The mythological reshaping

One of the most intriguing instances of contemporary film-making involves the deliberate reshaping of biblical mythological constructs. Perhaps the best popular example of this is to be found within the cult-TV series *Hercules: The Legendary Journeys* and *Xena: Warrior Princess*, which commenced on TV in America in 1994–1995. These series have enjoyed phenomenal success, and as such demonstrates the extent to which mythological reconstructions of this sort have become hot property in the media world. Two episodes from *Xena: Warrior Princess* will serve to illustrate the extent to which a biblical base underlies the basic story line. One is from the first season of the series and is entitled 'Cradle of Hope' (1995). This is an intriguing reworking of the story of the birth of Moses, combined with elements of the Christmas story of the birth of Jesus Christ, lightly mixed together with elements of Graeco-Roman mythology such as Pandora's fateful box. A second example occurs in an episode from the second season entitled 'Giant Killer' in which the biblical story of David's clash with the Philistine champion Goliath is reworked (Xena engineers the slaying of Goliath; David writes the twenty-third Psalm in anticipation of it). As the film credits announce at the end of the episode: 'No Bible myths or icons were irreparably mangled during the production of this motion picture.'

References and further reading

Babington, Bruce and Peter William Evans (1993) *Biblical Epics: Sacred Narrative in the Hollywood Cinema*, Manchester: University of Manchester Press.

Bach, Alice (ed.) (1996) *Semeia 74: Biblical Glamour and Hollywood Glitz*, Atlanta: Scholars Press.

Campbell, Richard H. and Michael R. Pitts (1981) *The Bible on Film: A Checklist, 1897–1980*, London: The Scarecrow Press.

Chilton, Bruce (2000) *Rabbi Jesus: An Intimate Biography*, New York: Doubleday.

Exum, J. Cheryl (1996) *Plotted, Shot and Painted: Cultural Representations of Biblical Women*, Sheffield: Sheffield Academic Press.

Fraser, George Macdonald (1988) *The Hollywood History of the World*, London: Michael Joseph.

Fraser, Peter (1998) *Images of the Passion: The Sacramental Mode in Film*, Trowbridge: Flicks Books.

Jewett, Robert (1993) *Saint Paul at the Movies: The Apostle's Dialogue with American Culture*, Louisville: Westminster/John Knox.

Kinnard, Roy and Tim Davis (1992) *Divine Images: A History of Jesus on the Screen*, New York: Citadel Press.

Kreitzer, Larry J. (1993) *The New Testament in Fiction and Film: On Reversing the Hermeneutical Flow*, Sheffield: Sheffield Academic Pres.

—— (1994) *The Old Testament in Fiction and Film: On Reversing the Hermeneutical Flow*, Sheffield: Sheffield Academic Press.

—— (1998) *Pauline Images in Fiction and Film: On Reversing the Hermeneutical Flow*, Sheffield: Sheffield Academic Press.

Marsh, Clive and Gaye Ortiz (eds.) (1997) *Explorations in Theology and Film*, Oxford: Blackwell.

Martin, Joel W. and Conrad E. Oswalt Jr. (eds.) (1995) *Screening the Sacred: Religion, Myth and Ideology in Popular American Film*, Boulder, CO: Westview Press.

Tatum, W. Barnes (1997) *Jesus at the Movies: A Guide to the First Hundred Years*, Santa Rosa, CA: Polebridge Press.

Telford, W.R. (1995) 'The New Testament in Fiction and Film: A Biblical Scholar's Perspective,' pp. 360–94 in *Words Remembered, Texts Renewed: Essays in Honour of John F.A. Sawyer*, JSOTSup 195, Jon Davies, Graham Harvey, and Wilfred G.E. Watson (eds.), Sheffield: Sheffield Academic Press.

LARRY J. KREITZER

FITZMYER, JOSEPH A. (1920–)

Joseph A. Fitzmyer was born on November 4, 1920 in Philadelphia. In 1938 he entered the Society of Jesus at the Novitiate of St. Isaac Jogues in Wernersville, PA. After spending two years as a novice and subsequently giving his vow to the society, Fitzmyer went on to study Greek, Latin, and scholastic philosophy. He received his B.A. and M.A. from Loyola University in Chicago and taught Greek, Latin, and German at Gonzaga High School in Washington, DC. After four years of further training at Woodstock College in Maryland and at the Facultés St-Albert de Louvain in Belgium, he received the degree of Licentiate in Sacred Theology (1952). Fitzmyer received his Ph.D. from Johns Hopkins University in 1956 and the degree of Licentiate in Sacred Scripture in 1957.

His teaching experience at various colleges and universities has been extensive. He began as an assistant professor of New Testament and biblical languages at Woodstock College in 1958, rising to full professor in 1964. Fitzmyer served as a visiting lecturer at Johns Hopkins from 1958 to 1961 and visiting professor from 1968 to 1969. He served as professor of Aramaic and Hebrew at the University of Chicago (1969–1971), and professor of New Testament and biblical languages at Fordham University (1971–1974). From 1974 to 1976 he served as both professor of New Testament and Biblical Languages at the Weston School of Theology in Cambridge, MA, and as Speaker's Lecturer in Biblical Studies at Oxford University. From 1976 until he retired, in 1986, Fitzmyer was professor of New Testament at the Catholic University of America.

He received several honorary degrees, including L.H.D. from the University of Scranton, Litt.D. from the College of the Holy Cross, L.H.D. from Fairfield University, and Teol.H.Dr. from Lund University. In 1984 he received the Burkett Medal for Biblical Studies from the British Academy, and in 1985 he was appointed to the Pontifical Biblical Commission.

He has been a past president of both the Society of Biblical Literature (1978–1979) and the Catholic Biblical Association of America (1969–1970).

Fitzmyer's importance in modern biblical studies may be seen in two areas. First, he has supported historical-critical study of the Bible among Catholic scholars. In 1943 the encyclical *Divino Afflante Spiritu* was issued by Pope Pius XII, which gave a cautious endorsement for historical-critical study. During the Second Vatican Council efforts were made to counter this. This included the document *Dogmatic Constitution on Divine Revelation*, written several months before the Council. This document, which opposed certain aspects of scriptural teaching, was rejected and rewritten by the order of Pope John XXIII, thereby encouraging historical-critical study. Fitzmyer became one of the foremost patrons of New Testament studies as a result. Second, Fitzmyer is widely recognized for his important Semitic, Aramaic, and background studies (including Qumran studies) for interpreting the New Testament. Two of his best-known works include *The Semitic Background of the New Testament* (1997), and *To Advance the Gospel* (1981). He has also published major commentaries on Luke, Acts, and Romans in the Anchor Bible series.

References and further reading

Fitzmyer, Joseph A. (1971) *Essays on the Semitic Background of the New Testament*, London: G. Chapman.

—— (1979) *A Wandering Aramean: Collected Aramaic Essays*, SBL MS 25, Atlanta: Scholars Press.

—— (1981) *To Advance the Gospel: New Testament Studies*, New York: Crossroad.

—— (1981–1985) *The Gospel According to Luke*, 2 Vols., AB 28, 28A, Garden City, NY: Doubleday.

—— (1993) *Romans*, AB 33, Garden City, NY: Doubleday.

—— (1997) *The Semitic Background of the New Testament*, Grand Rapids: Eerdmans.

—— (1998) *The Acts of the Apostles*, AB 31, New York: Doubleday.

S.R. GUNDERSON

FORM CRITICISM

1 Introduction: Gunkel and the origins of form criticism
2 Form criticism and the Hebrew Bible
3 Form criticism and the New Testament
4 Form criticism: Retrospect and prospect

1 Introduction: Gunkel and the origins of form criticism

'Form criticism' (FC) is an English rendering of the German term *Formgeschichte*, literally 'history of the form,' a critical research methodology that seeks to understand ancient texts – especially the Bible – by giving careful attention to their 'forms,' i.e., typical genres of verbal discourse. The origins of FC are generally traced back to the Old Testament scholar H. Gunkel (1862–1932), whose work was at the same time a critical response to the source criticism of Wellhausen and an adaptation of folklore studies to the biblical materials. Let us consider each element in turn. By the nineteenth century, scholars had long recognized that the Pentateuch was composed of diverse materials that reflected differing sources and viewpoints. Wellhausen's great accomplishment was to explain clearly this diversity by isolating four hypothetical literary sources in the Pentateuch, each the product of a different author working in a distinct historical context (on these four sources, known by the sigla JEDP, see Pentateuch, this volume). While Gunkel found some merit in this approach, he concluded that Wellhausen's four-source thesis was only half of the answer. Israel had originated as a primitive oral society, and it followed that any effort to recover the Pentateuch's composition history would need to peer behind its literary sources to the smaller oral traditions from which the literature was eventually composed. It was this observation that spawned Gunkel's interest in folklore studies.

During the nineteenth century, the Brothers Grimm assembled and catalogued their famous corpus of oral German folktales. Gunkel surmised that the forms of these tales were comparable to stories in the biblical narrative and so concluded that the Grimm tales, and similar traditions, could be used as the basis for positing the original oral contexts of tales in the Pentateuch (see Gunkel 1921; also J.G. Frazer 1923). Moreover, at about the same time, there was a strong belief emerging among folklorists that oral traditions followed very specific 'laws' (e.g., Olrik 1992) and that it was possible to trace the development of traditions from their 'primitive' oral origins to their more advanced literary forms (Jolles 1929). For Gunkel, the chief point of such an exercise in the Bible was not merely to recover the history of Israel's oral and literary traditions but rather something more ambitious: to reconstruct the social history of ancient Israel.

Essential to Gunkel's project was to identify the form of each individual tradition unit so that its genre might be correctly identified and then attached to a historical situation. This process of generic classification employed three key indices: *mood, form,* and *Sitz im Leben,* where 'mood' referred to the affective dispositions that inspired the tradition, form to the structure of its discourse, and *Sitz im Leben* to the 'life setting' or context that produced the genre (*Gattung*). In actual practice, however, it was *Sitz im Leben* that eventually took center stage in this analysis because history was the chief interest of the early form critics. Like other scholars during his age, Gunkel's view of genre presumed the neoclassical view that each form or genre reflected a single unique *Sitz im Leben.* While this inflexible equation made it deceptively easy to determine the context of a particular biblical pericope – one only needed to identify the form and the context followed – as we shall see, for later theorists the rigidity of FC would become the method's 'Achilles heel.'

Gunkel rigorously applied his method to both Genesis and the Hebrew Psalms, and although few scholars would now accept his conclusions at face value, it is fair to say that Gunkel's work produced lasting results. Modern scholars routinely accept his conclusion that Genesis contains etiological legends about the origins of Israel's institutions, and Gunkel's fivefold classification of the Psalms – hymns, communal laments, individual laments, individual thanksgiving songs, and royal

psalms – is still, with some variation, a mainstay in the study of that Hebrew collection. In sum, Gunkel succeeded in his effort to demonstrate that Genesis and the Psalms reflect a broad range of genres stemming from many different historical contexts.

2 Form criticism and the Hebrew Bible

European scholars were quick to apply Gunkel's new method to the Hebrew Bible, producing landmark studies of Hebrew law (Alt), the Pentateuch (Noth; Von Rad), the Deuteronomistic History/Chronicler (Noth), the prophetic books (Hölscher; Gunkel; Lindblom; see Westermann 1991), and the Psalms (Mowinckel). Gunkel's emphasis on the priority of orality in the Bible was subsequently taken up with gusto by the so-called 'Scandanavian school' (represented by H. Birkeland, I. Engnell, E. Nielsen, H.S. Nyberg, S. Mowinckel, *et al.*), which attributed nearly all the Hebrew Bible to oral composition (see Knight 1975). Although scholars continue to acknowledge the role of orality in biblical tradition, the far-reaching theory that the Bible originated orally is presently suspect in the view of most scholars. It is now more common to attribute the biblical materials to literary rather than oral processes, with signs of orality being increasingly attributed to the influences of oral patterns upon literary texts (Kirkpatrick 1988). One result of these developments is that FC's purview has been expanded gradually to include not only the Bible's smallest oral traditions but also its genres on a larger, literary scale, so that, for example, one may speak not only about the 'casuistic form' of a single law in Deuteronomy 15:12 but also of the 'treaty form' that characterizes the book of Deuteronomy as a whole. In recent years the use of FC in the study of the Hebrew Bible has undergone an extensive reevaluation, as we shall see.

3 Form criticism and the New Testament

The works of K.L. Schmidt, M. Dibelius, and R. Bultmann introduced FC into the study of the New Testament, with the focus centered mainly on the Gospels and life of Christ. According to these scholars, careful attention to form revealed that many units in the Jesus tradition originated in the life and preaching of the early church rather than during the actual life of Christ himself. It followed that the Gospels did not provide us with ready access to biographical details of Jesus' life and, where they did – mainly in Jesus' teachings and parables – these sources had to be carefully sifted to yield their historical fruit. Although not all scholars would share this skeptical view of the sources (e.g., Ellis 1999), an enduring result from the work of the early form critics is that the Gospel traditions are now used much more cautiously in the quest to produce a portrait of the historical Jesus.

Like their Old Testament counterparts, contemporary New Testament scholars are much more circumspect than their predecessors about FC's ability to uncover genres and their historical contexts. The result is that some traditions that formerly had a secure attachment to the historical Jesus, like the 'Passion narrative' (see Crossan 1988), are now matters of considerable debate. Moreover, again paralleling developments in Old Testament studies, the tendency in New Testament studies is to broaden the purview of FC so that it includes not only oral traditions but also literary genres in the broadest sense. This has spawned an interest in comparing Paul's letters to ancient epistolary literature (e.g., Doty 1973) and in comparing the book of Revelation with other apocalypses (e.g., Russell and many later scholars). However, FC has tended to be less important for New Testament studies because the generic types of the New Testament – gospels, letters, and apocalypse – are obviously far fewer than in the Hebrew tradition.

4 Form criticism: Retrospect and prospect

The importance of FC has been eclipsed in the last few decades by two new developments in biblical studies, postmodern reader-response criticism and redaction criticism. Reader-response criticism is interested primarily in the role of the text's final form in evoking responses in its readers. In such cases the critic has no interest in either the ostensible intentions of the text's author or in the oral and literary sources he may have used. This is not the place to discuss the relative merits of the reader-response approach, but it is obvious that such an interpretive posture precludes its value for answering the sociological and historical questions posited by many biblical scholars. As for redaction criticism, this was a natural response to the limitations of FC. Form critics were so preoccupied with the Bible's preliterary traditions that they often failed to consider how the traditions were finally combined by authors and editors to produce extended literary works like the Pentateuch and the Gospels. Redaction Criticism focuses attention on the important process of collecting, arranging, and organizing the text and hence has become, along with FC, an indispensable element in critical readings of the Bible.

In recent years FC has undergone an extensive reevaluation by biblical scholars, especially among scholars of the Hebrew Bible (see Koch 1969; Buss 1999; Sweeney and Ben Zvi 2003), but it is not clear that their critiques have generally appreciated the theoretical problems inherent in FC (for two exceptions, see Longman 2003; Van Leeuwen 2003). If we base our critique on the observations of modern generic theory (e.g., Hempfer 1973; Todorov 1978), it becomes clear that the primary problem with FC has been that its tendency to reify genres, to imagine that generic categories reflect hard, fixed realities rather than comparative taxonomies created by readers. For instance, traditional FC wanted to draw a sharp generic distinction between individual lament psalms and corporate laments, each a unique genre sporting its own distinctive *Sitz im Leben*. However, it is quite clear that on one level the two psalm types are of precisely the same genre (both are 'lament psalms'), while on another level it is also obvious that they are of entirely different genres (one was composed for individual use and the other not so). This reality is not a philosophical slight of hand but rather reflects the nature of 'analytical genre' as a classification system based on flexible criteria for identifying similarities and differences between texts. A related weakness of FC has been its struggle to account for the generic flexibility inherent in verbal discourse. For instance, how can the label 'individual lament' be permanently affixed to a psalm that will later be used in a corporate context? FC's traditionally rigid conceptual link between genre and *Sitz im Leben* does adequately explain variations like this, in which a text's 'intrinsic genre' (or, actual genre) changes as it passes through the successive hands of new readers. In sum, traditional FC has generally failed to appreciate the nature of both analytical and intrinsic genres, and it has multiplied the problems by inadvertently blending together these two conceptually distinct aspects of generic study.

By focusing our attention on the importance of genre in interpretation, FC has made a lasting contribution to the study of the Hebrew Bible and New Testament. If biblical scholars will hear the critiques of FC offered by modern generic theory, as they seem poised to do, then the prospects of FC are bright indeed. The reason is that, according to most modern generic theories, all interpretation is based on acts of generic comparison, so that, in the end, there is no aspect of interpretation that cannot be subsumed under the rubric of 'form criticism.' However, in order to avoid expected confusion, it is perhaps helpful to refer to this new, more broadly conceived version of FC with fresh labels, such as 'genre criticism' or 'literary competence.'

References and further reading

Blum, E. (2003) 'Formgeschichte – A Misleading Category? Some Critical Remarks,' pp. 32–45 in *The Changing Face of Form Criticism for the Twenty-First Century*, M.A. Sweeney and E. Ben Zvi (eds.), Grand Rapids: Eerdmans.

Crossan, J. D. (1988) *The Cross that Spoke: The Origins of the Passion Narrative*, San Francisco: Harper & Row.

Bultmann, R.K. (1988) *Die Geschichte der synoptischen Tradition*, Göttingen: Vandenhoeck & Ruprech (4th edn. *The History of the Synoptic Tradition*).

Buss, M.J. (1999) *Biblical Form Criticism in Its Context*, JSOTSup 274, Sheffield: Sheffield Academic Press.

Dibelius, M. (1959) *Die Formgeschichte des Evangeliums*, Tübingen: Mohr (3rd edn. *From Tradition to Gospel*).

Doty, W.G. (1973) *Letters in Primitive Christianity*, Philadelphia: Fortress Press.

Ellis, E.E. (1999) *The Making of the New Testament Documents*, Biblical Interpretation 39, Leiden: Brill.

Frazer, J.G. (1923) *Folktale in the Old Testament*, New York: Macmillan.

Garber, F. *et al.* (1993) 'Genre,' *The New Princeton Encyclopedia of Poetry and Poetics*, Princeton: Princeton University Press.

Gunkel, H. (1921) *Das Märchen im Alten Testament*, Tübingen: J.C.B. Mohr (*The Folktale in the Old Testament*).

Güttgemanns, E. (1979) *Candid Questions Concerning Gospel Form Criticism: A Methodological Sketch of the Fundamental Problematics of Form and Redaction Criticism*, Pittsburgh: Pickwick.

Hayes, J.H. (ed.) (1974) *Old Testament Form Criticism*, San Antonio: Trinity University Press.

Hempfer, K. (1973) *Gattungstheorie*, Munich: Funk.

Jolles, A. (1929) *Einfache Formen*, Halle: Niemeyer.

Knight, D.A. (1975) *Rediscovering the Traditions of Israel*, SBLDS 9, Missoula: Scholars Press, rev. edn.

Kirkpatrick, P.G. (1988) *The Old Testament and Folklore Study*, JSOTSup 62, Sheffield: Sheffield Academic Press.

Knierim, R. (1973) 'Old Testament Form Criticism Reconsidered,' *Interpretation* 27: 435–48.

Koch, K. (1969) *The Growth of the Biblical Tradition: The Form-Critical Method*, New York: Scribner's.

Longman III, T. (2003) 'Israelite Genres in Their Ancient Near Eastern Context,' pp. 177–95 in *The Changing Face of Form Criticism for the Twenty-First Century*, M.A. Sweeney and E. Ben Zvi (eds.), Grand Rapids: Eerdmans.

Olrik, A. (1992) *Principles for Oral Narrative Research*, trans. K. Wolf and J. Jensen, Folklore Studies in Translation, Bloomington: Indiana University Press, (orig. *Nogle Grundsaetninger for Sagnforskning*, 1921).

Russell, D.S. (1964) *The Method and Message of Jewish Apocalyptic*, Philadelphia: Westminster Press.

Schmidt, K.L. (1919) *Der Rahmen der Geschichte Jesu: Literarkritische Untersuchungen zur ältesten Jesusüberlieferung*, Berlin: Trowitzsch.

Sweeney, M.A. and E. Ben Zvi (eds.) (2003) *The Changing Face of Form Criticism for the Twenty-First Century*, Grand Rapids: Eerdmans.

Todorov, T. (1978) *Genres in Discourse*, Cambridge: Cambridge University Press.

Tucker, G.M. (1971) *Form Criticism of the Old Testament*, Philadelphia: Fortress Press.

Van Leeuwen, R. (2003) 'Form Criticism, Wisdom, and Psalms 111–112,' pp. 65–84 in *The Changing Face of Form Criticism for the Twenty-First Century*, M.A. Sweeney and E. Ben Zvi (eds.), Grand Rapids: Eerdmans.

Westermann, C. *Basic Forms of Prophetic Speech*, Louisville: Westminster/John Knox.

KENTON L. SPARKS

FORMALIST/NEW CRITICAL INTERPRETATION

Formalist/New Critical biblical interpretation is a development and refinement of the New Criticism that made its appearance in the 1930s among interpreters of secular literature and which dominated American literary criticism until late in the 1960s. New Critics (also called formalist critics) engage in 'close reading' or 'explication' of particular literary texts, which are regarded as autonomous objects separable from the design and purpose of the author ('intentional fallacy') and from the effects of the work on readers ('affective fallacy'). New Criticism is an alternative to historical-critical hegemony, which focused primarily on the social and historical contexts of texts, and audience-oriented forms of literary criticism, which dealt with the effects of a work on actual readers. Instead, formalists contend that the proper concern of literary criticism is not external circumstances, but the work itself, an independent and self-sufficient verbal object. New Critics insist that the meaning of a text is inseparable from its form, and therefore they focus on detailed and subtle nuances within texts: ambiguities, paradox, irony, tension (tightly inter-related elements), tropes, symbols, images, and so forth. Formalists also recognize the importance of the unity of a work, which must be understood as an organic whole with its parts in harmonious relationship to this whole.

Biblical New Criticism employs the methods and techniques of formalist critics but does not ignore the historical, social, and cultural backgrounds of texts, or the effects of texts on readers. Biblical formalists value close readings of texts: the sinuousness of form and content; nuances of words; the contribution of the parts to the whole; and the necessity of interpreting the work as an organic unity. The biblical formalist critic is not primarily concerned with authorial intention, or the historical, cultural, and social influences on the author of a work, although these factors may be considered in a close analysis of a text. Nor is the biblical formalist critic primarily concerned with the effect of the work on the reader, although some forms of formalist criticism – notably narrative criticism – do consider the work's effect on an implied reader. Rather biblical formalists regard the self-contained, unified text as the *primary* focus of interpretation. Early examples of formalist criticism of the Bible include Phyllis Trible on Ruth, Jean Starobinski on Mark 5, and J.L. Resseguie on John 9. More recently, formalist criticism takes the form of biblical narrative criticism, which reads biblical texts as artfully constructed unified narratives and analyzes them as stories with characters, setting, rhetoric, plot, and point of view. For examples of narrative criticism see R. Alan Culpepper on John, David Rhoads, Joanna Dewey, and Donald Michie on Mark, and J.L. Resseguie on the book of Revelation.

A brief close reading of the arrest of Jesus in John 18:1–11 will illustrate the method of biblical New Criticism. The *setting* is a garden across the Kidron Valley from Jerusalem, a walled open-air space similar to the sheepfold of John 10, which must be read with this narrative. The sheepfold is safe space that protects the sheep from outside threats such as wolves, thieves, and bandits. A mediating character, the good shepherd, leads the sheep in and out of the pen, and lays down his life for the sheep – unlike the hired hand who runs away (10:11–14). The garden recalls this setting. The *characters*, Jesus and the disciples, enter the safe space (18:1), while others, a menacing posse of soldiers and Judas, come like thieves and bandits to raid the pen (garden). (Judas is called a thief in 12:6.) Jesus, the mediating character who moves freely between safety inside and danger outside, goes out to protect the sheep within the pen (18:4). The *point of view* of the narrative develops and reinforces the perspective that Jesus is completely in charge of the sequence of events. The contrast between the disaffected disciple, Judas, who comes with all the power that he can muster (a 'cohort' of soldiers, normally 600 men), and Jesus, who goes out to single-handedly foil the redoubtable threat, is intentional. Despite the superior advantage of the raiding party, Jesus controls the circumstances of the arrest. He is prescient of his fate (18:4); he takes charge of the investigation (18:4); he fells the cohort of soldiers with the divine sobriquet, 'I Am' (18:6); and he chides Peter for interfering with God's ineluctable plan (18:10–11). Clearly, Jesus is sovereign over what happens in *this* pen. Whereas the self-protective hireling flees as 'wolves' approach (10:12), Jesus steps forward and voluntarily lays down his life for the sheep (cf. 10:11; 18:8). Jesus' actions illustrate the *ideological point of view* of the narrative: 'I did not lose a single one of those whom you gave me' (18:9). He alone determines the conditions of the release of the disciples. The *spatial stance* of Judas in the narrative highlights his disaffiliation. After receiving the sop at the Last Supper he left

the security of the pen (13:30); in this narrative his physical position leaves little doubt where his loyalties lie. The deceptively simple annotation of 18:5 underscores his resolve: 'Judas, who betrayed him, was standing with them.' He does not stand with Jesus or the disciples; rather he stands 'with them,' i.e., the soldiers and police. The *plot* of betrayal or denial is summarized in this simple action: where one stands in relation to Jesus (cf. also Peter in 18:18).

References and further reading

Abrams, M.H. (1993) 'New Criticism,' pp. 246–8 in *A Glossary of Literary Terms*, Fort Worth: Harcourt Brace College Publishers, 6th edn.

Brooks, Cleanth (1951) 'The Formalist Critics,' *The Kenyon Review* 13: 72–81.

Culpepper, R. Alan (1983) *Anatomy of the Fourth Gospel: A Study in Literary Design*, Philadelphia: Fortress Press.

Poland, Lynn M. (1985) *Literary Criticism and Biblical Hermeneutics: A Critique of Formalist Approaches*, Chico: Scholars Press.

Resseguie, James L. (1982) 'John 9: A Literary-Critical Analysis,' in K. Gros Louis (ed.), *Literary Interpretations of Biblical Narrative*, II, Nashville: Abingdon Press (reprinted in *The Gospel of John as Literature: An Anthology of Twentieth-Century Perspectives*, Mark W.G. Stibbe (ed.), Leiden: Brill, 1993, pp. 115–22).

—— (1998) *Revelation Unsealed: A Narrative Critical Approach to John's Apocalypse*, Leiden: Brill.

Rhoads, David, Joanna Dewey, and Donald Michie (1999) *Mark as Story: An Introduction to the Narrative of a Gospel*, Minneapolis: Fortress Press, 2nd edn.

Stibbe, Mark W.G. (1992) *John as Storyteller: Narrative Criticism and the Fourth Gospel*, Cambridge: Cambridge University Press.

Starobinski, Jean (1972/73) 'The Struggle with Legion: A Literary Analysis of Mark 5:1–20,' *New Literary History* 4: 331–56.

Trible, Phyllis (1978) 'A Human Comedy,' pp. 166–99 in *God and the Rhetoric of Sexuality*, Philadelphia: Fortress Press.

JAMES L. RESSEGUIE

FORMER PROPHETS

1 Introduction

The second of the Hebrew canon's three major divisions is known as the 'Prophets' (*nebi'im*) and is divided into the 'Former Prophets' (FP) and 'Latter Prophets' (LP). The reason for this designation is clear enough in LP, which contains the books of Isaiah, Jeremiah, Ezekiel, and the book of the Twelve, but the application of a prophetic title to FP is less transparent to modern readers because, generically speaking, FP includes the historical books of Joshua, Judges, Samuel, and Kings. The presence of these narratives in the prophetic corpus stems from the Jewish tradition that a series of prophets composed these books. Such a belief is reflected even in the canon itself, when the Hebrew Chronicler attributed his historical sources to prophetic authors (e.g., 1 Chron. 29:29 *et al.*).

2 The Former Prophets in modern research

The dominant views of FP in modern scholarship have been shaped by the works of M. Noth and F.M. Cross. Noth argued that FP should be viewed as a 'Deuteronomistic History' (DtrH; also 'Deuteronomistic Historian') because it presented the history of Israel and Judah as it might appear through the theological lens of Deuteronomy. DtrH added an introduction and conclusion to the book of Deuteronomy (Deut. 1–3, 27–34) and in this way folded the law book into his new composition, which began in Deuteronomy 1 and ended with the Exile in 2 Kings 25. The purpose of this composition was to explain the cause of Judah's exile to Babylon (586 BC), which DtrH blamed on the nation's disregard for the Deuteronomic law. Deuteronomy forbade the worship of foreign gods and idols, under threat of exile, and on this basis DtrH took the destruction of the northern kingdom (2 Kings 17) and the south's exile to Babylon (2 Kings 25) as the consequences of their idolatry. Noth's basic approach to FP still has many adherents (e.g., Peckham; Hoffman) and naturally presumes that DtrH was composed no earlier than the Babylonian Exile, although it is now common to postulate that a series of exilic and postexilic editorial layers were added to this original work (e.g., Smend 1971; Dietrich 1972; Veijola 1977; Klein 1983).

Cross agreed with Noth's assessments of FP in many respects, but he believed that a first edition of DtrH was composed *before* the Exile during the reign of Josiah, when the 'book of the Law' – apparently an edition of Deuteronomy – unexpectedly turned up in the Jerusalem temple (see 2 Kings 22–23). This first edition of DtrH assumed that the Davidic dynasty would endure forever (2 Sam. 7) and encouraged Judah to follow God's law as enumerated in Deuteronomy. The eventual fall of David's dynasty in 597 BC and the destruc-

tion of Jerusalem in 586 BC necessitated a second edition of DtrH, which explained the fall of David's house by conditioning God's promises to David on the obedience of his generally disobedient progeny (1 Kings 2:1–12). Psalm 89 suggests that some Jews found this solution unsatisfying. Because Cross's view assumes both preexilic and exilic editions of DtrH, his position has been conveniently labeled the 'double redaction' approach (see also Nelson 1981).

Three recent developments in the modern study of DtrH should be noted. First, there are some scholars who question the very existence of such a work, citing as evidence a lack of thematic unity in the text and the obvious form-critical differences between Joshua, Judges, Samuel, and Kings (Knauf 1996; Westermann 1994). But scholars have long attributed the form-critical differences in these books to the sources used by DtrH, and the thematic unity of DtrH is transparent to most scholars. Second, there is an emerging tendency to view the four books of FP as part of a larger composition rather than a work in itself. One increasingly influential theory postulates a 'greater DtrH composition' that stretched from Exodus 2 to 2 Kings 25 (Schmid 1999), while other scholars would add Genesis to this larger composition, thus forming a nine-book 'Enneateuch' (the Pentateuch plus FP; see H.-C. Schmitt 2003). This nine-book composition, known also to scholars as the 'Primary History' indeed reflects some clear signs of compositional unity, but the special affinities between Deuteronomy and FP suggest that it is more sensible to imagine that the original DtrH included only Deuteronomy and the four books of FP (Römer 2003). Third, there is a continuing debate about the extent to which DtrH depended on his sources. Most scholars believe that DtrH followed his sources closely and merely stitched them together through minor editing, but scholars in increasing numbers are granting a more creative role to DtrH, which implies that large portions of his history were composed as creative fiction (e.g., Hoffman 1980; Van Seters 1983).

Let us briefly consider the individual books of FP in more detail.

3 The book of Joshua

This segment of FP provides an account of early Israel's successful invasion of Palestine, its settlement there, and its ongoing struggle to secure the land in the face of resistance from the land's native inhabitants. Central to the narrative is Yahweh's role as a divine warrior who fights alongside Israel in its battles. Scholars are fairly certain that this account does not rest on early written sources but was instead composed by combining Israelite tradition – which may or may not preserve much history – with inferences that the author could draw in his own day. It is fairly clear that Joshua was composed by DtrH because of its many thematic connections with Deuteronomy (Josh. 1:3–5 and Deut. 11:24–25; Josh. ch. 2; 6:20–25 and Deut. 7:1–6; ch. 20; Josh. ch. 7 and Deut. 13:12–18; Josh. 8:30–35 and Deut. ch. 27; Josh. 9:1–27 and Deut. ch. 20; Josh. 10:12–27 and Deut. 21:22–23). If we date Deuteronomy to Josiah's reign, this suggests that Joshua dates no earlier than the seventh century BC. This first-millennium date for Joshua is reinforced by several other features. Archaeology suggests that many of the cities conquered in Joshua were not inhabited during the period of Israel's emergence in the land (*c.* 1200 BC; see Dever 1992), and these sites and regions correlate best with first-millennium epigraphic sources from Palestine (cf. Num. 26:29–34; Josh. 17:1–3; Renz and Rolling 2003). There is also good evidence that Joshua's conquest account was modeled after first-millennium neo-Assyrian conquest accounts (Van Seters 1990; cf. Younger 1990). We can surmise from this evidence that DtrH wrote at a time when there were no longer Canaanites in the land and that he took the ruins scattered across Palestine's countryside as evidence of Israel's early successes in battle.

Two peculiar features in Joshua lead us to other insights about the book's composition. First, the book actually contains two concluding speeches by Joshua, one that clearly belongs to DtrH and another that appears to have been appended to the book. The added speech is often attributed to the Yahwist author of the Pentateuch and probably reflects an effort to integrate Joshua's conquest with that Pentateuchal source. There is an ongoing debate about whether this means that the Yahwist was written after DtrH or before it. The second peculiar feature is that, although the first half of the book provides DtrH's description of a complete victory over the native Canaanites (chs 1 ff.), the second half depicts only partial success, with much land left to conquer and many Canaanites remaining in the land. Two pieces of evidence suggest that this part of Joshua should be associated with priestly materials in the Pentateuch (see Van Seters 1983). The Priestly Writer worked during the postexilic period, when sociological and religious conflicts between the returning exiles and the 'people of the land' would fit the notion that 'Canaanites' were still present in Palestine, and the use of lot-casting to divide the conquered territories – so conspicuous in this part of Joshua – is a practice found almost exclusively in the postexilic priestly materials. In sum, although Joshua provides an account of Israel's earliest national history, the book itself seems to be a relatively late composition by DtrH that was somehow edited to fit it into two other editions of Israel's history, that of the Yahwist and of the Priestly Writer.

4 The book of Judges

According to this portion of FP, early Israel was ruled by a series of military leaders called 'judges,' whom Yahweh called to deliver Israel from its enemies. Israel's history during this period mirrored its relationship with Yahweh in a repetitive four-stroke cycle that included: Israel's idolatry; divine punishment through foreign oppression; Israel's repentance; and deliverance by Yahweh's judge. Religious conditions in Israel gradually eroded during this period, as the author attempted to show by ending this sequence with the hapless judge Samson and by appending to the book a series of grisly tales about Israel's evil (chs 17–21). As a whole, the book's author wanted to prepare the reader for the rise of the monarchy in Samuel, a task that he accomplished by showing that the judges' institution did not offer the religious benefits of a more permanent royal monarchy: 'In those days there was no king, and everyone did what was right in his own eyes' (Judg. 17:6; 21:25; cf. 19:1). In order to make this point, the author needed the judges to rule over the entire nation of Israel, but a cursory examination of the book's tales reveals that each judge exercised authority over a rather small geographical area. From this we should conclude that the author of judges took up a series of local-hero tales and reshaped them to create an all-Israel scheme.

Two kinds of judge figures appear in the book, those who are the protagonists of its stories (the major judges) and those who are merely listed by the author (the minor judges). All the major judges, save Jephthah, ruled for twenty, forty or eighty years, while the reigns of minor judges were of varied lengths (e.g., twenty-three, twenty-two, seven years). Moreover, the minor judges appear to be nested together in the middle of the major judge sequence (Judg. 10–12). From this scholars have deduced that the author of Judges used two primary sources for his history of early Israel: a list of minor judges that included chronology but no stories, and a series of heroic tales about the major judges that included no detailed chronology. What prompted the author to join these two sources? There is only one major judge who seems also to have been in the minor judge list, and that is Jephthah. So it appears that Jephthah served as the lynchpin to join together the major and minor judge sources.

5 The book of Samuel

This third installment of FP provides an account of Israel's last judge (Samuel) and of the emergence of the united monarchy under Saul, David, and Solomon. Although some scholars believe that these narratives are late fictions, most conclude that DtrH's account of the nascent monarchy was based on old sources from close to the period that it describes. The most important evidence for this is that the narratives give the strong impression of providing propaganda for David and Solomon in their struggle to supplant the royal house of Saul (McKenzie 2000; Halpern 2001). The trajectory of this propaganda suggests that it was crafted to answer the impression that David and Solomon were illegitimate, murderous usurpers who violently assassinated Saul and his sons. In answer to this impression, the book of Samuel averred that God had chosen David as Saul's replacement and that in the deaths of Saul and his family/regime. David and Solomon were either entirely innocent or participated only because they were forced to do so (cf. 1 Sam. 24; 26; 31; 2 Sam. 1; 3–4; 9; 21; 1 Kings 2). It is reasonable to suppose that David and Solomon were less innocent in these deaths than the apologetic sources used by DtrH might indicate.

There is an ongoing discussion about whether the accounts in Samuel were composed by DtrH himself, using old but disparate sources, or whether full-blown narratives about Israel's early kings already existed before DtrH took up his pen. The latter is perhaps the most common approach and assumes that there were two old compositions from the time of the early monarchy, the 'Story of David's Rise' (1 Sam. 16–2; Sam. 6) and the 'Succession narrative' of Solomon (2 Sam. 9–1; Kings 2; see Rost 1926; Whybray 1968). Both were works of royal propaganda. Many scholars also believe that DtrH utilized two parallel sources from the time of Saul (see Halpern 2001), a conclusion that follows from the chronological and narrative tensions of the Saul story and from the fact that it contains propaganda from his regime, especially the accounts of Saul's divine election (see 1 Sam. 9–11). Some or all of these sources were already integrated into the Davidic/Solomonic propaganda and so accounted for Saul's being disqualified from kingship (1 Sam. 13), but DtrH edited this account to ensure that Saul's disqualification was occasioned not only by his impiety but, more specifically, by his infractions against the Deuteronomic law (1 Sam. 15; cf. Deut. 20).

6 The book of Kings

The concluding book of FP picks up with Solomon's ascension to the throne and provides a synchronistic account of the two Hebrew kingdoms until their respective falls. Here the Deuteronomistic flavor of FP is most pronounced, as each king is judged in turn according to the dictates of Deuteronomy's laws. Good kings are depicted as devoted followers of Yahweh who maintain his temple in Jerusalem as the only legitimate place for sacrifices and worship; by way of contrast, evil kings sponsor idolatry and permit worship at multiple 'high places,' in this way eschewing Deuteronomy's command

for a central cult site. Solomon is the first offender of the royal household, breaking Deuteronomy's law of the king (cf. Deut. 17: 14–20; 1 Kings 10:14–11:13) and consequently falling into idolatry. His punishment was a divided kingdom (Israel in the North; Judah in the South). The first king in the north, Jeroboam I, provided the paradigm for all subsequent northern kings, who 'walked in the ways of Jeroboam.' Jeroboam established idolatrous shrines at Dan and Bethel and instituted other cultic festivals to compete with the Jerusalem cult. Because other northern kings perpetuated these policies, Yahweh eventually sent Assyria to destroy the north and exile its inhabitants (722 BC; see 1 Kings 17). As for the south, DtrH depicted its kings in varied stripes, with some displaying great righteousness (e.g., Hezekiah; Josiah) but most others sponsoring idolatry. The evil southern counterpart to Jeroboam was Manasseh, who practiced human sacrifice and so became a chief cause of Jerusalem's destruction and Judah's exile to Babylon in 586 BC (cf. 2 Kings 21; 23:26). DtrH's account of the Hebrew kingdoms concludes with a message of hope, as the Jehoiachin king of Judah was released from his prison cell in Babylon.

Before considering the composition of Kings in more detail, we should note in passing the prophetic tales about Elijah and Elisha nested in 1 Kings 17–2 Kings 13. Although a superficial reading of the two prophetic cycles might create the impression that they are similar, there are important literary and ideological differences between them. The Elisha materials preserve a cycle of heroic legends that extolled the life of that celebrated prophet. DtrH's inclusion of this material is evidence of his antiquarian interest in preserving tradition and reminds us that, as a historian, more than theology motivated his work. In contrast to the Elisha stories, the Elijah stories do not focus on the prophet himself but were crafted instead to teach theology, especially a monotheistic devotion to Yahweh. Although this theological agenda suits DtrH well, the linguistic features of the Elijah materials, and of the Elisha cycle, reflect their origins in the north well before DtrH was assembled (Schniedewind and Sivan 1937; Rendsburg 2002). Many scholars take this as evidence that the monotheistic Deuteronomic movement originated in the northern kingdom, a conclusion that is reinforced by evidence for the northern prophet Hosea and by the northern flavor of Deuteronomy (e.g., Deut. 27).

How did DtrH compose the book of Kings? DtrH's presented his history of the two monarchies as a series of panels that treated each king in chronological order, alternating as necessary between the north and south. This arrangement is very similar to that found in the Neo-Babylonian Chronicle Series and suggests that DtrH's work was based on chronistic sources from Israel and Judah, a conclusion that is confirmed by the fact that he mentions such sources and by the fact that his regnal formula for the northern and southern kings differ (suggesting he had access to two separate chronistic sources; cf. Rendsburg 2002). DtrH supplemented the framework provided by his chronistic sources with other traditional sources (such as the stories about Solomon's wisdom, the Elisha tales) and then shaped the whole to accent his Deuteronomistic theological message.

7 Conclusions

Although Jewish tradition attributes FP to a series of prophetic authors, the modern scholarly view is that these four books were essentially the work of a single author (DtrH) who worked either just before or just after the Babylonian Exile. This author was not a historian in the modern sense, but it is clear enough that he consulted sources and that he adhered to them in such a way as to create occasional tensions and chronological problems. While DtrH's historical effort was overtly theological, his inclusion of material that did not promote this Deuteronomistic agenda – such as his list of minor judges and the Elisha cycle – attests to a parallel interest in preserving the traditions of his people. DtrH was eventually modified by later editors, but there is an ongoing debate about the extent and date of this editorial work.

The basic shape of DtrH suggests that he was familiar with and followed Mesopotamian literary conventions (Römer 2003). The book of Deuteronomy itself, which served as the basis for his history, was composed to mimic neo-Assyrian political treaties, and DtrH's conquest account in Joshua also echoes neo-Assyrian tradition. Near-Eastern literary conventions are similarly visible in the account of Solomon's temple construction (Hurowitz 1992) and in the overall chronistic arrangement of Kings. While it is possible that the imitative character of DtrH in these instances reflects an unconscious adoption of ancient scribal convention, the fact that DtrH was either composed or edited in the Babylonian Exile makes it more likely that the author intentionally followed Mesopotamian patterns in order to bestow upon his people a historical pedigree like that of his neighbors to the East.

References and further reading

Cross, F.M. (1973) *Canaanite Myth and Hebrew Epic*, Cambridge: Harvard University Press.

Dever, W.G. (1992) 'Archaeology and the Israelite "Conquest,"' *ABD* 3: 545–58.

Dietrich, W. (1972) *Prophetie und Geschichte; eine redaktionsgeschichtliche Untersuchung zum deuteronomistischen Geschichtswerk*, FRLANT 108, Göttingen: Vandenhoeck & Ruprecht.

Halpern, B. (2001) *David's Secret Demons: Messiah, Murderer, Traitor, King*, Grand Rapids: Eerdmans.

Hoffmann, H.-D. (1980) *Reform und Reformen: Untersuchungen zu einem Grundthema der deuteronomistischen Geschichtsschreibung*, ATANT 66, Zürich: Theologischer Verlag.

Hurowitz, V.A. (1992) *I Have Built You an Exalted House: Temple Building in the Bible in Light of Mesopotamian and Northwest Semitic Writings*, JSOTSup 115, Sheffield: Sheffield Academic Press.

Klein, R. (1983) *1 Samuel*, WBC 10, Waco: Word.

Knauf, E.A. (1996) 'L "'historiographie deutéronomiste" (DtrG) existe-t-elle?' pp. 409–18 in *Israël construit son histoire: L'historiographie deutéronomiste à la lumière des recherches récentes*, A. de Pury, T. Römer, and J.-D. Macchi (eds.), MdB 34, Geneva: Labor et Fides.

McKenzie, S.L. (2000) *King David: A Biography*, Oxford: Oxford University Press.

Nelson, R.D. (1981) *The Double Redaction of the Deuteronomistic History*, JSOTSup 18, Sheffield: Sheffield Academic Press.

Noth, M. (1981) *The Deuteronomistic History*, JSOTSup 15, Sheffield: Sheffield Academic Press.

Peckam, B. (1983) 'The Composition of Deuteronomy 5–11,' pp. 217–40 in *The Word of the Lord Shall Go Forth: Essays in Honor of David Noel Freedman in Celebration of His Sixtieth Birthday*, C.L. Meyers and M. O'Connor (eds.), Winona Lake: Eisenbrauns.

Rendsburg, G.A. (2002) *Israelian Hebrew in the Book of Kings*, Bethesda: CDL.

Renz, J. and W. Röllig (1995–2003) *Die althebräischen Inschriften*, 4 Vols., Darmstadt: Wissenschaftliche Buchgesellschaft.

Römer, T. (2003) 'The Form-Critical Problem of the So-Called Deuteronomistic History,' pp. 240–52 in *The Changing Face of Form Criticism for the Twenty-First Century*, M.A. Sweeney and E. Ben Zvi (eds.), Grand Rapids: Eerdmans.

Rost, L. (1926) *Die Überlieferung von der Thronnachfolge Davids*, BWANT 6, Stuttgart: Kohlhammer.

Schmid, K. (1999) *Erzväter und Exodus: Untersuchungen zur doppelten Begründung der Ursprünge Israels innerhalb der Geschichtsbücher des Alten Testaments*, WMANT 81, Neukircken-Vluyn: Neukirchener Verlag.

Schmitt, H.-C. (2003) 'Spätdeuteronomistisches Geschichtswerk und Priesterschrift in Deuteronomium 34,' pp. 407–24 in *Textarbeit: Studien zu Texten und ihrer Rezeption aus dem Alten Testament und der Umwelt Israels: Festschrift für Peter Weimar*, AOAT 294, Münster: Ugarit-Verlag.

Schniedewind, W. and D. Sivan (1997) 'The Elijah-Elisha Narratives: A Test Case for the Northern Dialect of Hebrew,' *Jewish Quarterly Review* 87: 303–37.

Smend, R. (1971) 'Das Gesetz und die Völker: Ein Beitrag zur deuteronomischen Redaktionsgeschichte,' pp. 494–505 in *Probleme biblischer Theologie: Gerhard von Rad zum 70. Geburtstag*, H.W. Wolff (ed.), München: Kaiser.

Van Seters, J. (1983) *In Search of History: Historiography in the Ancient World and the Origins of Biblical History*, New Haven: Yale University Press.

—— (1990) 'Joshua's Campaign of Canaan and Near Eastern Historiography,' *Scandinavian Journal of the Old Testament* 2: 1–12.

Veijola, T. (1975) *Die ewige Dynastie: David und die Enstehung seiner Dynastie nach der deuteronomistischen Darstellung*, Helsinki: Suomalainen Tiedeakatemia.

—— (1977) *Das Königtum in der Beurteilung der deuteronomistischen Historiographie: eine redaktionsgeschichtliche Untersuchung*, Helsinki: Suomalainen Tiedeakatemia.

Westermann, (1994) *Die Geschichtsbücher des Alten Testaments: gab es ein deuteronomistisches Geschichtswerk?* TB 87, Gütersloh: Kaiser.

Whybray, R.N. (1968) *The Succession Narrative: A Study of II Samuel 9–20; 1 Kings 1 and 2*, SBT, Second Series, 9, London: SCM Press.

Younger, Jr., K.L. (1990) *Ancient Conquest Accounts: A Study in Ancient Near Eastern and Biblical History Writing*, JSOTSup 98, Sheffield: Sheffield Academic Press.

KENTON L. SPARKS

FOUCAULT, MICHEL (1926–1984)

As a philosopher, Michel Foucault followed Jean-Paul Sartre as France's cultural hero. He is best known for analyzing power and the subject, and the conceptual/practical connection between the two terms.

To Foucault, every social relation is a power relation. Prior to his analysis, power was conceived as a scarce substance and its exchange was modeled on a zero-sum game. He challenged that view of power and focused not on what power is but on how it operates as energy, he thought, that constantly moves through the social world, and which everyone has access to and influence upon – power as a form of action in which we govern the actions of others.

He called his description a perspectival concept that permits people to see what power is doing in various social relations and wrote 'a history of the present' to reveal its three major patterns: sovereign power, pastoral power, and disciplinary power. Sovereign power is associated with feudalism in the West, pastoral power with the rise of Christianity, and disciplinary power with the economics of the Industrial Revolution. Foucault claimed that sovereign, pastoral, and disciplinary power are present in everyday social relations in which people become devoid of human value, distracted from self-knowledge, and incapable of self-generated action.

Foucault examined power, not by focusing on those who wield it but by observing those suspended in its webs. Following Foucault's gaze, we observe Jesus curing people who did not ask for help (Luke 6:6–11; 8:42b–48; 13:10–17; 14:1–6). He reached into their subjectivity – a worldview rife with expectations of what they could not think possible – and healed their diseases. He interrupted the order of things in the temple to question an established economic pattern that prescribed who could and could not offer worship and did so to awaken passion for God's house as a house of prayer (Matt. 21:12–13).

The question of subjectivity is central to Foucault's work. The term had two possible meanings: we may be subject to someone else by control and dependence, or we may be tied to our own identities by conscience or self-knowledge. Both meanings imply an exercise of power that subjugates people and keeps them under external authority. In the first case, external authority is literally another person or group; in the second case, external authority enters the body (like a parasite) so that a subject attends to that voice, rather than its own, does not know its self authentically, and is caught in what it is described as, e.g., an abnormal body.

Not only is the subject ambiguous, Foucault has an ambiguous relationship with the term. On the one hand, it is the core of his intellectual inquiry. It was the subject not power that was most important to him. He created a 'history of the different modes by which. . . human beings are made subjects' (Foucault 1982: 212). On the other hand, his work announced the death of the subject, i.e., the end of a concept for man [sic] that informed the modern period and, to him, was unique to it. In announcing its death, Foucault referred to the demise of modernity's rules for speaking about the subject. He developed the first sense of the subject (as constituted through an exercise of power that permits the subject to resist domination) and constantly fended off attacks for proposing the second, i.e., the death of man (Foucault 1973: 210).

On the strength of his interpretation of the subject, he came to assert that power is not domination. While asymmetry exists in every social relation, power refuses to dominate. In domination, an imbalance of force allows one person to govern another person's actions and cuts off resistance. In power relations, resistance is always possible, even if difficult. Foucault directed attention to sites for organizing resistance so that power is operating and domination is addressed. Like Socrates, he wanted to awaken people to care for themselves by resisting domination, including the self-imposed, but since we are human we will always be subject to some form of power's exercise.

Foucault retained an awareness of domination that prevented him from affirming the possibility of

Habermas' ideal speech community. To him, domination is inevitable in social relations and, though nothing is wrong with one person knowing more than another (e.g., in a teaching relation), he heralded our responsibility for self-care so that power would not degenerate into domination – in our own actions as well as in the actions of others toward us.

References and further reading

Arac, J. (1988) *After Foucault: Humanistic Knowledge and Postmodern Challenges*, London: Rutgers University Press.

Armstrong, T. (1992) *Michel Foucault: Philosopher*, New York: Routledge.

Deleuze, G. (1986) *Foucault*, Sean Hand trans. and ed., Minneapolis: University of Minnesota Press.

Eribon, D. (1991) *Michel Foucault*, trans. B. Wing, Cambridge, MA: Harvard University Press.

Foucault, M. (1973) *The Order of Things*, New York: Vintage Books.

—— (1979a) *Discipline and Punish*, New York: Vintage Books.

—— (1979b) 'Governmentality,' *Ideology and Consciousness*, 6: 5–21.

—— (1980) *Power/Knowledge: Interviews 1972–1977*, trans. C. Gordon *et al.*, C. Gordon (ed.), New York: Pantheon Books.

—— (1982) 'The Subject and Power,' in *Michel Foucault: Beyond Structuralism and Hermeneutics*, H. Dreyfus and P. Rabinow (eds.), Chicago: University of Chicago Press.

—— (1988a) *Madness and Civilization*, trans. R. Howard, New York: Vintage Books.

—— (1988b) 'The Ethic of Care for the Self as a Practice of Freedom,' in *The Final Foucault*, D. Bernauer and D. Rasmussen (eds.), Cambridge: The MIT Press.

—— (1990) *The History of Sexuality Vol. 1*, trans. R. Hurly, New York: Vintage Books.

Kant, I. (1991) 'An Answer to the Question: "What is Enlightenment,"' in *Kant: Political Writings*, Cambridge: Cambridge University Press.

Miller, J. (1991) *The Passion of Michel Foucault*, New York: Simon and Schuster.

Seigel, J. (1990) 'Avoiding the Subject,' *Journal of the History of Ideas* 51(2): 271–99.

Taylor, C. (1986) 'Foucault on Freedom and Truth,' in *Foucault: A Critical Reader*, New York: Blackwell.

JOYCE E. BELLOUS

FUCHS, ERNST (1903–1983)

German New Testament Protestant (Lutheran) scholar (prosecuted in Hitler's time) who taught at the universities of Bonn, Berlin, Tübingen, and Marburg; one of the students of Bultmann who revised some of their teacher's principles and developed a new methodology (see G. Ebeling, E. Käsemann, H. Conzelmann). He also influenced the debate in systematic theology. He has published several monographs (*Christus und der Geist bei Paulus*/Christ and Spirit in Paul, 1932; *Die Freiheit des Glaubens*/The Freedom of Faith, 1949) and numerous articles (*Gesammelte Aufsätze*/Collected Essays, I–III, 1959–1965). He made a particular contribution in the field of hermeneutics (*Hermeneutik*, 1954; *Marburger Hermeneutik*, 1968; from 1962 he was co-editor of the monograph series 'Hermeneutische Untersuchungen zur Theologie'/Hermeneutical Investigations in Theology).

His work in the field of hermeneutics is a monumental attempt at a combination of existential interpretation and diachronic text analysis. Like, for example, P. Ricoeur, he stressed the fact that an authentic interpretation aims at a new self-understanding of the reader (hearer) as well as of the interpreter himself.

Since the New Testament texts derive their authority from Jesus, Fuchs concluded that faith has to interpret the historical Jesus. The reason for this new interest in the historical Jesus (the new quest of the historical Jesus) is not to deliver evidence or a legitimization of faith. Instead, faith motivates interest in the earthly Jesus. Thus Fuchs moved the discussion beyond the Bultmannian impasse. He did not deny Easter as a reconfirmation of Jesus' attitude toward God. However, according to him, not only the mere 'that' of Jesus' earthly existence, which was included in the Easter faith, is the basic datum of Christianity, but also the faith of the earthly Jesus (cf. W. Herrmann) in all its dimensions (the basic one being love). There is an *analogia fidei* between the present Christian and the earthly Jesus.

The earthly Jesus is accessible in the language shape of the biblical text. And the relation of a text to history (it bears the signs of the time of its origin and of the time it relates to) corresponds to the character of God's revelation in its relation to a special point of history. Fuchs did not realize all the dimensions of language as a system and he did not discuss the theological problem of history. Nevertheless, as one of the pioneers of the new quest he opened up the problem of the personal engagement (of faith) and the orientation in time. In this respect he is the antipode of the postmodern attitude. (Information about Fuchs' hermeneutics is in Robinson 1964, Achtemeier 1969, and Keck 1971.)

Fuchs influenced contemporary theology with his thesis that Jesus was not only a teller of parables, but that through his attitude and behaviour (*Verhalten*) he himself also became a parable of God (*Gesammelte Aufsätze II*, orig. 1956). This idea of Jesus as a parable or metaphor of God has been taken over by numerous theologians like Bultmann, Schillebeeckx, Keck, Sölle, Jüngel or Ed. Schweizer.

References and further reading

Achtemeier, Paul J. (1969) *An Introduction to the New Hermeneutic*, Philadelphia: Westminster Press.

Keck, Leander E. (1971) *A Future for the Historical Jesus: The Place of Jesus in Preaching and Theology*, Nashville: Abingdon Press.

Robinson, James M. (1964) *The New Hermeneutic*, New Frontiers in Theology 2, New York: Harper & Row.

PETR POKORNÝ

G

GADAMER, HANS-GEORG (1900–2002)

Gadamer developed a distinctively dialogical approach that has become a major contribution to the development of twentieth-century hermeneutics. His name has become synonymous with philosophical hermeneutics, and although he was not explicitly a religious thinker his work has had a broad impact in many circles including theology and biblical criticism. Gadamer's most influential work, *Truth and Method* (*Wahrheit und Methode*, 1960, ET 1975), has the dual purpose of confronting narrow views of scientific method as the sole route to truth and offering an extension of Martin Heidegger's Dasein ontology. *Truth and Method* is an account of what Gadamer takes to be the universal hermeneutic experience of understanding in which he emphasizes language and tradition.

Philosophical hermeneutics exemplifies a shift from conceptualizing 'understanding' as a methodology toward a philosophical 'universality' of understanding and interpretation. Gadamer does *not* prescribe norms and rules for interpretation but describes the hermeneutical experience as a dialogical 'play' between the past and present, text and interpreter, that is, not reducible to technique but an ongoing process with no final completion. Understanding in interpretation occurs through the 'fusion of horizons' between the subject matter and the interpreter's initial position, that is, one's own historically situated horizon of knowledge and experience, and the historical horizon of a text. Interpretation is a gradual, perpetual, and creative interplay between horizons.

Gadamer argues that the objective, as idealized in scientific method, can only provide a limited degree of certainty and can never fully capture the intended or original meaning of a text. What is present in a text has become detached from the placement of its origin and author. For Gadamer, interpretation is a living dynamic in which one does not merely follow rules in the scrutiny and interrogation of passive texts but also allows them to draw one into their own world, while the interpreter remains rooted in the present. Since each reading of a text is grounded in its own context, no one reading offers a definitive or final interpretation of the text. Gadamer's interpretation of history and thought denies that there is a single true interpretation transcending all viewpoints and also denies that we are restricted to our own subjective interpretation.

Perhaps most controversial is his defense of our prior hermeneutical situatedness, since understanding always occurs in a larger historical context. Gadamer develops his understanding of the hermeneutical context through his notion of 'effective historical consciousness,' and works out the role of this 'effective history' as it manifests itself in our prejudices (or 'pre-judgments') that are themselves what open us up to what is to be understood. What matters most for Gadamer is our present involvement or relationship with a text, particularly as a response to our own questions that are themselves influenced by our 'effective history.'

Gadamer's philosophical hermeneutic is never about static and absolute interpretations but is a current dialogue, the universality of which binds together language, tradition, experience, and our effective history in the comprehensiveness of the hermeneutical experience.

References and further reading

Gadamer, Hans-Georg (2002) *Truth and Method*, trans. Joel Weinsheimer and Donald G. Marshall, New York: Continuum, 2nd rev. edn.

Thiselton, Anthony C. (1980) *The Two Horizons: New Testament Hermeneutics and Philosophical Description*, Grand Rapids: Eerdmans.

J.C. ROBINSON

GENERAL EPISTLES

1 Common issues
2 James
3 1 Peter
4 2 Peter–Jude

The General Epistles, with the exception of 1 Peter, were accepted into the canon late. Although well-accepted from the fourth to the sixteenth century, since then they have often been viewed as the stepchildren of the New Testament. Until recently they have been almost ignored in New Testament studies, but now because of a willingness to hear their distinctive voice these works are coming into their own in contemporary biblical studies.

1 Common issues

While each of these works presents its own unique challenges, there are a number of issues in common that may be discussed together. First, since the eighteenth century each of these works has frequently been considered a product of the second century. Only recently has there been more of a willingness to view them as products of the first century (even the third-quarter of the first century). Second, none of the works is from a significant body of literature by a given author. As a result, we lack the historical references and theological comparisons that we have in the Pauline epistles and, in another form, in the Gospels. Nor is any of the works set in a context extensively discussed in Acts. Third, some of these works are Jewish-Christian (James and Jude) and others have been wrongly thought to be Jewish-Christian (1 and 2 Peter). That means that they come from a church context that is foreign to modern interpreters and only in the last decades has been again described with the fullness that is needed.

2 James

Although sometimes still viewed as a post-Pauline polemic against Paul (Hengel 1987), James stems from the Jewish-Christian church in Jerusalem and therefore reflects a law-abiding community for whom Judaism and Christianity were not mutually exclusive. Unlike Paul's community, this community had no law–grace tension for they were already Jews when they became believers in Jesus and thus had no issue with circumcision or other Jewish practices. The letter presents itself as a Diaspora letter; that is, a letter written from the central 'Jewish' authorities in Jerusalem to Jewish communities in the Diaspora (Davids 1999). This means that the letter must be read against such a background and not in the context of the Pauline mission.

2.1 Use of the Jesus material
The Catholic tradition has welcomed James because of its extensive use of the Jesus tradition (in its Matthean form). One can identify at least thirty-six parallels (an average of five per chapter) of which twenty-five are to the Sermon on the Mount (Davids 1982: 47–8). Thus James must be read with the assumption that the readers are expected to know the appropriate sayings of Jesus (e.g., James 1:2 and Matt. 5:11–12). Even when James cites Jewish material, it is likely mediated to him and colored by its use by Jesus (e.g., James 1:19–20 reflects Proverbs and the wisdom tradition in general, but Jesus

uses this tradition in Matt. 5:22). Thus it is appropriate to read James as an application of the Jesus tradition to issues that arose in the Jewish-Christian church.

2.2 Use of the Old Testament
James quotes both legal material (James 2:8 = Lev. 19:18; James 2:11 = Exod. 20:13, 14) and wisdom (James 4:6 = Prov. 3:34) from the Hebrew scriptures, always identical in form to the Septuagint. He sometimes alludes to prophetic material (e.g., James 5:4 and 'Lord Sabaoth,' used repeatedly by Isaiah). When it comes to his use of narratives, however, he filters the four that he refers to (Abraham, Rahab, Job, Elijah) through the lens of contemporary Jewish interpretation. For example, his Abraham is the one tested by Satan rather than by God (James can write 1:13 because he reads Gen. 22:1 through the lens of the story of Job). His Rahab is the archetypal proselyte, who also showed hospitality. His Job is the patient Job of the *Testament of Job* rather than the frustrated Job of the canonical book (Davids 1978). In other words, James reads the teaching of the Hebrew scriptures through the lens of the teaching of Jesus and the stories through the lens of contemporary Jewish retelling (midrash). Ironically, in Christian interpretation such phrases as 'the patience of Job' have been read back into canonical Job rather than pointing to the contribution of James and his context in Judaism.

2.3 Structure
James has often been considered unstructured paraenesis (Dibelius and Heinrich 1976: 1–11). However, while James is an editing together of sayings and homilies attributed to James, recent study has shown that there is an organizing pattern according to which topics are introduced in the first chapter (1:2–11 being mirrored and advanced in 1:12–27) and then taken up in the body of the letter (2:1–5:6) in reverse order to their appearance in the letter opening. The conclusion includes a summary (5:7–11), a statement on oaths (5:12), a substitute for a health wish (5:13–18), and a purpose statement (5:19–20). Both the overall structure and especially the items in the closing were known letter structures in antiquity (Davids 1982: 22–8). Furthermore, this structure is found in some literary Diaspora letters. Within the structure come coherent smaller units, especially James 2:1–13; 2:14–26. Often termed a diatribe, these are a Jewish homiletic outline consisting of an opening topic statement and a brief narrative that sets the problem. This introductory section is followed by a theological argument supported by two scriptural texts. Finally, the sermon ends with a summary statement. Thus viewed structurally the Epistle fits into its Jewish-Christian environment.

2.4 Historical–cultural situation
The setting of the work is the Jewish Christianity that existed in Judaea in the sixth decade of the first century. Wealth is concentrated in the hands of rich landowners,

who work their land through tenant farmers. These same people also control the political and religious life of the people. Meanwhile the church exists as a movement within Judaism, one that is despised by many of the leaders of the nation, but has not yet separated from the synagogue. Furthermore, Christianity drew significant strength from the disenfranchised, whether they were the lower levels of the priestly hierarchy, the poor of the people, or aged pilgrims who had come to Judaea to live out their lives. The result was that the church was largely a church of the poor (cf. the collection for Jerusalem that is so important to Paul, e.g., Rom. 15:25–27) that was vulnerable to persecution by the wealthy and powerful, partly because its members were Christians and partly because they were poor. This tension between rich and poor was part of the inner dynamic of Judaism in the period leading up to the first revolt against Rome (AD 66–70). Thus one interprets James against a background of economic persecution. This type of persecution is low-grade, but constant. For the community the result was two related sets of problems: a struggle for economic security seen in trying to keep rather than share and to gain the favor of those few community members who were wealthier, and internal conflict in which Christians criticized each other. Both of these are typical responses to economic pressure in any culture. James is trying to maintain communal solidarity in the face of external pressure and its resultant internal friction.

2.5 James and Paul

A final critical issue in James is his relationship with Paul's thought. While James 2:14–26 and especially 20–24 appear to be directed against Paul's ideas embodied in Galatian's 3, a closer reading reveals a different situation. James' works are works of charity, while Paul's 'works of the law' are Jewish ethnic markers such as circumcision and dietary rules. In this passage 'faith' means adherence to an orthodox creed (the *Shema*, 2:19), while in Paul and elsewhere in James it means trust in or commitment to Christ/God. And James uses the traditional meaning of *dikaioō/dikaiosunē* (show to be or consider righteous), while Paul uses a new meaning (make the unrighteous righteous). As a result, we have three options: James totally misunderstands Paul; James has never seen a Pauline letter but is reacting to a distorted Paulinism (that he may not know comes from Paul) used to justify a lack of charity, or James is reacting to an independent teaching with roots in Judaism. Of the three options, only the latter two take all the data into account, and they also fit with the date and setting of James as proposed above (Davids 1993).

3 1 Peter

1 Peter is a letter written from Rome to a group of Christians personally unknown to the author who lived in northwest Asia Minor. The work therefore applies Christian teaching that was common to much of the church. The addressees are Gentile believers, who were experiencing persecution in the shape of social ostracism, slander, and other forms of loss of status. While there does not yet appear to be official persecution, this suffering was none the less serious in that honor was the chief positive value of their society and shame the chief negative one. Thus they may well have considered the experience as worse than death. The whole letter is aimed at giving Christians a sense of security and especially a place of belonging, minimizing conflict with the culture around them, and reframing their experiences in terms of identification with Christ.

3.1 Paulinism of 1 Peter

It is clear that 1 Peter uses a number of expressions in common with Paul, however, no literary dependence is evident (Michaels 1988: s.v. 'Literary Affinities'). Peter also lacks key Pauline ideas such as 'justification,' 'the cross,' and any Jew–Gentile tension. As a result it is unlikely that the work was written by a disciple of Paul, although it may reflect a common milieu in either its place of writing (Rome) or the sources of its theology (Antioch has been suggested, due to Peter's relationship to Matthean concepts).

3.2 Social code in 1 Peter

The social code in 2:13–3:22 is one item 1 Peter has in common with Pauline literature. Peter's adaptation of this code reflects two factors: first, Christianity was accused of undermining the social order in that it invited women, slaves, and children to embrace a faith that did not accord with the wishes of the male head of the family (this new faith was also exclusive and did not allow its members to participate in the pagan rites ordered by the family head), and, second, unlike the Pauline social codes 1 Peter addresses slaves and wives with non-Christian masters or husbands. Only in 3:7 does Peter address a Christian husband, and in that case he assumes that his wife is a believer (which would usually be the case when the head of a family converted). The Epistle makes the best of a difficult situation: in each case the societal value is upheld, but reframed in terms of obedience to the Lord. Thus Peter wants nothing to happen that would be disobedient to the Lord, but as much as possible to find a way of life that yields a peaceable relationship to unbelievers.

3.3 Use of Hebrew scriptures in 1 Peter

In 1 Peter we frequently encounter the Old Testament. In 2:4–10 there is not only a string of Old Testament passages quoted, but also Old Testament titles for Israel are applied to these Gentile believers. Thus the theology of 1 Peter often comes out in how the Old Testament is used. A more difficult passage is 1 Peter 3:18–22. The reference to the physical death of Christ and his being raised in a glorified body ('made alive in the spiritual sphere') is reasonably clear, but what about the spirits in prison? Here 1 Peter like James reads the Old Testament through the lens of Jewish interpretation. In this case Genesis 6:1–4 is read according to the understanding in *1 Enoch* (cited explicitly in Jude) that refers to the imprisonment of the angelic beings of Noah's day. The picture is one of the ascending Christ proclaiming his triumph. A second issue in this passage is that of salvation through baptism. Here we have typological interpretation. The image of Noah being saved by going through water is reflected in the Christian's being saved by baptism (that is, baptism was the point at which one officially made one's commitment to Christ, much as a wedding is when one makes a commitment to a spouse). Peter does not interpret every detail of the Noah story, but only notes the general resemblance, for his point is that Christians will escape judgment and that while they may go through execution like Christ, they will also rise and reign like Christ.

4 2 Peter – Jude

In fourth-century discussions of canon both of these works were disputed. In the past 200 years both have frequently been relegated to the second century as legalistic and legendary. However, recently a more nuanced reading views Jude and 2 Peter as related works that fit into two different worlds. Jude, the earlier work, comes from the Jewish-Christian community in Judaea. Like James it is a pre-AD 70 work and likely also a Diaspora letter. The letter is a prophetic denunciation of antinomian teachers and their practices (Bauckham 1983). Second Peter adapts Jude as the central portion of the book, but presents itself as a final testament from Peter addressed to largely Gentile communities (Charles 1997). The problem addressed is similar, however, and thus his use of Jude. In his case he must also combat the doctrinal position that made the antinomian teaching possible, namely, the idea that there would be no final judgment.

4.1 Jude

4.1.1 Jude's use of scripture
While citing a number of Old Testament narratives, Jude significantly cites them in groups of three, giving himself three witnesses and indicating his interest in the total effect of condemnation rather than in the details of the various stories. Scriptural images are also alluded to (e.g., Jude 12 alludes to Ezek. 34). This use of scripture expects the reader to know the Old Testament well.

4.1.2 Jude's use of noncanonical literature
Jude's significant citations of non-canonical literature (e.g., *1 Enoch* 1:9 in Jude 13–14; the *Testament/Assumption of Moses* in Jude 9) are often seen as a critical problem. This problem is anachronistic. Canon

consciousness arose significantly later than Jude, so while he is surely aware that these were not among the main books being read regularly in the synagogue, he had no reason to avoid them. He cites the stories just as he does the biblical stories without any consciousness of difference.

4.2 2 Peter

4.2.1 2 Peter's use of Greek ideas
Due to his use of Hellenistic terminology, most notably his references to 'godliness' (1:3, 6) and 'participation in the divine nature' (1:4), 2 Peter is often dated late. It is clear that such ideas were 'in the air' in the Gentile world in which 2 Peter was written, but we must be careful about trying to be more specific than that. That is, nothing indicates that he is intending to pick up a specific philosophical position. Such expressions need to be defined by their context in 2 Peter; however, they do tell us something about the culture in which 2 Peter was written and best fit a provenance outside of Palestine.

4.2.2 2 Peter's use of Jude
Not only does 2 Peter use Hellenistic terminology, but he also uses Jude. While it is not that unusual for one passage in scripture to be copied from another (it happens several times in the Old Testament; Matthew and Luke incorporate large sections of Mark), it is interesting that 2 Peter appears to have a strategy in his use of Jude. In 2:4 he removes the explicit reference to *1 Enoch* and in 2:10–11 does the same with the reference to the *Assumption of Moses*. Yet he retains the basic information. It appears that 2 Peter did not expect his readers to know the noncanonical literature that Jude uses and so edits Jude's material.

4.2.3 2 Peter's place in canon history
Paul's letters are referred to as 'scripture' in 2 Peter (3:16). However, it is easy to read too much into this statement. 2 Peter comes before any formal process of canonization, so he refers to Paul much as Jude refers to *1 Enoch*. Jude is not aware that *1 Enoch* will not be included in the canon, and 2 Peter is not aware that Paul will eventually be bound together with the Old Testament. What he does show is the knowledge that Paul has written more than one letter (but not necessarily of a collection of those letters), that at least one of his letters had been sent to the people he is addressing, and that Paul's letters were being misused. We see here the impulses that eventually led to collecting the Pauline letters and including them in the canon, but only the impulses, not the finished process.

References and further reading

Bauckham, Richard J. (1983) *Jude, 2 Peter*, WBC 50, Waco: Word Books.

Charles, J. Daryl (1997) *Virtue Amidst Vice: The Catalogue of Virtues in 2 Peter 1*, JSNTSup 150, Sheffield: Sheffield Academic Press.

Davids, Peter H. (1978) 'Tradition and Citation in the Epistle of James,' pp. 113–26 in *Scripture, Tradition and Interpretation*, W.W. Gasque and W.S. LaSor (eds.), Grand Rapids: Eerdmans.

—— (1982) *The Epistle of James: A Commentary on the Greek Text*, NIGTC, Grand Rapids: Eerdmans.

—— (1990) *The First Epistle of Peter*, NICNT, Grand Rapids: Eerdmans.

—— (1993) 'James and Paul,' pp. 457–61 in *Dictionary of Paul and His Letters*, G.F. Hawthorne, R.P. Martin, and D.G. Reid (eds.), Downers Grove: IV.

—— (1999) 'Palestinian Traditions in the Epistle of James,' pp. 33–57 in *James the Just and Christian Origins*, B. Chilton and C.A. Evans (eds.), NovT Sup 98, Leiden: Brill.

Dibelius, Martin, and Heinrich Greeven (1976) *James*, Hermeneia, Philadelphia: Fortress Press.

Hengel, Martin (1987) 'Der Jakobusbrief als antipaulinische Polemik,' pp. 248–78 in *Tradition and Interpretation in the New Testament*, G.F. Hawthorne and O. Betz (eds.), Grand Rapids: Eerdmans.

Martin, Ralph P. (1988) *James*, WBC 48, Waco: Word Books.

Michaels, J. Ramsey (1988) *1 Peter*, WBC 49, Waco: Word Books.

PETER H. DAVIDS

GNOSTICISM

1 Introduction

There are well-known problems about what precisely constitutes 'Gnostic' thought; the 'Bible' available to Gnostics (and others) was probably in a state of some flux; and it is not clear how far Gnostic (however defined) uses of the biblical material are attempting to provide an 'interpretation' of that material.

In line with an emerging scholarly consensus, I shall take 'Gnostic' to refer to the developed systems of speculative mythology and thought known to us through attacks from the Church Fathers and, more recently, through several of the texts now available to us in the Nag Hammadi library. However, one should note that not all the Nag Hammadi texts are necessarily Gnostic. Nor is it easy to subsume all Gnostic texts under a single banner in this respect. Gnostic thought is nothing

if not diverse (cf. the many attempts to identify and distinguish between, for example, 'Sethian,' 'Valentinian,' and other forms of Gnosticism); and attitudes to, and use of, the Bible are no exception. Clearly we see in Gnostic texts a range of very different attitudes to, and interpretations of, the Bible.

The dating of Gnostic texts is notoriously uncertain. The attacks on Gnostic ideas by the Church Fathers indicate that such ideas were prevalent in the second century AD and later. Whether Gnostic ideas can be traced back into an earlier period is much debated. Clearly though in the second century AD, there was no clearly defined 'New Testament,' and even Jewish scripture (the so-called 'Old Testament') may not have been definitively demarcated. In treating the topic of 'Gnostic interpretation of the Bible,' we should perhaps distinguish between Gnostic use of Jewish scripture and Gnostic use of Christian traditions (i.e., traditions which later became part of the Bible in the 'New Testament').

2 Gnostic interpretation of Jewish scripture

Gnostic use of Jewish scripture displays an enormous variety, and very different attitudes to scripture are discernible in different texts and/or writers. In some respects, Gnosticism is overtly hostile to all that Judaism stands for: above all, its denigration of the material world and of the creator of this world stands irreconcilably opposed to the traditional Jewish affirmation of the one God, the Creator of the world.

Yet it is also clear that Gnostics felt the need to justify their beliefs on the basis of a reading of Jewish scripture. Much of Gnostic mythology is focused on the origins of the universe and of the human race, and the nature of human beings, this being intimately connected with beliefs about human destiny. It is then in one way not surprising to find that large parts of Gnostic discussions of the origins of the world are in the form of a reading, or an interpretation, of the Genesis accounts in Jewish scripture. Given the radically different slant that is put on these accounts, it is uncertain whether they should be described as 'interpretations.' The reading involved often demands taking the text in a way that is radically different from any kind of exegesis that would be considered acceptable in 'normative' Judaism. Nevertheless it seems clear that the existence of such readings (or rereadings) of Jewish scriptural texts were regarded as important by Gnostic writers. As such it would appear that Gnosticism may have had deep roots within Judaism and may indeed have emerged from Judaism as some kind of 'protest' movement.

There is a great variety of attitudes shown toward Jewish scripture. However, at the very least one should note the enormous number of Gnostic texts that existed (or are said to have existed) which are clearly somehow related to Old Testament figures. (Many of these have not survived but there seem to have been books associated with figures such as Adam, Eve, Seth, Abraham, Moses, and several others.) Some Gnostic texts show an almost totally negative attitude to Jewish scripture and Jewish history. Thus the *Treat. Seth* (NHC 7.2) dismisses almost all the famous figures of the Old Testament as a 'laughing stock,' as well as dismissing the God of the Old Testament in the same way (though even this text, like a number of others, claims that the figure of Seth, Adam's third son [cf. Gen. 5:3], is to be regarded thoroughly positively, as the forerunner and origin of the race of true Gnostics). By contrast, the tractate *Exeg. Soul* (NHC 2.6) quotes extensively and positively from Jewish scripture (notably the prophets) to find descriptions (in allegorical form) of the odyssey of the soul (cf. 129.35ff., citing Jer., Hosea, and Ezek.)

More 'typical' (if anything here is typical!) may be the kind of attitude reflected in texts like the *Ap. John* (NHC 2.1, 3.1, 4.1 BG 2), the *Hyp. Arch.* (NHC 2.4), and *Orig. World* (NHC 2.5), and analyzed more explicitly in Ptolemy's *Letter to Flora* (in Epiphanius, *Pan.* 33.3). In the last, the whole question of the validity of the Law is raised and a mixed attitude is advocated. The Law is divided into three parts: one part derives from God himself, one part is from Moses, and one part is from 'the elders of the people.' (This is defended by appealing to Jesus' own discussion of divorce legislation.) Further, the Law of God can be subdivided into three: one part is fulfilled by Jesus' intensification ('fulfilment') of the commands (e.g., in some of the antitheses of Matt. 5:21ff.), one part is abolished by Jesus (e.g., the law on retaliation), one part is to be interpreted allegorically.

How far such a well thought out rationale is accepted by all Gnostic writers is not clear. Nevertheless it does seem to be the case that such an ambivalent attitude to Jewish scripture – accepting some parts, rejecting others, and providing a radically different interpretation of yet other parts – is reflected in many of the rewritings of the Genesis story that are evidently so important in the Gnostic myths of the origin of the world. One of the central tenets of Gnostic writers is of course a radical separation between the ultimate supreme God and the creator God of Jewish scripture. Judaism was famed for its monotheistic claims, its belief in the one, unique God. In many Gnostic rewritings of the Genesis story this claim is radically reinterpreted. The precise details of what happens before the creation of the world vary from one Gnostic text to another, though often some kind of disaster or rebellion (often associated with the figure of Sophia) is recounted. As a result, Sophia's offspring (sometimes called Ialdabaoth, sometimes by other names, e.g., Saklas or Samael) creates the world, but does so in a state of ignorance of his true status and of the existence of other powers over and above him. The great text of Jewish monotheism Isaiah 45:21 ('I am God, there is no other God beside me') is then

sometimes placed on the lips of Ialdabaoth, not to show his supremacy or uniqueness, but to show his total ignorance and/or arrogance (cf., e.g., *Ap. John* [NHC 2.1] 11.20; *Hyp. Arch.* [NHC 2.4] 94.20).

So too the story of the 'Fall' of Adam and Eve in Genesis 3 is radically rewritten. The act of eating from the tree of 'knowledge' is seen far more positively, and the prohibition by the 'God' of the story (taken as the creator God Ialdabaoth) is interpreted correspondingly negatively. Similarly the 'serpent' of the story is interpreted in a variety of ways. Some patristic writers speak of Gnostic groups giving an extremely high evaluation of the serpent (hence the description of some groups as 'Ophites,' cf. the Greek word *ophis* meaning serpent). However, in the texts from Nag Hammadi, the role of the serpent can vary considerably from being very positive (cf. *Test. Truth* [NHC 9.3] 45.23ff.) to being regarded as simply the vehicle taken over by the true 'instructor' in a docetic-type manner (*Hyp. Arch.* [NHC 2.4] 89.31ff.).

3 Gnostic interpretation of the 'New Testament'

Gnostic interpretation of the 'New Testament' is equally varied. One must beware of potential anachronism, since there may not have been a clearly defined 'New Testament' at the time of many Gnostic texts (i.e., in the second century AD or perhaps even earlier). However, traditions about Jesus and the writings of Paul were evidently known and valued by some Gnostic writers, though whether they were regarded as 'scriptural' remains unclear. How far the Christian elements are fundamental to Gnostic thought is much debated though it appears that quite often Christian features in Gnostic texts represent secondary additions to an earlier tradition which lacked explicitly Christian elements. (Cf. the case of *Soph. Jes. Christ* [NHC 3.4], which represents a Christianizing of *Eugnostos* [NHC 3.3] by adding questions by Christian disciples to an earlier unitary discourse.)

Jesus traditions were evidently known, probably from the canonical gospels (whether directly or indirectly: cf. Tuckett 1986). The issue of whether Gnostic writers knew of traditions about Jesus independent of the canonical Gospels is much debated, especially in relation to a text like *Gos. Thom.* (NHC 2.5), but also in relation to a text like *Ap. Jas.* (NHC 1.2): cf. the parable of the palm tree in 7.22ff., which some have seen as possibly a genuine parable of Jesus, otherwise unattested. Quite often Jesus traditions are simply echoed with no clear sustained attempt to 'interpret' them explicitly as part of a sacred text. Sometimes they are explicitly referred to (cf., e.g., *Ap. Jas.* [NHC 1.2] 8.6ff., referring apparently to a number of Jesus' parables by name) and sometimes they receive a specific allegorical interpretation (cf. the interpretation of the parable of lost sheep in *Gos. Truth* [NHC 1.3] 31.35ff., or in Ptolemy, according to Irenaeus, *A.H.* 1.8.4). So too, as we have already seen, Jesus' own attitude to the Jewish law can be adduced, to determine contemporary attitudes to the Law (cf. above on Ptolemy's *Letter to Flora*).

Along with a negative attitude to the created order, some Gnostics tended to regard Jesus as a purely heavenly being, and the reality of the incarnation was clearly difficult for some. Hence Jesus' death on the cross caused difficulties for some, and there are thus attempts at times to rewrite the Passion narratives (similar to the rewritings of the Genesis story) to bring out the 'true' facts of the matter; however, as always there is no uniformity among Gnostic writers. For example, the *Treat. Seth* ([NHC 7.2] 55.9ff.) retells the story so that the Savior watches and laughs as Simon of Cyrene is crucified in his place; however, in *Melch.* (NHC 9.1) the full reality of the humanity and the suffering of Jesus is emphasized (cf. 5.1ff.; 25.1ff.).

One text that evidently did give rise to sustained exegesis or 'interpretation' by Gnostics was the Gospel of John and especially the Prologue. Irenaeus (*A.H.* 1.8.5) tells of Ptolemy's detailed exposition of the Johannine Prologue in terms of the developed mythology of the emanation of the various aeons postulated; and elsewhere he refers to the extensive use of John by Valentinians (*A.H.* 3.11.7). Clearly John's Gospel was a text that was very highly regarded by Gnostic writers and formed the basis for their mythology and ideas (see further Pagels 1973).

Other writings which later became part of the New Testament were also clearly valued by other Christian Gnostic writers. The letters of Paul, for example, were clearly highly regarded and the authority of Paul was appealed to in order to buttress the claims made. Thus the author of *Hyp. Arch.* at the very start of his work identifies the 'archons,' who are responsible for the creation of the world as the evil spiritual forces of the universe mentioned by 'Paul' in Colossians 1:13 and Ephesians 6:12. The author of *Exeg. Soul* (NHC 2.6) cites Paul extensively (130.30ff.) and the author of the *Treat. Res.* (NHC 1.4) explicitly claims Pauline support for his assertion of the present reality of resurrection life (45.25ff.: 'we suffered with him, we rose with him, we went to heaven with him,' probably referring to Rom. 8:17 and Eph. 2:5–6). Allusion to, and indebtedness to, the Pauline letters may also underlie a number of other passages and extended arguments in Gnostic texts (see Pagels 1975).

4 Conclusion

The extensive use of the Bible – at times highly sustained, at times quite detailed, but also extremely varied when comparing one Gnostic writer with another – shows the importance attached to the Jewish and/or Christian tradition by Gnostic writers. Gnosticism would appear to have had firm roots in Judaism and (at least in some cases) Christianity, which Gnostic writers

evidently felt it was important to assert at the same time as they showed their own distinctive ideas by their reinterpretation of the scriptures they shared with others.

References and further reading

Pagels, E. (1973) *The Johannine Gospel in Gnostic Exegesis*, Nashville and New York: Abingdon Press.

—— (1975) *The Gnostic Paul: Gnostic Exegesis of the Pauline Letters*, Philadelphia: Fortress Press.

Pearson, B.A. (1988) 'Use, Authority and Exegesis of Mikra in Gnostic Literature,' pp. 635–52 in *Mikra: Text, Translation, Reading and Interpretation of the Hebrew Bible in Ancient Judaism and Early Christianity*, CRINT II.1, M.J. Mulder (ed.), Assen: Van Gorcum/Philadelphia: Fortress Press.

—— (1990) *Gnosticism, Judaism and Egyptian Christianity*, Minneapolis: Fortress Press.

Tuckett, C.M. (1986) *Nag Hammadi and the Gospel Tradition*, Edinburgh: T.&T. Clark.

CHRISTOPHER TUCKETT

GOSPEL: GENRE

> 1 Historical overview
> 2 The Gospels as ancient biography
> 3 Implications for interpretation

1 Historical overview

Before we can read the Gospels we have to discover what kind of books they might be. Differing understandings of their genre will have differing implications for their interpretation. For much of the ancient and medieval periods, the Gospels, like the rest of the Bible, could be interpreted on several levels: the literal meaning would provide facts about what actually happened, while an allegorical interpretation could apply any text to the story of redemption; the use of scripture for moral purposes would provide direct instruction for behavior and an anagogical or mystical reading would relate the text to the reader's own spiritual pilgrimage.

The Reformers rejected all levels of reading except for the literal, and on this basis the Gospels were interpreted as history – the stories of Jesus, even seen in terms of biographies. However, during the nineteenth century, biographies began to explain the character of a great person by considering his or her upbringing, formative years, schooling, psychological development, and so on. The Gospels began to look unlike such biographies.

Accordingly, during the 1920s, scholars like Karl Ludwig Schmidt and Rudolf Bultmann rejected any notion that the Gospels were biographies. Instead, the

Gospels were seen as popular folk literature, collections of stories handed down orally over time (see Bultmann 1972: 371–4). Furthermore, the development of form-critical approaches to the Gospels meant that they were no longer interpreted as whole narratives. Instead, they concentrated on each individual pericope, and the focus for interpretation moved more to the passage's *Sitz im Leben* in the early church.

The rise of redaction criticism half a century later led to more interpretation of each Gospel's theological interests and the development of theories about the communities which produced them. Once the Gospels were seen as a type of 'community' documents, then their interpretation focused on the development of groups like the Johannine or Matthean communities (see, for example, the work of R.E. Brown). However, redaction critics also saw the writers of the Gospels as individual theologians and the development of new literary approaches to the Gospels viewed them as conscious literary artists. This reopened the question of the genre of the Gospels and their place within the context of first-century literature, with scholars like Talbert and Aune beginning to treat the Gospels as biographies.

2 The Gospels as ancient biography

In order to determine whether the Gospels are a form of ancient biography, it is necessary to examine the generic features shared by ancient 'lives' or *bioi* – the word *biographia* does not appear until the ninth-century writer, Photius. From the formal or structural perspective, they are written in continuous prose narrative, between 10,000 and 20,000 words in length – the amount on a typical scroll of about 30–35 feet in length. Unlike modern biographies, Graeco-Roman lives do not cover a person's whole life in chronological sequence, and have no psychological analysis of the subject's character. They may begin with a brief mention of the hero's ancestry, family or city, his birth and an occasional anecdote about his upbringing; but usually the narrative moves rapidly on to his public debut later in life. Accounts of generals, politicians, or statesmen are more chronologically ordered, recounting their great deeds and virtues, while lives of philosophers, writers, or thinkers tend to be more anecdotal, arranged topically around collections of material to display their ideas and teachings. While the author may claim to provide information about his subject, often his underlying aims may include apologetic, polemic, or didactic. Many ancient biographies cover the subject's death in great detail, since here he reveals his true character, gives his definitive teaching, or does his greatest deed. Finally, detailed analysis of the verbal structure of ancient biographies reveals another generic feature. While most narratives have a wide variety of subjects, it is characteristic of biography that attention stays focused on one particular person with a quarter to a third of the verbs

dominated by the subject, while another 15 percent to 30 percent occur in sayings, speeches, or quotations from the person (see Burridge 1992: 261–74).

Like other ancient biographies, the Gospels are continuous prose narratives of the length of a single scroll, composed of stories, anecdotes, sayings, and speeches. Their concentration on Jesus' public ministry from his baptism to death, and on his teaching and great deeds, is not very different from the content of other ancient biographies. Similarly, the amount of space given to the last week of Jesus' life, his death, and the resurrection reflects that given to the subject's death and subsequent events in works by Plutarch, Tacitus, Nepos, and Philostratus. Verbal analysis demonstrates that Jesus is the subject of a quarter of the verbs in Mark's Gospel, with a further fifth spoken by him in his teaching and parables. About half of the verbs in the other Gospels either have Jesus as the subject or are on his lips: like other ancient biographies, Jesus' deeds and words are of vital importance for the evangelists' portraits of Jesus. Therefore these marked similarities of form and content demonstrate that the Gospels have the generic features of ancient biographies.

3 Implications for interpretation

This has several implications for their interpretation. First and foremost, they are portraits of a person and they must be interpreted in a biographical manner. Given that space is limited to a single scroll – ranging from Mark's 11,250 words to Luke's 19,500 – every story, pericope, or passage has to contribute to the overall picture of Jesus according to each evangelist. Thus Christology becomes central to the interpretation of the Gospels. Each evangelist builds up their account of Jesus through the selection, redaction, and ordering of their material. The key question for the interpretation of any verse or section is what this tells us about Jesus and the writer's understanding of him. Thus the motif of the failure of the disciples to understand Jesus in Mark is not to be interpreted in terms of polemic against differing groups and leaders within the early church, as often happens as a result of a more form-critical approach to the Gospels. Instead it is part of Mark's portrayal of Jesus as hard to understand and tough to follow – and therefore readers should not be surprised to find the Christian life difficult sometimes. Therefore, interpretation of the Gospels requires a thorough understanding of the Christology of each of the evangelists, while each section must be exegeted in the context of its place in the developing narrative as a whole.

Furthermore, it is significant that Jesus seems to have been the only first-century Jewish teacher about whom such *bioi* were written. It is quite common to compare individual Gospel pericopes with stories and anecdotes preserved in the rabbinic material. Thus the question about the greatest commandment in Mark 12.28–34 and parallels may be studied in the light of the famous story from the Babylonian Talmud, *Shabbat* 31A, of the differing reactions of Shammai and Hillel when asked to teach the whole law to a Gentile inquirer standing on one leg. If the Gospels are seen merely as a collection of such stories strung together like beads, we might expect similar works to be constructed about Hillel, Shammai, or the others. Yet this is precisely what we do not find. Both Jacob Neusner and Philip Alexander have explored various reasons why there is nothing like the Gospels in the rabbinic traditions. Burridge (2000: 155–6) has argued that to write a biography is to focus on a person center stage, where only the Torah should be; therefore the biographical genre of the Gospels is making an explicit theological claim about the centrality of Jesus.

Finally, the biographical genre of the Gospels has implications for their function and social setting. Form-critical approaches stressed the Gospels' *Sitz im Leben*, while redaction criticism led to the development of theories about the communities within which and for which the Gospels were produced. Further study of the way ancient lives functioned across a wide range of social levels in the ancient world cautions against too limited a view of the Gospels' audiences. The Gospels may well have been read aloud in large sections, or even in their entirety at meetings or in worship at the Eucharist in a manner similar to the public reading of lives at social gatherings or meal times in Graeco-Roman society. The scholarly consensus about the uniqueness of the Gospels' genre which dominated most of the twentieth century saw them as a communication produced 'by committees, for communities, about theological ideas'! Burridge has argued instead that their biographical genre means that they must be interpreted as 'by people, for people, about a person' (1998: 115, 144). As biographies, they are composed by one person, the evangelist, with a clear understanding of the Jesus he wishes to portray to a wide range of possible readers. Thus genre is the key to interpretation – and the biographical genre of the Gospels is crucial to any proper understanding of them today.

References and further reading

Alexander, Philip S. (1984) 'Rabbinic Biography and the Biography of Jesus: A Survey of the Evidence,' pp. 19–50 in *Synoptic Studies: The Ampleforth Conferences of 1982 and 1983*, JSNTSup 7, C.M. Tuckett (ed.), Sheffield: JSOT Press.

Aune, David E. (1987) *The New Testament in Its Literary Environment*, Philadelphia: Westminster.

Brown, Raymond E., SS, (1979) *The Community of the Beloved Disciple*, London: Geoffrey Chapman.

Bultmann, Rudolf (1972) *The History of the Synoptic Tradition*, trans. John Marsh, rev. edn. with supplement, Oxford: Blackwell.

Burridge, Richard A. (1998) 'About People, by People, for People: Gospel Genre and Audiences,' pp. 113–45, in *The Gospels for All Christians*, R. Bauckham (ed.), Grand Rapids: Eerdmans.

—— (2000) 'Gospel Genre, Christological Controversy and the Absence of Rabbinic Biography: Some Implications of the Biographical Hypothesis,' pp. 137–56 in *Christology, Controversy and Community: New Testament Essays in Honour of David Catchpole*, C. M. Tuckett and D.G. Horrell (eds.), Leiden: Brill.

—— (2004a) *Four Gospels, One Jesus? A Symbolic Reading*, London: SPCK/Grand Rapids: Eerdmans, rev. 2nd edn.

—— (2004b) *What are the Gospels? A Comparison with Graeco-Roman Biography*, Grand Rapids: Eerdmans, rev. updated 2nd edn. (orig. 1992).

Neusner, Jacob (1984) *In Search of Talmudic Biography: The Problem of the Attributed Saying*, Brown Judaic Studies 70, Chico: Scholars.

—— (1988) *Why No Gospels in Talmudic Judaism?* Atlanta: Scholars Press.

Talbert, Charles H. (1977) *What is a Gospel? The Genre of the Canonical Gospels*, Philadelphia: Fortress Press.

RICHARD A. BURRIDGE

GOSPELS: INTERPRETATION

1 Terminology
2 History of research
3 Questions and methods of interpreting the Gospels

1 Terminology

The English word 'gospel' is derived from the Anglo-Saxon 'godspel' and means 'good word.' It is a translation of the Greek term *euangelion*, i.e., 'good message.' The term *euangelion* occurs forty-eight times in the authentic Pauline letters. It is used as a technical term for the oral announcement of the eschatological function of Jesus' passion, death and resurrection. In the Gospels of Mark (1:14–15; 8:35, etc.) and Matthew (4:23; 9:35, etc.) it is either related to 'kingdom' (*basileia*) and 'God' (*theos*) or it occurs in an absolute way as the object of 'faith' (*pistis*) (e.g., Mark 1:15). Since Justin, and in continuity with Mark 1:1, the term *euangelion* has classified a specific type of literature within the Christian scriptures. It denotes such scriptures which contain traditions about Jesus (cf. Koester 1990, 1999). The first three Gospels (Matthew, Mark, and Luke) are classified as 'Synoptic Gospels' since J.J. Griesbach presented them in parallel print: his so-called synopsis (1776).

2 *History of research*

2.1 Origin of the 'synoptic problem'

The 'synoptic problem' is based on the plurality of the Gospel literature in the New Testament canon *and* on noticing the differences between the Gospels of Mark, Matthew, Luke, and John. The Gospels of Matthew, Mark, and Luke seem to describe Jesus' life, deeds and death similarly, whereas the Gospel of John represents an independent concept of narration. Although the Fathers of the Church had already made theological and philological remarks on this problem (Merkel 1971, 1978), the critical interpretation of the Gospels in a modern fashion began in the eighteenth century (Schmithals 1985: 47ff.). This originated from the perceived historical distance between the New Testament literature and the modern world (Lessing 1777; Overbeck 1994). G.E. Lessing (1729–1781), one of the first critical interpreters of the Gospels, proposed a theory of the Gospels' formation by which he explained the similarities of the first three Gospels and their differences from John: Matthew, Mark, and Luke, with the exception of John, were different translations of a common 'Nazareen source' (Lessing 1778: §47ff.; cf. Schmithals 1982, 1985). Lessing laid the foundations for literary criticism by interpreting the Gospels as literary works which reflect oral or literary sources. Lessing's 'Ur-Gospel' hypothesis was modified by K. Lachmann and C.G. Wilke in the first half of the nineteenth century. Lachmann and Wilke proposed the priority of Mark and its use by Matthew and Luke. H.J. Holtzmann (1863) extended this hypothesis. According to his proposal Matthew and Luke used another source in addition to the Gospel of Mark which contained words of Jesus. This source was later called Q (=Quelle) (cf. Schnelle 1998). The 'two-source' theory offers a provisional solution to the synoptic problem. It explains the congruence of Matthew, Mark and Luke, as well as the correspondence of Luke and Matthew in opposition to Mark: Matthew and Luke use Mark as one source and Q as the other source. Further extensions or modifications of the two-source theory have explained differences between Matthew and Luke or explained why Matthew and Luke differ from the Gospel of Mark, if they indeed used Mark as a source (cf. Becker 2004b).

The research on the Synoptic Gospels has been a distinct field in New Testament studies ever since. The interpretation of the Gospel of John, however, is influenced by research on the Johannine corpus (1–3 John; Revelation).

2.2 Research on the Synoptic Gospels in the twentieth century

The interpretation of the Synoptic Gospels in the nineteenth century concentrated on literary-critical and source-critical studies. In the first half of the twentieth century, historical research on the Gospels was dominated by approaches which placed the Gospels in the context of ancient religion and ancient literature. Literary criticism was also supplemented by studies of the 'history of religion' school (Gunkel and Bousset) and by studies in form criticism: Dibelius (1934) and Bultmann (1968) paid attention to the specific *forms* (words, deeds, etc.) in which the Jesus tradition had been transmitted before the oldest Gospel was written down (cf. Kümmel 1975). From this perspective, form criticism is similar to tradition criticism and transmission criticism. As well as examining the Jesus *tradition*, redaction criticism is focused on the intention (i.e., the theology) the evangelists had (Wrede 1971) and the literary techniques they used while transforming the traditions into the genre of a written Gospel (e.g., Conzelmann 1960; Marxsen 1969; cf. Bornkamm 1958: 751ff.). The *historical* method of analyzing the Synoptic Gospels differentiates between *tradition* and the evangelist's *redaction* (cf. Schmithals 1982: 600ff.). It has directed the diachronic methods of Gospel exegesis up to the present (cf. Theissen 1995). Another aspect of the historical approach to the Synoptic Gospels is historical Jesus research. Instead of interpreting the Gospels' literary form and theological character, Jesus research focuses on the reconstruction of the historical person and message of Jesus.

In the 1960s the interpretation of the Gospels was under the influence of empiricism and linguistics. This follows a reduction of interest in pure historical research. Many synchronic methods were tested (e.g., narrative criticism, literary criticism, etc.) with the methodological aim of taking the approach and results of literary and linguistic theories into Gospel exegesis (cf. *RGG⁴*-Art. Methoden der Bibelkritik; Porter 1997). Behind the synchronic approach lies the intention of interpreting the Gospels as contemporary literature (cf. Wischmeyer 2004).

2.3 State of Gospel research – tendencies – desiderata

The *state of research* in the Synoptic Gospels until the 1980s is given by Frankemölle and Dormeyer (1984). The present state of Gospel research based on considering form, that is, genre criticism, is represented in Koester (1999: 1736ff.): This article presents recent developments in describing the literary types and forms of the Gospels.

In addition to this, the present *tendencies* concerning the methods and fields of Gospel research can be summarized in some aspects:

(1) The 'International Q-Project' suggested an extensive reconstruction of the range, content, and growth of the Q tradition (e.g., Robinson, Hoffmann, and Kloppenborg 2000; Kloppenborg Verbin 2000). Therefore a process of growth in the stages of redaction within the 'logien-source' can be assumed (cf.

Lindemann 2001). Besides the reconstruction of Q, several studies examine the composition of Q (e.g., Schröter 1997; Kirk 1998), and others examine Q's language and style (e.g., Casey 2002).

(2) Historical Jesus research has worked out new criteria to differentiate between historical Jesus tradition and early Christian traditions about Jesus as found within the Gospel literature (e.g., Theissen and Winter 2002; Schröter and Brucker 2002).

(3) Some approaches develop the methods of historical exegesis: studies in social history and local context attempt to locate the Synoptic traditions in the context of the Jesus movement (e.g., Theissen 1991).

(4) Continuing source and redaction criticism, some studies focus on the different Synoptic sources (e.g., Hultgren 2002), redactional methods, and interests of the Gospel writer who arranged the Synoptic traditions (e.g., Blackburn 1991). Other studies using redaction criticism concentrate on the structure of the Gospel's community (e.g., Peterson 2000).

(5) Regarding form criticism, several studies concentrate on comparing Gospels with similar genres of ancient literature which deal with the narration of an important person's life. One way this is done is by comparing various types of ancient biography with the Gospel literature (e.g., Dormeyer 1999). Another way is by comparing the Markan genre with the Jewish and Hellenistic novel literature (Vines 2002).

(6) A new debate about the mythical concepts behind the composition of Gospel literature is opened in several monographs (Mack 1995; Klumbies 2001).

(7) Different types of narrative criticism attempt to respect narrative aspects and their theological function as the Gospel recounts Jesus' life and death (Best 1984; Klauck 1997).

(8) There is also much traditional work: several exegetical studies of particular pericopes in the Synoptic Gospels aim at interpreting the historical background of the Gospel writers and their theological proposals (e.g., Repschinski 2000).

Research in the Gospel of John concentrates on defining its relationship to the Synoptic Gospels (e.g., Denaux 1992) as well as on interpreting the Fourth Gospel for what it is. Studies in literary composition or in exegetical-theological topics (e.g., Frey 1997–2000) are at the centre of discussion.

Although Synoptic Gospel research has produced a plurality of methods and interest in interpreting Gospel literature since the 1980s, at least two examples concerning the exegesis of Markan literature may show today's desiderata of Gospel interpretation:

(1) The research in the pre-Markan collections, such as has been done (e.g., Kuhn 1970), has not led to further studies in the history of Markan sources. Beyond the examination of one specific tradition (e.g., Mark 13 or Mark 14–16), research in the Gospel of Mark should pay attention to the question of whether or not the pre-Markan traditions can be classified as sources or as collections with a definite structure. Research in the prehistory of the Gospel of Mark, as is done in Q research, should be intensified to lead towards a precise definition of form and structure of that which has been presented by the redactor of the Gospel of Mark.

(2) The genre of the Gospel of Mark has not been defined precisely (cf. Koester 1990: 26ff.). The approach of comparing the Synoptic Gospels with similar literary genres in ancient literature (e.g., biography, novel) should be extended to other possible literary analogies. The proposal that Christian historiography begins with the Lukan scriptures (Gospel and Acts) (e.g., Marguerat 2002) should be considered and supplemented by comparing the earliest Gospel of Mark with historiographic literature (cf. Becker 2006).

3 Questions and methods of interpreting the Gospels

3.1 An uncompleted task

The interpretation of the Gospels is based on different questions concerning the authors of the Gospels, their addressees, that is, the community the evangelists write for, the date, the historical context and the place of their writing, the literary form and structure of the Gospels, and their main theological emphases. The state of research in these areas is represented in the so-called critical introduction (e.g., Schnelle 1998). It presents the consensus of what exegesis finds out about author, date, community, etc.

Interpretation of the Gospels, however – like Pauline exegesis, for example – cannot come to a status quo. Exegesis of the Gospels has to do with a specific kind of ancient literature which is characterized by anonymity: the canonical Gospels are written anonymously and did not appear with headlines which entitle the Gospels with apostolic names until the second century AD (cf. Schmithals 1985: 31ff.). The authentic Pauline letters and the Revelation of John are the only orthonymously written texts in the New Testament canon. The anonymity of the Gospels causes most difficulty when attempting to date and locate them. Each attempt to put the Gospels into the chronology of ancient history and literature will remain a hypothesis. Therefore interpretation of the Gospels cannot lead to certain results but should study the texts with methods of interpretation that are used in other disciplines that engage in textual interpretation.

3.2 Synchronic and diachronic methods

New Testament exegesis has developed a large inventory of methods during the twentieth century. Some of these methods reflect previous scholarship, others are derived from linguistics and from literary theory. The distinction between 'synchronic' and 'diachronic' was first introduced by de Saussure. The intent was to differentiate between the origins and development of European language and the system of language. The terms were transferred to the interpretation of texts (cf. Wischmeyer 2004). Use of both terms (synchronic/diachronic) in New Testament exegesis reveals the differences in understanding the concept of a 'text.' The synchronic approach understands the 'text' in relation to itself: the meaning of the text does not lie behind or outside the text, but inside the text itself. The diachronic approach, on the other hand, pays attention to the historical and literary processes of text formation (cf. Egger 1996). One hermeneutical difference between the synchronic and the diachronic approach can be recognized in the way the different approaches perceive the relationship between author–text–interpreter: the synchronic approach concentrates on the text in its entirety as the object of interpretation. The author of a text only occurs as its producer. The diachronic approach examines the existing text as well as the history of its formation and its origins. The author of the text occurs as an individual and historical person (cf. Becker 2004a).

3.3 The synchronic method of Gospel interpretation

The synchronic method of interpreting the Gospels (cf. Egger 1996; Porter 1997), like the diachronic method, presupposes the results of *textual criticism*: The exegesis of Gospel literature in detail starts by analyzing the philological form of the original text. Observations of *language and syntax* help to uncover the formal structure of the text. The examination of the *text semantics* and studies in the semantic content of specific terms and words of the text open up its semantic propositions. The aim of *narrative criticism* is to analyse the Gospel narration with regard to narrative structure, their characters and settings, and the point of view of the events. Using this method the similarities or differences between the four Gospels' narrations of the same story can be detected. Analyses of *text types* describe the form and function of a narrative text in relation to the forms and genres which are classified by literary science and linguistics (cf. Brinker 2001). This differs from form criticism because the analysis of text types is not interested in the development of forms but in describing the existent text without considering its oral or literary prehistory.

Apart from these synchronic methods there are methods of Gospel exegesis (e.g., *literary criticism, rhetorical criticism*) which actually presuppose a synchronic approach to Gospel texts and their interpretation.

3.4 The diachronic method of Gospel interpretation

The diachronic method of interpreting the Gospels is concerned with the history of text formation (cf. Schnelle 2000). *Source criticism* treats the 'synoptic problem': it examines the different sources of a Synoptic text, i.e., Mark and Q, Lukan or Matthean 'special material' and – in case of the exegesis of a Markan text – the pre-Markan sources. *Form criticism* and *tradition criticism* reconstruct the history of the oral and, subsequently, the literary form of the Synoptic traditions and their so-called *Sitz im Leben* within the context of missionary activities or community life of the earliest Christians. *Religious history* places the Synoptic text or its specific vocabulary (*history of motifs and terms*) into the context of ancient religious literature. Searching for analogies to the Gospel texts in ancient religions reveals the religious and theological proprium of the Gospel texts. Finally, *redaction criticism* uncovers the interests specific to the Gospel writers who shaped the Synoptic traditions in their own way. Interpreting the Gospel of John using redaction criticism means something different: it analyzes later additions and interpolations (e.g., John 21) to the Gospel's text.

References and further reading

Becker, E.-M. (2004a) *Pauline Letter Hermeneutics in 2 Corinthians*, trans. Helen Heron, JSNTS 279, London: Continuum.

—— (2004b) "Die synoptischen Evangelien und ihre Quellen. Ein Beitrag zur Terminologie und Methodologie der neutestamentlichen Exegese," in *Quelle: zwischen Ursprung und Konstrukt*, Beiheft der Zeitschrift für Deutsche Philologie, T. Rathmann and N. Wegmann (eds.), Berlin: Erich Schmidt Verlag.

—— (2006) *Das Markus-Evangelium in Rahmen antiker Historiographie*, WUNT 194, Tübingen: Mohr Siebeck.

Best, E. (1984) *Mark: The Gospel As Story*, Edinburgh: T.&T. Clark.

Blackburn, B. (1991) *Theios Aner and the Markan Miracle Traditions*, WUNT 2.40, Tübingen: Mohr Siebeck.

Bornkamm, G. (1958) "Evangelien, formgeschichtlich/Evangelien, synoptische," *RGG*[3] 2: 749–66.

Brinker, K. (2001) *Linguistische Textanalyse. Eine Einführung in Grundbegriffe und Methoden*, Berlin: Erich Schmidt Verlag.

Bultmann, R. (1968) *The History of the Synoptic Tradition*, trans. John Marsh, New York: Harper & Row, 2nd edn.

Casey, M. (2002) *An Aramaic Approach to Q. Sources for the Gospels of Matthew and Luke*, SNTSMS 122, Cambridge: Cambridge University Press.

Conzelmann, H. (1960) *The Theology of St Luke*, London: Faber.

Denaux, A. (ed.) (1992) *John and the Synoptics*, BEthL 101, Leuven: Peeters.

Dibelius, M. (1934) *From Tradition to Gospel*, trans. B.L. Woolf, London: Ivor Nicholson and Watson.

Dormeyer, D. (1999) *Das Markusevangelium als Idealbiographie von Jesus Christus, dem Nazarener*, SBB 43, Stuttgart: Verlag Katholisches Bibelwerk.

Egger, W. (1996) *How to Read the New Testament: An Introduction to Linguistic and Historical-Critical Methodology*, trans. P. Heinegg, H. Boers (ed.), Peabody, MA: Hendrickson.

Frankemölle, H. and D. Dormeyer (1984) "Evangelium als literarischer und theologischer Begriff," *Aufstieg und Niedergang der römischen Welt* II.25.2: 1, 541–704.

Frey, J. (1997–2000) *Die johanneische Eschatologie*, Vol. I–III, WUNT 96/110/117, Tübingen: Mohr Siebeck.

Holtzmann, H.J. (1863) *Die Synoptischen Evangelien: Ihr Ursprung und geschichtlicher Charakter*, Leipzig: Engelmann.

Hultgren, S. (2002) *Narrative Elements in the Double Tradition: A Study of Their Place within the Framework of the Gospel Narrative*, BZNW 113, Berlin: de Gruyter.

Kirk, A. (1998) *The Composition of the Saying Source: Genre, Synchrony, and Wisdom Redaction in Q*, Leiden: Brill.

Klauck, H.-J. (1997) *Vorspiel im Himmel? Erzähltechnik und Theologie im Markusprolog*, BThSt 32, Neukirchen-Vluyn: Neukirchener Verlag.

Kloppenborg Verbin, J.S. (2000) *Excavating Q: The History and Setting of the Sayings Gospel*, Edinburgh: T.&T. Clark.

Klumbies, P.-G. (2001) *Der Mythos bei Markus*, BZNW 108, Berlin: de Gruyter.

Koester, H. (1990) *Ancient Christian Gospels: Their History and Development*, Philadelphia: Trinity Press International.

—— (1999) "Evangelium I/II," *RGG⁴* 2: 735–41.

Kümmel, W.G. (1975) *Introduction to the New Testament*, Nashville: Abingdon Press, rev. trans.

Kuhn, H.W. (1970) *Ältere Sammlungen im Markusevangelium*, StUNT 8, Göttingen: Vandenhoeck & Ruprecht.

Lessing, G.E. (*c.* 1776) *Theses aus der Kirchengeschichte*.

—— (1777) *Ueber den Beweis des Geistes und der Kraft*.

—— (1778) *Neue Hypothese über die Evangelisten als bloß menschliche Geschichtsschreiber betrachtet*.

Lindemann, A. (ed.) (2001) *The Sayings Source and the Historical Jesus*, BEThL 158, Leuven: Peeters.

Mack, B.L. (1995) *Who wrote the New Testament?: The Making of the Christian Myth*, San Francisco: HarperCollins.

Marguerat, D. (2002) *The First Christian Historian*, SNTSMS 121, Cambridge: Cambridge University Press.

Marxsen, W. (1969) *Mark the Evangelist: Studies on the Redaction History of the Gospel*, trans. James Boyce et al., Nashville: Abingdon Press.

Merkel, H. (1971) *Die Widersprüche zwischen den Evangelien. Ihre polemische und apologetische Behandlung in der Alten Kirche bis zu Augustin*, WUNT 13, Tübingen: Mohr Siebeck.

—— (1978) *Die Pluralität der Evangelien als theologisches und exegetisches Problem in der Alten Kirche*, Traditio christiana 3, Bern: P. Lang.

Overbeck, F. (1994) "Ueber Entstehung und Recht einer rein historischen Betrachtung der Neutestamentlichen Schriften in der Theologie," pp. 83–113 in *Franz Overbeck, Werke und Nachlass*, 1, Stuttgart and Weimar: J.B. Metzler Verlag.

Peterson, D.N. (2000) *The Origins of Mark: The Markan Community in Current Debate*, Biblical Interpretation Series 48, Leiden: Brill.

Porter S.E. (ed.) (1997) *Handbook to Exegesis of the New Testament*, Leiden: Brill.

Repschinski, B. (2000) *The Controversy Stories in the Gospel of Matthew: Their Redaction, Form, Relevance for the Relationship Between the Matthean Community and Formative Judaism*, FRLANT 189, Göttingen: Vandenhoeck & Ruprecht.

Robinson, J.M., P. Hoffmann, and J.S. Kloppenborg (2000) *The Critical Edition of Q*, Leuven: Peeters.

Schmithals, W. (1982) "Evangelien," *TRE* 10: 570–626.

—— (1985) *Einleitung in die drei ersten Evangelien*, Berlin: de Gruyter.

Schnelle, U. (1998) *The History and Theology of the New Testament Writings*, trans. M.E. Boring, London: SCM Press.

—— (2000) *Einführung in die neutestamentliche Exegese*, UTB 1253, Göttingen: Vandenhoeck & Ruprecht.

Schröter, J. (1997) *Erinnerung an Jesu Worte. Studien zur Rezeption der Logienüberlieferung in Markus, Q und Thomas*, WMANT 76, Neukirchen-Vluyn: Neukirchener Verlag.

Schröter, J. and R. Brucker (eds.) (2002) *Der historische Jesus. Tendenzen und Perspektiven der gegenwaertigen Forschung*, BZNW 114, Berlin: de Guyter.

Theissen, G. (1991) *The Gospels in Context: Social and Political History in the Synoptic Tradition*, trans. Linda M. Maloney, Minneapolis: Fortress Press.

—— (1995) "Die Erforschung der synoptischen Tradition seit R. Bultmann. Ein Überblick über die formgeschichtliche Arbeit im 20. Jahrhundert," pp. 409–52 in *R. Bultmann: Die Geschichte der synoptischen Tradition*, Göttingen: Vandenhoeck & Ruprecht.

Theissen, G. and A. Merz (1998) *The Historical Jesus: A Comprehensive Guide*, trans. John Bowden, Minneapolis: Fortress Press.

Theissen, G. and D. Winter (2002) *The Quest for the Plausible Jesus: The Question of Criteria*, trans. M.E. Boring, Louisville: Westminster/John Knox.

Vines, M.E. (2002) *The Problem of Markan Genre: The Gospel of Mark and the Jewish Novel*, Leiden: Brill.

Wischmeyer, O. (2004) *Hermeneutik des Neuen Testaments. Ein Lehrbuch*, Tübingen and Basel: Francke Verlag.

Wrede, W. (1971) *The Messianic Secret*, Cambridge: Clarke (orig. German edn 1901).

EVE-MARIE BECKER

GOULDER, MICHAEL D. (1927–)

Michael D. Goulder, Emeritus Professor of Biblical Studies at the University of Birmingham, UK, has broadly contributed studies ranging from the Psalms to the Gospels and Acts to the Pauline epistles, by publishing numerous books, chapters, articles, and book reviews. He is best known for being a leading exponent of those who reject form criticism and challenge the existence of the hypothetical document Q. Goulder has also done work on the Old Testament, particularly in recreating contexts and use in liturgy.

Goulder's work extends that of Austin Farrer, who wrote the article 'On Dispensing with Q,' in which the key is Lukan knowledge of Matthew. Three theories that are central to Goulder's work were presented in *Midrash and Lectikon in Matthew* (1974): Luke's knowledge of Matthew, the evangelists' use of their imagination/creativity, and the lectionary theory, which stresses the liturgical backgrounds of primarily Matthew and Luke, but also Mark. In his article 'On Putting Q to the Test' (1978b), Goulder attempts to deliver a direct deathblow to the Q theory. His *Luke: A New Paradigm* (1989) is the leading commentary that supports the view that Luke used Mark and Matthew, and that there was no Q or L (Luke's special material). In *Luke*, he revises his lectionary theory and drops the term 'midrash' for the Gospel authors' creativity, but maintains that the technique of embroidering sacred texts was widespread, regardless of the terminology.

Goulder expands F.C. Baur's theory that there was a rivalry between two groups: one headed by Paul and the other headed by James, Peter, and John. Goulder proposes his 'two mission hypothesis' as the overarching theory to explain how the New Testament came to be, in opposition to the Q hypothesis. In his popular paperback *St. Paul Versus St. Peter: A Tale of Two Missions*, he asserts it is 'a master key to open every lock' (1995: 157). In *Paul and the Competing Mission in Corinth* (2001), Goulder writes an academic apologia that elaborates the hypothesis, especially as reflected in the Corinthian letters, and states that there will need to be a second volume to develop the issues surrounding the two missions more fully. The two missions were the Gentile-focused Pauline group on the one side and the Jewish Petrines on the other. The development of the early church was characterized by an extreme conflict between the two missions. Mark is pro-Pauline, Matthew revises Mark for Jewish sensibilities, and Luke-Acts reasserts Pauline theology. The final form of the New Testament is a product and result of the spoils going to the victor: the Pauline mission.

Goulder's approach and style merit some comment. Controversial and provocative, his literary style, wit, and rhetorical abilities are ubiquitous in his work. He is equally adept in public lectures, debates, and conferences. However, his advocates and critics portray him respectively as either living on the cutting edge or the lunatic fringe of biblical studies. His challenge of the majority view of form criticism, his glib dismissal of historicity, his own liberal use of creativity and imagination, the inability to fit him easily into any slot or category, and his confrontational approach disturb and stimulate the synoptic discussion.

References and further reading

Farrer, A. (1955) 'On Dispensing with Q,' pp. 55–88 in *Studies in the Gospels: Essays in Memory of R.H. Lightfoot*, D.E. Nineham (ed.), Oxford: Blackwell.

Goodacre, M.S. (1996) *Goulder and the Gospels: An Examination of a New Paradigm*, Sheffield: Sheffield Academic Press.

Goulder, M.D. (1964) *Type and History in Acts*, London: SPCK.

—— (1974) *Midrash and Lection in Matthew*, London: SPCK.

—— (1978a) *The Evangelists' Calendar*, London: SPCK.

—— (1978b) 'On Putting Q to the Test,' *New Testament Studies* 24: 218–34.

—— (ed.) (1979) *Incarnation and Myth*, London: SCM Press.

—— (1982) *The Psalms of the Sons of Korah*, Sheffield: JSOT Press.

—— (1986) *The Song of Fourteen Songs*, Sheffield: JSOT Press.

—— (1989) *Luke: A New Paradigm*, 2 Vols., Sheffield: JSOT Press.

—— (1990) *The Prayers of David (Psalms 51–72)*, Sheffield: JSOT Press.

—— (1995) *St. Paul Versus St. Peter: A Tale of Two Missions*, London: SCM Press.

—— (2001) *Paul and the Competing Mission in Corinth*, Peabody, MA: Hendrickson.

—— (2004) *Isaiah as Liturgy*, Aldershot: Ashgate Publishing Company.

—— and J. Hick (1983) *Why Believe in God?* London: SCM Press.

Rollston, C.A. (ed.) (2002) *The Gospels according to Michael Goulder*, Harrisburg, PA: Trinity.

CYNTHIA LONG WESTFALL

GREEK GRAMMAR AND LEXICOGRAPHY

1 Introduction
2 Greek grammar
3 Greek lexicography
4 Implications for biblical interpretation

1 Introduction

In previous periods of biblical interpretation, it was assumed that the biblical interpreter would be adept at Greek – perhaps originally trained in the classical languages before turning to biblical studies. Such is no longer the case. However, along with the decrease in knowledge of the ancient language, there has not apparently been commensurate attention paid to the latest research in the Greek language. The result has been a tendency to view knowledge of Greek as static, and to rely simply upon categories of thought assumed from rudimentary study of the language. There have been a number of significant developments in Greek grammar and lexicography over the past several centuries that are worth noting, especially as they have bearing on biblical criticism and interpretation.

2 Greek grammar

Greek grammatical study has undergone at least four periods (see Porter 1989, 1996).

The first was study by the ancients themselves (besides above, see Sluiter 1990; Wouters 1979; Porter 2000). There are a number of incidental comments made by the ancient Greeks concerning their language. Some of these were significant, such as differentiating between saying and signifying (Heraclitus), differentiating past, present, and future (Homer), and distinguishing kind of action (Plato and Aristotle). Plato was the first to offer descriptive categories such as nominal and verbal elements, and Aristotle posited that the verb indicated time. It was only during the Hellenistic period that what might be termed philology was developed. Dionysius the Grammarian (Thrax) (second century BC) wrote his *Technē*, the only extant Greek grammatical manual, which provides a taxonomy of grammatical phenomena. The Stoics responded to Dionysius, with the scholiast Stephanus drawing major distinctions between time and kind of action in the use of the verb. Apollonius Dyscolus (second century AD) moved from classification to exemplification in terms of ancient authors. Even though there are a number of suggestive statements by the ancients – the most insightful being Stephanus' distinction between time and kind of action – they lack the kind of critical or methodological rigor required in modern language study.

The second period of study has been labeled the rationalist period. During this period, grammarians of New Testament Greek, in response to the growing scientism of the Enlightenment, attempted to systematically categorize usage according to formally based paradigms. These categories of usage, reminiscent of the kinds of taxonomies suggested by Dionysius in ancient times, ensured that any framework or grid not only was filled with requisite forms, but that there was a logically consistent definition offered for each form as well.

This grammatical discussion was also highly influenced by Latin grammatical categories, since Latin had been the language of scholarship for centuries. Georg Winer's grammar (originally published in 1822, but with many subsequent editions, both in German and in English, up to 1894) provides an excellent example. He insists that the tense forms express time in all of their occurrences, and that what might seem to be an aberration is one in appearance only (*sic*). Whereas most advanced reference works have moved beyond the work of Winer, his framework is still widely utilized in a number of elementary Greek grammars, where the rationalist framework is still intact.

The third period is that of the comparative philologists. In the late nineteenth century, with growth in scientific and cultural knowledge, linguistic investigation took a decidedly historical turn. It was discovered that there were a number of genetic relationships that existed among languages, and that a number of these languages shared a common ancestry. This development of historical linguistics led to the positing of Proto-Indo-European and the various languages that had developed from it. As a result, the relations between languages were studied, often focusing upon a particular grammatical category and its development in comparison with related languages. This diachronic approach led to the recognition that the various formal paradigms, such as the cases or tense forms, often had looked differently at different times in the history of their development. Georg Curtius inaugurated such work, but the most important credit goes to Karl Brugmann. One of his many innovations was the notion of *Aktionsart*, the theory that there were various types of objective ways that actions took place and that these were captured by the various tense forms. One of the results of his study was the classification of the various ways in which actions occur, and how these are exemplified in various languages comparatively studied. The major reference grammars in New Testament Greek grammatical study still utilize the comparative philological framework. These include Friedrich Blass' grammar (including its continued German versions and its well-known translation by Funk), which draws heavily upon comparison with earlier classical Greek; James Hope Moulton's grammar (especially volume one of the four volume set, the last two volumes reflecting a competing approach), in which the terminology of *Aktionsart* was introduced to the English-speaking world, as well as introducing useful reference to the contemporary papyrological evidence; and A.T. Robertson's massive comparative grammar.

The fourth period is that of modern linguistics. The lectures in linguistics by the late de Saussure are often credited with inaugurating modern linguistics, in which the historical framework was replaced by one that emphasized synchronic study. Instead of comparing isolated linguistic phenomena across languages, emphasis was placed upon systems within a given language, such as the verbal system, the case system, the voice system, and the like. It is only within the last thirty or so years that modern linguistic approaches have been applied to the Greek of the New Testament. Some of the developments include work in: Greek verbal structure by Porter (1989), Buist Fanning (1990), K.L. McKay (1994), Rodney Decker (2001), and Trevor Evans (2001); case structure by Simon Wong (1997) and Paul Danove (2001); and connective words by Stephanie Black (2002). As a result, for example, recent analysis shows that the Greek tense-system is not time-based but is concerned with the author's choice regarding depicting the action, or that connecting words are not merely continuative or disjunctive, but provide degrees of continuity in shaping the discourse. One of the most important recent developments has been the development of discourse analysis or text linguistics. Discourse analysis is a multidisciplinary approach in which the data from various levels of linguistic study are incorporated into a model for analysis of an entire discourse (see Reed 1997). There are a number of different approaches to discourse linguistics, some beginning with the smallest units of substance and others beginning with text types and genres, but they all are concerned to examine and place emphasis upon units of linguistic structure larger than the sentence. The variety of insights to be gained from discourse analysis is represented in various recent works (see Porter and Reed 1999, a collection of essays by a variety of scholars).

3 Greek lexicography

The recent survey and analysis by John Lee (2003) makes clear that Greek lexicography is a discipline in crisis, but without easy and simple resolution.

There have been many lexicons of the Greek language written over the past several centuries, with the earliest of significance usually being attributed to Pasor in 1619, and culminating most recently in the revised Walter Bauer lexicon by Frederick Danker in 2000. At first glance, these lexicons appear to be monuments to learning and industry, since many of them present accumulations of not only biblical references, but more references to extrabiblical primary literature and some secondary literature.

As Lee makes clear, however, the tradition is univocal and methodologically flawed in at least three major ways (2003: esp. 40–1, but *passim*). The major deficiencies that he chronicles include the high dependence of successive lexicons upon the previous lexicons, so that there are large periods of time when there is little to no significant or new information added to lexical entries. A check of some of the information that is transmitted also indicates that not all of it is reliable. Some of the references are not accurate, while others do not establish the definitional point that is being

made. A second difficulty is the fact that most lexicons have traditionally used a gloss as an indicator of meaning. That is, most lexicons simply utilize word-for-word equivalents to give the meaning of a word, rather than actually creating lexical meanings that describe the semantics of the word usage. A third and final deficiency is that these word-for-word equivalents are often highly dependent upon the major translations, including both Latin and English, rather than being based upon establishing the lexical meaning independent of the translations, which themselves end up acting as lexicons.

One of the few exceptions to the situation is the Louw-Nida lexicon (1988). This lexicon, first developed for translators, brings a number of innovations to New Testament lexicography. There are a number of deficiencies here as well, and these include failure to go outside the New Testament for usage, and a still heavy dependence upon the 'meanings' as established by previous lexicons. Nevertheless, the lexicon provides two significant steps forward. One is the utilization of the notion of semantic domains. Whereas most previous lexicons are alphabetically arranged (most by individual lexical items, although some lexicons have been classified by stem, similar to some Hebrew lexicons), the Louw-Nida lexicon arranges its entries by semantic domains. In other words, domains of meaning are defined, and the individual words that are related to this domain are all arranged together. In this way, one can establish the relations between the usage of words on the basis of concept, rather than simply on the basis of orthography. The use of semantic domains has been rightly scrutinized, since there are a number of assumptions at play in defining and determining the individual domains, and in how one determines whether a given lexical item belongs in the domain. Nevertheless, it would appear that such a system of classification is the way forward in lexicography. A second innovation is the use of lexical meanings, rather than glosses. Lee notes that this is entirely appropriate for a lexicon for translators, who must find the individual word that they will need to use in their receptor language, on the basis of the lexical meaning provided. There are still limitations to the use of these lexical meanings, since one needs to be descriptive yet concise. Some have advocated the use of other forms of description, such as componential notation (in which individual components of meaning are specified), used in the recent Spanish–Greek lexicon (by Mateos and Peláez 2000–). Such components need to be justified, but would seem to hold potential for further development in attempting to define words.

Some of the other means forward in lexicography, some of them suggested by Lee (2003: 182–8), include the following. One would be the utilization of the resources of corpus linguistics in developing an appropriate corpus of material for use. If the database were appropriately annotated, there would be the possibility for significant syntactical and other analysis. Ideally, texts from outside the New Testament would be included in the database so that the Greek of the New Testament can be seen in terms of other contemporary Greek usage, especially including that of papyri and literary authors, but also inscriptions.

4 Implications for biblical interpretation

As the discussion of these two areas has shown, there is much important work to be done to be able to appropriate recent linguistic insights into biblical interpretation. This may come as a surprise, since the use of Greek is often overlooked in the study of the biblical documents. If Lee is right regarding New Testament lexicography, there needs to be a complete revisioning and recasting of biblical lexicography. This is needed to ensure that the resources brought to the task of interpretation and translation accurately reflect the meanings of the words involved. In terms of Greek grammar, what is clear is that most of the comments made on the Greek text are governed by outdated or at least questionable models of Greek grammar. Rather than simply assuming that matters of Greek grammar are settled, one needs to incorporate the insights of recent work in Greek grammar and linguistics into textual analysis. For example, rather than relying upon seeing the tense-forms merely as ciphers for temporal values, interpreters need to see them as indicating how an author shapes the action of the text.

References and further reading

Black, S.L. (2002) *Sentence Conjunctions in the Gospel of Matthew*, Sheffield: Sheffield Academic Press.

Danove, P.L. (2001) *Linguistics and Exegesis in the Gospel of Mark: Applications of a Case Frame Analysis and Lexicon*, Sheffield: Sheffield Academic Press.

Decker, R.J. (2001) *Temporal Deixis of the Greek Verb in the Gospel of Mark with Reference to Verbal Aspect*, New York: Lang.

Evans, T.V. (2001) *Verbal Syntax in the Greek Pentateuch*, Oxford: Oxford University Press.

Fanning, B.M. (1990) *Verbal Aspect in New Testament Greek*, Oxford: Clarendon.

Lee, J.A.L. (2003) *A History of New Testament Lexicography*, New York: Lang.

Louw, J.P. and E.A. Nida (1988) *A Greek-English Lexicon of the New Testament Based on Semantic Domains*, New York: UBS.

McKay, K.L. (1994) *A New Syntax of the Verb in New Testament Greek*, New York: Lang.

Mateos, J. and J. Peláez (2000–) *Diccionario Griego-Español del Nuevo Testamento*, Córdoba: Edición El Almendro.

Porter, S.E. (1989) *Verbal Aspect in the Greek of the New Testament with Reference to Tense and Mood*, New York: Lang.

—— (1996) *Studies in the Greek New Testament: Theory and Practice*, New York: Lang.

—— (2000) 'Grammarians, Hellenistic Greek,' pp. 418–21 in *Dictionary of New Testament Background*, C.A. Evans and S.E. Porter (eds.), Downers Grove: IVP.

—— and J.T. Reed (eds.) (1999) *Discourse Analysis and the New Testament*, Sheffield: Sheffield Academic Press.

Reed, J.T. (1997) *A Discourse Analysis of Philippians*, Sheffield: Sheffield Academic Press.

Sluiter, I. (1990) *Ancient Grammar in Context*, Amsterdam: VU University Press.

Wong, S. (1997) *A Classification of Semantic Case-Relations in the Pauline Epistles*, New York: Lang.

Wouters, A. (1979) *The Grammatical Papyri from Greco-Roman Egypt: Contributions to the Study of the 'Ars Grammatica' in Antiquity*, Brussels: Paleis der Academi'n.

STANLEY E. PORTER

GREEK LANGUAGE

1 Linear B: the earliest records
2 The dialects of ancient Greek
3 Literary dialects and the rise of Attic
4 The Koine: Greek in the Hellenistic and Roman imperial periods
5 The Koine and Atticism
6 Biblical Greek
7 Later Christian literature
8 Medieval Greek: the Byzantine Empire
9 Greek in the Ottoman Empire
10 Modern Greek

1 Linear B: the earliest records

Greek is believed to be the product of contact, around 2000 BC, between Indo-European invaders and the indigenous populations of the Balkan peninsula. It has the longest recorded history of any European language, beginning with the Mycenaean dialect of the Linear B tablets from the second millennium BC (recording economic activity at the 'palaces' of southern Greece and Crete), which are written in a syllabary unrelated to the later Greek alphabet.

2 The dialects of ancient Greek

Writing disappeared with the collapse of the Mycenaean civilization *c.* 1200 BC, but from the eighth century BC we again start to find inscriptions (initially on pottery, later on stone and bronze), written in an adaptation of the Phoenician script in which redundant consonant signs were used for vowels, thus creating a true alphabet.

Since the Greek world of the archaic and classical periods (i.e., down to the latter part of the fourth century BC) was politically fragmented, each city used its own dialect for official purposes, and we have a rich store of information about the regional diversity of Greek in antiquity. The principal division is between East and West Greek. East Greek has two subgroups: (a) Attic (the dialect of Athens and the surrounding district of Attica) and Ionic (spoken in the central and northern Aegean and much of the Asia Minor littoral), and (b) Arcadian (spoken in the central Peloponnese) and Cypriot (carried east by colonists). Mycenaean is of East Greek type, and Arcadian and Cypriot are its close descendants, with Attic and Ionic showing more radical development in the period after the Mycenaean collapse. West Greek comprises (a) Peloponnesian Doric (spoken, outside Arcadia, throughout the Peloponnese, in many southern Aegean islands and much of Sicily and southern Italy) and (b) North West Greek. The Aeolic dialects of Thessaly, Boeotia, and the island of Lesbos (plus adjacent territory in Asia Minor) seem originally to have been of West Greek type, with early East Greek admixture followed by independent development in the immediate post-Mycenaean period.

3 Literary dialects and the rise of Attic

In the absence of a 'standard' form of Greek, early literature also shows a dialectal quality, and each genre employs a variety that loosely reflects the speech of the area where it acquired its definitive form, with all writers, regardless of their origins, following the established dialectal conventions. The Homeric epics, for example, as products of an oral tradition culminating in Ionia in the mid-eighth century BC, are composed in Ionic. But the epic tradition originated in the Mycenaean period, and many archaisms were preserved alongside material adopted from a parallel Aeolic tradition. This blending of old and new, Aeolic and Ionic, distanced the work from the dialect of any one region and gave it a stylized quality that set the aesthetic standard for all subsequent literary dialects, which similarly avoided narrow linguistic parochialism.

This situation began to change during the fifth century BC when Athens became a major imperial power and the foremost cultural center of the age. The resulting prestige of literary Attic, developed under the influence of Ionic (the dialect first used for prose writing in the sixth century), was such that by the fourth century BC it had become the norm for all serious prose writing throughout the Greek world. However, literary standardization now went hand-in-hand with the wider use of a more basic Attic as an administrative language, first in the territories of the Athenian empire, and then more widely. Since most of the cities of the empire were Ionic-speaking, this extended variety (Great Attic) was also influenced by Ionic, and in this 'international' form

it soon came to be used in place of local dialects as the default language of interstate administration.

4 The Koine: Greek in the Hellenistic and Roman imperial periods

The crucial step in the evolution of Great Attic into a national standard (the Koine, or 'common dialect') came with its adoption by the Macedonians, anxious to acquire cultural credentials to match the growing power of their kingdom. During the fourth century BC, Macedonia came to control first the Greek cities and then, with the conquests of Alexander the Great, an empire ranging from Egypt to the borders of India. The Attic-Koine was imposed as the official language throughout this new 'Hellenistic' world, where there was no incentive to learn any other variety, and colonists from the old Greek world quickly assimilated to the norm. In Greece itself diglossia (local dialect for local functions, Attic for international business) gradually gave way to a situation in which the local dialects, becoming steadily more Atticized, eventually ceased to have a distinctive identity or credible role. This situation was reinforced by the Romans, who took over the Hellenistic world during the last two centuries BC, but who 'adopted' ancient Greek culture and continued to use the contemporary Koine as an official language in the East, so that for many bilingualism became the norm.

5 The Koine and Atticism

Inevitably, the Koine of business and everyday communication began to diverge from the Attic of high literature, fixed by the classical canon. Though the 'practical' Koine was felt to be a satisfactory medium for technical writing, belletristic writers increasingly sought artistic validation in the ancient classics. By the end of the first century BC, this trend, supported by the perception that what the Romans really admired was 'ancient' Greece, had led to the establishment of the Atticist movement, dedicated to the restoration of ancient Attic 'purity' in literary composition.

Henceforth the history of Greek is characterized by a new diglossia in which the literary norm was an Atticizing style inspired by the authors of the fifth and fourth centuries BC, while all other functions were met by the Koine, itself partly re-Atticized in its higher written registers (administration, scientific writing, etc.) but otherwise evolving fairly naturally, especially among the mass of the population, where the impact of formal training was marginal and any attempt at writing reflected contemporary speech more directly.

6 Biblical Greek

Important sources for this everyday Koine include low-level administrative and personal inscriptions, ostraca, and (from Egypt) papyri. Careful study has shown that the language of the Septuagint, once thought to be a special 'Jewish' dialect, is broadly typical of the vernacular Greek of the Hellenistic world as a whole, though there is clear interference from the Hebrew original. Similar remarks apply to the Greek of the New Testament (the 'language of fishermen' according to Lactantius), where Biblical Hebrew, Aramaic, and Mishnaic Hebrew influences have been detected. In general, however, both texts reflect local varieties of the Koine, though the style varies widely with the educational level and aspirations of individual authors, ranging at the extremes from near-Atticizing (e.g., 4 Macc.) to vulgar/substandard (e.g., Revelation).

7 Later Christian literature

The earliest Christian writers continued to use a simple contemporary style, partly to show their contempt for the pagan tradition, partly in recognition of the needs of their audience. But as Christianity gained ground, achieving official status and imperial patronage, there was a need to develop doctrine in a style acceptable to a more privileged audience. From the third century AD Christian intellectuals such as Clement of Alexandria, Origen, and Eusebius began to adapt elements of the pagan philosophical and rhetorical traditions to this purpose, employing a highly Atticized Koine suited to their readership. In a different world, the 'humble' origins of Christianity might have validated a refined vernacular Greek as a prestigious vehicle for serious writing. Instead, though a simple Koine continued to be used for saints' lives and chronicles aimed at a popular audience, the adoption of Christianity by the Roman establishment effectively guaranteed the perpetuation of the diglossia initiated by the Atticists down into the Middle Ages and beyond.

8 Medieval Greek: the Byzantine Empire

The Roman Empire was divided in AD 395, and Roman government in the West ceased in AD 476. Thereafter the eastern provinces, with their capital at Constantinople (Byzantium), remained the sole 'Roman' state until its remnants fell to the Ottoman Turks in 1453.

The Byzantine establishment favored the high style as a symbol of imperial and cultural continuity, and classical revivals typically coincided with periods of prosperity, though more basic forms of Koine, evolving in a continuous compromise with changes in the vernacular, were used for administration, technical writing, and popular Christian literature. By the twelfth century, however, the empire had been greatly reduced, and most of its inhabitants were native speakers of Greek. The beginnings of a Greek national consciousness can now be detected, and while some sought to express this identity through a return to strict Atticism, others

began to experiment, for the first time, with literary versions of the vernacular, specifically in epic/romance and satire. This creativity disappeared with the sack of Constantinople by crusaders in 1204, when most of the empire was divided among the 'Latin' powers, though vernacular romances and chronicles reappeared in the fourteenth century under the impact of Western models, only to disappear finally under Ottoman rule.

9 Greek in the Ottoman Empire

The absence of a Greek-speaking state after 1453 inhibited the development of a modern standard, particularly as the Orthodox Church, the sole surviving 'Greek' institution, vigorously promoted its ancient traditions as a symbol of religious and cultural continuity. Most forms of written Greek therefore remained remote from the regional vernaculars in use from southern Italy to eastern Anatolia, which now began to diverge strongly in the more peripheral areas.

By the eighteenth century, however, intellectuals were agreed that a standard written language was essential in any Greek state that might emerge from the declining Ottoman Empire. The debate as to the form this should take was conducted in a style that had evolved out of earlier administrative usage through the incorporation of selected lexical and grammatical innovations into educated speech. Some advocated this as the basis for a modern standard, others opted for the more archaizing usage of church bureacracy, others still for a 'purification' of the language in the direction of ancient Attic (some even opting for Attic itself!). Only a radical minority, influenced by practice in the West, argued for a written language based directly on contemporary speech.

10 Modern Greek

The issue remained unresolved when, in 1833, Greek insurgents secured the establishment of an autonomous Greek kingdom. The written style of the intelligentsia was adopted by default, though ideologues, influenced by the admiration of Western powers for ancient Greece, quickly set about antiquing this variety, which soon came to be known as *katharevousa* ('purifying [language]'). Yet opponents of the written use of the vernacular had greatly exaggerated the difficulties. The Greek upper classes spoke a fairly uniform variety, and this had already been successfully employed in 'progressive' educational literature. Furthermore, while the more remote spoken dialects had developed autonomously, those of the Greek kingdom were phonologically and grammatically quite close to the educated standard. By the end of the nineteenth century, therefore, many creative writers had turned their backs on the increasingly artificial *katharevousa* and used forms of demotic ('[language] of the people') instead.

The history of Greek in the twentieth century centers around the resolution of this final phase of diglossia. The outcome, after decades of sterile wrangling and horrendous politicization of the issues (set in the context of extraordinary economic, military, and political difficulties), was the acceptance of 'demotic' as the official language of the state in 1976. This variety, however, is a compromise rather than the 'pure' language of the people that earlier proponents of demoticism had advocated. Thus the contemporary standard, while grounded in the natural evolution of Greek within the modern state, has accepted, and continues to accept, elements from the learned tradition that had long been normal in an institutional environment that supported *katharevousa*. Greeks, however, remain highly sensitive to linguistic issues, and the relationship between modern and ancient Greek remains a live political and educational issue.

References and further reading

Blass, F. and A. Debrunner (1984) *Grammatik des neutestamentlischen Griechisch*, Göttingen: Vandenhock & Ruprecht; ET. of the tenth edn by R. Funk (1961), *A Greek Grammar of the New Testament and Other Early Christian Literature*, Chicago: University of Chicago Press.

Browning, R. (1983) *Medieval and Modern Greek*, Cambridge: Cambridge University Press.

Horrocks, G.C. (1997) *Greek: A History of the Language and its Speakers*, London and New York: Addison Wesley Longman.

Palmer, L.R. (1980) *The Greek Language*, London: Faber.

GEOFFREY HORROCKS

H

HABERMAS, JÜRGEN (1929–)

Jürgen Habermas was born in Düsseldorf in 1929 and grew up in Gummersbach, some 50 km west of Cologne. From 1949 to 1954 he studied at the universities of Göttingen, Zürich, and Bonn, in the last of which he gained a doctorate in 1954 for a thesis on Schelling's philosophy of history. In 1956 he became the *Assistent* to T.W. Adorno in the Institute for Social Research in Frankfurt, and began to prepare his Habilitation, the additional doctoral thesis needed for a university post. Opposition from within the institute led to his removal to Marburg where, in 1962, he completed his Habilitation under the openly left-wing Wolfgang Abendroth on the subject of 'The Structural Transformation of the Public Sphere.' A post as professor of philosophy in Heidelberg preceded Habermas' return to Frankfurt in 1964, where he succeeded Max Horkheimer as professor of philosophy, and where he remained until 1971. This period not only saw the publication of *Theory and Practice* (1963) and *Knowledge and Human Interest* (1968), it was also the period of student protest in German universities, protest led by some of Habermas' students. While sympathizing with the protesters' aims, Habermas was deeply disturbed by what he saw as a desire on the part of some protesters to attain their aims without proper conceptualization or discussion. From 1971 to 1983 Habermas was director of the Max Planck Institute in Starnberg, and it was during this period that he published *Theory of Communicative Action* (1982), which marked a paradigm shift in his work from a philosophy of consciousness to a philosophy of language. He returned to Frankfurt in 1983, where be taught until his retirement.

Both Habermas' early and post-1982 work is based upon his conviction that the desire for an ideal world is implicit in the possession by the human race of language. Language not only makes communication between people possible, it is also a means of understanding and appreciating differing viewpoints; and by appealing to the force of the better argument it involves a willingness to reach agreement that transcends personal interests. The reality, however, is that communication between humans is distorted and frustrated by interests that produce and maintain an oppressive and class-dominated world, with all its manifest injustices. Working from a neo-Marxist standpoint, Habermas has sought to expose and analyze the forces that subvert what is implicit in ideal speech relationships; and in his recent work on discourse or communicative ethics he has sharply criticized the cultural relativism of postmodernism. There is what might be called a strongly salvific element in Habermas' work, in the sense that he has an ideal view of what it means to be human and seeks to expose and correct the structural and other factors that subvert this ideal. For this reason his work has appealed to some theologians; and although biblical scholars have been slower to use his work, his theory of discourse ethics has suggested new ways in which the ethical content of the Bible might be approached and appreciated.

References and further reading

Arens, E. (1989) *Habermas und die Theologie*, Düsseldorf: Patmos.
Outhwaite, W. (1994) *Habermas: A Critical Introduction*, Cambridge: Polity Press.
Pusey, M. (1987) *Habermas*, Chichester: Ellis Horwood/ New York: Tavistock.
White, S.K. (1995) *The Cambridge Companion to Habermas*, Cambridge: Cambridge University Press.
Wiggershaus, R. (1994) *The Frankfurt School: Its History, Theories and Political Significance*, Cambridge: Polity Press.

JOHN ROGERSON

HARNACK, ADOLF VON (1851–1930)

At the end of the nineteenth century Adolf von Harnack was regarded as the most brilliant, outstanding, and influential Church historian in Germany. In the realm of Patristic scholarship probably only two men were his peers – Theodor Zahn and J.B. Lightfoot.

Harnack's father, Theodosius Harnack, was a well-known conservative Lutheran scholar and Professor of Church History at Dorpat (present-day Tartu in

Estonia), where Adolf was born in 1851. During his study at the University of Dorpat, Adolf moved away from the conservative theological views of his father, especially after transferring to Leipzig in the autumn of 1872. Here he was influenced by the writings of the Tübingen school and by the far more radical Franz Overbeck, Nietzsche's friend at Basel. In 1874 he was appointed lecturer in the theological faculty at Leipzig, and in this same year journeyed to Göttingen where he met Albrecht Ritschl, perhaps the most influential theologian of the day. From that time a close theological relationship was established between the two men which lasted to Ritschl's death in 1889. In 1879 Harnack was appointed professor at the newly rejuvenated (Ritschlian) theological faculty at Giessen. Here in partnership with Emil Schürer he founded the *Theologische Literaturzeitung*, which quickly became the most important review of theological literature in Germany.

By now Harnack had completely abandoned his former conservative theological viewpoint. He no longer believed in a Trinity or a preexistent Christ. Such views in his opinion were the products of Greek metaphysics. The Christology of the early church was the result of the so-called Hellenization of Christianity; the doctrines of the Virgin Birth of Christ and his bodily resurrection were also consigned to the realm of metaphysics, views expressed somewhat vaguely in his seven-volume *History of Dogma*, the first volume of which appeared in 1886.

With such heterodox views it was not surprising that Harnack encountered opposition. Even his own father repudiated the liberal principles that he expressed. There was also opposition to his promotion in the university world. In Prussia the conservative theological faculties resisted his appointment, but the Prussian Ministry of Education, which at that period espoused a liberal viewpoint, wanted to appoint him to a professorship at Berlin, the highest theological position in Germany. The decision turned into a political struggle between the government with its liberal policies and Kaiser Wilhelm II, who in the end was forced to give way. Harnack was appointed professor at Berlin in 1889.

Four theological controversies creating widespread sensation arose during his years in Berlin. In 1892 he became embroiled in a dispute over the Apostles' Creed, whose doctrinal content he believed to be based on erroneous metaphysical speculation. What Harnack said in effect was that the Creed was doctrinally worthless, although it should not be done away with, that the clergy ought to support it, even though they did not agree with it, and that they should be free to dissent from certain statements so long as they expressed their views openly.

The second controversy concerned the Person of Christ. In the winter semester of 1899/1900, Harnack gave a series of sixteen public lectures on the essence of Christianity. In the second of these lectures he denied that Jesus was part of the Gospel. He meant that God was a loving Father who would forgive the sins of his erring children and that Jesus only informed mankind of this fact. The traditional view of Jesus as the Son of God, who had first to die for sins before God could forgive them was in the eyes of Harnack no part of the original Gospel, but the product of Hellenistic development and therefore irrelevant.

In 1911 Karl Jatho, a Lutheran clergyman who had openly denied the fundamental beliefs of the Lutheran Church, was in the process of being dismissed from his position. Harnack wrote a brochure generally supporting the governing body of the church which declared that Jatho's theology was irreconcilable with his position in the church. Harnack added, however, that even though Jatho's theology was 'unbearable' he should not be dismissed. Jatho in turn protested that his views were essentially no different from those of Harnack, who was now condemning him.

Hard on the heels of the Jatho affair came the case of Gottfried Traub in Dortmund, another Lutheran clergyman. Traub, an avowed deist, pantheist or atheist, not only denied all the traditional doctrines of the church, but poured out scathing attacks on his superiors in the church. In 1912 he was dismissed by the church authorities. Harnack, perhaps wanting to make amends for his ineffectual support of Jatho, now wrote a small brochure encouraging Traub and criticizing the continuing necessity of accepting the Apostles' Creed.

Harnack was a prolific writer in the field of the history of the early church. The number of his publications in this field is enormous. With Oscar von Gebhardt he founded the series called 'Texts and Investigations for the History of Early Christian Literature' (Texte und Untersuchungen zur Geschichte der altchristlichen Literatur). From 1905 he was Director of the Royal Library in Berlin and a close friend of the Kaiser. From 1910 and after the war he was President of the Kaiser Wilhelm Foundation, which spearheaded scientific and cultural research in Germany.

Harnack encountered with dismay the rise of the dialectical theology of Karl Barth in the post-First World War years. When Barth gave a lecture at Aarau in 1920 Harnack was in the audience. 'The effect on Harnack,' wrote Harnack's daughter, 'was shattering. There was not one sentence, not one thought which he could make his own. He acknowledged the seriousness with which Barth spoke, but this theology horrified him' (Zahn-Harnack 1936: 532). In the end, for Harnack, there was no revelation from a God outside of space and time, no irruption of God into history, no incarnation and bodily resurrection of Christ. This fact needs to be clearly understood when assessing Harnack's historical writings and his whole interpretation of events in the early church.

References and further reading

Relevant entries in *Oxford Dictionary of the Christian Church*, 736–7.

Busch, E. (1976) *Karl Barth: His Life From Letters and Autobiographical Texts*, trans. John Bowden, London: SCM Press.

Glick, G.W. (1967) *The Reality of Christ: A Study of Adolf von Harnack as Historian and Theologian*, New York: Harper & Row.

Rumscheidt, Martin (ed.) (1989) *Adolf von Harnack: Liberal Theology at its Height*, London: Collins Liturgical Publications.

Zahn-Harnack, A. (1936) *Adolf von Harnack*, Berlin: De Gruyter.

HORTON HARRIS

HEBREW AND ARAMAIC GRAMMAR AND LEXICOGRAPHY

1 Introduction

This article comprises a basic introduction to the Hebrew of standard editions of the Bible and surveys a number of common or striking features, without any pretense of exhaustiveness. Because the Hebrew Bible comprises material that is diverse in genre, date, and provenance, the term 'Biblical Hebrew' is something of a fiction. Nonetheless, from the Persian period through to the early Middle Ages, from which time our standard editions derive, this diverse material underwent a process of linguistic homogenization, which has tended to reinforce both the actual and the perceived linguistic unity of the corpus.

The ethnic, linguistic, and literary intertwining of Hebrew and Aramaic dates from the very beginnings of Israel's history (cf. Gen. 31:47; Deut. 26:5) and continued through the intertestamental period and into the Middle Ages. At various times and places Aramaic has replaced Hebrew as the vernacular or as a literary language. Many lexemes in the Aramaic portions of the Bible (Dan. 2:4–7:28; Ezra 4:8–6:18; 7:12–26) have recognizable cognates in the Hebrew sections and there are numerous Aramaisms in Biblical Hebrew (and Hebraisms in Biblical Aramaic). Nonetheless, Aramaic and Hebrew are not mutually intelligible dialects, but separate languages, each with a wealth of literary and spoken traditions that go well beyond the evidence of the Bible. Biblical Aramaic and Biblical Hebrew (often

via Aramaic) each contain a significant proportion of foreign loanwords.

2 Reading Hebrew

Biblical Hebrew (and Aramaic), like other varieties of the language, is read from right to left and employs twenty-two letters of a purely consonantal alphabet:

א, ב, ג, ד, ה, ה, ו, ז, ז, ח, ט, י, כ, ל, מ, נ, ס, ע, פ, צ, ק, ר, ש, ת

', b, g, d, h, w, z, ḥ, ṭ y, k, l, m, n, s, ʿ, p, ṣ, q, r, ś/š, t

In 'pointed' texts (that is, texts in which vowels and other guides to pronunciation are included), ש can be either שׂ (ś) or שׁ (š), making twenty-three consonants in all (*'alef, bet, gimel, dalet, he, waw, zayin, ḥet, ṭet, yod, kaf, lamed, mem, nun, samekh, ʿayin, pe, ṣade, qof, resh, śin, šin, taw*). The letters כ, מ, נ, פ, צ (k, m, n, p, ṣ) have special forms, ך, ם, ן, ף, ץ, when they occur at the end of a word. The original phonetic distinction between s (ס) and ś (ש) is unclear, and many words alternate between the two. Of the consonants not familiar to English-speakers, ' (א) represents a glottal stop, in practice only perceptible in the middle of a word; ḥ (ח), if Arabic is a guide, was pronounced like the 'j' in Spanish *julio* rather than the 'ch' in Scottish *loch*; ṭ (ט) and ṣ (צ) may have been pronounced like English 't' and 's,' but with the tongue tip nearer the teeth themselves than the alveolar ridge; q (ק) is similar to 'k' (כ) but with the back of the tongue against the uvula; ʿ (ע) represents a sound produced by tightening the throat and forcing air through it; š (ש) is pronounced 'sh.' Traditional rules of pronunciation say that ב, ג, ד, כ, פ, and ת are usually pronounced just like their English counterparts (b, g, d, k, p, t) when they do not follow a vowel but as ḇ (something like English 'v'), ḡ (as in 'Baghdad'), ḏ (as in 'this'), ḵ (as in 'loch'), p̄ (as in 'Philip'), and ṯ (as in 'thin') when they do.

In principle, Hebrew orthography, as shown here, could represent only consonants, meaning, in effect, that command of the written language required prior competence in the spoken language (or in the oral tradition of the language, once it had ceased to be spoken). Vowel signs were, therefore, introduced into the biblical text below, above, or within consonants, to facilitate its correct reading. In the Tiberian system of pointing (employed in standard editions of the Bible), nine basic vowel signs, each on its own or in combination with another vowel sign or a consonant represent fourteen or fifteen different sounds. Although vowel length (long, short, ultrashort/murmured) is clearly represented within this system, gaps and duplications strongly suggest that length was no longer primary in distinguishing one vowel from another.

The basic (or 'dictionary') form of most Hebrew words tends to be either mono- or bisyllabic. In the Tiberian system words are generally stressed on the final syllable, although there are many indications that stress was originally penultimate. A syllable must have a consonant (C) in first position and a vowel (v) in second position. If there is an additional consonant in third position (thus, CvC), the syllable is closed (by the second consonant), with the vowel inside it short if the syllable is unstressed, but short or long if it is stressed. Otherwise, the syllable remains open (Cv), with the final vowel long. Exceptions to this simple syllabic structure are rare.

3 Nouns

A large class of nouns, known as segolates (containing in their final syllable the vowel *segol* or 'e,' e.g., **ʿebed** 'servant,' **melek** 'king'), is (still) accented on the penultimate. Case-endings (for nominative, accusative, or genitive) are not used in the Hebrew noun. Noun compounding is rare, except in the so-called 'construct chain,' whereby a genitive relationship is expressed by placing the 'possessed' noun before the 'possessor.' For word-stress purposes the construct chain forms a single unit, with the first noun losing its stress and often, consequently, undergoing a change in vocalization, e.g., **deḇar ʾĕlōhīm** 'word [**dāḇār**] of God,' **bēṯ hā-ʾīš** 'house [**bayiṯ**] of the man.' The 'construct' form of the possessed noun can also be attached to special, suffixed, forms of the various personal pronouns, e.g., **deḇār-ī** 'my word,' **bēṯ-ō** 'his house.'

Hebrew has two genders, unmarked (masculine) and marked (feminine). Typical 'feminine' markers are -**ā** or -**eṯ** in the singular and -**ōṯ** (as against 'masculine' -**īm**) in the plural. However, because some 'feminine' words appear to be 'masculine' and *vice versa*, it is only when a noun is, for example, modified by an adjective (which is also marked for gender and number) that the gender of a noun is decisively exhibited. In the numbers three to ten, 'masculine' nouns usually take a 'feminine' form of the number and *vice versa*, e.g., **šelōšā bānīm** 'three sons,' **šālōš bānōṯ** 'three daughters.'

4 Verbs

Central elements of the Hebrew verb include the 'perfect' (generally referring to completed, past, actions or states) and 'imperfect' (for incomplete actions or states, typically rendered by present, future, conditional, or subjunctive). There are also two additional conjugations, which, despite their morphological appearance and traditional grammatical statements, are better regarded as separate conjugations, not derived, either historically or in their usage, from the 'perfect' and 'imperfect' conjugations. The best-known feature of these so-called *waw*-consecutive forms is, broadly

speaking, that the conjugation that looks most like the 'imperfect' functions as though it were a 'perfect' and *vice versa*. However, the predominance of their use in narrative prose and especially at the beginning of a narrative, where there is no preceding action to trigger their use (according to traditional explanations) is striking. Generally, in the context of narrative prose, the use of all the different forms of the Hebrew verb, although often broadly coterminous with distinctions of time, should be seen as dictated mainly by often subtle constraints of (a) word order (especially the class of word that begins a particular sentence and the placement of the ubiquitous particle **we-/wa-** 'and') and (b) of previous choices in the verbal system.

The 'perfect' verb employs just suffixes to denote its subject (e.g., **dibbar-tā** 'you spoke'), whereas the 'imperfect' is characterized by its use of prefixes as well (e.g., **te-dabbēr** 'you [will] speak'). As in the noun, forms of personal pronouns can be suffixed to verbs to indicate an accusative (or dative) relationship (e.g., **had-dāḇār ʾăšer lō dibber-ō** 'the word that he did not speak [it]').

A series of 'derived conjugations,' in which the basic, typically triconsonantal, form of a verb is modified by the addition of prefixes, duplication of consonants, or changes of vowels, allows Hebrew to express regular modifications of meaning (passive, reflexive, reciprocal, causative, intensive, etc.), e.g., **šābar** (simple conjugation) 'he broke,' **šibbar** (intensive) 'he shattered.' Often, though, verbs are only or mainly found in the 'derived' conjugations (e.g., standard words for 'speak,' 'fight,' and 'prophesy'). Moreover, a derived conjugation can express different modifications of meaning with different verbs, a particular modification may be expressed by two or more derived conjugations, and sometimes one conjugation is used in the 'perfect' and another in the 'imperfect.'

Verbless sentences, in which a subject and complement are simply juxtaposed, without the verb 'to be,' are common, as are 'stative' (or 'adjectival') verbs: 'be big,' 'be old,' etc. Hebrew has a variety of conjunctions, although to some extent it eschews clause embedding in favor of coordination of clauses with **we-** 'and,' which develops a wide range of grammatical functions. Adverbial complementation is frequently expressed by means of a preposition followed by an infinitive plus possessive pronoun, e.g., **ba-ʿăśōṯ-ō** 'in his doing' (i.e., 'when he did,' 'while he was doing,' 'as he did').

5 Aramaic

Obvious features that distinguish Biblical Aramaic from Hebrew include Aramaic's use of a suffixed – rather than prefixed – definite article, e.g., **bayt-ā** 'the house' (Hebrew **hab-bayit**), infinitives prefixed by **m**-, e.g., **le-miḇnē** 'to build' (Hebrew **li-ḇnōt**) or, in the derived conjugations, suffixed by -**ā**, e.g., **le-baqqārā** 'to seek' (Hebrew **le-baqqēr**), relative particle **dī** 'which, that, because' (Hebrew ˀᵃšer), interrogative **mān** 'who?' (Hebrew **mī**), masculine possessive or accusative pronoun ('his, him') in -ēh (Hebrew -ō), negative **lā** (Hebrew **lō**), the regular employment of 'jussive' lᵉ- before the third person masculine 'imperfect' of the verb 'to be' (**lehᵉᵂē** [contracted from **lᵉ-yehᵉwē**] for Hebrew **yihyè** 'he will be' [imperfect] or **yᵉhī** 'may he be' [jussive]), first person singular 'perfect' suffix in -ēṭ, not -tī (**hᵃwēṭ** for Hebrew **hāyītī** 'I was'), object marker **lᵉ-** (rarely **yāṭ**) rather than Hebrew 'eṭ-, and **ˀītay** 'there is' (for Hebrew **yēš**). Biblical Aramaic words without cognates in Biblical Hebrew include **mārē'** 'lord,' **zᵉban** 'acquire,' and **nᵉp̄aq** 'go out.'

References and further reading

(See also the references to the entry: Hebrew and Aramaic Languages).

Hadas-Lebel, Mireille (1995) *Histoire de la Langue Hébraïque: des Origines à l'Époque de la Mishna*, Collection de la Revue des Études Juives 21, Paris and Leuven: E. Peeters, 2nd edn.

Joüon, Paul, (1993) *A Grammar of Biblical Hebrew*, T. Muraoka (trans. and ed.), Subsidia Biblica 14.1–2, Rome: Editrice Pontificio Istituto Biblico, corrected 4th edn.

Koehler, Ludwig and Walter Baumgartner (1994–2000) *The Hebrew and Aramaic Lexicon of the Old Testament*, 5 Vols., trans. M.E.J. Richardson, Leiden: Brill.

Landis Gogel, Sandra (1998) *A Grammar of Epigraphic Hebrew*, SBL Resources for Biblical Studies 23, Atlanta: Scholars Press.

Rosenthal, Franz (1995) *A Grammar of Biblical Aramaic*, Porta Linguarum Orientalium, NS 5, Wiesbaden: Otto Harrasowitz, 6th rev. edn.

J.F. ELWOLDE

HEBREW AND ARAMAIC LANGUAGES

1 Introduction

This article focuses on the period from the second century BC to AD 135, from which we possess substantial documentary evidence in Hebrew, namely the Dead Sea Scrolls and the Bar Kockba archive. The article does not extend to the earliest phases of Hebrew or to Hebrew after the Mishnah, nor does it attempt to describe linguistic features of dialects or genres. For such topics as well as more elaborate treatment of the issues raised here, the reader is directed to References and further reading, which comprises works with a

primary or substantial historical interest as well as studies of nonbiblical Hebrew and Aramaic material. In this article, Aramaic is discussed only in its relationship to Hebrew, but again the References should help the interested reader.

2 The Hebrew of the biblical period

With regard to analysis of the Bible itself, linguistic chronology is hampered by such structural problems as the dating of our standard Hebrew text of the Bible to only as far back as the ninth century AD; the serial process of redaction and homogenization that the entire Bible, including any genuinely preexilic composition, has undergone; and the existence of non- or pre-Masoretic traditions (such as those represented by the Isaiah Scroll from Qumran or the Samaritan Pentateuch) and of non-Tiberian vocalizations and reading traditions of the Masoretic text (Babylonian, Yemenite, etc.).

Nonetheless, external and internal data give us some clear leads. From the seventh to sixth centuries BC in particular we have military correspondence on ostraca from Arad and Lachish written in a form of Hebrew not strikingly dissimilar to that found in the prose of, say, Samuel. It may, then, be assumed that before the Exile Hebrew flourished as a literary language and there is no positive evidence to suggest that the spoken language was significantly different, at least in the south. The study of direct speech in biblical narrative (through 'discourse analysis') could help to cast light on this topic. It is usually assumed that the remnants of early poetry found in the Bible, which employ a diction and grammar that make it stand out from standard preexilic prose, represent a northern literary idiom that reflects contact with the language and literature of Israel's Canaanite antecedents and Aramaic-speaking neighbors.

However, after the Exile there is practically no documentary evidence for the use of Hebrew beyond that of the postexilic biblical texts themselves (which may, in view of the evidence presented below, be assumed to represent nothing more – and nothing less! – than the skilful handling of a dead language) and there is positive evidence both for ignorance of Hebrew and for the encroachment of Aramaic on spoken and literary usage. In contrast, though, there are numerous instances of a non-classical, apparently vernacular, form of Hebrew in postexilic texts (the pervasiveness of such usage being in proportion to an author's ability to adhere to the preexilic classical literary idiom). This strongly indicates to most scholars the existence of a contemporary spoken dialect of Hebrew, albeit strongly Aramaized, that found its literary continuation in the Mishnah and subsequent tannaitic literature.

Nehemiah 13:24 is witness to the apparent decline of spoken Hebrew around 428 BC even among the Judaean populace that had not suffered exile. It is possible that some thirty years earlier Nehemiah 8:8 speaks of the necessity of translating the Torah into Aramaic for those who had returned from exile (although others date the incident described to 398 BC). If so, we can see that from the very beginning of the Second Temple period the survival of Hebrew as a spoken, or nonliterary written, medium was under attack both by the Aramaization in exile of the community leaders and by the natural encroachment of Aramaic (and possibly other Semitic dialects) into formerly Hebrew-speaking territory.

In the Diaspora as well, the linguistic ephemera of the Second Temple period suggest that Hebrew was in decline, being replaced for the practical purposes of life by Aramaic (in the east) and Greek (in the west). To this evidence we can also add the Aramaic forms of the New Testament (e.g., *talitha, sabachthani, Maranatha*) and the Aramaic legends on coins of Alexander Jannaeus (first century BC). In the period 300 BC to AD 700, the use of Hebrew in grave inscriptions, where it might have been expected, is very limited in comparison with Aramaic (and especially Greek), even in the Holy Land (van der Horst 1991: 22–4). How different this was to the situation in 701 BC, where Aramaic is presented as a language known only to the highest echelons of society and even foreigners deigned to speak in 'Judaean' (2 Kings 18:26–28).

As a literary language, Biblical Hebrew fared better. Scholars standardly separate, for example, late biblical prose (the Nehemiah memoirs, Esther, and the non-parallel parts of Chronicles) from early, or 'standard,' prose (e.g., Samuel-Kings), and have isolated grammatical and lexical features that tend to distinguish earlier from later usage. 'Later' features, it is argued, are due to influence from both literary and spoken Aramaic on writers attempting to imitate earlier prose, as well as from a nonliterary form of Hebrew (itself strongly influenced by spoken Aramaic) that had survived among those who did not undergo exile (see above).

The later books of the Bible are followed in the second and first centuries BC by the Dead Sea Scrolls, which provide abundant evidence of the continued use of Biblical Hebrew (albeit with linguistic differences, especially in morphophonology) in sectarian and para-biblical literature. However, the composition in Aramaic of several major Dead Sea texts and the production elsewhere of apocrypha and pseudepigrapha in Aramaic (and Greek) indicate not only the linguistic dominance of Aramaic but also its religious acceptability. These features are foreshadowed in the biblical Second Temple period, where we see the use of Aramaic for a substantial portion of scripture (Dan. 2–7). It has been suggested (Lemaire 1988) that biblical and postbiblical works concerned with Job, Daniel, Tobit, and Enoch result from the 'Judaization' of formerly Aramaic literary characters (note, e.g., the ending of LXX Job). In any case, at the purely linguistic level, Aramaic influence pervades postexilic Hebrew literature.

3 The emergence of Mishnaic Hebrew

Many scholars argue that the rather consistent morphological and syntactic idiosyncracies (with regard to the standard biblical tradition of Hebrew) of 'Qumran Hebrew' or 'the Hebrew of the Dead Sea Scrolls' are the reflex of a living, spoken dialect, closer to Biblical Hebrew than to Mishnaic Hebrew, that has influenced the scribes in their literary composition (e.g., Muraoka 2000). On this hypothesis, we might envisage a gradual process, commencing before the Exile, whereby the spoken language in the south grew apart from the official literary language preserved in Jerusalem. This would have resulted in part from the inherent conservatism of scribal practice and, in contrast, the natural tendency of the spoken language to develop, and in part from the influence of nonsouthern Hebrew dialects and Aramaic (both by natural encroachment and via the Exile). In any event, access to the (hypothetical) southern vernacular of Qumran is largely hindered by the consciously literary, and, more specifically, biblicizing, nature of the material. At every turn of style and thought, the Qumran writers are informed by the Bible, so that the idiom of the Bible does not simply influence, but virtually becomes, their natural literary language. Against this background, linguistic creativity consists primarily in the adaptation of biblical elements, including their application to contexts in which they are not found in the Bible.

If not before, then at least by, the time of Bar Kockba (AD 132–35), it is apparent that 'Biblical Hebrew,' even as a literary language in the south, was the domain only of the religious professional, for Bar Kockba and his correspondents have no qualms in writing in a form of Hebrew that is closer in some ways to the Mishnah than to the Bible. If the Dead Sea text abbreviated as MMT is indeed a 'halakhic letter,' written to a Pharisee, 'probably between 159–152 BCE' (Qimron and Strugnell 1994: 121), its increased use (as compared to that in other Dead Sea Scrolls) of forms known from the Mishnah would tend, along with the evidence of the Hebrew Bar Kockba material, to confirm the standard view that the Mishnah is a literary crystallization of the language in which the Pharisees had taught. This in turn is assumed by many to be a vernacular dialect of Hebrew, perhaps dating back even to preexilic times as a northern spoken counterpart to literary 'Biblical' Hebrew. The Dead Sea Scrolls may allude on various occasions to Pharisaic use of the vernacular, a blasphemy in the eyes of the sectarians (Rabin 1957: 67–9). Traces of this vernacular (or 'proto-Mishnaic') language have been noted in many postexilic biblical books (see above) and in some cases correspond to non-standard features (notably the particle **še-** for **ʾašer** 'who, which, that') found in preexilic passages assumed to have a northern provenience.

However, as already indicated, there is no nonbiblical documentary evidence for the use of such a vernacular during the biblical postexilic period, whereas there is explicit internal biblical evidence for the ignorance of Hebrew, and the growing prevalence of Aramaic is seen everywhere. Moreover, by the time of the composition of the Mishnah in the first half of the third century AD, even the vernacular Hebrew tradition the Mishnah might encapsulate had itself died out among any sizeable part of the population under the pressure of Aramaic and in the wake of the social and cultural devastation that followed the major Jewish revolts of the first and second centuries AD. A detailed study of a Bar Kockba document (G.W. Nebe in Muraoka and Elwolde 1997: 150–7) clearly shows the all-pervading influence of Aramaic on Hebrew legal composition of the period. Of the thirty-five legal documents in the Babatha archive, from the period just before the Bar Kockba revolt, there are none in Hebrew, three in Aramaic, and twenty-six in Greek (Yadin 1971: 229). Because so many documents associated with Bar Kockba are written in Aramaic, it has been suggested that the use of Hebrew in others was the result of a linguistic policy in support of Bar Kockba's fledgling state (Yadin 1971: 124, 181). This might explain why in a certain letter sent from one Bar Kockba supporter to another it is said that the letter has been composed in Greek because in the sender's non-Jewish camp there was nobody who knew Hebrew (Yadin 1971: 130), perhaps an implied apology for this linguistic breach of faith (although 'Hebrew' in this context may cover 'Aramaic' as well); in any case, we see that Greek was at least the language of last resort. However, an ostracon recording a conveyance of property and recently found at Qumran seems, at least on one reading (Yardeni 1997), to employ some typically 'Mishnaic' lexical forms within an otherwise quite biblical form of the language. This is evidence, albeit slight, for southern (Judaean) use of Hebrew in a nonliterary context in the century before Bar Kockba as well as for a natural, if not entirely linear, development from 'Biblical' to 'Mishnaic' Hebrew.

Indeed, we should not overstate the difference between the Hebrew of the Bible and that of the Mishnah. In many respects what is commonplace at the level of syntax, morphology, and lexis in the Mishnah is clearly foreshadowed in earlier postexilic Hebrew literature (including Ben Sira and the Dead Sea Scrolls). There is, to that extent, a continuum between Bible and Mishnah, although the Hebrew of the Mishnah also exhibits a more radical break with that of the Bible. First, in its mode of composition the Mishnah eschews a biblicizing model and consequently embraces a myriad of contemporary linguistic features (including, naturally, numerous Aramaic and Greek loans) that are alien to the Bible. Secondly, the Mishnah develops its own idiosyncratic, rather compressed, literary style for the expression of its dominant subject matter: the transmission of detailed rules for living in accordance with the word and spirit of Torah.

References and further reading

(See also the references to the entry: Hebrew and Aramaic Grammar and Lexicography).

Beyer, Klaus (1986) *The Aramaic Language: Its Distribution and Subdivisions*, trans. J.F. Healey, Göttingen: Vandenhoeck & Ruprecht.

Clines, D.J.A. (ed.) (1993–) *The Dictionary of Classical Hebrew*, 8 Vols., Sheffield: Sheffield Academic Press.

Dalman, Gustaf (1927) *Grammatik des jüdisch-palästinischen Aramäisch [und] aramäische Dialektproben*, Leipzig: J.C. Hinrichs Verlag, 2nd edn (reprinted Darmstadt: Wissenschaftliche Buchgesellschaft, 1978).

Fitzmyer, Joseph A. (1979) 'The Phases of the Aramaic Language,' pp. 57–84 in *A Wandering Aramean: Collected Aramaic Essays*, SBLMS 25, Missoula: Scholars Press.

—— and Daniel J. Harrington (1994) *A Manual of Palestinian Aramaic Texts (Second Century BC – Second Century AD)*, Biblica et Orientalia 34, Roma: Editrice Pontificio Istituto Biblico.

Horbury, William (ed.) (1999) *Hebrew Study from Ezra to Ben-Yehuda*, Edinburgh: T.&T. Clark.

Horst, Pieter W. van der (1991) *Ancient Jewish Epitaphs*, Contributions to Biblical Exegesis and Theology 2, Kampen: Kok Pharos.

Lemaire, André (1988) 'Aramaic Literature and Hebrew: Contacts and Influences in the First Millennium BCE,' pp. 9–24 in *Proceedings of the Ninth World Congress of Jewish Studies, Jerusalem, August 4–12, 1985; Panel Sessions: Hebrew and Aramaic*, Moshe Bar-Asher (ed.), Jerusalem: World Union of Jewish Studies.

Muraoka, T. (2000) 'Hebrew,' 1.340a–45b in *Encyclopaedia of the Dead Sea Scrolls*, Lawrence H. Schiffman and James C. VanderKam (eds.), Oxford: Oxford University Press.

—— and J.F. Elwolde (eds.) (1997) *The Hebrew of the Dead Sea Scrolls and Ben Sira: Proceedings of a Symposium held at Leiden University, 11–14 December 1995*, STDJ 26, Leiden: Brill.

—— (1999) *Sirach, Scrolls, and Sages: Proceedings of a Second International Symposium on the Hebrew of the Dead Sea Scrolls, Ben Sira, and the Mishnah, held at Leiden University, 15–17 December 1997*, STDJ 33, Leiden: Brill.

—— (2000) *Diggers at the Well: Proceedings of a Third International Symposium on the Hebrew of the Dead Sea Scrolls and Ben Sira, held at Ben-Gurion University of the Negev, Beer-Sheva, 10–15 October 1999*, STDJ, Leiden: Brill.

Muraoka, T. and Bezalel Porten (1998) *A Grammar of Egyptian Aramaic*, Handbuch der Orientalistik 1.23, Leiden: Brill.

Peursen, W.Th. van (1999) 'The Verbal System in the Hebrew Text of Ben Sira,' Ph.D. dissertation, Leiden University.

Pérez Fernández, Miguel (1997) *An Introductory Grammar of Rabbinic Hebrew*, trans. J.F. Elwolde, Leiden: Brill.

Qimron, Elisha (1986) *The Hebrew of the Dead Sea Scrolls*, HSS 29, Atlanta: Scholars Press.

—— and John Strugnell (1994) *Qumran Cave 4; V: Miqsat Maʿaśe ha-Torah*, DJD 10, Oxford: Clarendon Press.

Rabin, Chaim (1957) 'The Sect and its Opponents,' pp. 53–70 in *Qumran Studies*, Scripta Judaica 2, Oxford: Oxford University Press.

Ridzewski, Beate (1992) *Neuhebräische Grammatik auf Grund der ältesten Handschriften und Inschriften*, Heidelberger orientalische Studien 21, Frankfurt a.M.: Peter Lang.

Rosenthal, Franz (ed.) (1967) *An Aramaic Handbook*, 2 parts, Porta Linguarum Orientalium, NS 10; Wiesbaden: Otto Harrasowitz.

Sáenz-Badillos, Ángel (1993) *A History of the Hebrew Language*, trans. J.F. Elwolde, Cambridge: Cambridge University Press.

Yadin, Yigael (1971) *Bar-Kokhba: The Rediscovery of the Legendary Hero of the Last Jewish Revolt against Imperial Rome*, London: Weidenfeld and Nicholson.

Yardeni, Ada (1997) 'A Draft of a Deed on an Ostracon from Khirbet Qumrân,' *Israel Exploration Journal* 47: 233–37.

J.F. ELWOLDE

HEIDEGGER, MARTIN (1889–1976)

Martin Heidegger is one of the most influential and controversial philosophers of the twentieth century. He was raised as a Roman Catholic and even studied two years for the priesthood, but left to pursue philosophy at the University of Freiburg. By the 1920s Heidegger had rejected religion entirely. He received his Ph.D. in 1915, was professor at Marburg from 1923 to 1928, and then Freiburg. At Marburg Heidegger was a colleague of Rudolf Otto, Rudolf Bultmann, and Paul Tillich, among others. Between 1933 and 1934, after replacing Husserl as professor of philosophy at Freiburg, Heidegger became the first National Socialist rector of the university. His specific politics have been debated by scholars but his involvement with National Socialism is undisputed. After the war, Heidegger continued writing and teaching philosophy at Freiburg until his death.

In his notoriously difficult work *Being and Time* (*Sein und Zeit*, 1927), with its strained and obscure syntax, Heidegger places the question of understanding in a revolutionarily new context. His interest is the ontological foundation of hermeneutics and he concludes that both human understanding and existence are themselves hermeneutic.

Humanity, in Heidegger's view, has fallen into a state of crisis due to its parochial approach to the world that manifests through technologically conditioned ways of thinking and an ignorance of the question of 'the meaning of being.' The question of the meaning of being has not been authentically asked, and because of our ignorance and forgetfulness of what being is, and what we ourselves are, the world has been darkened. The 'being question' is an investigation of the 'being of beings,' that is, the ontological difference between the two. What is the meaning of 'to be'? To answer this, he proposes an existential analytic of *Dasein* ('human being' – literally 'to be there'). The path to the meaning is through *Dasein* that provides the place and occasion for the being of beings.

Heidegger's fundamental ambition, as the quest for being, denies the subject-object schema prevalent in prior philosophy. To be a thing is to be objectively present, but to be *Dasein* is characteristically different. Heidegger's hermeneutic points to an event of understanding, not towards methods or theories of interpretation. Though not a self-proclaimed existentialist, Heidegger's thought brings together traditional ontology and existential humanism in a dramatic new way. With him, hermeneutics became more fundamental as an existential understanding – an ontological process rather than one of consciousness or methodology. According to Heidegger, human existence itself has a hermeneutical structure that underlies all our interpretations, including those of the natural sciences. Understanding cannot be objectively grasped or employed as a faculty of the mind because it is the fundamental mode of 'being in the world' – in and through which one exists.

Dasein is an event, an occurrence, wherein understanding is primarily pragmatic, temporal, intentional, and historical. Being exists in time with conditioned understanding from previous understanding. All existence is basically interpretative and all judgments take place within a context of interpretation mediated by culture and language. Language is as primordial as understanding because understanding is linguistic. Like understanding, language is not a tool to be used but is the 'house of being' by which we are 'owned' rather than owners.

Dasein has no determinate essence but consists in its possibilities. 'To be' means there is always something outstanding. *Dasein* aims toward what is not yet; it is always reaching out of itself. We find ourselves as a 'thrown project' – as already in a world at a certain time and place – with foreknowledge from previous experience building upon itself as we work through the ontological hermeneutic circle from our existential situatedness to a self-conscious interpretative stance. It is a stance, however, that is historical and finite and, consequently, always incomplete. We are constantly understanding and interpreting what it means 'to be' as we think more fundamentally than do objective and methodological sciences, letting being reveal itself.

References and further reading

Heidegger, Martin (1982) *The Basic Problems of Phenomenology*, trans. Albert Hofstadter, Bloomington: Indiana University Press.

—— (1996) *Being and Time*, trans. Joan Stambaugh, New York: State University of New York Press.

Palmer, Richard E. (1969) *Hermeneutics: Interpretation Theory in Schleiermacher, Dilthey, Heidegger and Gadamer*, Evanston: Northwestern University Press.

Thiselton, Anthony C. (1980) *The Two Horizons: New Testament Hermeneutics and Philosophical Description*, Grand Rapids: Eerdmans.

J.C. ROBINSON

HELLENISTIC MORAL PHILOSOPHY AND THE NEW TESTAMENT

1 Hellenistic moral philosophy
2 Parallels
3 Conclusions

1 Hellenistic moral philosophy

The goal of Hellenistic philosophy was the attainment of happiness (*eudaimonia*). We will consider the most important of these traditions for New Testament studies. Since there is little philosophical speculation in the New Testament, we will concentrate on ethics.

1.1 Pythagoreans

The Pythagorean tradition is generally divided into Early Pythagoreanism, Hellenistic Pythagoreanism, and Neopythagoreanism. It only existed as an identifiable school during the early period. None of Pythagoras' (*c.* 582–500 BC) writings survive (DL 8.6). His views were transmitted orally in the *akousmata* that his followers memorized (DL 8.17–18). He thought that the soul was a fallen divinity trapped in a bodily tomb in a cycle of reincarnation (metempsychosis), but was capable of purification through ascetic practices. His interest in numbers lived on in the arithmologies that his followers and writers like Philo of Alexandria found fascinating.

During the Hellenistic and Roman periods there were individuals who identified themselves as Pythagoreans but did not have any formal institutional organization. The major sources for the Hellenistic period are a series of pseudonymous letters (perhaps later) and *The Golden Verses*. The most interesting letters are those attributed to or addressed to women. *The Golden Verses* was a sacred work that was probably used for the instruction of the younger or new members of the tradition.

The Neopythagorean movement began in the first century BC. Major figures include Nigidius Figulus (100–45 BC), Quintus Sextius (fl. 30 BC–AD 14), Apollonius of Tyana, Moderatus of Gades, and Nichomachus of Gerasa. Since the end of the third century, Philostratus' *Life of Apollonius* has been used as a point of comparison with the life of Jesus in the Gospels (see the debate between Hierocles and Eusebius of Caesarea). The idealized descriptions of the Pythagorean communities that we find in Iamblichus probably stand in the same literary tradition as the idealic summaries of the Jerusalem community in Acts (Acts 2:41–47; 4:32–35; 5:12–16; Iamblichus, *VP* 96–100; cf. also Chaeremon in Porphyry, *De abstinentia* 4.6–8; Arrian, *Indica* 11.1–8; Philostratus, *VA* 3.10–51; 6.6; and the various descriptions of the Essenes). The asceticism of the Pythagoreans had an impact on early Christian asceticism, e.g., Porphyry, *Life of Pythagoras* 34–35, 33 and Anthanasius, *Life of Anthony* 14.

1.2 Middle Platonists

The Platonic tradition, as distinct from the works of Plato, is typically divided into the Old Academy (347–267 BC), the New Academy (267–80 BC), Middle Platonism (80 BC–AD 220), and Neoplatonism (AD 220–). The Old Academy is associated with Plato's immediate successors who expounded his thought over against Aristotle and the Peripatetics. A break occurred in the tradition when Arcesilaus (fl. *c.* 273–*c.* 242 BC) expressed an epistemological reserve that undermined the dogmatism of the Old Academy. His skepticism became the defining mark of the New Academy.

Middle Platonism developed when Antiochus of Ascalon (*c.* 130–68 BC), broke with his teacher Philo of Larissa (*c.* 160–79 BC) the last scholiarch of the Academy, over the history of the tradition. As a member of the New Academy, Philo's skepticism led him to discard the Old Academy's attempts to expound Plato. Antiochus embraced the Old Academy and Aristotle in a return to a more positive epistemology. He extended the tradition to include the Stoics whom he considered heirs of the Old Academy. Unsurprisingly, many Middle Platonists accepted a great deal of Stoic ethical teaching. While there was no official Academy during the period, there were a significant number of Middle Platonic thinkers: Eudorus (fl. *c.* 25 BC), Pseudo-Timaeus (*c.* 25 BC–*c.* AD 100), Thrasyllus (fl. AD 14–36), Ammonius (fl. *c.* 66), Plutarch (*c.* 50–120), Apuleius (*c.* 123–post 161), Maximus of Tyre (*c.* 125–185), Numenius of Apamea (fl. second century), Albinus (fl. *c.* 150), Alcinous (fl. *c.* 150), Atticus (*c.* 150–200), Celsus (fl. *c.* 180), and Galen (*c.* 129–199). We should also mention Philo of Alexandria who was not a Middle Platonist but attests many of the basic views.

There is an enormous amount of relevant material in authors such as Philo of Alexandria and Plutarch, who touch on virtually all ethical questions discussed in the New Testament. This ethical material is not necessarily distinctively Platonic and for this reason may represent what was more widely held among moral philosophers. The Middle Platonists are also important as a source for the development of Christian theology. This is unquestionably true for Alexandrian Christianity and may even reach back into some New Testament texts, e.g., the use of prepositional metaphysics in Christological texts (John 1:3–4; Rom. 11:36; 1 Cor. 8:6; Col. 1:16–17; Heb. 1:2) and the use of Platonic ontology in Hebrews (e.g., 8:5) and John (e.g., the shift in tenses from 1:1–2 to 1:3).

1.3 Epicureans

The Epicureans are one of the two philosophical traditions mentioned in the New Testament (Acts 17:18). The tradition is closely tied to the founder of the Garden, Epicurus (341–241/40 BC) who was revered by his disciples. Epicurus' three letters and the *Key Doctrines* in Diogenes Laertius 10 still constitute one of the most important sources for the tradition. Epicurus taught that pleasure was 'the beginning and end of the blessed life' (*Ep. Men.* in DL 10.128). By pleasure he meant freedom from physical pain (*aponia*) and freedom from mental anguish (*ataraxia*). Pleasure was therefore a state of mind. Virtues were valuable to the extent that they assisted in producing this state. The most notable gift is friendship (*KD* 27 in DL 10.148).

Later Epicureans preserved and extended his thought. The most important of these for the New Testament was Philodemus who, with a benefaction from Julius Caesar's father-in-law, set up a school in Herculaneum (110–40 BC). Although the library of this school was discovered in 1752, scholars are still working on the carbonized remains. The Villa of the Papyri contained works of Epicurus, Philodemus' notes from his teachers (Demetrius of Laconia and Zeno of Sidon), Philodemus' own works, and the writings of subsequent Epicureans. These papyri along with Lucretius' *On the Nature of Things* and Diogenes of Oenoanda's monumental inscription constitute the evidence that we have for Epicurean thought during the time the New Testament was produced.

The Epicureans are valuable both for the ways in which they help us to understand how a philosophical community attempted to nourish itself as a community and for their treatment of specific topoi, e.g., friendship, frank or bold speech, anger, and household management.

1.4 Cynics

The most colorful group of philosophers was the Cynics. It is a matter of dispute whether Antisthenes (446–366 BC) or Diogenes of Sinope (404–323 BC) was the first Cynic. The former was a student of Socrates; the latter provided the inspiration for the movement through his disregard for convention (Epictetus 2.13.24; 2.16.35; DL 7.2–3). Plato's description of Diogenes as 'Socrates gone mad' (DL 6.54) is not far from the mark. He is said to have slept in a tub in the Metroon in Athens (DL 6.23, 43). On one occasion he lit a lamp in broad daylight and went around saying, 'I am looking for a man' (DL 6.41). On another occasion when Alexander the Great came to him as he was enjoying the sun and offered him any benefaction that he wanted, he said: 'Get out of my light' (DL 6.38; Plutarch, *Alex.* 14). These and other more salacious stories probably inspired the name Cynic from 'dog' (*kyon*) (Scholiast on Aristotle's *Categories*), although there is another tradition that associates the name with a gymnasium where Antisthenes taught (DL 6.13).

Diogenes' critique of convention became the trademark of the movement. The lack of regard for institutions meant that there was no institutional structure. There are, however, a large number of known Cynics, especially in the fourth and third centuries BC and the first and second centuries AD. Epictetus has a famous description of the Cynic (3.22) which bears some striking resemblances to some of the characteristics of the disciples in the mission discourse of Q (Matt. 10:5–42//Luke 10:2–16). The popular descriptions of the Cynics suggest that they wore threadbare cloaks and carried a staff and a begging bag, although their appearance was not uniform (Lucian, *Demonax* 19, 48; DL 6.13, 22–23, 83, 93).

While the Cynics are generally known for their criticisms of social conventions, especially wealth, they did have a concept of virtue – even if they did not articulate it systematically. For the Cynics happiness was achieved by living in harmony with nature. This required self-mastery, which was best displayed under adverse circumstances. Happiness thus had little to do with the factors that were conventionally associated with it; it was a matter of an individual's character.

The Cynics are important for a number of areas of New Testament research. Their itinerant lifestyle and critiques of conventions have led a large number of scholars to compare the historical Jesus, the Jesus movement, and the apostles with them. While most would still find it more credible to think of the historical Jesus and his followers in Jewish categories (e.g., a prophet), the presentation of Jesus in the Gospels may well reflect Cynic values. Paul certainly knew and used Cynic strategies. It is generally worth exploring Cynic material when considering any antisocial statement in New Testament texts.

1.5 Stoics

The other group of philosophers explicitly mentioned in the New Testament is the Stoics (Acts 17:18). An offshoot of the Cynics, the Stoics took their name from the painted colonnade (*stoa poikilē*) in Athens where the founder, Zeno (*c.* 334–262 BC) taught. The tradition is conventionally divided into the Early, Middle, and Late Stoa. The Early and Middle Stoa are poorly represented (i.e., there is not a single full work extant from any of the significant figures), although the thought of Zeno and Chrysippus (*c.* 280–206 BC), the second founder of the Stoa, was important for the entire tradition.

The Late Stoa is easily the best represented period. There are a number of major representatives. Several were highly placed in Roman society. Seneca (4 BC–AD 65), the political advisor to Nero, wrote a number of moral essays and a series of letters that cover almost all aspects of ethics. Musonius Rufus (ante 30–c. AD 102), who had a tumultuous career that included at least three banishments from Rome, held some of the most enlightened views of any ancient philosopher, especially with regard to women. Epictetus (c. 55–c. 135), a freed slave of Epaphroditus who attended the lectures of Musonius Rufus and then gave his own at Nicopolis, provides a fascinating window into the social world of a philosopher and his students. Finally, Marcus Aurelius (121–180), the emperor of Rome, wrote his personal *Meditations* while on campaign. They were transcribed from his notebooks posthumously.

The Stoics thought that humans had a natural instinct towards virtue (*oikeiōsis*). Humans should therefore 'live in harmony with nature.' They accepted the Socratic principle that knowledge was the equivalent of virtue. Passions are an irrational and unnatural movement of the soul (DL 7.110). Virtue, on the other hand, is a 'harmonious disposition' (DL 7.89); it requires equanimity and an agreeable course of life (Seneca, *Ep.* 31.8). The Stoics conceived of virtue in unitary terms: if you had one virtue, you had them all (Plutarch, *Mor.* 1046e–f). Correspondingly, they held that all sins were equal since they were all a result of poor judgment (*SVF* 3.524–43). They did not, however, think that all sins were equally tolerable (Cicero, *Fin.* 4.56). While this suggests that there are only the virtuous, who were in reality only an abstract ideal, and the vicious, the Stoics argued that there could be progress as one moved away from vice toward wisdom.

The Stoics are of great importance for the New Testament. The attractiveness of members of the late Stoa was so great to early Christians that they christened them: Seneca (Tertullian, *De anima* 20; Jerome, *Ad Jovem* 1.49; the fourth-century fictitious correspondence between Paul and Seneca), Epictetus (Origen, *Ag. Celsus* 6.2), and Musonius Rufus (Justin Martyr, *2 Apol.* 8.1; Origen, *Ag. Celsus* 3.66) were all converted posthumously by Christians who admired them.

2 Parallels

There are a number of areas of common concern between the different traditions of Hellenistic philosophy and early Christianity. These are not restricted to a single tradition, but span multiple traditions.

2.1 Psychagogy

Ancient philosophers were concerned with moral development. At the broadest level this was known as psy-

chagogy ('guidance of the soul'). The term is taken from the *Phaedrus* where Plato used it to replace a false rhetoric that deceives with a true rhetoric that guides the soul to self-knowledge (261a–b, 271d–272a). Later philosophers wrote a number of treatises that developed the concept, although they did not always explicitly use the term *psychagogia*, e.g., Philo, *Congr.*, *Ios.*; Plutarch, *Mor.* 14e–37b, 37c–48d, 48e–74e, Philodemus, *On Frank Speaking*; Dio Chrysostom 77/78; the *Cynic Epistles*; Seneca, *Ep.* 6, 16, 32, 34, 52, 64, 90, 94, 95, 112, 120; Musonius Rufus; Epictetus 1.4, 15, 18, 28; 2.9; 3.2; 4.5, 8; and Pseudo-Plutarch, *Mor.* 75b–86a.

The basic elements of psychagogy are the recognition of different classes of hearers (Cicero, *Tusc.* 4.32, 81; Seneca, *Ep.* 52.3–4; 71.30–37; 94.50–51), the use of multiple forms of exhortation/instruction (Plutarch, *Mor.* 70f, 71b; Seneca, *Ep.* 94, 95; Dio 77/78.38), the alignment of the appropriate class of hearer with the appropriate speech, and the delivery of the material on the appropriate occasion (Plutarch, *Mor.* 68c–74e). Such strategies were used in the New Testament. At its basic level it appears in statements like 1 Thessalonians 5:14: 'We exhort you, brothers and sisters, admonish the disorderly, encourage the faint-hearted, strengthen the weak, be long-suffering to all' (cf. also Jude 22–23). On a more sophisticated level, it probably controlled the ways in which Paul related to his churches.

2.2 Modes of discourse

Related to psychagogy were the different ways in which philosophers spoke. While philosophers used the available range of rhetorical modes, they gave some a particular slant that is important for understanding the New Testament. In most cases, these modes of discourse led to the development of literary forms that often use the same name, a phenomenon that has led to a great deal of confusion. We will consider only two, although there are others, e.g., protreptic speech.

The first is the diatribe, a technique of speaking that philosophers developed and refined within the context of their schools. The best example of the term is Arrian who entitled his notes of Epictetus' lectures as *diatribai*. While this use suggests that it is a genre, it primarily refers to the dialogical method associated with Socrates that used censure and persuasion in a give-and-take fashion. Platonists (Plutarch, Maximus of Tyre), Cynics (Dio Chrysostom), and Stoics (Seneca, Musonius Rufus, Epictetus) all used it as did Jewish authors who were influenced by philosophical traditions (Wisdom of Solomon and Philo). The hallmarks of the diatribe are the use of an imaginary opponent and the anticipation of false conclusions. Paul used it extensively in Romans (e.g., the interlocutor [2:17–29; 3:1–9; 3:27–4:2] and objections [6:1, 15; 7:7, 13; 9:14, 19; 11:1, 11, 19) and less frequently elsewhere (e.g., 1 Cor. 6:12–20). James also made use of it (objection [2:18] and rhetorical questions [2:2–7, 14–16; 3:20–21; 4:4, 12).

Another mode of discourse is paraenesis. Again, this can refer to a form (a paraenetic letter or a paraenetic section within a letter) or a style. Pseudo-Libanius, an ancient epistolographer, defined the style in these words: 'The paraenetic style is that by which we exhort someone by urging him to undertake something or to avoid something' (5). The style was widely used in philosophical circles, e.g., Seneca (94.25, 39, 49; 95.1, 65) provides explicit references. Some of the major features include the use of examples, antitheses, imperatives, standard literary forms that inculcate virtue, and a loose structure. These features are common in New Testament letters that address moral formation especially in Paul, e.g., paraenetic language (e.g., 1 Thess. 2:11–12) and personal example (e.g., 1 Cor. 4:16).

2.3 Literary forms
There are a significant number of literary forms that early Christians appropriated from the philosophical traditions. One of the more important is the use of the epistolary traditions common in philosophy. Ancient epistolography incorporated a wide range of material as the works of Pseudo-Demetrius and Pseudo-Libanius show. Philosophers often adapted epistolary conventions for their own purposes. A substantial number of their letters are extant: there are thirteen letters attributed to Plato (although a number are pseudonymous); three letters of Epicurus that summarize his thought (DL 10.35–83, 84–116, 122–135), fragments of four other letters from Epicurus to communities and more than twenty to individuals; a body of pseudonymous Cynic letters; and a significant number of Pythagorean letters. New Testament letters resemble a number of these: there are apologetic (Gal.), paraenetic (1 Thess., 1 Peter), friendship (Phil.), and protreptic (Rom.) letters within the New Testament.

A second major form is the epitome. It is possible to consider the Sermon on the Mount as a summary of Jesus' teaching in the same way that philosophers used epitomes to summarize their teaching, e.g., *The Golden Verses* of the Pythagoreans, the *Main Doctrines* (DL 10.139–154) of Epicureans, or Arrian's *Encheiridion* of Epictetus. While the Sermon on the Mount is one of five sermons in Matthew and the epitomes were independent works, the Sermon on the Mount has functioned in the same way for Christians that these *epitomai* did for philosophical groups.

There are a number of minor forms. The virtue and vice lists in the New Testament are very similar to the lists that we find in the moral philosophers. The Stoa frequently took the main virtues and the corresponding vices and then subordinated other virtues and vices to them (e.g., *SVF* 3.262–294). The use of lists was a commonplace, e.g., Dio Chrysostom has more than eighty. The New Testament has eighteen independent vice lists (that include ninety-one vices), sixteen independent virtue lists (that include fifty-four virtues), and

four compound lists. These lists have numerous functions within the text.

Paul used hardship lists (Rom. 8:35–39; 1 Cor. 4:9–13; 2 Cor. 4:8–9; 6:4–10; 11:23–28; 12:10; Phil. 4:11–12; 2 Tim. 3:11) to stress the divine power at work in his life. They are strikingly similar in form to the hardship lists (*peristaseis*) that we find in the philosophers, e.g., 2 Corinthians 4:8–9 and Plutarch, *Mor.* 1057e.

Another form is the household code (Col. 3:18–4:1; Eph. 5:21–6:9; Titus 2:1–10; 1 Pet. 2:13–3:12). Almost everyone recognizes that these came from the philosophical tradition, although the way in which Christians came into contact with them is disputed. The discussion began with Aristotle's *Politics* 1.1253b1–14 (cf. also *EN* 8.1160b23–1161a10; 5.1134b9–18). After the Stagirite, discussions of household management became a commonplace in philosophical traditions: Pythagoreans (the letters of *Bryson, Callicratidas, Phintys,* and *Perictione*); Platonists (Pseudo-Plutarch, *Mor.* 7e), Epicureans (Philodemus, *On Household Management*), Cynics (Dio Chrysostom 4.91), and Stoics (Seneca, *Ep.* 94.1–3; Epictetus 2.10.1–13; 2.14.8; 2.17.31) all addressed the issue. Such discussions were taken up by Jews prior to and at the same time as Christians appropriated them (Pseudo-Phocylides 175–225; Philo, *Dec.* 165–167; *Hypoth.* 8.7.3; Josephus, *Ag. Apion* 2.189–209).

2.4 Content
The acceptance of forms such as household codes points to the fact that New Testament moral exhortation shares a good deal of content with Hellenistic moral philosophy. This is evident in the use of *topoi* (conventional subjects) and specific statements. It is a relatively straightforward task to compare a subject that is developed at length in the New Testament with a similar *topos* in one of the moral essays or discourses of a philosopher. Previous research has concentrated on friendship and frank speech, but there are other *topoi* as well. For example, one could compare comments on anger (Philodemus, *On Anger*; Seneca, *On Anger* 1–3; Plutarch, *Mor.* 452f–464d; Epictetus 1.18, 28) or anxiety (Seneca, *On tranquillity of mind*; Plutarch, *Mor.* 464e–477f; Epictetus 2.2, 13) with a number of New Testament texts. More particularly, it is worthwhile to compare *topoi* in James with the same *topoi* in the philosophical tradition, e.g., the difficulty in controlling the tongue (3:1–12; Plutarch, *Mor.* 504f–515a). The same is true for specific statements, e.g., the necessity of practice with profession (1:22–25; Plutarch, *Mor.* 84b, 1033b).

3 Conclusion

At first glance, the prospect of understanding New Testament texts by comparing them with Hellenistic philosophical texts may seem improbable. New Testament texts rarely mention philosophy or philosophers explicitly and, when they do, it is generally in a negative context (Col. 2:9; Acts 17:18; although Acts 17:28 is positive). However, this is deceptive. New Testament texts could not avoid the use of Hellenistic philosophy. As minority members of a larger society they made use of the concepts of the larger world as their abilities and proclivities allowed. The recognition of this fact is a relatively recent phenomenon in the larger world of New Testament scholarship. There is a great deal to do both in the field of Hellenistic moral philosophy and in the comparison of this material with the New Testament.

References and further reading

Introductions

Malherbe, A. (1992) *Hellenistic Moralists and the New Testament*, ANRW, Berlin: DeGruyter, 2.26.1, 267–333.

Sterling, G.E. (1997) 'Hellenistic Philosophy and the New Testament,' pp. 313–58 in *Handbook to Exegesis of the New Testament*, NTTS, S.E. Porter (ed.), Leiden: Brill.

Hellenistic philosophy

Algra, Keimpe, Jonathan Barnes, Jaap Manfeld, and Malcolm Schofield (eds.) (1999) *The Cambridge History of Hellenistic Philosophy*, Cambridge: Cambridge University Press.

Armstrong, Arthur Hilary (ed.) (1967) *The Cambridge History of Later Greek and Early Medieval Philosophy*, Cambridge: Cambridge University Press.

Dillon, John M. (1977) *The Middle Platonists: 80 B.C. to A.D. 220*, Ithaca: Cornell University Press, 2nd edn. 1998.

Haase, Wolfgang (ed.) (1987–1994) *Philosophie, Wissenschaften, Technik*, ANRW 2.36.1–7, Berlin: De Gruyter.

Long, A.A. (1986) *Hellenistic Philosophy: Stoics, Epicureans, Sceptics*, Berkeley: University of California Press, 2nd edn.

—— and D.N. Sedley (1987) *The Hellenistic Philosophers*, 2 Vols.; Cambridge: Cambridge University Press.

Collections of parallels

Berger, Klaus and Carsten Kolpe (1987) *Religions-geschichtliches Textbuch zum Neuen Testament*, Göttingen: Vandenhoeck & Ruprecht.

Boring, M. Eugene, Klaus Berger, and Carsten Colpe (1995) *Hellenistic Commentary to the New Testament*, Nashville: Abingdon.

Malherbe, Abraham J. (1986) *Moral Exhortation, A Greco-Roman Sourcebook*, Library of Early Christianity, Philadelphia: Westminster.

Strecker, Georg and Udo Schnelle (eds.) (1997–1999) *Neuer Wettstein: Texte zum Neuen Testament aus Griechentum und Hellenismus*, 2 Vols., Berlin: Walter de Gruyter.

Wettstein, J.J. (1751–1752) *Novum Testamentum Graecum*, 2 Vols., Amsterdam, reprint, Graz, Austria: Akademische Druck- und Verlagsanstalt, 1962.

Specific comparisons

Almquist, H. (1946) *Plutarch und das neue Testament: Ein Beitrag zum Corpus Hellenisticum Novi Testament*, Uppsala: Appelberg.

Balch, David L. (1981) *Let Wives be Submissive: The Domestic Code in 1 Peter*, SBLMS 26, Chico: Scholars Press.

Betz, Hans Dieter (1961) *Lukian von Samosata und das Neue Testament: Religionsgeschichtliche und paranetische Parallelen. Ein Beitrag zum Corpus Hellenisticum Novi Testamenti*, TU 76, Berlin: Akademie-Verlag.

—— (ed.) (1975) *Plutarch's Theological Writings and Early Christian Literature*, SCHNT 3, Leiden: Brill.

—— (ed.) (1978) *Plutarch's Ethical Writings and Early Christian Literature*, SCHNT 4, Leiden: Brill.

De Witt, Norman Wentworth (1954) *St. Paul and Epicurus*, Minneapolis: University of Minnesota Press.

Downing, F. Gerald (1988) *Christ and the Cynics: Jesus and Other Radical Preachers in First-Century Tradition*, JSOT Manuals 4, Sheffield: Sheffield Academic Press.

—— (1992) *Cynics and Christian Origins*, Edinburgh: T.&T. Clark.

Ebner, Martin (1991) *Leidenslisten und Apostelbrief: Untersuchungen zu Form, Motivik und Funktion der Peristasenskataloge bei Paulus*, FB 66, Würzburg: Echter.

Fiore, Benjamin (1986) *The Function of Personal Example in the Socratic and Pastoral Epistles*, AnBib 105, Rome: Biblical Institute Press.

Fitzgerald, John T. (1988) *Cracks in an Earthen Vessel: An Examination of the Catalogues of Hardships in the Corinthian Correspondence*, SBLDS 99, Atlanta: Scholars Press.

—— (ed.) (1996) *Friendship, Flattery, and Frankness of Speech: Studies on Friendship in the New Testament World*, NovTSup 82, Leiden: Brill.

—— (ed.) (1997) *Greco-Roman Perspectives on Friendship*, SBLRBS 34, Atlanta: Scholars Press.

Glad, Clarence E. (1995) *Paul and Philodemus: Adaptability in Epicurean and Early Christian Psychagogy*, NovTSup 81, Leiden: Brill.

Hock, Ronald F. (1980) *The Social Context of Paul's Ministry*, Philadelphia: Fortress Press.

Malherbe, Abraham J. (1987) *Paul and the Thessalonians: The Philosophic Tradition of Pastoral Care*, Philadelphia: Fortress Press.

—— (1989) *Paul and the Popular Philosophers*, Minneapolis: Fortress Press.

Marshall, P. (1987) *Enmity in Corinth: Social Conventions in Paul's Relations with the Corinthians*, WUNT 2.23, Tübingen: J.C.B. Mohr.

Mussies, G. (1972) *Dio Chrysostom and the New Testament*, SCHNT 21, Leiden: Brill.

Petzke, Gerd (1970) *Die Traditionen über Apollonius von Tyana und das Neue Testament*, SCHNT 1, Leiden: Brill.

Sevenster, J.N. (1961) *Paul and Seneca*, NovTSup 4, Leiden: Brill.

Schmeller, Thomas (1989) *Paulus und die 'Diatribe': Eine vergleichende Stilinterpretation*, NAbh 19, Münster: Aschendorff.

Stowers, Stanley Kent (1981) *The Diatribe and Paul's Letter to the Romans*, SBLDS 57, Chico: Scholars Press.

van der Horst, Pieter Willem (1973) 'Macrobius and the New Testament: A Contribution to the Corpus Hellenisticum,' *Novum Testamentum* 15: 220–32.

—— (1974) 'Musonius Rufus and the New Testament,' *Novum Testamentum* 16: 306–15.

—— (1975) 'Hierocles the Stoic and the New Testament: A Contribution to the Corpus Hellenisticum,' *Novum Testamentum* 17: 156–60.

—— (1980) *Aelius Aristides and the New Testament*, SCHNT 6, Leiden: Brill.

—— (1981) 'Cornutus and the New Testament,' *Novum Testamentum* 23: 165–72.

Vögtle, A. (1936) *Die Tugend- und Lasterkataloge im Neuen Testament*, NTAbh 16.4–5, Münster: Aschendorff.

Winter, B. (2000) *Philo and Paul among the Sophists: Alexandrian and Corinthian Responses to a Julio-Claudian Movement*, Grand Rapids: Eerdmans, 2nd edn.

GREGORY STERLING

HENGEL, MARTIN (1926–)

German New Testament scholar, and a theologian who also contributed in the field of church history, classical antiquity, and archaeology. After a short period of service as a Protestant (Lutheran) vicar he divided his time between family business and an academic career at the University of Tübingen, and was successful in both areas. Since 1964 he has taught in Tübingen (and Erlangen 1967–1972), and from 1972 to 1992 he was also director of the Institute of Antique Judaism and History of Hellenistic Religions; from 1993–1994 he was president of the *Studiorum Novi Testamenti Societas*. As emeritus he was co-editor of several well-known series of monographs (AGJU; TSAJ; ÜTY Übersetzung des Talmud Yerushalmi; WUNT; WUNT 2), most of which he initiated himself.

Hengel has to date written the maximum number of scholarly monographs and articles a mortal can produce in such a period of time. The most important are: *Die Zeloten*, 1961 (ET 1989; Japanese translation 1986); *Nachfolge und Charisma*, 1968 (ET *The Charismatic Leader and His Followers*, 1981); *Judentum und Hellenismus*, 1969 (3rd edn, 1988, ET 1974 and 1981, Japanese translation 1983); *War Jesus Revolutionär?* 1970 (ET *Was Jesus a Revolutionist?* 1971, also translated into several other languages); *Gewalt und Gewaltlosigkeit*, 1971 (ET *Victory over Violence*, 1973); *Der Sohn Gottes*, 1975 (ET *The Son of God*, 1976); *Juden, Griechen und Barbaren*, 1976 (ET *Jews, Greeks and Barbarians*, 1980, other translations including Korean); *Zur urchristlichen Geschichtsschreibung*, 1979 (ET *Acts and the History of Earliest Christianity*, 1979 and 1980, other translations including Czech); *Die johanneische Frage*, 1993 (preliminary English version *The Johannine Question*, 1989); *Paulus zwischen Damascus und Antiochien* (with M.A. Schwemer), 1998 (shortened ET *Paul between Damascus and Antioch*, 1997); *Kleine Schriften I–II* (Collected Essays), 1996, 1999. Important selections of his numerous studies have been collected in English thematic volumes, e.g., *Between Jesus and Paul*, 1983, 1997; *The Atonement*, 1981; *Studies in the Gospel of Mark*, 1985; *The Cross of the Son of God*, 1986; *Studies in Early Christology*, 1995. For some volumes he is both the editor and the main author, e.g., *Die Septuaginta*, with M.A. Schwemer, 1994.

The first significant result of Hengel's work was the new image of the Mediterranean culture of Jesus' time. The traditional concept of a Jewish counterculture within the Hellenistic area has been definitely relativized by Hengel's reconstruction of a resurgent Hellenistic interest in vernacular barbarian cultures from the end of the second century BC, so that even Jewish restorative tendencies fit the general frame of Hellenism.

The second area of Hengel's research is gathering data from the history of early Christianity and reconstructing its context. The theological impact of this scholarly activity was already visible in his study 'Christologie und neutestamentliche Chronologie' (FS O. Cullmann), 1972 (see Hengel 1983), and is also present in the paper submitted to the Heidelberg Academy of Sciences 'Die Evangelienüberschriften,' 1984 (ET in Hengel 1985); furthermore, it dominates in his studies on Paul and the Johannine writings. Therefore Hengel is sometimes considered to be a conservative scholar. However, he shares most of the critical conclusions of New Testament research. His investigations in history are not considered a legitimization of faith. Nevertheless they convincingly exclude some inauthentic critical views. In this sense several of Hengel's monographs directly influenced the political and social debate.

References and further reading

Hengel, Martin (1974) *Judaism and Hellenismm*, trans. John Bowden, London: SCM Press.

—— (1981) *The Atonement: A Study of the Origins of the Doctrine in the New Testament*, London: SCM Press.

—— (1983) *Between Jesus and Paul: Studies in the Earliest History of Christianity*, trans. John Bowden, Philadelphia: Fortress Press.

—— (1985) *Studies in the Gospel of Mark*, trans. John Bowden, Philadelphia: Fortress Press.

—— (1986) *The Cross of the Son of God*, trans. John Bowden, London: SCM Press.

—— (1995) *Studies in Early Christology*, Edinburgh: T.&T. Clark.

PETR POKORNÝ

HISTORICAL APPROACHES

1 Description
2 History of the approach
3 Reactions to the approach
4 Modern applications

1 Description

Historical approaches to biblical interpretation involving the study of religion are grounded in the work of the *religionsgeschichtliche Schule* (loosely translated as the 'history of religions school'). The *religionsgeschichtliche Schule* flourished during the last decade of the nineteenth century and the first two decades of the twentieth century as part of a larger movement that investigated all religions as a product of human culture and human experience. Biblical scholars, particularly German Protestant scholars, sought to understand the religion of both the Old and New Testaments within the context of other religions. Members of the *religionsgeschichtliche Schule* attempted to be free from philosophical or theological assumptions, interpretations, and formulations of biblical questions. Rather than focus on doctrine, dogma, and theology, these scholars chose to investigate the Bible under the rubric of religion, particularly religious experience, cult, and practice. Guided by positivism, they focused almost exclusively upon historical and comparative analyses (deemed 'presuppositionless investigation'). The results of their work tended to be descriptive of the history and chronological development of biblical religion.

The rise of the *religionsgeschichtliche Schule* should be understood in relation to the advances within other disciplines at the time, including anthropology and ethnology. Particularly important was the burgeoning field of archaeology with its discoveries in the Near East and the deciphering of ancient languages. Evolutionary theory played a significant role in providing the theoretical framework of development from more primitive forms to highly developed forms within the natural world. For the *religionsgeschichtliche Schule* religious practice and belief were understood as developing along a similar continuum. Investigators also looked for parallel trends in various religions and were interested in the trajectory of influence. They were particularly concerned with the prehistory of Jewish and Christian practices and concepts.

2 History of the approach

It is unclear who coined the term *religionsgeschichtliche Schule* for the movement, although it first appears in the early 1900s, (Colpe 1961: 9 n.1). The roots of the movement, however, stretch throughout the nineteenth century. Julius Wellhausen brought together and synthesized the work of previous scholars in what has become known as the classical expression of the documentary hypothesis (JEPD; see his *Die Composition des Hexateuchs und der historischen Bücher des Alten Testaments*, 1889). The priestly legislation was seen as a late development, while the prophetic tradition came to the fore as the means whereby the religious beliefs of the Old Testament were created. Ancient Hebrew faith was compared to other 'primitive' religions and similar developments could be traced. Eventually, this line of investigation led to what has been termed the 'pan-Babylonian school,' which held that the religious ideas of the Babylonians were the source of the religious themes of all peoples of the ancient Near East.

Hermann Gunkel's *Schöpfung und Chaos in Urzeit und Endzeit* (1985) is seen as the inauguration of *religionsgeschichtliche Schule* research. In this and other works Gunkel investigated the development of the Old Testament in light of other religions of the time. He emphasized that the texts of the Old Testament were the result of long processes of oral transmission within the contexts of community life and institutional structures. Other Old Testament scholars such as Hugo Gressmann and Emil Friedrich Kautzsch pursued this interest in Israelite religion's beginnings, development, and relationships to other religions and particularly how its practices were conceived and developed (cf. Miller 1985: 201).

In New Testament studies, the *religionsgeschichtliche Schule* took hold at the University of Göttingen with the work of Albert Eichhorn. In *Das Abendmahl im Neuen Testament* (1898) Eichhorn argued that the presentation of the Lord's Supper in the New Testament reflects the dogma of the church rather than the original, historical event of Jesus. In order to explain the development from Jesus to the sacramental cult meal of the church one must employ the 'history of religions method' (Kümmel 1972: 253).

Gunkel moved from Old Testament studies to the New Testament to argue that the religion of the New Testament was influenced by Graeco-Roman religions by way of syncretistic Hellenistic Judaism (*Zum religionsgeschichtlichen Verstandnis des Neuen Testaments*, 1903). Thus, Christianity itself was a syncretistic religion. Similar themes appeared in other works such as those of Johannes Weiss. The influences on early Christianity were broadened to the mystery religions of antiquity through scholars such as Richard Reitzenstein, Alfred Loisy, and Wilhelm Bousset (see Ascough 1998: 50–9). Interestingly, although admitting the influence of Judaism, the mysteries, and Gnosticism upon the thinking and practices of the early church, these scholars often maintained that the actual gospel preached by Jesus remained untouched by such syncretism (cf. Kümmel 1972: 271).

Rudolph Bultmann represents the 'third generation' of the *religionsgeschichtliche Schule* that began to develop in the early 1920s. He was particularly interested in Gnosticism and its influence on earliest Christianity, but also moved the *religionsgeschichtliche Schule* into new methods such as form criticism, existential interpretation, and demythologization.

3 Reactions to the approach

The findings of the *religionsgeschichtliche Schule* scholars were disseminated in both academic and popular works. However, many came into conflict with ecclesiastical authorities and some even lost or left university positions. The work of the *religionsgeschichtliche Schule* 'tended to undercut theological work as it relativized the sacred literature out of which theological systems were constructed, challenging claims to uniqueness, absoluteness, revelation, and finality' (Miller 1985: 202). The *religionsgeschichtliche Schule*'s period of influence ceased after the First World War due to both social and theological shifts in Germany, particularly Karl Barth's dialectical theology. In its place there arose the biblical theology movement.

Early critics focused on the movement's propensity to explain Christianity in human terms without taking account of its supposed superiority to all other religions or of its uniqueness among the world's religions (see Kümmel 1972: 310; Malherbe 1989: 7). Others emphasized that the investigation of Christianity must be set within the life of faith, with belief in the incarnation as a precondition to historical investigation (see Kümmel 1972: 319). Still others suggested that the *religionsgeschichtliche Schule* failed to explain what made Christianity distinct and thus allowed it to flourish and eventually triumph where the other religions failed. Such critiques were aimed at preserving the perceived integrity of the Christian faith without engaging in the material presented by the *religionsgeschichtliche Schule* proponents. Later critics have recognized that the most serious mistake of the *religionsgeschichtliche Schule* 'was a kind of myopia which led them to believe that once they had traced the origin and development of an idea or of the entire religion, they had said fundamentally what needed to be or could be said' (Hayes and Prussner 1985: 134; see further Ascough 1998: 59–63).

On the positive side, advances made by the *religionsgeschichtliche Schule* led to the development and acceptance of various historical-critical methods such as form criticism and redaction criticism. A much greater understanding of the biblical texts and their social context was gained alongside a wider appreciation for Semitic

and Hellenistic religions and the various expressions of Christianity. Both Testaments were recognized as containing not one coherent religion but a variety of religions and religious documents. Revelation was seen as a product of human history and experience rather than a direct self-disclosure of God (Hayes and Prussner 1985: 137). Noncanonical material also began to draw serious attention as a source for the study of the religions of the Old and New Testaments.

4 Modern applications

Recently a new form of the *religionsgeschichtliche Schule* approach has been operative in biblical studies. In Old Testament studies since the 1960s there has been a shift from the post-Second World War emphasis on biblical theology to a renewed interest in the history of religion (Miller 1985: 201). Bolstered by archaeological discoveries of this century, the work of recent interpreters such as Claus Westermann and Frank Moore Cross has brought about greater awareness of the importance of setting the history of Israel within its larger context. While not losing sight of Babylon, there has also been a rise in interest in other nations surrounding Israel, such as Egypt, Phoenicia, Moab, and Ugarit. Rather than simplistic genealogical connections being made between Israel's religion and that of its neighbours, there is a growing 'recognition of a complex interaction with that world at many points, sometimes out of it, sometimes against it, often in a kind of creative tension that appropriates much from the milieu while giving it a new shape that may produce a rather sharp disjunction' (Miller 1985: 208).

New Testament studies in the 1960s and 1970s experienced a shift in the history of religions approach when scholars moved away from simply looking for the sources of the ideas and practices of Christianity. Through a broad comparative analysis, scholars recognized ways in which Christianity and Judaism confronted, conformed to, and were modified by their cultural environment. However, investigators often did not go far enough; Malherbe (1989: 11) suggests that 'the whole range of possible ways in which religions react when they meet, extending from opposition or rejection through amelioration to assimilation, conscious and unconscious, should be taken into consideration.'

A recent proponent of a new way of undertaking the history of religions approach is Jonathan Z. Smith. Smith advocates avoidance of arguments for the dependence of one religion upon another, the 'genealogical argument.' Rather, Smith proposes that biblical religions be compared to other religions analogically wherein the aim is not to find direct relationships. The comparative process serves to highlight similarities and differences. The connections rest in the mind of the interpreter and help the interpreter understand how things might be reimagined or redescribed. The comparison takes place around a specific set of options which is specified by the interpreter. This approach does not preclude the borrowing of aspects from one religion to another. However, rather than simply explain origins, Smith proposes that the setting beside one another of various facets of religion will lead to greater insight and awareness of both the religions being studied. Thus, ancient Mediterranean religions might be compared with modern Oceanic cargo cults in terms of myth and ritual. Clearly, one is not dependent upon the other, but examination of phenomena in both can lead to a greater understanding of each.

Work done recently on all aspects of ancient religions shows that it is no longer adequate to speak of 'Israelite religion,' or 'Hellenistic Judaism,' 'early Christianity,' or the like, as if these entities were monolithic, consolidated movements across time and geographical regions. In its place there is a growing recognition that one must speak, for example, of 'Israelite religions' or 'early Christianities,' thus giving recognition to diverse expressions and developments. This is true even at the microlevel where, for example, we might note that Paul's Galatian Christian community would not see itself having strong affinities with Paul's Philippian Christian community. Rather than claim that any one expression is 'unique' or 'pristine,' the differences among the biblical religions themselves, and between biblical religions and other ancient religions, invite 'negotiation, classification, and comparison' (Smith 1990: 42) in order to understand each more fully.

References and further reading

Ascough R.S. (1998) *What Are They Saying about the Formation of Pauline Churches?* New York and Mahwah: Paulist Press.

Colpe, C. (1961) *Die religionsgeschichtliche Schule. Darstellung und Kritik ihres Bildes vom gnostischen Erlösermythus*, FRLANT 60, Göttingen: Vandenhoeck & Ruprecht.

Hayes, John H. and Frederick Prussner (1985) *Old Testament Theology: Its History and Development*, Atlanta: John Knox.

Kümmel, W.G. (1972) *The New Testament: The History of the Investigation of Its Problems*, trans. S. McLean Gilmour and H.C. Kee, Nashville: Abingdon Press, 2nd edn.

Malherbe, A.J. (1989) 'Greco-Roman Religion and Philosophy and the New Testament,' pp. 3–26 in *The New Testament and Its Modern Interpreters*, E.J. Epp and G.W. MacRae (eds.), The Bible and Its Modern Interpreters 3, Philadelphia: Fortress Press/Atlanta: Scholars Press.

Metzger, B.M. (1968) 'Methodology in the Study of the Mystery Religions and Early Christianity,' in *Historical and Literal Studies: Pagan, Jewish and Christian*, NTTS 8, Grand Rapids: Eerdmans, pp. 1–24.

Miller, P.D. (1985) 'Israelite Religion,' pp. 201–37 in *The Hebrew Bible and Its Modern Interpreters*, D.A. Knight and G.M. Tucker (eds.), Philadelphia: Fortress Press/Chico: Scholars Press.

Smith, J.Z (1990) *Drudgery Divine: On the Comparison of Early Christianities and the Religions of Late Antiquity*, Chicago Studies in the History of Judaism, Chicago: University of Chicago Press.

RICHARD S. ASCOUGH

HISTORICAL JESUS

Jesus as a figure in history has emerged again, to the surprise of the academic world. Book after book has appeared, written for the most part by a generation of scholars who had been taught during their postgraduate studies that little could be known of the life of Jesus. The dictum of Rudolf Bultmann was often quoted: 'I do indeed think we can know almost nothing about the life and personality of Jesus' (1958: 8).The wisdom of our teachers was that the Gospels were written in order to inspire faith in Jesus as the Christ; therefore reliable information about him could not he discovered in them. Jesus is in the news again because many of us – such as John Dominic Crossan, Paula Fredricksen, Robert Funk, E.P. Sanders – have rebelled against our teachers.

Why the rebellion? As in the case of any insurrection, there has been a combination of internal discontent and destabilizing circumstances. The internal discontent was caused by a deep unease about the conventions of postgraduate education. The claims that Christianity makes about Jesus in the New Testament are obviously designed to awaken faith in him. But the argument of Albert Schweitzer, that 'the abiding and eternal in Jesus is absolutely independent of historical knowledge and can only be understood by contact with His spirit' (1910: 399), fed the insistence of Neo-Orthodoxy that readers could not get behind the New Testament's faith, which they just had to take or leave. Nonetheless, the New Testament's claims are made about a person who is located in history. It is intellectually dishonest not to include the study of Jesus in an account of how the New Testament and the Christian religion arose.

In fact, the old denial that Jesus could be known historically turned out to perform a service for the conservative waves of Christian practice, thought, and scholarship which flourished during the twentieth century. If Jesus could not be known in history, then the way was open to assert that only the teaching of the church could say anything about him. Both Protestant fundamentalism and Catholic papalism could easily live with scholars of the New Testament who had everything to say about the genre of the texts, and nothing to say about the person the texts spoke of. After the Second World War, a 'new quest of the historical Jesus' was pursued, but it focused on the philosophical appropriation of Jesus, to the virtual exclusion of the historical circumstances that produced him and in which he engaged.

Today the rebellion has succeeded in taking its first barricade: Jesus is acknowledged as a figure of history, not only in scholarship but also in popular discussion. Rebellions demand favorable conditions as well as sharp motivations in order to prevail. The discontent of scholars has long been obvious: what has galvanized them is the unearthing of new information. What is new is both literary documentation and archaeological evidence.

The discovery of new texts includes the Dead Sea Scrolls, which have shed new light on what Judaism in the time of Jesus was like, and above all on its diversity. Alongside those Jewish texts, manuscripts from the Gnostic library at Nag Hammadi in Egypt, from the fourth century, have shown us how different from traditional theology early Christian faith could be. These finds of new manuscripts turned scholars' attention to other ancient Jewish sources which had not been translated before.

The Targums are the Aramaic paraphrases of the Hebrew Bible that rendered the sacred scripture into the language of the people, and included large amounts of additional material. Chief among the additions there are repeated and emphatic hopes that one day 'the sovereignty of God' would be revealed: Israel would be vindicated over its enemies, and the world would be transformed. The sovereignty of God (traditionally translated as 'the kingdom of God') was also the center of Jesus' teaching. The Targums provide a key we need to understand what he meant, and all the Targums have now been translated into English, but only since 1987.

If the discoveries we had to cope with had only been textual, the present generation of scholars would still have been adjusting to more new information than any other generation in the discipline of New Testament since the Enlightenment. But that was only about half the challenge. At the same time that texts were being discovered, edited, translated, studied, and related to the question of Jesus and Christian origins, archaeology was making unprecedented progress in Israel. The temple, the administrative garrison town of Sepphoris in Galilee, as well as tiny Galilean hamlets (including Nazareth and Bethlehem nearby) were among the intentional excavations. And there were completely unplanned finds. In 1990, a bulldozer preparing a roadbed to the south of Jerusalem took the top off of a cave. Inside that cave, the tomb of the Caiaphas family – probably including the high priest who collaborated in the Roman execution of Jesus – was discovered.

So many new finds can be to scholars what too much power is to revolutionaries. Unfamiliar with what to do with it all, they sometimes try to push all the details into set ideologies, rather than wrestling with the complexities of a completely new situation. John Dominic Crossan and Robert Funk (alongside much of the work of Funk's 'Jesus Seminar') were the Robespierres of the Jesus revolution. Deeply concerned to contradict traditional theology and to take account of archaeological evidence, they used the excavation of Sepphoris, a Graeco-Roman city in Galilee, as the setting of Jesus. Their Hellenistic picture of Jesus did little justice to the Jewish environment which produced him, and largely ignored the simple fact that Jesus' activity was limited to rural Galilee and its small hamlets; he avoided cities such as Sepphoris, which he is never reported to have visited.

The necessity of a Judaic frame of reference for the understanding of Jesus has been established by the research of Ben F. Meyer, E.P. Sanders, the present writer, and now Paula Fredricksen. The publication of field reports of archaeological excavations in Galilee can today be brought to bear and has consistently confirmed that basic orientation.

We will come to terms with our own critical view of Jesus when we do more than recognize him as a figure within Jewish history. The Jesus of scholarship has remained two-dimensional; attention has been limited to the last three years of his public ministry, after his religious development had taken place. By that point, he already appears different enough from most Jews as to be somehow alien, an icon from another culture. But the archaeology of Galilee, as well as anthropological and textual research, now permits us to trace Jesus' development. Religion – specifically, Jewish religion – has been a missing dimension in the understanding of Jesus. If we put his religion together with his time and his place, we can tell the story of Jesus during the full course of his life, and tell it in the narrative terms that characterize true biography.

The way into Jesus' religious identity is through his own Judaism, the culture, the practice, the feeling, the politics, and the hardship involved in being a rabbi in Galilee during the first century. This focus on Jesus' unique development as a Galilean rabbi demands a new method of presentation. It will not do, as in the scholarly fashion since Schweitzer's doctoral thesis, to enter into an academic discussion of the vast secondary literature on Jesus, because that has not concerned Jesus' development within Judaism at all. Instead, the primary sources, the texts, and the archaeology that speak of him and his environment need to be accorded the precedence they deserve.

Three features are marking the emergence of the new profile of Jesus. First, scholars are taking his Judaism seriously, not only as historical context, but also as his cultural commitment. Second, the texts of the New Testament are no longer only read as being either historical or not, either propagandistic or not. They are evidently both of those, because they are the outcome of the rise of a religious movement centered on Jesus.

A historical picture of Jesus therefore involves the literary inference of what he must have taught and done to have generated that movement and its literature. Judaic context, as well as the literarily historical task of generative exegesis, is therefore basic to the current phase of work.

But the last feature proves to be the most explosive. Since the work of David Friedrich Strauss (first published in 1835), a persistent feature of scholarship has been to portray Jesus with only one, consistent persona, without regard to the human development – with its radical changes – that marks every significant biography. Unless the pivots of his life are discovered and explored, Jesus will never be known.

These key moments in his development, shaping how others have responded to him ever since, are rather clearly marked, both by the literary sources and by the analysis of early Judaism. The first transition took him from a boyhood which marginalized him within the Galilean community of Nazareth as a *mamzer* (an illegitimate child). Pilgrimage to the temple with his family brought this boy to an excited sense of the vastness of the Israel he was part of, as it did for many Jews. It also galvanized his youthful, mystical enthusiasm for the *Malkhuta delaha*, the sovereignty of God, which in the expectation of ancient Judaism was to replace every human authority. No wonder he ran away from his family, resolved – whatever the risk – to remain as near as he could to the temple, the promise of God's sovereignty on earth.

In Judaea, Jesus became the disciple (the *talmid*) of John the Baptist, a rabbi who taught how immersion in water purified Israel. From John, he learned this master's *kabbalah*, the mystical practice of ascent to the divine Throne, the seat of God's sovereignty. That practice was a guiding force for the rest of his life. He grew estranged from John, however, because Jesus taught that immersion was not always necessary prior to purification. That break was tragically completed by John's death at the hands of Herod Antipas. Jesus returned to Galilee after John's death for a prosperous but unsettled period of his life. His reputation as a rabbi, an expert in immersion and purity, returned with him to Galilee. His meals in his native Nazareth and its vicinity – following the pattern in Judaism of invoking God's presence with a cup of wine before eating – became celebrations of God's own sovereignty which verged on communal delirium, fueled by the public exorcisms which Jesus practiced from that time. Local fame was the result, but also deep controversy, conflict with his family, and even the threat of stoning in Nazareth.

Jesus responded to this crisis by returning to Jerusalem. He came into his own there as a healer in the tradition of other rabbis from Galilee and Judaea. He believed his practice of releasing sin and establishing the purity of a person brought about physical results. Conflict with the authorities in the temple – who believed that the means of forgiving sins lay in their hands alone – was the inevitable result, and Jesus withdrew again to Galilee, this time to Capernaum. There he gathered disciples and practiced the healings for which he became so widely renowned that Herod Antipas saw him as a political threat.

Jesus beat a retreat from Herod Antipas' kingdom into Syria. He sent twelve disciples back to Galilee, to function as his direct representatives in extending the sovereignty of God. Jesus was now the center of a recognizable religious movement, as John the Baptist had once been. In the wilderness near Caesarea Philippi, he went through a defining moment. Tempted to oppose Herod Antipas (and Rome) directly, by political and military revolt, Jesus came instead to view himself as especially gifted to receive divine revelation. He sought to manifest this revelation in the temple in Jerusalem. But disaster awaited him. Caiaphas, the high priest, had sanctioned a commercial market in sacrificial animals to be set up in the great court of the temple. That arrangement was not only untraditional; it also violated Jesus' principle that pure Israel was to be present before God in a direct, unmediated offering of what Israel itself produced. Jesus reacted with a large crowd and in force, occupying the great court and ejecting the vendors and the animals. Effectively, he challenged both the high priest and the Roman prefect who backed him, Pontius Pilate, and powerful resistance to him was inevitable from that moment.

The deadliness of the threat to him, however, was a function of political forces of which Jesus was only dimly aware. His execution followed because he was unfamiliar with the shifts of power in Rome that had altered the politics of Jerusalem, and because he began to celebrate his meals of fellowship as a replacement of sacrifice in the temple. He had premonitions of death. His visionary teaching, his instruction to his students how to conceive of and participate in the heavenly realm had long taken account of human mortality. Like other rabbis of his time, he pursued a characteristic depiction of the divine court, of Israel's relationship to the angels there, of how Israel might expect to be transformed by God. He conceived of resurrection as a change in bodily constitution, so that one became angelic, and that was his view of how – in one way or another – he would finally be raised to know God.

Having thoroughly taught that perspective during his life, groups of his disciples, especially those headed by Mary Magdalene, the Twelve, Simon Peter, Stephen, James (Jesus' elder brother), and Paul came to experience Jesus as risen from the dead after his death. Their different conceptions of how Jesus was raised from the dead resulted in the development of differing forms of the movement that became known as Christianity.

Archaeological, anthropological, and textual research permit us today to trace Jesus' development as a religious genius, provided we coordinate the insights of that scholarship. Each phase of his life brought his distinctive appropriation of Judaic practice – of seeing the sovereignty of God, immersing, communal feasting, exorcism, healing, heading up a group of *talmidim*, sacrifice, and envisioning God's transformation of humanity. Together they make up not only a coherent movement which became a new religion, but also a coherent life.

References and further reading

Bultmann, Rudolf (1958) *Jesus and the Word*, trans. L.P. Smith and E.H. Lantero, New York: Scribner's.

Chilton, Bruce (1992) *The Temple of Jesus: His Sacrificial Program within a Cultural History of Sacrifice*, University Park: Pennsylvania State University Press.

—— (1996) *Pure Kingdom: Jesus' Vision of God*, Studying the Historical Jesus 1, Grand Rapids: Eerdmans/London: SPCK.

—— (2000) *Rabbi Jesus: An Intimate Biography*, New York: Doubleday.

Crossan, John Dominic (1991) *The Historical Jesus: The Life of a Mediterranean Jewish Peasant*, San Francisco: Harper.

Fredricksen, Paula (1999) *Jesus of Nazareth, King of the Jews: A Jewish Life and the Emergence of Christianity*, New York: Knopf.

Funk, Robert W. (1996) *Honest to Jesus*, San Francisco: Harper.

Meyer, Ben F. (1979) *The Aims of Jesus*, London: SCM Press.

Sanders, E.P. (1985) *Jesus and Judaism*, London and Philadelphia: SCM and Fortress Press.

Schweitzer, Albert (1910) *The Quest of the Historical Jesus*, trans. W. Montgomery, London: A & C Black (from the German edn. of 1906).

Strauss, David Frierdrich (1972) *The Life of Jesus, Critically Examined*, trans. G. Eliot, Philadelphia: Fortress Press (from the German edn. of 1835–1836, although the translation is based on the 4th edn, 1840).

Telford, William R. (1994) 'Major Trends and Interpretive Issues in the Study of Jesus,' pp. 33–74 in *Studying the Historical Jesus: Evaluations of the State of Current Research*, NTTS 14, B.D. Chilton and C.A. Evans (eds.), Leiden: Brill.

BRUCE D. CHILTON

HISTORIOGRAPHICAL LITERATURE

1 Hebrew Bible of Israel

The arrangement of individual books from Genesis to 2 Kings (without Ruth?) provides a continuous narrative from the creation of the world to the end of the monarchy in Judah. Most of the narrative is the story of ancient Israel. Frequently there are minor narrative breaks or overlaps at the end and beginning of successive books from Genesis to 2 Kings. At some stages the action is rather static, particularly in Leviticus and Deuteronomy. However, the narrative structure is preserved in Leviticus by presenting religious laws in commandments of Yahweh to Moses, which he is to pass on to the people. And in the body of Deuteronomy 1–30 there is a minimal narrative framework for the three addresses of Moses, which are largely recapitulation of the wilderness wanderings followed by exhortation.

The narrative from Genesis to 2 Kings is predominantly prose, but includes poetic passages. The earlier stages contain particular types of material, such as the myths of Creation and Flood, aetiologies, genealogies, laws, and cultic instructions.

Ezra-Nehemiah comprises one book. Grabbe (1998) postulates that Ezra-Nehemiah is the result of conflation of three alternative traditions (Joshua and Zerubbabel; Ezra; Nehemiah) concerning rebuilding of the temple and restoration of the cult.

First and Second Chronicles appear to be a re-writing of biblical narrative from Genesis to 2 Kings with an extension. First Chronicles 1–9, largely by means of genealogies and lists, covers a period from Adam to the return from exile (depending on the interpretation of 1 Chron. 9:1–2). It is widely accepted that the main source for the body of Chronicles is Samuel-Kings. Attempts to base both Samuel-Kings and Chronicles on a common Deuteronomistic (or not really Deuteronomistic: Auld 1994) source have not proved convincing. Chronologically, the content of Ezra-Nehemiah follows that of Chronicles. This contradicts the usual arrangement of the books in the Hebrew Bible. Those manuscripts which put Chronicles at the beginning of the Writings (before Psalms) hardly solve the problem. On the other hand, any reader who reaches the end of Chronicles is directed to the beginning of Ezra-Nehemiah by the almost verbatim overlap between the two books: reference to the decree of Cyrus (2 Chron. 36:22–23; Ezra 1:1–3).

If the theory of Auld (1994) were accepted, the view that Chronicles is based on the so-called Deuteronomistic History (Joshua–2 Kings) would have to be reconsidered. In addition, however, a tendency for 'Deuteronomistic' viewpoints to be found in an increasing number of Jewish biblical books has been challenged in recent study: scholars should define what they mean by 'Deuteronomism' and should consider more carefully whether and to what extent there was a Deuteronomistic movement (see esp. Shearing and McKenzie 1999).

A fundamental challenge concerns the interrelated issues of the genre and the historical reliability of biblical narratives. Among prose narrative traditions, Thompson (1992a: 209; cf. 1992b: 397) distinguished historiography from aetiologies, traditional tales, fables, parables, legends, myths, tribal histories, genealogical tales, biographies, constitutional tales, origin stories, and ethnographies. According to Thompson (1992a: 209; 1992b: 377, cf. 397): 'Only very few Hebrew narratives involve historiography at a primary level.' However, it may be appropriate to allow ancient historiography to include not only the other items on Thompson's list, but also poetic forms.

Accounts of conquest and settlement of the Promised Land have been undermined, partly by inconsistency in the biblical material itself, but also by lack of archaeological confirmation. However, the biblical accounts themselves need to be treated as evidence. Moreover, even if it is assumed that there was no Egyptian sojourn, exodus, conquest, and settlement, or if these stories are regarded as foundation myths or legends, it still needs to be explained why these particular stories were composed and not others.

For some scholars, if a biblical narrative is not historically reliable, then it does not belong to the genre of historiography. For others, historical reliability is not an issue for determining genre, but for assessing sources for a modern history of ancient Israel. Scholarly distinctions between historiography and ideology and between historiography and literature have sometimes created the impression that these categories are intended to be mutually exclusive. However, there currently seems to be a more general acknowledgment that historiography is properly a *literary* genre, and that all historiography refracts an ideological stance.

As with other ancient historical writings, the biblical narratives frequently give prominence to individual leaders (patriarchs, judges, kings, prophets) and to battles. But the biblical narratives especially emphasize the one God as the prime motivator in history. In view of the features of the narratives, which have been considered, they may justifiably be regarded as belonging to a biblical genre of historiography.

2 Greek Bible of Israel

The earliest version of the Jewish Greek Bible was created in the third and second centuries BC, when the Hebrew text was still fluid. The additional Greek books which particularly deserve attention as historiography are 1 Esdras and 1 and 2 Maccabees.

A period from 622 to the late fifth or early fourth century BC is covered in 1 Esdras. The book begins and ends abruptly. Its (chronologically confused) account maintains a particular focus on the temple of Jerusalem. The period 175–134 BC is covered by 1 Maccabees, which focuses on the events leading up to the Maccabean revolt and subsequent campaigns. At least fifteen years down to 161 BC are covered by 2 Maccabees. The work has a consistent focus on oppressive Hellenization by the Seleucid rulers of Syria, which leads to a series of martyrdoms but is thwarted by the successful campaigns of Judas. After two prefixed letters, the book has a prologue (2 Macc. 2:19–32), in which the writer claims that the body of the work is a summary of an earlier history in five volumes.

All three of these writings have many of the features of the short historical monograph known in the Hellenistic and Roman periods. Each work consists of a single volume and focuses on one theme. First and Second Maccabees cover a limited period; the extensive period covered by 1 Esdras may be due to its theme of temple continuity. There is a concentration on one main figure in 1 Esdras and 2 Maccabees; and at least on one at a time (Judas, Jonathan, Simon, John) in the strict division of periods in 1 Maccabees. Only 2 Maccabees has a proper prologue. But narrative of past events is the basic method of all three writings; and they all contain speeches and quoted letters. First and Second Maccabees are largely concerned with battles. This is a feature not only of Greek and Roman historiography including monographs, but also of some narrative parts of the Hebrew Bible (and their Greek translations). With the latter, the Hellenistic Jewish writings share their monotheistic perspective.

3 Christian New Testament

The Gospels are properly biography rather than historiography. The Acts of the Apostles is best classified as a historical monograph, as it has often been regarded. Other views of Acts have been canvassed in the last two decades: Luke-Acts as biographical; Acts as a historical novel; Luke-Acts as 'apologetic historiography' giving a Hellenized version of the native traditions of a particular people; Luke and Acts understood against the background of technical treatises; Luke and Acts as a prose (adaptation of) epic. For critical discussion of these views see Palmer (1993, 2003).

Cancik (1997) regards Luke and Acts together as the history of 'the origin and spread of an institution,' the early church. The body of this article deals only with Acts. Cancik posits ten 'aspects' as defining the genre of 'institutional history.' However, these points are not all present in any one writing of 'ancient Western historiography,' from which Cancik seeks analogies for Acts. In particular there do not seem to be any adequate models of a Graeco-Roman history of the origins of a religious movement. (Lucian's satirical *Alexander*, decades later than Acts, is not a satisfactory example.) However, it is appropriate that Cancik sees Acts in the context of ancient historiography and sees it as concerned with 'the origin and spread' of a religious movement (though hardly of a highly structured institution).

Alexander (1998) places Acts on the borderline of fact and fiction. This is surprising after her earlier emphasis on Luke and Acts as belonging to the realm of technical treatises. Moreover, the term 'fiction' is sometimes used colloquially and in different senses as denoting 'unconfirmed report,' or 'non-fact' (1998: 385); but it is also used in discussion of the Greek novel (1998: 392–4) – although it is stated that 'fact' and 'fiction' are 'not generic categories at all' (1998: 394). The concluding assessment of Acts as 'fact or fiction' initially finds a number of 'fictional' (i.e., novelistic) features (1998: 394–5). But further examination tends to reverse this impression. Rather than there being in Acts 'a disturbing undercurrent which suggests that it might after all be intended as fact' (summary, 1998: 380), perhaps the writing was intended as seriously historiographical all along.

In conformity with the theory and practice of the contemporary Graeco-Roman world, Acts is best regarded as a short historical monograph. It is a single volume of moderate length, which covers a limited historical period and has a consistent focus on the one theme of the progress of the Christian mission. Luke does not concentrate on one individual throughout Acts, but he does tend to portray one missionary leader at a time (Peter, Stephen, Philip, Paul). Like other monographs, Acts includes the literary components of prologue, narrative, speeches, and quoted letters. Although Acts may be unprecedented in presenting the history of an incipient religious movement, the way had been prepared by the religious content of the Hellenistic Jewish historical monographs. Luke did not compose a novel, but a dramatic type of historical monograph, from which his readers could derive both profit and delight (see Plb. 1.4.11; 3.31.13).

References and further reading

Alexander, L.C.A. (1993) *The Preface to Luke's Gospel. Literary Convention and Social Context in Luke 1.1–4 and Acts 1.1*, SNTSMS 78, Cambridge: Cambridge University Press.

—— (1998) 'Fact, Fiction and the Genre of Acts,' *New Testament Studies* 44: 380–99.

Auld, A.G. (1994) *Kings without Privilege: David and Moses in the Story of the Bible's Kings*, Edinburgh: T.&T. Clark.

Bonz, M.P. (2000) *The Past as Legacy: Luke–Acts and Ancient Epic*, Minneapolis: Fortress Press.

Brettler, M.Z. (1995) *The Creation of History in Ancient Israel*, London: Routledge.

Cancik, H. (1997) 'The History of Culture, Religion, and Institutions in Ancient Historiography: Philological Observations Concerning Luke's History,' *Journal of Biblical Literature* 116: 673–95.

Davies, P.R. (1992) *In Search of 'Ancient Israel,'* JSOTSup 148, Sheffield: Sheffield Academic Press.

—— (1995) 'Method and Madness: Some Remarks on Doing History with the Bible,' *Journal of Biblical Literature* 114: 699–705.

de Pury, A., T. Römer and J.-D. Macchi (eds.) (2000) *Israel Constructs its History: Deuteronomistic Historiography in Recent Research*, JSOTSup 306, Sheffield: Sheffield Academic Press.

Grabbe, Lester L. (1998) *Ezra-Nehemiah*, London: Routledge.

—— (ed.) (2001) *Did Moses Speak Attic? Jewish Historiography and Scripture in the Hellenistic Period*, JSOTSup 317, European Seminar in Historical Methodology 3, Sheffield: Sheffield Academic Press.

Graham, M.P., K.G. Hoglund and S.L. McKenzie (eds.) (1997) *The Chronicler as Historian*, JSOTSup 238, Sheffield: Sheffield Academic Press.

Halpern, B. (1988) *The First Historians: The Hebrew Bible and History*, San Francisco: Harper & Row.

Lemche, N.P. (1998) *Prelude to Israel's Past: Background and Beginnings of Israelite History and Identity*, Peabody, MA: Hendrickson.

McKenzie, S.L., T. Römer and H.H. Schmid (eds.) (2000) *Rethinking the Foundations. Historiography in the Ancient World and in the Bible. Essays in Honour of John Van Seters*, BZAW 294, Berlin: Walter de Gruyter.

Müller, M. (1996) *The First Bible of the Church: A Plea for the Septuagint*, JSOTSup 206, Copenhagen International Seminar 1, Sheffield: Sheffield Academic Press.

Palmer, D.W. (1993) 'Acts and the Ancient Historical Monograph,' pp. 1–29 in *The Book of Acts in its First Century Setting, Volume 1: Ancient Literary Setting*, B.W. Winter and A.D. Clarke (eds.), Carlisle: Paternoster.

—— (2003) Review of Bonz (2000), *Australian Biblical Review* 51: 78–80.

Provan, I.W. (1995) 'Ideologies, Literary and Critical: Reflections on Recent Writing on the History of Israel,' *Journal of Biblical Literature* 114: 585–606.

Shearing, L.S. and S.L. McKenzie (eds.) (1999) *Those Elusive Deuteronomists: The Phenomenon of Pan-Deuteronomism*, JSOTSup 268, Sheffield: Sheffield Academic Press.

Thompson, T.L. (1992a) 'Israelite Historiography,' *ABD* 3.206–12.

—— (1992b) *Early History of the Israelite People: From the Written and Archaeological Sources*, Studies in the History of the Ancient Near East 4, Leiden: Brill.

Van Seters, J. (1992) *Prologue to History: The Yahwist as Historian in Genesis*, Louisville: Westminster/John Knox.

Wesselius, J.-W. (2002) *The Origin of the History of Israel: Herodotus's Histories as Blueprint for the First Books of the Bible*, JSOTSup 345, Sheffield: Sheffield Academic Press.

Witherington, B. (ed.) (1996) *History, Literature and Society in the Book of Acts*, Cambridge: Cambridge University Press.

DARRYL PALMER

HOLY SPIRIT AND INTERPRETATION

The role of the Spirit in the interpretation of scripture has long held a fascination for interpreters. Given the belief that the Spirit plays some role in the writing of scripture, many interpreters have assumed that the Spirit is necessary for a proper understanding of the biblical text. It is not uncommon to find statements by early Christian writers affirming the need for the reader to turn to the Spirit for assistance in the interpretive process. Such an attitude can be detected as early as the time of Origen, who identifies the need 'to turn the eyes of our mind toward him who ordered this to be written and to ask of him their meaning' (Origen 1979: 247). In fact, it is not uncommon for the Spirit to be regarded as the reader's teacher (Chrysostom 1983: 37). By the time of Augustine, it becomes necessary to defend the role of human teachers and the need for research on the interpreter's part owing to the fact that there were those who claimed no need for human teachers. Yet even with all his disclaimers Augustine prefaces his rules for interpretation noting that God presently aids and will continue to aid the interpreter in the task of understanding scripture.

With the Middle Ages came a suspicion of the need for the Spirit in the interpretation of scripture. This attitude can be seen in the work of Thomas Aquinas, who assigned pride of place to the power of reason in the interpretation of scripture. This preference is challenged by the Reformers Luther and Calvin. While insisting upon the need for a knowledge of history and original languages, these individuals regard the Spirit's role as indispensable to the interpretive process. Calvin can go so far as to say, 'The testimony of the Spirit is superior to all reason' (Calvin 1936: 1.90). The concept of the illumination of the interpreters by the Spirit is central to Luther and Calvin. A similar idea is found in Turretin and other writers of the period. Though avoiding the language of illumination, John Wesley also sees the Spirit's work as essential to this process.

With F. Schleiermacher, the Spirit's role in interpretation is strongly challenged in ways that continue to be felt in many contemporary approaches to interpretation, including some who approach scripture from a confessional location.

While a number of more contemporary interpreters continue to affirm, sometimes quite vigorously, the Spirit's role in interpretation, most of the discussions are quite ambiguous as to the concrete activity of the Spirit, using illumination language, or respecting this aspect of the Spirit's work as mysterious, or briefly describing the Spirit's activity in some other way.

Of those who offer a more detailed attempt to understand the Spirit's role in interpretation, three merit special attention. For J.D.G. Dunn the work of the Spirit allows a word spoken in a particular historical situation to speak to a different situation. In fact, the Spirit may speak a word through scripture which is not wholly in accord with the text's originally intended meaning. In addition to the *normative* authority of the Bible, which is more or less a straightforward reading of scripture, there is also a *directive* authority which results in the authoritative word speaking to particular situations today. This is produced by the 'interaction between the Spirit's inspiration then, and the mind of Christ now. . .' (Dunn 1987: 133). Thus, the Spirit speaks through the scripture as understood by the faithful.

Clark Pinnock suggests that the Spirit allows one to be involved with the Bible with an open receptivity to its message. Specifically, thinking about the text prayerfully allows one to be open to the direction and discernment that the Spirit gives. Like Dunn, Pinnock proposes that through the Spirit's activity texts can function as the Word of the Lord with a sense different from that which was originally intended. If the presence of the Spirit is essential in interpretation, then, Pinnock concludes, 'practitioners must be believers filled with the Spirit' (Pinnock 1984: 173).

Writing from a charismatic context, John MacKay likens the Spirit's role in interpretation to a drama into which the reader is invited to participate. Such participation is made possible owing to the shared experiences of the charismatic with the biblical characters. Specifically, the experience of Spirit Baptism enables the prophetic reader to enter into the text by means of the Spirit because after the experience of Spirit Baptism they have experienced the Spirit in similar ways to the biblical characters. For MacKay the experience of Spirit Baptism brings such a transformation in the reading of texts that one can speak of it using Paul's words: 'when the veil is taken away' (2 Cor. 3:16).

The role of the Spirit may also be discerned in the interpretive paradigm revealed in Acts 15, where one finds evidence of a dynamic interaction between the biblical text, the interpretive community, and the Holy Spirit. Here, the Spirit functions in several ways. First, the Spirit creates the context for the interpretation of scripture through his actions, namely, the inclusion of Gentiles into the church. Second, based on these actions, the Spirit guides the community in the selection of which texts are most relevant to this particular situation and how best to approach the texts. Third, it appears that the Spirit offers some guidance in the community's dialogue about the scripture in that the result 'seems good to us and to the Holy Spirit' (Acts 15: 28). Thus in this paradigm the Spirit's activity is not reduced to talk of illumination, but is given concrete expression.

References and further reading

Aquinas, T. (1989) *Summa Theologiae*, T. McDermott (ed.), Westminster, MD: Christian Classics.

Archer, K.J. (2004) *A Pentecostal Hermeneutic for the 21st Century: Spirit, Scripture, and Community*, JPTSup 28, London: T.&T. Clark.

Augustine (1958) *On Christian Doctrine*, trans. D.W. Robertson, New York: Bobbs-Merrill.

Calvin, J. (1936) *Institutes of the Christian Religion*, trans. J. Allen, Philadelphia: Presbyterian Board of Christian Education.

Chrysostom, J. (1983) 'Homilies on First and Second Corinthians,' in *The Nicene and Post-Nicene Fathers*, Grand Rapids: Eerdmans.

Dunn, J.D.G. (1987) *The Living Word*, London: SCM Press.

Johnson, L.T. (1983) *Decision Making in the Church: a Biblical Model*, Philadelphia: Fortress Press.

Luther, M. (1956–1959) *Luther's Works*, Vols. 13, 22, 23, J. Pelikan (ed.), St. Louis: Concordia.

MacKay, J. (1994) 'When the Veil is Taken Away: The Impact of Prophetic Experience on Biblical Interpretation,' *Journal of Pentecostal Theology* 5:17–40.

Oden, T.C. (1994) *John Wesley's Scriptural Christianity*, Grand Rapids: Baker.

Origen (1979) *On First Principles*, trans. R.A. Greer, New York: Paulist Press.

Pinnock, C. (1984) *The Scripture Principle*, San Francisco: Harper & Row.

Schleiermacher, F. (1977) *Hermeneutics: The Handwritten Manuscripts*, trans. J. Duke and J. Frostman, Missoula: Scholars Press.

Thomas, J.C. (1994) 'Women, Pentecostals, and the Bible: An Experiment in Pentecostal Hermeneutics,' *Journal of Pentecostal Theology*, 5: 41–56.

Turretin, F. (1981) *The Doctrine of Scripture*, trans. J.W. Beardslee III, Grand Rapids: Baker.

Wyckoff, J.W. (1990) 'The Relationship of the Holy Spirit to Biblical Hermeneutics,' Ph.D. dissertation, Baylor University.

JOHN CHRISTOPHER THOMAS

INTRA-BIBLICAL INTERPRETATION

> 1 Definition
> 2 The formation of biblical literature: Intra-biblical composition
> 3 The final form of the Christian Bible: Intra-canonical interpretation

1 Definition

The term 'intra-biblical interpretation' (and synonyms) entered the vocabulary of biblical scholarship as a broad reference to the various ways by which biblical writers presume the continuing authority of their scripture, whether cited or 'echoed' (so R. Hays 1989), when they interpret biblical tradition (*traditium*) as the Word of God (*traditio*) for their current readers/auditors (so M. Fishbane 1989).

J.A. Sanders' (1987) cautionary distinction between the 'stability' and 'adaptability' of biblical tradition, envisaged by scripture's own 'unrecorded hermeneutics,' is helpful in qualifying what Fishbane means by the transforming and generative powers of 'inner biblical exegesis.' On the one hand, it is no longer disputed that biblical writers found new and different meanings in their sacred texts and stories of their scripture from those originally scored by their authors for their first audiences. Indeed, the existential necessity and eschatological urgency of God's Word, mediated by this textual *traditium* is formative of theological understanding, yet constantly requires every faithful interpreter, ancient (including biblical writers) and contemporary, to seek out from the old, old Gospel story those new meanings (*traditio*) which are 'adaptable to the life' of today's believers who continue to submit to their scriptures as the Word of the Lord God Almighty.

On the other hand, this same biblical tradition is 'canonical' – a persistent and stable 'rule (*kanon*) of faith' and life for all God's people in each age and every place. The essential theological subject matter of the biblical word does not change: scripture in all its parts bears witness to one God, one salvation, one Gospel. The inherent subjectivity of the interpretive enterprise, by which the individual interpreter seeks out the meaning of scripture for a particular situation, is constrained not by consistent application of certain hermeneutical rules but by those core convictions about God disclosed through scripture's story of God's salvation (so Wall 1999). Biblical texts do not bear witness to the interpreter but to the interpreter's God, 'who was and who is and who is to come.'

2 The formation of Biblical literature: Intra-biblical composition

Even a cursory reading of scripture discloses the routine use the writers made of their own biblical witness. For example, earliest Christianity retained Jewish scriptures as the symbolic universe within which its faith and life took shape and found direction. Christian literature naturally reused, reinterpreted, and reapplied these sacred writings to bring clarity and direction to the new period of salvation they believed had dawned with Jesus. Indeed, earliest Christian interpreters inherited the Old Testament from Jesus and with Jesus; they were compelled in submission to their Lord to use his Bible to interpret his messiahship and themselves in relationship to it.

2.1 Jewish community of interpretation

What remains perplexing for the modern interpreter is *why* New Testament writers appropriate scripture so creatively, without due consideration of its 'original' meaning. In response to this problem and in keeping with critical scholarship's historical interest, standard discussions (Longenecker 1975; Ellis 1957; Vermes 1973; Patte 1975; Bruce 1959) are careful to locate the hermeneutics of New Testament writers/writings within an ancient Jewish interpretive culture.

Two qualifications should be added to make this consensus more precise: (a) while evincing the literary conventions and hermeneutical interests of Jewish exegesis, New Testament literature, like earliest Christianity, emerges from a Hellenistic world as well. 'The Christianity of the New Testament is a creative combination of Jewish and Hellenistic traditions transformed into a *tertium quid* ("a third something"): that is, a reality related to two known things but transcending them both' (Aune 1987: 12). (b) The same can be said of the (hellenized Judaism from which earliest Christianity emerged. In fact, the Judaism of the New Testament is hardly a monolithic movement, but is in J. Sanders' phrase, a 'pluralizing monotheism.' The fluidity of Jewish culture and of its canonical scriptures not yet stabilized in the first century, is generally reflected in its biblical tradition, still fluid, and exegetical practice, still experimental. Text-centered exegesis became the norm within the early church only after the canonical process resulted in a fixed text. Thus, what the reader of the New Testament will sometimes find is more like the 'rewritten Bible' of apocryphal literature, where the focus of the writer's use of a cited text is not the received text but a modified or supplemented one and where perceived 'gaps' in the biblical narrative are filled in by the writer in an attempt to complete the historical record.

2.2 Canon-consciousness of New Testament writers

Even if the boundaries around the biblical canon of its writers were not yet fixed when the New Testament literature was written, clearly they use their Bible as a normative guide to faith and witness; it is for them a sufficient and trusted medium of God's Word which communicated what it means to be God's people and to do as God's people ought. At no time is it possible for the interpreter to divorce the writer's citation of or allusion to scripture from these core convictions about scripture: the authority of the biblical text and the act of interpreting it are joined together. While demonstrating considerable creativity in adapting the meaning of their biblical texts to every new situation, biblical writers also reveal considerable selectivity in which texts are used and meticulous care in doing so – characteristics of what G. Sheppard has referred to as the writer's 'canon-consciousness' (1980: 109–19).

Further, the 'canon consciousness' of the New Testament writers must be a factor in determining the deeper logic of their exegetical activity. The biblical interpreter should not presume that New Testament writers thought of their stories or letters as literary creations, which arise *ex nihilo* as if every new historical event obligates a brand-new text to narrate or interpret it; rather, this literature is written in conceptual continuity with or mimesis of extant biblical tradition simply because its writers (and audiences) believed that the 'things that have happened among us' continue Israel's history and God's revelation, witnessed to by that tradition, into a new dispensation of God's promised salvation. New Testament writers are heirs of a sacred tradition, whose mind-set and methods are also nurtured within a living, dynamic interpretive culture. We make a mistake supposing that they picked up biblical texts to find a 'new' meaning for another audience in isolation from the prior interpretations of earlier tradents. The TaNaKh supplies the literary texts of a sacred tradition that is always received from others who have already found it to be Word of God for their own communities of believers.

2.3 Scripture as midrashic literature

Biblical writings are midrashic literature in this sense: they are written in response to the urgent needs and questions of the present moment under the light shed by antecedent texts, which writers deemed normative for faith and divine in origin (Bloch 1978). In particular, biblical writers find meaning in these canonical texts which not only coheres around the core convictions of a Christian theological tradition but also enters into a sometimes playful conversation with other interpretations of these same texts (Sanders 1987). This broader definition of midrash follows current literary theory which terms 'midrashic' any interpretive act that interprets earlier texts by means of narrative or discursive augmentation in a way that renders meaning in culturally and ideologically determined ways. Midrash is no longer limited by this definition to a particular exegetical method or literary genre (e.g., *aggadoth* or *halakoth*) which transmit determinate and timeless interpretations of specific, biblical texts to no particular audience. New Testament interpreters are increasingly apt to draw comparisons between the texts and topics of Old Testament literature with those of New Testament literature, ever more sensitive to the subtle and clever ways biblical writers appropriated these sacred traditions to make clearer and more authoritative their own words.

3 The final form of the Christian Bible: Intra-canonical interpretation

The intertextuality of New Testament writings is the literary precipitate of a Jewish interpretive culture in which these New Testament texts were written in conversation with a writer's antecedent sacred tradition in order to support and add an inherent depth of understanding to his reinterpretation of God's Word for the theological crisis of his day. Scripture's current address, however, is the Christian biblical canon. The ultimate referentiality of the biblical canon is not historical, with meanings posited at the point of origin, but theological, with meanings that result from scripture's performance as the Word of God for its canonical audience. The stakes of this discussion of intra-biblical interpretation acquire greater importance, then, if framed as a feature of scripture's ongoing mediation of God's Word.

That is, the intertextuality of scripture's final literary (or 'canonical') form is an inherent feature of its revelatory powers and must be understood by its current interpreters in terms other than a particular writer's exegetical strategy or, the intended meaning of his writing for his first readers/auditors (however, see Childs 1992: 76). The current reductionism of interpreting the Old Testament or New Testament in isolation from the other, thereby regarding the New Testament's relationship to the 'Hebrew Bible' as significant, is subverted by the New Testament's appeal to and exegesis of the Old Testament. Sharply put, the scriptures of the New Testament writers are 'neither superseded nor nullified but transformed into a witness of the gospel' (Hays 1989: 157); certainly on a canonical level of authority, this point funds the orienting concerns (rather than the exegetical methods per se) of a hermeneutical model for our ongoing consideration of the relationship between Old Testament and New Testament within the church's Christian Bible.

The Old Testament and New Testament each tell incomplete stories without the other (see Watson 1997). Together they form an irreducible and self-sufficient whole: we expect no third 'testament' beyond these two. Thus, what is 'new' about the New Testament's testimony to the Messiah's *kairos* and kerygma can be adequately discerned by the biblical interpreter only in relationship to what has become 'old' about the Old Testament as a result. Indeed, the Christian Bible, which narrates the beginnings of God's reconciliation of all things (Old Testament) that climaxes with Jesus' messianic mission (New Testament), heralds the consummation of this history with the coming triumph of God on earth as now in heaven, to which all scripture bears proleptic witness.

References and further reading

Aune, D. (1967) *The New Testament in its Literary Environment*, LEC, Philadelphia Westminster Press.

Bloch, R. (1978) 'Midrash' and 'Methodological Note for the Study of Rabbinic Literature,' pp. 29–50, 51–75 in *Approaches in Ancient Judaism*, W. Green (ed.), Missoula: Scholars Press.

Boyarin, D. (1990) *Intertextuality and the Reading of Midrash*, Bloomington: Indiana University Press.

Bruce, F.F. (1959) *Biblical Exegesis in the Qumran Texts*, Grand Rapids: Eerdmans.

Childs, B. (1992) *Biblical Theology of the Old and New Testaments: Theological Reflection on the Christian Bible*, Minneapolis: Fortress Press.

Ellis, E.E. (1957) *Paul's Use of the Old Testament*, Grand Rapids: Eerdmans.

Fishbane, M. (1989) *The Garments of Torah. Essays in Biblical Hermenuetics*, Bloomington: Indiana University Press.

Hays. R. (1989) *Echoes of Scripture in the Letters of Paul*, New Haven: Yale University Press.

Kugel, J.L. and R.E. Greer (1986) *Early Biblical Hermeneutic*, LEC, Philadelphia: Westminster Press.

Levenson, J. (1993) *The Hebrew Bible, the Old Testament, and Historical Criticism*, Louisville. Westminster/John Knox.

Longenecker, R. (1975) *Biblical Exegesis in the Apostolic Period*, Grand Rapids: Eerdmans.

Patte D. (1975) *Early Jewish Hermeneutic in Palestine*, SBLDS 22, Missoula: Scholars Press.

Sanders, J.A. (1987) *From Sacred Story to Sacred Text*, Philadelphia: Fortress Press.

Sheppard, G. (1980) *Wisdom as a Hermeneutical Construct*, BZAW 151, Berlin: Walter de Gruyter.

Vermes, G. (1973) *Scripture and Tradition in Judaism*, Leiden: Brill.

Wall, R.W. (1999) 'The "Rule of Faith" in Theological Hermeneutics,' pp. 88–107 in *Between Two Horizans*, J. Green and M. Turner (eds.), Grand Rapids: Eerdmans.

Watson, F. (1997) *Text and Truth: Redefining Biblical Theology*, Grand Rapids: Eerdmans.

ROBERT W. WALL

IRENAEUS (c. 140–202)

Irenaeus was born around 140 in Asia Minor, possibly near Smyrna. Most of the biographical information on him stems from Eusebius' *History of the Church*, which reports that in his youth Irenaeus had been a student of Polycarp. Around 170, he turns up in the city of Lugdunum in Gaul, the present Lyon, providing testimony to the cosmopolitan nature of the Roman Empire. Greek-speaking communities in the West, were, in fact, leaders in the early spread of Christianity. Irenaeus escaped the infamous persecutions of 177 in Lyon, being absent as an emissary in Rome seeking peace among Christian communities there. His mission had to do with the Montanists, a prophetic and spiritual movement, which had originated in Phrygia but had found a large following in Italy and North Africa as well. On his return to Lyon, Irenaeus became the successor of the martyred bishop Photinus. Irenaeus' name occurs again as a mediator in another conflict at Rome. In the period between 190–200, he urged moderation in the controversy about the date of Easter. Thereafter he vanishes from the pages of Eusebius, but in his *Historia Francorum*, the sixth-century writer Gregory of Tours reports that Irenaeus died in 202 as a martyr.

Two of Irenaeus' works have been fully preserved. The first is the five-volume *Refutation and Overturning of the Falsely So-called Knowledge*, more commonly known as *Against Heresies*. The text is mostly extant in an old Latin translation, while fragments of the Greek are preserved in later Christian writers. At the request of a friend, Irenaeus describes at length various 'Gnostic' systems, thereby providing important information – particularly on the teachings and beliefs of the Valentinians. One should, however, not take Irenaeus' report at face value since its intention was to be a refutation. The second writing, *The Demonstration of Apostolic Preaching*, was only known from its title until the discovery in 1904 of an Armenian translation. In its first part he deals with primary issues of Christian faith, such as the concept of God, the Trinity, Creation, the Fall, and salvation; in the second part he defends the truth of the apostolic teaching since it had been prophesied in the scriptures. The basic idea of Irenaeus' theology is that Adam, who had been created after the 'image and likeness' of God, was intended to be immortal, but because of his Fall, humanity received the fate of perishability. Through the incarnation and resurrection of Christ, human immortality was restored, and Christ became the second Adam, who restored with obedience the disobedience of the first ancestor. Through the Holy Spirit in baptism and eucharist, humanity was able to participate again in immortality. The unification and restoration of the divine and the human realms are the central elements in his theology. Irenaeus' conception of unity is epitomized in Ephesians 1:10, a text which has become a hallmark for his theology. His feast day is June 28.

References and further reading

Benoît, André (1960) *Saint Irénée; introduction à l'étude de sa théologie*, Paris: Presses universitaires de France.

Brox, Norbert (1966) *Offenbarung, Gnosis und gnostischer Mythos bei Irenaud von Lyon*, Salzburg: Pustet.

Grant, Robert M. (1997) *Irenaeus of Lyons*, London: Routledge.

Irenaeus (1920) *The Demonstration of the Apostolic Preaching*, trans. J. Armitage, London: SPCK.

—— (1992–) *St. Irenaeus of Lyons Against the Heresies*, trans. Dominic J. Unger, further revisions John J. Dillon, New York: Paulist Press.

Lawson, John (1948) *The Biblical Theology of Saint Irenaeus*, London: Epworth.

Minns, Denis (1994) *Irenaeus*, Washington, DC: Georgetown University Press.

Nielsen, Jan T. (1968) *Adam and Christ in the Theology of Irenaeus of Lyons*, Assen: Van Gorcum.

Sagnard, François (1947) *La gnose valentinienne et le témoignage de saint Irénée*, Paris: J. Vrin.

ANNEWIES VAN DEN HOEK

ISHMAEL (AD 90–135)

Rabbi Ishmael (ben Elisha) flourished in the first three decades of the second century AD and was a contemporary of the great Rabbi Aqiba. Neusner (1969) has suggested that the absence of names of Ishmael's disciples from the Mishnah may be due to their flight from Palestine to Babylonia at the outbreak of the Bar Kokhba revolt. Neusner's speculation is plausible and may account for early and significant transfer of rabbinic law and lore from Palestine to Babylonia, as comparison of the two Talmuds seems to suggest.

Ishmael and his school are given credit for *Mekilta deRabbi Ishmael* (on Exodus), *Sifre* Numbers, and part of *Sifre* Deuteronomy. Although Ishmael and his school are not credited with *Sifra* Leviticus, the so-called *Beraita deRabbi Ishmael* (consisting of one *parashah* and one *pereq*) preface this tannaitic work. Rabbinic literature often portrays Ishmael as the rival of the great Aqiba. Ishmael's name appears frequently in the mystical literature of the *hêkālôt*, although there is no early tradition that links this authority to *merkābâ* mysticism.

Ishmael and his school are also given credit for the formulation of 'thirteen' exegetical rules (or *middoth*). However, a more conventional numbering suggests sixteen *middoth*. They are expansions of six of the seven exegetical rules attributed to the school of Hillel (cf. *Beraita deRabbi Ishmael* §1). Ishmael's *middoth* include (a) 'light and heavy,' or what applies in the less important case will apply in the more important case; (b) 'an equivalent regulation,' where passages with common language may interpret one another; (c) 'constructing a father [i.e., principal rule] from one [passage]'; (d) 'constructing a father [i.e. principal rule] from two writings [or passages]'; (e) 'general and particular,' where what applies in a general case will apply in a particular case; (f) 'particular and general'; (g) 'general and particular and general'; (h) 'general, which requires the particular;' (i) 'particular, which requires the general'; (j) 'anything in the general and specified in order to teach (something) teaches not only about itself but also teaches about everything in the general'; (k) 'anything included in the general and specified as a requirement concerning another requirement in keeping with the general is specified in order to make (the second requirement) less strict and not more strict'; (l) 'anything included in the general and not specified as a requirement in the general and not specified as a requirement concerning another requirement not in keeping with the general is specified either to make less or more strict'; (m) anything included in the general and excepted from it by a new (provision), you may not return to (the provisions) of its (original) general statement unless scripture says you may do so'; (n) 'a matter is to be explained from its context'; (o) 'a matter is to be explained from what follows it'; and (p) 'two passages that contradict one another (may be reconciled by) a third passage.' Several of these *middoth* are explained throughout the remainder of the *beraita* credited to Ishmael. Porton (1977: 2.65) rightly concludes that this list in *Sifra* is composite. Ishmael's *middoth* are expanded still further, to thirty-two, in traditions credited to Eliezer ben Yose the Galilean, a generation or so after the defeat of Simon ben Kosiba.

Ishmael's first three *middoth* are identical, or almost identical, to Hillel's first three. The fourth through eleventh *middoth* of Ishmael partition and expand Hillel's fifth ('general and particular, and particular and general'), while Ishmael's twelfth *middah* is identical to Hillel's seventh. Ishmael's thirteenth through sixteenth *middoth* are new, with the final three representing rather conventional criteria for the interpretation of any text. But even the other *middoth*, if applied judiciously, approximate principles of contextual exegesis and biblical theology that most moderns find acceptable. Ishmael's *middoth*, as Hillel's earlier rules, were developed especially for the finer points of halakhic interpretation and its resultant rulings.

References and further reading

Abusch, R. (2003) 'Rabbi Ishmael's Miraculous Conception: Jewish Redemption History in Anti-Christian Polemic,' pp. 307–43 in *The Ways that Never Parted: Jews and Christians in Late Antiquity and the Early Middle Ages*, TSAJ 95, A.H. Becker and A.Y. Reed (eds.), Tübingen: Mohr Siebeck.

Goldenberg, R. (1992) 'Ishmael Rabbi,' *ABD* 3.513.

Neusner, J. (1969) *A History of the Jews in Babylonia*, Vol. 1, Leiden: Brill.

Porton, G. (1976–1982) *The Traditions of Rabbi Ishmael*, 4 Vols., SJLA 19, Leiden: Brill.

Strack, H.L. and G. Stemberger (1991/1992) *Introduction to the Talmud and Midrash*, Edinburgh: T.&T. Clark/Minneapolis: Fortress Press.

Yadin, A. (2003) '4QMMT, Rabbi Ishmael, and the Origins of Legal Midrash,' *Dead Sea Discoveries* 10: 130–49.

CRAIG A. EVANS

ISLAMIC INTERPRETATION

Although we cannot substantiate the claim that modern biblical criticism has its roots in medieval Islam (the theory of H. Lazarus-Yafeh), it is undeniable that after the eclipse of paganism, the first critical scrutiny of the biblical text was the work of Muslim scholars. Uncommitted to any theory of the Bible as the Word of God, many Muslims felt free to examine it in ways which Jews and Christians would have found religiously disturbing. They did so sometimes in order to convert its custodians, and sometimes to flesh out the somewhat exiguous prophetic biographies supplied by the Qur'ān and Ḥadīth.

The early Arab historians suggest that Muslim engagement with the Bible began with Islam itself. Ibn Saʿd (d. 845) relates that the Prophet asked his secretary to learn the 'script of the Jews,' and that he permitted another of his companions to read 'the Torah.' The Jewish convert Kaʿb al-Aḥbār is said to have taught 'the Torah' in the Madina mosque, and to have circulated biblical and aggadic lore among the Muslims; a task shared with the Prophet's cousin Ibn ʿAbbās, who enjoyed the soubriquet 'Rabbi of the Arabs' in consequence.

Justifying their activities with the hadith, 'Relate the tales of the Children of Israel,' such men proliferated until a class of storytellers (*quṣṣāṣ*) came into being, producing a popular literary genre of which the first extant example is the *Tales of the Prophets* by Ibn Bishr (d. 821). This literature influenced many standard Qur'ānic commentaries.

Nonetheless the Qur'ān itself (4:46, 6:91, etc.) implies that the biblical text had suffered processes of distortion (*taḥrīf*) or partial concealment (*kitmān*), and many Muslims held that the principal motivation had been to suppress foretellings of Muḥammad. The process was, however, incomplete, and a primary task of Muslim biblical criticism became the identification of surviving Muhammadan prophecies. Ibn Rabbān (d. 855) found 130 of these; but those commonly cited (for instance, in the dialogue between the caliph al-Mahdī (d. 785) and the Nestorian catholicos Timothy) were three: Muḥammad is the 'Rider on the Camel' (a variant of Isa. 21:7), he is the prophet 'like unto Moses' (Deut. 18:18), and he is the Paraclete (John 15:26). Qur'ān 61:6 attributes to Jesus the prediction of a prophet 'whose name will be Aḥmad,' and Muslim writers, beginning with Ibn Isḥāq (d. 763; his source probably being the Palestinian Syriac Lectionary), regard the Syriac *MNḤMNĀ*, 'comforter,' as cognate with the Prophet's Arabic names Muḥammad and Aḥmad.

This type of exegesis, which polemicists inferred from Qur'ān 5:47 ('let the people of the Gospel judge by what God has revealed in it'), coexisted uneasily with the theory of *taḥrīf*, which after the tenth century enjoyed almost universal acceptance. Muslims objected that unlike the Qur'ān, the Bible was not transmitted via *tawātur* (multiple lines of transmission through known authorities). The Moroccan Samaw'al (d. *c.* 1174) believed that Jewish history was too frequently disrupted by invasions for the Torah to have remained intact; while the greatest of all medieval Muslim Bible scholars, Ibn Ḥazm of Cordoba (d. 1064), added that the distortion was compounded by the reversion to idolatry of some Jewish kings. The text had been further destabilized by translation: ʿAbd al-Jabbār (d. 1025) believed that the original of the Gospels had been in Hebrew, while Ibn Ḥazm knew of the Septuagint and the Latin Bible.

Further evidence for *taḥrīf* was found in the theological impossibility of certain anthropomorphisms (God did not need to rest on the seventh day; He cannot be called 'Father'; Gen. 8:21 was originally 'God caused a pleasant smell to rise from the offering'). No true scripture could impugn prophetic morality, as the Bible does when narrating the stories of Lot's daughters, Jacob's adultery with Leah and his deceit of Isaac, and David's affair with Bathsheba.

Also decisive were New Testament attributions of divinity to Jesus. From the time of the historian Sayf ibn ʿUmar (d. 796 or 797) Muslims compared Paul's 'distortion' of Christianity to the alleged attempt by the Yemenite Jewish convert Ibn Saba' to spread exaggerated claims about the ontological and eschatological nature of Muhammad. Paul, the persecutor of the Christians, conspired with Jews to feign conversion, predicting that unless Christianity was destroyed the future of Jewry would be calamitous. Claiming visions, he convinced some Christians to discard the Jewish dietary laws, to reject violence, and to regard Jesus as God, thereby sowing the seeds for schism and dispute.

Muslims also used the Bible to prove to its followers that revelations may experience abrogation (*naskh*). For instance, Ibn Ḥazm cites Jacob's marriage to two sisters, a practice which was later 'abrogated' by Leviticus 18:18.

Others, like Ibn al-Jawzī (d. 1200), tried to reconstruct the original scriptures by excluding un-Islamic elements. Hence there exist Muslim 'psalters,' 'Torahs,' and 'scrolls of Abraham,' few of which have been the subject of scientific study.

In the modern period the medieval themes have proved remarkably tenacious. From the mid-nineteenth century some Muslims have used Western higher criticism to vindicate the theory of *taḥrīf*; a good example is the work of Maqsood (see references).

References and further reading

Adang, Camilla (1996) *Muslim Writers on Judaism and the Hebrew Bible*, Leiden: Brill.

Ferré, André (1977) 'L'historien al-Yaᶜqūbī et les Evangiles,' *Islamochristiana* 3: 65–83.

Gaudeul, Jean-Marie, and Robert Caspar (1980) 'Textes de la tradition musulmane concernant le *taḥrīf* (falsification) des Écritures,' *Islamochristiana* 6: 61–104.

Kairanawi, Rahmatullah (1989) *Izhar al-Haqq*, London: Ta-Ha.

Lazarus-Yafeh, Hava (1992) *Intertwined Worlds: Medieval Islam and Bible Criticism*, Princeton: Princeton University Press.

McAuliffe, Jane Dammen (1996) 'The Qur'ānic Context of Muslim Biblical scholarship,' *Islam and Christian Relations* 7: 141–58.

Maqsood, Ruqaiyyah (2000) *The Mysteries of Jesus: A Muslim Study of the Origins and Development of the Christian Church*, Oxford: Sakina Books.

Pulcini, Theodore (1998) *Exegesis as Polemical Discourse: Ibn Hazm on Jewish and Christian Scriptures*, Atlanta: Scholars Press.

Stern, S.M. (1968) ''Abd al-Jabbār's Account of How Christ's Religion was Falsified by the Adoption of Roman Customs,' *Journal of Theological Studies* 19: 128–85.

Tabarī, ᶜAlī b. Rabbān al- (1922) *The Book of Religion and Empire*, trans. A. Mingana, Manchester: Manchester University Press.

Thomas, David (1996) 'The Bible in Early Muslim Anti-Christian Polemic,' *Islam and Christian–Muslim Relations* 7: 29–38.

TIM WINTER

ISRAEL: HISTORY OF

1 Background

For much of the history of interpretation in both the church and synagogue, the subject of ancient Israel's history was accepted either as a straightforward reading of the Old Testament or Hebrew scriptures, or as an allegorical image from which various doctrines could be derived. Thus the historical value of this literature was not questioned. Briefly, this can be summarized as follows (with generally accepted dates included and the Jewish/Protestant canon followed). Israel's history began as the family of Abram, called out from Ur and Haran and given a covenant by God with the promise of becoming a great nation. Abram's grandson, Jacob, followed his son, Joseph, to Egypt where the family grew into a nation oppressed by Egypt. God miraculously led the nation forth and into the desert wilderness where he gave them a covenant as a permanent relationship between God and Israel. As a result of their lack of faith, Israel wandered in the wilderness for a generation. Upon the death of their leader, Moses, Israel followed Joshua into the Promised Land of Canaan and defeated their enemies. However, they soon became susceptible to foreign worship and that brought judgment in the form of oppression by foreigners. God raised up judges to deliver Israel from their enemies. After several generations, they requested a king. Saul was the first king but he was rejected by God's prophet, Samuel. David was chosen by divine decision and his dynasty was promised eternal rule in Jerusalem. His son Solomon saw the kingdom grow into an empire but this was lost and the original kingdom divided into northern and southern kingdoms soon after his death (c. 932 BC). The north, wealthier but more corrupt, succumbed to the Assyrian invasions of 733 and 722 BC. The south survived more than a century longer until it was also destroyed and exiled by the Babylonians in 586 BC. With the emergence of Persia and its conquest of Babylon, the Jews were allowed to return to Jerusalem and to resettle Judaea. The temple was rebuilt c. 517 BC and Ezra and Nehemiah instituted important religious reforms in the following century. Although some biblical texts may have been written after this, the narrative of the Old Testament ends at this point. The New Testament picks up the story with the coming of Jesus into a land dominated by the Roman Empire.

In addition to the Bible itself, classical sources such as Josephus were used to further enlighten readers' understanding of this period. However, the rise of higher criticism led to a reexamination of this literature in the light of different methods. Texts formerly thought to be unified were now understood as separable and identifiable from distinct sources. As a result diverse sources for the literature that formed the traditional view of Israel's history were identified. This led to a hierarchy of value in which some sources were more highly regarded as possessing historical value than others. The result was new descriptions of Israel's history in which some texts were reassigned to periods other than those the biblical context would suggest. With the discoveries of archaeology and the ancient Near East, a new dimension in recreating Israel's history became available. This allowed historians to fill in some gaps and provided understanding of obscure biblical texts and practices. It also added data to revise and further diversify the methods that historians applied to understanding Israel's history.

The modern age has witnessed several new approaches that scholars have applied to the biblical text for purposes of historical study. Literary analysis has produced refinements in critical investigations and reconstructions of the text (Miller 1998). It has also witnessed the emergence of postmodern trends in narrative history (Barstad 1997). Archaeology has ventured into new areas with emphases on social archaeology (Levy 1995) and on the analysis and comparison of ancient Near-Eastern literary forms and genres with similar ones from the Bible (Younger 1990; Hurowitz 1992; Hess 1997). Finally, an entirely new course has been plotted by those who emphasize a radical division between the biblical narrative and the history of ancient Palestine (Thompson 1992; Ahlström 1993; Davies 1995; Lemche 1998). Add to this the continuation of traditional 'straightforward' readings of the biblical literature as history (Merrill 1996; Kaiser 1998) and one has a wide selection of presuppositions involved in the identification, use, and reconstruction of the sources.

2 Critical issues

To understand the impact of these methods on the study of Israelite history a few representative texts or periods have been selected: the patriarchs (Gen. 12–36); the Exodus (Exod. 1–12); the appearance and settlement in Canaan (Josh.); the united monarchy of David and Solomon (2 Sam. 4–1 Kings 11); the Assyrian invasion during the reign of Hezekiah (2 Kings 18–20; Isa. 36–39); and the return from Exile (Ezra 1–6).

The supposed convergences that could be identified between social customs and linguistic data of the patriarchs and various Bronze Age archives (Bright 1981) were seriously challenged by Thompson (1974) and Van Seters (1975, 1992), for whom the narratives lacked any credibility as second-millennium BC sources and who found closer parallels with mid- and late first millennium BC textual sources. Lemche (1998) examines the city-state culture of Syria in the Middle and Late Bronze Ages, and concludes that the society so defined has no relation to that described in the Genesis narratives. Those who choose to find some historical value in the texts tend to view them in accordance with Alt (1989: 3–77), as preserving eponymic traditions of various tribes scattered throughout Palestine and worshipping deities who later became synthesized into the sole God, Yahweh (e.g., Ahlström 1993). However, the archival evidence in texts found at Alalakh, Nuzi, Mari, Ugarit, and elsewhere continues to suggest that at no other period in the ancient Near East are so many of the patriarchal customs and practices attested as c. 1500 BC (e.g., Alalakh, cf. Hess 1994a). In addition, challenges to specific parallels have proven groundless in some instances. So, for example, the parallel between Genesis 15 and treaty-making practices at Alalakh, where animals are also slain, remains. Upon examination, the objection to the parallel rests upon confusion of the texts and their publication (Hess 1994b). Finally, details such as the price of slaves and the specific grammatical structures of so many of the personal names among the patriarchs continue to be best explained by a date in the second millennium BC (Kitchen 1994).

The Exodus of Israel from Egypt has allowed a variety of Egyptologists the opportunity to address issues surrounding the history of Israel. Redford (1990) denies the presence of authentic Egyptian traditions from this period, preferring to date the origins of the story to the middle of the second millennium BC on the basis of parallels with Egyptian practices. Redford (1997) contends that there is no evidence for a West Semitic population, such as Israelites, living separately in any part of the routes of access from the Sinai to the Nile Valley. Lemche (1998) concurs. He pays particular attention to the mention of Pithom (Exod. 1:11) which cannot occur before the first millennium BC. Hoffmeier (1998) has reexamined the evidence and cites a great deal of evidence from Kitchen and others to support a historical exodus of Israel in the second millennium BC. This includes Egyptian names such as Moses and Phineas, which are attested in Ramesside Egypt. The excavations at the site of Tell ed-Dab'a have revealed a huge city in the eastern Delta, one that has much evidence of West Semitic occupation, and perhaps the one mentioned in a text that describes how Ramses II employed West Semitic (Hapiru) laborers to build a city. This is now identified as the city of (Pi-)Ramses.

The entrance into Canaan is a topic that has generated a huge discussion and no less than five interpretive approaches (Hess 1993). There is the traditional view of the conquest of Canaan by Israel through entering from outside the country and successfully waging holy war on its inhabitants. A second view argues for a nomadic immigration of Israelites into the highlands of Canaan and a gradual peaceful occupation

(Alt 1989: 133–67). An alternative approach suggests that pre-Israelites were the oppressed members of Canaanite city states who rebelled and declared their freedom by fleeing into the less populated hill country where they formed egalitarian communities (Gottwald 1979). More recently, Finkelstein's (1988) synthesis of the dramatic demographic change in hill country settlements in the twelfth century BC led him to argue that the Israelites were originally enclosed nomads who inhabited the hill country of Palestine and, for various reasons, changed their way of living from nomadic to sedentary in the twelfth century. A fifth alternative is to stress the political, economic, and environmental changes that were common at that time to the entire region and not merely the hill country. This view places an emphasis on similar demographic changes that may have occurred in Transjordan and the lowlands of Canaan. It suggests that there was nothing distinctive about the hill country; indeed, that there was no Israel or 'proto-Israel' in terms of any specifically recognizable archaeological evidence (Thompson 1992). In particular, this latter view is disputed by archaeologists, some of whom continue to affirm distinctive archaeological assemblages that they identify as somehow related to later Israelites (Dever 1995).

Much recent debate has revolved around the issue of the United Monarchy and the question of its existence. Historical criticism has traditionally found in the biblical texts from this period some of the earliest evidence for reliable and unbiased historical data, especially in the administrative lists and documents that are incorporated into the narratives of 2 Samuel, 1 Kings, and 1 and 2 Chronicles (Ahlström 1993; Soggin 1993). However, recent archaeological studies and discussions have argued against the presence of a recognizable period in the tenth century when a king in Jerusalem could have ruled a significant kingdom (see the survey in Knoppers 1997: 27–33). Much of the archaeological evidence traditionally assigned to the United Monarchy has been redated (the Jerusalem 'millo' to the Late Bronze Age, the southern Judaean forts to the Persian period, and the gates at Hazor, Megiddo, and Gezer to the ninth century). However, the redating of the gates is not established. As Knoppers (1997) and Millard (1997) have argued the paucity of archaeological evidence found to date implies nothing about the level of culture in tenth-century Israel any more than a similar absence of evidence in Kassite Babylonia or in Persian Jerusalem and Judaea intimates anything about the culture in those contexts.

The issues surrounding the invasion of Judah by the Assyrian king Sennacherib tend to reflect a greater interest in treating the biblical text as a historical source by asking how reliable the text can be. The views on this can be generally divided into three areas: historical approaches, critical approaches, literary approaches (Hess 1999). The historical approaches attempt to treat the entire narrative as chronologically sequential history. Thus the apparent discrepancy of 2 Kings 18:13b–16, where Sennacherib is paid tribute and retires from the battlefield, and 2 Kings 18:17–19:37, where Sennacherib's army is destroyed by divine visitation, is resolved by assuming two campaigns (Bright 1981). The critical approaches attempt to reconcile the discrepancy by assuming one or both texts to be nonhistorical. Clements (1980) illustrates this by arguing that 2 Kings 18:13b–16 contains the historical truth while 2 Kings 18:17–19:37 is a theological embellishment written at least eighty years after the event to propagate Josiah's view of Zion theology. The literary approach does not assume that the two texts are intended to be chronologically sequential but argues that the first text serves as a summary of the action which the second text describes in much greater detail (Hess 1999).

Like all periods of ancient Israel's history the exilic period has produced many issues that have evoked scholarly discussion. One of the more recent addresses the question as to whether or not there was an exile. Davies (1995) and Thompson (1992) have championed a view that this biblical literature was all composed centuries later in the Hellenistic period. It is not history but propaganda. That is, the concern of the writers is to create for the inhabitants of Palestine a history in order to give them an identity. This history never existed but is a creation derived from legends and various sources extending as far back as the Persian period. Thus the Babylonian and Assyrian deportations of peoples from Palestine and their subsequent resettlement of other peoples resulted in virtually a complete change of the population in terms of their ethnic identity. The inhabitants of Palestine in the ninth century BC bore no ethnic resemblance to those of the third century. Therefore the 'myth of the exile' was an attempt to incorporate these deportations into a story that would explain how the Jewish people had actually lived in the Promised Land from antiquity and therefore had a right to possess it. This approach contradicts the more traditional view that there was a real return from exile of Jewish people who could trace their ancestry to the Israel of the period of the monarchy. It is also challenged by Hoglund (1992: 18–20) who, though writing before the appearance of the works of Davies and Thompson, nevertheless provides several examples of peoples returning to their homeland during and around the time of Israel's return. Further, this can be integrated into larger geopolitical strategies of the Persian Empire. Thus the traditional interpretation remains a viable alternative.

3 Concluding observations

Thus recent tendencies in the study of ancient Israel's history have enjoyed substantial new discoveries in terms of historical sources as well as revised and refined methods. This has led to a much wider variety of interpretations in relation to the Hebrew texts than was available even a generation ago. Further, it appears that no single method or interpretive approach is likely to dominate scholarship or define studies for the next generation. Rather, the debate will continue in several areas: (a) the relationship of literary forms and purposes to the historical value of a written source; (b) the heuristic value of models derived from the social sciences and the degree to which they can reinterpret explicit statements in written texts; (c) the authenticity of biblical traditions in reflecting the historical times and places they purport to describe; and (d) the meaning and significance of epigraphic discoveries for the interpretation of Israel's history and their use in relation to the biblical account. The advent of new discoveries and new methods will continue to generate new dimensions in the interpretation of the history of ancient Israel.

References and further reading

Ahlström, Gösta W. (1993) *The History of Ancient Palestine from the Palaeolithic Period to Alexander's Conquest*, D. Edelman (ed.), JSOTSup 146, Sheffield: Sheffield Academic Press.

Alt, Albrecht (1989) *Essays on Old Testament History and Religion*, trans. R.A. Wilson, JSOT Seminar, Sheffield: Sheffield Academic Press.

Barstad, Hans M. (1997) 'History and the Hebrew Bible,' pp. 37–64 in *Can a 'History of Israel' Be Written?* European Seminar in Historical Methodology 1, JSOTSup 245, Lester L. Grabbe (ed.), Sheffield: Sheffield Academic Press.

Bright, John (1981) *A History of Israel*, Louisville: Westminster/John Knox, 3rd edn.

Clements, R.E. (1980) *Isaiah and the Deliverance of Jerusalem: A Study of the Interpretation of Prophecy in the Old Testament*, JSOTSup 13, Sheffield: Sheffield Academic Press.

Davies, Philip R. (ed.) (1991) *Second Temple Studies: 1. Persian Period*, JSOTSup 117, Sheffield: Sheffield Academic Press.

—— (1995) *In Search of 'Ancient Israel,'* JSOTSup 148, Sheffield: Sheffield Academic Press, 2nd edn.

Dever, William G. (1995) '"Will the Real Israel Please Stand Up?" Archaeology and Israelite Historiography: Part I,' *Bulletin of the American Schools of Oriental Research* 297: 61–81.

Finkelstein, Israel (1988) *The Archaeology of the Israelite Settlement*, Jerusalem: Israelite Exploration Society.

Gottwald, Norman K. (1979) *The Tribes of Yahweh: A Sociology of the Religion of Liberated Israel, 1250–1050 B.C.E.*, Maryknoll, NY: Orbis.

Halpern, Baruch (1988) *The First Historians: The Hebrew Bible and History*, San Francisco: Harper & Row.

Hess, Richard S. (1993) 'Early Israel in Canaan: A Survey of Recent Evidence and Interpretations,' *Palestine Exploration Quarterly* 126: 125–42.

—— (1994a) 'Alalakh Studies and the Bible: Obstacle or Contribution?' pp. 199–215 in *Scripture and Other Artifacts: Essays on the Bible and Archaeology in Honor of Philip J. King*, M.D. Coogan, J.C. Exum, and L.E. Stager (eds.), Louisville: Westminster/John Knox.

—— (1994b) 'The Slaughter of the Animals in Genesis 15: Genesis 15:8–21 and Its Ancient Near Eastern Context,' pp. 55–65 in *He Swore an Oath: Biblical Themes in Genesis 12–50*, R.S. Hess, G.J. Wenham, and P.E. Satterthwaite (eds.), Carlisle: Paternoster/Grand Rapids: Baker.

—— (1999) 'Hezekiah and Sennacherib in 2 Kings 18–20,' pp. 23–42 in *Zion, City of Our God*, R. Hess and G. Wenham (eds.), Grand Rapids: Eerdmans.

Hoffmeier, James K. (1997) *Israel in Egypt: The Evidence for the Authenticity of the Exodus Tradition*, Oxford: Oxford University Press.

Hoglund, Kenneth G. (1992) *Achaemenid Imperial Administration in Syria-Palestine and the Missions of Ezra and Nehemiah*, SBLDS 125, Atlanta: Scholars Press.

Kaiser, Walter C., Jr. (1998) *A History of Israel: From the Bronze Age through the Jewish Wars*, Nashville: Broadman & Holman.

Kitchen, Kenneth A. (1994) 'Genesis 12–50 in the Near Eastern World,' pp. 67–92 in *He Swore an Oath: Biblical Themes from Genesis 12–50*, R.S. Hess, G.J. Wenham, and P.E. Satterthwaite (eds.), Carlisle: Paternoster/Grand Rapids: Baker, 2nd edn.

—— (2003) *On the Reliability of the Old Testament*, Grand Rapids: Eerdmans.

Knoppers, G.N. (1993) *Two Nations under God: The Deuteronomistic History of Solomon and the Dual Monarchies. Volume 1: The Reign of Solomon and the Rise of Jeroboam*, HSS 52, Atlanta: Scholars Press.

—— (1997) 'The Vanishing Solomon: The Disappearance of the United Monarchy from Recent Histories of Ancient Israel,' *Journal of Biblical Literature* 116: 19–44.

Lemche, Niels Peter (1998) *Prelude to Israel's Past: Background and Beginnings of Israelite History and Identity*, trans. E.F. Maniscalco, Peabody, MA: Hendrickson.

Levy, Thomas E. (ed.) (1995) *The Archaeology of Society in the Holy Land*, New York: Facts on File.

Merrill, Eugene H. (1996) *Kingdom of Priests: A History of Old Testament Israel*, Grand Rapids: Baker.

Millard, A.R. (1995) 'The Knowledge of Writing in Iron Age Palestine,' *Tyndale Bulletin* 46: 207–17.

—— (1997) 'Assessing Solomon: History or Legend? King Solomon in His Ancient Context,' pp. 25–53 in *The Age of Solomon: Scholarship at the Turn of the Millennium*, SHANE 11, L.K. Handy (ed.), Leiden: Brill.

—— James K. Hoffmeier, and David W. Baker (eds.) (1994) *Faith, Tradition, and History: Old Testament*

Historiography in Its Ancient Near Eastern Context, Winona Lake: Eisenbrauns.

Miller, J. Maxwell (1998) *The History of Israel: An Essential Guide*, Nashville: Abingdon.

Na'aman, N. (1997) 'Cow Town or Royal Capital? Evidence for Iron Age Jerusalem,' *Biblical Archaeology Review* 23/4 (July/August): 43–7, 67.

Noth, Martin (1981) *The Deuteronomistic History*, JSOTSup 15, Sheffield: Sheffield Academic Press.

—— (1987) *The Chronicler's History*, trans. H.G.M. Williamson, JSOTSup 50, Sheffield: Sheffield Academic Press.

Redford, Donald B. (1990) *Egypt, Canaan, and Israel in Ancient Times*, Princeton: Princeton University Press.

—— (1997) 'The Sojourn of the Bene-Israel,' pp. 57–66 in *Exodus: The Egyptian Evidence*, Ernest S. Frerichs and Leonard H. Lesko (eds.), Winona Lake: Eisenbrauns.

Soggin, J. Alberto (1993) *An Introduction to the History of Israel and Judah*, Philadelphia: Trinity.

Thompson, T. L. (1974) *The Historicity of the Patriarchal Narratives: The Quest for the Historical Abraham*, BZAW 133, Berlin: Harrassowitz.

—— (1992) *Early History of the Israelite Peoples from the Written and Archaeological Sources*. SHANE 4. Leiden: Brill.

Van Seters, J. (1975) *Abraham in History and Tradition*, New Haven: Yale University Press.

—— (1992) *Prologue to History: The Yahwist as Historian in Genesis*, Louisville: Westminster/John Knox.

Whitelam, Keith W. (1996) *The Invention of Ancient Israel: The Silencing of Palestinian History*, London: Routledge.

Younger, K. Lawson, Jr. (1990) *Ancient Conquest Accounts: A Study in Ancient Near Eastern and Biblical History Writing*, JSOTSup 98, Sheffield: Sheffield Academic Press.

RICHARD S. HESS

J

JEREMIAS, JOACHIM (1900–1979)

Joachim Jeremias was born in Dresden, Germany, in 1900. As a youth, he spent five years in Jerusalem while his father was the provost of the Deutsche Gemeinde. Jeremias later studied oriental languages and theology at the University of Leipzig where he received a Ph.D. in 1922. He went on to serve as a professor at the University of Greifswald from 1929 to 1934, and then held the New Testament chair from 1935 to 1968 at the University of Göttingen. During his distinguished career Jeremias received several honorary doctorates from many prestigious universities, including Oxford, Uppsala, Leipzig, and St Andrews.

Jeremias was a prodigious writer, having authored over thirty books and more than 250 articles. A complete bibliography was printed in 1970 in his Festschrift, *Der Ruf Jesu und die Antwort der Gemeinde*.

Two of Jeremias' more significant works include *The Parables of Jesus* (1947) and *Jerusalem in the Time of Jesus* (1969). *The Parables of Jesus* was unique in that it challenged the popular assumptions of such scholars as Rudolph Bultmann who denied the possibility of discovering the historical Jesus in the New Testament. Although Jeremias acknowledged that the early church had altered the parables, he argued that it seemed possible to sift through the changes to hear the authentic words of Jesus in their original setting. Crucial to this interpretive process was acknowledging the inevitable change resulting in the translation from Aramaic to Greek, the use of Semitisms, and possible references or hints of the foundational first-century Palestinian context.

Jerusalem in the Time of Jesus is a comprehensive study of the social and economic conditions of Jerusalem in the New Testament period. There were four sections to his book including the economic conditions, economic status, social status, and the maintenance of social purity. The purpose of the book was to provide an interpretative background for the study of Jesus. This revealed that Jeremias thought that the New Testament writings must be interpreted within the setting, both historically and linguistically, of first-century Palestine. This meant that the study of rabbinic writings (along with archaeology) provided an important source for understanding Jesus and his message. Jeremias wrote several articles on both subjects.

Jeremias' contribution to the interpretative process would most certainly include the following. First, he insisted that any interpretion of Jesus must begin by recognizing his Jewish environment and by recognizing that he was speaking and teaching from a Jewish perspective. There is no question that Jesus' teachings were altered by the early church, but it was still possible (and necessary) to identify the original sayings of Jesus. Second, Jeremias thought that it was imperative that the interpreter understand Semitic languages. Finally, he taught that the interpreter should have an essential understanding of the historical setting of first-century Palestine. Some have faulted Jeremias for his uncritical use of first-century and rabbinical writings; nevertheless, he demonstrated the importance of their use for understanding the teachings of Jesus.

References and further reading

Jeremias, J. (1963) *The Parables of Jesus*, trans. S.H. Hooke, New York: Scribner's, rev. edn.
—— (1969) *Jerusalem in the Time of Jesus: An Investigation into Economic and Social Conditions During the New Testament Period*, trans. C.H. Cave and F.H. Cave, London: SCM Press.
Sider, J.W. (1983) 'Rediscovering the Parables: The Logic of the Jeremias Tradition,' *Journal of Biblical Literature* 102: 61–83.

S.R. GUNDERSON

JEROME (c. 347–420)

Jerome, Eusebius Hieronymus, is recognized as the best-equipped Christian scholar of the early church, known for his premier translation and expositions of scripture. He was born at Stridon in Dalmatia and received his secondary education of grammar and rhetoric in Rome from *c.* 360 to 366, where one of his teachers was the celebrated Latin grammarian, Aerlius Donatus. He received his baptism in Rome in 366. It may have been in Rome that Jerome began learning Greek.

After spending time in Trier and Aquileia, he devoted

himself to the ascetic life in the desert, near Chalcis in Syria. It is there that Jerome learned Hebrew from a converted Jew in order to read the Old Testament in its original language. Jerome attended lectures by Apollinaris of Laodicea and Gregory Nazianzus, who likely inspired Jerome to take an interest in Origen. Jerome's translation of Origen's homilies on Jeremiah and Ezekiel come from this period.

Jerome moved back to Rome in 382 where he served bishop Damasus as papal secretary. Upon the request of Damasus, Jerome consulted Greek codexes in order to correct previous Latin translations of the Gospels. Jerome also worked on the first of three translations of the Psalms in addition to two of Origen's homilies on the Song of Songs.

In 384 Damasus died, consequently Jerome's welcome in Rome was over. He moved to Bethlehem, where he co-founded a double monastery for both men and women; he would spend the rest of his life there. He continued to correspond with friends throughout the empire and the majority of his biblical work is from this period. While in Bethlehem he engaged in rigorous literary activity including translating the Bible, writing his own biblical commentaries, and translating the works of other biblical scholars. Additionally, Jerome was involved in a controversy over the orthodoxy of Origen.

Jerome is best known for his translations of most of the books of the Bible, which were collected by his friends into one volume later called the Vulgate. Originally, Jerome considered the Septuagint inspired but later recognized that only the original was inspired. Jerome began translating the Old Testament from the original Hebrew text (*Hebraica veritas*) with the assistance of several Jews from Palestine. During Jerome's life, his translation was the Bible of the learned and was not accepted by all, since it was a private initiative not commissioned by the church. Jerome's approach to translation was never to depart unnecessarily from while maintaining the true sense of the original. Jerome, although often hasty, was a great Latin stylist.

As a biblical commentator, Jerome wrote sixty-six volumes of commentaries and roughly 100 homilies for the religious community of Bethlehem. Jerome's commentaries included a translation of the Hebrew and the Septuagint along with literal commentary, textual notes, and references to other Greek translations and Jewish traditions. Often lacking originality, Jerome's commentaries are largely compilations of others' work, particularly Origen's, which he translated from Greek to Latin.

References and further reading

PL 22–30; E.C. Richardson (ed.), *De viris illustribus*, TU (1896); W.H. Fremantle *et al.*, trans., *Letters and Select Works*, NPNF, ser. 2 (1893), Vol. 6; *CCSL* (1958–1990), Vols. 72–80.

Hagendahl, Harald (1958) *Latin Fathers and the Classics: A Study on the Apologists, Jerome and Other Christian Writers*, Göteborg: Almqvist & Wiksell.

Kamesar, A. (1993) *Jerome, Greek Scholarship and the Hebrew Bible: A Study of the 'Quaestiones Hebraicae in Genesim,'* Oxford: Clarendon.

Kelly, J.N.D. (1975) *Jerome: His Life, Writings, and Controversies*, San Francisco: Harper & Row.

Murphy, F.X. (ed.) (1952) *A Monument to Saint Jerome: Essays on Some Aspects of His Life, Works and Influence*, New York: Sheed and Ward.

DALLAS B.N. FRIESEN

JESUS AS INTERPRETER OF THE BIBLE

Jesus as interpreter of the Bible refers primarily to Jesus' interpretation of the Old Testament. This topic is a subset of the subject, Jesus' use of the Old Testament, which is a subset of a larger topic, Jesus' teaching. In looking at Jesus' teaching and its use of the Old Testament, how does Jesus interpret the Old Testament?

Before one can answer the above question, there are several critical issues to consider. First and foremost, assessing Jesus' use of the Old Testament must be determined through the record of the Gospel writers. The question of the authenticity for the words of Jesus has to be addressed. While the reliability of the Gospels is highly contentious, the burden of proof is increasingly shifting to those who cast serious doubt on the veracity and historicity of the Gospels (Porter 2000). A key factor to consider in this debate is the fact that Jesus' use of the Old Testament is consistent across several traditions: Mark, Q, L(uke), M(atthew), and John.

Another critical issue is the fact that the language of the Gospels is Greek and the primary Old Testament text the Gospels cite is the Septuagint (LXX). Though recent research suggests Jesus most likely spoke Greek, Aramaic was probably his primary language (Porter 1993, 1994). Hence, it is questionable how much he would have quoted the LXX. The issue of translation from Aramaic or Hebrew into Greek then becomes a factor in assessing Jesus' original interpretation of the Old Testament.

As one examines the teaching of Jesus, the Old Testament is pervasive. It is there in his debates with his opponents, in his teaching in parables, in his instruction of the disciples and others, and in his witness to his own identity and mission. Yet, his teaching is not, in any way, a protracted exposition of or commentary on the sacred texts as that found in Jewish midrash, pesher, or targum (Chilton 1984: 187; Witherington 1990: 185–6). He does at times employ exegetical methods that are found in typical Jewish interpretation (such as *proem* and *yelammedenu* midrash) (Ellis 1991: 130–8). This is to be expected as he was a Jewish teacher, and was even called rabbi (Matt. 26:25; Mark.

9:5; 10:51; John. 1.38; 3:2; 20:16). Thus, if he wanted his listeners and followers to heed what he said, he would need to show congruity with the Torah in both his respect for it and in his handling of it.

Jesus' use of the Old Testament is complex in its uniqueness. At times he affirms the truth and authority of the Old Testament (Matt. 5:17–20); at other times he appears to reinterpret the Old Testament (Matt. 5:21–48); and at other times Jesus appears to break the law (Mark 2:23–38; 3:1–6). Jesus' multifaceted approach to the Old Testament suggests to some scholars that he is contravening or superseding the law; to others he is bringing it to an end by completing or fulfilling it. But the boundaries of his interpretation are always continuous with the law.

Jesus' handling of the Old Testament falls into three main approaches: legal, prophetic, and analogical (Evans 1992: 579–83). With regard to the legal aspect, he cites and interprets the Old Testament, generally affirming the original intent (Mark 12:29–31). On occasion he defends his own decrees by arguing from the Old Testament text itself (Matt. 18:16; Mark 10:6–8). He even at some places disparages oral tradition and refers back to the Old Testament text itself as the proper teaching on an issue (Mark 7:1–23). With regard to the prophetic aspect, he declares that Old Testament texts are fulfilled in his public ministry (Luke 4:18–19; 7:18–23), that certain texts interpret his life and ministry (Mark 14:27), and that certain texts will be fulfilled in the future (Mark 13:14; Luke 21:34–35). With regard to the analogical aspect, Jesus typologically identified Old Testament texts with himself (Luke 4:25–27; Matt. 12:40 or Luke 11:31–32); he alluded to Old Testament texts in his parabolic teaching, and he quoted Old Testament texts at significant transition points in his life (Matt. 4:1–11; Luke 23:34; Mark 15:34). However, as one surveys the entire scope of his use of the Old Testament, what stands out is his authoritative originality (Banks 1975: 237–63, France 1971: 200–1): 'We conclude that in his use of the Old Testament Jesus stood alone among his Jewish contemporaries, and that not because he took unusual liberties with the text (he was in general unusually faithful to its intended meaning), but because he believed that in him it found its fulfilment' (France 1971: 201).

References and further reading

Banks, R. (1975) *Jesus and the Law in the Synoptic Tradition*, SNTSMS 28, Cambridge: Cambridge University Press.

Chilton, B. (1984) *A Galilean Rabbi and His Bible: Jesus' Own Interpretation of Isaiah*, London: SPCK.

Ellis, E.E. (1991) *The Old Testament in Early Christianity: Canon and Interpretation in the Light of Modern Research*, WUNT 54, Tübingen: J.C.B. Mohr.

Evans, C.A. (1992) 'Old Testament in the Gospels,' pp. 579–90 in *Dictionary of Jesus and the Gospels*, J.B. Green, S. McKnight, and I.H. Marshall (eds.), Downers Grove: IVP.

France, R.T. (1971) *Jesus and the Old Testament: His Application of Old Testament Passages to Himself and His Mission*, London: Tyndale Press.

Kimball, C.A. (1994) *Jesus' Exposition of the Old Testament in Luke's Gospel*, JSNTSup 94, Sheffield: Sheffield Academic Press.

Loader, W.R.G. (1997) *Jesus' Attitude towards the Law: A Study of the Gospels*, WUNT 2.97, Tübingen: Mohr Siebeck.

Porter, S.E. (1993) 'Did Jesus Ever Teach in Greek?' *Tyndale Bulletin* 44(2): 199–235.

—— (1994) 'Jesus and the Use of Greek in Galilee,' pp. 123–54 in *Studying the Historical Jesus: Evaluations of the State of Current Research*, NTTS 19, B. Chilton and C.A. Evans (eds.), Leiden: Brill.

—— (2000) *The Criteria for Authenticity in Historical-Jesus Research: Previous Discussion and New Proposals*, JSNTSup 191, Sheffield: Sheffield Academic Press.

Powery, E.B. (2003) *Jesus Reads Scripture: The Function of Jesus' Use of Scripture in the Synoptic Gospels*, Biblical Interpretation Series 63, Leiden: Brill.

Witherington, III, B. (1997) *The Christology of Jesus*, Minneapolis: Fortress Press.

—— (1994) *Jesus the Sage: The Pilgrimage of Wisdom*, Edinburgh: T.&T. Clark.

DENNIS L. STAMPS

JESUS SEMINAR

Founded in 1985 by R.W. Funk, the Jesus Seminar of North America has gained media attention and notoriety for its negative pronouncements regarding the authenticity of the Gospels and even further notoriety for its unconventional portraits of the historical Jesus.

Angry over his sudden termination in 1980 as manager of Scholars Press, the publishing arm of the Society of Biblical Literature, and vowing never to attend another meeting or function of the SBL, Funk founded the Westar Institute and the Jesus Seminar in 1985. Hundreds of scholars were invited to join; initially some 300 did so. However, in due course the membership shrank to approximately eighty more or less active members.

The seminar created a media sensation by deciding the authenticity or inauthenticity of the sayings of Jesus by casting colored beads into a basket. The red bead indicated belief that the saying in question was authentic and accurately represented what Jesus said; the pink bead indicated belief that the saying was authentic but only approximated what Jesus said; the gray bead indicated doubt; while the black bead indicated the belief that the saying in question certainly did not originate with Jesus. The seminar has concluded (see R.W. Funk and R.W. Hoover 1993) that approximately 18 percent of the sayings originated with Jesus (i.e., either red or pink). A similar conclusion was reached with regard to the acts of Jesus (see R.W. Funk 1998).

The conclusions of the seminar have frequently been exaggerated and sometimes outright misrepresented in the popular press. This has only led to further misrepresentation in popular literature (whether supportive or critical), as well as scholarly literature. For attempts to set the record straight, one should consult R.W. Funk (1996) and R.J. Miller (1999).

One of the principal points of confusion concerns the extent to which the seminar's assumptions and findings reflect mainstream scholarship. Members of the seminar rightly insist that many of their views are unexceptional, even if not known by the average church-goer or admitted by the average seminary-trained pastor. These views include acceptance of Markan priority, the existence of the sayings source (i.e., Q), and the use of these sources by Matthew and Luke. Conventional also is the seminar's insistence that the Jesus tradition has been edited, often reflecting beliefs and issues in the life of the early church. Speculation about various layers of tradition in Q, including inferences about various 'communities' who edited and contributed to these layers, may be less conventional and less convincing, but they are not the exclusive domain of the seminar.

However, the seminar does hold to views that mainstream scholarship regards as dubious. These views include a high regard for the antiquity and independence of the extracanonical Gospels, such as the *Gospel of Thomas*, the Egerton Papyrus, and the much disputed 'Secret' Gospel of Mark (for a convenient collection of these and other texts, with brief introductions, see Miller 1992; Crossan 1985; 2nd edn, 1992). Also problematic is the tendency to situate Jesus at the very margins of Jewish Palestine and the Jewish faith. Jesus is seen as uninterested in Israel's scriptures, in Israel's redemption, in eschatology, and in messianism. It is assumed that these interests, well attested in the Gospels themselves, reflect emphases in the early church. How so much discontinuity emerged in such a short time is not convincingly explained. In the opinion of some, the Jesus Seminar reveals inadequate interest and expertise in archaeology, Judaica, and the Dead Sea Scrolls.

Critics of the Jesus Seminar must also realize that a diversity of opinion is to be found among its several members. Crossan's theological views are unexceptional, almost orthodox, yet his solution of the Synoptic Problem is quite unconventional. He argues that the extracanonical *Gospel of Peter* preserves a 'Cross Gospel' that pre-dates the four canonical Gospels and served as their principal source for the Passion narrative (Crossan 1988), that the Markan evangelist made direct use of the Egerton Papyrus, and that Secret Mark pre-dates canonical Mark. His tendency to compare Jesus with Cynicism

(1991) has also been roundly criticized. M.J. Borg (1987), on the other hand, holds to the conventional solution of the synoptic problem and tries to situate Jesus more squarely in a Jewish milieu, but thinks Jesus is best viewed not as a prophet or messiah but as a holy man, who may with profit be compared to Buddha. Some of the comments in Funk's writings sometimes reflect his flight from a fundamentalist upbringing.

The seminar is now addressing itself to the question of the Christian biblical canon and is openly asking if the canon should be altered. Though how open the seminar's leadership is on this question is itself an open question, as seen in its recent decision to refuse publication of a manuscript by L.M. McDonald, which the seminar had commissioned, for failing to reach preferred conclusions.

References and further reading

Bonilla, M. (2002) 'The Jesus Seminar, its Methodology and Philosophy: A Challenge to Catholic Biblical Theology,' *Science et esprit* 54: 313–35.

Borg, M.J. (1987) *Jesus: A New Vision*, San Francisco: Harper & Row.

Crossan, J.D. (1985) *Four Other Gospels: Shadows on the Contours of Canon*, New York: Harper & Row (2nd edn, Sonoma: Polebridge Press).

—— (1988) *The Cross that Spoke: The Origins of the Passion Narrative*, San Francisco: Harper & Row.

—— (1991) *The Historical Jesus: The Life of a Mediterranean Jewish Peasant*, San Francisco: HarperCollins.

Funk, R.W. (1996) *Honest to Jesus: Jesus for a New Millennium*, San Francisco: HarperCollins.

—— (ed.) (1998) *The Acts of Jesus: What Did Jesus Really Do? The Search for the Authentic Deeds of Jesus*, San Francisco: HarperCollins.

—— and R.W. Hoover (eds.) (1993) *The Five Gospels: The Search for the Authentic Words of Jesus*, Sonoma: Polebridge Press/New York: Macmillan.

Miller, R.J. (ed.) (1992) *The Complete Gospels*, Sonoma: Polebridge Press.

—— (1999) *The Jesus Seminar and its Critics*, Sonoma: Polebridge Press.

Veitch, J. (1999) 'The Jesus Seminar: What it is and What it isn't and Why it Matters,' *The Journal of Higher Criticism* 6: 186–209.

Wright, N.T. (1999) 'Five Gospels but no Gospel: Jesus and the Seminar,' pp. 83–120 in *Authenticating the Activities of Jesus*, NTTS 28/2, B.D. Chilton and C.A. Evans (eds.), Leiden: Brill.

CRAIG A. EVANS

JEWISH LITERATURE: NON-CANONICAL

Neither the Bible nor the history of Judaism and Christianity can be adequately studied without close consideration of 'extracanonical' or 'parabiblical' writings. Most notably, scholars have found the non-canonical literature of Second Temple Judaism (Early Judaism, Formative Judaism, or Intertestamental Judaism) to be indispensable for knowledge concerning the development of the history, culture, and religion of Early Judaism (250 BC–AD 200) and early Christianity (first–fourth centuries), including their respective importance as background to the New Testament. Since R.H. Charles' *Apocrypha and Pseudepigrapha* in 1913, the study of noncanonical Jewish literature has increased substantially. The more recent discovery of the manuscripts at Qumran represents another significant step toward the appreciation and scholarship of 'outside books' within the biblical tradition.

Apocryphal and pseudepigraphal literature includes a large number of ancient books, without fixed corpuses, which have affinities with the biblical tradition but did not become part of the canon. Both the Old Testament Apocrypha (*apokrypha*, a transliteration of a Greek neuter plural adjective that means 'hidden' or 'secret') in Protestant circles, or 'Deuterocanonical' books, considered inspired by Roman Catholics since the Council of Trent, and the Old Testament Pseudepigrapha (a transliteration of a Greek plural noun for writings 'with false superscription') form the main corpus of noncanonical Jewish literature presently being studied. For Protestants, the present use of the label 'apocryphal' as noncanonical literature, rather than used pejoratively for heretical literature, goes back to the time of Jerome. Added to the study of Old Testament Apocrypha or 'books between the Testaments' and the Old Testament Pseudepigrapha, are the Dead Sea (Qumran) Scrolls, the works of Josephus and Philo, and rabbinic (Talmudic) literature that has helped to bridge the Testaments, influence our understanding of early Jewish theologies and provide crucial insights into the traditions from which we have the Bible today.

Some of the most valuable contributions from 'outside books' come from their literary portraits of biblical tradition. This literature embodies developmental history of biblical themes, motifs, and ideas, particularly important between the third century BC and the late first century AD. The character and basic framework of many noncanonical Jewish writings reflect the common adoption of biblical style, structure, and content, including borrowed heroes, stories, and rhetoric. False ascription of authorship, for some, to biblical personalities such as Adam, Noah, Abraham, Moses, Elijah, Ezekiel, or Jeremiah, served to further emphasize biblical associations and foster confidence in the texts. The influence of historical biblical books on Judith or the widespread influence of the book of Daniel as a model for later apocalypses exemplify how biblical traditions and traits were carried forward, and how new developments, accentuations, and ways of interpreting the tradition come about. For example, *Jubilees* provides an expansion of biblical narratives by rewriting Genesis and Exodus stories.

The distinguished contribution of noncanonical Jewish literature to the interpretation of the Old Testament, an understanding of the intertestamental period, and as foundational to a perspective on the background to the New Testament cannot be dismissed. The study of these texts is an important and essential step for biblical scholarship that has already yielded large reward.

References and further reading

Charles, R.H. (ed.) (1913) *The Apocrypha and Pseudepigrapha of the Old Testament in English*, 2 Vols., Oxford: Clarendon Press (rep. 1963).

Charlesworth, J.H. (ed.) (1983–1985) *The Old Testament Pseudepigrapha*, 2 Vols., Garden City: Doubleday.

Harrington, Daniel J. (1999) *Invitation to the Apocrypha*, Grand Rapids: Eerdmans.

Metzger, B.M. (1957) *An Introduction to the Apocrypha*, Oxford: Oxford University Press.

Nickelsburg, George W. (1981) *Jewish Literature between the Bible and the Mishnah: A Historical and Literary Introduction*, Philadelphia: Fortress Press.

Pfeiffer, R.H. (1949) *History of New Testament Times, With an Introduction to the Apocrypha*, New York: Harper & Row.

J.C. ROBINSON

JOHANNINE LITERATURE

That the Fourth Gospel and three letters 'of John' belong in some sense together seems indisputable, with the epithet 'Johannine' dependent on the early church's eventual decision that they were the work of the apostle John. Ironically, the Apocalypse, eventually accepted by the church as part of the same author's corpus, is the only one of them to claim authorship by 'John' (Rev. 1:1). Despite some contacts in language which prompt some to speak of a Johannine 'school' (Hengel 1989, 1993), it is now generally recognized as so removed in thought, presuppositions, and probable context as not to be included in 'the Johannine literature.'

The Fourth Gospel has invited contention from the start. This is witnessed by the probable addition of Chapter 21 (or at least of the editorial comment in vv. 24–25), followed before long by the apologetic tone with which Clement of Alexandria describes it as the 'spiritual Gospel,' and by the affirmation, also found in the Muratorian canon, that its author, John, had the collegial support of his apostolic brethren. So too, it has attracted a wide range of interpreters – often cited is the gnostic Heracleon whose commentary on the prologue is known through Origen's refutation of it, while other early commentators include Augustine and Cyril of Alexandria (Wiles 1960). The epithet 'spiritual' to express its 'differentness,' since it allows a number of reapplications, has continued to dog the Gospel. Is the Gospel 'more theological,' a judgment challenged but not entirely annulled by the form- and redaction-critical consensus that all the Gospels are theological interpretations through the prism of faith? Or is it 'not historical,' thereby excluding those reconstructions of the 'historical Jesus' that draw heavily on the supposedly more mystical, and less jarringly 'apocalyptic' piety of its presentation? This assessment too has been challenged both by the reevaluation of Synoptic 'historicity' and by attempts to demonstrate John's indebtedness to scripture as well as his familiarity with Jerusalem's topography and with Jewish customs and exegesis otherwise known from postbiblical sources. Not all advocates of this position, however, would return to building 'a life of Jesus' around the Christology of the Gospel as the key to the inner or explicit workings of Jesus' intentions and mind (but see Robinson 1985). Nonetheless, the shift away from locating John in a thoroughly Hellenistic milieu – with particular affinities with Greek ideas of the 'logos' or perhaps with a Philonic Middle Platonism (Dodd 1954) – and toward affirming its thorough 'Jewishness,' however that be defined, a consequence also of the rediscovery of the variety within first-century Jewishness as well as its capacity for 'Hellenism,' seems unlikely to be reversed. It may well be that the Jewish roots of the Gospel belong not in Judaean – or Jerusalem – centered piety but in more marginal or sectarian trends – witnessed by some parallels with Samaritan or 'Qumranic' thought. This need not lead to a total rejection of an older perspective on 'spiritual,' that John is in some way 'gnostic,' or even that it draws on existing ideas of a descending heavenly redeemer (Bultmann 1971), even if earlier versions of this view which presupposed a highly developed gnostic redeemer myth no longer seem viable. The dualism, the emphasis on 'knowing' and on 'light,' the realized eschatology, and the contrast between below and above, where Jesus and those who believe belong, remain. Such ideas may not have been totally alien to a more Jewish context, and also owe something to the apocalyptic worldview, which has been more sympathetically studied in recent years: indeed John itself is evidence that apocalyptic and gnosticism have more than a little in common, while also indicating the continuing significance of wisdom categories, which are now seen as of primary importance for the Prologue (1:1–18) (Ashton 1991). Here too belongs the debate whether John is less committed to the physical conditions of Jesus' life ('docetic'), or to those of believers' experience (Käsemann 1968), through a realized eschatology or lack of interest in the sacraments – although the latter question has excited remarkably contrasting conclusions (Cullmann 1953). Finally, the characterization 'spiritual' provokes the question of the Fourth Gospel's relationship with the Synoptics, not just as possible sources but also within the canonical framework. The issue is not just did John know and even seek to replace one or more of the Synoptics, a question on which the jury is still out, but does the canonical context provide a necessary control on certain tendencies in the Gospel. These include its high Christology, which moves toward an undervaluing of the historical and human contingency of Jesus, and its dualistic determinism, which moves toward a realized and ahistorical idea of 'the church' (a term absent from the Gospel).

The 'Johannine community' interpretative framework, popular since the late 1960s, has offered a new solution to some of these enigmas (Martyn 2003): here a historical bridge to the earliest church, if not to Jesus himself, is constructed by an 'archaeological excavation' through the layers of experience exposed by a trench through the Gospel–Jewish (–Christian) origins, perhaps (see above) in non-Judaean Judaism, then Samaritan mission (ch. 4), next an opening to the Gentiles (12:20–22), a rift with 'the synagogue' (9:22) stimulated by an increasingly 'high' Christology (10:30–31; 5:18), resulting in a 'sectarian' mentality with clearly defined boundaries and tight inner cohesion (14–17). The resultant 'Johannine community' has commonly been presented as separate from, if not hostile to, other or 'mainstream' Christian groups, perhaps represented by the Beloved Disciple's relationship with Peter (especially 21:20–23), as possibly more egalitarian, and even more open to women (4; 11:20–27; 20:11–18) (Brown 1979). Such interpretations have sometimes been allied with a literary source analysis of the Gospel, chiefly with the attempt to isolate an earlier 'Signs Gospel' with a more primitive Christology. Proposals which reconstruct this (Fortna 1970), or other stages in the growth of the Gospel, have not achieved a consensus; arguments for the redactional editing of the Gospel, for example in an 'ecclesiastical' direction – a focus on future eschatology and sacraments – are not incompatible with such a reconstruction but are now less the focus of concern than they have been. The 'community history' approach has proved attractive because it anchors the Gospel in familiar waters and secures it against new tempests of more recent origin. Prime among these, particularly within the post-Holocaust growing sensitivity to the history and consequences of Christian anti-Judaism, has been the concern about the anti-Judaism or even (potential) anti-Semitism of the Gospel; its characteristic antithetical use of 'the Jews' (NB 8:34–47), hardly neutralized by appeals to 3:16 and 4:22, has earned it the epithet 'the father of the anti-Semitism of the Christians': (Bieringer 2001). Within a 'community' reconstruction, John's language is explained historically by the supposed historical situation of 'exclusion from the synagogue' (9:22) – no longer so confidently identified as the *birkat-haminim* or 'benediction against heretics' traditionally added to the Eighteen Benedictions in the AD 90s – and 'sociologically' by the bitterness of the child rejected by its parent, shaping its own identity by antithesis. 'The Jews' thus become the local 'synagogue' of the Gospel's own time and place, or specifically its leadership, while the dualistic mentality of the Gospel can be seen as characteristic of a sect establishing its own boundaries by mechanisms familiar in more recent times: here John has provided fertile ground for the sociological analysis popular from the 1970s. This response has become the seedbed of important hermeneutical debate: is historical reconstruction, if verifiable, sufficient solution to the (here anti-Jewish) problems of the text, or are not subsequent readings, the continuing history and influence of the text, and its evidential potential, also tasks for the interpreter to address?

Text-based and reader-based approaches, more characteristic from the 1980s on, which emphasize the way the text works in its rhetoric, narrative shape, and construction, or which focus on the role of the reader in the interpretative process, do indeed take the actual effect of the text rather than a putative 'original authorial intention' more seriously (Culpepper 1983; Stibbe 1993). However, these readings may address but do not resolve the issue of 'anti-Judaism,' for example, when they demonstrate that in the narrative context 'the Jews' refer only to the authorities, or when they reduce the Gospel's dynamic to that of the actors on a stage, forgotten when the curtain falls, or when they reintroduce the historical reconstruction by the back if not by the front door in order to recover the expectations of the original readers of the text. Yet such approaches have continued to be a dominant factor in the interpretation of John both through specific studies and in commentaries (Talbert 1992; Moloney 1998). Both 'community' and literary approaches to the Gospel focus particularly on narrative, and so have maintained one major thrust of recent study, namely, to pay less attention to the discourses and so to the theological ideas of the Gospel as a system independently from their narrative framework, and perhaps from their putative historical contextualization. As a corrective to the tendency to read the Gospel from the perspective of later doctrinal, especially trinitarian and Christological, development, this has been important, but it runs the risk of failing to address the ways in which the Gospel has been read for much of its history, and of failing to engage with the ways in which it continues to be used outside biblical scholarship. So, for example, the sources of and the appropriate way of understanding the relationship between Father and Son, or the nature and implications of the attitude to, perhaps engagement with, 'the world' continue to be significant in other arenas.

The history of the community approach has also allowed the Epistles to claim their own place in the story, instead of merely, as often in the past, being used to provide supporting footnotes to a theological or thematic analysis of the Gospel or of 'Johannine thought' (Lieu 1991). This has been aided by a growing consensus that the author of 1 John is to be distinguished from that of the Gospel, if not also from 'the elder' of 2 and 3 John, and by the still dominant but debated sequencing of the texts in that order. First John is not simply a diluted version of the Gospel, either before the latter attained or after it declined beyond its maturity; nor are 2 and 3 John merely affectionate postcards from the now aging disciple, beloved not just by Jesus but also by the churches he has founded – both ways in which they have been viewed in the past. First John, whose literary genre resists parallel, although celebrated by Augustine as the Epistle which teaches much, and all of it about love, has emerged from recent study as consigning to the realm of the Devil those who rejected (poorly defined) aspects of its Christology or soteriology, setting them beyond prayer and certainly beyond the boundaries of love and divine choice (1 John 3:9–15; 4:1–6) (Brown 1983). According to this interpretation, the increasingly enclosed community of the Gospel is now facing internal division, perhaps partly stimulated by opposing interpretations of and claims to that foundational text, and is responding by turning existing strategies of exclusion inwards and by a sharper focus on the cohesion and election of those who remain. Thus the letter is no longer seen, as in earlier interpretations, as defending an already defined 'pure' belief and as erecting a bastion against heretical Cerinthian docetism or gnostic libertinism; instead it demonstrates the process of rhetorically constructing a notion of 'orthodoxy,' with the potential negation of all dissent, dissent whose actual profile resists clear definition; so understood 1 John also provides challenges for the interpreter living in a more ecumenical age. Second and Third John have been located within the same trajectory; while at an interim stage they could be presented as witnesses to the tensions surrounding transitions in patterns of ministry and authority, perhaps from 'charismatic' to monarchical episcopal, more recently they have become worthy of monographs in their own right only by being seen to exhibit the next step, a retreat into name calling – the anonymous 'elder' refusing to enter into debate with those who react in the same way (2 John 10–11; 3 John 9–10) – which has perhaps seemed reassuring to those living in an age where such manoeuvres are all too common (Lieu 1986). Yet the preservation of letters presumably points not only to the victory of their sponsors but also to the eventual integration of the Johannine perspective within the wider church. Such reconstructions (and their highly hypothetical status can be too easily forgotten) offer implicit but hardly unique challenges to the concept of the canon; the earliest church took centuries to reach a consensus about the minor epistles at least, and the consensus may have been reached only on the basis of a confidence few would now accept about the apostolic authorship of any one of these texts. At times it may have seemed as if the interpretation of the Johannine literature has moved from celebration to apologetic; yet the quality and vibrancy of interpretative work indicates that these texts will continue to stimulate historical, literary and theological reflection.

References and further reading

The Gospel and Epistles of John are well represented in all the commentary series and have attracted the attention of many major scholars. The following list includes works referenced above, although in each case others could have been added, together with some (not all!) significant commentaries.

Ashton, J. (1991) *Understanding the Fourth Gospel*, Oxford: Clarendon.

Barrett, C.K. (1978) *The Gospel According to St. John*, London: SPCK, 2nd edn.

Bieringer, R. *et al.* (eds.) (2001) *AntiJudaism and the Fourth Gospel*, Assen: Van Gorcum.

Brown, R.E. (1971) *The Gospel According to John*, 2 Vols., AB, London: Chapman.

—— (1979) *The Community of the Beloved Disciple*, London: Chapman.

—— (1983) *The Epistles of John*, AB, London: Chapman.

Bultmann, R. (1971) *The Gospel of John*, Oxford: Blackwell.

Cullmann, O. (1953) *Early Christian Worship*, London: SCM Press.

Culpepper, R.A. (1983) *Anatomy of the Fourth Gospel: A Study in Literary Design*, Philadelphia: Fortress Press.

Dodd, C.H. (1954) *The Interpretation of the Fourth Gospel*, Cambridge: Cambridge University Press.

Fortna, R. (1970) *The Gospel of Signs*, Cambridge: Cambridge University Press.

Hengel, M. (1989) *The Johannine Question*, London: SCM Press.

—— (1993) *Die johanneische Frage. Ein Lösungsversuch mit einem Beitrag zur Apokalypse von Jörg Frey*, Tübingen: Mohr.

Käsemann, E. (1968) *The Testament of Jesus*, London: SCM Press.

Lieu J. (1986) *The Second and Third Epistles of John*, Edinburgh: T.&T. Clark.

—— (1991) *The Theology of the Johannine Epistles*, Cambridge: Cambridge University Press.

Martyn, J.L. (2003) *History and Theology in the Fourth Gospel*, Louisville: Westminster/John Knox, 3rd edn.

Moloney, F. (1998) *The Gospel of John*, Sacra Pagina, Collegeville: Liturgical.

Robinson, J. (1985) *The Priority of John*, J.F. Coakley (ed.), London: SCM Press.

Schnackenburg, R. (1982) *The Gospel According to St. John*, 3 Vols., New York: Crossroad.

—— (1992) *The Johannine Epistles: Introduction and Commentary*, Tunbridge Wells: Burns & Oates.

Stibbe, M. (ed.) (1993) *The Gospel of John as Literature*, Leiden: Brill.

Talbert, C. (1992) *Reading John: A Literary and Theological Commentary on the Fourth Gospel and Johannine Epistles*, London: SPCK.

Wiles, M. (1960) *The Spiritual Gospel: The Interpretation of the Fourth Gospel in the Early Church*, Cambridge: Cambridge University Press.

JUDITH LIEU

JOSEPHUS (37 BC–AD 100)

In AD 93–94 Josephus produced the *Jewish Antiquities*; in twenty books he wrote the history of the Jewish people from God's creation of the world to the outbreak of the war with the Romans. His source for the first eleven books was the Jewish scriptures, although there has been considerable dispute as to whether he used a Hebrew or a Greek text.

Despite the fact that Josephus, at the beginning of the *Jewish Antiquities*, declared that in his retelling of the biblical story he would neither add nor omit anything (*Ant.* 1.17), he did, in fact, both add a considerable number of haggadic stories and embellishments natural to his own interests, and omit a number of biblical incidents. It seems he recognized the problem his readers might have with this procedure, particularly with regard to the law of Moses, because, at the beginning of a major account of the law (*Ant.* 4.197), he defended the liberty he had taken to classify and rearrange the subject matter: Moses, he asserted, had left the written record in a scattered condition. Such an apologetic comment suggests that his use of scripture was outside the range of accepted interpretation of the period.

In the postbiblical development of Jewish literature we have evidence of a variety of literary forms in which parts of the Pentateuch were used. A number of Hebrew texts based on the Pentateuch, and usually classified by scholars as biblical interpretation or midrash, have been found among the Dead Sea Scrolls.

From the same period fragments of Greek writings also demonstrate ways in which the Pentateuch as a source was being used by Diaspora Jews. Ben Zion Wacholder has suggested that the attempt of the translators of the Septuagint to resolve some of the logical discrepancies in dates in the Pentateuchal text is related to a biblical chronographical school which flourished during the reign of Ptolemy IV Philopater (221–204 BC). The writings of Demetrius the Chronographer, Eupolemus, Pseudo-Eupolemos, and Artapanus have been identified with this school.

Josephus belonged to neither of these traditions. Rather he was the first to publish a comprehensive history of the Jewish people written in the form of Graeco-Roman national history. Maren R. Niehoff has described Josephus as the first to apply 'the sophisticated literary methods of rhetorical historiography' (1996: 31) to the retelling of scripture. Niehoff identifies Dionysius of Halicarnassus as the primary Graeco-Roman model for his undertaking.

Such a new venture in the use of scripture may have, in itself, called for a defensive strategy. Nonetheless, it is also possible that Josephus' specific use of the imperative mood in selected sections of the law of Moses (*Ant.* 4.199–301), by which we can see that the legal sanctions of the Torah have been reorganized to emphasize the social or secular laws as binding because they made up the *politeia* of the Jewish nation, would be in conflict with other contemporary interpretative traditions. In his version of the law, then, he minimized purity and holiness considerations which were still central to the religious lives of many of his Jewish contemporaries.

References and further reading

Attridge, Harold W. (1976) *The Interpretation of Biblical History in the Antiquitates Judaicae of Flavius Josephus*, Missoula: Scholars Press.

Bilde, Per (1988) *Flavius Josephus between Jerusalem and Rome*, JSPSup 2, Sheffield: Sheffield Academic Press.

Feldman, Louis H. (1986) *Josephus: A Supplementary Bibliography*, New York: Garland.

—— (1998a) *Josephus's Interpretation of the Bible*, Berkeley: University of California Press.

—— (1998b) *Studies in Josephus' Rewritten Bible*, Leiden: Brill.

—— (1999) *Judean Antiquities, Books 1–4*, Steve Mason (ed.), *Flavius Josephus* 3, Leiden: Brill.

Franxman, Thomas W. (1979) *Genesis and the 'Jewish Antiquities' of Flavius Josephus*, Rome: Biblical Institute Press.

Niehoff, Maren R. (1996) 'Two Examples of Josephus' Narrative Technique in His "Rewritten Bible",' *Journal for the Study of Judaism* 27: 31–45.

Rjak, Tessa (1984) *Josephus: The Historian and his Society*, Philadelphia: Fortress Press.

Wacholder, Ben Zion (1974) *Eupolemos: A Study of Judaeo-Greek Literature*, Cincinnati: Hebrew Union College.

DONNA R. RUNNALLS

K

KAISER JR., WALTER C. (1934–)

Kaiser received his education from Wheaton College (A.B.), Wheaton Graduate School (B.D.), and Brandeis University (M.A., Ph.D.). He taught at Wheaton College and Trinity Evangelical Divinity School. He is the recently retired President of Gordon-Conwell Theological Seminary where he also serves as professor of the Old Testament. He is the author of more than thirty books and numerous journal articles. His writing is marked by a desire for scholarship combined with a practical emphasis for the preacher in the church.

Kaiser is well known for a collection of 'Toward' books. The main purpose of these books is to enhance discussion on topics that have been generally ignored. In *Toward Old Testament Ethics*, he outlines five existing methods of approaching Old Testament ethics: sociological, moral theology, synchronic, diachronic, and central theme. Realizing the limitations of these approaches, Kaiser proposes a combined approach that he calls 'comprehensive.' It combines the approaches of synchronic (topical with categories derived from the Bible), the diachronic (chronological or developing ethics), and the central theme (for Kaiser, the Holiness of God), with exegetical studies of summarizing texts and apologetic analysis of moral difficulties within the Old Testament.

In *Toward an Exegetical Theology* Kaiser's desire is for preaching that takes scripture seriously in context and meaning while being applied in relevant ways to a modern audience. His methodology is an attempt to move beyond analyzing the text and toward the construction of a sermon that accurately reflects the meaning of the author.

Kaiser's foundation is built upon Karl A.G. Keil's 'Grammatico-historical' method of exegesis. Keil's method sought to establish the meaning of the author's words at a specific time and to a specific audience. Supposedly, the result would be the only meaning that the text could hold. Although agreeing with that perspective, Kaiser states that Keil's method does nothing to help the preacher transition from the authentic meaning of the text to the application or significance of the text today. Kaiser proposes an expanded method entitled the 'syntactical-theological' method.

Kaiser's method consists of five levels of analysis. First, the contextual analysis looks at the text from the canonical, book, sectional, and immediate context. Second, the syntactical analysis explores the type of composition, the paragraph divisions, and the kinds of clauses used. The analysis consists of a syntactical display or block diagram. The complicated diagram isolates each paragraph and its components or phrases to demonstrate the relationship between them. Third, the verbal analysis discusses the words used by the author to find the meaning behind them. The author's culture, figures of speech, parallel passages in this or another's work are compared, and key theological terms are used to enhance the understanding of the words. Fourth, the theological analysis begins the process of bringing the theological meaning of the text acquired in the previous three steps to a modern audience. Lastly, the homiletical analysis moves from the exegetical work to the application of the text in a sermon format.

References and further reading

Kaiser Jr., Walter C. (1981) *Toward an Exegetical Theology: Biblical Exegesis for Preaching and Teaching*, Grand Rapids: Baker Book House.
—— (1983) *Toward Old Testament Ethics*, Grand Rapids: Zondervan.
—— and Mosises Silva (1994) *An Introduction to Biblical Hermeneutics*, Grand Rapids: Zondervan.

H.C. JORGENSEN

KÜMMEL, WERNER GEORG (1905–1995)

Born in Heidelberg, Germany, on May 16, 1905, Kümmel was the son of a professor of medicine. He studied theology in Heidelberg, Berlin, and Marburg, and received his doctorate in Heidelberg in 1928. His dissertation, *Römer 7 und die Bekehrung des Paulus* ('Romans 7 and the Conversion of Paul') was published in 1929, and appeared in a second edition in 1974. From 1930 to 1932, he was an assistant to H. von Soden in Marburg; in 1932 he was appointed *ausserordentlicher* Professor of New Testament at Zurich and in 1946 as full professor. After a year at Mainz, he succeeded R. Bultmann at Marburg, where he served until his retirement in 1973, and where he died in 1995.

Kümmel's scholarly contribution was of two types: first, detailed and richly informed exegesis of important – often controversial – texts, and, second, perceptive analysis of the scholarly work of others in the field of Christian origins. Examples of the first type are his studies of Romans 7, which involved discerning examination of the background of Paul in Pharisaic Judaism, of his changing perception of the role of the law in the purpose of God, and of the anthropological terminology of Paul in which the human condition and the divine solution are perceived. Kümmel perceived that the discussion of the law in Romans was not a purely personal problem nor is it a digression in the letter. Rather, it reflects the conception of the law as central in the divine purpose as perceived by Jews and the transforming effect of his encounter with the risen Christ. Kümmel's examination of the concept of man in the New Testament was set forth in 1961 in *Das Bild des Menschen im Neuen Testament*. The enduring contribution of these studies to biblical scholarship is attested by the republication and revision of these two works in 1974 (*Römer 7 und das Bild des Menschen im Neuen Testament*), and the translation of the latter in a revised and enlarged edition in *Man in the New Testament* (1963).

Another major area of Kümmel's scholarly research was eschatology, which focused primarily on Jesus and his message of the coming kingdom of God: *Verheissung und Erfüllung* (3rd edn, 1956). An English translation appeared in 1957, *Promise and Fulfillment: The Eschatological Message of Jesus*. The study builds on careful analysis of Jesus' proclamation of the coming of the end of the age, examining the texts in the context of Jewish expectations, and avoiding the tactic popular in the mid-twentieth century of reducing the eschatological hope to inner personal experience, based on existentialist or liberal Protestant reductionism ('The kingdom of God is within you').

The compound results of this mode of careful exegetical analysis found expression in a major work of Kümmel, *Die Theologie des neuen Testaments*. The subtitle of this work in its English translation (see Kümmel 1973) reveals its scope and the diversity of theological viewpoints represented within the New Testament. The introduction to the volume notes that it is essential to discern the diversity of perceptions of Jesus and God's purpose through him as represented in the range of New Testament writings. There is no effort on the part of Kümmel to impose a unity or to establish theological norms. The analytical and interpretive strategy appropriate for the New Testament were set out by Kümmel in a joint work with Otto Kaiser, *Einführung in die exegetischen Methoden* (1975), which appeared in English translation in 1981 as *Exegetical Method: A Student's Handbook*. Kaiser's contribution concerns Old Testament exegesis, while Kümmel's focus is the point of view in New Testament exegesis, for which he provides analyses of methods and resources, as well as detailed examples.

Another major mode of scholarly contribution by Kümmel was his comprehensive surveys of New Testament scholarship. The first of these appeared in his *Das Neue Testament: Geschichte der Erforschung seiner Probleme* (1958, 1970), where he traces the prehistory of scholarly study, and then shows the rise of a range of historicocritical methods and the influence on them from the changing intellectual models operative. The book includes not only analyses of the theories of the scholars, but also detailed biographical information about them. An English translation was published in 1972. More direct impact from the wider scholarly world on Kümmel's perceptions of the New Testament appears in his *Einleitung in das Neue Testament* (1973), which was published in an English translation in 1975. There he describes the tools and methods for study of the New Testament, and provides detailed analyses of the books in it, as well as of the formation of the canon and of the textual history of the New Testament. Thus, on exegetical, theological, methodological, and historical grounds, Kümmel's contribution to New Testament scholarship is enduring.

References and further reading

Kaiser, Otto and W.G. Kümmel (1981) *Exegetical Method: A Student's Handbook*, trans. E.V.N. Goetschius and M.J. O'Connell, New York: Seabury, new rev. edn.

Kümmel, W.G. (1957) *Promise and Fulfillment: The Eschatological Message of Jesus*, trans. Dorothea M. Barton, SBT 23, London: SCM Press.

—— (1963) *Man in the New Testament*, trans. John J. Vincent, London: Epworth, rev. and enl. edn.

—— (1972) *The New Testament: The History of the Investigation of its Problems*, trans. S. McLean Gilmour and Howard C. Kee, Nashville: Abingdon Press.

—— (1973) *The Theology of the New Testament According to its Major Witnesses: Jesus – Paul – John*, trans. John E. Steely, Nashville: Abingdon Press.

—— (1975) *Introduction to the New Testament*, trans. Howard Clark Kee, London: SCM Press, rev. edn.

HOWARD CLARK KEE

L

LADD, GEORGE ELDON (1911–1982)

Born a Canadian in 1911, George Eldon Ladd moved to New England where he became an American citizen. His theological education began at Gordon Divinity School. His formal education was continued at Harvard from which he received a doctorate in 1949 for a study of eschatology in the Didache. A move to California followed with his acceptance of a post at Fuller Theological Seminary in 1950 where he remained until his retirement in 1978 and his death in 1982.

His sustained concerns for the church and his continuing commitment to Christian mission gave him the parameters within which he worked. He saw his vocation as preparing students for the ministry, with the vision of an informed clergy and an educated cadre of Christian workers. His impatience with ill-prepared students and insistence on careful exegesis, based on the original biblical texts, bore fruit in the number of students who proceeded to graduate study.

Links with Europe were to prove a formative factor in his thinking; yet he regretted that the rapport was onesided, and with some notable exceptions he found little encouragement from European colleagues. It was on the domestic front that his influence was mainly and deeply felt with the result that in the decade of 1970–1980 he was being hailed as the premier evangelical biblical scholar and writer in North America.

His published works reflected his deeply felt concerns and were a mirror image of the cultural shift occurring in the so-called 'new evangelicalism' of the postwar Protestant-evangelical world. His leading (and initial) interest was in eschatology and in particular the way in which he and his confreres were breaking free from the incubus of the once-dominant dispensational approach to biblical prophecy. His early books on the Parousia teaching both challenged these standpoints and paved the way for his lifelong study of the Kingdom of God in general and the teaching of Jesus in particular. In 1964 this interest bore fruit in his first substantial scholarly work, *Jesus and the Kingdom*, a title he later changed to reflect a revision but with no shift in position. That approach may be called one of proleptic eschatology where Jesus is said to have announced an imminent kingdom yet held out the promise of its future consummation.

The other chief contribution Ladd made was in a bid to cover the leading theological themes of the New Testament from the standpoint of salvation history, broadly following O. Cullmann and W.G. Kümmel. In this way Ladd attempted to come to terms with historical criticism and yet to insist that biblical theology was a prescriptive, not merely a descriptive, discipline of theology. The result appeared in 1974 in his monumental *A Theology of the New Testament*.

Ladd's influence is gauged by his personal effect on a generation of his students and the way in which he steered them (and the reading public) into a reasoned evangelicalism. He was less successful in fulfilling his cherished hopes when his books failed to make a lasting impact on the scholarly guild. His commitment to synthetic biblical theology came to publication as that movement was on the wane, and the appeal to *Heilsgeschichte* as the key to the Bible was put in serious question.

References and further reading

Ladd, G.E. (1964) *Jesus and the Kingdom of God*, New York: Harper.
—— (1974) *A Theology of the New Testament*, Grand Rapids: Eerdmans.
McDonald, L.M. (1998) 'George Eldon Ladd,' pp. 588–94 in *Historical Handbook of Major Biblical Interpreters*, D.M. McKim (ed.), Downers Grove: IVP (with further bibliography).

RALPH P. MARTIN

LATTER PROPHETS

The first stage in the history of the interpretation of prophetic books has to be recovered from the texts themselves in the form of glosses and explanatory and expansive comment. In some instances the process of incremental and cumulative rereading and reworking to which the texts have been subjected can easily be detected. Isaiah 16:12 is a hostile saying directed against Moab to which is added the codicil, 'this is the word that Yahveh spoke about Moab in the past, but now Yahveh says. . .' another equally hostile saying follows. We assume it was added by a scribe who considered himself authorized, perhaps even inspired, to update older prophecies. Isaiah 19:1–15 is a poem threatening Egypt of the Napatan (Ethiopian) dynasty of the eighth century BC with disaster, to which have been added five prose comments all with the common introduction 'on that day.' Four of these reflect the Jewish Diaspora in Egypt centuries later, including the Jewish settlement in the Heliopolis nome (cf. *Aristeas* 13; Josephus, *Ant.* 12:387–8; 13:62–73,283–7). They also manifest an astonishingly receptive attitude toward Assyria and Egypt, traditional evil empires, whose names serve in these addenda as a coded reference to the Seleucid and Ptolemaic Empires respectively.

Eventually the point was reached where such interpretative activity could no longer be carried on within the text but had to take the form of commentary distinct from it. The earliest commentaries on prophetic books known to us are the Qumran *pĕšārîm* (interpretations), mostly fragmentary, on Isaiah, Hosea, Micah, Nahum, and Habakkuk (García Martínez 1966: 185–207). They conform to the simple structure of citing the biblical text verse by verse followed by its *pešer*, and the purpose of the *pešer* is to apply the text to the situation of the sectarian group to which the commentator belongs. Allusions to the Assyrians in Isaiah are therefore taken to refer to the Romans under the code name *Kittim* (e.g., 4QpIsaᵃ = 4Q169 col.I). The angry lion of Nahum 2:12–14, in that prophetic book a figure of the Assyrians making their last stand at Nineveh, is reassigned to the Seleucid ruler Demetrius III who crucified his enemies and attempted to force his way into Jerusalem with the assistance of the Pharisees, sworn enemies of the sect (4QpNah = 4Q169 col.I). The best preserved of these commentaries, on Habakkuk 1–2, leaves the Neo-Babylonian period far behind in reading the biblical text as a running commentary on the persecution of the Legitimate (or Righteous) Teacher (*môreh haṣṣedeq*), the leader of the sect, by his opponent the Wicked Priest. At the point where Habakkuk is told by God to write the vision so that it can be read on the run, the interpreter makes this remarkable comment:

God told Habakkuk to write what was going to happen to the last generation, but he did not make known to him the end of the age. As for what he says, 'so that the one who reads may run,' its *pešer* concerns the Legitimate Teacher to whom God has revealed all the mysteries of the words of his servants the prophets. (1QpHab col.VII)

This is reading, interpretation, as *decryption*. The intention of the original author, even if we could grasp it, is irrelevant. On this view, a prophetic text is a form of automatic writing, a coded message whose referent is quite different from its ostensible meaning as established by the normal literary procedures.

The same interpretative principles are at work in the book of Daniel. The *text* can be a dream in the mind of a mad king (chapters 2 and 4), or in the interpreter's own mind (chapters 7 and 8), or an illegible graffito that appears suddenly on a wall (chapter 5), or a biblical text, Jeremiah 29:10 for example. The *interpretation* (*pĕšar, pišrāʾ* in Aramaic) encapsulates a mystery (*rāz*, Dan. 2:19, 27–28, 30) revealed to the sage by 'the God who reveals mysteries' (2:28). The basic formula elaborated in different ways in these narratives is quite simple and similar to that of the Qumran *pĕšārîm*: this is the dream, here is its interpretation (2:36; 4:18; 5:17, 25–26). All of this takes place in the typically sectarian atmosphere of prayer, fasting, trance experiences, and converse with angelic beings.

Unlike the Qumran community, the first generations of Christians did not produce biblical commentaries; for the first commentary on an Old Testament book we have to wait for Hippolytus' commentary on Daniel in the early third century. Why this is so is not apparent. Perhaps early Christian communities were not learned and textually oriented in the same way and to the same degree as were the Qumran sectarians, but in any case the new genre of gospel, in which the fulfilment of prophecy is a constituent element, substituted for commentary. A variation on the Qumran pattern can be detected in the Gospel of Matthew, especially in the opening chapters. It consists in a brief narrative linked with a prophetic citation by means of the formula 'this happened to fulfill what was spoken through the prophet' or something similar. Most of these units quote Isaiah (Matt. 1:18–23; 2:22–23?; 3:1–3; 4:12–16; 8:14–17; 12:15–21; 21:1–3), the most important of the prophets for early Christianity, but there are also quotes from Micah (2:1–6), Hosea (2:13–15), Jeremiah (2:16–18), and Zechariah (21:1–3).

A feature common to the Qumran *pĕšārîm* and the early Christian text-fulfilment pattern is that prophecy is no longer a matter of direct inspiration by which an individual receives a communication from the superhuman world and passes it on as divine utterance, for example, with the standard prophetic incipit 'thus says Yahveh.' That phenomenon is, of course, attested in the Graeco-Roman world, and even in early Christian churches, but it is at best a marginal phenomenon and, at worst, indistinguishable from the charlatanism that seems to accompany popular religion in all ages including our own. We know, too, from Cicero (*De Divinatione* 56-7), that the famous oracles (Delphi, Dodona, etc.) had long since fallen into disrepute. The question therefore arises: how is this scribalization or textualization of prophecy in early Judaism and, eventually, in early Christianity to be explained? One might think of the influence of Babylonian scribalism once Judah came under Babylonian control in the sixth century BC and, later, became a small part of the Babylon-Transeuphrates satrapy in the early Persian period. The loss of prestige that affected both professional *něbí'îm* (prophets) and free agents alike in the postdestruction period (see, for example, Neh. 6:7, 10–14; Zech. 13:2–6, and the gloss at Isa. 9:15b) would also have contributed to the sense that genuine prophecy was essentially a thing of the past. Optimistic prophets like Hananiah who predicted survival and well-being (Jer. 28:1–4) would obviously have lost their prophetic credentials and perhaps also their lives after the fall of Jerusalem in 586. But the experience of Jeremiah in the immediate postdestruction period shows that even the prophets of doom did not emerge with their reputations intact, on account of both their refusal to intercede and the demoralizing effect of their preaching. On one of the rare occasions in the Hebrew Bible where women get to speak on religious matters, they even accuse Jeremiah of responsibility for the disaster (Jer. 44:15–19).

The first clear indications of this attempt to neutralize the potentially disruptive and destabilizing impact of prophetic activity can be detected in Deuteronomy and the closely related Deuteronomistic History (hereafter the History *tout court*). The prophetic function and the scope of prophetic activity are authoritatively defined and delimited in the law book (Deut. 18:15–22). Prophecy is henceforth to be understood as an extension of the mission of Moses, and therefore in function of the law, a law now available in writing. This redefinition of the prophetic role is illustrated in the History in which 'his [Yahveh's] servants the prophets' play a crucial part in explaining how it all ended so badly: you, people of Israel and Judah, cannot blame God for the disaster since he sent his servants the prophets to warn you about the consequences of neglecting the law, and you disregarded their message. The point is made in the Historian's reflections on the fall of Samaria to the Assyrians:

> Yahveh warned Israel [and Judah] by every prophet and every seer, saying, 'Turn from your evil ways and keep my commandments and my statutes, in accordance with all the law that I commanded your ancestors, and that I sent to you by my servants the prophets.' (2 Kings 17:13)

Other indications of this redefinition can be detected in the History. The Historian mentions several prophets by name, but the prophets to whom books are assigned are conspicuously absent. Isaiah is indeed mentioned in 2 Kings 19–20, but as a man of God, a healer and miracle worker, a kinder and gentler version of Elisha, and therefore quite different from the Isaiah of the book who denounces abuses under Ahaz and Hezekiah in the most categoric terms. The Jonah ben Amittai who supported the campaigns of Jeroboam II of Israel (2 Kings 14:25) supplied a name for the antihero of the book of Jonah, but that is all they have in common.

Equally conspicuous is the the Historian's silence about social abuses, the kind castigated by the canonical prophets, as contributing to the fall of the kingdoms.

The promulgation of a written law, namely, the Deuteronomic law, governing all aspects of the political and religious life of the nation, itself renders the sporadic and often disruptive interventions of prophets unnecessary and undesirable. With a written law, political power, social leverage, and the control of the 'redemptive media' in the society pass into the hands of a class of legal specialists who claim the exclusive right to issue authoritative interpretations of the law. The attitude to prophecy in the Deuteronomic law (Deut. 18:15–22) and the History is a classic instantiation of Weber's theory of charismatic and bureaucratic authority, according to which 'a state of tension is characteristic of any stratum of learned men who are ritualistically oriented to a law book as against prophetic charismatics' (Weber 1982: 395). Reaction from the prophetic side can be heard in Jeremiah's complaint against 'handlers of the law' and the false pen of the scribes who have turned the law into a lie (Jer. 2:8; 8:8). While the prophetic voice was never completely silenced, the voice of legal authority spoke more loudly. The view of prophecy as essentially a phenomenon of the past crystallized into a dogma. Hence the many rabbinic assertions that prophecy came to an end either with the destruction of Solomon's temple (*b. B.Bat.* 12a; *b. Yoma* 21b), or with the death of Malachi, last of the prophets (*b. Yoma* 9b; *b. Sanh.* 11a; *b. B.Bat.* 14b). Only in the last days, the days of Messiah, will prophecy be revived (1 Macc. 4:46; 9:27; 14:41).

Another aspect of this relegation of prophecy to a past epoch can be seen in the growing interest in prophetic biography in the last days of the Kingdom of Judah and the early postdestruction period. A somewhat sketchy biography of Moses as lawgiver and protoprophet can be assembled from Deuteronomy and related texts in the Pentateuch, and the expanded version of the book of Jeremiah, generally attributed to Deuteronomic editors, betrays considerable biographical interest in Jeremiah himself. The book of Isaiah presents an interesting test case which has attracted less attention. In addition to numerous sayings from Isaiah himself and later anonymous authors, Isaiah 1–39 contains several passages which purport to provide biographical information about an Isaiah with a very different prophetic profile. The first of these (Isa. 7:1–17), describing Isaiah's relations with King Ahaz during the military crisis of 734 BC, is introduced in a form identical with 2 Kings 16:5. The second, in which Isaiah walks about naked and barefoot to simulate the fate of Assyrian prisoners of war (20:1–6), is thoroughly Deuteronomic in language and style. The longest of the passages (36–39) has been excerpted from the History (2 Kings 18–20) with minor adjustments, and the overall effect is to redirect attention away from the sayings, many of them extremely harsh, to the person of Isaiah. That the effort was successful can be seen from the ongoing development of what may be called the Isaian biographical tradition. For the author of Chronicles, Isaiah is primarily a historian (2 Chron. 26:22; 32:32) and not at all a critic of society, and about a century and a half later Ben Sira presents him as wonder worker, healer, and foreteller (Sir. 48:17–25). Josephus, too, omits the denunciations and presents Isaiah as a 'man of God' endowed with predictive, therapeutic, and thaumaturgical capacities (Feldman 1997: 583–608). By the time of *The Lives of the Prophets*, written late in the first century AD, a burial tradition in Jerusalem had developed (Hare 1988: 379–86), and the biographical pattern was rounded off with the detailed account of his death at the hands of Manasseh in *The Martyrdom of Isaiah*, a work which comes to us in Ethiopic as part of the Christian *Ascension of Isaiah*, but is acknowledged to be of Jewish origin, perhaps originating at the time of the martyrdom stories in 2 Maccabes 6–7. (Knibb 1985: 143–76).

The turn to biography is one aspect of the broadening range of meanings assigned to prophetic identity and activity and, correspondingly, to *nābî*, the standard term for 'prophet,' which came to be used of any great figure in the tradition, e.g., Abraham and Moses. Isaiah is only one of the prophetic historians on whom the author of Chronicles claims to have drawn; in fact he names prophetic sources so often as to leave little doubt that for him the writing of history was essentially a prophetic activity (1 Chron. 29:29; 2 Chron. 9:30; 12:15; 13:22). The same idea is present in Josephus and was exploited by him to reinforce his own standing as a historian. It explains how, eventually, the historical books came to be categorized as prophetic literature (Former Prophets). By the time of Chronicles, written probably in the last decades of Persian rule, the composition and rendition of liturgical music by Levitical guilds had also come to be regarded as a prophetic activity (1 Chron. 25:1–8). The tradition of David as prophetic musician and composer of Psalms arose in the same circles. A colophon to the Psalms Scroll from the eleventh Qumran cave (11QPs^a) informs us that by means of the prophetic gift he composed 4,050 psalms, and for the same reason early Christian authors could quote psalms as prophetic texts predictive of the momentous events to which the authors were testifying (e.g., Acts 1:20; 2:25–28, 34–35).

We can perhaps date the modern critical study of prophetic texts to the appearance of Heinrich Ewald's *Die Propheten des Alten Bundes* ('The Prophets of the Old Covenant') in 1840. In spite of all the criticisms leveled against the historical-critical method and its practitioners in recent years, it was to the credit of these scholars that the message of social regeneration preached by these dissident intellectuals of the eighth to the sixth century BC, more or less completely submerged as it was by Deuteronomic orthodoxy and its Jewish and Christian continuators, reemerged into the light of day.

References and further reading

Blenkinsopp, J. (1977) *Prophecy and Canon: A Contribution to the Study of Jewish Origins*, Notre Dame: University of Notre Dame Press.

Feldman, L.H. (1997) 'Josephus' Portrait of Isaiah', pp. 583–608 in *Writing and Reading the Scroll of Isaiah*, II, C.C. Broyles and C.A. Evans (eds.), Leiden: Brill.

García Martínez, F. (1996) *The Dead Sea Scrolls Translated: The Qumran Texts in English*, Leiden: Brill/Grand Rapids: Eerdmans, 2nd edn.

Hanson, R.P.C. (1970) 'Biblical Exegesis in the Early Church,' pp. 412–53 in *The Cambridge History of the Bible* I, P.R. Ackroyd and C.F. Evans (eds.), Cambridge: Cambridge University Press.

Hare, D.R.A. (1988) 'The Lives of the Prophets,' pp. 379–86 in *The Old Testament Pseudepigrapha*, II, J. Charlesworth (ed.), Garden City: Doubleday.

Knibb, M.A. (1985) 'Martyrdom and Ascension of Isaiah,' pp. 143–76 in *The Old Testament Pseudepigrapha*, II, J. Charlesworth (ed.), Garden City: Doubleday.

Sawyer, J.F.A. (1993) *Prophecy and the Biblical Prophets*, Oxford: Oxford University Press, 2nd edn.

Weber, M. (1952) *Ancient Judaism*, New York: The Free Press.

Wilson, R.R. (1998) 'The Prophetic Books,' pp. 212–25 in *The Cambridge Companion to Biblical Interpretation*, J. Barton (ed.), Cambridge: Cambridge University Press.

JOSEPH BLENKINSOPP

LAW

The study of the genre of law in the Bible must consider several dimensions: the forms of the laws themselves and the issues regarding the origins of these forms; the content, structure, and purpose of the legal collections found in the Bible, the context of these collections within the larger narrative of the Pentateuch and the purpose for this; and the validity of comparisons between the legal collections found in the biblical text and those occurring in surrounding cultures.

Although law is a recurring topic throughout the Bible, the genre of law is limited to the legal collections in the Pentateuch. Here laws are described and defined in some detail over many chapters of the texts.

Alt (1989) began modern study of the forms of biblical law with this 1934 essay that identified two types of laws: case and apodictic. Case law is that form common to modern law in which a case or situation is given in the apodosis of the stipulation. This is followed by a legal pronouncement regarding that case in the apodosis. Apodictic law is a shortened form of case law in which only the pronouncement (apodosis) is given. Thus it tends to be universal in scope, not limited to a specific case in which the apodosis occurs. The Ten Commandments are all apodictic in form. Alt went on to posit a nomadic origin for the apodictic laws and a source in the Canaanite city states for the case law. However, ancient Near-Eastern legal collections demonstrate a mixture of both forms of law as preserved in urban cultures.

Although individual laws are scattered throughout, the Pentateuch contains five separate legal collections that can be isolated: The Ten Commandments or Decalogue (Exod. 20:1–17; Deut. 5:6–21); the Book of the Covenant (Exod. 20:22–23:33); the Ritual Decalogue (Exod. 34:10–26); the Holiness Code (Lev. 17–26); and the Deuteronomic Code (Deut. 17–26). The Decalogue carries unique authority: it is repeated; it is the first of the legal collections; and it is given in a special way, written by God upon tablets (Deut. 3:14). These commands summarize the whole law. The first half deals with love for God through proper worship and handling of God's name, as well as societal reverence for parents who stand in the place of God (using the verb, 'to honour,' elsewhere used of devotion to God). The remaining laws describe love toward one's neighbor through the respect of life, marriage, property, and one's word. The final command goes to the heart of the others with its emphasis upon the interior disposition. The second half of the Decalogue also implies a hierarchy of values in which human life (forbidding murder) has the highest priority, marriage and societal covenants (forbidding adultery) come second, and property concerns (forbidding theft) are third in priority.

In a similar fashion, the Book of the Covenant begins with concern for the proper worship of God (Exod. 20:22–26 as love for God) and for the proper attitude toward fellow humans who are least able to defend themselves, i.e., slaves (Exod. 21:1–11 as love for one's neighbor). This is followed by societal laws that, as with the Decalogue, place the value of human life first, whether in terms of death (Exod. 21:12–17) or injury (Exod. 21:18–32).

The Ritual Decalogue is not so much ten laws but a collection of warnings regarding worship and involvement with other gods followed by a ritual calendar (Exod. 34:18–26), similar to the one that appears near the end of the Book of the Covenant (Exod. 23:10–19). Like the Ritual Decalogue, the Holiness Code is entirely devoted to laws regarding cultic matters and concerns for proper worship. Indeed, it may be appropriate to connect all the legislation from Exodus 25 to Leviticus 26 as one collection concerned with the Tabernacle, rituals, uncleanness, the cultic calendar, and promises and blessings (Wagner 1974).

The Deuteronomic Code most likely contains legal material arranged to approximate the order of the Decalogue (Wiener 1932; Kaufman 1979). Briefly, the general order is: right worship and rejection of apostasy (Deut. chs 12–14); the sabbath and other holy days (chs 15–16); societal authority (chs 17–18); homicide and war (chs 19–21); adultery and illicit mixtures (22:1–23:18); theft and property concerns (23:19–24:7); false witness and oppression (24:8–25:4); and (least likely as far as the structure) coveting (ch. 25).

The laws all occur in narrative contexts. Thus the Decalogue and the Book of the Covenant form the means by which Israel at Sinai becomes a holy people and actualizes its status as a special possession of God (Exod. 19 and 24). The Ritual Decalogue is a reaffirmation of Israel's covenant status after its idolatrous sin with the Golden Calf (Exod. 32). This apostasy and the ritual violations of Nadab and Abihu (Lev. 10) initiate the concerns for holiness and cultic cleanness throughout the priesthood and all of Israel in the Holiness Code. Finally, the Deuteronomic legislation forms part of Moses' farewell address to prepare a new generation of Israel for life in the Promised Land. It is part of the whole book of Deuteronomy, which itself is a covenant document.

Ancient Near-Eastern legal collections present similar laws as those found in the Pentateuch. All these collections date no later than the twelfth century BC. The similarities in some forms of law are offset by differences in priorities and values. The Code of Hammurabi, for example, begins with laws concerning theft of temple property. As a whole it is concerned to demonstrate the piety and justice of the Babylonian king before his divine sovereign. However, like the biblical legal collections, the ancient Near-Eastern texts are intended as representative models of justice. Their study provides examples for applications into the many specific circumstances that these laws do not address.

Legal material is also found in the treaties of the Hittites (fourteenth to twelfth centuries BC) and the Neo-Assyrian and Aramaic treaty texts. Despite recent objections, the Hittite suzereign-vassal treaties best parallel the covenant of Deuteronomy (Kitchen 1989). In addition to other common elements, both regularly contain historical prologues before the laws (designed to give evidence of advantages of loyalty to the treaty/covenant in the past; cf. Deut. 1–3) and blessings (for obedience) as well as curses (for disobedience) at the end of the treaty/covenant document (Deut. 28). The historical prologue and blessings sections appear unique to the second millennium BC treaty texts. Later treaties tended to omit these sections.

The legal genre continues to be studied in terms of literary patterns (Sprinkle 1994), ethics (Wright 1990; Matthews, Levinson, and Frymer-Kensky 1998), and its context in the area of ancient Near-Eastern law (Boecker 1980; Westbrook 1988; Hess 1999). The literary patterns can reveal palistrophic structures such as the one that Douglas (1993) identified in the Holiness Code of

Leviticus. The center of this structure, and the key point of significance, is Leviticus 19:18 and the command to 'love your neighbor as yourself.' The area of ethics is one of the most fruitful for the study of biblical laws. Wright (1990) identifies principles of justice and fellowship behind the focus of the covenant and law upon the land itself. Hoffner's recent edition of the Hittite laws is one example of the increasing number and type of parallels that can be identified with biblical laws (Hess 1999).

References and further reading

Alt, Albrecht (1989) 'The Origins of Israelite Law,' pp. 79–132 in *Essays on Old Testament History and Religion*, trans. R.A. Wilson, The Biblical Seminar, Sheffield: Sheffield Academic Press.

Boecker, Hans Jochen (1980) *Law and the Administration of Justice in the Old Testament and Ancient East*, trans. J. Moiser, Minneapolis: Augsburg.

Douglas, Mary (1993) 'The Forbidden Animals in Leviticus,' *Journal for the Study of the Old Testament* 59: 3–23.

Hess, Richard S. (1980) *The Structure of the Covenant Code: Exodus 20:22–23:33*, unpublished Th.M. thesis, Trinity Evangelical Divinity School, Deerfield, IL.

—— (1999) Review of H.A. Hoffner, Jr., *The Laws of the Hittites: A Critical Edition*, Leiden: Brill, 1997, *Journal of Biblical Literature* 118: 171–2.

Hoffner, Harry A., Jr. (1997) *The Laws of the Hittites: A Critical Edition*, Documenta et Monumenta Orientis Antiqui: Studies in Near Eastern Archaeology and Civilisation 23, Leiden: Brill.

Kaufman, Stephen A. (1979) 'The Structure of the Deuteronomic Law,' *Maarav* 1: 105–58.

Kitchen, K.A. (1969–1990) *Ramesside Inscriptions: Historical and Biographical*, 8 Vols., Oxford: Blackwell.

Matthews, Victor H., Bernard M. Levinson, and Tikva Frymer-Kensky (eds.) (1998) *Gender and Law in the Hebrew Bible and the Ancient Near East*, JSOTSup 262, Sheffield: Sheffield Academic Press.

Sprinkle, Joe M. (1994) *The Book of the Covenant: A Literary Approach*, JSOTSup 174, Sheffield: Sheffield Academic Press.

Wagner, Volker (1974) 'Zur Existenz des sogenannten "Heiligkeitsgesetzes",' *Zeitschrift für die alttestamentliche wissenschaft* 86: 307–16.

Westbrook, Raymond (1988) *Old Babylonian Marriage Law*, Archiv für Orientforschung Berheft 23, Horn: Ferdinand Berger & Söhne.

Wiener, Harold M. (1932) 'The Arrangement of Deuteronomy XII–XXVI,' pp. 26–36 in *Posthumous Essays*, H. Loewe (ed.), London: Humphrey Wilson.

Wright, Christopher J.H. (1990) *God's People in God's Land: Family, Land, and Property in the Old Testament*, Grand Rapids: Eerdmans/Carlisle: Paternoster.

RICHARD S. HESS

LETTERS

Summaries or portions of letters do exist in the Old Testament (e.g., 1 Kings 21:8–9; Ezra 4:11–22). However, when someone speaks of the biblical letter genre they are usually making reference to the twenty-one New Testament books that appear to be complete letters as they stand. Accordingly, the letters found in Acts 15:23–29 and 23:26–30, and those in Revelation 1–2, would be subsumed under the genre of the specific book in which they are found.

Research into the biblical letter genre is a product of the twentieth century. Previously, as part of sacred scripture, the New Testament letters were generally regarded as abstract theological and moral works rather than as addressing particular historical situations. This changed following the discoveries (nineeenth century and early twentieth century) of papyri containing Hellenistic letters. By comparing the biblical letters to other Hellenistic letters, the former began to be viewed as actual letters. Adolf Deissmann laid the groundwork for study in this area.

Based upon his observations Deissmann divided the New Testament letters into two categories: 'real' or 'nonliterary' letters and 'literary' letters (also called 'epistles'). Paul's letters (with the exception of the Pastoral Epistles) belong to the former category and the remaining belong to the latter. Real letters are those which are private, occasional, and artless. Literary letters, on the other hand, are public, artistic, and impersonal, and sometimes originated with several copies being produced. These general distinctions are still commonplace. However, these identifications should be considered more as poles along a continuum rather than as separate categories. The classifications of public (political) and private are also inappropriate because they are anachronistic. In actuality, Hellenistic realms of politics, family, and friendship were not clearly distinct. Hellenistic letters are better classified according to their particular purpose. For example, Philemon is a letter of mediation. Other types of letters include letters of introduction, recommendation, petition, rebuke, exhortation, and praise.

Like letters today, the general purpose of a Hellenistic letter was to inform a person who was elsewhere. Letters were written as a substitute for the author's presence and for live conversation. Particular occasions and circumstances relating to the sender and recipient necessitated their use. In the early stages they were mostly official letters, but later came to include private letters reflecting a need, and subsequently became more common for general purposes such as maintaining relational ties. Letters provided a means for giving instruction and information, dialogical interchange, and a permanent record of interaction (e.g., legal texts, official letters with government decrees). Although the letters were written, many of the New Testament letters would have been received orally (some read out loud in churches) because only 15 to 20 percent of men were literate.

Hellenistic letter writing developed from the fourth century BC and was an established practice by the Common Era. Accordingly, distinctive form and customary phraseology can be identified within the letters of this time. For example, the circumstances leading to a request are often presented using the genitive absolute and other participial constructions. Besides slight changes in form, New Testament letters differ from other Hellenistic letters due to their being Christianized. White has noted that 'The Apostle Paul appears to be the Christian leader who was responsible for first introducing Christian elements into the epistolary genre and for adapting existing epistolary conventions to express the special interests of the Christian community' (1986: 19).

Most New Testament letters are much longer than other Hellenistic letters, probably due to their instructional function (of those found among the Egyptian papyri the average length was 275 words). The New Testament letters do, however, follow the general form of Hellenistic letters, consisting of three parts: opening, body, and closing. The existence of distinct sections does not, of course, mean that the content of the letter and the author's thoughts are similarly divided. Pauline letters follow a modified pattern and consist of as many as five distinctive sections: opening, thanksgiving, body, paraenesis, and closing. It is debated whether or not the two additional sections should be considered distinct units.

The Hellenistic letter opening identified the sender and recipient, usually in the form of 'A to B greeting' (cf. Acts 15:23; James 1:1). Impersonal letters can be identified by the placement of the receiver's name first (although found mainly in letters of petition). All the New Testament letters (excluding the anonymous letters) identify the sender before the recipient. A lengthy opening or closing of a letter reveals a close relationship between the sender and recipient. Letters between close people tend to include a health wish (3 John contains the only clear New Testament example). Paul modifies the standard letter opening by occasionally mentioning a co-sender/author and by describing the sender or recipient in detail. Following this method, New Testament letter senders identify themselves as an 'apostle,' 'servant of Christ,' or 'elder.' The author might also remind the recipient of the status or privileges of Christians (e.g., 'set apart for the gospel'). Furthermore, rather than expressing 'greetings' or a health wish, Paul, and others following him, would express a desire for 'peace' (perhaps reflecting the Hebrew *Shalom*), 'grace,' or 'mercy.'

Hellenistic letters between friends or family might also include a prayer to god(s) on behalf of the recipient. Paul modifies this in his thanksgiving section. Here he gives thanks to God for the recipients' faithfulness. He might also encourage recipients and offer prayers to God on their behalf. This section sometimes foreshadows the topics of discussion found in the body of the letter. Second and Third John contain expressions of joy which perform a function similar to Paul's thanksgiving. That is, they put the recipients in a good mood to accept the message.

The body of a letter contains the primary information intended to be conveyed. In the New Testament this includes Christian doctrine, the occasion for writing, and the situation and relation between the sender and recipient.

The existence of body-openings, body-middles, and body-closings has been identified within the body of Hellenistic letters. Transitions between the units are noted by formulaic constructions. A body-opening generally employs two formulae such as 'I want you to know that.' In Hellenistic letters, authors expressed astonishment (*thaumazō*) to signify dissatisfaction that the receiver had not written for a while. Paul uses such phrases analogously to express dissatisfaction regarding a practice of the receivers. The body-closing generally includes three formulae: the reasons for writing, a phrase expressing or encouraging an expected response, and mention of further expected contact (e.g., a forthcoming visit). Paul uses a 'confidence' formula not used in other Hellenistic letters expressing that he is confident of the outcome of his writing (e.g. Philem. 21–22).

The existence of a distinct paraenetic section in Paul's writings is questionable. This supposed section consists of exhortations regarding Christian moral behavior. Of the Pauline letters, Romans possibly seems to exhibit this as a distinct section, but horatory material is also found elsewhere in the letter (cf. Stowers 1986: 23, contra Doty 1973: 37). In contrast to the view that Pauline letters exhibit distinct paraenetic sections, whole letters, such as 1 Thessalonians or 2 Timothy, might be regarded as paraenetic.

The closing of a Hellenistic letter might include another health wish, a parting word of 'goodbye' or 'farewell' (cf. Acts 15:29), and sometimes even a date. New Testament letters depart the most from the wider Hellenistic letter form in this area. None contains a health wish, a goodbye, or a date. Rather, we find greetings (e.g., 3 John), doxologies (e.g., Jude), benedictions (e.g., 1 Peter), or some combination of the three.

References and further reading

Aune, David E. (1987) *The New Testament in Its Literary Environment*, Philadelphia: Westminster Press.

Deissmann, Adolf (1978) *Light from the Ancient East: The New Testament Illustrated by Recently Discovered Texts of the Graeco-Roman World*, trans. Lionel R.M. Strachan, Grand Rapids: Baker, new and rev. edn (first German edition 1908).

Doty, William G. (1973) *Letters in Primitive Christianity*, Philadelphia: Fortress Press.

Exler, Francis X.J. (1923) *The Form of the Ancient Greek Letter of the Epistolary Papyri (3rd c. BC–3rd c. AD)*, Chicago: Ares.

Murphy-O'Connor, Jerome (1995) *Paul the Letter-Writer: His World, His Options, His Skills*, Good News Studies 41, Baltimore: Michael Glazier.

Stirewalt, M. Luther, Jr. (1993) *Studies in Ancient Greek Epistolography*, SBL Resources for Biblical Study 27, Atlanta: Scholars Press.

—— (2003) *Paul the Letter Writer*, Grand Rapids: Eerdmans.

Stowers, Stanley K. (1986) *Letter Writing in Greco-Roman Antiquity*, Library of Early Christianity 5, Philadelphia: Westminster Press.

White, John L. (1972a) *The Body of the Greek Letter: A Study in the Letter-Body in the Non-Literary Papyri and in Paul the Apostle*, SBL DS 2, Atlanta: Society of Biblical Literature.

—— (1972b) *The Form and Structure of the Official Petition: A Study in Greek Epistolography*, SBL DS 5, Atlanta: Society of Biblical Literature.

—— (1984) 'New Testament Epistolary Literature in the Framework of Ancient Epistolography,' in *Aufstieg und Niedergang der römischen Welt*, 2.25.2, 1730–1756, H. Temporini and W. Haase (eds.), Berlin: de Gruyter.

—— (1986) *Light from Ancient Letters*, Foundations and Facets: New Testament. Philadelphia: Fortress Press.

ANDREW K. GABRIEL

LEXICONS (THEOLOGICAL)

1 Introduction

Theological lexicography, in one sense, is as old as lexicography of the Bible, since the lexicons that were created from the outset were concerned with capturing the meanings of the words that were found within the biblical text. However, despite the limitations of biblical lexicography (especially New Testament lexicography, as noted in the entry on Greek grammar and lexicography), theological lexicography took on a more specialized sense as it came to be developed and exemplified especially in the twentieth century. As a result, a number of tools were developed that fit within the category of theological lexicography, and they have come to be associated with a particular type of lexicography that emphasizes the theological usage found within the biblical documents.

2 Development of theological lexicography

The theological lexicon in its more narrow and restricted sense is a product that developed along with the, largely American, biblical theology movement (see Childs 1970). Brevard Childs defines a number of major elements of the biblical theology movement (1970: 32–50). These include: the rediscovering of a theological dimension in the Bible, rather than seeing it simply in terms of the history of religions or purely historical criticism; the unity of the Bible as a whole, rather than seeing it in terms of the individual Testaments; the fact that God was revealed in history, allowing both the divine and human elements to be seen in the biblical accounts; the distinctiveness of the Bible against its environment, in which the Bible occupied a unique place in the history of ancient thought and development; and a distinctive biblical mentality, in which biblical writers were identified with a Hebraic mind-set that was created and shaped by the use of the Hebrew language, with its unique peculiarities, and in distinction from the Greek mind-set, created by the peculiarities of the Greek language. Thorlief Boman, reflective of this movement, wrote a book entitled *Hebrew Thought Compared with Greek*, in which he attempted to draw out these specific differences in terms of both language and mentality, in effect reflecting what has been called linguistic determinism, that is, one's language is determinative for thought processes. This notion was extended in the work of Oscar Cullmann on differences in conceptions of time, entitled *Christ and Time*. H. Wheeler Robinson and Aubrey Johnson, among others, emphasized the notion of corporate personality as fundamental to understanding the Semitic mentality, and, by extension, the biblical conception of the human in terms of corporate elements. Many of the characteristics of the biblical theology movement, and especially many of the elements of the language-mentality determinism, are reflected in several specific reference works, characterized by what Childs calls 'semantic theology' (Childs 1970: 47). These include Gerhard Kittel and Gerhard Friedrich's *Theological Dictionary of the New Testament* (1964–1976), Alan Richardson's *A Theological Word Book of the Bible* (1950), and J.-J. von Allmen's *Vocabulary of the Bible* (1958), among others.

The notions associated with theological lexicography, and especially some of the major works produced by the movement, have had a tremendous impact upon the study of the Bible in the second half of the twentieth century and beyond. This is so much the case that, in numerous instances, some of the highly doubtful presuppositions of the movement are still given the status of proven conclusions (see Porter 2003).

3 Criticism of theological lexicography

Most of the planks of the biblical theology movement have been severely attacked, if not fatally damaged, by subsequent research (see Childs 1970). As a result, for example, the notion of corporate personality has been shown to be mistaken in its formulation, definition, and exemplification within the biblical documents (see Rogerson 1970). The notion of complete linguistic determinism has also been called into serious question, since it is often based upon mistaken characterizations of the Hebrew and Greek languages, and neglects contrary evidence (see Porter 1997: 124–9). Most important, however, is the attack that James Barr marshaled in his *The Semantics of Biblical Language* (1961) and *Biblical Words for Time* (1962), in calling into serious question both the basis and the conclusions of the biblical theology movement in particular as they pertained to theological lexicography.

Barr in his 1961 work analyzed in detail the kind of work found in Cullmann's, Boman's, and especially Kittel and Friedrich's work, and disputed their methods of analysis and the results of their study. Thus, for example, he called into question the characterization of Hebrew as a dynamic language versus Greek as a static language, pointing out that their verbal systems have much more in common with regard to conceptualization of action than had been realized. Further, and more directly relevant for theological lexicography, Barr attacked the use of etymologies and related types of arguments. These were often used in theological lexicography to account for the meanings of words, but they often failed to take into account that these etymologies were either false etymologies or of no direct relevance to the contemporary usage of a word. Tracing the development of the theological lexicographical tradition of Kittel back to the work of Cremer, Barr pointed out that there were distinct efforts made to show the unique usage or meanings of words in the Bible. This went along with the assertion that such usage created the way that the biblical writers thought of the material they were writing, to the extent that the Greek words used in the New Testament became unique vehicles for the conveyance of Semitic thought. Barr showed in numerous ways – by disputing false etymologies, by noting the influence of later discoveries on the supposed uniqueness of the biblical usage, and especially by paying close attention to units larger than the word, including the sentence and context – that these kinds of results could and needed to be disputed. Along the way, he coined several terms that have come to be associated with the distortions or abuses of theological lexicography. These include 'illegitimate totality transfer,' where the total theological weight and significance of a word was transferred to a single instance of usage regardless of whether the context supported such transference (Barr 1961: 218); 'illegitimate identity transfer,' where the mistake is made of transferring identities of two things as if they were the same, simply because they may be referred to using the same word (Barr 1961: 218); and the equation of word and concept, in which lexical items are confused with the concepts that they can be made to represent. Others have followed in Barr's line continuing to criticize such theological lexicography. Despite the fact that Barr's work struck a death knell for such methodologically bankrupt work, there are those who, whether out of ignorance or outright wilfulness, continue to practice such methods, thus compromising the validity of the results of their work.

References and further reading

Barr, J. (1961) *The Semantics of Biblical Language*, Oxford: Oxford University Press.

—— (1962) *Biblical Words for Time*, London: SCM Press.

Boman, T. (1960 [1954]) *Hebrew Thought Compared with Greek*, London: SCM Press.

Childs, B.S. (1970) *Biblical Theology in Crisis*, Philadelphia: Westminster Press.

Cullmann, O. (1951 [1946]) *Christ and Time: The Primitive Christian Conception of Time and History*, London: SCM Press.

Johnson, A. (1949) *The Vitality of the Individual in the Thought of Ancient Israel*, Cardiff: University of Wales Press.

Kittel, G. and G. Friedrich (1964–1967 [1933–1973]) *Theological Dictionary of the New Testament*, trans. G.W. Bromiley, Grand Rapids: Eerdmans.

Porter, S.E. (1997) 'The Greek Language of the New Testament,' pp. 99–130 in *Handbook to Exegesis of the New Testament*, S.E. Porter (ed.), Leiden: Brill.

—— (2003) 'An Assessment of Some New Testament-Related Assumptions for Open Theism in the Writings of Clark Pinnock,' pp. 160–82 in *Semper Reformandum*, S.E. Porter and A.R. Cross (eds.), Carlisle: Paternoster.

Richardson, A. (ed.) (1950) *A Theological Word Book of the Bible*, London: SCM Press.

Robinson, H.W. (1981 [1936–1937]) *Corporate Personality in Ancient Israel*, C. Rodd (ed.), Edinburgh: T.&T. Clark, 2nd edn.

Rogerson, J. (1970) 'The Hebrew Conception of Corporate Personality: A Re-Examination,' *Journal of Theological Studies*, New Series 21: 1–16.

von Allmen, J.-J. (ed.) (1958 [1954]) *Vocabulary of the Bible*, London: Lutterworth.

STANLEY E. PORTER

LIBERATION THEOLOGICAL INTERPRETATION (LATIN AMERICA)

In 1492 the Bible arrived in Latin America hand in hand with the sword of Spanish conquistadors. Since then the way that the Bible has been read in Latin America has reflected the political allegiances of the church on the continent (Dussel 1992). During the colonial period (from the sixteenth to the beginning of the nineteenth century) interpretations of the Bible usually reflected the alliance between the Catholic Church and the Spanish or Portuguese crowns. Colonial interpretations spoke of the God-given authority of Iberian monarchs as the rightful rulers of the indigenous peoples of the New World. A notable exception to this was the Dominican Friar Bartolomé de las Casas, a sixteenth-century dissident appalled at the inhuman treatment of the Indians (Gutiérrez 1993).

After Latin American independence in the first two decades of the nineteenth century the church continued to seek political alliances with conservative social elites, and biblical interpretation continued to reflect a deeply conservative social ethic. It emphasized personal morality, individual piety, and ecclesial authority but had little to say about social injustice or political issues other than the rightful status of the church in society. It was not until the late 1960s in the aftermath of Vatican II that a significant minority of the Catholic Church shifted their political allegiance. In response to the social injustices of Latin American societies, the Latin American bishops adopted an 'option for the poor' at their Episcopal conferences at Medellín (1968) and Puebla (1979) (Cleary 1985; Smith 1991). Liberation theologians who committed themselves to solidarity with the people and their struggles offered new understandings of the Bible in terms of political and spiritual liberation (Gutiérrez 1973).

The liberationist approach to the Bible stressed the central message of social justice and holistic liberation to be found in Exodus, the Prophets, and the Gospels. Liberation theologians explored biblical themes alongside insights from the Catholic social tradition and contemporary social analysis – especially Marxism – that highlighted the political and economic nature of the biblical understanding of sin and salvation.

Liberation theology has also been distinctive in rejecting the common split between academic scholarship and the ordinary believer. Liberation theologians have sought an organic solidarity with the people by which their work can most directly serve the people's needs and be stimulated by what the people themselves have to say. This happened most often in the 'base ecclesial communities' (*comunidades eclesiales de base* or CEBs) that developed and spread throughout Latin America, In these small groups, which were particularly strong in Brazil, church members met together in neighborhood groups to read and reflect on the Bible together (Boff 1985). Usually the groups had someone who acted as a facilitator but the facilitator was not supposed to instruct but to provoke the discussion. This approach drew on the Catholic Action pastoral circle (commonly referred to as 'see-judge-act') and was influenced by the consciousness-raising (conscientization) pedagogy developed by the Brazilian educator Paulo Freire. Discussions of the Bible in the CEBs focused on the relevance of the texts to the group's everyday experiences and brought their own life situations to bear on the understanding of the Bible's message (Mesters 1989). These 'popular' interpretations complemented and stimulated the theologians and biblical scholars working at a 'professional' level in universities or seminaries. The mutual interaction between the popular and professional – usually mediated through pastoral agents of the church who acted as facilitators – rooted liberation readings of the Bible in Latin American reality as well as the world of biblical scholarship (Boff and Boff 1987).

Often these communal discussions of everyday experiences prompted by the text lead to a deeper understanding of wider structural issues in society. For example, in Brazil a discussion of hunger and personal poverty might eventually lead on to the consideration of the foreign debt and the systems of world trade. In Central American countries like Nicaragua and El Salvador, the experiences of repression and military conflict led to reflection on the structural reasons (political and economic) for the region's civil wars (Cardenal 1976–1982).

Much discussion of the liberationist approach has highlighted the selective means by which it focuses attention on political liberation and social justice. For example, in reading the Gospels particular emphasis is given to: the proclamation of the Kingdom of God; the promise to the poor; the role of Christ as liberator. However, liberation theologians suggest that neutrality is a spurious ideal for a Christian theologian or biblical scholar in Latin America. They say in contexts of institutionalized oppression such as Latin America it is not a matter of biblical scholarship *taking sides* but of *changing sides*.

The role of Marxist analysis and the readiness to move from the biblical word to the contemporary world have also been a center of the controversy surrounding liberation theology. In 1984 the dangers of Marxist reductionism were emphasized in a special Instruction issued by the Vatican that criticized certain aspects of liberation theology. It should, however, be said that the influence of Marxism was strongest in the earlier works of liberation theologians, and it has been given much less attention in works after the 1970s. This is partly because other concerns, for example, spirituality, culture, women's experience, and the environment, started to receive more attention in the 1980s and 1990s. Some of the most creative work of recent years has been done by women theologians in Latin America who have integrated feminist concerns into liberation theology at a much deeper level than any of their male colleagues (Tamez 1989).

The main proponents of liberation theology have been systematic theologians and committed parish priests (for example, Gustavo Gutiérrez, Leonardo and Clodovis Boff, Jon Sobrino, and Juan Segundo) rather than specialist biblical experts. Even biblical specialists such as Jorge Pixley and Elsa Tamez have difficulty in finding the time or resources to keep abreast of the very latest developments in biblical studies elsewhere, due to other pressures on their time. Some European and North American biblical critics have therefore questioned the scholarly depth and rigor of the liberationist approach to the Bible.

During the twentieth century the center of Christianity moved inexorably south as the numbers of Christians in Africa, Asia, and Latin America continued to rise and the numbers in Europe and North America have fallen. Latin American liberation theology and the CEBs confronted a crisis in the 1990s and are now much less prominent as organized movements (Vásquez 1998; Tombs 2002). However, the theological influence of the southern hemisphere is likely to increase further in years to come. In future the contextual theologies developed in Lima and São Paulo may rival the centers of theology in Europe and North America. Viewed from this perspective the rise of Latin American and other liberation theologies may only be a taste of what is to come in biblical studies.

References and further reading

Boff, Leonardo (1985) *Church: Charism and Power: Liberation Theology and the Institutional Church*, trans. J. Diercksmeier, New York: Crossroad/London: SCM Press.

Boff, Clodovis and Leonardo Boff (1987) *Introducing Liberation Theology*, trans. P. Burns, Maryknoll: Orbis /Tunbridge Wells: Burns & Oates.

Cardenal, Ernesto (1976–1982) *The Gospel in Solentiname*, trans. D.D. Walsh, 4 Vols., Maryknoll: Orbis.

Cleary, Edward L. (1985) *Crisis and Change: The Church in Latin America Today*, Maryknoll: Orbis Books.

Dussel, Enrique (ed.) (1992) *The Church in Latin America: 1492–1992*, trans. P. Burns, Maryknoll: Orbis/ Tunbridge Wells: Burns & Oates.

Gutiérrez, Gustavo (1973, 1974) *A Theology of Liberation: History, Politics and Salvation*, C. Inda and J. Eagleson (trans. and eds.), Maryknoll: Orbis/London: SCM Press.

—— (1993) *Las Casas: In Search of the Poor of Jesus Christ*, trans. R.R. Barr, Maryknoll: Orbis.

Mesters, Carlos (1989) *Defenseless Flower: A New Reading of the Bible*, Maryknoll: Orbis.

Pixley, George V. (1981) *God's Kingdom: A Guide for Biblical Study*, Maryknoll: Orbis/London: SCM Press.

Rowland, Christopher and Mark Corner (1990) *Liberating Exegesis: The Challenge of Liberation Theology to Biblical Studies*, London: SPCK.

Smith, Christian (1991) *The Emergence of Liberation Theology: Radical Religion and Social Movement Theory*, Chicago: University of Chicago Press.

Sobrino, Jon (1994) *Jesus the Liberator: A Historical-Theological View*, trans. P. Burns and F. McDonagh, Maryknoll: Orbis.

Tamez, Elsa (ed.) (1989) *Through her Eyes: Women's Theology from Latin America*, Maryknoll: Orbis.

Tombs, David (2002) *Latin American Liberation Theology*, Religion in the Americas Series 1, Leiden: Brill.

Vaage, Leif. E. (ed.) (1997) *Subversive Scriptures: Revolutionary Readings of the Christian Bible in Latin America*, Valley Forge, PA: Trinity Press International.

Vásquez, Manuel A. (1998) *The Brazilian Popular Church and the Crisis of Modernity*, Cambridge Studies in Ideology and Religion, Cambridge: Cambridge University Press.

DAVID TOMBS

LIETZMANN, HANS (1875–1942)

In the period between the First and Second World Wars, from 1919–1939, Hans Lietzmann was the leading liberal New Testament scholar in Germany. He was born in Dusseldorf but grew up in Wittenberg where he attended the local secondary school. During this time his first interest was in the natural sciences and especially astronomy. He was an avid observer of the night sky and in his later days even wrote a little book on the use of small telescopes in astronomical observations. His schoolteachers aroused his interest in classics and philology and Lietzmann devoted himself to a study of the classics and the New Testament. During this same period he encountered the higher-critical views, which undermined his faith in the scriptures. His former orthodox theology was also shaken by the teaching of the Jena zoologist Ernst Haeckel, the foremost proponent in Germany of Darwin's theory of evolution and foremost advocate of the new evolutionary explanations for the origin of the universe.

Lietzmann spent his first university year in 1892 at Jena where Haeckel was at the height of his career. Friedrich Nippold, the leading opponent of the Ritschlian school, was his main teacher, but after one year Lietzmann moved to Bonn where he became assistant to Hermann Usener (1834–1905), one of the leading lights behind the history of religions school. Usener believed that Christianity was an offshoot of the ancient mystery religions and that all the principal doctrines of Christianity were based on myths. It was Usener's teaching which finally caused Lietzmann to abandon the last remnants of any orthodox views of the Christian faith he might have retained. Henceforth he followed the liberal viewpoint of Harnack.

In the years 1905–1924 Lietzmann was professor of New Testament at Jena. He was called to Berlin as Harnack's successor in 1921, but declined the appointment. However, two years later in 1923, as the political situation in the Weimar Republic deteriorated, he accepted another call to the more conservative Prussian capital. Here he remained to the end of his life in 1942. From 1906 he edited the *Zeitschrift für die neutestamentliche Wissenschaft.*

Lietzmann's interpretation of the New Testament springs from his a-theological viewpoint, where God as a supernatural being is excluded from any involvement in the history of the early church. For Lietzmann the New Testament is basically the theological extension of primitive legends. Many stories about Jesus, he thought, had been grossly misunderstood. As an example he suggested that Jesus, arriving one day at Jerusalem exhausted by the journey, availed himself of a donkey to ride the last stages into the city. From this simple story the later myth of the Palm Sunday entry arose with its added messianic connotations. It is significant to note that Lietzmann's first major work was a study of the 'Son of Man.' Lietzmann claimed that Jesus never used this term to characterize himself, but that the early church ascribed it to him. Jesus called himself merely 'the Man.'

This liberal/rationalistic viewpoint formed the basis of all Lietzmann's investigations into the history of the New Testament and the early history of the church. Liberal interpretation for him meant primarily the freedom to interpret the Bible within a nonsupernatural framework. His whole investigation of the New Testament centered in effect on the question of how the early Christian doctrines could have arisen from nonsupernatural origins.

References and further reading

Lietzmann, *A History of the Early Church*, trans. Bertram Lee Woolf, 4 Vols., Cleveland: World Publishing.

—— (1962) Autobiography pp. 331–68. in *Kleine Schriften* III, *Texte und Untersuchungen* 74, Berlin: Akademie-Verlag.

—— (1979) *Glanz und Niedergang der deutschen Universität: 50 Jahre deutscher Wissenschaftsgeschichte in Briefen an und von Hans Lietzmann (1892–1942)*, Kurt Aland (ed.), Berlin: de Gruyter.

HORTON HARRIS

LINGUISTIC CRITICISM

1 Introduction
2 The principles of linguistic criticism
3 Examples of linguistic criticism
4 Implications for biblical criticism and interpretation

1 Introduction

Linguistic criticism is a label that aptly describes a number of different forms of biblical criticism that have their bases in the principles and practices of modern linguistics. The history of modern biblical criticism begins with the use of a grammar-based method that developed into higher criticism until sometime in the middle of the last century, when a variety of new forms of criticism began to be utilized. The rise of the use of these latter forms of criticism is linked to the development of many of these areas as new and emerging forms of scientific exploration. For example, modern linguistics is often dated to the seminal lectures of Ferdinand de Saussure, delivered at the beginning of the twentieth century and posthumously published in 1916. The use of modern linguistics in biblical criticism has developed relatively slowly, especially when compared with other forms of emerging criticisms, such as sociology. There are several reasons for this. One is that there is a widespread perception in biblical criticism that our knowledge of the ancient biblical languages is already exhausted, and that there is little need for further study. Such is clearly not the case, as new studies provide new insights into the languages. A second reason is that there is a perception that methods of interpretation developed within modern and contemporary contexts, such as the exploration of child language or of spoken dialects, have minimal value for biblical study. A third is that linguistics, like many other disciplines, comes with its own technical vocabulary, and this technical vocabulary is often seen as threatening, since it suggests that a scholar needs to learn a new form of critical discourse to participate. A fourth and final reason is that there is a mixed response that is at the same time suspicious of new readings of texts on the basis of new methods and easily dismisses any method that does not put forward significant and new results that challenge the older ones. Traditional critics in this instance fail to realize that providing a surer foundation for a traditional exegetical position can still constitute a significant contribution.

2 The principles of linguistic criticism

The principles that underlie linguistic criticism begin with the orientation of modern linguistics (see Cotterell and Turner 1989), but with a few noteworthy and significant differences. These differences include the recognition that only a finite corpus of texts is available for study, and that this corpus consists entirely of written documents, with no spoken stratum. Another is that there are no native speakers or informers to provide information regarding usage. All the analysis must be determined on the basis of comparative and other linguistic data. A last difference is that this study involves the numerous imponderables of the ancient world, thus excluding the kind of knowledge that is often present of the modern world.

In the light of these differences from linguistics in the modern world, those who are intending to utilize linguistic criticism tend to approach the biblical text with at least some of the following presuppositions in place. First, there is an important correlation between form and function. Without native speakers, it is often difficult to test one's results, unless one can establish a functional difference on the basis of difference in form. Another presupposition is that language is a complex system or set of systems, in which there is an intricate interplay between various elements. These systems are really the heart of the language under examination, because each element of the system enjoys a complex relationship with the other elements. These systems offer choices between forms and establish the meaningful relations between various component parts of the system. A third presupposition is that whereas there is much value in studying individual words and phrases of a language, there is an ever-increasing recognition that one must study units beyond the word and phrase, and even the sentence. This suggests that units larger than the word, such as the clause or sentence, or even larger units, are the basis for determining meaning in a text. A fourth and final presupposition is that recent developments in computer technology, including not only databases, retrieval systems, and annotated texts, but also the creation of structured corpora of ancient texts, provide a major resource for quantifying meaningful statements about the behavior of the language in question.

Even scholars not focused on linguistics recognize the contribution that Noam Chomsky (1957, 1965) has made to modern linguistic investigation, with his development of phrase structure grammar and then later forms of transformational grammar. Some of his work has been brought to bear on biblical interpretation, but other work has found that his framework is too constricting. However, there are a number of different models of linguistic analysis that have been applied to the Bible. These include tagmemics, systemic and functional linguistics, and construction grammar, to name a few.

3 Examples of linguistic criticism

There have been a number of examples of linguistic criticism that have been practiced in recent times on both the Old and New Testaments. Admittedly, few of those who have engaged in the following discussions would themselves label their method linguistic criticism, but their work nevertheless falls within the parameters of how that term is being defined here.

The first type of criticism is concerned with individual elements within the larger language system. The most important discussion has focused upon the Greek verbal structure. Whereas previous periods of scholarship had seen verbal structure in terms of time (when an event occurred) or the kind of action (*Aktionsart*), recent research in Greek verbal structure sees the verbs functioning as indicators of the perspective of the speaker on the action (see the work of Porter 1989; Fanning 1990; McKay 1994; Decker 2001). Concerning Greek verb structure, several of the ways in which linguistic criticism varies from previous grammatical analysis is in terms of recognizing that the individual tense-forms in Greek function as part of a larger verbal system. Another is the willingness to look beyond the traditional categories to those in apparent contradiction with those found in modern Western languages, such as German or English. Similar discussion has taken place regarding the Hebrew verbal system (see the work of S.R. Driver 1874 and more recently Niccacci 1990). Whereas previous analysis had seen the verbal forms as either time-based or in terms of comparative Semitic usage, recent scholarship has argued that the verbal forms are perspectival regarding the action.

Linguistic criticism is a fitting label to apply to a number of other recent grammatical investigations as well. These include the transitivity patterns in language (Martín-Asensio 2000), case grammar (Wong 1997; Danove 1993, 2001), corpus linguistics (O'Donnell in Porter and Reed 1999: 71–117), and speech act theory (Botha 1991), to name several important examples. There have also been a number of studies that have utilized the Chomskyan grammatical framework (Schmidt 1981; Louw 1982; Palmer 1995). Recent work has extended into the semantic realm in significant ways, promoting the pragmatically based theories of relevance (see Black 2002 on conjunctions).

The most inclusive form of Greek-language analysis that might be labeled linguistic criticism is the area referred to as discourse analysis (also known as text-linguistics). There have been major advances in discourse analysis, and it continues to offer potential for further study of both Testaments. Whereas other forms of grammatical analysis are often concerned with individual elements within language, such as the individual word or a particular phrase, discourse analysis goes much further and argues that the meaningful unit for textual analysis is the discourse. This shift in perspective is fundamental to interpretation. In the past, individual linguistic elements were often studied in isolation. However, discourse analysis requires that all of the various levels of language be drawn into the equation. This includes data from various structural units, including the word, clause, sentence. In fact, discourse analysis generates far too much potential data than can reasonably be analyzed. Once one has the data, the discourse analyst must determine whether to take a top-down approach or a bottom-up approach. The top-down approach starts from the largest recognizable unit of structure, such as the genre, and then investigates how the larger units exercise a controlling influence upon each of the individual smaller units. The bottom-up approach shifts the emphasis, with the result that each smaller unit becomes a building block for increasingly larger units of structure and meaning. To date, there have been only a few significant discourse analyses (e.g., Guthrie 1994; Cook 1995; Booth 1996; Reed 1997; Becker 2003; Dawson 1994; Heimerdinger 1999; cf. Porter and Reed 1999; Groom 2003; Levinsohn 1992; Black, Barnwell, and Levinsohn 1992), but these individual studies have had great significance, since they have opened up new ways of examining the biblical text.

4 Implications for biblical criticism and interpretation

Linguistic criticism is one of several emerging forms of criticism. In those few places where it has been applied, there have often been highly constructive results that have emerged. Some of these include the realization that the authors of the biblical texts have used a variety of linguistic means at their disposal to create, shape, and develop their writings, and that there are a variety of linguistically based means to analyze this usage. Rather than simply concentrating on individual words and phrases, linguistic criticism has drawn attention to a number of larger patterns of usage. Some of the results have threatened to overturn tried and true conclusions reached by other means. Even though linguistic criticism can possibly provide new and substantial support for traditional interpretation, linguistic criticism has often been dismissed because it dares to challenge the traditional perspective. One is compelled to see individual linguistic elements not in isolation but as a part of a complex system of individual but related elements. Like many of the other emerging criticisms, linguistic criticism tends to be much more self-consciously and overtly holistic and integrative in its approach than more traditional historical-critical methods.

References and further reading

Becker, E.-M. (2003) *Schreiben und Verstehen*, Tübingen: Francke.

Black, D.A. with K. Barnwell and S. Levinsohn (eds.), *Linguistics and New Testament Interpretation: Essays on Discourse Analysis*, Nashville: Broadman Press.

Black, S.L. (2002) *Sentence Conjunctions in the Gospel of Matthew*, Sheffield: Sheffield Academic Press.

Bodine, W. (ed.) (1995) *Discourse Analysis of Hebrew Literature*, Atlanta: Scholars Press.

Booth, S. (1996) *Selected Peak Marking Features in the Gospel of John*, New York: Lang.

Botha, J.E. (1991) *Jesus and the Samaritan Woman*, Leiden: Brill.

Chomsky, N. (1957) *Syntactic Structures*, The Hague: Mouton.

—— (1965) *Aspects of the Theory of Syntax*, Cambridge, MA: MIT Press.

Cook, J.G. (1995) *The Structure and Persuasive Power of Mark: A Linguistic Approach*, Atlanta: Scholars Press.

Cotterell, P. and M. Turner (1989) *Linguistics and Biblical Interpretation*, London: SPCK.

Danove, P.L. (1993) *The End of Mark's Story*, Leiden: Brill.

—— (2001) *Linguistics and Exegesis in the Gospel of Mark: Applications of a Case Frame Analysis and Lexicon*, Sheffield: Sheffield Academic Press.

Dawson, D.A. (1994) *Text-Linguistics and Biblical Hebrew*, Sheffield: JSOT Press.

Decker, R.J. (2001) *Temporal Deixis of the Greek Verb in the Gospel of Mark with Reference to Verbal Aspect*, New York: Lang.

de Saussure, F. (1959 [1916]) *Course in General Linguistics*, trans. W. Baskin, London: Collins.

Driver, S.R. (1998 [1874]) *A Treatise on the Use of the Tenses in Hebrew and Some Other Syntactical Questions*, Grand Rapids: Eerdmans.

Fanning, B.M. *Verbal Aspect in New Testament Greek*, Oxford: Clarendon.

Groom, S. (2003) *Linguistic Analysis of Biblical Hebrew*, Carlisle: Paternoster.

Guthrie, G.H. (1994) *The Structure of Hebrews: A Text-Linguistic Analysis*, Leiden: Brill.

Heimerdinger, J.-M. (1999) *Topic, Focus and Foreground in Ancient Hebrew Narratives*, Sheffield: Sheffield Academic Press.

Levinsohn, S.H. (1992) *Discourse Features of New Testament Greek*, Dallas: SIL.

Louw, J.P. (1982) *Semantics of New Testament Greek*, Philadelphia: Fortress Press.

McKay, K.L. (1994) *A New Syntax of the Verb in New Testament Greek: An Aspectual Approach*, New York: Lang.

Martín-Asensio, G. (2000) *Transitivity-Based Foregrounding in the Acts of the Apostles: A Functional-Grammatical Approach to the Lukan Perspective*, Sheffield: Sheffield Academic Press.

Niccacci, A. (1990) *The Syntax of the Verb in Classical Hebrew Prose*, Sheffield: JSOT Press.

Palmer, M.W. (1995) *Levels of Constituent Structure in New Testament Greek*, New York: Lang.

Porter, S.E. (1989) *Verbal Aspect in the Greek of the New Testament, with Reference to Tense and Mood*, New York: Lang.

—— and J.T. Reed (eds.) (1999) *Discourse Analysis and the New Testament*, Sheffield: Sheffield Academic Press.

Reed, J.T. (1997) *A Discourse Analysis of Philippians*, Sheffield: Sheffield Academic Press.

Schmidt, D.D. (1981) *Hellenistic Greek Grammar and Noam Chomsky*, Chico: Scholars Press.

Wong, S.S.M. (1997) *A Classification of Semantic Case-Relations in the Pauline Epistles*, New York: Lang.

STANLEY E. PORTER

LITERARY DEVICES

> 1 Biblical narrative (prose)
> 2 Biblical poetry

The literature of the Bible, like the literature of virtually any culture, is expressed in two main forms, prose and poetry, which are not always easily distinguishable. In general, prose more closely resembles the conventions of verbal speech, while poetry displays a higher degree of literary artifice and verbal craft.

1 Biblical narrative (prose)

Biblical prose narrative is similar in many ways to the literary conception of a story. Approaching it as one might approach a contemporary short story can often be enlightening, providing that one never loses sight of the primarily historical and theological nature of the text. All stories, to be stories at all, must have four basic elements: plot, character, setting, and point of view.

1.1 Plot

The term *plot* deals specifically with the events in a story, and how those events are rendered, arranged, and causally connected. Plot is made possible by the presence of conflict, or the oppositions of persons or forces. A plot will most commonly be constructed in such a way that it has a beginning (where the conflict is introduced), a middle (where the conflict is heightened), and an ending (where the conflict is addressed and often resolved). In the case of biblical narrative, where the events described are historical, these elements of plot may be difficult to delineate, but they are often present, as, for example, in the story of the Flood (Gen. 6:9–8:22).

In Genesis 6:11, the central conflict of the Flood story is introduced: God sees the wickedness of humanity and determines to destroy humankind. The conflict is heightened when Noah builds the ark, and the floodgates are opened (Gen. 7:11). The conflict is finally addressed and resolved when relations between God and humanity are restored; Noah sacrifices burnt

offerings to the Lord, and the Lord promises never again to destroy all living creatures

1.2 Character

For a plot conflict to be possible, at least one main character is necessary. This central, essential character, who is the focus of the story, is the protagonist. The protagonist may be either sympathetic or unsympathetic. If a story's conflict occurs between two characters, the character in opposition to the protagonist is commonly referred to as the antagonist.

Unlike contemporary examples of the story, biblical narrative does little to explore the psychology of personality of its characters. As is the case with folkloric tales, characters in biblical narrative are known primarily by their actions, not by their motives or personality. Little description or commentary is offered, and when it does occur, it tends to play an integral role on the level of plot, as is the case with Bathsheba's beauty (2 Sam. 11:2), Goliath's enormity (1 Sam. 17:4), or Samson's hair (Judg. 13:5). As Ryken points out, much of the characterization of biblical characters is left to the reader's inference. Readers must decide what the details revealed in the story tell them about the character; they must 'transform the particulars into an overall portrait of a person' and must also 'determine whether a character is good or bad . . . in a given trait or action' (Ryken 1987: 75).

In the case of the Flood story, the events of the plot clearly overshadow Noah as a character. Very little about Noah is revealed beyond his name and God's declaration that he is the most righteous man among his generation. Noah's motivation and personality are completely eclipsed by his actions. The reader is left to infer what Noah thought or felt at any point in the narrative. The other human characters in the story appear only as names.

1.3 Setting

Setting refers not only to the geographical and historical point at which the story occurs, but also to any other aspect of a story's physical environment. This may include time of day, locale, weather conditions, and many physical props.

The use of setting in biblical narrative serves literary as well as historical purposes. While the settings of biblical narrative are, of course, determined by where the events actually occurred, a great deal of latitude is seen in the degree of specificity and emphasis which various elements of setting receive. References to specific localities stress the historical veracity of the story, and when a setting is directly specified or developed with description, there is typically a correspondence between the setting and the character or event contained therein. Satan's temptation of Christ, for example, is an event completely dependent on its wilderness setting. Setting may also serve the important secondary purposes of creating atmosphere or acting symbolically, as is the case with the three days Jonah spent in the belly of the great fish.

The settings evoked in the Flood narrative work on several of these levels. The mention of Mount Ararat (Gen. 8:4) underscores the historical veracity of the account. The entire story relies on the ark as a setting, so a great deal of information about the dimensions of the ark and its construction is relayed. For the same reason, much time is also spent describing the weather conditions at many different points in the narrative. The floating ark and the rising waters also serve an explicitly symbolic function (1 Pet. 3:21).

1.4 Point of view

Except for a few rare occasions when the narrator of a biblical narrative takes part in the action (as is the case, for example, in the 'we' sections of Acts), biblical narratives are typically related from a fully omniscient, third-person point of view. The narrator stands apart from the events of the story; displays omniscience, in that he can reveal the thoughts and motives of any character; is omnipresent, in that he is not confined by time or space but is rather an invisible presence in all parts of the narrative. The fully omniscient, third-person narrator may also set the story aside to directly address the reader with some revelation, explanation, or ideological comment. As Longman points out, 'such a narrative strategy gives the impression of an all-knowing mind standing behind the stories of the Bible – a mind that in the context of the canon must be associated with God himself' (Longman 1993: 75).

In the story of the Flood, this God-like narrator is obvious. The narrator is able to reveal the thoughts of God (Gen. 6:11) and events that no human participant in the story could possibly know (Gen. 7:20). He is an invisible presence both *with* Noah on the ark and *apart* from Noah as the waters destroy every breathing creature not on the ark (Gen. 7:23).

2 Biblical poetry

As is the case in the literature of many cultures, the line that distinguishes biblical prose from biblical poetry is not clear. There are some features of language that are found much more frequently in what are clearly poetry books such as the Song of Solomon, which may serve to distinguish them from such narrative books as 1 Kings. Some of these common features of biblical poetry are parallelism, 'distilled' language, and figurative language.

2.1 Parallelism

The unit of construction in poetry varies from language to language, culture to culture, and is often derived from stressed features of a given language. Traditional English poetry, for example, is often constructed out of units of accentual syllabic verse. In other words, a line is commonly constructed of a certain number of units of stressed and unstressed syllables. In other languages, where stressed syllables play a lesser role, the basic unit of verse may be something else entirely.

With regard to biblical poetry, however, scholarly pursuit of a metric pattern has yielded no convincing conclusions. As Alter concludes, 'there is little evidence that the counting of stresses was actually observed as a governing norm for a poem . . .' (Alter 1985: 9). Rather than seeking a uniformity of syllables, Egyptian and Canaanite poetry, including Hebrew poetry, seeks a uniformity of units.

The Hebrew poetic line is often said to be composed of two or more *cola* (*colon*, in the singular), each of which is a short clause. The most common line is *bicoloic* and consists of two cola, each containing three words, though *monocolonic* and *tricolonic* lines are quite common, as are cola that contain two or four words. Alter finds such attempts at metric description misleading: 'the older scholarly term "hemistich" and the current "colon" (plural "cola") both have misleading links with Greek versification, the latter term also inadvertently calling up associations of intestinal organs and soft drinks' (Alter 1985: 9).

Similarly, rhyme, the other common trait of traditional English verse, is absent in biblical poetry. It has been argued, however, that the primary purpose of rhyme, which is to make verse more easily memorized, finds a parallel in the acrostics of biblical verse, where each successive unit of verse begins with a successive letter of the Hebrew alphabet. Psalms 9, 10, 25, and 34 are examples of such 'alphabet poems.'

While biblical poetry shows no clear metrical unit, much of it is constructed in units of thought, which is commonly called *parallelism*. Parallelism has often been misleadingly defined as a kind of repetition found in successive lines, but, as Longman writes, 'The new paradigm for understanding parallelism is development rather than equivalence. The biblical poet is doing more than saying the same thing twice. The second part always nuances the first in some way' (Longman 1993: 83).

Ryken defines parallelism as 'two or more lines that form a pattern based on repetition or balance of thought or grammar. The phrase *thought couplet* is a good working synonym' (Ryken 1987: 362).

Ryken distinguishes four main types of parallelism. 'Synonymous parallelism' consists of repeating an idea more than once in successive lines, using similar sentence construction (Ps. 47:5). In 'antithetic parallelism,' the second line makes the same point as the first in a contrasting way (Prov. 12:26). In 'climactic parallelism' the first part of the first line is repeated as the first part of the second, but is then completed differently (Ps. 96:7). What Ryken calls 'synthetic parallelism' may not seem like parallelism at all. It is when the second line expands or completes the thought introduced in the first, without any form of repetition (Ps. 103:13). Since there is no repetition in structure, this can only be called parallelism under Ryken's loose notion of a 'thought couplet.'

Also related to parallelism is the chiastic structure of two lines, which are placed in parallel structure. A chiasm occurs when the terms of a pair of parallel lines are reversed between the first and second lines to produce an AB/BA structure. Such is the case in Ecciesiastes 3:8: 'a time to love and a time to hate/a time for war and a time for peace,' where the positive and negative terms of 'love' and 'hate' are replaced, in reverse order, by their counterparts 'war' and 'peace.'

2.2 'Distilled' language

Another distinguishing feature of biblical poetry is the distilled language by which it is expressed. The language of Hebrew poetry is concise, terse, and often elliptical. It tends to forgo conjunctions, relative pronouns, and the direct object marker (Longman 1993: 82). Furthermore it frequently makes use of ellipses, or the omission of one or more words that are clearly implied but are not supplied. In Hebrew poetry, the ellipsis often takes place between the first and second of a pair of parallel lines, as is the case in Psalm 98:7: 'Let the sea resound, and everything in it,/the world, and all who live in it.'

2.3 Figurative language

Finally, biblical poetry is marked by its frequent use of figurative language. Figures of speech occur when a writer, for the sake of vividness, ignores the denotations of words to focus on the connotations, and thus to make a comparison that is not strictly logical but which may be very evocative. When we read 'Your hair is like royal tapestry' (Song of Sol. 7:5) we are invited not to ponder literal similarities, but rather similarities of connotation.

Such figures of speech abound in biblical poetry, in the form of simile (Ps. 1:3) and metaphor (Song of Sol. 1:15). Conceits, more elaborate and extended metaphors, also appear, as is the case in Psalm 23. Personification (Prov. 20:1) and apostrophe, the direct addressing of an absent person or personified thing (Ps. 14:6), are also frequently employed in biblical poetry.

References and further reading

Alter, Robert (1985) *The Art of Biblical Poetry*, New York: Basic Books.

Alter, Robert and Frank Kermode (1987) *The Literary Guide to the Bible*, Cambridge: Harvard University Press.

Caird, G.B. (1980) *The Language and Imagery of the Bible*, Grand Rapids: Eerdmans.

Long, Thomas G. (1989) *Preaching and the Literary Forms of the Bible*, Philadelphia: Fortress Press.

Longman, Tremper, III (1993) 'Biblical Poetry,' pp. 80–94 in *A Complete Literary Guide to the Bible*, Leland Ryken and Temper Longmann III (eds.), Grand Rapids: Zondervan Publishing House.

Ryken, Leland (1987) *Words of Delight: A Literary Introduction to the Bible*, 'Grand Rapids: Baker Book House.

—— and Tremper Longman III (eds.) (1993) *A Complete Literary Guide to the Bible*, Grand Rapids: Zondervan Publishing House.

Silderschlag, Eisig (1974) 'Hebrew Poetry,' in *Princeton Encyclopedia of Poetry and Poetics*, Princeton: Princeton University Press, enl. edn.

Sternberg, Meir (1985) *The Poetics of Biblical Narrative*, Bloomington: Indiana Univesity Press.

PAUL BUCHANAN

LITERATURE: BIBLICAL INFLUENCE

1 The influence of the Bible on English literature
2 The influence of the Bible on North American literature in English

As an influence on literature written in English, no other source approaches the profound and extensive influence of the Bible. Indeed, Northrop Frye, in his influential *Anatomy of Criticism*, calls the Bible 'the major informing influence on literary symbolism' (Frye 1957: 316). From the Anglo-Saxon period to the present day, the Bible continues to be the most frequently alluded to text in English-language literature.

C.S. Lewis distinguishes between the Bible as a literary *source*, which 'gives us things to write about' and a literary *influence*, which 'prompts us to write in a certain way' (1963: 15). As a *source*, the Bible has provided countless novels, poems, and plays with plot elements and characters – from Adam's Fall as told in *Paradise Lost* (1667) to his appearance in Robert Frost's (1874–1963) 'Never Again Would Birds' Songs be the Same' (1942). As an influence, the language, themes, and imagery of the Bible have become woven into every genre of literature. Indeed many universal symbols (symbols that do not derive their meaning solely from the text in which they appear) are clearly rooted in the Bible: the serpent, the dove, the rainbow, the lamb, the garden – the list goes on and on.

1 The influence of the Bible on English literature

Beginning in the Anglo-Saxon period, Caedmon (c. 658–680), called the earliest of English poets, based his first composition on the biblical account of Creation.

This poetic paraphrasing of biblical stories continues in the ninth and tenth centuries in works attributed to Cynewulf (ninth century), most notably the poem 'Christ.'

The influence of the Bible on English literature experienced a second upsurge in the fourteenth century, when two distinct threads of influence are distinguishable. At this point in history, many works continue to retell or paraphrase biblical events, but a second form of influence can be seen in contemporary treatments of vernacular literature. It is at this point that the Bible as both *source* and *influence* can first be readily distinguished. The Pearl Poet (writing 1365–1400) employs the Bible in both ways. Scripture is used as source in 'Patience,' a retelling of the story of Jonah, and as influence in 'Sir Gawain and the Green Knight,' which merely makes use of biblical themes.

The most notable poet of the fourteenth century, Geoffrey Chaucer (1342–1400), while not classed among those who relied on the Bible as a *source*, clearly falls into the category of those with a biblical *influence*. Work notes that as we listen to Chaucer's pilgrims in *Canterbury Tales* 'we hear them talking in the language of Scripture' (1917: 127).

In the fifteenth century, with the condemnation of Wycliffe's vernacular translation of the Bible, and the passage of laws designed to discourage other such translations, the influence of the scripture on literature waned, but resurged in the sixteenth century with the availability of a number of fresh Bible translations along with the Book of Common Prayer. The King James Version, completed in 1611, had an enormous effect on literature, which continues to this day.

The seventeenth century saw the Bible reach its apex in England as a foundational text for virtually every major writer of both poetry and drama. Biblical imagery is woven into the poetry of John Donne (1572–1631) and George Herbert (1593–1633), as it is in the plays of Christopher Marlowe (1564–1593) and William Shakespeare (1564–1616). John Milton's (1608–1674) *Paradise Lost* (1667) and *Paradise Regained* (1671) perhaps represent a high point in English literature inspired and informed by scripture.

In the late seventeenth century, however, with the onset of the Enlightenment and an increasing religious skepticism, biblical allusion virtually disappears from English literature, with the notable exception of John Bunyan (1628–1688).

By 1764, in *The Vicar of Wakefield*, we find Oliver Goldsmith (1730–1774) reflecting on a bygone era when the Bible was a social and literary force. Only rarely in the eighteenth century, among the likes of Isaac Watts (1674–1748) and Henry Fielding (1707–1754), did English writers make clear and extended allusions to scripture.

In the writings of William Blake (1757–1827) and in the works of the Romantics, the influence of the Bible again clearly appears, but the biblical text is made subservient to the poet's work. Scripture is *used* in Blake's *Songs of Experience* (1794) and *The Marriage of Heaven and Hell* (1793), but it no longer provides a moral or theological *foundation* for the literature, it is merely first among many sources of allusion.

In the Victorian period the Bible became more widely drawn upon as a source in English literary works, especially among the poets, as is the case with Robert Browning's (1812–1889) *Saul* (1847). Many authors of the period make extensive use of biblical sources in the service of antireligious themes, as is the case with George Eliot's (1819–1880) *Silas Marner* (1861) and Thomas Hardy's (1840–1928) *Jude the Obscure* (1897).

In the first half of the twentieth century, the Bible continued to be a primary source and influence in English literature, used in works ranging from Graham Greene's (1904–1991) *The Power and the Glory* (1940), which depicts the Christian church as indestructible, to William Butler Yeats' (1865–1939) 'The Second Coming' (1921), which predicts the imminent death of Christianity's influence.

Since the latter half of the twentieth century, the influence of the Bible on English literature has not been nearly as pervasive as its influence on North American literature.

2 The influence of the Bible on North American literature in English

The Puritans who settled the New England colonies in the New World brought with them both a high degree of literacy and a veneration for scripture. Puritan literature, mimicking the literature of scripture, was limited to historical chronicles, diaries, theological sermons, and poetry. Anne Bradstreet (1612–1672) and Edward Taylor (*c.* 1645–1729), preeminent among the American Puritan poets, wrote works rich in biblical allusion and idiom. The Puritans also developed a kind of typology wherein clear parallels were asserted between events in the New World and biblical history. This typological correspondence between the Puritan colonies and Eden or the New Canaan can be seen in the narratives of William Bradford (1590–1657) and John Winthrop (1588–1649), in Cotton Mather's (1663–1728) *Magnalia Christi Americana* (1702), and in the sermons of John Edwards (1703–1758).

With the increasing influence of Enlightenment thinking, biblical allusions in American writings diminished and were much less frequently found in the works of Benjamin Franklin (1706–1790) and Thomas Jefferson (1743–1826) than in those of their Puritan forbears.

The nineteenth century saw an upsurge in the influence of the Bible on American literature in every genre. Scripture clearly informs the works of such poets as John Greenleaf Whittier (1807–1892) and Henry

Wadsworth Longfellow (1807–1882), and it is at times cited to support the Transcendental philosophies of Ralph Waldo Emerson (1803–1882) and Henry David Thoreau (1817–1862). Nineteenth-century fiction also drew heavily from scripture. James Fenimore Cooper (1789–1851) drew parallels between the American frontier and the wanderings of the Israelites in search of a promised land in the five novels that make up his Leatherstocking Tales. Though anti-Christian in many respects, Nathanial Hawthorne (1804–1864), drawing upon his Puritan roots, makes frequent references to the Bible, though often in the service of parody. Herman Melville's (1819–1891) *Moby Dick* (1851) draws upon a broad variety of biblical narratives, most notably the Genesis account of the Fall, and his posthumously published *Billy Budd* (1924) draws clear parallels between its protagonist and Christ.

During this American Literary Renaissance the influence of the King James Version of the Bible was pervasive, but American religious thought had become largely antinomian. Poets like Walt Whitman (1819–1892) and Emily Dickinson (1830–1886) made extensive use of biblical idiom and diction, but, as Roger Lundin writes of Dickinson, 'the words of the Bible were evocative but unconvincing' (1998: 210).

In the late nineteenth century, realists continued to use biblical sources in a very secularized fashion. Mark Twain (1835–1910), for example, uses the story of Moses to inform Huck's delivering Jim from slavery in *Adventures of Huckleberry Finn* (1883). By the end of the nineteenth century, the Bible as both source and influence is nearly absent from 'serious' literature.

In the early twentieth century, T.S. Eliot's (1888–1965) conversion seemed to signal a renewal of interest in the Bible among poets and playwrights in the Modernist tradition. In fact, as Ryken notes, 'The prominence of the Bible in twentieth-century literature is all out of proportion to its relatively meager influence on secular society' (1998: 484). Marianne Moore (1887–1972) made frequent use of the Bible as source in such poems as 'Sojourn in a Whale' and 'Blessed is the Man.' The Harlem Renaissance was also marked by the use of biblical sources among African American poets, perhaps most notably Countee Cullen (1903–1946) in works such as 'Life to Love,' which draws from the book of Esther, and 'The Black Christ,' which depicts the lynching of an innocent Black youth. The Bible also served as both source and influence in many plays written in the first half of the twentieth century, including Archibald MacLeish's (1892–1982) *JB* (1958), which retells the story of Job, and Eugene O'Neill's (1888–1953) *Bellshazzar* (1915).

Among early twentieth-century novelists, the Bible also enjoyed a renewed interest as source in such works as William Faulkner's (1897–1962) *Go Down Moses* (1942), Zora Neale Hurston's (1891–1960) *Their Eyes Were Watching God* (1937), John Steinbeck's

(1902–1968) retelling of the Cain and Abel story in *East of Eden* (1952), and Ernest Hemingway's (1899–1961) use of a Christ figure in *The Old Man and the Sea* (1952).

In the latter half of the twentieth century and into the twenty-first century, the Bible as both source and influence continues to have a great impact on American literature. Among American fiction writers, few have been as influenced by scripture as Flannery O'Connor (1925–1964), who, in such stories as 'A Temple of the Holy Ghost' and 'The Displaced Person,' uses scripture as both source and influence. Ron Hansen's (1947–) *Atticus* (1996) recasts the parable of the Prodigal Son as a modern mystery, while John Updike (1932–) continues to plumb scriptural sources in works such as *Roger's Version* (1986) and *In the Beauty of the Lilies* (1996).

References and further reading

Bartel, Roland, James S. Ackerman, and Thayer S. Warshaw (eds.) (1975) *Biblical Images in Literature*, Nashville: Abingdon Press.

Fowler, David C. (1976) *The Bible in Early English Literature*, Seattle: University of Washington Press.

Frye, Northrop (1957) *Anatomy of Criticism*, Princeton: Princeton University Press.

Jeffrey, David Lyle (1992) *A Dictionary of Biblical Tradition in English Literature*, Grand Rapids: Eerdmans.

Lewis, C.S. (1963) *The Literary Impact of the Authorized Version*, Philadelphia: Fortress Press.

Lundin, Roger (1998) *Emily Dickinson and the Art of Belief*, Grand Rapids: Eerdmans.

Ryken, Leland (1993) 'The Literary Influence of The Bible,' pp. 473–88 in *A Complete Literary Guide to the Bible*, Leland Ryken and Tremper Longman III (eds.), Grand Rapids: Zondervan.

Work, Edgar Whitaker (1917) *The Bible in English Literature*, New York: Fleming H. Revell.

PAUL BUCHANAN

LITURGICAL INTERPRETATION

1 Introduction
2 Sources and documents
3 Shifting liturgies
4 Liturgical texts
5 Conclusion

1 Introduction

The term 'liturgy' comes from the, Greek verb, *leitourgeō*, with three meanings that have some bearing:

(a) at Athens, to serve public office at one's own cost; (b) to perform public duties or to serve the state; (c) to serve a master, to perform religious service, or to minister. In the Eastern church, 'liturgy' refers specifically to the eucharist (Communion or Lord's Table); in the Western church, 'liturgy' frequently includes the entire scope of the Christian service of worship. Yet, throughout the centuries of the Christian church, it is the texts and actions of the liturgy surrounding the eucharist, Lord's Table, or Communion that have been the most important elements of the liturgy.

Exodus 12:6–8, 24–27 describes the events and observance of the Passover in the Old Testament. The Gospel accounts place Jesus and the disciples in preparation for the Passover in the first instance of his blessing and sharing of the bread and wine with his disciples (Mark 14.12–26; Matt. 26:17–30; Luke 22:7–22). Other passages that speak about the breaking of bread and the manner in which one should partake of the Lord's Supper include 1 Corinthians 10:16–17, 21; 11:20–29 and Acts 2:42, 46.

In the Western sense of the word, many churches which do not think of themselves as liturgical do in fact have a liturgy. The form of their worship, the familiar words that are used, the order in which the service proceeds, and how Communion or the Lord's Supper is observed are all part of this liturgy. This becomes evident in a church that tries to change elements of its liturgy and meets with resistance from certain members.

Every liturgy, in some way, interprets the Bible – although not all do it consciously. Since the earliest records of the early church participating in the Lord's Supper (*Didache*, Justin Martyr, Hippolytus, see below), the actions, words, objects, and order of the proceedings have all played a part in interpreting the New Testament account and its Old Testament background, As the Christian church grew and spread, various interpretations of the New Testament accounts emphasized different elements as important, which was reflected in their liturgies. As some interpretations were thought to be heretical, church leaders assembled in several councils to deal with these supposedly deviant interpretations and to prevent their spreading through the formalization of doctrinal statements in creeds.

2 Sources and documents

The earliest document that gives some indication of how the early church observed the Lord's Supper and how its service of worship took place is the *Didache* (9–10, 14; late first or early second century). In *Didache* 9, instructions are given on how to observe the thanksgiving meal (literally, 'eucharist'). The cup is treated first, with a prayer of thanksgiving included in the document. The fragment of bread is then prayed over, distributed, and eaten, and then another fairly lengthy prayer of thanks follows the eating of the bread, 'when you have had enough to eat.'

The first known writer that discusses the Lord's Supper is Justin Martyr (*c.* 100–*c.* 165), in his *First Apology* (*c.* 155), written to Emperor Antoninus Plius, and then, later, in his *Dialogue* with Trypho, the Jew. We know from Justin Martyr's account that the early church celebrated the Eucharist each Sunday. It began with scripture reading, included a sermon by the president of the gathering, and had intercessions that finished with the kiss of peace. Bread, wine, and water were brought to the president, who offered a prayer of thanksgiving for them. About sixty years later comes the first text of the eucharistic prayer, found in Hippolytus, *The Apostolic Tradition* (*c.* 200). Although the original Greek text has not been found, and the version only exists in a composite of fifth-century Latin, with several other translations, it is clear that there was a prayer of thanksgiving, and the bread and wine were offered in memory of Christ's death and resurrection.

By the eleventh century, this liturgy, in its Roman form, included an introit (antiphon and psalm verses); *Kyrie eleison*; *Gloria in excelsis*; reading of an epistle; gradual (respond); alleluia; sequence; reading of a gospel; *Credo*; offertory (antiphon and prayer); preface; *Sanctus* and *Benedictus*; canon of the mass (that is, the eucharistic prayer); the Lord's Prayer; a versicle and response (pax); *Agnus Dei*; rite of peace; communion of the priest (with communion antiphon); postcommunion (prayer); and the dismissal, *Ite missa est* (Harper 1991).

3 Shifting liturgies

Ancient liturgies are often grouped and studied in 'families,' tracing the development of ancient liturgies, that is, the earliest Christian liturgies, toward their more recognizable forms today. These would include such liturgies as Alexandrian (leading to Ethiopic and Coptic); West Syrian (leading to Syrian Orthodox, Maronite, Malankarese); East Syrian (leading to Assyro-Chaldean, Mar Thoma, and Malabarese, as well as Armenian); Armenian (leading to Armenian Apostolic and Armenian Catholic); Basil/Chrysostom or Byzantine (leading to Orthodox, Ukrainian Catholic, Melkite); Roman (leading to Roman Catholic); North African; and Gallican, Celtic, Mozarabic, and Ambrosian leading to Toledo Cathedral, Spain, and the Milan Archdiocese, Italy (Jones *et al.* 1978; White 2000).

Later liturgies, stemming initially from the period of the Reformation, include Lutheran (leading to Evangelical Lutheran); Reformed (leading to Presbyterian); Anglican (leading to Episcopal); Anabaptist (leading to Mennonite); then Quaker (leading to Friends); Separatist and Puritan (leading to some Baptist, Congregationalist, other Free Church, and United Church of Christ); Methodist (leading to United Methodist); Frontier or Revival (leading to Southern

Baptist and numerous others); and Pentecostal (leading to Assemblies of God).

Each of these groups and the subsequent developments within them – and away from them – involves interpretation of scripture in the way each enacts and understands church practice, church texts and documents, church theology, etc.

As the early church grew, spread, and developed in numerous ways, it also began to deteriorate in various ways. Several by-now famous individuals became highly disillusioned with the corruption within the developed and formalized Roman Catholic Church, and these individuals desired, in some cases, radical reforms from within the church, or, in others, complete distancing from the church as it was currently known. These individuals became new interpreters of the Bible and, in many cases, wrote the documents that formed the new shape of the particular church with which they were associated. These include Martin Luther (*Formula Missae*, 1523, *Deutsche Messe*, 1526); Ulrich Zwingli (the Zwingli Liturgy: *Liturgy of the Word*, 1525, *Action or Use of the Lord's Supper*, 1525); Martin Bucer (the Strassburg Liturgy: *Psalter, with Complete Church Practice*, 1539); John Calvin (*The Form of Church Prayers*, Strassburg, 1545, Geneva, 1542); Thomas Cranmer (The First and Second Prayer Books of King Edward VI, The English Rite: *The Booke of the Common Prayer*, 1549, *The Book of Common Prayer*, 1552); John Knox (*The Forme of Prayers*, 1556); The Puritans (*A Booke of the Forme of Common Prayers*, 1586). Later, the Westminster Directory (*A Directory for the Publique Worship of God*, 1644), Richard Baxter's Savoy Liturgy (*The Reformation of the Liturgy*, 1661), and John Wesley's outline for Methodist worship (*The Sunday Service of the Methodists in North America*, 1784) all became fundamental documents for various strains of the Christian church and their subsequent liturgies. Each of the above clearly interprets the Bible in some way by outlining those practices and texts that would be retained and those that would be abandoned or destroyed. In some cases, the writer or interpreter explained the changes in detail; in others, simply introduced and enforced them.

4 Liturgical texts

The eucharistic prayer or canon of the Mass, also known as the *anaphora*, or the prayer of consecration, comes from the Greek verb, *anapherō*, meaning 'I carry up; I offer up (in sacrifice).' The oldest name for this prayer is, in fact, *eucharistia*, Greek for 'thanksgiving.' This prayer, during which the bread and wine are consecrated in the Mass or eucharist, is the most solemn part of the eucharist. Jesus' prayers over meals are thought to include the blessing (*berakah*) and the thanksgiving (*hodayah* or *todah*) of Jewish prayers, and this is echoed in the eucharistic prayer.

There does not seem to be an urtext, or one single text, of this prayer from the earliest days, but, rather, several similar prayers. The early eucharistic prayer begins with what is known as the *Sursum Corda*, an introductory dialogue. The priest begins, 'Lift up your hearts'; the people respond, 'we lift them up unto the Lord.' The Canons of Hippolytus include: priest: 'The Lord be with you all'; People: 'and with thy spirit'; Priest: 'Lift up your hearts'; People: 'we lift them up unto the Lord'; Priest: 'Let us give thanks unto the Lord'; People: 'It is meet and right to do so.' The same canons include: 'This is the body of Christ,' with the response, 'Amen'; and 'This is the blood of Christ,' with the response, 'Amen' (Hippolytus, *The Apostolic Tradition*).

The *Apostolic Constitutions* tell us that, following this, the eucharistic prayer contains a thanksgiving; narrative of the institution (the account of the Lord's Supper as found in the Synoptic Gospels and 1 Cor.); anamnesis ('remembrance'); epiclesis ('invocation'); and a concluding doxology (words expressing praise or glory to God, usually in trinitarian form, e.g., Lesser Doxology, 'Glory be to the Father and to the Son and to the Holy Spirit . . .'). Almost all anaphoras or eucharistic prayers of historic rites contain these basic categories and in this order. Exceptions include the mid-fourth-century Egyptian Anaphora of St Serapion (within which the narrative on institution and anamnesis are conflated) and the East Syrian Anaphora of the Holy Apostles Addai and Man, which is now missing the institution narrative.

Other texts that are used regularly in the liturgy include the *Magnificat*, which is from the New Testament. This is known as Mary's prayer in Luke 1:46–55, and has parallels to Hannah's prayer in 1 Samuel 2:1–10. This is one of the few Marian texts taken directly from the Bible. The *Pater noster*, or 'The Lord's Prayer,' comes directly from Matthew's Gospel where Jesus gives instructions on prayer (Matt. 5:9–13). As early as the *Didache* (see below), there are admonitions to pray this prayer, 'as the Lord commanded in his gospel' (*Apostolic Fathers*, I:429 LCL). The *Benedictus dominus* ('Blessed be the Lord') is Zechariah's prayer of prophecy from Luke 1:68–79. The *Nunc dimittis* ('Lord, now lettest thou thy servant depart') is Simeon's prayer and blessing from Luke 2:29–32.

The texts of the Ordinary of the Mass include the *Kyrie*, *Gloria*, *Credo*, *Sanctus* with *Benedictus*, and *Agnus Dei*. These texts are the ones most often set to music through the centuries by the greatest composers. Apart from the *Credo*, they were assembled between the fourth and eighth centuries for the celebration or observance of Mass in the Christian church. The *Credo* was not incorporated as a standard text until the eleventh century. Several of these texts are from the Bible, but not all, although they may be perceived as such by those who have heard them regularly in their liturgical setting.

The *Kyrie* is not exactly scripture. The three lines of this text, *Kyrie eleison, Christe eleison, Kyrie eieison* ('Lord, have mercy; Christ, have mercy; Lord, have mercy'), have generally remained in Greek even throughout the centuries of Latin observance of the Mass. The original form of this petition possibly had more to do with honoring a king and worshipping a sun-god than with calling upon Christ to have mercy. Nonetheless, this response, originally used in the liturgy to follow a litany, has become an oft-repeated prayer of the church, and expresses very simply the essence of a petition heard so often in the Psalms,

The *Gloria in excelsis Deo* ('Glory to God in the highest') is known as the Greater Doxology. It is a composite of scripture passages and other nonbiblical phrases. Luke 2:14, from the birth narrative, contains the phrases, 'Glory to God in the highest, and on earth peace among men with whom He is well pleased.' John 1:29, where John is speaking to Jesus, contains the exclamation, 'Behold, the Lamb of God who takes away the sin of the world!' Other sections of this text are not specifically drawn from scripture, although they use scripture-like language.

The *Credo in unum deum* ('I believe in one God') originated in an attempt to preserve a 'right' interpretation of biblical doctrines; concerns about accuracy and heresies led to the revisions in the councils of the fourth and fifth centuries. This text is not technically a biblical text at all, but from its conception, it attempts to interpret and present the most important tenets and facts of scripture relevant to the believer. There are four main sections to this text: the first expresses belief in God, the second expresses belief in the Lord Jesus Christ, the third expresses belief in the Holy Spirit, and the final section expresses belief in the holy Catholic Church. Composers throughout the history of the Christian church have used their musical settings of this, and other, liturgical texts to highlight those features that they deemed most important or outlined them in such a way as to present a certain view of them (see Porter 2003).

The *Sanctus* is from Isaiah 6:3, which is part of Isaiah's vision of the Lord: 'Holy, Holy, Holy, is the Lord of hosts, the whole earth is full of his glory.' Revelation 4:8 also uses this threefold statement, where the four living creatures never cease to say, 'Holy, Holy, Holy, is the Lord God, the Almighty, who was and who is and who is to come.'

The *Benedictus qui venit* ('Blessed is he who comes') was removed from the *Sanctus* during the Reformation. The statement suggested Christ's presence in the elements of the eucharist, so it was removed by some. Where the *Benedictus* is included with the *Sanctus*, it is clearly indicated, signifying the theological importance of this combination. *Benedictus qui venit* is from the triumphal entry of Jesus into Jerusalem in Matthew 21:9: 'Hosanna to the Son of David; Blessed is he who comes

in the name of the Lord; Hosanna in the highest!' Other relevant passages for this text are Luke 19:38, 'Blessed is the King who comes in the name of the Lord; peace in heaven and glory in the highest'; and Psalm. 118:26, 'Blessed is the one who comes in the name of the Lord.'

The *Agnus Dei* ('Lamb of God') consists of three lines: 'Lamb of God, that takes away the sin of the world, have mercy upon us. Lamb of God, that takes away the sin of the world, have mercy upon us. Lamb of God, that takes away the sin of the world, grant us peace.' The biblical background to the first section of each of these three lines is in John 1:29, 'Behold, the Lamb of God who takes away the sin of the world!' The phrase 'have mercy upon us' is not strictly biblical in its wording, although Matthew 18:33 does instruct the one who has been forgiven a debt to have mercy on a fellow slave, 'even as I [Jesus] had mercy on you.' Again, as with the *Kyrie*, the phrase reiterated here expresses the heart of a petition, such as one encounters in the Psalms or Lamentations. The final phrase of this tripartite plea, 'grant us peace,' was a later addition, when the prayer began to also accompany the kiss of peace that followed the breaking of the bread. Again, it is not strictly biblical in its wording. Scripture talks about granting life and loving kindness (Job 10:12), salvation (Ps. 85:7), and the desire of the righteous (Prov. 10.24). However, in the Old Testament, we encounter the blessing, 'The Lord bless you, and keep you; the Lord make his face shine on you, and be gracious to you; the Lord lift up his countenance on you, and give you peace' (Num. 6:24–26). In the New Testament, after Jesus' resurrection, Jesus stands in the midst of the disciples and says, 'Peace be with you,' and then again, 'Peace be with you; as the Father has sent me, I also send you.' Eight days later, Jesus appears once more to the disciples and begins, 'Peace be with you.'

Antiphons to Mary, such as *Alma redemptoris mater* ('Kind mother of the redeemer'); *Ave regina caelorum* ('Hail, O queen of heaven'); *Regina caeli* ('Queen of heaven'); and *Salve regina* ('Hail, O queen'), are not scripture texts, but do in fact interpret scripture with Mary as the object of worship.

The *Te Deum laudamus* ('We praise thee, O God') is another text that is not technically drawn from scripture itself, and is more like an extemporaneous prayer. This prayer of praise begins by addressing God, the Father everlasting, whom all the earth worships. About halfway through the prayer, it shifts to address Christ specifically: 'Thou art the King of glory O Christ. Thou art the everlasting Son of the Father.' This shift in subject is maintained to the end of the prayer. The very last line of this prayer also shifts person, in that the language throughout the prayer is 'we'; only in the last line does it shift to 'me': 'O Lord, in thee have I trusted, let me never be confounded.'

209

5 Conclusion

From the earliest known records of the celebration or observance of the Lord's Supper, the church in all its manifestations has been involved in interpreting the New Testament accounts of it. This has taken place through those scripture passages which are enshrined in the liturgy; the collage of scripture and nonscripture passages that are juxtaposed in other texts of the liturgy; the order and priorities of both specific actions and words in the liturgy; and even the musical settings used for certain set texts of the liturgy – all are a part of how the liturgy has been used to interpret scripture, whether intended or not.

References and further reading

Bradshaw, Paul (ed.) (2002) *The New Westminster Dictionary of Liturgy and Worship*, Louisville, Westminster/John Knox.

Davies, J.G. (ed.) (1972) *A Dictionary of Liturgy and Worship*, London: SCM Press.

Every, George (1961) *Basic Liturgy: A Study in the Structure of the Eucharistic Prayer*, London: The Faith Press.

Harper, John (1991) *The Forms and Orders of Western Liturgy from the Tenth to the Eighteenth Century*, Oxford: Clarendon.

Jones, Cheslyn, Geoffrey Wainwright, and Edward Yarnold (eds.) (1978) *The Study of Liturgy*, London: SPCK.

Porter, W.J. (2003) 'A Theory of Emphasis and Interpretation Applied to the Creed Settings of John Taverner, Christopher Tye, Thomas Tallis, John Sheppard and William Byrd,' Ph.D. thesis, University of Surrey, UK.

Thompson, Bard (ed.) (1961) *Liturgies of the Western Church*, Philadelphia: Fortress Press.

Warren, F.E. (1987) *The Liturgy and Ritual of the Ante-Nicene Church*, London: SPCK.

White, James F. (1989) *Protestant Worship: Traditions in Transition*, Louisville: Westminister/John Knox.

—— (2000) *Introduction to Christian Worship*, Nashville: Abingdon Press, 3rd edn.

WENDY J. PORTER

LUTHER, MARTIN (1483–1546)

Luther, the prophetic voice of the Protestant Reformation, was born to a German peasant family. His early university studies focused on Aristotelian philosophy and the nominalistic ideas of William Ockham. Luther's father wanted him to study law, but during an intense thunderstorm in 1505 Luther vowed to become a monk, out of fear and as a plea for his life. Two weeks later he entered the monastery and was subsequently ordained in 1507. Notwithstanding, he broke his vows when he married in 1525.

In 1508 Luther was invited to teach theology for a semester at the University of Wittenburg. Here Johannes von Staupitz encouraged him to study the Bible and later (1511) invited Luther to take his place as professor of the Bible. Luther received the doctor of theology degree from the university in 1512 and held his professorship until his death.

Luther is primarily known for emphasizing the Augustinian doctrine of justification by faith (*sola fide*). He found this doctrine to be in stark contrast to the Roman Church practice of indulgences. After expressing this view in his *Ninety-five Theses* (1517), he began to believe that church corruption, which the indulgences exemplified, could only be corrected by separating from the Roman Church.

Luther's theology was shaped through the preparation and delivery of his own lectures on the Psalms, then Romans, Galatians, Hebrews, and possibly Genesis (1513–1519). Luther based his lectures on the original biblical languages and employed the available exegetical tools to their fullest extent in his preparation. At first Luther followed scholastic hermeneutics (referred to as the *Quadriga*) to draw out four senses of scripture: literal, allegorical, tropological/moral, and anagogical/eschatological. Luther focused on the literal (including typological) and tropological senses of scripture, and had a distinct way of understanding the tropological sense. Rather than understanding it as a response to scriptures by human works, Luther understood it as the work of God in the believer.

Luther's concept of interpretation progressively reduced to his theory of the 'spirit and letter.' 'Spirit' referred to the spiritual/prophetic sense of scripture and 'letter' referred to the literal/historic sense. The former was given by the guidance of the Holy Spirit and pointed to the Christological content of the text. Luther believed that the Spirit was the best interpreter of that which the Spirit inspired. It was the Spirit who made the scriptures alive to one's contemporary existential situation. The 'spirit' and 'letter' where not absolutely antithetical, however, for the 'spirit' was contained in the 'letter.' This belief kept biblical interpretation from becoming arbitrary and is exemplified in Luther's conviction that the meaning of scripture could always be found in its grammatical sense unless the context suggested otherwise.

At the suggestion of Philip Melanchthon, Luther prepared a German translation of the Bible. He translated the New Testament in eleven weeks (1522) and, with colleagues at Wittenburg, completed the translation of the Bible, including the Apocrypha, by 1534. This translation, based upon the original languages, helped to standardize the German language. Fourteen German translations preceded Luther's but his became the standard due to its artistic and linguistic excellence and because the demand for a German Bible grew precisely when Luther was translating.

Luther prepared the translation because he desired that every believer would be able to study the Bible in his or her vernacular language. Behind this desire was the doctrine of *sola scriptura*, expressing the sole authority of the Bible. This doctrine was formed in reaction to the belief that the pope had primary teaching authority and that only he was able to properly interpret the scriptures (see Luther's *Appeal to the German Nobility*). In contrast, Luther believed that scripture was clear enough for any believer to interpret it. Nevertheless, through later theological conflicts with German peasants Luther came to believe that knowledge of Hebrew, Greek, and Latin was essential to interpret the Bible properly.

References and further reading

Bornkamm, Heinrich (1969) *Luther and the Old Testament*, trans. Eric W. and Ruth C. Gritsch, Victor I. Gruhn (ed.), Philadelphia: Fortress Press.

Brecht, Martin (1985) *Martin Luther: His Road to Reformation 1483–1521*, trans. James L. Schaaf, Philadelphia: Fortress Press.

Brendler, Gerhard (1991) *Martin Luther: Theology and Revolution*, trans. Claude R. Foster Jr., Oxford: Oxford University Press.

Ebeling, Gerhard (1970) *Luther: An Introduction to His Thought*, trans. R.A. Wilson, Philadelphia: Fortress Press.

Lohse, Bernhard (1986) *Martin Luther: An Introduction to His Life and Work*, trans. Robert C. Schulz, Philadelphia: Fortress Press.

—— (1999) *Martin Luther's Theology: Its Historical and Systematic Development*, Roy A. Harrisville (trans. and ed.), Minneapolis: Fortress Press.

Luther, Martin (1955–1986) *Luther's Works*, Jaroslav Pelikan and Helmut Lehmann (eds.), 55 Vols., St. Louis: Concordia, American edn.

Pelikan, Jaroslav (1959) *Luther the Expositor: Introduction to the Reformer's Exegetical Writings*, St. Louis: Concordia (Companion Volume to *Luther's Works*).

Tangely, Martin (2003) *Martin Luther: Overview and Bibliography*, New York: Nova Science.

ANDREW K. GABRIEL

M

MAIMONIDES (1135–1204)

Moses Maimonides is the Latinized name of Moses ben Maimon, known in rabbinical literature as 'Rambam' from the acronym for Rabbi Moses Ben Maimon. Maimonides was born into a line of distinguished rabbis and scholars in Cordoba, which was then part of Muslim Spain. As a result of religious persecution the Maimon family eventually left Cordoba in 1148. There is little accurate record of them and their wanderings until they reappear in Fez, Morocco in 1160. Here Maimonides began work on *Sirāj*, his commentary on the Mishnah. As far as we can tell, the five years that the Maimon family spent in Fez were a time of relative peace and security. All this changed in 1165 in the face of renewed persecutions and forced conversions. Rather than face execution, Moses Maimonides and family once again emigrated, eventually settling in Fostat, the Old City of Cairo – which was to become Maimonides' final home.

In 1168 Maimonides finished his first major work, the systematic commentary on the whole of the Mishnah. Its significance inheres both in its scope – bringing clear interpretation to the text for the general reader – as well as in the ethical, theological, and philosophical issues raised in the Mishnah and discussed in his introductory essays. Of particular importance are the thirteen Articles of Faith (found in his introduction to the 'sayings of the Fathers' in section IV) in which he crystallized the basic elements of Jewish faith. From roughly the time his family had settled in Fez, Maimonides had been supported by his younger brother David, who dealt in precious stones. In 1169 Maimonides' life was shaken once more with the tragic death of his brother whilst traveling on business. Rejecting any thought of taking a paid position as a rabbi to support himself, he severely denounced those who exploited the Torah for personal gain (Kobler 1952: 207). Thus Maimonides went on to become a physician and in time was appointed one of the physicians to al-Faḍil, Saladin's vizier in Egypt.

Having completed his Mishnah commentary in 1168, Maimonides took up his next great work: *Sefer ha-Mitzvot* ('Book of Commandments'), in which he both catalogued the 248 positive and 365 negative commandments from the Torah, as well as took issue with the work of his predecessors. In examining the 613 precepts Maimonides set out his fourteen guiding principles for including both positive and negative commandments in the Mosaic code. One of his innovations was to distinguish between binding *halakhic* and nonbinding *aggadic* material within the Talmud. *Sefer ha-Mitzvot*, finished shortly after 1170, did not remain an independent work but served as an introduction to his *Mishneh Torah* ('Repetition of the Law') over which he labored for ten years. His aim was to produce a work that expounded Jewish law 'in precise language and concise manner, so that the entire Oral Law may be made accessible to everyone without any arguments or counterarguments . . . so that no man shall have any need to resort to any other book on any point of Jewish law' (introduction to *Mishneh Torah*). Its great contribution to Jewish *halakhic* literature is the systematic treatment and taxonomy that Maimonides brought to the subject. Divided into fourteen books, each covering a separate category of Jewish law, never before had Mishnaic precepts been organized according to logical method. Although met in his own day with controversy, Maimonides' *Mishneh Torah* has continued to spawn debate and scholarship – even to the present time – unlike any other *halakhic* authority.

Even before *Mishneh Torah* appeared in 1180 Maimonides had begun work on the climax of his theological/philosophical career: *Dalālat-Hā'rīn* (*Guide of the Perplexed*). As this work belongs most properly to philosophy as opposed to biblical studies its discussion is beyond our scope here. However, it needs to be said that the *Guide* is significant not just for the truly great work that it is, but also for two important reasons: (a) it was through the *Guide* that Maimonides' well-deserved fame as a thinker became universal, extending beyond the Jewish community. Not only was it translated into Hebrew in Maimonides' lifetime (from Arabic), but also it was soon afterward translated into Latin and most other European languages as well; (b) As a consequence of its universal appeal 'Jews and Judaism may be said to have entered the orbit of the world's thinking' (Minkin 1957: 106) The impact of this work on Muslim, and particularly Christian, scholars cannot be overstated. Among the latter, scholastics such as William of Auvergne, Albertus Magnus, Roger Bacon, Thomas Aquinas, Meister Eckhart, and Duns Scotus have been influenced by Maimonides. The *Guide of the Perplexed* was completed around 1190, after which Maimonides' energies and writings were devoted almost exclusively to medicine and related topics. Even as his health failed, he continued in his role as leader of the Jewish community in Fostat and as court physician. Some time after his death, his remains were buried in Tiberias, Israel – as was his request – where his grave is still a shrine for pilgrims.

References and further reading

Encyclopaedia Judaica (1971) S.v. 'Maimonides,' Jerusalem: Keter.

Fox, Marvin (1990) *Interpreting Maimonides*, Chicago: University of Chicago Press.

Heschel, Abraham Joshua (1982) *Maimonides*, trans. Joachim Neugroschel, New York: Farrar, Straus, & Giroux.

Kobler, F. (ed.) (1952) *Letters of the Jews through the Ages*, Vol. 1, London: Ararat.

Minkin, Jacob S. (1957) *The World of Moses Maimonides*, New York: Thomas Yoselef.

JACK N. LAWSON

MANSON, T.W. (1893–1958)

Thomas Walter Manson was Rylands Professor of Biblical Criticism at the University of Manchester from 1936–1958. Preceded by C.H. Dodd and succeeded by F.F. Bruce, Manson continued a tradition of moderate British biblical scholarship and churchmanship.

He stood in opposition to the old and new 'quests for the historical Jesus.' He was clear in his presuppositions: 'The primary and vital interest of the Bible is that it records the authentic Word of God.' The task of criticism then becomes to determine 'the content of the revelation and the historical context within when it is first given' (Manson 1939: v.).

Born on July 22, 1893, and a graduate of Glasgow University, Manson received his theological training at Westminster College Cambridge, and then served three years (1922–1925) as Westminster's first senior tutor. He was ordained in the Presbyterian Church of England in 1925, serving for a year at the Jewish Mission in Bethnal Green. He then spent five years in a parish in Northumberland, where he met and married his wife Nora in 1926. During his parish years he wrote two foolscap pages a day, which culminated in his first and arguably most influential book, *The Teaching of Jesus: Studies of its Form and Content*. In 1932 he followed Dodd as Yates Professor of New Testament Greek and Exegesis at Mansfield College, Oxford.

In 1937, Manson wrote the 'Sayings of Jesus' section of *The Mission and Message of Jesus*. In 1938, he was one of the founders of Studiorum Novi Testamenti Societas. His paper 'The Idea of a Society for N.T. Studies' outlined the goals of the society and he was the chair of the steering committee from 1940 through its resumption after the Second World War in 1947. In 1939, the Society of Old Testament Study recommended Manson as the editor of *Companion to the Bible*.

He invested much time in ecclesiastical committees at the local and national level. In 1952 he was elected moderator of the General Assembly of the Presbyterian Church of England. This practical churchmanship spilled over into his scholarship. His presidential lecture to SNTS was entitled, 'The New Testament Basis of the Doctrine of the Church' (1949). His final book was *Ministry and Priesthood: Christ's and Ours* (1958). Matthew Black claimed 'for Manson the ministerial practice of Jesus was vastly more important than any apocalyptic or eschatological theory attributed to him' (Manson 1962: iv).

Manson was working on the New English Bible at the time of his death in 1958. Manchester University published a memorial volume *New Testament Essays* (Higgins 1959) and his Rylands Lectures, edited by his literary executor, Matthew Black: *Studies in the Gospels and Epistles* (1962). Black edited a final volume, *Paul and John: Some Selected Theological Themes*, in 1963.

Manson is best known for his work on the teachings and sayings of Jesus. He used the historical-critical method. He pursued what Brevard Childs labeled an 'eclectic perspective that combines historical development with a topical approach' (Childs 1970: 202).

He was disturbed by the radical skepticism of Bultmann. He held a more optimistic view of the historical reliability of the Gospel accounts. His review of Bultmann's *The Theology of the New Testament* demonstrated his fairness: 'We learn not least when we are forced to articulate why we disagree' (Manson 1956: 5). H.H. Rowley noted that Manson 'believed that liberal scholarship took a wrong turn early in this century and that it was necessary to go back to where it went astray and pursue a different line' (1962: xiv).

He was not enthusiastic about form criticism: 'A paragraph of Mark is not a penny the better or the worse as historical evidence for being labelled "Apothegm" or "Pronouncement Story" or "Paradigm"' (Manson 1962: 5). His former student Ralph Martin claims that Manson's *The Sayings of Jesus* should not be ignored, since it 'provides a virtual commentary on Jesus' teaching in this Gospel as understood in the pre-Bornkamm era' (Martin 1984: 58).

N.T. Wright takes him to task for his attempt 'to take the historical question seriously but without integrating the detailed work into a larger picture that would give direction to further study' (Wright 1996: 23). Childs warns that Manson's aversion to form criticism results in a 'method that does not satisfy either the historian or the theologian' (Childs 1970: 202).

Manson, along with Dodd and Vincent Taylor, are examples of the best of British scholarship in the middle of the twentieth century. He followed or founded no school. He quipped, 'Indeed, it may be said of all theological schools of thought: By their lives of Jesus ye shall know them' (Manson 1944: 92). His legacy is that of a scholar who sought to make the life and teachings of Jesus accessible.

References and further reading

Baird, William (2003) *The History of New Testament Research: From Jonathan Edwards to Rudolph Bultmann*, Vol. 2, Minneapolis: Fortress Press.

Childs, Brevard S. (1970) *Biblical Theology in Crisis*, Philadelphia: Westminster Press.

Higgins, A.J.B. (ed.) (1959) *New Testament Essays: Studies in Memory of Thomas Walter Manson*, Manchester: Manchester University Press.

Manson, T.W. (1931) *The Teaching of Jesus: Studies in its Form and Context*, Cambridge: Cambridge University Press.

—— (1937) 'The Sayings of Jesus,' pp. 301–639 in *The Mission and Message of Jesus*, H.D.A Major, T.W. Manson, and C.J. Wright (eds.), London: Nicholson and Watson (reissued as separate volume *The Sayings of Jesus*, London: SCM Press, 1949).

—— (ed.) (1939) *A Companion to the Bible*, Edinburgh: T.&T. Clark.

—— (1944) 'The Failure of Liberalism to Interpret the Bible as the Word of God,' pp. 92–107 in *The Interpretation of the Bible*, C.W. Dugmore (ed.), London: SPCK.

—— (1953) *The Servant Messiah: A Study of the Public Ministry of Jesus*, Cambridge: Cambridge University Press.

—— (1956) 'Review of Rudolf Bultmann's *The Theology of the New Testament*,' *Manchester Guardian* March 19: 5.

—— (1958) *Ministry and Priesthood: Christ's and Ours*, London: Epworth.

—— (1960) *Ethics and the Gospel*, London: SCM Press.

—— (1962) *Studies in the Gospels and Epistles*, M. Black (ed.), Manchester: University of Manchester Press.

—— (1963) *Paul and John. Some Selected Theological Themes*, London: SCM Press.

Martin, R.P. (1984) *New Testament Books for Pastor and Teacher*, Philadelphia: Westminster Press.

Wright, N.T. (1996) *Jesus and the Victory of God*, London: SPCK.

GREG ANDERSON

MARCION (c. 85–160)

Marcion was born in Sinope of Pontus located in Asia Minor where his father, who raised Marcion in the Christian faith, was bishop. Marcion was a wealthy shipbuilder and active as an established teacher in the church. In *c.* 140 when Marcion traveled to Rome, he came under the influence of the Gnostic teacher Cerdo. Although Marcion shared the Gnostic belief in two Gods, the evil nature of matter, and Docetism, there was also much dissimilarity. Marcion rejected the use of allegory and figurative language and held strictly to a literal interpretation of scripture. His teaching lacked philosophical speculation and mythological interest and centered on faith in Christ rather than knowledge as the way to salvation.

In Tertullian's *Against Marcion*, we gain access to a reconstruction of Marcion's canon and his book, *Antithesis*, which outlines the incompatibility of the Old Testament and its theology and practice with the New Testament. The Jewish God of the Old Testament was an inferior creator-God, the demiurge, who was a God of law, justice, and war who could be capricious and cruel. In contrast, the Christian God of the New Testament was unknown, gracious, the giver of mercy and salvation found in Christ, his son. Marcion held that Christ appeared at the age of thirty and that his sacrificial death bought humanity from the Old Testament God and made them the property of the New Testament God.

Marcion's teaching emphasizes Paul, whom he believed to be the only true apostle. He misunderstood Paul to teach that Christianity was a new religion of grace distinct from Judaism, the religion of law. The other apostles had been corrupted and did not teach this separation. As a consequence of his theology, Marcion believed that Christianity should have its own authorized scripture. He contended that while the Old Testament was a true account and revelation for the Jew it was not for the Christian. Therefore, in a sincere attempt to serve the Christian church, he rejected the Old Testament and assembled a Christian canon of scripture. Marcion's Canon is the first recorded New Testament canon and remains his biggest contribution to biblical scholarship. It served to hasten the church into establishing its canon, possibly the Muratorian Canon, and the formulation of doctrinal statements.

His canon consisted of two parts: the Gospel, an abbreviated version of Luke, having removed the first three chapters containing the birth narrative, and the Apostle, a collection of ten edited letters of Paul, excluding the Pastoral Epistles. Marcion's editing removed elements of Judaism that he felt were not incorporated by Paul. The letters were arranged according to length following Galatians that exemplified Paul's theology and the separation of Judaism from Christianity. Scholars continue to debate whether Marcion's selections were based on a previously known collection, or upon books he possessed rather than books he purposely rejected.

In 144, following excommunication from the church in Rome, Marcion established a church similar in structure and sacraments but containing ascetic elements including abstinence from marriage, sex, and wine for communion.

References and further reading

Blackman, E.C. (1948) *Marcion and His Influence*, London: SPCK.

Bruce, F.F. (1988) *The Canon of Scripture*, Downers Grove: IVP.

Harnack, Adolf Von (1990) *Marcion: The Gospel of the Alien God*, trans. John E. Steely and Lyle D. Bierma, Durham, NC: The Labyrinth Press.

Hoffmann, R. Joseph (1984) *Marcion: On the Restitution of Christianity*, Chico: Scholars Press.

Knox, John (1942) *Marcion and the New Testament*, Chicago: University of Chicago Press.

Tertullian (1972) *Adversus Marcionem*, Ernest Evans (ed. and trans.), 2 Vols., Oxford: Oxford University Press.

Williams, D.S. (1989) 'Reconsidering Marcion's Gospel,' *Journal of Biblical Literature* 108: 477–96.

H.C. JORGENSEN

METZGER, BRUCE MANNING (1914–)

Bruce Metzger was Professor of New Testament at Princeton Theological Seminary from 1943 to 1988. Among his twenty-one books are *Introduction to the Apocrypha* (1957), *Text of the New Testament* (1964, 3rd edn, 1992), *New Testament: Its Background, Growth, and Content* (1965, 3rd edn, 2003), *Textual Commentary on the Greek New Testament* (1971, 2nd edn, 1994), *Early Versions of the New Testament* (1977), *Manuscripts of the Greek Bible* (1981), *Canon of the New Testament* (1987), *Breaking the Code: Understanding the Book of Revelation* (1993), and *Bible in Translation: Ancient and English Versions* (2001).

Metzger is known primarily as a New Testament textual critic, but, in addition to the subjects of the above volumes, he has also published books and articles on Qumran, New Testament Greek, New Testament and early church bibliography, New Testament apocrypha, patristics, early church history, ancient mystery religions, and modern cults.

Metzger was one of the five editors of the Bible Societies' Greek text that is found in both the United Bible Societies' *Greek New Testament* (4th edn, 1993) and the Nestle-Aland *Novum Testamentum Graece* (27th edn, 1993) and is now the most widely used Greek text. It is based upon the textual theory called rational eclecticism that gives equal weight to external and internal evidence.

Metzger has also played a major role in twentieth-century Bible translation. He was a member of the committee that translated the RSV Apocrypha (1957). From 1964 to 1970 he was chairman of the American Bible Society's Committee on Translations, and from 1977 to 1990 of the NRSV translation committee. Still further he was the editor of the *Reader's Digest Bible* (1982).

Among Metzger's many honors are President of the Society of Biblical Literature (1971), President of the Studiorum Novi Testamenti Societas (1970–1971), five honorary doctorates, three festschriften, Corresponding Fellow of the British Academy, and the British Academy's Burkitt Medal in Biblical Studies.

Metzger was one of the more important New Testament scholars in the second half of the twentieth century for the following reasons. First, there is the quantity and quality of his publications. Second, his scholarship has extended to many different fields. Third, his teaching, writing, and work with other scholars has been irenic and constructive. Fourth, his technical scholarship has been accompanied by practical application. Fifth, he is not only a scholar but also a churchman who has treated biblical and theological problems with reverence and reserve. Sixth, despite all his accomplishments and honors, he is a man of great humility. And seventh, he has had a profound influence upon a multitude of both undergraduate and graduate students.

References and further reading

Brooks, James A. (1994) 'Bruce Metzger as textual critic', *Princeton Seminary Bulletin* ns 15(2): 158–64.

—— (1999) 'Bruce M. Metzger,' pp. 260–71 in *Bible Interpreters of the Twentieth Century*, W.A. Elwell and J.D. Weaver (eds.), Grand Rapids: Baker.

Metzger, Bruce M. (1997) *Reminiscences of an Octogenarian*, Peabody, MA: Hendrickson.

JAMES A. BROOKS

MIDDLE AGES

1 A definition of the Middle Ages
2 The proliferation of translations of the Bible
3 Biblical interpretation in the monastic context
4 Biblical interpretation in the university context
5 'Popular' biblical interpretation

A single word which encapsulates the overall substance of biblical interpretation in the Middle Ages is 'conservatism.' Innovation was generally frowned upon; what was esteemed was the intention of fidelity both to scripture and to the putatively authoritative interpretations propounded by the ecclesiastically approved commentators of the second to sixth centuries. This is not to suggest that innovation in biblical interpretation was absent from the Middle Ages, but that those who took new hermeneutical paths had to cover their tracks with rhetorical affirmations of obeisance to tradition. To trace this pattern of innovation within conservatism, it will be necessary to consider not only scholarly use of the biblical text, but also the geographical proliferation of Bible translations and the 'popular' use of the Bible.

This article is divided into five sections: a definition of the period 'the Middle Ages'; a discussion of the spread of translations; and three segments dealing with interpretation proper. The latter three units are organized in terms of institutional locus of interpretation, beginning with the monastery, shifting to the university, and finally to 'the street.' There is a sizeable degree of chronological overlap between these sections; the emergence of a new locus of interpretation did not necessitate the elimination of an older form. Monastic interpretation continued after the rise of the university; the university continues to function despite the democratization of biblical interpretation in modernity.

1 A definition of the Middle Ages

At the outset, one must consider the problem of the definition of the era now known as 'the Middle Ages.' The term, coined during the Renaissance, was derogatory, suggesting an era of intellectual stagnation, when serious thought was in a holding pattern between the glories of antiquity and the emerging splendor of humanist endeavor. The late twentieth century postmodernist challenge to the notion of Modernism as the zenith of learned inquiry is itself the high-water mark of an existing movement to reject early modern intellectual arrogance and to renew respect for the era between ancient Rome and the Reformation.

Suggested starting points for the Middle Ages span a full four centuries, from as early as the sack of 'the eternal city' of Rome in AD 410 to the coronation of Charlemagne as Holy Roman Emperor in AD 800. Each of these is a significant psychological moment, but a more precise definition takes into consideration the fall of Roman political institutions. The last Western emperor was deposed in AD 476, yet, in terms of biblical interpretation, this is still not the ideal indicator. In medieval Europe, institution and interpretation were most intimately linked, more so than in the periods immediately preceding and following. For much of the era, biblical interpretation was confined to monasteries, while the boundaries of orthodoxy were increasingly stipulated by the papacy. The rise of a new form of monasticism in the sixth century, marked by *The Rule of Benedict of Nursia* (*c.* 480–*c.* 543), coupled with the

elaboration of the papacy's theoretical basis and the practical extension of its power under Gregory 'the Great' (*c.* 540–604), suggests the early seventh century as a more useful date to reckon as the inception of the Middle Ages. The significance is not the mere chronological coincidence of the genesis of each institution; they shared an ideology, a rigidly hierarchical structure grounded in the concept of absolute obedience to earthly superiors. These two institutions set the parameters for medieval biblical interpretation.

The end of the Middle Ages is no more clearly demarcated. The earliest suitable terminus is the Renaissance, an era in which many ancient manuscripts were rediscovered after having been lost to the West for centuries and in which several allegedly ancient documents that had been known for centuries were unmasked as pious forgeries. Clearly each of these trends impacted biblical interpretation, but the Renaissance provides an imprecise landmark, as the new intellectual climate took more than a century from its first stirring in Italy until its successful spread to the transalpine north. Protestants may gravitate to AD 1517 (or some similar date, depending upon one's denominational commitment), but one must be careful not to overemphasize the abruptness of change. 'Medieval' conditions persisted in parts of southern Europe, Latin America, and among non-European groups in the East for centuries. It is perhaps best to suggest a fairly limited period, from 1492 to 1517, during which the institutions which defined the Middle Ages and shaped exegesis lost much of their power. The onset of this quarter century, 1492, is important in terms of biblical interpretation more for the expulsion from Iberia of Muslims and Jews who refused to convert to Christianity than for the discovery of the 'New World.' The midpoint of this pivotal period is typified by the emergence of Protestant-like opinion in France in the so-called 'Circle of Meaux.' This group exerted direct influence upon the Reformer John Calvin. The Reformation makes a reasonable terminal bookend for this period, as it swept away papal hegemony and undermined the pervasiveness of monasteries as a social institution. Both Spain of 1492 and Germany of 1517 exemplify the rise of national identity which fractured the unified European society and opened the floodgates for new intellectual currents.

2 The proliferation of translations of the Bible

For a text to be interpreted it must be available to potential interpreters. In the case of the Bible, this means not only access to the Hebrew and Greek texts, but also to translations into languages in common use. The determination had been made, two centuries before Christ, that the truth contained within the Hebrew scriptures was capable of translation into the main cultural and trade language of the day, Greek. The availability of the Septuagint was of incalculable value in preparing the way for the spread of the Christian evangel. When the Gospel proclamation encountered new areas or eras in which Greek was not the dominant tongue, translation into the vernacular proceeded without controversy. As Latin began to displace Greek as the dominant language in the Western Roman Empire in the third century (Latin was not spoken widely outside of the Italian peninsula before this), a number of Latin translations appeared. The inconsistent quality of many of these led Pope Damasus (c. 304–384) to commission a thorough translation by Jerome. The resulting 'Vulgate,' or common language translation, became the uncontested basis for interpretation and vernacular translation until the late Middle Ages.

The proliferation of vernacular translations in the Middle Ages falls into three rough phases: early mission work at or beyond the periphery of the Roman Empire until near the end of the first millennium, including liturgical items translated near the nadir of intellectual activity in the tenth century; the renewed scholarly and mendicant interest in the vernacular dating from the twelfth and thirteenth centuries; the burst of new editions created during the Renaissance as rising nationalism spurred demand for the Bible in local tongues.

In the early era, translations of at least portions of the Bible were made into several languages of folk living near the edge, or just outside, of the Roman Empire. On the Empire's southeastern fringe, a Syrian Church emerged. In AD 508, the entire Bible was translated into Jacobite Syrian. Only scraps of this *opus* remain. Centered in Persia and Mesopotamia, the Jacobite Syrian Church had links with churches in India formed by Syrian expatriates there. This tiny minority avoided religious assimilation for centuries, but at the cost of their liturgical language being cut off from daily life, becoming a fossilized technical language unrelated to anything beyond worship. This state of affairs continued until the onset of European colonization of the Indian subcontinent.

At the opposite extreme, at the northwestern frontier, the evangelization of England got underway in the late sixth century. It is misleading to refer to this process as 'reevangelization,' for while Roman missionaries entered the same geographical territory as their predecessors centuries earlier, it was not the same nation. The Celtic Britons, many of whom had been converted under Roman rule, were forced to the island's extremities (the word 'Cornwall' literally means 'the place where the Corns [i.e., Britons] rule') by invasions of Angles, Saxons, Kents, Mercians, and Jutes. The dominant ethnic stock changed; 'England' was the Teutonic tribal grouping which supplanted the Romano-Brittanic race. Although Britain had been part of the empire, England never had been, because its people came from outside and displaced the Celts. In this missionary setting, practical portions of scripture were translated for liturgical use. The monk-translator-historian Bede

(c. 672–735) is said to have translated the Gospel of John, while others rendered the Psalms and the Decalogue. Unlike the Syrians, the early Anglo-Saxons laid no plan to translate the whole Bible. The Psalter was translated into other dialects more than once over the next two centuries, up to the time of King Alfred the Great (848–901). There were two tenth-century translations of the Gospels into English, one by Ælfric, Abbot of Eynsham (c. 955–c. 1020). On the whole, efforts to render the Bible into the major Anglo-Saxon dialects were sporadic and disjointed. The first Germanic translation was by the Arian Ulfilas. This was not acceptable to the trinitarian evangelists arriving from England to evangelize the pagan cousins whom they had left behind a few generations earlier. Several German words which developed into technical terms were actually Anglo-Saxon neologisms. The most prominent is the German word for 'savior,' *Heiland*, a loanword derived from the Anglo-Saxon *Hælend*, a multivalent word used to render the personal name 'Jesus,' as well as meaning 'savior' and 'healer.' The Psalter was also translated into Dutch in the late tenth century.

On the northcentral frontier, missionaries from Byzantium extended mission work into what is now Central Europe. In the late ninth century, work began in the Slavic linguistic and cultural basin, as two brothers from Macedonia, Cyril (c. 826–869) and Methodius (c. 815–885), entered Great Moravia. There were so few differences then among the Slavic dialects that the variants were mutually intelligible. Reducing the Slavic tongue to a modified Greek notation, the Cyrillic alphabet still used in Slavic languages, these missionaries created a translation which would remain in use for almost a millennium. Roman missionaries from Germany put an end to this mission in 885, but the language endured. While many Slavic idioms evolved from what became known as Old Church Slavonic, that language continued to be used unmodified in Orthodox worship services throughout Eastern Europe. With the exception of minor tinkering in the sixteenth and seventeenth centuries, Cyril and Methodius' translation remained almost unchanged until it was replaced in the nineteenth century by Russian and other modern Slavic translations. It is ironic that translation of the Bible into the once vernacular tongues of Latin, Syriac, and Old Church Slavonic would lead later to those same languages becoming calcified liturgical forms, unintelligible to the common people.

The second period of Bible translation came in the early high Middle Ages, spurred on by the development of Scholasticism. Yet liturgical needs of the populace remained front and center at this time. It is important to remember that the mendicant (itinerant begging) orders of monks quickly developed strong academic traditions, so that these two statements are not contradictory. Again, the pragmatic basis of many of the translations meant that the entire Bible was translated infrequently, in favor of portions perceived to be useful liturgically. So, in twelfth-century France, the Psalter, as well as Kings, Revelation, and five chapters of John's Gospel were translated. Not all translations were well received by the hierarchy. In 1170 Peter Waldo rendered several portions, which were suppressed. Somewhere between 1226 and 1250, a team of translators at the University of Paris translated almost all the Bible into French. It was of inconsistent quality. Around the same time, several scholars attempted *correctoria* of the Vulgate. These early attempts at textual criticism failed miserably and tended to leave the textual situation even more muddled than before. There is an oblique reference in 1233 to a Spanish vernacular version, banned by the monarch. This royal ban was later reversed, and royal patronage was extended for the publication of a new edition. Several Jewish scholars also translated portions of the Old Testament into Castilian and Ladino (a Judaeo-Spanish idiom). An Arabic version appeared around 1250. At roughly the same time, Genesis to 2 Kings was converted into the Icelandic dialect. Portions in poetic form appeared in Dutch in 1271 (the *Rijmbijbel*), with a prose version following in the fourteenth century. Gospel harmonies appeared in Italian in the thirteenth and fourteenth centuries. The proto-Reformer Jan Hus (1369–1415) made use of a fourteenth-century Czech Psalter. Manuscripts of the Psalter circulated in Polish from the second half of the fourteenth century.

The third flurry of translation activity coincides roughly with the Renaissance, and is rooted in the rising importance of vernacular languages as literary vehicles. A market developed in the fourteenth century for lay literature, even for vernacular theological books. The first late medieval vernacular Bible translation was by John Wycliffe (*c.* 1325–1384) and his associates. Scholarship of the last century has challenged the degree to which Wycliffe contributed to the 1382 translation bearing his name; the more radical question his involvement at all. The project certainly dovetailed with Wycliffe's own concerns expressed elsewhere, particularly his conviction that there existed a clerical plot to keep the Bible out of the hands of the common people. Although still based on the Vulgate, this translation gave unprecedented lay access to biblical ideas. Wycliffe's subsequent condemnation led to the unfortunate English precedent of banning the vernacular Bible.

The invention of the moveable type printing press accelerated the emerging trends in the vernacular languages. It also increased the sense of permanence of the words. Whereas spoken words disappear immediately, alleged error in print endures. The first printed book was a Latin Bible, with no less than ninety-two editions of the Vulgate appearing before 1500. Access to less expensive Latin texts led to a demand for vernacular editions. Contrary to a belief commonly held among evangelicals, there was no systematic attempt to suppress vernacular translations of the Bible in the late Middle Ages. The only country not to have ready recourse to the Bible in the local parlance was England. The Wycliffite translation remained banned, but this was not the case elsewhere. The first Bible printed in a modern European tongue was a 1466 German edition. It too was based on the Vulgate; the first complete Bible translated from the original languages to the vernacular was that of Martin Luther, the Old Testament of which appeared in 1534. No less than twenty-two editions of the entire German Bible were issued before 1522. Just five years after the German edition (1471), an Italian version was published in Venice. Francophones received a vernacular New Testament by 1477, the Old Testament following by 1487. Dutch readers had the Old Testament, except the Psalms, in 1477, with the Psalter coming three years later. Oddly, the New Testament was not printed until 1522. A Spanish translation appeared in 1478, but it was banned and burned. Notably, this did not set a precedent as in England, with an approved Spanish translation produced by 1492. Two Czech Bibles appeared in 1488 and 1489. A harmony of the Gospels was produced in Portuguese by 1495, with liturgical portions into Serbo-Croat in the same year.

A common misunderstanding of the proliferation of vernacular translations in the Reformation era is that the Bible suddenly became readily available to 'common folk.' Even though the work of Wycliffe did aim in that direction, and the early Reformers succeeded in providing high-quality vernacular translations, this did not mean that the average Protestant possessed a Bible. Even though literacy rates continued to rise dramatically in the early sixteenth century, they still fell short of modern levels. Furthermore, the cost of a Bible remained prohibitively high (the cost of a good cow) for most people until the rise of the British and Foreign Bible Society in 1804, a development far beyond the scope here. What is true is that 'popular' interpretation becomes a reality as the laity gain access to vernacular translations both in public settings and through the kindness of neighbors who belonged to the emerging middle class and who allowed others to read or listen to the reading of their copies. Truth had become incarnated in the local tongue.

3 Biblical interpretation in the monastic context

For the most part, during the Middle Ages, interpretation of the scripture was the preserve of the clergy. This was partly a function of education, and partly the result of social, economic, and political factors which undermined the parish system and concentrated not only learning, but also much of the overall expression of spirituality, in the monasteries. No intellectual titans graced the church between Augustine of Hippo (354–430) and Anselm of Canterbury (*c.* 1033–1109).

The few significant thinkers in between were monks, who tended to play the role of custodians and translators of ancient texts. The preservation of knowledge hung by a thread in the West, and it is not absurd to suggest that apart from the efforts of a few Irish and Spanish monks, all formal knowledge would have disappeared from the West.

For the first half of the Middle Ages, *The Rule* of Benedict gained ascendancy, so that by the middle of the eleventh century, monasticism and Benedictine observance were virtually coextensive in the West. The second half of the era saw the emergence of new orders, and the resurrection of earlier canons or rules to govern them. The newer monastic orders tended to engage in direct service to the broader Christian church, particularly putting monks in the role of preacher. Whether monks lived a cloistered life or performed direct ministry among the populace, preaching became a more important task to them as the medieval era unfolded. Technically, this was the territory of the bishops, but for much of the early Middle Ages this power was exercised more in the breach than in the observance. Preaching was one of the most significant forms of biblical interpretation during this era.

Preservation and preaching met at the point of interpretation; the protected texts contained an interpretive method which provided the concern that was proclaimed. Until the rise of scholasticism, the emphasis was on practical application of knowledge, rather than its intellectual exploitation. This is not to say that the era is devoid of originality, but that whatever creativity was exercised among them occurred within carefully defined boundaries. The interpretive method was allegorical, rooted in the work of the Jewish philosopher Philo and adapted to the Christian scripture by thinkers such as Origen and Tyconius (d. *c.* 400). Augustine endorsed the Donatist Tyconius' method, which favored a spiritual exegesis over either historical or chiliastic elements. Augustine expanded this existing exegetical tradition, thereby providing a foundation for the development of medieval theology along allegorical lines. A famous example is Augustine's treatment of the fall of Jericho, interpreting the story at four levels of meaning. The first was the 'historicogrammatical,' that is, that the story of Joshua's capture of Jericho actually happened in history. Next came the 'moral' (or 'tropological') sense: walls of sin fall before the onslaught of faith. Third was the 'Christological' ('typological,' or 'allegorical') sense, in which the story is viewed as a prefiguration of Jesus' triumphal entry into Jerusalem. Last, most literally so, comes the 'eschatological' ('anagogical,' or 'mystagogical') sense, which Augustine read in this instance as a promise that at the sound of the last trumpet the world of sin will fall. In each of the allegorical senses, numbers or names mentioned in scripture could be pressed to reveal deeper levels of meaning. The utilization of the three 'spiritual' senses

of interpretation was formalized by the Second Council of Constantinople (Fifth Ecumenical Council, AD 553), which rejected the suggestion that nothing in the Old Testament refers expressly to Christ, and that any such identification of meaning is a later interpolation. This raised the status of allegorical interpretation above matters of taste or fashion, establishing the method as a necessary hermeneutical approach.

The pattern was followed, with precious little deviation, for the next six centuries. Gregory 'the Great' did not value originality. Not only were many of his homilies derivative, but he reveled in his conformity to the 'deposit' he had received. This was not plagiarism, even in the modern sense, as Gregory and those who followed him were usually quite willing to give credit to those whose work they reproduced. Others, such as Bede and Paul the Deacon (d. *c.* 800), would in turn reproduce Gregory's sermons. Paul was appointed in 792 by Charlemagne to compile a book of homilies. The 244 sermons he gathered, including fifty-seven by Bede, became a standard text for the next three centuries. The other figures represented (Ambrose [340–397], Augustine, Basil of Caesarea [*c.* 330–379], Caesarius of Arles [d. 542], Gregory 'the Great,' Hilary of Poitiers [*c.* 315–367], John Chrysostom and Origen) formed a *corpus* of authoritative interpreters whose work served to mark the limits of acceptable discourse. Much of Bede's work simply embodied quotations of these earlier sources. He generally eschewed novelty, although he wrote a commentary on the Acts of the Apostles (*c.* AD 709–716) which showed great originality. No Latin authority had penned a commentary on Acts and the few Greek commentaries on the book were not known in the West in the Middle Ages. Bede's own work was quickly pressed into service as an authority with which one was not to trifle. In the ninth century, the homily became a 'closed tradition,' the accepted body of sermonic literature almost gaining the sense of inviolability associated with scripture. Conformity so dominated preachers' outlooks that most pre-1200 orators appear to have spoken only in Latin. Despite an AD 812 decree permitting vernacular sermons, such were rare, as barbarous idioms were generally held to be incapable of expressing satisfactorily the essence of Christian truth. It is impossible to ascertain whether Latin texts from the era reflect a scholarly record of what was preached (that is, being either translations of a transcription or the base document from which the vernacular was preached), or whether sermons were simply read in Latin, with the sense that that fulfilled the obligation to preach. The result of building homily upon homily was a growing mass of self-referent and self-reinforcing texts, a transmittable package.

The spectacular exception to the lack of vernacular preaching was England. Bede's *Ecclesiastical History* notes routinely the monks' preaching to laity living in the vicinity of the monasteries. The tenth and eleventh centuries saw the development of a relatively strong homiletic thrust among English bishops, although Continental sermons appear to have been preached only in Latin at this time (there are no extant vernacular sermons on the Continent before the twelfth century). The sermons of folk such as Ælfric, Abbot of Eynsham, and Wulfstan, Archbishop of York (d. 1023), although preached in Anglo-Saxon, were also strongly derivative (but not completely so). Both men were steeped in the lore of the ancients, particularly the sermons of Augustine, Jerome, and Gregory. Wulfstan even borrowed from Ælfric's sermons, although making significant emendations to them. Roughly two-thirds of Ælfric's sermons are exegetical. They display a certain dynamism, with variants among authentic manuscripts indicating development of the same sermon over time, its adaptation to the particular audience addressed. That audience is not specified, but the tenor of Ælfric's preaching is edification of existing believers (i.e., monks), not evangelism.

If the formal content of Anglo-Saxon vernacular sermons was predictable and driven by tradition, the mode in which they were delivered was not. Extant sermons are culturally sensitive, showing an adept utilization of the rhetorical features of the language, especially alliteration. While Bede's style evinced his grounding in classic rhetoric and knowledge of Latin and Greek, Wulfstan's word stock and syntax are decidedly English. Wulfstan, in particular, avoided metaphor, simile, poetic imagery, and analogical interpretation of scripture. The few instances found in his sermons tend to be those copied from his sources, differing in style from what he himself wrote. Wulfstan's elevation to the archepiscopal see of York rendered him the equivalent of Prime Minister. His public sermons were directed at a rowdy populace containing many overly enthusiastic warrior-settlers from Scandinavia. Many were nominally Christian simply because they had been defeated in battle and mass-baptized by force. As their gods had failed to protect them, it behooved them to heed the warnings of the priests of their vanquishers. Thus it is not surprising to find that Wulfstan was a strong moralist, ready to castigate and scold any departure from socially acceptable behavior. All too aware of his listeners' limited capacity for abstract thought, he kept to simple, forceful, and idiomatic preaching. Preachers such as Wulfstan preferred to render their Latin sources 'sense from sense,' rather than providing a literal translation. This is not to hint that they were sloppy, for Old English preachers tended to place great emphasis on accuracy. It is to suggest, rather, that they worked with assumptions akin to the modern notion of 'dynamic equivalence,' using Anglo-Saxon social, political, and legal terminology to translate biblical concepts and relationships. For example, Old English translators portrayed Israel as governed by 'earls.' Other instances were less quaint and possibly jeopardized the

very biblical theological tradition which the monks sought to preserve. Along with Anglo-Saxon vocabulary, Teutonic values were imported into the Christian community. The elegant poem 'The Dream of the Rood' (i.e., the cross) portrays Christ as a Germanic battle hero, aggressively ascending the cross and nailing himself to it. Biblical virtues such as meekness and submission did not translate well into a warrior culture and language.

If one distinguishes between a homily as primarily exegetical and a sermon (with or without a key text) as focused on a subject, then Wulfstan differed from most ancients by preaching more sermons than homilies. Ælfric, on the other hand, was more the homilist, following Augustine and Bede's example, although Ælfric did not push the spiritual senses of the text as far as his sources. Yet this is not to say that Ælfric abandoned the method of finding a threefold spiritual sense behind most literal renderings. He explains, for example, that the Crossing of the Red Sea means more than the literal crossing of the Israelites from servitude to the Promised Land. Allegorically, it bespeaks the passage of Christ from earth to the Father; tropologically, it betokens the movement from a life of sin to one of virtue; and, anagogically, it points to crossing into the next life by resurrection in Christ. Eschatological connotations garnered much of Ælfric's attention, as he believed those educated in their mysteries gained an armory with which to equip themselves to face end-time terror. In this the Anglo-Saxon abbot probably followed Augustine's lead, who believed that one should not choose passages for popular sermons if their literal sense could not be readily understood. Even if Ælfric's self-conception was that of a mere translator, modern readers have a greater appreciation for his positive contribution; no innovator or speculator, but one capable of expounding the truths of Christianity in vital, vigorous vernacular.

Preaching began to take a new direction, with lay folk intentionally viewed as the preachers' prime audience. The eleventh century witnessed the rise of devotion to the Virgin Mary. Marian interpretations of the Song of Songs were propounded by monachists such as Rupert of Deutz (1070–c. 1129) and Bernard of Clairvaux (1090–1153). This new devotion would soon spread beyond the cloister as vernacular preaching became the *raison d'être* of the mendicant orders formed in the early thirteenth century. A new sense of optimism arose concerning the possibility for those outside of monasteries to receive salvation. Latin sermons did the general public little good, so the Dominicans (followers of Dominic de Guzman, 1170–1221) and the Franciscans (followers of Francis of Assisi, 1182–1226) began to present the claims of faith to the average person within Christendom. Missionary concern also led some mendicants to attempt to convert Muslims. After their founders' deaths, mendicants came to dominate theological faculties at the newly founded universities. The timing is far from coincidental. These orders offered a disciplined means to channel the energies of those distressed by the perceived spiritual threats posed by the new urban centers which began appearing in the late eleventh century. The same economic and demographic shifts which spurred the formation of new orders also created the conditions necessary for the university. Theological masters were expected not only to lead disputations, but also to preach sermons in their cities. This overlap created tension, which would continue to build until the time of John Wycliffe. He felt that the authorities' contention that only Latin allowed the precision of expression necessary for correct doctrine meant that the church had abandoned the hope of explaining the content of faith to the average believer. By 1380, he had moved theological controversy from the academy to the street, stirring vernacular discussion among the masses and gathering a sizeable lay following, much to the chagrin of the authorities. Controversy did not end with Wycliffe's death. The Lollards, his followers, encountered stiff persecution and were forced underground until the Reformation.

4 Biblical interpretation in the university context

The eleventh century witnessed the beginning of new trends in scholarship. In 1085, Muslim leaders in the Spanish city of Toledo offered to surrender without a fight in exchange for a promise not to destroy the city's library. This is one of the more dramatic incidents by which the West was reintroduced to ancient philosophical and scientific teaching that had been lost to it centuries earlier. In particular, Aristotle's philosophy was rediscovered. A new aspect of systematization in scholarship was initiated. Old arguments were arrayed in novel order. One of the earliest, and most significant, figures is Anselm of Canterbury. While he broke from precedent, not citing earlier authorities in his *Proslogion* and employing original forms of argumentation, his self-perception was that he was not innovating but refining existing understandings. Faith remained the prerequisite for scholarly study. Without well-developed faith, the mind is misdirected; when 'understanding' is given priority, error occurs. Purity of heart is necessary for clarity of mind; the person must be formed spiritually in order to study. Jews and pagans may have reason, but only revelation completes the picture. Others, such as the brothers Anselm (d. 1117) and Ralph (d. *c.* 1133) of Laon sought to provide systematic comments on the entire biblical text. Their work formed the basis of the *Glossa Ordinaria*, which became a textbook in the schools by 1150. At the same time, the discipline of Canon Law emerged. Gratian (d. before 1179) compiled a set of church laws, council decrees, episcopal opinions, and comments by the 'doctors' of the early church, attempting to resolve contradictions by deciding the issue in favor of the papacy. His method was bor-

rowed from secular law schools. Some, such as Guibert of Nogent (1053–1124), opined that if theology were taught well enough, allegory would not be necessary. Hugh of St. Victor (*c.* 1100–1141) and his followers, known as the Victorines, still validated the notion that theology properly dealt with the spiritual senses, but began to insist that meaning must be sought from within the text itself, not what external authorities have to say about the text. They began to consult Jewish Old Testament exegesis and several members had at least some knowledge of Hebrew. But deeper changes were afoot in education and biblical interpretation.

One of the most obvious differences between monastic education, and the type of interpretation it fostered, and university education is the setting. While monasteries generally were located in rural areas, universities were an urban phenomenon. Without the freedom from subsistence farming gained after 1050, the medieval city would not have been possible. The new urban economy required different structures than the feudal rural one. Workers in various trades organized themselves into guilds, organizations which regulated the training of workers and the labor pool. Masters controlled workshops, in which new members began as apprentices and, attaining a certain level of proficiency, became bachelors, fully trained workers not sufficiently established economically to afford their own households. When bachelors reached that level, they too became masters. The university initially developed as the trade guild of academic masters, bachelors, and apprentices. All students began in the faculty of arts, where six years' study led to the degree of bachelor. Theology students took another eight years beyond the arts degree, passing through three more bachelors' degrees, usually being thirty-five years old before attaining the degree of master (initially 'Master' and 'Doctor' were interchangeable). Early university centers included Bologna, Paris, and Oxford.

Scholarship based in universities differed not only in terms of location, but also in terms of method. The academy treated theology as a dispassionate 'science,' whose content may be accessed without a mind or heart formed by faith, and taught like any other art or science. Theology was not grounded in the experience of the theologian, but a body of objective and standardized knowledge available to anyone. The study of such an impersonal science was institutionalized in the university. Even in the Faculty of Theology, Aristotle's work both provided the rules to govern argument and debate, as well as setting out logical procedures for defining, distinguishing, and categorizing knowledge. Peter Abelard began to set out a 'dialectical' method. He had studied under Anselm of Laon, but thought the method of glossing to be old-fashioned. His *Sic et Non* assembled ancient texts which did not always agree. He did not attempt to resolve tensions, but to use them to promote logical thinking among students. Concepts

221

isolated from context supplanted the original sequential reading, a nonlinear approach to thought. Increasingly scholars believed that in order to understand an entire text, one must examine its components in minute detail. Peter Lombard (*c.* 1100–*c.* 1160) published *Four Books of Sentences*, a collection and ordering of opinions of the Church Fathers, in particular Augustine's. He developed a logical approach to resolving the tensions, but remained profoundly conservative, relying upon patristic argumentation. He was also interested in background issues, such as the authorship of biblical books. The Fourth Lateran Council approved a commentary on Lombard's *Sentences* for use in the universities; *The Sentences* joined the Bible as the core of the university curriculum. This new Aristotelan approach to scholarship became known as scholasticism.

Twelfth-century developments in academic method encouraged fragmentation of the text. Bachelors began as 'cursors,' teaching overviews of biblical passages and providing superficial comments. This work prepared them for the profoundly more difficult teaching methods employed by the masters, the lecture and the disputation. The lecture was literally a reading of a text by the professor, a necessary practice in the early days, when few students could afford their own copies of texts (changes in the twelfth century to the way books were produced did lower costs). The master then 'glossed' the reading, that is, commented on the salient features, weaving the comments into a grand interpretation of the whole work. As the master was the reputed source of wisdom, there was little discussion during lectures. In a disputation, the master set a thesis for discussion. He would then establish the 'state of the question,' that is, what had been discussed in the literature up to that point in time. He would then raise objections to the question, and a junior teacher, a bachelor, defended the thesis. The next lecturing day, the results were summarized in class and written up. Series of such questions could be discussed, to highlight critical areas of thought. There were two types of disputation, class and public. The distinction was that in a public lecture, not only the master responsible for giving the class, but also any other teaching master at the university, could take part in the debate, which often led to bitter contention. Understandably, not all masters held public disputes, but those who did posted lists of resolutions or theses to be debated, so others could prepare well. Thus Martin Luther's nailing of his theses on the cathedral door was no act of defiance, but a mundane announcement of an upcoming academic debate.

As the scholarly endeavor proceeded, a means to refer to precise, limited portions of long biblical books became imperative. Thus the twelfth century witnessed the completion of the division of the Bible into 'chapters,' divisions which had not existed previously. Further subdivision into verses began in the late thirteenth century but no standard division was accepted until after the invention of the moveable type printing press. Chapterization paved the way for a crucial hermeneutical development: the concordance. Often taken for granted by modern scholars and pastors, the concordance is more than a useful shortcut for locating passages quickly, although this was the main rationale for its creation. Concordances constitute a revolutionary rearrangement, an alternate (re)presentation, of the biblical text. Its order is distinct from that of the canonical text, yet it is a legitimate form of the text in and of itself. A concordance is a tool for exploring the logical relationship between different occurrences of a word; its use is governed by syntactic and semantic reason. It is important to understand that this radically restructured model of the text allowed scholars to explore new aspects of the Bible's meaning, highlighting otherwise unexploited features. This power could be positive, creating a more malleable text with the potential of bringing together significant scriptural themes or motifs not easily discerned by a linear reading of the text. The impact might also be negative, as concordances promote atomization of the text. Atomization entails the reading of increasingly smaller portions of text in isolation from their context, thus increasing the likelihood of interpretation unrelated to the original author's intent. The key point is that the new order of the text itself fosters a different thought process. This new orientation would flower in the work of scholars such as Thomas Aquinas.

Thomas Aquinas is the quintessential figure of scholasticism. During the third quarter of the thirteenth century, this Dominican friar formed a major theological system, still officially sanctioned by the Roman Catholic Church. Believing that truth emerges through the process of debate, Aquinas' twofold purpose was to strip off inessential elements of the argument, clearing the ground by settling rational objections people might propose against an article of faith, and then to add back what was helpful to clear understanding. Thomas did not believe that philosophy was necessary for theology, but if one used philosophy, it must be the best available. This built on the assumption that there was no essential conflict between reason and faith, and that any apparent conflict is the result of the improper or inadequate use of philosophy. He adopted an existing academic literary genre, the *Summa*, to promote his system. The *Summa* moved beyond the mere gloss, to deal with concepts in a systematic and comprehensive fashion, following the internal logical order of a doctrine, not the order of the text as penned by the ancient authorities. A *Summa* encapsulated the results of a particular type of public disputations, *Quodlibetal* debates ('Quodlibetal' means 'as you want to say'). They built a case step by step, so that students were not merely accepting the idea on the teacher's authority, but having followed the necessary steps of logic, the student could defend the idea himself.

The 'golden age' of Scholasticism ended in 1277 with the papal denunciation of a set of philosophical errors associated with the Arab philosopher Averroës (1126–1198). As the fourteenth and fifteenth centuries progressed, the philosophical and interpretive consensus broke down completely. Innovations by William of Ockham undermined what had been accepted, only a few years earlier, as virtual certainties. Thereafter no one set of ideas or school of thought dominated. During the fifteenth century, universities became less church institutions and more nationalist ones, further shaking the once monolithic culture of interpretation. Into this unsettled arena came scholars willing to challenge other long-held tenets. In 1512, the French humanist Jacques LeFèvre d'Étaples (c. 1460–1536) published a translation of Paul's Epistles, in which he developed a doctrine of justification by faith. This departure from tradition was tolerated until Luther's more aggressive championing of the idea. The circle of humanists at Meaux, of which d'Étaples was leader, broke up under threat of persecution, some retreating back to the safety of more traditional interpretations, while others, such as Guillaume Farel (1489–1565) and François Vatable (d. 1547), chose to seek substantial reform of the church. The spread of this new idea marked the end of an era.

5 'Popular' biblical interpretation

This section is predicated on the assumption that insufficient attention is generally paid to 'the view from below,' that is, the practical impact of biblical interpretation upon the common person. To understand properly biblical interpretation in any era, one must balance the more commonly studied 'view from above' with an examination of opinion in the 'street.' The distinction between scholarly and popular interpretation was perhaps not as pronounced in the Middle Ages as may appear to be the case today. Such a statement is counterintuitive, but rests upon an assertion made by no less a figure than Thomas Aquinas, who averred that the Gothic cathedral embodied in stone values similar to those that scholars enshrined in writing. Architect and philosopher shared elements of a common calling. In each case, the project aimed to oversee and coordinate the details of a vast plan designed to make biblical truth intelligible and accessible, what differed were the audience and the medium of expression. Other forms of 'popular' interpretation, either for or by the common people, include devotional art, the 'Modern Devotion,' and street theater.

The Gothic (also a later adjective, used pejoratively to suggest the style was barbaric) cathedral may be considered the 'Bible' of the illiterate. A discussion of the various factors which led to the emergence during the twelfth century of this new architectural style is not warranted here, what is worthy of attention is the impact of this innovation upon an average, illiterate medieval person. A salient feature of Gothic cathedrals is the high percentage of window space in the walls, space filled with stained glass. Aspects of Aristotelian philosophy accentuated an existing centuries-old Platonic-based theology of divine illumination. Several 'high' Gothic cathedrals had 2,000 or more individual images arranged in as many as 200 windows. Biblical scenes and persons flooded the eyes of the worshipper. These were complemented by a vast herd of saints, apostles, Old Testament figures, confessors, kings, bishops, and virgins depicted in myriad statues. Often grouped in cycles to portray a story in stone, the sculptures functioned as memory keys, entrance points to the recollection of the details of biblical tales. Emphasis in art paralleled that of the homilies, tending to fall not upon stimulation of sensations of personal satisfaction, but upon the calculated induction of fear of damnation. The Last Judgment, for example, appears in strikingly lurid detail in a frieze on the western façade of Notre Dame de Paris, over the main door through which the faithful entered. Even believers seem barely to escape the clutches of hoards of soul-devouring demons. The so-called 'smiling angel' at Rheims stands out in whimsical contrast to the vast majority of stern figures, a delightful exception to a gloomy rule. The fact remains that many urban late medieval illiterates knew the principal biblical figures and stories intimately as a result of 'reading' the fabric of a cathedral. Yet there is one downside to this Bible 'carved in stone.' Medieval representations of towns and cities in the Holy Land depict them as if they were in northern Europe. This indicates that there was virtually no sense of the cultural distance between the Palestine of Jesus' day and the Europe of postantiquity. The Gothic cathedral's statuary and stained-glass images would tend to reinforce a narrow world-view which assumed greater continuity between the two cultures than truly existed, a distortion which almost certainly was detrimental to effective biblical interpretation.

Devotional art also provided a key means of access to biblical stories for the illiterate laity. A common votive artifact still in use is the crèche, or manger scene, allegedly first used by Francis of Assisi as a memory aid. Another relatively common icon was the diptych. In the eleventh and twelfth centuries it was fashionable among the wealthier of the emerging urban population to carry small ivory diptychs. These were often ten or twelve centimeters square, or rectangular, being slightly taller than wide. Large numbers have been preserved. The two panels were hinged so that the item could be closed for safe transport, but then opened and set on a table or desk in order to serve as a focus for contemplation. Images were often in sets, depicting a series of events in a single story. Many diptychs contained two images per panel (one above the other), four in total, grouped around the incarnation, miracle stories, or the Crucifixion. Depictions became standardized, with certain details included to accentuate aspects of the story. As the Middle Ages drew to a close, the size and content of the diptychs evolved. By the fifteenth century, wooden panels served as the basis for paintings, often as large as thirty centimeters wide and fifty centimeters high. A common pairing were the *Mater Dolorosa* (Mary) and her son (Jesus). Mary usually appears on the left, gazing upon her suffering son. The figure of Jesus is either dead or resurrected but still clearly bearing the marks of death. As the fifteenth century progressed, the details became more gruesome: more thorns bit deeper into Jesus' flesh, the skin being more transparent; the drops of blood loom larger and more numerous; the face is more haggard. The intent is to draw the viewer deeper and deeper into contemplation of the agonies of Christ. Even those bereft of the ability to read could participate in profoundly introspective interpretations of the Bible.

The larger wooden diptychs were especially common among the followers of the *Devotio Moderna*, the 'Modern Devotion.' A late fourteenth-century movement founded in the Netherlands by Gerhard Groote (1340–1384), the Modern Devotion was a reaction to the perceived spiritual sterility of late Scholasticism. It extended and amplified existing trends in popular devotion and interpretation, emphasizing an increasingly interior approach to faith. The most widely known literature produced by the movement is *The Imitation of Christ* by Thomas à Kempis (1380–1471). This too promoted affective interpretation of the Passion narrative, encouraging personal identification with Christ's suffering. The movement also stimulated demand for vernacular translations of scripture to facilitate personal access to the text. The movement's impact continued into the Reformation era. The Modern Devotion exerted profound influence upon the Renaissance textual scholar and critic Desiderius Erasmus (1469–1536), whose early education was provided by the Brethren of the Common Life, one of the main organized expressions of the Modern Devotion. The Brethren's simple piety, mystical tendencies, and ethical emphasis left Erasmus with little patience for scholastic minutiae. His 1516 publication of a critical Greek New Testament renders him a transitional figure, intent upon remaining faithful to the church and its traditions, hence he became an implacable foe of Martin Luther, once the Saxon Reformer stepped outside the bounds of the papal church. The two carried on a pamphlet war for years. Yet, ironically, Erasmus provided grist for the Protestants' interpretive mills; the Reformation could not have progressed as it did without his standard edition of the original Greek New Testament. Erasmus' life attained a rare fusion of popular and academic interpretation.

A final example of popular biblical interpretation literally takes one 'to the street': the morality play cycles. The best-known of these are the York and Chester Cycles, named for the English cities where these street dramas were performed. The York Cycle was part of the *Corpus Christi* devotion which emerged in the late Middle Ages (Thomas Aquinas is said to have composed the most widely used liturgy for the celebration of this feast). Annually, the city's craft guilds each presented one of forty-seven plays. Often the guild was related to the content of the story (shipwrights brought Noah's adventure to life, bakers undertook the Last Supper), but sometimes there was no meaningful link (coopers staged the expulsion of Adam and Eve from Paradise). Performances were on stages mounted on wagons; plays were repeated at several stations in the city, the actors drawing the wagons between venues. The York Cycle began near dawn on *Corpus Christi* day, with the Creation, and ended around sunset, with the Last Judgment. The intervening plays portrayed salvation history as it unfolded between the two landmark events. Actors spoke ordinary English, giving the illiterate memorable access to an otherwise relatively inaccessible text. The intention was to cement basic ethical teaching into the hearts and minds of the urban audience. The Cycles' mnemonic effectiveness was acknowledged in a backhanded way by their suppression during the Reformation. The Cycles remained unperformed as complete sets until the 1970s.

References and further reading

Augustine (1955) *The Problem of Free Choice*, trans. Mark Pontifex, New York: Newman Press.

Baldwin, John W. (1971) *The Scholastic Culture of the Middle Ages 1000–1300*, Lexington, MA: D.C. Heath and Company.

Bray, Gerald (1996) *Biblical Interpretation Past & Present*, Downers Grove: IVP.

Hopkins, Jasper and Herbert Richardson (eds. and trans.) (1976) *Anselm of Canterbury, Volume Three*, Toronto and New York: The Edwin Mellen Press.

Hudson, Ann and Michael Wilks (eds.) (1987) *From Ockham to Wyclif*, Oxford: Blackwell.

McAuliffe, D., B.D. Walfish, and J.W. Goering (eds.) (2003) *With Reverence for the Word: Medieval Scripture Exegesis in Judaism, Christianity, and Islam*, Oxford: Oxford University Press.

Martin, Lawrence T. (ed. and trans.) (1989) *The Venerable Bede: Commentary on the Act of the Apostles*, Kalamazoo: Cistercian Publications.

Shanley, Brian J. (2002) *The Thomist Tradition*, Dordrecht/Boston/London: Kluwer Academic Publishers.

Weisheipl, James A. (1974) *Friar Thomas D'Aquino: His Life, Thought, and Work*, Garden City: Doubleday.

C. MARK STEINACHER

MIDRASH

1 Narrow understanding of midrash
2 Character of rabbinic midrash
3 Broad understanding of midrash

1 Narrow understanding of midrash

Discussion of midrash (pl. midrashim) suffers from a lack of definition. Some suggest (e.g., P.S. Alexander) that midrash should be defined only according to the characteristics of rabbinic midrash, since all agree that this is midrash. However, while this method clearly has merit, it will necessarily end with a definition limited to its test cases, and to the exclusion of all that is not rabbinic midrash. Nevertheless, midrash clearly includes the rabbinic interpretation of fixed canonical texts and the succeeding rabbinic writings (sometimes found as a compilation of commentaries) on the Hebrew scriptures. It might also refer to the method found within these interpretations.

Midrash is not an academic exercise. This is understood in light of the fact that it originated amidst Israel's postexilic need for stability. This was found in their earlier written, divinely prescribed laws – 'They read from the Book of the Law of God, making it clear and giving the meaning so that the people could understand what was being read' (Neh. 8:8). Midrash likely developed from this point, its traditions being preserved orally. Some of the traditions that were preserved include those of the oral Torah believed to have been revealed by God at Sinai when he gave the written Torah.

It is difficult to date the writing of midrash because editing and the interpolation of material resulted in several versions of (essentially) the same texts. However, most scholars agree that the writing and compilation of midrash began as early as the third century AD and continued into the Middle Ages. Some traditions claim that there had been a ban on the writing of rabbinic oral traditions previous to this.

2 Character of rabbinic midrash

Midrash may be classified as midrash halakhah (legal exposition on Exodus through Deuteronomy) and midrash haggadah (narrative exposition). Both forms may be found in one text so the categories remain fluid.

Midrashic interpretation consists of a quotation of an Old Testament passage followed by commentary which might include devotional comments, exhortations, and explanatory or exegetical comments. Exposition occasionally follows the rabbinical rules of interpretation but is certainly not restricted to them. Legal exposition was primarily performed with the aim of presenting and justifying applicable norms from the Torah using analogy. In practice, a general principle is identified from a literal interpretation of the text, from which contemporary 'laws,' or applications, are patterned. Narrative exposition is more hortative and didactic in nature, and is less strict in its interpretive methods. Its exposition seeks to explain the meaning of stories and the historical events found therein.

From a literary perspective, midrash occurs in two forms. First, expositional midrash provides a verse-by-verse, often word-by-word, commentary on biblical text. For example, *Genesis Rabbah (Bere'shit Rabba)* provides a commentary on the entire book of Genesis. The sequential character of such midrashim likely results from the work of editors since composition involved gathering comments from various sources (sometimes cited anonymously). Second, homiletical midrash develops a scriptural theme following a lectionary cycle. This does not provide a running commentary but focuses on a selection of verses. For example, *Leviticus Rabbah (Vayikra Rabbah)* consists of thirty-seven homilies appointed for festival readings.

Biblical interpretation was driven by a conviction that the entire text was the revelation of God, which had ongoing relevance. Midrash itself is not considered to have been guided by the gift of prophecy. Rather, the rabbis taught that the Holy Spirit left Israel after the Minor Prophets. Midrash is not scripture or its substitute. Accordingly, the text generally guides midrashic interpretation (exegesis). On the other hand, the rabbinical worldview is regularly read into the text (eisegesis) with the purpose of better explaining the text's contemporary significance and application. From this perspective, midrashic interpretation has affinities with contemporary reader-response criticism. In addition, some midrashim seek to justify oral rabbinical law from the Mishnah or Tosefta.

Expositional logic is often clearly displayed for the reader. Often the authors answer questions that they pose to the texts. Expositional elements of midrash draw extensively upon syntactical, lexicographical, and contextual elements. Every element was thought to have significant meaning, even multiple meanings, and was to be accounted for. *Genesis Rabbah* illustrates the way minute details are occasionally examined. Here, the author discusses the first letter of the first word in Genesis 1:1, *bereshit*: 'Why was the world created with a b? . . . Because it connotes a blessing.' This conclusion is made because the first letter of 'blessing' (*berakah*) is also 'b.' Furthermore, repetitions or seemingly superfluous elements were to be accounted for. Contradictions also had to be resolved. Sometimes this was done using scripture to explain scripture. Where information was lacking, midrash often fills in the gaps. For example, one might describe the emotions that a biblical character might have been feeling. The result is that midrash is often subjective.

D. Hoffman argues that there are two main schools of interpretation reflected in midrash: the schools of

Rabbi Aqiba and Rabbi Ishmael. The school of Ishmael is thought to have followed a more literal interpretation focusing on authorial intent, while the school of Aqiba was more imaginative, drawing interpretations that were likely not intended by the author. It is more likely, however, that the differences within midrash reflect those of their redactors (H.L. Strack and G. Stemberger 1991).

3 Broad understanding of midrash

The term 'midrash' has also been used to refer to any form of Jewish scriptural exposition. This definition follows the etymological meaning of its Hebrew root *drs*, meaning 'to seek, investigate, or elucidate' (e.g., G.G. Porten). From this perspective, the earliest midrashim can be found within the Hebrew Bible itself. The books of 1 and 2 Chronicles have been considered as midrash on 1 and 2 Kings, 1 and 2 Samuel, and the priestly document of the Torah. The works of the prophets have been viewed as midrash on the Torah. Pesher, Targums, the LXX, and the Rewritten Bible might be considered midrash. Midrash is also identified within the New Testament. For example, Galatians 3:16 could be considered midrash on Genesis 12:7 and 13:15. G.W. Buchanan has suggested that the whole of Hebrews is midrash on Psalm 110 (1972). M.D. Goulder, and others following him, suggested that the New Testament even contains midrash on itself. He argued that Matthew is midrash on Mark (1974). He later withdrew the term. Since the texts included in this broad definition are considered in other articles, they need not be considered here.

An objection to this broad definition is that many of these 'midrashim' do not follow the rabbinic midrashic form of quotation and commentary. They may, however, follow midrashic method. The disagreement over how to identify midrash stems from the uncertainty of it as a genre, an exegetical method, or both.

References and further reading

Alexander, Philip S. (1984) 'Midrash and the Gospels,' pp. 1–18 in *Synoptic Studies: The Ampleforth Conferences of 1982 and 1983*, C.M. Tuckett (ed.), JSNTSup 7, Sheffield: JSOT Press.

Bloch, Renée (1978) 'Midrash,' pp. 29–50 in *Approaches to Ancient Judaism: Theory and Practice*, William Scott Green (ed.), Missoula: Scholars Press.

Buchanan, G.W. (1972) *To the Hebrews*, AB, Garden City: Doubleday.

Fishbane, Michael (ed.) (1993) *The Midrashic Imagination: Jewish Exegesis, Thought and History*, Albany: State University of New York Press.

Goulder, M. (1974) *Midrash and Lection in Matthew*, London: SPCK.

Hartman, Geoffrey H. and Sanford Budick (eds.) (1986) *Midrash and Literature*, New Haven: Yale University Press.

Jacobs, Irving (1995) *The Midrashic Process: Tradition and Interpretation in Rabbinic Judaism*, Cambridge: Cambridge University Press.

Neusner, Jacob (1987) *Midrash as Literature: The Primacy of Documentary Discourse*, Studies in Judaism, New York: University Press of America.

—— (1989) *Invitation to Midrash: The Workings of Rabbinic Bible Interpretation*, San Francisco: Harper & Row.

Porten, Gary G. (1981) 'Defining Midrash,' pp. 55–92 in *The Study of Ancient Judaism I: Mishnah, Midrash, Siddur*, J. Neusner (ed.), New York: Ktav.

Stern, David (1991) *Parables in Midrash: Narrative Exegesis in Rabbinic Literature*, Cambridge: Harvard University Press.

—— (1996) *Midrash and Theory: Ancient Jewish Exegesis and Contemporary Literary Studies*, Evanston, IL: Northwestern University Press.

Strack, H.L. and G. Stemberger (1991) *Introduction to the Talmud and Midrash*, trans. Markus Bockmuehl, Edinburgh: T.&T. Clark.

Vermes, G. (1970) 'Bible and Midrash: Early Old Testament Exegesis,' pp. 199–231 in *The Cambridge History of the Bible, Volume 1, From the Beginnings to Jerome*, P.F. Ackroyd and C.F. Evans (eds.), Cambridge: Cambridge University Press (reprinted in Vermes, *Post-Biblical Jewish Studies*, Leiden: Brill, 1975, pp. 59–91).

ANDREW K. GABRIEL

MILLENARIANISM

> 1 Jewish origins
> 2 Christian millenarianism

Millenarianism (or millennialism, or chiliasm [Gk]), which gains its name from a particular interpretation of the 'thousand years' of Revelation 20:1–10, denotes an influential set of eschatological beliefs which can be traced to Jewish and Christian sources of the first and second centuries of the Christian era. In the twentieth century the name also came to be used as a sociological category which has been applied to various utopian movements in diverse cultures throughout history.

1 Jewish origins

Most forms of Jewish eschatology of the Second Temple period viewed the Old Testament prophets as foretelling a restoration of the land of promise and a blessed, worldwide rule of God's people, typically (though not exclusively) under a messiah figure (or figures). Some literature of Second Temple Judaism, such as *1 Enoch* 1–36 (chs 10–11), expressed this hope in terms of an unending, earthly reign. But by at least the end of the first century AD in works such as *4 Ezra* and *2 Apoc. Bar.*, there had evolved a clear temporal distinction between an interim, earthly restoration and a more transcendent, final state. The temporary nature of this interim kingdom (predictions ranging from 40 to 365,000 years are preserved) prior to the resurrection and the last judgment of the world is a defining element of ancient millenarianism (though not necessarily of its modern, sociological namesake). Thus this messianic kingdom belonged not to the 'age to come' but to 'this age,' or better, to the transition between the two (*2 Apoc. Bar.* 74.2; Irenaeus, *Adv. Haer.* 5.32.1). Jewish millenarianism strongly advocated a resurrection at the last day and held that the souls or spirits of the righteous would await that day in the chambers of sheol/hades and not in heaven (*4 Ezra* 4.42; 7.32; *2 Apoc. Bar.* 11.6; 21.23, etc.; *Bib. Ant.* 21.8–9; 23.13, etc.). Millenarianism was thus a pattern of beliefs, a fact which is also apparent when we observe its transference to Christianity.

2 Christian millenarianism

Millenarianism has at times been seen in many New Testament texts, but all agree that the key passage is Revelation 20:1–10, which depicts the binding and subsequent release of Satan, separated by a thousand-year reign of Christ and his saints. Interpreters have differed, however, over whether the millennium doctrine of Revelation 20 represents merely a minor Christian modification of, or a genuine, antithetical alternative to, Jewish millenarianism (Mealy 1992; Beale 1999). Revelation 20:1–10 certainly configures the rule of Christ and his saints in an explicitly Christian way which excludes many stock elements of Jewish millenarianism, such as a return of the lost tribes, restitution of the temple and sacrificial cult, earthly peace and fecundity, and a geopolitical sovereignty centered at Jerusalem. Revelation 20:4–6 in fact depicts a scene that appears to many to be heavenly, not earthly, and which has much in common with early Christian martyrological depictions of heaven (cf. *Asc. Isa.* 6–11; *Mart. Pol.* 14; 21; Cyprian, *Ad Fortunatum* 12). In Jewish millenarian eschatology the temporary messianic reign precedes the resurrection, but in Revelation those who rule with Christ have already passed out of death into life. What is more, a key trapping of Jewish millenarianism, the view of the righteous dead awaiting the resurrection in subearthly chambers, is replaced in Revelation by a vital and specifically Christian (Luke 23:43; 2 Cor. 5:6–10) notion of the saints already in heaven (cf. 6:9–11; 16:7; 18:20; 19:2) (Hill 1992). Revelation's view of the 'intermediate state' is characteristic of Christian non-millenarian eschatologies and contrasts to that of the millenarians Justin (*Dial.* 80), Irenaeus (*Adv. Haer.* 5.31.1–2), and Tertullian (*De anima* 55.2–4).

Nevertheless, from at least the 130s (Papias; the early Justin), a Christian millenarianism was invoking John's Revelation. The form known to Papias essentially Christianized the scheme of *2 Baruch*, as can be seen both in his description of the millennium (*2 Apoc. Bar.* 29.1–30.1; *Adv. Haer.* 5.30.3–4) and in his traditions about the intermediate state (*2 Bar.* 21.23, 76.2; *Adv. Haer.* 5.5.1). It is probable that a millenarianism of a similar kind was known to Justin shortly thereafter, who is the first on record to link it explicitly to John's Revelation. Finding millenarianism in Justin and Papias, Irenaeus employed it powerfully in his debate with gnosticism, which denied the goodness of the material creation and the bodily resurrection. His integration of Old Testament, New Testament, and Jewish sources in defense of millenarian eschatology in *Adv. Haer.* 5.30.4–36.3 is remarkably thorough and mature. Even with Tertullian, about three decades later, however, a corner is being turned. Tertullian modifies Irenaeus' millenarianism with more 'spiritual' exegesis (Heid 1993), and can no longer exclude all Christians from heaven: the martyrs (but they alone) may ascend before the resurrection (*De anima* 55.5–5). This tendency to blend Millenarian and nonmillenarian elements reaches its zenith in Methodius (late third century), who retains millenarian nomenclature but expresses an essentially nonmillenarian eschatology supported by allegorical exegesis.

It is now apparent that millenarianism was never the dominant form of Christian eschatology even in the second and third centuries (Hill 1992). It was, however, advocated by a number of very notable Christian writers, including Justin, Irenaeus, Tertullian, Victorinus, and Lactantius, and was accepted early on by Augustine. An early nonmillenarian eschatology, however, always present throughout the period, gained strength as literalism in prophetic interpretation declined and as millenarianism was increasingly perceived as favoring Jewish and not Christian messianic ideas. The exegetical efforts of Jerome, Tyconius, and Augustine combined to send Christian millenarianism virtually underground by the early fifth century.

References and further reading

Beale, G.K. (1999) *The Book of Revelation: A Commentary on the Greek Text*, Grand Rapids: Eerdmans.

Daley, B.E. (1991) *The Hope of the Early Church: A Handbook of Patristic Eschatology*, Cambridge: Cambridge University Press.

Heid, S. (1993) *Chiliasmus und Antichrist-Mythos: Eine frühchristliche Kontroverse um das Heilige Land*, Bonn: Borengässer.

Hill, C.E. (1992) *Regnum Caelorum: Patterns of Future Hope in Early Christianity*, Oxford: Oxford University Press (2nd edn Grand Rapids: Eerdmans, 2001).

Mealy, J.W. (1992) *After the Thousand Years: Resurrection and the Judgment in Revelatoin 20*, JSNTSup 70, Sheffield: JSOT Press.

CHARLES E. HILL

MORRIS, LEON L. (1914–2006)

Leon L. Morris represents the voice of a sane conservatism, not only in the field of biblical studies as a whole, but also in biblical theology in particular. His best work was not always as widely received by his academic colleagues as it might have been, partly because he wrote with deceptive simplicity, partly because a very substantial part of his prolific output was designed either to serve lay Christians or to be a mediating conduit between technical scholarship and well-trained pastors and other Christian leaders. His *New Testament Theology* is an excellent example of the latter. Doubtless his years of pastoral ministry in the Australian bush, combined with his years of teaching and administration at Ridley College, Melbourne, combined to reinforce these priorities.

Nevertheless, in two domains in particular Morris' contribution has been strategic. First, in addition to a score of essays on the subject, Morris wrote at length on the cross and the atonement. His three books on the subject – one technical, one a substantive survey, one popular – reflect the kind of work that was typical of him: painstaking word studies, grammatico-historical exegesis, and close attention to related themes. For instance, in Morris' view the great atonement passage Romans 3:21–26 cannot be abstracted from the argument of Romans 1:18–3:20, which is a damning indictment of Jews and Gentiles alike, both under 'the wrath of God' which is revealed from heaven against 'all the godlessness and wickedness of men who suppress the truth by their wickedness' (Rom. 1:18). This datum necessarily feeds into the analysis of Romans 3:21ff.: by God's design, what the cross achieves, amongst other things, is the setting aside of his own principled wrath, such that God himself is vindicated (i.e., his 'righteousness' is disclosed). These connections Morris traces through the canon. Although his views on these matters are not currently in vogue, any biblical theology of the cross that does not wrestle with them merely impoverishes itself.

The second domain in which Morris made important contributions is the field of Johannine studies. In a major commentary, a volume of critical studies, a useful theology of John, and several more popular works, Morris plowed a furrow in line with the earlier works of Hengstenberg and Westcott. In some ways he was helped by the discovery of the Dead Sea Scrolls, which have gone a long way in showing that the world of the Fourth Gospel by and large fits comfortably into the matrix of first-century Palestinian Judaism, rather than something much later and more esoteric. If he did not always advance the most original proposals, he was refreshing in his stubborn refusal to stray too far from the text. His theology of John is less interested in the outlook and religio-social world of the Johannine community than it is in the theology of the texts as we have them — a frustration to some critics and a breath of fresh air to many students.

One of Morris' contributions to biblical theology has less to do with innovative synthesis than with a sterling ability to write books helpful to students at the precise moment when faddish research is in danger of leading the discipline astray. When many were highly impressed by the thesis that liturgical cycles explain the structure of one or more of the canonical Gospels, Morris' study of Jewish lectionaries was one of the works that helped turn the tide. When apocalyptic was on everyone's lips, widely advanced as the 'mother' of primitive Christian thought, Morris' little book on apocalyptic helped many a student retain a sense of proportion. Neither work was the sort of thing destined to be milestones in biblical studies, but both exercised a strategic role at the time. Similarly, his many commentaries (he wrote commentaries on almost all the New Testament books, and on two of the Old Testament books) are marked by workman-like sobriety within historic confessionalism – which is surely a better place for students to begin than with the merely faddish, even if in due course they may choose to expand their horizons.

References and further reading

Morris, L.L. (1955) *The Apostolic Preaching of the Cross*, London: Tyndale.
—— (1964) *The New Testament and the Jewish Lectionaries*, London: Tyndale.
—— (1965) *The Cross in the New Testament*, Grand Rapids: Eerdmans.
—— (1969) *Studies in the Fourth Gospel*, Grand Rapids: Eerdmans/Exeter: Paternoster.
—— (1972) *Apocalyptic*, Grand Rapids: Eerdmans.
—— (1983) *The Atonement: Its Meaning and Significance*, Downers Grove: IVP.
—— (1986) *New Testament Theology*, Grand Rapids: Zondervan.
—— (1989) *Jesus Is the Christ: Studies in the Theology of John*, Grand Rapids: Eerdmans.
—— (1995a) *Bush Parson*, Melbourne: Acorn Press.
—— (1995b [1971]) *The Gospel According to John*, NICNT, Grand Rapids: Eerdmans.

D.A. CARSON

MOULE, C.F.D. (1908–)

The contribution of C.F.D. Moule to biblical theology has not so much been in the domain of sweeping synthesis (he has not written a 'New Testament Theology') as in three complementary domains.

First, over against many of his contemporaries, who picture the growth of primitive Christianity in essentially Hegelian terms (i.e., the conflict of thesis and antithesis, Peter against Paul, Jerusalem against Antioch, historical Jesus against resurrected Christ, and so forth), Moule has written at length in terms of organic development. Nowhere is this clearer than in two of his books. *The Birth of the New Testament* lays out a panoramic vision of how the New Testament documents came to be written, and came together. More important, perhaps, is *The Origin of Christology*, which seeks to avoid the Charybdis of fundamentalism and the Scylla of skepticism. Moule argues that although the full development of 'high' Christology took some decades to work out, and can in measure be traced across the New Testament documents, the kernel of the matter was already present from the very beginning. Just as the nature of the oak tree is genetically determined by the acorn, so the development of Christology was determined by who Jesus was, and what he said and did, from the very beginning. Moule thus avoids the anachronisms that pretend the fully developed oak is already present in the acorn, and the skeptical hiatus that supposes there is only accidental connection between the acorn and the tree.

Second, although his published essays are distributed over a large range of themes and texts, much of Moule's written work has revolved around a small number of important themes: the significance of the death of Jesus Christ (and with it the nature of forgiveness, the (in)appropriateness of the category of retribution, the connections between Jesus' death and the notion of 'sacrament'), the Holy Spirit, and miracles. In the first-mentioned, Moule has repeatedly maintained that for Christians, sacrament has replaced sacrifice, and that there is no essential element in the Gospel that requires the language of sacrifice in the strict, cultic sense, even though sacrifice continues to be a metaphor used in the New Testament and in Christian tradition. On some of these themes Moule's influence has perhaps proved less convincing to many colleagues than his work in other domains.

Third, exegetical rigor and clear thinking characterize so much of his handling of the biblical text. That has been a major reason why many of his essays, published willy-nilly, have been collected into books. *An Idiom-Book of New Testament Greek* is never far away from any serious student of the Greek New Testament, and his commentary on the Greek text of Colossians, written with students in mind, is a model of clarity and precision. Long into retirement and after reading countless 'creative' proposals regarding the meaning of 'son of man,' Moule could not restrain himself from publishing a short, trenchant essay that reminded everyone of the actual *facts* of the matter, which could only trim the more imaginative suggestions. Several of his essays argue for positions that have now become widely accepted. For instance, his essay on certain datives construed with *apothnēskein* (the verb 'to die') suggests that Paul created the constructions death *to sin*, death *to law*, and death *to the world* by analogy with *zēn* (the verb 'to live') followed by the dative in a relational sense (e.g., *zēn tō theō* 'to live to God,' 4 Macc. 7:19; 16:25; Luke 20:38). His observation that John's Gospel focuses more attention on the individual than do the Synoptics and that this may be part of the reason for a greater emphasis on realized eschatology is widely accepted. Moule's exegetical astuteness has contributed to biblical theology by focusing sober attention on the text.

But perhaps it would not be unfair to say that Moule's greatest contribution to the discipline of biblical theology has been through his students, not a few of whom have become internationally influential. Moule has been above all a teacher and mentor, both at Ridley Hall, Cambridge, where he began and ended his teaching career, and especially at Cambridge University, where he held the Lady Margaret Chair of Divinity from 1951 until his retirement. Knowledgeable observers note how many of his ideas have proved seminal in the minds of his students, who later enlarged, developed, and published them.

References and further reading

Moule, C.F.D. (1957) *The Epistles of Paul the Apostle to the Colossians and to Philemon*, The Cambridge Greek Testament Commentary, Cambridge: Cambridge University Press.
—— (1959 [1953]) *An Idiom-Book of New Testament Greek*, Cambridge: Cambridge University Press, 2nd edn.
—— (1962) 'The Individualism of the Fourth Gospel,' *Novum Testamentum* 5: 171–90.
—— (1967) *The Phenomenon of the New Testament: An Inquiry into the Implications of Certain Features of the New Testament*, SBT 1, London: SCM Press.
—— (1970) 'Death "to Sin", "to Law", and "to the World": a Note on Certain Datives,' pp. 367–75 in *Mélanges bibliques en hommage au Révérent Père Béda Rigaux*, A. Descamps and A. de Halleux (eds.), Gembloux: Duculot.
—— (1977) *The Origin of Christology*, Cambridge: Cambridge University Press.
—— (1981 [1962]) *The Birth of the New Testament*, London: Black, 3rd edn.
—— (1982) *Essays in New Testament Interpretation*, Cambridge: Cambridge University Press.
—— (1995) '"The Son of Man": Some of the Facts,' *New Testament Studies* 41: 277–9.
—— (1998) *Forgiveness and Reconciliation: And Other New Testament Themes*, London: SPCK.

D.A. CARSON

MOULTON, JAMES HOPE (1863–1917)

Moulton was an English Methodist clergyman, scholar, and pacifist, best known for his contributions to the understanding of the Greek New Testament in the light of papyrus publications; he was also a specialist on Zoroastrianism.

In 1890, the same year of his ordination, Moulton married Eliza Keeling Osborn (1867–1915). Moulton had been educated at the Leys School in Cambridge, the University of Cambridge (M.A.; Fellowship at King's College 1888, the first Cambridge fellowship awarded to a Nonconformist), and the University of London (D.Lit.).

After teaching at the Leys School, he moved in 1902 to Manchester as tutor in classics and mathematics at Didsbury College (Wesleyan Methodist); 1903–1915 he was tutor in New Testament language, literature, and classics. He maintained that appointment when also appointed to the Greenwood Lectureship in Hellenistic Greek at the University of Manchester in 1905, from which he was promoted in 1908 to Greenwood Professor of Hellenistic Greek and Indo-European Philology. In 1915, following the death of his wife, he went to India at the invitation of the YMCA to work among the Parsee community in Bombay. Illness led to the decision to return to England in 1917, but he died from exposure after his ship was torpedoed in the Mediterranean.

Four major intellectual influences on Moulton's life may be identified: his father, who was one of the Revisers, founding headmaster of the Leys School, and president of the Methodist Conference in England in 1890; J. Rendel Harris (1852–1941), quaker and scholar of Greek and Syriac MSS; E.B. Cowell, professor of Sanskrit at the University of Cambridge, who initiated Moulton into Avestan and Zoroastrian studies; and G.A. Deissmann (see entry), who regarded Moulton as his closest friend in England. From the first he gained a focus on the Bible and on Greek in particular; the second cemented his pacifist views, which Moulton appears to have held to the end despite the personal calamity of the death in action of his elder son in 1916. For Moulton's long-term reputation, however, the influence of Deissmann was decisive. Moulton's two best-known works, his *Grammar of the New Testament* and *Vocabulary of the Greek Testament*, were his initiatives and bear the stamp of his lively personality, although it was left to others to complete both.

After several preliminary studies (and taking his cue from his father's translation, with improvements, of Winer's *Grammar of New Testament Greek*), Moulton produced the *Prolegomena* (vol. 1) to his *Grammar* in 1906, the third edition of which (1908) was translated into German thanks to the active promotion of it by A. Thumb. It still stands up well as both informative and highly readable. Vol. 2, *Accidence*, was largely completed by him, but finished by his former pupil W.F.

Howard and published complete in 1929 (parts 1 and 2 appeared separately in 1919 and 1921). To the projected third volume on syntax (1963) was added a fourth on style (1976). These two volumes were entirely the work of N. Turner, and reflect a considerable departure from Moulton's own views of the nature of the Greek of the New Testament (Horsley 1989: 49–65).

For *Vocabulary* Moulton drew into collaboration G. Milligan (1860–1934), a Scottish Presbyterian minister who later held the Regius Chair of Divinity at Glasgow (1910–1932). Milligan was not his first choice: E.L. Hicks (1843–1919) and then Deissmann were approached first by Moulton (North 1997, modifying Horsley 1994: 197). The first two fascicules were published in 1914 and 1915 before Moulton's death, and it was left to Milligan to finish the remaining six (the last appearing in 1929) by drawing, often verbatim, on the long series of articles they produced jointly in *The Expositor* from 1908–1912. Moulton's distinctive stamp is once more in evidence: the lively, accessible style of the entries in *Vocabulary* made it highly popular and has kept it in print since the one-volume edition appeared in 1930. Yet its very readability veils a certain looseness in focus on what is actually being illustrated in each entry. The strongly papyrological orientation of the work (signaled by its subtitle) in part reflects a desire not to cover the same territory – viz., epigraphy – which Deissmann had intended for his own projected lexicon (Horsley 1994: 196). There were two unintended negative effects of *Vocabulary* on New Testament scholarship for the next two generations: it gave the impression that the papyri would not have much more to offer; and by their relative lack of mention the inference was frequently drawn that the inscriptions were of little relevance for the New Testament. It has taken a long time for these misconceptions to start to change.

An athletic and energetic individual, Moulton threw himself into tasks knowing he could rely on his strong philological training to produce work of substance. Yet he was also a popularizer (in the best sense); and the effect of the combination of his talents was that he had a propensity for somewhat cavalier progress. Milligan's more careful approach to the *Vocabulary* task helped ensure their joint work's lasting quality; Moulton's lasting contribution was to make it enjoyable.

A biography of Moulton and his intellectual circle is needed.

References and further reading

Horsley, G.H.R. (1989) *New Documents Illustrating Early Christianity*, Vol. 5: *Linguistic Essays*, Sydney, Macquarie Univ. Ancient History Documentary Research Centre.
—— (1994) 'The Origins and Scope of Moulton and Milligan's *Vocabulary of the Greek Testament*, and Deissmann's Planned New Testament Lexicon. Some

Unpublished Letters of G.A. Deissmann to J.H. Moulton,' *Bulletin of the John Rylands Library* 76(1): 187–216.

Moulton, H.K. (1963) *James Hope Moulton, 11th October 1863–7 April 1917*, London: Epworth Press.

Moulton, J.H. (1906–1976) *Grammar of New Testament Greek*, Edinburgh: T.&T. Clark (vol. 1 *Prolegomena*, 1906, 3rd edn 1908; other vols. completed or written by others).

—— (1913) *Early Zoroastrianism*, Hibbert Lectures 1912, London: Williams and Norgate.

—— and G. Milligan (1930) *The Vocabulary of the Greek Testament, illustrated from the papyri and other non-literary sources*, 8 fasc., London: Hodder & Stoughton 1914–1929 (one vol. edn 1930; freq. repr., the current imprint being at Peabody, MA: Hendrickson).

North, J.L. (1997) '"I sought a colleague": James Hope Moulton, Papyrologist, and Edward Lee Hicks, Epigraphist, 1903–1906,' *Bulletin of the John Rylands Library* 79(1): 195–205.

G.H.R. HORSLEY

MUSIC AND INTERPRETATION

1 Introduction

The composer of sacred music, to some degree in every century since the beginning of the Christian church, has interpreted the Bible and other liturgical texts through the musical–textual interrelationships of these compositions. These works shed light on the history of interpretation of the Bible at the time of their composition. Whether composers altered biblical and theological passages, juxtaposed biblical passages used nonbiblical texts to provide commentary on biblical ones, or specifically set individual words or phrases in a way that influences one's view of the larger text, each presents a particular view of the biblical passage and is itself an interpretation of it.

2 Third-century Christian hymn

An anonymous Christian hymn, the first to be found with accompanying musical notation, is dated to the latter part of the third century. This Greek musical fragment, P.Oxy. 1786, was found written on the back of a papyrus account for corn, in Oxyrhynchus, Egypt.

This early Christian hymn provides interesting evidence of early biblical interpretation through music. Fragments torn away from the manuscript and sections that are simply missing mean we do not know the full extent of this work. This musical work draws not only on the Old Testament, but also on the New. The fact that the hymn was written down may suggest that it had been known previously, for the passing on of music was largely by means of oral tradition and this would have been the means to preserve the hymn. In that case, it may represent biblical interpretation from the second or early third century; if the hymn was a new composition, it may represent slightly later interpretation.

Grenfell and Hunt summarize the hymn: 'Creation at large is called upon to join in a chorus of praise to Father, Son, and Holy Spirit, and the concluding passage is the usual ascription of power and glory to the "only giver of all good gifts"' (Grenfell and Hunt 1922; cf. West 1992; Werner 1962). The doxology at the end of this hymn fragment shows an integration of Old Testament-like sections within it, while placed clearly within the new Christian tradition, as the shift from terms like 'Lord' to 'Father, Son, and Holy Spirit' indicates. An integration of psalm passages, language that sounds like Revelation, and echoes of classical Greek hymns (e.g., Cleanthes, 'Hymn to Zeus') result in a hymn that synthesizes and reinterprets earlier documents in an unprecedented way.

3 Tenth-century New Testament lectionary

This Greek parchment codex (Austrian National Library Suppl. Gr. 121; Gregory-Aland 0105; see Gregory 1909: III, 1066–74; Hunger with Hannick 1994: 208; Porter and Porter forthcoming; cf. Porter forthcoming) contains the lectionary passages from John 6:71–7:46. Its ekphonetic (musical–rhetorical) notation and other markings give interpretive clues as to its musical presentation in a liturgical setting.

The surviving four folios (or eight pages) include headings that divide the units according to a liturgical calendar.

Ekphonetic notation varies from manuscript to manuscript, even where the pericopes are the same – here the liturgical hand provides clues to interpretation of these biblical passages (Wellesz 1961: 256; Tillyard 1935: 13). Scholars think the signs represent melodies or melodic formulae, passed down through oral tradition (Velimirovic 1960: 61–7). In this portion of the lectionary, the text is divided into four pericopes or scenarios, with only three of the four notated ekphonetically.

Although ekphonetic notation is still not entirely understood, nor the actual sounds that it represents, it is clear that the notation represents a specific interpretive plan for each passage as a whole. Single words or groups of two words often are given specific emphases. It is evident that the interpreter was involved in very close readings of the text; it seems to be understood that the person delivering these musical readings would accurately interpret and deliver the text according to the ekphonetic notation.

4 Sixteenth-century responsory by Sheppard

The choice of texts plays a role in musical interpretation of the Bible, such as the responsory of English composer John Sheppard (c. 1515–1558). The Latin text, Verbum caro factum est, 'The Word was made flesh' (Christ Church, Oxford: Mus. MS 979; see Hofman and Morehen 1987), a six-part respond-motet for Christmas Day, is one such choice.

Verbum caro factum est comes from two New Testament verses: John 1:14, 'The word was made flesh and dwelt among us: and we beheld his glory as of the only Son of the Father, full of grace and truth'; and John 1:1, 'In the beginning was the Word, and the Word was with God, and the Word was God,' combined with the Lesser Doxology, 'Glory be to the Father and to the Son and to the Holy Spirit.' Although the doxology is not technically scripture, in most musical-liturgical settings it is treated as scripture.

Prior to the sixteenth century, responsory settings were limited to a very small number of texts (Doe 1968–1969: 93–4). Sheppard, using a new distribution of polyphony and plainchant between the parts, reshapes and, essentially, reinterprets these texts. The form of the responsory and the pattern of repetition in the text emphasizes the last phrase of John 1:14, and juxtaposes others, which gives increasing attention to the second and third parts of this verse. Increasing prominence is given to the penultimate phrase, 'full of grace,' and even more prominence to the final repetitive phrase, 'of truth.' In the second setting, the conflated text now reads: 'In the beginning was the word and the word was with God and the word was God/we beheld his glory as of the only Son of the Father.' In the last section, 'and we beheld his glory as of the only Son of the Father/full of grace and truth' now reads 'Glory be to the Father and to the Son and to the Holy Spirit/full of grace and truth.' This draws attention back to John 1:14 and suggests that it is fundamental to the other two texts. Sheppard has taken a liturgical practice and applied it to a text that had not been set polyphonically in this way. In doing so, he presents a new perspective on this New Testament text.

5 Eighteenth-century motet by Bach

Johann Sebastian Bach (1685–1750) frequently interprets biblical passages through his music, whether passions, masses, cantatas, chorales, or motets, some would even say the instrumental music. Bach's notations in his Bible give evidence of his interest in interpreting it. One example is how he juxtaposes two verses from Romans 8 (vv. 26, 27) with a hymn from Martin Luther (Komm, Heiliger Geist, Herre Gott, 1524) in his motet, Der Geist hilft unsrer Schwachheit auf, 'The Spirit helps us in our weakness' (BWV 226). He uses this setting to interpret the Lord's nearness in the time of death and mourning, clearly articulating the feeling of sorrow, and contrasting this with the secure calm of the Holy Spirit's presence with the grieving believer.

The use of chromatic notes, the tritone, and minor seconds, all help to express the anguish of the text. As the biblical text shifts from the personal dimension and suffering to the 'mind of the Spirit' and 'God's will,' the musical writing becomes more straightforward and spacious.

The third section is the briefest. It brings the listener back to Luther's familiar hymn, in the familiar style of the Lutheran chorale. The verse, appropriate to the situation, speaks of help from the Holy Spirit – in keeping with the earlier Romans text – and of preparation for death, finding the grave a door or portal to God in heaven, and to life immortal. The concluding 'Halleluja, halleluja' at this point is oddly fitting and provides a victorious if brief conclusion to the work. Bach's setting of two verses in Romans and their transition to Luther's hymn takes one on a journey through suffering and pain to the mind of God and ultimately to a hymn that speaks of life immortal.

6 Nineteenth-century mass by Beethoven

The Missa Solemnis of Ludwig van Beethoven (1770–1827) clearly depicts one aspect of the Christ figure that has never been so evident before – the humanity of Christ. While the standard Credo text always has the phrase et homo factus est – 'and was made man' – Beethoven treats this statement in a new way. His division of the text, use of tempos, keys, and their interrelationships, attention to certain words and ideas in the various sections, and integration and contrast of soloists and chorus, all clearly interpret this phrase in an unprecedented way (Porter 1996).

Beethoven marks out fifteen independent sections in the text of the Credo. In doing this, he isolates phrases that Bach, for instance, does not, such as the separation of et homo factus est, 'and was made man,' from its preceding et incarnatus est, 'and was incarnate.' This gives deliberate emphasis to the role of Jesus becoming human. Part of Beethoven's genius is in the ambiguity about the central focus of his Credo: is it three or four sections? If three, et homo factus est is in the middle of the three. If four, then if crucifixus is central by intention, the symmetrical balance does not fully support this arrangement. The question relates partly to the passage that follows immediately after *crucifixus: et resurrexit*. In some ways *et resurrexit* seems to belong to the previous group and in some ways to the following group. It is unlikely that this ambiguity is unintentional.

The interaction and contrast of soloists with chorus clearly directs attention to the human image presented in *et incarnatus, et homo*, and *crucifixus*. The four soloists begin with a semispoken style, while the chorus enters *pianissimo*, also in a semispoken style of chant, creating a sense of underlying mystery that reinforces the inexplicable concept of how God could become human. From a quiet and intense chant section, the tenor emerges from the choir on the same note that the upper voices have been chanting. As the music abruptly changes from archaic mode into D major, the tenor moves up a tone to begin in earnest the full phrase, *et homo factus est*. In this shift, the sudden and rather unexpected change from minor chord to major (*tierce de picardie*) creates a dramatic transition from suppressed tension to bold release. The tenor line presents *et homo factus est* as though utterly thrilled to discover that he is human and truly alive. Beethoven fleshes out the Christ image by filling in the depth of his humanity. Indeed, his Christ figure seems to live and breathe, and even seems quite modern.

7 Twentieth-century motet by Poulenc

Although Francis Poulenc (1899–1962) is sometimes characterized as sentimental and nostalgic (Mellers 1962: 227), his *Tenebrae factae sunt*, 'It became dark,' is anything but these (Porter 2002). This third of four motets is deeply expressive – it seems to place the listener right at the Crucifixion and gives a vivid and profoundly moving interpretation of that event.

The text is the key to this powerful motet, a standard text for Holy Week. This is by no means a standard musical interpretation of it, however. *Tenebrae facta sunt* is a composite of the four Gospel accounts of the Crucifixion: 'It became dark when the Jews had crucified Jesus, and around the ninth hour Jesus exclaimed in a loud voice: "My God, why have you forsaken me?" and with inclined head he gave up the spirit. Crying out, Jesus with a loud voice said: "Father, into your hands I commend my spirit" and with inclined head he gave up the spirit.'

The first phrase is paraphrased from the three Synoptic Gospel accounts (Matt. 27:45; Mark 15:33; Luke 23:44), although they do not state that 'it became dark *when the Jews had crucified Jesus*,' only that it became dark. The second portion of the text follows Matthew 27:46 and Mark 15:34 closely. The next section comes from John 19:30, Matthew 27:50, with the final lines from Luke 23:46.

Poulenc mixes old with new in this work, bringing about a metamorphosis of the text and scene. The first muted notes of the motet give an impression of darkness and foreboding, setting the scene of the Crucifixion.

It is poignant that in Jesus' exclamation 'in a loud voice, "My God, my God, why have you forsaken me?"' it is only the first two words that are sung in that 'loud voice.' The rest are quiet, as though Jesus has used all the breath he can muster to speak the first two words. Their echo is much like the sound of a desperate, dying, and forsaken man: 'MY GOD ... my God ... why have you forsaken me ...?' Poulenc's choice of upper voices and notes on *Deus meus*, 'My God,' further suggests a strained sound, one that cannot be sustained and must subside. This suggestion of physical fatigue, pain, effort, and rejection is Poulenc's interpretation of Jesus' final moments on the cross (Hengel 1986: 93–185).

8 Twentieth-century mass by Stravinsky

Igor Stravinsky (1882–1971) had moved far from his *Rite of Spring* ballet of 1911 by the time he composed the *Mass* in the mid-1940s. He wrote the mass for liturgical use, not concert performance (Stravinsky and Craft 1959: 76), one of his few uncommissioned works, suggesting genuine piety.

Within this short *Mass*, Stravinsky uses classical symmetry as a formal arch, with the longest movement being the Credo. He chose Latin (Amy 1986: 196), although his native Russian would have been a natural choice, having rejoined the Russian Orthodox Church in the late 1920s. Stravinsky's pragmatic reason was that Russian Orthodoxy did not allow for musical instruments in its services, which he was not prepared to forgo. Written for children's and men's voices – Stravinsky expressed the belief that women's voices were too passionate for liturgical chant – the liturgical nature of the setting is evident throughout (Craft 1982: 246–7).

Stravinsky's Christ image in the Credo is somewhat two-dimensional and symbolic; certainly not sentimental in any way. The Credo is scored for voices in semichant and, in fact, the setting is one long, practically unbroken chant. The unusual instrumentation of oboes, cor anglais, bassoons, trumpets, and trombones creates a sound not unlike an organ. The dynamic range is narrow and the vocal range limited, with few dramatic effects or ornamentation (Siohan 1965: 129; Druskin 1983: 26). There are no soloists in the Credo – no one individual emerges in this section at all. Attention is focused on the function of the text, and, as a result, his mass creates an image of Christ that is almost featureless and flat. There is no sense of emotion to suggest the warmth of a living Christ. The image is a symbolic one that does not seem intended to display a natural lifelikeness, or an ethereal otherworldliness, but is simply functional (White 1979: 447; Walsh 1993: 193). This setting of the mass has an element of timelessness (White 1979: 100). Stravinsky seems to have been trying to transcend normal temporal boundaries, and in some ways to present the mass in the tradition of the great icon painters of the Orthodox Church.

9 Twentieth-century musical ikons by Tavener

The choral work, 'We Shall See Him as He Is' by John Tavener (1940–), represents the continuing musical and liturgical need to reinterpret biblical passages. Tavener uses Byzantine musical idioms and some theological ideas of the Eastern Christian Church, and brings them to an unusually receptive Western Christian Church. He attempts to present visual symbols and visual forms of ritual through his music, using ancient chant formulae and the terminology of 'ikons' (Burn 1992: 3). These ikons reflect his interest in the iconography of the Greek Orthodox Church. Tavener's musical settings are sometimes deceptively simple, often extreme in vocal and instrumental range, with minute changes in orchestration, ornamentation, or dynamics, and little development in the classical sense. The music is static and ritualistic. The idea of mosaic also exists in his musical timbres and in the compilation of the text.

Mother Thekla, of the Greek Orthodox Church, is the compiler and arranger of the text for this work. The New Testament images are not exactly rewritten, but the text is reductionistic, even minimalistic. While appearing at first to come from John's Gospel, the text conflates three books that tradition attributes to the same author, but which have very different styles of writing and very different roles in the New Testament: John's Gospel, the First Epistle of John, and Revelation or the Apocalypse of John. John is the perceived author and main character of this musical work. The interesting merging of texts is observed in the two phrases that form the refrain. The first, the title of this work, 'we shall see him as he is' (1 John 3:2), is combined with the second phrase of the refrain, 'Amen, come Lord Jesus,' from the penultimate verse in Revelation 22:20. The refrain is sung in Greek throughout the piece until the very last line of the work, where it is in English. The words outline a portrait without filling in the details.

The work is set out in eleven 'ikons' or pericopes from John's Gospel. An example of the abbreviated form of text is found in Ikon 1: 'I heard: Before time was. Time within. Time beyond. Created. Uncreated. Bodiless Body' (see John 1:1–4 and 1 John 1:1–2).

In a stylized way, Tavener provides insight into the twentieth-century penchant to reread and reinterpret old texts, rearranging them in new kaleidoscopic ways.

10 Conclusion

While having merely touched on these works, and each is only representative of a much larger body of works, it is evident that each one unveils and interprets unique facets of the biblical text through its musical setting. The works reveal composers in the role of interpreter of the Bible. Although the composition of sacred music in recent years has been seen as less creative than that of writing music for its own sake, in fact, the com-poser, in writing sacred music, has had the unique opportunity of engaging intellectually with the text at a theological level by composing a musical work that recreates the text in some new form. In this new form, the composer sets out for performance and for evaluation a personal or collective interpretation of the biblical text.

References and further reading

P.Oxy. 1786

Bischel, M.A. (1992) 'Hymns, Early Christian,' *ABD* 3.350–51.

Grenfell, B.P. and A.S. Hunt (1922) '1786. Christian Hymn with Musical Notation,' pp. 21–5. in *The Oxyrhynchus Papyri*, XV. London: Egypt Exploration Society.

McKinnon, J. (ed.) (1987) *Music in Early Christian Literature*, Cambridge: Cambridge University Press.

Mountford, J.F. (1929) 'Greek Music in the Papyri and Inscriptions,' pp. 146–83 in *New Chapters in the History of Greek Literature*, Second Series, J.U. Powell and E.A. Barber (eds.), Oxford: Clarendon Press.

Smith, J.A. (1984) 'The Ancient Synagogue, the Early Church and Singing,' *Music & Letters* 65(1): 1–16.

Wellesz, E. (1961) *A History of Byzantine Music and Hymnography*, Oxford: Clarendon Press, 2nd rev. edn.

Werner, E. (1962) 'Music,' pp. 457–69 in *The Interpreter's Dictionary of the Bible*, 4 Vols., G.A. Buttrick (ed.), Nashville: Abingdon Press.

West, M.L. (1992) 'Analecta Musica,' *Zeitschrift für Papyrologie und Epigraphik* 92: 1–54.

—— (1998) 'Texts with Musical Notation,' pp. 81–102 in *Oxyrhynchi Papyri*, LXV, M.W. Haslam *et al.* (eds.), London: Egypt Exploration Society.

Tenth-century lectionary

Gregory, C.R. (1909) *Textkritik des Neuen Testaments*, 3 Vols., Leipzig: Teubner.

Hunger, H. with C. Hannick (1994) *Katalog der Griechischen Handschriften der Österreichischen National-bibliothek*, Part 4, Vienna: Österreichischen Nationalbibliothek.

Porter, S.E. and W.J. Porter (forthcoming) *New Testament Greek Papyri and Parchments: New Editions*, Vienna: Österreichische Nationalbibliothek, no. 39.

Porter, W.J. (forthcoming) 'The Use of Ekphonetic Notation in Vienna New Testament Manuscripts,' in *Acts of the 23rd International Congress of Papyrology, Vienna, Austria, 23–28 July 2001*, H. Harrauer and B. Palme (eds.), Vienna: Österreichische Nationalbibliothek.

Tillyard, H.J.W. (1935) *Handbook of the Middle Byzantine Musical Notation*, Copenhagen: Levin & Mundsgaard.

Velimirovic, M.M. *Byzantine Elements in Early Slavonic Chant*, Copenhagen: Ejnar Munksgaard.

Wellesz, E. (1961 [1948]) *A History of Byzantine Music and Hymnography*, Oxford: Oxford University Press, 2nd edn.

Sheppard

Benham, H. (1977) *Latin Church Music in England 1460–1575*, London: Barrie & Jenkins.

Chadd, D. (trans. and ed.) (1977) *John Sheppard*: Vol. I: *Responsorial Music*, London: Stainer & Bell.

Doe, P. (1968–1969) 'Latin Polyphony under Henry VIII,' *Proceedings of the (Royal) Musical Association* 95: 81–95.

Harrison, F.L. (1980) *Music in Medieval Britain*, Buren, The Netherlands: Fritz Knuf.

Hofman, M. and J. Morehen (eds.) (1987) *Latin Music in British Sources c1485–c1610*, London: Stainer & Bell.

Hughes, A. (1982) *Medieval Manuscripts for Mass and Office: A Guide to their Organization and Terminology*, Toronto: University of Toronto Press.

le Huray, P. (1978) *Music and the Reformation in England 1549–1660*, Cambridge: Cambridge University Press.

Wulstan, D. (1994) 'Where there's a Will,' *Musical Times* 135: 25–7.

Bach

Butt, J. (1991) *Bach: Mass in B Minor*, Cambridge: Cambridge University Press.

Daw, S. (1981) *The Music of Johann Sebastian Bach: The Choral Works*, East Brunswick: Fairleigh Dickinson University Press/Associated University Presses.

Geiringer, K. (1967) *Johann Sebastian Bach: The Culmination of an Era*, London: George Allen and Unwin.

Hofmann, K. (1995) Preface, 'Bey Beerdigung des seel. Hn. Prof. und Rectoris Ernesti,' in *Johann Sebastian Bach Motetten Motets BWV 225–230*, K. Ameln (ed.), Kassel: Bärenreiter-Verlag.

McCaldin, D. (1971) 'The Choral Music,' pp. 387–410 in *The Beethoven Companion*, D. Arnold and N. Fortune (eds.), London: Faber and Faber.

Schweitzer, A. (1911) *J.S. Bach*, Vol. II, trans. E. Newman, 2 Vols., London: Breitkopf.

Spitta, P. (1889) *Johann Sebastian Bach: His Work and Influence on the Music of Germany, 1685–1750*, Vol. II, trans. C. Bell and J.A. Fuller-Maitland, 3 Vols., London: Novello (repr. New York: Dover, 1951).

Terry, C.S. (1933) *The Music of Bach: An Introduction*, London: Oxford University Press.

Wolff, C. (1991) *Bach: Essays on his Life and Music*, Cambridge: Harvard University Press.

Beethoven

Cooper, B. (1990) *Beethoven and the Creative Process*, Oxford: Clarendon Press.

Fiske, R. (1979) *Beethoven's Missa Solemnis*, London: Paul Elek.

Kirkendale, W. (1970) 'New Roads to Old Ideas in Beethoven's *Missa Solemnis*,' *Musical Quarterly* 56: 676–700.

Porter, W.J. (1996) 'Bach, Beethoven and Stravinsky Masses: Images of Christ in the Credo,' pp. 375–98 in *Images of Christ: Ancient and Modern*, S.E. Porter, M.A. Hayes, and D. Tombs (eds.), Sheffield: Sheffield Academic Press.

Solomon, M. (1988) 'Beethoven: The Quest for Faith,' pp. 216–29 in *Beethoven Essays*, Cambridge: Harvard University Press.

Poulenc

Daniel, K.W. (1980, 1982) *Francis Poulenc: His Artistic Development and Musical Style*, Ann Arbor: UMI Research Press.

Hengel, M. (1986) *The Cross of the Son of God: Containing The Son of God, Crucifixion, The Atonement*, trans. J. Bowden, London: SCM Press.

Mellers, W. (1962) *Man and his Music: The Story of Musical Experience in the West: Romanticism and the Twentieth Century*, Vol. IV, London: Barrie & Rockliff.

Porter, W.J. (2002) 'The Composer of Sacred Music as an Interpreter of the Bible,' pp. 126–53 in *Borders, Boundaries and the Bible*, M. O'Kane (ed.), Sheffield: Sheffield Academic Press.

Poulenc, F. (1978 [1963]) *My Friends and Myself*, conversations assembled by S. Audel, trans. J. Harding, London: Dennis Dobson.

Stravinsky

Amy, G. (1986) 'Aspects of the Religious Music of Igor Stravinsky,' pp. 195–206 in *Confronting Stravinsky: Man, Musician, and Modernist*, J. Pasler (ed.), Berkeley: University of California Press.

Craft, R. (ed.) (1982) *Stravinsky: Selected Correspondence*, Vol. I, London: Faber and Faber.

Druskin, M. (1983) *Igor Stravinsky: His Life, Works and Views*, trans. M. Cooper, Cambridge: Cambridge University Press.

Siohan, R. (1965) *Stravinsky*, trans. E.W. White, London: Calder and Boyars.

Stravinsky, I. and R. Craft (1959) *Igor Stravinsky: Expositions and Developments*, London: Faber and Faber.

Walsh, S. (1993) *The Music of Stravinsky*, Oxford: Clarendon Press.

White, E.W. (1979) *Stravinsky: The Composer and his Works*, London: Faber and Faber.

Tavener

Burn, A. (1992) notes, 'John Tavener: "We Shall See Him as He Is",' Chandos Chan 9128.

Porter, W.J. (2001) 'Sacred Music at the Turn of the Millennia,' pp. 423–44 in *Faith in the Millennium*, S.E. Porter, M.A. Hayes, and D. Tombs (eds.), Sheffield: Sheffield Academic Press.

Smith, R.L. (1992) 'Review, "A Winning Path",' *Musical Times* 133: 475–6.

WENDY J. PORTER

N

NARRATIVE

Biblical narratives, story accounts that connect events in order of happenings, have nurtured faiths, instructed theologies and challenged imaginations for centuries. At the heart of Christianity and Judaism are artistic and poetic stories from scripture that shape our convictions and theological ideas. Valuable Christian expressions like creeds, baptism, communion, symbols, liturgies, etc., all have their basis primarily in biblical narratives. While these artistic writings come from ancient, prescientific, and alien worldviews, they continue to reach across cultural and historical distance to influence our beliefs and practices today.

As a literary genre, narratives compose a considerable portion of both New Testament and Hebrew scriptures. However, narratives are significant not only because of their volume but also their relational nature. Most people are introduced to religious ideas through stories because stories resonate with common experiences of life. Whether the narrative is a portion of a text or an entire book, even the most fantastical of biblical stories connect readily with readers in exceptional ways. Through the tension, drama, and power of unfolding narratives, readers are caught up in the message. And while the study of narratives may seem in contradiction to this sense of 'just reading the text,' narrative scholarship is essential to our understanding of their meanings.

The study of narratives, how thinkers read them, and then subsequently arrive at justifications for various theological ideas reflect both narrative study and systematic reflection – literary, historical, and theological concerns. Previous scholarship has sometimes erred in approaching biblical narratives by imposing contemporary literary models without appreciating the narratives in their own right, or by supposing sacred literature to be so unlike other texts that it could not be examined appropriately as literary work. The kinds of truth claims we think stories make, the sorts of questions we ask of them, and the method and historical assumptions we make in reading and interpreting biblical narratives will profoundly shape our lives, faith, and practices. The value of narrative scholarship is clear.

While narrative is an essential genre of the Bible it can also be difficult to interpret. More than detailed accounts of life experiences in which historical accuracy could be mistaken as the fully intended meaning of texts, biblical narratives were created by writers as stories and fables. Some authors chose to narrate factual information with little elaboration while others displayed great literary art and crafting through various forms of description, plot development, characterization, perspective (often of an omniscient narrator), dialogue, wordplay, ordering of events, dramatic tension, etc. Narrative authors desired above all to convey meaning and purpose to their readers rather than stringent obedience to facts.

The generally recognized sparcity of narrative details, i.e., characters, events, and settings, has been judged by some scholars as a sign of the crude and elemental nature of biblical narratives. However, contemporary scholarship has increasingly recognized the art of biblical narrative and the sophistication of literary skill involved. As a consequence, narratives should not be hastily classified, defined, or thematically categorized. The genre has many different motifs, themes, story patterns, intentions, linguistic and generic features. While biblical stories are typically identified as having events, characters, and settings, the relative complexities of their forms make defining all-inclusive criteria for the genre challenging – if not foolish.

One of the most demanding problems for the interpretation of narratives is the classification of historicity or pseudohistoricity. This difficulty often occurs when one segregates narratives by their historical or nonhistorical character without appreciating the highly fictionalized nature of much of the materials. By sacrificing historical detail for the sake of conveying theological truth, narrators often frustrate any simple definition of their own sense of historicity as evident in the texts. The combination of both history and theology in story format does not easily admit to the modern reader the type of information we might like. The task of interpreting biblical narrative is the discovery of meaning in the historical-theological text of the story and not necessarily the reduction of the story to the specific truth of an original event. The historicity or pseudohistoricity of narratives is a complex issue that reveals itself more and more because of a desire to place scientific categories and literary models on ancient cultures and texts.

If we approach the genre with the intention of merely employing it as an instrument for formulating propositional truths about God or historical facts, we will miss a great deal that it has to offer us. Narratives do not consist of sets of doctrines or propositions for normative guidance in life and belief but present us with rich stories in which the reader can participate. One of the mistaken prejudices of previous scholarship has been to emphasize literary, historical, or theological concerns to the detriment of a coherent and justified approach to scripture. The present task is to seek new ways in which these different concerns may dialogue with and do justice to one another.

Since the late 1960s, increasing numbers of scholars have suggested that many methods of the traditional historical-critical approaches, e.g., source and form analysis, have come to a relative standstill. Following the desire for new approaches to studying biblical literature, literary criticism has developed into many forms like that of narrative criticism. As a critical methodology, narrative criticism of biblical texts is the hermeneutical endeavor that seeks to understand the various factors that combine for a close reading of a text's narrative world without being arbitrary and subjective. Narrative criticism attempts to appreciate the aesthetic nature of stories as both a literary and historical concern within the larger context of the stories or books themselves rather than isolated segments on their own. Compared to other schools of biblical criticism, narrative criticism generally places less stress on specific theological ideas, historical reference, grammar, and lexicographical matters. Instead, narrative criticism emphasizes analysis of plot, theme, motifs, characterization, style, figures of speech, symbols, repetition, etc. In cases of integrated approaches to the Bible – such as the combination of reader-response theories with narrative criticism – the result is often quite positive.

References and further reading

Alter, R. (1981) *The Art of Biblical Narrative: A Critical Introduction*, New York: Basic.

Clines, David J.A., David M. Gunn, and Alan J. Hauser (eds.) (1982) *Art and Meaning: Rhetoric in Biblical Literature*, Sheffield: JSOT Press.

Frei, Hans W. (1974) *The Eclipse of Biblical Narrative: A Study in Eighteenth and Nineteenth Century Hermeneutics*, London: Yale University Press.

Goldbert, Michael (1982) *Theology and Narrative: A Critical Introduction*, Nashville: Abingdon Press.

McConnell, Frank (ed.) (1986) *The Bible and the Narrative Tradition*, Oxford: Oxford University Press.

J.C. ROBINSON

NARRATIVE CRITICISM

Narrative criticism is often treated as a subcategory of literary criticism. However, the 1980s provided a watershed, when narrative criticism came to be regarded as a critical method of biblical studies in its own right. Robert Alter's publication of *The Art of Biblical Narrative* appears to be the turning point in 1981. While the term 'narrative criticism' is more common in New Testament studies than among Hebrew Bible scholars, there has been parallel work in the application of methodology, with Hebrew Bible scholars usually leading the way in the application of current trends in secular literary criticism. Narrative criticism in Hebrew Bible and New Testament studies can also be distinguished respectively by an interest in poetry versus an interest in ancient rhetoric.

Narrative critics read biblical narratives as literature or story, taking a 'fictive' approach, which treats the text as art or poetry. They interpret the text in its final form in terms of its own story world. A narrative critic's 'close reading' assumes literary integrity and reads the text holistically. The text is processed sequentially, and the parts are related to the whole. The approach is in contrast, for example, with traditional treatments of the Gospels where studies isolate individual pericopes or scholars create synopses that combine all four Gospels into one account. Narrative criticism is also a reaction against historical criticism which attempts to reconstruct sources and recreate an editorial history of the text, and focuses on the original setting, recipients, and the author's or editor's intentions. Narrative critics deplore the historical critics' tendency to segment the text. They claim to advocate a 'restorationist biblicism' that respects the text and provides a better basis for its religious use.

The methodology of narrative criticism is complex and by no means unified, but may be summarized in four steps that are not necessarily taken by a critic in a sequential manner. First, the *form* of the text is analyzed and categorized according to formal and conventional literary aspects and genres. Literary aspect includes the categories of fiction, nonfiction, prose, and poetry. Literary narrative genres include categories such as history, legend, and myth. Second, the literary *structure* of the text is analyzed in terms of setting, plot, language play, and theme. The setting consists of the basic context given in the narrative in which the plot and the characters develop. It includes geographical, temporal, social, and historical information. The plot includes the story's beginning, a sequence of events that build to the climax, and the ending. Plot can be studied at a macro (the whole text) or micro (pericope) level. It involves attention to narrative time, which is regarded as literary arrangement of the order of events rather than historical sequence. Conversely, attention is given to temporal or thematic discontinuity, due to the assumption that gaps, suspense, or inconsistency contribute to the meaning of the story. Language play provides implicit commentary that guides the reader through the story and includes devices such as irony, comedy, symbolism, repetition, and omission. Third, the *characters* are studied. Conventional roles such as protagonists and antagonists are identified as well as motives and change. The use of characterization is significant: how the author develops interesting personalities with whom the reader identifies is key to the narrative. Fourth, the *narrative perspective* or points of view taken by various characters are identified. Among some narrative critics, there is a distinction between the real author, the implied author, and the narrator. The narrator is the person within the story that is telling the story, and the implied narrator is the perspective from which the text is written. In the Gospel of John, the narrator is the 'beloved disciple,' and the implied narrator is John. The perspectives from which the text is told include the use of the first or third person, the temporal location and the omniscience and/or omnipresence of the author/narrator who is able to interpret events from a future perspective and provide the reader with 'inside' information about characters' thoughts, motivations, reasons, and private conversations. There is a similar distinction made by some between the real reader, the narratee, and the implied reader. The implied readers are the group of readers that the text addresses who share certain presuppositions and knowledge of certain information. The real reader is meant to agree to accept the dynamic of the story world created by the author, temporarily adopting the faith commitments and value systems indicated by the text in order to associate with the feelings of the implied readers and determine the effect of the text, which is the intended response. The application of the four steps of narrative criticism is directed toward the detection of an overarching or encapsulating theme.

Narrative criticism is characterized by a remarkable diversity of approach. There is a growing interest in intertextuality, which is interconnection with texts outside of a narrative's immediate contextual boundaries. There is considerable disagreement about narratorial reliability (omniscience), the role of texts, contexts and readers, and the implications of interpretations. Even if all can be brought to agree on the facts, what is made of the facts is entirely different. Therefore, there has been a growing recognition that a uniform system of reading cannot guarantee uniform interpretation. Some narrative critics are combining reader-response criticism with narrative criticism through paying attention to the role of the reader in making meaning and studying how the text interprets the readers by helping them to understand themselves and their experiences. Literary criticism and narrative criticism are also combined with other current literary and sociological trends such as deconstruction, feminist criticism, political criticism, and psychoanalytic criticism.

References and further reading

Alter, R. (1981) *The Art of Biblical Narrative*, New York: Basic.

—— (1985) *The Art of Biblical Poetry*, New York: Basic.

Amit, Y. (2001) *Reading Biblical Narratives: Literary Criticism and the Hebrew Bible*, Minneapolis: Fortress Press.

Bal, M. (1991) *On Story-Telling: Essays in Narratology*, David Jobling (ed.), Sonoma: Polebridge.

Bauer, D.R. (1988) *The Structure of Matthew's Gospel: A Study in Literary Design*, Sheffield: Almond.

Camery-Hoggatt, J. (1992) *Irony in Mark's Gospel: Text and Subtext*, Cambridge: Cambridge University Press.

Culpepper, R.A. (1983) *Anatomy of the Fourth Gospel: A Study in Literary Design*, Philadelphia: Fortress Press.

Darr, J.A. (1992) *On Character Building: The Reader and the Rhetoric of Characterization in Luke-Acts*, Louisville: Westminster/John Knox.

Duke, P. (1985) *Irony in the Fourth Gospel*, Atlanta: John Knox.

Fokkelman, J.P. (1999) *Reading Biblical Narrative: An Introductory Guide*, trans. I. Smit, Louisville: Westminster/John Knox.

—— (2001) *Reading Biblical Poetry: An Introductory Guide*, trans. I. Smit, Louisville: Westminster/John Knox.

Gunn, D.M. (1999) 'Narrative Criticism', pp. 201–29 in *To Each Its Own Meaning: An Introduction to Biblical Criticisms and their Applications, Revised and Expanded*, S.L. McKenzie and S.R. Haynes (eds.), Louisville: Westminster/John Knox.

—— and D.N. Fewell (1993) *Narrative in the Hebrew Bible*, Oxford: Oxford University Press.

Heil, J.P. (1991) *The Death and Resurrection of Jesus: A Narrative-Critical Reading of Matthew 26–28*, Minneapolis: Fortress Press.

Howell, D.B. (1990) *Matthew's Inclusive Story: A Study in the Narrative Rhetoric of the First Gospel*, Sheffield: JSOT Press.

Karris, R.J. (1989) *Luke, Artist and Theologian: Luke's Passion Account as Literature*, New York: Paulist.

Kingsbury, J.D. (1988) *Matthew as Story*, Philadelphia: Fortress Press, 2nd edn.

—— (1989) *Conflict in Mark: Jesus, Authorities, Disciples*, Philadelphia: Fortress Press.

—— (1991) *Conflict in Luke: Jesus, Authorities, Disciples*, Minneapolis: Fortress Press.

Kurz, W.S. (1993) *Reading Luke-Acts: Dynamics of Biblical Narrative*, Louisville: Westminster/John Knox.

Malbon, E.S. (1986) *Narrative Space and Mythic Meaning in Mark*, San Francisco: Harper & Row.

Moore, S. (1989) *Literary Criticism and the Gospels: The Theoretical Challenge*, New Haven: Yale University Press.

O'Day, G.R. (1986) *Revelation in the Fourth Gospel: Narrative Mode and Theological Claim*, Philadelphia: Fortress Press.

Osborne, G.R. (1991) *The Hermeneutical Spiral: A Comprehensive Introduction to Biblical Interpretation*, Downers Grove: InterVarsity Press.

Powell, M.A. (1990) *What is Narrative Criticism?* Minneapolis: Fortress Press.

Rhoads, D. and D. Michie (1982) *Mark as Story: An Introduction to the Narrative of a Gospel*, Minneapolis: Fortress Press.

Sheely, S.M. (1992) *Narrative Asides in Luke-Acts*, Sheffield: JSOT Press.

Staley, J.L. (1988) *The Print's First Kiss: A Rhetorical Investigation of the Implied Reader in the Fourth Gospel*, Atlanta: Scholars.

Sternberg, M. (1985) *The Poetics of Biblical Narrative*, Bloomington: Indiana University Press.

Stibbe, M.W.G. (1992) *John as Storyteller: Narrative Criticism and the Fourth Gospel*, Cambridge: Cambridge University Press.

Tannehill, R.C. (1986, 1990) *The Narrative Unity of Luke-Acts: A Literary Interpretation*, 2 Vols., Philadelphia: Fortress Press.

Weaver, D.J. (1990) *Matthew's Missionary Discourse: A Literary-Critical Analysis*, Philadelphia: Fortress Press.

CYNTHIA LONG WESTFALL

NEOPLATONISM

Beginning in the third century AD, Neoplatonism has had a significant and lasting influence on Western metaphysics, mysticism, and Christianity. As the last great school of antiquity, Neoplatonism generally refers to philosophical and religious doctrines developed and synthesized from Platonic metaphysical ideas. Having maintained its essentially Greek character, Neoplatonism is philosophically diverse and has experienced resurgence in medieval, Renaissance, and modern metaphysical theories.

The term 'Neoplatonism' is a relatively new one. It was not until the mid-nineteenth century that scholars made a sharp distinction between Platonism and Neoplatonism. Consequently, many who may have thought of themselves as Platonist are now labeled as Neoplatonist. Many of these Neoplatonists would have also considered themselves to be interpreters and their works as further elaborations of Plato's thought rather than distinct and separate from it, as they are now often seen.

In contradiction to the common dualistic interpretations of Plato, that is, Plato's dualism of Idea and Matter – the realm of Matter (finite world of humans, animals, objects) is separate from the realm of Ideas (infinite world) – Neoplatonism modified and developed a form of idealistic monism in which the One (e.g., God) is not separate from the finite world. This modified Platonism proposes a single source from which all forms of existence emanate – the One itself is above being. Ultimate reality is an infinite, unknowable, and perfect One. The natural world is a series of emanations from the One. Neoplatonists adopted many nonmaterialist elements of previous schools like the Pythagoreans, Peripatetics, and Stoics in their own interpretation and development of Platonic thought – a development often sharing little with the thought of Plato himself.

Neoplatonism is both an experiential and rational approach in which the soul seeks mystical union with the source of all, attained through the ascent of mystical exaltation. The aversion to the sensible world, developed primarily from Plato's dualism of thought and matter, became an opposition of the spiritual and carnal in Neoplatonic philosophy. The soul existed before its union with the body and will return to the One when it gains knowledge of the deceptive illusions that now separate them. To return and to achieve ecstatic union, one must be liberated from a life of physical sense through rigorous ascetic discipline. Through this discipline one moves toward the One (analogously 'the Good') as the object of universal desire. Composed of both body and soul, our duty is to return to the One by eliminating everything that is material and that separates us from the all-sufficient unity.

The most important of early Platonists were Plotinus (AD 204–270), Porphyry (232–302) in Rome, Iamblichus (260–330) in Syria, and Proclus (d. 485) in Athens. Plotinus, a Greek philosopher, likely a Hellenized Egyptian, is the founder of Neoplatonism. After Plotinus' death it was his student Porphyry who collected and published his fifty-four treatises called the *Enneads*, the first and most important of Neoplatonic writings. Plotinus' distinctively systematic thinking reflects strong influences from Platonic, Aristotelian, Neopythagorean, and Stoic schools in his own unique form of idealist Platonism.

Like Plato, Plotinus believed that we must know the world as it is in order to live good lives. To that end, Plotinus produced a comprehensive metaphysical cosmology of what he perceived to be Plato's philosophy. Plotinus' quasimystical philosophy attempted to establish an intellectual basis for a rational and good life concerned for the well-being of the human soul. Like Plato and Aristotle before him, Plotinus believed that the theoretical life takes primacy over the practical, including the search for physical and emotional well-being.

Plotinus rejected the dualism of two differing realms of being (material and transcendental, good and evil). Unlike Plato who divided all reality into two realms, Plotinus concluded that there is only one order containing all levels and kinds of existence. For Plotinus, there are three transcendental sources (hypostases): the One, the Intelligence (*nous* – intellect, spirit, mind), and the Soul. The similarity to the Christian notion of the Trinity is clear. However, while Plotinus unquestionably held a threefold notion of God, it was not trinitarian in the sense of maintaining the equality of all three. The One is beyond thinking and being, to which the other two are subordinate.

Plotinus proposed that 'the real' is the One, the absolute, infinite, incomprehensible, all-sufficient unity from which everything derives and to which everything returns. In this sense, the entire universe is an overflow of the One. This is expressed in Plotinus' now-famous aphoristic description of the One that 'has its center everywhere but its circumference nowhere.' The Intelligence, by a process of emanation from the One (the flowing of One into all), contains archetypal matter and forms, living intelligences, of individuals. The Soul (or World-Soul) emanates from the Intelligence, as mediator between the material and intellectual world, containing forces such as individual human, animal, and even plant souls. The Soul is an image of the Intelligence like the Intelligence is an image of the One. The Intelligence and Soul transmit the power of the One as mediating agencies. The central concept of the relation of all three as 'emanation,' or 'effulguration,' is particularly important and ambiguous in Plotinus' philosophy.

Neoplatonism has deeply influenced theologians like Origen, Augustine, and Pseudo-Dionysius, who created a synthesis of Platonic philosophy and Christian theology that carried Neoplatonic ideas to many medieval philosophers like Thomas Aquinas. Early on, Christian thinkers discovered in Plato a powerful affirmation of a spiritual world more real than the world of matter. In Neoplatonism, many Christians found elements of asceticism and unworldliness that they found appealing, particularly those that confirmed their beliefs and helped defend against pagan materialism. It is not surprising that many Christians found Neoplatonism to be supportive of their theology, especially when the One is identified with the God of scripture. Even so, many Neoplatonist aspects fit well with Gnosticism and other heretical schools of thought that were employed in opposition to Christianity and in defense of paganism.

References and further reading

Blumenthal, Henry J. and Robert A. Markus (eds.) (1981) *Neoplatonism and Early Christian Thought: Essays in Honour of A.H. Armstrong*, London: Variorum Publications Ltd.

Lloyd, A.C. (1990) *The Anatomy of Neoplatonism*, Oxford: Oxford University Press.

O'Meara, D.J. (1993) *Plotinus: An Introduction to the Enneads*, Oxford: Oxford University Press.

Rist, J.M. (1967) *Plotinus: The Road to Reality*, London: Cambridge University Press.

Wallis, R.T. (1995) *Neoplatonism*, Indiana: Hackett Publishing, 2nd edn.

J.C. ROBINSON

NEW ACADEMY, ATHENS

In ancient Athens the *Academia* was a public garden or grove of one of its suburbs named after its benefactor Academus or Hecademus. Within it, Plato established a school and the place became known by this name. His later successors from early in the third century BC under the influence of Pyrrhonian skepticism had adopted a style of inquiry highlighting the skeptical aspects of Plato's dialogues. This attitude had been exemplified in Plato's description of Socrates' interpretation of the Delphic Oracle in the *Apology* where the wisest among mortals confess their ignorance. Other passages from Plato's dialogues conveying the fundamental limitation of human knowledge included: the *Crito*, the *Euthyphro*, and the *Laches*. Further characteristics were detected in the *Parmenides*, which questions universals; pessimism with respect to the virtues of common sense, along with the open quality of the dialogue form, allowing for multiple interpretations of texts, also reflected this style of inquiry. Much later, Cicero would offer an apologia for Academic skepticism based upon Plato's use of dialectic, one in which positive statements were eschewed along with subjugation of every matter to critical inquiry and the renunciation of ultimate truth claims.

The skepticism of the Academy traces its roots to Arcesilaus (*c.* 315–241 BC), who served as its head during an era known as 'the Middle Academy.' In many respects this approach was adopted in order to combat the influence of Stoicism. Arcesilaus was determined to discredit the Stoic epistemology of 'cataleptic' impression (*kataleptike phantasia*) which, on account of their clarity in the mind, reveals truth with absolute certainty. Arcesilaus disputed this claim as without foundation and therefore not delivering the guarantee of truth which it claimed.

The 'New Academy' begins with Carneades (*c.* 213–128 BC) as a distant successor of Arcesilaus. According to a quotation by Numenius in Eusebius' *Preparatio Evangelica* (Book 14), Carneades was acclaimed for his success in debate. In arguing against the Stoic cataleptic notion Carneades asserted that because such experiences sometimes produce false impressions they cannot serve as a criterion for certain knowledge. In addition, based upon an analogy of light which both illumines and reveals itself, experience itself is mixed with that which is purported to be objectively known. Subjectivity and objectivity stand in inseparable relation within the mind and, therefore, appeal to the mere contents of the mind cannot deliver purely objective truth. Like other skeptics, the only resort of the mind is to suspend judgment with respect to demands for absolute certainty. Having done so however, one can proceed to the weighing of claims as to their relative merit, as to greater or lesser persuasiveness based upon available evidences, and their degree of plausibility.

A summary of Carneades' views can be found in Sextus' 'Against the Logicians' in which is recounted the former's adoption of the principle of *pithanon* (the 'plausible') as a practical criterion for judging impressions ranging from implausible, plausible, to irreversible – on account of a variety of impressions, and tested – where irreversible judgments have been tested in a variety of ways by multiple persons. Thus, Carneades' views might actually be regarded as an adoption and refinement of Stoic epistemology where knowledge criteria not only pass a test of being 'clear and distinct' mental notions but should also be irreversible and tested. Having noted this, however, it must be kept in mind that the framework of all this is not the establishment of truth but of plausibility and as such it remains a species of skepticism.

The question arises as to whether Carneades worked with the category of the plausible merely for the sake of argument – to offer practical demonstration of the possibility of living without the category of absolute truth. Carneades would then be viewed as a dialectician only eschewing every definitive position, even skepticism, as a philosophical approach. If so, Carneades as 'skeptic' would only be one in a very limited sense of avoiding philosophical commitment regarded as necessary for living. Carneades seems to have succeeded, perhaps in a way that anticipates Ockham's razor, of eliminating unnecessary concepts in the interest of reasoning only at those points where the human is capable of making a decisive difference in life. The principle of parsimony at work in this tradition certainly contributes to development of the scientific method in Bacon and others. This way of reasoning also contributed to a sense of cultural undecideability of religious differences in seventeenth-century Europe among theologians and the likes of early Enlightenment thinkers such as Bayle and Simon. Pressed to an extreme, it influenced the work of Hume and finally the significant consequences his approach would have on religious interpretations of scripture texts.

Indebted to Carneades, Cicero's *Academica* 2.78 argues that whereas the former regarded the truth as unavailable, it is nevertheless imperative to adopt sound opinions over against unsound ones. Cicero claims, however, that the adoption of an opinion took place only for dialectical purposes and not for higher purposes of arriving at guidance for living (cf. *Academica* 2.139). It remains a point of unresolved dispute as to what Carneades actually intended in arguing any matter.

Carneades' successor in the Academy was Clitomachus (d. 110/9 BC). Following Clitomachus, the head of the Academy was Philo of Larissa (*c.* 160–79 BC), Cicero's teacher, who taught, on the basis of the Carneadean notion of 'plausible' impressions, an epistemology which allowed an academic to respond to disputed questions by adopting whatever position seemed most plausible after a thorough examination of the arguments on all sides. One did so on the understanding that one was not claiming to have established certain truth, or to *know* that any doctrine was the truth. One only held a position as rationally best-supported and, therefore, most worth believing. In this way, one held a position to be true without claiming to know that this was so. As is evident in the philosophical writings of Philo's pupil Cicero, this in practice meant the adoption (in a tentative spirit) of many Stoic points of view.

What is crucial for understanding the New Academy of the ancient world into the time of the rise of Christianity was the psychological practice of suspending judgment in pursuit of a quality of mind akin to 'equanimity' (*isostheneia*). The responsibility of the ancient academic was to render each position in argument as having equal force in opposition to arguments of another position leading to 'undecideability' (*ataraxia*). Arriving at such a state of suspended judgment would render beliefs modest at best as to their force and thus passionate belief in any human account of certainty would be rendered untenable.

Much of modern epistemology is indebted to such background intellectual style. The attractiveness of this or similar positions is undeterred by claims of inconsistency, i.e., that true skepticism would require the suspension of thought and assertion itself. The eschewment, again, is relegated to absolute claims not relative ones. Dogmatic realists might press New Academy skeptics on such binary as the certain knowledge of the objective existence of the world but the latter could respond that even agreeing with such minimal propositions only results in trivial knowledge, nothing which is sufficient to ground certain knowledge of complex relations. The New Academy asserted that the only requirement for functional participation in the world was assessment and response to the appearances with which one must deal. Modern arguments for realism then would simply have been regarded as an overdetermination of data from sense experience.

References and further reading

Annas, Julia and Jonathan Barnes (1985) *The Modes of Scepticism: Ancient Texts and Modern Interpretations*, New York: Cambridge University Press.

Brittain, Charles (2001) *Philo of Larissa: The Last of the Academic Sceptics*, Oxford Classical Monographs, Oxford: Clarendon Press.

Caton, Hiram (1973) *The Origin of Subjectivity: An Essay on Descartes*, New Haven: Yale University Press.

Couissin, P. (1983) 'The Stoicism of the New Academy,' pp. 31–63 in *The Skeptical Tradition*, Myles Burnyeat (ed.), Berkeley: University of California Press.

Eusebius (1981) *Preparation for the Gospel*, trans. Edwin Hamilton Gifford, 2 Vols., Grand Rapids: Baker Book House (reprint of the 1903 Clarendon edition).

Hankinson, R.J. (1995) *The Sceptics*, New York: Routledge.

Kirk, G., J.E. Raven, and M. Schofield (1983) *The Pre-Socratic Philosophers*, New York: Cambridge University Press.

Popkin, Richard H. (2003) *The History of Scepticism: from Savonarola to Bayle*, New York: Oxford University Press.

Schofield, Malcolm, Myles Burnyeat, and Jonathan Barnes (1980) *Doubt and Dogmatism: Studies in Hellenistic Epistemology*, Oxford: Clarendon Press.

Stough, C.L. (1969) *Greek Scepticism: A Study in Epistemology*, Berkeley: University of California Press.

Tarrant, H. (1985) *Scepticism or Platonism? The Philosophy of the Fourth Academy*, Cambridge Classical Studies, Cambridge: Cambridge University Press.

Wittgenstein, Ludwig (1969) *On Certainty*, G.E.M. Anscombe and G.H. von Wright (eds.), Evanston: Harper & Row.

KURT A. RICHARDSON

NEW HERMENEUTIC

The New Hermeneutic was a movement associated with students of Rudolf Bultmann, especially Ernst Fuchs and Gerhard Ebeling, which changed the hermeneutical dialectic from language (or myth) versus understanding of existence to language versus language-event or word-event. Fuchs and Ebeling saw language as the key to solving the problem of historical, cultural, and linguistic 'distance' in interpretation.

Fuchs used the expression 'language-event' to describe the occurrence of language, the event of Being (to use the conceptualization of Martin Heidegger) that is the actual content of language. Language not only creates Being but also brings forth Being as an event that remains present, at least potentially, in language (Fuchs 1959: 126–7). When this is translated into Christian conceptualization, Pauline theology becomes the master example that Christian faith has enriched language itself. The language-event in the theology of Paul was a word of possibility of faith for all, and the language-gain that produced the literary style of the Gospel is distinguished in the fact that 'it made the language of the people serviceable for the highest, for the discourse of God' (Fuchs 1960: 181). Because of the language of Jesus, new Being before God is an actual and continuing possibility. The vocation of the church is the bringing to language once again of the person and work of Jesus, and this is to be understood in terms of the challenge of freedom and love.

Gerhard Ebeling used the expression 'word-event' to speak of the process whereby texts from a distant age and a strange context are enabled to utter a relevant message in a new age and a new context. 'In dealing with a text,' according to Ebeling,

there is a transition from an exposition *of* the text to an exposition *by* the text (i.e., that one is concerned to be taught the truth about oneself by the text) ... For the text is not there for its own sake, but for the sake of the word-event which is the origin and also the future of the text. Word-event is the exposition-event which is carried out by the Word. ... For the Word, which once happened and which has been recorded in the form of a text as an event which has occurred, must with the help of the text again become Word, and so come into being as the expounding Word.

(1966: 28–9)

The New Hermeneutic has been criticized for importing a theory of language and meaning to distinguish between the meaning of a text and the direct significance of the words through which the meaning comes to expression or to justify the translation of an intentionality or meaning that once presented itself through a particular set of words but no longer does so (for example, Dillenberger 1964; Verhaar 1969; and Zuck 1972). A.C. Thiselton, however, utilizes the work of J.L. Austin and Ludwig Wittgenstein to corroborate Fuchs' concept of language and language-event. In the language-event of Fuchs and the performative utterance of Austin, 'the issuing of the utterance is the performing of an action' (Thiselton 1970). Thiselton suggests that the later work of Wittgenstein may help to bridge the gap between the function of language on the purely cognitive level and the function of language on the deeper level, the function of exposing or reorienting attitudes and presuppositions. Thiselton admits that Fuchs may press his ideas too far, but he declares that the work of Wittgenstein and Austin has confirmed that, in general outline, Fuchs' understanding of language-event stresses, or at least gropes after, important points in biblical hermeneutics.

References and further reading

Dillenberger, John (1964) 'On Broadening the New Hermeneutic,' pp. 147–63 in *The New Hermeneutic*, New Frontiers in Theology 2, James M. Robinson and John B. Cobb, Jr. (eds.), New York: Harper & Row.

Ebeling, Gerhard (1963) *Word and Faith*, London: SCM Press.

—— (1966) *Theology and Proclamation*, London: Collins.

Fuchs, Ernst (1959) *Zum Hermeneutischen Problem in der Theologie*, Gesammelte Aufsätze 1, Tübingen: J.C.B. Mohr.

—— (1960) *Zur Frage nach dem historischen Jesus*, Gesammelte Aufsätze 2, Tübingen: J.C.B. Mohr.

Thiselton, A.C. (1970) 'The Parables as Language-Event: Some Comments on Fuchs's Hermeneutics in the Light of Linguistic Philosophy,' *Scottish Journal of Theology* 23: 437–68.

Verhaar, J. (1969) 'Language and Theological Method,' *Continuum* 7: 3–29.

Zuck, John E. (1972) 'The New Hermeneutic on Language: A Critical Appraisal,' *Journal of Religion* 52: 397–416.

E.V. MCKNIGHT

NEW HISTORICISM

New historicism is a method of literary criticism which takes into account the historical power relations, context, and politics of a text as an integral part of the production of meaning, while recognizing the subjectivity of the reader. Cultural materialism is a second mode of literary study which is sometimes used synonymously with new historicism. The difference is the anthropological emphasis in new historicism where cultural materialism exhibits much greater Marxist influence (Brannigan 1998: 6–11). The practice was established in the early 1980s following some foundational thinking in different areas.

Clifford Geertz, an anthropologist, set the stage through his observation of the interconnectedness of contexts. There is no fixed location from which meaning emerges clearly from within history because there is a greater context for each location, complicating it as a definitive source for meaning. He uses the term 'thick description' to signal that scrutiny of textual relationships will reveal dialogue and development of meaning rather than random variation. Texts must be respected for their distinction from other production sites and simultaneously be seen as sources of context. Furthermore, Geertz asserts that the theorist looking at history will similarly come from a social context that will produce a subjectivity which will then be imposed on the historical setting. This recognition of one's own agency in the construction of meaning must be acknowledged as well in order to sift how a document is understood. This is what set Geertz apart from earlier anthropologists.

Michel Foucault's critical approach to power also informed the development of new historicism. He rejected the idea of the impartial theorist who might be capable of standing outside his own subjectivity to form objective systematic theories. He further rejected the text as a product and understood it more clearly as a process. In both cases power dynamics and manipulation of power blur the voice of the author. In this way Foucault offered a much more complicated view of history. In place of the traditional linear model, he painted any historical era as hosting many different ideologies, arenas of discourse (for example, medical, political, economic), and fluid word meanings. He also looked beyond what was present in the text to what was also absent.

It was through studies of Renaissance literature that key poststructuralist ideas were brought to literary

theory, which also contributed to new historicism. Stephen Greenblatt clarifies the distance between historicism, which continues to be contained within the discipline of history, and new historicism which has become a practice of literary criticism. Where the former assumes inevitability around the unfolding of history and takes an abstract universal position of the context, new historicism embraces the agency of individual voices within the contexts. Each character will be affected by his or her gender, class, nationality, race, and religion, and will be effecting change rather then merely reacting to an inevitable direction being taken because history is unfolding. Each person will not only reflect the details of his/her context but will also affect these same details. A second distinction is that historicism claims the ability to suspend judgment of history and lay aside one's own values, whereas new historicism assumes this task to be impossible. Many new historicists have made it a priority to write about their own subject position (see Louis Montrose, Don Wayne, Catherine Gallagher), while others such as Greenblatt consciously strive for transparency of their subject position through the examples and comparisons they use in their writing, which are deliberately reflective of the values they have in relation to the experiences found in their own contexts (Greenblatt 1990: 74–9). A third response is to historicism's veneration of historical texts. This attitude sets before the historian the task of defending and celebrating the greatness of a text, assuming its accuracy and its ability to reveal the universal position. New historicism consciously receives and legitimates all texts from history. The goal is to not focus solely on the texts that represent the 'center' of the culture, but to deliberately include equally the voices found at the margins of the context (Greenblatt 1990: 74–9). At the same time all artifacts are received as texts that will communicate meaning. A tent, a cup, a prison, a receipt for a consumer transaction, a medical record, a literary work: all are given permission to inform, to be in dialogue with each other, and to contribute to the formation of discourse. How cultural forces are at work in situations is considered rather than which forces are at work (Hens-Piazza 2002: 6).

The usefulness of new historicism within biblical studies is quickly evident. Where historicism approached biblical texts as scripture, new historicism approaches them as literature. New historicist practice opens up space for biblical literature to be in dialogue with its cultural setting. What is absent can become as informative as what is present.

Self-reflexivity is a core ingredient in new historicist practice. It requires that the reader not only exegete the text, but also exegete his/her own cultural location. This is critical in accepting that our own subjectivity will necessarily be present in the reading of the text. Hens-Piazza argues that this has indeed been done before but that self-exegesis has been minimal and that its depth must match the depth of textual exegesis. The initiative in this area has been taken by feminist, minority, and Third World readers who have had to wrestle with the differences between their understandings of texts, specifically biblical texts, and more traditional First World, white, male readings of the text. The location of the reader will affect all faculties of interpretation, including his/her understanding of word meanings, identification of sympathetic characters, familiarity with similar experience, and the questions the reader chooses to ask about the text. According to Hens-Piazza, 'self-reflexivity is a refusal to hide behind the "original author" or the original audience of the text' (2002: 47). New historicism provides a wide lens through which we might understand biblical texts and the cultural texts with which they are in dialogue.

References and further reading

Brannigan, John (1998) *New Historicism and Cultural Materialism*, New York: St. Martin's Press.

Colebrook, Claire (1997) *New Literary Histories: New Historicism and Contemporary Criticism*, Manchester: Manchester University Press.

Gallagher, Catherine and Stephen Greenblatt (2000) *Practicing New Historicism*, Chicago: University of Chicago Press.

Geertz, C. (1973) *The Interpretation of Cultures*, New York: Basic Books.

Greenblatt, Stephen (1990) 'Resonance and Wonder,' pp. 74–9 in *Literary Theory Today*, Peter Collier and Helga Geyer-Ryan (eds.), Cambridge: Polity Press.

Hamilton, Paul (1996) *Historicism*, London: Routledge.

Hens-Piazza, Gina (2002) *The New Historicism*, Minneapolis: Fortress Press.

JENN BURNETT

NEW RELIGIOUS MOVEMENTS AND INTERPRETATION

New Religious Movements (NRMs), otherwise designated as 'alternative religions,' are generally viewed as religious phenomena emerging particularly from the 1960s. It is evident that the appeal of the Bible as a source of doctrine and praxis for some categories of NRMs is an enduring aspect. While there are pre-Christian forms including paganism, witchcraft, magic, and satanism, which largely deny any biblical legitimacy, other strands of NRMs may be rather ambiguous in their attitude or endorse at least certain parts of the scriptures. In turn, the extent to which the scriptures are accepted, and how they are interpreted, is frequently determined by a number of discernible variables including their proximity to orthodox Christianity, their sectarian or cultist nature, their syncretic form, and the needs of a movement's leadership.

Some contemporary expressions of Christianity may be said to fall within the remit of New Religious Movements. Perhaps the most obvious is the Charismatic Renewal Movement, which shares the Bible, along with historical Christianity, as its fundamental source of literary inspiration. However, the movement stresses certain scriptures as particularly important. Doctrines of the Second Baptism in the Spirit and the emphasis upon the charismata (glossolalia, prophecy, etc.) provide the 'badge' of belonging which occasionally belies a tendency toward sectarianism in the creation of boundaries with what is sometimes regarded as 'nominal' Christianity. Another stance, taken by certain strands of the Charismatic Movement, such as the community-based Jesus Fellowship in Britain, is to castigate mainline Christianity for practicing what the Bible *does not* appear to teach. This includes the celebrations of Christmas and Easter, which are regarded as pagan in origin.

Another frequently discernible element of the more sectarian form of New Religious Movements is the emphasis upon eschatological and millenarian themes. Hence, for such broadly Christian NRMs as the Messianic Communities in the USA (a movement arising from the Californian Jesus Movement of the late 1960s) there is an accent particularly on the book of Revelation and the more prophetic books of the Old Testament. On the extremes of the millenarian-oriented movements are such notorious and ill-fated cults as the People's Temple led by the self-assigned prophet Jim Jones. Here, biblical apocalyptic text was fed back to enforce a distinct premillenarianism, dualism, and conspiratorial view of the outside persecuting world. This also tends to be true of far less violent NRMs. For instance, Rastafarianism reads the text into the worldly experience of its adherents. In many ways a retreatist religion, Rastafarianism sees itself in battle with the 'oppressive' forces of white-dominated society. Growing since the 1970s, it seeks a destruction of this world ('Babylon') and the triumph of 'Zion,' which will free Black people from exploitation and oppression.

In their more overtly cultist manifestation, the biblical inspiration for some NRMs may be merged with syncretic tendencies. In Japan, several new quasi-Christian movements have emerged out of the interaction between Christianity and traditional religion including Shinto and Buddhist beliefs and rituals. For instance, the infamous Aum Shinrikyo movement (frequently designated a 'doomsday' cult), which was responsible for the gas attack on the Tokyo metro system in 1995, has constantly emphasized biblical Christian apocalyptic themes including the battle of Armageddon.

Another mode of syncretic development includes those NRMs who rely heavily on biblical text, but follow older movements such as Jehovah's Witnesses and the Mormons, in typically legitimating a literary source which functions as a kind of accessory to the biblical canon. Indeed, it is through such extrabiblical sources that the Bible is read and interpreted. For instance, the scriptural interpretation of the Children of God (now the 'Family') is supplemented by the authority of the many literary works of its late cultist charismatic leader, Mo David. These works often brought a controversial reinterpretation of the scriptures. The erroneous practice of 'flirty fishing' by the Children of God – a form of prostitution in order to win converts – was justified by Christ's statement 'I will make you fishers of men' (Matt. 4:19).

An alternative way biblical text may be supplemented by the more cultist-oriented groups is through prophetic revelation – especially that uttered by the movement's leadership. Typically, such esoteric phenomena take precedence over scripture in a manner reminiscent of ancient Gnosticism. One example is that of Rev. Sun Myung Moon, the charismatic leader of the Unification Church (the 'Moonies'). Although it regards itself as 'Christian,' the Unification Church has moved a very considerable distance from mainstream Christianity and is typical of the syncretic form of many NRMs. Given equal weight to the Bible is the 'further revelation' of Moon that can be found in his book, *Divine Principle* (1973), where he is seen to triumph over both the spiritual and physical world and where Christ is alleged to have instructed Moon to build His kingdom on earth.

Another feature of some NRMs is that, while accepting the validity of the scriptures, there is the denial of their infallibility. In turn, this allows the scriptures to be selectively gleaned in order to construct a new belief system. The Unification Church, for instance, insists that the Judaic-Christian Bible is the inspired Word of God. However, it does not regard the scriptures as word-for-word infallible. Rather, they were written down, copied, and edited by fallible men, each with his personal motivations. This means that the scriptures, through further prophetic revelation, can be given their 'true' interpretation. We may cite the Unification Church's rendering of the story of Adam and Eve, which is embellished so that Satan is seen as copulating with Eve and so destroying God's ideal of the perfect family. Thus, Jesus did not come to offer an atonement but to reestablish the lost ideal family. In 1992, Moon made the formal declaration that he was the Messiah, not divine, but neither was Jesus. A messiah had to come again to finish Christ's mission, to marry, and reestablish the true family.

In the New Age movement there is a discernible 'Christian' wing which converges biblical text with esoteric New Age inspiration and in doing so frequently denies the fallibility of the Bible. A key teaching is that the advent of the New Age will be apocalyptic and characterized by terrestrial and social upheaval in what is typically a premillenarian form of Christianity. Christ's physical return follows a period of catastrophes which inaugurate the New Age millennium. One such expression, the Church Universal and Triumphant (originating

in the late 1950s), sees Jesus as a great 'Ascended Master' in his time on earth but that his teachings were corrupted by the New Testament writers. Two important publications, *The Lost Years of Jesus* and *The Lost Teachings of Jesus*, identify strongly with the Judaic-Christian tradition, while also stressing New Age esoteric experience where God the Father becomes the 'I AM presence,' and the 'Holy Christ Self' (or Higher Consciousness) is reduced to 'the Kingdom of God within.'

Most brands of new religions based upon Eastern mysticism may make no references to the Bible, while others may dip into it to legitimate their beliefs and in doing so even further dilute its teachings. For instance, ECKANKAR (which holds the ancient teachings of ECK to be the source of all religions) sees Jesus and St. Paul as ECK masters of soul-travel and mysticism, and culls ideas of Satan as God of the lower worlds and ruler of the negative forces. Then, at perhaps the most esoteric pole of new religiosity, the Aetherius Society (derived from the flying saucer cults of the 1950s) partakes in aspects of Christianity and includes a new version of the Lord's Prayer and the belief that Christ was a great 'Cosmic Master' who came to earth from Venus. Here, biblical reference and interpretation are expressed in perhaps their most bizarre form.

References and further reading

Barrett, L. (1977) *The Rastafarians: The Dreadlocks of Jamaica*, Jamaica: Sangster's Book Stores.

Brockway, A. and P. Rajasheker (eds.) (1987) *New Religious Movements and the Churches*, Geneva: WCC Publications.

Chryssides, G. (1991) *The Advent of Sun Myung Moon: The Origins, Beliefs and Practices of the Unification Church*, London: Macmillan.

Hunt, S. (1998) 'The Radical Kingdom of the Jesus Fellowship,' *Pneuma* 20(1): 21–42.

—— (2003) *Alternative Religions: A Sociological Introduction*, London: Hurst Publishers.

Reader, I. (2001) 'Violent Millenarianism with a Christian Touch: Syncretic Themes in the Millennial Perspective of Aum Shinrikyo,' in *Christian Millenarianism*, S. Hunt (ed.), London: Hurst Publishers.

York, M. (1995) 'The Church Universal and Triumphant,' *Journal of Contemporary Religion* 10(1): 62–71.

STEPHEN HUNT

NEW RHETORIC

During the middle decades of the last century, biblical scholars became increasingly dissatisfied with form and redaction criticisms' failure to offer effective interpretive paradigms. James Muilenburg articulated the dissatisfaction in his 1968 presidential address to the Society of Biblical Literature, 'After Form Criticism What?' Rhetorical criticism, 'that's what!' (Amador 1999a: 16). This critical structure is not new, however. Many scholars (e.g. Wuellner 1987: 451; Mack 1990: 12; Watson and Hauser 1994: 9, 107; Amador 1999a: 11) point to Muilenburg's paper as the event that reintroduced rhetoric as an interpretive structure.

Using classical paradigms, as identified by Plato, Aristotle, Cicero, and Quintilian, scripture was studied under the three major types of oral or written communication: judicial – the legal presentation of accusation and defense; deliberative – an effort to effect change in action in the future; and epideictic – attributing positive or negative value to someone or something (Kennedy 1984: 36). Classical rhetoric was concerned with the structure and style of the presentation, with little concern for the context of either the speaker or audience (or, writer or reader).

Rhetorical criticism is anything but new – it enjoys a rich and long heritage, almost as long as the texts themselves. Origen and Augustine, for example, assumed rhetoric provided the interpretive framework for the scriptures (Mack 1990: 10). Bede, an English scholar of the late seventh century, equated style with rhetoric as he analyzed figures and tropes in his *De schematibus et tropis*. The Reformers Luther, Calvin, Erasmus, and Melanchthon, too, wrote rhetorical commentaries on many of Paul's letters. And, as language studies developed over the last three centuries, rhetorical analysis of the original languages was applied to produce exegetical aids – lexica, grammars, and the like.

With the emphasis on other critical paradigms – e.g., form (source) and redaction criticism – through the nineteenth and until the mid-twentieth centuries the use of rhetoric as a critical methodology waned. Not only was rhetoric ignored as a critical method, exegetical (e.g., K. Barth) and existential (e.g., R. Bultmann) theologies, and the American focus on Jesus as teacher of a humane, social ethic were openly hostile to taking the words of the New Testament writers literally as rhetoric (Mack 1990: 12).

It was a full decade after Muilenburg's address, however, before a rigorous rhetorical commentary was written. Hans Dieter Betz produced his commentary on Galatians (1979) aware that he was producing a new interpretation based upon the assumption that 'the letter is composed in accordance with the conventions of Greco-Roman rhetoric and epistolography' (1979: xiv). Betz' commentary marks a modern rediscovery of rhetorical criticism. He stands securely on classical analysis, and reminds biblical scholars that rhetoric, virtually absent from interpretive paradigms during the early and mid-decades of the last century, formed many of the communicative norms by which the New Testament writers wrote (Mack 1990: 9–11).

However, both Betz' and Kennedy's work in the late 1970s and early 1980s still followed the Graeco-Roman paradigm. Their work was antiquarian – only rhetorical handbooks from second century BC to second century AD were consulted – and tropological – focusing on the identification of structure and style (Amador 1999b: 195): i.e., still classical rhetorical criticism. This may have been too narrow an interpretation for even the classical rhetors. As S.E. Porter suggests in his essay, 'The Theoretical Justification for Application of Rhetorical Categories to Pauline Epistolary Literature' (1993), the rhetors of the Graeco-Roman world allowed and recognized a breadth of adaptation of the classical rules. That is, applying the classical rules stringently to the New Testament texts limits the interpretation and assumes the writer sat down with a rhetorical handbook before composing his letter or gospel. Porter added his voice to those scholars suggesting that even classical rhetoric is somewhat limiting or unsatisfying as a critical paradigm.

'New' was added when biblical critics appreciated and applied the work of Chaim Perelman and L. Olbrechts-Tyteca. Their seminal work, *The New Rhetoric: A Treatise on Argumentation*, defined rhetoric as argumentation considering essential both ornamental style (classical) *and* the social context of the interplay between speaker and listener. In their analysis, the reader of the text is not just a passive recipient, but becomes an active – creative and productive – agent (Wuellner 1987: 461). Thus the door was opened for texts to be analyzed from a far broader rhetorical point of view.

The union of classical and modern rhetorical analysis marks a reinvention of rhetoric with far-reaching implications (Amador 1999a: 14). The text is far more than simply a medium to communicate an argument, but is a description of socially significant relationships between the writer and reader, regardless of historical contexts. Further, the reader has actual power and influence in determining the meaning of the text 'thereby granting the [reader] the freedom to determine what expressions best represent its convictions' (Amador 1999a: 18). Each time a text is read, or a performance is enacted, there is dialogical interaction between writer and reader producing a new meaning based upon the sociocultural context of the event (Amador 1999a: 20). In this respect, the text has 'power' that influences institutions, societies, and cultures with each reading. And so the rhetorical critic understands the sociocultural setting of the reading as being as important as the sociocultural setting of the original writing.

Vernon K. Robbins (1992), for example, rethought the book of Mark, specifically the social environment of Jesus and his disciples, and developed his 'sociorhetorical' framework. In the introduction to the paperback edition of the book, he explained his thinking: 'We know that a primary rhetorical aspect of stories is their beginning, middle, and end. But I had not been taught to think ... about the beginning, middle, and end of a social environment' (1992: xix).

Another example is S. E. Porter's rethinking of some of the redaction critic's discoveries in light of a rhetorical paradigm. Some textual variants were 'accidental and unconscious, but others conscious and intentional' (2002: 405). These others, Porter suggests, need to be considered rhetorically significant.

In the above examples, Robbins and Porter stand in the 'New Rhetoric' by taking seriously the discoveries of the sociohistorical and the redaction critic respectively, *and* interpreting those discoveries through the framework of the rhetorical. Thereby they provide new interpretations and revaluing of other critical disciplines.

'The New Rhetoric' is, then, a broad and inclusive analytical paradigm that continues to consider the classics, but takes equally seriously modern rhetorical thought. So, as Robbins suggests, biblical rhetorical scholars are increasingly recognizing 'that texts are performances of language, and language is a part of the inner fabric of society, culture, ideology and religion' (1996: 1–3). In response to this growing awareness, there has been a call for serious dialogue between rhetorical interpreters and those who focus on historical, social, cultural, theological, and ideological interpretations (Amador 1999a: 196ff.).

References and further reading

Amador, J. David Hester (1999a) *Academic Constraints in Rhetorical Criticism of the New Testament*, JSNTSup 174, Sheffield: Sheffield Academic Press.

—— (1999b) 'Where Could Rhetorical Criticism (Still) Take Us?' *Currents in Research: Biblical Studies* 7: 195–221.

Betz, Hans Deiter (1979) *Galatians*, Philadelphia: Fortress Press.

Kennedy, George A. (1984) *New Testament Interpretation through Rhetorical Criticism*, Chapel Hill: University of North Carolina Press.

Mack, Burton L. (1990) *Rhetoric and the New Testament*, Minneapolis: Fortress Press.

Perelman, Chaim and L. Olbrechts-Tyteca (1969) *The New Rhetoric: A Treatise on Argumentation*, Notre Dame: University of Notre Dame Press.

Porter, Stanley E. (1993) 'The Theoretical Justification for Application of Rhetorical Categories to Pauline Epistolary Literature,' pp. 100–22 in *Rhetoric and the New Testament: Essays from the 1992 Heidelberg Conference*, S.E. Porter and T.H. Olbricht (eds.), JSNTSup 90, Sheffield: Sheffield Academic Press.

—— (2002) 'The Rhetorical Scribe: Textual Variants in Romans and their Possible Rhetorical Purpose,' pp. 403–19 in *Rhetorical Criticism and the Bible*, S.E. Porter and D.L. Stamps (eds.), JSNTSup 195, Sheffield: Sheffield Academic Press.

Robbins, Vernon K. (1984, 1992) *Jesus the Teacher: A Socio-Rhetorical Interpretation of Mark*, Minneapolis: Fortress Press.

—— (1996) *The Tapestry of Early Christian Discourse: Rhetoric, Society and Ideology*, London: Routledge.

Watson, Duane F. and Alan J. Hauser (1994) *Rhetorical Criticism of the Bible: A Comprehensive Bibliography with Notes on History and Method*, Leiden: Brill.

Wuellner, Wilhelm (1987) 'Where is Rhetorical Criticism Taking Us?' *Catholic Biblical Quarterly* 49(3): 448–63.

C. DAVID DONALDSON

NUMISMATICS

The importance of numismatics as one arrow in the quiver of archaeology has long been recognized, particularly among those who have attempted to apply the discipline to an understanding of the biblical texts. Yet at one level the results of such an application have not yielded the fruit that one might have expected. It is rare to find much of a dialogue being undertaken between biblical scholars, on the one hand, and numismatic specialists in the ancient Near East or the Graeco-Roman world, on the other. This is not to suggest that there has been a lack of serious research and investigation into the field of numismatics, but merely to note that this is not an area in which many biblical specialists have demonstrated much interest. Studies of coinage illustrative of the Jewish revolt of AD 66–73 are perhaps the exception to the rule in this regard.

Thankfully a growing number of serious investigations into biblical backgrounds have woken up to the benefits that the field of numismatics can provide. Yet there are still many instances in which presuppositions among many competent interpreters of both the Old Testament and New Testament need to be challenged on the basis of a more careful study of the numismatic evidence itself. Two recent examples are worth citing in this regard. The first concerns the famous 'Yehud' coins of the Persian period, coins which have often been invoked as primary evidence for a reconstruction of the importance of the Jewish high priesthood within the institutional structures of the nation as a whole. Recent interpretation of this numismatic evidence suggests that great potential exists for misinterpretation, and the question of the place and position of the priesthood as an institutional feature of Israel's national life is once again an open matter. Similarly, the interpretation of the famous 'Noah' coinage of Apameia in Phrygia has long been a staple in asserting the importance of Jewish influence in regions of Asia Minor within the New Testament period. Yet recent interpretations of the coinage question whether this is a methodologically sound basis on which to proceed.

In short, numismatic evidence has frequently been overlooked within biblical studies, and this is to the detriment of all parties concerned. The time has come for a more thorough application of the fruits of numismatic research to be applied to the study and interpretation of both the Old Testament and the New Testament, even if it means that some cherished assumptions need to be jettisoned as a result. Nowhere is this more true than in the matter of local coin issues, both citywide issues and those from larger geographical regions or areas. The fact of the matter is that biblical scholarship seems largely ignorant of, or uninterested in, what numismatics might reveal to us about the geographical areas and local contexts in which many of the Old Testament and New Testament texts arose. Research students in search of a topic combining archaeological and hermeneutical expertise would be well advised to consider this a fruitful area of investigation. The field of numismatics is ripe unto harvest and crying out for reapers!

References and further reading

Hart, H. St J. (1952) 'Judaea and Rome: The Official Commentary,' *Journal of Theological Studies* 3: 172–98.

Kreitzer, Larry J. (1996) *Striking New Images: Roman Imperial Coinage and the New Testament World*, Sheffield: Sheffield Academic Press.

—— (1999) 'On Board the Eschatological Ark of God: Noah–Deucalion and the "Phrygian Connection" in 1 Peter 3.19–22,' pp. 228–72 in *Baptism, the New Testament and the Church: Historical and Contemporary Studies in Honour of R.E.O. White*, Stanley E. Porter and Anthony R. Cross (eds.), Sheffield: Sheffield Academic Press.

Rooke, Deborah W. (2000) *Zadok's Heirs: The Role and Development of High Priesthood in Ancient Israel*, Oxford: Oxford University Press.

LARRY J. KREITZER

O

ORIGEN (c. 185–253 AD)

Origen, who lived from about 185 to 255 AD, was one of the most influential of all Christian theologians, in spite of a long phase in which he was considered a heretic. Most of the information about his life is provided by Eusebius in book VI of his *Ecclesiastical History* and by Gregory Thaumaturgus in his *Panegyric on Origen*. Gregory was a student and an important link between Origen and the Cappadocians. According to Eusebius, Origen was brought up a Christian in Alexandria but also received a traditional Greek education. His father was martyred in 202, and thereafter Origen became a teacher and soon the head of a Christian school, where he remained until 231.

Eusebius reports that Origen traveled to places such as Rome, Athens, Arabia, and Palestine. He became a celebrity, even being invited by the mother of the emperor, Julia Mammaea, for an audience in Antioch. During a visit to Caesarea, he was ordained as presbyter, arousing the hostility of the bishop of Alexandria. This forced him to move to Palestine, where he established a new school. The most important part of his work ended up in the library of Caesarea, along with the books that he had brought from Alexandria – particularly the works of Philo. Origen debated major theological questions in public encounters, for example, in 244 with the Monarchians and in 245 with the Arabian Church. He suffered during the persecutions of Decius and died around 253 in Tyre.

According to Jerome who visited the library in Caesarea, Origen wrote some 2,000 treatises. A rich patron named Ambrose provided stenographers and copyists. Controversies about his teachings began during his lifetime and escalated during the fourth century and thereafter. Only a small part of his works has survived in Greek, while more remains in Latin translation either by Rufinus or Jerome. Most of Origen's works deal with the interpretation of scripture. In an attempt to come to a critical text of the Bible, he devised the Hexapla, of which only a few fragments survived. The biblical text was laid out in six columns, one in Hebrew, one in a Greek transcription of the Hebrew, followed by the translations of Aquila and Symmachus, the LXX, and the translation of Theodotion. Origen used editorial marks in this work like those employed in Homeric scholarship in Alexandria.

His works of biblical interpretation consist of commentaries, homilies, and scholia; the last of which are mostly preserved in catenae. Origen dealt with most books of the LXX but only a fraction of this work is left. Extensive parts of the Latin translation of his commentary on the Song of Songs are extant. Much of his commentaries on the Gospels of Matthew and John have been preserved in Greek.

His further writings consist of *Contra Celsum*, an apologetic work, responding to the arguments of the philosopher Celsus against the Christians; *De Principiis*, in which Origen tried to give an overview of Christian teachings. Books three and four have been preserved in Greek through the *Philocalia*, an anthology of Origen's works, composed by Basil and Gregory of Nazianzus. Some letters and shorter treatises, including *De Oratione* and *De Pascha*, have been preserved in Greek.

References and further reading

Crouzel, H. (1982) *Bibliographie critique d'Origène*, Suppl. I, Steenbrugge: Abbatia Sancti Petri.
—— (1989) *Origen*, trans. A.S. Worall, San Francisco: Harper & Row.
—— (1996) *Bibliographie critique d'Origène*, Suppl. II, Steenbrugge: Abbatia Sancti Petri.
Daniélou, J. (1955) *Origen*, New York: Sheed & Ward.
Hanson, R.P.C. (1954) *Origen's Doctrine of Tradition*, London: SPCK.
Nautin, P. (1977) *Origène: sa vie et son oeuvre*, Paris: Beauchesne.
Trigg, J.W. (1998) *Origen*, London and New York: Routledge.
Various Acts of the International Colloquia for Origen Studies (1973–) *Origeniana 1*.

ANNEWIES VAN DEN HOEK

P

PAPYROLOGY AND EPIGRAPHY

1 Introduction

Papyrology and epigraphy are concerned with the written artifacts of the ancient world as they are preserved on their original materials. Papyrology refers to ephemeral writing on a variety of surfaces, including papyrus, animal skins, stones, bone, pieces of broken pottery, and the like, and are often referred to in terms of documentary and literary papyri. Epigraphy comprises writing that was designed to be durable and lasting, and hence the writing was done on such substances as stone, clay (fired or not), glass, and metal. These are not hard and fast categories, since, for example, some manuscripts on skins or clay tablets were designed to be preserved, but they offer some insight into the original purpose for which the ancient artifact was created (see Bagnall 1995). The importance of papyrology and epigraphy for biblical criticism and interpretation is found in their contribution to establishing and deciphering the historical and textual basis for the biblical documents and their surrounding world (see Bodel 2001). The significance of papyri and inscriptions for study of the ancient world has, unfortunately, led to what many believe are the creation of a number of forged documents.

2 Papyrology

If the nineteenth century was the age of inscriptions (see below), the twentieth century was that of papyrology. Beginning with the end of the nineteenth century and extending through the twentieth century, vast hoards of papyri manuscripts were found. The major findings took place in Egypt, but there have been other significant finds in Palestine, and elsewhere. These have had relevance for the study of both the Old and New Testaments. Many of the same issues apply in studying the papyri as for studying inscriptions. The major differ-

ence is that the manuscripts were rarely written with the intention of lasting in the same way as inscriptions were. This adds a number of difficulties to the task of using them for biblical criticism and interpretation. These include the fact that many were disposed of after use, since they were not deemed to be worth retaining, and have been damaged as a result; their context and often their date of composition are obscured; many of the documents are concerned with trivial matters, and therefore do not have clear points of cross-reference; and the damage that resulted from disposal has made the task of reconstruction more difficult, especially where the text has no known literary author.

As mentioned above, the major distinction in papyri is between documentary and literary papyri. Documentary papyri are concerned with ephemeral texts, including wills, receipts, other business transactions, and, especially, letters. Literary papyri are concerned with known and newly discovered (in the papyri) literary authors. The major literary papyri for study of both the Old and New Testaments are manuscripts of the biblical documents themselves. These are found in abundance.

Important papyri for the study of the Old Testament include the following (besides sources above, see Würthwein 1979): receipts on ostraca from Samaria (eighth century BC); the Elephantine papyri (fifth century BC), attesting to a Jewish community in Egypt (on the island of Elephantine) that worshipped Yahweh; the Samaria papyri found near Jericho (fourth century BC), attesting to people and events in the Persian period; the Hebrew Dead Sea documents (second to first centuries BC), evidencing the biblical textual tradition, including the Isaiah Scrolls, the Habbakuk commentary, the Psalm Scroll, among many other manuscripts; Greek biblical manuscripts (second century BC on), with the earliest being significant fragments from Deuteronomy and the Minor Prophets Scroll, as well as many later documents (some of these Greek fragments from Qumran), including the major codexes Sinaiticus and Vaticanus (fourth century AD); various Hebrew genizah documents attesting to the developing and transmitted Old Testament text, as well as various other types of texts, such as incantations; the Aramaic targum traditions, attesting to later interpretation of the Hebrew Bible; the major Masoretic Hebrew Bible codexes, Leningrad (eleventh century AD) and Aleppo (tenth century AD); the Samaritan Pentateuch, in Hebrew and in its Greek translation (the Samariticon); and the papyri of various other biblical versions, including not only Greek (Septuagint and later Greek interpreters), but also Latin, Coptic, Ethiopic, Armenian, and Arabic, among others.

New Testament papyri of importance include many of the same papyri noted above when they touch upon the New Testament textual tradition. Similar literary papyri are to be found for the Greek New Testament, including the earliest Greek fragment of John (second century AD), a number of significant other New Testament papyri (there are now around 120 that have been published), the major Greek codexes from the fourth century on (Sinaiticus, Vaticanus, Alexandrinus, and Bezae, to name only a few), as well as manuscripts of the various biblical versions, including especially Latin, Syriac, and Coptic, but also Armenian, Georgian, Ethiopic, Gothic, and Old Church Slavonic, among others. A number of documentary papyri are also of interest for the study of the New Testament (see Barrett 1987). These include: the Zenon papyri (third century BC), the largest documentary archive, attesting to the social and financial situation in Egypt and Palestine during this time; a papyrus record of Claudius' edict regarding the Jews at Alexandria (AD 41); the Bar Kokhba letters in Greek (second century AD), attesting to the use of Greek in the eastern Mediterranean; the Babatha archive (second century AD), containing a number of legal and financial documents that illustrate financial conditions, including the role of women in society of the time; the Theon letter (second/third century AD), a letter representative of many such letters from the ancient world, this one from a disgruntled and petulant child to his father; and the Fayyum fragment (third century AD), one of several apocryphal Gospel fragments found, this one containing a conflation of Mark 14:26–30 and Matthew 26:30–34.

3 Epigraphy

In 1822, the Rosetta stone, first discovered in 1798, was deciphered, which allowed for understanding of Egyptian hieroglyphs (and Demotic) on the basis of the parallel Greek text, and, in 1847, the decipherment of the trilingual Behistun inscriptions led to unraveling the mysteries of the cuneiform script. These two major accomplishments played significant roles in terms of the nineteenth century coming to be called the age of epigraphy or inscriptions. During this century, as the field of archaeology was developed, numerous inscriptions found in a variety of ancient sites throughout the Mediterranean world and eastward were deciphered, published, and utilized in reconstructing the ancient world. These ancient artifacts attested to the written cultures of the ancient world, but, more than that,

provided important evidence for reconstructing the ancient biblical world, of both the Old and New Testaments, in terms of their history and its textual basis.

Through inscriptions significant insights have been gained (see Bodel 2001) into the political structures of the ancient world, including government and its positions; social structures, including the family; the names, identities, titles, and positions held by various people, including both those with status and those without; the legal structure, including the laws and practices of the society; the religious institutions, including the practices and people involved; and, perhaps most importantly, individual events from the ancient world and when and how they occurred. Inscriptions also give insight into the languages used in the ancient world, including various dialects that were found within language groups. There was also a wide range of conventions for writing inscriptions, depending upon time and place. Some of these were formal conventions (spacing of letters) but others were related to the skill and care taken by the inscriber. Inscriptions were written for all sorts of events, including celebratory and mundane, but the most common type of inscription from the ancient world is that of the grave epitaph.

It is to be welcomed when an inscription is found intact, but that occurrence is rarer than one would hope for. Most inscriptions are found in a damaged condition, either through neglect (they have fallen down or have simply eroded), reuse for other purposes (such as in a wall or as part of a fountain), or outright abuse (some have been reinscribed, but others have been defaced). As a result, some of the major tasks in the use of inscriptions for biblical interpretation include: identification of the inscription, in terms of its language and its text type, such as a legal decree; reconstruction of as much of the text as is possible to enable gaining the largest amount of data from it; dating and contextual study to establish provenance and significance, recognizing that the means of dating are often imprecise and based upon subjective features such as letter forms; decipherment, transcription, and translation, often aided by reliance upon formulaic language found in similar inscriptions; and interpretation and application to biblical issues so that the biblical world is enhanced through knowledge of the inscription. Due caution must be exercised by the epigrapher in order not to press the evidence further than it will reach, since each stage in the process requires a number of subjective judgments. This overreaching has been referred to as doing history from square brackets, when the reconstructed part of the text becomes the basis for historical judgments (see Bodel 2001: 52).

Epigraphy related to the Old Testament requires expertise in a number of languages and the cultures from which they arise, some languages of which have yet to be deciphered and whose texts have yet to be determined. The languages include pictographic languages such as Egyptian hieroglyphs and ancient Sumerian; the various cuneiform-based languages (cuneiform being a form of ancient writing developed from pictographs), such as Hittite, Babylonian (Old and New), Assyrian, Ugaritic, and Old Persian; and the alphabetic languages (also derived from earlier pictographs), such as Phoenician, Hebrew, and Aramaic (and Greek).

The number of inscriptions illuminating the study of the Old Testament is large, with some coming from Palestine and some from surrounding nations (see Wiseman 1958; Pritchard 1958; Winton Thomas 1958). These include a number of commemorative inscriptions, as well as many clay tablets (e.g., from Ebla, Mari, Nuzi, and Hittite). Some of the most important include the following (in chronological order): Hammurabi's code of laws from Babylon (eighteenth century BC); the Ras Shamra tablets (fourteenth century BC), describing Canaanite religion; stele of Mernehptah from Egypt (thirteenth century BC), the only inscription of the time mentioning Israel; Gezer calendar (tenth century BC); the 'house of David' inscription (ninth century AD); a black limestone obelisk from Nimrud (ninth century BC), depicting King Jehu bowing to the Assyrian king, Shalmaneser III; Mesha inscription (ninth century BC), recording the Moabite king's victories over Israel; Siloam tunnel inscription in Jerusalem (eighth century BC); cuneiform tablets from Nineveh containing the creation story of Enuma elish and the flood story of Gilgamesh (seventh century BC); a cuneiform prism from Nineveh (seventh century BC), recording the Assyrian King Sennacherib's invasion of Israel; cuneiform Babylonian Chronicle (sixth century BC), recording events around the exile; cuneiform Cyrus cylinder (sixth century BC), containing his edict regarding returning Babylonian exiles to their native lands; and the Rosetta stone (second century BC), which, as a trilingual inscription, led to decipherment of hieroglyphs and Demotic on the basis of knowing Greek. Though not meant for lasting preservation, several other important epigraphic sources should also be mentioned (and could be listed under papyri): the cuneiform Amarna tablets (fifteenth century BC), letters from officials in Palestine to Egypt asking for aid against the invading Habiru; and Hebrew Lachish tablets (sixth century BC), which record correspondence between the commander of the city and the commander of an outpost during the time of the Babylonian invasion.

New Testament epigraphy includes contemporary materials in Hebrew and Aramaic, and related languages, as well as Greek and Latin. One important source of information is coins, which in their composition, style, and inscriptions provide evidence regarding the religious, civil, and economic conditions of the time. Coins of importance would include those by the Greek kingdoms of Alexander's successors, the Romans, the Herods, and various Jewish rulers, such as the Maccabees and Simon bar Kokhba (see Numismatics).

Inscriptions of relevance for study of the New Testament are large in number, and could theoretically include a variety of inscriptions found throughout Asia Minor and Greece (see Wiseman 1958; Boffo 1994). Those of more particular significance include the following (in chronological order): so-called Priene inscription (9 BC), one of several versions of a calendar inscription that celebrates Augustus as savior and the beginning of good news for the world; a Latin inscription (c. first century AD) attesting to Quirinius' term as governor of Syria; a Greek ordinance of a Caesar forbidding grave robbery (first century AD); the Greek temple inscription (first century AD), forbidding entrance into the Herodian temple by those other than Jews; the Latin Pilate inscription from Caesarea (first century AD), indicating Pilate as prefect of Judaea; the Greek Theodotos inscription (first century AD), which provides the earliest evidence for a synagogue; the Gallio inscription from Delphi (first century AD), indicating the date of his proconsulship; various Aramaic inscriptions, including grave inscriptions such as the so-called James ossuary (see Evans 2003); a Greek inscription from Thessalonica (second century AD), indicating that the term politarch was the correct designation during Paul's time for a certain type of civic official; Beth Shearim grave inscriptions (first to sixth century AD), providing evidence of Jewish burial practices; and the Aphrodisias inscription (third to fourth century AD), attesting to those known as 'godfearers.'

4 Implications for biblical interpretation

One can see that the epigraphic and papyrological remains provide a crucial foundation for biblical studies. It is often through these documents that the textual basis of biblical study is ascertained, established, and charted in its development. For example, the Dead Sea Hebrew texts have pushed back the textual basis for the Old Testament to the second century BC. However, these documents also illustrate that the textual tradition was more varied than the Masoretic tradition attests, to which the Greek Septuagint documents also testify. Further, the extrabiblical documents provide various types of reference points. Some of them, such as the Gallio inscription, help to determine with some exactness the dating of a particular event. The Gallio inscription is widely viewed as providing one of the relatively firm dates for establishing a Pauline chronology. Others provide the type of context in which one can place the various biblical events, such as attesting to rival ancient Near-Eastern powers, such as the Assyrians and Babylonians, the return of exiles under Cyrus, and the like. One of the major cautions to keep in mind, however, is that the artifacts themselves require interpretation. They provide one – although an admittedly important – piece in a complex puzzle that is assembled from a variety of considerations both ancient and modern.

References and further reading

Aland, K. and B. Aland (1989) *The Text of the New Testament*, Grand Rapids: Eerdmans.

Bagnall, R.S. (1995) *Reading Papyri, Writing Ancient History*, London: Routledge.

Barrett, C.K. (1987) *The New Testament Background: Selected Documents*, New York: Harper, 2nd edn.

Bodel, J. (ed.) (2001) *Epigraphic Evidence: Ancient History from Inscriptions*, London: Routledge.

Boffo, L. (1994) *Iscrizioni Greche e Latine per lo Studio della Bibbia*, Brescia: Paideia.

Brown, R.E. (1983) *Recent Discoveries and the Biblical World*, Wilmington, DE: Glazier.

Evans, C.A. (2003) *Jesus and the Ossuaries*, Waco, TX: Baylor University Press.

Pritchard, J.B. (ed.) (1958) *The Ancient Near East: An Anthology of Texts and Pictures*, Princeton: Princeton University Press.

Winton Thomas, D. (ed.) (1958) *Documents from Old Testament Times*, New York: Harper.

Wiseman, D.J. (1958) *Illustrations from Biblical Archaeology*, London: Tyndale.

Woodhead, A.G. (1981) *The Study of Greek Inscriptions*, Cambridge: Cambridge University Press, 2nd edn.

Würthwein, E. (1979) *The Text of the Old Testament*, Grand Rapids: Eerdmans.

STANLEY E. PORTER

PARABLES

The Hebrew term rendered by Greek *parabolē* and English 'parable' is *mashal*, which basically refers to a comparison. For that reason, the genre as a whole is an exploration of metaphorical possibilities, as is evidenced, for example, in the book of Proverbs (which in Hebrew is called *meshalim*, illustrating that the term *mashal* has a wider sense than any single term in English conveys).

The book of Ezekiel represents the wide range of meaning involved. In the name of the LORD, the prophet says, 'There is nothing for you in parabling [*moshlim*] this parable [*mashal*]. The fathers ate sour grapes and the children's teeth stand on edge' (Ezek. 18:2). Evidently, there is no requirement of a strong narrative element within the metaphorical image for the 'parable' to stand as such. Its gist is transparent, and that is precisely what the prophet is objecting to and refuting. Yet within the same book, a parable is developed in such an elaborate way that it may be styled an allegory (complete with explanation), in which the fate of Israel between Babylon and Egypt is addressed by comparison to two eagles and a sprig of cedar (Ezek. 17). It is fortunate the chapter includes interpretation, because this particular parable (which is translated 'allegory' at 17:2 in the New Revised Standard Version) is complicated, opaque, and unrealistic. Nathan's parable of the ewe lamb in 2 Samuel 12:1–15 is a more successful development of narrative allegory and interpretation, and it is not in the least surprising that David got the point of the parable, because a certain didacticism is evident here (as in the narrative parable of Ezek. 17).

Jesus was known as a master of the genre of parable in its full extent, from simple adage to complicated – sometimes, as we shall see, even surreal – narrative. For that reason, it is only to be expected that the parabolic tradition attributed to him will have been the outcome of considerable embellishment during the course of transmission. The interest here is not in attribution, but in the depth and range of the development of the genre.

Taxed with the charge that his exorcisms were performed by the power of Satan, Jesus replied with the observation that no kingdom or home divided against itself can stand (Mark 3:22–25; Matt. 12:24–25; Luke 11:15–17). That double maxim is devastating enough to have lived on within the proverbial tradition of many languages (with a meaning usually unrelated to its original context!), but the Gospels also add a parable with a narrative element, the comparison with attempting to rob a strong man's house (Mark 3:27; Matt. 12:29; developed more fully in Luke 11:21–22). Such examples instance not only the range of the genre, but also the ease with which one sort of parable might be associated with another. (For that reason, unlike some recent treatments, no hard and fast rule is suggested here between simple, embellished, and narrative parables, since a single *mashal* can easily participate in several features of the genre overall.) The narrative element which was perennially an option within the genre is exploited, complete with an interpretation of the allegory in the parable of the sower (Mark 4:3–8, 13–20; Matt. 13:3–8, 18–23; Luke 8:5–8, 11–15). Although no less didactic than the parable in Ezekiel 17, a certain vivid mastery is instanced.

In his remarkable work on rabbinic parables in relation to Jesus, David Flusser has debunked the widely held position that rabbinic parables were always exegetical, in the nature of commentaries. He instances the parable of Yochanan ben Zakkai (*Shabbat* 153a), who told of a king who invited his servants to a feast, without announcing the hour of the meal. Wise servants attired themselves properly, and waited at the door of the king's house. Foolish servants expected definite signs of the meal's preparation, and went about their work until they should see them. When the king appeared without further notice, the wise enjoyed a fine meal, and the foolish, work-soiled servants were made to stand and watch.

The motif of a festal banquet is central within Jesus' parables and sayings, and the Matthean parable of the wedding feast (Matt. 22:1–14; cf. Luke 14:16–24) especially invites comparison with Yochanan's. Matthew's subplot concerning the appropriate wedding garment (vv. 11–13) provides another point of similarity. Still, the meanings generated by the two parables are distinctive. Where Yochanan speaks of servants who either are or are not prudent in their assessment of the king's capacity, Jesus speaks of guests invited to a feast who respond with extraordinarily bad and finally violent behavior, which is answered in kind. Beneath that distinction, of course, there is a thematic similarity. The readiness to accept and act upon the invitation is called for, especially since the king is none other than God. But each parable urges a particular kind of response upon the hearer. Yochanan's narrative involves dropping normal obligations to await God's promised banquet, while Jesus' parable of recalcitrant guests is more fraught in its warning against obstinacy.

Perhaps most importantly, comparison with rabbinic parables reveals what has frequently been overlooked: there is a surrealism possible within the genre, from Ezekiel through Jesus and on to Yochanan ben Zakkai. Parables are not just lively stories taken from nature; the point can often turn on what is striking, peculiar, unpredictable. Even in Jesus' parables of growth, elements of hyperbole are plain. In the narrative of the man, the seed, and the earth (Mark 4:26–29), action is abrupt and unmotivated. The man sleeps for no apparent reason, and puts in his sickle 'immediately'; the seed sprouts in no stated time, and the earth produces 'as of itself.' Similarly, mustard seed becomes a 'tree' (Matt. 13:31–32; Luke 13:18–19), or makes 'big branches' (Mark 4:30–32) without an interval of time being indicated. The point lies in the contrast of beginning and result, miraculous transformation rather than predictable process. The hyperbolic comparison of start and finish is also evident in the parable of the leaven (Matt. 13:33; Luke 13:20–21). The parables of the hidden treasure and pearl (Matt. 13:44–46) are surprising, rather than hyperbolic, when they concern the discovery of what is valuable, but the reaction of those who find them, in selling everything to acquire them, is exaggerated. In these cases, also, ethical themes are especially conveyed by the least realistic motifs.

References and further reading

Chilton, Bruce and J.I.H. McDonald (1987) *Jesus and the Ethics of the Kingdom*, London: SPCK/Grand Rapids: Eerdmans.

Crossan, John Dominic (1992) *In Parables: The Challenge of the Historical Jesus*, Santa Rosa: Polebridge.

Flusser, David (1981) *Die rabbinischen Gleichnisse und der Gleichniserzähler Jesus*, New York: Peter Lang.

Funk, Robert W. (1982) *Parables and Presence: Forms of the New Testament Tradition*, Santa Rosa: Polebridge.

Hultgren, Arland (2000) *The Parables of Jesus: A Commentary*, Grand Rapids: Eerdmans.

Perrin, Norman (1985) *Jesus and the Language of the Kingdom: Symbol and Metaphor in New Testament Interpretation*, Philadelphia: Fortress Press.

Scott, Bernard Brandon (1989) *Hear then the Parable: A Commentary on the Parables of Jesus*, Minneapolis: Fortress Press.

Snodgrass, Klyne (2004) 'Modern Approaches to the Parables,' pp. 177–90 in *The Face of New Testament Studies: A Survey of Recent Research*, Scot McKnight and Grant R. Osbourne (eds.), Grand Rapids: Baker.

BRUCE D. CHILTON

PATRISTIC INTERPRETATION

> 1 Scripture as literal truths embodying general principles (halakhah)
> 2 Scripture as that which, though historically true, narrates events and persons that are types of eternal and future realities (antitypes)
> 3 The narratives as redemptive allegories

There were approximately three possible modes of understanding the sacred texts of the Old and New Testament open to the various early Christian groups. They believed that a certain collection of texts, first the Old Testament and subsequently the New Testament, constituted divine revelation. But those texts consisted of a variety of works and genres, including historical narrative, addressed to a particular historical situation. In consequence, the following possibilities of interpreting divine revelation opened themselves:

(1) The historical contexts and narratives of the Old and New Testament were literally true, and the events, persons, and words that they described enabled the derivation of general principles, and also role models, whether for good or for evil.

(2) The historical contexts and narratives were true but the events and persons described were mysterious. Events and persons were not exactly what they seemed: behind the literal, an eternal story was unfolding in which type gave way to antitype, and the present was to be fulfilled in the future.

(3) The texts themselves are misunderstood if they are believed to be literal and historical, or paraenetic, poetic, or prophetic products addressed to a specific historical situation: rather they are allegories in which each person and event of the story is a cipher for the eternal drama of salvation. Redemption will be achieved by whoever grasps the true meaning of the allegory or redeeming story.

These three approaches have their roots in exegesis as found in the various forms of Judaism before the uniformity imposed by what became orthodox rabbinic

Judaism, perhaps at Jabneh around AD 95. In (1) we find the purpose of halakhah as a system of deriving decisions about particular contemporary issues from the sacred text regarded as literal. In (2) we find the haggadic method, in which a midrash or retelling of a sacred story involved developments and additions in order to make it applicable to a contemporary situation. Midrash led also to pesher interpretations, characteristic of the Qumran community, in which the obscurities and vagueness of narrative passages either describing past event or prophecies are exploited as mysteriously applying to the present. For example, the *Kittim* of Habakkuk 1:8–9 are identified in 1Qp II–IV with the Romans, thus transferring the significance of the text from one historical situation to another. In (3) we find the characteristic method of Philo who exhorts: 'Let us not, then be misled by the actual words, but look at the allegorical meaning that lies beneath them' (*Cong. Quaer.* 172).

Philo, like Origen his Christian successor, modified an extreme position of allegorical interpretation by insisting that the story, though capable of a proper allegorical interpretation, was nevertheless literally true (*Praem.* 11.61). Indeed Origen in his biblical commentaries gives first, briefly, the literal meaning of the text, which he calls the historical or corporeal meaning, on which he can draw geographical, philological, medical knowledge, and natural history in order to elucidate the text. He then goes on to draw out the spiritual or allegorical meaning. Just as there is body, soul, and spirit, so too, he insists, we must interpret the scriptures in three ways, literally or corporeally, psychically, and spiritually (Or. *Princ.* IV.2.4; *Philocal.* 1.11). In that respect he may be thought, like Philo, to have sought to systematize all three methods into a coherent method of exegesis. However, in practice such a system was never consistently applied. Origen himself appears to deny the historicity of Genesis 1–3 and of Matthew 4:8 when he claims that no one of intelligence could accept that there could be a day of creation without sun, moon, and stars, or that Jesus literally had to be taken up to a high mountain and physically saw all the kingdoms of the world (Or. *Princ.* IV.3.1; *Philocal.* 1.17).

Origen does not stand alone in such inconsistency but rather is symptomatic of the existence of three distinct and separate approaches to biblical interpretation in early Christian literature that are ultimately irreconcilable. Indeed the New Testament itself bears witness to the separateness of such approaches and must bear responsibility for their continuation. Let us see some central examples of these three additional approaches.

1 Scripture as literal truths embodying general principles (halakhah)

Many sayings of Jesus are in this category as when, according to Mark 12:35–37, Jesus concludes that if in Psalm 109:1 (LXX) 'David' calls the Christ (anointed

Messiah) his Lord, then the Messiah cannot be David's son. For another example see Mark 12:28–34.

In the letter of the Church of Rome to the Church at Corinth, written by Clement *c.* AD 95, we find a continuance of such exegesis uninformed by neither a typology nor allegorization. The famous passage on Church Order (*1 Clem.* 40.5) may initially be thought to represent a typology in which the Israelite high priest stands for the Christian bishop, the sons of Aaron for the presbyters, the Levites for the deacons. But this is clearly not the case since Clement assumes a plurality of presbyter-bishops whose legitimacy is guaranteed not by an exact Old Testament typological correspondence, but by a lineal episcopal succession initiated by the apostles themselves (*1 Clem.* 44.1–2) in fulfilment of a prooftext loosely derived from Isaiah 40:17 (*1 Clem.* 42.5). His allusions to Old Testament liturgies are simply one example of divine order amongst others, which include a stoically conceived cosmos (*1 Clem.* 20.1–3) or indeed the Roman army (*1 Clem.* 37.1–3).

With Clement's exposition of the general principles of ministerial order from the Old Testament we may compare that found in *c.* AD 265, in *Didasc.* chs 8–9 (= *CA*, ed. Funk, II.25.7–26.8) of that document. Here we find a different exegetical method from that of Clement where the principle of provision from sacrifices preserved for the upkeep of the ministry of the Old Testament Tabernacle is applied to payment for a professionally organized and paid clergy. However, the Didascaliast goes beyond using the Old Testament for the provision of general principles of church government. Instead he deploys a typology in which high priest, priests, and Levites are types of the threefold order of bishop, priests, and deacons, with the Holy Spirit as type of the deaconess. The use of *patros* by the Didascaliast is here, by contrast with Ignatius of Antioch, indicative of a different exegetical method. Although Ignatius uses the term *patros* (of bishops, priests, and deacons), he does not regard ecclesial structure as derived exegetically from the Old Testament. Rather he regarded the bishop as 'type of the Father,' the presbyterate that liturgically encircled the bishop, the spirit filled 'council of the apostles,' and the deacons as types of Christ (Ign. *Magn.* 6.1; *Trall.* 3.1). Thus the three ecclesiastical orders are images or models of the persons of the Trinity, and thus reflect the mystery of the transcendent godhead, rather than constituting antitypes of Old Testament types.

The Old Testament is not for Clement, any more than for Ignatius, a mysterious typology but a book of historical characters providing models for Christians, or embodying principles illustrative of the divine order of the world and society. Cain and Abel, Jacob, Esau, and Joseph, Moses, Aaron and Miriam, Korah, Dathan, and Abiram are each examples of what happens when jealousy upsets the peace of the community (*1 Clem.* 4.1–13). Enoch, Abraham, Lot and Noah, and Rahab are principally models of grace and single-mindedness (*1 Clem.* 9.3–4; 10–12). Clement allows himself to see in Rahab's scarlet thread 'redemption through the blood of Christ' but this is an example of 'not only faith but prophecy in the woman' (*1 Clem.* 12.8) rather than an indication of a future mystery unfolding behind the literal and historical text.

There is, however, a problem for the concept of historical revelation which avoids typology and denies allegory as valid exegetical methods. In the light of the finality of the sacrifice of Christ, what is to become of the laws of sacrifice, ritual, and food in the Old Testament, let alone descriptions of divine action that are morally abhorrent? If it is not to be allowed that Old Testament sacrifices are typological, mysterious prior runs of the act of Christ the true redeemer, least of all ahistorical, allegorical expressions of these, then there are few general principles to be derived from the texts that are ceremonial and sacrificial. The *Didascalia*, without the availability of a general typological or allegorical exegesis, had accordingly to produce a doctrine of the *deuterosis* (or second legislation) in order to distinguish Old Testament principles and practices that were specific to Israel, and those of which were general and universally applicable for all time.

Paul in Galatians 3:13 had referred to the law as a schoolmaster bringing us to Christ and had argued that the reason why the law has no more dominion over us is because we have died with Christ who was made a curse for us under the law in accordance with Deuteronomy 21:22ff. The Didascaliast goes much further than this. His claim is that subsequent to the Ten Commandments, the remaining law had been given in order to punish the Jews for making with Aaron the Golden Calf. Sacrifices, food laws, ritual purification were not rudimentary preparations for redemption by Christ but were punishments that effected nothing. God commands such things merely 'as though he had need of these things.' Deuteronomy 21:22 is interpreted in this context as divine deception so that Christ is made to appear cursed in order that the Jews might not receive him. Christ therefore affirms the first legislation but abolishes the punishment for idolatry that was the *deuterosis* or second legislation (*Didasc.* p. 222.5–34– p. 223.7 [= *CA*, ed. Funk, VI.16.6–27.1]).

It is interesting to compare this approach to exegesis with that which emerges in the Pseudo-Clementines. For the Didascaliast the *deuterosis* was clearly of relevance in itself as divine revelation, albeit as the revealed commandments whose intentions were solely punishment upon the Jews and therefore intended for no one else. There is no hint here, as we shall see shortly was the case with Barnabas, of divine revelation in the form of allegory misunderstood and reconstructed literally as a First and Jewish Covenant. But in the Pseudo-Clementines what is problematic in the Old Testament in terms of divinely revealed prescriptions is dealt with

by an alternative method that is reminiscent of a kind of nascent, nineteenth-century higher criticism. Here what is acceptable is distinguished from the unacceptable by claiming that the relevant texts are false interpolations that have distorted the sense and meaning. It is a method of coping with unacceptable passages rather akin to those used by both Clement of Rome and Justin Martyr. The former is quite capable of devising additional Old Testament quotations to suit his desire to find the principle of episcopacy in the prophets (*1 Clem.* 42.5). Certainly both Justin and Trypho indulge in mutual accusations regarding who has changed or interpolated which Old Testament passage, and indeed over the use of the LXX (Just. *Dial.* 67.1–2; 71.1–2; 72–73).

In (Ps.) Clem. *Hom.* III.43.1–4, in reply to Simon Magus, Peter claims that amongst false expressions (*fōnai pseudei*) are descriptions of God reasoning with himself as if he needed to make up his mind, or tempting Abraham, or having to descend from heaven in order to see human wickedness (Gen. 22:1; 11:7). The exegetical or even editorial principle proposed is: 'As many expressions as accuse God of ignorance or any other grave offence are convicted of being false reconstructions by other expressions which state the opposite' (*Hom.* III.43.3). If God can prophesy the future to Abraham or Moses, clearly he does not need to reason with himself or to descend from heaven to see what has come about (*Hom.* III.44.1–2). God did not desire animal sacrifices or first fruits (*Hom.* III.45.1–4). Moses as prophet is infallible but his words were entrusted orally to the seventy elders. His alleged written works clearly come from another writer after his death, which is recorded in Deuteronomy 34:5 (*Hom.* III.47.1–3).

Finally, in the fourth and fifth centuries, Theodore of Mopsuestia and his school represent literal and critical exegesis in its last and final form. Theodore was the pupil of Diodore, who became bishop of Tarsus in AD 378. Unfortunately we have lost the theoretical treatment of exegesis in Diodore of Tarsus' *On the Difference between Allegoria and Theoria*, and Theodore's own work *On Allegory and History*. But we do have Diodore's commentary on the Psalms, in the prologue to which he distinguishes between *historia*, *theoria*, and *allegoria* (Diod. *Com.Ps.* prol. 123–162). Superficially, Alexandrian exegesis, like that of Philo, had subscribed to the three senses of scripture that we considered in our introduction. But Diodore limits the use of *theoria* and *allegoria* by the prescription that *theoria* must follow from the literal meaning of the text: there must exist a true *anagoge* or justifiable analogy. Without such an *anagoge*, *historia* dissolves into *allegoria*, which Diodore is anxious to reject (*Com.Ps.* prol. 125). Accordingly he claims that Paul's use of *allegoria* (Gal. 4:24) is really equivalent in meaning to *theoria*, or the observation of the spiritual antitype in the literal events or words of scripture (*Com.Ps.* prol. 133–135). Pure allegorization was exegesis that leads to heresy and paganism (*Com.Ps.* prol. 141).

A consequence of this prescription that limited typological interpretation by the literal features of the text led Diodore to regard only Psalms such as 2, 8, and 45(44) as referring to Christ. But he regards that reference as one of prophetic vision (*Com.Ps.* 2.1:'The second psalm is prophecy regarding the Lord'). His literalist exegesis led him to reject Psalm 22(21) as in total referring to Christ's suffering and exaltation, but rather to David's own: 'it does not accord with the Lord; for David appears mindful of his own sins, and attributes the causes of his sufferings to his sin' (*Com.Ps.* 22(21).1). The LXX of Psalm 22(21):2b said: 'The reckoning of my offences are far from my salvation.' Furthermore, the quest for the literal meaning led Diodore to investigate the historical background and chronology in which to set the Old Testament text. Thus Psalm 5 refers to the sin with Bathsheba, Psalm 41(40) to Hezekiah, Psalms 31(30), 43(42), and 48(47) to Babylon. Indeed, *Com.Ps.* 51(50).1 argues typically an exilic provenance in direct contradiction to the claim of the inscription that it applies to David when he had heard Nathan's condemnation of him over Bathsheba. Psalms 14(13), 15(14), 20(19), 27–30(26–29), 31–34(30–33) are ascribed to the reign of Hezekiah despite the claims of their inscriptions. A Psalm such as 44(43) actually refers to the period of the Maccabees.

Theodore as Diodore's pupil continued the Antiochene exegetical tradition, particularly regarding the Psalms. He used the Hebrew text rather than the Septuagint. Unfortunately his works survive only in fragmentary form. According to the Acts of the Fifth Ecumenical Council at Constance (AD 553), Theodore had in a letter rejected the canonicity of Canticles, although that letter refers to this work more as a problem text that fits neither into the category of prophecy nor of history and which is unsuitable for public reading (*PG* 66.699). Clearly if the history of the allegorical interpretation of that work, which had begun with the genuine Hippolytus, *c.* AD 225, were rejected, such a text became of questionable value. Leontius of Byzantium (*c.* AD 500) also claims that Theodore rejected this work (Leont. B. *Nest. et Eutych.* 3.16) as well as Job (3.13), Ezra, and Chronicles (3.17). He also rejected James in the New Testament (3.14), even though the latter was in the canon of the Syrian Church as witnessed by its presence in the Peshitta version. He denied that Psalms 22(21) and 69(68) could apply to Christ, for similar reasons as those given by Diodore, due to the psalmist's indications of his sins in the former, and applicability of the latter to the Maccabees (Thdr.Mops. *Ps.* 21.1–2; 68.1–2).

Cosmas Indicopleustes (*c.* 535) was a follower of Theodore's exegetical method. A navigator and traveler, in his *Topographia Christiana* he finds messianic references only to Psalms 2, 8, and 110(109) (Cosm. Ind. *Top.* 5.252 A; 5.251 D; 5.256 C). Where a messianic reference is made in a New Testament passage

such as to Psalm 22(21):19, 68(67):18, or 69(68):21–22, Cosmas simply claims that what is applied to Christ's servants can selectively be applied to him. His justification is that Paul adopts a similar exegetical principle in Romans 10:6 when he transforms Deuteronomy 30:12 into a messianic reference (*Top.* 5.256 C–260 A).

It is possible to regard this critical and historical approach to the Old Testament as a rejection of the ambiguities of the allegorical approach that had led to Arian exegesis. However, we have seen the pre-Arian roots of that literalist exegesis in the third-century *Didascalia* and its concept of the *deuterosis*. Undoubtedly the eclipse of the nascent critical approach of Theodore and his school was their relegation to the Nestorian side of the two natures debate, and the condemnation of Origenism. Pope Vigilius (AD 537–555) specifically rejects Theodore's claim that Psalm 22(21) cannot refer directly to Christ (Vigil. *Const. Trib. Cap.* 21–24).

Such, then, was the literal approach to the Old Testament and its development over the first five centuries. But let us look at precisely what were the other two distinct approaches to exegesis (with which we began) that this literalist movement had threatened.

2 Scripture as that which, though historically true, narrates events and persons that are types of eternal and future realities (antitypes)

Paul in his references to the pillar, the cloud, the manna, and the rock in the wilderness (1 Cor. 10:1–4) or to Sara, and Hagar (Gal. 4:21–31) did not deny the historical character of any of these scenes. Rather he claimed that they had happened, and that they embodied mysterious and prophetic messages regarding what was to come: 'These have become our types [*tauta de tupoi hēmōn egenēthēsan*]' (1 Cor. 10:6). The message that they bore was of the spiritual and eucharistic food that is Christ seen in the water from the rock, and the spiritual food that was the manna, and Christian baptism seen in the cloud and the passing through the sea. It was essentially this kind of exegesis that was to find its development in the writings of Justin Martyr (AD 110–167).

There is clearly no sense of allegory as a substitute here for the literal truth of the events. Rather in the events in all their facticity the mystery of Christ as the cosmic savior was unfolding. Theophilus of Antioch (AD 169), as representative of the tradition of the Eastern Church of the mid-second century, in his three volumes addressed to Autolychus quotes from the Old Testament in a manner that conforms to such a principle. In Genesis 1:1, at the literal Creation, the Logos of God was operative, and the divine Sophia who foresees all things, and speaks through the prophets, was literally present in space and time (Thphl. Ant. *Autolycum* 2.10). Indeed, it is the literal truth of the Old Testament that makes the Christian message superior to that of Greek poets and philosophers who never got the history of the past right in the way that Genesis does. What is older is superior to what is more recent, and Moses can be shown to be more ancient than Solon, and indeed even than the reign of Zeus in Crete and the Trojan War (*Autolycum.* 2,29–33; 3, 26–29). Justin Martyr, who wrote at Rome between AD 150–160, was to continue such an exegetical tradition.

Justin's view was that Christ the Logos had preexisted not only as the Word of the Lord that came to the prophets but also as the angel of the Lord in the Pentateuch. As such the preexistence of the Logos could be personal. God's 'logos-like power [*logikē dunamis*]' which God generated as the first principle [*archē*] 'is called by the Holy Spirit sometimes the glory [*doxa*] of the Lord, and sometimes Son, and sometimes Wisdom, and sometimes an angel, and sometimes God, and sometimes Lord and Logos' (*Just. Dial.* 61.3). Indeed he appeared in human form to Joshua as the Leader of the Host (*architstratēgos*) (*Dial.* 62.5). Justin will insist that if scripture appears to be at variance with itself, it is due to the limits of human understanding (*Dial.* 65). Clearly Justin required a mystical rather than a literal interpretation of scripture to preserve his exegetical method from the conclusions which the Pseudo-Clementines and Theodore's school were later to draw.

Theodore was interested in prophecy as divine inspiration capable of the test of veracity in terms of fulfilment. Justin appears to adopt that principle without accepting what Theodore was to conclude from it. For him all the Old Testament was prophecy since it involved the activity of the preincarnational Logos. Such a case applies not only to the *Dialogue* with Trypho but also to the *Apologia* addressed to a pagan audience. Thus he will focus upon the prophetic writings as evidential for Christianity, with Moses included as the first prophet (*1 Apol.* 33.6). Justin knows the Synoptic Gospels, and will quote from them for his account of Christ's birth, life of healing and teaching. But when he focuses on Christ's death, resurrection, and second coming, he prefers to tell the narrative through Old Testament quotations rather than those from the Synoptic Gospels. After all, it is better to have Christ's *ipsissima verba* that he speaks before the incarnation as the preexistent Logos, rather than the secondhand accounts of the Gospel writers themselves. He will quote an amalgamation of Luke 1:32 and Matthew 1:21 for a virgin birth without the intervention of sexual intercourse with a human-like Jupiter, but most of the narrative will be told from Genesis 49:10, Isaiah 11:1 and 7:14, and Micah 5:2. Here is described the star of Jesse, with robes of blood, born of a virgin so that, with the exception of the latter, no quotes about Wise Men or angelic promises of death and anguish need be given from the Gospels (*Just. 1 Apol.* 32–34). Indeed, when he describes the Passion he has no direct quotes from the Synoptists either on the Triumphal Entry or Crucifixion scene, but rather the

Passion according to Isaiah, Zechariah, and the Psalms (Isa. 9:6, 65:2, 58:2, Zech. 9:9, and Ps. 22:16 [*1 Apol.* 35.1–8, 10–11]). Indeed, his claimed source for corroboration for his pagan audience is the lost *Acts of Pontius Pilate* (*1 Apol.* 35.9).

It is important therefore to note that this is the general character of Justin's exegesis – preferring to tell the story of Jesus from the Old Testament with but minor support from the New – and not simply anti-Jewish apologetic when used in the *Dialogue*. When challenged regarding Malachi 4:5, he quotes Matthew 3:11–12, 11:12–15, 17:12 and Luke 3:16–17, 16:16 as showing John as the Elijah to come (*Dial.* 50–51). It is to be emphasized here that Justin will not see Elijah as an allegory of John, but both are literal and historical persons. The dilemma of how there can be, as it were, two Elijahs is resolved by Justin's claim that the same spirit that was in Elijah was also in John, just as Moses transmitted his spirit to Joshua, in a confused reference to Numbers 11:17 and 27:18. He will quote Luke 20:35–36 on the resurrection body (*Dial.* 81), and, for the Virgin Birth, Luke 1:35 in fulfilment of Isaiah 7:14 (*Dial.* 66 and 100). In the conclusion of the *Dialogue* he will quote Luke 6:35 on loving one's enemies (*Dial.* 96), Matthew 11:27 on Christ's claim of oneness with the Father (*Dial.* 100), and Matthew 16:21 in which Christ himself is prophet of his own Passion. He will continue such quotes up until the agony in the garden itself described in Matthew 26:39 (= Luke 22:42). But on the Triumphal Entry, or the Passion, and Resurrection narratives themselves there are simply allusions and no direct quotes, save one from Luke 23:46. The preexistent Logos speaking in prophecy can be allowed to tell the story in his own and direct words found in Psalm 22, Isaiah 53, Jonah 4:10, and in many other such Old Testament passages (*Dial.* 101–107).

In view of the quotes from Luke 1:35, 23:46, and Matthew 26:29, we cannot hypothesize the existence of a sayings source such as Q available to Justin without a birth or Passion narrative. His allusions to the text are rather to be explained by his belief in the superiority of the Old Testament as the spoken prophecy of the preexistent Logos. As such his exegesis involves typology but not allegory. Indeed, his comments at various points say as much. The object of his exegesis, he specifically states, is what was 'spoken in a hidden way [*apokekalummenōs*] and in parables [*en parabolais*] or in mysteries [*en mustēriois*], or again in symbolic actions [*en sumbolois ergōn*]' (*Dial.* 68.6). He speaks of his Old Testament subject matter, rather as the Fourth Evangelist describes the miracles of Jesus, as signs or *sēmeia*, as when Moses sets up the serpent in the wilderness. With both writers, whether of a miracle of Jesus or of an Old Testament happening, 'sign' is clearly a reference to the spiritual or eternal message of the Logos mysteriously concealed in the event. As such it is synonymous with *tupos* or 'type.' The latter terms, however, have a more predictive significance, and seem always to be fulfilled in what others would later call an 'anti-type,' although Justin never uses this specific term (e.g., Gregory Nazianzen, *Orat.* 45.22; Epiph. *Haer.* LI.31.2).

Melito of Sardis (*c.* AD 160) systematically developed such a use of type fulfilled in antitype in his exegesis of the Old Testament. Melito on Abraham's offering of Isaac speaks of the latter as the type of Christ, and the scene on Mount Moriah excites astonishment and fear as it is a 'strange mystery' (Mel. *Frg.* 9.10). In the course of his homily on the Passover, he describes accurately how he regards the Old Testament in relation to Christ (Mel. *Pasc.* 33–35). The word 'type' in Greek can mean both 'model' and 'picture.' The Old Testament contains for Melito the 'preliminary sketch' or 'preliminary structure,' in wax, or clay, or wood, in contrast to the finished work that will arise 'taller in height, and stronger in power, and beautiful in form, and rich in its construction' (*Pasc.* 227–234). Melito refines this typological exegesis that he otherwise shares with Justin so as to produce a systematic parallelism between Old and New Testaments. This exegetical parallelism was centered on the Pascal Lamb and Christ (*Pasc.* 769–780). But Melito can also reason in terms of antitheses of fulfilment, as opposed to Marcion's follower, Apelles' antitheses of contradiction. From Deuteronomy 28:66 he derives the antitheses 'He who hung the earth is hanging, he who fixed the stars has been fixed, he who fastened the universe has been fastened to a tree' (*Pasc.* 711–713).

Clearly such a method of exegesis was reinforced by the controversy with Marcion conducted by Irenaeus and Tertullian. For Irenaeus there is both an Adam-Christ and an Eve-Mary typology (Iren. *Praed.* 31 and 33; *Haer.* III.22.3; V.19.1). On the one hand, his insistence on the literal character of the Old Testament enables him to reject the scriptural evidence for Gnostic claims based upon an excessive reliance on allegory. On the other hand, his typological fulfilment enables him to refute Marcionite claims that the descriptions of the Old Testament God show him to be morally defective. Unlike the Gnostics, he can normally insist on literal interpretations of the New Testament that complete and fulfil the Old, and in which mystery vanishes into what is clear and definitive (Iren. *Haer.* IV.2.1–5; III.11.5). He does, however, on occasions interpret the New Testament as he does the Old, regarding, for example, the unjust judge of the parable as a type of the Antichrist (Luke 18:2), or the widow at the temple as a symbol of the earthly Jerusalem (*Haer.* V.25.4). Irenaeus also reveals his debt to Justin in his use of the Old Testament to reveal the work of the preexistent Logos before the incarnation (*Praed.* 45; cf. Just. *Dial.* 56–60).

One writer in the Hippolytan school is an heir of both the Old Testament Christological exegesis of Justin, Athenagoras, and Irenaeus, and of Melito's concept of antithetical fulfilment. Hippolytus, *Contra Noetum* (10.4) identifies Logos/Wisdom with the pre-existent Christ in Isaiah 40:12 and Proverbs 8:22, even though, unlike in Justin's case, the 'unfleshed logos [*logos asarkos*]' is not completely personal before the incarnation when it becomes perfected by being born from the Virgin as 'perfect Son [*teleios huios*]' (*CN* 4:10–13; 15.7). The prooftext in question is Daniel 7:13. Unlike his predecessor in (Ps.) Hippolytus, *Refutatio* (X.33.11), therefore, Hippolytus did not cite Psalm 109:3 in evidence that Christ was already 'first born son of the father [*prōtogonos partros pais*], the voice before the dawn-bringing morning star [*hē pro heōsforou fōsforos fonē*].' But both writers were in this respect within the general tradition of a typology of preexistence. The genuine Hippolytus, in writing *De Antichristo*, also deployed an antithetical exegesis in order to draw a picture of Antichrist in contrast to Christ. Just as Christ is a lion (Rev. 5:5) so the Antichrist is called a lion (Dan. = Antichrist in Deut. 33:22). Christ is king, as is Antichrist (John 18:37; cf. Gen. 49:16). Christ is born from Judah, the Antichrist from Daniel, etc. (Hipp. *Antichr.* XIV–XV).

Both Tertullian and Cyprian continue the typological approach to exegesis.

Tertullian mentions disparagingly pagan, allegorical interpretations of the myth of Saturn in *Ad Nationes* (II.12.17), but uses typological exegesis against both Jews and Marcion. It was the latter's literalist 'method of errors [*rationem errorum*]' that had concealed from him the true meaning of Isaiah 53 (Tert. *Marc.* III.7.1–2), as well the example of the serpent of bronze in Numbers 21:8–9 amongst many others (*Marc.* III.18). Here we find examples of what we understand as typology rather than allegory. Tertullian uses the words *allegoria* and *allegorizare* of his exegetical method (*Marc.* IV.17.12), but apparently equivalently with *figura* (*tupos*), as well as *parabola* and *ainigma*, expressive of the mystery of literal historical events which are nevertheless mysterious and other than they seem rather than pure allegories (*Marc.* IV.25.1). 'The facts [*res*] are contained in the letters [*in litteris*], the letters are read in the facts. Thus not always and in every instance have the speech of the prophets an allegorical form, but only seldom and in certain of them' (Tert. *Res.* 20.9).

Cyprian has left in his *Ad Quirinum* a large collection of Old Testament testimonies interpreted typologically. There is, however, a far greater use of Old Testament typology in defence of Cyprian's view of the nature of the church in his writings. In Cyprian (*Ep.* LXIX.6,1–3) Novatian is compared with Jeroboam and his schism with the two nations, only one of which possessed a valid sanctuary. However, the New Testament antitype of the Old Testament type in this case is Matthew 10:5 ('Do not go into the way of the gentiles, and do not enter any city of the Samaritans'). But in this case it is the type that gives clarity to the vagueness and mysteriousness of the antitype, and not the other way around. It is thus curious that Cyprian's exegesis often regards the Old Testament as fulfilling the New rather than vice versa.

Within the writings of the Hippolytan school, however, in the generation before Cyprian, we witness a definite movement in exegetical method from the typological toward that of allegory. In his exegesis of Daniel, which, in Theodotian's version of the Greek Old Testament, has the history of Susanna as a preface to the text, the author begins with a strictly historical treatment in which he relates Josiah to Jehoiakin, Susanna's husband. Susanna in turn is the sister of the prophet Jeremiah and her father, Helkesiah, was the priest who discovered the lost book of the law in the time of Josiah (Hipp. *In Dan.* 1.12). But the writer clearly believes that the history comes from a vision of Daniel about events that are to him in the future. In consequence, he is able to apply a systematically typological interpretation that approaches pure allegory. Susanna becomes a type of the church, Jehoiakin that of Christ. The garden of this rich man represents the society of saints, Babylon is the present age, and the two elders are the two peoples who conspire against the church, namely, the Circumcision and the Uncircumcision. Susanna's bath represents baptism, etc. (*In Dan.* 1.14–17). Here types are not occasional and isolated mysterious events but are woven together in a continuous narrative that becomes more allegorical than typological. Thus we can now turn to our third category of exegetical method.

3 The narratives as redemptive allegories

We shall now see that the allegorical approach to exegesis has it roots in some parts of the New Testament as the two other approaches that we have considered have their roots in others.

One of the strange paradoxes of the Fourth Gospel is that however committed the writer is to the doctrine of the enfleshment of the divine Logos (John 1:14), his actual description of Jesus' humanity is highly ambiguous (John 6:20–21). Similarly, if he is committed to that doctrine, it would suggest something like Justin's doctrine of the Old Testament as literal events embodying nevertheless mysterious appearances of the preincarnate Logos. Yet the exegesis of scripture attributed to Christ himself is at times purely allegorical. In the discourse arising from the Feeding of the Five Thousand, the Jews refer to Moses feeding them miraculously with the manna in the wilderness, and suggest that Jesus does the same. Jesus then replies: 'Your fathers ate the manna in the wilderness and they died. This is the bread which comes down from heaven that a man may eat of it and not die' (John 6:49–50). Here Jesus appears to deny the historical character of the text of Exodus. If the Jews of Moses' time had eaten the true

manna, they would still be alive. Old Testament references to this event were therefore intended to be read allegorically and not literally, as the Jews had done as the representatives of a world of darkness and error.

Such an exegetical method was reminiscent of Philo who nevertheless, as we have seen, did not deny the literal as one valid level of interpretation as this allegorical strategy appears to do. It is reflected moreover both in the speech attributed to Stephen in Acts 7 as well as Hebrews. Stephen attacks the building of the Temple of Solomon as the result of a gross misinterpretation of what God had intended. The story of the Tabernacle in the wilderness had been an allegory of the heavenly realm: it was constructed 'according to the pattern [*kata ton tupon*]' of what Moses had seen (Acts 7:44). Solomon in building a house had failed to understand that 'the Most High does not dwell in houses made with hands' (7:47–48). Similarly, and representing a similarly Hellenistic milieu, Hebrews will regard the true significance of the Tabernacle in the wilderness as a pattern of the heavenly order (Heb. 8:6). 'The Law possessing a shadow of good things to come, was not the express image of actual things' (10:1). While the author does not deny the actuality of patriarchal history (11), he nevertheless denies any efficacy for the temple ritual itself. It was only to the one sacrifice of Calvary that such ritual pointed, since its need for repetition revealed its inadequacy. His final conclusion drawn from such a line of reasoning is that: 'it was impossible for the blood of bulls and of goats to take away sin' (10:4).

Such New Testament approaches that draw typological conclusions very close to allegorical ones become even more blatant in (Ps.) Barnabas. Circumcision in the flesh was not commanded to Abraham since Egyptians, Syrians, Arabians, and idolatrous priests are also circumcised. Abraham's words were prophetic of Jesus, and his words are therefore to be interpreted allegorically ([Ps.] Barn. *Ep.* 9.6–7). The food laws moreover were never intended to be taken literally. Being forbidden to eat pork, hare, falcon, or fish without scales was really an injunction not to have qualities of men who have the moral characteristics of these animals (*Ep.* 10.1–9). It was not simply that God provided, as Hebrews had claimed, a new, eternal, and more real Second Covenant. Rather there was only ever one Covenant, and it was Jewish misunderstanding that claimed the Old Testament for themselves, rather than seeing it as prophetic allegory for the future (*Ep.* 13.1–7a). Here there is no doctrine of the *deuterosis* that we have witnessed in the later *Didascalia*, in which certain laws and customs are not efficacious but were actually and historically given as a punishment. God had spoken allegories to Moses, which were converted by the perversity of Jewish understanding into ceremonial and sacrificial laws. Allegorization thus solved the Didascaliast's difficulty of regarding the Old Testament as divine revelation in a different way.

Justin and Irenaeus had resisted a thoroughgoing allegorical method of scriptural interpretation since it was this method that was deployed by the Gnostics for both Old Testament and New Testament texts, unless they were Gnostics or Marcionites who denied that the Old Testament was the revelation of the supreme and perfect God. But with Clement of Alexandria and his associates and successors, the allegorical method was to become of fundamental importance, however much the literal exegesis may have been acknowledged as well as part of the tradition. Clement was to draw out and refine further the implication that had been implicit in Justin's view of the appearances of the Logos in various Old Testament passages as the preexistent Christ. Since the Logos has revealed himself in the Burning Bush, in the cloud, and in the prophets, and has given the Law through Moses (Clem. Alex. *Prot.* I.8.1–3; *Paed.* I.7.60.1), 'the Logos becomes flesh again' (Clem. Alex. *Exc. ex Theod.* 19.2; *Paed.* I.9.88.2–3). Thus arises Clement's doctrine of a double incarnation.

To read the Old Testament therefore is like confronting the incarnation, the Logos veiled in flesh. Thus 'enigma [*ainigma*],' 'allegory [*allēgoria*],' 'parable [*parabolē*],' or 'symbol [*sumbolon*]' are his terms for the characteristics of the Old Testament as the experience of the mystery of the incarnation. Exegesis involves finding 'the saving words [*tē tōn sōtēriōn logōn heuresei*]' and expounding 'the concealed sense [*ton . . . kekrummenon noun*]' (Clem. Alex. *Strom.* VI.15.126.1; *Dives* 5.2). Scripture, whether Old Testament or New Testament, thus constitutes both body and soul: the aim of the interpreter is to move from the former to the latter. The true Gnostic embraces the teaching of Christ as Logos in scripture, as opposed to the simple believer (*Strom.* VII.16.95.9). The final end of exegesis thus leads to the contemplation (*epopteia*), which is a full initiation into the mysteries, whether pagan or Christian, leading to the attainment of the 'divine rational form [*theologikon eidos*]' (*Strom.* IV.1.3.2). Thus for him Old Testament narratives, despite the literal and typological aspects that he will acknowledge, are nevertheless primarily redemptive allegories in which knowledge that grasps the mysterious nature of the incarnate Logos transforms the knower.

At this point Clement parallels in his hermeneutic his pagan, Middle Platonist background. Indeed, his quotation from Numenius, 'What is Plato but Moses speaking Attic Greek?' (*Strom.* I.21.150.4), shows the means by which he will justify a Middle Platonist allegorical exegesis as one strand in his hermeneutic. We see in such writers as Philostratus and Diogenes Laertius an argument for the validity of a philosophical tradition in terms of the antiquity of its historical origin. Philostratus will not concede that philosophy originated in Egypt, despite Plato's reference to the Egyptian priest from whom he had learned his doctrines. Rather the true philosophy comes from India and the gym

nosophists (Philost. *Vit. Apoll.* 8.7). Laertius, on the other hand, will locate the origins of philosophy purely within Hellenism in the Seven Wise Men of Ancient Greece and their philosopher successors (Diogenes Laertius 1.1–2 and 1.12). Clement is arguing the superiority of the Old Testament in terms of an account both of antiquity and ultimate origin that shows its rivals to be copies of it and therefore inferior to it.

Clement, as Justin before him, claims that Moses is older than Plato, and the latter's philosophy was derived from the former, helped of course by Philo's Platonist and Stoic exegesis of the Pentateuch. The Stoics were able to allegorize obscene fables such as the castration of Ouranos that the highest principle of refined fire does not need genitals in order to procreate (Cicero *Nat. Deor.* 2.63–64). If the aetherial, refined, fiery Logos was the imminent divine principle of reason permeating all matter and life, and giving to them order and rationality, then indeed there was an inner light incarnated in all cultures concealed behind myths that might seem childish and without substance. A Middle Platonist such as Plutarch could read the story of Isis and Osiris in the light of his version of Plato's philosophy (Plut. *Is. et Os.* 372E, 53 and 373A–B, 54).

Origen was Clement of Alexandria's successor, whether of a definite school, or simply a tradition of ideas. He too will insist that Jesus is not present in the world only through the incarnation, since he has previously sojourned in the world in the form of the preexistent Logos to which the Old Testament as prophecy testifies (Or. *Hom. In Jer.* IX.1.20–25). Thus, all that followed from this fact for Clement did so also for Origen. Origen, as we stated in our introduction, distinguishes three levels of meaning of which scriptural exegesis will take account, the corporeal, the psychological, and the spiritual. But here Origen will distinguish between literal readings of the Old Testament and those of the New Testament. Literalism regarding the Old Testament could lead to Marcionite heresy, or a God of human passions and mood swings. But in the case of the New Testament, literalism is never damaging, though it must lead to a higher, spiritual interpretation (Or. *Princ.* IV.2.1). The Sadducees were in error in interpreting the resurrection in a different way from what can be expressed as historical truth (Or. *Com. In Matt.* X.20.4–10). Some events or laws found in the Old Testament cannot be given a literal meaning since this would make them either impossible or morally scandalous. But such features of the Old Testament have been deliberately implanted there by divine providence to perform an educative role. If all parts of scripture had been literal and clear, there would be no stimulus for the spiritual believer to advance beyond the literate to the spiritual meaning veiled and incarnate in the text (Or. *Princ.* IV.2.8–9; 3.5). To admit that such impossibilities or scandals could be part of the literal meaning of the text would be to breach the principle that scripture forms a harmonious whole, not one part of which ought to be interpreted as at variance with another. Thus Origen will not support the idea of the Clementine *Homilies* that the *falsae voces* are pernicious interpolations, nor of the later Theodore and his school. His exegetical position became generally accepted within the church before the rise of higher criticism at the Enlightenment, as Article XX of the Church of England at the Reformation shows, where it says of the church: 'neither may it expound one place of Scripture that it be repugnant to another.'

Rather than removing by editorial fiat texts that expressed theologically unsound content, Origen was able thus to engage in the kind of primitive textual criticism represented by the Hexapla. Here along with the Hebrew text and its Greek transliteration stood the LXX along with the Greek versions of Aquila, Symmachus, and Theodotion and two others. He placed obelisks beside passages in the LXX which did not appear in Hebrew, and asterisks besides Hebrew passages that did not occur in the LXX. Believing in the full inspiration of every text of scripture, he clearly shows sensitivity to the problem of the necessity to establish the correct text of inspired revelation. His problem was that there were variant readings of the LXX, which he sought to correct from the Hebrew particularly where this might agree with other Greek versions (Or. *Ep. In Afric.* 6–7). However, his method of exegesis in such cases assumed a maximizing approach. He will accept the Hebrew version as the true reading but will nevertheless also give the LXX reading as well if it expands the meaning of the Hebrew so that he conflates two interpretations of a text. In Origen's *Homilia In Psalmis* (2.12) we find that the LXX has added 'right' to 'lest you perish from the [right] way.' He will also interpret passages marked with an obelisk which he admits has therefore no corresponding Hebrew version. His justification appears to be that such omissions or additions are the work of divine providence, which thus assists the exegete in multiplying the interpretations of the words of God who wills to say many different things (Or. *Ep. In Afric.* 8).

It is important to note that Origen in none of his surviving works mentions the *Letter to Aristeas* and the belief that the LXX was itself a divinely inspired translation. This is of great importance, since Origen's distinctive approach to exegesis was to prevail within Christianity up until the Enlightenment and the rise of higher criticism. All scripture is divinely inspired, but its spiritual message completes and perfects its literal narrative rather than being at variance with it. Nevertheless, critical research regarding the state of those texts is essential given that human hands capable of human error must transmit those texts.

We find that Ambrose will deploy the allegorical method as will Jerome, subject to Origen's restraints, and Jerome will additionally engage in textual criticism.

The alternative, embryonically higher-critical stance of Theodore was not to prevail. A clear indication that it was not to do so can be seen from the fact that Diodore of Tarsus was the teacher of John Chrysostom. The latter delivered a panegyric in his honor in 392. John rarely interprets allegorically anything that it is not clear by the context that scripture itself acknowledges as allegory. In *Hom. In Is.* 6.4 John makes it clear that whilst an allegorical meaning can be given of Isaiah's vision as an eschatological image of the Last Judgment, he prefers to interpret the passage literally and historically.

It was the Cappadocian Fathers, Gregory Nazianzus and Basil of Caesarea, who compiled the collection of Origen's writings known as the *Philocalia* between 360 and 378. Basil's own commentary on the days of Creation, the *Hexameron*, had been literalist and arguably influenced by Diodore. But clearly by the time of writing the *Philocalia* he had become Origenist in his exegesis. But his brother, Gregory of Nyssa, was further committed to Origenist exegesis, in particular in his work on the Psalm titles and Ecclesiastes (Gr. Nyss. *Pss.Titt.*; *Hom. 1–8 In Eccl.*). In *Hom. 1–15 In Cant.* 6 Gregory argues that the voice of the bridegroom is Philosophy addressing the soul. In *Vit. Mos.* (PG 44.327–329) the birth of Moses subsequent to the pharaoh's decree to kill male children requires a deeper understanding than the literal sense. Gregory proceeds to expound the passage as a psychological allegory about the hostility of vice to virtue struggling to be born.

Jerome was to continue Origen's influence in the West with particular emphasis on the latter's textual criticism. In 386–390 Jerome worked on the Old Latin (*Vetus Latina*) text of the Bible, which he proceeded with the use of the Hexapla to make closer to the text of LXX. But in 389, in his commentary on Ecclesiastes, he began to use the Hebrew text and to make his Latin version far closer to that than the LXX. Thus he came to challenge the view that the LXX was itself an inspired translation or even, as Origen claimed, a providential aid. Jerome challenged the legend of the seventy, and, in his commentary on the Pentateuch (398), he held that they were men of education but not of prophecy (Jer. *Praef. In Pent.*). Whilst accepting that allegory was a legitimate means of interpretation, his philological work reveals an interest in the literal or historical meaning of the texts, which he takes sufficiently seriously to find contradictions such as the conflicting genealogies between Matthew and Luke an intractable problem. He falls back on the principle that whatever may be incredible to the human imagination is so due to the limitations of human knowledge (Jer. *Ep.* LVII.9.1).

Augustine clashed with Jerome's newfound faith in the Hebrew original, the *veritas Hebraica*, and claimed that the LXX was the divinely authorized translation (Aug. *Civ. Dei* XV.14.48 and XVIII.43.1–50). To ignore the LXX would place in danger the apostolic tradition, and put Greek and Latin Christendom at variance with each other (Aug. *Ep.* LXXI.2.4; *Doctr. Chris.* II.15.22). Jerome had insisted that language was the key to the sense of scripture: 'We must not think that the Gospel is found in the words of the Scripture, but in its meaning' (Jer. *Com. In Gal.* I.1.386). But Augustine regards Jerome's philology as indicative of a theory of meaning that equates words with their meanings and ultimately with their truth. Undoubtedly Jerome did call the Hebrew language the *matrix omnium linguarum* (Jer. *Soph. Proph.* III.14–18.540). But to regard Hebrew as the most accurate human language in recording the truth of divine revelation is not equivalent to regarding truth and word to be one and the same.

Language for Augustine, as for the Stoics, was a sign rather than a symbol embodying in itself the truth of that to which it made reference (Aug. *Doctr. Chris.* II.2–4.4; II.1.1–8.8). When a spoken word is written down, then it becomes a sign for what was originally itself a sign (*Doctr. Chris.* II.4.5.1–4). Thus any human language, by its very nature, is one or two removes away from the real and true and only erroneously identified with what is true itself. As the Tower of Babel shows, languages are themselves a judgment of God upon human sinfulness, and the means of preventing too close an access to God (*Doctr. Chris.* II.4.5.5). The God who inspires the sacred text has, in accordance with this punishment, placed there deliberately obscure passages and concepts in order to obstruct human pride (Aug. *Confess.* XII.14.17–25; 25.35; XI.3.5). The mystery of their meaning results from the action of grace rather than of nature so that scientific philology and linguistic translation have their limitations. Augustine really did need therefore the translation of the LXX duly inspired and kept immune from error by divine grace for there to be a written revelation.

Augustine's intellectual conversion through hearing the sermons of Ambrose involved his acceptance of the validity of the allegorical method. As a Manichean he had spurned the Old Testament as depicting a lesser God who changed his mind, who required the 'sweet savour' of an animal sacrifice, who robbed the Egyptians, etc. (*Confess.* III.5.; III–V). Ambrose's method of exegesis was allegorical, as shown in his works in which the images of the individual soul in quest for God are united with images of the church. In Ambrose's *Isaac* 1–2, Isaac as the soul finds in Rachel the heavenly Jerusalem and receives in figure the waters of baptism from Rachel's well. Indeed Ambrose uses allegory in a way that has a greater orientation toward issues of Church Order and discipline than appears in his predecessors. Certainly in Ambrose's *Hexam.* I.8.30 and III.7.32 the goodness of Creation by Father and Son is asserted specifically against the Manicheans. In Ambrose's *Noe* 22.78 it is asserted that Noah's sacrifice was one of thanksgiving on his part and not by God's command, who was not therefore 'greedy for reward.' Here also the allegorical character of the Old Testament,

as Ambrose presented it, convinced Augustine that it was after all 'a matter concealed from the proud . . . and veiled in mysteries' (Aug. *Confess.* III.5.9).

Thus Augustine, in work composed AD 388–389, claims that what is written can only be devoutly understood 'figuratively and enigmatically [*figurate atque in aenigmatibus*]' (Aug. *Gen. Con. Manich.* II.2.3 [= *Gen. Litt.* 8.2]). Later, however (*c.* 393), Augustine (*Gen. Litt. Impf.* 3.1) emphasizes to the contrary that the account 'must be accepted according to history [*secundum historiam accipiendum*].' But he was even later to express his rejection of this thesis with the momentary wish to destroy the book altogether (Aug. *Retract.* II.24). Later still, in 401, in *Gen. Litt.* 8.1, whilst still holding to the principle *secundum historiam*, Augustine will modify the rejection of his early allegorism. The serpent, like the garden of Eden, although not part of usual everyday experiences, is nevertheless to be interpreted *secundum historiam* except where the literal sense is absurd, as with the prediction that 'your eyes will be opened.' Their eyes could not have been literally closed before otherwise they could not have witnessed and spoke about all that went before. Within the narrative that is historical and literal there may be instances where literal interpretation would be illogical or impious and so here understanding in terms of metaphor or even allegory may be used, as in anthropomorphic expression of divine activity. In this case it is permitted to the reader to consider 'in what significance and sense what is written is written.' But the principle remains that 'everything cannot be accepted figuratively [*nec. . . figurate accipiendum est*] on account of the transferred meaning of one word [*propter unius verbi translationem*]' (*Gen. Litt.* 11.31). Here he was prepared to hold fast to the implications of Philo's and Origen's tripartite approach to exegesis where, at least in theory, the three levels of the physical or literal, the psychical, and the allegorical. The narrative of Genesis 1–3 is not for Augustine allegorical like Canticles. Adam is literally the father of Cain and Abel, and Eden as much a literal creation as the world itself, however much the experience of creation is not of an everyday character (*Gen. Litt.* 8.1).

Augustine did however have the intellectual honesty to admit that literal interpretation frequently raises problems to which it gives only provisional and doubtful solutions (*Retract.* II.24.1). Thus he articulated the enduring dilemma of the church's official and formal exegesis before the Enlightenment and the rise of critical biblical scholarship.

References and further reading

Bammel, C.P. (1995) *Tradition and Exegesis in Early Christian Writers*, Aldershot: Variorum.

Barnard, L.W. (1964) 'The Old Testament and Judaism in the Writings of Justin Martyr,' *Vetus Testamentum* 14: 395–406.

Boeft, J. den and M.L. Van Poll (eds.) (1999) *The Impact of Scripture in Early Christianity*, VCSup 44, Leiden: Brill.

Brent A. (1989) 'History and Eschatological Mysticism in Ignatius of Antioch,' *Ephemerides theologicae lovanienses* 65(4): 309–29.

—— (1993) 'Diogenes Laertios and the Apostolic Succession,' *Journal of Ecclesiastical History* 44(3): 367–89.

—— (2000) 'Cyprian's Exegesis and Roman Political Rhetoric,' *L'Esegesi dei Padri Latini dale origini a Gregorio Magno, Studia Ephemeridis Augustinianum* 68: 145–58.

Bultmann, R. (1984) *Die Exegese des Theodor von Mopsuestia*, Stuttgart: Kohlhammer.

Carleton Paget, J.N.B. (1994) *The Epistle of Barnabas: Outlook and Background*, WUNT 2.64, Tübingen: Mohr Siebeck.

—— (1996) 'The Christian Exegesis of the Old Testament in the Alexandrian Tradition,' pp. 478–542 in *Hebrew Bible/Old Testament*, M. Sæbø (ed.), Göttingen: Vandenhoeck & Ruprecht.

Crouzel, H. (1989) *Origen*, trans. A.S. Worrall, Edinburgh: T.&T. Clark.

Daniélou, J. (1962) 'Figure et événement chex Méliton,' in *Neotestamentica et Patristica, Festschrift für O. Cullmann*, H. Baltensweiler and B. Reicke (eds.), Leiden: Brill.

Fahey, M.A. (1971) *Cyprian and the Bible: A Study in Third-Century Exegesis*, Beiträge zur Geschichte der Biblischen Hermeneutik, Tübingen: Mohr Siebeck.

Greer, R.A. (1961) *Theodore of Mopsuestia, Exegete and Theologian*, Westminster: Faith Press.

Hagner D.A. (1973) *The Use of the Old and New Testaments in Clement of Rome*, NovTSup 34, Leiden: Brill.

Hanson, R.P.C. (1959) *Allegory and Event: A Study in the Sources and Significance of Origen's Interpretation of Scripture*, London: SPCK.

Hidal, S. (1996) 'Exegesis of the Old Testament in the Antiochene School with its Prevalent Literal and Historical Method,' pp. 543–68 in *Hebrew Bible/Old Testament*, M. Sæbø (ed.), Göttingen: Vandenhoeck & Ruprecht.

Hoek van den, A. (1988) *Clement of Alexandria and his use of Philo in the Stromateis: An Early Christian Reshaping of a Jewish Model*, VCSup 3, Leiden: Brill.

Jacob, C. (1996) 'The Reception of the Origenist Tradition in Latin Exegesis,' pp. 682–700 in *Hebrew Bible/Old Testament*, M. Sæbø (ed.), Göttingen: Vandenhoeck & Ruprecht.

Kieffer, R. (1996) 'Jerome: His Exegesis and Hermeneutics,' pp. 663–81 in *Hebrew Bible/Old Testament*, M. Sæbø (ed.), Göttingen: Vandenhoeck & Ruprecht.

Osborn, E.F. (1973) *Justin Martyr*, Beiträge zur historischen Theologie 47, Tübingen: Mohr Siebeck.

Mayer, H.T. (1971) 'Clement of Rome and His Use of Scripture,' *Concordia Theological Monthly* 42: 536–40.

Prigent, P. (1964) *Justin et l'Ancien Testament*, Paris: LeCoffre.

Prokopé, J.F. (1996) 'Greek Philosophy, Hermeneutics and Alexandrian Understanding of the Old Testament,' pp. 451–77 in *Hebrew Bible/Old Testament*, M. Sæbø (ed.), Göttingen: Vandenhoeck & Ruprecht.

Sæbø, M. (1996) *Hebrew Bible/Old Testament: The History of Its Interpretation, Vol. I: From the Beginnings to the Middle Ages (Until 1300), Part 1: Antiquity*, Göttingen: Vandenhoeck & Ruprecht.

Schoedel, W. (1984) 'Theological Method in Irenaeus,' *Journal of Theological Studies* 35: 31–49.

Schulz-Flügel, E. (1996) 'The Latin Old Testament Tradition,' pp. 642–62 in *Hebrew Bible/Old Testament*, M. Sæbø (ed.), Göttingen: Vandenhoeck & Ruprecht.

Schweizer, E. (1941–1942) 'Diodor von Tarsus als Exeget,' *Zeitschrift für die neutestamentliche Wissenschaft* 40: 33ff.

Shotwell, W.A. (1965) *The Biblical Exegesis of Justin Martyr*, London: SPCK.

Simonetti, M. (1985) 'Lettera e/o allegoria. Un contributo alla storia dell'esegesi patristica,' *Studia Ephemeridis Augustinianum* 32.

—— (1994) *Biblical Interpretation in the Early Church: An Historical Introduction to Patristic Exegesis*, trans. J.A. Hughes, Edinburgh: T.&T. Clark.

Skarsaune, O. (1996) 'The Development of Scriptural Interpretation in the Second and Third Centuries – except Clement and Origen,' pp. 373–442 in *Hebrew Bible/Old Testament*, M. Sæbø (ed.), Göttingen: Vandenhoeck & Ruprecht.

Torrance, T.F. (1995) *Divine Meaning: Studies in Patristic Hermeneutics*, Edinburgh: T.&T. Clark.

Wright, D.F. (1996) 'Augustine: His Exegesis and Hermeneutics,' pp. 701–30 in *Hebrew Bible/Old Testament*, M. Sæbø (ed.), Göttingen: Vandenhoeck & Ruprecht.

Wazink, J.H. (1979) 'Tertullian's Principles and Methods of Exegesis,' in *Early Christian Literature and the Classical Intellectual Tradition* (Festschrift for R.M. Grant), W.R. Schoedel and R.L. Wilken (eds.), Théologique Historique 53, Paris: Éditions Beauchesne.

Zaharopopoulos, D.Z. (1989) *Theodore of Mopsuestia on the Bible: A Study of his Old Testament Exegesis*, New York: Paulist.

PAUL AS INTERPRETER OF THE BIBLE

Paul's Bible consists of the Jewish scriptures as these had come to be generally recognized by the first century AD in Israel. Paul's use of these scriptures in his Epistles can be categorized under four headings: quotations, allusions, echoes, and language structures. Consideration of

Paul's explicit quotations requires attention to the textual tradition of his citations. A large number of Paul's quotations are in substantial agreement with the common Hebrew traditions and the LXX (approximately 40 percent), and a significant group of quotations agree with neither the Hebrew nor the LXX (some over 30 percent). Where the Hebrew traditions and the LXX vary, Paul in a few cases agrees with the Hebrew, but more often he reflects the Greek text.

Paul's basic pattern of explicit citation is opening theological statement, introductory formula, and scriptural quotation(s). Frequently, an interpretation, application, or instruction based on the scriptural text follows the quotation, as the apostle weaves images together and develops his particular argument. Paul in some cases also indicates that what was shown to be 'true' in scripture is 'true' now (e.g., Rom. 3:10–18; 10:18–20), that scriptural characters or events are typologically connected to contemporary characters or events (Rom. 5:14; 1 Cor. 10:6, 11), and that the meaning of scripture is to be uncovered by means of allegory (Gal. 4:24). Still, Paul's use of scripture is not exhausted by the direct quotations, for he himself often alludes to texts and material from the scriptures, whereas at other times texts and images from scripture appear to echo through Paul's writing. In still other cases, the structure of Paul's own language and thought appears to be shaped according to scriptural language patterns, as biblical language contributes to the generation and formation of specific theological discussions. These four types of biblical usage are not discrete, nor are they easily distinguishable, but commonly overlap in Paul's interpretation of scripture.

Paul interprets scripture from the perspective of his belief that Jesus is the crucified and risen Messiah who appeared to him on the Damascus Road and commissioned him to be apostle to the Gentiles. For Paul, scripture points forward to Christ and the Gospel (Rom. 1:1–2; 3:21; 1 Cor. 15:3–4; Gal. 3:6–9), but he does not normally use scripture in his Epistles to establish the church's claim that Jesus is the Christ (cf. Acts 17:2–3; 28:23). The issues that prompt Paul to quote scripture directly most often relate to matters of Jew–Gentile concern: righteousness by faith, works of law, and the place of Israel in the scope of salvation (see especially Rom. 4, 9–11; Gal. 3–4). Paul uses scripture in the service of his missionary work among the Gentiles and of the church, as it awaits Christ's imminent return. Though many scholars reject the idea that Paul juxtaposes two different interpretive methods in 2 Corinthians 3:1–4:6 (letter versus spirit), it is the case that, for him, to understand scripture merely as inscribed text is to misunderstand it. In the 'ministry of the spirit,' there is a new orientation to the scriptures of Israel; and in this 'ministry of the spirit,' Paul's experience with Christ and his interpretation of Israel's scriptures are intimately linked.

References and further reading

Aageson, James W. (1993) *Written Also for Our Sake: Paul and the Art of Biblical Interpretation*, Louisville: Westminster/John Knox.

Hays, Richard B. (1989) *Echoes of Scripture in the Letters of Paul*, New Haven: Yale University Press.

Stanley, Christopher D. (1992) *Paul and the Language of Scripture: Citation Technique in the Pauline Epistles and Contemporary Literature*, Cambridge: Cambridge University Press.

JAMES W. AAGESON

PAULINE LETTERS

1 Exegetical issues in the interpretation of the Pauline corpus
2 History of interpretation
3 Modern interpretative approaches
4 Future issues in Pauline interpretation

The Pauline letters are central to Christian history and theology. The letters attributed to Paul comprise the largest corpus in comparison with all the other New Testament authors. They are the earliest witness to the life and faith of the first Christians, pre-dating the writing of the canonical Gospels. As such, they present firsthand insight into the expansion of Christianity beyond the borders of Palestine into the wider Mediterranean world. These letters also provide the foundation for many of the central Christian beliefs and statements of faith, with Paul himself regarded as one of the first and one of the greatest Christian theologians.

Understanding and interpreting the Pauline letters has occupied a key place in the life and theology of the church since the late first century AD until today. In order to survey the interpretation of these letters, four key issues will be surveyed: exegetical issues in the interpretation of the Pauline corpus, the history of interpretation of Paul, modern interpretative approaches, and future issues in Pauline interpretation.

1 Exegetical issues in the interpretation of the Pauline corpus

Thirteen letters list Paul as the author in the epistolary opening. Scholarship since the early critical period of biblical interpretation (the seventeenth century) has questioned the authorship of some of these letters. Seven are generally regarded as authentic, Romans, 1 and 2 Corinthians, Galatians, Philippians, 1 Thessalonians, and Philemon. The authorship of 2 Thessalonians, Colossians, and Ephesians is highly debated, with the Pastorals (1 and 2 Timothy and Titus) generally regarded as inauthentic. The letters that bear Paul's name but which are regarded as written by someone else are considered as pseudepigraphic (deliberately written under Paul's name) and as post-Pauline (a continuation of the Pauline tradition after his death by disciples of Paul). Other issues like the dating or chronology, sequence, and provenance of the letters is affected by the dispute over the authorship of the Pauline letters.

The debate over the authorship of the six doubtful letters is based on a number of issues like the supposed lack of theological and grammatical consistency of the disputed letters with the undisputed letters. Also central to this debate is whether the practice of pseudepigraphy is endemic to the literary tradition of the biblical writings. The Old Testament in both the Pentateuch and the Prophets shows evidence of redaction in which later anonymous writers expanded and developed existing tradition. But this is not the same as creating a document and attributing it to a pseudonym. In addition, some non-canonical inter-testamental Jewish writings appear to be pseudepigraphic (*1 Enoch*, *4 Ezra*) and their exclusion from the canon is partly based on this fact.

Pseudepigraphy was not received without question in the ancient world. Establishing the authorial authenticity was important for many kinds of literature. Within the New Testament canon, it appears that pseudepigraphy was the basis for rejecting some post-New Testament writings like 3 Corinthians and the *Gospel of Peter*. This means that any pseudonymous writing in the New Testament canon must have been included because the deception was undetected or overlooked. But the matter of deception is more than authorship with the post-Pauline letters. The so-called inauthentic letters are personal and situational, meaning that the details about Paul's life in these letters and the situation which frames these letters is fictional, making them more forgeries than a continuation of Pauline thought. The burden of proof, therefore, is on those who dispute the authenticity of the named sender in the Pauline letters. The matter of Pauline pseudepigraphy is still an important interpretative issue.

It is widely acknowledged that the thirteen extant letters represent a selection of the letters Paul wrote. Paul himself alludes to other letters: 1 Corinthians 5:9; 2 Corinthians 2:4; Colossians 4:16. The issue of epistolary integrity and interpolations also affects the extent of the authentic Pauline corpus. Some scholars suggest that 2 Corinthians 10–13 is the lost, tearful letter referred to in 2 Corinthians 2:4, thus making 2 Corinthians a combination of several letters. There is also debate as to whether Romans 16 is authentic to the original letter to the Romans, even if it is Pauline. The integrity of the canonical form of Philippians and 1 Thessalonians is often questioned as well. Some scholars detect interpolations in Paul's letters, insertions of a non-Pauline text into a letter, such as Romans 3:24–26; 13:1–7; 1

Corinthians 11:2–16; 14:34–35; 2 Corinthians 6:14–7:1; 1 Thessalonians 2:13–16; 5:1–11. The arguments for interpolations, however, have not gained widespread acceptance. A tangential and neglected issue related to the determination of the Pauline corpus is how and why the Pauline letters were collected, circulated, and eventually formed into an acceptable 'canon.'

Another important issue in interpreting Paul's letters is understanding their literary nature and form. There is still debate as to whether Paul's writings are letters (real or true) or epistles (literary), a distinction that Deissmann made in 1901. Presently, scholarship recognizes that ancient letters operate more on a continuum according to various factors including language, content, style, and the use of various epistolary conventions. A great deal of work has been done on analyzing the various literary forms used in ancient letters, such as the opening, thanksgiving, judgment forms, travelogue or visit narrative, paraenesis, benediction and doxology, greeting formulae, and closing. There is ongoing debate over the general structure of the Pauline letters as to whether the structure includes three to five parts: opening, body and closing, or opening, thanksgiving, body, paraenesis, closing.

The extent, authorship, integrity, and literary form of the Pauline letters are ongoing as important critical and interpretative issues for the Pauline letters.

2 History of interpretation

The earliest critical comment on Paul's writings comes from 2 Peter 3:15b–16:

> So also our beloved brother Paul wrote to you according to the wisdom given him, speaking of this as he does in all his letters. There are some things in them hard to understand, which the ignorant and unstable twist to their own destruction, as they do the other scriptures.

During the late first century through to the end of the second century, Clement of Rome, Ignatius of Antioch, and Irenaeus offered comments on some of Paul's letters. Marcion was a keen advocate of Paul, but only a Paul who emerged after expunging anything in his writings which suggested continuity with Judaism. Gnostic writers also drew upon Paul to support their esoteric beliefs. Patristic writers like Origen, Victorinus, John Chrysostom, Theodore of Mopsuestia, and Jerome provided commentary on Paul's writings. Perhaps most significant was Augustine who drew primarily upon Paul in order to substantiate his doctrine of original sin, free will, and predestination. The early and late medieval writers in a revival of patristic studies also wrote exegetical commentaries on Paul. Reformation scholars like Erasmus, Luther, and Calvin wrote commentaries on Paul's letters, forging interpretations that corresponded to their theological perspective. In all these different periods, the interpretation of Paul tended toward a substantiation of the church's doctrines as understood by each theologian or by the theological tradition they represented.

In the Enlightenment period of critical scholarship, the interpretation of the Pauline writings turned away from a dogmatic interpretation which served the church and embarked on a more rational, historical, and literary approach that strived to be independent from the church's dogma and from any supernaturalism. Within this sphere of research and study, the work of F.C. Baur in the early nineteenth century transformed Pauline studies and in many ways determined the agenda which still controls present Pauline interpretation.

Methodologically, Baur approached the study of Paul on a purely historical level. Drawing upon Hegel's dialectical philosophy of history, thesis – antithesis – synthesis, Baur posited that in response to the law-dominated Jewish exclusivism of the Jerusalem apostles (thesis), Paul countered with a law-free, universal, Hellenistically shaped message (antithesis). In essence, the opposition in the New Testament was between two primary Christian parties, the Petrine/Jewish and the Pauline/Gentile. The move toward resolution of this conflict in what became the orthodoxy of the late second century is the synthesis. According to this schema, only Romans, Galatians, and 1 Corinthians can be considered authentic to Paul. This radical historical approach promoted by Baur and his associates was labeled the Tübingen school.

The Tübingen school dominated German biblical studies in the nineteenth century. The 'Cambridge school,' J.B. Lightfoot, F.J.A. Hort, and B.F. Westcott, was more influential in the English-speaking world. They responded by offering a powerful critique of Baur's theory of the way in which orthodoxy emerged in the church. In their historical analysis, there was no division between the Jerusalem apostles and Paul. The opponents of Paul could be identified as Pharisaic Judaizers in Galatians, 2 Corinthians, and Philippians, and a 'Christian Essene' proto-Gnostic movement in Romans, 1 Corinthians, Colossians, and the Pastorals. In this scenario, Paul faced several different opponents in his letters, and though they may have been Christians, they were not aligned with the Jerusalem apostles.

At the beginning of the twentieth century a new school emerged, the *religionsgeschichtliche Schule* or history of religions school. This equally historical and rationalistic approach suggested that early pre-Pauline Christianity in Antioch and other places outside Jerusalem was influenced by Hellenistic Gnostic and mystery-religion ideas. This resulted in a reconstruction of Christianity's development along two streams, Palestinian and Hellenistic. Paul drew upon both traditions but was primarily influenced by Hellenistic Christianity and Hellenistic mysticism. Key scholars in this school were W. Bousset, R. Reitzenstein, and R.

Bultmann. Out of this perspective, Bultmann wrote one of the most influential evaluations of Paul's theology from an anthropological or human-centered point of view. The history of religions school, however, failed to explain all aspects of Paul's theology such as his view on the law and eschatology, and it could never establish any full-blown pre-Christian Gnosticism from any sources before the second or third centuries.

A key issue implicit in this historical development is where to align Paul in terms of the locus of his thought-world and his religious orientation. Both the Tübingen school and the history of religions school emphasized Hellenism, and they saw Paul countering the salvation by 'works' model in Judaism with the justification by faith in Christ. While there was always a strand in Pauline studies which emphasized the Jewish influence on Paul, A. Schweitzer's book in the 1930s, *The Mysticism of Paul the Apostle*, was a catalyst in reorienting Pauline studies along the Jewish axis. This was taken further by W.D. Davies who advocated that Paul belonged within the mainstream of first-century Judaism and that his development of Christianity represented the 'full flowering' of Judaism or its intended fulfilment. Since the 1950s, Pauline studies has been dominated by the perspective that Paul's roots were primarily, if not exclusively, within the orb of first-century Judaism.

Invariably, aligning Paul with Judaism raises the issue of Paul's continuity and discontinuity with Judaism after his conversion to Christianity. This issue is particularly focused on Paul's understanding of the law in the new age or under the new covenant inaugurated by Jesus Christ. Identifying Paul with Judaism meant such interpreters had to find a way to understand what appear to be rather negative aspersions concerning the law in Paul's writings. How did his faith in Christ change his understanding of Judaism, especially in terms of how one is saved?

But the whole paradigm of salvation by works of the law versus justification by faith which had been at the heart of Pauline studies since the Reformation was severely challenged by E.P. Sanders. In his landmark book, *Paul and Palestinian Judaism*, he assesses first-century Judaism and questions the assumption of legalism or works-righteousness as the basis for earning God's favor, suggesting rather that a covenant relationship is at the center. A Jew, therefore, keeps the law out of gratitude and in order to stay within this relationship, what Sanders labels as covenantal nomism. For Sanders, Paul does not abandon Judaism because it is inferior, but because he recognizes that God has provided salvation in a new way, through 'participationist eschatology,' a mystical-sacramental union with Christ. Paul, thus, recognizes that it is not necessary for Gentiles to conform to the demands of the Torah in order to become part of the eschatological community of faith.

For many scholars, Sanders' reassessment of Second Temple Judaism provided the leverage to reassess the issue of Paul's continuity and discontinuity with regard to the law. If Sanders is correct about Judaism, then it is possible to maintain that Paul remains continuous with Judaism and that his criticism is not of Judaism, but a corruption of Judaism. J.D.G. Dunn and others offered an expansion of Sanders' work as a 'new perspective' on Paul. In essence, for these scholars the new paradigm is that Judaism is not legalistic and that the law/Gospel antithesis no longer applies to Paul. Where Paul is critical of the law, he is criticizing a distorting tendency toward nationalistic exclusivism in Judaism which locates ethnic Judaism in 'works of the law': circumcision, sabbath keeping, and purity regulations.

The new perspective has not convinced everyone and there is much work being done to reassess Sanders' reconstruction of first-century Judaism. Equally, exegetical debate about the meaning of 'works of the Law' and other key phrases in Paul's discussion of the law is vociferous. Into this discussion has come a revival of Baur's thesis, albeit a modified one by C.K. Barrett and Michael Goulder that Paul's opponents are related to a Petrine party. It is fair to say that through the centuries the interpretation and understanding of Paul's writings have not reached any general consensus.

3 Modern interpretative approaches

While a historical-critical approach continues to dominate the interpretation of Paul, in the latter part of the twentieth century various interpretative approaches emerged which gave a particular slant or emphasis to the historical-critical perspective. Foremost have been the sociological and anthropological methods. These employ modern social-scientific theory as a means of reconstructing social systems operative at the time of writing. Groundbreaking studies which provide a description of the social world of the New Testament times include, E.A. Judge (1960), J.G. Gager (1975), and W.A. Meeks (1983). Then there are those that are not only descriptive but also analytical: G. Theissen (1982), for instance, provides an analysis of the social strata of the Corinthian Church as a way to understand the problem of division at the Lord's Supper. B. Holmberg, in his 1978 study, analyzes the way the early church ordered power relations in a social structure. All these studies easily complement and even enhance the historical method.

Another influential interpretative approach is rhetorical criticism. It utilizes a literary and historical approach to analyze the persuasive means of Paul's letters in the context of the communication conventions used in the first century AD. The dominant approach used by most scholars is treating Paul's letters as ancient speeches and categorizing the argumentative units and methods according to ancient classical or Graeco-Roman rhetor-

ical theory as found in ancient rhetorical handbooks. Numerous rhetorical-critical studies have focused on Galatians. H.D. Betz (1979) suggested it was an apologetic or forensic letter with seven parts: epistolary prescript (1:1–5), exordium (1:6–11), narratio (1:12–2:14), propositio (2:15–21), probatio (3:1–4:31), exhortatio (5:1–6:10), epistolary postscript (6:11–18). G.A. Kennedy (1984), however, classified Galatians as a deliberative rhetoric with five parts: salutation (1:1–5), proem (1:6–10), proof (1:11–5:1), exhortation (5:2–6:10), epilogue (6:11–14). R. Longenecker (1990) proposed a combination of forensic and deliberative with four parts: salutation (1:1–5); forensic rhetoric section (1:6–4:11), which includes an exordium (1:6–10), narration (1:11–2:14), proposition (2:15–21), probatio (3:1–4:11); deliberative rhetoric section (4:12–6:10), which includes exhortatio 1 (4:12–5:12) and exhortatio 2 (5:13–6:10); and subscription (6:11–18). The advantage of this method is that it goes beyond using history to explain meaning or content to highlight the persuasive techniques employed in response to a particular historical contingency.

A growing methodology applies a form of narrative theory to Paul with some interesting insights. The studies are less literary in nature and more philosophical or hermeneutical, suggesting that narrative is the means by which Paul constructed his worldview or symbolic world. In essence, Paul's theology (or macronarrative) is built upon a substratum of other micronarratives such as Paul's narrative constructs related to (a) God and Creation, (b) Israel, (c) Jesus, (d) his own story – Paul. Key studies include, R.B. Hays (1983), N. Petersen (1985), B. Witherington III (1994), B. Longenecker (2002). By using a narrative perspective, traditional aspects of Paul's theology are illuminated and understood from a different point of view.

Numerous other perspectives have also been applied to Paul. G. Theissen analyzes Paul's theology from the basis of psychological theory (1987). N. Elliot offers a political critique of Paul's theology (1995). Feminist interpretations are still few but growing in number: A.-J. Levine (2003) is an example.

The application of various interpretative methodologies to Paul's letters provides new insights and is an important ongoing area in Pauline studies.

4 Future issues in Pauline interpretation

In many ways, most interpretative issues remain open in Pauline studies. The issues of authorship and pseudepigraphy as well as the extent of Paul's corpus are still unresolved, as are the related issues of the chronology of Paul's life and the dating of his writings. The relationship of the epistolary form to rhetoric and the impact of form and rhetoric on shaping the content of Paul's letters requires further exploration. In addition, the situational nature of Paul's letters in terms of the relationship between the occasion (the historical context) and their purpose (the author's aim) remains a fruitful area of further research.

Furthermore, Baur's agenda still remains open, identifying the opponents of Paul, assessing Paul's continuity and discontinuity with Judaism and Hellenism, and hence his understanding of the law and his use of the Old Testament. Coterminous with the law issue is the relationship between Jesus and Paul or, more specifically, the knowledge of and use of the Jesus tradition in Paul and how his understanding of this tradition corresponds to the Jerusalem or Palestinian Christian tradition. Also if Paul is a Hellenistic Jew, why do biblical scholars continue to neglect the Graeco-Roman milieu for understanding Paul, and is it possible to identify the primary locus for Paul's thought and religious ideas?

New methodological approaches to Paul's writings provide new insights and there remains important work to be done in both applying these methods and assessing their conclusions. In particular, rhetorical criticism has shifted the interpretative emphasis from the content alone to include the manner and method of Paul's argumentation. In addition there are other methodologies which have not impacted significantly on Pauline studies. Paul's writings still have not had any major interpretation according to contextual ideological perspectives like Black theology or postcolonial and other Third World perspectives. While there have been a number of forays into Paul's writings by literary critics, there is still more one should expect in this regard.

While not discussed, a fundamental area of further study relates to identifying a center for Paul's theology. Is this even possible and what is the appropriate method to use? An important challenge in this regard is maintaining the situational nature of his theology while discerning the core convictions and pervasive concerns.

Most issues in the interpretation of Pauline studies remain open for further study and for new assessment.

References and further reading

Barrett, C.K. (1994) *Paul: An Introduction to His Thought*, London: Chapman.

Beker, J.C. (1980) *Paul the Apostle: The Triumph of God in Life and Thought*, Philadelphia: Fortress Press.

Betz, H.D. (1979) *Galatians: A Commentary on Paul's Letter to the Churches in Galatia*, Hermeneia, Philadelphia: Fortress Press.

Bruce, F.F. (1977) *Paul: Apostle of the Heart Set Free*, Grand Rapids: Eerdmans.

Bultmann, R. (1951–1955) *Theology of the New Testament*, trans. K. Grobel, 2 Vols., London: SCM Press.

Davies, W.D. (1980) *Paul and Rabbinic Judaism: Some Rabbinic Elements in Pauline Theology*, Philadelphia: Fortress Press, 4th edn.

Deissmann, A. (1901) *Bible Studies*, trans. A. Grieve, Edinburgh: T.&T. Clark.

Dunn, J.D.G. (1998) *The Theology of Paul the Apostle*, Grand Rapids: Eerdmans.

Elliot, N. (1995) *Liberating Paul: The Justice of God and the Politics of the Apostle*, Sheffield: Sheffield Academic Press.

Gager, J.G. (1975) *Kingdom and Community: The Social World of Early Christianity*, Englewood Cliffs: Prentice-Hall.

Harris, H. (1990) *The Tübingen School: A Historical and Theological Investigation of the School of F.C. Baur*, Grand Rapids: Baker.

Hays, R.B. (1983) *The Faith of Jesus Christ: An Investigation of the Narrative Substructure of Galatians 3:1–4:1*, SBLDS 56, Chico: Scholars Press.

Hengel, M. with R. Deines (1991) *The Pre-Christian Paul*, trans. J. Bowden, London: SCM Press.

Holmberg, B. (1978) *Paul and Power: The Structure of Authority in the Primitive Church as Reflected in the Pauline Epistles*, Philadelphia: Fortress Press.

Judge, E.A. (1960) *The Social Pattern of Christian Groups in the First Century*, London: Tyndale.

Kennedy, G.A. (1984) *New Testament Interpretation through Rhetorical Criticism*, Chapel Hill: University of North Carolina Press.

Kim, S. (1981) *The Origin of Paul's Gospel*, Grand Rapids: Eerdmans.

Levine, A.-J. (ed.) (2003) *A Feminist Companion to Paul: Deutero-Pauline Writings*, Sheffield: Continuum.

Longenecker, B. (ed.) (2002) *Narrative Dynamics in Paul: A Critical Assessment*, Louisville: Westminister/John Knox.

Longenecker, R.N. (1990) *Galatians*, WBC 41, Dallas: Word.

Meeks, W.A. (1983) *The First Urban Christians: The Social World of the Apostle Paul*, New Haven: Yale University Press.

Pagels, E. (1975) *The Gnostic Paul: Gnostic Exegesis of the Pauline Letters*, Philadelphia: Fortress Press.

Petersen, N. (1985) *Rediscovering Paul: Philemon and the Sociology of Paul's Narrative World*, Philadelphia: Fortress Press.

Porter, S.E. and C.A. Evans (eds.) (1995) *The Pauline Writings: A Sheffield Reader*, Sheffield: Sheffield Academic Press.

Sanders, E.P. (1977) *Paul and Palestinian Judaism: A Comparison of Patterns of Religion*, Philadelphia: Fortress Press.

Schweitzer, A. (1931) *The Mysticism of Paul the Apostle*, New York: H. Holt.

Smalley, B. (1941) *The Study of the Bible in the Middle Ages*, Oxford: Clarendon Press.

Sumney, J.L. (1990) *Identifying Paul's Opponents: The Question of Method in 2 Corinthians*, JSNTSup 40, Sheffield: Sheffield Academic Press.

Stowers, S.K. (1986) *Letter Writing in Greco-Roman Antiquity*, LEC, Philadelphia: Westminster.

Theissen, G. (1982) *The Social Setting of Pauline Christianity*, Philadelphia: Fortress Press.

—— (1987) *Psychological Aspects of Pauline Theology*, Philadelphia: Fortress Press.

Trobisch, D. (1994) *Paul's Letter Collection: Tracing the Origins*, Minneapolis: Fortress Press.

Westerholm, S. (1988) *Israel's Law and the Church's Faith: Paul and His Recent Interpreters*, Grand Rapids: Eerdmans.

Wiles, M.F. (1967) *The Divine Apostle: The Interpretation of St. Paul's Epistles in the Early Church*, Cambridge: Cambridge University Press.

Witherington III, B. (1994) *Paul's Narrative Thought World: The Tapestry of Tragedy and Triumph*, Louisville: Westminster/John Knox.

Ziesler, J. (1983) *Pauline Christianity*, Oxford: Oxford University Press.

DENNIS L. STAMPS

PENTATEUCH

1 Jewish interpretation
2 Samaritan interpretation
3 Christian interpretation

1 Jewish interpretation

For orthodox Jews the Pentateuch (Genesis to Deuteronomy) is the most sacred part of the Bible, containing laws and narratives revealed by God to Moses on Mount Sinai. It is often referred to as the Torah (the law), although the Hebrew word 'Torah' has many other meanings such as 'teaching' or 'instruction.' Judaism is a religion of practical observance of God's laws, and the Pentateuch is the major source for these. According to traditional Jewish teaching it contains 613 commandments in positive and negative forms of which the first, 'be fruitful and multiply' (Genesis 1:28), puts the obligation upon males from the age of eighteen to marry and have children. All other commandments are obligatory from the age of thirteen. These commandments cover such matters as clean and unclean foods, times of prayer, and observance of the sabbath. The festivals of Passover (commemorating the Exodus from Egypt), Weeks (commemorating the giving of the law to Moses on Mt. Sinai), and Booths (commemorating God's protection of the people during the wilderness wanderings) are not only based upon Pentateuchal narratives describing the events that these festivals celebrate, but these narratives also contain regulations about how the festivals are to be observed. The most important Jewish prayer, the *Shema* (hear, O Israel!), uses the words of Deuteronomy 6:4–9, 11:13–21, and Numbers 15:37–41.

In addition to providing the legal and historical basis for the distinctive observances of Judaism, the Pentateuch sets the faith within the universal context of the world as created by the God of Israel, a God who chose Israel to be his special people. The Pentateuch is thus also the source of Judaism's theology, a theology that is explored and elaborated in the midrashim, compositions which date from the second half of the first millennium AD, and which use biblical texts as the starting point for theological investigation and discussion.

Although orthodox Judaism remains committed to the Mosaic, and thus the divine, origin of the Pentateuch, Jewish interpretation has been far from rigid. The Middle Ages witnessed a distinguished succession of scholars who were guided by the rediscovered philosophy of Aristotle, and who interpreted the Bible in the light of the scientific knowledge of the day. Their greatest representative was Moses Maimonides. In his *Guide of the Perplexed* Maimonides explained how language about God should be understood as implying that he had human parts and passions when, of course, he did not. Maimonides also laid down the principle, based upon Genesis 15:1 ('the word of the Lord came to Abraham in a vision'), that all divine communications took place on the basis of visions. This principle also covered difficult miraculous passages, such as Baalam's speaking ass in Numbers 22:28–30. Because this encounter with God had taken place in a vision, the talking ass did not violate the natural order.

In modern times, movements, such as Reform and Liberal Judaism, have emerged which accept many of the conclusions of modern critical scholarship about the origin of the Pentateuch, but which try to uphold the spirit of the Pentateuchal commandments. Also, the traditional festivals are observed within these movements as fundamental parts of Judaism. Orthodox Judaism has continued to interpret the Pentateuch so as to provide solutions to moral dilemmas such as abortion, suicide, and artificial insemination, thus demonstrating the resourcefulness of the eternal Torah.

2 Samaritan interpretation

The Pentateuch preserved by the Samaritan community, although, like the traditional Hebrew text, a medieval text in its present form, derives from an ancient textual tradition. In hundreds of small instances it is probably superior to the Hebrew text. It is estimated to contain some 6,000 divergences from the traditional Hebrew text, in around 1,900 of which it is supported by the ancient Greek translation known as the Septuagint. Among places where it is held to preserve a superior text are Genesis 2:2, where it agrees with the Septuagint and the Syriac Peshitta that God completed the Creation on the sixth day, and Genesis 4:8, where, in the story of Cain and Abel it adds, with the ancient Greek, Latin, and Syriac versions, 'let us go out into the field.' Another passage, crucial for Samaritan beliefs, where its Pentateuch probably has the correct text is at Deuteronomy 27:4, where God commands the Israelites to build an altar on Mount Gerizim when they have crossed over the Jordan. Strangely, although many commentators believe that the Samaritan Pentateuch preserves the correct reading at this point, English translations (but not the German *Einheitsübersetzung*) persist with the Hebrew reading 'Mount Ebal.'

For the Samaritans, the Pentateuch is the only authoritative and infallible scripture, because it was written by God himself (cf. Exod. 32:16). The remainder of the Hebrew Bible is rejected. Moreover, Moses occupies a unique place in their faith, as the one to whom the sacred writings were given. While, therefore, the Samaritan Pentateuch undoubtedly preserves readings superior to those in the traditional Hebrew text, it also contains many altered readings designed to support distinctive Samaritan beliefs. Two of these, the sanctity of Mount Gerizim and the supremacy of Moses, can be briefly illustrated. The Samaritan version of the Ten Commandments has, as the tenth, a command based upon Deuteronomy 27:2–4 to build an altar on Mount Gerizim. In twenty-one instances where the Hebrew speaks of the place that God *will* choose, the Samaritan reads 'has chosen.' At Exodus 29:42 and Numbers 17:19 the Hebrew plural 'you' in 'I will meet with you' (at the tent of meeting) is a singular 'you,' indicating that Moses alone is meant. Moses and Gerizim figure prominently in the way in which biblical passages are understood by the Samaritan Targum and Samaritan interpreters. The claim in Exodus 4:24 that God sought to kill Moses is taken to mean that God merely frightened or disturbed him. Again, because it was inconceivable that God could be angry with Moses the text that said that he was (Deut. 3:26) was paraphrased in the Targum as 'the Lord passed by my entreaty.' Mount Gerizim became a central theme of interpretation. From it flowed the rivers that watered the garden of Eden; the passage 'Enoch walked with God' (Gen. 5:24) meant that he hastened to Mount Gerizim. Salem, where Abram offered tithes to Melchizedek (Gen. 14:18–20) was Mount Gerizim, as was Bethel where Jacob had his dream (Gen. 28:19). In the story of the binding of Isaac (Gen. 22) the words 'Jehovah jireh' (v. 14) are taken to mean 'in the mountain the Lord was seen,' the mountain being Gerizim. Also located there was the cave of Machpelah, the burial place of Abraham and Sarah. Other Samaritan interpretation was devoted to clarifying obscure passages and interpreting laws and commandments in ways distinctive to Samaritan belief.

3 Christian interpretation

Early Christian interpretation sought to justify Christian beliefs. The plural 'let us make humankind in our image after our likeness' (Gen. 1:26) was taken as evidence for the Trinity, as was the appearance of the three men to Abraham in Genesis 18. In the letter to the Hebrews the Levitical sacrificial system was expounded in such as way as to show that the death of Jesus had been a sacrificial, high priestly ministry, which was continued by the risen Christ. Little reference was made to the legal parts of the Pentateuch, following the Pauline view that the commandments were summed up in the injunction to love one's neighbors as oneself (Rom. 13:9). With Augustine in the fifth century AD, the opening chapters were viewed in the light of contemporary scientific knowledge, and problems such as the creation of light before the sun and the fact that men live to be over 900 years old in Genesis 5 were addressed. Indeed, such was the importance attached to the opening chapters of Genesis that no expositor worth his salt could avoid dealing with the hexameron – the six days of Creation. Another concern was the nonsacrificial laws in the Pentateuch, and the extent to which they were binding upon Christians. One solution was to try to identify which commandments exhibited the natural moral law, and were therefore universally binding on humankind. In the Middle Ages, and under the influence of the great Jewish philosopher Moses Maimonides, Thomas Aquinas argued that the Old Testament sacrifices enabled the Israelites to avoid idolatry. At the same time, these sacrifices symbolized and pointed forward to the sacrifice of Christ.

At the Reformation, especially in the Reformed (i.e., Calvinist) tradition there was a renewed interest in applying the nonsacrificial laws of the Pentateuch not only to Christians individually but also to Christian nations. The death penalty was urged not only for offenses such as murder, but also for blasphemy, violation of the sabbath (i.e., Sunday), adultery, rape, and certain kinds of false testimony. Calvin's exposition of the Ten Commandments in his *Institutes of the Christian Religion* is a masterly example of how to apply their implications to many practical situations. There was also continued interest in the opening chapters of Genesis, especially in the light of scientific discoveries. Calvin, for example, knowing that astronomy had shown that the moon was not one of the two greatest objects in the sky (cf. Gen. 1:16) argued that Genesis 1 described the universe as it appeared to an observer on earth using the naked eye. It was not a manual for physics or astronomy. Inevitably, however, the opening chapters of Genesis came increasingly under pressure from new discoveries, beginning with Genesis 10. This chapter had been held to describe the complete geography of the world, a view that was challenged by the voyages of Drake and others around the world. In the early part of the nineteenth century Lyall's geological discoveries called into question the accepted age of the world (just under 6,000 years) based upon biblical chronology. In the previous century, polygenism (the view that the human race had originated in more than one part of the world) had challenged the story of Adam and Eve as the sole ancestors of the human race. Darwin's *The Descent of Man* (1871) arguably presented more of a challenge to traditional interpretations of Genesis than *The Origin of Species* (1859).

From within biblical scholarship, the historical-critical investigation of the Pentateuch had discerned two sources in Genesis in 1753, and for the next century and a half the analysis was refined to the point of the four-document hypothesis: a 'J' source (using the divine name Jahweh), an 'E' source (using the Hebrew word for God, *'elohim*), 'D' (the book of Deuteronomy), and 'P' (priestly material). The publication, from 1871, of Babylonian texts similar to the Genesis accounts of the Creation and of the Flood, and the discovery, in 1901, of the laws of Hammurabi king of Babylon in the seventeenth century BC, laws which closely paralleled Exodus 21–24, meant that the Pentateuch had to be understood within its ancient Near-Eastern context. Further, historical investigation in the nineteenth century had proposed that Abraham, Isaac, and Jacob were not historical personages, but founders or heroes of 'tribes.' Stories about the individual patriarchs, it was argued, reflected relationships between tribes and other groups.

In 'creationist' circles, especially in the United States, vigorous attempts to assert the truth of Genesis 1 over against scientific theories continue unabated. In critical scholarship, theological attention had turned to the narratives as testimony to the faith of those who wrote them, and to the way in which laws taken over by Old Testament legislators from neighboring peoples were redrafted to show God's compassion for the poor, and the necessity to give them practical help. The ecological implications of the fact that Genesis 1:30 describes the Creation as vegetarian have been much discussed, and laws enjoining compassion for animals have been highlighted (e.g., Exod. 23:12). The way in which Genesis 3:16 has been used to achieve the subordination of women to men has provoked much discussion. The Exodus story has been a main inspiration for liberation theology. The potential of the Pentateuch to provoke and challenge is far from exhausted.

References and further reading

Houtman, C. (1999) 'Pentateuchal Criticism,' pp. 257–62 in *Dictionary of Biblical Interpretation*, Vol. 2, J.H. Hayes (ed.), Nashville: Abingdon Press.

Lowy, S. (1977) *The Principles of Samaritan Bible Exegesis*, Studia Post-biblical 28, Leiden: Brill.

Macdonald, J. (1964) *The Theology of the Samaritans*, London: SCM Press.

Pearl, C. (1970) *Rashi, Commentaries on the Pentateuch*, New York: Viking Press.

Plaut, W.G. (ed.) (1981) *The Torah: A Modern Commentary*, New York: Union of American Hebrew Congregations.

Rogerson, J. (1988) 'The Old Testament,' pp. 1–150 in *The Study and Use of the Bible*, J. Rogerson, C. Rowland, and B. Lindars (eds.), Basingstoke: Marshall Pickering/Grand Rapids: Eerdmans.

—— (ed.) (2001) *The Oxford Illustrated History of the Bible*, Oxford: Oxford University Press.

Talmage, F.E. and David Kimhi (1975) *The Man and the Commentaries*, Cambridge: Harvard University Press.

JOHN ROGERSON

PERRIN, NORMAN (1920–1976)

Norman Perrin was born in Wellingborough, Northamptonshire, United Kingdom, in 1920, the son of a factory worker. He graduated from the Hinckley Grammar School in 1936 and then helped to support his family. The implementation of his plan to study biblical theology was interrupted by the Second World War. From 1940 to 1945, he was an intelligence officer in the Royal Air Force, analyzing aerial photographs in North Africa. There he learned Greek in a military canteen within earshot of Rommel's Afrika Corps.

After the war, Perrin visited Israel and resumed his academic and ecclesiastic pursuits. At the University of Manchester he studied with T.W. Manson and graduated with a B.A. in Theology in 1949. He married Rosemary Watson and, while pastor of the Westbourne Park Baptist Church in London, enrolled as an external student at the University of London. He received his Bachelor of Divinity in 1952 and was ordained in the Baptist Union of Great Britain and Ireland in 1953. He continued as an external student while serving his second pastorate at the Sketty Baptist Church, Swansea, South Wales, and received his Master of Theology from London in 1955.

In 1956 Perrin attended Berlin's Kirchliche Hochschule. The following year he went to the University of Göttingen to study with the distinguished Semiticist and interpreter of Jesus' parables, Joachim Jeremias. In 1959 he graduated *magna cum laude* and emigrated to the United States where he joined the faculty of the Candler School of Theology at Emory University in Atlanta. His revised Göttingen dissertation was published as *The Kingdom of God in the Teaching of Jesus* in 1963.

In 1964 Perrin accepted a position at the Divinity School of the University of Chicago. Increasingly absorbed by Bultmannian hermeneutics, popular at Emory, he now came under the influence of Eliade's studies of myth, and Ricoeur's hermeneutics. He became an American citizen in 1967, divorced, and married Nancy Denney. Though he was diagnosed with cancer and had a kidney removed in 1969, he died unexpectedly of a heart attack on Thanksgiving Day, 1976.

Perrin's professional academic career lasted only seventeen years. Yet, he wrote eight books, thirty articles, and forty book reviews. He also translated two articles and three books from German. Perrin was a specialist in form criticism, redaction criticism, and Bultmannian existentialist hermeneutics. He helped to pioneer 'new' literary criticism. He made major contributions to the study of the Kingdom of God; the Son of Man; the historical Jesus; parables; the Gospel of Mark; New Testament Christology; and myth and symbol in the New Testament. He also wrote *The New Testament: An Introduction* (1974). He was a Guggenheim Fellow and in 1973 was honored as President of the Society of Biblical Literature.

Perrin's life and work later became the subject of a dissertation and several articles by Calvin Mercer. His legacy was celebrated in video, lecture, and personal reminiscence at a special session of the Society of Biblical Literature on November 25, 1996, the twentieth anniversary of his untimely death.

References and further reading

Betz, H.D. (1971) *Christology and a Modern Pilgrimage: A Discussion with Norman Perrin*, Atlanta: Society of Biblical Literature.

Duling, D. (1984) 'Norman Perrin and the Kingdom of God: Review and Response,' *The Journal of Religion* 64(4): 468–83.

——— and M. Santiago (1998) *Norman Perrin (1920–1976): A Tribute*, Atlanta: SBL (video).

Kelber, W. (1984) 'The Work of Norman Perrin: An Intellectual Pilgrimage,' *Journal of Religion* 64(4): 452–67.

Mercer, C. (1986) *Norman Perrin's Interpretation of the New Testament: From 'Exegetical Method' to 'Hermeneutical Process,'* Macon, GA: Mercer University Press.

DENNIS C. DULING

PESHER

1 The term pesher
2 Pesher as method

1 The term pesher

The Hebrew word pesher (pl. pesharim) is a noun derived from the Semitic root pšr, which is found in several languages with the principal meaning of 'loosen,' and the extended meaning of 'interpret.' In Biblical Hebrew the term only occurs as a noun (Eccles. 8:1; cf. Sir 38:14), but in Biblical Aramaic, where it is particularly associated with the interpretation of dreams, it is found both as a noun (e.g., Dan. 4:3; 5:15, 26) and as a verb (Dan. 5:12, 16).

Since the discovery of the scrolls in the caves at and near Qumran, the term pesher has been used by scholars to describe a literary genre (most fully delineated by Horgan 1979: Part II; and Brooke 1979). This genre is commonly divided into two subgroups of texts (since Carmignac 1970: 360–2): continuous pesharim (such as 1QpHab; running commentary on a scriptural text section by section with few or no omissions) and thematic pesharim (such as 4Q174; commentary based on scriptural excerpts in order to illustrate a theological theme). Many scholars add a third group consisting of small units of interpretation in which use is made of a formula including the word pšr (Dimant 1992: 248; Berrin 2000: 646). However, in only one surviving very fragmentary manuscript can the term be construed as a generic label: in 4Q180 1 1, 7 (the so-called 'Ages of Creation' or 'Pesher on the Periods') the term introduces whole units of summarized interpretation. The fragments of the Pesher on the Periods are generally ordered according to the allusions they contain to the Pentateuch, which seems to be interpreted as a review of sacred history arranged in periods, a feature known in various sectarian compositions from Qumran and in some apocalyptic writings. Even if pesher may be suitably described as a literary genre of scriptural exegesis, it is just one among several found in the Qumran sectarian texts (Gabrion 1979; Fishbane 1988).

2 Pesher as method

The term pesher should properly be used to refer to the kind of interpretation found in a wide range of compositions, in which scriptural text and interpretation are linked by a formula containing the word. These formulae include 'the interpretation of the matter concerns' (pšr hdbr ʿl) and 'its interpretation concerns' (pšrw ʿl). The key matter in these interpretations is identification. The words of the ancients, which they themselves did not understand, are to be identified with the present and future experiences of the community, which are thus shown to be part of God's purposes. The interpretation of the prophets in the pesharim is thus largely consolatory, though frequent references to divine judgment might also encourage in the reader loyalty to the community's view of things. In all cases where pesher is used in a formula in a composition found in one of the Qumran caves various features are present.

(1) The term is only applied to the interpretation of texts. There is no evidence in the sectarian manuscripts found at Qumran of any continuation of the practice of technical interpretations being given to the dream experiences or ecstatic utterances of any member of the

community. What is to be identified is to be found exclusively in texts.

(2) The texts which are interpreted with pesher are all to be found amongst those which were later included in the Hebrew Bible. Nearly all these authoritative scriptural texts being interpreted through pesher are some kind of blessing, curse, prophetic oracle, or prediction which was understood by the interpreter as not yet fulfilled. They were treated like dreams needing interpretation. There may be a few possible exceptions to this, such as the probable interpretation of Leviticus 16:1 in 4QOrdinances fragment 5. However, it should also be remembered that not every unfulfilled scriptural text is given interpretation introduced by a pesher formula. It is notable, for example, that there are no extant pesharim at Qumran on any sections of Jeremiah or Ezekiel, though rewritten forms of those works have survived. The identification is thus between what is unfulfilled and its fulfilment, but pesher is not the only way that such identification can be made.

(3) The interpretation following the use of the formula seems to have been understood as itself carrying some authority, even revelatory authority (Betz 1960). That authority rested in two interrelated matters. On the one hand, as with much interpretation, the status of the interpreter was considered important. So, according to 1QpHab 2.8 it is the priest in whose heart God sets 'understanding that he might interpret [lpšwr] all the words of his servants the prophets.' This priest can be readily identified with the Teacher of Righteousness to whom God 'made known all the mysteries of the words of his servants the prophets' (1QpHab 7.4–5). It would be inadvisable to restrict the activity of giving pesher to the Teacher of Righteousness alone, even though many scholars have claimed that the pesharim are autograph compositions of the teacher himself.

In addition to the authority of the interpreter the authority of the interpretation rests in the way that it is demonstrably connected with the text being interpreted. The interpreter is not free to say anything by way of identifying the meaning of the text, but interprets within certain parameters and by means of various methods which would be verifiable by his audiences or readers. Those methods have been particularly summarized as atomistic (Bruce 1959: 11), picking on only detailed features of the text considered out of context, but pesher is more complex than that, since it shows that scripture cannot be understood either monochromatically or superficially. The interpretative techniques used include the use of catchwords (linking supplementary texts by analogy with the main text which is being interpreted, as in 4Q174), paronomasia (exploiting the polyvalence of some Hebrew roots: e.g., the Hebrew mšl of Hab. 2:6, there meaning 'proverb,' is understood as 'rule' [1QpHab 8:9], which the same three letters can indeed signify), anagram (e.g., the consonants hykl,

'temple' [Hab. 2:20] are rearranged in the interpretation as yklh, 'he will destroy' [1QpHab 13:4]) (Brownlee 1979; Brooke 1985: 166–9, 283–92). The later rabbinic approach of 'al tiqre' ('don't read this, but read that') is anticipated in the pesharim. The use of soubriquets in the pesharim is particularly indicative of the dehumanizing both of the subject matter and also of the implied reader which can also be found in other Qumran texts.

(4) Like much interpretation of authoritative texts in any age, pesher reflects the interdependence of text and interpretation in several ways. From text to commentary the interdependence is visible in the ways the interpretation may borrow the terminology of the text, either directly or through recontextualizing it, and may reflect the structure of the text (such as in 1QpHab where all the woes of Hab. 2:6–20 are applied to the community's enemies). From commentary to text the interdependence may be reflected in the choice of reading provided in the scriptural lemma, and it can even be argued (in cases where there is no other textual witness to the variant in the extract) that occasionally the interpreter alters his quoted extract to fit his interpretation all the better.

The interpretation of the Old Testament in the New is never pesher in the strict sense; it is at best 'pesheresque' (Lim 1997).

References and further reading

Berrin, S. (2000) 'Pesharim,' 2.644–47 in *Encyclopedia of the Dead Sea Scrolls*, L.H. Schiffman and J.C. VanderKam (eds.), New York: Oxford University Press.

Betz, O. (1960) *Offenbarung und Schriftforschung in der Qumransekte*, WUNT 6, Tübingen: Mohr.

Brooke, G.J. (1979–1981) 'Qumran Pesher: Towards the Redefinition of a Genre,' *Revue de Qumran* 10: 483–503.

—— (1985) *Exegesis at Qumran: 4QFlorilegium in its Jewish Context*, JSOTSup 29, Sheffield: JSOT Press.

Brownlee, W.H. (1979) *The Midrash Pesher of Habakkuk*, SBLMS 24, Missoula: Scholars Press.

Bruce, F.F. (1959) *Biblical Exegesis in the Qumran Texts*, Exegetica 3/1, Den Haag: van Keulen/Grand Rapids: Eerdmans.

Carmignac, J. (1969–1971) 'Le document de Qumrân sur Melkisédeq,' *Revue de Qumran* 7: 343–78.

Dimant, D. (1992) 'Pesharim, Qumran,' *ABD*. 244–51.

Fishbane, M. (1988) 'Use, Authority and Interpretation of Mikra at Qumran,' pp. 339–77 in *Mikra: Text, Translation, Reading and Interpretation of the Hebrew Bible in Ancient Judaism and Early Christianity*, CRINT 2/1, M.J. Mulder (ed.), Assen: van Gorcum/ Philadelphia: Fortress Press.

Gabrion, H. (1979) 'L'interprétation de l'Écriture dans la littérature de Qumrân,' *Aufstieg und Niedergang der römischen welt* 2.19.1: 779–848.

Horgan, M.P. (1979) *Pesharim: Qumran Interpretations of Biblical Books*, CBQMS 8, Washington, DC: Catholic Biblical Association of America.

Lim, T.H. (1997) *Holy Scripture in the Qumran Commentaries and Pauline Letters*, Oxford: Clarendon Press.

GEORGE J. BROOKE

PHILO (c. 20 BC–AD 50)

Philo of Alexandria or Philo Judaeus was a Jewish philosopher and theologian, who lived from about 20 BC to AD 50. Information about his life is scarce, coming from his own writings, from Eusebius, and from Jerome. It appears that Philo both received a Greek education and was well versed in Greek Jewish scripture. He was also a respected member of his community, heading a mission to Emperor Caligula in Rome in AD 39–40 to ask for recognition of the Jewish privileges and exemption from the imperial cult.

Philo represents a high point in a tradition that started long before his time and produced the Greek translation of the Hebrew Bible. This tradition connected Greek education and philosophy with Jewish culture and, in particular, with the interpretation of the Bible. In this Judaism of the Diaspora many elements of the surrounding culture were adapted, perhaps most importantly allegorical interpretation, which had been used by Stoics in their interpretation of mythology. Other influences came from contemporary Platonism. Philo perceived the human soul as the central element in the ascent to divine contemplation. He considered the divine revelation manifest in the scriptures equal to the highest form of philosophy. Another distinctive element of his thought was his perception of the divine Logos and its role in the creation of the world. The Logos, the active principle of God's thought, was at times perceived as the creator of the cosmos and at other times as the mediator between God and the world.

Scholars have debated at length which of the two, the philosophical or the exegetical aspects, were more dominant in Philo's writing. The question as formulated is overly simplified and therefore difficult to answer. Both aspects are important for Philo, but the majority of his treatises consist of allegorical commentaries on the Pentateuch. For that reason the biblical commentaries may be considered the basis of his interests.

Most of his many treatises have been preserved. They can be divided into three groups: exegetical, historical-apologetical, and philosophical. The exegetical writings form the vast majority. 'The Allegorical Commentary' interprets the book of Genesis and touches on other texts of the Pentateuch. 'The Exposition of the Law' deals with the creation of the world and the lives of the patriarchs. The *Questions and Answers on Genesis and Exodus* are brief commentaries in the form of questions and answers on the first two books of the Pentateuch. All but a small part of the latter works are lost in Greek but remain in an Armenian translation.

The small group of historical and apologetical treatises defends various aspects of Jewish culture; they were written on the occasion of specific historical events, such as Philo's mission to Rome. These writings include *On Contemplative Life*, *Against Flaccus,* and *The Embassy to Gaius*. The philosophical tractates form another small group, which deals directly with philosophical issues without much reference to the Bible. They include *About the Eternity of the World*, *About Providence*, and *That Every Good Man is Free*.

Philo's writing style has a rich vocabulary and an excellent command of rhetorical techniques. His influence on later Judaism has been negligible but his impact on early Christian writing, particularly that of Clement and Origen, has been substantial.

References and further reading

Goodenough, E.R. (1935) *By Light, Light*, New Haven: Yale University Press.

Nikiprowetzky, V. (1977) *Le commentaire de l'écriture chez Philon d'Alexandrie*, Leiden: Brill.

Philo of Alexandria (1961–1992) *Les oeuvres de Philon d'Alexandrie*, Paris: Éditions du Cerf.

Radice, R. and D. Runia (1992) *Philo of Alexandria: An Annotated Bibliography, 1937–1986*, Leiden: Brill, 2nd edn.

Runia, D. (1995) *Philo in Early Christian Literature*, Leiden: Brill.

Sandmel, S. (1979) *Philo of Alexandria: An Introduction*, New York: Oxford University Press.

Wolfson, H.A. (1948) *Philo*, Cambridge: Harvard University Press.

ANNEWIES VAN DEN HOEK

PHILOSOPHICAL HERMENEUTICS

Philosophical hermeneutics carries out a reflection on the nature and conditions of human understanding. While the problem of understanding and misunderstanding is perennial, it emerged with special prominence with the invention of writing. Oral utterances usually connect immediately with their contemporary life world, but utterances fixed in writing can persist or travel into a significantly different life world. Usually, a culture takes the trouble to transmit only texts that have legal or religious importance or poetry central to a culture's identity and self-understanding. But just as, with writing, a distance opens between such texts and their originators, so also a distance opens between them and their later readers. The texts are highly valued but puzzling, and they must be reconnected to their readers' world. In its original, limited sense, 'hermeneutics' articulated the rules for understanding puzzling texts or correcting misinterpretations of them.

Over many centuries, a variety of techniques were developed for reintegrating texts into the contemporary life world, and each reveals something about understanding more generally. Grammarians provided glosses or elucidations of textual features that had become unfamiliar as texts traveled in space and persisted in time. These included, for example, geographical terms, archaic diction, allusions, metric patterns, and methods of organizing or sequencing texts. The need for such explanations reveals that specific background knowledge and linguistic competencies come into play in understanding, even in the case of texts that seem unproblematic.

Various methods of allegorical interpretation provided, with varying motives, bridges to texts that had become puzzling. Euhemeristic interpretation treated myths as distorted presentations of historical fact. It thus made texts less alien but tended to dissipate their aura by reducing them to the terms of the everyday life world.

Moral allegory translated texts into ethical ideas. Interpretations inspired by one or another philosophical system used texts as bases for the presentation of doctrine. Both moral and doctrinal interpretation presumed a split between the apparent surface meaning of a text and an esoteric meaning.

The moral allegorist usually claimed that the surface vehicle, attractive for its narrative interest or vivid imagery, could draw young people or those not able to grasp moral principles in abstract terms and convey to them moral ideas in a way that assured emotional commitment to applying them ('gilding' or 'sugar-coating' the pill of moral instruction). Critics of moral allegory argued that the text's surface meaning was often contrary to the extracted moral doctrine and that such texts were a poor foundation for steadfast moral action.

Doctrinal allegorists often asserted that the esoteric meaning was deliberately concealed, either to challenge readers to make the effort to discover it (and in that process, to take it seriously) or to conceal the true meaning from those unworthy of it. Or they might assert that doctrines beyond the grasp of the mortal mind had to be presented in a more concrete, if only approximate, manner. The distinction of 'apparent' vs. 'hidden' meaning was thus coordinated with an ethical and social contrast between ignorant outsiders and morally worthy initiates.

The emergence of Christianity posed a tremendous problem of interpretation. Christianity could itself be seen as an interpretation of Jesus' life and teachings in relation to the Hebrew scriptures. With the emergence of Christian scriptures, techniques were devised for connecting the Old and New Testaments, notably figural interpretation, which saw specific events in the Old Testament as prefiguring events in the life of Jesus in the Gospels. Both Hebrew and Greek scriptures were written in ways divergent from the rhetorical and poetic ideals of the Greeks and Romans. Christian converts thus experienced a sharp cultural conflict. Pagan texts presupposed cultural values incompatible with Christianity and inculcated standards by which Christian scriptures seemed poorly written. But how could Christians dispense with pagan texts that were central to their own cultural formation and to learning the language of the New Testament? A double movement emerged: scripture was defended against negative pagan judgments of its style; and interpretations were devised that extracted Christian meanings from valued or unavoidable pagan texts, thus allowing Christians to make use of them. The real point, however, is that Christians discovered that the very act of understanding a text drew one into a commitment to the cultural values it necessarily presupposed and thus into the community to and for whom it spoke.

The Reformation centered on another controversy over interpretation. Luther insisted that scripture interpreted itself and that scripture alone was sufficient for salvation. The Roman Catholic Church asserted the legitimacy of its accumulated interpretations and argued that the authority of its teaching tradition (*magisterium*) was needed to decide the correct interpretation of doubtful passages. This conflict made evident that understanding calls on institutional power or authority to control interpretation and the social practices legitimated by it.

Modern rationalism challenged scripture in another way. Baruch Spinoza divided scripture into moral precepts, whose validity was subject to judgment by a reason able to attain moral insight independently, and everything else. The latter turned out to be a mass of fables and strange customs, which he explained as belonging to the history and comparatively primitive state of its era. This distinction paved the way for the elaboration of historical techniques for understanding the origin and meaning of texts both sacred and secular. It also widened the problem of understanding from texts to history itself.

The problem of interpreting textual meaning thus revealed a number of philosophical issues. One was the role of background knowledge in understanding language. Another was the capacity of words to mean something other or more than what they say, figured as 'surface' and 'depth' meaning or 'apparent' and 'hidden.' Another was that words presupposed cultural values which could conflict with those of readers or even corrupt them. Moreover, understanding a text rested in practice on institutionalized authority. And finally, to 'understand' a text might mean relating it to the immediate historical world in which it was created and denying it any validity as a guide and standard for present-day life.

In the wake of historical interpretation and the Enlightenment critique of all authority based on mere texts handed down from the past, a fresh effort to legitimate the importance of past texts for contemporary life led to a widening of the scope of hermeneutics. Friedrich Schleiermacher is a key figure. On the one hand, he consolidated the techniques for interpreting a text in the light of its linguistic and historical context. This he called 'grammatical' interpretation. On the other hand, he tried to grasp the particular authorial intuition that a text preserved and transmitted and which could be shared directly by the reader. This he called 'psychological' or 'divinatory' interpretation. Both kinds of interpretation set an infinite task for an interpreter, but understanding could be achieved, as it was in everyday life, through mutual interchange, on the model of conversation or dialogue. At its heart, understanding exercised an ethical capacity and presupposed an ethical development on the part of the interpreter.

Schleiermacher thus posed the problem of understanding less in terms of its techniques than in terms of its epistemological and ethical conditions. Over the course of the nineteenth century, various thinkers pursued the critical analysis (in the Kantian sense) of the conditions of textual and historical understanding. The culmination of this pursuit is the work of Martin Heidegger, who argues that understanding is the constitutive structure of human being itself. It thus belongs to our temporality as mortal beings. Human beings are situated in a past that manifests itself by opening the future possibilities specific to their present existence. Tradition is not an inheritance but a task, a call to become the beings who understand it. Tradition is not memory but conscience (Yves Congar). The task of understanding thus reveals the limits of the self and of self-subsisting reason.

Heidegger's position is fully elaborated by Hans-Georg Gadamer in *Truth and Method*. For Gadamer, hermeneutics is not just a collection of methods or techniques for uncovering the meaning of puzzling texts. Its nature is dialogue and its medium is language. Because our being as humans is constituted by understanding, understanding texts that come down from the past necessarily draws on and in that very process critically tests and reconstitutes who and what we are. As a result, the problems posed by hermeneutics, that is, by the task of bridging through understanding the gap that separates us from meaningful texts passed down to us, reveals its full philosophical scope and power to make us aware of our nature and capacity as human beings.

References and further reading

Bleicher, Josef (1980) *Contemporary Hermeneutics: Hermeneutics as Method, Philosophy and Critique*, London: Routledge.

Bruns, Gerald (1992) *Hermeneutics Ancient and Modern*, New Haven: Yale University Press.

Gadamer, Hans-Georg (1976) *Philosophical Hermeneutics*, trans. David E. Linge, Berkeley: University of California Press.

—— (1989) *Truth and Method*, trans. rev. Joel Weinsheimer and Donald G. Marshall, New York: Crossroad, 2nd rev. edn.

Grondin, Jean (1994) *Introduction to Philosophical Hermeneutics*, trans. Joel Weinsheimer, New Haven: Yale University Press.

Heidegger, Martin (1962) *Being and Time*, trans. John Macquarrie and Edward Robinson, New York: Harper.

Krajewski, Bruce (ed.) (2004) *Gadamer's Repercussions: Reconsidering Philosophical Hermeneutics*, Berkeley: University of California Press.

Mueller-Volmer, Kurt (ed.) (1985) *The Hermeneutics Reader: Texts of the German Tradition from the Enlightenment to the Present*, New York: Continuum.

Palmer, Richard E. (1969) *Hermeneutics: Interpretation Theory in Schleiermacher, Dilthey, Heidegger, and Gadamer*, Evanston, IL: Northwestern University Press.

Pokorný, Peter and Jan Roskovec (ed.) (2002) *Philosophical Hermeneutics and Biblical Exegesis*, WUNT 153, Tübingen: Mohr Siebeck.

Schleiermacher, Friedrich (1977) *Hermeneutics: The Handwritten Manuscripts*, Heinz Kimmerle (ed.), trans. James Duke and Jack Forstman, Missoula: Scholars Press.

Spinoza, Baruch (1951) *A Theologico-Political Treatise*, trans. R.H.M. Elwes, New York: Dover.

DONALD G. MARSHALL

PLATO (429–347 BC)

Plato and the Platonists influenced the history of interpretation of both Testaments, as well as certain features of various New Testament documents. Several of these Platonic traits were found in Hellenistic Judaism with Philo of Alexandria as a chief representative. These characteristics had to do with philosophical outlooks, lifestyle, and the literary features of moral philosophy: the diatribe, paraenesis, and protreptic, as well as pathos.

In the Platonic vision true reality resides beyond the empirical world and is far superior to it. The world experienced through the senses is only a pale reflection of the realm where ideal forms exist, and therefore the transcendent may only be understood metaphorically or through allegories. Philo often interpreted those parts of the Torah which ran counter to Middle Platonistic allegorically. The Stoics likewise contributed to the use of allegory, even though they did not share the Platonic view of transcendental reality. Echoes of metaphorical positioning may be found especially in Hebrews 9, Colossians 1:15–20, and John 1:1–18. A philosophical lifestyle as found in those influenced by Platonic asceticism has likewise been utilized as a model for understanding Jesus of Nazareth.

Rudolf Bultmann highlighted the diatribe as a means of understanding certain New Testament materials, especially in the Epistles of Paul. The dialogues of Plato, as also represented in Plutarch and Maximus of Tyre, were the means for discovering truth. The form itself, however, later influenced, if only indirectly, the argumentative methods of the rabbis and Paul, especially Romans 3–6 (with special dependence upon Epictetus), and the literary features of the Epistle of James.

Philosophical paraenesis, that is, encouragement or exhortation to a certain lifestyle, was common among the Middle Platonists, as well as the Cynics, Stoics, and Epicureans. Paraenesis may also be found in the Pauline letters and other Epistles. Similarities and differences are important. Paul, for example, employed the approach of the philosophers in encouraging the imitation of himself, but insofar as he himself modeled the crucified Christ (1 Cor. 10:31–11:1; Rom. 14:13–18). The philosophers, in contrast, heralded idealistic or natural rules ontologically based. Paraenesis is also a philosophical style of moral exhortation through the employment of lists. Elaborated lists of virtues and vices were especially influenced by Plato. Plato set out four cardinal virtues: prudence, moderation, justice, and courage. Later philosophers listed the opposites and offered numerous breakdowns under each virtue and vice. Such lists may be found in the New Testament, for example, of virtues: 2 Peter 1:5–7; Philippians 4:8; Titus 2:2–10; and of vices: Mark 7:21–22; Romans 1:29–31; 2 Corinthians 12:20–21.

Another strategy of the popular philosophers was an argument designated protreptic (*protreptikos*). The philosophers pointed out the problems inherent in their auditor's way of life and extolled the manner in which a philosophical life could rectify them. Plato criticized the Sophists for their protreptic speeches, for example, in the *Gorgias*, but he wrote several himself in the *Phaedo* and *Epinomis*. It has been suggested by D.E. Aune that Paul, utilizing protreptic as a model, opened Romans with relentless criticism, but ended by offering new hope through the life empowered by Christ and the Holy Spirit.

Plato, in the *Gorgias* and *Phraedrus* on rhetoric, and in the *Philebus* on the emotions, provided perspectives which might be employed in examining biblical texts in respect to ethical proof (*ēthos*) and the emotions (*pathos*). Even though Plato did not provide catalogues of character and the emotions and how they affect different persons, he nevertheless thought that rhetoricians should provide such breakdowns. In his early years, Plato recognized the strong emotive dimension to human existence, but thought it something to be purged. Later, however, he came to terms with feeling, and admitted to it having an honorific contribution. In his later mixed, unified perspective, he even accepted a noetic content to human character and pathos. The employment of the writer's own character as well as pathos so as to move readers to conviction and action is obvious in most biblical texts.

References and further reading

Aune, D.E. (1991) 'Romans as a *Logos Protreptikos*,' pp. 278–96 in *The Romans Debate*, K.P. Donfried (ed.), Peabody, MA: Hendrickson, 2nd edn.

Bultmann, R. (1910) *Der Stil der paulinischen Predigt und die kynisch-stoische Diatribe*, FRLANT 13, Göttingen: Vandenhoeck & Ruprecht.

Dillon, J. (1977) *The Middle Platonists*, Ithaca: Cornell University Press.

Fitzgerald, J.T. (1997) 'The Catalogue in Ancient Greek Literature,' pp. 275–93 in *The Rhetorical Analysis of Scripture: Essays from the 1995 London Conference*, S.E. Porter and T.H. Olbricht (eds.), Sheffield: Sheffield Academic Press.

Frede, D. (1996) 'Mixed Feelings in Aristotle's Rhetoric,' pp. 258–85 in *Essays on Aristotle's Rhetoric*, Amélie Oksenberg Rorty (ed.), Berkeley: University of California Press.

Malherbe, A.J. (1987) *Paul and the Thessalonians: The Philosophic Tradition of Pastoral Care*, Philadelphia: Fortress Press.

Sterling, G.E. (1997) 'Hellenistic Philosophy and the New Testament,' pp. 313–58 in *Handbook to Exegesis of the New Testament*, S.E. Porter (ed.), Leiden: Brill.

Stowers, S. (1992) 'Diatribe,' *ABD* 2.19.

T.H. OLBRICHT

POETRY

'A distinctive literary feature of the Hebrew Bible is its propensity for mixing prose and poetry' (Watts 1992: 11). Accordingly, the crucial questions to be discussed in this entry are: first, whether it is significant for interpreting a text to know whether it is written in poetry (or verse), and second, how to understand poetry once it has been so identified. This in turn entails a further preliminary question: how does one differentiate prose from verse in Hebrew? In general, the answer is that certain books are largely in prose but may include longer or shorter stretches of verse (the Pentateuch, Joshua, Judges, 1–2 Samuel, 1–2 Kings, etc.), some books are completely in verse (Psalms, Proverbs, Song, Lamentations, etc.), and others are mostly in verse with a few passages in prose (Isaiah, Jeremiah, Ezekiel, Amos, etc.). In spite of such an evident distinction, in recent years more and more research has been focused on analyzing prose as narrative verse. However, while it is true that more prose passages are now considered to be verse than previously accepted, the broad picture remains much the same, with some books largely or exclusively in prose and others only in verse.

Even beyond Hebrew verse the whole issue of differentiating prose from poetry has also led to some blurring of the lines (e.g., in Native American Indian texts; cf. Watson 1994b: 31–44). However, some biblical scholars take issue with such an apparently lax approach (Niccacci 1997: 92, n.62). According to Niccacci (1997: 77–8), poetry differs from prose with respect to communication, parallelism, and the verbal system. Nevertheless, the distinction between verse and prose may not always be as clear-cut as we might wish, although it is very evident in prose books which include sections in verse. In this respect, Watts (1992) has shown how certain hymns (e.g., Exod. 15:1–21; 1 Sam. 2:1–20) occur at crucial moments in the narrative.

Should it, in fact, matter whether a 'prose' text is recognized as 'verse'? In verse a greater degree of micro- and macrostructure imposed by the author is acceptable than in prose. This in turn leads to various patterns being proposed for understanding such texts. On the other hand, since most prose is narrative, the general rules of narrative apply to prose, whereas there is little narrative verse. Furthermore, Koopmans (1990: 415–8) makes the point that a passage is not necessarily without historical value simply because it is in verse and as an example cites Joshua 24, which is probably narrative verse. Is Psalm 105 any less historical than the account of the same events in Genesis and Exodus? If, as some claim, the book of Ruth is narrative verse, is it any less or more historical than the books of Samuel and Kings or the book of Jonah, generally conceded to be a fictional tale? These are questions to be answered in interpreting verse.

In general, whereas more linguistic analysis has been applied to prose texts than to those in verse, the opposite is true with respect to detailed structural analysis. Kort (1975: 18) states: 'narratives, unlike lyric poems, do not, with some exceptions or except for some passages, lend themselves to close verbal analysis.' However, the work of Fokkelman on the books of Genesis and Samuel (Fokkelman 1975 and 1981/1986/1990) has shown that prose texts can be better understood if analyzed in this way. Similarly Kim (1993) on Judges.

Perhaps the best example for determining the significance for interpretation of the prosaic or poetic nature of a text is supplied by Judges 4 and 5. Judges 4 is a prose account of the events also described in the poem in Judges 5 and comparison between them provides key material for the topic in hand. For example, Fokkelman (1975: 596, n.4) comments: 'In contrast to the disembodied voice of the narrator who is responsible for narrative prose [i.e., Judg. 4], we have here in Judges 5 the highly visible and active voice of the lyrical "I" who is mainly looking back to a military event and the eve and aftermath of the battle.' Here, the lyrical 'I' consists of the combined voices of Deborah and Barak. 'The psalm does not repeat so much as supplement the prose account with added details, emotions, scenes and characterizations' (Watts 1992: 92). According to Niccacci (1997: 78, n.5), the prose version is an account of the battle whereas the poem is a celebration of victory. It would seem, then, that they are different not because one is prose and the other verse, but because they focus on different aspects of the same event. Hence the vehicle (prose or verse) is irrelevant once it has been interpreted according to the rules that apply to that vehicle. Almost the reverse of these parallel accounts is the use of Psalm 18 (in modified form) in 2 Samuel 22, a poem missing from 1 Chronicles. While not contributing directly to the plot its purpose seems to be to focus on David the king as an individual addressing God (cf. Watts 1992: 117). Similar is the presence of Hezekiah's Psalm in Isaiah 38:9–20, although it is not present in 2 Kings 20. Although such verse inserts appear, therefore, to be optional extras, nevertheless they still require interpretation and perhaps the best approach is to consider these passages as integral parts of the whole and interpret accordingly.

To conclude then, the way remains open for two improvements in the interpretation of Hebrew verse. One is to analyze prose passages in much the same way as verse is analyzed (as in Fokkelman 1998). Although this has been done for a number of books, there are still many which have not been studied in such detail. This will enable some comparison with the results already available from the study of verse. The other improvement is better linguistic analysis of the verse passages of the Hebrew Bible, particularly using the techniques of discourse analysis and information theory (see, e.g., Niccacci 1996, on Jonah). Once such studies are on a par with those already conducted on prose we shall be better able to answer some of the questions raised concerning the interpretation of verse.

References and further reading

Fokkelman, Jan P. (1975) *Narrative Art in Genesis: Specimens of Stylistic and Structural Analysis*, SSN 17, Assen and Amsterdam: Van Gorcum.

—— (1981, 1986, 1990) *Narrative Art and Poetry in the Books of Samuel*, Vols. 1–3, Assen: Van Gorcum.

—— (1998) *Major Poems of the Hebrew Bible at the Interface of Hermeneutics and Structural Analysis. Volume I: Ex. 15, Deut. 32, and Job 3*, SSN 37, Assen: Van Gorcum.

—— (2003) *Reading Biblical Poetry: An Introductory Guide*, Louisville: John Knox.

Klaus, Nathan (1999) *Pivot Patterns in the Former Prophets*, JSOTSup 247, Sheffield: Sheffield Academic Press.

Kim, Jichan (1993) *The Structure of the Samson Cycle*, Kampen: Kok Pharos Publishing House.

Koopmans, William T. (1990) *Joshua 24 as Poetic Narrative*, JSOTSup 93, Sheffield: Sheffield Academic Press.

Korpel, Marjo C.A. and Johannes C. de Moor (1998) *The Structure of Classical Hebrew Poetry: Isaiah 40–55*, OTS 41, Leiden: Brill.

Kort, Wesley A. (1975) *Narrative Elements and Religious Meanings*, Philadelphia: Fortress Press.

Loretz, Oswald (1975) 'Poetische Abschnitte im Ruth-Buch,' *Ugarit-Forschungen* 7: 580–2.

Moor, Johannes C. de (1984) 'The Poetry of the Book of Ruth, I,' *Orientalie* 53: 262–83.

—— (1986) 'The Poetry of the Book of Ruth, II,' *Orientalie* 55: 255–61.

—— and Wilfred G.E. Watson (1993) *Verse in Ancient Near Eastern Prose*, AOAT 42, Kevelaer: Verlag Butzon & Bercker/Neukirchen-Vluyn: Neukirchener Verlag.

Niccacci, Alviero (1996) 'Syntactic Analysis of Jonah,' *Liber Annuus* 46: 9–32.

—— (1997) 'Analysing Biblical Hebrew Poetry,' *Journal for the Study of the Old Testament* 74: 77–93.

Talstra, E. (1999) 'Reading Biblical Hebrew Poetry – Linguistic Structure or Rhetorical Device?' *Journal of Northwest Semitic Languages* 25: 101–26.

Watson, Wilfred G.E. (1994a) *Classical Hebrew Poetry: A Guide to its Techniques*, JSOTSup 26, Sheffield: Sheffield Academic Press, 3rd edn.

—— (1994b) *Traditional Techniques in Classical Hebrew Verse*, JSOTSup 170, Sheffield: Sheffield Academic Press.

Watts, James W. (1992) *Psalm and Story: Inset Hymns in Hebrew Narrative*, JSOTSup 139, Sheffield: Sheffield Academic Press.

WILFRED G.E. WATSON

POST-ENLIGHTENMENT CRITICISM

1 The Enlightenment: definitions and consequences

The Enlightenment is usually understood as a movement among intellectuals in Europe beginning in the seventeenth century. For various historical and religious reasons the movement was not uniform. The vanguard was led by Britain and the Netherlands in the seventeenth century, while from the middle of the eighteenth century it was German scholarship that took the leading role. What happened at the Enlightenment was that human reason became the standard by which everything was measured. This altered the way in which people read and used the Bible. Prior to the Enlightenment the Bible was regarded as an authoritative, or even infallible, source book of information about

the origins, history, and geography of the world, as well as of the nature of God and the destiny of the world and its inhabitants. The Enlightenment shift to the primacy of human reason meant that intellectuals were no longer willing to accept statements in the Bible as true merely because they were in the Bible. The question 'is this piece of information in the Bible true?' could only be answered by appeal to the canons of human reason; and if biblical statements failed the test of that appeal, their truth claims were rejected.

It would be wrong to suppose that it was the Enlightenment that first introduced the use of human reason into biblical interpretation. In fact, from the very beginnings biblical scholars applied reason to such matters as establishing the correct text of the biblical books, translating the text into other languages, identifying place names in the Bible, and discussing passages in which the Bible appeared to contradict itself, or what was known about the world, human growth, and development. It was noted very early on that light is created before the sun in Genesis 1 and that men live to be over 900 years in Genesis 5, in some cases not having children until they are over 100. Such statements were not accepted at face value but discussed in the light of human reason. What made the post-Enlightenment period different from the pre-Enlightenment period was not the use of human reason in the former, but the use of reason as the sole arbiter of what was true. This meant that, in the post-Enlightenment period, thinkers were prepared to challenge the central doctrines of Christianity and to interpret the Bible in ways that contradicted these beliefs. This did not mean that all post-Enlightenment interpretation was anti-Christian, although some undoubtedly was and still is. It meant that interpreters of the Bible did not feel bound to interpret it in ways that committed them to affirming traditional Christian doctrines. In many cases the result was a positive rediscovery of the Bible leading to attempts to understand it as relevant to contemporary needs.

2 The seventeenth century

The best-known critical interpreters of this period included the Dutch Jew Benedict Spinoza, the English philosopher Thomas Hobbes, and the French Catholic priest Richard Simon. Needless to say, they approached the Bible with very different agendas, yet they were united in challenging traditional assumptions about when and by whom the various books of the Bible had been written. All three denied that Moses was the sole author of the first five books of the Bible, with Simon attributing them to scribal schools. Spinoza revived the rationalist tradition in Judaism that had received classical expression in the work of Maimonides, and called the biblical miracles into question. Hobbes noted that the prologue and epilogue of the book of Job did not fit easily with the central poetic section and presumed that they were added as a preface and epilogue. Hobbes also identified Deuteronomy 11–27 as the law book discovered in the temple by Hilkiah during the reign of Josiah (2 Kings 22:8) – Hobbes being prepared to regard Moses as the author of this particular part of the Pentateuch. The seventeenth-century criticism can be summarized as a set of acute observations based upon the biblical text, by writers who, for various reasons, did not feel constrained by traditional Jewish and Christian views of who had written the Bible. Many of these observations have become commonplace in modern scholarship. At the same time, no radically new theories about the Bible were advanced.

3 The eighteenth century

The first half of this century was dominated by the Deists in Britain. The second half of the century saw the beginnings of biblical criticism in Germany, beginnings that would lead to radical breakthroughs. The Deists believed that the existence of God, the immortality of the soul, and the divine punishment of the wicked and the reward of the righteous could be established by reason alone. There was therefore no need for a biblical revelation especially when, in its Old Testament form, it entailed animal sacrifice and immoral actions such as Joshua's wholesale slaughter of Canaanites. Deist scholars began to attack the credibility of Old Testament narratives. John Toland, in 1720, explained the pillar of cloud by day that accompanied the Israelites through the wilderness in purely natural terms. It was a smoking, burning, brazier carried by a pathfinder. Antony Collins (1676–1729) argued that prophecies in the Old Testament were not predictions of the coming of Christ, but pronouncements that had to be understood in their strict historical sense. Thomas Morgan went even further in 1737 by trying to discredit Old Testament prophecy entirely. While Morgan argued, with some plausibility, that there was a struggle throughout Old Testament history between the kings and the prophets, he argued that the prophets had largely failed in their primary task, which was to uphold and propagate the religion of reason. Nowhere was their failure more clearly illustrated than in their championing of David, a man who had committed adultery and murder. The purpose of Morgan's attack was to discredit the Old Testament as divine revelation, to the benefit of Jesus and Paul who were seen as upholders of the principles of nature and reason.

A more political use of the Old Testament was made by Moses Lowman in 1745, a year that saw the revolt of prince Charles Edward against the English crown. Lowman used the Old Testament to consider the circumstances under which it was legitimate to initiate revolt. Those prophets who had opposed kings Jeroboam, Baasha, Omri, and Ahab, and who had insti-

gated Jehu to carry out a coup d'état, had been justified in their actions, because these kings had led the nation away from loyalty to the God of Israel. This established the principle that revolt was justified if it was directed against a monarch who was unfaithful to God. In the case of Britain the established religion was Protestantism, and Prince Charles Edward's revolt was not justified because it was carried out in the name of his Roman Catholic ancestor, James II. As well as critical scholarship that was driven by Deist philosophical (Morgan) and national political (Lowman) agendas, this period saw the work of Humphry Prideaux (1716–1718) and Samuel Shuckford (1728) who produced histories of Israel that were connected with what was known about the history of Egypt and Mesopotamia. They became standard works and were reprinted until well into the nineteenth century. They exhibited considerable critical acumen in the handling of the source material although, convinced of the inerrancy of the biblical text, they privileged the latter where it appeared to clash with nonbiblical sources. A pioneering work around the middle of this century was Robert Lowth's *Lectures on the Sacred Poetry of the Hebrew* (1753), which used criteria from secular poetry to illumine the poetry of the Old Testament and, indeed, which alerted the world of scholarship to the fact that, whatever else they were, many prophetic passages were cast in the form of poetry. Lowth was also a representative of another feature of eighteenth-century scholarship, the development of textual criticism. Benjamin Kennicott scoured museums in Britain and abroad for Hebrew manuscripts of the Old Testament, which he collated in his attempts to achieve the best possible text. At the same time, scholars such as Lowth and C. Houbigant did not hesitate to propose conjectural emendations to the text where it appeared to be corrupt, emendations which in some cases have become received wisdom.

After 1750 the initiative in critical scholarship passed to Protestant Germany, albeit a Germany that had taken full cognizance of what had been going on in British scholarship. Lowth's work on Hebrew poetry, for example, was particularly influential. The big advance in scholarship came in the area of source criticism. In 1780–1783, J.G. Eichhorn's German *Introduction to the Old Testament*, building on the work of the French Catholic Jean Astruc (1753), divided the book of Genesis into two sources, based upon alterations in the use of the divine name. In 1798, K.D. Ilgen carried out further source analysis and divided the story of Joseph in Genesis into two sources. By the end of the eighteenth century, therefore, scholarship had achieved much of what would become the Documentary Hypothesis of the late second half of the nineteenth century. Other results of critical scholarship included the suggestion of J.B. Koppe (1780) that Isaiah 40–66 had been written during the Babylonian Exile, that what Bernhard Duhm (in 1892) would later call the 'Suffering Servant Songs' in Isaiah were four passages that belonged specially together (the proposal was made by E.F.K. Rosenmüller in 1793) and that Isaiah 24–27 came from a later prophet. The unity of the book of Zechariah was disputed as was the unity of the book of Daniel.

The historical value of the Bible was questioned from two different angles: a repudiation of its factual claims about history, and a demythologizing of its references to the supernatural. The attack on the Bible's historical narratives was mounted by the Hamburg Orientalist S.H. Reimarus in papers published by G.E. Lessing from 1777, after Reimarus' death. The first attack questioned the credibility of the statement in Exodus 12:37 that 600,000 men (excluding women, children, cattle, flocks, and herds) had left Egypt at the time of the Exodus. By spelling out the implications of these numbers, Reimarus showed that the account was not credible. The length of the column of Israelites and their animals and carts would, he estimated, have been over 800 miles! Reimarus also attacked the New Testament account of the resurrection, although his aim was the, for him, positive one of showing that the apostles had corrupted the teaching of Jesus, which Reimarus held in high regard, and had invented the resurrection in order to bolster their own aims.

The demythologizing of the Bible in order to strip what were taken to be crude, supernatural elements from them was undertaken by a group known as Neologists, scholars who had a high regard for the Bible, and who applied to it an extension of the ancient principle of accommodation. As far back as at least Augustine, scholars had argued that, in revealing himself to humankind, God had accommodated the revelation to the particular mental and moral stage of development that the human race had reached. Thus, statements to the effect that God repented that he had created the human race (Gen. 6:6–7) were not to be taken literally. They were phrased in accordance with human understanding. The same argument can be found in Calvin. The Neologists, men such as J.S. Semler, J.G. Eichhorn, and J.P. Gabler, believed that the earliest Hebrews were similar in mentality to what was known at the end of the eighteenth century about so-called primitive peoples. They thus interpreted biblical narratives from the standpoint that the Hebrews saw God directly at work in phenomena that are explained today in scientific ways. Their interpretation of Genesis 3 saw it as a true account of the experiences of the first human couple whose sexual awareness was aroused when they ate the fruit of a semipoisonous tree. A thunderstorm that seemed like the voice of God drove them in panic from their garden, to which they could not find their way back. New Testament narratives could be treated similarly. The story in Luke 22:43–44 about an angel appearing to Jesus in the Garden of Gethsemane was not literally true. It could have arisen in two ways, either by Jesus telling his disciples that he

felt as though he was being strengthened by an angel, or by someone observing him in prayer and conceptualizing the incident in terms of the presence of an angel. Studies that concentrated upon the supernatural elements in the stories included the investigation of the role of oral tradition in introducing and inflating references to the supernatural.

Three other German scholars need to be mentioned briefly. J.D. Michaelis believed that Arabic dialects were closely related to ancient Hebrew and that they could be used to elucidate difficult Hebrew words. He was instrumental in persuading the king of Denmark to send an expedition to Arabia in 1762 in order to bring back scientific information that would shed light on the Bible; and in a four-volume work on the laws of Moses (1770–1775) he drew extensively upon studies of the laws and customs of many peoples. Herder wrote about Hebrew poetry and how it embodied the distinctive spirit (*Geist*) of the Hebrews. He also included a section on Israelite history in his *Reflections on the Philosophy of the History of Mankind*, and argued that Christianity originated in an oral proclamation about Jesus the Messiah, which was later written down. J.J. Griesbach laid the foundations for the study of the synoptic problem by printing Matthew, Mark, and Luke in parallel columns. He became famous for the so-called Griesbach hypothesis (although he was not the first to present it) according to which Mark was dependent upon both Matthew and Luke. Herder's view was that Mark best reproduced the original oral gospel.

4 The nineteenth century

In 1804 a young man of twenty-four presented a doctoral thesis to the University of Jena, which changed the face of critical biblical scholarship. His name was Wilhelm M.L. de Wette and the thesis argued that Deuteronomy had been written later than the other books of the Pentateuch. It contained a long footnote, however, which suggested that the actual history of Israelite religion and sacrifice had been different from that presented in the Old Testament. According to the latter, Moses had instigated a full-blown sacrificial and priestly system of religion at the outset of the history of the people, following the Exodus. According to de Wette's footnote, the actual course of events had been quite different, the full-blown Mosaic system being the end-product of a long process of development, and not something that was present from the beginning. De Wette followed up his doctoral thesis with a two-volume *Contributions to Old Testament Introduction* (1806–1807), which made two points in particular. First, the books of Chronicles, which attributed Israel's religious institutions to ancient founders, especially David, were based upon the books of Samuel and Kings, and contained no reliable information about the origins of these religious institutions. Second, the Pentateuch was mythical in the sense that it provided evidence only for the religious faith of its authors rather than historical information about the beginnings of Israel's religion. These seemingly negative results of de Wette's critical acumen represented part of his attempt to regain a faith that had been lost as a teenager and further hindered by his rationalist teachers in Jena. His championing of the importance of aesthetics and symbolism in religion over history was part of the legacy of the eighteenth century, which preferred the assured truths of reason over the contingent (i.e., provisional and therefore subject to change) truths of history. Whatever his reasons, de Wette inaugurated a new period in critical biblical scholarship by maintaining that the Bible contained essentially source material which scholarship could use to reconstruct Israel's history and Christian origins according to modern canons of historical investigation.

Modern canons of historical investigation were, and are, human constructs influenced by human agenda, a fact which is illustrated by the path taken by New Testament scholarship with the publication in 1835–1836 of D.F. Strauss' *Life of Jesus*. This was a radical attack on traditional ways of studying the Gospels. Strauss demolished the credibility of St. John's Gospel as the work of an eyewitness apostle, and argued that it was the climax of a synthesizing tendency that could be found in all the Gospels, a process that transformed the life of the Jewish teacher from Nazareth into the supernatural Christ of Christian faith. Strauss believed that the essence of Christianity was based upon eternal truths, and that this freed him from the need to hold back in his critical investigation of the origin and growth of the Gospels. At the same time that Strauss was working out his criticism of the Gospels, his one-time teacher F.C. Baur was investigating Christian origins from a different angle, that of the conflict apparent in the letters of Paul between a Jewish Christianity championed by James and Peter, and a more open, Gentile, Christianity championed by Paul. Although Baur was to suggest datings for some of the New Testament writings that placed them well into the second century AD, a conclusion that has not survived the verdict of scholarship, his observation that human conflict between different parties profoundly influenced the development of Christianity and the composition of the New Testament has become a commonplace of modern scholarship. Strauss' theories have faded from view.

From roughly the mid-1840s to the early 1860s critical scholarship took a breather from the hectic progress it had made in the nineteenth century. This was partly because Germany was the scene of the growing influence of orthodox pietist circles, while Britain's theological climate was heavily influenced by evangelicals and the Catholicizing high church movement in the Church of England. Also, conservative German biblical scholars such as E.W. Henstenberg wielded a good deal of power, and critical German scholars such as Heinrich

Ewald advanced much more traditional reconstructions of Israel's religion and Christian origins than de Wette, Strauss and Baur. From the 1860s, however, critical scholarship got its second wind. *Essays and Reviews* published in 1861 by a prominent British churchman, and Bishop J.W. Colenso's *The Pentateuch and Joshua, Part I* of 1862, while making no new contributions to critical scholarship, indicated the dissatisfaction in some establishment British circles with traditional biblical scholarship. In Germany, the researches undertaken by de Wette were repeated, confirming his results. A consensus emerging from the work of the Dutch scholar Abraham Kuenen and the Scot William Robertson Smith found classical expression in the German Julius Wellhausen's *History of Israel*, first published in 1878, but better known to history in its second, 1883, manifestation as the *Prolegomena to the History of Israel*. Wellhausen brought together a modified version of de Wette's reconstruction of the history of Israelite religion with the so-called new documentary hypothesis which, however, owed much to its eighteenth-century predecessor. In Wellhausen's reconstruction the presumed documentary sources of the Pentateuch corresponded to three stages in the development of Israelite religion. The sources J and E (so named because of the Hebrew name for God that they characteristically used) had been composed in the ninth–eighth centureis BC in the southern kingdom, Judah, and the northern kingdom, Israel, respectively. They were to be found in the books of Genesis, Exodus, and Numbers (as well as parts of Joshua, Judges, Samuel, and Kings). They reflected the religious conditions of their time, in which there were many Israelite sanctuaries and priests, and when celebrations such as the Passover were local, family occasions presided over by the male head of the family. This was the period of the great prophets such as Isaiah, Hosea, Amos, and Micah, who proclaimed ethical monotheism. The source D (most of Deuteronomy) dated from the seventh century, when the attempt was made to consolidate the preaching of the prophets into a law book, which became the basis for a religious reformation during the reign of Josiah in 622 BC. The effect of the reform was to close down all Israelite sanctuaries, except Jerusalem. It was the first stage in establishing centralized control over what had been a varied and spontaneous form of religion. Because Jerusalem became the only sanctuary at which sacrificial animals could be killed, the Passover ceased to be a local festival and became a national celebration, held in Jerusalem. The third phase in the development of Israel's religion was the priestly phase, corresponding to that source of the Pentateuch called P (the priestly code). P was present in Genesis, Exodus, and Numbers, and above all in Leviticus. It represented the religion of the postexilic community centered on Jerusalem, a community which, because it had lost political independence, had become a religious community led by priests.

Its concentration upon the temple and its sacrificial rituals was due to conditions in postexilic Jerusalem and to the sense of guilt engendered by the belief that the Babylonian Exile had been God's punishment of Israel for its unfaithfulness to God.

Wellhausen's synthesis gained steady support in Germany. In Britain it was enthusiastically advocated by Robertson Smith (it cost him his post at the Free Church College in Aberdeen in 1881) and later embraced by the influential professor of Hebrew in Oxford, S.R. Driver. In the United States it found support from scholars such as C.A. Briggs (who was tried, and suspended from the Presbyterian ministry, in 1893). Despite many attempts to disprove it, it remained and remains a formidably cogent account of the origin and development of Israelite religion.

In New Testament scholarship attention focused upon the historical Jesus from the late nineteenth century until well into the next century, with emphasis placed by scholars such as A. von Harnack and Albrecht Ritschl upon his ethical teaching. The decipherment of cuneiform and the translation and publication of Babylonian and Assyrian texts in the latter part of the century inaugurated the study of the Bible from the standpoint of the history of religions. Babylonian accounts of the Creation and Flood which exhibited similarities with the biblical accounts required a complete reassessment of the opening chapters of Genesis.

5 The twentieth century

The discovery in 1901 of the laws of Hammurabi, king of Babylon in the seventeenth century BC, laws that were very similar to those in Exodus 21–24, further demonstrated how much the Old Testament owed to its world of origin. Research into the Hellenistic world into which Christianity was born, and particularly into Gnosticism and the mystery religions, ensured that the New Testament was also viewed from the perspective of the history of religions. A new departure in method, however, was the application of form criticism to the Bible, a procedure that concentrated on the oral traditions and units that underlay written sources, and which attempted to find their 'settings in life.' In due course biblical narratives (especially those in Genesis), psalms, prophetic oracles, and the sayings of Jesus were investigated by form criticism, and the resulting units were compared with literary genres known from literature in general, such as sagas, folktales, riddles, and legends. One of the results of these procedures was to indicate that the traditions were collections of similar types of material, such as parables, miracle stories, and confrontation stories. This led scholars such as R. Bultmann to draw negative conclusions about how much could actually be known about the history of Jesus, and up to around 1950 British New Testament scholars were reluctant to embrace form criticism, likening it to

cutting the string that held together the beads of a necklace. British scholarship became much more concerned with the impact of Albert Schweitzer's *Quest of the Historical Jesus* (English edition 1910), which presented Jesus as a preacher of the imminent end of the world – a very different Jesus from the ethical teacher proposed by Harnack and Ritschl. Studies of the parables by A. Jülicher and C.H. Dodd led to a compromise picture of Jesus, one who proclaimed that the long-awaited Kingdom of God was already decisively present in the world, as indicated by his miracles of healing.

Old Testament scholarship witnessed attempts to provide a fuller account of Israel's origins than that allowed by Wellhausen's thesis. On the basis of Palestinian archaeology and ancient Near-Eastern texts, American scholars led by W.F. Albright believed that they could verify and roughly date the existence of the patriarchs (Abraham, Isaac, and Jacob), and events such as the Exodus from Egypt and the conquests of Canaan under Joshua. This confidence was maintained as late as the early 1960s in G.E. Wright's *Biblical Archaeology* (revised edn 1962) and John Bright's *A History of Israel* (1960). In Germany, Albrecht Alt and Martin Noth used ancient inscriptions and Greek models in order to reconstruct the religion of the patriarchs, and to account for the origin of Israel's twelve-tribe system in terms of Greek amphictyonic leagues (tribes centered upon particular holy places). That David and Solomon had established a small Israelite empire at the beginning of the tenth century BC was undisputed, and Solomon's reign was identified as the likely period in which Israel's writing of its own history, or thus of the Old Testament, had begun. British and Scandinavian scholarship pursued a different line by regarding the worship of the Solomonic temple and the symbolic roles undertaken by the king in that worship, as the formative location of Israelite religion. Reconstructions of the first temple's rites offered by S.H. Hooke and S. Mowinckel drew heavily upon information about the Babylonian new year festival. Other British scholars, heavily influenced by nineteenth-century evolutionistic theories in social anthropology, looked to find evidence in the Old Testament for the gradual development of Israelite religion from animism (the worship of spirits believed to inhabit stories, trees, and water) to monotheism via polytheism (belief in many gods) and henotheism (belief in a supreme god among other gods).

Critical biblical scholarship did not escape the turbulent events of the first half of the twentieth century, namely, the First World War and the establishment in Germany of the so-called Third Reich. Indeed, these events cast doubt on the adequacy of human reason to be the sole arbiter in matters of truth, while the attempts of the anti-Jewish 'German Christians' to rid the church of the Old Testament and all Jewish influences led to brave and determined attempts to rehabilitate the Old Testament as a document of fundamental theological importance. Karl Barth was a vital catalyst in this process, while, beginning in 1933, the Swiss Old Testament scholar Walther Eichrodt produced a massive theology of the Old Testament organized around the concept of covenant. This was a defiant answer to the question of whether it was any longer possible to write an Old Testament theology, given the many known similarities between the Old Testament and the religions of Israel's neighbors. New Testament scholars did not lag behind in this regard. Ethelbert Stauffer completed a New Testament theology in 1938 (it was published in 1941), while Rudolf Bultmann began to publish a theology as soon as postwar conditions allowed, in 1948. Another feature of the immediate postwar period was the so-called biblical theology movement. While it had its origins in the prewar German theological word books of the Bible, with their detailed studies of distinctive Hebrew and Greek words, the movement was prominent in Britain and the United States. Among other things, it was a reaction against the history of religions approach of the earlier part of the century, and it tried to emphasize what it believed to be unique, and therefore authoritative, about biblical words and thought categories. It enabled scholars to write about the 'biblical view' of time, work, faith, love, ethics, and similar matters. Gerhard von Rad's Old Testament theology, begun in 1964, marked the end of this phase of scholarship and demonstrated how the basic methods of critical scholarship – form, source, and redaction criticism – could be used creatively in the hands of a scholar committed to theology and to preaching. Although it expounded the theologies contained in the Old Testament as opposed to attempting to find or impose one overall theology, it owed much to the central idea of confession – the confession of Israel's faith in worship and in the retelling of stories that expressed and embodied faith.

Up to the end of the 1960s there was broadly one main method in critical study of the Bible – historical criticism, with its ancillary disciplines of textual criticism, comparative philology, various types of literary criticism, and archaeology and studies of Israel's neighboring peoples. The new phase of scholarship that began at the end of the 1960s did not make historical criticism obsolete or unnecessary, but it did challenge the all-sufficiency of the method, and was increasingly characterized by a plurality of methods.

The first was literary structuralism, which was based upon structural linguistics, and focused attention on the biblical texts themselves as opposed to these texts being means to ends, such as the scholarly reconstruction of Israel's history, or the life of Jesus. The literary artistry of texts was pointed out, as was the use of plot and character in biblical narratives. Instead of the Synoptic Gospels being read in order to yield the sources Mark and the 'Q' tradition of Jesus' sayings, each Gospel was seen to be a literary work in its own right, and to be

read as such. In Old Testament study, features of narratives that had previously been used to identify different literary sources were now seen as creative juxtapositions within a unified story. For example, in Exodus 7–11 it is said both that Pharaoh hardened his heart against letting the Hebrews go free under Moses, and that God hardened Pharaoh's heart. Source criticism assigned these two different reasons for Pharaoh's stubbornness to two different literary sources. New literary methods applied to the story, however, suggested that this apparent contradiction enabled the problem of divine causation and human responsibility to be explored in the narrative.

The next new method was liberation theology, popularized by Gustavo Gutiérrez' A Theology of Liberation (English edition 1973), in which the story of the Exodus assumed particular importance in the claim that salvation in the Bible was primarily a political and social phenomenon rather than something purely spiritual. Liberation theology, with its quasi-Marxist but overtly political assumptions, challenged the view that critical-biblical scholarship was a value-free and neutral search for the truth. In doing this it also challenged one of the basic assumptions of the whole enterprise of biblical scholarship since the Enlightenment, namely, the all-sufficiency of human reason as the arbiter of what was true. Liberation theology argued that the concept of human reason implied in this enterprise was, in fact, the reason of privileged and wealthy human beings. While it is highly doubtful that there are different types of reason among human beings depending upon their class or gender, there was undoubtedly truth in the claim that people's political commitments, or lack of them, may well be an important factor in shaping their priorities in biblical interpretation.

Hot on the heels of liberation theology came feminist criticism, and in common with liberation theology, it eventually took three forms. There were feminist writers who believed that the Bible could sensitively reflect women's interests if scholarship became aware of its male preponderance and bias, and if justice were done to the female characters in the Bible. A second viewpoint regarded the Bible primarily as source material for rediscovering women's roles in ancient Israel and the early church. Because the Bible had been written by men, it reflected male interests, and women had been overlooked or their voice had not been allowed to be heard. It was the task of feminist biblical criticism to redress this situation. According to a third approach the Bible was so overwhelmingly the product of patriarchal societies that it could offer nothing to women. The task of feminist scholarship was to expose the irredeemable patriarchy of the Bible and to expose how it has subsequently been used to oppress women. Liberation theologians similarly used the Bible positively as an agent of liberation among oppressed peoples, or used it to recover the history of those who were oppressed in ancient Israel and the world of Christian origins, or argued that a text produced by ruling classes could have no liberating potential. One of the outcomes of the third type of feminist approach was the charge, taken particularly seriously in Germany, that it was anti-Jewish to write off the Old Testament as irredeemably patriarchal. In German circles, attempts were made to formulate a feminist approach that was sensitive to the need to respect Judaism.

Two other types of criticism entered the academy of critical biblical scholarship in the latter part of the twentieth century – deconstruction and ideological criticism, and it was also widely accepted that critical studies must now operate in the era of postmodernism. Deconstruction derived from the theories of the French philosopher Jacques Derrida and became, in biblical studies, a method of close reading of biblical texts in order to discover in them elements that undermined what they appeared to be saying. This approach went hand-in-hand with belief in the indeterminacy of meaning, as well as with the view that texts did not have meanings intended by their authors. While some of the results of deconstructive readings of biblical texts were negative, they also drew attention to features of texts that were otherwise easily overlooked, and they had the merit of focusing attention on the texts themselves, rather than on the texts as means to other ends. Ideological criticism took its cue from the Marxist understanding of ideology as a false consciousness that blinded people to reality, and which needed to be brought to their awareness. As applied to the Bible it sought to uncover the interests of the powerful groups who, it was assumed, had written the Bible. It was therefore a kind of political interpretation but one that was not necessarily intended to achieve the kind of liberation looked for in liberation theology. Indeed, ideological criticism often assumed barely concealed antitheological forms. The belief that scholarship was operating in a postmodern era, one in which grand, explanatory narratives no longer had a place, and in which there was a profound distrust of human reason, helped to give credibility to some of the extreme forms of feminism, deconstruction, and ideological criticism. It is also necessary to point out, however, that one fundamental distinction ran like a fault line through these various approaches. Structuralism had brought with it the view that, in order to have meaning, languages and texts do not have to refer to an outside world. Meaning is something immanent within, and determined by, systems of sounds and signs. This had the implication that the Bible did not refer to extralinguistic realities such as God and Jesus Christ, but that these were to be seen as characters within narratives. This viewpoint was often a valuable means of enabling the literary character of texts to be appreciated, and theologically it avoided the problem that the God of the Old Testament orders the slaughter of the populations of Canaanite

cities, and Jesus in the New Testament curses the fig tree and warns that those who are angry with others will be in danger of hellfire. If God and Jesus are simply characters in a narrative, they do not say anything about the nature of God or of the Jesus of history. Of the approaches mentioned above, deconstruction and ideological criticism were primarily concerned with the texts as such, and not with anything that they might say about the world. Some feminist readings also concentrated upon the women characters in narratives, and how their treatment could be evaluated positively or negatively. For liberation theologians, on the other hand, it was vital that the biblical text yielded information about the world and God. The Exodus was a real event in which God had delivered the Israelites from slavery. It showed that God was on the side of the poor and oppressed. Similarly, a positive picture of the historical Jesus was important for liberationists, a Jesus who also opposed the powerful of his day, identifying himself with the poor.

What this discussion has indicated is that there is now a bewildering plurality of methods in biblical scholarship as compared with the early 1960s. That these methods have contributed many insights cannot be denied. What future they have is more difficult to determine. The bell is already tolling for the demise of postmodernism, while there are limits to what can be achieved by feminist and ideological criticism. The conclusion here will deal, therefore, with the more traditional methods of biblical criticism, which have certainly not been ousted by the structuralist and poststructuralist approaches.

In Old Testament study a significant development has been a complete reassessment of the dating of biblical sources and of the reconstruction of Israelite history compared with 1960. This has partly been affected by developments in Palestinian archaeology, which have necessitated a revision of earlier 'assured results.' Thus, it is becoming clear that the kingdoms of Judah and Israel began to emerge as 'states' after the time of David and Solomon, and that the same is true of the neighboring kingdoms of Edom, Moab, and Ammon. Whereas scholars previously saw the reign of Solomon as the time when Israelite history began to be recorded, several experts have seriously questioned whether David or Solomon ever existed. The reign of Hezekiah (727–698 BC) is increasingly favored as the period in which the Old Testament began to be written, and sources such as J and E which used to be dated to the ninth to eighth centuries are increasingly dated to the late sixth to fifth centuries. A bitter controversy has developed between 'maximalists' who believe that it is still possible to reconstruct a traditional history of Israel based primarily on the Old Testament with the assistance of archaeology, and 'minimalists' who argue that any reconstruction must be based primarily on the archaeological data. The upheavals in biblical scholarship have not dealt a fatal blow to theologies of the Old Testament, and scholars such as Otto Kaiser, Rolf Rendtorff, and Walter Brueggemann contributed to this genre in the 1990s.

In New Testament studies the quest for the historical Jesus has returned with confusing vengeance. Major, and often contradictory, reconstructions of Jesus have been offered by scholars such as G. Theissen, E.P. Sanders, J.D. Crossan, and N.T. Wright. Jesus has been seen as a kind of Stoic, a Wisdom teacher, a charismatic healer, or an opponent of the temple and of Jewish purity laws. The question of the extent to which Jesus was an apocalyptic prophet proclaiming the imminent end of the world has remained controversial.

A short, and therefore necessarily inadequate, overview such as is presented here may well create the impression that post-Enlightenment biblical criticism has been diverse and varied in a way that pre-Enlightenment scholarship was not. This would be a false impression. Both before and after the Enlightenment, scholars wrestled with the Bible in ways that were profoundly affected by the cultural, scientific, and political realities of their days. The post-Enlightenment period was less constrained by theological and ecclesiastical agendas. Through both periods, however, the Bible has shown that it can withstand the most searching criticism, and can continue to inspire and give hope to anyone sincerely seeking to hear its message.

References and further reading

Drury, J. (ed.) (1989) *Critics of the Bible 1724–1873*, Cambridge: Cambridge University Press.

Hayes, John H. (ed.) (1999) *Dictionary of Biblical Interpretation*, 2 Vols., Nashville: Abingdon Press.

Henning Reventlow, Graf (1984) *The Authority of the Bible and the Rise of the Modern World*, London: SCM Press.

Rogerson, J. (1984) *Old Testament Criticism in the Nineteenth Century: England and Germany*, London: SPCK.

—— (ed.) (2001) *The Oxford Illustrated History of the Bible*, Oxford: Oxford University Press.

Scholder, K. (1990) *The Birth of Modern Critical Theology: Origins and Problems of Biblical Criticism in the Seventeenth Century*, London: SCM Press/Philadelphia: Trinity Press.

Schottroff, L., S. Schroer, and M.-T. Wacker (eds.) (1998) *Feminist Interpretation: The Bible in Women's Perspective*, Minneapolis: Fortress Press.

JOHN ROGERSON

POSTSTRUCTURALISM, DECONSTRUCTION

1 The endless play of texts
2 Analytics of power
3 Ethics and the face of the Other

Poststructuralism and deconstruction are terms that have come to describe a philosophical movement that seeks to question totalizing or 'transcendental' descriptions of linguistic, cultural, and historical structures, as well as the traditional metaphysical grounds of 'Being' or subjectivity. This philosophical movement has drastically rethought common approaches to philosophical categories, to text, to history, to power, to 'the subject,' and to ethics. While biblical scholars tend to be once removed from the philosophical front of the poststructural project, a number of poststructural strands have been taken up in biblical studies, following the work of theorists such as Julia Kristeva, Jacques Derrida, Luce Irigaray, Michel Foucault, Gayatri Spivak, Jacques Lacan, Roland Barthes, Michel de Certeau, Edmond Jabès, Homi Bhabha. Poststructuralist themes in biblical studies might be grouped in the following way (though this list is by no means definitive or exclusive): (a) the endless play of texts; (b) an analytics of power; (c) ethics and the face of the Other. The first of these (the endless play of texts) has appeared most prevalently in biblical studies because it is text centered; however, the other two currents reflect extremely important aspects of the poststructuralist project, and their appearance in biblical studies must be commented upon, if more briefly. For overviews of poststructuralism and deconstruction written within biblical studies see: Detweiler (1982); Moore (1994); Castelli *et al.* (1995).

1 The endless play of texts

Attractive but troubling ideas for biblical scholars have been Barthes' conception of a writerly (plural, open, reversible, indeterminate) text (1974: 4–6, 260); Kristeva's intertextuality, that 'intersection of textual surfaces' (1982: 65) in which text is endlessly augmented by the transposition of other texts into it; and Derrida's understanding of text as a fabric of endlessly deferring traces (1979: 84) 'constituted on the basis of the trace within it of the other elements of the chain or system' (1981: 26). Thinking of *texts as infinitely intersecting and endlessly playing* enables scholars to get beyond defining the text's 'real' meaning, history, or structure, and begin thinking about how other texts – whether they be canonical, cultural, or historical – play an active role in the reading process and the production of meaning (see Fewell 1992; Beal 1997; Aichele 2001).

Beyond showing that readings of biblical texts conform to a notion of text as unstable, endlessly referring and deferring chains of signifiers, a number of biblical scholars have found useful Derrida's notion of the *undecidable*, though somewhat detached from its philosophical bearings. An undecidable is an image or term that 'escapes from inclusion in the philosophical (binary) opposition and which nonetheless inhabits[s] it, resist[s] it, and disorganize[s] it but without ever constituting a third term, without ever occasioning a solution' (Derrida 1981: 43). The notion of the undecidable has not only been used to complicate the larger discussion of textual determinacy (Phillips 1995), but also in specific readings of texts (Sherwood 1996; Runions 1998). Scholars have looked at those ambiguous points in a text that have 'a double and opposite meaning, which allows (indeed invites) the reader to read the text against the grain of its main argument' (Sherwood 1996: 177). This enables scholars to begin to critique some of the oppressive colonial and patriarchal aspects of biblical texts, by using them against themselves. Now the oppressive binary oppositions highlighted by biblical scholars doing structuralist analysis (for examples see the structuralist studies of Gen. 1–3 outlined in Milne 1993) can be looked at in another way, in order to see what escapes to disorganize such oppositions.

Biblical scholars have also drawn upon the related notions of *trace* and *abject*. For Derrida, the trace is what is required for philosophical discourses to get started, but then is excluded from those very discourses. One might say that the trace is the absence upon which presence establishes itself; it is the movement of *différance*, the continually deferred and differing movement of signification (Derrida 1974: 61–73). Similarly, for Kristeva, the abject is that which is jettisoned, radically excluded, yet still visible; it '*shows me* what I permanently thrust aside in order to live' (1982: 3). The abject, like the trace, comes back as excess to 'disturb identity, system, order' (1982: 4). In employing these ideas, biblical scholars have begun to look at the absences within texts, or the signs of what has been excluded, in order to reflect upon the disturbing deferral and supplement that these exclusions provoke. In other words, the process of exclusion leaves its mark, which threatens to both add to and replace (supplementation) the identities or dominant figures in a text, and therefore has habitually been thrust away (deferral), creating new disturbing, abjected traces (see Linafelt 2000; Beal 1997; Black 2001).

2 Analytics of power

Biblical scholars have also drawn on Foucault's rethinking of power relations. For Foucault, power is not from above, but is rather a 'multiplicity of force relations' (1990: 92–3); 'it flows through the social body politic as blood circulates through an organism, capillary rather than controlling . . . [this] creates the possibility of agency for the occupants of the subordinate position in a hierarchical relationship' (Castelli 1992: 203). Power for Foucault is invested through techniques of knowledge: 'between techniques of knowledge and strategies of power there is no exteriority' (1990: 98). Further, Foucault is particularly concerned with the workings of power as it is mediated through the self-regulation of disciplinary practices of individual bodies. Such an understanding of power/knowledge has been productive for scholars of early Christian texts as they look at the ways in which the (self-) disciplining of early Christian bodies is related to the production of power relations and of claims to truth (Castelli 1991, 2004). And following Foucault, whose description of power and knowledge is developed through historical analysis, the power relations read in early Christian texts can also be read back onto their social contexts, producing slightly different understandings of early Christian history (Castelli 1991, 1992; Moore 1994).

3 Ethics and the face of the Other

Inspired by poststructural readings of Levinas, biblical scholars have begun to attend to the call of the wholly Other in the text and in interpretation. For Levinas, ethics is 'a radical obligation which precedes and infuses every act of critical thinking' (Phillips and Fewell 1997a: 4). This obligation 'is the demand made by the face of the Other' (Levinas 1985: 52). For Levinas, and for biblical scholars, the biblical text illuminates the face of the Other (Levinas 1985: 117; Phillips and Fewell 1997a: 7–10). Reading biblical text therefore means attending to the face of the Other presented there (Phillips and Fewell 1997b: 7). Deconstructive tactics, attention to the trace, the abject, and the undecidable can open up the text to reveal the obligating Other (Pippin 1993; Phillips and Fewell 1997b). Scholars have also begun to see the face of the Other through voices of biblical interpretations that have traditionally been excluded, residing on the margins (see Segovia and Tolbert 1993; West and Dube 1996; Sakenfeld and Ringe 1997).

References and further reading

Aichele, George (2001) *The Control of Biblical Meaning: Canon as Semiotic Mechanism*, Harrisburg: Trinity Press International.

Barthes, Roland (1974 [1970]) *S/Z*, trans. Richard Miller, New York: Noonday.

Beal, Timothy K. (1997) *The Book of Hiding: Gender, Ethnicity, Annihilation and Esther*, Biblical Limits, London and New York: Routledge.

Black, Fiona (2001) 'Nocturnal Egression: Exploring Some Margins in the Song of Songs,' in *Postmodern Interpretations of the Bible: A Reader*, A.K.M. Adams (ed.), St. Louis: Chalice.

Castelli, Elizabeth (1991) *Imitating Paul: A Discourse of Power*, Literary Currents in Biblical Interpretation, Louisville: Westminster/John Knox.

—— (1992) 'Interpretations of Power in 1 Corinthians,' *Semeia* 54: 197–222.

——, Stephen D. Moore, Gary A. Phillips, and Regina M. Schwartz (eds.) (1995) 'Poststructuralist Criticism,' in *The Postmodern Bible*, New Haven: Yale University Press.

—— (2004) *Martyrdom and Memory: Early Christian Culture Making*, New York: Columbia University Press.

Derrida, Jacques (1974 [1967]) *Of Grammatology*, trans. Gayatri Chakravorty Spivak, Baltimore and London: Johns Hopkins University Press.

—— (1979) 'Living on: *Border lines*,' in *Deconstruction and Criticism*, Harold Bloom (ed.), New York: Continuum.

—— (1981 [1972]) *Positions*, trans. Alan Bass, Chicago: University of Chicago Press.

Detweiler, Robert (ed.) (1982) *Derrida and Biblical Studies*, Semeia 23, Atlanta: Scholars Press.

Fewell, Danna Nolan (ed.) (1992) *Reading between Texts: Intertextuality and the Hebrew Bible*, Louisville: Westminster.

Foucault, Michel (1990 [1976]) *History of Sexuality. Volume 1: An Introduction*, trans. Robert Hurley, New York: Vintage.

Jobling, David and Stephen D. Moore (eds.) (1992) *Poststructuralism as Exegesis*, Semeia 54, Atlanta: Scholars Press.

Kristeva, Julia (1982 [1980]) *Powers of Horror: An Essay on Abjection*, trans. Leon S. Roudiez, New York: Columbia University Press.

Levinas, Emmanuel (1985 [1982]) *Ethics and Infinity: Conversations with Phillippe Nemo*, trans. R. Cohen, Pittsburgh: Duquesne University Press.

Linafelt, Tod (2000) *Surviving Lamentations: Catastrophe, Lament and Protest in the Afterlife of a Biblical Book*, Chicago: University of Chicago Press.

Longenecker, Bruce W. (2003) 'Evil at Odds with Itself (Matthew 12:22–29): Demonising Rhetoric and Deconstructive Potential in the Matthean Narrative,' *Biblical Interpretation* 11: 503–14.

Milne, Pamela J. (1993) 'The Patriarchal Stamp of Scripture: The Implication of Structural Analyses for Feminist Hermeneutics,' in *A Feminist Companion to Genesis*, Athalya Brenner (ed.), Sheffield: Sheffield Academic Press.

Moore, Stephen D. (1994) *Poststructuralism and the New Testament: Derrida and Foucault at the Foot of the Cross*, Minneapolis: Fortress Press.

Phillips, Gary A. (1995) '"You are Either Here, Here, Here, or Here": Deconstruction's Troublesome Interplay,' *Semeia* 71: 193–213.

—— and Danna Nolan Fewell (1997a) 'Ethics, Bible Reading as If,' *Semeia* 77: 1–22.

—— (1997b) 'Drawn to Excess or Reading Beyond Bethrothal,' *Semeia* 77: 23–58.

Pippin, Tina (1993) '"And I Will Strike Her Children Dead": Death and the Deconstruction of Social Location,' in *Reading from this Place: Vol. 1, Social Location and Biblical Interpretation in the United States*, F.F. Segovia and M.A. Tolbert (eds.), Minneapolis: Fortress Press.

Runions, Erin (1998) 'Zion is Burning: "Gender Fuck" in Micah,' *Semeia* 82: 225–46.

Sakenfeld, Katherine Doob and Sharon H. Ringe (eds.) (1997) *Reading the Bible as Women: Perspectives from Africa, Asia and Latin America*, Semeia 78, Atlanta: Scholars Press.

Segovia, Fernando F. and Mary Ann Tolbert (eds.) (1993) *Reading from this Place: Vol. 2, Social Location and Biblical Interpretation in Global Perspective*, Minneapolis: Fortress Press.

Sherwood, Yvonne (1996) *The Prostitute and the Prophet: Hosea's Marriage in Literary-theoretical Perspective*, JSOTSup 212, Gender, Culture, Theory 2, Sheffield: Sheffield Academic Press.

—— (ed.) (2004) *Derrida's Bible: (Reading a Page of Scripture with a Little Help from Derrida)*, New York: Palgrave.

Via, Dan O. (2003) 'Revelation, Atonement, and the Scope of Faith in the Epistle to the Hebrews: A Deconstructive and Reader-Response Interpretation,' *Biblical Interpretation* 11: 515–30.

West, Gerald and Musa W. Dube (eds.) (1996) *Reading With: An Exploration and Interface Between Critical and Ordinary Readings of the Bible*, Semeia 73, Atlanta: Scholars Press.

ERIN RUNIONS

PROPHETIC LITERATURE

1 Approaches to genre
2 Prophecy in the ancient Near East
3 Micro forms of prophecy in Israel
4 Macro forms of prophecy in Israel
5 Later forms of prophecy in Israel
6 Conclusion

1 Approaches to genre

The genre of prophecy in the biblical corpus has been the focus of much scholarship over the past two centuries. Beginning in earnest in the nineteenth century, genre was considered indispensable for the historical-critical enterprise. As materials from the ancient Near East were uncovered through archaeological digs, scholars increasingly noted points of similarity between ancient non-Israelite texts and the prophetic texts in the Hebrew tradition. The refinement of form-critical methodologies in the latter part of the same century led in the twentieth century to the careful cataloguing of the basic types of prophetic literature as well as the elements that made each type unique. Form-critical scholars also sought after the life setting (*Sitz im Leben*) of the prophetic messages now encased in their literary corpora. This was helpful to isolate the oral foundations of prophecy and also assisted biblical scholars in isolating the smallest oral units from which the written text had been constructed. The form-critical agenda soon gave way to closer attention to the rhetoric of the prophetic literature and so genre was investigated not primarily as a window into the original historical moment of oral prophecy, but rather as a signal of the appropriate reading strategy for interpretation. Genre analysis was thus essential to isolate the building blocks of the particular prophetic message. The focus on these building blocks, however, was only to isolate the basic units in order to highlight the way the prophetic poet uniquely combined these standard units into a new and creative whole. Additionally, genre analysis was helpful by providing a larger interpretive context so that passages could be read not only in the literary context of the book in which they were found, but also in the broader literary context of the genre which they evince.

2 Prophecy in the ancient Near East

As already noted, some of the earliest uses of genre analysis in modern study were in comparisons between Hebrew prophecy and texts from the ancient Near East. It is clear that prophecy was not the unique possession of Israel among its ancient neighbors (cf. Jer. 27:1–15), for most of the surrounding nations attest to divine messenger functionaries within their ranks whether that was in Phoenicia, Aram, Ammon, Anatolia, Babylonia, Assyria, or Mari. Such prophecies addressed the king, focusing on national affairs, and could be either an encouragement or a warning (cf. Huffmon 1992; Nissinen 2000; Nissinen *et al.* 2003; Baker 1999; Walton 1989: 201–216).

3 Micro forms of prophecy in Israel

Passages in the prophetic books are composed in both poetry and prose, the latter of which can be narrative as well as sermonic. Employing these literary types, the prophets communicated their message through a variety of forms (*Gattungen*).

These forms can be divided into three basic groups, arranged according to avenues of experience: action, vision, utterance (see further Sweeney 1995). First of all, there are various types of actions experienced and communicated by the prophet. The prototypical prophetic call narrative can be discerned in the calling of Moses in Exodus 3–4, elements of which appear in the prophetic literature in Isaiah 6, Jeremiah 1, and Ezekiel 1–3; cf. Isaiah 40:1–11 (Habel 1965). The

prophets also employed sign-act reports (e.g., Jer. 19) which followed the pattern: exhortation (God commands the prophet to do an action), execution (the prophet relates the fulfilment of the action), and explanation (the prophet declares the significance of the action; cf. Fohrer 1952, 1968; Friebel 1999). Finally, there are passages in the prophetic corpus that suggest the prophet's participation in a liturgical event (prophetic description of the calamitous conditions, communal lament, prophetic approach to Yahweh asking for an answer, divine answer: judgment or salvation; cf. Boda 2001).

Second, prophets, sometimes denoted as 'seers' (*hōzēh, rō'ēh*), also received and communicated visionary experiences. The 'oracle-vision' type (Jer. 24) involved a dialogue between God and the prophet which was instigated by a vision and resulted in an oracle, while in the 'dramatic word vision' form (Amos 7:1–6) the prophet sees a heavenly scene depicting a future event to be announced by the prophet (cf. Horst 1960; Long 1976; Niditch 1983).

Third, prophets were known above all as communicators of divine words, something clear from the fact that even the former two categories (action, vision) are only known to us because of their verbal phase. Prophetic utterances are generally divided into two fundamental groups based on their mood: the negative forms (condemnation) and the positive forms (promise), categories suggested in the call of Jeremiah (1:10) which reveals that prophets were called to both 'tear down' (condemnation) and to 'build up' (promise). Not surprisingly the dominant of the two moods is the negative as prophets were often called to confront their generation (cf. Westermann 1991a). Such confrontation was delivered often through the Announcement of Judgment (depiction of the situation, messenger formula, 'therefore,' prediction of judgment; cf. Mic. 1:2–7), but also through the Cry of Woe ('woe,' addressee, depiction of situation, messenger formula, 'therefore,' prediction of judgment; cf. Isa. 5:8–25), and the Covenant Prosecution of Sin (preparations for trial, cross-examination questions, accusatory address, declaration of guilt, condemnation threats or positive instructions; cf. Mic. 6:1–8). Less common, but extremely creative, are the use of Praise (praising the just character of God to warn the people of God's character, cf. the Doxologies of Judgment in Amos 4:13; 5:8–9; 9:5–6), Remorse (singing a funeral dirge in order to announce that the end was near, call to hear, dirge, messenger formula, prediction of judgment; cf. Amos 5:1–3), Questions (asking the people questions and awaiting a response: assertion of God's character/people's action toward God, question, answer, command/warning/promise; cf. Amos 3:3–8; 9:7; Mal.), Quotation (citing a saying among the people to set up a condemnation, in Jer. 31:29–30; Ezek. 12:21–25, 26–28; 18:1–4; Hag. 1:2–11), or Sermon (cf. Zech. 1:1–6a).

The prophets, however, also offered hope through promise (Westermann 1991b). The most common form employed was that of the Announcement of Salvation (declaration of human need/divine character, announcement of salvation, purpose of salvation; cf. Isa. 44:1–5) and the Denouncement of Foreign Nations (by judging the foreign nations, the prophets were offering hope to Israel; cf. Obad.). However, as Praise could be used for condemnation it could also be employed for promise (cf. Isa. 12:1–3).

4 Macro forms of prophecy in Israel

The many original formal units of prophecy drawn from the career of the Hebrew prophets (or in some cases written as an echo of prophetic experience) were brought together by editors into collections which resulted in the prophetic books in the canon (cf. Collins 1993; Clements 1996). In some ways this work on the macrolevel reflects further genre categories. For instance, Floyd has noted that Haggai 1 is 'Prophetic History,' which he defines as 'a type of literary narrative that is both historiographic and prophetic' (Floyd 2000: 401–22. Many have noted striking similarities in the overall structure of some of the prophetic books: oracles pertaining to the immediate historical situation of Judah, oracles against foreign nations, oracles of future eschatological blessing (Isaiah, Ezekiel, LXX of Jeremiah, Zephaniah, Joel; cf. Dillard and Longman 1994: 320, 419). Furthermore, the use of date/messenger formulae to structure a prophetic book can be discerned in Ezekiel, Haggai, and Zechariah. Such evidence suggests that the category of genre can be used to refer to the smaller (and in some cases) originally oral units of prophecy, but also to the larger (and most assuredly) originally written collections of prophecy.

5 Later forms of prophecy in Israel

The later history of prophecy evidences the enduring use not only of forms from the earlier age (cf. Amos 7–8 with Zech. 1:7–6:9; Amos 3:3–8 with Mal.), but also of content from earlier prophecy (e.g., Zech. 9–14; cf. Boda and Floyd 2003). It is in this phase that the foundations are laid for the emergence of apocalyptic as a literary genre that draws on the visionary-narrative quality of some prophetic material (e.g., Zech. 1–8) as well as the eschatological quality of others (e.g., Zech. 9–14; cf. Hanson 1979; Collins 1979; Murphy 1994; Cook 1995).

6 Conclusion

Although similar in form to the broader ancient Near-Eastern context, the prophetic collections that survived in Israel clearly evidence a tradition all their own. They are enduring witness to the creative power of genre to capture the imagination of an audience, offering both challenge and hope even to readers separated by immense temporal, cultural, and geographical gaps.

References and further reading

Baker, David W. (1999) 'Israelite Prophets and Prophecy,' pp. 266–94 in *The Face of Old Testament Studies: A Survey of Contemporary Approaches*, David W. Baker and Bill T. Arnold (eds.), Grand Rapids: Baker.

Ben Zvi, Ehud and Michael H. Floyd (eds.) (2000) *Writings and Speech in Israelite Prophecy and Ancient Near Eastern Prophecy*, Symposium, Atlanta: Society of Biblical Literature.

Boda, Mark J. (2001) 'From Complaint to Contrition: Peering through the Liturgical Window of Jer 14,1–15,4,' *Zeitschrift für die alttestamentliche Wissenschaft* 113: 186–97.

—— and Michael H. Floyd (eds.) (2003) *Bringing out the Treasure: Inner Biblical Allusion and Zechariah 9–14*, JSOTSup 370, Sheffield: Sheffield Academic Press.

Clements, R.E. (1996) *Old Testament Prophecy: From Oracles to Canon*, Louisville: Westminster/John Knox.

Collins, John J. (ed.) (1979) *Apocalypse: The Morphology of a Genre*, Semeia 14, Missoula: Scholars Press.

Collins, T. (1993) *The Mantle of Elijah: The Redaction Criticism of the Prophetical Books*, The Biblical Seminar 20, Sheffield: JSOT.

Cook, Stephen L. (1995) *Prophecy & Apocalypticism: The Postexilic Social Setting*, Minneapolis: Fortress Press.

Dillard, Raymond B. and Tremper Longman III (1994) *An Introduction to the Old Testament*, Grand Rapids: Zondervan.

Floyd, Michael H. (1995) 'The Nature of the Narrative and the Evidence of Redaction in Haggai,' *Vetus Testamentum* 45(4): 470–90.

Floyd, Michael H. (2000) *Minor Prophets, Part 2*, Forms of Old Testament Literature 22, Grand Rapids: Eerdmans.

Fohrer, G. (1952) 'Die Gattung der Berichte über symbolische Handlungen der Propheten,' *Zeitschrift für die alttestamentliche Wissenschaft* 64: 101–20.

—— (1968) *Die symbolische Handlungen der Propheten*, Abhandlungen zur Theologie des Alten und Neuen Testaments 54, Zurich: Zwingli Verlag, 2nd edn.

Friebel, Kelvin G. (1999) *Jeremiah's and Ezekiel's Sign-acts*, JSOTSup 283, Sheffield: Sheffield Academic Press.

Habel, N. (1965) 'The Form and Significance of the Call Narratives,' *Zeitschrift für die alttestamentliche Wissenschaft* 77: 297–323.

Hanson, Paul D. (1979) *The Dawn of Apocalyptic: The Historical and Sociological Roots of Jewish Apocalyptic Eschatology*, Philadelphia: Fortress Press, rev. edn.

Horst, F. (1960) 'Die Visionsschilderungen der alttestamentlichen Propheten,' *Evangelische Theologie* 20: 193–205.

Huffmon, H.B. (1992) 'Prophecy (ANE),' *ABD* 5.477–82.

Lohfink, N. (1978) 'Die Gattung der "Historischen Kurzgeschichte" in den letzten Jahren von Juda und in der Zeit des Babylonischen Exils,' *Zeitschrift für die alttestamentliche Wissenschaft* 90: 319–47.

Long, Burke O. (1976) 'Reports of Visions Among the Prophets,' *Journal of Biblical Literature* 95: 353–65.

March, W.E. (1974) 'Prophecy,' pp. 251–66 in *Old Testament Form Criticism*, J.H. Hayes (ed.), Trinity University Monograph Series in Religion 2, San Antonio: Trinity University Press.

Murphy, Frederick J. (1994) 'Apocalypses and Apocalypticism: The State of the Question,' *Currents in Research: Biblical Studies* 2: 147–80.

Niditch, Susan (1983) *The Symbolic Vision in Biblical Tradition*, Chico: Scholars Press.

Nissinen, Martti (ed.) (2000) *Prophecy in its Ancient Near Eastern Context: Mesopotamian, Biblical, and Arabian Perspectives*, Symposium, Atlanta: Society of Biblical Literature.

——, C.L. Seow, and Robert K. Ritner (2003) *Prophets and Prophecy in the Ancient Near East*, Writings from the Ancient World, Atlanta: Society of Biblical Literature.

Petersen, David L. (1984) *Haggai and Zechariah 1–8: A Commentary*, Old Testament Library, London: SCM.

Sweeney, M.A. (1995) 'Formation and Forms in Prophetic Literature,' pp. 113–26 in *Old Testament Interpretation: Past, Present, and Future: Essays in Honor of Gene M. Tucker*, J.L. Mays, D.L. Petersen, and K.H. Richards (eds.), Nashville: Abingdon Press.

Walton, John H. (1989) *Ancient Israelite Literature in its Cultural Context: A Survey of Parallels between Biblical and Ancient Near Eastern Texts*, Library of Biblical Interpretation, Grand Rapids: Regency Reference Library.

Westermann, Claus (1991a) *Basic Forms of Prophetic Speech*, Cambridge: Lutterworth/Louisville: Westminster/John Knox.

—— (1991b) *Prophetic Oracles of Salvation in the Old Testament*, Louisville: Westminster/John Knox.

MARK J. BODA

PROVERB/WISDOM

The English term 'proverb' is one which most people have a 'sense' about, but which becomes very slippery when it comes to definition. Proverb comes to us from Latin *prōverbium*, which basically means 'a set of words put forth.' Yet it is this Latin root which is used to translate the Hebrew *māšāl*. Sadly, *māšāl* doesn't help us a lot, as its etymology is disputed, but in any case can be associated with the idea of 'comparison' and also with the Proto-Semitic 'rule' (Botterweck *et al.* 1998: s.v. *māšāl*). The denominative verb has meanings of 'be like,' 'become like,' and 'compare,' perhaps due to the extensive employment of simile/metaphor within biblical proverbs. ('In the light of the king's countenance is life; his favour is like a spring-cloud in the spring' Prov. 16:15; 'A soothing word is a tree of life, but a mischievous tongue breaks the spirit' Prov. 15:4.) However, etymology alone can no more provide a comprehensive understanding for the proverb in ancient Israelite society than it can for modern proverbs.

Archer Taylor writes, 'The definition of a proverb is too difficult to repay the undertaking; and should we fortunately combine in a single definition all the essential elements and give each the proper emphasis, we should not even then have a touchstone . . . An incommunicable quality tells us this sentence is proverbial and that one is not . . . Let us be content with recognizing that a proverb is a saying current among the folk' (Taylor 1962: 3). I suppose this is not unlike Louis Armstrong's response to the question 'What is jazz?': 'If you gotta ask, don't bother.' In other words, a proverb, like jazz, must evoke an immediacy of response and recognition amongst the hearers. To try to define what makes a saying 'proverbial' is nearly as futile as trying to explain what makes a joke funny: it obtains both in the telling and in the hearing, and perhaps in the context as well. 'The proverb assumes a certain degree of equality on the part of user and hearer, since the hearer is called upon to affirm the message of the proverb' (Fontaine 1982: 17).

In any event, the English term 'proverb' is at the same time both too specific and too general to do justice to the literature we associate with it in the Hebrew Bible. Specifically, the term *māšāl*/proverb appears in the superscription to the book of Proverbs in the construct plural form (*mišlê šĕlōmōh*). Even a cursory examination of the book of Proverbs reveals it to be a compendium of various types of instructive literature organized under the term *māšāl*. Although popularly associated with 'wisdom,' due to its grouping with Job and Ecclesiastes within the Christian canon, the category of 'wisdom literature' is a modern designation and has no basis in the Jewish division of the canon. In the opening verses of Proverbs we are confronted with what can be understood as either synonyms or categories of *māšāl*: satire (mockery), words of the wise and riddles (enigmas, obscure problems). Within the book there are a number of separate collections, each bearing its own characteristics: moral discourse, wise sayings (often in two parallel *stichoi*), admonitions, and even musings concerning life and wisdom.

As regards the specific connection between proverb and wisdom, we find that the Hebrew term for wisdom, *hokmāh*, is as elusive as *māšāl*, the English term 'wisdom' being only an approximation of the Hebrew. *Hokmāh* may be defined as a realistic approach to the problems of life, including all the practical skills and technical arts of civilization. The term *hākām*, 'sage, wise man,' is variously applied throughout the Old Testament: for the artist, craftsman, musician and singer, and even the sailor. To cite only a few, Bezalel, the skilled craftsman who built the Tabernacle in the wilderness, as well as all his associates, are called 'wise of heart' (Exod. 35:31; 36:2). Weavers (Exod. 35:35), goldsmiths (Jer. 10:9), women skilled in lamentation (Jer. 9:17), and sailors (Ps. 107:27) are *hākām*. The same epithet is used of diviners and soothsayers (Gen. 41:8; 1 Kings 4:30–32; Isa. 44:25). In rabbinic Hebrew *hakamah* is also applied to the midwife. Above all, there is an integral relationship between the term wisdom and the arts of poetry and music – both vocal and instrumental. This relationship between wisdom and song is so close that often no distinction was drawn between the two (Gordis 1978: 17). Thus 1 Kings 4:30–32: 'Solomon's wisdom surpassed of all the men of the east and of all Egypt. For he was wiser than any man . . . his fame spread among all the surrounding nations. He propounded three thousand proverbs, and his songs numbered a thousand and five.' Although the general consensus of scholarship would no longer accept Solomonic authorship for the book of Proverbs, we may safely assume that this attribution is an indication of the value placed on wisdom/proverbs and the importance this genre held with those who compiled and preserved the canon. It should be noted in regard to the Hebrew wisdom genre that 'The similarities in form and content between Israelite and Egyptian didactic wisdom literature have been so well established that there can be no doubt that Israelite wisdom is part of an international genre . . . and cannot be properly studied in isolation' (Fox 1980: 120).

However, it must be stated that proverbs in the Bible are not limited to formal collections. In Westermann's estimation the occurrence of a proverb in a collection clearly represents a secondary stage of transmission, when the wisdom contained in a given saying has been evaluated and consciously preserved (Westermann 1971: 74–5). Beginning with Eissfeldt, many scholars have held that the term *māšāl* is a secondary and overarching rubric for popular sayings and maxims (Eissfeldt 1913: 26; McKane 1970: 31). The Old Testament is rife with such examples outside the 'wisdom' literature. There are those which are explicitly categorized as *māšāl*, such as the one following Saul's being taken up in prophetic ecstasy: hence the proverb, 'is Saul among the prophets?' (1 Sam. 10:12 [19:24]; other examples being: 1 Sam. 24:13; Ezek. 12:22; 18:2). We also find sayings which are introduced by phrases such as 'therefore it is said,' e.g., Genesis 10:9 'He was outstanding as a mighty hunter' – therefore it is said, 'like Nimrod, outstanding as a mighty hunter before the Lord.' (See also 2 Sam. 5:8; 20:18; Isa. 40:27; Zeph. 1:12; Ezek. 9:9; 18:25, 29; 33:10, 17, 20; 37:11.) Many other sayings have the 'ring' of a proverb (e g., Judg. 8:21; 1 Sam. 24:14; 1 Kings 20:11; Isa. 22:13; Jer. 8:22). There are those who would dispute whether such (folk) sayings are to be considered proverbs in a formal sense (e.g., Jolles 1965: 150–5), but as stated at the beginning, *māšāl* covers a broad range of literary types.

In sum, we can say that from the 'wisdom' point of view, the proverb serves to instruct, to impart 'a practical knowledge of the laws of life and of the world, based upon experience' (von Rad 1962: 418). The other Old Testament 'proverbs' – be they aphorism, maxim, folk saying, riddle – serve the same purposes they do today: entertainment, jibe, paraenesis. For a saying to become proverbial, it must have currency among the folk, and it must succinctly capture in its form – be it rhyme or simple choice of words – a common human experience, which gives it its currency and durability.

References and further reading

Botterweck, G., H. Ringgren, and H.-J. Fasoy (eds.) (1998) *Theological Dictionary of the Old Testament*, Vol. 9, trans. D. Green, Grand Rapids: Eerdmans.

Eissfeldt, Otto (1913) *Der Maschal im Alten Testament*, BZAW 24, Giessen: Alfred Töpelmann.

Fontaine, Carole (1982) *Tradition Sayings in the Old Testament*, Sheffield: The Almond Press.

Fox, Michael (1980) 'Two Decades of Research in Egyptian Wisdom Literature,' *Zeitschrift für ägyptische Sprache und Altertumskunde* 107: 120.

Gordis, Robert (1978) *Koheleth – the Man and His World*, New York: Schocken Books.

Jolles, André (1965) *Einfache Formen*, Tübingen: Max Niemeyer Verlag, 3rd edn.

McKane, William (1970) *Proverbs: A New Approach*, London: SCM Press.

Taylor, Archer (1962) *The Proverb and an Index to the Proverb*, Hatboro: Rosenkilde & Baggers.

Thompson, John M. (1974) *The Form and Function of Proverbs in Ancient Israel*, The Hague: Mouton.

von Rad, Gerhard (1962) *Old Testament Theology*, I, trans. D.M.G. Stalker, San Francisco: Harper.

Westermann, Claus (1971) 'Weisheit im Sprichwort,' in *Schalom: Studien zu Glaube und Geschichte Israels*, Festschrift Alfred Jepsen zum 70. Geburtstag, Karl-Heinz Bernhardt (ed.), Stuttgart: Calwer Verlag.

JACK N. LAWSON

PSALMS

Gunkel's work on the form criticism of the Psalms (1998 [1933]) was one of his greatest contributions to the understanding of the Old Testament. He was able to sort out its heterogeneous poetry into a coherent group of categories and to analyze the elements of each category in ways which to a large extent have stood the test of time. His work was refined at an important point by Mowinckel (1961 [1921], 1: 137–59, [1924], 6: 8–36). Whereas Gunkel (1998 [1933]: 20–1, 123–30) considered that texts were composed in a noncultic setting on the model of earlier cultic prototypes, Mowinckel used internal evidence to claim that in most cases their own social setting or *Sitz im Leben* was the temple.

Gunkel postulated five big types of psalm. The most common is the lament, which is represented by communal and individual forms. His term 'lament' is derived from the lamenting description of crisis that dominates the first half of such poems. Kraus (1988: 26, 47–8) observed that its Hebrew equivalent is *těpillâ* 'prayer,' found for instance in the superscription of Psalm 102. This term focuses on the second and main element, the petitions for divine intervention and deliverance to which the description of crisis forms the persuasive background, and indeed on the general orientation of the laments as prayer language, directed to God. More recently, Broyles (1989) has shown that the communal and individual laments subdivide into a larger category of persuasive prayer (e.g., Ps. 54) and a smaller, more radical variety which engages in protesting complaints that God has failed to honor divine traditions of answering prayer and delivering or even caused the crisis (e.g., Ps. 22:1–21). The second of Gunkel's types is the thanksgiving song, also crisis related, but now celebrating resolution and interpreting it as an answer to the lament prayer (e.g., Ps. 116). Typically it is spoken by an individual, though communal adaptations of the genre are found (Pss. 124; 129). It was associated with a thanksgiving service at which individuals testified to God's help and offered their thanksgiving prayer and also brought a thanks offering sacrifice, all in fulfilment of the vows offered at the close of a lament (e.g., 56:12).

The third and most common of the genres after the lament is the hymn, which celebrates God's self-revelation in the history of Israel (e.g., Ps. 105) or in Creation (e.g., Ps. 104). It is communal, sometimes in a solo form, and reflects use in temple services. It typically consists of a call to praise and a statement of grounds for praise, though grounds for praise can also be expressed by means of participles (cf. Crüsemann 1969: 19–154). It has a number of subtypes, such as hymns sung at the thanksgiving service (e.g., Pss. 100; 103), songs of Zion which indirectly praise Zion's God (e.g., Pss. 46; 48), and hymns of divine kingship (e.g., Pss. 96–99). The fourth genre is that of the royal psalms, which, however, are united only by their focus on the Davidic king and can take various shapes, such as a royal lament (Ps. 89) or a royal thanksgiving (Psalm 18). The last of Gunkel's big five is the category of wisdom poems, which in origin reflects a noncultic setting, the wisdom 'schools,' and is allied with the wisdom books of Proverbs, Job, and Ecclesiastes. Apart from pure wisdom poems (e.g., Ps. 112), there are cultic versions written under wisdom influence (e.g., Ps. 73). There are also other genres less often represented, such as the affirmation of confidence (e.g., Pss. 16; 23) and priestly liturgies on entering (Ps. 15) or leaving (Ps. 121) the temple.

Hermeneutical light has been shed on the Psalms by interpreting them in terms of broader life-settings, the different seasons of human life they represent, whether that of orientation, disorientation, or reorientation (Brueggemann 1980, 1984: 15–23). This perspective has form-critical implications: Psalm 30:6–11, reflecting these seasons, ties reorientation to the thanksgiving song, disorientation to the lament, and orientation to a precrisis (or, better, extracrisis) period which is defined in terms of what appears to be a motto of orientation psalms, 'shall never (or not) be moved' (Allen 1986a: 711). The range of this motto identifies orientation psalms as the hymn (e.g., 93:1), the affirmation of confidence (16:8), the priestly liturgies (15:5; 121:3), a relevant royal psalm (21:7), and a normative wisdom psalm (112:6). The sequence of seasons, in which reorientation is eventually followed by more mature orientation and so on, comprises a spiral of development in human experience (Goldingay 1981).

The book of Psalms as a literary whole attests two distinct form-critical trajectories. The first is a hymnic one. Division into five smaller books is marked by closing doxologies. Psalm 150 has such a role for the fifth book and the Psalter. The doxology at 106:48 is already presupposed in 1 Chronicles 16:36. A doxology corresponds to the first half of a hymn; the second half, grounds for praise, is meant to be gleaned from the psalms which precede in the book. The Psalms en masse are thus transposed into a literary medium of theological praise. This trajectory is furthered by the structural position of royal psalms: for instance, Psalm 2 is in a prominent place, while Psalm 89 (now prized for its hymnic and oracular content) appears at the end of the third book (cf. Wilson 1985: 207–8). At this stage they have an eschatological role, affirming God's future purposes (Westermann 1981: 257–8). Our title for the book, 'Psalms,' comes from the LXX; the Hebrew title, *těhillîm*, 'praises' or 'hymns,' marks the climax of this theological trajectory. The second literary trajectory is ethically oriented. It is announced by the introductory Psalm 1, which commends the Psalter as God's veritable 'torah' or written revelation, given to impart ethical teaching which may be gleaned from each psalm (Childs 1979: 513). This trajectory takes its cue from the ethical teaching of the wisdom psalms. It regards as the believer's role models God (Ps. 112 after Ps. 111) and David (Ps. 19 after Ps. 18 [Allen 1986b]; the historicizing Davidic superscriptions [Childs 1979: 520–2]). We can only speculate about the social settings associated with these literary, genre-related trajectories of theology and ethics, but Gunkel's postcultic assessment of the Psalms has turned out to be relevant for their later roles.

References and further reading

Allen, L.C. (1986a) 'Review of Brueggemann's *The Message of the Psalms*,' *Journal of Biblical Literature* 105: 710–11.

—— (1986b) 'David as Exemplar of Spirituality: The Redactional Function of Psalm 19,' *Biblica* 67: 544–6.

Broyles, C.C. (1989) *The Conflict of Faith and Experience in the Psalms: A Form-Critical and Theological Study*, JSOTSup 52, Sheffield: JSOT Press.

Brueggemann, W. (1980) 'Psalms and the Life of Faith: A Suggested Typology of Function,' *Journal for the Study of the Old Testament* 17: 3–32 (repr. in *The Psalms and the Life of Faith*, P.D. Miller [ed.], Minneapolis: Fortress Press, 1995, pp. 3–32).

—— (1984) *The Message of the Psalms: A Theological Commentary*, Minneapolis: Augsburg.

Childs, B.S. (1979) *Introduction to the Old Testament as Scripture*, London: SCM Press.

Crüsemann, F. (1969) *Studien zur Formgeschichte von Hymnus und Danklied in Israel*, WMANT 32, Neukirchen-Vluyn: Neukirchener Verlag.

Goldingay, J. (1981) 'The Dynamic Cycle of Praise and Prayer in the Psalms,' *Journal for the Study of the Old Testament* 20: 85–90.

Gunkel, H. and J. Begrich (1998) *Introduction to Psalms: The Genres of the Religious Lyric of Israel*, trans. J.D. Nogalski from 4th edn of a work published in 1933, Macon: Mercer University Press.

Kraus, H.-J. (1988) *Psalms 1–59: A Commentary*, trans. H.C. Oswald, Minneapolis: Augsburg.

Mowinckel, S. (1961 [1921–1924]) *Psalmenstudien*, 6 Vols., Amsterdam: P. Schippers.

Westermann, C. (1981) *Praise and Lament in the Psalms*, trans. K.R. Crim and R. Soulen, Richmond: John Knox.

Wilson, G.H. (1985) *The Editing of the Hebrew Bible*, SBLDS 76, Chico: Scholars Press.

LESLIE C. ALLEN

Q

QUOTATION AND ALLUSION

It appears that from the earliest stages of canonization, long before the turn of the Common Era, inner-biblical connections were essential to interpretation. Later texts in the Old Testament as well as texts in the New Testament provided a precedent for an approach to interpretation within the church that would be called 'scripture interpreting scripture,' based on the conviction that there was a deep interconnectedness between the various books of the Bible.

Critical study of the Old Testament has long recognized this interconnectedness between its texts. This can be discerned in the development of tradition-historical method, which was designed to trace the evolution of the various traditions of Israel's history largely through oral transference from generation to generation (Rast 1972; Knight 1975, 1992). A distinction was made in this critical method between the 'traditum' (the traditions themselves) and the 'traditio' (the process by which they are transferred between generations). Reflection on this 'traditio' led to the discovery that similar processes were also evident when these traditions were transferred on the written level (Fishbane 1985). Although there is more rigidity to the passing of a tradition on the written level than there is on the oral level, such transference does indicate ongoing growth in the tradition.

This application of traditiohistorical methodology to written tradition led to new appreciation for the literary interconnectedness of the Hebrew Bible. It was demonstrated that prayers such as Psalms 105, 106, and Nehemiah 9 lean heavily upon the Torah's narrative material by weaving together a pastiche of quotation and allusion to leverage the ancient story for a new generation (Boda 1999). Even when there are direct quotations of the Torah material, however, this is not mere replication, but rather reflects interpretation that shapes the tradition in new ways. So also passages such as Ezra 9 and Nehemiah 10 have been shown to draw upon the Torah's legal material through quotation and allusion to bring old legal precedents to bear on new realities (Milgrom 1976: 72–73; Clines 1981; Bautch 2003: 86–7). Reliance on earlier material is also evident in later prophetic material such as Zechariah, made expli-

cit in chs 1–8 through references to the 'earlier prophets' and to their tradition (1:4; 7:7–10; 8:16–17; Boda 2003), yet implicit in chs 9–14 through a fusion of literary allusions to these same prophets (Boda and Floyd 2003a). The various techniques used by biblical authors to connect with earlier materials have been tagged by many terms, demonstrated poignantly in Beal's list: 'allusion, echo, inner biblical exegesis, intertextuality, intertext, intratextuality, poetic influence, and trace' (Beal 1992: 21–4; so Petersen 2003). Petersen has recently offered some direction for those pursuing relationships between texts by drawing from the work of Gerard Genette, who identifies various forms of 'transtextuality' which include: 'intertextuality' (quotation, plagiarism, allusion), 'paratextuality' (a title, terminal notes, chapter headings, marginalia, forewords), 'metatextuality' (commentary), 'hypertextuality' (imitation), and 'architextuality' (genre).

By citing the work of Genette it is clear that recent work on quotation and allusion has moved to a whole new level through the incorporation of paradigms from the study of 'intertextuality' (Draisma 1989; Fewell 1992; Hatina 1999). In large measure the approaches identified to this point here would be considered historical approaches to intertextuality (diachronic), that is, approaches that seek to discover how a text 'evokes its antecedents,' thus, focusing on the author–text relationship. In contrast, more recent approaches to intertextuality (synchronic) focus 'not on the author of a text but either on the text itself . . . or on the reader.' In this way, quotation and allusion are ultimately categories in the reader's mind and are imposed upon the text from our modern context (cf. the work of Kristeva 1980). Such an approach has been heralded as a new way forward for the study of biblical theology, especially for the relationship between the Old and New Testaments (Martens 2001). Part of the attraction may lie in the fact that a reader-centered hermeneutic alleviates perceived instances of tension between the original intention of the Old Testament author and the ultimate intention of the New Testament reader, a problem that is often cited in studies of the New Testament appropriation of the Old.

Concerns, however, over this shift to reader-orientation are evident in recent work on the 'allusive' character of the book of Isaiah. Sommer (1998) makes a clear distinction between two streams of scholars, one which focuses on 'influence/allusion' and the other on 'intertextuality.' The former is diachronic in character focusing on the relationship between the antecedent text and the author, while the latter is synchronic focussing on the relationship between the text and the reader. Sommer prefers the diachronic approach due to the character of the texts in Isaiah that appear to call attention to the allusions (contrast Eslinger 1992). Schultz (1999) adopts both diachronic and synchronic phases to his analysis, the first investigating the historical processes that resulted in the citation/allusion (antecedent text as well as context of author) and the second investigating the impact of the resultant text on the reader. Similar debate is evident also in the study of quotation and allusion in the New Testament as seen in articles by Hays and Green (1995), Litwak (1998), as well as volumes by Marguerat and Curtis (2000) and Moyise (2000). A powerful case study is that of allusions in the book of Revelation (Beale 1999, 2001; Moyise 1999; Paulien 2001).

While synchronic intertextuality may be helpful at some stage in interpretation, one cannot avoid the fact that biblical instances of quotation and allusion, especially noticeable in the New Testament, are presented in a way that demands diachronic sensibilities. The point of drawing on earlier tradition is to provide a strong foundation for a statement in the new experience of the reader. A critical methodology for the study of quotation and allusion in the biblical texts, therefore, should include both diachronic and synchronic phases. In the diachronic phase the interpreter should identify inner-biblical connections (with attention to the lexical and structural similarities between the two texts), study the larger contexts of the two texts (antecedent and text under study) to understand their meaning, and then reflect on the way in which the antecedent is being used within the later text. In the synchronic phase, the interpreter must read the later text to discern the impact that such intertextual insight makes upon the reading of this text in its final form, especially within its final textual context (cf. Boda 2003b).

References and further reading

Bautch, Richard J. (2003) *Developments in Genre between Post-Exilic Penitential Prayers and the Psalms of Communal Lament*, SBLAB, Atlanta: Society of Biblical Literature.

Beal, T.K. (1992) 'Glossary,' pp. 21–4 in *Reading Between Texts: Intertextuality and the Hebrew Bible*, Danna Nolan Fewell (ed.), Louisville: Westminster/John Knox.

Beale, G.K. (1999) *John's Use of the Old Testament in Revelation*, JSNTSup 166, Sheffield: Sheffield Academic Press.

—— (1999) 'Questions of Authorial Intent, Epistemology, and Presuppositions and Their Bearing on the Study of the Old Testament in the New: A Rejoinder to Steve Moyise,' *Irish Biblical Studies* 21: 152–80.

—— (2001) 'A Response to Jon Paulien on the Use of the Old Testament in Revelation,' *Andrews University Seminary Studies* 39(1): 23–34.

Boda, Mark J. (1999) *Praying the Tradition: The Origin and Use of Tradition in Nehemiah 9*, BZAW 277, O. Kaiser (ed.), Berlin: Walter de Gruyter.

—— (2003a) 'Zechariah: Master Mason or Penitential Prophet?' pp. 5, 49–69 in *Yahwism after the Exile: Perspectives on Israelite Religion in the Persian Era*, Bob Becking and Rainer Albertz (eds.), Assen: Royal van Gorcum.

—— (2003b) 'Reading between the Lines: Zechariah 11:4–16 in its Literary Contexts,' pp. 277–91 in *Bringing out the Treasure: Inner Biblical Allusion and Zechariah 9–14*, Mark J. Boda and Michael H. Floyd (eds.), JSOTSup 370, Sheffield: Sheffield Academic Press.

—— and Michael H. Floyd (eds.) (2003c) *Bringing out the Treasure: Inner Biblical Allusion and Zechariah 9–14*, JSOTSup 370, Sheffield: Sheffield Academic Press.

Clines, David J.A. (1981) 'Nehemiah 10 as an example of early Jewish biblical exegesis,' *Journal for the Study of the Old Testament* 21: 111–17.

Draisma, S. (ed.) (1989) *Intertextuality in Biblical Writings*, Kampen: Kok.

Eslinger, Lyle (1992) 'Inner-Biblical Exegesis and Inner-Biblical Allusion: The Question of Category,' *Vetus Testamentum* 42(1): 47–58.

Fewell, Danna Nolan (1992) *Reading between Texts: Intertextuality and the Hebrew Bible*, Literary Currents in Biblical Interpretation, Louisville: Westminster/John Knox.

Fishbane, Michael A. (1985) *Biblical Interpretation in Ancient Israel*, Oxford: Clarendon Press.

Hatina, Thomas R. (1999) 'Intertextuality and Historical Criticism in New Testament Studies: Is there a Relationship?' *Biblical Interpretation* 7(1): 28–43.

Hays, Richard B. and Joel B. Green (1995) 'The Use of the Old Testament by New Testament Writers,' pp. 224–38 in *Hearing the New Testament: Strategies for Interpretation*, Joel B. Green (ed.), Grand Rapids: Eerdmans.

Knight, D.A. (1975) *Rediscovering the Tradition of Israel: The Development of the Traditio-Historical Research of the Old Testament, with Special Consideration of Scandinavian Contributions*, SBLDS 9, Missoula: University of Montana Press, rev. edn.

Knight, D.A. (1992) 'Tradition History,' *ABD* 6.633–8.

Kristeva, Julia (1980) *Desire in Language: A Semiotic Approach to Literature and Art*, New York: Columbia University Press.

Litwak, Kenneth D. (1998) 'Echoes of Scripture? A Critical Survey of Recent Works on Paul's Use of the Old Testament,' *Currents in Research: Biblical Studies* 6: 260–88.

Marguerat, Daniel and Adrian Curtis (eds.) (2000) *Intertextualités: La Bible en échos*, La monde de la Bible 40, Geneva: Labor et Fides.

Martens, Elmer (2001) 'Reaching for a Biblical Theology of the Whole Bible,' pp. 83–101 in *Reclaiming the Old Testament: Essays in Honour of Waldemar Janzen*, Gordon Zerbe (ed.), Winnipeg: CMBC Publications.

Milgrom, Jacob (1976) *Cult and Conscience: The Asham and the Priestly Doctrine of Repentance*, Studies in Judaism in Late Antiquity 18, Leiden: Brill.

Moyise, Steve (1999) 'The Language of the Old Testament in the Apocalypse,' *Journal for the Study of the New Testament* 76: 97–113.

—— (ed.) (2000) *The Old Testament in the New Testament: Essays in Honour of J.L. North*, JSNTSup 189, Sheffield: Sheffield Academic Press.

Newman, Judith H. (1999) *Praying by the Book: The Scripturalization of Prayer in Second Temple Judaism*, SBLEJL 14, J.C. Reeves (ed.), Atlanta: Scholars.

Paulien, Jon (2001) 'Dreading the Whirlwind: Intertextuality and the Use of the Old Testament in Revelation,' *Andrews University Seminary Studies* 39(1): 5–22.

Petersen, David L. (2003) 'Zechariah 9–14: Methodological Reflections,' pp. 210–24 in *Bringing out the Treasure: Inner Biblical Allusion and Zechariah 9–14*, Mark J. Boda and Michael H. Floyd (eds.), JSOTSup 370, Sheffield: Sheffield Academic Press.

Pröbstl, V. (1997) *Nehemia 9, Psalm 106 und Psalms 136 und die Rezeption des Pentateuchs*, Göttingen: Cuvillier Verlag.

Rast, Walter E. (1971) *Tradition History and the Old Testament*, Philadelphia: Fortress Press.

Schultz, Richard L. (1999) *The Search for Quotation: Verbal Parallels in the Prophets*, JSOTSup 180, Sheffield: Sheffield Academic Press.

Snyman, Gerrie (1996) 'Who is Speaking? Intertextuality and Textual Influence,' *Neotestamentica* 30(2): 427–49.

Sommer, Benjamin D. (1996) 'Exegesis, Allusion and Intertextuality in the Hebrew Bible: A Response to Lyle Eslinger,' *Vetus Testamentum* 46(4): 479–89.

—— (1998) *A Prophet Reads Scripture: Allusion in Isaiah 40–66*, The Contraversions Series, Stanford: Stanford University Press.

MARK J. BODA

R

RABBINIC JUDAISM

The rabbinic movement in its earliest phase is to be identified with Pharisaism. The Pharisees are portrayed by Josephus as being critical of the Hasmonean priesthood. Their expression was at first political (Josephus, *Ant.* 13 §§ 88–298) and could extend to violent action, as in the demand that the counselors who advised Alexander Jannaeus to kill some of their sympathizers should themselves be executed (Josephus, *War* 1.110–113) At base, however, the orientation of the Pharisees was towards the achievement and maintenance of purity. The purity they strived for had fundamentally to do with making offerings, people, and priests fit for the cult of sacrifice in the temple. For that reason, the issues of the personnel of the priesthood, the sorts of animals and goods that might be brought, and their permitted proximity to all sources of uncleanness were vitally important.

By the dawn of the Common Era, the Pharisees found a distinguished teacher in Jerusalem in the person of Hillel. Hillel is justly famous for the dictum, uttered some twenty years before Jesus, 'That which you hate, do not do to your fellow; that is the whole Torah, while all the rest is commentary thereon' (*b. Shab.* 31a). The story is striking, but it can also be misleading. First, Hillel in the tale is talking to an impatient proselyte, who wished to learn the Torah while standing on one foot; his impatience has just won him a cuff with a measuring rod from Shammai, the rabbi with whom Hillel is programmatically contrasted in Mishnah. Obviously, Hillel has no overt desire to reduce the Torah on the grounds of principle, and he goes on to tell the proselyte, 'Go and learn it.' In other words, the Gentile is told that the revelation to Moses is the expression of the best ethics, and for that reason the whole should be mastered.

In any case, Hillel was understood among the Pharisees as having come to prominence for adjudicating quite a distinct issue: whether the Passover could be sacrificed on the sabbath. Hillel first offers a scriptural argument for accepting the practice: since other forms of priestly service are permitted, so is the slaying of the lamb. His hearers are unimpressed, until he simply states that he learned the position in Babylon, from

Shemaiah and Abtalion, distinguished predecessors in the movement. Their authority is sufficient to displace the current leaders of Pharisaic opinion, the sons of Bathyra (cf. *t. Pesah.* 4:13, 14; *y. Pesah.* 6:1; *b. Shabb.* 19:1; *b. Pesah.* 66a, b).

This story may appear arcane, but it is redolent of Pharisaic culture. Throughout the history of the rabbinic movement, biblical interpretation was not conducted for its own sake, nor was it properly speaking the purpose of discussion. The aim was rather to discover the Torah in both the traditions of the sages and in the sacred scripture. Hillel consistently involved himself in cultic questions and disputes in Jerusalem. His position also is said to have convinced another teacher, Baba ben Buta, to provide cultically correct beasts in great numbers for slaughter, with the stipulation (against the school of Shammai) that the offerer must lay hands on the victim immediately prior to the killing (cf. *t. Ḥag.* 2:11; *y. Ḥag.* 2:3; *y. Beṣa* 2:4; *h. Beṣa* 20a, b).

The basis of Hillel's authority was not as much scriptural expertise as his mastery of what he had been taught by previous masters. He embodies the Pharisaic principle that the 'chains' of their tradition were normative for purity. Such chains were understood to have been developed from Moses to Ezra, after that by 'the men of the great congregation,' and then by teachers who were generally invoked as 'pairs' (*m. Avoth* 1:1–18). The last 'pair' was Hillel and Shammai, from which point the Pharisees acknowledged that division increased in Israel (*b. Soṭa* 47b; *b Sanh.* 88h; *t. Soṭa* 14:9; *t. Ḥag.* 2:9; *t. Sanh.* 7:1; *y. Ḥag.* 2:2; *y. Sanh.* 1:4). The notion of primeval unity disturbed by recent faction is probably mythical, but it is plain that the Pharisees developed their oral tradition by means of a structured understanding of the past as well as by mnemonic techniques.

The term 'Pharisee' is probably an outsiders' name for the movement, and may mean 'separatist' or 'purist'; participants in the movement appear to have referred to their ancient predecessors (after Ezra) as 'the sages' or 'the wise,' and to their more recent predecessors and contemporaries as 'teachers' (cf. *rab* in *m. Aboth* 1:6, 16; *sophistes* in Josephus, *War* 1.648). The normal, respectful address of a teacher was 'my great one,' or 'my master,' rabbi. Jesus is so addressed in the Gospels more than by any other designation; moreover, he had a characteristic interest in purity, and a dispute concerning appropriate sacrifice in the temple cost him his life. That Jesus' followers called him 'rabbi' (Matt. 26:25, 49; Mark 9:5; 10:51; 11:21; 14:45; John 1:38, 49; 3:2; 4:31; 6:25; 9:2; 11:8) is a straightforward deduction from the Gospels as they stand; that he is most naturally (if broadly) to be categorized among the Pharisees of his period is an equally straightforward inference. When, during the course of the twentieth century, scholars have expressed reservations in respect of that finding, they have had in mind the danger of identifying Jesus with the rabbinic movement after AD 70, which was more systematized than before that time, and which amounted to the established power within Judaism. Unfortunately, anxiety in respect of that anachronism can result in the far greater error of bracketing Jesus within 'sectarian' Judaism (as if 'orthodoxy' existed in early, pluralized Judaism), or – worse still – of placing him within no Judaism at all.

During the time of Hillel and Shammai, and until AD 70, Pharisaic teaching was targeted at the conduct of the cult in the temple, but its influence was limited. Nonetheless, Pharisees appear to have succeeded reasonably well in towns and villages, even in Galilee, where they urged local populations to maintain the sort of purity which would permit them to participate rightly in the cult. Josephus' colleague in the armed resistance against Rome (and archrival), John of Gischala, may well have been representing Pharisaic interests when he arranged for Jews in Syria to purchase oil exclusively from Galilean sources (*War* 2.591–593). In any case, it does appear plain that some Pharisees supported the revolt of 66, while others did not. But while many priests and Essenes perished in the internecine strife of the revolt and in the war with the Romans, and while the aristocracy of scribes and elders in Jerusalem was discredited and decimated, the Pharisees survived the war better than any other single group. They were well accepted locally, had long ago accommodated to some marginality, and survived with their personnel and their traditions comparatively intact.

Rabbinic literature itself personifies the survival of the movement in a story concerning Rabbi Yochanan ben Zakkai. According to the story, Yochanan had himself been borne out of Jerusalem on the pretense he was dead, only to hail Vespasian as king; when he really did ascend to power, Vespasian granted Yochanan his wish of settlement in the town of Yavneh, the group of Rabbi Gamaliel, and medical attention for Rabbi Zadok (cf. *b. Gittin* 56a, b). In that Josephus claims similarly to have flattered Vespasian (*War* 2.399–408), and to have seen in his coming the fulfilment of messianic prophecy (*War* 6.310–315), the tale is obviously to be used with caution, but it remains expressive of the rabbinic ethos.

With the foundation of academies such as the one at Yavneh after AD 70, we may speak of the transition of Pharisaism to Rabbinic Judaism. The rabbis, those who directly contributed to rabbinic literature and to the Judaism which is framed by that literature, belonged to a movement much changed from the popular puritanism of the Pharisees, initially for reasons not of their own making. The sort of leadership which a Yochanan ben Zakkai might offer became suddenly attractive, in the absence of priestly, Essene, or scribal alternatives. The target of the tradition's application became correspondingly wider, as the pharisaic/rabbinic programme was applied, not simply to issues of purity and sacrifice, but to worship generally, ethics, and daily living. To Yochanan is explicitly attributed the view that the world, which had been sustained by the law, the temple, and deeds of faithful love, now was to be supported only by the last two of the three (*Aboth R. Nat.* 4). Moreover, he specifically adjudicated, on the basis of his tradition and scripture, how feasts might be kept in the gathering for reading, prayer, and discussion which was called a 'congregation' or 'synagogue' (*kenesset*, also applied to buildings erected for the purpose of such gatherings; cf. *m. Sukk.* 3:12; *m. Rosh Hash.* 4:1, 3, 4). The development of that sort of worship, as a replacement for activity within the temple, was not without analogy during the period prior to AD 70. Mishnah (*m. Ta'an.* 4:2) envisages a system in which Priests, Levites, and lay people alike gathered in local synagogues while their representatives were in Jerusalem. The priestly system of 'courses' of service was perhaps the germ of such piety: it allowed for a substantial population of priests, which it divided into twenty-four courses. While a few priests from each group were chosen to officiate in Jerusalem during the course of the week which the group was appointed to cover, the remainder may have gathered and read the appropriate lections in the villages of Judaea and Galilee where they normally lived (1 Chron. 24:1–19; Josephus, *Ant.* 7.365). The inclusion of the faithful in Israel generally in such meetings was a natural development under the rabbis, and general meetings for prayer and instruction had long been a customary feature of Judaism in the Diaspora. The development of worship in synagogues as something of a replacement for worship in the temple was therefore natural, although dramatic.

The transition from Pharisaism to Rabbinic Judaism, however, was not accomplished immediately after AD 70, nor was it only a matter of the same movement with the same personnel carrying on in a totally new environment. The environment *was* new, of course, and favored the emerging authority of rabbis uniquely. But the Pharisees of the period before 70 also were sufficiently flexible to accommodate an influx of priests and scribes into their ranks. The priestly interest of the Pharisaic movement, of course, was historic and organic, and the references to priests in stories and teachings from the time of Yochanan (cf. Rabbi Yosi the Priest, *m. Aboth* 2:8) and well into the second century is striking. Moreover, the consolidation of the rabbis' power after AD 70, predicated as it was on local influence, could only be assured by means of the control of local adjudication, as well as worship and study. The tendency of scribes to align themselves with the Pharisees, together with priestly adherents and sympathizers with the movement, assured the emergence and the success of the rabbis. At the same time, the triumph of rabbinic authority assured the continuing influence of the priests in decisions regarding purity, in blessings, and in receipts of payment of redemption and of tithe, while scribal influence, in the production of written materials and the convocation of formal courts, is also striking. Nonetheless, the functional consolidation of the power of the old groups and factions was only achieved during the time of Rabbi Judah during the second century, with the emergence of a patriarchate recognized and supported by the Romans.

In the wake of AD 70 and the Roman confiscation of the tax formerly paid for the temple, neither Jerusalem nor its environs were amenable to the maintenance of a hub of the movement, and even Yavneh was eclipsed during the second century by centers in prosperous Galilee, such as Usha and Beth She'arim. Later, metropolitan cities such as Sepphoris and Tiberias were the foci of leadership. There was at first nothing like a central leadership, or even a common policy, but Rabbinic Judaism was constituted in the Pharisaic, priestly, and scribal quest for the purity of the nation. The health of the movement required a shift from the highly personal authority of the Pharisees to some notion of learned consensus. Just that shift is reflected in a Talmudic story concerning a great teacher, Rabbi Eliezer ben Hyrcanus. The story has it that, against a majority of his colleagues, Eliezer held that a ceramic stove, once polluted, might be reassembled, provided the tiles were separated by sand. The majority taught that the result would be unclean; such materials should never be used again. Eliezer's correctness was demonstrated by a tree which was uprooted at his behest, by a stream which ran backwards at his command, by a building he similarly demolished, and by a voice from heaven. Despite all that, the majority held that its decision was binding (*b. B. Meṣ.* 59a, b). As the rudiments of an institution emerged, Eliezer's personal authority clearly diminished; the rabbis of the second century were to stress a rational, consensual achievement of purity, and by the time of the Talmud that was held to be a greater purity than charismatic authority could achieve.

The historic concern for the temple as the actual focus of purity nonetheless resulted in a final, and nearly disastrous, attempt – encouraged by some rabbis – to free and restore the holy site. The most prominent rabbinic supporter of that attempt was a student of Eliezer's

renowned for his expertise in the tradition, Aqiba. Aqiba supported the claims of one Simon bar Kosiba to be the new prince of Israel, acting in conjunction with a Priest named Eleazar. Simon's supporters referred to him as Bar Kokhba, 'son of a star,' projecting onto him the messianic expectations of Numbers 24:17, while his detractors came to know him as Bar Koziba, 'son of a lie.' His initial success and military acumen are attested in letters he sent to his commanders during his revolt and regime, which lasted from AD 132 until 135. In the shape of Hadrian, the response of the empire was even more definitive than it had been in AD 70. The remnants of the temple were taken apart, and new shrines – idols according to the principles of Judaism – were built in the city; Jerusalem itself was now called Aelia Capitolina, Jews were denied entry, and Judaea became Syria Palaestina.

The rabbis survived by disowning the aspirations embodied by Aqiba, but keeping much of his teaching. 'Aqiba, grass will grow out of your jaw, before the son of David comes' (*y. Ta'an.* 4:7; *Lamentations Rabbah* 2.2.4); that is to say, the Messiah is to be of David, not of humanity's choosing, and his time cannot be pressed. But the greatness of the rabbinic response to national defeat, and their consequent redefinition of Judaism consisted less in their formulation of a particular teaching regarding messianism (which emerges in any case from time to time in many forms of Judaism) than in their textual constitution of a form of thought, discipline, and life, the Mishnah.

Rabbis such as Aqiba had taught their own norms, which came to be known as *halakhoth* (from *halakhah*, 'way'), and had their disciples learn them by heart. A disciple (*talmid*) might himself internalize what he learned, his teacher's *mishnah* ('repetition'), and proceed to promulgate both it and his own *halakhoth*. But after the failure of Bar Kokhba, the rabbis engaged in an extraordinary, synthetic effort, under Rabbi Judah ha-Nasi (or, 'the Prince,' albeit in stark contrast to Bar Kokhba's aspirations), to combine the *mishnayoth* commonly held to be worthy.

Certain features of the work are both striking and of paradigmatic importance for Rabbinic Judaism. First and foremost, the Mishnah represents earlier traditions pressed into a dialectical relationship; argument exists in an eternal present between positions which previously had been separated by time and/or geography. Precisely that invitation to dialectical reasoning concerning purity, unconstrained by history or chronology, is the principal contribution of Mishnah. Then, however, it must be said that the often uneven synthesis is presented in a definite plan of tractates, which typically address the topic of their title, arranged within orders (*sedarim*). Each order presupposes the agricultural activity the rabbis came to see as normal and normative for Israel. As rabbis, they implied, we speak of the purity we may achieve for a temple which should always have been, but we do so in the knowledge that the Israel we address and which supports us is more a collection of farms than a nation. Paradoxically, however, Rabbi Judah's move from Beth She'arim to Sepphoris signaled the emergence of rabbinic authority within cities, and in close association with Roman power. In reading the Mishnah, anachronism must be taken into account at several levels.

The radical centralization accomplished under Rabbi Judah ranks with Ezra's reform among formative events in the history of Judaism. But where Ezra's programme was located in a particular city (which could only be Jerusalem), Judah's was headquartered in one or another (whether Beth She'arim or Sepphoris), but located in the mind. The Mishnah which emerged was a pattern of reflection which enabled any rabbi anywhere to join in the reflection and the discipline of keeping or making Israel pure. Sanctity in that sense could become the project of the learned in any place. The emergence of Mishnah, of course, called into question its status as compared to scripture, and the revolt under Bar Kokhba radically raised the issue of the status of those works which had promised the speedy rebuilding of the temple after AD 70 (cf. 2 Esdras and the Targum of Isaiah). The priestly canon, represented (although oddly counted) by Josephus (*Against Apion* 1 § 39), had already called for the recognition of twenty-four books, and the rabbis could both invoke the support of that group and control messianic yearnings by insisting that those who read books 'outside' that canon would have no part in the world to come (*m. Sanh.* 10:1). Nonetheless, the issue of messianism was more accidental than systemic: it needed to be addressed by the rabbis, and it was definitively addressed, but the crucial matter was the relationship between scripture and Mishnah. That relationship required several centuries to resolve.

Midrash may be said to be a category of thought and literature which seeks the resolution of scripture with the teaching of the rabbis. It is true – as is frequently reported – that the noun derives from the verb *darash*, which means to 'inquire,' but that fact is largely beside the point. Formally, any midrash will cite the scriptural locus under consideration, somewhat in the manner of the *pesherim* of Qumran, but typically exegesis is not the point of the exercise. Rather, the citation becomes an occasion to invoke the rabbinic teaching which may be associated with scripture at that juncture. The relative autonomy of that teaching from any text is usually apparent in what are called the Tannaitic or halakhic midrashim. 'Tannaitic' refers to the Tannaim ('repeaters' the rabbis of the Mishnaic period, although the ascription is traditional), while 'Halakhic' refers to the substance of their teaching. Such documents include two midrashim on Exodus, each called the *Mekhilta* (which means 'measure'); one is ascribed to R. Ishmael and another to R. Simeon ben Yochai, both of whom lived during the second century. Leviticus receives similar treatment in *Sifra*, and Numbers and Deuteronomy in *Sifre*.

The influence of R. Ishmael is apparent in the attribution to him (as to Hillel earlier) of 'rules' (*middoth*) of interpretation. The rules by no means govern what rabbis may teach, but they do represent the evolving grammar of the association of that teaching with scripture. Formally, the *middoth* set out the patterns of similarity, analogy, and logical categorization which might permit scriptural patterns to be adduced in support of a given teaching or assertion. Their application may be observed within rabbinic discussion, but they are more in the nature of a description of the sort of inference involved in interpretation than they are the programme by which that association was effected. The clear impression conveyed by *Mekhilta* (in both traditions), *Sifra*, and *Sifre* is that the biblical text is an occasion for the exposition of fundamentally rabbinic ideas and modes of thought.

Despite the triumph of Rabbi Judah's experiment, the third century saw a crisis in the understanding of what might be done with Mishnah. The crisis is visible in two dilemmas. The first dilemma concerned scripture, as discussed above. The second was even more basic, in that it involved how the discussion occasioned by Mishnah was to be handled. If the former question turned on the issue of the rabbis' authority in respect of the past, as embodied in the canon, the latter question turned on the issue of their authority in respect of that of their successors. Mishnah undertook a dialectic of eternal purity, but how was that dialectic, once it was consigned to writing, to be related to rabbinic discussion in the present? Both dilemmas receive a tentative treatment in the Tosefta. The term means 'addition,' in that the corpus was seen as an addendum to the Mishnah in later centuries. In fact, however, the Tosefta is to some extent a fresh Mishnah, which incorporates the work of later rabbis, and brings their views into a pattern of discussion with those of the Tannaim. Nonetheless, the Tosefta is essentially conservative, in its reliance upon the materials of Mishnah, and it does not promulgate the radical notion – adumbrated in *Aboth*, a tractate appended to the Mishnah around AD 250 – that, alongside the Torah written in scripture, Moses received an oral Torah, which was passed on through the prophets and sages, and finally to the rabbis. Tosefta represents a greater comprehensiveness in its supplementation of the Mishnah, but it points to the necessity of the daring it lacks, to elevate rabbis not merely by including their teaching, but also by permitting them to engage directly in dialogue with their illustrious predecessors in scripture and memory.

The relative comprehensiveness of the Tosefta did not assure its triumph. Mishnah was not superseded by it, nor by any subsequent work within the rabbinic tradition. Moreover, the rabbis implicitly and formally accorded scripture privilege, in that the capacity to cite a text in order to demonstrate or illustrate a point was acknowledged. The problem of how to address the present with the eternal truth of the tradition (and vice versa) was met by means of an innovation. The rabbis, as expositors (Amoraim, as distinct from Tannaim), undertook to treat Mishnah as scripture, that is, to generate a commentary on Mishnah, which became known as Talmud (a noun which means 'learning'). The 'commentary' (as in the case of midrash) is more a matter of using text as an occasion on which to associate teaching than it is an exposition or exegesis, but the Amoraim triumphantly accomplished what the rabbis of the Tosefta did not: Mishnah was preserved, and at the same time its generative activity and logic were perpetuated in the present. The ideological advance which allowed that accomplishment was the doctrine that Torah was known orally, not only in writing.

The Talmud of Jerusalem (c. 400), or the Yerushalmi, was the last, great product of Rabbinic Judaism in Palestine (as it came to be called in the Roman period). Sociologically, it was difficult to maintain the sort of discipline of purity the rabbis practiced, and wished others to practice, in a territory recently vanquished by the Romans. The Hadrianic prohibition of circumcision may or may not have been a great impediment (depending upon time and place within the history of the Empire), but the incursion of Roman institutions and culture, even at a local level, was a reality from the second century in a way it was not earlier. Toward the end of the period of the Palestinian Amoraim, the very patriarchate which had sealed the victory of the rabbis, in the redaction of Mishnah, appears to have been more aligned with the local aristocracy. Progressive urbanization was not congenial to the maintenance of rabbinic power in Palestine. Moreover, Babylonia during the third century saw the rise of the Sassanids and their form of Zoroastrianism, whose policy toward the practice of Judaism was relatively tolerant. The economic life of the Jews in Babylon, in largely autonomous towns and villages, supported by agriculture, was better suited to the rabbinic ethos than the increasing syncretism of the Roman Empire from the second century. Particularly, the Sassanids encouraged or tolerated (in varying degrees over time) the formation of the academies which were the dynamos of rabbinic discussion, in places such as Sura, Pumbeditha, and Nehardea.

The rabbis of Babylon gave Judaism its distinctive character, at least until the modern period, which was and is conveyed in their monument (probably completed during the sixth century), the Babylonian Talmud, or the Babli. It is a more comprehensive and subtle treatment of the Mishnah than the Yerushalmi, often employing rich, narrative means which permit the contemporization of the rabbinic ethos. Each rabbi is here to some extent a Moses of his own, as when Moses himself is said to visit the academy of Aqiba, and to observe to God that the discussion is so complex, his

own unworthiness is obvious (b. Menaḥ. 29b). But the rabbis are also respectful tradents, as when Rab Joseph of Pumbeditha, the blind master, acknowledges that, without the Targum, he would not understand scripture (b. Sanh. 94b). Their knowledge and expertise is functionally infinite: a rabbi can be consulted regarding the vision of God's chariot, how to make love, or to relieve constipation. Although the Talmud (and Babli, for practical purposes, is the Talmud) is vast, its very range is a succinct statement of its intent to transform the whole of life with the light of the Torah as interpreted by the rabbis.

Their energy and their resources enabled the rabbis of Babylon to see to the completion of the standard recension of the Targumim (Aramaic paraphrases of the Bible), and to the publication of as definitive a form of the midrash as was ever produced. Midrash Rabbah presents not only the biblical books used for festal and commemorative occasions (Esther, Ruth, Song of Songs, Ecclesiastes, Lamentations), but also the Pentateuch. The confidence of the rabbis of Babylonia in their own ethos was so great that the 'comment' upon scripture might include explicit narrative concerning rabbis, as well as exposition and discourse. Midrash Rabbah was likely completed during the eighth century, and it represents the confidence that Torah, whether in scripture or Talmud, is fundamentally one. The interweaving of scripture and rabbinic teaching is also represented in the homiletic midrashim of a later period, the Pesiqta Rabbati, the Pesiqta de-Rab Kahana, and Tanḥuma.

The rabbinic period closes with the rise of Islam, and the subsequent reaction of the Geonim, the successors of the rabbis who maintained and extended rabbinic Judaism with a distinctively academic and sometimes rationalistic bent. Increasingly, their work is of a literary nature, and takes the rabbinic canon as a fact to be acknowledged, rather than achieved; moreover, a tendency toward philosophy and esoterism becomes manifest. The Sefer Yeṣirah, or 'book of formation,' is a good representative of a work which is transitional between the Amoraim and the Geonim, and was perhaps composed during the seventh century. It builds upon a mystical tradition which reaches back at least until Yohanan ben Zakkai, according to which it is possible to see the chariot (the 'Merkabah') of Ezekiel 1, and to know the structure of the Creation. But where the rabbis held that such experiments were a matter for private exposition (and then under tight controls, cf. b. Shab. 80b; b. Ḥag. 11b, 13a, 14b), the Sefer Yeṣirah commences a tradition of literary and rational esoterism, which is more typical of the Kabbalah of the Middle Ages than of the Judaism of the rabbis. The dialectic of the rabbis was rooted in the oral argument which produced their literature, and which their literature was designed to serve; when the logic of literary discourse takes over, the constitution of the Judaism which is reflected is no longer, strictly speaking, rabbinic.

References and further reading

Boyarin, Daniel (1990) *Intertextuality and the Reading of Midrash*, Bloomington: Indiana University Press.

Braude, William G. (1968) *Pesikta Rabbati: Discourses for Feasts, Fasts, and Special Sabbaths*, New Haven: Yale University Press.

—— and Israel J. Epstein (1975) *Pesikta de-Rab Kahana: R. Kahana's Compilation of Discourses for Sabbaths and Special Days*, Philadelphia: Jewish Publication Society.

Brewer, David Instone (1992) *Techniques and Assumptions in Jewish Exegesis before 70 CE*, Texte und Studien zum Antiken Judentum 30, Tübingen: Mohr Siebeck.

Carson, D.A. and H.G.M. Williamson (eds.) (1988) *It is Written: Scripture Citing Scripture, Essays in Honour of Barnabas Lindars*, Cambridge: Cambridge University Press.

Chilton, Bruce (1984) *A Galilean Rabbi and His Bible: Jesus' Use of the Interpreted Scripture of His Time*, Wilmington: Glazier (also published with the subtitle, *Jesus' own Interpretation of Isaiah*, London: SPCK).

—— *The Isaiah Targum. Introduction, Translation, Apparatus, and Notes*, The Aramaic Bible 11, Wilmington: Glazier/Edinburgh: T.&T. Clark.

—— 'Targums,' pp. 880–4 in *Dictionary of Jesus and the Gospels*, J.B. Green and S. McKnight (eds.), Downers Grover: IVP.

Epstein, Isidore (ed.) (1936–1948) *The Babylonian Talmud . . . Translated with Notes, Glossary, and Indices*, London: Soncino.

Fitzmyer, Joseph A. (1974) 'The Bar Cochba Period,' pp. 305–54 in *Essays on the Semitic Background of the New Testament*, Sources for Biblical Study 5, Missoula: Scholars Press.

Freedman, H. and Maurice Simon (1983) *Midrash Rabbah, translated into English with Notes, Glossary and Indices*, London: Soncino.

Goldin, Judah (1974) *The Fathers according to Rabbi Nathan*, New York: Schocken.

Lauterbach, Jacob Zallel (1976) *Mekilta de-Rabbi Ishmael*, Philadelphia: Jewish Publication Society.

Levine, Lee I. (1989) *The Rabbinic Class of Roman Palestine in Late Antiquity*, New York: The Jewish Theological Seminary.

Neusner, Jacob N. (1973) *The Pharisees: Rabbinic Perspectives*, Hoboken: Ktav.

—— (1982–) *Talmud of the Land of Israel*, Chicago: University of Chicago Press.

—— (1985a) *The Peripatetic Saying: The Problem of the Thrice-Told Tale in Talmudic Literature*, Brown Judaic Studies 89, Chico: Scholars Press.

—— (1985b) *Torah: From Scroll to Symbol in Formative Judaism*, The Foundations of Judaism, Philadelphia: Fortress Press.

—— (1988a) *The Mishnah: A New Translation*, New Haven: Yale University Press.

—— (1988b) *Sifre: An Analytic Translation*, Brown Judaic Studies 138, Atlanta: Scholars Press.

Schürer, Emil (1973–1987) *A History of the Jewish People in the Age of Jesus Christ*, G. Vermes, F. Millar, *et al.* (eds.), Edinburgh: T.&T. Clark.

BRUCE D. CHILTON

RABBINIC RULES OF INTERPRETATION

Rabbinic tradition holds that biblical interpretation was pursued by following seven rules (or 'measurements,' *middoth*) promulgated by Hillel the Elder (*c.* 50 BC–AD 10; cf. *t. Sanh.* 7.11; *'Abot R. Nat.* [A] 37.10). That attribution is considered suspect; yet according to *Sifre Deut.* §2 (on 1:3) even Moses is said to have taught several of these rules. The seven are as follows:

(1) *Qal wa-homer* (lit. 'light and heavy'). According to this rule, what is true or applicable in a 'light' (or less important) instance is surely true or applicable in a 'heavy' (or more important) instance. Such a principle is at work when Jesus assures his disciples (cf. Matt. 6:26 = Luke 12:24) that because God cares for the birds, as taught in scripture (cf. Ps. 147:9; *Pss. Sol.* 5:8–19), they can be sure that he cares for them. A similar saying is attributed to Rabbi Simeon ben Eleazar: 'Have you ever seen a wild animal or a bird who has a trade?' (*m. Qid.* 4:14).

(2) *Gezera shawa* (lit. 'an equivalent regulation'). According to this rule one passage may be explained by another, if similar words or phrases are present. When Jesus took action in the temple precincts, he quoted phrases from Isaiah 56:7 and Jeremiah 7:11: 'Is it not written that: my house shall be called a house of prayer for all the Gentiles? But you have made it a thugs' lair' (Mark 11:17). What has drawn these two passages together is the word, 'house,' which appears in the quotation drawn from Isaiah 56:7 and also appears in the part of Jeremiah 7:11 not quoted. Jeremiah 7 qualifies the sense of Isaiah 56. Examples of *gezera shawa* are common among the rabbis. Because 'its appointed time' is used of the daily sacrifice (Num. 28:2) and of Passover (Num. 9:2), one may infer that what applies to the one applies to the other (*b. Pesah.* 66a). This rule was applied to haggadic interpretation. Several of the comparisons between Moses and Elijah delineated in *Pesiq. R.* 4.2 are based on the principle. For example, the appearance of the verb 'send' in Exodus 3:10 ('I will send you to Pharaoh') and Malachi 3:23 ('I will send you Elijah') legitimates comparison between these two great prophets. Both are called 'man of God' in Deuteronomy 33:1 and 1 Kings 17:18. Both were taken up to heaven, as implied by the use of the verb 'to go up' in Exodus 19:3 and 2 Kings 2:1.

(3) *Binyan 'ab mikkatub 'ehad* (lit. 'constructing a father [i.e., principal rule] from one passage'). According to this *middah* a general principle may be established from one verse or phrase. Other verses, which contain this key phrase, can be viewed as belonging to a family.

Since God is not the God of the dead, but of the living, the revelation at the Burning Bush, 'I am the God of Abraham' (Exod. 3:14–15), implies that Abraham is alive. From this one text one may further infer, as Jesus did (Mark 12:26; Matt. 22:31; Luke 20:37), the truth of the general resurrection. Similarly, the rabbis taught that people who are to be put to death for the various offenses described in Leviticus 20:10–21 should be stoned, because the phrase 'their blood be upon them' that appears in these verses (vv. 11, 13, 16) also appears in a verse (v. 27) that describes an offense for which stoning is specifically commanded (*Sifra Lev.* §209 [on 20:13–16]). From Deuteronomy 19:15 ('by the mouth of two witnesses or by the mouth of three witnesses shall a matter be confirmed') Rabbi Simeon ben Shetach concluded that 'Whenever the Mosaic law speaks of a "witness" it refers to two unless it specifies one' (*b. Mak.* 5b).

(4)   *Binyan 'ab mishene kethubim* (lit. 'constructing a father [i.e., principal rule] from two writings'). This *middah* functions as the one above, except that it constructs its general principle from two passages. When Paul argues that as an apostle of Christ he deserves his food (1 Cor. 9:1–14), he appeals to the general principle that the treading ox must be allowed to eat of the grain (Deut. 25:4) and to scripture's specific command that the priests receive a share of the burnt offering (Deut. 18:1–8). For a rabbinic example of this rule of interpretation, see *Mek.* on Exodus 21:26–27 (*Neziqin* §9), where on the basis of the two commands to compensate a slave for having lost either an eye or a tooth, one may infer that for any irreplaceable loss a slave must be set free.

(5)   *Kelal uperat uperat ukelal –* (lit. 'general and particular, and particular and general'). This *middah* is based on the assumption that general principles can be inferred from specific statements in scripture, or that specific principles can be inferred from general statements. When Jesus replied that the greatest commandment is to love the Lord with all one's heart (Deut. 6:4–5) and to love one's neighbor as one's self (Lev. 19:18), he summed up in one 'general' commandment all the 'particular' commandments (Mark 12:28–34; Matt. 22:34–40). Commenting on Leviticus 19:18, Aqiba is reported to have said: 'That is the greatest principle in the Law' (*Sifra Lev.* §200 [on 19:15–19]).

(6)   *Kayyoṣe bo bemaqom 'aḥer* (lit. 'to which something [is] similar in another place'). This *middah* is similar to the principle of *gezera shawa*, excepting that whereas the latter is limited to a common word or phrase, the former takes into account similar ideas or events, as well as common vocabulary. The principle is well illustrated in a Tannaitic discussion of the dividing of the sea. According to Rabbi Shemaiah: 'The faith with which their father Abraham believed in me is reason enough that I should divide the sea for them, as it is written: "And he believed in the Lord" [Gen. 15:6].'

To this Rabbi Abtalyon adds: 'The faith with which they believed in me is reason enough that I should divide the sea for them, as it is written: "And the people believed" [Exod. 4:31]' (*Mek.* on Exod. 14:15 [*Beshallaḥ* §4]; cf. *Exod. Rab.* 23.5 [on 15:1]). Comparison with Galatians 3:6–9 is straightforward.

(7)   *Dabar halamed me'inyano* (lit. 'a word of instruction from its context [or subject]'). According to this *middah* the meaning of a given passage may be clarified from its context. Rabbi Aqiba explained it accordingly: 'Every Scripture passage which is close to another must be interpreted with respect to it' (*Sifre Deut.* §131 [on 16:4]).

The *middoth* are essentially a compilation of the logical processes which had long been involved in the systematic correlation between scripture and tradition among the rabbis. How could the written text be held to support and embody the oral teaching? Once the theology of the single Torah was operative (even before it was fully articulated), the relationship between text and tradition was obviously crucial. The *middoth* distill logical operations by which that relationship was worked out.

The formulation of the *middoth* comport well with their purpose. If scripture is Torah, then there must be coherent principles which may be inferred from one passage and applied to another. Small matters may illuminate weighty ones (the first *middah*); commensurate wordings imply commensurate meanings (the second *middah*); one or two passages may enunciate a systemic truth (the third and fourth *middoth*); the general and the particular are coordinate statements (the fifth *middah*); similarity between passages implies an identity of topic (the sixth *middah*); proximity between passages implies a shared context of meaning (the seventh *middah*). Such logical operations of inference and synthesis permit what is written and what is taught together to embody the single Torah, given to Moses and eternal in heaven.

The *middoth* find their natural center and purpose within Rabbinic Judaism The logical operations which they relate alone certainly could not have produced the varieties of midrash which are extant, nor would they have resulted in the coherent focus on the single Torah which is characteristic of Rabbinic Judaism. Both the variety and the coherence of the sources is explicable when it is appreciated that the *middoth* are a means to an end. The end is the synthesis of the teachings of the rabbinic sages with the Hebrew Bible: the systemic relation between the two is the axiom and the product of rabbinic interpretation.

References and further reading

Chilton, B.D. and C.A. Evans (1994) 'Jesus and Israel's Scriptures,' pp. 281–335 in *Studying the Historical Jesus: Evaluations of the State of Current Research*, B.D.

Chilton and C.A. Evans (eds.), *NTTS* 19, Leiden: Brill.

Doeve, J. (1954) *Jewish Hermeneutics in the Synoptic Gospels and Acts*, Assen: Van Gorcum.

Ellis, E.E. (1988) 'Biblical Interpretation in the New Testament Church,' pp. 691–725 in *Mikra: Text, Translation, Reading and Interpretation of the Hebrew Bible in Ancient Judaism and Early Christianity*, CRINT 2.1, M.J. Mulder (ed.), Philadelphia: Fortress Press.

Evans, Craig (2004) 'The Old Testament in the New,' pp. 130–45 in *The Face of New Testament Studies: A Survey of Recent Research*, Scot McKnight and Grant R. Osborne (eds.), Grand Rapids: Baker.

Finkel, A. (1964) *The Pharisees and the Teacher of Nazareth: A Study of Their Background, Their Halachic and Midrashic Teachings, the Similarities and Differences*, AGJU 4, Leiden: Brill.

Kasher, R. (1988) 'The Interpretation of Scripture in Rabbinic Literature,' pp. 547–94 in *Mikra: Text, Translation, Reading and Interpretation of the Hebrew Bible in Ancient Judaism and Early Christianity*, CRINT 2.1, M.J. Mulder (ed.), Philadelphia: Fortress Press.

Neusner, J. (1992) *The Foundations of the Theology of Judaism, An Anthology*, Part II: *TORAH*, SFSHJ 44, Atlanta: Scholars Press.

Zeitlin, S. (1963–1964) 'Hillel and the Hermeneutical Rules,' *Jewish Quarterly Review* 54: 161–73.

BRUCE D. CHILTON

RAD, GERHARD VON (1901–1971)

Born in Nuremburg, Germany, on October 21, 1901. He studied theology at Erlangen and Tübingen. He completed his doctorate at Erlangen in 1928 and then was a tutor there from 1929 to 1930. He finished his Habilitation at Leipzig under A. Alt in 1930 and then worked as *Dozent* and *ausserordentlicher* professor from 1930 to 1934. He was appointed a full professor of Old Testament at Jena in 1934. As a Franconian-Bavarian Lutheran, he struggled to defend the Old Testament during the rise of National Socialism and served the Confessing Church by traveling extensively to lecture and preach. Following military conscription, during which he was an American prisoner of war, he returned to academia as professor at Göttingen in 1945. In 1949, he was appointed professor at Heidelberg, retiring as professor emeritus in 1967. He died October 31, 1971 in Heidelberg.

Von Rad is one of the most influential Old Testament scholars of the twentieth century. His genius was to combine a thoroughgoing tradition-historical approach with a theological analysis of the Old Testament based on a salvation history (*Heilsgeschichte*) perspective. The culmination of this approach was expressed in his two-volume theology of the Old Testament published in the latter part of his career. This approach was an effort to preserve history as the interpretative control for any Old Testament theological analysis, thereby following the work of A. Alt and M. Noth. His approach was a counter to the rising biblical theology found in W. Eichrodt and others which used a theological theme as the interpretative center for an Old Testament theology.

The key feature of his Old Testament theology was a concentration on the historical development of Israel's history and the message each chronological stage or the various cultic institutions or traditions propounded. His Old Testament theology was an attempt to posit successive historical traditions as they grew and developed showing how each generation appropriated and developed previous tradition to their own new context. For von Rad, given the historical development of the Old Testament traditions, it was inappropriate to conceive a theological core as the key to the Old Testament's message or even to survey the Old Testament content according to theological themes. The Old Testament was composed of many different theologies related to the historical layers and the specific situation of each redactor. What von Rad's analysis led him to conclude theologically was that the primary witness of each historical redactor or tradition was to the mighty acts of God in history, salvation history. Using critical interpretative methods, von Rad reconstructed the historical traditions and their development which lie behind the canonical text and he explicated the witness of each tradition to *Heilsgeschichte*.

However, his influence was significant before he wrote his Old Testament theology. Through his pioneering application of redaction criticism alongside form criticism, he layered the historical traditions of the Pentateuch (or the Hexateuch as he preferred, adding the settlement texts as the sixth book). He proposed that the Deuteronomic tradition began with a small historical credo, such as Deuteronomy 26:5b–9; 6:20–24; or Joshua 24:2b–13. These creeds were composed of three historical events: (a) the promise to the patriarchs; (b) the Exodus from Egypt; and (c) the settlement in the Promised Land. The absence of the Sinai tradition suggested to him that this was a wholly separate and independent second tradition. Von Rad located these two traditions in a cultic context that was both ritualistic and institutional. The early Deuteronomic creedal tradition was actualized in the annual Festival of Weeks originally located at the Gilgal shrine. The Sinai tradition was commemorated in the autumn Feast of Booths (Succoth) originally placed in Shechem. As these traditions were loosed from their cultic milieu and imbibed in new contexts through retelling and adaptation, they were eventually combined, written down, and prefaced with the primeval history of Genesis 1–11 by the Yahwist. Eventually they found their final form through the redaction of various literary and cultic traditions which continued to retell and appropriate these historical 'confessions.' Through this tradition-history process, von Rad identified the Pentateuch (Hexateuch) as 'salvation history' in which historical events and religious faith blended into one.

His tradition-history criticism and his salvation-history perspective also posited a reevaluation of the prophetic tradition as more than a reappropriation of the Pentateuch Creed, but as an entirely new set of elective demands upon Israel which stemmed from their failure to keep the law. Later, von Rad came to interpret the wisdom literature, and his study of this tradition took a new turn, abandoning the kind of historicism he had employed for the law and prophets, resulting in the surprising book, *Wisdom in Israel.*

Part of von Rad's influence stems from his authoritative and charismatic style as well as his scholarly erudition. Von Rad set the agenda and dominated Old Testament studies in the twentieth century. However, as to be expected, many of his specific historical conclusions were critiqued, challenged, and supplanted by other historical theories. Toward the end of the twentieth century, Old Testament studies moved on from the kind of historicism he practiced and a new agenda emerged.

References and further reading

Bray, G. (1996) *Biblical Interpretation Past and Present,* Leicester: Apollos.

Crenshaw, J.L. (1978) *Gerhard von Rad,* Makers of Modern Theology, Waco: Word.

Goldingay, J. (1981) *Approaches to Old Testament Interpretation,* Issues in Contemporary Theology, Downers Grove: IVP.

Hayes, J.H. and F.C. Prussner (1985) *Old Testament Theology: Its History and Development,* Atlanta: John Knox.

Knight, D.A. and G.M. Tucker (eds.) (1985) *The Hebrew Bible & Its Modern Interpreters,* The Bible and Its Modern Interpreters, 1, Philadelphia: Fortress Press/ Decatur: Scholars Press.

McKim, D.K. (ed.) (1998) *Historical Handbook of Major Biblical Interpreters,* Downers Grove: IVP.

Rad, Gerhard von (1929) *Das Gottesvolk im Deuteronomium,* BWANT 47, Stuttgart: W. Kohlhammer.

—— (1930) *Das Geschichtsbild des chronistischen Werkes,* BWANT 54, Stuttgart: W. Kohlhammer.

—— (1934) *Die Priesterschrift im Hexateuch,* BWANT 65, Stuttgart: W. Kohlhammer.

—— (1938) *Das formgeschichtliche Problem des Hexateuch,* BWANT 78, Stuttgart: W. Kohlhammer (ET *The Problem of the Hexateuch and Other Essays,* New York: McGraw-Hill, 1966).

—— (1947) *Deuteronomium-Studien,* BRLANT 58, Göttingen: Vandenhoeck & Ruprecht (ET *Studies in Deuteronomy,* SBT 9, London: SCM Press, 1953).

—— (1951) *Der heilige Krieg im alten Israel,* Zürich: Zwingli-Verlag (ET *Holy War in Ancient Israel,* Grand Rapids: Eerdmans, 1991).

—— (1952–1953) *Das erste Buch Mose: Genesis,* ATD 2–4, Göttingen: Vandenhoeck & Ruprecht (ET *Genesis: A Commentary,* OTL, London: SCM Press, 1972).

—— (1957) *Theologie des Alten Testaments 1,* Munich: Chr. Kaiser (ET *Old Testament Theology,* New York: Harper, 1962).

—— (1960) *Theologie des Alten Testaments 2,* Munich: Chr. Kaiser (ET *Old Testament Theology,* New York: Harper, 1965).

—— (1964) *Das fünfte Buch Mose: Deuteronomium,* ATD 8, Göttingen: Vandenhoeck & Ruprecht (ET *Deuteronomy: A Commentary,* OTL, Philadelphia: Westminster Press, 1966).

—— (1971) *Das Opfer des Abraham,* München: C. Kaiser.

—— (1972) *Weisheit in Israel,* Neukirchen-Vluyn: Neukirchener Verlag (ET *Wisdom in Israel,* Nashville: Abingdon Press, 1972).

Spriggs, D.G. (1974) *Two Old Testament Theologies: A Comparative Evaluation of the Contributions of Eichrodt and von Rad to our Understanding of the Nature of Old Testament Theology,* London: SCM Press.

DENNIS L. STAMPS

RAMSAY, WILLIAM MITCHELL (1851–1939)

Ramsay was born March 15, 1851 in Glasgow, Scotland. He received his formal education at the University of Aberdeen (M.A.), where he majored in Greek and archaeology. During his later studies, at Oxford University, he gained an interest in the study of Paul and the book of Galatians. Ramsay taught classics and archaeology at both Aberdeen and Oxford.

Ramsay was able to combine his education and scholarly pursuits with his love for travel when he was given the opportunity to do archaeological research in Greece, Asia Minor, and Italy. From these experiences, he wrote a number of books concerning the history and geography of Rome and Asia Minor, and how they related to the religious situation of the first two centuries AD. His knowledge of those areas was extensive and formed the background for his work in the New Testament and specifically his thinking concerning the missionary trips of Paul. While tracing Paul's missionary trips he was able to describe in detail the geography, history, and importance of the various cities Paul visited.

During his study of the book of Acts, Ramsay became convinced that Acts was a fine example of recorded history and was trustworthy in every detail from topography to descriptions of society and the political and religious structures of the day. Accordingly, he hailed Luke as a preeminent historian concerned with writing an uncolored recital of important facts without personal feelings and preferences. No attempt was made by the author of Acts at pointing to a moral or a lesson to be learned. Ramsay held that the author of Acts was a historian, not an ethicist, or a theologian.

One of the problems Ramsay encountered in his pursuit of historical accuracy, in the book of Acts, occurred in the harmonizing of the details of Paul's missionary trips with the letter Paul wrote to the Galatians. Under the then accepted Northern Galatians theory, the book of Galatians was written to the ethnic people of Galatia, located in the north, but Ramsay felt that too many incongruities and inconsistencies existed in this theory to present Acts as trustworthy. Ramsay argued three main reasons why the Galatians were Christians living in the southern region. First, Paul's second missionary trip appears to have taken him through the southern region not the northern region. Second, in writing to the Galatians Paul mentions Barnabas who only traveled with Paul on his first trip through the southern region. Finally, the geographical character of the north could not support a large population nor large city centers in which Paul could establish churches. This is confirmed by the lack of any reported churches in the north at that time. By accepting the Southern Galatians theory, the book of Acts could be brought in line with the Epistle to the Galatians. Having resolved the problem of harmonization to his satisfaction, Ramsay became the leading proponent of the Southern Galatians theory and wrote extensively concerning it in his commentary on Galatians.

References and further reading

Ramsay, William M. (1900) *A Historical Commentary on St. Paul's Epistle to the Galatians*, New York: G.P. Putnam's Sons.
—— (1906) *Pauline and Other Studies in Early Christian History*, London: Hodder & Stoughton, 2nd edn.
—— (1908) *Luke the Physician: and Other Studies in the History of Religion*, London: Hodder & Stoughton.
—— (1911) *The Church in the Roman Empire Before A.D. 170*, London: G.P. Putnam's Sons.
—— (1920) *The Bearing of Recent Discoveries on the Trustworthiness of the New Testament*, London: Hodder & Stoughton, 2nd edn.
—— (1966) *St. Paul the Traveller and the Roman Citizen*, Grand Rapids: Baker Book House.

H.C. JORGENSEN

RASHI (1040–1105)

Rashi, an acronym for Rabbi Shlomo ben Yiṣḥaq, is virtually synonymous with Jewish commentary. He wrote commentaries on most – if not all – of the books of the Hebrew Bible. Those few commentaries that have been disputed might have been augmented or rewritten by his students. Rashi's commentary on the Pentateuch is the earliest known Hebrew work to have benefited from the printing press (1475) and his commentary on the Talmud was included in the first printed edition of that work.

Born in Troyes, a major commercial center of the Champagne region of France, Rashi was drawn to the old Rhenish centers of Jewish learning in Mainz and Worms. Around 1065 Rashi returned to Troyes whilst retaining close relations with his teachers. In about 1070 he established his own school which began the eclipse of the Rhenish institutions of his former teachers. Not only did Rashi's school outshine those of his teachers, but his contributions to Talmudic thought also broke the hegemony the Babylonian academies had held over Jewish moral and intellectual life since the formation of the Talmuds. Before Rashi, whenever students of the Talmud encountered difficult and obscure passages, their questions would be referred to the Geonim in Babylonia. Rashi's comprehensive commentary on the Talmud emancipated Jewish scholarship from dependence on the Geonim, whose office began to decline from that time (Heschel 1973: 55).

Rashi's scholarship, biblical and talmudic, was not born of splendid isolation; rather he was a winegrower by trade and the unofficial leader of the Jewish community in Troyes. Perhaps because of his practical business interests Rashi's commentary style is marked by the 'common touch' – straightforward, simple language – even to the point of rendering difficult words or phrases into the French vernacular to aid his readers in understanding a text. Rashi's aim was to help the student of the Bible get at the 'literal' or 'plain meaning' of the text, *peshat* in Hebrew. Rashi was well aware that there were those who thirsted for *derash* – the homiletic exposition of a text – but he professed to resort to *derash* or *aggadah* (rabbinic legend) only when it could serve to explicate the plain sense of the text (Gen. 3:8). There are occasions in his commentaries, however, when it is clear that he could take delight in *aggadah* for its own sake (Gen. 1:26).

Rashi did not cite the sources for his commentaries, but for the most part he worked from the Targums. Rashi's commentary on the Pentateuch was heavily derived from the Targum Onqelos. Such was Rashi's influence that when his version differed from that of Onqelos, subsequent publishers emended the Targum to reflect Rashi's version.

Because of the clarity of his commentaries, Rashi has been called a democratizer of the Bible (Heschel 1973: 56); yet there is some debate on this issue. Some scholars feel that Rashi's straightforward approach, rather than being tailored for the general reader of the Bible, was made with the assumption that his readers were fully acquainted with the relevant details (*Enc. Jud.* 13:1562). In any case, Rashi's commentaries 'have had the most profound influence on Jewish life and letters and it would be difficult to point to any single post-talmudic work which has had such an influence' (Pearl 1988: 91).

References and further reading

Encyclopaedia Judaica (1971) S.v. 'Rashi,' Jerusalem: Keter.

Federbush, Simon (1958) Rashi: His Teachings and Personality, New York: World Jewish Congress.

Heschel, Abraham Joshua (1973) 'The Study of Torah,' pp. 55–61 in Understanding Jewish Theology, Jacob Neusner (ed.), New York: Ktav.

Mielziner, M. (1925) Introduction to the Talmud, New York: Bloch.

Oesterley, W.O.E. (1973) A Short Survey of the Literature of Rabbinical and Mediaeval Judaism, New York: Lenox Hill.

Pearl, Chaim (1988) Rashi, London: Peter Halban.

Shereshevsky, Esra (1982) Rashi: the Man and His World, New York: Sepher-Hermon.

JACK N. LAWSON

READER-ORIENTED APPROACHES

Variously referred to as pragmatic, audience-oriented, reader-response, or (more rarely) rhetorical criticism, reader-oriented approaches focus more critical attention on the identities and roles of readers (or hearers) in the production of literary meaning than have historical, sociological, or (other) literary approaches. Following certain trends within general literary theory over the past three decades, a significant minority of biblical literary critics have moved beyond the formalist (or objectivist) notion that texts are transhistorical, self-evidencing, and autotelic aesthetic objects, and embraced the cogent arguments that (a) literary meaning is produced only when readers read texts and, therefore, that (b) what readers bring to texts and how they process texts must be taken fully into account by the critic. In short, the reader (and all the human variables implied thereby) becomes a prime factor in the interpretive equation.

A convenient means of distinguishing among reader-oriented approaches is to place them along an imaginary spectrum between the poles of text and reader, the criterion for placement being where each approach locates the production of meaning. Wary of descending into subjectivism and relativity, many biblical scholars have followed the lead of early reader critics like W. Booth (1961) who envisioned a 'mock' or 'implied' reader in the text. In such cases a reading role is wholly structured and controlled by the text (which is, in turn, controlled by the author); real readers are invited to accept this role, but have no further input or creative function in the reading process. At the other end of the spectrum are the relatively few biblical critics who have adopted theories by S. Fish (1980: 13–14) and

others who argue that the text is in the reader or the reading community. Readers or reading cultures engender and control meaning; texts as independent voices are muted. A recent logical development of this kind of reader-oriented criticism is the move to auto-biography: the critic is the reader, the reader is the font of meaning, and so one writes one's own story, even if the purported subject matter is a biblical story (Staley 1995).

Perhaps most reader-oriented biblical scholars would locate their approaches somewhere near the middle of the spectrum between text and reader. These critics take their cue from W. Iser, who argues that 'one must take into account not only the actual text, but also and in equal measure, the actions involved in responding to that text' (1972: 279). In the reading process the reader is a full participant with the text, rather than merely another feature of the text. For Iser and his followers, the text is real and constant, but also schematic, full of indeterminacies, blanks, and gaps. In order to produce a literary work (to be distinguished from the text alone), the reader must fill these textual lacunae in the temporal, sequential act of cognition we call reading. 'Actualization' (or 'concretization') occurs only with the convergence of the rhetorical structures of the text and the interpretive capacities (imagination, experience, conventional knowledge) of a reader. The interpretive focus, then, is shifted from text alone, or reader alone, to the act of reading, that is, to the reader reading the text. An aspect of Iser's approach that has attracted biblical critics is its ability to embrace at one and the same time the possibility (indeed, probability) of divergent readings (because the text is schematic) and a means by which one can adjudicate among and delimit valid readings (the text as constant along with a set theory of reading). One thus, it would seem, avoids objective determinism, on the one hand, and sheer relativism, on the other.

In Iser's theoretical approach the critic interprets neither an object nor an agent in isolation, but rather a mental activity, a complex sequence of cognitive acts elicited and guided by an ordered set of stimuli. To interpret is to follow and explicate the delicate dance among reader, text, and extratextual repertoire (the conventional social and literary knowledge expected of readers). Reading activities that reader-oriented biblical interpreters have begun to take into account are: (a) anticipation and retrospection; (b) consistency building; (c) identification and distancing; and (d) defamiliarization. Anticipation and retrospection are complementary, continuing activities. Moving forward through the text, the reader is constantly forming expectations and opinions, and then reassessing and revising them in light of new insights and data. Each new word or sentence establishes expectations about what is to come and also illuminates what has already been read. Consistency building refers to the proclivity of readers 'to fit everything together in a consistent pattern' (Iser 1972: 288). In other words, readers attempt to correlate discrete and schematic textual elements into consistent, meaningful patterns and will seek the most logical and efficient means of doing so. Identification and distancing involve the reader's tendency to form positive or negative opinions of narrators or characters. The reader's ability to perceive new significance when the familiar (conventional norms, values, and traditions) is placed in an unfamiliar context is referred to as defamiliarization.

Reader-oriented biblical criticism is yet in its infancy. Its proponents have been neither theoretically innovative nor particularly agreeable concerning how best to adopt and adapt recent literary theory to ancient biblical texts. It has become common practice to select and apply only discrete elements of various theories with little regard for overall systems or philosophical underpinnings. Somewhat influential has been the derivative but integrated approach of J. Darr (1992: 11–59; 1998: 18–136), who takes as starting points Booth (texts as rhetorical) and Iser (texts as gapped but constant, basic notions about the reading process), but moves beyond them to stress (a) the critic's role in formulating readers as heuristic devices, and (b) the crucial role of extratextual repertoires (the literary, social, and cultural conventions readers bring to the text) in the production of meaning. Darr, followed by K. Darr (1994), R. Tannehill (1994), and others, advocates reconstructing the extratextual repertoires of the authorial (original, intended) audiences of biblical writings. History, a topic much neglected among biblical literary critics, is thus reintroduced as a vital element in interpretation, though not necessarily in a way that traditional historical critics would immediately recognize.

References and further reading

Booth, W. (1961) *The Rhetoric of Fiction*, Chicago: University of Chicago Press.

Darr, J. (1992) *On Character Building: The Reader and the Rhetoric of Characterization in Luke-Acts*, Louisville: Westminster/John Knox Press.

—— (1998) *Herod the Fox: Audience Criticism and Lukan Characterization*, JSNTSup 163, Sheffield: Sheffield Academic Press.

Darr, K. (1994) *Isaiah's Vision and the Family of God*, Louisville: Westminster/John Knox.

Fish, S. (1980) *Is There a Text in this Class? The Authority of Interpretive Communities*, Cambridge: Harvard University Press.

Iser, W. (1972) 'The Reading Process: A Phenomenological Approach,' *New Literary History* 3: 279–99.

Staley, J. (1995) *Reading with a Passion: Rhetoric, Autobiography, and the American West in the Gospel of John*, New York: Continuum.

Tannehill, R. (1994) '"Cornelius" and "Tabitha" Encounter Luke's Jesus,' *Interpretation* 48: 347–56.

JOHN A. DARR

REDACTION CRITICISM

In general usage a 'redactor' is another word for an editor, but in biblical and related studies the word has come to specify one who chooses, arranges, expands, curtails (any or all of these) older written or oral matter in detail or more extensively to express his or her own views and understanding. Redaction criticism is then an endeavor to discern such a process and interpret its results. We may also attempt to discover and evaluate the older sources that the redactor seems to have used, and redaction criticism may help in that quest, but that is not its main aim.

Thus, for example, we may be persuaded that the authors of Matthew and Luke used the written Gospel of Mark as an important resource for their own respective expanded versions of that work; and we may also hold that Mark himself deployed earlier, and likely oral matter (see Source Criticism this volume). We may then note, for example, that where Mark 16:7 has the angel at the tomb recall Jesus' promise to go ahead 'to Galilee' (Mark 14:28), Luke has no such promise, but at 24:6 has two messengers at the tomb recall some other teaching as having been given 'in Galilee.' We then see that Luke has the disciples told to wait in Jerusalem, which is to be the base from which the movement spreads. We may then wonder whether each locality may have a different symbolic significance for these two writers. We may recall that Jerusalem figures early in the Lukan Gospel narrative, as well as at the end, and again frequently in Acts. Perhaps as well as providing narrative unity, this focus helps to place the Christian movement at the heart of the ancient Jewish tradition, and so claim a share in the respect that antiquity accords. On the other hand, it might be that in Mark the insistence on Galilee (short for 'the circuit of the Gentiles') is added to convey a different understanding of outreach to the Gentile world, away from the heart of Judaism.

An interest in the evangelists as redactors got under way with work in the 1950s by G. Bornkamm, H. Conzelmann, and W. Marxsen, though significant studies had appeared earlier from R.H. Lightfoot, who expressed a debt to E. Lohmeyer. Where the evangelists had been seen by the form critics as collectors, stringing items together almost haphazardly, they were now seen as narrative theologians, creating coherent sequences, with considerable control over their material at large and in detail.

Redaction criticism of canonical and other Jewish texts followed a little later. The most obvious choice, and the most studied is 1 and 2 Chronicles, where it is common to assume there has been a redaction of Samuel-Kings, or at least of the sources of the latter. Here we may find, for example, that the Chronicler's omission of David's domestic failings and his bunching of David's military campaigns allows him to lead up to a triumphant climax in David's preparation for the building of the temple, for which the disastrous census of 2 Samuel 24 becomes now the crucial first step. But redaction need not be once-for-all. It can be argued for a later period that 'the Laws of the Damascus Document continued to be *revised and brought up to date*' by the community, rather than merely copied (Hempel 1998: 191; original emphasis), just as Christian communities continued 'to copy and revise, or copy for the sake of revising, Jewish texts.'

In many cases, as with Exodus or Mark, we may reasonably assume that older sources have been used, even though none survives. We may still attempt to discriminate between what looks older to us, and what seems to be the work of the final author: but now the results are necessarily more tenuous. So, in the example given above, the promise to go ahead to Galilee may seem to be inserted in Mark 14:27–31, but could still be part of a tradition Mark reproduced without himself paying it much attention. Of course we can discern the tendencies of works read on their own, as critics have done for much longer, and we can appraise their theological and general ideological drift, and their narrative or other rhetorical procedures (see Narrative Criticism this volume). But the lack of any objective comparison with a source in front of us makes our conclusions that much less secure. As another example we may also ask how Paul is redacting the passages of scripture that he cites, but then have to admit that we cannot be sure whether any of the textual traditions that have come down to us represent the text from which he started or which he thought he remembered (Stanley 1992).

Redaction criticism becomes still more rarified when the document we are appraising is itself a hypothetical reconstruction: for instance, the sayings gospel 'Q,' the supposed common source of matter Matthew and Luke share but which does not appear in Mark. If we accept the hypothesis, firmly, or even just for the sake of argument, we may note how Matthew and Luke keep in step or separate, and when they separate we may sometimes at least try to decide whether one or both is departing from their shared original. But then, on the basis of supposed breaks or turns in the flow of thought in the reconstructed original, we have recently found it further being argued that we may see how this collection itself was assembled out of more or less disparate strata. In particular it is argued by some that a strongly eschatological stratum has been imposed by a redactor upon timeless wisdom sayings.

There are in fact a number of skeptical issues to be faced. First, the method assumes that we know quite well that people in the ancient world always meant much the same when they used the same or a very similar sequence of words, and always meant something different if they changed some words in a given sequence. Further, if we ourselves detect a change of topic, that must indicate the work of another, a redactor. Neither of these assumptions can be relied on, at least, not in the Graeco-Roman period (Downing 2000: 61–74). Here we find writers frequently claiming to be reproducing trustworthy sources accurately, while they had been schooled to do so in fresh words of their own as much as possible. So Josephus rewriting the *Letter of Aristeas* only twice reproduces exactly a sequence of ten or more words, yet for the rest will readily interchange synonyms. None of this tells you by itself whether he meant to say what he thought his original said or not. In fact, he insists his paraphrase of Jewish scripture reproduces it with total accuracy. As we need to recognize, it was widely and firmly believed that words simply named ideas, and so 'the same idea' could often be named (and conveyed) by a variety of words. But more than this, persuasion then as now involves amplification and digression: any given author may go off on various tacks that seem coherent enough to him or her at the time, even if to us some phrase may look like an addition by a not very bright or even hostile redactor (Downing 2000: 57–69).

An example from Q may be in order. In the very similar sequences Luke 12:22–31 and Matthew 6:25–34 it seems to some that comparing life and food, body and clothes, fits ill with the general injunction against worry; and also that the note about worry's failure to extend life sunders the paired examples from birds and plants: so a second, redactional hand must have been at work. Yet sets of ideas about worry similar to all that we find here appear in other near contemporary authors, with no apparent strain (just as none is evinced by Matthew or Luke). In the light of this we should be very cautious in ascribing anything in a piece in front of us to redactional revision, unless we actually have for comparison the source(s) used. And even if we are agreed that we have an author's source(s), our interpretation of the implications of detailed changes or of exact quotation should remain tentative, and subject to an argued intepretation of the work as a whole (Downing 2000: 58–61).

Initially redaction criticism depended heavily on discerning the distinct and distinctive oral 'forms' in which the early gospel tradition was held to have appeared. 'Interference' with a pure form indicated redaction. More generally, issues of genre continue to be widely discussed, and may seem to have some bearing on our discerning and interpreting redaction: perhaps we may think we have found one genre superimposed on an earlier one, by a fresh redactor. Or, on the other hand, if we can show that a work follows consistently one recognized model in its structure at various levels, in its content and mood, then we may seem justified in claiming it as the work of a single redactor, as Alan Kirk has done for Q (Kirk 1998). But again we must take due note of the fact that contemporaries in the ancient Graeco-Roman world discussed a much smaller range of genres than current scholars find, and made it clear that they were not bound even by these. None cite Kirk's 'instructional speech genre,' nor the generalized subheadings he imposes. Nor can a hard division between firm oral forms and subsequent literary activity be assured. The forms are fluid, and writers compose for oral performance (Downing 2000: 75–94).

A second critical issue presents itself at two levels of generality. We have of late been offered a range of 'intertextual' studies. We find it argued that there seems to have been interaction one way or another between, say, the book of Jeremiah and some of the Psalms; or between Paul in Romans 1–2, and Hellenistic Jewish apologetics: allusion, rather than quotation. In this sense many scriptural authors are redactors of elements of earlier scripture or wider oral tradition. But recent literary and philosophical critics have argued further than this, that all that we utter is in a still broader sense 'intertextual' (Bannet 1989: 244–5). We are all redactors of our complex traditions, as well as ourselves being redacted by those with whom we converse. And if we accept even just the first level of 'intertextuality' as valid, we may ask why we should bother to focus on just one limited patch of such a vast field. The pragmatic response, however, would be much as with any critical historical investigation: we work tentatively with what is clearest, rather than get lost in what is diffuse and opaque.

And that brings us to a third critical issue. Redactional arguments on their own can be used to support competing accounts of the relationships between Matthew, Mark, and Luke (Source Criticism this volume), and so might seem to leave it equally uncertain as to who is redacting what, and undermine even what might seem to be one of our clearest examples. But such indeterminate discussions seem to depend on ignoring the compositional conventions and scribal procedures taken for granted in the ancient Mediterranean world. It is clear that even sophisticated ancient redactors (Plutarch is our best example) had learned from school days to work very simply, in difficult scribal conditions. Only the conclusion that Mark and Q were redacted by Matthew and Luke working independently matches these conventions. All the other solutions ask us to

imagine redactional practices of unprecedented complexity invented by authors whose schooling would have prepared them to redact as simply and straightforwardly as possible (Johnson 1991; Downing 2000: 152–97).

The overall but still provisional conclusion must be that redaction criticism has some force where we are reasonably sure we have for comparison the original the redactor used, but then only when such appraisal is deployed as part of an interpretation of the whole of the second work, and still with the caution indicated above. Imagining an author before us redacting a work lost to us may, of course, suggest interesting possibilities but it affords us no objective criteria for choice among them, and we are clearly left to appraise the work as it stands.

References and further reading

Bannet, E.T. (1989) *Structuralism and the Logic of Dissent: Barthes, Derrida, Foucault, Lacan*, Houndsmill: Macmillan.

Blenkinsopp, J. (2000–2003) *Isaiah*, 3 Vols., AB 19, 19a, 19b, New York: Doubleday.

Downing, F.G. (2000) *Doing Things with Words in the First Christian Century*, JSNTSup 200, Sheffield: Sheffield Academic Press).

Graham, M.P. and S.L. McKenzie (1999) *The Chronicler as Author: Studies in Text and Texture*, JSOTSup 263, Sheffield: Sheffield Academic Press.

Hempel, C. (1998) *The Laws of the Damascus Document: Sources, Tradition and Redaction*, Leiden: Brill.

Johnson S.E. (1991) *The Griesbach Hypothesis and Redaction Criticism*, SBLMS 41, Atlanta: Scholars Press.

Kirk, A. (1998) *The Composition of the Sayings Source. Genre, Synchrony, and Wisdom Redaction in Q*, Leiden: Brill.

Kloppenborg Verbin, J.S. (2000) *Excavating Q: The History and Setting of the Sayings Gospel*, Minneapolis: Fortress Press.

Lightfoot, R.H. (1938) *Locality and Doctrine in the Gospels*, London: Hodder & Stoughton.

Perrin, N. (1970) *What is Redaction Criticism?*, London: SPCK.

Repschinski, B. (2000) *The Controversy Stories in the Gospel of Matthew: Their Redaction, Form and Relevance for the Relationship between the Matthaean Community and Formative Judaism*, FRLANT 189, Göttingen: Vandenhoeck & Ruprecht.

Sabbe, M. (ed.) (1988) *L'évangile selon Marc: Tradition et redaction*, Leuven: Peeters.

Stanley, C.D. (1992) *Paul and the Language of Scripture*, SNTSMS, Cambridge: Cambridge University Press.

F. GERALD DOWNING

REFORMATIONS
(SIXTEENTH CENTURY)

1 Key factors in sixteenth-century Bible interpretation
2 Hermeneutics in the reformations

1 Key factors in sixteenth-century Bible interpretation

1.1 Philological and textual tools

Sixteenth-century biblical exegesis was precritical (which must not be misconstrued as uncritical) and is not to be understood as the beginning of the historical-critical method, which is a child of the 'Age of Reason' (Bray 1996: 225; cf. R.A. Muller and J.L. Thompson in Muller and Thompson 1996: 335–45; and Steinmetz 1980b). Rather it was textual, philological, and theological, the historical sense being identified as the literal and grammatical meaning. As such, 'the Reformation . . . period had more in common with medieval and patristic exegesis than with the modern higher-critical interpretation of the Bible' (R.A. Muller in McKim 1998: 124). This is an important corrective to the older form of scholarship (represented by, e.g., Farrar 1961 and Lampe 1969) which drew a sharp distinction between Reformation exegesis and both pre- and post-Reformation exegesis (see the essays in Muller and Thompson 1996 and on p. 343).

The Renaissance humanists' watchword, *ad fontes* ('back to the sources'), summarizes their concern to return to the founding documents of the Christian faith, primarily the canonical scriptures, but also the writings of the early Church Fathers, and it was they who began the textual work to recover the original Hebrew and Greek texts of both Testaments and developed the philological tools needed to interpret them. It is also important to note that, to varying degrees, the Christian humanists and their programme had a major impact on reformers and Catholics alike and influenced them in the development of their understanding of the scriptures.

Medieval exegesis was based on the Latin Vulgate, though there were some thirteenth-century attempts to revise it from the Hebrew and Greek originals (on which see Evans 1985: 70–3). While there had been medieval translations of parts or the whole of scripture into the vernacular, the Vulgate had achieved de facto status as sacred language, and vernacular translations were regarded with suspicion as the gateway to heresy (as reflected in the church's condemnation of the Waldensians, Cathars, and John Wycliffe and the Lollards). Therefore, at the beginning of the sixteenth century, most people's approach to the Bible was mediated through the Latin Vulgate, but also the books of sentences (handbooks of predominantly patristic quotations on a wide range of scriptural subjects), the best-known of which is Peter Lombard's (*c.* 1095–1169) *Libri Quatuor Sententiarum* (*Four Books of Sentences*), the *Historia Scholastica* of Peter Comestor (*c.* 1100–*c.* 1180), the *Glossa Ordinaria* (the *Ordinary Gloss*, a running commentary on scripture), and the *postillae* (from *post illa* meaning 'after that/after those things,' which complemented the *Glossa*). For the humanists, reliance on medieval tools such as these, with all their limitations, was wholly unacceptable. To fulfil their goal to achieve written and spoken eloquence (*eloquentia*) after the manner of the classical writers of the ancient world whom they admired and sought to emulate, the humanists needed to learn the classical languages, including Hebrew and Greek. Implicit within this whole programme was the need to restore and interpret the original texts of scripture and also the writings of the Fathers (many of the humanists and reformers provided fresh translations of the patristic writers, the best-known being Desiderius Erasmus).

Giovanni Pico della Mirandola (1463–1494) was fluent in both biblical languages and exposed many translation errors in the Vulgate Old Testament and thereby the need for its revision. A member of a humanist group in Basle, Conrad Pellican (1478–1556, later a fellow reformer in Zürich with Huldrych Zwingli [1484–1531]) was the first to produce a Hebrew textbook (*De modo legendi et intelligendi Hebraeum*, 1504), but the most important Hebrew grammar, *De Rudimentis Hebraicis* (1506), was the work of Johannes Reuchlin (1455–1522). Both the Wittenberg reformers, Andreas Bodenstein von Karlstadt (*c.* 1477–1541) and Martin Luther, used this work, which was eventually adopted by the University as part of the theology curriculum in 1518, though it was influential on all the reformers who managed to master the language (Zwingli and Philip Melanchthon [1497–1560] included). Developments in the understanding of Hebrew and the resulting translation of parts or the whole of the Old Testament were greatly aided by the study of Jewish materials and the conversion to Christianity of Jews who brought with them their linguistic skills, such as Alphonso of Alcala, Alphonso of Zamora, and Paul Coronel who edited the Hebrew text and Targum of Onqelos printed in the Complutensian Polyglott (printed in Alcala [the old name of which was Complutum], Spain, in 1513–1517 but not published until 1520).

In the fifteenth century, Lorenzo Valla's (1407–1457) work on Greek demonstrated to him the inadequacy of the Vulgate New Testament and, by extension, the theology based on it. In 1504, Erasmus discovered Valla's manuscript, the *Annotations* (notes on the Greek text of the Gospels, Epistles, and Revelation), which had lain untouched in a Premonstratensian monastery for nearly a century. Valla is best known for his successful employment of text-critical methods to demonstrate that the *Donation of Constantine*, on which the temporal claims of the papacy were based, was a forgery and also that the works of Dionysius the Areopagite were written pseudonymously in the fifth century and not by the convert of Paul (Acts 17:34). Valla's work was published by Erasmus as *Adnotationes in Novum Testamentum* in 1505 and it formed the basis of his own work on the Greek of the New Testament. His own edition of the Greek New Testament (printed alongside a fresh Latin translation) appeared in 1516 under the title *Novum Instrumentum omne*, and, in so doing, Erasmus made readily available the text-critical tools and the basic text itself which was to form the foundation for so much of the biblical work of the Protestant reformers. A further factor in the development of the knowledge of Greek was the influx into Western Europe of many Byzantine scholars (the Byzantine Church had always used the Bible in Greek) who were fleeing from the Muslim invasion of the East.

By the early sixteenth century, then, it was no longer possible simply to appeal to either the authority of the church or its official version of the Bible, the Vulgate, on matters of theology and interpretation. The issue of accuracy of translation was championed by Erasmus who in many instances followed the earlier work of Valla. Of many possible examples, there is the translation of Mark 1:14, where, at the commencement of his ministry, Jesus says, 'Repent (Greek *metanoeite*) for the kingdom of God is at hand.' The Vulgate, however, translated 'repent' as *poenitentiam agite*, 'do penance,' and used it as a prooftext for the sacrament of penance (for other examples, see McGrath 1987: 133–5). The underlying assumption of this sixteenth-century text-critical work was the belief that only an accurate text could provide the basis for accurate interpretation which would therefore lead to theological truth and right ecclesiastical and moral practice.

Between 1516 and 1517 Jacques Lefèvre d'Étaples (*c.* 1460–1536) and Erasmus clashed over the translation of Psalm 8:5, which, in Hebrews 2:7, follows the Septuagint form instead of the Hebrew, thereby stating that Christ was 'made a little lower than the angels.' D'Étaples, in his *Quincuplex Psalterium* (*Fivefold Psalter*, 1509, an edition of the Psalms in four old Latin versions and a new Latin one), amended the Psalms text to read 'made a little lower than God' on the basis that the God-man Christ, to whom he took the verse to be referring, could not be lower than the angels. In the *Annotations* to his 1516 Greek text, Erasmus opposed the alteration of the Hebrew text, maintaining that the word 'little' should be translated 'for a short time,' which was a valid rendering of the Greek original of Hebrews and referred to the short time Christ lived on the earth (see Augustijn 1991: 113–15). However, other factors were also involved in establishing the texts in their original languages and subsequent translations. One of the best-known examples is to be found in Erasmus who, in the first edition of his New Testament, omitted the explicitly trinitarian 'Johannine comma' (1 John 5:7b–8a, 'in heaven: the Father, the Word and the Holy Spirit, and these three are One. And there are three that testify on earth') because he did not find them in his Greek manuscripts. For this his orthodoxy was seriously called into question and he was accused of Arianism. But after a manuscript including it had appeared in England, Erasmus included this section in his third edition of 1522, though this turned out to be a forgery made two years earlier in order to discredit him.

McGrath sees the importance of the d'Étaples– Erasmus exchange in the way that it exemplifies the emerging understanding of the nature of textual criticism and exegesis. Earlier exegetes had contented themselves with repeating the views of accepted authorities, such as the *Glossa Ordinaria*, but this was insufficient for the humanists and the reformers who looked to the original texts in the original languages. Such debates did not go unnoticed (for instance, Wendelin Steinbach of Tübingen [d. 1519] sided with d'Étaples, Luther with Erasmus), and the growing awareness of the limitations of the Vulgate raised the issues of its theological reliability and authority, so that '[u]nless theology and exegesis were to become divorced, as disciplines of no relevance to each other, it was clear that some accommodation to the new humanist exegetical methods was necessary' (McGrath 1999: 134–5). That this in fact happened on both sides of the reformations is shown by the number of Protestant and Catholic scholars whose works reflect these developments: the Protestant scholars Musculus, Robert Estienne (Stephanus, 1503–1559, whose 1550 edition of the New Testament was the first to include critical apparatus which formed the basis of the Textus Receptus and who introduced the form of versification followed in contemporary Bibles), and Theodore Beza (1519–1605, Calvin's successor in Geneva and biographer), and the Catholics Jacopo Sadoleto (1477–1547) and Claude Guillard (1493–1551) (on whom see Bray 1996: 177, 179–81).

The importance of competency in Greek is also highlighted by, for example, Melanchthon, Luther's colleague, Reuchlin's great nephew and the leading humanist of the Lutheran reformers, who stressed that it was impossible to return *ad fontes* without an understanding of Greek, which he believed could express the highest truths (see his *Oratio de studiis linguae graecae* [1549] and McGrath 1987: 128). It was, in fact, Melanchthon who taught Luther Greek in 1519.

1.2 Bible translation

It was inevitable that once the inadequacies of the Vulgate became known that Renaissance humanists would turn their attention to translating the Bible into Latin and the vernacular and also correcting the existing translations. Such had been the work of the thirteenth-century Dominican correctories who were engaged in extensive editorial work comparing the Latin with

Hebrew and Greek texts. With the humanistic emphasis on *ad fontes* and the philological developments in both biblical languages, the work of Bible translation began to blossom. One of the most significant events for this work of translation was the invention of the printing press, the first substantial book ever to be printed being the Gutenberg Bible in 1456. In the fifteenth and early-sixteenth centuries, humanist scholars produced many editions of the Bible, at first editions of the Vulgate.

Vernacular translations, though known before the reformations, were clearly characteristic of them. Luther, Zwingli, William Tyndale, Miles Coverdale (1488–1569), and Castellio all produced Bibles in their native languages. The many commentaries and theological books published during this period also provided translations of scripture and their influence must not be underestimated.

1.3 Sola scriptura

Sola scriptura ('by scripture alone') was not simply one of the great slogans of the sixteenth-century Protestant reformers, but also the principle by which they sought to rediscover the faith and practices of the early church and thereby reform and reinvigorate the contemporary church. The understanding of *sola scriptura* was not to deny the place of tradition, merely to make it subject to scripture (on the scripture–tradition relationship, see Oberman 1967: 53–66, and McGrath 1987: 140–51). However, scripture needed to be interpreted and this proved less straightforward and more contentious than expected. The irony of the humanists' and reformers' emphasis on the biblical languages as necessary for the correct interpretation of scripture was that it precluded the common people and made them dependent on theologians and philologists, thereby replacing the medieval Catholic mediators between God and the common people (the church, various books of sentences, glosses, and the like), with Protestant mediators, specifically the Protestant leaders themselves and the books they provided for their less able students and the ordinary people, for example, Luther's *Shorter Catechism* (1529).

2 Hermeneutics in the reformations

Throughout the Middle Ages the claim that the authority to interpret the scriptures, under the guidance of the Spirit, rested with the [Roman Catholic] church had come to be increasingly challenged. This is evidenced by the growth of various reform movements, some of which remained within the church (most clearly seen in the conciliar movement and its attempts to reform the papacy, originating in the twelfth century, but particularly during the Great Schism [1378–1417], and whose leading proponents were Marsiglio of Padua [*c.* 1275–1342] and William of Ockham), others were on the periphery (such included John Wycliffe during his lifetime), while others were regarded as heretical

(the Waldensians, Cathars, and Hussites). This developing pluralism was fueled by the Renaissance humanists who, in their circumvention of the 'Middle Ages' in their quest to return *ad fontes*, encouraged a questioning attitude on all matters, not least when the limitations of the Vulgate had become clear and such a document as the *Donation of Constantine* had been exposed as forgeries.

In common with the precritical exegesis of the patristic and medieval periods, the reformers believed that the meaning of a text was not to be identified solely with its literal and grammatical meaning. If it was, then huge portions of the Old Testament would have nothing to say to their own age. With the Roman Catholics, they accepted the inspiration and authority of scripture, though they challenged, on the one hand, the Catholic teaching that its authority rested with the church and the church's tradition, and, on the other, the subjective appeal to the authority of personal experience, characterized by the spiritualist radicals (such as Sebastian Franck [1499–1542] and Sebastian Castellio).

The *Quadriga* ('fourfold sense of scripture'), which had originated in the patristic era, dominated medieval hermeneutics and was based on the belief that there were four different senses to scripture: the literal, allegorical, tropological, and anagogical, the last three corresponding respectively to doctrine, morals, and Christian hope. However, this did not mean that employment of the *Quadriga* precluded an interest in the literal interpretation of the text. The three nonliteral senses were grounded in the literal as the primary meaning of the text, as the writings of Thomas Aquinas and Nicholas of Lyra (*c.* 1270–1349) show.

2.1 Hermeneutics and the Lutheran reformation

As far as the Wittenberg reformer Martin Luther was concerned, the Word of God is first and foremost Christ. Only secondarily is it the proclaimed Word, and only then is it the Bible, which he described as 'the swaddling clothes and the manger in which Christ lies.' While the swaddling clothes and manger are 'simple and lowly,' 'dear is the treasure, Christ, who lies in them' (*LW* 35: 236). According to Luther, 'all the Scriptures point to Christ alone' (*LW* 35: 132). Further, he maintained that the Bible contains two opposing but complementary elements, the law and the gospel, promise and fulfilment. It was not simply that law was contained in the Old Testament and gospel in the New, but rather that God judges and is merciful and 'this twofold dimension of the Word of God must be taken into account in [the] interpretation of Scripture' (Lohse 1987: 157). Law and gospel exist in a dialectical relationship which links the past with the present. It was for this reason that he rejected the canonicity of the book of James, describing it as 'an epistle of straw' because it had 'nothing of the nature of the gospel about it' and opposed Paul's doctrine of justification

315

sola fide with justification by works (*LW* 35: 362, 396). For Luther, authority did not lie in the biblical canon but in the gospel revealed within scripture.

The proper way to interpret any particular text is in its context with a view to discerning the author's intention. This was equally true of the whole of scripture, where every passage is to be interpreted within the overall context of the Bible and its author, the Holy Spirit. He was also convinced of the clarity of scripture: 'The meaning of Scripture is, in and of Scripture itself, so certain, accessible, and clear that Scripture interprets itself and tests, judges, and illuminates everything else' (*WA* 7: 97, 23–4). This work of interpretation needs the guidance of the Spirit. Here he was in clear conflict with the Roman Catholic Church for whom scripture could only be interpreted by the church itself, but equally with the radicals (Luther called them *Schwärmer*, enthusiasts), who claimed that there was a revelation of the Spirit separate from scripture. Against both positions, Luther insisted that the Spirit, the scriptures' author, does not contradict the teaching of the gospel revealed in scripture (cf. *LW* 35: 29).

The groundwork of Luther's exegetical method can be seen in his *Lectures on the Psalms* (1513–1515) in which he asserted that the proper key to understanding scripture is the recognition of the distinction between spirit and letter, though he could not separate the two as 'the spirit is hidden in the letter.' Understanding the Bible does not come through human cleverness but is a gift of the Spirit to the church, so while the biblical languages are important, they are not the total of the matter. He rejected, for instance, the monastic practice of repeating the Psalms in the liturgy and divine office, believing that the Psalms themselves were nothing more than letter without the inner understanding of the Spirit (Oberman 1989: 250–2 and Lohse 1987: 146–7).

While the reformers and many humanists formally rejected the *Quadriga*, they nevertheless frequently employed both its terms and followed its method. Luther had been schooled in its use as is illustrated, for example, in his *Lectures on Galatians* (1535) in which, on Galatians 4:6, Jerusalem 'literally signified the city of that name; tropologically a pure conscience; allegorically, the church militant; and anagogically, our heavenly fatherland or the church triumphant.' However, he believed that such interpretations 'tore Scripture apart into many meanings,' depriving people of reliable instruction (*LW* 26: 440). He did not dismiss allegory altogether, for he knew that the New Testament itself employed allegory (e.g., in Gal. 4:21–31), but he used it sparingly for the purpose of illustrating a doctrine, never establishing one (see, e.g., his Genesis commentary, *WA* 44: 93), and anagogy even less because he was convinced that the Parousia was imminent (Oberman 1989: 252).

For Luther, the tropological sense was concerned with faith, not in the sense of true doctrine, but trust in God's promises, and therefore focused on the individual's relationship to Christ. But Luther's primary concern was with the literal sense. Following the work of Nicholas of Lyra in the fourteenth century, Luther accepted a double literal sense of scripture, whereby the meaning of an Old Testament passage applies to the time of writing (the literal-historical sense) but also to the time of Christ and the New Testament (the literal-prophetic sense). For Luther, scripture has one simple sense and this is Christ (Lohse 1987: 156–7). He also calls this the 'grammatical-historical sense' because it 'drives home Christ.' Christ himself had provided the key to interpreting the scriptures when he said that believers are to study the scriptures 'so that in it you discover me' (*WA* 51: 2; cf. John 5:39, on which see Oberman 1989: 251). The literal sense, then, is also the spiritual sense, though at times he lapsed into literalism, most significantly in his interpretation of Matthew 26:26, 'This *is* my body' (see, e.g., McGrath 1999: 178–80). This, he believed, showed the real presence of Christ in the eucharist and led to his breach with Zwingli which prevented the unification of Protestantism at the Marburg Colloquy in 1529. Building on the work of d'Étaples, Luther insisted on the literal-prophetic sense of the Psalms and this enabled him to interpret them Christologically, unless there was overwhelming exegetical reasons to think otherwise. Therefore, in emphasizing the tropological and literal senses, then, Luther was able to focus his exegetical work on the relationship between Christ and the believer (D.C. Steinmetz in Hayes 1999: 97).

In his work of translating the Bible into German the influence of humanism is clear. He learned both biblical languages and used Reuchlin's work on the Hebrew and Erasmus' Greek New Testament to produce his New Testament in 1522, the complete Bible following in 1534. But translation was not simply a matter of grammar and philology alone, for the translator needed to know the substance of the text. In this Luther followed Augustine's distinction between knowledge and wisdom, and cognition and faith (Oberman 1989: 309). The end result was Luther's use of 'living, colloquial German,' the language of the common people as the conveyor of the language of God (Oberman 1989: 305).

Philip Melanchthon was the great systematizer of Lutheran theology. Trained in humanism, and a classical linguist, he knew the three biblical languages (though he was no expert in Hebrew), and was renowned throughout Europe for his expertise in Greek, writing a Greek grammar which was widely used and commentaries on a number of biblical books, including one on Romans (on Romans see T.J. Wengert in Muller and Thompson 1996: 118–40). Unlike many other humanists and reformers, he was not concerned with textual issues but rather with interpreting the received text, which he approached through rhetorical analysis (on which see, e.g., J.R. Schneider in Maag 1999:

141–59), as evidenced in his early *De Rhetorica Libri Tres* (*Three Books on Rhetoric*), which he had almost completed before he arrived in Wittenberg in 1518 and was published the following year. Rhetoric, he believed, would elucidate both the structure of any given biblical book and its main theological topics (*loci*). For Melanchthon, '[t]he first goal of rhetoric is to provide the linguistic abilities to understand and consider scholarly issues critically. Rhetoric as an analytical tool benefits scriptural exegesis, yet the ability to communicate is … the key' (N. Kuropka in Maag 1999: 166). In contrast to the other commentaries by reformers, Melanchthon's were not verse-by-verse expositions but studies of the major *loci* of the passage.

In his most famous work, the *Loci Communes Theologici* (*Common Places of Theology*, first edition 1521, last edition 1551), he followed the Aristotelian method of discovering the *loci* which he believed represent the meaning of the text (Parker 1993: 66). 'He … believed that the writers of Scripture had themselves knowingly written according to fixed, classical rhetorical rules. The authors had selected ("invented") primary topics or *loci communes*, arranged ("disposed") them in the manner prescribed for standard species of writings, and thus offered arguments in the technical rhetorical senses of that term to prove ("confirm") their points' (J.R. Schneider in McKim 1998: 228). This rhetorical analysis of the various biblical books, focusing on the structure of each book and examining its theological *loci* (these two emphases are also prominent in the work of Heinrich Bullinger [1504–1575]) proved to be his major contribution to exegesis in this period. He followed Luther on the true and clear sense of scripture and believed all scripture to be either law or the promise of grace, or both. In his Preface to Luther's *Operationes in Psalmos* (*Second Lectures on Psalms*, 1519) he commented that not all sacred and canonical books were of the same rank, that certain ones were read more often than others and 'such is their composition that they are able to act as interpreters, or commentaries on the rest … among the Pauline epistles, the one to Romans is a scopus … which points the way into the rest' (*WA*: 5: 24, cited by Schneider in Maag 1999: 154). He employed allegory, but only as an expression of the *loci communes* that were clearly taught elsewhere. The literal sense, as understood by Luther, was clear to all who employed the rhetorical method he explicated (Schneider in McKim 1998: 228–9), and no one 'was so single-minded as he about proving the single (Lutheran) sense of Scripture as evident in every nook and corner of the Bible' (Schneider in McKim 1998: 230).

2.2 Hermeneutics and the Reformed reformation

The leader of the early Reformed Church was Huldrych Zwingli, the people's priest of Zürich from 1519 to his death in 1531. The center of his theology was the conviction that the Bible is the Word of God and that this is what makes it authoritative. He believed in the perspicuity of scripture – clear to all who were humbly willing to be taught by God (*theodidacti*) – and that it can only be properly understood with the prayerful aid of the Holy Spirit who opens it to those who are otherwise unreceptive to its meaning and without whom people are prone to read into it what they want. This did not, however, mean that the Spirit replaces scripture: for such views he opposed the radical reformers. For Zwingli, faith was his principal hermeneutical criterion, as it is the reason people leave behind human wisdom and seek God through his Word (see Zwingli's *Of the Clarity and Certainty or Power of the Word of God* [1522], in Bromiley 1953: 88–9).

Greatly influenced by Erasmian humanism from his formative years (1514–1519) onwards, Zwingli, in time, mastered Greek and Hebrew and paid particular attention to the literary nature of scripture. While he drew a fundamental distinction between scripture and the traditions of the church in which scripture was the bar against which the Fathers were to be assessed, he nevertheless used the Fathers, various church councils, and even non-Christian writers in order to support his own position, but also to find common ground with those with whom he was debating. He was no literalist, but recognized the different genres within the Bible and also that the various writers employed many figures of speech. This became clear in his dispute with Luther over the eucharist and the interpretation of Matthew 26:26 (on which see Stephens 1986: 218–59, and McGrath 1999: 182–6). Luther asserted that 'this *is* my body' should be interpreted literally, while Zwingli insisted that it was nonliteral and, in fact, is an example of alloiosis (the sharing/interchange of properties), thus meaning 'this *signifies* my body,' and he supported this from other scriptures which declared that Jesus was now at the right hand of the Father. This shows how Zwingli insisted on the unity and consistency of scripture, refusing to accept disharmony, for while it was written by many different authors it was nevertheless inspired by God's Spirit. This meant that at times he indulged in the harmonization of seemingly inconsistent passages. Further, he frequently compared passages which discuss the same theme, setting individual passages within their broader context and enabling difficult passages to be elucidated by clearer ones.

Zwingli used a modified form of the *Quadriga*, following Origen's threefold sense of scripture: the natural, moral, and mystical senses (see Stephens 1986: 73–7). Künzli (1905–) has shown that for Zwingli the natural sense is the literal sense once the idioms and figures of speech have been taken into account, hence his attention to such rhetorical devices as metonymy, alloiosis, synedoche, and catachresis. The early days of the Zürich reformation focused a great deal on moral rather than doctrinal reform and, like Erasmus, Zwingli was deeply concerned for the moral interpretation and application of scripture. On the basis of 1 Corinthians 10:11 he believed that the Old Testament provided examples and warnings for Christians to learn from. Using Paul's teaching in 1 Corinthians 10:6 and 11, Zwingli further believed that everything in the Old Testament was historical but also symbolic, and the method to hand for such exegesis was allegory (the legitimacy for which was Paul's use of it in Gal. 4:21–30), though he used it with caution, insisting that allegory could only be legitimately used to confirm what was elsewhere clearly set out. In keeping with his conviction that the relationship between the Old and New Testaments was one of promise and fulfilment, he employed typology which had a double referent: the Old Testament type represented the historical situation but also pointed to its antitype in the New Testament, as in Israel and the church respectively (covenant theology being a major theme in Zwingli's theology). This use of typology also showed both similarity and dissimilarity between the Testaments: for example, Genesis 22 shows that in their preparedness to sacrifice their sons, Abraham was the type and God the antitype, while Isaac's not dying contrasts with Christ's death.

Zwingli's colleague and successor in Zürich, Bullinger, was also heavily influenced by humanism. His most important work on hermeneutical method, the *Studiorum Ratio, sive Hominis addictis studiis Institutio* (*Method for Students, or Training for Men Devoted to Study*), written in 1527, set out his belief that because scripture is from God it has to be studied in a spirit of reverence and devotion, and that this is aided by a number of factors. First is the need for linguistic skills additional to Latin, namely, Hebrew and Greek. Second, the intention (*scopus*) of scripture must be understood, by which he meant the two-sided covenant between God and humanity which he believed runs throughout all the books of the Bible. For Bullinger, 'the sum of Scripture is the covenant, and Jesus Christ is its guarantor' (R.L. Peterson in McKim 1998: 167). He thus sees this covenantal continuity as supporting the hermeneutical (and soteriological) unity of both Testaments (A.E. McGrath in Hayes 1999: 1.148). Further, four considerations needed to be taken into account: the context of the passage, which also included the author's distinctive characteristics of style and perspective and the differences of historical period; the circumstances surrounding the book's writing; comparison of one passage with another by the reader; and the point at issue, that is, the chief subject of the discussion and on which the argument is based. In all this, Bullinger was concerned with discovering the author's meaning. While he accepted the use of allegory, he was careful to ensure that this did not lead to invention or the allegorizing of everything in scripture, limiting its use to where the passage was clearly typological and where it could be squared with what scripture taught elsewhere (Parker 1993: 74–6).

Martin Bucer (1491–1551), the Strasbourg reformer, built on his humanist foundations and his goal was to discover the natural sense of scripture. While his *Instruction on How the Holy Scriptures Should Be Handled in Preaching* (1531) is of little help, his 1527 commentaries, *Gospels* (revised 1530) and *Romans*, reveal his understanding of scripture and how it should be interpreted. Bucer believed that the fullness of the truth of scripture could only be attained by those who were born again, the light of faith being necessary for the understanding of the text. Bucer's method, as revealed in his *Romans*, included *metaphrasis* (a free translation of the passage), *expositio* (exposition), *interpretatio* (interpretation), and *observatio* (observation). Like other reformers and humanists, he too recognized the existence of various figures of speech, including metaphor, allegory, metonymy, parables, and images, though he rejected allegorism, seeing it as an ancient abuse, an insult to the Spirit and a means of Satan to lure believers away from the true efficacious teachings and example of Christ. For Bucer, the primary goal of the interpreter of the Gospels, for example, is to discover the intention (*scopus*) of the Gospels, which is to explain the life of Christ so that the believer might have eternal life (D.F. Wright in McKim 1998: 160). Bucer condemned the speculative nature of allegory, though he did employ typology; for instance, he sees in Adam, Noah, Melchizedek, and Abraham a likeness and shadow of Christ (Wright in McKim 1998: 162).

In the preface to his first biblical commentary, *Romans* (1540), Calvin expressed his admiration for the earlier work of both Melanchthon and Bucer, though he criticized the former for what he judged to be some important omissions and Bucer for his verbosity and obscurity (Parker 1993: 87–8). Through his early studies in the law and the influence of the humanists Calvin's exegetical work focused on the historical context of the scriptures and the literary and linguistic features of the text. The form he employed in his first commentary on Seneca's *De Clementia*, written in 1532 prior to his evangelical conversion and which he hoped would establish his reputation as a humanist writer, set the pattern he was to follow in his biblical commentaries throughout his life. The original text is printed first and followed by systematic expositions of each sentence, so that by 'a continuous exegesis and exposition of the language' he was able to arrive at an understanding of the passage's meaning (Parker 1986: 85). While Calvin did not systematically set out his exegetical method, eight exegetical principles have been identified (Kraus 1977: 12–18).

In his dedicatory letter to *Romans*, Calvin discloses his views on method. For him, method is secondary, while the primary concern is that the scriptures are understood and explained. Then he identified the 'best virtues' of the exegete as 'clarity and brevity' (*perspicua* and *brevitas*, e.g., CR 38.403, also Parker 1993: 85–93, and Gamble 1987) and these came to have the sense of 'illumination' and 'relevance' (Parker 1986: 91). The primary task is the interpretation of the text, for which knowledge of Hebrew and Greek is necessary. Elaborate interpretations cloud the text's meaning, when all that is needed is clarity and brevity. Calvin attacked the arbitrary use of allegory. For example, he rejected the many allegorical meanings given to the details of the construction and furnishings of the Tabernacle in Exodus 26. He stated that it 'was not at all God's purpose to include a mystery in each hook and loop. Even if every part contained its mystical sense – which no sane man would admit – it is still better to confess ignorance than play parlour guessing games.' He appealed to the writer of Hebrews as one who, when he set out the analogy between 'the shadows of the Law and the truth revealed in Christ,' only touched 'on the chief points, and that sparingly. By this moderate procedure he holds us back from over-much enquiry and deep speculations.' Instead, Calvin interprets the passage in a literal sense, adopting a 'simple treatment' which will edify his readers (CR 24.415, in Parker 1986: 70–1).

Second, Calvin's concern was to discover the author's intention: 'almost [the commentator's] only duty is to lay open the mind of the writer whom he has undertaken to explain' and not to do so is to deviate from the commentator's mark (CR 10b.403). The text is the representation of the writer's thoughts and the text, he asserted, was both the dictation of the Holy Spirit (therefore inspired) and the work of the writers. In the Bible, God reveals himself to humanity (Parker 1986: 92–6). Calvin believed that the text, written in Hebrew, Greek, or Aramaic by a human writer who was effectively an amanuensis, is the 'speech' of the Holy Spirit whose mind is understood when the text is understood. But the texts also show that this inspiration did not circumvent the various authors' personalities through whom the Spirit worked. However, this understanding of the text does not come naturally, for it 'is not conceived naturally nor apprehended by an intellectual movement, but it depends entirely on the revelation of the Spirit' (CR 49.342 on 1 Cor. 2:12). In other words, 'it is possible to "understand" the New Testament without "understanding" it' (Parker 1993: 107–8). Third, in the process of discovering the author's intention the background to the passages – historical, geographical, religious, and cultural – has to be taken into account.

Fourth, once the setting has been determined it is possible to set out the 'real meaning' of the text, which he also calls the 'original meaning,' 'true meaning,' 'simple meaning,' or 'grammatical meaning.' For instance, the emnity between the serpent and the woman and their seeds in Genesis 3:15 was traditionally interpreted as the 'protoevangelium,' anticipation of the gospel. Calvin opposed this, stating, 'however much I would like to agree with [the interpretation],

[it] does too much violence to the word "seed". Who could insist that this collective noun here refers to only a single individual [Christ]? Rather the meaning must be that the struggle between Satan and man will be unceasing, but in the course of time mankind will be victorious' (CR 51.71, cited by Kraus 1977: 15). To justify such a 'transference' (transitum facere) from the serpent to the Devil, Calvin had to claim that this was 'not only a comparison but a true literal anagogue' (CR 23.70). Though he used the same term as used in the Quadriga, he meant by it something different. Parker argues that this is 'a transference or application of a Biblical person or event to some theological truth,' and it is 'not merely a comparison that happens to arise in the expositor's mind, but an application that is demanded by the letter of the text,' and sometimes his use comes close to analogia, similarity. 'The important element is that, if the Old Testament is allowed to stand in its own right and not be dissolved into time-less spirituality or even into Christianity, it is inevitable that in the first instance it will have to be treated on its own; therefore, a certain gap will have to be bridged, a transference made,' and this bridging is anagogical (Parker 1986: 72–3).

Fifth, Calvin believed that many exegetical difficulties could be explained when the context of a passage ('connection' or 'special circumstances') was investigated (Institutes 3.17.14). Further, as each passage is to be seen in its context, so too each biblical book has to be understood within the context of the whole of scripture. Sixth, Calvin's goal was to find the literal sense of scripture, but he did not equate this with the grammatical sense, for he recognized the presence of rhetorical devices which are used in everyday language within scripture – anagoge, allusion, figure, similitude, and allegory. To this end, he sought to discern how far exegesis could legitimately go beyond the literal wording of scripture: this was clearly not without its inherent dangers, and led to the seventh point on how to interpret metaphorical expressions and figures of speech. Calvin's references to allegory are usually negative, and the object of his criticisms is the view that believes 'there could be a secondary meaning, not expressed directly in words' (Parker 1993: 102). He believed that metaphor is not allegory, even if allegory occurs in scripture, for the interpreter is not to go beyond the rules permitted by scripture. This clearly had implications for his understanding of the eucharist and in particular the words of consecration (see, e.g., Institutes 4.17.21). But neither is allegory hyperbole, which is a poetic device where an 'exaggerated wordiness' is legitimate (cf. CR 59.172 and Kraus 1977: 17). Calvin also believed that certain persons, institutions, and events were types or figures or images (words he uses interchangeably). This was not to imply that the historical person of Moses, for instance, had no reality of his own, but that he corresponds to Christ. Such resemblances are no accident but have been set up by God. While typology could easily descend into allegory, Calvin's use is 'restrained and practical' (Parker 1986: 76, see the broader discussion of typology pp. 74–81).

Calvin, then, was no literalist, because literalism is the misrepresentation of metaphorical language, and, to this end, knowledge of the original languages and historical background is necessary. For him, the literal sense 'means the plain straightforward understanding of a passage according to its grammatical and rhetorical structure, and that any interpretation that does violence to this literal sense is inadmissable' (Parker 1993: 104).

Finally, Calvin believed that the sole purpose of exegesis is to find Christ in the text: 'Exegesis is to be carried out with [Christ] as its goal – seeking him and finding him' (Kraus 1977: 17, citing *CR* 47.125 and Col. 2:3). In short, 'Illumination by the Holy Spirit and philological expertise were both needed by the biblical exegete' (Puckett in McKim 1998: 176).

Theodore Beza succeeded to the leadership of the Genevan Church on Calvin's death. He too was humanist trained, and while his Hebrew was weak, he was a master of Greek and also a text critic, for which his legacy is perpetuated in the collection of fourth- and fifth-century manuscripts representing the Western text which he discovered in 1562, known as the Codex Bezae. He is best known for his ten critical editions of the Greek New Testament, the last published posthumously in 1611. Beza believed that the true author of the Bible is the Holy Spirit, therefore exegesis must be careful and sober, and this led him to show harmony among the various canonical writings. His approach is grammatical, philological, and historical, and he insisted that passages be interpreted contextually and when he does use allegory (as with the Song of Songs) the historical and sociological context governs it. The goal of exegesis is to enable believers to hear the truth of God's Word (J.L. Farthing in McKim 1998: 154–5).

2.3 Hermeneutics and the Radical reformations

Among all the reformers, 'no group took more seriously the principle of *sola scriptura* in matters of doctrine and discipline as did the Anabaptists' (Estep 1975: 140, see pp. 140–5). With the magisterial reformers, they rejected the twofold authority of the Roman Catholic Church, scripture and tradition, but they departed from them, and even among themselves, in formulating their understanding of the authority of scripture. In line with their biblicist principles, the Anabaptists asserted that whatever is not clearly found in scripture is to be rejected (see the letter of September 5, 1524, from Conrad Grebel [*c.* 1498–1526] to Thomas Müntzer [before *c.* 1489–1525] in Baylor 1991: 38), though they were not always consistent in this regard (see Baylor 1991: 40), whereas the magisterial reformers only rejected what scripture explicitly rejected.

The radicals fall into three broad groupings: the evangelical Anabaptists, the spiritualists, and the evangelical rationalists/anti-trinitarians. The spiritualists emphasized the Spirit as central to their life and thought, but as far as exegesis is concerned, they believed that while scripture was inspired by the Spirit, the immediate inspiration of the Spirit is superior to any written record, including the Bible. The Anabaptists in particular believed the Bible to be God's Word and that the Holy Spirit would aid them in their exegetical work (Williams 1962: 829). Two problems, however, face the reconstruction of the radicals' hermeneutics: they were predominantly a persecuted and underground movements and their extant works are comparatively few compared to other reformers; and their leaders rarely survived long enough to write much. Combined with the fact that a strong anticlericalism characterized the movements, they believed that, in line with their views on the priesthood of all believers, all had the right to interpret the scriptures for themselves – one exception being the apocalyptist, Melchior Hoffmann (*c.* 1493/95–1543), who believed that only leaders and prophets could undertake difficult exegesis (see Williams 1962: 831). As a result, the radicals were predominantly lay movements whose leaders were often uneducated, therefore illiterate.

The Swiss Brethren emerged out of the Swiss reformation in 1525, being former disciples of Zwingli, who became convinced that the reformer was not rigorous enough in his application of the *sola scriptura* principle. As such, they were influenced by humanism and its emphasis on *ad fontes*. The South German Anabaptists, who emerged around 1526, were deeply influenced by forms of medieval mysticism and apocalypticism, while the early Dutch Anabaptists were predominantly an apocalyptic movement until the debacle at Münster in 1534–1535.

In many respects the Anabaptists followed the other reformers in believing in the perspicuity of the scriptures (see Grebel to Müntzer in Baylor 1991: 38) and that scripture should be interpreted by scripture. This was clearly of advantage to a lay movement that lacked the linguistic knowledge and scholarly training that distinguished so many of the reformers and thus enabled the radicals to interpret the Old Testament by the New. This was of great importance to the radicals for whom 'the core of the hermeneutical problem was how to interpret the Old Testament evangelically, because, for the most part, unlike the classical Protestants, the Radicals did not accept the Scriptures of the Old Testament without a radical reconception of their meaning for reborn Christians' (Williams 1962: 828). For instance, they rejected the magisterial reformers' arguments from the Old Testament for the continuation of the church–state relationship: a position the radicals completely rejected. The Tyrolese Anabaptist, Pilgram Marpeck (*c.* 1495–1556), distinguished between the Testaments, so that, for example, he countered the claim of the magisterial reformers who argued that the covenant inaugurated by circumcision was sealed with baptism on the grounds that the second covenant is a new one, discontinuous with the old, as shown by the Fourth Gospel's teaching (John 7:39 and 16:7) that the Holy Spirit's indwelling of the believer is possible only after the glorification of Christ (Marpeck, *The Admonition* [1542] 225–28, cited by J. Rempel in McKim 1998: 223).

The magisterial reformers rejected on principle, though not in practice, the Catholic Church's use of nonliteral senses of scripture so that they could approach the Bible as a unity and could interpret it literally, as evidenced by the important forms of covenant theology played in the theologies of so many of the leading magisterial reformers. Like the Catholic Church, however, the Anabaptists employed a number of hermeneutical approaches and dispensational schemes in order to distinguish between the Testaments, while the spiritualists and evangelical rationalists, though closer to the magisterial reformers in this matter, nevertheless located the unifying feature of the Bible in the God who transcended the written word (see Williams 1962: 828).

The Anabaptists were, as far as the New Testament was concerned, literalists. Some Anabaptists, on the basis of Matthew 10:9–10, wandered the countryside without weapons, girdle, or money, while others, based on Matthew 10:27, literally preached from the rooftops, though leaders, such as Balthasar Hubmaier (c. 1485–1528), Marpeck, and Menno Simons (1496–1561), opposed such literalism (Williams 1962: 829–30). As far as the Old Testament was concerned, the Anabaptists only interpreted it literally when the plain sense supported their belief that they were the righteous remnant. The rest of the time they resorted to allegory, concordance, typology, and other nonliteral methods in order to understand otherwise difficult passages (Williams 1962: 830).

Hoffmann argued that the two Testaments were one, and he justified this by interpreting Leviticus 11:3's image of a clean animal who has 'cloven claws' typologically (cf. Deut. 14:6; see his *The Ordinance of God* [1530], in Williams and Mergal 1957: 202–3, and Deppermann 1987: 241–62, especially pp. 241–5). He saw Old Testament events as types of New Testament ones and contended that all God's words are double/twofold. In seeing figures and events in the Old Testament as prototypes of the New, 'Hoffmann created the impression that a single developing principle unites the two. The Old Testament could remain a sacred text without being absolutely binding' (Deppermann 1987: 244). Convinced that the Spirit indwelt him, Hoffmann believed that he was divinely authorized to interpret the scriptures and that difficult passages could also be interpreted by himself and other prophets and

prophetesses like him. By the application of allegory and the principle of the 'cloven claw,' he 'was able to make biblical characters the bearers of his own ideas. If he felt inclined to do so, he could rationalize or spiritualize biblical passages so as to do away with their literal meaning' (Deppermann 1987: 244). In Münster such ideas were drawn on to support the Anabaptist takeover of the city in 1534–1535, which led to such disastrous consequences for the city in particular and the radicals in general (see Williams 1962: 355–60). In 1534, Obbe Philips (b. 1500), who agreed with Hoffmann on other matters, managed to convince Jacob van Campen, the bishop of Amsterdam, of the errors of Hoffmann's typological hermeneutics. Philips argued that the writing of the two Testaments stood on one hoof and were not to be excessively allegorized, but rather that the only legitimate interpretation was the literal one. In so doing, Philips prevented Campen from leading his city along a similar path to that taken by the radical apocalyptists of Münster who were using Hoffmann's twofold principle to justify their violent takeover of the city, which was finally crushed by a combined Protestant and Roman Catholic army (Williams 1962: 830–1).

Finally, it should be noted that the Anabaptists believed that scripture could only be genuinely interpreted by those true disciples who were committed to keeping it. 'There could be no knowing of the truth without also doing it' (W. Klaassen in McKim 1998: 35).

2.4 Hermeneutics and the English reformation

Foremost among the English reformers who translated the Bible and wrote commentaries on it, was William Tyndale (c. 1494–1536), the translator of the first New Testament to be published in English, in 1525, whose work of translation (1525–1535) was continued by his colleague, Miles Coverdale, and 'Thomas Matthew' (real name John Rogers, c. 1550–1555), and greatly influenced the Great Bible (1539) and, in time, the King James Version/Authorized Version (1611) (see Bruce 1979: 24–112). Tyndale's contribution to the interpretation of scripture has often been eclipsed by his work as a translator, but his 'work as an exegete rested upon the very skills that made him an exceptional translator, namely, his capacity for language' (N.P. Feldmeth in McKim 1998: 235). While little is known about his early years, it is likely that humanism was an important factor in his development, as is suggested by his translation of Erasmus' *Enchiridion Militis Christiani* (*Christian Soldiers' Handbook*), his use of Erasmus' Greek New Testament (1522 edition), his linguistic skills (he mastered seven languages, including Latin, Greek, and Hebrew), and the fact that he gave his life for the translation of the original text of the scriptures.

Tyndale insisted that scripture has only one sense – the literal sense, or what is also called the natural or normal sense, and this is that which the author intended: 'Thou shalt understand, therefore, that the scripture hath but one sense which is the literal sense. And that literal sense is the root and ground of all, and the anchor that never faileth, whereunto if thou cleave thou canst never err or go out of the way. And if thou leave the literal sense: thou canst not but go out of the way. Never the later the scripture useth proverbs, similitude, riddles or allegories as all other speeches do, but that which the proverb, similitude, riddle or allegory signifieth is ever the literal sense, which thou must seek out diligently. As in the English we borrow words and sentences of one thing and apply them to another and give them new significations' (*The Obedience of a Christian Man* [1528], cited by Daniell 1994: 239). The exegete's task, then, is to discover the author's intention, the literal sense which is the spiritual sense, since, ultimately, the Holy Spirit is the divine author of scripture (cf. *Doctrinal Treatises* 305, 309, in Hughes 1997: 43–4).

Tyndale was no mere literalist as his recognition of the presence of figures of speech shows. The longest section of the whole of his *The Obedience of a Christian Man* (1528) Tyndale gave over to an extended discussion of the *Quadriga*, in which he rejects allegory, which he believed included tropology and anagogy: 'this word allegory comprehendeth them both . . . For tropological is but an allegory of manners, and anagogical is an allegory of hope' (*Doctrinal Treatises* 303–304, in Hughes 1997: 43). He condemned allegory as 'The greatest cause of which captivity and the decay of the faith, and this blindness wherein we now are, sprang first of allegories,' laying the blame at the feet of Origen and those who had followed him, 'till they at last forgot the order and process of the text, supposing that the Scripture served but to feign [invent] allegories upon; insomuch that twenty doctors expound one text twenty ways . . . Yea, they [sophisters with their anagogical and chopological – Tyndale's word for logic-chopping/ironic effect, which is a mocking replacement for tropological – sense] are come unto such blindness that they not only say the literal sense profiteth not, but also that it is hurtful, and noisome, and killeth the soul' (*Doctrinal Treatises* 307–308, in Hughes 1997: 43). The proper use of allegories and metaphors, however, was the way in which they made the text clear. They were not the building blocks of truth and could prove nothing, but could illustrate what was openly taught elsewhere in the Bible (McKim 1998: 237).

In his 1533 study, *Exposition of Matthew V–VII*, Tyndale developed his idea of the conditional nature of the covenant promises and the normativity of God's law. This influenced his interpretation of the Bible, in that he contended that the proper understanding of the law is the key to scripture. To support this he employed typology in order to understand the relationship between the two Testaments. The scapegoat, bronze serpent, ox burned outside the gate, and the Passover lambs, for example, were the types, 'the secrets of Christ,' by which God showed Moses 'the very manner of his death' (*Prologue to Leviticus* [1530] 1.422, in McKim 1998: 237–8).

The most serious departure from the literal sense of scripture, Tyndale believed, was the way the pope used Jesus' words to Peter in Matthew 16:18 and other passages to justify the papacy's claim to dominical authority and sanction. Tyndale's objection reflects the conviction of many reformers that the Bible interprets itself in the sense that any text cannot stand apart from the teaching of the rest of scripture. He wrote: 'Now the Scripture giveth record to himself, and ever expoundeth itself by another open text. If the pope then cannot bring for his exposition the practising of Christ or of the apostles and prophets or an open text, then is his exposition false doctrine' (cited by Daniell 1994: 240).

2.5 Hermeneutics and the Catholic reformation

The Protestant reformers were not the only ones to stress the necessity of using the biblical languages and returning *ad fontes* to the foundation documents of Christianity – the Bible and the writings of the Fathers. It must not be forgotten that Erasmus remained a Roman Catholic, committed to the internal reform of the Catholic Church. In 1527, Tommaso de Vio Cajetan (1469–1534) translated the Psalms from Hebrew not the Vulgate and relied on the help of a Christian Hebraist and a Jewish scholar because he himself did not know the language. He also wrote commentaries based on the Greek text, comparing his work with Erasmus' 1516 Greek New Testament, of the Gospels, Acts, and the Epistles between 1527–1532, which set out to discover the literal sense of each book, rejecting the tradition of spiritual exegesis. Other leading Catholic commentators include Jacopo Sadoleto, whose 1535 commentary on Romans was regarded by many as almost Protestant, though he used the Epistle to support the papacy against Luther, and Andreas Masius (1514–1573), whose commentary on Joshua (1574) was the first to speak of a book's compilation which had undergone a later redaction (Bray 1996: 181–2).

Jacques Lefèvre d'Étaples (also known by his Latin name, Faber Stapulensis) was a Roman Catholic humanist who admired the work of Zwingli, the French reformer William Farel (1489–1565, who persuaded Calvin to stay in Geneva), and Calvin, and while he corresponded with them, he never moved over to the Protestant side. He wrote widely, editing and translating many classical and patristic texts as well as the works of Aristotle. In 1509 he published his *Fivefold Psalter*, followed by his commentary on Paul's letters (1512) and a Latin commentary on the Gospels in 1521, which he followed up with a French translation of the Gospels in 1523. His New Testament came next and also the Psalms (1524), and in 1530 a translation of the whole Bible appeared, though he needed help with his

Hebrew. D'Étaples accepted the twofold literal sense advocated by Nicholas of Lyra, though he took him to task on his distinction between the literal-historical and literal-prophetic senses of the Psalms, insisting on the latter as the primary literal sense, which for him is Christological, and arguing that the former sense is distorted. He argued, 'It is impossible for us to believe this one to be the literal sense . . . which makes David a historian rather than a prophet. Instead, let us call that the literal sense which is in accord with the Spirit and is pointed out by the Spirit. "We know," says Paul . . . , "that the law is spiritual," [Rom. 7:14] and if it *is* spiritual, how could the literal sense, if it is really to be the sense of the law, not be spiritual? Therefore the literal sense and the spiritual sense coincide. This true sense is not what is called the allegorical or tropological sense, but rather the sense the Holy Spirit intends as He speaks through the prophet [in this case, David]. It has been our total purpose to draw out of this sense all that the Holy Spirit has put into it' (Oberman 1967: 300). D'Étaples did not dismiss the *Quadriga*, for there were times when it was called for by a particular passage of scripture, but for him, Christ is the key to understanding the Psalms and what David wrote (P.D.W. Krey in McKim 1998: 206–7).

In his *Aurea Rosa* (1503, especially the section 'The Rules for the Exegesis of Scripture'), the Dominican Sylvester Mazzolini Prierias (d. 1523), advisor to Pope Leo X, and Luther's first literary opponent, rejected d'Étaples' identification of the literal and spiritual senses in favor of the argument of Nicholas of Lyra that there is only one literal sense which is subject to human investigation and another which comes from the teaching of the church. In his 1518 attack on Luther, Prierias made the implications of his view explicit: 'Whoever does not rely on the teaching of the Roman Pontiff as the infallible rule of faith, from which also Holy Scripture draws its power and authority, is a heretic' (cited by Oberman 1967: 292; cf. Oberman 1989: 42–3, 193–5).

This was the position ratified at the fourth session of the Council of Trent (April 8, 1546; see McGrath 1999: 165–7). The 'Decree Concerning the Canonical Scriptures' and 'Decree Concerning the Edition and Use of the Sacred Books' made five major points: that scripture and tradition are equally authoritative for faith and conduct – 'that the purity of the gospel may be preserved in the church after the errors have been removed. This [gospel] . . . [is] the source at once of all saving truth and rules of conduct. It also clearly perceives that these truths and rules are contained in the written books and in the unwritten traditions, which, received by the apostles from the mouth of Christ himself, or from the apostles themselves, the Holy Ghost dictating, have come down to us, transmitted as it were from hand to hand.' Further, the extent of the canon included the books of the Apocrypha/Deuterocanonical

books, that the Vulgate was the authoritative translation of scripture, and no Roman Catholic was to publish any interpretation of the Bible without 'the permission of ecclesiastical superiors.' On the authority of the church as the interpreter of scripture, it was declared that

no one relying on his own judgement shall, in matters of faith and morals pertaining to the edification of Christian doctrine, distorting the holy Scriptures in accordance with his own conceptions, presume to interpret them contrary to that sense which holy mother church, to whom it belongs to judge of their true sense and interpretation, has held and holds, or even contrary to the unanimous teaching of the fathers, even though such interpretations should not at any time be published. (Noll 1991: 170–3)

References and further reading

Aldridge, J.W. (1966) *The Hermeneutic of Erasmus*, Winterthur: P.G. Keller/Richmond: John Knox Press.

Augustijn, C. (1991) *Erasmus: His Life, Works, and Influence*, Toronto: University of Toronto Press.

Baylor, M.G. (1991) *The Radical Reformation*, Cambridge Texts in the History of Political Thought, Cambridge: Cambridge University Press.

Bornkamm, H. (1969) *Luther and the Old Testament*, Philadelphia: Fortress Press.

Bray, G. (1996) *Biblical Interpretation: Past and Present*, Leicester: Apollos.

Bromiley, G.W. (ed.) (1953) *Zwingli and Bullinger*, Library of Christian Classics 24, Philadelphia: Westminster Press.

Bruce, F.F. (1979) *History of the Bible in English*, Cambridge: Lutterworth Press, 3rd edn.

Cameron, R. (1969) 'The Attack on the Biblical Work of Lefèvre d'Étaples, 1514–1521,' *Church History* 38: 9–24.

—— (1970) 'The Charges of Lutheranism Brought Against Jacques Lefèvre d'Étaples (1520–1529),' *Harvard Theological Review* 63: 119–49.

CR: *Corpus Reformatorum*, Berlin/Leipzig/Zürich, 1834–.

Daniell, D. (1994) *William Tyndale: A Biography*, New Haven: Yale University Press.

de Greef, W. (1993) *The Writings of John Calvin: An Introductory Guide*, Grand Rapids: Baker.

Deppermann, K. (1987) *Melchior Hoffmann: Social Unrest and Apocalyptic Visions in the Age of the Reformation*, Edinburgh: T.&T. Clark.

Estep, W.R. (1975) *The Anabaptist Story*, Grand Rapids: Eerdmans, 2nd edn.

Evans, G.R. (1985) *The Language and Logic of the Bible: The Road to Reformation*, Cambridge: Cambridge University Press.

Farrar, F.W. (1961) *History of Interpretation* (orig. 1886).

Furcha, E.J. and H.W. Pipkin (eds.) (1984a) *Huldrych Zwingli Writings*, 2 Vols., Allison Park, PA: Pickwick.

—— and H.W. Pipkin (eds.) (1984b) *Prophet, Pastor, Protestant*, Allison Park, PA: Pickwick.

Gamble, R.C. (1987) 'Exposition and Method in Calvin,' *Westminster Theological Journal* 49: 153–65.

Greenslade, S.L. (ed.) (1963) *The Cambridge History of the Bible. Volume 3: The West from the Reformation to the Present Day*, Cambridge: Cambridge University Press.

Haroutunian, J. (ed.) (1958) *Calvin: Commentaries*, Library of Christian Classics 23, Philadelphia: Westminster Press.

Hayes, J.H. (ed.) (1999) *Dictionary of Biblical Interpretation*, 2 Vols., Nashville: Abingdon Press.

Hoffmann, M. (1994) *Rhetoric and Theology: The Hermeneutic of Erasmus*, Toronto: University of Toronto Press.

Hughes, P.E. (1997) *Theology of the English Reformers*, Abington: Horseradish, 3rd edn.

Kraus, H.-J. (1977) 'Calvin's Exegetical Principles,' *Interpretation* 31: 8–18.

Künzli, E. (1905–) 'Zwingli als Ausleger des Alten Testamentes,' pp. 869–99 in *Huldrych Zwinglis Sämtliche Werke*, Corpus Reformatorum 14, E. Egli (ed.), Leipzig: Heinsius.

Lampe, G.W.H. (ed.) (1969) *The Cambridge History of the Bible. Volume 2: The West from the Fathers to the Reformation*, Cambridge: Cambridge University Press.

Lohse, B. (1987) *Martin Luther: An Introduction to His Life and Work*, Edinburgh: T.&T. Clark.

LW: Pelikan, J. and H.T. Lehmann (eds.) (1955–1986) *Luther's Works*, 55 Vols., St. Louis: Concordia.

Maag, K. (ed.) (1999) *Melanchthon in Europe: His Work and Influence beyond Wittenberg*, Texts and Studies in Reformation and Post-Reformation Thought, Grand Rapids: Baker Books/Carlisle: Paternoster.

McGrath, A.E. (1987) *The Intellectual Origins of the European Reformation*, Oxford: Blackwell.

—— (1999) *Reformation Thought: An Introduction*, Oxford: Blackwell, 3rd edn.

McKim, D.K. (ed.) (1998) *Historical Handbook of Major Biblical Interpreters*, Downers Grove: IVP.

McNeil, J.T. (ed.) (1960) *Institutes of the Christian Religion*, Library of Christian Classics 21–22, Philadelphia: Westminster Press.

Muller, R.A. and J.L. Thompson (eds.) (1996) *Biblical Interpretation in the Era of the Reformation: Essays Presented to David C. Steinmetz in Honor of His Sixtieth Birthday*, Grand Rapids: Eerdmans.

Noll, M.A. (ed.) (1991) *Confessions and Catechisms of the Reformation*, Leicester: Apollos.

Oberman, H.A. (1967) *Forerunners of the Reformation: The Shape of Late Medieval Thought*, London: Lutterworth Press.

—— (1989) *Luther: Man between God and the Devil*, New Haven: Yale University Press.

—— (1992) *The Dawn of the Reformation: Essays in Late Medieval and Early Reformation Thought*, Edinburgh: T.&T. Clark.

—— (1994) *The Impact of the Reformation*, Grand Rapids: Eerdmans.

Parker, T.H.L. (1986) *Calvin's Old Testament Commentaries*, Edinburgh: T.&T. Clark.

—— (1992) *Calvin's Preaching*, Edinburgh: T.&T. Clark.

—— (1993) *Calvin's New Testament Commentaries*, Edinburgh: T.&T. Clark, 2nd edn.

Pauck, W. (ed.) (1969) *Melanchthon and Bucer*, Library of Christian Classics 19, London: SCM Press.

—— (ed.) (1971) *Luther: Lecture on Romans*, Library of Christian Classics 15, London: SCM Press.

Payne, J.B. (1969) 'Toward the Hermeneutics of Erasmus,' pp. 13–49 in *Scrinium Erasmianum* II, J. Coppens (ed.), Leiden: Brill.

—— (1974) 'Erasmus and Lefèvre d'Étaples as Interpreters of Paul,' *Archiv für Reformationsgeschichte* 65: 54–83.

Pelikan, J. (1959) *Luther the Expositor*, St. Louis: Concordia.

—— (1996) *The Reformation of the Bible – The Bible of the Reformation*, New Haven: Yale University Press.

Potter, G.R. (1976) *Zwingli*, Cambridge: Cambridge University Press.

Puckett, D.L. (1995) *John Calvin's Exegesis of the Old Testament*, Louisville: Westminster/John Knox.

Rabil, Jr., A. (1972) *Erasmus and the New Testament: The Mind of a Christian Humanist*, San Antonio: Trinity University Press.

Rogers, J.B. and D.K. McKim (eds.) (1979) *The Authority and Interpretation of the Bible: An Historical Approach*, San Francisco: Harper & Row.

Schneider, J.R. (1990) *Melanchthon's Rhetorical Construal of Biblical Authority: Oratio Sacra*, Lewiston: Edwin Mellen.

Shuger, D.K. (1994) *The Renaissance Bible: Scholarship, Sacrifice, and Subjectivity*, Berkeley: University of California Press.

Snyder, A. (1995) *Anabaptist History and Theology: An Introduction*, Kitchener: Pandora.

Steinmetz, D.C. (1980a) *Luther and Staupitz: An Essay in the Intellectual Origins of the Protestant Reformation*, Durham: Duke University Press.

—— (1980b) 'The Superiority of Pre-Critical Exegesis,' *Theology Today* 37: 27–38.

—— (ed.) (1990) *The Bible in the Sixteenth Century*, Durham: Duke University Press.

Stephens, W.P. (1986) *The Theology of Huldrych Zwingli*, Oxford: Clarendon.

Stupperich, R. (1965) *Melanchthon*, Philadelphia: Westminster.

Swartley, W. (ed.) (1984) *Essays on Biblical Interpretation: Anabaptist-Mennonite Perspectives*, Text Reader 1, Elkhart: Institute of Mennonite Studies.

Thompson, Mark D. (2004) *A Sure Ground on Which to Stand: The Relation of Authority and Interpretive Method in Luther's Approach to Scripture*, Studies in Christian History and Thought, Carlisle: Paternoster.

Torrance, D.W. and T.F. Torrance (eds.) (1959–1972) *Calvin's Commentaries*, 12 Vols., Grand Rapids: Eerdmans.

Torrance, T.F. (1988) *The Hermeneutics of John Calvin*, Edinburgh: Scottish Academic Press.

WA: Knaake, J.K.F., G. Kawerau *et al.* (eds.) (1883–1983) *D. Martin Luthers Werke: Kritische Gesamtausgabe*, 61 Vols., Weimar: Hermann Böhlaus Nachfolger.

Walter, H. (ed.) (1948) William Tyndale, *Doctrinal Treatises . . .* , Vol. 1. Parker Society, Cambridge: Cambridge University Press.

Wengert, T.J. and M.P. Graham (eds.) (1997) *Philipp Melanchthon and the Commentary*, Sheffield: Sheffield Academic Press.

Williams, G.H. (1962) *The Radical Reformation*, Philadelphia: Westminster Press.

—— and A.M. Mergal (eds.) (1957) *Spiritual and Anabaptist Writers*, Library of Christian Classics 25, Philadelphia: Westminster Press.

Yoder, J.H. (1967) 'The Hermeneutics of the Anabaptists,' *Mennonite Quarterly Review* 42: 291–308.

ANTHONY R. CROSS

REIMARUS, HERMANN SAMUEL (1694–1768)

Hermann Samuel Reimarus, a Hamburg professor of Oriental languages, lived during the German Enlightenment amidst an evolving discussion on the relation of reason and revelation. His biblical interpretation reflects this context. The philosopher Christian Wolff provided the dominant synthesis of the time: (a) that revelation may be above reason but not contrary to reason, and (b) that reason establishes the criteria by which revelation may be judged. Wolff's synthesis was attacked from two directions. On the one side, Neology contended that (a) revelation is real but its content is not different from that of natural religion in general, and (b) reason may eliminate those individual doctrines of Christian revelation which are not identical with reason. On the other side, rationalism contended that reason's criteria judge revelation to be false, leaving reason to exist alone. Reimarus' public views attempted to show that the demands of natural religion and those of Christianity complemented one another. Natural religion prepares for Christianity. His private views were those of rationalism, the total displacement of revelation by reason. There are, he argued, two criteria by which every alleged revelation must be tested. First, revelation must be necessary. It must contain knowledge not attainable by natural means but only by miracle. Second, it must be free both from contradictions of the laws of nature and from inner contradictions. Reimarus argued that (a) it is possible to trace the natural origins of Christianity, and (b) the supposed revelation is filled with contradictions. Reason's criteria, therefore, undermine the claims of the alleged Christian revelation.

In his *Apology* Reimarus assumed the traditional churchly view of the Gospels' authorship, regarding Matthew and John as by apostles. He, therefore, used these two Gospels most frequently, filling in with Mark and Luke. Apart from authorship, however, Reimarus' views of the sources were far from traditional. He believed the Gospels to be colored by the later church's point of view. He accepted as authentic Jesus material only what had escaped the church's redaction, an incipient criterion of discontinuity. He thus drew attention to the distinction between the preaching of Jesus and that of the early church, to the fact that the latter colors the former, and to the need for some criterion to decide which is which. Jesus, he argued, taught none of the three central doctrines of Christianity: atonement, resurrection, and second coming. These teachings were created by Jesus' followers after his death. Jesus was a this-worldly Messianic claimant who failed. Neither miracle reports nor proofs from prophecy are to be believed. Rather than being paragons of virtue, the apostles were just the opposite. Christianity's origins are based on apostolic fraud. Since the revelation is not necessary and since contradictions abound in it, it is false.

References and further reading

Schweitzer, Albert (1910) *The Quest of the Historical Jesus*, London: A.&C. Black.

Strauss, David F. (1877) *Hermann Samuel Reimarus und seine Schutzschrift für die vernünftigen Verehrer Gottes*, Bonn: Emil Strauss, 2nd edn.

Talbert, Charles H. (ed.) (1970) *Reimarus: Fragments*, Philadelphia: Fortress Press.

CHARLES H. TALBERT

RHETORICAL CRITICISM

In the Hellenistic world, training in rhetoric followed upon rudimentary grammatical education. Rhetoric therefore made at least a cursory impression upon certain biblical authors from the third century BC. Some of the earliest efforts at interpreting the scriptures involved aspects of rhetoric having to do with style and literary figures. By the time Augustine completed *De Doctrina Christiana* (AD 427), rhetorical approaches to interpretation of scripture were somewhat common. Rhetorical criticism flourished in the time of the Renaissance and

Reformation in the works of Erasmus and Melanchthon; in the latter half of the eighteenth century and into the nineteenth in the writings of J.A. Ernesti, K. Bauer, and C. Wilke; then again at the end of the nineteenth century in the works of F. Blass, J. Weiss, and E. Norden. Each of these authors drew heavily upon classical Graeco-Roman rhetoric. Classical rhetorical analysis achieved a resurgence in the latter half of the twentieth century in works by J. Muilenburg, H.D. Betz, W. Wuellner, and G.A. Kennedy.

The major extant works of classical rhetoric are: Aristotle *The Rhetoric* (*c.* AD 335); Demetrius *On Style* (*c.* second century, BC); the *Rhetorica ad Herennium* (*c.* 85 BC); Cicero *De Inventione* (*c.* 89 BC) and *De Oratore* (55 BC); Longinus *On the Sublime* (*c.* first century, AD); and Quintilian *Institutio Oratoria* (*c.* AD 92).

The Graeco-Roman rhetoricians set out, not so much to lay the foundations for rhetorical criticism, but to provide insight and practical guidelines for those engaged in speaking and writing. They limited their observations to discourse in the law courts (forensic or juridica, *dikanikon*), the political assemblies (deliberative *sumbouleutikon*), and ceremonial occasions (demonstrative or epideictic, *deiktikon*). These are the three famous genres of classical rhetoric. Aristotle declared that there were many other types of discourse which he did not subsume under the rubric of rhetoric.

The observations of the classical rhetoricians may therefore be somewhat limited in value for biblical critics since the classical rhetoricians did not experience nor comment upon speaking in synagogues and churches. They focused on speeches, both oral and written, and viewed each speech as a total discourse. They did not apply rhetorical analysis to smaller units (pericope) as if they were complete discourses within larger documents. Only after the third century AD were insights from rhetoric thought useful in commenting on letters, histories, apocalypses, or dialogues.

The five classical canons or parts of rhetoric, first declared in the *Rhetorica ad Herennium*, are: invention, arrangement, style, memory, and delivery. Certain of these canons have been given more emphasis than others in certain historical periods. Through medieval times, rhetorical analysis chiefly assessed style, including tropes and figures. In the eighteenth century rhetorical critics turned to speakers and audiences. In America in the twentieth century, rhetoricians who taught speech and composition stressed invention and rhetorical proofs. Beginning with Muilenburg (1958), biblical scholars approaching the scriptures rhetorically have focused chiefly on structure (*taxis*), that is, arrangement. Since the Renaissance little comment has been made upon memory in rhetorical criticism, but because of recent discussions of memory in the ancient world, certain observations are possible (Olbricht 1997). The criticism of delivery, of course, requires preferably both hearing and seeing the speaker and therefore is not a component of criticism when ancient documents are discussed, unless of course a contemporary wrote observations about the delivery.

Rhetorical criticism of biblical documents extrapolated from classical precepts may therefore proceed (step 1) with a determination of genre, whether forensic, deliberative, or epideictic. (Kennedy 1984: 3–8 offers a somewhat different set of steps.) Such identification is often inconclusive and controverted and in the end not especially efficacious in providing new insights. Next, the canons of rhetoric are taken up in order, beginning with invention (*heurēsis*). Invention assesses both the status of the question (*stasis*) and the proofs (*pisteis*). Hermagorus in *Art of Rhetoric* (*c.* 150 BC) expounded a theory of stasis. Determining the stasis (step 2) has to do with basic issues involving fact, definition, quality, and jurisdiction. The proofs (*pisteis*) were divided into nonartistic (*atexnoi*) and artistic (*entexnoi*). The former consisted of what in the courtroom are called exhibits such as objects, contracts, and witnesses. The citation of biblical texts belongs in this category. The speaker or writer also invents artistic proofs, that is, they select these with a specific audience in mind. There are three types of artistic proofs: logical argument and evidence (*logos*), the speaker's character (*ēthos*), and emotive appeal (*pathos*).

The assessment of the logical argument (step 3) consists of examining enthymemes (*enthumēmata*) and examples (*paradeigma*). Aristotle argued that philosophical arguments proceeded from syllogisms based on universally declared premises. The premises of rhetors, however, are probable and derive from presuppositions of the specific auditors addressed. The determination of enthymemes therefore requires picking out the assumptions in the speech, and ascertaining whether they correspond with the presuppositions of the audience. The speaker does not set these forth, Aristotle declared, as a complete syllogism. From examples in a speech, the speaker induces conclusions which in turn often become premises in enthymemes. Examples are of two kinds: those that have happened, which we may designate historical, and those invented, that is, comparisons (*parabolē*) or fables (*logos*) (Aristotle, *The Rhetoric* 2.20.3). One should consult the rhetoricians for observations on how the forms of proof differ from genre to genre.

The critic is now (step 4) ready to turn to ethical proof, which is based on the character of the speaker. The speaker often stands before his auditors with a certain reputation. But in addition to what the speakers bring to the situation, in the speech itself, they seek to establish themselves as persons of worthy character by their goodwill, virtue, good sense, and liberality. The examination of ethical proof is followed by the assessment (step 5) of pathos. Aristotle in *The Rhetoric* set forth six emotions and their opposites: anger and mildness, love and hate, fear and confidence, shame and benevolence, pity and indignation, and envy and emulation.

The parts (step 6) of arrangement (*taxis*) in their fullest classical expression are: exordium, narration, proposition, partition, proof, refutation, digression, and peroration. Some of these parts may be omitted in specific discourses. The third canon (step 7) is style (*lexis*). Aristotle declared that good style should be characterized by perspicuity, purity, loftiness, and propriety. Various of the rhetoricians on style wrote of three levels, the plain, the grand, and the middle styles, and later of the styles of the first and second sophistic. The critics reflected on words (diction), how they were put together (synthesis), and the various literary figures and tropes. Memory (step 8) is more difficult to assess but attention can be given to whether items might be arranged according to placement on a landscape or chronologically.

While analyzing biblical documents according to the dictates of classical rhetoric may be of some help, even more helpful may be approaching the biblical documents as a separate genre, since it makes as much sense to declare a separate genre for these religious discourses as it does a separate genre for political assemblies, courts, and occasional discourses of praise and blame. The rhetoric of the 'biblical' genre will be generated through scrutiny of biblical texts and their unique features. For example, the special powers of quotations from earlier texts, metaphors, and narratives in biblical materials may differ in construction as well as in content because of the conviction that the maker of heaven and earth revealed himself in human history through word and deed.

References and further reading

Kennedy, G.A., *New Testament Interpretation through Rhetorical Criticism*, Chapel Hill: University of North Carolina Press.

Lausberg, H. (1998) *Handbook of Literary Rhetoric: A Foundation for Literary Study*, trans. M.T. Bliss, A. Jansen, and D.E. Orton; D.E. Orton and R.D. Anderson (eds.), Leiden: Brill.

Muilenburg, J. (1969) 'Form Criticism and Beyond,' *Journal of Biblical Literature* 88 1–18.

Olbricht, T.H. 'Delivery and Memory,' pp. 159–67 in *Handbook of Classical Rhetoric in the Hellenistic Period 330 BC–AD 400*, S.E. Porter (ed.), Leiden: Brill.

Porter, S.E., and T.H. Olbricht (eds.) (1993) *Rhetoric and the New Testament: Essays from the 1992 Heidelberg Conference*, Sheffield: Sheffield Academic Press.

—— (1996) *Rhetoric, Scripture and Theology: Essays from the 1994 Pretoria Conference*, Sheffield: Sheffield Academic Press.

—— (1997) *The Rhetorical Analysis of Scripture: Essays from the 1995 London Conference*, Sheffield: Sheffield Academic Press.

Porter, S.E., and D.L. Stamps (eds.) (1999) *The Rhetorical Interpretation of Scripture: Essays from the 1996 Malibu Conference*, Sheffield: Sheffield Academic Press.

Watson, D.F. and A.J. Hauser (1994) *Rhetorical Criticism of the Bible: A Comprehensive Bibliography with Notes on History and Method*, Leiden: Brill.

Wuellner W. (1976) 'Paul's Rhetoric of Argumentation in Romans: An Alternative to the Donfried-Karris Debate Over Romans,' *Catholic Biblical Quarterly*, 38: 330–51 (repr. in Karl Donfried [ed.], *The Romans Debate*, Philadelphia: Fortress Press).

T.H. OLBRICHT

RICOEUR, PAUL (1913–2005)

French philosopher and Christian activist, Ricoeur held dual appointments at the Universities of Paris (Nanterre) and Chicago through the 1970s and 1980s and is best known for a hermeneutical approach to philosophy that enabled him to contribute to a number of disciplines.

Ricoeur stands in a long tradition of philosophers interested in human subjectivity; he is above all an exegete of human being. Kant's philosophy, for instance, aimed at understanding human beings by seeking answers to certain basic questions: 'What can I know?' 'What should I do?' 'What may I hope?' Ricoeur's questions are every bit as fundamental: 'Who am I?' 'What can I do?' 'What may I become?' Under the influence of G. Marcel and J. Nabert, Ricoeur came to reject the phenomenological or direct approach to the study of consciousness and became convinced that self-understanding is obtained indirectly, through an interpretation of the signs and acts that disclose it. Hermeneutics thus becomes the 'long route' to the 'promised land' of ontology (Ricoeur 1974: 24). The manifesto of hermeneutic philosophy is 'existence via semantics': human beings attain self-understanding only through the exegesis of every cultural artifact.

The Bible is the preeminent cultural artifact of the West. Ricoeur's study of the human will led him to grapple with the meaning of various myths, including the Adam narrative, which symbolize the origin of human evil. While the philosopher cannot accept the literal or historical meaning of such texts, it does not follow that they are without meaning. Indeed, only by interpreting such stories can we gain a full grasp of the human condition. The symbol – of creation, of fall, of redemption – 'gives rise to thought.'

Ricoeur confronts a number of critical approaches – historical criticism, Freudian criticism, structuralism, atheism – and argues in each case that there is something in the symbol, and the text, that survives critical suspicion. He commends not a precritical but a postcritical 'second naiveté' open to a meaning beyond that of the literal.

Hermeneutics bridges the various kinds of distance that separate readers from a meaningful encounter with texts. Yet texts, precisely because they are written, gain an autonomy from their authors, and their original situations, and launch out on a career of their own. Interpretation involves more than a re-creation of the original sense; it explores a text's trajectory of meaning.

Central to Ricoeur's interpretation theory is his notion of the text. A text is neither a mirror to the past, nor a self-contained entity, but rather a world-bearing or world-projecting dynamism. The Adam narrative may not be about a literal prehistorical figure, but it does not follow that the text is not 'about' anything. Ricoeur sees a parallel between the way metaphors and narratives refer: both are types of creative language that project a meaning beyond any possible literal reference. Metaphors refer to being as possibility; narratives refer to ways of human being-in-time, to human possibilities. The Adam narrative describes the paradox of a freedom that corrupts itself, a notion difficult to express coherently with concepts.

Ricoeur's 'Biblical Hermeneutics' (1975) treats Jesus' parables as metaphoric narratives that are about the ways in which the Kingdom of God opens up new possibilities for human social existence. Similarly, each of the literary genres in scripture refers to or 'refigures' the world in its own irreducible manner, all of which 'call for thought.' Interpretation is the process by which the world of human possibilities revealed by different kinds of texts are appropriated by the reader. Exegesis demands appropriation, for the purpose of hermeneutics is to overcome the distance between readers and the 'world of the text.' (For an important critique of Ricoeur's preference for 'textual sense' rather than 'authorial intention,' see Wolterstorff 1995: 130–52.)

Where Descartes elevates the 'ego' and Derrida deconstructs it, Ricoeur prefers to situate and interpret the ego 'in front of' the text. This is the wager of faith: that we will come to a better understanding of the human condition, and of our own selves, by interpreting narratives about others.

All poetic texts, and not the Bible only, 'reveal' the 'transcendent' in the sense that the worlds they project open up possible ways of being-in-the-world which, if appropriated, can transform the world of the reader. What then is unique about scripture? And what might 'theological interpretation' mean for Ricoeur?

All biblical interpretation is at one and the same time self-interpretation, for all self-understanding is mediated through the ensemble or canon of texts that refigure human existence. Some see Ricoeur's hermeneutics as having particular affinities with Barth (Wallace 1990), Bultmann (Vanhoozer 1990), and Hauerwas (Fodor 1995) respectively. 'God' is the referent of the medley of biblical genres, taken together in all their irreducible plurality. God is not a univocal concept so much as the index of incompleteness of human discourse, and the mystery of human being. Human being is constituted by the 'word' that summons it, yet it is unclear whether this word – and the possibility of transformed life projected by the biblical text – is human or divine.

References and further reading

Fodor, J. (1995) *Christian Hermeneutics: Paul Ricoeur and the Refiguring of Theology*, Oxford: Clarendon.

Kearney, R. (ed.) (1996) *Paul Ricoeur: The Hermeneutics of Action*, London: Sage.

Laughery, Gregory J. (2002) *Living Hermeneutics in Motion: An Analysis and Evaluation of Paul Ricoeur's Contribution to Biblical Hermeneutics*, Lanham: University Press of America.

Ricoeur, P. (1967) *The Symbolism of Evil*, Boston: Beacon Press.

—— (1974) *The Conflict of Interpretations*, Evanston: Northwestern University Press.

—— (1975) 'Biblical Hermeneutics,' *Semeia* 4: 27–148.

—— (1976) *Interpretation Theory: Discourse and the Surplus of Meaning*, Fort Worth: Texas Christian University Press.

—— (1980) *Essays on Biblical Interpretation*, Philadelphia: Fortress Press.

—— (1991) *A Ricoeur Reader: Reflection and Imagination*, M.J. Valdes (ed.), New York: Harvester Wheatsheaf.

—— (1992) *Oneself as Another*, Chicago: University of Chicago Press.

—— (1995) *Figuring the Sacred: Religion, Narrative, and Imagination*, Philadelphia: Fortress Press.

—— (1998) *Thinking Biblically: Exegetical and Hermeneutical Studies*, Chicago: University of Chicago Press.

Stiver, Dan R. (2001) *Theology after Ricoeur: New Directions in Hermeneutical Theology*, Louisville: Westminster/John Knox.

Van den Hengel, J. (1982) *The Home of Meaning: The Hermeneutics of the Subject of Paul Ricoeur*, Washington: University Press of America.

Vanhoozer, K.J. (1990) *Biblical Narrative in the Philosophy of Paul Ricoeur*, Cambridge: Cambridge University Press.

Wallace, M. (1990) *The Second Naiveté: Barth, Ricoeur, and the New Yale Theology*, Macon, GA: Mercer University Press.

Wolterstorff, N. (1995) *Divine Discourse*, Cambridge: Cambridge University Press.

KEVIN J. VANHOOZER

S

SCHLEIERMACHER, FRIEDRICH D.E. (1768–1834)

Schleiermacher's thought was influenced especially by three factors: a desire to offer a credible theological response to the challenge of Kant's transcendental philosophy; his upbringing in Christian pietism and retention of many (but not all) of its elements; and his sympathetic resonance with emerging Romanticism. The first factor led to a new era in theology (often regarded as the beginning of 'modern' theology), namely, engaging with grounds for the very *possibility* of theology and the nature of understanding (*Verstehen*) as such. Transcendental philosophy asks not simply what we know, but on what basis we may claim to know at all. Schleiermacher redefined hermeneutics as a study of the conditions for the possibility of understanding. Second, his debt to pietism led him to emphasize the role of experience, relationality, and a sense of immediate dependence upon God as a given, from which Christian doctrine is derivative. This is more than a mere 'feeling,' but an immediacy in which the infinite finds expression in the finite, contingent, and historical. Third, with Romanticist writers he stressed the creativity and livingness of understanding. Texts, in effect, become what is left behind in the wake of creative vision, and interpretation seeks to recapture the living vision that gives rise to the text.

All this leads to a distinctive view of the relation between biblical criticism and the task of interpretation. First, hermeneutics stands upon its own feet as an independent discipline. It is not a mere service tool brought in to justify some prior theology or exegesis. 'Hermeneutics is part of the art of thinking' (Schleiermacher 1977 [1819]: 97). Anticipating Gadamer in this respect, Schleiermacher insists that the interpreter must not force the text into his or her prior categories of understanding. Preliminary understanding (*Vorverständnis*) is necessary but open to correction. 'In interpretation it is essential that one be able to step out of one's own frame of mind into that of the author' (Schleiermacher 1977 [1805]: 42). Second, anticipating Bultmann, he insists that historical criticism and 'Introduction to the New Testament' serve the task of interpretation, not the other way around. 'Introduction to the New Testament,' he writes, gathers and assesses

historical knowledge in order to place us 'in the position of the original readers for whom the New Testament authors wrote' (Schleiermacher 1977 [1829]: 38). Third, interpretation necessitates interaction between two distinct methods: 'divinatory [*divinatorische*] knowledge is the feminine strength in knowing people . . . a receptivity to the uniqueness of every . . . person'; scientific, critical, or 'comparative' method is the masculine feature of checking and evaluating through the general, abstract, and transpersonal (Schleiermacher 1977 [1826–1827]: 150).

Schleiermacher also developed and refined F. Ast's formulation of the hermeneutical circle. To understand the elements of a text presupposes a provisional understanding of the whole, yet an understanding of the whole presupposes careful critical attention to its parts. Further, understanding begins with partial, provisional, preliminary 'preunderstanding,' which in turn undergoes correction and development in the light of dawning understanding. If the interpreter has fully engaged with historical, linguistic, and theological or ideological data more fully than had entered the consciousness of the author, in principle it is possible to understand a text 'better' or more fully than the author who produced it.

Three common misunderstandings of Schleiermacher are to be avoided. First, while Schleiermacher does indeed regard interpretation as following the path from the finished composition to what called it forth, it is an oversimplification to call this a 'genetic' theory of hermeneutics. For he regards it as a matter of *strategy* in relation to given questions whether hermeneutics begins with the author, or the text, or even the effects to which the text gives rise. Second, it is a mistake to accept G.W.F. Hegel's criticism that everything depends on precritical, nonconceptual 'feeling.' Schleiermacher's emphasis on the *immediacy* of *Gefühl* (feeling) has an ontological grounding and is never isolated from his 'masculine' principle of critical evaluation and comparison. Third, D.F. Strauss' dismissal of Schleiermacher as too 'churchly' overlooks his epoch-making contribution of setting up hermeneutics as an independent discipline for the first time in the history of the subject. His *Brief Outline of the Study of Theology* (1966 [1811 and 1830]) underlines attention to theoretical, critical, and scientific issues; while his *Hermeneutics* (1977

[1803–35]) underlines his concern for 'listening' to the living quasipersonal voice of the text. His exegetical work on 1 Timothy (1807 reprinted in Schleiermacher 1834–1864) reveals a rigorously critical approach to the problem of authorship and pseudonymity, while placing a range of hermeneutical questions before the text in the service of interpretation. His work is more complex and sophisticated than most writers seem to appreciate, even if it is not without flaws.

References and further reading

Clements, K.W. (1990) *Friedrich Schleiermacher*, Edinburgh: T.&T. Clark.

De Vries, D. (1998) 'Schleiermacher,' pp. 350–5 in *Historical Handbook of Major Biblical Interpreters*, D.K. McKim (ed.), Leicester, IVP.

Schleiermacher, F.D.E. (1834–1864) *Sammtliche Werke*, 31 Vols., G. Wolde (ed.), Berlin: Reimer.

—— (1928) *The Christian Faith*, Edinburgh: T.&T. Clark (orig. 1821–1822; 2nd edn 1830–1831).

—— (1966) *Brief Outline on the Study of Theology*, Richmond: Knox (reissued Lewiston, NY: Mellen, 1989; orig. 1811; 2nd edn 1830).

—— (1977) *Hermeneutics: The Handwritten Manuscripts*, AAR & Translation Series 1, Missoula: Scholars Press (six MSS 1803–1835 ed. H. Kimmerle).

Thiselton, A.C. (1992) 'Schleiermacher's Hermeneutics,' in *New Horizons in Hermeneutics*, London: Harper-Collins/Grand Rapids: Zondervan (reissued Carlisle: Paternoster).

ANTHONY C. THISELTON

SCHWEITZER, ALBERT (1875–1965)

New Testament lecturer in Strasbourg (1902), medical missionary in Africa (1913), and Nobel Peace Prize recipient (1952), Schweitzer marks a turning point in the study of Jesus and Paul. Among his numerous works in many fields (philosophy, theology, music, medicine), those of most abiding interest in New Testament studies are *The Quest of the Historical Jesus* (ET 1910), *Paul and His Interpreters* (ET 1912), and *The Mysticism of Paul the Apostle* (ET 1931).

Schweitzer bade an end to all modernizing and spiritualizing of Jesus (theology must give way to history). Jesus' primary motivation in action and speech was his imminent expectation of the end of the world in his own messianic establishment of God's Kingdom (Matt. 10:23). Living to see these hopes fail, he died to force their fulfilment (the first in a long line of theological readjustments to the 'delay of the Parousia'). Paul was similarly driven by eschatological dogma. Fitting Jesus into the scheme of his prior expectations, Paul formed his doctrine of 'being-in-Christ,' of participating in Jesus' dying and rising and thus anticipating in the final days of the old age the life of the new (ultimately

showing modern theology the way back to the distant historical Jesus).

Schweitzer's influence is still felt, in principle if not always in detail. Although his treatment of the Synoptic sources, of Jesus' messianic self-consciousness, and of Paul's precise eschatological scheme has not carried conviction, an eschatological interpretation of Jesus and Paul is now standard; and his 'participatory' reading of Paul has made a direct impact on Pauline studies. At the end of the twentieth century and into the twenty-first, the 'third quest' of the historical Jesus and the 'new perspective' on Paul attest to Schweitzer's influence. (Is the 'eschatological Jesus' authentic or the invention of early Christians? Is 'justification by faith' or 'participation in Christ' most characteristic of Paul's theology?)

Schweitzer established 'history of interpretation' as a matter of critical interest in its own right (even if for him it is still a means to an end, and should end with him). In the process, his history/theology antithesis had a decisive effect on the disciplinary rhetoric of biblical studies. Though he took himself simply to be showing how the problems of biblical criticism unfold themselves in history, his work is now more readily seen as a construction – and, as such, it is both enabling and constraining. His relative silence on hermeneutics/philosophy of religious language masks assumptions with which subsequent criticism could not rest content. Yet he displayed a keen intuitive sensitivity to hermeneutical shifts in modern biblical criticism, and his work raised a question of lasting interest: does the significance of Jesus and Paul die with the failure of their hopes, or does there come to expression amidst those hopes a human striving with which we might still identify?

References and further reading

Grässer, E. (1999) 'Schweitzer, Albert,' pp. 449–50 in *Dictionary of Biblical Interpretation*, J.H. Hayes (ed.), Vol. 2, Nashville: Abingdon.

Matlock, R.B. (1996) *Unveiling the Apocalyptic Paul*, Sheffield: Sheffield Academic Press.

R.B. MATLOCK

SECOND TEMPLE PERIOD

1 Introduction
2 Quotations and allusions
3 Translation
4 'Rewritten Bible'
5 Commentary
6 Allegory
7 'Parabiblical' exegesis
8 Conclusions

1 Introduction

With the development of a concept of scripture and further stages on the road to a canon of Jewish writings during the Second Temple period (539 BC to AD 70), biblical interpretation became a sophisticated endeavor on the part of many Jews. A number of the Jewish techniques were picked up by the Christian church and used but were also reused and developed in a particular way to create uniquely Christian ways of scriptural interpretation. The purpose of this article is to survey some of the main types of Jewish biblical interpretation attested in the Second Temple period. Before looking at the specific sorts of exegesis attested in the Jewish context of the Second Temple period, however, some preliminary comments on methodology need to be considered.

First, a Hebrew canon in our sense of the word may not have come into existence until the end of the Second Temple period or even afterward. Therefore, it will be obvious that scriptural interpretation as such could not begin until there was a body of writings conceived of as scripture. When this situation first pertained is a moot point, but it seems unlikely that 'intrascriptural exegesis' had really begun before the Exile. The reason is that the concept of authoritative scripture appears to be a development of the Persian period (Grabbe 2004: 331–43). Some point to Nehemiah 8 as an example of public biblical interpretation associated with the public reading by Ezra (e.g., Fishbane 1985: 107–13). There are difficulties with this understanding, however, partly because the passage does not seem to be very early and partly to do with lack of agreement on what is going on beyond the public reading (cf. Grabbe 2004: 334–37). Yet the concept of authoritative writings seems to have been in existence already as early as the Persian period, with the accepted body of such writings to include the Pentateuch, the Former Prophets (Joshua to 2 Kings), the Major and Minor Prophets, and some of the Writings (Job, 1 and 2 Chronicles) by the time of Ben Sira (c. 200 BC).

Second, we know that an oral tradition can be subtly revised and reformulated as it is passed on, but this also applies to many writings that go through a period when their text is easily revised and altered before eventually taking on a more fixed form. At a time when the tradition was still quite fluid, it could be adapted and reshaped in various contexts according to one's understanding. It is only when the text becomes fixed and authoritative that interpretation becomes a way to create new meanings.

Third, it has been suggested (using Chronicles as a major example) that the Jewish writings of the postexilic period were mainly interpretations of scripture rather than original writings. As a general statement, this does not stand up to investigation. There are many Second Temple works that have little or nothing to do with

the Hebrew Bible we know (e.g., Ben Sira, Tobit, Judith, 1 Enoch, the books of Maccabees). Some of these are 'parabiblical' traditions which parallel in some way the biblical text but may not be connected to it directly or straightforwardly (see further below). Yet it is true that literature from Ben Sira on becomes permeated with a knowledge of portions of the Hebrew Bible in a form similar to or the same as we now use. We also find many examples of biblical exegesis in the two or three centuries before the fall of Jerusalem in AD 70.

The rest of this entry will explore some of the main ways in which the Bible was interpreted in early Jewish literature, including quotations and allusions, translation, 'rewritten Bible,' commentary and midrash, and allegory. Also included is a section on 'parabiblical writings' and the question of their relationship to the biblical text.

2 Quotations and allusions

The topic of intertextuality has become a major enterprise in Hebrew Bible scholarship. Sometimes this is interpreted widely to include the context of a biblical passage in the broad context of the prevailing culture and a variety of media. More frequently, though, it applies to the connection between literary passages that show dependence one on the other through allusion or – less frequently – precise quotation. This issue is sometimes more complicated than at first realized because many passages show resemblances not because of direct interdependence but because all have made use of a common stock of ideas, oral and literary traditions, and linguistic phraseology. One suspects that this is generally the case in writings associated with the pre-exilic period when a body of authoritative writings had not developed or was still in its embryonic stages.

One of the earliest writings in which clear allusions and even quotations from a developing canon are to be found is the book of Ben Sira or Ecclesiasticus, dating from about 200 BC. Ben Sira himself does not normally give explicit quotations, and he can in many ways be considered a continuator of an old wisdom tradition which had its own language and concepts not necessarily dependent on the biblical text. That is, Ben Sira was a wisdom teacher who incorporated the Torah, rather than a Torah teacher who incorporated the wisdom tradition. Nevertheless, there are many passages with parallels to the current text of the Old Testament, not least in Ben Sira 44–49, which lists the heroes of Israel from Adam to the high priest Simon (II) in Ben Sira's own time. In this section Ben Sira has summarized in outline form much of the contents of the present Torah and Prophets sections of the Hebrew Bible. He gives a close paraphrase and even a partial quotation from a number of passages (e.g., Gen. 5:24; 6:9; 15:18; 1 Sam. 7:10; 12:3–4; Hag. 2:23; and Mal. 3:23–24).

As time goes on Jewish writings contain an increasing number of quotations. A book such as the Wisdom of Solomon (first century BC) has many such passages. Philo of Alexandria of course quotes a good deal of Genesis, as well as other parts of the Pentateuch, though this usually precedes a commentary on the passage. Many of the Qumran writings are filled with quotations, as are sections of the New Testament.

3 Translation

One activity with the text that is often overlooked is that of translation. At first sight, this might not seem to be a form of biblical interpretation, but it can be an important one. The first aim of a translation is usually to transfer contents of the text into another language which is better understood by readers. Yet there is no such thing as a completely neutral translation. The translator makes decisions about the meaning of the original text at every point in the translation process. A translation therefore represents also an interpretation – whether to a greater or lesser extent – and may well be the first stage in a longer interpretative tradition.

Possibly the earliest example of translation is the so-called Septuagint (LXX), a translation of the Pentateuch into Greek in Alexandria in the mid-third century BC. The translation is fairly literal, but there are many small differences from the Masoretic text. Some of these are due to the use of a Hebrew text that differed from our present Masoretic text, at a time when the text was still fluid to some extent and several different versions of many books and passages circulated. Later on we find the scroll of the Minor Prophets in Greek that was found in the Judaean Desert. It contains a fairly literal translation of a text very close to the Masoretic text, known as the *kaige*. This was followed somewhat later by the three Greek Minor Versions of Aquila, Theodotion, and Symmachus. Although these are associated with specific translators from the second century AD on, Theodotion at least seems to be a revision of the *kaige*, showing that his was not a new translation; however, arguments can be made that Aquila and Symmachus were original translations.

We also have a number of translations of parts of the Hebrew Bible into Aramaic. The best known of these are the Targums, though as we now have them they are the products of the rabbinic period. Although the Targum Onqelos and Targum Jonathan to the Prophets are fairly literal translations, they still have many interpretative passages, while Targum Pseudo-Jonathan on the Pentateuch often includes a good deal of additional material. These are all from about the third century AD or later, though it has been proposed that they depend on an earlier 'Palestinian Targum' created before AD 70. There is little evidence of such an early Targum, but we do have some evidence of earlier Aramaic translations from Qumran (4Q Targum Job

and 4Q Targum Leviticus), though the preserved examples are quite literal translations. Yet even if the Aramaic translations of the Second Temple period are usually literal, they still sometimes indicate the Jewish understanding of particular passages.

4 'Rewritten Bible'

In the mind of many, one of the first major acts of interpretation was the production of the books of Chronicles. Although it has recently been suggested that they both revised a common source, Chronicles has usually been seen as a retelling of the story in Samuel-Kings (and also in some sense a retelling of the story of Genesis to Judges by means of the genealogies in 1 Chron. 1–9). If Chronicles is a rewriting of Samuel-Kings, it is a good example of one of the main means of interpretation in the Second Temple period: the retelling of the biblical account, now often known as 'rewritten Bible.'

We have many examples of 'rewritten Bible' among the Second Temple Jewish writings. In some cases, the writer accepted the authority of scripture and was only trying to supplement it. This would apply to Josephus' *Antiquities of the Jews*, the first ten books of which are more or less a paraphrase of biblical texts. However, the authors of 'rewritten Bible' no doubt always had a purpose, which was to clarify and explain the biblical text according to their understanding of it. In the case of Josephus, he brings in many interpretative traditions as well as his own rationalization of the text, but one of his main aims was to make Jewish history palatable to Graeco-Roman readers. One might ask whether many Romans or Greeks read his work, though he claims that the emperors Vespasian and Titus read his history of the *War of the Jews* (*Life* 65 §§361–63; *Ag. Apion* 1.9 §50). But it is clear that he uses apologetic devices to make Judaism look philosophically respectable to Stoics and others among the Greek and Roman population. For example, certain discreditable episodes are omitted (such as the Golden Calf incident) and, whereas many Roman writers saw Jewish customs as strange and barbaric, Josephus tries to present Jewish law as idealistic and admirable to educated Greeks and Romans.

A work such as *Jubilees* may have had a different aim from just supplementing the biblical text, however. Some have suggested that it was meant to be a substitute or replacement for Genesis, since it is presented as a divine revelation to Moses. Regardless of this, the author certainly wishes to advocate the use of the jubilee cycle (here interpreted as forty-nine years) and the solar calendar. A number of passages add material to the Genesis story that tell about customs and events of the writer's own time (e.g., the observance of the Passover in ch. 49). Of particular interest is a detailed account of the war between Jacob and the Amorites (*Jub.* 34:1–9), which seems based on the enigmatic statement in Genesis 48:22. Also taking a prominent place in *Jubilees* is a fight to the death between Jacob and Esau (*Jub.* 37–38; cf. also *T. Judah* 9). This might reflect conflicts between Jews and the Idumeans in the second century BC when *Jubilees* is likely to have been composed.

The Targums were discussed above under 'Translation,' but there is not always a clear-cut division between translation and 'rewritten Bible.' As noted, some of the Targums include a good deal of interpretative material in addition to the original text. A good example of this is the Targum Pseudo-Jonathan on the Pentateuch. This is a very late work, perhaps toward the end of the first millennium AD, but the literary form is parallel to Josephus and other writings we call 'rewritten Bible.' It looks almost like a stage between a translation of the text and a retelling of Genesis in such a writing as the *Genesis Apocryphon*. The reason is that 'rewritten Bible' takes a variety of forms.

'Rewritten Bible' is a bit of a problematic category because it could include so much. *The Book of Biblical Antiquities* (also known as Pseudo-Philo) is a paraphrase of the biblical text from Genesis to the death of Saul. Where the biblical text is detailed, it tends to be short, but at other times it expands the story greatly. This suggests that it was meant to be read alongside the biblical text almost as a commentary. On the other hand, the various Fragmentary Jewish Writings in Greek appear in a number of different literary forms. Granted, they all seem to be addressing themselves to biblical themes and interpretation (e.g., trying to resolve 'difficulties' in the text), yet their approach varies greatly. One example of this is the Exodus drama of Ezekiel the Tragedian. We have only a few quotations from this intriguing work, yet it seems to have been a drama in typical Greek form but with the biblical story of the Exodus as the subject and source. The chonography of Demetrius, on the other hand, seems mainly concerned with telling the story of Jacob in such a way as to work out a rational chronological scheme, including how to resolve some textual difficulties.

It can paraphrase the biblical text, shortening or expanding it, leaving out some parts or adding additional information. It is argued that some 'rewritten Bible' writings are based on a single verse or short passage in which a whole story is developed from an enigmatic biblical statement. For example, much of the *Apocalypse of Abraham* seems to be a development of the revelation to Jacob in Genesis 15. However, there may be a different way of understanding some of these writings: they may not be biblical interpretation at all but traditions that are parallel to but independent of the biblical text, or 'parabiblical writings' (discussed below).

5 Commentary

One of the most ubiquitous forms of biblical interpretation through history has been commentary, though this is not as widespread in early Judaism as it becomes in later Judaism and Christianity. The term 'midrash' is widely used as a synonym, though there are problems with using this term promiscuously to designate any sort of ancient commentary (cf. Porton 1981). *Midrash* is a Hebrew word meaning 'exposition' derived from the root *drš* 'to seek, search, examine.' The earliest reference of the noun *midrash* is apparently to a book (2 Chron. 13:22; 24:27), but in rabbinic literature the term takes on the meaning 'scriptural commentary or interpretation.' Midrash is a specific form of commentary, to be defined as follows (Porton 1981: 62; 1992: 819):

a type of literature, oral or written, which has its starting point in a fixed, canonical text, considered the revealed word of God by the midrashist and his audience, and in which the original verse is explicitly cited or clearly alluded to.

By this definition there is very little prerabbinic midrash (Porten 1981: 67).

One type of interpretation known solely from Qumran is '*pesher* exegesis.' This is found in the Qumran commentaries known as *pesharim* (from *pšr* 'interpret'). Some have wanted to label it 'midrash' and, indeed, it seems to fit Porton's definition above. In some ways, it is more a form-critical category than a type of exegesis, since it is identified by a literary formula: the quotation of a biblical passage and then an explication beginning with the phrase, 'its meaning concerns' (*pišrô 'al*) or 'its meaning is that' (*pešer 'ǎer*). However, the special characteristic of pesher exegesis is often thought to be the interpretation of biblical passages as the contemporary history of the community in coded form. A number of examples can be found in the *pesharim* from Qumran. A good example of this sort of exegesis is found in the Qumran Habakkuk commentary (1QpHab):

(7:3) And that he said, 'So that the one who reads it may run' [Hab. 2:2], (7:4) its interpretation concerns the Teacher of Righteousness to whom God made known (7:5) all the mysteries of the words of his servants the prophets. 'For again the vision (7:6) is for an appointed time, and it hastens to the end and will not lie' [Hab. 2:3]: (7:7) its interpretation is that the final age will be extended and will exceed all (7:8) which the prophets spoke, for the mysteries of God are miraculous. ... (8:7) 'They will say, "Woe, the one who amasses what is not his. How long will he multiply for himself (8:8) debts?"' [Hab. 2:6]. Its interpretation concerns the Wicked Priest who (8:9) was called concerning the name of truth at the beginning of his office, and when he ruled (8:10) in Israel his heart was lifted up, and he forsook God and betrayed the commandments for (8:11) wealth, and he seized and amassed the wealth of violent men who rebelled against God. (8:12) The wealth of peoples he took, increasing his iniquity.

An example in a Hellenistic context is the midrash on the plagues of the Exodus in the Wisdom of Solomon. The term 'Hellenistic Jewish midrash' seems to be appropriate in this particular instance. That is, it makes use of biblical examples evidently taken from the canonical text (and thus serving as an implicit textual citation) and draws on the known Jewish tradition. On the other hand, there is much in the context which has been derived from Greek literature and rhetoric. There are actually two midrashim in Wisdom of Solomon 10–19, though the first runs without a clear break into the second. The formal structure of the two is different, however. The first covers only ch. 10 and follows the fortunes of biblical history to the time of Moses. The other is the midrash on the plagues of the Exodus (11:1–14; 16:1–19:22). Although it follows seamlessly from the survey of history in Wisdom of Solomon 10, it has a different literary form and can for this reason be considered a separate midrash. It is in the form of a *synkresis*, a set of antitheses contrasting the sufferings of the Egyptians in the plagues and the parallels. It shows how the Bible could be interpreted in a Hellenistic context.

A good portion of Philo's writings are commentary of one sort or another. The *Questions and Answers on Genesis and Exodus* take the form of citing a passage and then expounding it, in classic commentary fashion. In his other commentaries, though, there is more of a continuous narrative, even if quotation and comment on the quotation are still the foundation of the format of his writings. Philo is known for his allegorical commentary (see below) but often refers to the 'literal' meaning as well.

6 Allegory

A form of interpretation known from some early Jewish texts which became quite popular in early Christian circles is allegory. Allegory already occurs in the Bible in such passages as Ezekiel 16 and 23. Some have alleged that the Song of Songs is allegorical, though most modern scholars would see any allegorical interpretation as a later imposition rather than one present in the book from its final composition. But despite some Jewish precedents, the main examples of allegory in Second Temple Jewish literature most likely owe their existence to Greek models (Grabbe 1988: 66–87). There are really only two writers who use allegory to any extent, and they both show a great deal of Hellenistic influence. These are Aristobulus and Philo. The first postbiblical writer to use allegory extensively was Aristobulus (second century BC), but, unfortunately, we know of him only from a few quotations in later writers; however, he shows a number of allegorical techniques

well-known from Philo (e.g., the etymology of Hebrew names and number symbolism).

Judging from Philo's statements, we can surmise that allegory was especially characteristic of interpreters in Alexandria of the first century or so BC and AD. We know of this from statements made in Philo, since none of the other interpreters has been preserved, as far as we know. In some cases, Philo used a 'literal' form of interpretation; since this is not his favorite method, one suspects that there were certain schools that specialized in this method of interpretation. If so, Philo probably borrowed it from a particular school of interpretation. He also talks about those who (like him) looked for hidden symbolism in the text but, once they found it, felt it was unnecessary to follow the letter of the law. Philo castigates these 'extreme allegorists' and makes it clear that Jewish law should be followed even if the exegesis found a much deeper meaning. Not all Alexandrian interpreters were allegorists. For example, even though allegory may be alluded to in the Wisdom of Solomon (18:24, probably written just about the time Philo was born), the nearest thing to an actual allegory is the passage on God's armor, reminiscent of Ephesians 6:14–17 but certainly earlier (5:17–20).

Allegory is not one of Josephus' normal techniques, but he has one example in which the dress of the high priest is allegorized as a model of the cosmos (*Ant.* 3.7.7 §§184–87). It so happens that Philo had earlier written on the meaning of the high priestly robes at even greater length and in a very similar vein (*Vita Mosis* 2.117–26): there is 'in it as a whole and in its parts a typical representation of the world and its particular parts' (2.117). The robe is the atmosphere and air. The earth is represented by the flowers at the ankles, and water by the pomegranates. These three elements represent life since all living things come from and exist in them. The ephod is a symbol of heaven, with the stones on the shoulder piece representing the sun and moon or the two hemispheres of the sky. The twelve stones are the signs of the zodiac.

Some have wanted to emphasize the use of 'typology' as an exegetical device, usually in contrast with allegory which is castigated. It is doubtful that such a distinction can be made. Typology is simply a form of allegory. For example, one could refer to the children of Hagar and Sarah as types of the two covenants in Christian terms (Gal. 4:21–31), just as Adam is a 'type' of Christ (Rom. 5:14). Yet the symbolism of Hagar and Sarah is specifically said to be an allegory. If one rejects the use of allegory as inappropriate for interpretation, it hardly seems legitimate to reintroduce it through the backdoor by calling it typology.

7 'Parabiblical' exegesis

As noted above, we quickly come up against the problem of a number of writings which seem related to the Bible in some way but are not clearly interpretations of it in any normal sense of the word. In some cases, an exegete may have developed a whole writing out of a brief biblical statement or tradition, but often the actual origin of the writing is debatable. The writer may be continuing or developing old traditions or religious interpretations that did not make it into the canonical collection, though they still addressed issues important to the Jewish people. These traditions may have paralleled the biblical account but were ultimately independent of it. We might call this process 'parabiblical.' Some of the texts in this category have been considered examples of 'rewritten Bible,' even though they have a content quite different from the Bible. For example, much of the Enoch tradition might well fall into this category. Some see the *Book of Watchers* (*1 Enoch* 1–36) as an interpretation of Genesis 6:1–4, but the evidence is against it. More likely is the view that the Genesis passage is only a reflex of an old tradition more fully given in *1 Enoch*. Whether other texts whose contents are by and large different from the biblical text might bear this designation (instead of 'rewritten Bible') is a moot point (e.g., *4 Ezra*, the Adam and Eve literature, *Testament of Abraham*, *Testament of Moses*). A number of 'parabiblical' texts from Qumran have been published in volumes from Cave 4 (see the series 'Discoveries in the Judaean Desert,' Oxford University Press, volumes 13, 19, 22). We also have many halakhic traditions whose relationship to the Pentateuch is unlikely to be one of simple interpretation (cf. examples in Neusner 1981).

The fact that some important Jewish religious writings have only a loose relationship to the biblical text should alert us to the dangers of focusing on the various techniques or the exegetical wrappings in which interpretation is presented. The main reason is that much 'biblical interpretation' was rather a different activity than that with which we are familiar. It might well involve developing parabiblical material rather than being an actual attempt to understand a particular biblical passage. Also, even when we can identify the connection with a specific biblical passage with reasonable confidence, we must recognize that (a) ancient exegesis was not primarily concerned with the original literal meaning of the text, and (b) it was almost always atomistic in nature (cf. Grabbe 1988: 45–8, 115–19).

Thus, what we are inclined to label 'exegesis' or 'interpretation' may be nothing more than building bridges between the biblical text and some other set of intellectual information that the writer wants to legitimate. For example, a writer such as Philo is clearly interested in finding his theologicophilosophical system (a form of Platonism) in the text of the LXX (cf. Grabbe 1988: 115–19). This system did not arise primarily from study of the Bible, but Philo still wants to find it in the text. Allegory helps him do it, including the use of various devices such as the etymologies of Hebrew names. Similarly, the Qumran writers were able to find contemporary references to their community and history in some biblical texts, again by focusing on minute details of the text. When writers rewrite sections of the biblical text or produce stories that run alongside the biblical text, they may also simply be discovering in the text what they want to discover.

This does not suggest that the biblical text was not used to find new information. On the contrary, it was often the vehicle to develop a new ruling, especially in matters about personal conduct (halakhah) or law. There was also a strong belief in many circles that the text was a code with secret information, especially information about the future. The writers of the Qumran *pesharim* not only find their own past history encrypted into the text, but they also think their future is there as well, just waiting to be deciphered. Philo also seems to treat the text in the same way. The last thing we should be doing in such cases is trying to find 'rules of interpretation' because they do not exist in the conventional sense of the expression.

8 Conclusions

The following are some of the points that arise when ancient biblical interpretation is studied:

(1) Scriptural interpretation became an important activity in the latter part of the Second Temple period, though how early it began is debatable. Many would see little if any before the Greek period, and many Jewish writings which have something in common with biblical characters or passages seem to be something other than just interpretation in the strict sense of the word.

(2) A canon in the later sense may have taken a long time to develop, perhaps not until the end of the Second Temple period. Nevertheless, the rather fluid tradition could still be enormously productive in generating new traditions, insights, and views without involving strict biblical interpretation in the later canonical sense of the word.

(3) One reason for biblical interpretation was to seek information on various subjects: the cult, festival observance, purity regulations, theological concepts and ideals. It would be expected that God's revelation generally included such vital information. However, although it is often assumed that this was the primary function of scripture – as a source of information – other purposes were in fact often more important to the individual person or group.

(4) Scriptural interpretation was often a way of justifying or legitimating a particular belief or idea. That is, the writer came to certain views by another route (perhaps even subconsciously) but then wants to justify them by appeal to sacred writings. Philo is a good example of one who uses exegesis to find in scripture what is in fact a Platonic-based theologicophilosophical

system, but he is only one of many. Much of what has been called 'Jewish exegesis' seems actually to be in this category rather than a straightforward attempt to understand the text in its literal form. Most ancient exegesis was atomistic and ignores the original context of the passage being interpreted.

(5) Even at a time when scripture was developing toward a canon, we find many writings that parallel biblical writings in certain ways but may be more or less independent (e.g., *1 Enoch*). These 'parabiblical' writings did not become a part of the canon, but this may be due more to a historical accident than anything else. In any case, they often tell us a good deal about Jewish views about religion, theology, and interpretation.

References and further reading

Fishbane, Michael (1985) *Biblical Interpretation in Ancient Israel*, Oxford: Clarendon (repr. with addenda 1989).

Grabbe, Lester L. (1988) *Etymology in Early Jewish Interpretation: The Hebrew Names in Philo*, Brown Judaic Studies 115; Atlanta: Scholars Press.

—— (2004) *Yehud: A History of the Persian Province of Judah*, London/New York: T.&T. Clark International.

Harrington, Daniel J. (1986) 'The Bible Rewritten (Narratives),' pp. 239–47 in *Early Judaism and its Modern Interpreters*, SBLBMI 2, R.A. Kraft and G.W.E. Nickelsburg (eds.), Atlanta: Scholars Press/Philadelphia: Fortress Press.

Hay, David M. (1979–1980) *Both Literal and Allegorical: Studies in Philo of Alexandria's Questions and Answers on Genesis and Exodus*, Brown Judaic Studies 232, Atlanta: Scholars Press.

Horgan, M.P. (1979) *Pesharim: Qumran Interpretations of Biblical Books*, CBQMS 8, Washington, DC: Catholic Biblical Association.

Mulder, Martin Jan, and Harry Sysling (eds.) (1988) *Mikra: Text, Translation, Reading and Interpretation of the Hebrew Bible in Ancient Judaism and Early Christianity*, CRINT 2/1, Assen and Maastricht: Van Gorcum/Minneapolis: Fortress Press.

Neusner, Jacob (1981) *Judaism: The Evidence of the Mishnah*, Chicago: University of Chicago Press.

Porton, G.G. (1981) 'Defining Midrash,' 1.55–92 in *The Ancient Study of Judaism*, J. Neusner (ed.) New York: Ktav.

—— (1992) 'Midrash,' *ABD* 4.818–22.

Sæbø, Magne (ed.) (1996) *Hebrew Bible/Old Testament: The History of its Interpretation, Volume I: From the Beginnings to the Middle Ages (Until 1300), Part 1: Antiquity*, in cooperation with Chris Brekelmans and Menahem Haran, Göttingen: Vandenhoeck & Ruprecht.

Trebolle Barrera, Julio (1998) *The Jewish Bible and the Christian Bible: An Introduction to the History of the Bible*, trans. W.G.E. Watson, Leiden: Brill/Grand Rapids: Eerdmans.

LESTER L. GRABBE

SMITH, WILLIAM ROBERTSON (1846–1894)

William Robertson Smith was born on November 8, 1846 in Keig, near Aberdeen, his father being a minster of the Free Church, which had broken from the Church of Scotland in 1843. Educated initially by his father, he attended the universities of Aberdeen and Edinburgh, at the latter of which he worked as assistant to the eminent physicist P.G. Tait. Smith could have enjoyed a successful career as a mathematician or physicist but chose to study theology in Edinburgh in order to enter the ministry of the Free Church.

Barely out of his student days he was appointed, in 1870, to a professorship in Old Testament at the Free Church College in Aberdeen and was also ordained. Prior to this appointment he had already begun to visit Germany regularly, and in 1872 he went to Göttingen to study Arabic with Paul de Lagarde. Smith's aim was to master the pre-Islamic Arabian literature thought at that time to embody the most primitive forms of Semitic religion, so that he could demonstrate the uniqueness of Hebrew religion as divine revelation. At the same time, he was convinced, as a committed evangelical, that the newly-developmg biblical criticism that was being spear-headed in Germany and Holland was a genuine development within the tradition of Reformation, and that the church needed to take it on board. Unfortunately, his church did not share this view, and following the publication of the article 'Bible' in the innovative ninth edition of the *Encyclopaedia Britannica* in December 1875, Smith was accused of undermining belief in the inspiration and infallible truth of the Bible. He was acquitted and admonished by the General Assembly in 1880, but two articles that appeared shortly afterwards (they had been in press during his first trial) led to renewed charges and suspension. Smith defended himself in a series of public lectures that were published in 1881 as *The Old Testament in the Jewish Church*. This remains one of the most brilliant and persuasive presentations of what is called the Wellhausen hypothesis, although Smith had made his own contribution to its development, and his mode of presentation was distinctively his own.

Dismissed from his post in Aberdeen in 1881, Smith moved to Cambridge in 1883 where he later became Professor of Arabic (1889). Here he published *The Prophets of Israel*. His crowning work was the Burnett Lectures delivered in Aberdeen from 1888 to 1891. Published as *Lectures on the Religion of the Semites* the first series exerted enormous influence on the social-scientific study of religion as well as on Old Testament studies. Smith's death on March 31, 1894 prevented publication of the second and third series of these lectures, and it was not until 1995 that the labors of John Day enabled them to appear in publishable form.

Smith was a crucial figure in the history of biblical criticism. His sincere evangelicalism demonstrated that biblical criticism was not incompatible with Christian faith, and this encouraged other scholars to take biblical criticism seriously. To the end of his life, Smith remained convinced that biblical religion could not possibly be a mere human development, and he used his exceptional intellectual gifts to defend this viewpoint.

References and further reading

Black, J.S. and G. Chrystal (1912) *The Life of William Robertson Smith*, London: Adam and Charles Black.

Day, J. (ed.) (1995) *Lectures on the Religion of the Semites by William Robertson Smith, Second and Third Series*, JSOTSup 183, Sheffield: Sheffield Academic Press.

Johnstone, W. (1995) *William Robertson Smith: Essays in Reassessment*, JSOTSup 189, Sheffield: Sheffield Academic Press.

Rogerson, J.W. (1995) *The Bible and Criticism in Victorian Britain: Profiles of F.D. Maurice and William Robertson Smith*, JSOTSup 201, Sheffield: Sheffield Academic Press.

JOHN ROGERSON

SOCIAL-SCIENTIFIC APPROACHES

1 What is social-scientific interpretation?
2 Landmarks in social-scientific interpretation
3 Various approaches to social–scientific interpretation
4 The future

1 What is social-scientific interpretation?

Social-scientific interpretation refers to biblical interpretation which draws upon ideas and perspectives from social sciences such as anthropology, sociology, social psychology, economics, and so on. There are a number of recent useful discussions (Esler 1994: 1–18; Horrell 1999: 3–27). It is a (common) misnomer to describe this enterprise as 'sociological' since that word only designates one of the social sciences involved, especially when anthropology is now equally if not more prominent in the exercise.

This type of interpretation is usually practiced by exegetes interested in trying to determine what the biblical texts meant to the original audiences, and to

that extent it represents a development of the historical-critical method. Nevertheless, recent developments have raised the prospect of its use in bringing out contemporary applications in biblical texts, as discussed below.

Social-scientific interpretation is usefully distinguished from 'social history' practiced by certain biblical interpreters, since that approach, although also concerned with historical issues, seeks to examine social dimensions of biblical texts without the explicit use of ideas from the social sciences.

Why do we use the social sciences to help us interpret biblical texts? The answer to this is that we cannot open a single biblical text without encountering issues relating to how human beings live together in social groups. The Bible is not a work of abstract or abstruse theologizing, for the theological issues found within it have a social embodiment. As the Fourth Evangelist says, the Word was not only made flesh, but 'lived amongst us' (John 1:14). In view of the social context of every sentence in the Bible, many interpreters have considered it appropriate to turn for assistance to the writings of those who have specialized in the disciplined examination of social questions in contemporary cultures; that is, these interpreters have gone to social scientists for help. For interpreters who take this route, it seems as essential to draw upon the fruits of social-scientific research conducted during the last century or so as it is to learn the biblical languages. Why have resources available which are directly relevant to the social setting of the Bible, and to the interrelationship between that setting and the ideas it contains, and not utilize them?

2 Landmarks in social-scientific interpretation

Interpreters began making this move in the 1970s, especially in relation to the New Testament and with sociology the main social science employed. In 1972 Wayne Meeks published a superlative essay on the descending and ascending Son of Man motif in the Fourth Gospel, which introduced to the field important ideas contained in *The Social Construction of Reality* (1966) by Peter Berger and Thomas Luckmann, a work which has been widely employed since, as has a closely related work published by Berger in 1969, *The Sacred Canopy* (Esler 1987; Elliott 1990). In 1973 Gerd Theissen produced the first of his seminal contributions on early Palestinian and then diaspora Christianity with an essay on wandering charismatics, which used various sociological ideas (Theissen 1973; for the fruits of this research see Theissen 1978 and 1982). The year 1975 saw the publication of a book by John G. Gager (1978) which introduced a variety of social-scientific ideas to the field, including millenarianism, cognitive dissonance, and charismatic authority. Millenarianism has been frequently taken up in later research (for example, Jewett

1986 and Esler 1994: 92–409) and so too has cognitive dissonance (for example, Esler 1994: 110–30). In 1975 there also appeared an important article by Robin Scroggs (1975) exploring the application of sectarian theory to early Christian communities, a perspective which has proved very useful since (see Esler 1987; Elliott 1990). By 1980 it was becoming possible to write survey articles on social-scientific interpretation, although that year was more notable for the publication of Bengt Holmberg's application of Max Weber's theory of authority to the Pauline corpus (Holmberg 1980).

During the late 1970s Bruce J. Malina inaugurated in a number of essays what was to become a fundamentally important project of applying contemporary anthropological research into the Mediterranean as a way of modeling the culture of the region. This research culminated in 1981 in *The New Testament World: Insights from Cultural Anthropology* (revised edition 1993). In the same year John H. Elliott published *A Home for the Homeless*, a close analysis of 1 Peter from the viewpoint of sectarianism (revised edition 1990).

Yet the Old Testament was not being forgotten in this revolution in biblical interpretation. Even before the developments in the 1970s the Old Testament had been the subject of investigation from certain anthropological perspectives (Rogerson 1970). But in 1979 two important works appeared, Norman Gottwald's *The Tribes of Yahweh* and Robert Carroll's *When Prophecy Failed*. Gottwald's book sought to trace the connections between Israelite society and religion in the period 1250–1050 BC using macrosociological theory drawn from Durkheim, Weber, and Marx, together with a wealth of other social-science material, and it convinced most Old Testament researchers that Israelite history could hardly be contemplated henceforward without such assistance. One sign of the influence of Gottwald's book was its being given a twenty-year retrospective at the 1999 Society of Biblical Literature Conference in Boston. Robert Carroll's book also played a major role in demonstrating the usefulness of social theory.

Subsequent landmarks in Old Testament social-scientific interpretation include Bernhard Lang's collection of essays by various writers (1985), Thomas Overholt's application of contemporary Third World prophetic phenomena to Old Testament prophecy (1986), John Rogerson's study of anthropological approaches to the Old Testament (1987), and the increasing use of Mediterranean anthropology (particularly as modeled by Malina) to explicate various aspects of the text. In Mary Douglas we have an anthropologist who has brought social-scientific methodology to bear on biblical texts (1993). Other notable volumes or collections devoted partially or exclusively to social-scientific interpretation include Chalcraft (1997), Carter and Meyers (1996), and Carroll R. (2000). These works utilize the social sciences to investigate social roles (such as prophet and king), cultural values (especially honor

and shame) and codes (including purity), institutional organization and ethos, identity, gender, and so on (Carroll 2000: 15).

The 1980s witnessed a rich flowering of social-scientific interpretation. Wayne Meeks' *The First Urban Christians* (1983) has been widely appreciated for its merging of an eclectic mix of sociological ideas with a social-history style of thoroughness in its account of the first century Graeco-Roman world, even though some criticized Meeks' lack of engagement with the distinctive contours of Mediterranean culture from an anthropological point of view. In 1985 Norman Petersen published a sociological and literary critical reading of Philemon. The year 1986 saw Malina producing a significant theoretical contribution, Elliott editing an influential collection of essays, and Douglas Oakman publishing his study of Jesus and first-century Palestinian economics. The following year, 1987, saw the publication of Esler's study of Luke-Acts largely from the perspective of the legitimation theory of Berger and Luckmann and the sociology of sectarianism, while in 1988 Neyrey published his study of Johannine Christology from a social-scientific perspective, Moxnes brought out his study of Luke's Gospel from the perspective of preindustrial economics, and Malina and Neyrey published a work on Matthew from the perspective of labeling theory. In 1989 Richard Horsley considered sociological perspectives in relation to the Jesus movement.

The rate of production has increased even more in the last ten years. While the decade began with Holmberg's perceptive assessment of sociological contributions (1990), the most productive area proved to be the use of Mediterranean anthropology associated with the Context Group of scholars (a group discussed in *Biblical Interpretation* [1993] 1: 250–1). Books utilizing this perspective published by this group or people associated with it include (to name only a few) Esler (1994 and 1995), Hanson and Oakman (1998), and Pilch (2000). A recent development has been the introduction of that part of social psychology known as social identity theory associated with Henri Tajfel, who worked at the University of Bristol in the 1970s and 1980s.

3 Various approaches to social-scientific interpretation

Although critics have used a wide variety of social-scientific ideas and perspectives to investigate biblical texts from both Testaments, in recent years something of a distinction has opened between those who favour explicit use of models and those who do not. Models have been described in detail on several occasions (Malina 1986; Esler 1987: 6–12; 1995: 4–8) and may be loosely defined as a simplification and accentuation of certain empirical phenomena structured in such a way as to serve as an instrument for organizing and interpreting a complex body of data. They are, in short, heuristic tools; they spark the imagination, enabling one to put a new range of questions to the data which would otherwise not be available. While one may ask of models whether they are useful or not, to inquire whether they are 'true' or 'false,' or to seek to 'verify' them against data, entails a fundamental misunderstanding of the method.

Models of Mediterranean culture derived from contemporary anthropological research into that region have become particularly prominent in Old and New Testament research as a result of Malina's 1981 work *The New Testament in Its Cultural World.* Those who employ such models seek to read biblical texts with social scenarios originating in a group-oriented and honor-focused culture, where all goods are thought to exist in limited quantities and patron–client relations are entered into as a way of coping with such features. Such inquiries frequently produce extremely fresh readings of the texts as compared with traditional approaches which are often unconsciously committed to modern, individualistic ways of understanding the world. This use of models involves a belief that the members of any particular culture are socialized to accept its values, structures, and institutions as usual, expected and even normative, so that models based on them will provide a better framework for exploration than the ethnocentric and anachronistic perspectives derived from modern Northern European or North American culture we would otherwise bring to the texts. This does not mean that human beings are not free to diverge from these values and institutions, only that usually they do not do so and, if they do, the divergences are only comprehensible in the context of the typical and conventional. Efforts by astute scholars like David Horrell (2000) to argue, in his case on the basis of the sociology of Anthony Giddens, that such a view is contradicted by the way in which individuals transform rather than reproduce their social environment are arguably themselves a victim of the modern individualism that model users seek to avoid (Esler 2000).

Another approach to social-scientific interpretation has been inspired by the 'interpretivism' of anthropologist Clifford Geertz. Its exponents, who have produced fine exegesis, tend to eschew model use since they regard it as nomothetic and insufficiently sensitive to ethnographic particularity and the indigenous point of view. The debate may be seen by comparing Garrett (1992) and Esler (1995: 4–9). One problem with interpretivism is that it rests ultimately upon a highly detailed understanding of a foreign culture, thus producing what Geertz has called a 'thick description,' and it is difficult to see how one could ever acquire this degree of familiarity with historical phenomena for which participant observation is impossible. At the same time, the use of models is not normally as positivist or 'objec-tive' as portrayed by interpretivists. Models are heuristic tools, not social laws.

4 Future

Hitherto social-scientific interpretation has largely been regarded as contributing to historical criticism. Yet it seems likely that those interested in how the biblical documents produce meaning for contemporary readers will increasingly utilize this approach. On one view, the distance opened up between our biblical ancestors in faith and ourselves as a result of social-scientific interpretation is a necessary precursor to their words having any real effect in our lives. The possibility is emerging of a social hermeneutic in which the vigorous dialogue between our culture and theirs, the experience of culture shock when we return to our culture having been deeply immersed in theirs, will stimulate a lively and enriching sense of our distinctive values and destiny, of our identity itself.

References and further reading

Berger, Peter L. (1969) *The Sacred Canopy: Elements of a Sociological Theory of Religion,* New York: Anchor.

—— and Thomas Luckmann (1966) *The Social Construction of Reality: A Treatise in the Sociology of Knowledge,* London: Pelican.

Carroll, Robert P. (1979) *When Prophecy Failed: Cognitive Dissonance in the Prophetic Traditions of the Old Testament,* New York: Seabury.

Carroll R. and M. Daniel (eds.) (2000) *Rethinking Contexts, Rereading Texts: Contributions from the Social Sciences to Biblical Interpretation,* JSOTSup 299, Sheffield: Sheffield Academic Press.

Carter, C.E. and C.L. Meyers (eds.) (1996) *Community, Identity, and Ideology: Social Science Approaches to the Hebrew Bible,* SBTS 6, Winona Lake: Eisenbrauns.

Chalcraft, D.J. (ed.) (1997) *Social Scientific Old Testament Criticism,* Sheffield: JSOT Press.

Douglas, Mary (1993) *In the Wilderness: The Doctrine of Defilement in the Book of Numbers,* JSOTSup 158, Sheffield: Sheffield Academic Press.

Elliott, John H. (ed.) (1986) *Social-Scientific Criticism of the New Testament and Its Social World,* Semeia 35, Decatur: Scholars Press.

—— (1990 [1981]) *A Home for the Homeless: A Social-Scientific Criticism of 1 Peter, Its Situation and Strategy, With a New Introduction,* Minneapolis: Fortress Press, rev. and expanded edn.

Esler, Philip F. (1987) *Community and Gospel in Luke-Acts: The Social and Political Motivations of Lucan Theology,* Cambridge: Cambridge University Press.

—— (1994) *The First Christians in Their Social Worlds: Social-Scientific Approaches to New Testament Interpretation,* London and New York: Routledge.

—— (ed.) (1995) *Modelling Early Christianity: Social-Scientific Studies of the New Testament in Its Context*, London and New York: Routledge.

—— (2000) 'Models in New Testament Interpretation: A Reply to David Horrell,' *Journal for the Study of the New Testament* 78: 107–13.

—— (2004) *Conflict and Identity in Romans: The Social Setting of Paul's Letter*, Minneapolis: Fortress Press.

Gager, John G. (1978) *Kingdom and Community: The Social World of Early Christianity*, Englewood Cliffs: Prentice-Hall (see review by D.L. Bartlett, *Zygon* [1978] 13: 131–5).

Garrett, Susan R. (1992) 'Sociology of Early Christianity,' *ABD* 6.89–99.

Gottwald, Norman K. (1979) *The Tribes of Yahweh: A Sociology of the Religion of Liberated Israel 1250–1050 BC*, Maryknoll: Orbis.

Hanson, K.C. and Douglas E. Oakman (1998) *Palestine in the Time of Jesus*, Minneapolis: Fortress Press.

Holmberg, Bengt (1980) *Paul and Power: The Structure of Authority in the Primitive Church as Reflected in the Pauline Epistles*, Philadelphia: Fortress Press.

—— (1990) *Sociology and the New Testament: An Appraisal*, Minneapolis: Fortress Press.

Horrell, David G. (ed.) (1999) *Social-Scientific Approaches to New Testament Interpretation*, Edinburgh: T.&T. Clark.

—— (2000) 'Models and Methods in Social-Scientific Interpretation: A Response to Philip Esler,' *Journal for the Study of the New Testament* 78: 83–105.

Horsley, Richard A. (1989) *Sociology and the Jesus Movement*, New York: Crossroad.

Jewett, Robert (1986) *The Thessalonian Correspondence: Pauline Rhetoric and Millenarian Piety*, Foundations and Facets, Philadelphia: Fortress Press.

Lang, Bernhard (ed.) (1985) *Anthropological Approaches to the Old Testament*, Issues in Religion and Theology 8, Philadelphia: Fortress Press/London: SPCK.

Malina, Bruce J. (1986) *Christian Origins and Cultural Anthropology: Practical Models for Biblical Interpretation*, Atlanta: John Knox.

—— (1993 [1981]) *The New Testament World: Insights from Cultural Anthropology*, Louisville: Westminster/John Knox.

—— and Jerome H. Neyrey (1988) *Calling Jesus Names: The Social Value of Labels in Matthew*, Foundations and Facets, Social Facets, Sonoma: Polebridge Press.

Meeks, Wayne A. (1972) 'The Man from heaven in Johannine Sectarianism,' *Journal of Biblical Literature* 91: 44–72.

—— (1983) *The First Urban Christians: The Social World of the Apostle Paul*, New Haven: Yale University Press.

Moxnes, Halvor (1988) *The Economy of the Kingdom: Social Conflict and Economic Relations in Luke's Gospel*, Overtures to Biblical Theology, Philadelphia: Fortress Press.

Neyrey, Jerome H. (1988) *An Ideology of Revolt: John's Christology in Social-Science Perspective*, Philadelphia: Fortress Press.

Oakman, Douglas E. (1986) *Jesus and the Economic Questions of His Day*, Lewiston: Edwin Mellen Press.

Overholt, Thomas W. (1986) *Prophecy in Cross-Cultural Perspective*, Atlanta: Scholars Press.

Petersen, Norman R. (1985) *Rediscovering Paul: Philemon and the Sociology of Paul's Narrative World*, Philadelphia: Fortress Press.

Pilch, John J. (2000) *Healing in the New Testament: Insights from Medical and Mediterranean Anthropology*, Minneapolis: Fortress Press.

Rogerson, J. (1970) 'Structural Anthropology and The Old Testament,' *Bulletin of the School of Oriental and African Studies* 33: 49–500.

Scroggs, Robin (1975) 'The Earliest Christian Communities as Sectarian Movement,' pp. 1–23 in *Christianity, Judaism and Other Greco-Roman Cults: Studies for Morton Smith at Sixty*, Part II: *Early Christianity*, J. Neusner (ed.), Leiden: Brill.

Theissen, Gerd (1973) 'Wanderradikalismus: Literatursoziologische Aspekte der Überlieferung von Worten Jesu im Urchristentum,' *Zeitschrift für Theologie und Kirche* 70: 245–71 (ET 'Itinerant Radicalism: The Tradition of Jesus Sayings from the Perspective of the Sociology of Literature,' [1975] *Radical Religion* 2/2–3: 84–93).

—— (1978) *Sociology of Early Christian Palestinian Christianity*, Philadelphia: Fortress Press (orig. *Soziologie der Jesusbewegung*, 1977; published in Great Britain as *The First Followers of Jesus*, London: SCM Press, 1978).

—— (1982) *The Social Setting of Pauline Christianity: Essays on Corinth*, trans. and with an introduction by John H. Schütz (ed.), Philadelphia: Fortress Press.

PHILIP F. ESLER

SOURCE CRITICISM

1 Introduction

Formerly called 'literary criticism' (*Literarkritik*), source criticism has as its purpose the detection and, in some cases, reconstruction, of documentary sources which were used by various biblical authors in composing their works. When the profile of source documents can be established in some detail, it has been possible to date these documents and to analyze their literary genres, dominant ideologies, and provenances. Source criticism has been used extensively in the analysis of the Pentateuch, the Synoptic Gospels, and the Fourth Gospel, but also in such other books as Isaiah, Jeremiah, Acts, and the Apocalypse.

The pursuit of written sources for books of the Hebrew Bible and the New Testament is not based on any *a priori* conviction that such sources existed. Rather, it arose out of the effort to write a history of Israelite religion (Wellhausen) and to understand the historical relationship of four somewhat divergent Gospels to one another, to the historical Jesus, and to subsequent elaboration of Christian doctrine. These historical investigations quickly identified inconsistencies, doublets, and stylistic variations that were most easily explained as the result of the combination of discrete documentary sources.

2 Hebrew Bible

Source criticism proceeds in two distinct operations: first, the identification of composite accounts and the isolation of discrete fragments of source materials embedded in a biblical account, and second, the grouping of individual fragments from various biblical episodes or books into one or more coherent sources, normally by criteria of coherence (narrative style, vocabulary, common perspective).

The *criteria* for isolating discrete documentary fragments within an account arise from features of the Hebrew text itself and can be grouped under three headings: *aporiae*; doublets; and stylistic variations.

Aporiae or inconsistencies include contradictions in details, odd repetitions, rough narrative transitions, and odd shifts in perspective, style, idiom, or rhetorical posture. For example, 1 Samuel 16–17 offers two divergent accounts of David's introduction to Saul. First Samuel 16:1–13 introduces Jesse and his sons and Samuel's choice of David. David, a shepherd, is described as stalwart and a 'man of war.' As a musician he endeared himself to Saul and then became the king's armor bearer (1 Sam. 16:20–23). In that capacity, he received Saul's permission to fight Goliath (1 Sam. 17:37). In 1 Samuel 17:12, however, David and his family are presented again, as if for the first time, and the account suggests that David happened on the battlefield only because he was sent to provision his brothers (1 Sam. 17:14–19). Moreover, as a 'lad' (*naʿar*) he was unaccustomed to fighting in soldier's gear (1 Sam. 17:38–40). Moreover, 1 Samuel 17:55–58 indicates that even after the killing of Goliath, neither Saul nor Abner knew David, directly contradicting 1 Samuel 16. The matter is made yet more complicated by the fact that the LXX[B] lacks 1 Samuel 17:12–31, 41, 48b, 50, 51[a–a], 55–58, and 18:1–5, that is, the elements belonging to the second story. These data suggest that 1 Samuel 16–17 is a composite account, and that the

second story was inserted into the first at a relatively late date.

In other instances, details of one account conflict with chronological or genealogical data of another. The expulsion of Hagar and Ishmael, still a child in Genesis 21, conflicts with chronological details of Genesis 16:16; 17:1, and 21:5, which would make Ishmael at least fourteen years old. Such conflicts may be resolved by ascribing conflicting details to two separate sources.

Doublets (or multiple parallel accounts) provide one of the clearest indications of the combination of discrete sources. For example, Exodus 24:9–18 contains three versions of Moses' ascent of Sinai, each of which has an invitation for Moses to come up the mountain. In the first (24:1, 9–11), Moses ascends with Aaron, Nadab, Abihu, and seventy elders; they see *ʾElohê yisraʾel*; and they eat in God's presence. In the second (24:12–15a), only Moses and Joshua ascend the mountain, and the account focuses on God's giving of the 'teaching and commandments.' In the third account (24:15b–18), Moses is seemingly alone. God's glory (*kᵉbôd YHWH*) rather than God himself is what is seen and even this is obscured by a cloud and manifest as a 'consuming fire.' Each account focuses on different aspects of the theophany, and implies somewhat differing views of God's relationship to Israel.

The most obvious of the doublets is the double creation account, the first in Genesus 1:1–2:4a (P), and the second in Genesus 2:4b–25 (non-P or JE). The first has a highly formulaic and repetitive style; it is organized on a seven-day schema and focuses on divine commands; and it employs a set of distinctive vocabulary: *baraʾ*, 'create'; *ʾElohim*, 'God'; *ʾadam*, 'humankind'; *zakar ûneqebah*, 'male and female'; *bᵉṣalmenû kidmûtenû*, 'in our image and after our likeness.' The second account treats Creation not as a series of discrete events, but synthetically, focusing on the relationship among the characters and employing picturesque language. Unlike the first account, it uses *yaṣar* for 'create,' *YHWH ʾElohim* for God, and the phrase *ʾadam uᵉʾištô*, 'the man and his wife.' The perspective of the first account is a world created and ordered by God's command in accord with a pattern that establishes the Sabbath. The second focuses more on God's care for humankind and freely employs anthropomorphisms in its description of God's activities.

Stylistic variations and distinctive vocabulary in discrete strands and blocks also point to the presence of sources. The best-known of these variations are the names for God. One Pentateuchal strand, now identified as the priestly source, uses the generic *ʾElohim* or the title *ʾEl Šaddai* from Genesis 1 to Exodus 6:3, the point at which Moses is first told God's name (YHWH). The first Creation account (Gen. 1:1–2:4a), which belongs to this strand, uses *ʾElohim*, as does the theophany to Abraham in Genesis 17:1 where God reveals himself as *ʾEl Šaddai*. But in another strand (non-P or JE), represented by the theophany in Genesis 15:7 and the second Creation account (Gen. 2:4b–25), the Tetragrammaton appears. Similarly, one of the theophanies to Jacob uses *'El Šaddai* as God's name and *'Elohim* in the surrounding narrative (Gen. 35:1–13 [P]) while a parallel account in Genesis 28:10–19 (non-P or JE) uses YHWH.

The strands delineated through attention to the use of divine names display other stylistic and vocabularic characteristics and this has allowed the assembling of relatively clear stylistic profiles for the priestly writer (Driver 1913: 131–5; McEvenue 1971). The book of Deuteronomy displays a different but equally recognizable style. The work of this Deuteronomist is related to various elements found in the so-called Deuteronomistic History (Joshua–2 Kings) (Weinfeld 1972).

Once individual fragments and strands are isolated, they can be grouped together into discrete sources. This is normally achieved by appeal to principles of stylistic, vocabularic, and ideological coherence. Wellhausen identified three basic sources, the Jehovist (JE, combining the Yahwist [J] and the Elohist [E]), the Priestly source (P), and the Deuteronomist (D), but standard Old Testament introductions (Eissfeldt 1965: 158–241; Fohrer 1968: 103–95) normally refer to four documents (J, E, D, P). D is usually placed in the seventh century and P, despite some efforts to date it earlier, in the exilic or postexilic period. J, once placed in the tenth century, has more recently been dated by Van Seters (1975; cf. Schmid 1976) to the late exilic period. E has been variously dated to the eighth, ninth, and tenth centuries BC.

Despite the seeming consensus of a generation ago, many questions linger. Should J be subdivided further? Is E, the most fragmentary of the four, a documentary source at all or simply materials used by the Yahwist? Are most of the non-P texts in Exodus–Numbers the work of a late Yahwist (Van Seters 1994)? Is the Holiness Code (Lev. 17–26) an independent source within P? The relation of P to the non-P material is highly problematic: earlier critics regarded it as a discrete source; some now think that P was the framework into which the JE material was inserted; others suggest that P is an edition or revision of JE (Cross 1973), and Carr (1996) suggests that P was a separate composition, but one that knew the non-P sources and was intended to displace them. There have been, moreover, more fundamental challenges to the documentary hypothesis by Blum (1990), who accounts for the Pentateuch by appeal not to sources, but to two composers, a Deuteronomistic composer (K^D) and a slightly later priestly composer (K^P), who together are responsible for most of the elements that the older documentary analyses ascribed respectively to the D and P documents.

3 New Testament

Doublets, variations in style and vocabulary, and contradictory details in Luke 1–2, Acts, and the Apocalypse

have encouraged the search for literary sources underlying these books, much along the same lines that source criticism proceeded in the Pentateuch. The most sustained discussions, however, have concerned the sources of the Synoptics and of the Fourth Gospel.

3.1 Synoptic Gospels

3.1.1 Markan priority and the two document hypothesis
Synoptic criticism is aided greatly by the fact that we have three discrete and partially overlapping accounts whose agreements in sequence and wording imply some form of literary interdependence. Careful comparison of the Synoptics has identified four sets of data that are key to understanding the literary relations among the three:

(1) In the Triple tradition [TT] – those pericopes where Mark stands in parallel to Matthew and Luke – there are triple verbatim agreements, agreements of Matthew with Mark against Luke, agreements of Mark and Luke against Matthew, but a relatively small number of Matthew–Luke agreements against Mark (the so-called 'minor agreements').

(2) In the relative sequence of the TT, the same pattern obtains, except that there are *no* pericopes in which Matthew and Luke agree in placement against Mark.

(3) In the Double tradition [DT] – material where Matthew and Luke agree in the absence of Mark – Matthew and Luke sometimes display near verbatim agreement and sometimes lower, though on balance the agreement is slightly higher in the DT than in the TT (Carlston and Norlin 1971, 1999).

(4) Despite their sometimes high verbatim agreement, Matthew and Luke never agree in the placement of the DT material *relative to Mark* after Matthew 4:1–11 and Luke 4:1–13 (Kloppenborg 2000: ch. 1).

These data permit some inferences. First, the non-agreement of Matthew and Luke against Mark in the sequence of the TT implies that Mark is medial: either the link between Matthew and Luke, or their common source, or the conflation of the two (Neville 1994). Second, the nonagreement of Matthew and Luke in placing the DT suggests that Matthew has had no direct contact with Luke (and *vice versa*), since Luke's arrangement of the DT has apparently had no influence on Matthew's placement and *vice versa*. The only alternative is to provide a convincing redactional explanation of Luke's thorough displacement of the DT from its Matthean settings, something that has been attempted by McNicol (1996) within the framework of the Griesbach (Two Gospel) hypothesis, and by Goulder (1989), a proponent of the view that Matthew used Mark, and Luke used both. But both of these attempts, owing to the sheer scale of Luke's disagreement with Matthew in the placement of the DT, create as many difficulties as they solve. Moreover, it is difficult to account for Luke's near complete avoidance of distinctively Matthean vocabulary.

If Matthew and Luke are independent and Mark is medial, the simplest hypothesis by which to account for these inferences is to posit Mark (or something very like Mark) as the source of Matthew and Luke. In order to account for the DT, for Matthew and Luke's verbatim agreements but their near complete disagreement in the placement of the DT, and for the fact that about 40 percent of the DT pericopes (27/67) occur in the same relative order (despite the fact that they are combined differently with Mark: Kloppenborg 2000: ch. 2), it is necessary to posit a *documentary source* to which Matthew and Luke had access. This is normally called 'Q' (=*Quelle*, source). The hypothesis that asserts the priority of Mark, the independence of Matthew and Luke, and the existence of a second documentary source of sayings for Matthew and Luke is called the 'Two Document (or Source) hypothesis' (2DH).

3.1.2 The Q source

Since Matthew and Luke agree in 51–54 percent of the DT vocabulary (Kloppenborg 1988: 209) and in 40 percent of its sequence, the general shape of the document is relatively clear. Reconstructive attempts normally proceed by an adaptation of text-critical principles: deviational probability and coherence with 'minimal Q' (i.e., the Matt.=Luke agreements) (Robinson, Hoffmann, and Kloppenborg 2000). Special problems are raised by *Sondergut*, which may represent Q material that either Matthew or Luke has omitted (Vassiliadis 1978), and by TT material where there are important minor agreements which might signal a Q version parallel to Mark, for example, Matthew 3:16–17/Luke 3:21–22 (Mark 1:9–11).

According to most reconstructions (Kloppenborg 1988) Q contained between 4,000 and 4,600 words (approximately 235–260 verses, or the size of 2 Corinthians). Q displays a distinctive form-critical profile when compared with Mark (Jacobson 1982) and evinces a relatively coherent literary structure and topic arrangement. Its genre has been variously characterized as prophetic book (Sato 1988) or an instruction expanded into a chriae collection (Kloppenborg 1987) but there is general agreement on the dominance of sayings materials, the lack of a passion account, and the lack of a strong narrative outline.

3.1.3 Proto-Luke and Ur-Markus

Two other source-critical issues arise in the framework of the 2DH. First, the nature of the deployment of Q and non-Q, non-Markan material, particularly in Luke 9:51–18:14, has suggested to some that prior to Luke's incorporation of Q, Q had already been combined with special material into an intermediate document, normally called 'Proto-Luke.' This is sometimes thought to have contained an alternate version of the Passion narrative, thus accounting for non-Markan aspects of Luke's Passion account (Weiss 1907; Streeter

1924: 199–222; Taylor 1926). Others treat the special material appearing in Luke 3–19 as a discrete document, L (Paffenroth 1997).

Second, some textual features of the Synoptics have encouraged the view that Mark existed in at least two recensions and that Matthew and Luke used either an earlier (*Ur-Markus*) or later (*Deutero-Markus*) recension. The matter is now even more complicated with the discovery of the Secret Gospel of Mark, which might represent an early pre- or post-Markan recension of Mark (Koester 1983). Earlier or later recensions of Mark are normally posited in order to account for the minor agreements (Ennulat 1994), or Luke's omission of Mark 6:45–8:22, or the alleged agreement of Matthew and Luke in placing the Sermon on the Mount/Plain at Mark 3:19/20.

3.2 The Fourth Gospel

The double ending of the Fourth Gospel (FG) (20:30–31; 21:25), a variety of thematic, narrative, and chronological *aporiae*, and significant stylistic variations have served as the bases for positing one or more sources underlying the FG. Bultmann (1941) posited the existence of three sources, a 'revelation discourse source' to account for the monologue speeches in the FG, a 'signs source' to account for the miracle stories and call of the disciples, and a Passion source parallel to but not dependent on the Synoptic Passion. Subsequent criticism has cast doubt on a discourse source, but a pre-Johannine 'Signs Gospel,' containing the call of the disciples, seven miracles, and a Passion account has been isolated by R.T. Fortna (1970, 1988) and shown to display a discrete vocabularic and ideological profile when compared with the rest of the FG.

4 Conclusion

Originally intended to account for the literary composition of various biblical books, source criticism has more recently created the basis for a nuanced and diversified 'map' of the history of Israelite religion and the prehistory of the Gospels. To the extent that documentary sources are treated as works in their own right, with discrete genres, ideological proclivities, and social locations, they constitute both an enrichment of the resources available for comprehending the history of literature and theology in the Bible, and a challenge for incorporating pluriform and sometimes divergent ideologies and social formations.

References and further reading

Bultmann, R. (1941) *Das Evangelium des Johannes*, MeyerK, Göttingen: Vandenhoeck & Ruprecht.

Blum, E. (1990) *Studien zur Komposition des Pentateuch*, BZAW 189, Berlin: Walter de Gruyter.

Carlston, C.E. and D. Norlin (1971) 'Once More – Statistics and Q,' *Harvard Theological Review* 64: 59–78.

—— (1999) 'Statistics and Q – Some Further Observations,' *Novum Testamentum* 41: 108–23.

Carr, D.M. (1996) *Reading the Fractures of Genesis*, Louisville: Westminster/John Knox.

Cross, F.M. (1973) *Canaanite Myth and Hebrew Epic*, Cambridge: Harvard University Press.

Driver, S.R. (1913) *Introduction to the Literature of the Old Testament*, Edinburgh: T.&T. Clark.

Eissfeldt, O. (1965) *The Old Testament: An Introduction*, trans. P.R. Ackroyd, Oxford: Blackwell.

Ennulat, A. (1994) *Die 'Minor Agreements': Untersuchung zu einer offenen Frage des synoptischen Problems*, WUNT 2.62, Tübingen: Mohr Siebeck.

Farmer, W.R. (1964) *The Synoptic Problem: A Critical Analysis*, New York: Macmillan.

Fohrer, G. (1968) *Introduction to the Old Testament*, trans. David Green, Nashville: Abingdon Press/London: SPCK.

Fortna, R.T. (1970) *The Gospel of Signs*, SNTSMS 11, Cambridge: Cambridge University Press.

—— (1988) *The Fourth Gospel and Its Predecessor*, Philadelphia: Fortress Press.

Goulder, M.D. (1989) *Luke: A New Paradigm*, JSNTSup 20, Sheffield: JSOT Press.

Jacobson, A.D. (1982) 'The Literary Unity of Q,' *Journal of Biblical Literature* 101: 365–89.

Kloppenborg, J.S. (1987) *The Formation of Q*, Studies in Antiquity and Christianity, Philadelphia: Fortress Press (2nd edn Harrisburg: Trinity Press International, 2000).

—— (1988) *Q Parallels*, Foundations and Facets, New Testament, Sonoma: Polebridge Press.

—— (2000) *Excavating Q*, Minneapolis: Fortress Press.

Koester, H. (1983) 'History and Development of Mark's Gospel,' pp. 35–57 in *Colloquy on New Testament Studies*, B. Corley (ed.), Macon, GA: Mercer University Press.

McEvenue, S. (1971) *The Narrative Style of the Priestly Writer*, AnBib 50, Rome: Pontifical Biblical Institute.

McNicol, A.J. (1996) *Beyond the Q Impasse – Luke's Use of Matthew*, Valley Forge: Trinity Press International.

Neville, D.J. (1994) *Arguments from Order in Synoptic Source Criticism*, New Gospel Studies 7, Leuven: Peeters/Macon, GA: Mercer University Press.

Paffenroth, K (1997) *The Story of Jesus According to L*, JSNTSup 147, Sheffield: Sheffield Academic Press.

Robinson, J.M., P. Hoffmann, and J.S. Kloppenborg (eds.) (2000) *The Critical Edition of Q*, M.C. Moreland (gen. ed.). Hermeneia Supplements, Leuven: Peeters/Minneapolis: Fortress Press.

Sato, M. (1988) *Q und Prophetie*, WUNT 2.29, Tübingen: Mohr Siebeck.

Schmid, H.H. (1976) *Der sogenannte Jahwist*, Zürich: Theologischer Verlag.

Streeter, B.H. (1924) *The Four Gospels*, London: Macmillan.

Taylor, V. (1926) *Behind the Third Gospel*, Oxford: Clarendon.

Van Seters, J. (1975) *Abraham in History and Tradition*, New Haven: Yale University Press.

—— (1994) *The Life of Moses*, Louisville: Westminster/John Knox.

—— (1999) *The Pentateuch: A Social-Scientific Commentary*, Trajectories 1, Sheffield: Sheffield Academic Press.

Vassiliadis, P. (1978) 'The Nature and Extent of the Q Document,' *Novum Testamentum* 20: 49–73.

Weinfeld, M. (1972) *Deuteronomy and the Deuteronomic School*, Oxford: Clarendon.

Weiss, B. (1907) *Die Quellen des Lukasevangeliums*, Stuttgart and Berlin: Cotta.

Wellhausen, J. (1885) *Prolegomena to the History of Israel*, Edinburgh: T.&T. Clark.

JOHN S. KLOPPENBORG

STRAUSS, DAVID FRIEDRICH (1808–1874)

Assuming both Hegel's replacement of a personal God by an impersonal Idea and Enlightenment cosmology whose world was a closed system of natural laws allowing no supernatural intervention, Strauss attacked Christianity. The vehicle was his *Life of Jesus* (first edn 1835). Strauss focused on the stories of Jesus' life, examining each unit independently to test its historical credibility. Do the parallel accounts contradict one another? Do they violate the known, universal laws of nature? Do they give evidence of the presence of myth? He played off supernaturalists and rationalists to make room for his mythical interpretation. Myths, he believed, were expressions in story form of temporally conditioned religious ideas. Miracle stories, for example, were neither historical records of supernatural interventions nor natural events interpreted supernaturally but myths, stories constructed by the Christian imagination out of such materials as Old Testament prophecies. Like Reimarus, Strauss offered a history of Christian origins that required no supernatural explanation. Unlike Reimarus, he resorted not to apostolic fraud as the basis for his explanation but appealed instead to religious imagination.

The Jesus that emerged from Strauss' *Life* varied, depending on the edition. In the first, second, and fourth editions, Jesus is an apocalyptic fanatic who cannot have been the God-man of orthodox faith. The reconstruction of Christology by speculative philosophy is not contingent on the particular founding events of Christianity. Once the mind has grasped the unity of God and humanity philosophically, Jesus ceases to be essential and may be discarded. In the third edition (1838), Christ is a religious genius who raised the development of Spirit in humanity to higher levels. Another may come, however, who will be equal or superior to Christ. In the *New Life* (1864) Strauss distinguished between the historical and the ideal Christ, the latter being the exemplar of human moral perfection. This exemplar has only gradually reached its fuller development. Every person of moral preeminence has contributed to the ideal. Among such stands Jesus. He was not the first nor will he be the last. For salvation one looks to the ideal Christ, that moral pattern of which Jesus did bring to light many features. So in Strauss' most radical phase (first, second, fourth edn), Jesus' value is only negative. He is a proof that theology must be cut loose from its historical roots. In Strauss' more accommodating phases (third edn; *New Life*), the historical Jesus has a positive, if limited, role. Jesus was a catalyst for the development of the moral ideal but only one among many and one that can be transcended by later catalysts.

For Strauss, the best nonsupernatural explanation of the accounts of Jesus was the mythical interpretation. Having begun with disbelief in a personal God, Strauss explained, with his mythical reading of the Gospels, the origins of Christianity in nonsupernaturalistic terms.

References and further reading

Harris, Horton (1974) *David Friedrich Strauss and His Theology*, Cambridge: Cambridge University Press.

Strauss, David Friedrich (1972) *The Life of Jesus Critically Examined*, trans. George Eliot, Peter Hodgson (ed.), Philadelphia: Fortress Press.

Zeller, Eduard (1874) *David Friedrich Strauss in seinem Leben und seinen Schriften*, Bonn: E. Strauss.

CHARLES H. TALBERT

STRUCTURALISM

Though there are no universally accepted definitions for structuralism, the general viewpoint is that it is a practice dedicated to discerning the meanings behind language, both written and spoken, based not upon the author, original intent, audience, or historical location; but rather recognizing the structure of the language itself as being central to the message being communicated. The structuralist is not primarily concerned with the 'surface structure' analysis of literature (syntax, grammar, narrative themes, etc.) but with the 'deep structure' (foundational truths that span culture, time, and language) that provides the motivation and identity to the more obvious elements. The deep structures are seen as the engine driving the vehicle that is the message.

The ideology of structuralism is not confined strictly to literary criticism but is finding acceptance in the fields of philosophy, anthropology, mathematics, and political science, to name a few. All social activity is governed by underlying principles that mediate human interaction regardless of cultural or chronological differences. The man who does not wear his housecoat to the office may not consciously choose not to wear it, but he is acting under certain societal restraints whether he is consciously aware of them or not (Hayes and Holladay 1987: 121).

In order to discover these underlying structures the interpreter needs to view the text in question in an 'ahistorical' setting. The concern is only with the final version of the text, not with the journey it took to get there. Common practices such as discerning historical relevance, later additions, political climate, syntactical and linguistic growth are seen as irrelevant when attempting to discern the deep truths that lie below the surface.

The methodologies differ largely as some practitioners view structuralism as a scientific method (Ferdinand de Saussure, A.J. Greimas), while others believe it to be literary/artistic in nature (Roman Jakobson, Viktor Shlovsky). Though this debate is ongoing, a general conclusion is being sought that sees structuralism as a combination of both. With that in mind, what follows can be viewed as a basic outline of structural methodologies:

(1) It is not concerned with textual meaning but with seeing the various kinds of structures within the writing itself. The 'value of language' (Greenwood 1985: 5), as de Saussure put it, is found in the structures.

(2) It is to be used to complement other critical interpretation methods, not replace them.

(3) The approach that suits the practice best is the coupling of paradigmatic and syntagmatic methods. The paradigmatic method is less interested in words as they appear in relation to their set groupings (i.e., sentences or grammatical units) and more interested in how that word relates to other words that could have been used in its place. On a chart the syntagmatic method would run horizontally as the interpreter attempts to see each word as it relates to those around it. The paradigmatic axis would be vertical as it attempts to understand why that specific word was selected when several other words could easily have been chosen as well. (The term synonyms is not completely appropriate here; though the words are similar in meaning, no two words can ever share an identical definition. However, it is helpful to use the term to assist in clarifying the point.) Therefore the words and sentences are given their identity through the duality of combination (relation to other words in the unit) and choice (the motives behind the selection of each individual word).

Swiss linguist Ferdinand de Saussure (1857–1913) is largely credited with originating the linguistic school of structuralism that most directly influences biblical interpretation. He contributed to the field by defining the syntagmatic and paradigmatic methods as well as stating the difference between synchrony and diachrony; in other words, the fact that structuralism is concerned with the language at the time of interpretation, not its development throughout history (which would be the diachronic approach). De Saussure taught that linguistic signs are arbitrary in their identity and that all language is based on a finite amount of humanmade sounds. The key to their meanings is not in the sounds themselves but in discovering the various combinations of these sounds used by the differing linguistic groups.

It is these same principles that govern written language. Though the symbols differ from those in spoken language it is in deciphering the order of the symbols, which represent spoken language, that the interpreter unlocks the mystery of the true meaning of the text.

Another major contributor to this field is French anthropologist Claude Levi-Strauss (1908–) who found that myth, prose, narrative, and poetry could be understood through the decoding of the 'binary oppositions' within the story. These diametrically opposed themes are arranged in the text on both the surface and deep levels and appear to be conducive to all human writing. To Levi-Strauss these underlying (deep) structures of hardship/ease, enemy/friend, light/darkness and, despair/hope etc. impact the reader on a subconscious level and allow him or her to identify with the text (whether it be narrative, like Jacob wrestling the angel, or poetic in nature, like the Psalms). In addition to this he discerned that all myths seem to have recurring typical roles within their narrative structure; he called these roles 'actants.' These actants appear in most stories, and though not every character is evident in every story, variations are quite frequent. One of the more common actants is the theme of a world that is somehow disrupted and the remainder of the story deals with the reinstating of that world to its former order.

Vladimir Propp (1895–1970) was instrumental in deciphering Russian folklore and it has been argued that he may actually be the historic precursor to de Saussure. Both he and Levi-Strauss shared reservations about applying their principles of discerning myth and folklore to biblical interpretation. Some of the problems he noted were that biblical and Russian folklore have differing agendas in their telling, and in addition to this the biblical tales do not appear to be based on a single model, as do Russian folk stories. Propp also found it too difficult to discern which tales are actually to be considered in this genre; for example, while the tale of Samson has numerous mythic actants, stories like Ruth and Jonah cannot be so easily identified and categorized as such.

Through varying techniques the structuralist attempts to discern the messages in the text based solely on the text itself. These structures, if they can be detected, allow the text to speak for itself, independent of its author, its timeframe, or even its story line: 'In experimenting with structural exegesis, we need to resist asking historical questions ... and instead look for general structures in the text, for examples of binary opposition, and for the deep structures reflective of universal interests and concerns' (Hayes and Holladay 1987: 119).

References and further reading

Clarke, Simon (1981) *The Foundations of Structuralism*, New Jersey: Harvester.

DeGeorge, Richard T. and Fernande M. DeGeorge (1972) *The Structuralists: From Marx to Levi-Strauss*, New York: Anchor.

De Saussure, Ferdinand (1959) *Course in General Linguistics*, trans. Wade Baskin, London: Peter Owen.

Fee, Gordon D. (1993) *New Testament Exegesis: Revised Edition*, Louisville: Westminster/John Knox.

Greenwood, David (1985) *Structuralism and the Biblical Text*, New York: Mouton.

Hayes, John H. and Carl R. Holladay (1987) *Biblical Exegesis: A Beginner's Handbook*, Atlanta: John Knox Press.

Levi-Strauss, Claude. (1976) *Structural Anthropology: Vol. II*, trans Monique Layton, New York Basic.

Sturrock, John (1993) *Structuralism: Second Edition*, London: Fontana.

J.T. ROBERTSON

T

TARGUM

The Aramaic translations of Hebrew scripture are known as Targums. They shed important light on biblical interpretation in Jewish circles in late antiquity and as such are part of a very important interpretive method that developed then, in which scripture was translated, paraphrased, and rewritten.

1 Origin of Targums

How early Hebrew scripture was translated into Aramaic is unknown. Most of the extant Targums are products of the rabbinic period, dating from the fourth to tenth centuries AD. However, the discovery of at least one Targum at Qumran (i.e., 11QtgJob) and possibly two others (i.e., 4QtgLeviticus, 4QtgJob) demonstrates that some Targums existed in the first century BC, perhaps even earlier. The impulse to translate Hebrew scripture into Greek (i.e., the Septuagint, or LXX) for one Jewish constituency, which began in the third century BC, may have coincided with a similar impulse to render scripture into Aramaic for another constituency.

The Aramaic translation became known as *targum* (pl. *targumim*), a Hebrew and Aramaic word that means 'translation.' There are extant Targums of every book of scripture, with the exceptions of Ezra, Nehemiah, and Daniel. These books may not have been translated into Aramaic because parts of them are already in Aramaic.

The Targums originated in the synagogue and perhaps also the rabbinical academies as homiletical and interpretive paraphrases of the passage of Hebrew scripture that was to be read (such as the *haftarah*). Following the Babylonian and Persian Exile (*c.* 600–500 BC) many of the Jewish people spoke Aramaic with greater ease than the cognate Hebrew, the language of scripture. Therefore, it became useful to translate Hebrew scripture into Aramaic (cf. Neh. 8, where Ezra the scribe translates Hebrew scripture into Aramaic; cf. *b. Meg.* 3a). The translator was called the *meturgeman* ('translator'). He recited his translation after the reading of the Hebrew passage.

2 Classifications of Targums

Targums fall into three basic classifications: (a) Targums to the Pentateuch, (b) Targums to the Prophets, and (c) Targums to the Writings (or Hagiographa). These Targums exemplify individual characteristics and should be studied accordingly.

2.1 Targums to the Pentateuch

The major extant Targums to the Pentateuch include the traditional Onqelos (see Sperber 1959–1973: vol. 1), the much later Pseudo-Jonathan (see Clarke 1984), the Fragment Targum (see Klein 1980), and the recently discovered Neophyti (or Neofiti; see Díez Macho 1968–1978). Of these, the last is considered to reflect the oldest language and interpretive tradition. The so-called Fragment Targum is in reality a Targum made up of selected readings. Its name is a minomer; it would have been better to have called it the Excerpt Targum.

2.2 Targums to the Prophets

At one time it was commonplace to refer to Targum Jonathan to the Prophets, as if the whole corpus reflected a single school or tradition. Recent study has made it clear that the Prophets should be studied individually, for each reveals a character of its own (in the 'Aramaic Bible' series, see the introductory essays by Chilton, on Isaiah; Hayward, on Jeremiah; Levey, on Ezekiel; and Cathcart and Saldarini, on the Twelve all in McNamara *et al.* 1987–1989, 1990–). Chilton (1982) has concluded that the exegetical framework of the Isaiah Targum took shape between the two great Jewish wars for liberation (i.e., from AD 70 to 132). There are indications that the other Prophets Targums took shape in this approximate period.

2.3 Targums to the Writings

The Targums to the Writings are individualistic; indeed, there are two Targums to Esther. These Targums are quite midrashic and often accommodate large insertions of interpretive or homiletical material (e.g., Tg. Ruth 1.1, which contains a homily concerning ten great famines in Israel's history). The most difficult of these Targums are those to Job and the Psalms, for there is no fixed text for either. Also puzzling is the relationship of the Targum to the Proverbs and the Syriac version of this book.

3 Character of Targums

The Targums are sometimes literal in their translation, but more often they are paraphrastic and interpretive. Targums are part of the phenomenon sometimes called 'rewritten Bible,' though not identical to it. Rewritten Bible, as seen, for example, in *Jubilees* or Pseudo-Philo's *Biblical Antiquities*, freely omits, rearranges, and radically alters the biblical text. In comparison, Targums are more conservative, following the text. Concern to update the text, answer questions raised by the text, even correct the text, is seen in the Targums.

4 Targumic tradition in the New Testament

At several points Jesus' utterances and interpretation cohere with Targumic tradition, especially as seen in the extant Isaiah Targum. Jesus' allusion to Isaiah 6:9–10 in Mark 4:12 reflects the Targumic diction ('forgive') not Hebrew or Greek ('heal'). Jesus' saying about the perishing by the sword (Matt. 26:52) reflects Isaiah 50:11 in the Aramaic, while linkage of Gehenna with Isaiah 66:24 in Mark 9:47–48 also reflects Aramaic tradition. Jesus' admonition to his followers to be 'merciful, as your Father in heaven is merciful' (Luke 6:36=Matt. 5:48) coheres with Levitius 22:28 in Aramaic (i.e., Pseudo-Jonathan). Jesus' parabolic understanding of Isaiah's Song of the Vineyard (Isa. 5:1–7) and his use of it against the temple establishment in his similar parable (Mark 12:1–12 and parallels) once again reflects acquaintance with the Aramaic tradition. The antiquity of this tradition is attested at Qumran (cf. 4Q500). Jesus' allusion to Levitius 18:5 in reference to 'eternal life' (cf. Luke 10:25–28) once again reflects the Aramaic tradition and once again is attested at Qumran (CD 3:12–20).

The opening words of the Fourth Gospel, 'In the beginning was the Word . . . All things came into being by Him' (John 1:1–3), probably reflect an Aramaic paraphrase of Genesis 1:1, 'In the beginning with wisdom the Word of the Lord created . . .'. The bitter polemic of John 8:44 ('You are of your father the devil . . . He was a murderer from the beginning') probably reflects targumic tradition in which it was believed the Devil had fathered Cain, who then in turn murdered his brother Abel (cf. 1 John 3:12).

Targumic tradition is echoed in Paul as well. Perhaps the most important instance is seen in Romans 10, where the apostle creatively applies Deuteronomy 30:11–12 to Christ. At many points Paul's allusive paraphrase and exegesis cohere with the Aramaic paraphrase, especially as seen in Neofiti (where instead of crossing the sea to fetch the law, we have reference to Jonah descending into the depths to bring it up).

Targumic traditions are echoed in many other places in the New Testament writings, including the Deutero-Paulines, Hebrews, and the book of Revelation. Although most of the tradition preserved in the Targums is too late to be of use in New Testament interpretation, there is much that reaches back to the first century and earlier and therefore should be taken into consideration.

References and further reading

Aramaic texts

Clark, E.G. (1984) *Targum Pseudo-Jonathan of the Pentateuch: Text and Concordance*, Hoboken: Ktav.

Díez Macho, A. (ed.) (1968–1978) *Neophyti 1: Targum Palestinense*, 6 Vols., Madrid: Consejo Superior de Investigaciones Científicas.

Klein, M.L. (1980) *The Fragment-Targums of the Pentateuch: According to their Extant Sources*, Vol. I: *Texts, Indices, and Introductory Essays*, AnBib 76, Rome: Pontifical Biblical Institute Press.

Sperber, A. (1959–1973) *The Bible in Aramaic Based on Old Manuscripts and Printed Texts*, 5 Vols., Leiden: Brill.

English translations

Grelot, P. (1992) *What Are the Targums? Selected Texts*, Collegeville: Liturgical Press.

McNamara, M.J. et al. (eds.) (1987–1989, 1990–) *The Aramaic Bible*, Wilmington: Michael Glazier/ Collegeville: Liturgical Press.

Studies

Beattie, D.R.G. and M.J. McNamara (eds.) (1994) *The Aramaic Bible: Targums in their Historical Context*, JSOTSup 166, Sheffield: JSOT Press.

Bowker, J. (1969) *The Targums and Rabbinic Literature*, Cambridge: Cambridge University Press.

Cathcart, K.J. and M. Maher (eds.) (1996) *Targumic and Cognate Studies: Essays in Honour of Martin McNamara*, JSOTSup 230, Sheffield: Sheffield Academic Press.

Chilton, B. (1982) *The Glory of Israel: The Theology and Provenience of the Isaiah Targum*, JSOTSup 23, Sheffield: JSOT Press.

—— (1984) *A Galilean Rabbi and His Bible: Jesus' Use of the Interpreted Scripture of His Time*, GNS 8, Wilmington: Glazier.

—— (2004) 'From Aramaic Paraphrase to Greek Testament,' pp. 23–43 in *From Prophecy to Testament: The Function of the Old Testament in the New*, C.A. Evans (ed.), Peabody, MA: Hendrickson.

Churgin, P. (1927) *Targum Jonathan to the Prophets*, Yale Oriental Series 14, New Haven: Yale University Press.

Evans, C.A. (2004) 'The Aramaic Psalter and the New Testament,' pp. 44–91 in *From Prophecy to Testament: The Function of the Old Testament in the New*, Peabody, MA: Hendrickson.

Flesher, P.V.M. (ed.) (1992–1998) *Targum Studies*, 2 Vols., Atlanta: Scholars Press.

Forestell, J.T. (1979) *Targumic Traditions and the New Testament*, SBL Aramaic Studies 4, Missoula: Scholars Press.

Kasher, R. (1999) 'Metaphor and Allegory in the Aramaic Translations of the Bible,' *Journal for the Aramaic Bible* 1: 53–77.

Levey, S.H. (1974) *The Messiah: An Aramaic Interpretation: The Messianic Exegesis of the Targum*, MHUC 2, Cincinnati: Hebrew Union College Press.

McNamara, M. (1972) *Targum and Testament: Aramaic Paraphrases of the Hebrew Bible: A Light on the New Testament*, Shannon: Irish University Press/Grand Rapids: Eerdmans.

—— (1978) *The New Testament and the Palestinian Targum to the Pentateuch*, AnBib 27A, Rome: Pontifical Biblical Institute, 2nd edn.

York, A.D. (1974) 'The Dating of Targumic Literature,' *Journal for the Study of Judaism* 5: 49–62.

—— (1979) 'The Targum in the Synagogue and the School,' *Journal for the Study of Judaism* 10: 74–86.

CRAIG A. EVANS

TERTULLIAN (c. 160–c. 220)

Tertullian, Quintus Septimius Florens, is recognized as having founded theology and exegesis in the Latin tradition. There are thirty-one extant treatises, which, in addition to accounts by Jerome and Eusebius of Caesarea, give us the little biographical information we know about Tertullian. There are fifteen, possibly eighteen, titles of lost works as well as spurious works attributed to his name. Born in North Africa to a centurion just after the first half of the second century AD, Tertullian received a classical education in rhetoric, Roman law, and philosophy. He converted to Christianity, probably at midlife, around 193 to 195 and no later than 197, and was, contrary to Jerome's assumption, never made presbyter of the church.

His writings indicate a comprehensive knowledge of literature, philosophy, and medicine. Tertullian was inventive and fervent as a debater and his technique places him within the Second Sophistic movement. He was influenced by Stoic philosophy; nevertheless the Bible remained a priority and was used abundantly.

Tertullian wrote treatises in both Greek and Latin against pagans, heretics, Jews, and ethically lax Christians. His writings are often divided into three categories: apologies, treatises on Christian living, and antiheretical writings. Later in his life, Tertullian became an adherent of the Montanist sect and wrote with a leaning toward Montanism, although he never fully separated from the Church of Carthage. Nevertheless, he spoke out against Gnosticism and Marcionism, influencing Cyprian and Augustine and later Latin authors.

He probably used a Latin version of the scriptures that was possibly translated in his lifetime from the Septuagint. He considered the Greek authoritative and some believe that Tertullian, with his bilingualism, worked from the Greek, translating the quotes he used into Latin. Tertullian's only commentary, *On Prayer*, is a short exposition on the Lord's Prayer. His works are full of exegesis and he often wrote about scripture in forensic terms. He believed that scripture belonged entirely to the church, therefore heretics had no right to use scripture. Christianity, for Tertullian, was based on revelation and the gift of God. He believed that scripture was the source of the revelation but that scripture also needed to be sifted through rationally by incorporating a literal and historical interpretation of it. Tertullian also used allegory and typology but avoided esoteric meanings. He implemented and transformed his rhetorical background to further develop precision and formulaic technique in scriptural interpretation.

Tertullian's work epitomizes the discussion of the relation between revelation and reason. He is well known for posing the question, 'What has Jerusalem to do with Athens, the church with the academy, the Christian with the heretic?' Tertullian masterfully utilizes rhetorical and sophistical devices to cleverly undermine his opponents' reasoning. He defended Christianity from the culture of the day; nevertheless, scholars disagree about Tertullian's belief regarding the compatibility of Christianity and classical culture.

His creativity in using Latin and his colorful word pictures were a tremendous influence on Latin theological thought and language, sufficiently warranting the title, father of Latin theology.

References and further reading

CCSL (1953), vols. 1–2; *ANF* (1956), vols. 3–4; Eusebius, *Church History* 2.2.4; Jerome, *Lives of Illustrious Men* 53.

Barnes, T.D. (1985) *Tertullian: A Historical and Literary Study*, Oxford: Oxford University Press, 2nd edn.

O'Malley, T.P. (1967) *Tertullian and the Bible: Language-Imagery-Exegesis*, Nijmegen: Dekker & Van de Vegt.

Rankin, David (1955) *Tertullian and the Church*, Cambridge: Cambridge University Press.

Snider, R.D. (1971) *Ancient Rhetoric and the Art of Tertullian*, Oxford: Oxford University Press.

Waszink, J.H. (1979) 'Tertullian's Principles and Methods of Exegesis,' pp. 17–31 in *Early Christian Literature and the Classical Intellectual Tradition: In Honorem Robert M. Grant*, W.R. Schoedel and R.L. Wilken (eds.), Paris: Éditions Beauchesne.

DALLAS B.N. FRIESEN

TESTAMENT RELATIONSHIPS

1 General patterns construing the Old Testament–New Testament relationship
2 The use of the Old Testament in the New Testament

The study of the Old Testament–New Testament relationship entails an investigation of general approaches to the question as well as a survey of the distinctive approaches to the Old Testament by various New Testament authors.

1 General patterns of construing the Old Testament–New Testament relationship

The relationship between the Old Testament and the New Testament has been variously described as following a pattern of disunity/discontinuity or unity/continuity (Hasel 1978; Baker 1991). Various mediating approaches attempting to balance elements of continuity and discontinuity have been proposed as well. Disunity/discontinuity is advocated in an extreme form by the second-century heretic Marcion, who completely dissociated the two Testaments and rejected the Old Testament in its entirety (as well as parts of the New Testament) owing to what he perceived as its inferior presentation of God. Others, more recently, while less radical, have nonetheless asserted the superiority of the New Testament while minimizing the Old Testament's importance. According to Bultmann (cited in Hasel 1978: 175), the Old Testament depicts the 'failure of history'; 'the history of Israel is not history of revelation'; and the Old Testament is nothing but 'the presupposition of the New.' On the opposite side of the spectrum, some have underemphasized the New Testament while overstating the importance of the Old Testament. The Reformed scholar Vischer, for example, claims that the Old Testament is Christological to such an extent that Jesus' biography can be reconstructed from its data. However, either extreme is of doubtful value.

Those identifying a pattern of unity/continuity find that 'the Old Testament continually looks forward to something beyond itself' while 'the New Testament continually looks back to the Old' (Rowley 1953: 95). Scholars favoring this approach view the Old Testament–New Testament relationship as reciprocal. While the Old Testament cannot be fully understood without the New Testament, the New Testament, without the Old Testament, would lack its proper foundation. The continuity can be traced along the following lines (Hasel 1978: 186–96): (a) *salvation history*: the history of God's people encompasses both the history of Israel and the history of the New Testament church; (b) *scripture*: the New Testament writers frequently cite, allude to, or echo Old Testament passages, utilizing distinctive hermeneutical axioms and appropriation techniques (Moo 1983: 374–87; Longenecker 1999); (c) *terminology*: Jesus and the New Testament writers frequently draw on Old Testament language; the study of significant New Testament theological terms requires an investigation of their Old Testament background; (d) *themes*: beyond the verbal level, the Old Testament and the New Testament are united by important themes such as creation, sin, promise, covenant, salvation, or Messiah; (e) *typology* (Goppelt 1982 [1939]): the New Testament features antitypes (escalated patterns) of Old Testament types, be it events (the Exodus), characters (Elijah), or institutions (the sacrificial system); (f) *promise fulfilment*: the New Testament records the fulfilment of countless Old Testament promises in and through the Lord Jesus Christ (e.g., the Matthean and Johannine 'fulfilment quotations'; see below); and (g) *perspective*: both the Old Testament and the New Testament look forward to an eschatological consummation of the redemptive purposes of God.

While these patterns of unity/continuity are undeniable, however, unity ought not to be misconstrued as uniformity and the biblical witness ought to be viewed within a framework that allows for development and diversity (Köstenberger 2002a: 144–58) and even discontinuity (though not disunity), properly understood. An element of discontinuity is introduced into the biblical record through the presence of initially undisclosed but subsequently revealed salvation truths, such as Paul's formulation of the *mystērion* of the body of Christ encompassing both Jews and Gentiles (Rom. 16:25–27; Eph. 3:1–6; Col. 1:25–27; Bockmühl 1990). Progressive dispensationalists and others also point to the distinct identities of Israel and the church, contending that the church does not replace Israel in God's plan and that there remains a future for ethnic Israel (Rom. 11:25–32; Blaising and Bock 1992).

2 The use of the Old Testament in the New Testament

Jesus claimed to be the Messiah predicted in the Old Testament and interpreted both Old Testament types and predictions with reference to himself. He variously affirmed (Matt. 5:17), sharpened (Matt. 5:27–28), or even suspended the Old Testament (Mark 7:19). Jesus' use of scripture became a model for the interpretation of the Old Testament by the early church (France 1971). The New Testament includes over 250 Old Testament quotations, plus thousands of allusions and echoes (Hays 1989). The New Testament writers concur that God's revelation in Jesus is final and definitive (John 1:1–18; Heb. 1:1–3). Most frequently cited are the Pentateuch, the Psalms, and Isaiah. The following discussion will briefly survey the distinctive uses of the Old Testament by the various New Testament authors (Carson and Williamson 1988: 205–336).

2.1 Matthew

Matthew's Gospel (and hence the New Testament) opens with a genealogy of Jesus Christ, identifying him as the son of Abraham and David. Matthew's 'fulfilment quotations' (1:22–23; 2:15, 17–18, 23; 4:14–16; 8:17; 12:17–21; 13:35; 21:4–5; 27:9–10; cf. 2:5) demonstrate the fulfilment of Old Testament scripture in virtually every significant aspect of the life of Christ. From the Virgin Birth and Jesus' name and birthplace to Jesus' substitutionary death, burial, and resurrection, Matthew provides ample scriptural evidence that Jesus is the Messiah predicted in the Hebrew scriptures.

2.2 Mark

Mark's use of the Old Testament centers primarily around the ministry of John the Baptist (1:2–3 citing Mal. 3:1; Isa. 40:3); the rejection of Jesus' message and ministry by the Jews (4:12 citing Isa. 6:9–10; 7:6–7 citing Isa. 29:13); and the sufferings and ultimate rejection of Jesus (12:1 alluding to Isa. 5:1–2; 12:10–11 citing Ps. 118:22–23; 15:36 citing Ps. 22:1). While probably writing to a Gentile Roman audience, Mark roots the key elements of the gospel of Jesus Christ firmly in the Old Testament scriptures.

2.3 Luke–Acts

Luke's most distinctive (though not first) Old Testament reference is found in 4:18–19 where Jesus is presented as the Spirit-anointed messenger of good news to the poor in keeping with Isaiah's portrait of the Servant of the Lord (61:1–2). The remainder of Luke's Gospel shows Jesus as a compassionate healer and Savior who reaches out particularly to those of low social status. The two other distinctive Lukan Old Testament references are found in 24:27 and 44–49 where Jesus is shown to fulfil the Old Testament scriptures in their entirety.

Prominent Old Testament references in the book of Acts include those found in Peter's Pentecost sermon (2:17–21, citing Joel 2:28–32); Stephen's speech before the Sanhedrin (ch. 7); Philip's ministry to the Ethiopian eunuch (8:32–33 citing Isa. 53:7–8); Paul's sermon at Pisidian Antioch (13:33–35, 41, 47 citing Ps. 2:7; Isa. 55:3; Ps. 16:10; Hab. 1:5; Isa. 49:6); James' speech at

the Jerusalem Council (15:16–18, citing Amos 9:11–12); and Paul's preaching first to the Jews, then to the Gentiles (28:26–27 citing Isa. 6:9–10).

2.4 John

Explicit Old Testament quotations in John's Gospel are relatively rare. The most significant clusters of Old Testament references are found at 12:38–40 (where the evangelist adduces Isa. 53:1 and 6:10 in support of his contention that the Jewish people's rejection of Jesus as Messiah fulfilled Old Testament scripture) and in the Passion narrative (19:24, 36, 37, referring to Ps. 22:18; Exod. 12:46 or Num. 9:12; and Zech. 12:10). Notable is the switch in pattern to fulfilment quotations starting with 12:38. Beyond these explicit citations there are many scriptural allusions and references involving Old Testament symbolism, such as the depiction of Jesus as the 'good shepherd' and the 'true vine' in chapters 10 and 15 (cf. Ezek. 34; Isa. 5; Köstenberger 2002b: 67–96). Jesus is also shown to fulfil the symbolism underlying Jewish festivals such as Passover (ch. 6) or Tabernacles (chs 7–8).

2.5 Paul

About half of the Old Testament references in Paul's writings occur in the book of Romans, with half of these clustered in Romans 9–11 and a quarter in Romans 1–4. The thematic verse 1:17 roots Paul's Gospel in Habakkuk 2:4, which Paul interprets as indicating that righteousness is from (divine) faith(fulness) to (human) faith (Dunn 1988: 43–6). Using the rabbinic technique of pearlstringing (3:10–18, citing mostly from various Pss.), Paul shows that all humanity is guilty of sin and in need of redemption. Abraham is the paradigmatic example of saving faith (4:3 citing Gen. 15:6), while Adam serves as a type of Jesus (5:12–21).

In Romans 9–11 the apostle, addressing the question of whether the lack of Jewish response to Jesus marks the failure of God's Old Testament promises to Israel (9:6), adduces the scriptural motif of the faithful remnant as proof that inclusion among God's people was never merely a function of ethnicity but always required faith (9:27–29 citing Isa. 10:22–23; 1:9). Paul also seeks to show that the Old Testament envisioned the inclusion of Gentiles into God's covenant community (9:25–26 citing Hos. 2:23; 1:10) and affirms God's sovereign elective purposes (9:15 citing Exod. 33:19; 11:33–36 citing Isa. 40:13; Job 41:1).

Paul's argument in Galatians (esp. 3:6–14) over against the Judaizers, likewise, draws significantly on the Old Testament (esp. Gen. 15:6 and Hab. 2:4, both of which are also quoted in Rom.). According to Paul, the scriptures foresaw that God would justify the Gentiles by faith and announced the gospel in advance to Abraham (3:8; cf. Gen. 12:3), and Christ redeemed us from the curse of the law by becoming a curse for us (3:13; cf. Deut. 21:23). God's salvific purposes always focused on faith (3:14); the law was added only as a temporary structure (3:15–25). Thus both Jews and Gentiles must believe in Christ to be saved (3:28).

Paul's other writings are not devoid of scriptural references, yet since Jewish–Gentile issues are less at the forefront than in Romans and Galatians, the use of the Old Testament there is less pronounced and pervasive.

2.6 General Epistles and Revelation

In the General Epistles it is particularly the book of Hebrews that is closely wedded to the Old Testament scriptures. Hebrews (probably addressed to a Jewish Christian congregation in Rome) features Jesus as superior to Old Testament Judaism, including Moses, Joshua, and the Aaronic priesthood. Jesus is presented as an eternal high priest according to the order of Melchizedek (5:6; 7:17, 21 citing Ps. 110:4), who instituted the new covenant envisaged by the prophet Jeremiah (8:8–12 citing Jer. 31:31–34; cf. 10:15–18). The non-Christian recipients in the audience are warned that the rejection of so great a salvation will result in eternal damnation (e.g., 2:1–4), just as the disobedience of Israel's wilderness generation prevented its entry into the Promised Land (6:4–6). The faith of selected Old Testament characters is showcased to serve as inspiration for believers in Christ (ch. 11).

James' Epistle, similarly, adduces the examples of Abraham (2:21–23), Rahab (2:25), Job (5:11), and Elijah (5:17–18), and includes frequent Old Testament references and allusions. In Peter's first epistle it is particularly chapter 2 that features a series of 'stone testimonia' and other Old Testament references (1 Pet. 2:6–9 citing Isa. 28:16; Ps. 118:22; Isa. 8:14; and alluding to Isa. 43:20–21; Exod. 19:5–6) describing God's new covenant community in terms originally applied to Israel. In 1 Peter 2:21–25 Jesus is presented as the Suffering Servant of Isaiah 53. Jude, while not featuring any explicit Old Testament quotes, provides a midrash on various Old Testament types of God's punishment as paradigmatic of his impending judgment of false teachers in Jude's day (5–7, 11). The book of Revelation, too, evinces a nonformal approach in its use of the Old Testament. The seer's visions are cast against the backdrop of imagery supplied by the Hebrew scriptures, which provide the raw material for John's depiction of the endtimes, including Christ's return and God's judgment of the wicked.

References and further reading

Baker, David L. (1991) *Two Testaments, One Bible: A Study of the Theological Relationships between the Old and New Testaments*, Downers Grove: IVP, rev. edn.

Blaising, Craig A. and Darrell L. Bock (eds.) (1992) *Dispensationalism, Israel and the Church: The Search for Definition*, Grand Rapids: Zondervan.

Bockmühl, M.N.A. (1990) *Revelation and Mystery in Ancient Judaism and Pauline Christianity*, WUNT 2.36, Tübingen: Mohr Siebeck.

Carson, D.A. and H.G.M. Williamson (eds.) (1988) *It Is Written: Scripture Citing Scripture: Essays in Honour of Barnabas Lindars*, Cambridge: Cambridge University Press.

Dunn, James D.G. (1988) *Romans 1–8*, WBC 38A, Dallas: Word.

France, R.T. (1971) *Jesus and the Old Testament*, London: Tyndale.

Goppelt, Leonhard (1982 [1939]) *Typos: The Typological Interpretation of the Old Testament in the New*, Grand Rapids: Eerdmans.

Hasel, Gerhard (1978) *New Testament Theology: Basic Issues in the Current Debate*, Grand Rapids: Eerdmans.

Hays, R.B. (1989) *Echoes of Scripture in the Letters of Paul*, New Haven/London: Yale University Press.

Köstenberger, Andreas J. (2002a) 'Diversity and Unity in the New Testament,' pp. 144–58 in *Biblical Theology: Retrospect and Prospect*, Scott J. Hafemann (ed.), Downers Grove: IVP.

—— (2002b) 'Jesus the Good Shepherd Who Will Also Bring Other Sheep (John 10:16): The Old Testament Background of a Familiar Metaphor,' *Bulletin for Biblical Research* 12: 67–96.

Longenecker, Richard N. (1999) *Biblical Exegesis in the Apostolic Period*, Grand Rapids: Eerdmans, 2nd edn.

Moo, Douglas J. (1983) *The Old Testament in the Gospel Passion Narratives*, Sheffield: Almond.

Rowley, H.H. (1953) *The Unity of the Bible*, London: Cary Kingsgate.

ANDREAS J. KÖSTENBERGER

TEXTUAL CRITICISM (NEW TESTAMENT)

1 Introduction
2 The texts of the New Testament
3 The principles of textual criticism
4 Implications for biblical criticism and interpretation

1 Introduction

Textual criticism, sometimes referred to as lower criticism (as opposed to higher criticism), is foundational for interpretation of the Bible, since it is on the basis of textual criticism that the interpreted text is established. Interest in textual criticism has ebbed and flowed during the last several hundred years. In the nineteenth century, in the light of advancements in biblical studies, and especially as knowledge of ancient manuscripts grew through discovery and rediscovery, modern textual criticism was born. The enthusiasm of the nineteenth century, however, gave way to a more passive and less critical acceptance of the supposed assured results of textual criticism. It is only within the last several decades that interest in textual criticism has reawakened. This new interest has emerged out of consideration of new manuscripts of both canonical and noncanonical texts. The result of such study is twofold. On the one hand, there is the assurance that the textual tradition of the New Testament is more firmly established than that of virtually any other ancient text, with well over 5,000 ancient manuscripts for the Greek New Testament now known, including around 120 papyri, numerous majuscule manuscripts, and an assortment of minuscules and lectionaries (see Bruce 1960: 13–20). On the other hand, with the increased knowledge of the textual world of the New Testament – including the ways in which manuscripts were copied and transmitted, the numbers and significance of a range of variants, and questions raised about scribal practices – has come recognitions of the limitations of textual criticism to establish the certainty of the text. In any event, unless a surprising turn of events occurs, New Testament textual criticism, no matter how early the manuscripts now known are, will almost assuredly never be concerned with the autographs, but will need to reconstruct such autographs on the basis of later copies. This presents the ongoing challenge of textual criticism for biblical criticism and interpretation.

1 The texts of the New Testament

The history of the development of the modern Greek New Testament has taken a number of twists and turns (see Metzger 1968; Aland and Aland 1989). In the sixteenth century, the Complutensian New Testament was first printed (1514) but was not distributed. This distinction fell to Erasmus, who published the first edition of his Greek New Testament in 1516. This edition was based upon a relatively small number of late minuscule manuscripts from around the tenth to thirteenth centuries. Nevertheless, this became the basis of the so-called Textus Receptus, and reflected the Byzantine textual tradition. It dominated textual criticism for nearly 400 years, and provided the textual basis for numerous translations, most notably the text that lay behind the King James Version. In the nineteenth century, there was growing dissatisfaction with this text, in the light of the development of critical thought and greater textual knowledge. As a result of the work of such people as Johann Jakob Griesbach, Karl Lachmann, Constantin Tischendorf, and especially B.F. Westcott and F.J.A. Hort, the domination of the Textus Receptus was broken, and new principles of textual criticism were developed. These led to the development of the eclectic text, which was a principled edition of a text thought to approximate the original on the basis of the evi-

dence from a variety of later manuscripts, often categorized by textual type or family (these are explained briefly below). The eclectic text developed by Nestle, on the basis of comparison of texts by Tischendorf, Westcott and Hort, and first Weymouth and later Weiss, became the basis of the modern critical edition widely used in the twentieth and into the twenty-first centuries.

2.1 Reasoned eclecticism

There were a number of different types of eclectic texts that were developed especially in the twentieth century, but the most popular was the reasoned eclectic text that was based upon the major codex manuscripts, Sinaiticus and Vaticanus, supplemented by evidence from the growing number of papyri, and other codexes and later texts. Reasoned eclecticism used a combination of this textual evidence with a commonly agreed and utilized set of principles of textual criticism to reconstruct a text that was not matched in all of its readings by any ancient document but that was thought to best approximate the autograph. Optimism for the text created by reasoned eclecticism reached the point where some defenders of it were willing to claim that modern scholarship had found what was tantamount to the original text. This kind of belief was reflected in ratings assigned to variants in some editions, in which there was shown to be a noteworthy increase in the ratings given in subsequent editions, even though the textual evidence had not significantly changed (see Clarke 1997). The eclectic text is still used in the Nestle–Aland and United Bible Societies' *Greek New Testament*, the texts of which now are the same.

2.2 Byzantine text

The Byzantine text is sometimes equated with the Textus Receptus. Whereas it is true that the Textus Receptus in most instances resembles the Byzantine text, the two are not exactly the same (one should also distinguish the Majority Text; see Wallace in Ehrman and Holmes 1993: 293–8). In modern text-critical scholarship, a number of textual types have been identified. Those most commonly referred to are the Alexandrian, the Western, and the Byzantine. There is less attempt made today to locate these particular texts or textual types, since most of the distinctive readings of these manuscript types are found in manuscripts from various locations. Instead, these manuscripts are identified by the type and character of their readings. The vast majority of manuscripts of the New Testament are classified as Byzantine in nature. The number of manuscripts, as well as a number of the readings found in them, as well as the widespread use of this manuscript type (e.g., in the Textus Receptus) has led a number of scholars to argue for a very important position to be occupied by the Byzantine text in text-critical studies, although most scholars do not hold to this position.

The Textus Receptus is still available and used by some, while a recent edition of the Majority Byzantine text has been published by Hodges and Farstad.

2.3 Single manuscript

The clear majority of scholars today use the reasoned eclectic text that utilizes the Alexandrian textual tradition as its basis, whereas some scholars wish to revive interest in the Byzantine text type. A third alternative, argued for lately, is the utilization of a single manuscript, such as Sinaiticus or Vaticanus. The argument is that the reasoned eclectic text is the product of nineteenth- and twentieth-century critical scholarship. As noted above, despite the efforts of textual critics to reason their way to the earliest text, their conclusions are not reflected in any single ancient manuscript. Similarly, even though there is a vast majority of Byzantine manuscripts, the simple process of counting does not establish reliability or originality, especially since the Byzantine text type appears to be the youngest, and the largest number of manuscripts are later. Instead, the single manuscript proponents argue that the use of a single early manuscript reflects actual usage by a Christian community of the ancient world, even if that world is that of the fourth century (or some other time period). Whereas for the entire New Testament an Alexandrian manuscript is usually the one endorsed, for certain books, such as Acts, some wish to argue for use of the Western text as found in Codex Bezae.

3 The principles of textual criticism

Griesbach was the first to formulate principles of textual criticism. These were further developed by such scholars as Lachmann, and Westcott and Hort. In many circles, the commonly agreed principles of textual criticism have been tacitly accepted as providing a firm basis for text-critical decisions. The kinds of variants are typically classified into unintentional and intentional errors. The kinds of evidence that derive from the manuscripts themselves, since Westcott and Hort, are typically ascribed to transcriptional probabilities (that is, probabilities determined the way that scribes tended to write) and intrinsic probabilities (that is, probabilities determined by the way that authors tended to write) (see Metzger 1968: 209–10). What must be realized about these discussions of the principles of textual criticism is that they are products of Enlightenment rationalistic thinking, and such thinking is evident in their very formulations. For example, one of the basic principles of textual criticism, since the time of Griesbach, is that the shorter reading is to be preferred over the longer reading. The argument is that a scribe would tend to add words rather than subtract them. Even when Griesbach formulated this principle, he was careful to qualify it in a number of ways, including equating it with the more difficult reading (see Metzger 1968: 120).

This principle is subject to criticism on several fronts, however. The first is the logical one of whether the shortest and most difficult reading can in fact be thought original if it is so short and difficult as not to make sense. There is the further difficulty that much recent Gospel criticism has shown that in fact there is not a necessary tendency toward scribal expansion of an account. Similarly, the principle of the more difficult reading is often used, but is also subject to scrutiny. Metzger ends up qualifying this principle in a number of ways. He formulates it in terms of the more difficult reading being preferred 'when the sense appears on the surface to be erroneous, but on more mature consideration proves itself to be correct' (1968: 209). Besides the possibility of an ad hominem argument regarding what constitutes mature consideration, this develops into a logical conundrum, as it becomes difficult to determine what makes the best sense or what is in fact difficult nonsense. Criticisms of this sort can also be marshaled against other principles of textual criticism.

4 Implications for biblical criticism and interpretation

Knowledge of textual criticism has several implications for the entire enterprise of biblical criticism and interpretation. One is that it forces scholars to come to terms with the messiness of ancient manuscripts and their transmission. Rather than hoping to discover the autograph, or even an ideal manuscript, the textual critic is forced to appreciate the variances in the textual tradition. Along with this must come the recognition that the standards by which text-critical decisions are made must also be subject to scrutiny, to ensure that the principles used actually serve the purpose for which they were designed. One should not be either overly optimistic or unduly pessimistic regarding the function and ability of textual criticism. Nevertheless, text-critical decisions are fundamental to the interpretive enterprise and must be made at the outset so that the text used for subsequent interpretation can be established.

References and further reading

Aland, K. and B. Aland (1989) *The Text of the New Testament,* trans. E.F. Rhodes, Grand Rapids: Eerdmans.

Bruce, F.F. (1960) *The New Testament Documents: Are They Reliable?* Grand Rapids: Eerdmans, 5th edn.

Clarke, K.D. (1997) *Textual Optimism: A Critique of the United Bible Societies' Greek New Testament,* Sheffield: Sheffield Academic Press.

Ehrman, B. and M.W. Holmes (eds.) (1995) *The Text of the New Testament in Contemporary Research: Essays on the Status Quaestionis,* Grand Rapids: Eerdmans.

Ewert, D. (1983) *From Ancient Tablets to Modern Translations*, Grand Rapids: Zondervan.

Metzger, B.M. (1968) *The Text of the New Testament*, New York: Oxford University Press.

Porter, S.E. (2003) 'Why So Many Holes in the Papyrological Evidence for the Greek New Testament?' pp. 167–86 in *The Bible as Book: The Transmission of the Greek Text*, S. McKendrick and O.A. O'Sullivan (eds.), London: British Library.

STANLEY E. PORTER

TEXTUAL CRITICISM (OLD TESTAMENT)

Textual criticism exists because the Old Testament or Hebrew Bible is attested in more than one ancient manuscript and these manuscripts differ in their witness to the text. The purpose of textual criticism is to understand the relationship among these differences and to explain how they came into being. The result of this study may be to arrive at the original text but the question of what constitutes the original text is debated. This is because it is not always clear at what point the writing and subsequent redacting of a text ceases, at what point the text is recognized as part of a fixed canon, and at what point the text is given religious significance by a religious authority. For example, the decision of Barthélemy (1992) to identify the text to be studied as that one received by religious authorities is only one among several possibilities in the history and development of the biblical text.

Differences between texts are variants. A specific variant within an extant text is a reading. Manuscripts that possess similar readings (in comparison to other manuscripts) can form a text tradition. The manuscripts and the text traditions that they represent can be grouped according to the language in which they are written: Hebrew, Greek, Aramaic, and Latin. Although each of these is represented by many manuscripts a few of the most important may be noted.

The earliest Hebrew text that resembles something found in the Bible is the Ketef Hinnom silver 'amulet.' Two of these were found in excavations of a burial at Jerusalem dating from the end of the first Temple period (*c.* 600 BC). They record part of the Aaronic blessing from Numbers 6:24–26. These texts may be quotations from a larger biblical source.

The Nash papyrus dates from the second century BC. It contains the Ten Commandments and Deuteronomy 6:4–7. For many years this was the earliest biblical manuscript in existence. However, it is possible that some of the texts found among the Dead Sea Scrolls are contemporary with it.

The discovery of the Dead Sea Scrolls in 1947, and the ongoing publication of these texts over more than fifty years, has revolutionized the field of Hebrew Bible textual criticism by providing a much larger corpus of texts older by 1,000 years than the Masoretic texts. These are predominantly Hebrew texts of every book of the Bible with the exception of Esther. Some of these books are attested only by fragments. However, other texts include the whole book, such as the two scrolls of Isaiah. The Dead Sea Scrolls date between the second century BC and the first century AD. From the same period, though farther south along the Dead Sea, come those fragments of biblical texts that were buried by the last Jewish inhabitants at Masada, before it fell to the Romans in AD 73. Also in the Judaean Desert, though from the second century AD, are the biblical texts found in the caves along the Wadi Murabba'at.

Many biblical texts were discovered more than a century ago in the geniza of the Old Cairo Synagogue. Among the hundreds of thousands of Hebrew fragments there are biblical manuscripts dating from as early as the fifth century AD.

Until the discovery of the Dead Sea Scrolls the most reliable manuscript witnesses to the Hebrew Bible were the texts copied by the Masoretes in the eighth through eleventh centuries AD. Initially based in Tiberias, the Ben Asher family and others produced the first extant manuscripts with the vowels written into what was originally a consonantal text. Codex Cairensis is one of the earliest (AD 895), as is St Petersburg Codex of the Prophets (AD 916). Codex Leningrad, dating from AD 1008, is the manuscript that forms the basis for the Hebrew Bible that most students and scholars use today. An important exemplar of the Masoretic text is the Aleppo Codex from the early tenth century AD.

The Samaritan Bible forms a separate but related Hebrew witness to the first five books of the Bible. The earliest manuscripts do not pre-date the eleventh century BC. In general, it is not regarded as a more reliable witness to earlier traditions than the Masoretic texts.

The second century BC *Letter of Aristeas* records the tradition that the Pentateuch was translated into Greek in Alexandria during the reign of Ptolemy II, in the first half of the third century BC. Eventually the entire Hebrew Bible would be translated into Greek, the lingua franca of the Eastern Mediterranean. Among the earliest manuscripts of the Septuagint, as it came to be known, are the papyri from Egypt that form part of the collection housed at the John Rylands Library in Manchester. These date from the second century BC. An important collection of Greek translations is that preserved by the second-century Christian scholar, Origen, in the *Hexapla*. The six columns of this text each contain a version of the Old Testament: the Hebrew text, a Greek transliteration of the Hebrew, Aquila's Greek translation (*c.* AD 130), the translation of Symmachus (*c.* AD 170), the Septuagint, and the Greek translation of Theodotion (second century AD). Although only preserved in fragments, it is an important witness to four Greek translations of the Old Testament in the second century AD.

The most important manuscripts of the Septuagint are the Codex Sinaiticus, Codex Vaticanus, and the Codex Alexandrinus. The first two date from the fourth century AD and the third from the fifth. They are in book form (i.e., codices) and are written with upper-case Greek letters (uncials). They form the earliest complete (although there are some gaps in the manuscripts that are not preserved) texts of the entire Old Testament.

The Aramaic manuscripts can be divided into two groups: Jewish and Christian. The Jewish Aramaic texts are made up of homiletical paraphrases of the Hebrew Bible known as Targums. While not as literal as some of the Greek translations, they do reflect and suggest readings of the Hebrew manuscripts from which they were copied. Although the Targum manuscripts are medieval in date, they are copies of earlier manuscripts that may go back to the early centuries of this era and thus reflect Hebrew witnesses from a period before the Masoretic text. Some of the best-known Targums of the Pentateuch include Pseudo-Jonathan and Onqelos. Other Targums include Neofiti, Jonathan on the Prophets, and the Fragment Targums. In addition, there is a Samaritan Targum that reflects the Samaritan text of the Pentateuch. Christian Aramaic is attested in the Syriac language and texts. The Syriac Old Testament is the Peshitta. Its manuscripts date as early as the fifth century AD.

In the fifth century AD Jerome translated the Hebrew Bible into Latin and thus created the Vulgate. However, earlier Latin translations of the Old Testament witness to Septuagint traditions that are especially important in the historical books of the Old Testament.

Earlier in this century there were generally thought to be three manuscript traditions, as described by the three centers of early Jewish settlement: Egypt, Palestine, and Babylon. However, recent discoveries, especially those of the Dead Sea Scrolls, suggest that this model is oversimplified and that there was influence between multiple textual traditions. Thus, although the Dead Sea Scrolls often witness to the Masoretic tradition (e.g., the Isaiah Scroll 1QIsᵃ) there are important manuscripts that are closer to the Septuagint (e.g., the books of Samuel), and there are others that bear distinctive readings. An example of the latter is the appearance of a Dead Sea Scroll fragment that contains a different order to Joshua 5:1 and 8:30–35 and that also incorporates a heretofore unrecognized text as part of the biblical narrative. This as well as omissions in another fragment of texts from the book of Judges raises not only textual issues, but also canonical questions about the time and process of forming a fixed Old Testament text (Hess 1997). Thus, although the Septuagint and the Masoretic traditions continue to provide dominant guides for later centuries, the earlier periods, as exemplified by the Dead Sea Scrolls, do not provide clear textual traditions.

The actual practice of textual criticism is an art as well as a science. It is dangerous to follow without exception any text critical principles that automatically prefer one Old Testament reading over another. For example, there is the 'rule' that the more difficult reading is preferred. However, this rule begs the question as to which reading is more difficult. Such principles should be used with caution because many exceptions exist. Much more important is a careful study of the particular biblical book under examination and the translation style used by the Greek, Aramaic, Latin, or other translators in rendering it.

References and further reading

Barthélemy, Dominique (1992) *Critique textuelle de l'Ancien Testament: Tome 3, Ézéchiel, Daniel et les 12 Prophètes*, OBO 50/3, Fribourg: Éditions Universitaires/Göttingen: Vandenhoeck & Ruprecht.

Brotzman, Ellis R. (1994) *Old Testament Textual Criticism: A Practical Introduction*, Grand Rapids: Baker.

Deist, F.E. (1988) *Witnesses to the Old Testament: Introducing Old Testament Textual Criticism*, The Literature of the Old Testament 5, Pretoria: NG Kerkboekhandel.

Hess, Richard S. (1997) 'The Dead Sea Scrolls and Higher Criticism of the Hebrew Bible: The Case of 4QJudgᵃ,' pp. 122–8 in *The Scrolls and the Scriptures: Qumran Fifty Years After*, S.E. Porter and C.A. Evans (eds.), JSPSup 26, Roehampton Institute London Papers 3, Sheffield: Sheffield Academic Press, 1997.

Jobes, Karen H. and Moisés Silva (2000) *Invitation to the Septuagint*, Grand Rapids: Baker Academic.

Szek, Heidi M. (1992) *Translation Technique in the Peshitta to Job: A Model for Evaluating a Text, with Documentation from the Peshitta to Job*, SBLDS 137, Atlanta: Scholars Press.

Tov, E. (1981) *The Text-Critical Use of the Septuagint in Biblical Research*, Jerusalem Biblical Studies 3, Jerusalem: Simor.

—— (1992) *Textual Criticism of the Hebrew Bible*, Minneapolis: Fortress Press.

Würthwein, E. (1979) *The Text of the Old Testament*, trans. E.F. Rhodes, Grand Rapids: Eerdmans.

RICHARD S. HESS

THISELTON, ANTHONY C. (1937–)

Anthony C. Thiselton was born in Woking, Surrey, on July 13, 1937. He attended London University where he received his B.D. and his M.Th. He received his Ph.D. from the University of Sheffield. Thiselton has had a long and distinguished career, beginning in 1963 as a Recognized Teacher in Theology at the University of Bristol. In 1970 he became a Sir Henry Stephenson Fellow at the University of Sheffield, and in 1971 a lecturer in biblical studies at the same university. In

1979 he was appointed senior lecturer at the University of Sheffield, a post which he held until 1985. From 1982–1983 Thiselton served as visiting professor and fellow at Calvin College, Grand Rapids, Michigan in the USA. From 1985 until 1988 he was principal of St. John's College, Nottingham, from 1986 Special Lecturer in Theology at the University of Nottingham, and from 1988 to 1992 principal of St John's College, Durham, and Honorary Professor of Theology at the University of Durham. From 1992–2000 he served as Professor of Christian Theology and head of the department of Theology at the University of Nottingham. In 2001 he was appointed Emeritus Professor of Christian Theology in Residence at the University of Nottingham. Thiselton has been Canon Theologian of Leicester Cathedral since 1994, and Canon Theologian of Southwell Minster since 2000.

Thiselton has been a member of several learned societies including the Society of Biblical Literature, the Society for the Study of Theology (president, 1998–2000), the American Academy of Religion, and *Studiorum Novi Testamenti Societas*.

He has been a prodigious writer with several books on hermeneutics and biblical interpretation, and a major commentary on the Greek text of 1 Corinthians. He has written over fifty articles and chapters for various journals, dictionaries, commentaries, and books.

In the field of hermeneutics and biblical interpretation Thiselton is probably most noted for his *The Two Horizons* (1980), and *New Horizons in Hermeneutics* (1992). In *The Two Horizons* Thiselton questions the old view of hermeneutics which was concerned with the formation of rules to ensure that a particular understanding of a text was an accurate one. The old view disregards the presuppositions and preunderstandings of the interpreter, which influence the interpretation of a text. Thiselton disagreed with skeptics who had argued that this preunderstanding (the interpreter's theology and tradition) made accurate and unbiased interpretation impossible. Thiselton argued for an engagement of what he calls the 'historical conditionedness' of the text and of the modern reader. These are the 'two horizons' which must be considered in any hermeneutical task. Thiselton argues that the merging of these two horizons must be a basic element in all explanatory interpretation.

Thiselton's book *New Horizons in Hermeneutics* is a wide-ranging volume which has contributed to the understanding of such issues as the legacy of patristic and reformational hermeneutics and the hermeneutics of Black, Marxist, feminist, and liberation theologies. There are also sections on the theory of texts, semiotics, and reader-response theories.

References and further reading

Thiselton, A.C. (1980) *The Two Horizons: New Testament Hermeneutics and Philosophical Description with Special Reference to Heidegger, Bultmann, Gadamer and Wittgenstein*, Grand Rapids: Eerdmans.

—— (1992) *New Horizons in Hermeneutics: The Theory and Practice of Transforming Biblical Reading*, Grand Rapids: Zondervan.

—— (1995) *Interpreting God and the Postmodern Self: On Meaning, Manipulation, and Promise*, Grand Rapids: Eerdmans.

—— (1999) *The Promise of Hermeneutics*, with Roger Lundin and Clarence Walhout, Grand Rapids: Eerdmans.

—— (2000) *The First Epistle to the Corinthians: A Commentary on the Greek Text*, The New International Greek Testament Commentary, Grand Rapids: Eerdmans.

—— (2006) *Thiselton on Hermeneutics: Collected Writings and New Essays*, Grand Rapids: Eerdmans.

STEVEN R. GUNDERSON

TISCHENDORF, CONSTANTIN (1815–1874)

Lobegott Friedrich Constantin von Tischendorf laid the foundation for modern textual criticism. He studied at Leipzig under Johann G.B. Winer and held a position at Leipzig for his entire academic career, though he took numerous leaves of absence as he traveled throughout Europe and the Middle East. His goals were to search for New Testament manuscripts and to produce the best possible critical edition of the Greek New Testament.

Tischendorf discovered, collected, edited, and published vast quantities of manuscripts, but none was as important as the two major Alexandrian manuscripts: the Codex Sinaiticus and the Codex Vaticanus. His most significant discovery was the fourth-century Codex Sinaiticus, which includes a large portion of the Old Testament, the complete New Testament, plus the *Epistle of Barnabas*, and the *Shepherd of Hermas*. He found the manuscript at St Catherine's Monastery at Sinai and was able to procure it in two parts after several journeys. The part of the codex which he found in 1844 is housed in Leipzig. Tischendorf secured the larger part for the Czar of Russia, who sponsored the more productive expedition in 1859, but it was purchased by the London Museum in 1933. Tischendorf is also responsible for accessing, copying, and publishing a reliable edition of the other great fourth-century manuscript of the Greek Bible: Codex Vaticanus, which was housed in the Vatican library. Accounts of how these two manuscripts were accessed indicate a rather callous facility for undercover operations on Tischendorf's part.

He published eight editions of the Greek New Testament. The second edition presented the Greek text which would be used in later editions. In the prologue, he elucidated his text-critical principles. The eighth edition contained his fourth principal recension, and was his greatest achievement. The Greek text has been relatively unchanged from this point on, and his extensive critical apparatus is still used by scholars. It was published in two volumes; the prolegomena were added after his death as a third volume, which incorporated and elaborated on his earlier prolegomena.

In addition to his work with manuscripts and the Greek Bible, Tischendorf was interested in defending the reliability of the biblical text. His *Wann würden unsere Evangelien verfasst?* (1865) utilized his knowledge of the history of transmission of the New Testament and of the writings of the early Church Fathers to argue against the theory that John's Gospel is a late and tendentious development of Christian tradition, and to maintain that all four Gospels were firmly established as scripture by the middle of the second century. It was translated into Danish, Dutch, English, French, Italian, Russian, Swedish, and Turkish.

No scholar can rival Tischendorf in volume of manuscripts discovered and published, in his recension of the Greek texts, and in the detail and usefulness of his critical apparatus. His methods of evaluating variants and the classification of manuscripts into families moved the discussion forward. Many agree that textual critics are most indebted to Tischendorf.

References and further reading

Aland, K. and B. Aland (1987) *The Text of the New Testament: An Introduction to the Critical Editions and to the Theory and Practice of Modern Textual Criticism,* trans. Erroll F. Rhodes, Grand Rapids: Eerdmans.

Bentley, J. (1986) *Secrets of Mount Sinai: The Story of the Oldest Bible – Codex Sinaiticus,* New York: Doubleday.

Black, M. and R. Davidson (1981) *Constantin von Tischendorf and the Greek New Testament,* Glasgow: University of Glasgow Press.

Metzger, B.M. (1968) *The Text of the New Testament: Its Transmission, Corruption and Restoration,* New York: Oxford University Press, 2nd edn.

Moir, I.A. (1976) 'Tischendorf and the Codex Sinaiticus,' *New Testament Studies* 23: 108–15.

Tischendorf, C. (n.d.) *Codex Sinaiticus: The Ancient Biblical Manuscript Now in the British Museum,* London: Lutterworth, Press.

—— (1884) *Novum Testametnum Graece ad antiquissimos testes denuo recensuit, apparatum criticum omni studio perfectum apposuit, commentationem isagogicam praetexuit Constantinus Tischendorf. Editio octava critica maior, Volumen III: Prolegomena scripsit Casparus Renatus Gregory, additis curis Ezrae Abbot,* Leipzig: J.C. Hinrichs.

—— (1865) *Wann würden unsere Evangelien verfasst?* Leipzig: J.C. Hinrichs (4th edn 1880; ET *Origin of the Four Gospels,* trans. William L. Gage, Boston: American Tract Society 1866).

CYNTHIA LONG WESTFALL

TORREY, CHARLES CUTLER (1863–1956)

Torrey was born on December 20, 1863 in East Hardwick, Vermont. He received his B.A. from Bowdoin College in 1884. He continued his studies at Andover Theological Seminary and Strasbourg University, receiving his Ph.D. in 1892. Torrey taught Latin at Bowdoin (1885–1886), Semitic languages at Andover (1892–1900), and was appointed Professor of Semitic philosophy and comparative grammar at Yale University in 1900. Here Torrey also served as chairman of the department of Semitic and Biblical languages, literature, and history until his retirement in 1932.

Torrey's knowledge of languages was extensive, including Hebrew, Aramaic, Arabic, Ethiopic, Phoenician, Syriac, Akkadian, and Persian. He was a founding member and director of the American School of Oriental Research in Jerusalem. His studies in the Arabic language allowed him to contribute to works such as the *Encyclopaedia of Islam.* Torrey was a fellow of the American Academy of Arts and Sciences and the Deutsche Morganländisches Gesellschaft. He was also an archaeologist. He received honorary degrees from Yale, Chicago College of Jewish Studies, the Jewish Institute of Religion, and the Jewish Theological Seminary. Torrey served as president of the Society of Biblical Literature in 1915 where he was noted for his combative style of debate.

Torrey is remembered for holding several controversial beliefs. He believed strongly that the Gospels and Revelation were primarily direct translations from Aramaic originals. He reasoned that Greek was despised because it was the language of oppressors and therefore, although knowledge of Greek was necessary, the common people in first-century Palestine would only have received these writings in Aramaic. Since part of the purpose of the Gospels was to persuade the Jewish people that Jesus was the long expected Messiah, it seemed foolish to Torrey to compose these writings in what he called the 'detested language of the enemy.' He went on to compose *The Four Gospels: A New Translation* (1933), which was essentially his translation of the Greek back into the Aramaic and then into English. Torrey also believed that the Ezra-Nehemiah texts were basically fictions created by a Chronicler as propaganda against the Samaritans. He believed that the books of Second Isaiah, Jeremiah, and Ezekiel were part of a sacred library that had been formed by prophets during the third century BC, and that Ezekiel was essentially a pseudepigraphic response to Alexander the Great's conquest of the East written sometime around 230 BC. Torrey's view on Jeremiah was that its connection with the seventh century BC was certainly fictitious and that it was mainly a literary device.

Some of his views have been accepted, including the idea that Isaiah 40–66 forms a unit and that chapters 34–35 serve as an introduction. Although many of Torrey's innovative views have been rejected, his contributions to biblical scholarship have been considerable, especially his views on the origin and purpose of many of the prophetic books. At the very least, Torrey's views have been used as starting points for the study of these important issues.

References and further reading

Burrows, M. (1953) 'A Sketch of C.C.T's Career,' *Bulletin of the American Schools of Oriental Research* 132: 6–8.

Torrey, C.C. (1928) *The Second Isaiah: A New Interpretation*, Edinburgh: T.&T. Clark.

—— (1930) *Pseudo-Ezekiel and the Original Prophecy*, Yale Oriental Series: Researches 18, New Haven: Yale University Press.

—— (1933) *The Four Gospels: A New Translation*, New York: Harper.

—— (1936) *Our Translated Gospels: Some New Evidence*, New York: Harper.

S.R. GUNDERSON

TRADITION-HISTORICAL INTERPRETATION

1 Tradition-historical interpretation as a subdiscipline of historical criticism
2 Terminological ambiguity
3 Tradition-historical interpretation as intertextuality
4 Tradition-historical interpretation as intellectual history
5 Critique and prospect

1 Tradition-historical interpretation as a subdiscipline of historical criticism

Historical criticism is primarily concerned with reconstructing the events and history lying behind the biblical texts. As such, the broad discipline of historical criticism covers a number of subcategories within biblical studies, including textual criticism, source criticism, form criticism, and redaction criticism. Tradition-historical interpretation (also known as tradition criticism

and tradition history) has established itself as another important subdiscipline of historical criticism within biblical studies.

2 Terminological ambiguity

Tradition history is variously understood in the literature because of the inherent ambiguity of the term 'tradition.' Some scholars understand 'tradition' as *traditio*, referring to the process of the transmission of materials, whereas others define 'tradition' from *traditum*, referring to the conceptual contents of what is transmitted (Steck 1998: 124). Another approach is to see 'tradition history' as moving back from the written sources to the oral traditions that make them up (*traditio*), whereas 'inner-biblical exegesis' begins with the received scripture (an authoritative and relatively fixed *traditum*, the final of many oral stages of *traditio*) and moves forward to the interpretations based on it (Fishbane 1985: 7). For the purposes of the present article, we shall define 'tradition history' as the specific literary or oral developments that led up to the biblical literature in its present form (Knight 1992: 634). The following discussion is divided into two main sections: (a) tradition history as intertextuality and (b) tradition history as intellectual history. As we shall see, the distinction is not hard and fast.

3 Tradition-historical interpretation as intertextuality

In this sense of the term, tradition history proceeds from the observation that texts and textual fragments are taken up, (re)interpreted, and included in later texts.

The phenomenon of intertextuality pertains to the imbedding of fragments of an earlier text within a later one. Whether this embedding occurs in the form of a direct citation, an allusion, or a somewhat fainter 'echo' (rigorous distinctions along this spectrum cannot be maintained), there is in each case some clear evidence in the text that distinctly points to another passage.

Intertextuality is an important factor in communities that appeal to scripture as an authoritative basis for faith and practice. In these social contexts, the embedded scriptural text reverberates in the later text, even though frequently the scriptural text is also changed in the process of being incorporated into the new passage. As Michael Fishbane (1985, 1986: 36) has shown, intertextuality already occurs in the biblical texts themselves and continues throughout the whole process of canonization:

One may say that the entire corpus of Scripture remains open to these invasive procedures and strategic reworkings up to the close of the canon in the early rabbinic period, and so the received text is complexly compacted of teachings and their subversion, of rules and their extension, of topoi and their revision. Within ancient Israel, as long as the textual corpus remained open, Revelation and Tradition were thickly interwoven and interdependent, and the received Hebrew Bible is itself, therefore, the product of an interpretive tradition.

Emphasizing again that the received biblical text was always read in light of traditional interpretations and is itself the product of an interpretive tradition, James Kugel's book, *Traditions of the Bible* (1998), gives eloquent testimony to Pentateuchal interpretive traditions that find their way into both early Judaism and early Christianity alike. With new resources at our disposal, such as the whole Dead Sea Scrolls library of biblical texts (cf. Abegg, Flint, Ulrich 1999), more work can and must be done to trace the history of these interpretive traditions across the divides that have been traditionally erected. Moreover, the exact nature of these interpretive traditions is frequently more complicated than a simplistic model of intertextuality may allow. Whether, for example, the Temple Scroll, the *Book of Jubilees*, and the *Biblical Antiquities* of Pseudo-Philo should be described as 'rewritten Bibles' or independent accounts drawn from a common tradition remains unclear. Perhaps the truth lies somewhere between these two possibilities. In any case, we seem to be poised on the threshold of some important discoveries in this murky and complicated field of research.

When we read the New Testament writers in light of these interpretive traditions and trajectories, we begin to understand that they belong to one broad river of Old Testament/Jewish tradition and are actually part of the same fluid canonical process (cf. Stuhlmacher 1999: 303–4 *passim*). In a history of more than a millennium, this one river constantly had smaller and larger tributaries feeding into it, without losing its identity as the one river, although it also kept bringing change in the process, and distributaries occasionally branched off from the mainstream. From this perspective, we might expect to find more continuity, say, from Jesus to Paul than many critics reckon.

If, as was mentioned, the received biblical text was always read in light of traditional interpretations and is itself the product of an interpretive tradition, tradition history in the sense of intertextuality cannot be strictly separated from the history of intellectual traditions in general. To the latter we now turn.

4 Tradition-historical interpretation as intellectual history

In this second sense of the term, tradition history is not necessarily bound to any particular preexisting text(s); it proceeds from the assumption that an author lives in an intellectual world of presupposed ideas and conceptual complexes that are more or less fixed. Tradition history asks the degree to which the contents of the

author's statements are either determined by preexisting elements from the author's intellectual world or deviate from them. In John 9, for example, the disciples' question to Jesus, 'Rabbi, who sinned, this man or his parents, that he was born blind?' (v. 2), partakes of two received traditions. On the one hand, the notion that the cause of the man's blindness could have been his own sin stems from a pervasive tradition that can be called retributive justice – the belief that a person's behavior receives its just deserts. Despite the book of Job, the old notion of a direct causal relationship between sin and bodily infirmity was still a living tradition in the first century (e.g., 1 Cor. 11:30). On the other hand, the notion that the cause of the man's blindness could have been his parents' sins stems from the tradition that punishment for the parents' sins could be transmitted to their children, even to the third and fourth generations (Exod. 20:5; 34:7; Num. 14:18; Deut. 5:9). According to John 9, Jesus rejected both possibilities as applicable to the blind man's specific situation, emphasizing the divine purpose of the blindness (*hina*) rather than its causation: 'Neither this man nor his parents sinned; he was born blind so that God's works might be revealed in him' (v. 3). The latter aspect of Jesus' answer may reflect the famous story of Tobit, a righteous man who was accidentally afflicted with blindness (2:10) but was later healed (11:10–15); for the angel Raphael exhorts him and his son Tobias to 'reveal the works of God' (12:7, 11). Alternatively, the latter aspect of Jesus' answer may reflect a common tradition.

Since traditions frequently constitute a complex of ideas or beliefs, it is important not to isolate one particular element of a tradition from the other constituent members of the complex. As O.H. Steck (1967) has shown, for example, the idea that Israel killed the prophets (e.g., 1 Kings 18:13; Neh. 9:26; Matt. 23:37/Luke 13:34) cannot be properly understood in isolation; it must be seen in light of the larger tradition of the Deuteronomic view of Israel's history, which contained a complex of several more-or-less fixed elements that grew and developed over the course of several centuries, right down to the time of the New Testament (cf. Scott 1993). By the same token, the mention of one element within a tradition may be enough to evoke the memory of the entire complex. Thus, even a single key word or phrase may signify more than it would at first appear. For example, the twofold covenant formula in 2 Corinthians 6:16 ('I will be their God, and they will be my people') signifies more than a bilateral relationship between God and his people; it recalls a relatively defined set of traditional associations about the expected restoration of Israel (cf. Scott 1994; Rendtorff 1998).

Given the nature of our sources, there is an inherent difficulty in tradition-historical investigation that is sometimes difficult to avoid, especially in weakly attested traditions. Since our only access to ancient Jewish and

Christian traditions is usually through written sources, we can become caught in the vicious circle of inferring a *traditio* from a received *traditum*, and using the reconstructed *traditio*, in turn, as a principal means for ascertaining the components of that same *traditum*. In general, however, the stronger the received tradition, the better we can understand the constituent components of the underlying complex.

5 Critique and prospect

Today, scholars who emphasize the synchronic level of the text assert that diachronic study and the inquiry into the biblical text's process of transmission, as endorsed by historical criticism, has led to a focus concerned with microscopic analysis rather than telescopic analysis. In other words, the individual sources, traditions, literary forms, redactional units, and even lone words have been considered more important, and, in fact, have been singled out for biblical interpretation over and above the completed and final canonical form of the text.

It may be argued in response, however, that only insofar as we grasp the traditions in and behind the text will we be able to perceive the organic growth and therefore the inherent interrelationship of texts within the biblical canon (e.g., Steck 1993). The point here is not that one overarching theme (e.g., covenant, salvation history, the biblical idea of time) unifies either the Old Testament or the New Testament or both, but rather that a complex tissue of interrelated traditions connects and supports the whole. Tradition-historical investigation, done on a comprehensive scale and with proper attention also to the final form of the text and to its subsequent influence, may be our best hope for constructing a biblical theology that is sensitive both to the underpinnings of the text and to the ultimate coherence of its message. It seems increasingly probable, for example, that exegetical and intellectual traditions relating to the restoration of Israel provide an important matrix for constructing a biblical theology of the New Testament.

References and further reading

Abegg, Martin, Jr., Peter Flint, and Eugene Ulrich (eds. and trans.) (1999) *The Dead Sea Scrolls Bible: The Oldest Known Bible Translated for the First Time into English*, New York: HarperCollins.

Betz, Otto (1990) 'Die traditionsgeschichtliche Exegese als Beitrag zur theologischen Toleranz', pp. 407–24 in *Jesus, Der Herr der Kirche. Aufsätze zur biblischen Theologie II*, WUNT 52, Tübingen: Mohr Siebeck.

Catchpole, David R. (1977) 'Tradition History,' pp. 165–80 in *New Testament Interpretation: Essays on Principles and Methods*, I. Howard Marshall (ed.), Grand Rapids: Eerdmans.

Ellis, E. Earle (1999) *The Making of the New Testament Documents*, Biblical Interpretation Series 39, Leiden: Brill.

Fishbane, Michael (1985) *Biblical Interpretation in Ancient Israel*, Oxford: Clarendon.

—— (1986) 'Inner-Biblical Exegesis: Types and Strategies of Interpretation in Ancient Israel,' pp. 19–37 in *Midrash and Literature*, G.H. Hartman and S. Budick (eds.), New Haven: Yale University Press.

Knight, Douglas A. (1973) *Rediscovering the Traditions of Israel: The Development of the Traditio-Historical Research of the Old Testament, with Special Consideration of Scandinavian Contributions*, SBLDS 9, Missoula: Scholars Press.

—— (1992) 'Tradition History,' *ABD* 6.633–8.

Kugel, James L. (1998) *Traditions of the Bible: A Guide to the Bible as It Was at the Start of the Common Era*, Cambridge: Harvard University Press.

Rendtorff, Rolf (1994) 'Martin Noth and Tradition Criticism,' pp. 91–100 in *The History of Israel's Traditions: The Heritage of Martin Noth*, S.L. McKenzie and M. Patrick Graham (eds.), JSOTSup 182, Sheffield: Sheffield Academic Press.

—— (1998) *The Covenant Formula: An Exegetical and Theological Investigation*, Old Testament Studies, Edinburgh: T.&T. Clark.

Scott, James M. (1993) 'Paul's Use of Deuteronomic Tradition,' *Journal of Biblical Literature* 112: 645–65.

—— (1994) 'The Use of Scripture in 2 Corinthians 6.16c–18 and Paul's Restoration Theology,' *Journal for the Study of the New Testament* 56: 73–99.

Steck, Odil Hannes (1967) *Israel und das gewaltsame Geschick der Propheten. Untersuchungen zur Überlieferung des deuteronomistischen Geschichtsbildes im Alten Testament, Spätjudentum und Urchristentum*, WMANT 23, Neukirchen-Vluyn: Neukirchener Verlag.

—— (1968) 'Das Problem theologischer Strömungen in nachexilischer Zeit,' *Evangelische Theologie* 28: 445–58.

—— (1993) *Das apokryphe Baruchbuch. Studien zu Rezeption und Konzentration 'kanonischer' Überlieferung*, FRLANT 160, Göttingen: Vandenhoeck & Ruprecht.

—— (1998) *Old Testament Exegesis: A Guide to the Methodology*, trans. James D. Nogalski, SBLRBS 39, Atlanta: Scholars Press.

Stuhlmacher, Peter (1999) *Biblische Theologie des Neuen Testaments, Band II: Von der Paulusschule bis zur Johannesoffenbarung. Der Kanon und seine Auslegung*, Göttingen: Vandenhoeck & Ruprecht.

Thompson, M.B. (1993) 'Tradition,' pp. 943–5 in *Dictionary of Paul and His Letters*, G.F. Hawthorne and R.P. Martin (eds.), Downers Grove IVP.

JAMES M. SCOTT

TRANSLATIONS OF THE BIBLE (SINCE THE KJV)

1 Introduction

One of the most important means of biblical interpretation is translation. As discussed elsewhere in this dictionary, the Septuagint, the translation of the Hebrew Bible into Greek, played a fundamental role in how Judaism and Christianity interpreted some of their crucial texts; and the Latin translations, especially of Jerome, had a decisive influence upon later Christian interpretation of the Bible. With the increase in vernacular translations as a result of the Reformation, translation as a form of biblical interpretation took on new dimensions, as increasing numbers of language groups gained direct access to the biblical text through their own native language. This pattern of rendering the biblical text into vernaculars has continued and come to be identified with the Bible translation movement. While the Bible translation movement continues to progress, rendering for the first time previously unwritten languages into a graphic form, there also continue to be ever increasing numbers of translations being made for language groups that already have a written form of the Bible. This is especially so in the English-speaking world, where in the twentieth century it has been estimated that there were well over 100 Old and New Testament portions or complete versions rendered into English alone (cf. Ewert 1983: 250–1). In the course of the production of an increasing number of Bible translations into the vernacular, there has been a corresponding development of theories regarding Bible translation. There has also been the important question raised regarding what the interpretive implications are for such renderings.

2 Major movements in Bible translation

As is widely known, the King James or Authorized Version of the Bible was not the first, and not even the first widely used, English version. For example, there were the translations of Tyndale (1526), Coverdale (1535), and Rogers (1537), and the so-called Great Bible (1539), Geneva Bible (1560), and Bishops' Bible (1568). Nevertheless, publication in 1611 of the King James Version marks a watershed in Bible translation. In a very real sense, every English version produced since the King James has been a response to it. This response can be chronicled into the following periods.

2.1 The dominance of the King James Version

Many language groups have an equivalent of the King James Version of the Bible. For example, Luther's rendering of the Bible into German (1522 New Testament; 1534 Old Testament) marks the beginning of modern German. A translation such as this, often the first significant one into the language, frequently became the model for all subsequent translations – although many other language groups than English had vernacular translations from the early Middle Ages on. At first, the King James Version was not accepted, especially since there were other translations available, but due to its many strengths, and the political and theological climate of the times, the King James Version became the recognized translation of the English-speaking world in the second part of the seventeenth century. From this time until the late nineteenth century, and in many circles even after this time, the King James was the recognized standard for English translations. Its strengths included its having been produced by many of the finest biblical scholars of the time gathered from both the church and the academy, and drawing upon the many virtues of previous translations, including especially Tyndale's translation, which still has an elegance and grace rarely matched by other translations.

Despite the dominance of the King James Version, however, there were a number of other translations that were produced between the seventeenth and late nineteenth centuries that are worth noting. Virtually all of these were personal translations. There were upwards of seventy of these produced during this time. Some of the translators include John Wesley the churchman (1775), Charles Thomson the patriot (1808–1809), Noah Webster the lexicographer (1833), Henry Alford the biblical scholar (1869), and Julia Smith the first woman to translate the Bible into English (1876).

During the time of the ascendancy of the King James Version, however, there was a major change that took place in interpretation of the Bible. Beginning during the eighteenth century and in conjunction with the Enlightenment, but increasing during the nineteenth century, there was growth in the higher-critical method of biblical interpretation. As is recounted elsewhere in this volume, the rise of higher criticism had an influence upon how scholars, in particular, began to view the biblical text and how it should be understood. One of the important critical developments of this time was the formalization of rules of textual criticism, as scholars explored the fact that their biblical documents were the products of textual development. Further, the principles by which the text was to be analyzed and interpreted underwent development, as scholars became aware of and appreciated the influence and relationship of other religions and languages of the time. Concurrently with this change in critical perspective came increasing knowledge of the material world of the Bible. This knowledge encompassed the material remains from archaeology, and the discoveries in the area of epigraphy and papyrology. The result was an increase in knowledge of the physical environment of the Bible, and especially of the actual manuscripts that stood behind the text of the Bible. This was especially the case for the New Testament where there were increasingly greater numbers of early Greek biblical manuscripts found (rather than the few relatively late manuscripts that had been the basis for the King James Version).

These developments created an atmosphere in which it was increasingly recognized by scholars that revision of the King James Version was required. Efforts along such lines can be classified in two major categories, those by committees and those by individuals (some scholars, such as Metzger 2001, divide the scene differently).

2.2 Committee translations of the Bible

The first major effort to revise the King James Version, the (British) Revised Version, was the product of a significant committee effort, involving various denominations and an American committee, and including some of the premier scholars of the day. Despite the effort (1881 New Testament; 1885 Old Testament; 1895 Apocrypha; 1901 for American Standard Version), the Revised Version was not a general overall success for the major reason that it was caught between conservatism and innovation. At the same time, there were too many instances that retained the features of the King James Version, as well as too many occasions when cherished passages or truths were seen to be compromised. Nevertheless, this version marked the beginning of numerous efforts to translate the Bible into English over the next 100 plus years, an effort that is still ongoing. The first half of the twentieth century was apparently dominated more by personal translations than by committee-based translations. Perhaps this was in part as a reaction against the perceived failings of a committee, even such an august one as was marshaled for the Revised Version, to succeed in the light of the necessary compromises that are demanded in committee work. To this day, however, most of the translations that are recognized and used are the product of committee work.

Several of the most important committee-based translations, and what makes them distinctive, are worth noting briefly.

The Revised Standard Version was begun in 1937 as an attempt to revive the programme of the American Standard Version. This project availed itself of a broad range of denominational representation and scholarly support. The latest advances in biblical criticism were also incorporated, including use of the Dead Sea Scrolls once they became available, and the latest Hebrew and Greek scholarly critical texts. When published (1946 New Testament; 1952 complete Bible), the Revised Standard Version met with some criticism over its rendering of some theological concepts, but has persisted

to this day as a significant and widely used version. Revisions include a revised edition of 1962, a Catholic version with Apocrypha in 1957, a common Bible for Orthodox churches in 1973, and major revision including gender-inclusive language in 1989, the New Revised Standard Version. The English Standard Version (2001) is an attempt to retain literalness based upon the RSV. A conservative attempt to retain the flavor of the American Standard Version but in a new translation resulted in the New American Standard Bible (1963 New Testament; 1971 complete Bible; revised 1995), but the literalness of this version did not attract widespread use especially for public reading. The RSV held sway until publication of the New International Version (1973 New Testament; 1978 complete Bible). In many ways the more conservative counterpart to the RSV, and drawing upon scholars from English-speaking countries worldwide, this version has had huge success, but also generated controversy, especially when a gender-inclusive version was proposed. One was published in the UK (1995–1996), but was resisted in the USA until the TNIV (Today's NIV) New Testament was published in 2002. As will be noted below, this publication has prompted much discussion.

The New English Bible benefited from the Old Testament scholarship of G.R. Driver and the New Testament scholarship of C.H. Dodd. However, not everyone was pleased with all the results of their work (1961 New Testament; 1970 complete Bible with Apocrypha). They issued an edition of the eclectic Greek text that was used in the project (1964), but, perhaps more noteworthy, there was attention drawn to how Driver's comparative philological method was reflected at numerous text-critical points, especially the use of Arabic in interpreting the Hebrew text. There was further criticism for the relatively free literary style used in the translation. The Revised English Bible was published in 1989. A significant Catholic version was produced by French scholars in Jerusalem (1956), and this version provided the basis for the English-language initiative known as the Jerusalem Bible (1966). This version was revised and published as the New Jerusalem Bible in 1985. This is not the only Catholic version in use, the other being the Confraternity Bible, revised as the New American Bible (1941 New Testament translated from the Vulgate; 1969 Old Testament; 1970 New Testament from Greek). The NET Bible is a translation that began on the Internet (1996), but is now available in printed form (2001), with plenty of footnotes to help readers understand the original languages.

The last committee-based translation to mention here is the Good News Bible or Today's English Version. Dependent upon the dynamic or functional equivalence translational methods of Eugene Nida (see discussion below), the New Testament was actually a personal translation by Robert Bratcher (1966), to which the Old Testament was added (1976; 1979 Apocrypha).

Originally designed for nonnative English users, the translation has had a tremendous impact upon the entire Bible translation movement, because of its exemplification of the principles that Nida espouses. The Contemporary English Version (1995) was designed, consistent with dynamic equivalence translation theory, as an updating of the Good News Bible, but with self-conscious attention to its being at the end of a grand tradition of translation going back at least to the King James Version.

The two major issues that emerge from the committee translations is how much and in what ways they will be faithful to and depart from previous translations and the established translational tradition. There appears to be some flexibility – in fact translations are expected to 'modernize' their sound in some ways – but there are boundaries that should not be crossed. The other issue is how much of modern critical scholarship is evident in the translation. More overt expressions of such scholarship are less well received than a more subtle integration of scholarly advances in the translational process itself.

2.3 Personal translations of the Bible

There have been a number of personal translations of the Bible since the time of the Revised Version. In fact, some of the most important translations of the first half of last century were personal translations.

The most noteworthy are the following: Richard Weymouth's of the New Testament based upon his own Greek text (1903); Edgar J. Goodspeed with J.M.P. Smith's *An American Translation*, which drew upon the latest New Testament papyrological evidence (1923 New Testament; 1927 Old Testament), but was branded as liberal because of Goodspeed's association with the University of Chicago; Ronald Knox's revision of the Douai-Rheims-Challoner Version (1945 New Testament; 1949 Old Testament), though mitigated by its dependence upon the Vulgate; J.B. Phillips's so-called paraphrase (1947–1958; revised 1972); Gerrit Verkuyl's Berkeley Version (1945 New Testament; 1959 complete Bible); Hugh Schonfield's Jewish translation of the New Testament (1955); E.V. and C.H. Rieu's translation of the Gospels (1952) and Acts (1957), performed by classical scholars; Richmond Lattimore's rendering (1962, 1982), again by a classical scholar; Kenneth Taylor's so-called paraphrase *The Living Bible* (1971), now revised on the basis of the Hebrew and Greek texts as the *New Living Translation* (1996); and Eugene Peterson's *The Message* (1993 New Testament; 2002 complete Bible), a very free and sometimes highly fluid translation.

In many ways, the most important personal translation insofar as incorporating and exemplifying advances in higher criticism, however, was James Moffatt's second translation. Moffatt translated his Historical New Testament in 1901, but his New Translation (1913

New Testament; 1924 Old Testament) has a number of important features that no doubt contributed to its being a very popular and important modern language version. Moffatt was determined to present a modern translation in both form and substance. As a result, he paid attention to the literary characteristics of his translation, and his translation has been commended for the liveliness and vividness of his renderings. However, he was also concerned to ensure that the translation was faithful to critical biblical knowledge. As a result, within both testaments he used graphic conventions to illustrate what he considered the state of critical consensus. Thus, the Old Testament begins with a portion of Genesis 2:4 before 1:1, and Genesis 2:4b–4:26 is in italics, rather than roman font, to indicate a different source from what precedes and follows. Moffatt also indicated where there were gaps in the text, showing that the textual basis was less than secure.

Personal translations clearly move further away from the established translational norm than do committee translations, often in the interests of clarifying the meaning of the biblical text in the language of contemporary readers. Few have gone to the lengths that Moffatt did to reflect critical scholarship directly in the means of textual display. Of course, the danger of such a choice is that if the critical consensus changes – as it is bound to do – then the version loses currency.

3 Theories regarding Bible translation

The field of biblical translation has been very important in the development of the larger field of translation studies. It is traditionally closely related to work in classical languages, but also to developments regarding modern languages. However, there is often an added emotional element when the Bible is concerned. These perceptions regarding the sacred text have clearly focused attention on theories of translation.

3.1 Formal vs. dynamic equivalence

The traditional approach to Bible translation reflects what has been called formal equivalence. Found in such versions mentioned above as the King James Version, the Revised/American Standard Version, Revised Standard Version, English Standard Version, and New American Standard Bible, formal equivalence is distinguished by a number of features: individual word based translation; retention of word-order and other features of the source text, even at the expense of clarity; consistency in rendering of vocabulary; and retention of biblical-sounding language.

The translational work of Eugene Nida marked a significant departure from this perspective, when in 1964 he consolidated previous research and advocated what has come to be called dynamic or functional equivalence translation theory (Nida 1964; Nida and Taber 1965; de Waard and Nida 1986). This theory has undergone continuing development by Nida and others, but is distinguished by the following features: recognition of the individual characteristics of each language; acknowledgment that some features can and others cannot be rendered from one language to another; an attempt to make the translation as understandable to its audience as the source language was to the original readers; the desire to find the closest natural equivalent in the receptor language; and emphasis upon the preservation of meaning over the form of language.

Debates will no doubt continue over the principles of dynamic equivalence translation. Some wish to move further in their methodological development. For example, some translational theorists contend that Nida does not take his theories far enough. He is still concentrating upon the sentence level in translation (e.g., his use of Mark 1:4, 'John preached a baptism of repentance for the forgiveness of sins,' as a template), rather than appreciating that a text must be understood, analyzed, and hence translated at the level of the entire discourse (Hatim and Mason 1990) or in terms of pragmatic principles of relevance (Gutt 1991). Others, however, believe that Nida has gone too far, and wish to return to a more literalistic translational method. They contend that the source language must take priority, since some of the tenets of dynamic equivalence – such as mutual intelligibility and emphasis upon the receptor – detract from the centrality of the sacred text (see Ryken 2002). Others contend that Nida's methods of translation amount to the practice of Western cultural hegemony (see Venuti 1995).

3.2 Gender and translation

One of the major hotbeds of recent discussion, and one that touches upon what has just been said above regarding formal versus dynamic equivalence translation, is the issue of gender in language. Virtually all translators of the Bible, whether professional or merely those using the original language as tangential to some other task, soon recognize that there are a number of gender-related issues that are important in creating translations. Some of these issues stem from the fact that the Old Testament and New Testament worlds were heavily gendered and androcentric. Others of these issues stem from the fact that languages themselves sometimes contain elements that are construed as being more than simply grammatically gendered but that reflect gender bias. The problem becomes how this is handled when one is rendering an ancient text into a modern context that has a differing set of sensibilities regarding such issues.

There are a number of Bible translators and scholars who argue that the original and gendered nature of the language of the original text must be maintained (e.g., Poythress and Grudem 2000). This would include such instances as preserving translation of the word *anthrōpos* as 'man' or *adelphoi* as 'brothers.' The emphasis for many who would wish to retain such language is that the

biblical text reflects the culture of the world in which it was written, and this gendered nature must be preserved. There are those, however, who reject such argumentation for several reasons (e.g., Carson 1998; Strauss 1998). One line of argument is that some of the language that is often endorsed as being gendered is in fact not as gendered in the original language as it is in modern translations. For whatever reason, and perhaps it includes modern gender bias, some of these words are rendered in gendered ways as a means of continuing to assert gender bias. Thus, the word *anthrōpos*, so it is argued, may well have represented 'human' to the original authors, rather than 'man,' and *adelphoi* would have included women as well and thus be legitimately rendered as 'brothers and sisters.' Another line of argument is that modern languages and perceptions are changing and that these changes need to be reflected in modern biblical translations in order to keep the text current and in meaningful contact with its contemporary audience (e.g., one cannot use 'he' in the same way as earlier, but must use 'they' or some other equivalent).

The debate over these issues has at times been vociferous, and no doubt will continue to be highly contentious, since more is involved than simply the rendering of vocabulary items. An entire theory of translation lurks behind the kinds of translational decisions that are made when so-called gendered language is rendered.

4 Implications for biblical interpretation

The implications for biblical interpretation of translation are many. The first, and perhaps most important, is the realization that the biblical text, in order to retain its voice in the contemporary world, must be rendered so that it communicates with this world. This assumption alone means that interpretive decisions must be made regarding the biblical documents and how they are transformed from their ancient form into a modern one. This linguistic transformation might well address new and innovative ways to translate the text as audiences change, and even as the technologies available develop (see Kee 1993).

The second implication is the realization that biblical interpretation takes place on several different levels in relation to translation. The first begins before the text is actually translated, when one realizes that the choice of text (e.g., which ending of Mark's Gospel is included), particular text-critical decisions, certain cultural and historical assumptions, and, most importantly, the kinds of critical stances that one takes in regard to the text have a formative influence on the translational process. The second level of interpretation is in terms of the actual translation of the text. This is related to the critical stances that one assumes in approaching the text, but is more obvious in how one chooses to render particular units of text, what kind of consistency one displays in rendering vocabulary, and the kind of textual cohesion and coherence one sees in the flow of the narrative or exposition. The oft-repeated phrase 'a translator is a traitor' could have the effect of stifling and retarding translational efforts if one cannot get beyond the fact that, indeed, translation involves the inevitability of making interpretive decisions. However, the failure to make such decisions means that one does not even become a translator, and that could have the effect of rendering the text mute to a new generation of those seeking its understanding.

Dr. Eugene Nida has prepared this treatment of the history of translation of the Lord's Prayer as an example of what has transpired in the wake of the King James Version in rendering this apparently short and simple passage. Dr. Nida's article is presented here as more detailed evidence of the ongoing interpretation that occurs in the act of translation.

Appendix: Liturgical structure and translation of the Lord's Prayer, by Eugene A. Nida

The growth of rhetorical structures is amply illustrated by the Lukan and Matthean Greek texts of the 'Lord's Prayer,' which is, however, a seriously misleading title, because this prayer is not what Jesus prayed, but what he taught his disciples to pray. Nevertheless, this title is retained despite its being grammatically incorrect. This should not, however, be surprising because the names of many objects are often logically wrong. Names are names, and only linguists worry about such matters.

The history of this prayer in Luke 11:2b–4 and Matthew 6:9b–13 illustrates a basic principle of liturgical texts to grow and expand, both in their Greek and English forms. Most comparisons of the Lukan and Matthean Greek texts mention only six petitions in Luke and seven in Matthew. In Luke, however, there are really only five because the fifth line of the text, 'because we have forgiven everyone indebted to us' or 'everyone who has wronged us' is related to the preceding line as a causal restriction. Similarly, in the Matthean form of the prayer the corresponding eighth line is a conditional extension of the seventh line, namely, 'as we have forgiven those indebted to us' or 'who have wronged us.'

Most analysts of these two forms of the prayer regard the Lukan form as being earlier and the Matthean form as being a later rhetorical expansion, especially in view of the tendency in Greek rhetoric to employ three rather than two elements to indicate totality. But there is also an interesting extension of expressions consisting of nine syllables. For example, in Luke the first two requests contain nine syllables, and in Matthew there are nine syllables for all three requests. In fact there are nine syllables in each of the first five lines of the Matthean form of the prayer. We cannot, however, be completely certain about the patterns of elision, but the

parallelism of syllable length in the first five lines is surely rhetorically significant. In the Lukan form of the prayer, the initial *pater* is not included in the nine syllable unit, but in Matthew the vocative form is included within the metrical unit of nine syllables, in view of the probable elision of omicron and epsilon.

In the Lukan form of the prayer the last three lines alternate between 12 and 15 syllables in a pattern of 12, 15, 12, and in the corresponding lines of the Matthean form of the prayer the alternations involve lines consisting of 15, 12, 15, 12, 12, despite the fact that terminology differs considerably. Such parallelism cannot be merely a matter of chance.

Of the first five lines of the Matthean form of the prayer, lines 2, 3, and 4 have completely parallel grammatical structure: a passive imperative, followed by an article, a noun, and the second-person singular pronoun. And the Lukan form also has this same grammatical structure. Evidently, the Lukan structure formed the basis for the expansion in Matthew by the addition of a third request, followed by a succinct way of speaking about God's will being expressed in both heaven and earth.

Since there is every evidence that early believers repeated this prayer many times in private and public worship, the development of balanced lengths of utterance must be carefully reckoned with, especially since we know that the Gospel of Matthew was by far the most often quoted Gospel. This can be readily shown by analyzing the quotations by the early Church Fathers. Even when they were presumably quoting a passage from Luke, they often mistakenly followed the wording of Matthew.

Such growth of ritual utterances is not at all unusual. Note what happens with catechetical texts and even with official pronouncements of faith and practice. One Protestant denomination decided that they would reduce their official statement of doctrine to only what was found in scripture and they succeeded in eliminating almost 35 percent. But essentially the same type of ritual expansions occurs in indigenous religious expression, for example, songs of healing in Navajo and in the ritual of the Cherubim and Seraphim Church of West Africa.

Evidently some early Christians felt that the end of the prayer was entirely too abrupt, especially when the last words referred either to 'evil' or 'the evil one,' which occurs in three of the best ancient uncials: Sinaiticus, Vaticanus, and D. Numerous Byzantine-type uncials, as well as many minuscules, add the words 'because yours is the kingdom and the power and the glory forever, Amen.' This doxology was soon introduced into texts in Syriac, Coptic, Gothic, Armenian, Ethiopic, and Georgian, perhaps because it is such an appropriate echo of 1 Chronicles 29:11–13.

This addition was not accepted into the Vulgate, and accordingly it is not found in the translation of Wycliffe

(1389) nor in Tyndale (1526), but both do add the form 'Amen.' The King James Version of 1611 does have 'For thine is the kingdom, and the power, and the glory, for ever. Amen,' since this doxology also existed in other earlier English translations. The King James translators stated in their introduction that they did not seek to provide an entirely new text of the Bible but to incorporate widely received renderings in various existing English translations.

Issues of interpretation also have an interesting history involving numerous fluctuations. Wycliffe's translation, which follows the Vulgate closely, has 'And forgeue to us oure dettis, as we forgeue to oure dettours,' but Tyndale, who was much more concerned about making the text meaningful for average English-speaking people, translated 'And forgeve us oure treaspases, even as we forgeve them which treaspas us.' This use of *treaspas* as a transitive verb is unusual.

The King James Version goes back to the tradition of Wycliffe and other English versions and has 'And forgive us our debts, as we forgive our debtors,' but such a rendering has been the object of great controversy. In the first place, it seems more like a commercial transaction than a matter of forgiving wrongs. And in view of the use of the Greek term for 'sins' in the first part of the corresponding prayer in Luke, some constituencies have insisted on 'trespasses.' This became an important factor in separating Methodism from the Anglican and Presbyterian traditions. In fact, some persons have joked about Presbyterians for having retained *debts* and *debtors* because they seemingly would prefer to have their debts forgiven and could leave their sins for later consideration.

Another serious drawback in the King James Version was the use of italic letters for English words that did not correspond literally to words in Greek, but were required by English grammar. This resulted in calling special attention to words that marked only formal relations rather than lexical content. Such italicized words were the source of serious theological controversies, and were only eliminated in the latter part of the twentieth century.

The conservative attitudes with regard to changes in the text of the scriptures were particularly strong up to the twentieth century, although more than 500 translations of at least one book of the Bible into English were published between the time of the King James Version and the publication of the Revised Standard Version (1946). But relatively few of these translations had a significant circulation. The English Revised Version of 1895 and the American Standard Version of 1901 were certainly superior in terms of the underlying Hebrew and Greek texts that were the basis for interpretation, but the style of language was terribly academic and stodgy. The use of old-fashioned language of *thee, thou, thine, hath, oft* (especially in prayer) and the literal grammatical rendering of the Epistles found

an acceptance in seminaries training pastors and scholars, but these revisions of the King James Bible were largely rejected by the general public. But the controversies over traditional versus new translations, for example, the American Standard Version and Goodspeed's *American Translation*, became a matter of widespread concern, and some of the most hotly contended issues involved the Lord's Prayer in the Matthean text.

'Our Father which art' seemed doubly wrong. First, the relative pronoun *which*, in place of *who*, seemed out of place in referring to God, and the old-fashioned third-person singular *art* of the verb *to be* was completely misleading. What did this verse have to do with 'art in heaven,' people asked. But the most serious problem was the use of *hallowed*, pronounced not as two syllables in speaking of *hallowed ground* (a way of talking about a cemetery), but as three syllables that no one really understood. Some people heard the word as *hollowed*, and some even concluded that it was a proper name, perhaps *Harold*.

Through the years I have asked hundreds of people to explain to me the meaning of *hallowed* in the Lord's Prayer, and not one person has been able to even come close. One pastor tried to explain its meaning, but actually only described the meaning of the underlying Greek term, not the meaning of the English.

To make matters worse 'hallowed be' is a passive imperative, a grammatical construction that is no longer used in English, except for such fixed grammatical remnants as 'be damned if I would.' The underlying Greek term is a passive aorist imperative referring to 'being made holy,' but this is semantically contradictory to the passage, since God is the very essence of holiness. Accordingly, how can he be made holy? Obviously, only in the minds of those who are willing to recognize his holiness.

The text, however, refers to *name*, and how can a name be made holy? The answer, of course, exists in the fact that in referring to Deity there was a tendency in Hebrew and subsequently in Greek to use words such as *name, heaven, the almighty, the highest* to refer to God without employing his name, regarded as too powerful to utter in any but the most exalted contexts, as when the high priest in ancient Judaism uttered the tetragrammaton (the name with four Hebrew letters) once a year when blood was offered in the Holy of Holies for the sins of the people.

The term *name* must of course refer to God, but the Greek verb referring to being made holy must be the recognition of his holiness on the part of people. The New Testament in Modern English has 'may your name be honoured' and Today's English Version has 'May your holy name be honored'; the Contemporary English Version, however, has 'help us to honor your name,' but it could also be rendered as 'show people that you are the one true God'or 'that you alone are God.'

The second petition in the King James Version is 'Thy kingdom come,' but this statement is not only awkward in the use of 'thy' instead of 'your,' but also kingdoms do not 'come,' although they can be said 'to come into existence.' Some translators employ 'May your kingdom come' but the auxiliary *may* normally suggests uncertainty, and accordingly the Contemporary English Version has 'Come and set up your kingdom.'

The petition 'Thy will be done on earth' is far less understood than most preachers realize. But a change to 'Your will be done on earth' does not solve the issue, because most people only understand 'will' as the future tense auxiliary of the verb *to be*, and if they do not think of that, they assume that this 'will' is the final will and testament that people write before dying. 'Will' in the sense of 'what you desire' or 'what you want' is seldom what people understand by 'will.' In fact, they often assume that this must be the inexorable will of a vengeful deity.

The succinct expression 'your will be done on earth, as it is in heaven' may need some expansion, as in the Contemporary English Version where this phrase is considered to be a purpose clause 'so that everyone on earth will obey you as you are obeyed in heaven.'

For verse 11 most translations recognize that the adjective qualifying 'bread' can mean 'daily' or 'needed.' With the exception of one papyrus, this word occurs nowhere else in Hellenistic literature, except for the writings of early Christians who were likewise not able to explain its meaning.

But a reference to bread can have an important cultural significance, because bread may be a rare and expensive commodity. Quechua Indians of Bolivia questioned the use of the Spanish term for bread in their New Testament because they felt that praying for bread would mean that they wanted to be rich while all they really wanted to pray for was 'something to eat.'

The issue of 'debts' and 'debtors' has already been discussed, but there is a serious problem in the traditional rendering of 6:13, in which the prayer asks God not to 'lead into temptation.' This is a possible interpretation of the Greek text, but most modern exegetes interpret the Greek word *peirasmos* as referring to 'trial' or 'testing,' since such an interpretation seems more in keeping with the context. After all, the believers were regarded as worshipping a man condemned to death for causing an uprising among the people. Not long after the death of Jesus, his followers could be arrested and summarily tortured and killed for belonging to an outlawed movement. What Christians must have feared greatly was the denial of their Lord under pressure of torture. The New Revised Standard Version makes this interpretation quite clear by rendering this final clause as 'do not bring us to the time of trial,' while Today's English Version has 'do not bring us to hard testing.'

Although many modern translators render the final petition as 'deliver us from evil' or 'protect us from evil,' most are more concerned with the plight of early Christians and therefore render this final petition as 'rescue us from the evil one' (New Revised Standard Version) or 'Keep us safe from the Evil One' (Today's English Version).

Most translators are increasingly aware of the liturgical character of certain passages in the New Testament that represent direct quotations or literary echoes of the Old Testament, for example, Matthew 12:18–21 and 13:14b–15, and they are also willing to consider Philippians 2:6–11 as an early creedal proclamation of the church, but La Bible de Jérusalem (1974) rendered Ephesians 1:3–14 (condemned by some as the sentence that didn't know when to stop) as a liturgical expression of faith. Since that time a number of other translations have clearly recognized the liturgical nature of this passage.

One particularly important aspect of present-day development in Bible translating is the effort to make sense of a Bible passage, whether translators follow a largely Byzantine text or are willing to accept a more scientific text based on early and broadly representative manuscript evidence. This idea of making the Bible as meaningful to present-day readers as it was to Hebrew and Greek speakers some 2,000 years ago is an important development during this last century. As one Jesuit friend of mine said, 'This idea of making the scriptures fully understandable to everyone is the most important development since the Reformation.'

References and further reading

Bruce, F.F. (1978) *History of the Bible in English: From the Earliest Versions*, New York: Oxford University Press, 3rd edn.

Carson, D.A. (1998) *The Inclusive Language Debate: A Plea for Realism*, Downers Grove: IVP.

de Waard, J. and E.A. Nida (1986) *From One Language to Another: Functional Equivalence in Bible Translating*, Nashville: Nelson.

Ewert, D. (1983) *From Ancient Tablets to Modern Translations*, Grand Rapids: Zondervan.

Gutt, E.-A. (1991) *Translation and Relevance: Cognition and Context*, Oxford: Blackwell.

Hatim, B. and I. Mason (1990) *Discourse and the Translator*, London: Longman.

Kee, H.C. (ed.) (1993) *The Bible in the Twenty-First Century*, Philadelphia: Trinity Press International.

Metzger, Bruce M. (2001) *The Bible in Translation*, Grand Rapids: Baker.

Nida, E.A. (1964) *Toward a Science of Translating*, Leiden: Brill.

—— and C.R. Taber (1969) *The Theory and Practice of Translation*, Leiden: Brill.

Orlinsky, H.M. and R.G. Bratcher (1981) *A History of Bible Translation and the North American Contribution*, Atlanta: Scholars Press.

Porter, S.E. (2001a) 'Some Issues in Modern Translation Theory and Study of the Greek New Testament,' *Currents in Research: Biblical Studies* 9: 350–82.

—— (2001b) 'Modern Translations,' pp. 134–61 in *The Oxford Illustrated History of the Bible*, J. Rogerson (ed.), Oxford: Oxford University Press.

—— and R.S. Hess (eds.) (1999) *Translating the Bible: Problems and Prospects*, Sheffield: Sheffield Academic Press.

Poythress, V.S. and W.A. Grudem (2000) *The Gender-Neutral Bible Controversy: Muting the Masculinity of God's Words*, Nashville: Broadman & Holman.

Ryken, L. (2002) *The Word of God in English: Criteria for Excellence in Bible Translation*, Wheaton, IL: Crossway.

Scorgie, G.G., M.L. Strauss, and S.M. Voth (eds.) (2003) *The Challenge of Bible Translation: Communicating God's Word to the World*, Grand Rapids: Zondervan.

Strauss, M.L. (1998) *Distorting Scripture? The Challenge of Bible Translation and Gender Accuracy*, Downers Grove: IVP.

Venuti, L. (1995) *The Translator's Invisibility: A History of Translation*, London: Routledge.

STANLEY E. PORTER

TRANSLATION AS INTERPRETATION

The authority of the Hebrew Bible persisted both within the Jewish and Christian cultures even when the Hebrew language did not. When the vernacular of the Hebrew Bible was no longer the vernacular of the synagogue and church, the Hebrew Bible was translated into languages like Aramaic, Greek, Syriac, and Latin. A form of those early translations has survived so that today we may read ancient translations like the Targumim, the Septuagint, the Samaritan Pentateuch, the Peshitta, and the Vulgate. The ancient versions may be studied in a number of ways. We may view them as independent pieces of literature, as tools via which to discover an earlier form of the Hebrew text, or as commentaries that offer interpretation of the parent text.

It is possible to examine the linguistic elements, the literary quality, and the rhetorical flavor of the translated text without consideration of its source. While finding rebirth in a new culture, the translation may take on a life of its own animated by the literary style, the theological concerns, the sociological realities, and the history of the receiving community. Thus it is completely legitimate to study the ancient versions as independent literary works. The ancient versions may also be used to reconstruct the parent text that lies behind them. This is the goal of lower text criticism. Because no complete witness to the pre-Tiberian text exists, these scholars attempt to reconstruct such a *Vorlage* by retroverting the ancient versions.

The third way of using the ancient versions is our focus here. This approach views the ancient versions as commentaries. Since we are unable to interview a member of the ancient interpretive community, we are unable to directly inquire about their interpretation of a particular Hebrew story or piece of poetry. But we do have the translation of those stories and that poetry. And in those translations, we may find clues that indicate how they understood those texts. For it is a truism that every act of translation is also an act of interpretation (Wevers 1996: 87; Brock 1988: 87). Changes occur during the translation process not only because they are demanded by differing language structures between the parent and original text, but also because translators might pursue their own artistic and rhetorical intentions. At times they sought to preserve the tone and message of the original by carefully mimicking the cues of the parent text. At other times, the translation reveals a literary and rhetorical dynamic foreign to the original audience but one that sheds light on the interpretive community which produced the translation. Thus a translated text may be approximately the same length as the original or may blossom like the Greek Esther, a text that is more than twice the length of its Hebrew counterpart. In either case, the act of translation is at the same time an act of interpretation. That means every translation is also a commentary.

We obtain access to this ancient interpretation when we investigate the translation techniques of the ancient translators. Of all the ancient versions, the one that has enjoyed the most attention is the Septuagint. During the last 100 years, there has been a prominent trend in assessing the translation technique of the Septuagint. Scholars pursuing the practice of lower text criticism have sought to define the 'literalness' of this ancient version. That measurement for literalness is really a measure of 'consistency' (Tov and Wright 1985: 153). And the consistency of the translator most frequently pursued is *linguistic* consistency (Beck 2000: 17–21). This approach to translation-technique analysis offers the interpreter insights that are intriguing but incomplete. The data drawn from linguistic research tell only part of the story since texts are much more than strings of loosely connected sentences filled with linguistic phenomena. Barnstone cautions us against viewing translations in a mechanistic way where translators first disassemble and then reassemble meaning word by word:

Some think the oral or graphic words of the past can really be heard, seen, and transported intact, word by word, note by note, brick by brick to a new site and erected again in stunning duplication. But the words of the singer, the poet, the Bible-maker, and scribe is different, and the carriers of the word stumble at every step on the road to revelation. Their way is as crooked as a butterfly's ruler. (Barnstone 1993: 4)

The translated story like the original is much more than just a string of words and grammar. It is literature filled with art, intuition, and mystery.

Thus scholars have expanded translation-technique analysis and the interpretation of the translated versions to include literary analysis. Rabassa observes that 'language learning and the study of literature are two completely different things, and translation has to be part of the latter if it is to receive the breadth that is inherent in it' (Rabassa 1984: 27). Barnstone sounds a similar tone:

> Writing is translation and translation is writing. The very essence of the activity of writing is that at every millisecond of the writing process the writer is simultaneously interpreting, transforming, encoding and translating data into meaningful letters and words, and at every millisecond of the translation process the translator is the writer, performing the same activities. Because literary translation is a work of literature, its existence and formation can be studied only within a theory of literature. (Barnstone 1993: 7–8)

When we analyze the translation through the lens of literary analysis, we will be observing the way in which the translator directed or at times redirected the translation in order to impact the reader. With regard to the original text, Alter observes that 'the literary vehicle is so much the necessary medium through which the Hebrew writers realized their meanings that we will grasp their meanings at best imperfectly if we ignore their fine articulations as literature' (Alter 1992: 63–4).

The same may be said for the translated text which has a literary soul and life of its own. By comparing and contrasting the literary analysis of the parent and translated text, the translator's interpretation of the text will become apparent (Beck 2000: 1–5).

When the translators are viewed as both language and literary artists, then a new set of questions percolates up with regard to their translation. We will not just ask how consistently they have preserved the independent personal pronoun but how they have shaped the twists and turns of the plot. We will not just ask how consistently they translated the Hebrew participles, but through which devices of characterization we meet the participants in the plot. We will not just compare the number of morphemes present in the original and translated text but inquire about the way the narrator has shaped our experience with the story. We will not just measure the translator's consistency in replicating the paratactic clause structure of the parent text but also examine the paralleling of syntactic elements and replicating of gaps in the poetic structure.

Fundamental to our appreciation of the translator's work is the realization that they have options that influence both *what* they say and *how* they say it. If we are to really appreciate and understand their translation, we must see them as self-conscious composers who carefully select the content and manipulate the form to shape the reading experience. When we measure their product with both linguistic and literary sensitivity, we will have a sharper sense of the way they understood the text they were translating.

Consider the Greek edition of Esther as it characterizes Vashti. A narrative critical analysis of Vashti's character shows that the Vashti we meet in the Greek edition is a very different Vashti from the one we meet in the Hebrew edition of the story. That change is largely brought about by just three words in the first chapter. In the Hebrew edition, Queen Vashti is summoned by King Xerxes to appear at a drunken party in order to display her beauty before the guests. She 'refuses' the invitation and subsequently is removed from office. The characterization of the Hebrew Vashti gives her a sense of dignity and decorum that allows her to rise above the men at the drunken party. The reader is invited to like her and empathize with her actions.

We meet a very different Vashti in the Greek edition of this story. That recharacterization is animated by three changes in the translated text. First of all, the drunken royal party becomes the wedding reception for the king and queen (1:5). Second, at this reception, the Greek Xerxes summons Vashti in order to enthrone her as queen before the people (1:11). Third, the Greek translator states that Vashti 'disobeyed' a direct order of the king. This is a moral interpretation of the Hebrew text that says she 'refused' to come to the banquet. Although these three changes are small by linguistic standards, they make a major shift in the literary character of this chapter. A literary analysis of the translated text shows the translator has changed both the context and nature of Vashti's action. She is a woman who disobeys her husband at their wedding reception at just the moment he wishes to present her as queen to his subjects. Those changes present the Greek reader with a more negative characterization of Vashti than the Hebrew edition warrants and reveal a translator interpreting the text.

When translation-technique analysis of the ancient versions addresses both the linguistic and literary dimensions of the text, we may see the translators as both storytellers and poets. This form of analysis will deepen our appreciation of their literary artistry and open a commentary that reveals how they interpreted the parent text.

Reference and further reading

Aejmelaeus, A. (1993) *On the Trail of the Septuagint Translators*, Kampen, The Netherlands: KOK Pharos.

Alter, R. (1992) *The World of Biblical Literature*, New York: Basic Books.

Barnstone, W. (1993) *The Poetics of Translation: History, Theory, Practice*, New Haven: Yale University Press.

Beck, J.A. (2000) *Translators as Storytellers: A Study in Septuagint Translation Technique*, New York: Peter Lang.

Brock, S.P. (1988) 'Translating the Old Testament', in *It Is Written*, D. Carson and H. Williamson (eds.), Cambridge: Cambridge University Press.

Olofsson, S. (1990) *The LXX Version: A Guide to the Translation Technique of the Septuagint*, Stockholm: Almqvist and Wiksell International.

Greenberg, M. (1978) 'The Use of the Ancient Versions for Interpreting the Hebrew Bible,' in *Congress Volume Göttingen 1977*, Leiden: Brill.

Rabassa, G. (1984) 'If This be Treason: Translation and its Possibilities,' in *Translation: Literary, Linguistic and Philosophical Perspectives*, W. Frawley (ed.), Newark: University of Delaware Press.

Schogt, H.G. (1988) *Linguistics, Literary Analysis and Literary Translation*, Toronto: University of Toronto Press.

Tov, E. (1987) 'The Nature and Study of the Translation Technique of the LXX in the Past and Present,' in *Sixth Congress of the International Organization for Septuagint and Cognate Studies*, C.E. Cox (ed.), Atlanta: Scholars Press.

—— and B.G. Wright (1985) 'Computer-assisted Study of the Criteria for Assessing the Literalness of Translation Units in the LXX,' *Textus* 12: 149–87.

Wevers, J.W. (1996) 'The Interpretive Character and Significance of the Septuagint Version,' in *Hebrew Bible/Old Testament, the History of Its Interpretation, Vol. 1 From the Beginnings to the Middle Ages*, M. Saebo (ed.), Göttingen: Vandenhoeck & Ruprecht.

JOHN A. BECK

TWENTIETH CENTURY INTERPRETATION

1 Introduction

In the twentieth century the plethora of approaches and associated methods for the interpretation of the Bible grew ever faster to reach a peak at the turn of the millennium. As the century progressed, it gradually became clear that none of the newly introduced perspectives from which the Bible can be approached would supplant the existing dominance of the principal modes of reading the Bible. On the one hand, the Bible continued to be seen as God's Word revealed for the salvation of the world and as the norm for faithful living. On the other hand, the firmly established scholarly insight into the historical character of both content and expression remained the determining factor for the critical interpretation of the Bible as an old collection of even older materials. Especially since the Second World War, this began to develop into the situation with which biblical interpretation sees itself confronted at the beginning of the twenty-first century: many perspectives, approaches, and methods add themselves to the existing repertoire without rendering previous ones obsolete (despite often claiming to do that).

Since interpretation concerns the Bible as the fundamental scriptures of Judaism and Christianity, it is no wonder that the methods for the interpretation and criticism of both the Old and the New Testaments continue to parallel each other – as it had always been in principle. Often, for instance, in the development of form criticism, Old Testament scholarship has led the way in developing new methods and techniques within the dominant historical way of reading the Bible. But sometimes, for instance, in the major contribution of Rudolf Bultmann, it was the other way around. This dual development has been further amplified by theological models for the unity of 'the' (or rather 'a') Christian canon, e.g., the classic pattern of promise and fulfilment or newer canonical readings of the 'whole Bible.' The existence of several major series of commentaries on both Testaments (e.g., *The Anchor Bible* and the German series *ATD* and *NTD*) amply illustrates the parallel ways of the two disciplines. Nevertheless, as will become clear in the two major parts of this article, the issues involved differ sufficiently to warrant separate treatments of the Testaments.

In the case of New Testament scholarship, it seems best to organize the discussion around the dominant paradigm, historical criticism, to show how it developed its techniques and methods and how it eventually came to be challenged and amplified by newer approaches, all of which amounts to a more or less chronological description. In the case of the Old Testament, however, the vast spectrum of perspectives, approaches, methods, and readings, running as they do concurrently to a large extent, can better be ordered according to their situation within the communication process: are they oriented toward the origin of the text (author-based methods), toward the text lying before us (text-focused methods), or toward the receivers of the text (reader-oriented methods)?

Interpretation seeks to understand the text. As a scholarly activity, it is often called 'exegesis' in theological jargon. But interpretation is present wherever people seek to understand the meaning of the Bible and does not necessarily have to be scholarly. *Criticism* of the Bible also seeks to contribute to the understanding of the Bible, but adds a technical dimension. The word is not intended to convey anything negative, like fault-finding or carping, but is a term roughly equivalent to 'scholarly inquiry,' the testing and weighing of evidence in order to reach scholarly arguable answers to questions of history, form, and content. Such critical study of the Bible was certainly enhanced by the rational principle of the Enlightenment, but the principle harks back to the Reformation in that it does not uncritically accept the official church interpretation, but reserves the right to research the Bible and reach its own answers. Our focus is on this kind of interpretation, that is, scholarly work in the fields of both Testaments, although occasional reference to other modes of interpretation may be made.

2 Old Testament criticism and interpretation

Twentieth-century Old Testament scholarship can be viewed as both the culmination of and the backlash to its own achievements in the course of the nineteenth century. First, the developments of historical criticism, particularly to be seen in Pentateuchal studies, were refined and progressed further. But growing concern over the tendency of the historical perspective to eclipse other dimensions of the text led to the emergence of alternative approaches, mostly of a literary character, but, mainly in the latter decades of the century, also informed by sociology and contextual considerations. However, all of this was dependent on a number of ancillary disciplines. 'Ancillary' does not suggest a lesser status – in fact, scholarly interpretation would be impossible without them. Their ancillary status within the theological domain only means that they literally serve the cause of biblical interpretation – which is often stated in the prefaces to such publications.

The basic tools used by critical scholars were improved on an impressive scale during the twentieth century. First, the several editions of the Hebrew Bible have enabled scholars to achieve the results they did. The editions of R. Kittel's *Biblia Hebraica* (I/II 1905–1937) were from 1968 overhauled by K. Elliger and others under the title *Biblia Hebraica Stuttgartensia*. This improved many defects of the older edition but still tended to present matters of classic literary criticism as though they were textual criticism, i.e., an aspect of interpretation itself is often confused with the preparatory discipline of establishing the most reliable text that can be achieved. Nevertheless, it still is the standard scholarly edition.

Following E. Würthwein's text-critical introduction to the Kittel Bible (English 1957), similar introductions to the Stuttgart Bible (e.g., W.R. Scott 1987; R. Wonneberger 1990), and highly specialized works (e.g., J. Barr 1989), E. Tov produced in 1992 (second edition 2001) what is probably today the standard work in the field. The biblical texts among the many scrolls from Qumran, published at Oxford since 1955 in an ongoing series, have become an indispensable tool in textual criticism, as has work on the Septuagint (the 1935 Württemberg edition by A. Rahlfs and the comprehensive edition of the Göttingen Septuagint Project, appearing since 1931).

The lexicons to Biblical Hebrew (editions of F. Brown, S.R. Driver, and C.A. Briggs since 1907 and the 1958 Leiden edition of the lexicon by L. Koehler and W. Baumgartner) have profoundly influenced Old Testament interpretation. They are now being updated or replaced by the new Leiden edition (1967–) and a dictionary of classical Hebrew by D.J.A. Clines (1993–). In turn, the great theological dictionaries of the twentieth century have been subjected to severe methodological criticism, but have nevertheless allowed scholars access to otherwise unsystematized material (G. Kittel and G. Friedrich, *TDNT*, containing as it does an abundance of material on the Old Testament [1964–1976; orig. German edn 1933–1979], G.J. Botterweck and H. Ringgren's *TDOT* [1970–], as well as the smaller one by E. Jenni and C. Westerman [1971–1975, ET 1997]). A similar subsidiary but indispensable role was played by several new concordances to the Hebrew Bible (G. Lisowski and A. Even-Shoshan), a role that is now being assumed by electronic media.

The advances in the independent disciplines of linguistics, Semitics, and archaeology that have steadily been taking place throughout the twentieth century have been of great significance to critical study of the Bible. This can be seen particularly in the influence of archaeological results on historical criticism and of structural linguistics on literary interpretation.

In the twentieth century the dominant model for interpreting the Old Testament was the historical-critical one, which is still the overall situation. Its primary interest is the origin and growth of the text. Classical historical criticism is not alone in this, for the question as to the production of the text can also be posed from a *sociological* point of view.

Historical criticism proper poses the question as to how the text before us reached its present stage, which traditions lie embedded within it, and how it was edited in different stages under different circumstances for different reasons. But that does not entail that historical criticism lacks concern for the *meaning* of the texts so studied, as is often alleged. Its activities (detecting tensions within a text, describing different theologies of different sources, etc.) imply, on the contrary, close attention to the *sense* made by the text. That includes rather than excludes primary interest in the historical meaning of the text and its earlier phases. Therefore historical criticism has spent the whole twentieth century sifting through the Old Testament in search of what its texts *originally* meant. This explains the mass of commentaries, Old Testament theologies, and theological dictionaries written within this paradigm concerning the *sense* made by the Old Testament. A concomitant issue is the allegation that historical criticism has been unconcerned with the *literary* character of the Old Testament. In the latter part of the century this resulted in some of the methods mentioned below calling themselves 'literary criticism' as opposed to historical criticism –

despite the fact that German historical criticism has always retained this very term (*Literarkritik*) to denote its central activity. But the historical-critical enterprise has been distinguished for sharp analyses of style, point of view, story line, choice of vocabulary, and other literary aspects of the text. The first real literary analysis of the Old Testament in general, E. König's German work on the *Stylistics, Rhetorics and Poetics of Biblical Literature* (1900), was consciously written within the historical-critical paradigm and deeply influenced many historical critics throughout the century.

Historical criticism has different aspects and has developed different methods by means of which to address these. The first is usually called *source criticism* in English, but German scholarship has always called it *literary criticism*. It traditionally seeks to identify sources within a stratified text, but has in the latter stages of its development come to apply all available literary criteria to investigate the unity of a text, whether it has been worked over by other hand(s) or not at all. This method has been applied to various parts of the Old Testament. So the Deuteronomistic History (DH, Deuteronomy–2 Kings) and the books it comprises have been found to contain traces of several sources behind them (M. Noth, F.M. Cross, R. Smend), some of which were reconstructed, e.g., the Succession narrative of 2 Samuel 9–20 plus 2 Kings 1 (L. Rost, E. Würthwein, T. Veijola). But Pentateuchal criticism remained the flagship of source criticism. The 'Four Sources hypothesis' inherited from the nineteenth century (Jahwist [J], Elohist [E], Deuteronomist [D], Priestly document [P]) was developed in several directions. The problem of E's existence (O. Procksch, P. Volz, W. Rudolph), the further division of the J document (O. Eissfeldt, G. Fohrer), and the extension of the sources beyond the Pentateuch were investigated (Eissfeldt, R.H. Pfeiffer, Fohrer). But unease with source criticism, especially its atomizing effect, grew as the century continued. Although source criticism as a method is still defended (e.g., W.H. Schmidt), it is gradually being subsumed into another aspect of historical criticism, namely, redaction criticism.

Redaction criticism works with the principles of historical criticism and is not to be confused with so-called synchronic literary criticism (see below). It is concerned with the larger literary complexes in the Bible and poses the question as to whether and how the different strata, sources, and secondary editions within one or more books were worked into larger complexes with recognizable theological profiles, such as the Pentateuch, DH, or the whole canon. It is within this field that historical criticism has made most of its salient contributions to interpretation in the latter decades of the century. The Pentateuch, DH, and the canon have been among the key areas in which criticism has endeavored to show how the Old Testament texts hang together. Recent theories on the redaction of the Pentateuch can roughly be divided into three groups, sometimes closely related. All three question the ability of traditional source criticism (*not* historical criticism in principle) to adequately address all problems of the growth of the Old Testament. First, R. Rendtorff took up the lead of forerunners like H.H. Schmid and rejected the validity of the 'Four Sources hypothesis' in favor of a so-called 'new fragmentary hypothesis.' Supported by others (e.g., E. Blum) this hypothesis claims that, whereas the individual books of the Pentateuch carry their own theological hallmarks, several sections of Genesis to Numbers show the influence of the exilic DH, so that the overall theological stamp of the whole Pentateuch is clearly recognizable. The second tendency (e.g., J. van Seters; R.N. Whybray) is to likewise relate the Pentateuch to DH from the sixth century BC, and to argue that the nonpriestly parts of the Pentateuch had been a 'preface' to DH, and were then added to the Pentateuch and given a priestly overhaul. The third tendency (O. Kaiser, E. Zenger) is to retain the idea of documentary sources, but to also accept that these were first composed from gradually accumulating traditions as a prepriestly reflection on Israel's history (eighth century), a law collection in Deuteronomy (seventh century), and a priestly document (sixth century), which were subsequently edited repeatedly. The counterpart of Pentateuchal criticism is the work on DH. In 1943 M. Noth first identified this encompassing work (including Deuteronomy) and interpreted it as a single work by one author to justify Israel's exile. His interpretation of its overall meaning was criticized by G. von Rad (a history of hope) and H.W. Wolff (a call to repentance). Theories were advanced to show that a complex redactional process occurred either by one (e.g., G. Hölscher, H.-D. Hoffmann, J. van Seters) or more redactors (e.g., A. Jepsen, R. Smend, T. Veijola), or that the work was a reworking of several existing documents (e.g., F.M. Cross, B. Halpern). Similar investigations into the redaction history of the prophetic books, the Psalms, and wisdom literature have extended these trends into the other bodies of literature.

A third aspect of historical-critical interpretation is *tradition criticism* (usually called 'tradition *history*' in German literature). Here the theologies and thought complexes in the Old Testament are analyzed and reconstructed in their historical contexts. This is done with specific phenomena, e.g., the cult, or with the ideas of whole movements, such as the preexilic Deuteronomic movement (M. Weinfeld) and the so-called Zion theology during the latter years of the Kingdom of Judah. Thus interest lies in traditions *behind* the texts and testified to by them.

Since H. Gunkel this has been going hand in glove with another historical-critical technique, *form criticism*. This aspect of interpretation establishes the various literary forms (genres) and identifies their place (and therefore *meaning*) in Israel's social institutions. The most famous example is perhaps Gunkel's description of the psalm forms as laments, hymns, songs of thanksgiving, etc. In his work on Genesis (1910) he combined this with the classic source hypothesis, as did others who followed the form-critical line (e.g., A. Alt on legal types, M. Noth and G. von Rad on narrative texts). S. Mowinckel and other Nordic scholars continued in this strain. In mid-century a school developed in Scandinavia that emphasized the importance of oral tradition, often in opposition to literary criticism (e.g., A. Bentzen, E. Nielsen, G. Widengren, I. Engnell). As with source criticism, tradition and form criticism have tended to be subsumed in redaction criticism, of which a clear illustration can be seen in recent Old Testament introductions.

Far from being irrelevant for interpreting the meaning of the Old Testament, historical criticism did not always succeed in making this apparent. The sheer mass of mutually opposing opinions is often experienced as confusing. But neither the proliferation of detailed knowledge nor lack of consensus is foreign to other sciences, detrimental to the search for truth, or bad in principle. The task of interpretation *includes* extracting essentials and presenting them in a way suitable for theological digestion, rather than rejecting an arsenal of interpretive methods that have produced such impressive results.

Form-critical interest in the social location of texts pointed to another way of handling texts from a historical perspective: the *sociohistorical interpretation* of the Bible. This approach is as much critical as it is historical, but is not usually called 'historical-critical,' in order to distinguish it from historical criticism 'proper.' Its establishment within the fold of standard Old Testament interpretive procedures was driven by at least three forces: the impulse of form criticism, the impact of recent archaeological results, and the influence of Marxist philosophy. Although archaeology has concentrated on Israelite history in the Late Bronze and Early Iron Ages, it has tended to focus on 'ordinary' locations inhabited by 'ordinary' people other than the 'literary' upper classes. Study of the demography, social organization, and economy of Palestine has begun to focus on the concerns of day-to-day life in the ancient societies of the region. This bears directly on the interpretation of the Old Testament. Issues such as the intermingling of cultures and the question as to what extent a state structure in early monarchial times could have been possible have far-reaching implications for interpretation of especially the historical books. Not only are many texts 'illumined' by archaeological evidence (S.M. Paul, W.G. Dever, A. Negev, M. Avi-Yonah, E. Stern), but they can now also be interpreted in the light of the ideological conflicts that helped to produce them (e.g., R.P. Carroll and R.R. Wilson on prophecy, and P.D. Hanson on apocalyptic literature). N.K. Gottwald has produced a comprehensive introduction to the Old Testament from a sociological perspective,

and the abundant writings by W. Brueggemann, especially since the 1980s, testify to the way in which interpretation from a sociological angle impacts on the meaning of the Old Testament for theology today.

As in recent archaeology, emphasis on the 'ordinary folk' is often featured in sociohistorical readings of the Old Testament (e.g., W. Schottroff, W. Stegemann, F. Golka). Although sociological interpretation is not necessarily 'Marxist,' much of it has a base in the philosophical premise of Karl Marx that socioeconomic circumstances condition the production of texts and that texts feed back into society either to stabilize or to destabilize power structures (e.g., F. Crüsemann, Brueggemann). This has joined forces with reader-based liberation methods (see below). The topical nature of this method is obvious, but other questions can also be put to the text, for which other modes of interpretation are necessary.

Especially since the Second World War uneasiness with historical criticism has been mounting. It was felt that this approach neglects the Bible as *literature*, that its *meaning* is not taken seriously, and that it consequently is not really interpretation. This censure is not justified in principle, but it can be understood as comment on the way in which historical criticism has managed its own enterprise. The methods orienting themselves by the text itself as opposed to its production or reception were influenced by the view of language developing in linguistics. This in turn was indebted to French structuralist philosophy (C. Levi-Strauss), which not only influenced linguistics, but also anthropology and other humanities.

Linguistically oriented interpretation has established itself as a distinctive minority school in the German-speaking world and came to prominence in the 1970s. Initially it did not deny its compatibility with elements from the historical-critical fold (so W. Richter), but later became more self-contained and mathematical (e.g., H. Schweitzer and American discourse analysis applied in biblical studies). After a development from ideas espoused in early structuralist linguistics (F. de Saussure 1913/14), the referential character of language was rejected, which means that texts no longer referred to things outside themselves (e.g., E. Güttgemanns). Therefore texts, by using language, create their own world and only refer within this world (text-immanent meaning). That necessitates discarding the extratextual historical dimension as well as the idea that the truth of linguistic utterances can reside in a reality outside themselves (H.F. Plett). Although this is a theoretically possible position, it requires that language become absolute, having no relation with the intentions of the people who use it. For the purposes of interpretation, its advantage is its attention to details of the linguistic aspect of texts. Syntactic analyses, word patterns, statistics, etc. can be of great help in this respect. Its disadvantages as a method in biblical interpretation are equally clear. Doing away with all aspects of texts' historicity is questionable. While it is quite possible to interpret a text without reference to its diachronic (developmental) facet, the references within the text at least have to be understood synchronically, which does not mean a-chronic reading (without any regard for the historical dimension of the text). It does entail understanding a text in the world within which it has meaning. Since this world, even if fictional, exists in time, it has a historical dimension.

The approach known since 1910 by the umbrella designation of *new (literary) criticism*, sometimes bluntly called 'the' synchronic approach, is typical of the English-speaking contribution to biblical interpretation. Not so much a method as a basket of methods working broadly along common lines, it was appropriated in biblical interpretation especially in America. Paralleled by related Israeli and European literary approaches (e.g., Y. Zakovitsch, the German 'Werkinterpretation,' L. Alonso-Schökel [stylistics of poetry], and J.P. Fokkelman [stylistics of narrative]), North American scholarship continues to play a leading role in this field. New criticism is concerned with the organization, structure and style of the text surface as opposed to the genetic interest of historical criticism. Within biblical studies it is also referred to as the '*Bible-as-Literature-Movement*' and sometimes simply as 'biblical structuralism' (R.M. Polzin). Toward the end of the century, literary critics also began to incorporate reader-centered interpretation in their work (e.g., D.J.A. Clines, C. Exum), so that the two approaches cannot always be kept apart.

In the 1960s one of New Criticism's most influential expressions in America, *rhetorical criticism*, gave literary interpretation of the Old Testament considerable impetus under the leadership of J. Muilenburg. It focuses on the communicative aspect of texts, and studies the rhetorical devices of a text in terms of 'speech act theory,' that is, treating language not on the linguistic level alone, but rather as it actively operates on the level of extended literary texts. Distinguishing content and discourse within a text, it concentrates on the latter in order to get to the argumentative thrust of a text. But this implies that the intentional aspect of texts does play a role and that the method therefore does have a hermeneutical character (communicating people's intentions to other people). Moreover, the argumentative function of texts implies social conventions by which readers can be convinced. Since this in turn tends toward a communication model (sender–text–receiver), it is not surprising that rhetorical criticism is also open to reader-response criticism (see below). A closely related literary method, *narrative criticism* (T.S. Bar-Efrat, M.A. Powell), is sometimes regarded as no more than a branch of rhetorical criticism. Here too the use of rhetorical strategies, point of view, setting, etc. is central, and the concept of the 'narrative universe,' the self-contained world created by the text, forms the basis of interpretation (R. Alter). Since the text does not refer to things in the nonliterary world, the intention of the author (as opposed to the rhetorical construct called the 'Narrator') becomes irrelevant. A feature of narrative criticism as well as other literary strategies is the 'close reading' of the text surface. The structural patterns, stylistic devices, and symbols are painstakingly analyzed (R.M. Polzin). But a rhetorical element lurks here too. The analysis of plots into which stories are organized in order to 'convince' readers to identify or reject reveals a hermeneutical element, notably the desire to communicate a value or truth – which has to come from outside the text. An appeal is made to the reader to accept the perspective from which the narrative is told, i.e., a message is conveyed.

The advantages of the 'literary' interpretation of the Bible are obvious. The linguistic, structural, stylistic, and narratological organization of texts is systematically studied and has brought a wealth of insights in both the poetry and the prose of the Old Testament. On the negative side it has to be admitted that there are many tensions in our texts that cannot so easily be covered up by the axiomatic presupposition that everything makes perfect sense in a perfect 'final text.' Expressed positively: a consistently 'synchronic' literary reading reveals the necessity of a 'diachronic' historical reading as a complementary partner.

The hugely influential *canon criticism* is here subsumed, as usual, under the literary approaches, but only for lack of an alternative. Its preoccupation with the 'final' text of the 'whole' canon, with what it *means* rather than with what it *meant*, its appreciation of structural, rhetorical, and other literary techniques, and its animosity toward historical criticism as atomistic and destructive (B.S. Childs, R. Alter) seem to warrant this grouping. On the other hand, both brands of canon criticism also display fundamental differences from mainline literary interpretations of the Bible. Childs has a *theological* programme, designed to heal the crisis in biblical theology purported to have been caused by historical criticism. This is a confessional and not in the first place a literary undertaking. But here too the supposed renunciation of extratextual criteria in favor of text-immanent interpretation is not carried out. Canon criticism is only possible when there already *is* a canon, however, the basic issues (*which* canon, *what* it is, *how* its final form is constituted) are not text-immanent interpretive issues, but imposed on the text from without. Childs' idea that the Masoretic text is 'right' from the perspective of the common Jewish and Christian traditions contradicts his literary presupposition because it comes from extratextual historical reality (relationships of faith communities). The type of canon criticism espoused by J.A. Sanders is of a different ilk. Here canon is not so much a text as a *process* functioning in a community, even though this form of canonical interpretation may also work with 'literary' phenomena such as composition, structure, and style (which has always been done by historical criticism as well). Sanders studies transformation processes within the canonical process, the continuing adaptation of the tradition under different circumstances, and this is a *historical* undertaking. Therefore it is not surprising to notice a convergence of canonical interest with redactional criticism (e.g., the team around E. Zenger). Neither is it coincidental that the Childs version of canon criticism and the Rendtorff version of redaction criticism appreciate each other so highly. It is because all of these combine regard for literary composition with the historical dimension of the text. Its inconsistencies notwithstanding, canon criticism's penchant for the overarching complexes in the Bible and its insistence on interpretation as a theological enterprise within a faith community have salutary effects in that it retains the relevance of the overall picture instead of stumbling over details. But this applies to redaction criticism as well. Therefore the canonical approach's unnecessary animosity to historical criticism, tending as it does to attract allies from fundamentalist currents into its fold, is all the more to be regretted. More important is the serious theological problem of substantiating *which* canon is to be interpreted – that of the early church and a major portion of present-day Christianity, or that of the Masoretes and another portion of Christianity. This is especially pressing, since the extent, form, and composition of a 'final' text is basic to its meaning. Can *biblical* interpretation uphold the views of both Paul's Septuagint and the Reformation's Bible?

A third group of approaches to biblical interpretation is *oriented toward the readers* or receivers. One philosophical root of this approach is the postmodern concept of 'context' and the pluriformity of truth: there is no absolute truth, since truth is bound to the context of the people who understand it relative to their situations. Therefore a text's meaning is assigned by its receivers. The other root was provided from quite another angle by H.-G. Gadamer (1960): The 'horizons' of ancient texts (what they meant) and those of the later receivers (what they mean) 'merge,' so that understanding has a history (because this happens time and again in history). Gadamer's idea of *Wirkungsgeschichte* (the history of the effects of the text) accordingly requires interpretation to take cognizance of the earlier ways in which people have interpreted the Bible.

The first of such interpretive strategies is appropriately called *reader-response criticism*. It is itself an assortment of methods and often has links with 'New Criticism' (close reading, narrative strategies, distinction between story and discourse, etc.; see above) and as such has a certain affinity with the German school of *reception aesthetics* (W. Iser). Readers respond to the directives encoded within the text that invite them to interpret its significance in their own situations. Therefore a reciprocal relationship between the direc-

tives of the text and the assumptions of the readers brings about a dynamic that results in meaning being ascribed to the text. This kind of approach has many similarities to rabbinic biblical interpretation (different possible senses in different circumstances), but has not as yet acquired an established foothold in modern biblical interpretation. It can be radicalized in the direction of *deconstruction*, originally a French way of showing that all texts are ultimately flawed against themselves so that all claims to their 'truth' can be deconstructed (J. Derrida).

Other forms of radicalizing the basic tenets of this approach have become firmly established in the arsenal of strategies for understanding the Bible. *Liberation theology* has developed its own typical style of interpretation by applying the context of oppressed people to the text rather than applying the text to this situation (G. Gutiérrez). Because of the obvious usefulness of social-historical interpretation in addressing social issues (see above), liberationist readings of the Bible are usually indebted to this kind of historical criticism (e.g., W. Schottroff, W. Stegemann, N.K. Gottwald), but they are essentially of another provenance. Liberationists gladly zoom in on 'special' texts, especially the Exodus narrative, that can be *used* for their cause (J.S. Croatto). Their interpretation has been immensely meaningful, mostly in the Third World, and has had reverberations in the First (F. Crüsemann). But it has a downside as well. The doublesidedness of text and user has evoked a discrepancy between the Bible and the contextualized reader. On the one hand, the Bible is used in order to give authority to its argument, and, on the other, it claims that authority to decide what is 'right' resides with the reader. A special expression of the liberation approach is to be seen in the widely practiced *feminist exegesis*. Increasing awareness of the necessity of the liberation of women from discriminatory restrictions by male-dominated societies developed a theological branch in feminism, of which biblical interpretation is an aspect. The hermeneutics are basically the same as that of other brands of liberationist interpretation, but it often avoids many of the pitfalls of liberation theology and has reached a high level of sophistication. Within the Old Testament discipline its programme is not only to focus on the historical (even when fictional) women of the Bible, but also to rid the text of the layers of patriarchal reinterpretation that have made the Bible even more androcentric than it already was. Male editing should be uncovered (not unrelated to procedures of redaction criticism). Where the result is palpably patriarchal, this should be unmasked and criticized (E. Schüssler Fiorenza, R.R. Ruether, P. Trible). Apart from the achievements of raising the consciousness of women and the contribution to their liberation from oppressive structures, feminist interpretation also helps women to identify with the biblical content. A contribution of importance to biblical interpretation in general is its insistence that the distinction between human and divine word be taken seriously. What Israel (and the early church) *did* according to the Bible is by no means to be identified with the Word of God.

There are more reader-oriented interpretations, e.g., various psychological (A.A. Bucher) and symbolic (R. Volp) approaches, and still others are beginning to appear, such as cognitive (E. van Wolde) and 'virtual' (C. Exum) readings, but those described above are representative of the mainstream currents.

The overwhelming mass of interpretations, methods, and results poses the question as to how this is to be evaluated. The newer approaches have not *eliminated* the disturbing effect of the lack of consensus perceived to be the fault of historical criticism, but have *added* to it. This forces the question: is consensus achievable? The history of interpretation suggests an unequivocal 'no.' Is it necessary? The same history suggests a negative answer again. Many strategies have, despite their weaknesses, produced insights that others could not have produced. These are exposed to each other, thereby critically limiting and complementing each other – and pointing each other to modesty. Since the Bible is the classical document for defining Christian faith, it must remain central in theology, whatever the reading strategy. *Mutatis mutandis* the same goes for Jewish faith (cf. M. Weiss, M. Fishbane). And ultimately this should be welcome, since God's truth cannot be encapsulated, not even by the Bible.

3 New Testament criticism and interpretation

The task of New Testament *exegesis* is to interpret the texts of the New Testament. During the long history of exegesis, the methods of interpretation have changed. Old methods have been maintained; new ones have been added. Since it began (with the ancient interpretation of Homer), exegesis has been using the *philological method* that integrates textual criticism, grammar, semantics, rhetoric, and the study of realia. The philological method is meant to clarify the literal sense (*sensus litteralis*) of the texts in their original language. The Age of Enlightenment transformed the philological criticism into *historical criticism*. In the nineteenth century, historical-critical exegesis became established as a new successful set of questions. Here, the methodological tools of historical scholarship were applied, and the focus was no longer the literal sense, but shifted to sources (historical approach) and the original form and meaning of the texts (critical approach), without dogmatic presuppositions. Traditional views of authorship regarding the Gospels and the letters were doubted. The image of Jesus that is given by the Synoptic Gospels was questioned. The canon of the New Testament was no longer considered as dogma but merely as a historical entity. Hence, the New Testament writings were interpreted as tendentious writings authored by various groups of early Christians.

The aim of exegesis has been and still is the appropriate 'reconstruction and interpretation of the New Testament writings' as it was defined in the nineteenth century: the reconstruction of the original texts and their historical contexts, and the interpretation of their messages, prescriptions, and religious meaning. The work of reconstruction is critical in every field. The assumption is always made that original traditions or texts have a history that alters or distorts the initial shape of the text in some way. The aim of historical criticism is to expose the original shape since only that is viewed as genuine and important. This critical approach, rooted in the Age of Enlightenment, deconstructs the present text in order to get to the respective 'Ur-text' (original text). The history of a text is seen as an undesirable development rather than as a way of appropriating and interpreting the text. Historical-critical exegesis became stuck in this narrow self-definition and increasingly lost its critical potential over the twentieth century. In this situation, structuralism, linguistics, and the study of literature, on the one hand, and engaged ways of reading, on the other hand, opened up new possibilities for understanding texts. This is the point of departure for the interpretations that were developed during the second half of the twentieth century.

Historical criticism interprets texts in their definitive versions and it has three objectives: to show and explain, with respect to form and content, the development of the texts from their initial shape up to their definitive versions; to interpret the definitive text version; to understand the steps of development of the text, its definitive version included, as interpretations of the 'Ur-text' (original text).

Historical-critical exegesis works within the framework of *New Testament scholarship*. In the twentieth century, New Testament studies developed into an expansive, independent scientific discipline, working on a broad field of interests, with an ever increasing differentiation and specialization. Its scope is the collection of canonical writings of the New Testament, considered in the context of the contemporary early Jewish and pagan environments. Five subdisciplines became established: text interpretation – customarily called *exegesis* – with its different methods; *introduction* into New Testament textual and literary problems (*Einleitungswissenschaften*); *contemporary history*, or the reconstruction of the environment of the New Testament; *history of early Christianity;* and *theology of the New Testament.* The main task of New Testament studies lies in the exegetical field and consists of interpreting and commenting on the individual New Testament writings. The European and North American standard series of commentaries (with Catholic, Protestant, or non-denominational background) are the results of the intensive explanation and interpretation of New Testament texts by mainly Catholic and Protestant biblical scholars.

Biblical interpretation always includes explicit and implicit hermeneutics. Two disciplines set the standards of biblical interpretation: contemporary theology, especially doctrines about scripture, and contemporary humanities, especially philosophy. Friedrich D.E. Schleiermacher joined together both impulses. Schleiermacher's *Hermeneutics* is a product of his theology and has at the same time influenced the philosophical-philological hermeneutics of the nineteenth and twentieth centuries up to Hans-Georg Gadamer. The hermeneutical approach of Rudolf Bultmann is the most important contribution of New Testament studies to the hermeneutical discussion during the twentieth century. It is shaped by Martin Heidegger's existential philosophy but did not have an influence beyond the boundaries of New Testament exegesis. The hermeneutical works of today adopt impulses from history, text linguistics, and the study of literature, that is, literary theory.

In the twentieth century, biblical interpretation kept the impulses of both historical and critical interpretation, and the historical hermeneutics that the eighteenth and nineteenth centuries had established. Still, it was not possible to come to a scholarly understanding of the New Testament texts without historical criticism. W.-G. Kümmel writes: 'The ancient text in itself is mute and can be revived to speak to a lesser or greater extent only by scientific operation' (Kümmel 1981). For Kümmel and the New Testament scholarship to follow, historical interpretation had this 'scientific' claim.

This claim manifested itself in the development of the individual *exegetical methods* whose problem-orientation and achievements continually grew in importance. The development took place gradually and in stages. Well-tested questions and methods were retained whereas others were added which modified the former. Old questions were raised again. As to methods, Old Testament exegesis was often ahead of New Testament scholarship in the first part of the twentieth century. Old Testament form criticism, tradition criticism, history of religions, and redaction criticism influenced New Testament exegesis. The well-tested historical criticism of sources and traditions was extended by impulses from religious studies (*religionsgeschichtliche Schule*) at the beginning of the twentieth century. German Protestant exegesis was especially influenced by systematic theology after the First World War (factual criticism – *Sachkritik* – and demythologization). After the Second World War, redaction criticism formulated a new interest in the final version of the text and its author. In the last third of the twentieth century, methodological influences and appropriation of other fields of study increased. Works on social history and psychological interpretations continued the 'empirical turn.' Furthermore, theological trends and social for-

mations aspired to take part in biblical exegesis, especially liberation theology (contextual theologies) and feminism. The linguistic turn was also (slowly) adopted by New Testament exegesis. Since the 1970s, different methodological questions derived from linguistics and the study of literature have become important. These very divergent impulses were integrated into New Testament interpretation after considerable argument. Historical criticism, with its set of methodological questions, lost its exclusive rule and was seen as the 'diachronic method' that was now joined by the 'synchronic method,' with its set of questions from text linguistics, the study of literature, and applied hermeneutics. One tendency can be seen over the whole of the twentieth century: every new question got into a dispute with the predominant paradigm, which was the historically oriented exegesis that developed into the so-called 'historical-critical method.' These arguments had a double result: historical-critical exegesis was strengthened and enhanced. In the second half of the twentieth century, it developed into a self-reflective method, organized according to methodological steps and taught through student textbooks. (This methodization was an effect of the growing theorization of the humanities since the 1960s.) Thus, the historical-critical method attained a monopoly that could be challenged, and its limitations were made visible. The new questions that were directed against historical criticism were either self-reflected in terms of method (like social theory, e.g., whose point of departure was social history), and in this case they blamed historical criticism for being undertheorized; or they started as enemies of theory (like feminism) and took a stance against the arrogance of the historical-critical method. Later on, they developed their own methods. Thus they secured their lasting and accepted participation in New Testament studies. The success of a new method was granted at the time it was integrated into student textbooks, created its own works on exegetical method, and, finally, with the introduction of a commentary series applying this method.

After a century of scientific professionalization, the modernized historical criticism has not been superseded (but has been significantly modified) as the dominant paradigm in the eyes of most New Testament scholars. New Testament exegesis regards itself as an integrative combination of methods that adopts and successfully appropriates elements of diverse new methodological approaches. The historical (diachronic) approach and the analytical (synchronic) description of texts stand side-by-side and presuppose models from text theory and literary theory (the world before the texts, the world beside the texts, the world after the texts).

In the twentieth century, prominent *instruments of study* for New Testament exegesis were created which serve as the basis of textual interpretation and are internationally acknowledged. First, works that give access to the *inventory of texts*: the standard edition of New Testament sources is the so-called *Nestle* (*Novum Testamentum Graece*, 27th edn, Aland 1993). In 1997, work toward the complete edition (*Editio Critica Maior* of the *Novum Testamentum Graece*, ed. B. Aland *et al.*) began. Prerequisite for comparative access to the text of the four Gospels is the *Synopsis Quattuor Evangeliorum* (15th edn, Aland 1996). Those and other important works are compiled at the Institut für neutestamentliche Textforschung in Münster, Germany.

Other works present the *semantic inventory* of the New Testament, first, the so-called *BDAG* (*A Greek-English Lexicon of the New Testament and Other Early Christian Literature*). The standard ancient Greek reference dictionary is still the *Liddell-Scott* (*A Greek-English Lexicon*, H.G. Liddell, R. Scott, H.S. Jones 1996). *The Vocabulary of the Greek Testament Illustrated from the Papyri and other Non-Literary Sources* (J.H. Moulton and G. Milligan 1914–1929) gives a special introduction to the environment of the New Testament. The most important terms of the New Testament are given a vast historical and semantic explanation in the *Theological Dictionary of the New Testament* (Kittel and Friedrich 1964–1976). The complete occurrence of New Testament vocabulary on the basis of the *Nestle* edition is presented by the *Vollständige Konkordanz zum Griechischen Neuen Testament* (K. Aland 1975). The new and monumental *Synoptic Concordance* (Hoffmann *et al.* 1999–2000) presents the complete vocabulary of the first three Gospels in their respective synoptic contexts.

In the second half of the twentieth century, interest focused on the *sources* of the Jesus traditions. Efforts were made to reconstruct the Sayings Source Q, which chiefly transmits the oral preaching of Jesus. The outcome of those efforts is *The Critical Edition of Q* (J.M. Robinson, P. Hoffmann, J.S. Kloppenborg 2000). The *Critical Edition* is one of the groundbreaking works in current New Testament studies. Several publications have followed. Since 2001, the *Documenta Q* (J.M. Robinson, P. Hoffmann, J.S. Kloppenborg) has been published in single volumes. A small textbook edition (*The Sayings Gospel Q in Greek and English with Parallels from the Gospels of Mark and Thomas*, Robinson *et al.* 2002) is meant to make the new text known to the common reader.

The following works are introductions into the *environment* of the New Testament: *Strack-Billerbeck* (*Kommentar zum Neuen Testament aus Talmud und Midrasch*, H.L. Strack and P. Billerbeck 1978) and *Der Neue Wettstein* (G. Strecker and U. Schnelle 2001) – a voluminous collection of Greek and Hellenistic texts related to the New Testament. The series *New Documents Illustrating Early Christianity* (9 vols.) has opened up the field of ancient inscriptions and papyri with respect to New Testament terms and texts.

The *whole field* of New Testament studies has been explained by standard encyclopaedias and student intro-

ductions: *The Anchor Bible Dictionary* (Freedman 1992, 6 vols.) was published in 1992. It covers the whole of biblical studies on a high scientific level. *Interpreting the New Testament*, by H. Conzelmann and A. Lindemann (2000), introduces students to New Testament studies and into the subdisciplines: methods, contemporary history and environment, the problems of the individual New Testament writings (introduction) and the history of early Christianity. There is also a chapter on the historical Jesus, but none on the theology of the New Testament (H. Conzelmann wrote a *Theology of the New Testament* that parallels this introduction). Stanley Porter's *Handbook to Exegesis of the New Testament* (1997) gives a comprehensive introduction into the well-established methods, but especially into the more modern methods, of New Testament exegesis. The handbook is indispensable to anyone who works in the field of exegesis.

During the twentieth century, historical-critical exegesis was found refining itself and reflecting the objectives of reconstruction and interpretation.

Exegesis begins with the reconstruction of the original texts of the individual New Testament writings. The first manuscripts of the New Testament texts (autographs) have not been preserved. We have only copies from which we can deduce the originals. The copies date from the second to the fifteenth century. Work in this area is called *textual criticism*. Textual criticism progressed immensely during the twentieth century. About 120 papyri have been discovered, some of which contain the oldest witnesses to the text of the New Testament (e.g., P[apyrus] 52 from the first half of the second century, containing a fragment of John 18). At the moment, we know *c.* 300 majuscules (parchment codexes) and *c.* 3,000 minuscules. Presently, a critical edition of all individual writings of the New Testament is being prepared along with a history of the origin and development of the different text forms, all of which is based on a vast amount of textual material. The aim of the critical edition is not the 'Ur-text,' which must remain hypothetical, but rather a reconstruction of the oldest text versions.

Different approaches and methods have developed on the basis of which historical-critical exegesis has up to now been working.

Source criticism (*Literarkritik*) seeks after the text in its respective context, and after the homogeneity of the text or 'disruptions' in the text. Proceeding from this question, it looks for sources that might stand behind the text. It also asks questions regarding the author, place, and time of composition. In other words, literary criticism reads the texts in a critical-historical way in the sense that it explores the literary and preliterary history along with the historical dimensions of a text. Within New Testament exegesis, source criticism is an important part of literary criticism. The Gospel of Mark was identified as a source for the Gospels of Matthew and Luke. From the text material shared by Matthew and Luke, but not found in Mark, the (hypothetical) Sayings Source Q was postulated and reconstructed – a great achievement of twentieth century's exegesis of the New Testament. As to the Gospel of John, Rudolf Bultmann postulated a Passion source, a *semeia* (miracles) source, and a source with Jesus' speeches. Adolf von Harnack observed three sources in Acts: A (based in Jerusalem or Caesarea), B (Acts 2 and 5), and C (the so-called Antioch source in Acts 6–15). As to the New Testament letters, literary criticism has been applied primarily to the Pauline letters. Various hypotheses exist regarding their divisions, especially regarding 1 and 2 Corinthians, Philippians, and Romans (ch. 16 as an independent letter). These letters are understood as compilations of several, originally independent, shorter writings of Paul. The assumption also exists that Revelation consists of several individual sources.

The method of *form criticism* (*Formgeschichte*) was introduced to New Testament studies by Karl Ludwig Schmidt, Martin Dibelius, and Rudolf Bultmann, on the basis of the works of Old Testament scholar Hermann Gunkel. An inaugural advance was the division between the frame of Jesus history and the narrative and speech units – thus, traditions of the early church communities were singled out from the redacting work of the evangelists. The traditional topics of the forms were postulated from the needs of the Christian communities in different situations (Dibelius: sermons and catechisms) or gained by a formal analysis and subsequently connected with possible settings in the life of the communities (Bultmann: apophthegms, words of the Lord, miracle stories, historical narrative and legend). *History of forms/form criticism* presupposed that the communities were a contributing factor to the shape of early Christian tradition in its preliterary and literary forms. These units had a certain history before they were integrated into the Gospels' redaction as traditions.

The ideas of a *Sitz im Leben* ('setting in life') of the individual literary forms and of the productivity of the communities were subsequently questioned. New methods were added to *form criticism*. In due course, it developed into *tradition criticism* (*Überlieferungsgeschichte*) and *redaction criticism* (*Redaktionsgeschichte*). *Tradition criticism* follows up by reconstructing the development process of the Jesus tradition and of the different early Christian community traditions, from their original shape up to the final literary formulation in the Gospels. This leads one to question the originality of the Jesus traditions. Gerd Theissen (Theissen and Winter 2002) has formulated the 'criterion of historical plausibility': we can regard as historically correct those traditions that can be understood as an effect of Jesus and that can be imagined only in a Jewish context. This has superseded Hans Conzelmann's 'criterion of dissimilarity' (1959). The latter defines the original Jesus tradition as anything that cannot be integrated into Jewish thinking or

into ideologies of the later Christian communities. At the same time, form criticism was transformed into *literary genre criticism* (*Gattungsgeschichte*). Literary genres are literary forms that can be identified by characteristic structural features – but these are not based on a *Sitz im Leben* (i.e., a social community and its needs as to a group-specific literature) but rather on the inner laws of literature. Apart from the smaller genres, in the last thirty years the genres of Gospel (especially H. Koester) and of letter (especially H.D. Betz and H.-J. Klauck) have received most of the attention. *Redaction criticism* has especially been applied successfully in Synoptic Gospel research over the last forty years (H. Conzelmann, W. Marxsen, G. Bornkamm). The question here concerns the way the evangelist handles his sources and traditions, his literary style, and narration, his outlook on Jesus, his ethos, and the way he directs his readers. The evangelists who do not only collect and write down traditions, but also create a Jesus narrative themselves, are seen as authors in their own right. The reconstruction of the theology of the evangelists (especially their Christology and ethics) is of special importance.

Terms, the combination of words, and religious language is another topic in exegesis. During the twentieth century, the *history of (theological) terms* has become established. The monumental ten–volume *Theological Dictionary of the New Testament* (Kittel and Friedrich 1964–1976) presents the history of all important Greek lexemes in the New Testament within their Greek and Jewish contexts of meaning. The history of meanings is close to the 'history of religions school,' which has been very important for New Testament exegesis since the great works of H. Gunkel, W. Bousset, J. Weiss, and W. Wrede, but without developing a method of its own. The so-called 'history-of-religions comparison' is less a method but rather a question of comparison and an individual research task. Here, the questions concern religious elements in the language, literary genres, mind, ethos, rites, cult, and institutions of early Christianity and its literature. Gerd Theissen reformulates this question under the modified conditions of structuralist religious studies (Theissen 1999).

Historical criticism had to react to the changes in historical scholarship. French historians introduced the 'social' as a historical category (*Annales* school since 1929) that came to dominate historical scholarship throughout the twentieth century. The work of G. Theissen, E.A. Judge, W.E. Meeks, and their followers has made questions of social history and history of consciousness fruitful for New Testament exegesis by exploring the social conditions of the Jesus tradition and the social structure of the Pauline communities.

Feminist exegesis developed with a certain degree of closeness to the socio-historical approach. Feminist discourse on society was applied to the writings of the New Testament. Feminist exegesis is characterized by a radical-critical and theology-of-liberation approach which takes an explicit stance against oppression and discrimination of women, colonialism, racism, and Christian anti-Judaism, and criticizes those tendencies in the New Testament. At the same time, feminist exegesis unearths the hidden or oppressed history of early Christian women from the New Testament writings.

Sociohistorical and feminist exegeses are related to the historical paradigm in spite of their radicalization or methodological differentiation. At present, they are firmly established in exegesis as part of the network of methods that New Testament scholars regularly use. A very different paradigm is represented by the synchronic methods that were developed by the study of literature and by text linguistics in the second half of the twentieth century. These have been adopted by New Testament exegesis through various stages. In the study of literature and in text linguistics, theories were developed that in time turned into established methods or certain analytical forms.

Text-linguistics ('discourse analysis') has focused on the text since the 1970s. Textual structure, textual function, and textual genres have been explored. Text linguistics has developed several methods to describe texts: syntactic, semantic, and pragmatic *textual analysis*. It investigates the structure (cohesion and coherence) of a text, its meaning, and its intended impact on the original readers. At present, textual analysis is also part of the standard procedures in New Testament exegesis.

Two further approaches that deal with the text on the synchronic level are derived from the study of literature. *Narrative analysis/narrative criticism* is based on narrative theory which has been developed since the 1960s. It describes the different ways of narrating and the functions of the narrative process between narrator and hearer, that is, the reader. Narrative analysis is especially applied in Synoptic Gospel research. *Rhetorical or argumentative analysis/rhetorical criticism* takes into account the prominent role of rhetoric in Hellenistic-Roman antiquity. As public judicial speech, it necessarily influenced the culture of speech and writing. Topic, disposition, and style of a speech can be found also in non-rhetorical genres of literature. H.D. Betz has made rhetorical analysis fruitful for the letters of the New Testament as well as for the Gospels (*Galatians*, 1979; in German *Der Galaterbrief*, 1988). To a degree, New Testament letters can be understood and analyzed as rhetorical documents (H.-J. Klauck; M.M. Mitchell).

Reception criticism/reader-response criticism leads from the initial to the later readers – an aspect of modern literary theory. Literature is seen as a process of communication during which every reader must formulate the meaning of the text anew. Thus, the interpretation of the text is opened up for every reader. At this point, there is a connection between reader-response criticism and feminist exegesis: The reader is constitutive for every interpretation, and the history of interpretation becomes an essential part of exegesis. The

German Evangelisch-Katholischer Kommentar interprets according to this method. At the same time, reader-response criticism has connections with the diachronic methods and opens up the historical dimension of the New Testament texts as well as New Testament exegesis.

References and further reading

The text of the Old Testament

Barr, James (1989) *Variable Spellings of the Hebrew Bible*, Schweich Lectures 1986, Oxford: Oxford University Press.

Brenton, L.C.L. (ed.) (1972) *The Septuagint Version of the Old Testament and Apocrypha, with an English Translation*, Grand Rapids: Zondervan.

Rahlfs, A. (ed.) (1950) *Septuaginta*, Stuttgart: Württembergische Bibelanstalt, 4th edn.

Rudolph, W. and H.P. Rüger (eds.) (1983) *Biblia Hebraica Stuttgartensia*, Stuttgart: Deutsche Bibelstiftung, 2nd corr. edn (Editio Minor, 1984).

Scott, W.R. (1987) *A Simplified Guide to BHS: Critical Apparatus, Masora, Accents, Unusual Letters and Other Markings*, N. Richland Hills, Tx: Bibal.

Snaith, N.H. (ed.) (1958) *Torah, Nevi'im u-Khetuvim*, London: British and Foreign Bible Society.

Tov, E. (2001) *Textual Criticism of the Hebrew Bible*, Minneapolis: Fortress Press.

Wonneberger, R. (1990) *Understanding BHS*, Winona Lake: Eisenbrauns.

Source editions related to the Old Testament

Charlesworth, J.H. (1983–1985) *Old Testament Pseudepigrapha*, Garden City: Doubleday.

Pritchard, J.B. (ed.) (1969) *Ancient Near Eastern Texts Relating to the Old Testament*, Princeton: Princeton University Press, 3rd edn with supplement.

Vermes, G. (1987) *The Dead Sea Scrolls in English*, Sheffield: JSOT Press, 3rd edn.

New Testament text editions

Aland, B. *et al.* (1997) *Novum Testamentum Graecum editio Critica Maior*, Stuttgart: Deutsche Bibelgesellschaft.

Aland, K. (ed.) (1993) *Novum Testamentum Graece*, New York: American Bible Society, 27th edn.

—— (ed.) (1996) *Synopsis Quattuor Evangeliorum*, Stuttgart: Deutsche Bibelgesellschaft, 15th edn.

Source editions related to the New Testament

Horsley, G.H.R. and S.R. Llewelyn (1976–2002) *New Documents Illustrating Early Christianity I–IX*, Grand Rapids: Eerdmans.

Robinson, J.M., P. Hoffmann, and J.S. Kloppenborg (eds.) (2000) *The Critical Edition of Q: Synopsis including the Gospels of Matthew and Luke, Mark and Thomas with English, German, and French Translations of Q and Thomas*, Leuven: Peeters.

—— (eds.) (2002) *The Sayings Gospel Q in Greek and English with Parallels from the Gospels of Mark and Thomas*, Minneapolis: Fortress Press.

Dictionaries and concordances (OT)
Anderson, F.I. and A.D. Forbes (1989) *The Vocabulary of the Old Testament*, Rome: Pontifical Institute.
Botterweck, G.J. and H. Ringgren (eds.) (1974–) *Theological Dictionary of the Old Testament*, trans. J.T. Willis, Grand Rapids: Eerdmans.
Brown, F., S.R. Driver, and C.A. Briggs (1957) *A Hebrew and English Lexicon of the Old Testament*, Oxford: Clarendon.
Even-Shoshan, A. (1985) *A New Concordance of the Old Testament*, Jerusalem: Kiryat Sefer.
Hatch, E. and H.A. Redpath (1954) *A Concordance to the Septuagint and the other Greek Versions of the Old Testamente*, including the Apocryphal Books, Graz: Akademische Verlagsanstalt.
Holladay, W.L. (1971) *A Concise Hebrew and Aramaic Lexicon of the Old Testament based on the Lexical Work of Ludwig Koehler and Walter Baumgartner*, Leiden: Brill.
Koehler, L. and W. Baumgartner (1958) *Lexicon in Veteris Testameni libros* (German and English), Leiden: Brill.

Dictionaries and concordances (New Testament)
Aland, K. (1975) *Vollständige Konkordanz zum Griechischen Neuen Testament*, Berlin: de Gruyter.
Bauer, W. (2000) *A Greek-English Lexicon of the New Testament and Other Early Christian Literature*, F.W. Danker (ed. and trans.), Chicago: University of Chicago Press (abbreviation: BDAG).
Hoffmann, P., U. Bauer, and T. Hieke (eds.) (1999–2000) *Synoptic Concordance: A Greek Concordance to the First Three Gospels in Synoptic Arrangement, Statistically Evaluated, Including Occurrences in Acts*, 4 Vols., New York: de Gruyter.
Jenni, E. and C. Westermann (1997) *Theological Lexicon of the Old Testament*, Peabody, MA: Hendrickson.
Kittel, G. and G. Friedrich (eds.) (1964–1976) *Theological Dictionary of the New Testament*, 10 Vols., Grand Rapids: Eerdmans.
Liddell, H.G., R. Scott, H.S. Jones, with R. McKenzie and S. Liddell (1996) *A Greek-English Lexicon*, Oxford: Clarendon.
Moulton, J.H. and G. Milligan (eds.) (1914–1929) *The Vocabulary of the Greek Testament Illustrated from the Papyri and other Non-Literary Sources*, London: Hodder & Stoughton.
Strack, H.L. and P. Billerbeck (1978) *Kommentar zum Neuen Testament aus Talmud und Midrasch*, München: Beck, 7th edn.
Strecker, G. and U. Schnelle (eds.) (2001) *Der Neue Wettstein*, Berlin: de Gruyter.

Dictionaries and concordances (General)
Buttrick, G.A. (ed.) (1962) *The Interpreter's Dictionary of the Bible*, New York: Abingdon Press (supplementary volume ed. K. Crim, Nashville: Abingdon Press, 1976).
Coggins, R.J. and J.L. Houlden (eds.) (1990) *A Dictionary of Biblical Interpretation*, Philadelphia: Trinity Press.
Freedman, D.N. (ed.) (1992) *The Anchor Bible Dictionary*, New York: Doubleday.

Literature on interpretation and hermeneutics
Alonso-Schökel, L. (1988) *A Manual of Biblical Poetics*, Rome: Pontifical Institute.
Alter, R. and F. Kermode (eds.) (1987) *The Literary Guide to the Bible*, London: Collins.
Barton, J. (ed.) (2003) *The Cambridge Companion to Biblical Interpretation*, Cambridge: Cambridge University Press.
Bauckham, R. (1989) *The Bible in Politics: How to Read the Bible Politically*, London: SPCK.
Carter, C.E. and C.L. Meyers (1996) *Community, Identity and Ideology: Social Science Approaches to the Hebrew Bible*, Winona Lake: Eisenbrauns.
Frymer-Kensky, T. (2002) *Reading the Women of the Bible: A New Interpretation of their Stories*, New York: Schocken.
Gunn, D.M. and D.N. Fewell (1993) *Narrative in the Hebrew Bible*, Oxford: Oxford University Press.
Kugel, J. (1981) *The Idea of Biblical Poetry*, New Haven: Yale University Press.
Noble, P.R. (1995) *The Canonical Approach: A Critical Reconstruction of the Hermeneutics of Brevard S. Childs*, Leiden: Brill.
Soulen, R.N. and R. Kendall (2001) *Handbook of Biblical Criticism*, Louisville: Westminster/John Knox, 3rd edn.
Thiselton, A.C. (1995) *New Horizons in Hermeneutics*, Carlisle: Paternoster.
Whybray, N. (1995) *Introduction to the Pentateuch*, Grand Rapids: Eerdmans.
Wischmeyer, O. (2004) *Hermeneutik des Neuen Testaments. Ein Lehrbuch*, Tübingen: Francke.

Commentaries
The Anchor Bible (1964–), Garden City: Doubleday.
Evangelisch-Katholischer Kommentar zum Neuen Testament (1975–), Zürich: Benzinger.
Hermeneia (1971–), Philadelphia: Fortress Press.
International Critical Commentary on the Holy Scriptures of the Old and New Testaments (1895–), Edinburgh: T&T Clark.
The Interpreter's Bible (1951–1957), New York: Abingdon Press.
Kritisch-exegetischer Kommentar über das Neue Testament (Meyers Kommentar) (1832–), Göttingen: Vandenhoeck und Ruprecht.

The New Century Bible Commentary (1971–) Grand Rapids: Eerdmans.

Other literature

Aland, K. and B. Aland (1981) *The Text of the New Testament*, trans. E.F. Rhodes, Grand Rapids: Eerdmans, rev. edn.

Betz, H.D. (1979) *Galatians*, Philadelphia: Fortress Press.

Conzelmann, H. (1959) *Art.* 'Jesus Christus,' pp. 619–53 in *Die Religion in Geschichte und Gegenwart*, Vol. 3, Tübingen: Mohr Siebeck, 3rd edn.

—— (1969) *An Outline of the Theology of the New Testament*, trans. John Bowden, London: SCM Press (latest 6th German edition: *Grundriß der Theologie des Neuen Testaments*, UTB 1446, Tübingen: Mohr Siebeck, 1997).

—— and A. Lindemann (1988) *Interpreting the New Testament: An Introduction to the Principles and Methods of New Testament Exegesis*, trans. S.S. Schatzmann, Peabody, MA: Hendrickson (latest 13th German edition: *Arbeitsbuch zum Neuen Testament*, UTB 52, Tübingen: Mohr Siebeck, 2000).

Gunkel, H. (1997) *Genesis*, trans. Mark E. Biddle, Mercer Library of Biblical Studies, Macon, GA: Mercer University Press (orig. 1910).

Kümmel, W.G. (1981) 'New Testament Exegesis,' pp. 43–76 in *Exegetical Method: A Student Handbook*, O. Kaiser and W.G. Kümmel, trans. E.V.N. Goetschius and M.J. O'Connell, New York: Seabury, rev. edn.

Metzger, B.M. (1994) *A Textual Commentary on the Greek New Testament*, Stuttgart: Deutsche Bibelgesellschaft, 4th edn.

Newsom, C. and S.H. Ringe (eds.) (1998) *The Women's Bible Commentary*, Louisville: Westminster/John Knox, exp. edn.

Porter, S.E. (ed.) (1997) *Handbook to Exegesis of the New Testament*, Leiden: Brill.

Robinson, J.M., P. Hoffmann, and J.S. Kloppenborg (eds.) (1996–) *Documenta Q: Reconstructions of Q through Two Centuries of Gospel Research Excerpted, Sorted and Evaluated*, Leuven: Peeters.

Schottroff, L. and M.-T. Wacker (eds.) (1998) *Kompendium Feministische Bibelauslegung*, Gütersloh: Gütersloher Verlagshaus.

Schüssler Fiorenza, E. (ed.) (1993–1994) *Searching the Scriptures: A Feminist Introduction*, 2 Vols., New York: Crossroad.

Stegemann, E.W., P. Fiedler, L. Schottroff, and K. Wengst (eds.) (2000–) *Theologischer Kommentar zum Neuen Testament*, Stuttgart: Kohlhammer Verlag.

Theissen, G. (1999) *A Theory of Primitive Christian Religion*, trans. John Bowden, London: SCM Press.

—— and A. Merz (1998) *The Historical Jesus: A Comprehensive Guide,* trans. John Bowden, Minneapolis: Fortress Press.

—— and D. Winter (2002) *The Quest for the Plausible Jesus: The Question of Criteria*, trans. M.E. Boring, Louisville: Westminster/John Knox.

JAMES ALFRED LOADER (I, II) AND
ODA WISCHMEYER (III)

W

WESTCOTT, LIGHTFOOT, AND HORT

In the second half of the nineteenth century Westcott, Lightfoot, and Hort, known as the Cambridge trio, dominated English New Testament scholarship. Lightfoot with his commentaries on the Pauline Epistles was the preeminent name in this field, the depth of his knowledge producing admiration not only throughout the English-speaking world but also on the Continent. Westcott and Hort were renowned for their work on the Greek text of the New Testament, with Westcott contributing lengthy commentaries on the Fourth Gospel, the Epistles of John, and the Epistle to the Hebrews. Hort was less widely known, but the breadth of his knowledge inspired awe among all who knew him. William Sanday, writing after his death, declared that Hort was 'our greatest English theologian of the century' (1897).

Brooke Foss Westcott (1825–1901) came from Birmingham. He was three years senior to both Lightfoot and Hort, and in fact was Lightfoot's tutor when Lightfoot first arrived in Cambridge in 1848. Westcott's brilliance lay in his understanding of Greek poetry and drama where he was always placed first amongst his peers. After three years as a fellow of Trinity College he was ordained in 1851, and in 1852 appointed assistant master at Harrow. He remained there for seventeen years until 1869 when he was appointed residentiary canon at Peterborough and in 1870 Regius Professor of Divinity at Cambridge. Here at Cambridge he worked with Hort on the Greek text of the New Testament, which became known as the Westcott and Hort edition first published in 1881. In 1890 he succeeded Lightfoot as bishop of Durham, where he remained until his death in 1901. He was acclaimed for his success in negotiating a settlement between owners and workers in the great Durham coal strike of 1892.

Joseph Barber Lightfoot (1828–1889) was born in Liverpool and educated at King Edward's School in Birmingham. It is not generally known that he was an enthusiastic mountaineer and that with Hort he was one of the first Englishmen to ascend the Jungfrau in the Swiss Alps. He was without doubt the greatest of the three Cambridge scholars in the realm of the New Testament and its historical background. His vast knowledge of the classics and confidence of interpretation (it is said that in his undergraduate examinations in Cambridge he never made a single mistake) assured that he ascended the Cambridge University hierarchy with virtually no opposition or competition, becoming Hulsean Professor of Divinity in 1861 and Lady Margaret Professor in 1875. In 1879 he became bishop of Durham and for ten years exercised a very positive influence on the spiritual life of the diocese, being well loved by both priests and parishioners.

It is, however, in his commentaries on the Pauline Epistles that his most enduring influence lies. By his repudiation of the historical views of the Tübingen School Lightfoot provided a bastion against the German higher criticism for half a century. His attack on Baur and his followers runs through the great commentaries on Galatians (1865), Philippians (1868), Colossians with Philemon (1875), and elsewhere. From his profound knowledge of the Apostolic Fathers Lightfoot demonstrated that the Tübingen viewpoint represented a quite perverted interpretation of the historical evidence. This was shown especially in his edition of the Epistles of Ignatius (1885). Theodor Zahn had already reached the same conclusions earlier in 1873, but Lightfoot so confirmed and buttressed Zahn's findings that from this time forth the authenticity of the Ignatian Epistles (and as a direct consequence, the refutation of the Tübingen hypothesis) was virtually incontrovertible.

Fenton John Anthony Hort (1828–1892) was born in Dublin and educated at Rugby School and at Trinity College, Cambridge. He had a prodigious mind, not only in the classics, but also in the scientific field, where he excelled in natural history, physiology, and especially botany. He was also well versed on seaweeds. Geology was another of his interests and he was an accomplished mountaineer, frequently climbing high peaks in the Swiss and French Alps. In his early years he was influenced by F.D. Maurice, but later became more aware of Maurice's heretical tendencies (for Maurice, God was not an objective personal Being, but simply 'the Spirit of truth and love').

From 1852–1857 Hort was a fellow of Trinity. After his marriage in 1857 he spent the next fifteen years as the vicar of St Ippolyts near Hitchin. From 1872 until his death he was back in Cambridge where he held various lectureships. With Westcott he worked on the Greek text of the New Testament for their joint edition mentioned above. His published works were disappointingly small in number, the most important being probably an unfinished commentary on James, and his book *The Way, the Truth and the Life*.

In order to comprehend adequately the significance of the Cambridge trio one must understand the nature of the higher-critical viewpoint which at the time was seeping into Britain from Germany, where the dominant 'school' of New Testament criticism was the Tübingen school of Ferdinand Christian Baur. There were two aspects to the Tübingen investigation including both a theological and a historical perspective. The Tübingen theological perspective, based on the rationalism of the Enlightenment, was a-theistic (excluding God), rather then atheistic (denying God). This had a corresponding historical perspective, which issued in a completely nonmiraculous interpretation of the New Testament. Central to this historical perspective was Baur's view that a Gentile-Christian community with Paul at its head stood over against, and hostile to, a Jewish-Christian community led by Peter. The resulting antagonism, according to Baur, was only resolved at the end of the second century in the irenical mediating position of the followers of John.

Lightfoot's examination of the Pauline Epistles discovered no trace of such an interpretation. Westcott and Hort were completely agreed with him. Theology for all three had to be based on the scriptures as trustworthy historical documents, which could not be sacrificed to the philosophical views and ideologies of those who declined to hold to this reliability.

The work of the Cambridge trio steadied orthodox conservative scholarship against the inroads of higher criticism. In 1877 Lightfoot devoted his attention to an anonymous work entitled *Supernatural Religion* (later revealed to have been written by W.R. Cassels), which was founded on the higher-critical principles enunciated by the Tübingen school. Lightfoot's painstaking demonstrations of the errors of this work retarded the growth and spread of higher criticism, in the New Testament at least, for the following three decades. During the lifetime of the trio the higher-critical ideas permeated into Britain mostly through the translation of German theological books and the teaching of Old Testament scholars such as William Robertson Smith and Samuel Driver. Only after the turn of the century, when all three Cambridge scholars had died, did German New Testament scholarship become more dominant in Britain.

The Cambridge opposition to this higher-critical viewpoint, however, did not mean that there was no place for biblical criticism. Textual criticism, for all three, was not only permissible, but also absolutely essential. Each of them held in varying degrees that scripture was neither infallible nor inerrant in every word, precisely because the original text of scripture was not always known with certainty. Within the sphere of reliability, therefore, there was marked off a specific area of uncertainty. In this sphere it was up to the scholar, working according to defined principles of textual criticism, to determine the most reliable text. Infallibility and inerrancy were to this degree uncertain and dependent on textual criticism. It was a parallel to Werner Heisenberg's uncertainty principle in the field of quantum mechanics in which within the limits of every quantum level there is always a certain freedom. So too, in the view of the Cambridge trio, there was also freedom for investigation in the matter of textual criticism within the limits of a general trustworthiness of scripture, as well as free investigation of particular aspects or interpretations within theological doctrines.

This freedom of interpretation within the traditional doctrinal formulations of the church comes to view most conspicuously in the doctrine of the atonement, where both Westcott and Hort had serious questions about certain aspects or facets of it (Lightfoot seems not to have been troubled by any such theological concerns). Hort expressed his views in an exchange of letters in 1871 when the bishop of Ely asked him to become his examining chaplain. 'About the manner of the Atonement,' wrote Hort, 'we must all feel that it lies in a region into which we can have only glimpses, and that all figures taken from things below are of necessity partial and imperfect. It is the vain attempt to bring the Divine truth down to the level of our own understandings that has created all the dark perversions of the Atonement which have justly offended sensitive consciences, and so given occasion to the denial of the truth itself.' On the other hand, he could also write: 'Christian peace comes not from sin denied, or sin ignored, but sin washed away. If it was not washed effectually away once for all upon the Cross, an awakened conscience has no refuge but in futile efforts after a heathenish self-atonement' (Hort 1896: 157).

Westcott fully believed that Christ gave His life as a ransom for the sin of the world, as was explicitly stated in the scriptures, but was uncertain whether this involved such concepts as punishment, satisfaction, and substitution. He regarded these concepts as a human attempt to provide a coherent explanation, but whether such an explanation was possible he could not be sure.

This example from the doctrine of the atonement may be paralleled within various facets of other Christian doctrines. The concerns and perplexities for which Westcott, and especially Hort, sought solutions illustrate once again the principle of freedom within limits, uncertainty within reliability, interpretative freedom of individual aspects within each doctrine, while still upholding the essential doctrine itself and not rejecting it on a priori philosophical presuppositions.

All of the trio were leading members of the committee appointed to revise the Authorized (King James) Version of the Bible during the 1870s. The resulting

Revised Version, however, which appeared in the years 1881–1885, did not find wide acceptance. This was partly because of doubts about the Westcott and Hort edition of the Greek text on which the Revised Version was based and which had been so strongly condemned by J.W. Burgon, Dean of Chichester. In the view of Burgon, one of the greatest scholars in the field of textual criticism, the Textus Receptus of Erasmus was the most reliable text. This had been brought to Basel from Byzantium in the fourteenth century by John of Ragusa and was regarded as the standard text of the New Testament. The work of John Mills, Lachmann, and Tregelles, however, put forward the theory that the fourth-century uncials Vaticanus and Alexandrinus were to be preferred to the Byzantine text because they were earlier and, therefore, supposedly less prone to copying errors and alleged interpolations. When Tischendorf obtained the Codex Sinaiticus at St Catherine's Monastery at Mount Sinai in 1859 a new impetus was given to the eclectic principle of ascertaining the original text from the earlier codexes. Westcott and Hort adopted the same principle that these fourth-century codexes were earlier and therefore more trustworthy than the Byzantine text. Vaticanus and Sinaiticus were called 'neutral texts' and made the standard by which all the other manuscripts were to be evaluated. Burgon, however, demonstrated that these versions were less reliable than the Received Text, which was supported by the citations in the works of John Chrysostom in the fourth century. This showed that although the manuscripts of the Byzantine text date from the fourteenth century, the original text itself stemmed from the second half of the fourth century, a fact also admitted by Hort.

All three were brilliant scholars in their own fields and certainly equal to the best that Germany could produce. Doubtless Hort possessed in general the most extensive knowledge and deepest understanding of theological issues, while Westcott excelled in his New Testament commentaries. Lightfoot was the most profound in the realm of classical and biblical learning.

References and further reading

Relevant articles in the *Oxford Dictionary of the Christian Church*

Barrett, C.K. (1972) 'J.B. Lightfoot,' *Durham University Journal* 64: 192–204.

Benson, A.C. (1911) *The Leaves of a Tree: Studies in Biography*, London: Smith, Elder.

Burgon, D.J.W. (1883) *The Revision Revised: A Refutation of Westcott and Hort's False Greek Text and Theory*, Collingswood: Dean Burgon Society.

Chadwick, H. (1961) *The Vindication of Christianity in Westcott's Thought*, Cambridge: Cambridge University Press.

Chadwick, W.O. (1970) *The Victorian Church*, II, London: Adam and Charles Black.

Elton, G.R. and F.C. Macdonald (1932) *Lightfoot of Durham*, Cambridge: Cambridge University Press.

Hort, A.F. (1896) *Life and Letters of F.J.A. Hort*, London: Macmillan.

Patrick, G.A. (1988) *F.J.A. Hort: Eminent Victorian*, Sheffield: Sheffield Academic Press.

Sanday, W. (1897) *American Journal of Theology* 1: 95–117.

Watkins, H.W. (1893) 'J.B. Lightfoot,' *Quarterly Review* 176: 73–105.

Westcott, A. (1903) *Life and Letters of B.F. Westcott*, London: Macmillan.

HORTON HARRIS

WETTE, W.M.L. DE (1780–1849)

Wilhelm Martin Leberecht de Wette was born on January 12, 1780 in the village of Ullaa near Weimar, the son of a Lutheran pastor. Among the schools he attended was the *Gymnasium* (grammar school) in Weimar, where he was taught by J.G. Herder. In 1798 he enrolled at the University of Jena, where his boyhood reservations about Christian belief were both fortified and shaken by his exposure to Kantian philosophy and the aesthetics of Schelling. In 1804 he gained his doctorate in philosophy with a thesis on the authorship of Deuteronomy which contained, in a long footnote, the essence of the view of the history of Israel's religion that would be given classical formulation in 1878 by Julius Wellhausen. This maintained that the sacrificial and priestly systems attributed in the Old Testament to Moses were in fact late developments, and that Israel's religion had earlier enjoyed considerable variety based upon many local shrines and local priesthoods. De Wette followed this with a two-volume *Beiträge zur Enleitung in das A.T.* (1806–1807), in the first volume of which he argued for the untrustworthiness of the history of Israel's religion as presented in the books of Chronicles. This contribution would also play a part in the development of Wellhausen's synthesis.

From 1807 to 1810 de Wette taught in Heidelberg, where he began a lifelong friendship with philosopher J.F. Fries, and adopted the latter's aesthetic-philosophical view of religion. A commentary on the Psalms from this period anticipated the later form-critical work of Gunkel. In 1810 he was appointed to the newly founded University of Berlin where his main colleague and rival was F.D.E. Schleiermacher. Here he published works on biblical dogmatics and theology, but his faith took a new direction when he saw the life of Christ as an expression of the Absolute within the limitations of human history. From this point he was a positive, if not entirely orthodox, Christian believer.

His career in Berlin was cruelly cut short in 1819 when he was dismissed for writing a letter of sympathy to the mother of Karl Ludwig Sand, a radical theological student who had carried out a high-profile political assassination. Unemployed, he returned to Weimar. The unanimous decision of the St Katharine Church in Braunschweig to appoint him to a pastorate was blocked by the government of Hanover, and in desperation de Wette accepted a post in Basel in 1821. Here he remained until his death on June 16, 1849. In Basel he published commentaries on the Greek text of the whole New Testament, as well as works on ethics, comparative religion, and Christian doctrine. He also produced the first critical edition of the letters of Martin Luther.

De Wette's main contribution to biblical scholarship was his early critical work in Jena. Thereafter his banishment to Basel and the predominance of neoorthodoxy in Prussia marginalized him, until his work was rediscovered and to some extent repeated in the 1870s, leading to Wellhausen. However, he remained an important figure, not least because of the philosophical, literate, and aesthetic insights that he brought to biblical scholarship.

References and further reading

Mathys, H.P. and K. Seybold (eds.) (2001) *Wilhelm Martin Leberecht de Wette. Ein Universaltheologie des 19. Jahrhunderts*, Studien zur Geschichte der Wissenschaften in Basel, Neue Folge 1, Basel: Schwase & Co. Verlag.

Rogerson, J.W. (1992) *W.M.L. de Wette: Founder of Modern Biblical Criticism*, JSOTSup 126, Sheffield: Sheffield Academic Press.

JOHN ROGERSON

WILLIAM OF OCKHAM (c. 1287–1347)

One of the chief scholastic philosophers of the medieval period; a member of the Franciscan order. Ockham studied and would later teach at Oxford. His contribution to logic and semantics and significance for biblical interpretation is of particular interest. His nominalist logic and philosophy (denying the existence of universal entities) would lead him to suggest methods of scriptural interpretation abstracted from tradition, the latter of course regarded by the church of his day as the sum of all knowledge. His philosophy contributed to interpretive methods of scriptural texts correlated with a kind of direct experience as a source of knowledge.

Ockham introduced a number of important semantic ideas, the most basic of which is 'signification' in the use of terms. A term 'signifies' when it corresponds to specific contents of thought. Terms are not generalities but they can become attached to anything, even nonexistent or immaterial things.

While his ideas were consonant with late medieval semantic theory on the topic of 'supposition' Ockham expanded upon it with his account of signification. Terms were understood to have supposition only in the context of a proposition. Ockham identified signification as a psychological, cognitive relation, and as such it became a key building block to modern theories of reference. For Ockham, there are three main kinds of supposition: (a) personal supposition, in which a term refers to what it signifies, e.g., 'every house is a building'; (b) simple supposition, in which a term refers to a concept it does not signify, 'this house is a building,' – but not all buildings are houses, etc; (c) material supposition, in which a term refers to a spoken or written expression it does not signify, e.g., 'a house has an entry,' where house is a material supposition.

Ockham developed his philosophy further through accounts of mental language, synonymy, and connotation. His discussion of language isolates three types: written, spoken, and mental language, with the written kind dependent on the spoken, and the spoken dependent upon mental language. Mental language – thought itself – is construed as the most primitive and basic level of language. For mental language, concepts are its terms and its propositions are mental judgments. Whereas the signification of terms in spoken and written language is purely conventional and can be changed (from English to Chinese), the signification of terms (concepts) in mental language is established by nature once and for all. Concepts 'naturally signify' what they are concepts of.

In effect, Ockham created a culture of interpretation which sought to eliminate interpretations which multiplied meanings, e.g., allegorical, where every feature of a text could become an allusion to the religious institution, ritual, and personal life of its readers; or anagogical, where every dimension of ethical life could be read off of the text. Ockham contributed to this trend by eliminating 'putative entities' from philosophical discourse with respect to semantic ideas and in general. By denying 'abstract entities,' the chief characteristic of ontological parsimony, reflected in the motto attributed to him but nowhere found in his texts, 'Don't multiply entities beyond necessity,' the interpreter is constantly sorting out references to nonexisting or unnecessary matters in the interest of strict and precise attention to any matter of inquiry. If there is no demonstrated need for a particular entity, there should be no reference to it.

Conditions for reference in knowledge of a particular thing follow a set of three positive evidences as reflected in his assertion in Sent. I, dist. 30, q. 1: 'For nothing ought to be posited without a reason given, unless it is self-evident (literally, known through itself) or known by experience or proved by the authority of Sacred Scripture.' No reference here is made to tradition which could only be derived, multiple, varying, and therefore fallible. In terms of the elimination of entities, this has a fundamentally scientific application in text-critical work: the search for the best source and the competition between variant readings. Using as an instrument of 'ontological reduction' he attempts to remove all need for entities beyond the categories of substance and quality, and a few entities in the category of relation, for reasons pertaining to the theology of the Trinity, the Incarnation and the Lord's Supper.

By making faith foundational to Christian truth, Ockham in many respects intensifies the ecclesiastical positivism of Augustine and Duns Scotus. Faith must be accepted as a whole and as it is taught and mediated by the church. Reason is entitled to question the church's teaching, but in the end Christians accept what they are taught. Acceptance is dependent upon the gift of 'infused faith,' is always necessary to realize the reason for the church's authority, and is learned only by authority, rather than by reason, experience, or logic. Church authority is founded upon scripture and the infallible teachings it has generated for itself. Ockham claimed that for salvation, nothing other than the content of scripture or inferences from it were necessary. The possible link to Martin Luther's own theological reasoning here is unmistakable. In his theology, Ockham assumes or tries to show that the authority of the Fathers and of the Roman Catholic Church are functionally coequal with that of the scripture. But a perceptible disconnect existed in the logical, semantic, and hermeneutical principles which he so technically developed.

References and further reading

Adams, Marilyn McCord (1989) *William Ockham*, Notre Dame, IN: University of Notre Dame Press.

Copley, Paul (ed.) (2001) *Companion to Linguistics and Semiotics*, London: Routledge.

Pasnau, Robert (1997) *Theories of Cognition in the Later Middle Ages*, Cambridge: Cambridge University Press.

Thijssen, J.M.M.H. (1998) *Censure and Heresy at the University of Paris 1200–1400*, Philadelphia: University of Pennsylvania Press.

William of Ockham (1967–1988) *Op. Philosophica et Theologica, cura Instituti Franciscani Universitatis S. Bonventurae*, 7 Vols., New York: St Bonaventure.

—— (1998) *Quodlibetal Questions*, New Haven: Yale University Press.

—— (1999) *Ockham's Theory of Propositions: Summa Logicae and Theory of Terms: Summa Logicae*, trans. Michael J. Loux, Alfred J. Freddoso, and Henry Schuurman, South Bend, IN: St Augustine's Press.

KURT A. RICHARDSON

WREDE, WILLIAM (1859–1906)

A son of the manse (b. May 10, 1859 in Bücken, near Hanover), William Wrede was both a scholar and a pastor. After theological studies at Leipzig and Göttingen (1877–1881), and a period of college teaching and pastoral ministry thereafter, he became *Privatdozent* in New Testament at Göttingen in 1891 and subsequently Professor of New Testament at Breslau (1893–1906). He died there on November 23, 1906. Among the influences operating on him was the contemporary 'history of religions school' (with its emphasis on New Testament texts as the bearers not so much of the history but of the ideology of the religious communities which produced them), and among the scholars to whom he acknowledged a debt were A. Eichhorn, A. von Harnack, C. Krüger, P. Lagarde, and A. Ritschl. Wrede's own publications were few but influential, comprising three major pieces of work on New Testament theology, Mark and Paul (as well as some secondary writings): *Über die Aufgabe und Methode der sogenannten neutestamentlichen Theologie* (1897); *Das Messiasgeheimnis in den Evangelien* (1901; ET *The Messianic Secret*, 1971); *Paulus* (1904; ET 1907).

Applying history of religions insights to the Gospels, Wrede challenged the prevailing Liberal Life of Jesus assumption that these texts furnished an accurate historical and psychological picture of Christianity's founder, and in particular the view that Jesus had thought of himself as Messiah. The Gospel texts had been shaped by theology (or dogma), he argued, rather than by history. In the case of Mark's Gospel, it is to the early church and the evangelist that we owe the portrait of a Jesus who veils the developing consciousness of his messianic status in secrecy. In reality, Jesus' life was unmessianic, and the so-called 'Messianic secret' is a construction whereby the church's subsequent theological claims on his behalf have been retrojected into the account of his life. Scholars have reacted to Wrede's controversial thesis in three main ways, some attacking it head-on (but vainly) by attempting to defend Mark's presentation of Jesus as historical, and others more subtly by questioning the extent (or even existence) of the motif itself. Most have been swayed, however, by Wrede's approach, anticipating as it did later developments such as form and redaction criticism, although many would prefer to modify his thesis by claiming that the secrecy motif 'is a theme pursued by the evangelist Mark, not in order to introduce a christological motif into the tradition, but rather to correct one already present' (Perrin 1976: 799).

Radical in the field of Gospel studies, Wrede proved even more so where Pauline studies were concerned. If post-Easter Christology could shape the historical Jesus tradition as it had done in the case of Mark, then it had almost overwhelmed it in the case of Paul. In his influential little book, *Paul*, Wrede addressed the perennial question of the relation between the apostle and Jesus. For Paul, the *theologian* with a background in syncretistic Judaism, the Christ of faith was more important than the Jesus of history. Paul's conception of this Christ, Wrede maintained, owed far less to the historical Jesus tradition and far more to the ideas that he had entertained as a first-century Jew on the nature of the Messiah. Uninfluenced by Jesus' personality or teaching, Paul transferred to Jesus those inherited ideas. In a celebrated dictum, Wrede claimed that 'Paul believed in such a celestial being, in a divine Christ, before he believed in Jesus' (cited in Kümmel 1973: 297). To that extent, he became the second (or even the real) founder of Christianity,

Wrede's sensitivity to the boundary between history and dogma is also to be seen in his contribution to the debate over what constitutes a 'theology of the New Testament.' In opposition to those who confined themselves to the New Testament canon, and saw the discipline as an analytical or synthetic discipline which laid the foundation, in turn, for a dogmatic (or systematic) theology operating in the service of the church or Christian faith, Wrede took a 'history of ideas' approach, arguing that New Testament theology was a historical-descriptive exercise whose purpose it was to illumine the nature, origin, and development of the religious ideas of early Christianity, and which should not he restricted, therefore, to the canonical writings.

Almost a century after Wrede's sparse but consequential output, his legacy is still with us. Apart from the influence it exerted over R. Bultmann and other major scholars, the trace of his work can still be discerned today. Issues raised by him still confront those seeking to understand early Christianity, pursuing the quest for the historical Jesus, or assessing Paul's contribution to early Christianity. The approach he took to New Testament texts, setting them within their religio-historical context and exposing their ideological presuppositions, is now commonplace. Few now approach the Gospels without an application of the redactional or literary approaches of which he was a precursor, or without an awareness of the theology reflected in them, and the limitations imposed thereby on historical reconstruction.

References and further reading

Blevins, J.L. (1981) *The Messianic Secret in Markan Research 1901–1976*, Washington, DC: University Press of America.

Kümmel, W.G. (1973) *The New Testament: The History of the Investigation of its Problems*, New Testament Library, London: SCM Press.

Lührmann, D. (1990) 'Wrede, W,' p. 734 in *A Dictionary of Biblical Interpretation*, R.J. Coggins and J.L. Houlden (eds.), London: SCM Press/Philadelphia: Trinity Press International.

Morgan, R.C. (1973) *The Nature of New Testament Theology: The Contribution of William Wrede and Adolf Schlatter*, SBT, Second series 25, London: SCM Press.

Perrin, N. (1976) 'Secret, Messianic,' pp. 789–9 in *The Interpreter's Dictionary of the Bible, Supplementary Volume*, K. Crim (ed.), Nashville: Abingdon Press.

Strecker, G. (1960) 'William Wrede. Zur hundertsten Wiederkehr seines Geburtstages,' *Zeitschrift für Theologie und Kirche* 57: 67–91.

Schweitzer, A. (1998) *The Quest of the Historical Jesus: A Critical Study of its Progress from Reimarus to Wrede*, Baltimore and London: Johns Hopkins University Press/Albert Schweitzer Institute.

W.R. TELFORD

WRITINGS

In order to discuss the interpretation of the Writings as a whole, one cannot avoid first asking questions related to their place in the canon. Of the Hebrew Bible's three divisions: the Law (Torah), the Prophets, and the Writings, it is the last one which is most difficult to typify. Although there is great diversity within the first two divisions (narrative, historiography, poetry, etc.), in simple terms they are bound together by thematic unity: the Law sets the standards for the faith and life of the Jewish community, and the Prophets is a collection of God's revealed Word to his people. However, the Writings are not so easily categorized. One could even say that 'Writings' is at worst a noncategory or at best a catchall category, which includes Psalms, the 'wisdom' writings of Job and Proverbs, the Five Scrolls: Ruth (short story), the Song of Songs (love poetry), Ecclesiastes (also wisdom), Lamentations (poetic lament liturgy), Esther (short story) which are associated with cultic calendar festivals, the apocalyptic book of Daniel, and the historiographical works of Chronicles, Ezra and Nehemiah. Such wide a variety of literary genres does not easily yield to a single interpretation, except in the question of canonicity, i.e., what brought all these miscellaneous works together? What themes or ideas within these texts would have secured their place in the canon?

Later Jewish tradition as enshrined in the Babylonian Talmud, *Baba Batra* 14b, provides us with a major clue toward understanding the reason for including those books found within the Writings: prophetic inspiration. This passage seems to work on the assumption that a prophetic author is to be found either in the titles of books or in their sequence within the canon. Thus Moses, who in rabbinic tradition is regarded as a prophet, is credited with having written the books of the Law (and Job). Joshua, Samuel, and the Prophets are given credit for having written the books which are attributed to them or bear their names – remembering that in the Jewish canon the Prophets also contain

Judges and 1–2 Kings, thought to have been written by Samuel and Jeremiah respectively. (It should be noted that *B. Bat.* 14b credits Hezekiah and his colleagues with the written versions of Isaiah, Proverbs, Song of Songs, and Ecclesiastes. The 'Men of the Great Synagogue' [*B. Bat.* 15a] are credited with having set down in writing Ezekiel, the Twelve Minor Prophets, Daniel, and Esther.) As regards the Writings, according to *Baba Batra* 14b, Samuel is the author of Ruth, Jeremiah is thought to have written Lamentations and Ezra the scribe is attributed with the book which bears his name (Nehemiah being considered part of the same work [*B. Bat.* 15]) and Chronicles. David is of course considered the author of Psalms, and to Solomon are assigned Proverbs, Song of Songs, and Ecclesiastes. It would seem that as the narratives concerning David and Solomon are contained within the books of Samuel and Kings (i.e., 'prophetic' works), there is per force an unbroken chain of 'prophetic' authorship from Moses to Malachi. Esther, although not having a prophetic author, finds itself included in the tradition inasmuch as Mordecai was venerated in Jewish tradition as having been a prophet contemporary with Haggai, Zechariah, and Malachi. Further, according to various rabbinic sources (*Yoma* 80a; *Shab.* 104a; *Meg.* 2a), the Great Synagogue had numerous prophets among its members who saw to it that the story of Esther was written down. This apparent criterion for prophetic authorship – and its anachronizing tendency to make great figures of ancient times 'prophets' – lends some support for positing an original twofold canon of the Law and the Prophets as supported by New Testament references (Harrison 1973: 267; Barr 1983: 54–6; the rabbinic tendency to cast familiar figures from the past in the role of prophet [i.e., divinely inspired] finds its precursor in Chronicles, which even cites temple singers as prophets: 1 Chron. 25:1–8; 2 Chron. 20:13–17, 20; 29:25–30; 35:15.). It is reasonable to assume that the Prophetic group of scripture was not a closed 'canon' until well within the first century of the Christian era and that many of the books we recognize today as Writings could well have been within the Prophetic corpus.

In any event, the Hebrew Bible we have received has a threefold division. Given that the Writings were the last to receive their canonical status, one could naturally assume that this chronology also reflects the relative importance, in descending order, of each division within scripture. Indisputably, the Torah holds the predominant place within Judaism. The Prophets are important theologically, and also have their place within Jewish liturgy. Then come the Writings. However, this ranking on the basis of relative importance loses ground when one takes into consideration the fact that the Five Scrolls are read at certain prominent festivals: Song of Songs is read at Passover, Ruth at the Feast of Weeks/Pentecost, Lamentations at Tisha b'Av (ninth of Av: a day of commemoration/mourning for the destruction

of the temple), and Esther is read at Purim. These, along with many of the Psalms, have been and are exceedingly familiar in Jewish life. Thus, the gradation in importance of the three divisions does not work out in fact.

The order of the books within the Writings varied considerably in Hebrew manuscripts before taking the canonical shape we know today. No explicit reason is given in the *Gemara* of *Baba Batra* 14b, but it can be noted that historical context/chronology seemingly influenced the order of the books. Of the eight main variations, six preserve the basic chronological order. Ruth, with its genealogy of David, precedes Psalms, which has been ascribed to David. Next comes Job, presumably because of the tradition (*B. Bat.* 15b) which places Job in the time of the Queen of Sheba. Proverbs, Ecclesiastes, and Song of Songs were attributed to Solomon; Lamentations was considered the work of Jeremiah; Daniel was located in the exilic period; and Esther, Ezra-Nehemiah, and Chronicles were of the postexilic, Persian era. In all the manuscripts, Job, Psalms, and Proverbs are grouped together. This close association has led to a tradition of referring to them as the Book of Truth, an acrostic formed by the initial letters of each book: א (איוב-Job) מ (משלי-Proverbs) ת (תהלים-Psalms) (אמת 'truth' in Hebrew). The greatest variance within the order is to be found with the Five Scrolls. Nowhere in rabbinic sources are the five listed in immediate succession (*Encyclopaedia Judaica* 1971: 829). This canonical sequence is obviously based on the later tradition of reading these scrolls on festival days (above). Chronicles presents the greatest puzzle as to location within the order, appearing either at the beginning or the end of the corpus. The fact that Chronicles has found itself in the final position is remarkable due to the fact that Ezra-Nehemiah follows seamlessly the narrative chronology of the former. Why this canonical order? We can only speculate as others have done (e.g., Gottwald 1985: 108; *Encyclopaedia Judaica* 1971: 831) that Genesis and Chronicles form an inclusio around the canonical scriptures, as both begin with the creation of humanity and both end with God's promise of redemption and return to the land of Israel. In fact, Chronicles presents the reader with a compressed history (Adam to Saul in nine chapters!) of the Jewish people from Creation to the rebuilding of the temple. As no fewer than twenty-nine chapters of 1–2 Chronicles deal with David, Solomon, and the preparation for building and staffing the temple, one could easily interpret these books as a history of the rise and fall of the temple cult. In addition, inasmuch as Ezra-Nehemiah ends on a somewhat dour note regarding the dubious success of Nehemiah's religious reforms, it would thus seem that Chronicles makes for a more fitting ending to the Hebrew Bible as it closes with the positive report of Cyrus' edict for the rebuilding of the temple in Jerusalem and its message of hope.

The interpretation of the Writings becomes vexed once we leave questions surrounding their place and shape within the canon. This is due, once again, to the great diversity of literature within the corpus. However, we can make some logical assumptions based on the late arrival of the Writings to canonical status, coupled with the status of Judah and Judaism between the second century BC and the second century AD, when Judah was a 'client state' or occupied territory under one foreign power or another. As a great deal of the Writings were produced during or shortly after the Exile, there is strength in the argument that these books provided both hope and a model for Jewish life in the Diaspora. This is especially so for the books of Esther, Daniel, Ezra-Nehemiah. It is within foreign courts or under foreign patronage that these heroes act. In this setting, the possibility of a rewarding and creative life is affirmed. Such a life is not without its dangers, as is clearly depicted in Esther and Daniel, yet nevertheless, each book makes clear that one can meet adversity and still remain a loyal Jew – even within a pagan setting (Humphreys 1973: 211–23; Morgan 1990). In this vein, Ezra-Nehemiah chronicles the successful re-establishment of the Jewish community within the sphere of foreign domination. In concert with 1–2 Chronicles, Ezra-Nehemiah has seemingly gathered together all the essential elements of monarchic life along with the temple cults it bequeathed, such that the postexilic community became the true inheritors – or indeed embodiment – of the entire monarchic/priestly tradition within their current *Sitz im Leben*. This holds true whether or not the author(s) of the Chronicler's History envisaged a revival of the Davidic monarchy. Thus Chronicles and Ezra-Nehemiah posit the restored community as an obedient counterpart to the initial contributions of David and Solomon, but without the need for national sovereignty.

> By drawing so straight and unerring a line from Moses through David to the restored and freshly reformed postexilic community C[hronicler's] H[istory] validates a vigorous recovery of national traditions and communal practices that was both a form of accommodation to the colonial status under Persia and also an act of national resistance by marking off a religiocultural identity for Jews that was drawn so tightly that in the end it excluded fellow Jews, such as the Samaritans, who did not succumb to the reform leadership in Judah. (Gottwald 1985: 521–2)

What of contributions made by wisdom literature to life in the Diaspora? That the 'wisdom' genre was an international phenomenon in the ancient Near East is now well-recognized. Perhaps due to this international scope, we find that one of the most striking characteristics of the Hebrew wisdom literature is the absence of subjects considered typically Israelite and Jewish: e.g., no mention of the promise to the patriarchs, the Exodus,

Moses, the covenant, and Sinai. The exceptions to this are late and are found outside the canonical books (Sir 44–50 and Wis 11–19) (Murphy 1990: 1). Although not necessarily a late characteristic, lack of reference to distinctively Jewish elements makes the wisdom literature all the more 'workable' in the pluralistic, postexilic world. There is what could be described as a 'survivalist' attitude within the wisdom genre; a realist's sense that whatever one's hopes and aspirations might be, one still has to deal with the powers that be. Proverbs is characterized by an exalted, yet workable, morality, a sagacious understanding of human nature, and a clear interest in the happiness of the individual in the here and now. 'Job and Ecclesiastes are distinguished by their fearless use of reason in confronting the most fundamental issues of life, their refusal to pretend to certainty where none is to be had, and their unswerving allegiance to truth, whatever the cost' (Gordis 1978: 37–8). Their existence within the canon is testimony to an internal dialogue within the canon: if the Law and the Prophets are based upon Sinai, the covenant, the monarchy, etc. then Job and Ecclesiastes are the results of a search for meaning when all external props and hope have been taken away. Certainly Job serves a corrective to any simplistic or dogmatic belief in a mechanistic moral universe: that the innocent suffer (nations or individuals) is an indisputable, if inexplicable, reality. One can see why such literature would have the resonance of 'truth' about it for the restored community in Judah.

The role that two of the Five Scrolls (Ecclesiastes and Esther) could have played in the restored community has been mentioned above. Regarding the other three, Lamentations, as the name indicates, consists of poems which have been gathered together around the common theme of lament for the destruction of Jerusalem and the temple. These dirges or poems of lament were most probably used for public fast days, which apparently began shortly after Jerusalem's destruction in 587 or 586 (Jer. 41:5). In any event, these poems took on more poignant meaning following the destruction of the second temple by the Romans in AD 70, following which they became part of the canon. Lamentations is now read yearly on Tisha b'Av, the date when the destruction of both temples is commemorated. Song of Songs holds a unique place within the canon of both the Hebrew Bible and New Testament scriptures as it is quite simply erotic love poetry of the highest order. (The Hebrew name, which is rendered literally as 'Song of Songs,' is in fact the superlative: 'the Best or Most Excellent of Songs.') This caused discomfort for certain groups within both Judaism and Christianity during the early part of the Common Era, and thus allegorical interpretations were favored by many. For Jewish readers, the lovers were God and Israel, whereas for Christians they represented God/Christ and the church or the soul of the believer.

Rabbinic sources would seem to indicate that the allegorical interpretation helped secure Song of Songs' place in the canon (t. Sanh. 12.10). However, there is nothing within the Song nor anything from similar works among extrabiblical sources which would support a purely allegorical interpretation. Nevertheless, lively debate has continued over the centuries regarding the appropriateness of the Song's canonicity: is it to be understood literally, is it drama, is it liturgical (based on earlier pagan sacred marriage mythology), is it a collection of wedding songs, etc.? Whatever the interpretation, one cannot escape the rich and sensual language, the absence of allusions to marriage, and the unashamedly joyful expression of human sexuality. It served the Jewish and Christian communities in all the aforementioned capacities, and continues to do so. The last of the Five Scrolls, Ruth, stands as a paradigm for storytelling and the economy of the Hebrew language as its four short chapters are packed with poignancy, irony, humor, and social critique, which have all combined to create an enduring tale. Although set in the period of the Judges, debate still continues regarding the date of composition: ranging from the period of the United Monarchy to the time of Ezra-Nehemiah. The debate focuses on things such as linguistic usage: grammar, syntax, spelling, dialect; social customs and legal prescriptions (gleaning, levirate marriage, etc.); and even the theme of the story. Although these are beyond the scope here, it is worth mentioning the theme: Ruth herself. Not only is she a Moabite (which some critics see as evidence of its late composition: opposition to the exclusivist policy of Ezra, regarding putting away foreign wives), but Ruth, in coalition with her mother-in-law Naomi, acts as a woman alone in a man's world (Trible 1978: 166–99). In this regard, the story of Ruth stands as an intricate piece of countercultural social critique, which is as applicable in the early monarchic period as it is in postexilic Judah. It also carries the poignant message of restoration following a period of intense trial, which is echoed in Job and Chronicles.

We now end where the Writings begin: with Psalms (the title of the book comes to us from the Greek *psalmoi* or 'songs sung to or played on a stringed instrument'). Like so many titles of books in the Old Testament, we are dealing with the Greek translation of a Hebrew term, but in this case it is not completely accurate. The Hebrew title for the book is *sefer tehilîm*, 'Book of Praises,' itself divided into five 'books.' The Greek title more closely approximates the Hebrew מזמור *mizmôr* ('melody,' 'song'), a superscription which occurs fifty-seven times throughout the book. In any case, both *psalmos* and *mizmôr* provide us with the sense that many (but perhaps not all) of these poems of praise were meant to be sung, thus indicating a liturgical role within Judaism. As such, one finds instructions to the (choir) director, notes regarding instruments to be used, etc. However, not all of the psalms are simply 'hymns.'

Some of the Psalms are referred to as prayers (Hebrew *tĕphillâ*: Pss. 17, 86, 90, 102, 142) and Book II ends with the postscript: 'Here end the prayers of David, son of Jesse' (72:20). Since Gunkel's groundbreaking form-critical study of the Psalms was published in 1929, scholars have debated the number of different types of Psalms, e.g., hymns, laments (communal, individual), thanksgiving (communal, individual), royal psalms, etc. We cannot say for certain that the object of collecting these poetic prayers was simply liturgical. What becomes clear upon reading the Psalms is that they cover the entire spectrum of human emotion within religious experience from joy and blessing to lament and cursing as well as everything in between (e.g., wisdom and prophetic oracle). They in no way hold back from expressing extremes in human emotion (e.g., Ps. 137:9). The poetic expression of religious sentiment appears throughout the Hebrew Bible and was no doubt always a part of their tradition, as with other ancient Near-Eastern societies. The book of Psalms contains material from the time of the First Temple through the time of the Second Temple. That there were psalms which did not get absorbed into the canonical book is clear from the discoveries at Qumran. In the final analysis, Psalms were written throughout the life of Israel and were not inextricably linked to either temple or monarchy. Thus the real key to their survival consisted in their eloquence and genuine expression of the human condition which transcended any institution and have remained applicable since their fixture in the canon. The same could be said of the Writings in general, which have provided the beginnings of a tradition of exposition and testing of the traditions laid down in the Law and the Prophets.

References and further reading

Barr, James (1983) *Holy Scripture: Canon, Authority, Criticism*, Oxford: Clarendon.

Encyclopaedia Judaica (1971) S.v. 'Bible: Canon, Texts and Editions,' by Nahum Sarna, Jerusalem: Keter.

Gordis, Robert (1978) *Koheleth – the Man and His World*, New York: Schocken.

Gottwald, Norman (1985) *The Hebrew Bible – A Socio-Literary Introduction*, Philadelphia: Fortress Press.

Harrison, R.K. (1973) *Introduction to the Old Testament*, Grand Rapids: Eerdmans.

Humphreys, W.L. (1973) 'A Life-Style for the Diaspora: A Study of the Tales of Esther and Daniel,' *Journal of Biblical Literature* 92: 211–23.

Morgan, D. (1990) *Between Text and Community*, Minneapolis: Fortress Press.

Murphy, Roland (1990) *The Tree of Life*, New York: Doubleday.

Trible, Phyllis (1978) *God and the Rhetoric of Sexuality*, Philadelphia: Fortress Press.

JACK N. LAWSON

Index

Related titles from Routledge

The Church in the Age of Constantine
The Theological Challenges

Johannes Roldanus

The Church in the Age of Constantine provides a refined theological screening of the doctrinal and ethical thinking during the fourth century.

Relating biblical essentials to ancient cosmology and anthropology, Roldanus uses the concept of 'contextualisation' to appreciate this process. He makes clear that, however much the winning positions were dependent on the interfering of the State, the theological reflection went nevertheless its proper way, conditioned as it was by various understandings of salvation-in-Christ. There was a natural concern to relate salvation to the most important elements of the existing culture.

Providing models for reflection on inculturation, this study helps students to focus on the essentials and to form and unprejudiced opinion on this crucial period of history.

ISBN10: 0–415–0903–9 (hbk)
ISBN10: 0–415–0904–7 (pbk)

ISBN13: 978–0–415–0903–2 (hbk)
ISBN13: 978–0–415–0904–9 (pbk)

Available at all good bookshops
For ordering and further information please visit:
www.routledge.com

Related titles from Routledge

Early Christianity

Mark Humphries

Examining sources and case studies, this accessible book explores early Christianity, how it was studied, how it is studied now, and how Judaeo-Christian values came to form the ideological bedrock of modern western culture.

Looking at the diverse source materials available, from the earliest New Testament texts and the complex treaties of third century authors such as Lactantius, to archaeology, epigraphy and papyrology, the book examines what is needed to study the subject, what materials are available, how useful they are, and how the study of the subject may be approached.

Case study chapters focus on important problems in the study of early Christianity including:

- the book of Acts as a text revelatory of the social dynamics of cities and as a text about the inherent tensions in Hellenistic Judaism
- Orthodoxy and Organization in early Christianity
- Early Christianity and the Roman Empire.

Also including a comprehensive guide for students that lists major collections of literary and non-literary sources, major journals and series, and major text books, it is an excellent aid to the study of Christianity in history.

ISBN10: 0–415–20538–7 (hbk)
ISBN10: 0–415–20539–5 (pbk)

ISBN13: 978–0–415–20538–2 (hbk)
ISBN13: 978–0–415–20539–9 (pbk)

Available at all good bookshops
For ordering and further information please visit:
www.routledge.com